2nd Conference of the Asia-Pacific Chapter of the Association for Computational Linguistics and the 12th International Joint Conference on Natural Language Processing (AACL-IJCNLP 2022)

Findings of the Association for Computational Linguistics:
AACL-IJCNLP 2022

Online
20-23 November 2022

ISBN: 978-1-7138-6316-8

Printed from e-media with permission by:

Curran Associates, Inc.
57 Morehouse Lane
Red Hook, NY 12571

Some format issues inherent in the e-media version may also appear in this print version.

Printed with permission by Curran Associates, Inc. (2023)

For permission requests, please contact the Association for Computational Linguistics at the address below.

Association for Computational Linguistics
209 N. Eighth Street
Stroudsburg, Pennsylvania 18360

Phone: 1-570-476-8006
Fax: 1-570-476-0860

acl@aclweb.org

Additional copies of this publication are available from:

Curran Associates, Inc.
57 Morehouse Lane
Red Hook, NY 12571 USA
Phone: 845-758-0400
Fax: 845-758-2633
Email: curran@proceedings.com
Web: www.proceedings.com

AACL-IJCNLP 2022

The 2nd Conference of the Asia-Pacific Chapter of the Association for Computational Linguistics and the 12th International Joint Conference on Natural Language Processing

Findings of the Association for Computational Linguistics: AACL-IJCNLP 2022

November 20-23, 2022

Preface by the General Chair

Welcome to AACL-IJCNLP 2022, the 2nd Conference of the Asia-Pacific Chapter of the Association for Computational Linguistics and the 12th International Joint Conference on Natural Language Processing! The conference will be held online on November 20-23, 2022.

AACL-IJCNLP 2022 was originally scheduled to take place in Taipei, Taiwan. We had a discussion with AACL executive board early this year whether to hold the conference entirely in the virtual mode due to the strict COVID quarantine rule imposed by the Taiwan government. We later decided to wait until the mid of June to re-evaluate the situation. In early June, the Central Epidemic Command Center in Taiwan announced that starting from 15 June 2022, the mandatory quarantine period for international arrivals in Taiwan would be reduced from 7 to 3 days. After a discussion with both the Program Chairs and the Local Organization Chair, we decided to wait further until August to see if we could have a hybrid conference in the hope that Taiwan will open its border fully in November. But we eventually made a difficult decision to hold the conference entirely online at mid of August as the quarantine rule and the travel ban imposed on foreign nationals were still in place in Taiwan. This was rather disappointed. Nevertheless, our Program Chairs have put together a very interesting conference program. I hope to see many of you joining our conference online.

AACL-IJCNLP 2022 adopted a dual paper submission system that authors can choose to submit their papers to the "ACL Rolling Review (ARR)" or submit to the softconf submission site in a conventional way. For the latter, authors had a chance to respond to reviewers' comments. One innovation our Program Chairs introduced is to allow authors to run additional experiments and upload revised papers during the rebuttal period to address reviewers' comments. This required additional efforts from our reviewers, area chairs and senior area chairs to check the revised submissions. But it gave authors better opportunities to address reviewers' criticism. Another innovation is to introduce poster lightning talks in the main conference. We hope these efforts will be followed in future conferences.

AACL-IJCNLP 2022 would not be possible without the contribution from a large number of volunteers who are willing to spend tremendous time and effort. These include the members of our organisation committee and various people from the ACL community. In particular, I would like to thank:

- the three Program Co-Chairs, Heng Ji, Sujian Li, and Yang Liu, who managed the whole conference paper submission and review process, and assembled the conference program with new initiatives such as a debate on "*Is there more to NLP than Deep Learning?*" and the "7 NLP Dissertation Topics for Next 7 Years";
- the Local Organisation Chair, Chia-Hui Chang, who was in charge of venue booking when we initially planned for a hybrid conference and coordinated the setup of a registration site. She was supported by a great local organisation team, including the Financial Chair, Lun-Wei Ku, the Local Arrangement Chair, Kuan-Yu (Menphis) Chen, the Online Conference Coordinator, Richard Tzong-Han Tsai, and the Registration Chair, Hsiu-Min Chuang;
- the Publication Co-Chairs, Min-Yuh Day, Hen-Hsen Huang, and Jheng-Long Wu, who prepared the instruction for proceedings compilation and coordinated with our workshop/tutorial/demo/student research workshop chairs to assemble all papers into our conference proceedings;
- the Workshop Co-chairs, Soujanya Poria and Chenghua Lin, who selected 5 workshops for the conference and ensured all the workshops could successfully run virtually;
- the Tutorial Co-Chairs, Miguel A. Alonso and Zhongyu Wei, who selected 6 tutorials to be presented at the conference and prepared the tutorial abstract proceedings;

- the Demonstration Co-Chairs, Wray Buntine and Maria Liakata, who manged the demo paper submission and review process;
- the Special Theme Co-Chairs, Monab Diab and Isabelle Augenstein, who handled paper submissions to the Special Theme on Fairness in Natural Language Processing;
- the Student Research Workshop (SRW) Co-Chairs, Hanqi Yan and Zonghan Yang, who organised the student workshop under the guidance our our SRW Faculty Co-Advisors, Sebastian Ruder and Xiaojun Wan;
- the Publicity Co-chairs, Pengfei Liu, Gabriele Pergola,and Ruifeng Xu, who communicated the information about the conference to the community using various social media channels;
- the Website Chair, Miguel Arana Catania and Yung-Chun Chang, who ensured that the AACL-IJCNLP 2022 website contains all up-to-date information;
- the Diversity & Inclusion (D&I) Chairs, Ruihong Huang and Jing Li, who have worked tirelessly to make AACL-IJCNLP 2022 as welcoming and inclusive as possible for all participants. They were supported by the D&I committee members, Yuji Zhang, Yuanyuan Lei, and Ayesha Qamar;
- the Sponsorship Coordinators, Hiroya Takamura, Wen-Hsiang Lu, and Deyi Xiong, who reached out institutions and corporations to collect funds to support our conference;
- the Communication Chairs, Zheng Fang, Jiazheng Li, and Xingwei Tan, who stepped in with a short notice to help Program Co-Chairs deal with a large number of email enquires;
- Priscilla Rasmussen, who stayed as a consultant for ACL, and Jennifer Rachford, the ACL Business Manager, for helping with various conference matters;
- the Chair of the AACL, Keh-Yih Su, and all the AACL executive board members, that have provided guidance regarding various decisions;
- the ACL executive board including the President, Tim Baldwin, for linking us with the right support; the ACL Sponsorship Director, Chris Callison-Burch, for providing guidance to our Sponsorship Chairs; and the ACL Treasurer, David Yarowsky, who negotiated a contract with Underline for supporting our virtual conference;
- Rich Gerber from Softconf, who set up the AACL-IJCNLP conference submission site, has always been responsive to our queries.

I would also like to express gratitude to our sponsors, whose generous support has been invaluable in building up AACL-IJCNLP to what it is now. These include our Diamond-level sponsors - GTCOM, LivePerson, Tourism Bureau, the Ministry of Science and Technology, the Ministry of Education and National Central University in Taiwan; our Platinum-level sponsor - Baidu; our Gold-level sponsors - Bloomberg; and our Bronze-level sponsors - Adobe.

Finally, I would like to thank all authors, senior area chairs, area chairs, reviewers, invited speakers and panelists, the volunteers organizing and chairing various sessions in the conference, and all attendees, for making this hopefully another successful NLP conference!

Hope you all enjoy AACL-IJCNLP 2022!

AACL-IJCNLP 2022 General Chair
Yulan He, King's College London, UK

Preface by the Program Committee Co-Chairs

We welcome you to AACL-IJCNLP 2022, the 2nd Conference of the Asia-Pacific Chapter of the Association for Computational Linguistics (AACL) and the 12th International Joint Conference on Natural Language Processing (IJCNLP)! Due to the strict COVID quarantine rule imposed by the local government, AACL-IJCNLP 2022 has to be held fully virtual. However, conference organizers have worked very hard to simulate an in-person meeting setting, thanks to the relatively mature virtual conference infrastructures that have been built by our community.

AACL-IJCNLP 2022 has utilized two submission platforms SoftConf and ACL Rolling Review (ARR)-OpenReview, and received 554 submissions in total (518 from SoftConf and 36 from ARR) for the main conference. We have accepted 147 papers (87 long and 60 short) for the main conference and 44 papers for the Findings. The submissions came from all over the world. Among the 191 accepted papers, according to the information of the main contact, 84 were from the Asia-Pacific region (23 from China mainland, 18 from India, 16 from Japan, 7 from South Korea, 5 from Australia, 3 from Singapore, 3 from Taiwan, 3 from Bangladesh, 2 from New Zealand, 1 from Sri Lanka, 1 from Nepal, 1 from Malaysia, and 1 from HongKong), 42 were from the America (36 from the USA, 5 from Canada, 1 from Chile), and 65 from Europe and the Middle East (18 from the UK, 12 from Germany, 9 from France, 5 from Netherlands, 4 from Switzerland, 4 from Italy, 3 from Norway, 2 from Egypt, 2 from Spain, 1 from Estonia, 1 from Denmark, 1 from Finland,1 from Iron, 1 from Bulgaria and 1 from Czech).

We have developed the following new attempts this year for paper submission:

- We created a new special theme "Fairness in Natural Language Processing".
- We added a new function during paper rebuttal to allow authors to upload their revised papers so that some responses can be more clearly presented and elaborated.

AACL-IJCNLP2022 does have a great program, thanks to all of you! We have put up a very exciting program with many new plenary sessions:

- We have invited four wonderful keynote speakers this year: Chris Callison-Burch (University of Pennsylvania), Eduard Hovy (University of Melbourne and Carnegie Mellon University), Juanzi Li (Tsinghua University), and Prem Natarajan (Amazon Alexa AI).
- A promised-to-be-heated debate: "Is there more to NLP than Deep Learning?" between "Yes" team: Eduard Hovy (Team Lead), Kathleen McKeown, Dan Roth, Eric Xing and "No" team: Kyunghyun Cho (Team Lead), Danqi Chen, Manling Li, Graham Neubig, to be moderated by Rada Mihalcea.
- "7 NLP Dissertation Topics for Next 7 Years" by Kevin Duh, Fei Huang, Smaranda Muresan, Preslav Nakov, Nanyun Peng, Joel Tetreault and Lu Wang.
- A panel on the special theme "Fairness in Natural Language Processing", moderated by our special theme chairs Mona Diab and Isabelle Augenstein.
- A Global Women in NLP session "Finding Your Purpose, Findign Your Voice - Professional Growth in the Age of Deep AI" led by Pascale Fung.

We are very grateful for all of these speakers and panelists on accepting our invitations! We will also have a special best paper award session and a lighting talk session for posters, following the successes of previous ACL and NAACL conferences. The excellence of the overall AACL-IJCNLP2022 program is thanks to all the chairs and organizers. We especially thank the 47 Senior Area Chairs, 84 Area Chairs and reviewers for their hard work. We are grateful to Amanda Stent, Goran Glavaš, Graham Neubig, and Harold Rubio for their invaluable support in the commitment of papers reviewed by ARR to AACL-IJCNLP 2022. We appreciate Rich Gerber's prompt responses and support whenever we request any fix or adding new functions. It has been an enormous privilege for us to see the scientific advances that will be presented at this conference. Congratulations to all authors!

We hope you will enjoy AACL-IJCNLP 2022, and look forward to seeing many of you online!

AACL-IJCNLP 2020 Program Committee Co-Chairs
Heng Ji (University of Illinois Urbana-Champaign and Amazon Scholar)
Yang Liu (Tsinghua University)
Sujian Li (Peking University)

Preface by the Local Chair

Since winning the bid for organising AACL-IJCNLP 2022 conference in Taiwan, the local team has worked hard to get subsidies from Ministry of Science and Technology, Ministry of Education, Bureau of Foreign Trade, and National Central University, Taiwan. We also planned to co-host AACL-IJCNLP 2022 with ROCLING 2022, the annual meeting of the Association for Computational Linguistics of Chinese Language Processing in Taiwan. We, Yung-Chun Chang, Kuan-Yu (Menphis) Chen and I, envisioned that even if only half the registrants can come to Taiwan due to COVID-19, the conference will still be lively with ROCLING participants.

Even at the end of June, we remained optimistic that a hybrid conference would be possible. However, Taiwan's border control were not lifted and passengers entering Taiwan still needed to be quarantined for three plus four days after August, which will deter most international participants. Thus, we had to adopt a purely online mode at last.

It was a great experience to co-host the AACL-IJCNLP 2022 conference with the international team. On behalf of the local organising team: Yung-Chun Chang, Kuan-Yu (Menphis) Chen, Hsiu-Min Chuang, Min-Yuh Day, Hen-Hsen Huang, Lun-Wei Ku, Wen-Hsiang Lu, Tzong-Han Tsai, and Jheng-Long Wu, we would like to thank our general chair, Yulan He, program co-chairs, Heng Ji, Yang Liu, Sujian Li, and the international team. Yulan's leadership and the international team made the conference go smoothly. Without you, it would be impossible to accomplish so many tasks. I also learned a lot from it. Hope we can meet physically in the near future.

AACL-IJCNLP 2022 Local Chair
Chia-Hui Chang (National Central University)

Organizing Committee

General Chair
Yulan He, King's College London, UK

Program Committee Co-Chairs
Heng Ji, Unversity of Illinois at Urbana-Champaign, USA
Yang Liu, Tsinghua University, China
Sujian Li, Peking Unversity, China

Local Organisation Chair
Chia-Hui Chang, National Central University, Taiwan

Workshop Co-Chairs
Soujanya Poria, Singapore University of technology and Design, Singapore
Chenghua Lin, University of Sheffield, UK

Tutorial Co-Chairs
Miguel A. Alonso, Universidade da Coruña, Spain
Zhongyu Wei, Fudan University, China

Demo Co-Chairs
Wray Buntine, VinUniversity, Vietnam
Maria Liakata, Queen Maty University of London, UK

Student Research Workshop Co-Chairs
Hanqi Yan, University of Warwick, UK
Zonghan Yang, Tisnghua University, China

Student Research Workshop Faculty Co-Advisors
Sebastian Ruder, DeepMind, Uk
Xiaojun Wan, Peking University, China

Publication Co-Chairs
Min-Yuh Day, National Taipei University, Taiwan
Hen-Hsen Huang, Academia Sinica, Taiwan
Jheng-Long Wu, Soochow University, Taiwan

Publicity Co-Chairs
Pengfei Liu, Carnegie Mellon University, USA
Ruifeng Xu, Harbin Institute of Technology, Shenzhen, China
Garbriele Pergola, University of Warwick, UK

Diversity & Inclusion Co-Chairs

Ruihong Huang, Texas A&M University, USA
Jing Li, Hong Kong Polytechnic University, China

Financial Chair

Lun-Wei Ku, Academia Sinca, Taiwan

Local Arrangement Chair

Kuan-Yu (Menphis) Chen, National Taiwan University of Science and Technology, Taiwan

Online Conference Coordinator

Richard Tzong-Han Tsai, National Central University, Taiwan

Sponsorship Co-ordinators

Wen-Hsiang Lu, National Chiao Tung University, Taiwan
Hiroya Takamura, Tokyo Institute of Technology, Japan
Deyi Xiong, Tianjin University, China

Webmaster

Yung-Chun Chang, Taipei Medical University, Taiwan
Miguel Arana-Catania, University of Warwick, UK

Communication Chairs

Xingwei Tan, University of Warwick, UK
Zheng Fang, University of Warwick, UK
Jiazheng Li, University of Warwick, UK

Special Theme co-chairs

Mona Diab, Facebook AI, USA
Isabelle Augenstein, University of Copenhagen, Denmark

Program Committee

Program Committee Co-chairs
Heng Ji, University of Illinois at Urbana-Champaign, USA
Sujian Li, Peking University, China
Yang Liu, Tsinghua University, China

Computational Social Science and Cultural Analytics
Senior Area Chairs: Chenhao Tan, Binyang Li
Area Chairs: Kenny Joseph, Fei Li, Xu Tong

Dialogue and Interactive Systems
Senior Area Chairs: Mahdi Namzifar, Spandana Gella
Area Chairs: Andrea Madotto, Yi-Chia Wang, Saab Mansour, Lili Mou, Saleh Soltan

Discourse and Pragmatics
Senior Area Chairs: Vincent Ng, Yang Liu
Area Chairs: Hen-Hsen Huang, Naoya Inoue, Sharid Loáiciga

Generation
Senior Area Chairs: Meng Jiang, Nanyun Peng, Victoria Lin
Area Chairs: Qingbao Huang, Lianhui Qin, Chenguang Zhu

Information Extraction
Senior Area Chairs: Marius Pasca, Radu Florian
Area Chairs: Qiang Ning, Minjoon Seo

Information Retrieval and Text Mining
Senior Area Chairs: Jing Jiang, Scott Wen-tau Yih, Yixin Cao
Area Chairs: Xu Chen, Muhao Chen, Xiang Wang, Weinan Zhang, Fuli Feng

Interpretability and Analysis of Models for NLP
Senior Area Chairs: Xipeng Qiu, Kevin Duh
Area Chairs: Jasmijn Bastings, Hassan Sajjad, Baotian Hu

Language Modeling
Senior Area Chairs: Han Zhao, Lena Voita
Area Chairs: Ilia Kulikov, Marjan Ghazvininejad, Wenhu Chen

Machine Learning for NLP
Senior Area Chairs: William Wang , Zhiting Hu, Bo Li
Area Chairs: Zichao Yang, Hao Peng, Xin Eric Wang, Boxin Wang, Kai-Wei Chang

Machine Translation and Multilinguality
Senior Area Chairs: Fei Huang, Yang Feng, Sid Patwardhan
Area Chairs: Boxing Chen, Jun Xie, Weihua Luo, Kehai Chen, Junhui Li, Marta R. Costa-jussà

NLP Applications
Senior Area Chairs: Deyi Xiong, Preslav Nakov, Tao Ge
Area Chairs: Zhouhan Lin, Lei Sha, Karin Verspoor, Christian Hardmeier, Yoshi Suhara

Phonology, Morphology, and Word Segmentation
Senior Area Chairs: Mark Hasegawa-Johnson, Peng Li
Area Chairs: Hai Zhao, Sakriani Sakti, Yan Song, Suma Bhat

Question Answering
Senior Area Chairs: Avi Sil , Dian Yu
Area Chairs: Mo Yu, Kai Sun, Jing Liu, Yiming Cui, Jaydeep Sen, Qiang Ning

Resources and Evaluation
Senior Area Chairs: Joel Tetreault, Masayuki Asahara
Area Chairs: Mamoru Komachi, Courtney Napoles, Anne Lauscher, Sudha Rao

Semantics
Senior Area Chairs: Jonathan May, Wenbin Jiang
Area Chairs: Zheng Lin, Meishan Zhang, Mingxuan Wang, Zhiyang Teng

Sentiment Analysis, Stylistic Analysis, and Argument Mining
Senior Area Chairs: Shuai Wang, Alexandra Balahur
Area Chairs: Rui Xia, Serena Villata, Lun-Wei Ku, Ruifeng Xu

Speech and Multimodality Processing
Senior Area Chairs: Nancy Chen, JiaJun Zhang
Area Chairs: Hung Le, Hungyi Lee, Hanwang Zhang, Florian Metz, Jing Liu, Haoran Li, Tianzhu Zhang

Summarization
Senior Area Chairs: Ziqiang Cao, Fei Liu
Area Chairs: Wenhao Wu, Ruifeng Yuan

Syntax: Tagging, Chunking and Parsing
Senior Area Chairs: Barbara Plank, Kewei Tu
Area Chairs: Carlos Gómez-Rodríguez, Joakim Nivre, Yusuke Miyao

Theme: "Fairness in Natural Language Processing"
Senior Area Chairs: Margaret Mitchell, Hal Daumé III
Area Chairs: Su Lin Blodgett, Emily Dinan, Kai-Wei Chang, Kellie Webster, Marta R. Costa-jussà, Timothy Baldwin, Zeerak Talat, Tanmoy Chakraborty, Yun-Nung Chen

Linguistic diversity
Senior Area Chairs: Steven Bird, Constantine Lignos
Area Chairs: Alexis Palmer, Antonios Anastasopoulos

Reviewers

Sadaf Abdul Rauf, Sallam Abualhaija, Piush Aggarwal, Chunhui Ai, Akiko Aizawa, Mohammad Akbari, Md. Shad Akhtar, Ahmad Al Sallab, Fahad AlGhamdi, Bashar Alhafni, Hamed Alhoori, Ahmed Ali, Hend Al-Khalifa, Hussein Al-Olimat, Miguel A. Alonso, Shehzadi Ambreen, Haozhe An, Jisun An, Antonios Anastasopoulos, M. Hidayath Ansari, Rahul Aralikatte, Yuki Arase, Fawaz Arfaj, Arturo Argueta, Arnav Arora, Masayuki Asahara, Aitziber Atutxa Salazar, Isabelle Augenstein, Lukasz Augustyniak, Abhijeet Awasthi, Parul Awasthy, Fahima Ayub Khan

NGUYEN BACH, Xuefeng Bai, JinYeong Bak, Alexandra Balahur, Timothy Baldwin, Ramy Baly, Ritwik Banerjee, rong bao, Mohamad Hardyman Barawi, Maria Barrett, Christine Basta, Mohaddeseh Bastan, Jasmijn Bastings, Lee Becker, Emily M. Bender, Gábor Berend, Sabine Bergler, Gabriel Bernier-Colborne, Thales Bertaglia, Dario Bertero, Chandra Bhagavatula, Suma Bhat, Parminder Bhatia, Arnab Bhattacharya, Sudha Bhingardive, Chris Biemann, Yi Bin, Steven Bird, Debmalya Biswas, Johanna Björklund, Nate Blaylock, Su Lin Blodgett, Michael Bloodgood, Victoria Bobicev, Sravan Bodapati, Nadjet Bouayad-Agha, Florian Boudin, Pierrette Bouillon, Zied Bouraoui, Siddhartha Brahma, Ana Brassard, Wray Buntine

José G. C. de Souza, Aoife Cahill, Deng Cai, Agostina Calabrese, Chris Callison-Burch, John Calvo Martinez, William Campbell, Shuyang Cao, Yang Trista Cao, Yixin Cao, Ziqiang Cao, Spencer Caplan, Giovanni Cassani, Taylor Cassidy, Damir Cavar, Mauro Cettolo, Joyce Chai, Tanmoy Chakraborty, Yllias Chali, Hou Pong Chan, Ashis Chanda, Senthil Chandramohan, Kai-Wei Chang, Rochana Chaturvedi, Jiahao Chen, John Chen, Hsin-Hsi Chen, Xiaoli Chen, Zhousi Chen, Xiang Chen, Qian Chen, Luoxin Chen, Chung-Chi Chen, Kai Chen, Yun-Nung Chen, Yue Chen, Qiang Chen, Fuxiang Chen, Xinchi Chen, Kuan-Yu Chen, Boxing Chen, Nancy Chen, Xu Chen, Muhao Chen, Wenhu Chen, Kehai Chen, Dhivya Chinnappa, Luis Chiruzzo, Hyundong Cho, Eleanor Chodroff, KEY-SUN CHOI, Monojit Choudhury, Chenhui Chu, Hsiu-Min Chuang, Jin-Woo Chung, Abu Nowshed Chy, Elizabeth Clark, Marta R. Costa-juss, Josep Crego, Alina Maria Cristea, Yiming Cui, Rossana Cunha

Daniel Dakota, Ankit Dangi, Falavigna Daniele, Aswarth Abhilash Dara, Avisha Das, Sarthak Dash, Pradeep Dasigi, Vidas Daudaravicius, Hal Daumé III, Gaël de Chalendar, Renato De Mori, Mathieu Dehouck, Luciano Del Corro, Vera Demberg, Michael Denkowski, Sunipa Dev, Chris Develder, Kuntal Dey, Jwala Dhamala, Kaustubh Dhole, Mona Diab, Emily Dinan, Haibo Ding, Chenchen Ding, Nemanja Djuric, Simon Dobnik, Tobias Domhan, Miguel Domingo, Daxiang Dong, Li Dong, Shuyan Dong, Qianqian Dong, Zi-Yi Dou, Rotem Dror, Aleksandr Drozd, Yuhao Du, Cunxiao Du, Junwen Duan, Pablo Duboue, Kevin Duh, Jonathan Dunn

Hiroshi Echizen'ya, Sauleh Eetemadi, Steffen Eger, Ismail El Maarouf, Akiko Eriguchi, Liana Ermakova, Andrea Esuli, Saad Ezzini

Marzieh Fadaee, Wei Fan, Michael Färber, Chen Feiyang, Fuli Feng, Yang Feng, Paulo Fernandes, Daniel Fernández-González, Elisabetta Fersini, Mauajama Firdaus, Margaret Fleck, Radu Florian, Karën Fort, Thomas François, Dayne Freitag, Jesse Freitas, Peng Fu, Atsushi Fujita

Byron Galbraith, Björn Gambäck, Leilei Gan, Xibin Gao, Wei Gao, Yuze Gao, Yang Gao, Utpal Garain, Miguel Ángel García-Cumbreras, Guillermo Garrido, Susan Gauch, Tao Ge, Spandana Gella, Debela Gemechu, Carlos Gemmell, lei geng, Marjan Ghazvininejad, Kripabandhu Ghosh, Michael Giancola, Jose Manuel Gomez-Perez, Carlos Gómez-Rodríguez, Samuel González-López, Jesús González-Rubio, Colin Gordon, Isao Goto, Navita Goyal, Natalia Grabar, Floriana Grasso, Eleni Gregoromichelaki, Shuhao Gu, Yi Guan, Tunga Güngör, Peiming Guo, Vivek Gupta

Udo Hahn, Zhen Hai, Felix Hamborg, Michael Hammond, Na-Rae Han, Xudong Han, Jie Hao, Yongchang Hao, Junheng Hao, Rejwanul Haque, Christian Hardmeier, John Harvill, Sadid A. Hasan, Maram Hasanain, Mark Hasegawa-Johnson, Hiroaki Hayashi, Yoshihiko Hayashi, Shirley Anugrah Hayati, Bin He, Jie He, Delia Irazú Hernández Farías, Tsutomu Hirao, Tosho Hirasawa, Keikichi Hirose, Nora Hollenstein,

Ales Horak, Dirk Hovy, Shu-Kai Hsieh, Chan-Jan Hsu, Yi-Li Hsu, Po Hu, Qinmin Vivian Hu, Huang Hu, han hu, zhiyuan hu, Pengwei Hu, Zhiting Hu, Baotian Hu, Hang Hua, Kaiyu Huang, Jiangping Huang, Chung-Chi Huang, Fei Huang, Hen-Hsen Huang, Qingbao Huang, Muhammad Humayoun

Ebuka Ibeke, Adrian Iftene, Filip Ilievski, Dmitry Ilvovsky, Koji Inoue, Naoya Inoue, Takashi Inui, Hitoshi Isahara, Etsuko Ishii, Hayate Iso, Julia Ive

Mona Jalal, Abhik Jana, Hyeju Jang, Zongcheng Ji, Xiaowen Ji, Yuxiang Jia, Lavender Jiang, Chengyue Jiang, Jyun-Yu Jiang, Shuoran Jiang, Zhuoxuan Jiang, Meng Jiang, Jing Jiang, Jing Jiang, Wenbin Jiang, Zhanming Jie, Lifeng Jin, Baoyu Jing, Kristiina Jokinen, Gareth Jones, Kenneth Joseph, Dhanya Jothimani

Vimal Kumar K, Besim Kabashi, Indika Kahanda, Tomoyuki Kajiwara, Surya Kallumadi, Lis Kanashiro Pereira, Diptesh Kanojia, Mladen Karan, Börje Karlsson, Shubhra Kanti Karmaker, Sanjeev Kumar Karn, Omid Kashefi, Daisuke Kawahara, arefeh kazemi, Casey Kennington, Katia Lida Kermanidis, Salam Khalifa, Halil Kilicoglu, Sunghwan Mac Kim, Hwichan Kim, David King, Tracy Holloway King, Julien Kloetzer, Jordan Kodner, Mamoru Komachi, Kanako Komiya, Myoung-Wan Koo, Mikhail Kopotev, Valia Kordoni, Yannis Korkontzelos, Katsunori Kotani, Venelin Kovatchev, Pavel Kral, Satyapriya Krishna, Nikhil Krishnaswamy, Lun-Wei Ku, Roland Kuhn, Ilia Kulikov, Saurabh Kulshreshtha, Murathan Kurfalı, Haewoon Kwak

Hemank Lamba, Phillippe Langlais, Ekaterina Lapshinova-Koltunski, Stefan Larson, Anne Lauscher, Alberto Lavelli, Julia Lavid-López, Phong Le, Hung Le, Claudia Leacock, Young-Suk Lee, Lung-Hao Lee, Roy Ka-Wei Lee, Hung-yi Lee, Gurpreet Lehal, Yang Lei, Yikun Lei, João Leite, Alessandro Lenci, Yves Lepage, Tomer Levinboim, Gina-Anne Levow, Xiang Li, Yanyang Li, Zhi Li, Si Li, Fei Li, Bangzheng Li, Jinpeng Li, Haibo Li, Liangyou Li, Yitong Li, Zuchao Li, Juan Li, Sheng Li, Moxin Li, mingda Li, Xiaonan Li, Jiaqi Li, Junyi Li, Weikang Li, Dongfang Li, Tao Li, Yuan Li, Binyang Li, Bo Li, Shuangyin Li, Junhui Li, Baoli LI, Peng Li, Haoran Li, Vladislav Lialin, Chao-Chun Liang, Jindřich Libovický, Mohamed Lichouri, Constantine Lignos, ZhiChao Lin, Chu-Cheng Lin, Xi Victoria Lin, Zhouhan Lin, Zheng Lin, Yuan Ling, Marina Litvak, Ting Liu, Yiqun Liu, Bang Liu, Jiangming Liu, Han Liu, Maofu Liu, Zhuang Liu, Zitao Liu, Nelson F. Liu, Tengxiao Liu, Zhiyuan Liu, Qun Liu, Dexi Liu, Changsong Liu, Fenglin Liu, Guangyi Liu, Yue Liu, Yongbin Liu, Yang Liu, Tianyi Liu, Fei Liu, Jing Liu, Jing Liu, Sharid Loáiciga, Robert L Logan IV, Usha Lokala, Yunfei Long, Henrique Lopes Cardoso, Jaime Lorenzo-Trueba, Natalia Loukachevitch, Ismini Lourentzou, Yanbin Lu, Sidi Lu, Di Lu, Yichao Lu, Ling Luo, Wencan Luo, Weihua Luo, qi Lv

Xuezhe Ma, Liqun Ma, Jing Ma, Zhengrui Ma, Long-Long Ma, Nishtha Madaan, Aman Madaan, Andrea Madotto, Peter Makarov, Andreas Maletti, Valentin Malykh, Saab Mansour, Jianguo Mao, Mitchell Marcus, Edison Marrese-Taylor, Eugenio Martínez-Cámara, Bruno Martins, David Martins de Matos, Takuya Matsuzaki, Jonathan May, Sahisnu Mazumder, Stephen McGregor, Bridget McInnes, Ninareh Mehrabi, Rui Meng, Fanchao Meng, Kourosh Meshgi, Florian Metze, Ivan Vladimir Meza Ruiz, Meryem M'hamdi, Haitao Mi, Stuart Middleton, Margot Mieskes, Claudiu Mihăilă, Erxue Min, Koji Mineshima, SeyedAbolghasem Mirroshandel, Abhijit Mishra, Margaret Mitchell, Sudip Mittal, Yusuke Miyao, Daniela Moctezuma, Ashutosh Modi, Alaa Mohasseb, Diego Molla, Manuel Montes, Hajime Morita, Larry Moss, Lili Mou, Ahmed Mourad, Diego Moussallem, Pramod Kaushik Mudrakarta, Matthew Mulholland, Emir Munoz, Saliha Muradoglu, Yugo Murawaki

Masaaki Nagata, Tetsuji Nakagawa, Preslav Nakov, Mahdi Namazifar, Courtney Napoles, Diane Napolitano, Vincent Ng, Axel-Cyrille Ngonga Ngomo, Kiet Nguyen, Nhung Nguyen, Jian Ni, Eric Nichols, Irina Nikishina, Qiang Ning, Takashi Ninomiya, Masaaki Nishino, Sergiu Nisioi, Tong Niu, Joakim Nivre, Pierre Nugues

Tim Oates, Alexander O'Connor, Maciej Ogrodniczuk, Tsuyoshi Okita, Oleg Okun, Antoni Oliver, Ethel Ong, Abigail Oppong, Naoki Otani, Hiroki Ouchi

Deepak P, Avinesh P.V.S, Ankur Padia, Chester Palen-Michel, Alexis Palmer, Alessio Palmero Aprosio, Youcheng Pan, Yi-Cheng Pan, Nikos Papasarantopoulos, Ivandré Paraboni, Kunwoo Park, Lucy Park, Marius Pasca, Vaishnavi Patil, Siddharth Patwardhan, Sarah Payne, Hengzhi Pei, Wei Peng, Nanyun Peng, Hao Peng, Gerald Penn, Gabriele Pergola, Scott Piao, Flammie Pirinen, Barbara Plank, Andrei Popescu-Belis, Fred Popowich, Christopher Potts, Morteza Pourreza Shahri, Animesh Prasad, Emily Prud'hommeaux

Chen Qian, Lianhui Qin, Xinying Qiu, Long Qiu, Xipeng Qiu, Chen Qu

Alexandre Rademaker, Sunny Rai, Taraka Rama, Lakshmi Ramachandran, Shihao Ran, Surangika Ranathunga, Peter A. Rankel, Sudha Rao, Ari Rappoport, Traian Rebedea, Hanumant Redkar, Navid Rekabsaz, Yuqi Ren, Corentin Ribeyre, Tharathorn Rimchala, Annette Rios, Anthony Rios, Paul Rodrigues, Lina M. Rojas Barahona, Andrew Rosenberg, Sophie Rosset, Bryan Routledge, Irene Russo

Fatiha Sadat, Sylvie Saget, Monjoy Saha, Saurav Sahay, Sunil Kumar Sahu, Hassan Sajjad, Sakriani Sakti, Elizabeth Salesky, Jonne Saleva, Avneesh Saluja, Germán Sanchis-Trilles, Hugo Sanjurjo-González, Ananth Sankar, Diana Santos, Bishal Santra, Soumya Sanyal, Naomi Saphra, Kamal Sarkar, Anoop Sarkar, Shota Sasaki, Felix Sasaki, Ryohei Sasano, Asad Sayeed, Shigehiko Schamoni, Helmut Schmid, William Schuler, Lane Schwartz, Nasredine Semmar, Gregory Senay, Minjoon Seo, Lei Sha, Swair Shah, Cory Shain, Mingyue Shang, Yunfan Shao, Soumya Sharma, Ravi Shekhar, Tianxiao Shen, Bowen Shen, Tianhao Shen, Yuming Shen, Aili Shen, Michael Sheng, Tian Shi, Yangyang Shi, xiaodong shi, Tomohide Shibata, Yutaro Shigeto, Takahiro Shinozaki, Raphael Shu, Chenglei Si, Maryam Siahbani, Avi Sil, Carina Silberer, Diego Silva, Stefano Silvestri, Patrick Simianer, Dan Simonson, Edwin Simpson, Keshav Singh, Sahib Singh, Amando Jr. Singun, Olivier Siohan, Kevin Small, Luca Soldaini, Saleh Soltan, Xingyi Song, Yan Song, Dongjin Song, Siqi Song, Yan Song, Anna Sotnikova, Marlo Souza, Felix Stahlberg, Efstathios Stamatatos, Shane Steinert-Threlkeld, Pontus Stenetorp, Kristina Striegnitz, Keh-Yih Su, Aparna Subramanian, Katsuhito Sudoh, Yoshi Suhara, Derwin Suhartono, Ming Sun, Shichao Sun, Kai Sun

Zeerak Talat, George Tambouratzis, Akihiro Tamura, Fei Tan, Bowen Tan, Chenhao Tan, Yuka Tateisi, Marta Tatu, Tatiane Tavares, Selma Tekir, Irina Temnikova, Zhiyang Teng, Joel Tetreault, Krishnaprasad Thirunarayan, Yufei Tian, Erik Tjong Kim Sang, Takenobu Tokunaga, Marwan Torki, Samia Touileb, Trang Tran, Aashka Trivedi, Yuen-Hsien Tseng, Kewei Tu

Kiyotaka Uchimoto, L. Alfonso Ureña-López, Masao Utiyama

Rob van der Goot, Oskar van der Wal, Clara Vania, Shikhar Vashishth, Rakesh Verma, Karin Verspoor, David Vilar, Jesús Vilares, Martin Villalba, Serena Villata, Esau Villatoro-Tello, Elena Voita, Thuy Vu, Henning Wachsmuth

Xinhao Wang, Han Wang, Junfeng Wang, Haoyu Wang, Hongfei Wang, Qian Wang, Xin Wang, Yanshan Wang, Ping Wang, Hsin-Min Wang, Lei Wang, zili Wang, Rui Wang, Hao Wang, Tong Wang, Weiyue Wang, Wei Wang, Wei Wang, Jin Wang, Xintong Wang, Yufei Wang, Zhaowei Wang, Xiaojie WANG, Guangtao Wang, Jianzong Wang, Xuezhi Wang, Hao Wang, Wenqi Wang, William Yang Wang, Shuai Wang, Yi-Chia Wang, Yi-Chia Wang, Xiang Wang, Xin Wang, Boxin Wang, Mingxuan Wang, Shuo Wang, Xiting Wang, Koichiro Watanabe, Taro Watanabe, Shinji Watanabe, Roger Wattenhofer, Kellie Webster, Feng Wei, Xiangpeng Wei, Charles Welch, Simon Wells, Derry Tanti Wijaya, Gijs Wijnholds, Rodrigo Wilkens, Adina Williams, Jennifer Williams, Tak-sum Wong, Kam-Fai Wong, Alina Wróblewska, Zhiyong Wu, Xianchao Wu, Chien-Sheng Wu, Fangzhao Wu, Stephen Wu, Ji Wu, Mengyue Wu, Wenhao Wu

Heming Xia, Rui Xia, Ruicheng Xian, Min Xiao, Yuqing Xie, Yiqing Xie, Jun Xie, Yujie Xing, Zhenchang Xing, Chao Xiong, Deyi Xiong, Chejian Xu, Benfeng Xu, Yueshen Xu, Song Xu, Canwen Xu, Qiongkai Xu, Hongfei Xu, Ruifeng Xu, Dongkuan Xu, Tong Xu

Shuntaro Yada, Ming Yan, Xu Yan, Muqiao Yang, Longfei Yang, Haiqin Yang, Eugene Yang, Wei Yang, Ze Yang, Erguang Yang, Ziqing Yang, Zichao Yang, Roman Yangarber, Tae Yano, Wenlin Yao, Kaisheng Yao, Wen-tau Yih, Lang Yin, Seunghyun Yoon, Masaharu Yoshioka, Liang-Chih Yu, Heng Yu, Dian Yu, Mo Yu, Zhaoquan Yuan, Ruifeng Yuan, Chuan Yue, Frances Yung

Fadi Zaraket, Zhiyuan Zeng, Xingshan Zeng, Qingcheng Zeng, Torsten Zesch, Deniz Zeyrek, Shuang (Sophie) Zhai, Yuxiang Zhang, Zeyu Zhang, Zizheng Zhang, Xiaohan Zhang, Chengzhi Zhang, Jingsen Zhang, Ningyu Zhang, Guangwei Zhang, Dongyu Zhang, Zhuosheng Zhang, Ke Zhang, Biao Zhang, Jinnian Zhang, Chenwei Zhang, Shuai Zhang, Jiajun Zhang, Wei-Nan Zhang, Meishan Zhang, Hanwang Zhang, tianzhu zhang, Hai Zhao, Chao Zhao, Jieyu Zhao, Xiaobing Zhao, Dongyan Zhao, Lin Zhao, Sendong Zhao, Han Zhao, Rui Zheng, Xiaoqing Zheng, Wenxuan Zhou, Qiang Zhou, Jingbo Zhou, Lina Zhou, Su Zhu, Junnan Zhu, Shaolin Zhu, Chenguang Zhu, Caleb Ziems, Michael Zock, Bowei Zou, Vilém Zouhar, Arkaitz Zubiaga, Ingrid Zukerman

Table of Contents

Efficient Entity Embedding Construction from Type Knowledge for BERT

Yukun Feng[1,*], **Amir Fayazi**[2], **Abhinav Rastogi**[2], **Manabu Okumura**[1]
[1]Tokyo Institute of Technology
[2]Google Research
{yukun,oku}@lr.pi.titech.ac.jp
{amiraf,abhirast}@google.com

Abstract

Recent work has shown advantages of incorporating knowledge graphs (KGs) into BERT (Devlin et al., 2019) for various NLP tasks. One common way is to feed entity embeddings as an additional input during pre-training. There are two limitations to such a method. First, to train the entity embeddings to include rich information of factual knowledge, it typically requires access to the entire KG. This is challenging for KGs with daily changes (e.g., Wikidata). Second, it requires a large scale pre-training corpus with entity annotations and high computational cost during pre-training. In this work, we efficiently construct entity embeddings only from the type knowledge, that does not require access to the entire KG. Although the entity embeddings contain only local information, they perform very well when combined with context. Furthermore, we show that our entity embeddings, constructed from BERT's input embeddings, can be directly incorporated into the fine-tuning phase without requiring any specialized pre-training. In addition, these entity embeddings can also be constructed on the fly without requiring a large memory footprint to store them. Finally, we propose task-specific models that incorporate our entity embeddings for entity linking, entity typing, and relation classification. Experiments show that our models have comparable or superior performance to existing models while being more resource efficient.

1 Introduction

Many studies have attempted to enhance pre-trained language models with knowledge such as ERNIE (Zhang et al., 2019), KnowBert (Peters et al., 2019), K-ADAPTER (Wang et al., 2020), E-BERT (Poerner et al., 2020), and KEPLER (Wang et al., 2021). Among them, ERNIE, KnowBert, E-BERT, and KEPLER are typical work that do so by incorporating entity embeddings. The entity embeddings are usually trained by methods that model the global graph structure, such as TransE (Bordes et al., 2013a) used in ERNIE and TuckER (Balažević et al., 2019) used in KnowBert. These entity-incorporated pre-trained language models have shown to be powerful on various natural language processing (NLP) tasks, such as entity linking, entity typing, and relation classification.

In this paper, we investigate whether we can construct entity embeddings by considering only local entity features. This is motivated by the observation that the context itself usually provides good information for the right answer. A number of examples are shown in Table 1. Instead of heavily relying on entity embeddings that encode global information, we simply tell the model what these entities are by using local features to help the model infer the answer from the context more easily. For example, if we can know 'Cartí Sugtupu' is a place in the relation classification example in Table 1, the task may be easier. To utilize such information for an entity, we select entity-type knowledge from Wikidata as a local feature for the entity. Specifically, we propose to encode the labels of neighboring nodes of the entity connected through *instance_of* edges in Wikidata. Figure 1 shows an example. These labels can informatively tell the entity type and are usually short, which enables them to be efficiently encoded by simple methods, that we mention later.

One big advantage of utilizing only local features of entities is that we can update our entity embeddings very fast once the knowledge graph (KG) is changed, which is a desirable feature for KGs with rapid updates. We can construct the entity embeddings even on the fly to significantly reduce memory consumption and parameters since a number of tasks (e.g., entity linking) easily involve millions of entities. A disadvantage is that it is hard to infer the answer if large amounts of information are missing. For example, the LAnguage Model Analysis (LAMA) task (Petroni et al., 2019) re-

*Work was extended after the internship with Google.

Findings of the Association for Computational Linguistics: AACL-IJCNLP 2022, pages 1–10
November 20–23, 2022.

quires a [MASK] placeholder in the given sentence "Sullivan was born in Chippewa Falls, Wisconsin in [MASK]" to be filled. The type knowledge may not be able to answer this question. Thus, we do not focus on such tasks. Instead, we apply our method on several typical entity-focused tasks, which were also chosen by related work.

To construct the entity embeddings, we simply average BERT's WordPiece embeddings from the type label of the entity as there are only 2.8 or 2.96 WordPiece tokens on average per label depending on our tasks. Thus, our method is very fast and can be used to construct the entity embeddings on the fly without much cost to save memory and reduce parameters. For example, E-BERT requires six hours to train its entity embeddings, while our method takes only about 1 minute to prepare the entity embeddings for our downstream tasks. The trained entity embeddings of E-BERT take up around 30GB in size[1]. Thus, storing these embeddings requires a large memory footprint, and the size continues to grow linearly if new entities are added. However, our method does not require such extra space for entity embeddings.

For incorporation, previous work incorporates their entity embeddings during both fine-tuning and pre-training (ERNIE and KnowBert). However, pre-training language models is a cumbersome and resource-intensive task. We show simply incorporating our entity embeddings during fine-tuning without any pre-training works well. One reason may be that these entity embeddings are directly constructed through averaging BERT's WordPiece embeddings, so that they look like BERT's WordPiece embeddings, which may be helpful for incorporation for BERT.

Finally, we propose task-specific models to incorporate our entity embeddings[2]. For entity linking, we propose a model that incorporates entity embeddings into the output; for entity typing and relation classification, the proposed model incorporates entity embeddings into the input. We show that our entity embeddings and incorporation method are simple and can achieve comparable or superior performance to existing methods on entity linking, entity typing, and relation classification. The contribution of this work can be summarized as follows:

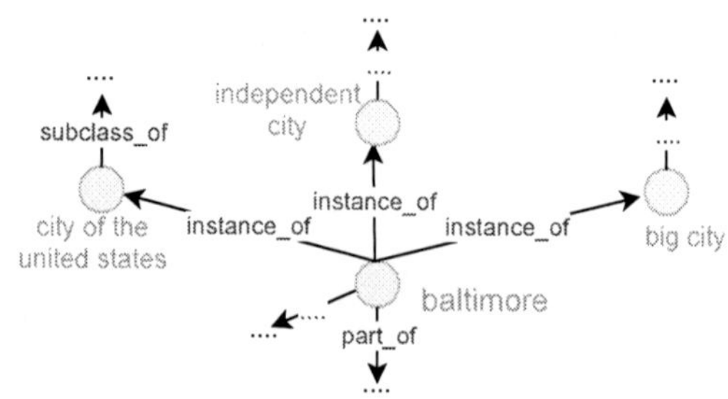

Figure 1: An example of connected entity nodes from Wikidata. The circles are entity nodes with blue texts as their labels. We encode the labels of the neighboring nodes of "baltimore" connected through *instance_of* edges to construct its entity embedding.

- We propose an efficient method to construct entity embeddings that are particularly a good fit for BERT, and they work well without any pre-training step during incorporation.
- Our entity embeddings can be constructed on the fly for BERT. We do not need a large memory footprint to store entity embeddings, which is often required by other work.
- We propose task-specific models to incorporate our entity embeddings for entity linking, entity typing and relation classification.

2 Related Work

ERNIE (Zhang et al., 2019), KnowBert (Peters et al., 2019), E-BERT (Poerner et al., 2020), and our model are all based on Google $\text{BERT}_{\text{BASE}}$ and aim to incorporate entity embeddings into them. The main differences between the models are the methods for constructing entity embeddings and incorporating them.

For entity embeddings, ERNIE uses the one trained on Wikidata by TransE (Bordes et al., 2013b). KnowBert uses TuckER (Balazevic et al., 2019) embeddings, and E-BERT incorporates Wikipedia2Vec entity embeddings (Yamada et al., 2016).These entity embeddings were trained with consideration for a KG structure and have to be trained again if new updates need to be incorporated from KGs, which further requires additional pre-training of ERNIE and KnowBert. When only local features are used to construct the entity embeddings, the aforementioned issues can be avoided. In addition, our entity embeddings are simply obtained by averaging BERT WordPiece embeddings and can be constructed on the fly to save a large memory footprint usually required by

[1]This size here is from the downloaded embeddings provided by the author.

[2]Our code is available at `https://github.com/yukunfeng/efficient_bert_ent_emb`

Task	Example	Label
Entity linking	Cricket - **England** beat **Pakistan** by 107 runs in second one-dayer.	England_cricket_team Pakistan_national_cricket_team
Entity typing	GM is a publicly traded company that releases every bit of news **they** have	organization
Relation classification	**Cartí Sugtupu** can be reached by boat from the nearby onshore settlement of Carti and the **Carti Airstrip**.	place_served_by_transport_hub

Table 1: Examples of entity linking, entity typing, and relation classification. The text in bold is the entity of interest. In these examples, we can infer the label from the context.

other work. We found that although our entity embeddings contain only local information, they perform well when combined with context. However, ERNIE, KnowBert or E-BERT are supposed to work better than ours where large amounts of information are missing such as in LAMA task.

For the incorporation, ERNIE and KnowBert both use new encoder layers to feed the entity embeddings, which requires pre-training. In contrast, E-BERT achieves comparable results without pre-training by directly incorporating its entity embeddings into the standard BERT model during task-specific fine-tuning. One proposal from E-BERT is to align the entity and BERT WordPiece embeddings in the same space. To do so, it first trains word and entity embeddings jointly and then learns a linear mapping from word to BERT WordPiece embeddings. The final entity embeddings can be obtained by applying this learned linear mapping so that they look like BERT WordPiece embeddings. This mapping helps improve 4.4 micro F1 score on the test data on entity linking task. To learn this mapping, E-BERT needs to train both word and entity embeddings, which are 30GB in size. Our method for constructing entity embeddings shares the similar spirit, but it is an averaging method from BERT WordPiece embeddings.

K-ADAPTER (Wang et al., 2020) and KEPLER (Wang et al., 2021) are both trained using multi-task learning based on RoBERTa (Liu et al., 2019) in relation classification and knowledge base completion and do not rely on entity embeddings.

Outside the area of incorporating entity embedding into pretrained language model, there are a number of work that propose to use entity types from KGs on various tasks. For example, on entity linking task, some work use entity types together with entity descriptions or entity embedding trained over whole KG (Francis-Landau et al., 2016; Gupta et al., 2017; Gillick et al., 2019; Hou et al., 2020; Tianran et al., 2021). Some work use only entity types on entity linking task (Sun et al., 2015; Le and Titov, 2019; Raiman, 2022). Khosla and Rose (2020) use entity type embeddings for coreference resolution. The main difference between our work with them is that we mainly design our method for constructing entity embedding and our incorporation method for BERT. As introduced before, we simply create entity embeddings from the BERT's internal WordPiece embeddings. When incorporating our entity embeddings into BERT, we also propose a model that makes use of BERT's position embeddings on entity typing and relation classification task (mentioned in Sec. 5.2).

3 Entity Embedding Construction

We take the labels of the neighboring nodes for an entity obtained from Wikidata as local features. Since these labels are usually very short, as shown in Figure 1, we can efficiently obtain label embeddings by averaging WordPiece embeddings in the label. The final entity embeddings are then obtained by averaging the label embeddings. We denote $\mathbf{m}_{ij}$ as the j-th WordPiece embeddings in the i-th label of an entity. The entity embeddings $\mathbf{e}$ are computed as follows:

$$\mathbf{e} = \frac{1}{M}\sum_{i=1}^{M}\frac{1}{N_i}\sum_{j=1}^{N_i}\mathbf{m}_{ij}, \tag{1}$$

where M and N_i are the number of labels and that of WordPiece tokens in the i-th label, respectively. Please note that M and N_i are small in our relation classification task (1.27 and 2.96, respectively, on average). Finally, the generated entity embeddings are updated in the task-specific fine-tuning.

4 Entity Linking

4.1 Task Description

Entity linking (EL) is the task of recognizing named entities and linking them to a knowledge base. In this paper, we focus on an end-to-end EL system that includes detecting the entities and then disambiguating them to the correct entity IDs.

	Train	Dev.	Test
#Tokens	222K	56K	51K
#Gold entities	18454	4778	4778
#Unique generated entities	230K	154K	148K
#Conversion rate	0.8	0.80	0.81

Table 2: Data statistics of AIDA and found unique entities by generator. The conversion rate is the ratio of found entities that we can link to Wikidata.

Following the same setting of E-BERT[3], we use KnowBert's candidate generator to first find all spans that might be potential entities in a sentence. These spans are matched in a precomputed span-entity co-occurrence table (Hoffart et al., 2011) and each span is annotated with linked entity candidate IDs associated with prior probabilities based on frequency. Note that the generator tends to over-generate and most found spans should be rejected according to our observation on the training dataset. Thus, given a span in a sentence, our model needs to learn to reject it or predict the correct one among its candidate IDs in accordance with the context. As with E-BERT, we formulate this task as a classification task where the model needs to classify the given input. The classified labels contain candidate IDs and a rejection label.

4.2 Dataset

We use the AIDA dataset (Hoffart et al., 2011), which was also chosen in related works. The gold named entities in AIDA and spans found by KnowBert's generator are identified with Wikipedia URLs. Due to this reason, we have to convert them to Wikidata IDs to determine the type knowledge of an annotated entity, in which a number are missing during conversion. The statistics of AIDA, found entities by generator, and conversion rates are shown in Table 2.

4.3 Model

Our model is based on $\text{BERT}_{\text{BASE}}$ and the architecture is shown in Figure 2. We describe the incorporation method, modeling, and training hyper-parameters in the following.

4.3.1 Incorporation Method

Given a span from the generator, we denote the embeddings of candidate entities as $\{\mathbf{c}_1, \mathbf{c}_2, ..., \mathbf{c}_N\}$ and corresponding prior probabilities as $\{p_1, p_2, ..., p_N\}$. The entity embeddings are computed by Eq. 1. Since different candidate entities may have the same type (e.g., the type 'country' may contain different entities), the model cannot distinguish these label embeddings in classification if we simply use the entity embeddings as the label embeddings. Note that this is not an issue when incorporating these entity embeddings into the input, as shown later in our entity typing and relation classification tasks, because the surface forms of entities included in the input can help distinguish between each embedding. Thus, to distinguish these label embeddings, we propose to combine the surface forms of entity candidates, which are still local features, and entity embeddings into label embeddings. The embeddings of surface forms of entities are denoted as $\{\mathbf{s}_1, \mathbf{s}_2, ..., \mathbf{s}_N\}$. $\mathbf{s}_i$ is simply computed by averaging the WordPiece embeddings in the surface form, which is the same way as computing our entity embeddings. Since large number of entities are involved in this task as shown in Table 2, we compute $\mathbf{s}_i$ and $\mathbf{c}_i$ both on the fly to save memory and reduce the parameters. This means the gradients will come to the WordPiece embeddings during backpropagation. To combine $\mathbf{s}_i$ and $\mathbf{c}_i$, we use a gate to learn to control the weight between $\mathbf{s}_i$ and $\mathbf{c}_i$, and label embedding $\mathbf{l}_i$ is computed as follows:

$$
\begin{aligned}
g &= \text{sigmoid}(\mathbf{W}\mathbf{c}_i), \\
\mathbf{l}_i &= (1-g) \odot \mathbf{c}_i + g \odot \mathbf{s}_i
\end{aligned} \tag{2}
$$

$\odot$ is element-wise multiplication and $\mathbf{W} \in \mathbb{R}^{d \times d}$ are trainable parameters where d is a BERT dimension. If $\mathbf{c}_i$ is not found during the aforementioned conversion, we only use $\mathbf{s}_i$.

4.3.2 Modeling

We denote the output vector from the BERT encoder at the position of '[ENT]' as $\mathbf{o}_{\text{ENT}}$. The value of the i-th candidate entity before the softmax function is computed as $\mathbf{l}_i^T \mathbf{o}_{\text{ENT}} + b_i$ where b_i is the bias of the i-th entity candidate. To incorporate the prior probabilities in the classification, we set b_i as $\log p_i$ so that the probability will be p_i if no other information is available (i.e., $\mathbf{l}_i^T \mathbf{o}_{\text{ENT}}$ equals zero). The bias of a rejection label will be learned from the training data. We use the standard cross entropy as our loss function.

4.3.3 Hyper-parameters

Since the dataset is quite small as shown in Table 2, we only train for maximum of four epochs, and the

[3]Our code is based on E-BERT, which is available from https://github.com/NPoe/ebert

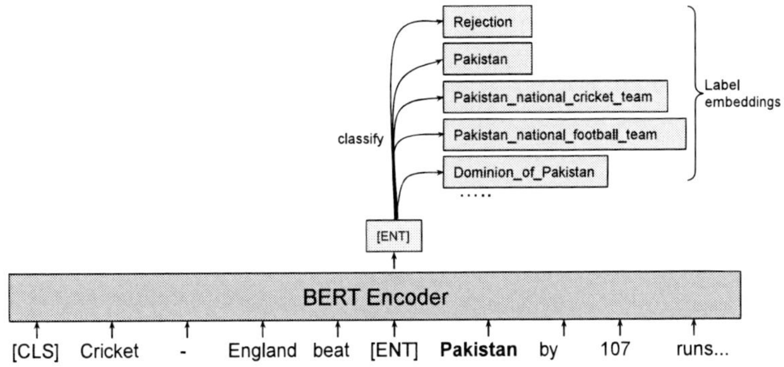

Figure 2: Model architecture for entity linking. The text in bold in the example is the span that the model needs to reject it as a named entity or accept it and link it to the correct entity entry in accordance with the context. A special symbol '[ENT]' is inserted before the span, and the output vector from it will be used for classification.

model with best micro F1 score on the valid dataset is chosen. The batch size is set to 16 and the default AdamW optimizer was used with a linear learning rate scheduler (10% warmup). The learning rate was chosen among {1e-5, 2e-5, 3e-5,} on a valid set.

4.4 Results

The results on the AIDA test set are shown in Table 3. We mainly compare our model with BERT-Random (introduced later), KnowBert and E-BERT as they also focus on incorporating entity embeddings to BERT. Note that we only include end-to-end EL models in this table, and the results are not comparable to ones of disambiguation-only EL models where the golden entity mentions are given.

We used BERT-Random as our baseline, which is the same as our model except that the label embeddings are randomly initialized and trained from scratch. Compared with BERT-Random, our model shows significant improvement, which suggests our proposed label embeddings are effective.

E-BERT incorporates its entity embeddings not only to the output but also to the input. The embedding of its '[ENT]' in the input is computed by averaging all embeddings of candidate entities. We also tried a similar strategy but found no obvious change in our model. Thus, we only focused on the output. In addition, E-BERT uses another strategy that iteratively refines predictions during inference. However, this strategy slows down the inference speed. The results, indicate that the local features work even better than global features used to train entity embeddings in E-BERT. This may suggest that we can utilize local features to

Models	Strong micro-F1	Strong macro-F1
Cao et al. (2021)	83.7	-
Kannan Ravi et al. (2021)	83.1	-
van Hulst et al. (2020)	-	81.3
Broscheit (2019)	79.3	-
Kolitsas et al. (2018)	82.6	82.4
Hoffart et al. (2011)	71.9	72.8
E-BERT (Poerner et al., 2020)	85.0	84.2
KnowBert (Peters et al., 2019)	73.7	-
Our model	**86.3**	**84.4**
BERT-Random	73.3	76.8

Table 3: Results on AIDA test set. BERT-Random use randomly initialized label embeddings trained from scratch.

construct entity embeddings in tasks where the context already contains a lot of information. Please also note that we can only convert around 80% of Wikipedia URLs to Wikidata IDs, and this may limit the performance of our model. Another advantage is that our label embeddings are constructed on the fly and thus save memory and reduce the number of training parameters. Finally, our model and E-BERT achieved the highest strong micro-F1 and macro-F1 scores among all models, indicating it may be a good way to incorporate knowledge through entity embeddings.

5 Entity Typing and Relation Classification

5.1 Task Description

The goal of entity typing is to predict the types of a given entity from its context. Note that it is not necessary that the mention of a given entity is a named entity. For example, the type 'they' is labeled as 'organization' as shown in the example of entity typing in Table 1. The formulation of relation classification is similar with the only difference being that there are two target entities in the sentence. We need to predict the relation of two given target entities together with the context. Thus, the application of our entity embeddings is similar for entity typing and relation classification. We introduce our incorporation method in the following section.

5.2 Incorporation Method

Unlike the EL task where we applied our entity embeddings to the output, we only incorporate entity embeddings to the input for these two tasks. To incorporate the entity embeddings, we propose a method that emphasizes target entities (e.g., in relation classification, there are two entity mentions). Specifically, for all entities, we first sum the embeddings of the entities and the corresponding BERT WordPiece tokens, and then feed them into the BERT model. For target entities, we explicitly insert the entity embeddings into the input of WordPiece token embeddings and make the entity embeddings share the same position embeddings with their corresponding WordPiece token embeddings, as if they are in the same position. Our model architecture is shown in Figure 3. We mathematically describe our method as follows.

We denote the number of WordPiece tokens in a sentence as T, and the i-th WordPiece token embedding, entity embedding, and position embedding as $\mathbf{w}_i$, $\mathbf{e}_i$, and $\mathbf{p}_i$, respectively. As shown in the figure, the entity embedding $\mathbf{e}_i$ is $\mathbf{0}$ if the i-th token is not the start token of an entity. For simplicity, we ignore token type embeddings here, although they are actually used in our model. We first obtain the input $\mathbf{x_i}$ to the BERT encoder by summing the entity embeddings with the other embeddings:

$$\mathbf{x_i} = \mathbf{e}_i + \mathbf{w}_i + \mathbf{p}_i. \quad (3)$$

Since target entities are usually more important than other entities in an entity-centric task, we explicitly insert target entity embeddings that have the same position embeddings as their aligned WordPiece embeddings, as if they are in the same position. For the relation classification task, there are two target entities, and thus the extra inserted inputs are $\mathbf{x_{T+1}}$ and $\mathbf{x_{T+2}}$, which are computed as follows:

$$\begin{aligned} \mathbf{x_{T+1}} &= \mathbf{e}_{k_1} + \mathbf{p}_{k_1}, \\ \mathbf{x_{T+2}} &= \mathbf{e}_{k_2} + \mathbf{p}_{k_2}, \end{aligned} \quad (4)$$

where k_1 and k_2 are the index of the first and second target entities, respectively.

5.3 Experiments

5.3.1 Entity Typing

We chose Open Entity (Choi et al., 2018) to evaluate our model. The dataset has several versions, and we chose the one that has nine general types (e.g., person, location, and object), which is the same as that in previous works. One example from this dataset is shown in Table 1. As previously mentioned, the entity mention in Open Entity is not limited to named entities, and pronoun mentions and common noun expressions are also included. We used a preprocessed version from ERNIE (Zhang et al., 2019). This preprocessed dataset was annotated with mentions of named entities and automatically linked to Wikidata by TAGME (Ferragina and Scaiella, 2010) so that we could find their type knowledge in Wikidata for all entities in Open Entity. We used the same annotated entities as the ones used in ERNIE by keeping the same confidence threshold to filter unreliable entity annotations. The statistics of this dataset are shown in Table 4. Most annotated entities are non-target because the entity mention in Open Entity is not limited to named entities. Our model needs to utilize the context together with the entity annotations to infer the types of the target entity. We can also see the type labels of entities are quite short (only 2.8 word pieces per label), and this may be one reason that our averaging method for constructing entity embeddings works. If the label is long (e.g., becoming a text description), the averaging method might be too simple to encode it. Since the involved entities are not that many, we did not construct the entity embeddings on the fly to speed up the training. That is, the entity embeddings are initialized by Eq. 1 and are updated in the training.

	Train	Dev.	Test
#Instances	2,000	2,000	2,000
#Target entities	122	107	94
#All entities	2573	2511	2603
#Labels per entity	1.56	1.56	1.63
#WordPieces per label	2.8	2.8	2.8

Table 4: Statistics of Open Entity dataset with nine label types. TAGME (Ferragina and Scaiella, 2010) is used to automatically annotate named entities in the dataset.

Our code was adapted from ERNIE,[4] and we

[4] https://github.com/thunlp/ERNIE

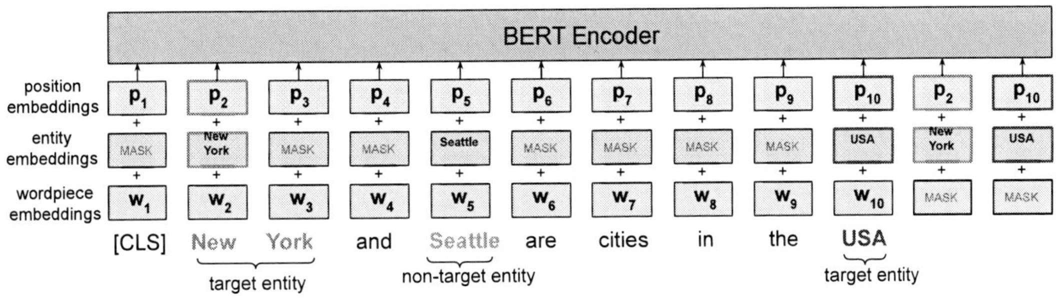

Figure 3: Overall architecture showing a sequence input to the BERT encoder for the relation classification task. The entity embeddings are obtained by encoding the labels of their neighboring nodes, as described in Sec. 3. Note that the entity and position embeddings for the two target entities are copied over to the end of the sequence.

used the same setup as it. For each instance, we used a special symbol to mark the span of a target entity and used the [CLS] vector in the last hidden layer from the BERT encoder for classification. For the hyper-parameters, we basically followed those of ERNIE. The learning rate was set to 2e-5 with the AdamW optimizer and a linear learning rate scheduler (10% warmup). The model was trained for 10 epochs with a batch size of 16. The results are shown in Table 5. Among the models in the BASE size, our model is comparable to or more effective than the related methods. Compared with KnowBert and ERNIE, the construction of our entity embeddings is more efficient and our model does not require pre-training. Further analysis of our model will be in the ablation study.

5.3.2 Relation Classification

We used a preprocessed relation classification dataset from ERNIE (Zhang et al., 2019) to evaluate our model. This dataset is from the FewRel corpus (Han et al., 2018) and was rearranged by Zhang et al. (2019) for the common relation classification setting. One example from this dataset is shown in Table 1. We used FewRel oracle entity IDs, which were also used in ERNIE and E-BERT (Poerner et al., 2020). These oracle entity IDs cover only target entities; there are no annotations for non-target entities. Our model needs to predict the relation of two given target entities with their annotations and context. The statistics of the FewRel dataset are shown in Table 6. Since oracle annotations were used, the statistics of annotated target entities are not shown in the table. Again, we can see the type labels are quite short, which enables them to be encoded with a simple averaging method. Since there are not many entities involved, we take these entity embeddings as parameters and do not construct them on the fly.

As with the entity typing task, special tokens [HD] and [TL] were used to mark the span of a head and tail entity, respectively. The [CLS] vector in the last hidden layer of the BERT encoder was used for relation classification. For the hyper-parameters, we basically followed those of ERNIE. The model is trained for 10 epochs with a batch size of 16. The default AdamW optimizer was used with a linear learning rate scheduler (10% warmup). The learning rate was set to 4e-5, which was chosen among {2e-5, 3e-5, 4e-5, 5e-5} on the valid dataset.

The results are shown in Table 7. ERNIE, E-BERT, and our model can be directly compared with because all the models are based on $\text{BERT}_{\text{BASE}}$ and used the same entity annotations. Our model achieves better results than ERNIE and E-BERT, indicating that our methods are effective while being cost-efficient. However, E-BERT reports that their entity coverage is about 90% (around 10% of entity embeddings are not found in their Wikipedia2Vec embeddings), while the entity coverage in our model and ERNIE is about 96%. This may put E-BERT at a disadvantage.

5.4 Ablation Study

To analyze the gain, we define three components in our model for entity typing and relation classification: *entityEmbs*, defined by Eq. 1, *sum*, defined by Eq. 3, and *insert*, defined by Eq. 4. When *entityEmbs* is not used, the entity embeddings are initialized randomly. The results for cases when independently excluding each component are shown in Table 8. When *entityEmbs* was removed, the performance of our model on two datasets dropped significantly, which indicates our method for con-

	Model	Architecture	P	R	F1
Incorporate KG in pre-training	ERNIE (Zhang et al., 2019)	$BERT_{BASE}$	78.42	72.90	75.56
	KnowBERT (Peters et al., 2019)	$BERT_{BASE}$	78.60	73.70	76.10
	K-ADAPTER (Wang et al., 2020)	$RoBERTa_{LARGE}$	79.30	75.84	77.53
	KEPLER (Wang et al., 2021)	$RoBERTa_{BASE}$	77.80	74.60	76.20
Fine-tuning only	$BERT_{BASE}$ (our reproduction)	$BERT_{BASE}$	79.78	70.90	75.08
	Our model	$BERT_{BASE}$	78.53	74.16	76.28

Table 5: Results of our model and related models on the entity typing dataset - Open Entity. Note that only K-ADAPTER is in the LARGE size, and ERNIE, KnowBERT, and K-ADAPTER also require incorporating knowledge during fine-tuning.

	Train	Dev.	Test
#Instances	8,000	16,000	16,000
#Labels per entity	1.27	1.25	1.25
#WordPieces per label	2.96	3.0	3.02

Table 6: Relation classification dataset FewRel with 80 relation types.

Model	P	R	F1
ERNIE (Zhang et al., 2019)	88.49	88.44	88.32
E-BERT (Poerner et al., 2020)	88.51	88.46	88.38
$BERT_{BASE}$ (our reproduction)	86.16	86.16	86.16
Our model	**88.93**	**88.93**	**88.93**

Table 7: Relation classification results on FewRel. Only ERNIE incorporates entity embeddings in both pre-training and fine-tuning steps.

Model	Open Entity	FewRel
Our model	76.28	88.93
w/o *entityEmbs*	74.03	84.98
w/o *sum*	75.83	88.81
w/o *insert*	75.62	87.99

Table 8: Ablation study with F1 scores. Each component in our model is excluded independently.

Model		P	R	F-1
Our model		78.53	74.16	76.28
w/o *sum*	*insert*	78.33	73.48	75.83
	insert for all	78.73	72.32	75.39
w/o *insert*	*sum* for only non-target	79.12	72.43	75.62

Table 9: Ablation study on Open Entity dataset.

structing entity embeddings is effective while maintaining cost-efficiency. Once *entityEmbs* was used, we can see that *sum* shows improvement on the two datasets. The performance can be further improved if *insert* was used together with *sum*, which suggests that *sum* does not make full use of the information for target entities, and emphasizing target entities explicitly by *insert* is effective.

To analyze how *insert* and *sum* separately work on target and non-target entities, we conducted another ablation study on Open Entity, and the results are shown in Table 9. Since there are no non-target entity annotations in FewRel, only Open Entity is included. If *insert* was applied for all entities, the performance degraded, which suggests that emphasizing non-target entities is not helpful, and it is more effective to incorporate entity embeddings for target and non-target entities in a different way. When *sum* was applied only to non-target entities without *insert*, its performance was better than that of $BERT_{BASE}$, indicating that incorporating the embeddings of non-target entities is useful.

6 Conclusion

In this paper, we proposed to construct entity embeddings using local features instead of training those with consideration of the whole KG for tasks where the context already contains large amounts of information. Utilizing local features to construct the entity embeddings is much faster than the methods mentioned in related work. The local features of an entity used in this paper are the labels of its neighboring nodes connected through *instance_of* edges in Wikidata. Since these labels are usually very short, we can simply encode them by averaging their WordPiece embeddings. The simple averaging method enables us to even construct entity embeddings on the fly without much cost. This is helpful for saving memory and reducing parameters in tasks where minions of entities may be involved. Finally, we proposed task-specific models to incorporate our entity embeddings. Unlike most previous works, our entity embeddings can be directly incorporated during fine-tuning without requiring any specialized pre-training. Our experiments on entity linking, entity typing, and relation classification show that our entity embeddings and incorporation method are simple and effective, and the proposed models have comparable or superior performance to existing models while having the aforementioned advantages.

References

Ivana Balažević, Carl Allen, and Timothy M Hospedales. 2019. Tucker: Tensor factorization for knowledge graph completion. In *Empirical Methods in Natural Language Processing*.

Ivana Balazevic, Carl Allen, and Timothy Hospedales. 2019. TuckER: Tensor factorization for knowledge graph completion. In *Proceedings of the 2019 Conference on Empirical Methods in Natural Language Processing and the 9th International Joint Conference on Natural Language Processing (EMNLP-IJCNLP)*, pages 5185–5194, Hong Kong, China. Association for Computational Linguistics.

Antoine Bordes, Nicolas Usunier, Alberto Garcia-Duran, Jason Weston, and Oksana Yakhnenko. 2013a. Translating embeddings for modeling multi-relational data. In *Advances in Neural Information Processing Systems*, volume 26. Curran Associates, Inc.

Antoine Bordes, Nicolas Usunier, Alberto Garcia-Duran, Jason Weston, and Oksana Yakhnenko. 2013b. Translating embeddings for modeling multi-relational data. In *Advances in neural information processing systems*, pages 2787–2795.

Samuel Broscheit. 2019. Investigating entity knowledge in BERT with simple neural end-to-end entity linking. In *Proceedings of the 23rd Conference on Computational Natural Language Learning (CoNLL)*, pages 677–685, Hong Kong, China. Association for Computational Linguistics.

Nicola De Cao, Gautier Izacard, Sebastian Riedel, and Fabio Petroni. 2021. Autoregressive entity retrieval. In *International Conference on Learning Representations*.

Eunsol Choi, Omer Levy, Yejin Choi, and Luke Zettlemoyer. 2018. Ultra-fine entity typing. In *Proceedings of the 56th Annual Meeting of the Association for Computational Linguistics (Volume 1: Long Papers)*, pages 87–96, Melbourne, Australia. Association for Computational Linguistics.

Jacob Devlin, Ming-Wei Chang, Kenton Lee, and Kristina Toutanova. 2019. BERT: Pre-training of deep bidirectional transformers for language understanding. In *Proceedings of the 2019 Conference of the North American Chapter of the Association for Computational Linguistics: Human Language Technologies, Volume 1 (Long and Short Papers)*, pages 4171–4186, Minneapolis, Minnesota. Association for Computational Linguistics.

Paolo Ferragina and Ugo Scaiella. 2010. Tagme: on-the-fly annotation of short text fragments (by wikipedia entities). In *Proceedings of the 19th ACM international conference on Information and knowledge management*, pages 1625–1628.

Matthew Francis-Landau, Greg Durrett, and Dan Klein. 2016. Capturing semantic similarity for entity linking with convolutional neural networks. In *Proceedings of the 2016 Conference of the North American Chapter of the Association for Computational Linguistics: Human Language Technologies*, pages 1256–1261, San Diego, California. Association for Computational Linguistics.

Daniel Gillick, Sayali Kulkarni, Larry Lansing, Alessandro Presta, Jason Baldridge, Eugene Ie, and Diego Garcia-Olano. 2019. Learning dense representations for entity retrieval. In *Proceedings of the 23rd Conference on Computational Natural Language Learning (CoNLL)*, pages 528–537, Hong Kong, China. Association for Computational Linguistics.

Nitish Gupta, Sameer Singh, and Dan Roth. 2017. Entity linking via joint encoding of types, descriptions, and context. In *Proceedings of the 2017 Conference on Empirical Methods in Natural Language Processing*, pages 2681–2690, Copenhagen, Denmark. Association for Computational Linguistics.

Xu Han, Hao Zhu, Pengfei Yu, Ziyun Wang, Yuan Yao, Zhiyuan Liu, and Maosong Sun. 2018. FewRel: A large-scale supervised few-shot relation classification dataset with state-of-the-art evaluation. In *Proceedings of the 2018 Conference on Empirical Methods in Natural Language Processing*, pages 4803–4809, Brussels, Belgium. Association for Computational Linguistics.

Johannes Hoffart, Mohamed Amir Yosef, Ilaria Bordino, Hagen Fürstenau, Manfred Pinkal, Marc Spaniol, Bilyana Taneva, Stefan Thater, and Gerhard Weikum. 2011. Robust disambiguation of named entities in text. In *Proceedings of the 2011 Conference on Empirical Methods in Natural Language Processing*, pages 782–792, Edinburgh, Scotland, UK. Association for Computational Linguistics.

Feng Hou, Ruili Wang, Jun He, and Yi Zhou. 2020. Improving entity linking through semantic reinforced entity embeddings. In *Proceedings of the 58th Annual Meeting of the Association for Computational Linguistics*, pages 6843–6848, Online. Association for Computational Linguistics.

Manoj Prabhakar Kannan Ravi, Kuldeep Singh, Isaiah Onando Mulang, Saeedeh Shekarpour, Johannes Hoffart, and Jens Lehmann. 2021. Cholan: A modular approach for neural entity linking on wikipedia and wikidata. In *Proceedings of the 16th Conference of the European Chapter of the Association for Computational Linguistics: Main Volume*.

Sopan Khosla and Carolyn Rose. 2020. Using type information to improve entity coreference resolution. In *Proceedings of the First Workshop on Computational Approaches to Discourse*, pages 20–31, Online. Association for Computational Linguistics.

Nikolaos Kolitsas, Octavian-Eugen Ganea, and Thomas Hofmann. 2018. End-to-end neural entity linking. In *Proceedings of the 22nd Conference on Computational Natural Language Learning*, pages 519–529, Brussels, Belgium. Association for Computational Linguistics.

Phong Le and Ivan Titov. 2019. Distant learning for entity linking with automatic noise detection. In *Proceedings of the 57th Annual Meeting of the Association for Computational Linguistics*, pages 4081–4090, Florence, Italy. Association for Computational Linguistics.

Yinhan Liu, Myle Ott, Naman Goyal, Jingfei Du, Mandar Joshi, Danqi Chen, Omer Levy, Mike Lewis, Luke Zettlemoyer, and Veselin Stoyanov. 2019. Roberta: A robustly optimized bert pretraining approach. *arXiv preprint arXiv:1907.11692*.

Matthew E. Peters, Mark Neumann, Robert Logan, Roy Schwartz, Vidur Joshi, Sameer Singh, and Noah A. Smith. 2019. Knowledge enhanced contextual word representations. In *Proceedings of the 2019 Conference on Empirical Methods in Natural Language Processing and the 9th International Joint Conference on Natural Language Processing (EMNLP-IJCNLP)*, pages 43–54, Hong Kong, China. Association for Computational Linguistics.

Fabio Petroni, Tim Rocktäschel, Sebastian Riedel, Patrick Lewis, Anton Bakhtin, Yuxiang Wu, and Alexander Miller. 2019. Language models as knowledge bases? In *Proceedings of the 2019 Conference on Empirical Methods in Natural Language Processing and the 9th International Joint Conference on Natural Language Processing (EMNLP-IJCNLP)*, pages 2463–2473, Hong Kong, China. Association for Computational Linguistics.

Nina Poerner, Ulli Waltinger, and Hinrich Schütze. 2020. E-BERT: Efficient-yet-effective entity embeddings for BERT. In *Findings of the Association for Computational Linguistics: EMNLP 2020*, pages 803–818, Online. Association for Computational Linguistics.

Jonathan Raiman. 2022. Deeptype 2: Superhuman entity linking, all you need is type interactions. *Proceedings of the AAAI Conference on Artificial Intelligence*, 36(7):8028–8035.

Yaming Sun, Lei Lin, Duyu Tang, Nan Yang, Zhenzhou Ji, and Xiaolong Wang. 2015. Modeling mention, context and entity with neural networks for entity disambiguation. In *Twenty-fourth international joint conference on artificial intelligence*.

Li Tianran, Yang Erguang, Zhang Yujie, Chen Yufeng, and Xu Jinan. 2021. Improving entity linking by encoding type information into entity embeddings. In *Proceedings of the 20th Chinese National Conference on Computational Linguistics*, pages 1087–1095, Huhhot, China. Chinese Information Processing Society of China.

Johannes M. van Hulst, Faegheh Hasibi, Koen Dercksen, Krisztian Balog, and Arjen P. de Vries. 2020. Rel: An entity linker standing on the shoulders of giants. *Proceedings of the 43rd International ACM SIGIR Conference on Research and Development in Information Retrieval*.

Ruize Wang, Duyu Tang, Nan Duan, Zhongyu Wei, Xuanjing Huang, Cuihong Cao, Daxin Jiang, Ming Zhou, et al. 2020. K-adapter: Infusing knowledge into pre-trained models with adapters. *arXiv preprint arXiv:2002.01808*.

Xiaozhi Wang, Tianyu Gao, Zhaocheng Zhu, Zhiyuan Liu, Juanzi Li, and Jian Tang. 2021. Kepler: A unified model for knowledge embedding and pre-trained language representation. *Transactions of the Association for Computational Linguistics*.

Ikuya Yamada, Hiroyuki Shindo, Hideaki Takeda, and Yoshiyasu Takefuji. 2016. Joint learning of the embedding of words and entities for named entity disambiguation. In *Proceedings of The 20th SIGNLL Conference on Computational Natural Language Learning*, pages 250–259, Berlin, Germany. Association for Computational Linguistics.

Zhengyan Zhang, Xu Han, Zhiyuan Liu, Xin Jiang, Maosong Sun, and Qun Liu. 2019. ERNIE: Enhanced language representation with informative entities. In *Proceedings of the 57th Annual Meeting of the Association for Computational Linguistics*, pages 1441–1451, Florence, Italy. Association for Computational Linguistics.

Spa: On the Sparsity of Virtual Adversarial Training for Dependency Parsing

Chao Lou[1], **Wenjuan Han**[2]*, **Kewei Tu**[1]*
[1]School of Information Science and Technology, ShanghaiTech University
Shanghai Engineering Research Center of Intelligent Vision and Imaging
[2]Beijing Jiaotong University, Beijing, China
{louchao,hanwj,tukw}@shanghaitech.edu.cn

Abstract

Virtual adversarial training (VAT) is a powerful approach to improving robustness and performance, leveraging both labeled and unlabeled data to compensate for the scarcity of labeled data. It is adopted on lots of vision and language classification tasks. However, for tasks with structured output (*e.g.*, dependency parsing), the application of VAT is nontrivial due to the intrinsic proprieties of structures: (1) the non-sparse problem and (2) exponential complexity. Against this background, we propose the **S**parse **P**arse **A**djustment algorithm (Spa) and successfully applied VAT to the dependency parsing task. Spa refers to the learning algorithm which combines the graph-based dependency parsing model with VAT in an exact computational manner and enhances the dependency parser with controllable and adjustable sparsity. Empirical studies show that the TreeCRF parser optimized using Spa outperforms other methods without sparsity regularization.

1 Introduction

Dependency parsing is a fundamental structured prediction task in natural language processing that aims to capture syntactic structures in sentences in the form of dependency relations between words. The application of dependency structures is mainly reflected in discourse parsing (Nishida and Nakayama, 2020; Zhang et al., 2021), machine translation (Shen et al., 2008), and many other tasks. While supervised learning is the ideal technique used to learn a dependency parser automatically, it requires the training sentences to be manually annotated with their gold parse trees. This brings the main bottleneck for learning a practical dependency parser — the lack of adequate training corpora with dependency trees. Annotations are both laborious and time costly. Multiple research directions (*i.e.*, unsupervised learning, semi-supervised learning and transfer learning, *etc.*) try to eliminate this bottleneck (Han et al., 2020a).

Virtual adversarial training (VAT) (Miyato et al., 2018), as a semi-supervised learning approach, utilizes both annotated training sentences and unlabeled data to compensate for the scarcity of labeled data. It extends adversarial training (AT) (Goodfellow et al., 2015) to unlabeled data. VAT encourages the output distributions to be similar on both an unlabeled sample and corresponding adversarial examples by adding a Kullback-Leibler (KL) divergence term in the training loss. In this way, VAT improves the performance and robustness of many tasks (Akhtar and Mian, 2018; Berthelot et al., 2019; Chen et al., 2020).

However, multiple technical challenges are faced by applying VAT on dependency parsing. Except for the general challenges related to gradient computation of discrete inputs, grammatical correctness, and meaning preservation (Zhang et al., 2019; Jia and Liang, 2017; Wang et al., 2019; Cheng et al., 2019, 2020) faced by all adversarial example generators, two potential but critical challenges exist because of the propriety of structured prediction: (1) the non-sparse problem and (2) exponential complexity. The non-sparse problem is naturally connected to unambiguity (Tu and Honavar, 2012), both highlighting that the number of plausible parses of a natural language sentence is relatively small compared with the huge number of possible parses. We are interested in predicting probabilities as small as possible for these unlikely trees rather than having an estimation of their actual probabilities. The fact that the Viterbi expectation-maximization algorithm (EM) outperforms Standard EM in previous work (Poon and Domingos, 2011; Tu and Honavar, 2012; Spitkovsky et al., 2010, 2011) also provides evidence of the advantage of implicitly utilizing the sparsity property. Although Chen et al. (2020) make VAT compatible with a linear-chain structured prediction model by

*Corresponding Author

Findings of the Association for Computational Linguistics: AACL-IJCNLP 2022, pages 11–21
November 20–23, 2022.

considering the probabilities of K most possible label sequences, which is a sparse approximation of the original distribution, they did not quantitatively investigate the impact of sparsity in the application of VAT. For the complexity challenge, different from conventional classification tasks with a fixed number of classes, computing the KL divergence of parse tree distributions by enumerating all possible parses is intractable because the number of possible parses for each sentence is exponential w.r.t. the sentence length. Therefore, conventional approaches can only estimate the KL divergence in the VAT loss rather than compute it exactly.

Against this background, we propose **S**parse **P**arse **A**djustment algorithm (`Spa`) and successfully applied VAT to dependency parsing. `Spa` refers to the learning algorithm which combines the graph-based dependency parsing model with VAT in an exact computational manner, overcoming the problem of enumerating, and enhances the dependency parser with controllable and adjustable sparsity. We applied VAT to a state-of-the-art parsing model: the Tree Conditional Random Field (TreeCRF) parser (Zhang et al., 2020). `Spa` incorporates into TreeCRF an inductive bias in favor of models that lead to a controllable sparsity. Adjusting the hyper-parameter can control sparsity to ease the non-sparse problem. Empirical studies show that the TreeCRF parser optimized using `Spa` outperforms other semi-supervised methods without sparsity regularization. Within `Spa`, our exact computational manner achieves competitive performance and enables faster training compared to the top-K approximate approach (Chen et al., 2020). The code can be found at: `https://github.com/LouChao98/struct-vat`.

2 Related Work

2.1 Semi-Supervised Learning

Semi-supervised learning is an important branch of machine learning to improve model performance when there is insufficient labeled data, which utilizes unlabeled data to get more information that might be beneficial for supervised tasks. A common semi-supervised learning approach is to train a generative model (Hinton et al., 2006; Maaløe et al., 2016; Wang and Tu, 2020a) which achieve state-of-the-art performance. However, these methods require additional hyperparameters, and the conditions under which the generative model will provide good supervised learning performance are poorly understood (Miyato et al., 2017b).

Self-training (Yarowsky, 1995) is another approach to semi-supervised learning, which has been successfully applied to natural language processing tasks. In self-training, the model acts as teacher and student iteratively. Recent approaches use soft targets from one or multiple teachers' output (Hinton et al., 2015), such as in tri-training (Zhi-Hua Zhou and Ming Li, 2005; Ruder and Plank, 2018).

Consistency training is also a branch of semi-supervised learning, forcing the model to make consistent predictions on different views of the same data. Cross-view training (CVT) (Clark et al., 2018) works on bidirectional LSTMs and constructs views by masking out neurons of one direction. R-drop (Liang et al., 2021) constructs views by *dropout-twice*, thus is compatible with transformers. Unsupervised Data Augmentation (Xie et al., 2019) changes the input tokens instead of hidden representations with the help of external models, e.g., a back-translator. Unlike others, VAT constructs views using a gradient-based attacker. Next, we will introduce VAT in detail.

2.2 Virtual Adversarial Training

Adversarial training (Goodfellow et al., 2015) is a method to improve model robustness, in which models are trained using not only labeled data but also perturbed samples generated by an adversarial attacker. As a consequence, model predictions would be consistent regardless of the perturbations. AT was demonstrated to be more effective than random attackers since its perturbations maximize model loss in a constrained length. Many previous works (Goodfellow et al., 2015; Miyato et al., 2017a; Yasunaga et al., 2018; Han et al., 2020c; Zhang et al., 2022) proved the effectiveness of AT on computer vision tasks and language tasks. To introduce AT into semi-supervised settings, Miyato et al. (2018) proposed virtual adversarial training. The idea of VAT can be seen as the combination of self-training (Yarowsky, 1995) and AT if we treat predictions on clean input as labels in AT. VAT can be applied to both labeled and unlabeled data because ground-truth labels are not required. VAT achieved state-of-the-art performance for image classification tasks (Miyato et al., 2018) and proved to be more efficient than previous semi-supervised approaches, such as entropy minimization (Grandvalet and Bengio, 2005) and self-training (Yarowsky, 1995). Chen et al. (2020)

proposed SeqVAT, which successfully makes VAT compatible with the linear-chain conditional random field (LinearChainCRF), and showed that VAT benefits from structure information. It combines VAT with LinearChainCRF and achieves significant improvements in sequence labeling. They estimate the KL divergence by only considering the K most possible label sequences and report that the performance of VAT on LinearChainCRF is better than that of VAT on token-level categorical distributions, which is used by works before SeqVAT. In this paper, we show VAT can be applied to dependency parsing with TreeCRF, which is a more complex structure.

3 Model

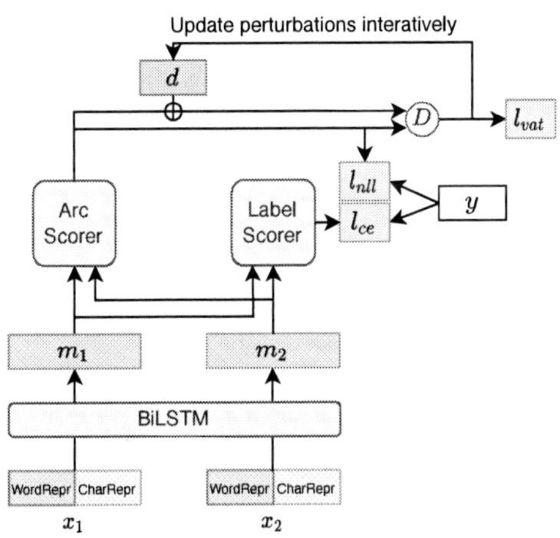

Figure 1: Model Architecture

Our model architecture is illustrated in Fig. 1. It adopts the basic architecture of the TreeCRF parser. We concatenate word embeddings with character features extracted by a LSTM layer as input features. Then, we feed input features into the scoring functions. Finally, TreeCRFs are constructed using scores.

Encoder The encoder includes both a word-based representation and a character-based representation inspired by character information capturing morphological features (Ma and Hovy, 2016; Zhang et al., 2020).

Word Representation We use 100-dimension GloVe (Pennington et al., 2014) as word representations for dependency parsing, following previous parsing work (Dozat and Manning, 2017; Zhang et al., 2020). Intuitively, a model could learn to make the perturbations in VAT insignificant by learning embeddings with a very large norm. To prevent this pathological situation, we follow the setting from Miyato et al. (2017b) and use normalized word embeddings $\hat{w}$ instead of raw vectors w. Formally, we use the representations as follows:

$$\hat{w}^{(i)} = \frac{w^{(i)} - \text{Mean}(w)}{\sqrt{\text{Var}(w)}}$$

$$\text{where Mean}(w) = \frac{1}{n}\sum_{i=1}^{n} w^{(i)}$$

$$\text{and Var}(w) = \frac{1}{n}\sum_{i=1}(w^{(i)} - \text{Mean}(w))^2$$

where n is the number of all tokens in the embedding space and $w^{(i)}$ is the embedding of the ith word in the vocabulary.

Character Representation Following Zhang et al. (2020), 50-dimension character embeddings and a bidirectional LSTM with 50 neurons per direction are used. Similar to word embeddings, we also apply normalization to the output vectors of the character LSTM.

Contextual Representation After transforming input tokens to vector representations, we use a three-layer bidirectional LSTM to capture contextual information with 400 neurons per direction. We also add Variational Dropout (Gal and Ghahramani, 2016) between LSTM layers for stable training.

Scoring Functions Following Zhang et al. (2020), we adopt a two-stage parsing strategy. The structure (whether arcs exist) and the labels of arcs are processed separately. The scores of structures are computed using deep biaffine functions. Let $m_{(\cdot)}$ be the output of LSTM and MLP be a multi-layer perceptron, the score of the arc from i to j is defined as follows:

$$h_{(\cdot)}^{h/d} = \text{MLP}^{h/d}(m_{(\cdot)})$$

$$\phi_{ij} = \text{Biaffine}(h_i^h, h_j^d)$$

Label scores ϕ_{ijl} of the arc from i to j with label l are defined similarly. Please refer to Zhang et al. (2020) for more details.

Decoder The arc scores are fed into TreeCRF, which defines the distribution over all possible trees of a sentence. For a tree y (a set of arcs) of sentence

x, its probability is defined as follows:

$$
\begin{aligned}
p(y|x) &= \frac{\phi(y)}{Z} \\
\phi(y) &= \prod_{(i,j)\in y} \phi_{ij} \\
Z &= \sum_{y'\in\mathcal{Y}(x)} \phi(y'),
\end{aligned}
$$

where $\phi(y)$ denotes the scores of the tree y, Z denotes the partition function and $\mathcal{Y}(x)$ denotes the set of possible trees of x. The supervised training loss L_{sup} consists of two parts. Negative log-likelihood L_{nll} is used as the supervised loss of structures and cross-entropy L_{ce} is used as the supervised loss of labels.

$$
\begin{aligned}
L_{nll} &= \log Z - \log \phi(\bar{y}) \\
L_{ce} &= \sum_{(i,j)\in\bar{y}} \mathcal{CE}(\text{Softmax}(\phi_{ij\cdot}), l_{ij}) \\
L_{sup} &= L_{nll} + L_{ce},
\end{aligned}
$$

where $\bar{y}$ is the gold tree and l_{ij} is the one-hot encoding of the gold label of arc from i to j.

4 Learning

4.1 Unsupervised Loss

In AT, the perturbations d_w, d_c bounded by δ_w, δ_c is generated by maximizing the training loss:

$$
\begin{aligned}
d_w &= \underset{\epsilon, \|\epsilon\| \leqslant \delta_w}{\arg\max}\, D(y; P(w+\epsilon, c)) \\
d_c &= \underset{\epsilon, \|\epsilon\| \leqslant \delta_c}{\arg\max}\, D(y; P(w, c+\epsilon))
\end{aligned}
$$

where D is an arbitrary distance measure or loss function, w, c are the normalized word and character representations respectively, and P is the model outputting TreeCRF distribution. AT can only be used in supervised settings because it requires y to generate the perturbations.

Miyato et al. (2018) proposed virtual adversarial training to extend AT to unlabeled data. Denote x, x_{adv} as a sample and its corresponding adversarial sample, and p_{orig}, p_{adv} as the distribution predicted by the model for x, x_{adv}. Then a natural choice of D in VAT is the KL divergence:

$$
D(p_{orig}; p_{adv}) = \mathcal{KL}(P(w,c)||P(w+d_w, c+d_c))
$$

Compared to AT, VAT can be seen as the "self-training" version of AT since VAT replaces the ground-truth y with the predicted p_{orig}. The perturbations d_w, d_c are now defined by:

$$
\begin{aligned}
d_w &= \underset{\epsilon, \|\epsilon\| \leqslant \delta_w}{\arg\min}\, \mathcal{KL}(P(w,c)||P(w+\epsilon, c)) \\
d_c &= \underset{\epsilon, \|\epsilon\| \leqslant \delta_c}{\arg\min}\, \mathcal{KL}(P(w,c)||P(w, c+\epsilon))
\end{aligned}
$$

Those two are still intractable for gradient descent. Miyato et al. (2018) propose to approximate perturbations by the second-order Taylor approximation and the power iteration method. The perturbations d_w, d_c can be estimated as follows:

$$
d_w = \frac{g_w}{\|g_w\|}\delta_w \quad d_c = \frac{g_c}{\|g_c\|}\delta_c
$$

where g_w, g_c are gradients of the distance w.r.t. perturbations:

$$
\begin{aligned}
g_w &= \nabla_\epsilon \mathcal{KL}(P(w,c)||P(w+\epsilon, c)) \\
g_c &= \nabla_\epsilon \mathcal{KL}(P(w,c)||P(w, c+\epsilon))
\end{aligned}
$$

We stop the gradient propagation through d_w, d_c when optimizing model parameters because they are adversarial attacks.

The full loss function of our model is a weighted summation of the supervised training loss and contrastive training loss:

$$
L = L_{sup} + \alpha D(p_{orig}; p_{adv}). \tag{1}
$$

Because p_{orig} is at least as good as p_{adv}, we do not want to optimize p_{orig} for the loss in terms of p_{adv}. In practical, we detach p_{orig} from the computational graph when optimizing the unsupervised loss, such that the entropy term $\mathcal{E}(p_{orig})$ in $D = \mathcal{KL}(p_{orig}||p_{adv}) = \mathcal{CE}(p_{orig}||p_{adv}) - \mathcal{E}(p_{orig})$ can be omitted because it will not contribute any gradients to trainable parameters.

4.2 Exact Computation

As Chen et al. (2020) mentioned, the computation of the KL divergence of two CRFs is nontrivial because of the exponential-size space. This section derives the polynomial-time exact computation for the TreeCRF using dynamic programming. A similar derivation for the entropy of constituency trees is documented in Hwa (2000).

We use the notation $N(i,j;y)$ to denote the quantity N (Tab. 1) of the tree y which covers the span $x_i \ldots x_j$ and $N(i,j)$ to denote the quantity N of all possible trees covering it. Similarly, we use the notation $N(i,j,k;y)$ to denote the quantity N of the tree y which, additionally, can be split

N	$N(\cdot)$	$N(\cdot; y)$	Explanation
ϕ_d	•	•	the tree score
p_d	○	•	the tree probability
h_d	•	○	the cross entropy

Table 1: Notations. •/○ means the quantity is defined/undefined for this form. $d \in \{p, q\}$ is the identifier of two distributions. We abuse some notations.

into two sub-trees at the point k. The left sub-tree covering $x_i \dots x_k$ is named as y_l and the right one covering $x_{k+1} \dots x_j$ as y_r. We do not decorate y_l, y_r with the span indices (e.g., i, j, k) because they can be understood from the context. $N(i, j, k)$ is the aggregated version of $N(i, j, k; y)$.

The KL divergence consists of the entropy and the cross-entropy. As the full KL divergence can be derived with little effort from the cross-entropy, we only show the derivation of the cross-entropy, $h(1, n) \equiv \mathcal{CE}(p, q)$, for the sake of simplicity. $h(i, j)$ can be written as the form of enumerating all possible trees $y \in \mathcal{Y}$.

$$h(i,j) = -\sum_{y} p_p(i,j;y) \log p_q(i,j;y) \quad (2)$$

The first step (Eq. 6) is to decompose y into sub-trees y_l, y_r and also an arc connecting the two sub-trees' roots $\mathcal{A}(y_l, y_r) \in \{root(y_l) \rightarrow root(y_r), root(y_r) \rightarrow root(y_l)\}$[1] where γ_d ($d \in \{p, q\}$) is the normalizer[2] (Eq. 5). After breaking the log-terms about q into three terms, the summation of y_l, y_r reduces p_q terms to h terms (Eq. 8). Specifically, there are two types of reduction: (1) reducing to cross entropy of trees covering smaller spans (e.g., Eq. 3); (2) and reducing to marginalization of possible trees (e.g., Eq. 4):

$$-\sum_{y_l} p_p(i,k;y_l) \log p_q(i,k;y_l) \equiv h(i,k) \quad (3)$$

$$\sum_{y_r} p_p(k+1,j;y_r) = \sum_{y_r} p(y_r|x_{[k+1:j]}) = 1 \quad (4)$$

Eq.8 is the state transition equation of dynamic programming, in which $h(i, j, k)$ is in terms of $h(i, k), h(k + 1, j)$, which are smaller problems, and $\gamma(\mathcal{A}(y_l, y_r))$ is in terms of $\phi_d(i, k), \phi_d(k + 1, j)$ and the potential score of $a \rightarrow b$ in d ($\phi_{d,ab}$).

$$\gamma_d(\mathcal{A}(y_l,y_r), y_l, y_r) = \gamma_d(a \rightarrow b, y_l, y_r) = \phi_{d,ab}\phi_d(i,k)\phi_d(k+1,j)/\phi_d(i,j,k) \quad (5)$$

4.3 CrossEntropy Semiring

The semiring parsing framework (Goodman, 1999; Li and Eisner, 2009) enables us to decouple the semantics (e.g., cross-entropy and MAP inference) from the routine (e.g., the inside algorithm).

The semiring parsing framework is a generalization of the sum-product algorithm where operators $+, \times$ are generalized to abstract operators $\oplus, \otimes$. Plugging in different semirings allows us to query different properties, e.g., partition and mode. To illustrate the cross-entropy semiring, we define the elements of the semiring as triplets indexed by positions i, j:

$$s(i,j) = (\phi_p(i,j),\ \phi_q(i,j),\ h(i,j)) \quad (9)$$

Because the first two elements can be solved by the inside algorithms, we focus on the third term. An abstract product $\otimes$ combines two sub-structures. After reordering terms in Eq. 8, we observes that:

$$h(i,j,k) = A(h(i,k) + h(k+1,j)) + B \quad (10)$$

where A, B are in terms of γ_d but irrelative to $h(i, k), h(k + 1, j)$. γ_d is available only after summation due to $\phi_d(i, j, k)$[3] in Eq. 5 , therefore we delay to resolve A, B and perform the summation of $h(i, k)$ and $h(k + 1, j)$ only (Eq. 11).

An abstract summation $\oplus$ aggregates all possible structures at the same position. In our case, there are two jobs: (1) resolve A, B (2) aggregate $h(i, j, k)$ to get $h(i, j)$. The computation is defined as Eq. 12. Let $s = [s_1, s_2, \dots]$ be a list of triplets, the cross-entropy semiring is defined as follows:

$$\otimes s = (\prod s[0],\ \prod s[1],\ \sum s[2]) \quad (11)$$

$$\oplus s = (\sum s[0],\ \sum s[1],\ f) \quad (12)$$

$$f = \sum\left(\frac{s[0]}{\sum s[0]} \times \left(s[2] - \log \frac{s[1]}{\sum s[1]}\right)\right)$$

$$\mathbf{1} = (0, 0, 1), \quad \mathbf{0} = (-\infty, -\infty, 0)$$

4.4 Sparsity Regularization

Motivated by the sparsity property, we would like to incorporate into the model a flexibly adjustable button in favor of sparsity adjustment. In our approach, this button is a adjustable hyperparameter.

One natural measurement of sparsity is the number of parse trees considered in leaning. We denote the number of parse trees K as this adjustable

[1] We use the Eisner algorithm (Eisner, 2000) as the routine (Sec.4.3), in which $\mathcal{A} = \{i \rightarrow j, j \rightarrow i\}$.

[2] We denote $\gamma_d(\mathcal{A}(y_l, y_r), y_l, y_r)$ as $\gamma_d(\mathcal{A}(y_l, y_r))$ for simplicity. One can read i, j, k from y_l, y_r.

[3] $\phi_d(i, j, k)$ can be obtained by summing the first two items in triplets.

$$
\begin{aligned}
&h(i,j,k)\\
&= - \sum_{(y_l,y_r,\mathcal{A})} \left[p_p(i,k;y_l)p_p(k+1,j;y_r)\gamma_p(\mathcal{A}(y_l,y_r))\log[p_q(i,k;y_l)p_q(k+1,j;y_r)\gamma_q(\mathcal{A}(y_l,y_r))]\right] \quad (6)\\
&= \underbrace{\sum_{\mathcal{A}}\gamma_p(\mathcal{A}(y_l,y_r))}_{\substack{\text{Only depends on i,j}\\ \text{(Eq. 5 and Fn. 1.)}}} \underbrace{\sum_{y_r} p_p(k+1,j;y_r)}_{\text{Eq. 4}} \underbrace{\Big(-\sum_{y_l} p_p(i,k;y_l)\log p_q(i,k;y_l)\Big)}_{\text{Eq. 3}} \quad (7)\\
&\quad + \sum_{\mathcal{A}}\gamma_p(\mathcal{A}(y_l,y_r))\sum_{y_l} p_p(i,k;y_l)\Big(-\sum_{y_r} p_p(k+1,j;y_r)\log p_q(k+1,j;y_r)\Big)\\
&\quad + \sum_{y_l} p_p(i,k;y_l)\sum_{y_r} p_p(k+1,j;y_r)\Big(-\sum_{\mathcal{A}}\gamma_p(\mathcal{A}(y_l,y_r))\log\gamma_p(\mathcal{A}(y_l,y_r))\Big)\\
&= \sum_{\mathcal{A}}\left[\gamma_p(\mathcal{A}(y_l,y_r))h(i,k) + \gamma_p(\mathcal{A}(y_l,y_r))h(k+1,j) - \gamma_p(\mathcal{A}(y_l,y_r))\log\gamma_q(\mathcal{A}(y_l,y_r))\right] \quad (8)
\end{aligned}
$$

hyperparameter. Specifically, the sparsity of the model is controlled by the value of the non-negative parameter K. Following Chen et al. (2020), we provide an approximate probability distribution with "$K+1$ dimensions" to estimates the KL divergence. In addition to the K most possible label predictions, the rest predicted labels are represented as the additional $+1$ dimension. We could modify K in the objective function to favor different degrees of sparsity. We refer this sparsity regularization as *Top-K* approach.

While *Top-K* estimates the KL divergence by designing an approximate distribution, the full probability distributions actually can be exactly computed as shown in Sec. 4.2. We manipulate the sparsity degree based on the exact computation by temperature control following Hinton et al. (2015). Specifically, we divide the logits of probability distributions by a temperature in the objective. A higher temperature results in softer probability distributions and often results in better KD performance. However, there is an opposite view of temperature. Grandvalet and Bengio (2004) applied a low temperature to sharpen predictions, which leads to a lower entropy, and showed that regularizing the predictions to have low entropy could be beneficial. When setting the two temperatures T_{orig} and T_{adv} (which refer to the temperatures of p_{orig} and p_{adv} respectively), we could adjust the sparsity degree in a more flexible way. Specifically, the sparsity of our model is controlled by the value of the non-negative parameter T_{orig} and T_{adv}. A smaller value of T_{orig} corresponds to a stronger sparsity in favor of an unambiguous model. When T_{orig} is set to 1, the learning algorithm can be considered as the exact computation. When $T_{orig} < 1$, our approach becomes a sparse version. When $T_{orig} > 1$, our approach falls into a smoother version. Models do not have a fixed degree of sparsity when targeting different datasets. For a given dataset, different models should be set different hyperparameters. Therefore, it is unclear how to choose an optimal temperature. To make it more flexible, we use different temperatures T_{orig} and T_{adv} for the two terms in KL. We refer to this sparsity regularization as *Temp-*(T_{orig},T_{adv}) approach. *ExactComp-*(T_{orig},T_{adv}) denotes applying *Temp-*(T_{orig},T_{adv}) on TreeCRF with exact computation and *HeadSelect-*(T_{orig},T_{adv}) denotes applying *Temp-*(T_{orig},T_{adv}) on the head selection model Dozat and Manning (2017).

5 Experiments

5.1 Dataset

We evaluate our methods on the Wall Street Journal (WSJ) corpus with default training/development/test split (Cohen et al., 2008) for dependency parsing by unlabeled and labeled attachment score (UAS/LAS) (Han et al., 2020b).

We use Stanford dependencies 3.3 (Manning et al., 2014) to preprocess the WSJ corpus as in previous work. We consider several settings including full labeled WSJ data with extra unlabeled BLLIP corpus[4], and $x\%$ in WSJ as labeled data and the rest $(1-x)\%$ as unlabeled data. We use BLLIP as the unlabeled data pool, which has the

[4]Brown Laboratory for Linguistic Information Processing (BLLIP) 1987-89 WSJ Corpus Release 1

Setting	Labeled	Unlabeled
WSJ(10%/90%)	3,983	35,849
WSJ(30%/70%)	11,950	27,882
WSJ(50%/50%)	19,916	19,916
WSJ+BLLIP	39,832	650,000

Table 2: Statistic analysis of labeled and unlabeled training data. WSJ($x\%/(1-x)\%$) means $x\%$ of sentences are annotated while the remaining $(1-x)\%$ are not.

same data source as WSJ but contains much more sentences than the WSJ corpus. We drop sentences in BLLIP with length >20 to speed up training and balance the number of labeled and unlabeled data. All dataset settings we used to evaluate our method are listed in Tab. 2.

5.2 Setting

We directly adopt most hyper-parameters from Zhang et al. (2020). We train our supervised baseline for 200 epochs. For other models, we run semi-supervised training for 100 epochs after 100 epochs of purely supervised training.

5.3 Main Results

We report the averaged score over four random restarts for each model[5] and compare our models on dependency parsing. We tune hyperparameters and choose models according to the LAS score on th validation set. The results of small training data are shown in Tab. 3 on WSJ test data, including two settings: supervised learning and semi-supervised learning.

We focus on the semi-supervised settings and list supervised learning[6] for reference. We have three strong baselines reported in previous work: (1) Self-Training is the conventional self-training approach that uses the predicted data as extra labeled training data; (2) NCRFAE is the semi-supervised version of a neural CRF autoencoder (Cai et al., 2017)[7]. (3) Arc-Factored Sup/Semi are the supervised/semi-supervised version of the model from Wang and Tu (2020b). It can be seen that two variants of Spa generally outperform these three baselines with a margin. For example, *Top-2* outperforms Self-Training by 1.04% and Arc-Factored Sup by 0.31%. *ExactComp-*(0.3,2) outperforms Self-Training by 1.0% and Arc-Factored Sup by 0.27%.

There are also some interesting observations from different settings. We also apply VAT on the head selection distribution of each token (Dozat and Manning, 2017) (denoted as *HeadSelect-*(1,1)), in the sense that TreeCRF is not used, to show the efficiency of adversarial training without the tree structure constraint. Here two 1 in *HeadSelect-*(1,1) mean that sparsity adjustment is not used. In semi-supervised settings, *HeadSelect-*(1,1) is competitive and even outperforms some baselines with the structure constraint by a large margin. We suspect that it may be because of our good hyperparameters. Then after we set $T_{orig} = 0.3$ and $T_{adv} = 2$, an improvement is observed from 92.23% to 92.60%. It reveals the benefit of sparsity bias in the head selection model.

The second evidence of the benefit of sparsity bias lays on the *Top-K* Sparsity rows. All variants of *Top-K* including *Top-2*, *Top-3*, *Top-5*, and *Top-7* outperform the strong baselines.

Finally, a similar improvement can also been seen from *ExactComp-*(1,1) to *ExactComp-*(0.3,2). This empirical result provides another piece of evidence for the superiority of Spa. Results show that *ExactComp-*(0.3,2) with both exact computation and sparsity adjustment consistently performs well, regardless of the different settings. This demonstrates that the non-sparsity problem limits the power of VAT.

In Tab. 4, models are fed with sufficient labeled data as well as unlabeled data. Results show that VAT provides consistent improvement, especially the model without sparsity regularization, *ExactComp-*(1,1). Later analysis (Tab 6) also shows that a large amount of labeled data weakens the significance of the sparsity regularization. We argue that in this case, we have high quality p_{orig} such that no much inaccurate information is required to be ruled out.

5.4 Results of Different K

The value of K in Spa is an important hyperparameter. If the value of K is too large, the model may consider too much possibilities of parses and hence the model is very likely to be misled. If

[5]If a setting requires to sample data, e.g., WSJ(10%/90%), we randomly sample data twice and run models using two randomly chosen seeds for each data. Otherwise, we run models using four randomly chosen seeds.

[6]The TreeCRF parser in this paper is different from the original version by an additional embedding normalization.

[7]We develop this neural version of CRF autoencoder dependency parser by Cai et al. (2017). For the self-training setting, we use the parser to predict parse trees of the unlabeled data iteratively and use the pseudo labeled data to update the model.

Approach		UAS	LAS
Supervised Learning			
Arc-Factored VAE Sup* (Wang and Tu, 2020b)		92.00	-
TreeCRF (Zhang et al., 2020)		92.11	89.51
Semi-supervised Learning			
Self-Training*		91.82	-
NCRFAE*		91.94	-
Arc-Factored VAE Semi* (Wang and Tu, 2020b)		92.55	-
W/O Sparsity	*HeadSelect-*(1,1)	92.23	89.80
	ExactComp-(1,1)	92.36	89.99
Top-K Sparsity	*Top-2*	**92.86**	90.38
	Top-3	92.76	90.36
	Top-5	92.74	90.35
	Top-7	92.79	90.45
Temp-(T_{orig},T_{adv}) Sparsity	*HeadSelect-*(0.3,2)	92.60	90.19
	ExactComp-(0.3,2)	**92.82**	90.45

Table 3: Results on Test data for a typical semi-supervised setting – 10% labeled WSJ+90% unlabeled WSJ. W/O Sparsity: Without Sparsity Adjustment. Result with a star * are reported by Wang and Tu (2020b).

Approach	UAS
Supervised Learning	
Zhang et al. (2020)	95.82
Semi-supervised Learning	
Top-3	95.92
ExactComp-(1,1)	95.99
ExactComp-(0.3,2)	95.84

Table 4: UAS Results on Test data for the semi-supervised setting – WSJ+BLIIP650k.

the value of K is too small, the model loses the benefit of expressiveness. As Tab. 5 illustrates, value of $K = 3$ leads to the best parsing accuracy, while other values produce lower parsing accuracy probably because of inappropriate sparsity degrees.

6 Analysis

6.1 Ablation Study

In this section we study the effectiveness of our two sparsity adjustment on different settings: exact computation to ease the computation errors and sparsity adjustment to add a prior of sparsity property. As show in Tab. 6, the sparsity adjustment is not only successfully applied on low-resource setting, namely the 10%WSJ+90%WSJ setting, but also works on other settings (*i.e.*, 30%WSJ+70%WSJ and 50%WSJ+50%WSJ).

Exact computation is capable of improving

	10%+90%	30%+70%	50%+50%
Supervised Learning			
Sup	92.00	93.94	94.38
TreeCRF	92.11	94.43	95.28
Semi-supervised Learning			
Semi	92.55	94.15	94.41
Top-2	92.86	94.74	95.47
Top-3	92.76	95.00	95.54
Top-5	92.74	94.93	95.35
Top-7	92.79	94.76	95.51

Table 5: UAS Results of different K in various semi-supervised setting. **X%+Y%**: X% labled WSJ+Y% unlabled WSJ. Sup: Arc-Factored VAE Sup (Wang and Tu, 2020b). Semi: Arc-Factored VAE Semi (Wang and Tu, 2020b). TreeCRF: (Zhang et al., 2020).

		10%+90%	30%+70%	50%+50%
W/O	*HeadSelect-*(1,1)	92.23	94.65	95.11
	ExactComp-(1,1)	92.36	94.66	**95.47**
W	*HeadSelect-*(0.3,2)	92.60	94.83	95.31
	ExactComp-(0.3,2)	**92.82**	**94.85**	**95.47**

Table 6: With Sparsity *vs*. Without Sparsity. in various semi-supervised setting. W/O: W/O Sparsity. W: *Temp-*(T_{orig},T_{adv}). **X%+Y%**: X% labled WSJ+Y% unlabled WSJ.

the parsing result on all the settings (including 10%WSJ+90%WSJ, 30%WSJ+70%WSJ and 50%WSJ+50%WSJ). It shows that the model takes advantage of eliminating the approximation problem. When simultaneously combining the sparsity adjustment and the sparsity adjustment, we observe a further improvement on the final result in the *ExactComp-*(0.3,2) row.

We provide other results, including inspection of non-sparse problems and speed comparison, in the Appendix.

7 Conclusion and Further Work

In this paper, we propose **S**parse **P**arse **A**djustment algorithm (Spa). We successfully applied VAT to the dependency parsing task using this Spa algorithm. We use Spa to enhance the TreeCRF parser with exact computation and sparsity adjustment. Further empirical study indicates that Spa has strong effects in semi-supervised settings and time and space efficiency. Furthermore, this approach has broad applications on other structured prediction tasks. The exact computation for the TreeCRF can be easily transferred to general structured prediction architectures, *e.g.*, LinearChain-CRF. We will leave it as a further work.

Acknowledgment

This work was supported by the National Natural Science Foundation of China (61976139). Wenjuan Han has been supported by the National Key R&D Program of China (2020AAA0108005) and the National Nature Science Foundation of China (No. 61976015, 61976016, 61876198 and 61370130). The authors would like to thank the anonymous reviewers for their valuable comments and suggestions to improve this paper.

References

Naveed Akhtar and Ajmal Mian. 2018. Threat of adversarial attacks on deep learning in computer vision: A survey. *Ieee Access*, 6:14410–14430.

David Berthelot, Nicholas Carlini, Ian Goodfellow, Nicolas Papernot, Avital Oliver, and Colin A Raffel. 2019. Mixmatch: A holistic approach to semi-supervised learning. *Advances in Neural Information Processing Systems*, 32.

Jiong Cai, Yong Jiang, and Kewei Tu. 2017. Crf autoencoder for unsupervised dependency parsing. In *Proceedings of the 2017 Conference on Empirical Methods in Natural Language Processing*, pages 1638–1643.

Luoxin Chen, Weitong Ruan, Xinyue Liu, and Jianhua Lu. 2020. SeqVAT: Virtual adversarial training for semi-supervised sequence labeling. In *Proceedings of the 58th Annual Meeting of the Association for Computational Linguistics*, pages 8801–8811, Online. Association for Computational Linguistics.

Yong Cheng, Lu Jiang, and Wolfgang Macherey. 2019. Robust neural machine translation with doubly adversarial inputs. In *Proceedings of the 57th Annual Meeting of the Association for Computational Linguistics*, pages 4324–4333, Florence, Italy. Association for Computational Linguistics.

Yong Cheng, Lu Jiang, Wolfgang Macherey, and Jacob Eisenstein. 2020. AdvAug: Robust adversarial augmentation for neural machine translation. In *Proceedings of the 58th Annual Meeting of the Association for Computational Linguistics*, pages 5961–5970, Online. Association for Computational Linguistics.

Kevin Clark, Minh-Thang Luong, Christopher D. Manning, and Quoc Le. 2018. Semi-supervised sequence modeling with cross-view training. In *Proceedings of the 2018 Conference on Empirical Methods in Natural Language Processing*, pages 1914–1925, Brussels, Belgium. Association for Computational Linguistics.

Shay B Cohen, Kevin Gimpel, and Noah A Smith. 2008. Logistic normal priors for unsupervised probabilistic grammar induction. In *Advances in Neural Information Processing Systems*, pages 321–328.

Timothy Dozat and Christopher D. Manning. 2017. Deep biaffine attention for neural dependency parsing.

Jason Eisner. 2000. Bilexical grammars and their cubic-time parsing algorithms. In *Advances in probabilistic and other parsing technologies*, pages 29–61. Springer.

Yarin Gal and Zoubin Ghahramani. 2016. A theoretically grounded application of dropout in recurrent neural networks. *Advances in neural information processing systems*, 29.

Ian J. Goodfellow, Jonathon Shlens, and Christian Szegedy. 2015. Explaining and harnessing adversarial examples.

Joshua Goodman. 1999. Semiring parsing. *Computational Linguistics*, 25(4):573–606.

Yves Grandvalet and Yoshua Bengio. 2004. Semi-supervised learning by entropy minimization. In *Proceedings of the 17th International Conference on Neural Information Processing Systems*, NIPS'04, page 529–536, Cambridge, MA, USA. MIT Press.

Yves Grandvalet and Yoshua Bengio. 2005. Semi-supervised learning by entropy minimization. In *Advances in Neural Information Processing Systems*, volume 17, pages 529–536. MIT Press.

Wenjuan Han, Yong Jiang, Hwee Tou Ng, and Kewei Tu. 2020a. A survey of unsupervised dependency parsing. In *Proceedings of the 28th International Conference on Computational Linguistics*, pages 2522–2533, Barcelona, Spain (Online). International Committee on Computational Linguistics.

Wenjuan Han, Yong Jiang, Hwee Tou Ng, and Kewei Tu. 2020b. A survey of unsupervised dependency parsing. In *Proceedings of the 28th International Conference on Computational Linguistics*, pages 2522–2533.

Wenjuan Han, Liwen Zhang, Yong Jiang, and Kewei Tu. 2020c. Adversarial attack and defense of structured prediction models. In *Proceedings of the 2020 Conference on Empirical Methods in Natural Language Processing (EMNLP)*, pages 2327–2338, Online. Association for Computational Linguistics.

Geoffrey Hinton, Oriol Vinyals, and Jeff Dean. 2015. Distilling the knowledge in a neural network.

Geoffrey E. Hinton, Simon Osindero, and Yee Whye Teh. 2006. A fast learning algorithm for deep belief nets. *Neural Comput.*, 18(7):1527–1554.

Rebecca Hwa. 2000. Sample selection for statistical grammar induction. In *2000 Joint SIGDAT Conference on Empirical Methods in Natural Language Processing and Very Large Corpora*, pages 45–52, Hong Kong, China. Association for Computational Linguistics.

Robin Jia and Percy Liang. 2017. Adversarial examples for evaluating reading comprehension systems. In *Proceedings of the 2017 Conference on Empirical Methods in Natural Language Processing*, pages 2021–2031.

Zhifei Li and Jason Eisner. 2009. First- and second-order expectation semirings with applications to minimum-risk training on translation forests. In *Proceedings of the 2009 Conference on Empirical Methods in Natural Language Processing*, pages 40–51, Singapore. Association for Computational Linguistics.

Xiaobo* Liang, Lijun* Wu, Juntao Li, Yue Wang, Qi Meng, Tao Qin, Wei Chen, Min Zhang, and Tie-Yan Liu. 2021. R-drop: Regularized dropout for neural networks. In *NeurIPS*.

Xuezhe Ma and Eduard Hovy. 2016. End-to-end sequence labeling via bi-directional LSTM-CNNs-CRF. In *Proceedings of the 54th Annual Meeting of the Association for Computational Linguistics (Volume 1: Long Papers)*, pages 1064–1074, Berlin, Germany. Association for Computational Linguistics.

Lars Maaløe, Casper Kaae Sønderby, Søren Kaae Sønderby, and Ole Winther. 2016. Auxiliary deep generative models.

Christopher D Manning, Mihai Surdeanu, John Bauer, Jenny Rose Finkel, Steven Bethard, and David McClosky. 2014. The stanford corenlp natural language processing toolkit. In *Proceedings of 52nd annual meeting of the association for computational linguistics: system demonstrations*, pages 55–60.

Takeru Miyato, Andrew M. Dai, and Ian Goodfellow. 2017a. Adversarial training methods for semi-supervised text classification.

Takeru Miyato, Andrew M. Dai, and Ian J. Goodfellow. 2017b. Adversarial training methods for semi-supervised text classification. In *5th International Conference on Learning Representations, ICLR 2017, Toulon, France, April 24-26, 2017, Conference Track Proceedings*. OpenReview.net.

Takeru Miyato, Shin ichi Maeda, Masanori Koyama, and Shin Ishii. 2018. Virtual adversarial training: A regularization method for supervised and semi-supervised learning.

Noriki Nishida and Hideki Nakayama. 2020. Unsupervised discourse constituency parsing using viterbi em. *Transactions of the Association for Computational Linguistics*, 8:215–230.

Jeffrey Pennington, Richard Socher, and Christopher D. Manning. 2014. Glove: Global vectors for word representation. In *Empirical Methods in Natural Language Processing (EMNLP)*, pages 1532–1543.

Hoifung Poon and Pedro Domingos. 2011. Sum-product networks: A new deep architecture. In *2011 IEEE International Conference on Computer Vision Workshops (ICCV Workshops)*, pages 689–690. IEEE.

Sebastian Ruder and Barbara Plank. 2018. Strong baselines for neural semi-supervised learning under domain shift. In *Proceedings of the 56th Annual Meeting of the Association for Computational Linguistics (Volume 1: Long Papers)*, pages 1044–1054. Association for Computational Linguistics.

Libin Shen, Jinxi Xu, and Ralph Weischedel. 2008. A new string-to-dependency machine translation algorithm with a target dependency language model. In *Proceedings of ACL-08: HLT*, pages 577–585.

Valentin I Spitkovsky, Hiyan Alshawi, and Daniel Jurafsky. 2011. Lateen em: Unsupervised training with multiple objectives, applied to dependency grammar induction. In *EMNLP*.

Valentin I Spitkovsky, Hiyan Alshawi, Daniel Jurafsky, and Christopher D Manning. 2010. Viterbi training improves unsupervised dependency parsing. In *CoNLL*.

Kewei Tu and Vasant Honavar. 2012. Unambiguity regularization for unsupervised learning of probabilistic grammars. In *Proceedings of the 2012 Joint Conference on Empirical Methods in Natural Language Processing and Computational Natural Language Learning*, pages 1324–1334.

Dilin Wang, Chengyue Gong, and Qiang Liu. 2019. Improving neural language modeling via adversarial training. In *International Conference on Machine Learning*, pages 6555–6565.

Ge Wang and Kewei Tu. 2020a. Semi-supervised dependency parsing with arc-factored variational autoencoding. In *Proceedings of the 28th International Conference on Computational Linguistics*, pages 2485–2496, Barcelona, Spain (Online). International Committee on Computational Linguistics.

Ge Wang and Kewei Tu. 2020b. Semi-supervised dependency parsing with arc-factored variational autoencoding. In *Proceedings of the 28th International Conference on Computational Linguistics*, pages 2485–2496.

Qizhe Xie, Zihang Dai, Eduard Hovy, Minh-Thang Luong, and Quoc V Le. 2019. Unsupervised data augmentation for consistency training. *arXiv preprint arXiv:1904.12848*.

David Yarowsky. 1995. Unsupervised word sense disambiguation rivaling supervised methods. In *33rd Annual Meeting of the Association for Computational Linguistics*, pages 189–196, Cambridge, Massachusetts, USA. Association for Computational Linguistics.

Michihiro Yasunaga, Jungo Kasai, and Dragomir Radev. 2018. Robust multilingual part-of-speech tagging via adversarial training. In *Proceedings of the 2018 Conference of the North American Chapter of the Association for Computational Linguistics: Human Language Technologies, Volume 1 (Long Papers)*, pages 976–986, New Orleans, Louisiana. Association for Computational Linguistics.

Huangzhao Zhang, Hao Zhou, Ning Miao, and Lei Li. 2019. Generating fluent adversarial examples for natural languages. In *Proceedings of the 57th Annual Meeting of the Association for Computational Linguistics*, pages 5564–5569, Florence, Italy. Association for Computational Linguistics.

Liwen Zhang, Zixia Jia, Wenjuan Han, Zilong Zheng, and Kewei Tu. 2022. SHARP: Search-based adversarial attack for structured prediction. In *Findings of the Association for Computational Linguistics: NAACL 2022*, pages 950–961, Seattle, United States. Association for Computational Linguistics.

Liwen Zhang, Ge Wang, Wenjuan Han, and Kewei Tu. 2021. Adapting unsupervised syntactic parsing methodology for discourse dependency parsing. In *Proceedings of the 59th Annual Meeting of the Association for Computational Linguistics and the 11th International Joint Conference on Natural Language Processing (Volume 1: Long Papers)*, pages 5782–5794, Online. Association for Computational Linguistics.

Yu Zhang, Zhenghua Li, and Min Zhang. 2020. Efficient second-order TreeCRF for neural dependency parsing. In *Proceedings of the 58th Annual Meeting of the Association for Computational Linguistics*, pages 3295–3305, Online. Association for Computational Linguistics.

Zhi-Hua Zhou and Ming Li. 2005. Tri-training: exploiting unlabeled data using three classifiers. *IEEE Transactions on Knowledge and Data Engineering*, 17(11):1529–1541.

A Hyper-Parameters Setting

We adopt most hyperparameters of the TreeCRF parser (Zhang et al., 2020). We only list parameters different from them and VAT-specific parameters in Table 7.

Name	Value
Base model	
Maximum epochs	$\{200, 100 + 100\}$
VAT-specific	
Update steps for d_w, d_c	1
α	1
ξ in Miyato et al. (2018)	0.5
ϵ in Miyato et al. (2018)	0.1
Normalization on	Token
Temperature of p, q	$\{0.3, 0.7, 1, 2\}$

Table 7: Hyper-parameters of our methods.

B Other Results

B.1 Speed Comparison

Computing the *Top-K* distribution cost more and time than our exact computation, since the former has to record the *Top-K* candidates at each step in the routine. We report the training time per epoch of several methods (Tab. 8) on WSJ(10%/90%) running on one Nvidia RTX3090.

Method	Time/epoch
Supervised	27s
HeadSelect-(1,1)	1min9s
Top-3	2min36s
ExactComp-(1,1)	1min41s

Table 8: Training speed of *Top-K* and our exact computation with batch size 64.

B.2 Analysis of Sparsity

We conduct an experiments about the motivation of sparsity adjustment. Fig.2 shows the number of the gold parse tree in the *Top-K* beams. We can see that most of the gold parses are existed in the *Top-10* parse trees. Quantitatively, we find that the number of the parses increase roughly before 4. After K reaches a large number, *e.g.*, 7, the leaning may not be easy. This observation is consistent with our empirical experiments and further suggests that natural language parsing are indeed should be adjusted in favor of sparsity.

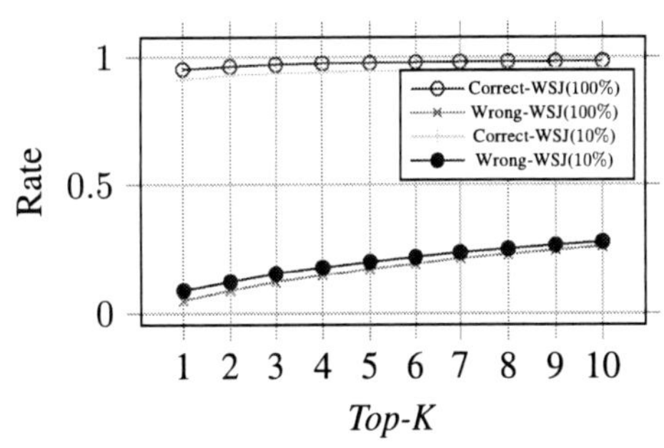

Figure 2: Correct-*: #(all arcs of *Top-K* trees ∩ gold arcs) / #tokens. Wrong-*: #(all arcs of *Top-K* trees - gold arcs) / #tokens. *-WSJ(100%)/*-WSJ(10%): the model train on the full/10% WSJ training set. We only count sentences with length⩾ 5.

KreolMorisienMT: A Dataset for Mauritian Creole Machine Translation

Raj Dabre
NICT, Japan
raj.dabre@nict.gp.jp

Aneerav Sukhoo
University of Mauritius, Mauritius
aneeravsukhoo@yahoo.com

Abstract

In this paper, we describe KreolMorisienMT, a dataset for benchmarking machine translation quality of Mauritian Creole. Mauritian Creole (Kreol Morisien) is a French-based creole and a lingua franca of the Republic of Mauritius. KreolMorisienMT consists of a parallel corpus between English and Kreol Morisien, French and Kreol Morisien and a monolingual corpus for Kreol Morisien. We first give an overview of Kreol Morisien and then describe the steps taken to create the corpora. Thereafter, we benchmark Kreol Morisien↔English and Kreol Morisien↔French models leveraging pre-trained models and multilingual transfer learning. Human evaluation reveals our systems' high translation quality.

1 Introduction

Creoles[1] are natural languages that develop from the simplifying and mixing of different languages into a new one within a fairly brief period of time. Most creoles are highly related to a widely spoken language, and in this paper, we focus on Mauritian Creole, which is a French based creole. Mauritian Creole, or Kreol Morisien, is widely spoken in the republic of Mauritius by approximately 1.2 million people. Kreol Morisien is an important language from the perspective of tourism because Mauritius is a country well known for its tourism industry. Therefore, enabling tourists and locals to easily communicate with each other should not only help the tourism industry, but also improve cultural understanding. Machine translation of Creoles is quite under researched, mainly due to the lack of publicly available datasets. Although research has been conducted on Kreol Morisien translation in the past (Dabre et al., 2014; Boodeea and Pudaruth, 2020), datasets were not released publicly, making it difficult to reproduce and continue research.

In this paper, we describe KreolMorisienMT, a dataset containing standardized evaluation sets for benchmarking Kreol Morisien↔English and Kreol Morisien↔French translation. We first give an overview of Kreol Morisien followed by the description of the dataset creation process. We then use the evaluation sets to benchmark strong Neural machine translation (NMT) (Bahdanau et al., 2015) baselines trained using the created parallel corpora. We mainly rely on transfer learning (Zoph et al., 2016) through multilingual (Dabre et al., 2020) fine-tuning of pre-trained models based on mBART. By leveraging transfer learning, we can obtain a translation quality of about 23-25 BLEU for Kreol Morisien–English and about 20-23 BLEU for Kreol Morisien–French. We manually evaluate translations to better understand the impact of transfer learning. Our results show that there is significant room for innovation for Kreol Morisien NMT and Kreol Morisien NLP in general. Our datasets, models and human evaluation annotations are publicly available[2].

2 Related Work

This paper mainly focuses on the creation of datasets for under resourced languages, specifically creoles, as well as leveraging multilingualism and transfer learning to improve translation quality.

Mauritius is a part of East Africa, and KreolMorisienMT falls under the broad area of research focusing on African language machine translation. The Masakhane[3] community heavily focuses on African language NLP (Nekoto et al., 2020), a heavily under resourced area. With regard to creole translation, Haitian creole was the first creole language to receive substantial attention (Lewis, 2010) and was featured in a WMT shared task[4]. Work

[1] https://en.wikipedia.org/wiki/Creole_language

[2] https://github.com/prajdabre/KreolMorisienNLG

[3] https://www.masakhane.io/

[4] https://www.statmt.org/wmt11/

Findings of the Association for Computational Linguistics: AACL-IJCNLP 2022, pages 22–29
November 20–23, 2022.

French	Kreol Morisien	English
avion	avion	airplane
bon	bon	good
gaz	gaz	gas
anormalité	anomali	abnormality
colère	koler	anger
méditation	meditasion	meditation

Table 1: Similarities (top half) and differences (bottom half) between English, French and Kreol Morisien.

on Kreol Morisien itself was focused on a bit later by Sukhoo et al. (2014), Dabre et al. (2014), and Boodeea and Pudaruth (2020) but unlike us, they did not release their datasets. Motivated by work on Cree (Teodorescu et al., 2022), we decided to focus on the creation of publicly available standardized datasets for Kreol Morisien to/from English and French translation. On a related note, Lent et al. (2021) work on language models for Nigerian Pidgin and Haitian creole.

Kreol Morisien is a low-resource language where multilingualism (Dabre et al., 2020; Firat et al., 2016) and transfer learning approaches involving fine-tuning (Zoph et al., 2016) are most relevant. Self-supervised pre-trained models such as mBART (Liu et al., 2020) can be used, but they are not explicitly trained on Kreol Morisien. However, Dabre et al. (2022) showed that mBART like pre-trained models can be useful for unseen related languages, and we explore this possibility in this paper. Once strong baselines are trained, approaches such as back-translation (Sennrich et al., 2016) may be used to further improve translation quality, but we do not explore this given our limited size of monolingual corpus for Kreol Morisien.

3 Kreol Morisien

Kreol Morisien is spoken in Mauritius and Rodrigues islands, and a variant is also spoken in Seychelles. Mauritius was colonized successively by the Dutch, French and British. Although the British took over the island from the French in the early 1800, French remained as a dominant language and as such Kreol Morisien shares many features with French.

featured-translation-task.html

3.1 Kreol Morisien, English and French Similarities

Table 1 contains examples of words from French, Kreol Morisien and English. The same alphabet is used for all 3 languages, and in several cases words are either written or pronounced similarly. There are several words that are either identical, nearly identical or cognate pairs (Kanojia et al., 2020) between the 3 languages such *gaz* (gas) *avion* (airplane), *bon* (good), etc. On the other hand, despite similar pronunciations, in written French there is a heavy usage of accents which is absent in Kreol Morisien. An example is *anormalité* in French, which stands for *anomali* in Kreol Morisien meaning abnormality.

3.2 Kreol Morisien Grammar

The grammar of Kreol Morisien has been published in 2011 by Daniella Police-Michel in the book Gramer Kreol Morisien (Police-Michel et al., 2012). Kreol Morisien sentence structure follows the subject-verb-object order, the same as English and French. However, some similarities and differences with English and French can be noted as follows:

Adjective placement: Like French but unlike English, adjectives are sometimes placed after the object rather than before. *The brown bird* is translated as: *Zwazo maron-la*. Here, *maron* stands for *brown* and is moved after the object (Zwazo). The article *la* which stands for *the* is moved at the end of the sentence. On the other hand, the French translation would be *L'oiseau maron* which shows that Kreol Morisien is more grammatically similar to French in terms of adjective placement but differs in terms of article placement.

Singular-plural forms: Singular and plural forms are different between English and Kreol Morisien. *There are many birds* is translated as *Ena boukou zwazo* where the plural form *zwazo* does not take the suffix *s* as in English. Instead, the word *boukou* indicates *many* and therefore, it can be deduced that there are many birds. In French, the translated sentence is *Il y a beaucoup d'oiseaux* which has the same grammatical construction as in Kreol Morisien.

Verb dropping: Verbs are sometimes dropped in Kreol Morisien. *He is bad* is translated as *Li move* where *He* is translated to *Li* and *bad* to *move*. The verb *is* is dropped. Furthermore, in French, the translated sentence becomes *Il est méchant*, where the verb is retained, indicating a difference from Kreol Morisien.

4 KreolMorisienMT

KreolMorisienMT is a mixed-domain dataset which was either created by manual translation of parts of Kreol Morisien and English books or by manual alignment of content in books that were already translated.

4.1 Data Sources

Our major sources are the holy Bible and story books. We used the online Bible from here[5]. Kreol Morisien sentences were manually aligned to their English and French counterparts to ensure high quality. Similarly, we had at our disposal 5 story books which were available in Kreol Morisien and English. However since we did not have PDF equivalents for most of the books, we ended up transcribing them. One such book which is available online is *The Flame Tree*[6] but manual alignment was done to ensure quality. We also created dictionaries, basic sentences and useful expressions manually from scratch for all 3 languages which account for most of the data. We expect dictionaries[7] to aid language learners. We included approximately 1500 basic expressions covering the following cases:, greetings, getting medical help, obtaining food from restaurants or supermarkets, simple conversations (weather, talking about oneself or others), money, accommodation.

The basic expressions should be useful for language learning as well as for use in a tourism setting. Due to the lack of human capital, not all content is translated into 3 languages, and there is more Kreol Morisien–English data than Kreol Morisien–French data. There is also a small amount of Kreol Morisien monolingual corpus, which we extracted mainly from untranslated books and online[8] articles. In the end, we obtained 23,310 and 16,739 pairs for English–Kreol Morisien and French–Kreol Morisien, respectively, as well as 45,364 Kreol Morisien monolingual sentences. The monolingual sentences are not in the Kreol Morisien side of the parallel corpus.

English–Kreol Morisien					
split	**L**	**AL-s**	**AL-t**	**U-s**	**U-t**
train	21,810	6.5	5.8	28,004	28,232
dev	500	16.9	16.2	2,330	2,164
test	1,000	17.0	16.0	3,700	3,323
French–Kreol Morisien					
split	**L**	**AL-s**	**AL-t**	**U-s**	**U-t**
train	15,239	2.6	2.0	16,171	16,754
dev	500	18.0	16.2	2,817	2,164
test	1,000	18.0	16.0	4,566	3,323
Kreol Morisien Monolingual					
split	**L**	**AL**	-		
-	45,364	15.8	-	52,425	-

Table 2: Corpora statistics for KreolMorisienMT. L, AL, U and -s/-t indicate #lines, average sentence length, #unique words and source/target language, respectively.

4.2 Dataset Statistics and Evaluation Splits

Of the 23,310 pairs for English–Kreol Morisien, 12,467 were dictionary entries. Similarly, for French–Kreol Morisien, of 16,739 pairs 12,424 were dictionary entries. Since the main goal is to develop translation systems that can translate full sentences, we decided to choose the longest sentences for the development and test sets. Furthermore, we decided to have trilingual evaluation sets following Guzmán et al. (2019) and Goyal et al. (2021). To this end, we first extracted a trilingual corpus of 13,861 sentences, sorted the corpora according to the number of words on the Kreol Morisien side and chose the top 1,500 ones representing the longest sentences. We then randomly chose 500 for the development set and 1,000 for the test set, both of which are trilingual. We remove the pairs from the English–Kreol Morisien, French–Kreol Morisien and Kreol Morisien corpora that overlap with the development and test set, resulting in 21,810, 15,239 sentence pairs and 45,364 sentences, respectively.

Table 2 contains an overview of the corpora. It is evident that there is a big mismatch between the length distributions of training and evaluation sets, but we prioritize the evaluation of medium to longer length sentences, so we have little choice.

5 Experiments

We describe the experimental settings including datasets used, training details, and models.

[5] https://www2.bible.com/en-GB/bible/344/MAT.1.NTKM2009

[6] https://shawkutis.weebly.com/uploads/1/9/7/4/19747661/flame_tree_lane_final.pdf

[7] Google translate is often used as a dictionary and we expect our dictionaries to enable out MT systems to act as dictionaries too.

[8] https://www.lalitmauritius.org/

5.1 Datasets

In addition to the parallel corpora from Kreol-MorisienMT, we use 5M randomly sampled sentence pairs from the UN corpus for French–English (Ziemski et al., 2016) which we use for pre-training a French↔English bidirectional NMT model which we contrast with the mBART-50 pre-trained denoising/MT models (Tang et al., 2021).

5.2 Training details

We train transformer (Vaswani et al., 2017) models using the YANMTT toolkit (Dabre and Sumita, 2021) which is based on the HuggingFace transformers library (Wolf et al., 2020). We use the training sets of KreolMorisienMT to create a joint English, French, Kreol Morisien 16,000 sub-words tokenizer using sentencepiece (Kudo and Richardson, 2018) for all our experiments except for fine-tuning mBART-50 based models. We do not extend the mBART-50 vocabulary. We tune hyperparameters as applicable (See Appendix A). Multilingual models are trained using the language indicator token proposed by Johnson et al. (2017). All models are trained to convergence on the relevant development sets, where convergence is said to take place if the development set BLEU score does not increase for 20 consecutive evaluations. BLEU scores are calculated using sacreBLEU with default parameters (Post, 2018). For decoding, we choose the model checkpoint with the highest validation set BLEU score and use a default beam size of 4 and length penalty of 0.8.

5.3 Models trained

We train and evaluate models for Kreol Morisien to English, English to Kreol Morisien, French to Kreol Morisien and Kreol Morisien to French. For each direction, we train:

Scratch: Unidirectional models.

Fine-tuned: Unidirectional and multilingual multiway models. We use 3 types of pre-trained models: our own English↔French models, denoising mBART-50 and its many-to-many fine-tuned version for MT from Tang et al. (2021).

6 Results

Table 6 compares unidirectional and multiway models trained from scratch and via fine-tuning.

Baselines: Owing to the tiny training set, most of which is a dictionary, unidirectional baseline models without any pre-training show poor performance of <10 BLEU. This is especially the case for translation involving French and Kreol Morisien. However, multiway models improve by up to 3.5 BLEU indicating the value of multilingualism.

Type	PT	Direction			
		cr-en	en-cr	cr-fr	fr-cr
Uni	-	9.1	9.9	4.6	5.6
Multi	-	11.1	11.5	7.9	9.3
Uni	Fr↔En	22.9	22.6	17.9	19.2
Multi	Fr↔En	22.7	22.5	19.9	22.4
Uni	MB-D	21.5	20.1	15.4	16.4
Multi	MB-D	22.3	20.8	18.3	21.0
Uni	MB-T	24.3	22.0	19.0	19.8
Multi	MB-T	**24.9**	**22.8**	**20.4**	**22.8**

Table 3: Unidirectional (Uni) and Multiway (Multi) model sacreBLEU scores with and without pre-training (PT) for translation involving Kreol Morisien (cr), English (en) and French (fr). Pre-trained models are: our own (Fr↔En), mBART-50 denoising (MB-D), and the many-to-many fine-tuned version of mBART-50 (MB-T) from Tang et al. (2021).

Fine-tuning: Both unidirectional and multilingual fine-tuning of the French↔English model trained on the UN corpus as well as the mBART-50 models leads to large improvements of >10 BLEU compared to their baseline counterparts. Especially, the performance of fine-tuning the mBART-50 models is impressive. mBART-50's vocabulary does not explicitly cover Kreol Morisien, but models fine-tuned on them still are comparable to or even outperform the French↔English model, which does. This shows the impressive power of massively multilingual models.

Denoising vs Translation Pre-training: Comparing the results of fine-tuning on the mBART-50 denoising model (MB-D) and its many-to-many translation version (MB-T) as well as the French↔English model (Fr↔En), we can see that in the absence of Kreol Morisien monolingual corpora for denoising pre-training, it is better to consider translation models for fine-tuning. However, denoising models perform reasonably well.

6.1 Human Evaluation

We randomly sample 50 examples from the test set for each translation direction and ask a native speaker of Kreol Morisien, French and English to rate the adequacy and fluency (Snover et al., 2009) of translations on a scale of 1 to 5. Additionally,

Input	Ena mem ki tom lor bann serviter, maltret zot e touy zot.
Reference	Others grabbed the servants, then beat them up and killed them.
Baseline	Some have been agreed on those servants, and they are murdered.
Fine-Tuned	Some people even fall on servants, maltreat them and kill them.
Input	"E natirelman mo prezant mo bon kamarad, Mourgat", Madam Ourit finn kontinie.
Reference	Mrs Octopus continued, "And naturally, I present my good friend Mr Squid".
Baseline	"Hey, I've got a good friends, Mr Octopus."
Fine-Tuned	"Hey obviously I present my good friend, Squid", Mrs Octopus went on.

Table 4: Examples for Kreol Morisien to English translation.

Direction	Adequacy	Fluency	#Perfect
cr-en	3.44	4.44	26
en-cr	3.73	4.35	40
cr-fr	2.64	3.70	12
fr-cr	3.30	4.24	26

Table 5: Adequacy, fluency and number of perfect translations out of 50 examples rated by a native speaker.

we ask the speaker to mark perfect translations. Due to lack of human power, we only evaluate the best system from Table 3. Annotations are in our public repository. Table 5 contains the results. Comparing Tables 3 and 5, the human evaluation scores appear to be correlated with BLEU. Kreol Morisien to French translation was rated to be of poorer quality compared to other directions. This can be attributed to the smaller training data size, the higher linguistic complexity of French than Kreol Morisien. Additionally, more than half of the translations were rated perfect with room for improvement. This shows that BLEU might underestimate the quality of translations.

6.2 Translation Examples

Table 4 contains examples generated by our MT systems for Kreol Morisien to English translation.

In the first example, taken from the holy Bible, the baseline system mistakes the act of *grabbing the servants* for *agreeing with the servants* and misses the part where the *servants are beaten up*. On the other hand, the fine-tuned model manages to capture both phenomenon properly. Both systems make the mistake of translating *others* as *some*, but this is understandable because a translation of the word *ena* in Kreol Morisien in English is *some*. The fine-tuned system also uses the word *maltreat* instead of *beat* and while this does reduce the adequacy of the translation, the general meaning is conveyed properly.

In the second example, taken from a story book, and the baseline system completely mistranslates the Kreol Morisien sentence. However, the fine-tuned model, except for the placement of the phrase *Mrs Octopus went on* to the end of the sentence and the imprecise translation of *natirelman* to *obviously*, translates almost perfectly. In the reference, *Mrs Octopus continued* is at the beginning of the sentence, and in the translation, *Mrs Octopus went on* is at the end of the sentence. The equivalent of *Mrs Octopus went on* in Kreol Morisien, *Madam Ourit finn kontinie*, is also at the end of the sentence and this explains the positioning in the translation. Multiple references and metrics may help in better evaluation by not penalizing such translations.

7 Conclusion

We have presented KreolMorisienMT, a dataset for machine translation between Mauritian Creole (Kreol Morisien) to/from English and French. Our datasets contain dictionary and sentence pairs belonging to a mix of domains and their sizes range from roughly 17,000 to 23,000 pairs. We also provide a monolingual corpus for Kreol Morisien containing about 45,000 sentences. We conduct translation experiments using KreolMorisienMT in conjunction with large English–French corpora and mBART-50 pre-trained models, leading to improvements of up to 15 BLEU, despite most of the training data being dictionary pairs. Adequacy and Fluency based human evaluation indicates high translation quality, despite BLEU scores being in the range of 20 to 25, indicating the need for better metrics. In the future, we plan to expand KreolMorisienMT with additional data as well as on additional generation tasks for Kreol Morisien. The Kreol Morisien monolingual corpus will be used in the future to extend pre-trained denoising models via light-weight adapter pre-training (Üstün et al., 2021).

References

Dzmitry Bahdanau, Kyunghyun Cho, and Yoshua Bengio. 2015. Neural machine translation by jointly learning to align and translate. In *3rd International Conference on Learning Representations, ICLR 2015, San Diego, CA, USA, May 7-9, 2015, Conference Track Proceedings*.

Zaheenah Boodeea and Sameerchand Pudaruth. 2020. Kreol morisien to english and english to kreol morisien translation system using attention and transformer model. *International Journal of Computing and Digital Systems*, 09(6):1143–1153.

Raj Dabre, Chenhui Chu, and Anoop Kunchukuttan. 2020. A survey of multilingual neural machine translation. *ACM Comput. Surv.*, 53(5).

Raj Dabre, Himani Shrotriya, Anoop Kunchukuttan, Ratish Puduppully, Mitesh Khapra, and Pratyush Kumar. 2022. IndicBART: A pre-trained model for indic natural language generation. In *Findings of the Association for Computational Linguistics: ACL 2022*, pages 1849–1863, Dublin, Ireland. Association for Computational Linguistics.

Raj Dabre, Aneerav Sukhoo, and Pushpak Bhattacharyya. 2014. Anou tradir: Experiences in building statistical machine translation systems for mauritian languages – creole, English, French. In *Proceedings of the 11th International Conference on Natural Language Processing*, pages 82–88, Goa, India. NLP Association of India.

Raj Dabre and Eiichiro Sumita. 2021. YANMTT: yet another neural machine translation toolkit. *CoRR*, abs/2108.11126.

Orhan Firat, Kyunghyun Cho, and Yoshua Bengio. 2016. Multi-way, multilingual neural machine translation with a shared attention mechanism. In *Proceedings of the 2016 Conference of the North American Chapter of the Association for Computational Linguistics: Human Language Technologies*, pages 866–875, San Diego, California. Association for Computational Linguistics.

Naman Goyal, Cynthia Gao, Vishrav Chaudhary, Peng-Jen Chen, Guillaume Wenzek, Da Ju, Sanjana Krishnan, Marc'Aurelio Ranzato, Francisco Guzman, and Angela Fan. 2021. The flores-101 evaluation benchmark for low-resource and multilingual machine translation. Cite arxiv:2106.03193.

Francisco Guzmán, Peng-Jen Chen, Myle Ott, Juan Pino, Guillaume Lample, Philipp Koehn, Vishrav Chaudhary, and Marc'Aurelio Ranzato. 2019. The FLORES evaluation datasets for low-resource machine translation: Nepali–English and Sinhala–English. In *Proceedings of the 2019 Conference on Empirical Methods in Natural Language Processing and the 9th International Joint Conference on Natural Language Processing (EMNLP-IJCNLP)*, pages 6098–6111, Hong Kong, China. Association for Computational Linguistics.

Melvin Johnson, Mike Schuster, Quoc V. Le, Maxim Krikun, Yonghui Wu, Zhifeng Chen, Nikhil Thorat, Fernanda Viégas, Martin Wattenberg, Greg Corrado, Macduff Hughes, and Jeffrey Dean. 2017. Google's multilingual neural machine translation system: Enabling zero-shot translation. *Transactions of the Association for Computational Linguistics*, 5:339–351.

Diptesh Kanojia, Malhar Kulkarni, Pushpak Bhattacharyya, and Gholamreza Haffari. 2020. Challenge dataset of cognates and false friend pairs from Indian languages. In *Proceedings of the 12th Language Resources and Evaluation Conference*, pages 3096–3102, Marseille, France. European Language Resources Association.

Taku Kudo and John Richardson. 2018. SentencePiece: A simple and language independent subword tokenizer and detokenizer for neural text processing. In *Proceedings of the 2018 Conference on Empirical Methods in Natural Language Processing: System Demonstrations*, pages 66–71, Brussels, Belgium. Association for Computational Linguistics.

Heather Lent, Emanuele Bugliarello, Miryam de Lhoneux, Chen Qiu, and Anders Søgaard. 2021. On language models for creoles. In *Proceedings of the 25th Conference on Computational Natural Language Learning*, pages 58–71, Online. Association for Computational Linguistics.

William Lewis. 2010. Haitian Creole: How to build and ship an MT engine from scratch in 4 days, 17 hours, & 30 minutes. In *Proceedings of the 14th Annual conference of the European Association for Machine Translation*, Saint Raphaël, France. European Association for Machine Translation.

Yinhan Liu, Jiatao Gu, Naman Goyal, Xian Li, Sergey Edunov, Marjan Ghazvininejad, Mike Lewis, and Luke Zettlemoyer. 2020. Multilingual denoising pre-training for neural machine translation. *Transactions of the Association for Computational Linguistics*, 8:726–742.

Wilhelmina Nekoto, Vukosi Marivate, Tshinondiwa Matsila, Timi Fasubaa, Taiwo Fagbohungbe, Solomon Oluwole Akinola, Shamsuddeen Muhammad, Salomon Kabongo Kabenamualu, Salomey Osei, Freshia Sackey, Rubungo Andre Niyongabo, Ricky Macharm, Perez Ogayo, Orevaoghene Ahia, Musie Meressa Berhe, Mofetoluwa Adeyemi, Masabata Mokgesi-Selinga, Lawrence Okegbemi, Laura Martinus, Kolawole Tajudeen, Kevin Degila, Kelechi Ogueji, Kathleen Siminyu, Julia Kreutzer, Jason Webster, Jamiil Toure Ali, Jade Abbott, Iroro Orife, Ignatius Ezeani, Idris Abdulkadir Dangana, Herman Kamper, Hady Elsahar, Goodness Duru, Ghollah Kioko, Murhabazi Espoir, Elan van Biljon, Daniel Whitenack, Christopher Onyefuluchi, Chris Chinenye Emezue, Bonaventure F. P. Dossou, Blessing Sibanda, Blessing Bassey, Ayodele Olabiyi, Arshath Ramkilowan, Alp Öktem, Adewale Akinfaderin, and Abdallah Bashir. 2020. Participatory research for low-resourced machine translation: A case study in African languages. In *Findings of the Association for Computational Linguistics: EMNLP 2020*, pages 2144–2160, Online. Association for Computational Linguistics.

D. Police-Michel, A. Carpooran, and G. Florigny. 2012. *Gramer kreol morisien: volim I. Dokiman referans*. Number v. 1 in Gramer kreol morisien. Akademi Kreol Morisien, Ministry of Education and Human Resources.

Matt Post. 2018. A call for clarity in reporting BLEU scores. In *Proceedings of the Third Conference on Machine Translation: Research Papers*, pages 186–191, Belgium, Brussels. Association for Computational Linguistics.

Rico Sennrich, Barry Haddow, and Alexandra Birch. 2016. Neural machine translation of rare words with subword units. In *Proceedings of the 54th Annual Meeting of the Association for Computational Linguistics (Volume 1: Long Papers)*, pages 1715–1725, Berlin, Germany. Association for Computational Linguistics.

Matthew Snover, Nitin Madnani, Bonnie Dorr, and Richard Schwartz. 2009. Fluency, adequacy, or HTER? Exploring different human judgments with a tunable MT metric. In *Proceedings of the Fourth Workshop on Statistical Machine Translation*, pages 259–268, Athens, Greece. Association for Computational Linguistics.

Aneerav Sukhoo, Pushpak Bhattacharyya, and Mahen Soobron. 2014. Translation between english and mauritian creole: A statistical machine translation approach. *2014 IST-Africa Conference Proceedings*, pages 1–10.

Xu Tan, Jiale Chen, Di He, Yingce Xia, Tao Qin, and Tie-Yan Liu. 2019. Multilingual neural machine translation with language clustering. In *Proceedings of the 2019 Conference on Empirical Methods in Natural Language Processing and the 9th International Joint Conference on Natural Language Processing (EMNLP-IJCNLP)*, pages 963–973, Hong Kong, China. Association for Computational Linguistics.

Yuqing Tang, Chau Tran, Xian Li, Peng-Jen Chen, Naman Goyal, Vishrav Chaudhary, Jiatao Gu, and Angela Fan. 2021. Multilingual translation from denoising pre-training. In *Findings of the Association for Computational Linguistics: ACL-IJCNLP 2021*, pages 3450–3466, Online. Association for Computational Linguistics.

Daniela Teodorescu, Josie Matalski, Delaney Lothian, Denilson Barbosa, and Carrie Demmans Epp. 2022. Cree corpus: A collection of nêhiyawêwin resources. In *Proceedings of the 60th Annual Meeting of the Association for Computational Linguistics (Volume 1: Long Papers)*, pages 6354–6364, Dublin, Ireland. Association for Computational Linguistics.

Ahmet Üstün, Alexandre Berard, Laurent Besacier, and Matthias Gallé. 2021. Multilingual unsupervised neural machine translation with denoising adapters. In *Proceedings of the 2021 Conference on Empirical Methods in Natural Language Processing*, pages 6650–6662, Online and Punta Cana, Dominican Republic. Association for Computational Linguistics.

Ashish Vaswani, Noam Shazeer, Niki Parmar, Jakob Uszkoreit, Llion Jones, Aidan N Gomez, Ł ukasz Kaiser, and Illia Polosukhin. 2017. Attention is all you need. In I. Guyon, U. V. Luxburg, S. Bengio, H. Wallach, R. Fergus, S. Vishwanathan, and R. Garnett, editors, *Proceedings of the Advances in Neural Information Processing Systems 30*, pages 5998–6008. Curran Associates, Inc.

Thomas Wolf, Lysandre Debut, Victor Sanh, Julien Chaumond, Clement Delangue, Anthony Moi, Pierric Cistac, Tim Rault, Remi Louf, Morgan Funtowicz, Joe Davison, Sam Shleifer, Patrick von Platen, Clara Ma, Yacine Jernite, Julien Plu, Canwen Xu, Teven Le Scao, Sylvain Gugger, Mariama Drame, Quentin Lhoest, and Alexander Rush. 2020. Transformers: State-of-the-art natural language processing. In *Proceedings of the 2020 Conference on Empirical Methods in Natural Language Processing: System Demonstrations*, pages 38–45, Online. Association for Computational Linguistics.

Michał Ziemski, Marcin Junczys-Dowmunt, and Bruno Pouliquen. 2016. The United Nations parallel corpus v1.0. In *Proceedings of the Tenth International Conference on Language Resources and Evaluation (LREC'16)*, pages 3530–3534, Portorož, Slovenia. European Language Resources Association (ELRA).

Barret Zoph, Deniz Yuret, Jonathan May, and Kevin Knight. 2016. Transfer learning for low-resource neural machine translation. In *Proceedings of the 2016 Conference on Empirical Methods in Natural Language Processing*, pages 1568–1575, Austin, Texas. Association for Computational Linguistics.

A Training and Hyperparameter Tuning Details

Models trained from scratch use the transformer-base architecture (Vaswani et al., 2017) whereas the French$\leftrightarrow$English model uses the transformer-big architecture. For models trained from scratch and those fine-tuned on our French$\leftrightarrow$English models, we varied the dropout, label smoothing and ADAM optimizer learning rates. Dropout values we considered were 0.1, 0.2 and 0.3. Label smoothing values considered were 0.1, 0.2 and 0.3. Learning rate values we considered were 10^{-3}, $3{*}10^{-3}$, 10^{-4} and $3{*}10^{-4}$. We found that the optimal dropout, label smoothing and learning rate values were 0.2, 0.2 and 10^{-4}, respectively. For fine-tuning mBART-50 and the many-to-many fine-tuned version of mBART-50 from Tan et al. (2019), we found that learning rate of $3{*}10^{-5}$, label smoothing of 0.1 and dropouts of 0.3 worked best. For pre-training our French$\leftrightarrow$English model, we use a learning rate of 10^{-3}, dropout of 0.1 and label smoothing of 0.1.

LEATHER: A Framework for Learning to Generate Human-like Text in Dialogue

Anthony Sicilia[1] and **Malihe Alikhani**[1,2]
{anthonysicilia, malihe}@pitt.edu
[1]Intelligent Systems Program and [2]Computer Science Department
University of Pittsburgh, Pittsburgh, PA, USA

Abstract

Algorithms for text-generation in dialogue can be misguided. For example, in task-oriented settings, reinforcement learning that optimizes only task-success can lead to abysmal lexical diversity. We hypothesize this is due to poor theoretical understanding of the objectives in text-generation and their relation to the learning process (i.e., model training). To this end, we propose a new theoretical framework for learning to generate text in dialogue. Compared to existing theories of learning, our framework allows for analysis of the multi-faceted goals inherent to text-generation. We use our framework to develop theoretical guarantees for learners that adapt to unseen data. As an example, we apply our theory to study data-shift within a cooperative learning algorithm proposed for the *GuessWhat?!* visual dialogue game. From this insight, we propose a new algorithm, and empirically, we demonstrate our proposal improves both task-success and human-likeness of the generated text. Finally, we show statistics from our theory are empirically predictive of multiple qualities of the generated dialogue, suggesting our theory is useful for model-selection when human evaluations are not available.

1 Introduction

Generating coherent, human-like text for dialogue remains a challenge. Yet, it is an inseparable component of open domain and task oriented dialogue systems like Alexa and Siri. Undoubtedly, it is also a complex process to learn. Generation based on classification (e.g., next-word prediction) over-emphasizes the likelihood of text, leading to bland qualities, which are not human-like (Holtzman et al., 2019). Meanwhile, framing dialogue generation as a Markov decision process is highly data-inefficient when compared to classification (Kakade, 2003). Further, without careful design of rewards, models can suffer from mode-collapse in dialogue, producing repetitive behaviors that are not human-like (Shekhar et al., 2019). Even carefully designed rule-based systems are brittle in the presence of unforeseen data-shift.

Theoretical analyses of learning are imperative as they provide solutions to these issues. For example, traditional (PAC) learning theory (Valiant, 1984) studies similar issues arising from computational algorithms for learning to classify. Progress in our understanding has been impressive, ranging from comprehensive guarantees on data-efficiency (Shalev-Shwartz and Ben-David, 2014) to insights for algorithm-design when the learner is faced with data-shift (Zhao et al., 2019; Zhang et al., 2019b; Tachet des Combes et al., 2020). While traditional theory may be applicable to simple generation objectives like next-word prediction, it is unfortunately unable to model more diverse goals. That is to say, it is insufficient to study replication of the diverse qualities inherent to human dialogue.

The goal of this paper is to provide a new theory for analyzing the multi-faceted objectives in computational learning of dialogue generation. In particular, we propose LEATHER[1] based on existing theories of computational learning. We demonstrate the utility of LEATHER with a focus on understanding data-shift in learning algorithms. We also show empirical results for a task-oriented visual dialogue game. In detail, we contribute as follows:

1. In Section 3, we propose LEATHER, our novel theory for computational learning of dialogue generation. We use the *GuessWhat?!* visual dialogue game (De Vries et al., 2017) as an example to ground abstract terminology in practice. We conclude Section 3 by applying our theory to analyze a cooperative learning algorithm for *GuessWhat?!*. Our theory unveils harmful shifts in data-distribution that occur during training.
2. In Section 4, we use LEATHER to study the general problem of data-shift in text-generation. We provide new theoretical study that characterizes

[1]**LEA**rning **T**heory for **H**uman-like dialogue gen**ER**ation

Findings of the Association for Computational Linguistics: AACL-IJCNLP 2022, pages 30–53
November 20–23, 2022.

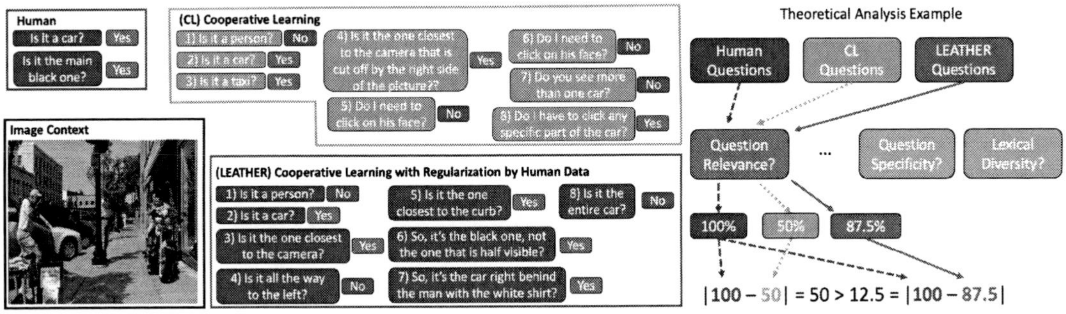

Figure 1: Examples of human and generated dialogue with original cooperative learning algorithm CL (Shekhar et al., 2019) and our learning algorithm motivated by our theory (LEATHER). Roughly, LEATHER works by applying a series of tests to generated dialogue and comparing the test results across the human and generated dialogue. Well-generated dialogue is expected to perform similarly to human dialogue on these tests. The example tests the % of relevant questions. Compared to CL, LEATHER asks more relevant questions and therefore behaves more human-like. Aggregate empirical results in Section 5 echo this trend.

statistical energy as an effective empirical tool for quantifying the impact of data-shift. Aptly, to conclude Section 4, we use energy to motivate an improved learning algorithm for our running example – the *GuessWhat?!* game.

3. In Section 5, empirically, we demonstrate the benefits of our LEATHER-inspired algorithm compared to common baselines. Importantly, we also show our proposed statistic (energy) is predictive of the quality of generated dialogue; i.e., we exhibit a linear relationship. This suggests LEATHER is useful, not only as a theoretical tool for algorithm design, but also as an empirical tool for model-selection.

Our framework is publicly available through experimental code and a Python package.[2]

2 Related Works

Theories of Learning to Generate Text Most widely, text-generation is framed as a classification problem, in which a model predicts the next word provided existing context (e.g., previous words). While common PAC learning analyses do apply to classification, this theory only describes the learner's ability at the next-word prediction task. In some specific cases, instead, PAC analysis has also been used to analyze high-level objectives and motivate conversational strategies (Sicilia et al., 2022b), but this analysis is problem-dependent. In contrast, our work offers a general problem-independent formalism for studying high-level qualities of generated text. Another frequent formalism comes from partially observable Markov decision processes (POMDPs) used to motivate reinforcement learning. For example, see Strub et al. (2017). While POMDPs remedy the issues of typical PAC analysis by supporting implementation of high-level objectives, as we are aware, there are no empirically verified theoretical studies of learning under data-shift in POMDPs. In contrast, we demonstrate LEATHER admits such a theory of learning, using it to predict the human-likeness of generated text under data-shift (where POMDPs fall short).

Theories of Learning with Data-Shift Early learning theoretic models of data-shift in classification and regression are due to Ben-David et al. (2010a,b) and Mansour et al. (2009). While modern approaches are generally similar in spirit, new statistics incorporate increasing information about the learning algorithm (Lipton et al., 2018; Kuroki et al., 2019; Germain et al., 2020; Sicilia et al., 2022a). Ultimately, such techniques tend to improve the predictive capabilities of a theory in practical application (Rabanser et al., 2019; Atwell et al., 2022). Diverse additional approaches to describing the impact of data-shift have also been proposed, for example, using integral probability metrics (Redko et al., 2017, 2020; Shen et al., 2018; Johansson et al., 2019). Unfortunately, existing works focus on classification and regression which, as discussed, are not directly applicable to dialogue generation. Further, this theory does not easily extend to generation (see Section 3.3). Ultimately, using LEATHER, our work derives a new statistic (energy) for predicting changes in model performance, which *is* applicable to dialogue generation.

Evaluation of Generated Text There are many automated metrics for evaluation of generated text including metrics based on n-grams such as BLEU

[2]github.com/anthonysicilia/LEATHER-AACL2022

(Papineni et al., 2002), ROUGE (Lin, 2004), and CIDEr (Vedantam et al., 2015). Automated metrics based on neural models are also becoming more prevalent including BLEURT (Sellam et al., 2020), BertScore (Zhang et al., 2019a), and COSMic (Inan et al., 2021). Bruni and Fernandez (2017) propose use of an adversary to discriminate between human and generated text, evaluating based on the generator's ability to fool the adversary. Human annotation and evaluation, of course, remains the gold-standard. Notably, our proposed framework encapsulates these techniques, since it is suitable for analyzing the impact of the learning process on *all of these evaluation strategies and more* (see Section 3 for examples).

3 Theory with Examples

In this section, we develop our new theoretical framework. To assist our exposition, we use the *GuessWhat?!* visual dialogue game – a variant of the child's game *I Spy* – as a running example. We first describe the game along with our modeling interests within the game. We continue with a description of our theory and then apply this theory to analyze an algorithm that learns to play the game.

3.1 *GuessWhat?!* Visual Dialogue Game

An image and **goal-object** within the image are both randomly chosen. A **question-player** with access to the image asks yes/no questions to an **answer-player** who has access to both the image and goal-object. The question-player's goal is to identify the goal-object. The answer-player's goal is to reveal the goal-object to the question-player by answering the yes/no questions appropriately. The question- and answer-player converse until the question-player is ready to make a guess or at most m questions have been asked.[3] The question-player then guesses which object was the secret goal.

Notation for Human Games To discuss this game within our theoretical framework next, we provide some notation. We assume the possible questions, answers, and objects are respectively confined to the sets $\mathcal{Q}$, $\mathcal{A}$, and $\mathcal{O}$. We also assume a set of possible images $\mathcal{I}$. A game between two human players can be represented by a series of random variables. The image-object pair is represented by the random tuple (I, O). The dialogue between the question- and answer-player is represented by the random-tuple $D = (Q_1, A_1, \ldots, Q_P, A_P)$ with some random length $P \leq m$. Each Q_i is a random question taking value from the set $\mathcal{Q}$ and each A_i is a random answer from the set $\mathcal{A}$.

Notation for Modeled Games From a modeling perspective, in this paper, we focus on the question-player and assume a human answer-player. We consider learning a model that generates the random dialogue $\hat{D} = (\hat{Q}_1, \tilde{A}_1, \ldots \hat{Q}_m, \tilde{A}_m)$ along with a predicted goal object $\hat{O}$.[4] For example, consider the model of Shekhar et al. (2019) we study later. It generates dialogue/predicted goal as below:

$$\begin{aligned} \hat{O} &= \texttt{Gues}_\alpha(\texttt{Enc}_\beta(I, \hat{D})) \\ \hat{Q}_{i+1} &= \texttt{QGen}_\theta(\texttt{Enc}_\beta(I, \hat{Q}_1, \tilde{A}_1, \ldots \hat{Q}_i, \tilde{A}_i) \end{aligned} \tag{1}$$

where, aptly, the neural-model $\texttt{QGen}_\theta : \mathbb{R}^d \to \mathcal{Q}$ is called the *question-generator* and the neural-model $\texttt{Gues}_\alpha : \mathbb{R}^d \to \mathcal{O}$ is called the *object-guesser*. The final neural-model $\texttt{Enc}_\beta : \mathcal{I} \times (\mathcal{Q} \times \mathcal{A})^* \to \mathbb{R}^d$ is called the *encoder* and captures pertinent features for the former models to share. Subscripts denote the parameters of each model (to be learned).

Modeling Goals There are two main objectives we consider. The first is task-oriented:

$$\min_{\alpha,\beta} \mathbf{E}[1\{\hat{O} \neq O\}] \tag{2}$$

which requires the predicted goal-object align with the true goal. The second objective is more elusive from a mathematical perspective: the generated dialogue $\hat{D}$ should be human-like. That is, it should be similar to the human dialogue D. As we see next, our theory is aimed at formalizing this objective.

3.2 Theoretical Framework (LEATHER)

Now, we present our proposed theory with examples from the *GuessWhat?!* game just discussed.

3.2.1 Terminology

Sets Assume a space $\mathcal{C}$, which encompasses the set of dialogue contexts, and a space $\mathcal{D}$, which encompasses the set of possible dialogues. In general, the structure of these sets and representation of elements therein are arbitrary to allow wide applicability to any dialogue system. For particular examples, consider the *Guess What?!* game: $c \in \mathcal{C}$ is an image-goal pair and $d \in \mathcal{D}$ is a list of question-answer pairs. Note, we also allow an additional, arbitrary space $\mathcal{U}$ to account for any unobserved effects on the test outputs (discussed next).

[3]By default, $m = 8$ following Shekhar et al. (2019).

[4]Notice, although the answer-player is still human, the answers may follow a distinct distribution due to dependence on the questions, so we demarcate this difference by $\tilde{\square}$.

Test Functions To evaluate generated text, we assume a group of fixed **test functions** $\{h_1 \dots h_L\}$ where for each $\ell \in [L]$ the function $h_\ell : \mathcal{D} \times \mathcal{U} \to [0,1]$ assigns a $[0,1]$-valued score that characterizes some high-level property of the dialogue. For example, a test function might be a binary value indicating presence of particular question-type, a continuous value indicating the proportion of clarification questions, a sentiment score, or some other user-evaluation. A test function can also be an automated metric like lexical diversity, for example.

Random Outputs As noted, the space $\mathcal{U}$ primarily allows the test h_ℓ to exhibit randomness due to unobserved effects. For example, this is the case when our test function is a human evaluation and randomness arises from the human annotator. To model this, we assume an unknown distribution $\mathbb{U}$ over $\mathcal{U}$, so that for $U \sim \mathbb{U}$ and dialogue $d \in \mathcal{D}$, the score $h_\ell(d, U)$ is a random variable. In general, we do not assume too much access to this randomness, since sampling from $\mathbb{U}$ can be costly; e.g., it can require recruiting new annotators or collecting new annotations. Note, U can also be used to encapsulate additional (observable) information needed to conduct the test h_ℓ (e.g., a reference dialogue).

Goal Distribution Next, we assume a **goal distribution** $\mathbb{G}$ over the set of contextualized dialogues; i.e., context-dialogue pairs in $\mathcal{C} \times \mathcal{D}$. Typically, $\mathbb{G}$ is the distribution of contextualized dialogues between human interlocutors. In the *GuessWhat?!* example, $\mathbb{G}$ is the distribution of the random, iterated tuple $((I, O), D)$. Recall, I is the random image and O is the random goal-object, which together form the context. $D = (Q_1, A_1 \dots Q_P, A_P)$ is the variable-length tuple of question-answer pairs produced by humans discussing the context (I, O).

Dialogue Learner and Environment We also assume some **dialogue learner** parameterized by $\theta \in \mathbb{R}^d$. The learner may only *partially* control each dialogue – e.g., the learner might only control a subset of the turns in each dialogue – and the mechanism through which this occurs is actually unimportant in the general setting; i.e., it will not be assumed in our theoretical results. Ultimately, we need only assume existence of some function $(\theta, c) \xrightarrow{\mathsf{E}} \mathbb{P}_\theta(c)$ where θ are the learned parameters, $c \in \mathcal{C}$ is the context, and $\mathbb{P}_\theta(c)$ is a distribution over dialogues $\mathcal{D}$. In the *GuessWhat?!* example discussed previously, the dialogue learner is $\texttt{QGen}_\theta$ and the function E is implicitly defined by Eq. (1). In particular, we have $\hat{D} \sim \mathbb{P}_\theta(I, O)$ where image I and object O are sampled from the goal-distribution of contextualized dialogues $((I, O), D) \sim \mathbb{G}$. We call E the **environment** of the learner and use $\mathsf{sans\ serif}$ in notation. In the *GuessWhat?!* example, the environment can change for a myriad of reasons: the answer-player could change strategies (inducing a new answer-distribution), the distribution of image I could change, or the distribution of the object O could change. All of which, can impact the function $(\theta, c) \xrightarrow{\mathsf{E}} \mathbb{P}_\theta(c)$. One implicit factor we encounter later is the dependence of the environment E on the encoder parameters β in Eq. (1). In discussion, we may explicitly write E_β to denote this dependence.

Formal Objective of Learner As discussed before, the conceptual task of the dialogue learner is to produce human-like text. To rephrase more formally: the task of the learner is to induce a contextualized dialogue distribution that is indistinguishable from the the goal distribution. Unfortunately, this objective is made difficult by the complexity of dialogue. In particular, it is unclear what features of the dialogue are important to measure: should we focus on the atomic structure of a dialogue, the overall semantics, or maybe just the fluency? Surely, the answer to this question is dependent on the application. For this reason, we suggest the general notion of a *test function*. Each test $\{h_1 \dots h_L\}$ can be hand selected prior to learning to emphasize a particular goal for the dialogue learner; e.g., as in Figure 1, h_1 can represent a user evaluation of question relevance, h_2 can capture lexical diversity, etc. Then, the quality of the contextualized dialogue distribution induced by the dialogue learner is measured by preservation of the output of the test functions. That is, the output of test functions should be similar when applied to human dialogue about the same context. We capture this idea through the **test divergence**:

$$\begin{aligned}
&\mathbf{TD}_{\mathsf{E}}(\theta) = \sum\nolimits_{\ell=1}^{L} \mathbf{TD}_{\mathsf{E}}^{\ell}(\theta) \\
&\text{where } \mathbf{TD}_{\mathsf{E}}^{\ell}(\theta) = \mathbf{E}[|h_\ell(D, U) - h_\ell(\hat{D}, U)|], \\
&\qquad (C, D) \sim \mathbb{G},\ \hat{D} \sim \mathbb{P}_\theta(C),\ U \sim \mathbb{U}.
\end{aligned} \tag{3}$$

Notice, the test divergence is not only dependent on the parameters of the dialogue learner, but also the environment E which governs the distribution $\mathbb{P}_\theta(C)$. Recall, this function is induced by the learner's environment and its role in eliciting generated dialogue. Finally, with all terms defined, the formal objective of the dialogue learner is typically to minimize the test divergence:

$$\min_\theta \ \mathbf{TD}_{\mathsf{E}}(\theta). \tag{4}$$

Example (BLEU/ROUGE) Useful examples of test divergence are traditional evaluation metrics, using a human reference – metrics like BLEU, ROUGE, or accuracy at next-word prediction. To see the connection, in Eq. (3), let $L = 1$, let h_1 be one of the metrics, and set $U = D$. Then, $h_1(D, U)$ computes some form of n-gram overlap between the human reference and itself, so it evaluates to 1 (full overlap). On the other hand, $h_1(\hat{D}, U)$ is the traditional notion of the metric (e.g., BLEU or ROUGE). So, the test divergence simply becomes 1 minus the average of the metric. Notice, this example shows how U can be used to encapsulate observable (random) information as well.

Example (*GuessWhat?!*) We can also consider a more complicated example in the *GuessWhat?!* game. Here, Shekhar et al. (2019) evaluate the human-likeness of dialogue with respect to the question strategies. Specifically, the authors consider a group of strategy classifiers $s_i : \mathcal{Q} \to \{0, 1\}, i \in [L]$ which each indicate presence of a particular strategy in the input question. For example, s_1 might identify if its input is a color question *"Is it blue?"* and s_2 might identify if its input is a spatial question *"Is it in the corner?"*. Then, one intuitive mathematical description of the question-strategy dissimilarity may be written

$$\mathbf{E}\Big[\sum_{i=1}^{\ell}\Big|\frac{1}{P}\sum_{j=1}^{P} s_i(Q_j) - \frac{1}{m}\sum_{k=1}^{m} s_i(\hat{Q}_k)\Big|\Big] \tag{5}$$

Above captures expected deviation in proportion of color/spatial questions from the human- to the generated-text. It also coincides with the definition of test divergence. To see this, note the above is Eq. (3) precisely when h_i returns the proportion of questions in a dialogue with type identified by s_i.

Example (Human Annotation) Human annotation is also an example, in which, human subjects are presented with two dialogue examples: one machine generated and one from a goal corpus with both dialogues pertaining to the same context. The human then annotates both examples with a score pertaining to the quality of the dialogue (e.g., the relevance of questions as in Figure 1). So, h_i is represented by the annotation process, using U to encapsulate any unobserved random effects. Then, the test divergence simply reports average absolute difference between annotations.

3.3 Application to a *GuessWhat?!* Algorithm

In this next part, we apply the theory just discussed to analyze a cooperative learning algorithm (`CL`) proposed by Shekhar et al. (2019). Recall Eq. (1), `CL` generates dialogue/predicted goal as below:

$$\begin{aligned}\hat{O} &= \mathtt{Gues}_\alpha(\mathtt{Enc}_\beta(I, \hat{D}))\\ \hat{Q}_{i+1} &= \mathtt{QGen}_\theta(\mathtt{Enc}_\beta(I, \hat{Q}_1, \tilde{A}_1, \ldots \hat{Q}_i, \tilde{A}_i)\end{aligned} \tag{6}$$

where $\mathtt{QGen}_\theta$ is the question-generator, $\mathtt{Gues}_\alpha$ is the object-guesser, and $\mathtt{Enc}_\beta$ is the encoder.

`CL` **Algorithm** Conceptually, cooperative learning encompasses a broad class of algorithms in which two or more independent model components coordinate during training to improve each other's performance. For example, this can involve a shared learning objective (Das et al., 2017). In the algorithm we consider, Shekhar et al. (2019) coordinate training of a shared encoder using two distinct learning phases. Written in the context of our theory, they are:

1. **Task-Oriented Learning**: Solve Eq. (2). Update α and β to minimize $\mathbf{E}[1\{\hat{O} \neq O\}]$.
2. **Language Learning**: Solve Eq. (4). Update θ and β to minimize $\mathbf{TD}_{\mathsf{E}_\beta}(\theta)$ where the test measures accuracy at next-word prediction.

The two phases repeat, alternating until training is finished. As is typical when training neural-networks, the parameter weights are updated using batch SGD with a differentiable surrogate loss. To do so in the **task-oriented learning phase**, $\mathtt{Gues}_\alpha$ is designed to output probability estimates for each object and the negative log-liklihood of this output distribution is minimized. In the **language learning phase**, $\mathtt{QGen}_\theta$ is designed to output probabilities for the individual utterances that compose each question. Then, the surrogate optimization is:

$$\begin{aligned}&\min_{\theta,\beta} \mathbf{E}\Big[\sum_{i+1 \leq P} \mathcal{L}(\hat{Q}_{i+1}, Q_{i+1})\Big] \quad \text{where}\\ &\hat{Q}_{i+1} = \mathtt{QGen}_\theta(\mathtt{Enc}_\beta(I, Q_1, A_1 \ldots Q_i, A_i)\end{aligned} \tag{7}$$

and $\mathcal{L}$ sums the negative logliklihood of the individual utterances. Notice, a form of *teacher-forcing* is used in this objective, so that the encoder and question-generator are conditioned on *only* human dialogue during the language learning phase. This fact will become important in the next part.

Problem Importantly, the encoder parameters β are updated in *both* the *task-oriented* and *language learning* phases. So, in the language learning phase, the dialogue learner selects θ to minimize the test divergence in cooperation with a *particular* choice of the encoder parameters – let us call these β^s. Then, in the task-oriented learning phase, the learned encoder parameters may change to a new setting β^t. Importantly, by changing the parameters in Eq. (1), we induce a *new* environment $\mathsf{E}_{\beta^t} \neq \mathsf{E}_{\beta^s}$, which governs a new generation process. For brevity, we set $\mathsf{T} = \mathsf{E}_{\beta^t}$ and $\mathsf{S} = \mathsf{E}_{\beta^s}$. This change brings us to our primary issue: the shift in learning environment *does not necessarily preserve the quality of the generated dialogue*. In terms of our formal theory, we rephrase:

$$\mathbf{TD}_{\mathsf{S}}(\theta) \stackrel{?}{=} \mathbf{TD}_{\mathsf{T}}(\theta). \tag{8}$$

Without controlling the *change* in test divergence across these two environments, it is possible the two learning phases are not "cooperating" at all.

LEATHER-Inspired Solution In general, it is clear equality will not hold, but we can still ask *how different* these quantities will be. If they are very different, the quality of the dialogue generation learned in the language learning phase may degrade substantially during the task-oriented learning phase. More generally, the problem we see here is a problem of data-shift. In learning theory, the study of data-shift is often referred to as *domain adaptation*. The test divergence on the environment S – in which we learn θ – is referred to as the **source error**, while the test divergence on the environment T – in which we evaluate θ – is referred to as the **target error**. The tool we use to quantify the change between the source error and the target error is an *adaptation bound*, in which we find a statistic Δ for which the following is true:[5]

$$\mathbf{TD}_{\mathsf{T}}(\theta) \lesssim \mathbf{TD}_{\mathsf{S}}(\theta) + \Delta. \tag{9}$$

Then, we can be sure the error in the new environment has not increased much more than Δ. In this sense, we say Δ is a **predictive statistic** because it predicts the magnitude of the target error $\mathbf{TD}_{\mathsf{T}}$ from the magnitude of the source error $\mathbf{TD}_{\mathsf{S}}$. To put it more concisely, it predicts the change in error from source to target. *When Δ is small, the change should be small too or the target error should be even lower than the source error. When Δ is large, we cannot necessarily come to this conclusion.* Importantly, for Δ to be useful in practice it should not rely on too much information. In dialogue generation, it is important for Δ to avoid reliance on the *test functions*, since these can often encompass costly sampling processes like human-evaluation.

As alluded in Section 2, many adaptation bounds exist, but as it turns out, none of them are directly applicable to dialogue generation contexts. This is because, as we are aware, computation of all previous bounds relies on efficient access to the test functions $\{h_1 \ldots h_L\}$ and samples $U \sim \mathbb{U}$, which is not always possible in dialogue. In particular, these functions, along with the sampling process $U \sim \mathbb{U}$, might represent a time-consuming, real-world processes like human-evaluation. For this reason, in the next section, we prove a new adaptation bound with new statistic Δ, which does not require access to the test functions.

[5]The inequality is approximate because there are often other statistics in the bound, but through reasonable assumptions, one statistic Δ is identified as the key quantity of interest. These assumptions should be carefully made to avoid undesirable results (Ben-David et al., 2010b; Zhao et al., 2019).

4 Text-Generation under Data-Shift

Motivated by the *GuessWhat?!* example and algorithm CL, we continue in this section with a general study of domain adaptation for dialogue generation. We begin by proposing a new (general) adaptation bound for LEATHER. We then apply this general bound to the *GuessWhat?!* algorithm CL, motivating fruitful modifications through our analysis.

4.1 A Novel Adaptation Bound for LEATHER

The Energy Statistic and Computation

Definition 4.1. *For any independent random variables A and B, the discrete energy distance is defined $\varepsilon_{01}(A, B)$ equal to*

$$2\mathbf{E}[1\{A \neq B\}] - \mathbf{E}[1\{A \neq A'\}] - \mathbf{E}[1\{B \neq B'\}] \tag{10}$$

where A' is an i.i.d copy of A, B' is an i.i.d. copy of B, and $1\{\cdot\}$ is the indicator function; i.e., it returns 1 for true arguments and 0 otherwise.

The *discrete energy distance* is a modification of the *energy distance* sometimes called the *statistical energy*. It was first proposed by Szekely (1989) and was studied extensively by Székely and Rizzo (2013) in the case where A and B are continuous variables admitting a probability density function. In general, and especially in dialogue, this is not the case. Aptly, our newly suggested form of the energy distance is more widely applicable to any variables A and B for which equality is defined. While general, this distance can be insensitive, especially when A and B take on many values. To remedy this, we introduce the following.

Definition 4.2. *Let $\mathcal{D}$ be any set. A coarsening function is a map $c : \mathcal{D} \to \mathcal{D}$ such that $c(\mathcal{D}) = \{c(d) \mid d \in \mathcal{D}\}$ is finite, and further, $|c(\mathcal{D})| < |\mathcal{D}|$.*

Since $\mathcal{D}$ is likely an immensely large set, this can make the signal $1\{a \neq b\}$ for $a, b \in \mathcal{D}$ overwhelming compared to the signal $1\{a = b\}$, and therefore, weaken the sensitivity of the discrete energy distance, overall. Coarsening functions allow us to alleviate this problem by effectively "shrinking" the set $\mathcal{D}$ to a smaller set. To do this, the role of the coarsening function is to exploit additional context to arrive at an appropriate *clustering* of the dialogues, which assigns conceptually "near" dialogues to the same cluster. So, the choice of $c(d)$ should be a "good" representation of d, in the sense that too much valuable information is not lost. As a general shorthand, for a coarsening function c and variables A, B, we write

$$\varepsilon_c(A, B) = \varepsilon_{01}(c(A), c(B)). \tag{11}$$

In this paper, we implement c using the results of a k-means clustering with details in Appendix A.

Adaptation Bound With these defined, we give the novel bound. Proof of a more general version of this bound – applicable beyond dialogue contexts (e.g., classification) – is provided in Appendix B Thm. B.1. Notably, our proof requires some technical results on the relationship between discrete energy and the characteristic functions of discrete probability distributions. These may also be of independent interest, outside the scope of this paper.

Theorem 4.1. *For any $\theta \in \mathbb{R}^d$, any coarsening function $c : \mathcal{D} \to \mathcal{D}$, and all $\ell \in [L]$*

$$\mathbf{TD}^{\ell}_{\mathsf{T}}(\theta) \leq \gamma + \varphi + \mathbf{TD}^{\ell}_{\mathsf{S}}(\theta) + \sqrt{\varepsilon_c(\tilde{D}_1, \tilde{D}_2) \times \delta} \tag{12}$$

where $\tilde{D}_1 \sim \mathbb{P}_\theta(C) = \mathsf{T}(\theta, C)$, $\tilde{D}_2 \sim \mathbb{Q}_\theta(C) = \mathsf{S}(\theta, C)$, $(C, D) \sim \mathbb{G}$, $U \sim \mathbb{U}$,[6]

$$\begin{aligned}
\gamma &= \sum\nolimits_{i \in \{1,2\}} \mathbf{E}[|h_\ell(c(\tilde{D}_i), U) - h_\ell(\tilde{D}_i, U)|] \\
g &\in \underset{f \in [0,1]^{\mathcal{D} \times \mathcal{U}}}{\arg\min} \sum\nolimits_i \mathbf{E}[|f(c(\tilde{D}_i), U) - h_\ell(D, U)|] \\
&\quad \textit{where} \quad [0,1]^{\mathcal{D} \times \mathcal{U}} = \{f \mid f : \mathcal{D} \times \mathcal{U} \to [0,1]\}. \qquad (13) \\
\varphi &= \sum\nolimits_{i \in \{1,2\}} \mathbf{E}[|g(c(\tilde{D}_i), U) - h_\ell(D, U)|] \\
\delta &= \mathbf{E}\Big[\sum\nolimits_{x \in c(\mathcal{D})} |g(x, U) - h_\ell(x, U)|\Big].
\end{aligned}$$

[6]For simplicity, let $\tilde{D}_1, \tilde{D}_2, U$ be pairwise-independent.

Unobserved Terms in Dialogue As noted, an important benefit of our theory is that we need not assume computationally efficient access to the test functions $\{h_1 \ldots h_L\}$ or samples $U \sim \mathbb{U}$. Yet, the reader likely notices a number of terms in Eq. (12) dependent on both of these. Similar to the traditional case, we argue that our theory is still predictive because it is often appropriate to assume these unobserved terms are small, or otherwise irrelevant. We address each of them in the following:

1. The term γ captures average change in test output as a function of the coarsening function c. Whenever $c(\tilde{D}_i)$ is a good representative of $\tilde{D}_i$ (i.e., it maintains information to which h_ℓ is sensitive) γ should be small.
2. The next term φ is the smallest sum of expected differences that *any* function of the coarsened dialogues $c(\tilde{D}_i)$ and the arbitrary randomness U can achieve in mimicking the true test scores $h_\ell(D, U)$. Since the set of all functions from $\mathcal{D} \times \mathcal{U}$ to $[0, 1]$ should be very expressive, this can be seen as another requirement on our coarsened dialogues $c(\tilde{D}_i)$. For example, when $c(\tilde{D}_i) = \tilde{D}_i \approx D$ this term can be close to zero. When instead $|c(\mathcal{D})|$ is much smaller than $|\mathcal{D}|$ (e.g., a singleton set), we expect φ to grow.
3. The last term δ can actually be large. Fortunately, since δ is multiplied by the energy distance, this issue is mitigated when the statistical energy is small enough. Ultimately, the energy is paramount in controlling the impact of this term on the bound's overall magnitude.

A Predictive Theory Granted the background above, our discussion reduces the predictive aspect of the bound to a single key quantity: the discrete energy distance $\varepsilon_c(\tilde{D}_1, \tilde{D}_2)$. In particular, besides the test divergence $\mathbf{TD}_{\mathsf{S}}$, all other terms can be assumed reasonably small by proper choice of the coarsening function, or otherwise controlled by the statistical energy through multiplication. Note, the first issue is discussed in Appendix A. Ultimately, the main takeaway is that statistical energy plays the role of Δ as discussed in Section 3.3.

4.2 A New Cooperative Learning Algorithm

With all theoretical tools in play, we return to the algorithm CL and the problem raised in Section 3.3.

LEATHER-Motivated Modification Recall, we are interested in quantifying and controlling the change in error from source $\mathbf{TD}_{\mathsf{S}}(\theta)$ to target $\mathbf{TD}_{\mathsf{T}}(\theta)$ across the training phases. Based on our

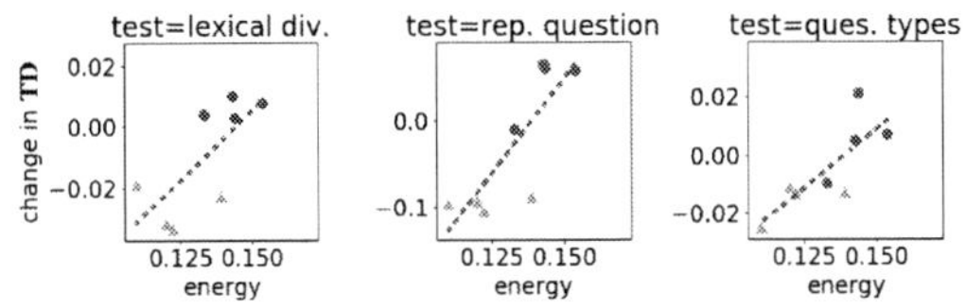

Figure 2: Energy between training phases. Energy is predictive of change in test divergence as desired. Dotted line is line of best fit. Blue circles (CL) indicate use of *only* generated dialogue in task-oriented learning phase. Orange triangles (LEATHER) indicate regularization with human data.

theory, we know we should decrease the statistical energy between dialogues to reduce this change. That is, we should reduce the distance between the generated dialogue distributions across learning phases. We hypothesize this may be done by incorporating human dialogue in the task-oriented learning phase. The encoder in CL sees *no* human dialogue when forming the prediction $\hat{O}$ that is compared to O during task-oriented learning – as seen in Eq. (1), only the generated dialogue $\hat{D}$ is used. In contrast, the encoder sees *only* the human dialogue D in the alternate language learning phase – i.e., as seen in the surrogate objective in Eq. (7). We hypothesize this stark contrast produces large shifts in the parameters $\beta^s \to \beta^t$ between phases. Instead, we propose to *regularize* the task-oriented learning phase with human dialogue as below:

$$\begin{aligned} &\min_{\alpha,\beta} \mathbf{E}[1[\hat{O} \neq O]] + \mathbf{E}[1[\hat{O}' \neq O]] \quad \text{where} \\ &\hat{O}' = \texttt{Gues}_\alpha(\texttt{Enc}_\beta(I, D)), \quad ((I, O), D) \sim \mathbb{G} \end{aligned} \tag{14}$$

and $\hat{O}$ is still as described in Eq. (1). Intuitively, this should constrain parameter shift from $\beta^s \to \beta^t$, thereby constraining the change in outputs of the encoder, and ultimately constraining the change in outputs of the question-generator, which is conditioned on the encoder outputs. As the generated dialogue distributions from distinct learning phases will be more similar by this constraint, we hypothesize the penultimate effect will be decreased statistical energy (i.e., since energy measures distance of distributions). Based on our theory, reduced energy provides resolution to our problem: test divergence should be preserved from source to target.

5 Experiments

5.1 Cooperative Learning via LEATHER

Setup In general, we use experimental settings of Shekhar et al. (2019) (e.g., hyperparameters, validation, etc.) with full details available in the code. CL denotes the original algorithm proposed by Shekhar et al. (2019) (Section 3.3). LEATHER denotes our LEATHER-inspired modification (Section 4.2).

Automated Metrics We report average accuracy **acc** of the guesser module in identifying the true goal-object across three random seeds as well as average lexical diversity (**lexdiv**; type/token ratio over all dialogues), average question diversity (**qdiv**; % unique questions over all dialogues), and average percent of dialogues with verbatim repeated questions (**repq**). **acc** quantifies task-success, while subsequent metrics are designed to quantify human-likeness of the generated dialogue. These metrics were all previously computed by Shekhar et al. (2019) with details in their code.

Human Evaluation We asked two annotators to help us further evaluate the results. Throughout the process, human subject guidelines from the authors' institution were followed and the task was approved by our institution human subject board. The annotators examined contextualized human dialogues and generated dialogues from a CL model and LEATHER model. All dialogues used the same image/goal context and annotators observed all dialogues for a specific context in random order without knowing how each dialogue was created. Across 50+ dialogues, average percentage of irrelevant questions per dialogue (**irrq**) was determined.[7] Average percentage of specific questions (**spcq**) was also determined.[8] We report **TD**, which gives the average *difference* in percentages from the corresponding human dialogue. Sans scaling, these **TD** metrics are examples of the test divergence in Eq. (3) using a human-evaluation test function. Qualitative analysis of errors was also conducted based on annotator remarks (provided later in this section).

Impact of LEATHER In Table 1, we compare the cooperative learning algorithms CL and LEATHER. The former uses only the generated dialogue during task-oriented learning, while the latter incorporates human data to regularize the change in parameters underlying the environmental shift. As predicted by our theory, regularization is very beneficial, improv-

[7] An *irrelevant* question ignores the image or current dialogue context. For example, in Figure 1, CL asks about the man's "face" (Q5) after learning the goal-object is a car, which ignores dialogue-context. CL also hallucinates an object "cut off" on the right side (Q4), which ignores image context.

[8] A *specific* question contains two or more modifiers of one or more nouns. For example, LEATHER modifies "car" with "behind" and "man" with "the white shirt" in Figure 1 Q7.

	acc ↑	lexdiv ↑	qdiv ↑	repq ↓	irrq(TD) ↓	spcq(TD) ↓	energy ↓
CL	57.1 (55.9)	9.98 (10.7)	13.5 (14.3)	55.9 (58.2)	30.5	23.3	0.143
LEATHER	58.4 (56.9)	11.4 (12.7)	13.1 (16.0)	53.6 (47.5)	26.2	19.5	0.123
RL	56.3	7.3	1.04	96.5	-	-	-

Table 1: Comparison of CL and our theory-motivated modification LEATHER. Best epoch based on validation **acc** is reported with last epoch in parentheses. Up/down arrows indicate objective. Metrics are on 100 point scale, excluding **energy**. The first 4 metrics are automated, the next 2 are from human evaluation, and the last is our proposed statistic. LEATHER improves accuracy and human-likeness of dialogue. Further, our proposed statistic **energy** is predictive of human-likeness.

ing task-success and human-likeness. For example, LEATHER decreases % of irrelevant questions by 4.8% compared to CL, which is more similar to human dialogue according to the test divergence (**TD**). Interestingly, LEATHER also decreased % of specific questions by 1.7%. Based on the **TD**, this is *also* more similar to human dialogue, indicating humans ask fewer specific questions too. The design of the **TD** allows us to capture these non-intuitive results. Notably, regularization inspired by LEATHER *allows us to train longer* without degrading task-success or suffering from mode collapse (i.e., repeated questions). Automated human-likeness metrics for the last epoch (in parentheses) show substantial improvements over CL in this case.

Cooperative vs. Reinforcement Learning In Table 1, we compare the two cooperative learning algorithms CL and LEATHER to the reinforcement learning algorithm (RL). We use the results reported by Shekhar et al. (2019) for RL, since we share an experimental setup. Compared to RL, both cooperative learning approaches improve task success and human-likeness. As noted in Section 2, the theoretical framework for RL (i.e., POMDPs) is not equipped to study interaction of the distinct learning phases within this algorithm (i.e., with respect to data-shift). Better theoretical understanding could explain poor performance and offer improvement as demonstrated with LEATHER, which improves human-likeness of CL.

Qualitative Analysis In dialogue generated by CL, questions with poor relevance ignored the image context (e.g., model hallucination). In dialogue generated by the LEATHER model, irrelevant questions ignored current dialogue context (e.g., a question which should already be inferred from existing answers). We hypothesize this may be due to poor faith in the automated answer-player used for training, which also has problems with model hallucination (e.g., Figure 1). Both models had issues with repeated questions. In human dialogue, issues were grammatical with few irrelevant questions.

5.2 LEATHER is Empirically Predictive

Here, we show statistical energy predicts test divergence, empirically. Computation of energy can be automated, so predictive ability is useful for model-selection when human evaluation is not available. We consider test divergence (**TD**) with 4 groups of tests: (**A**) the 9 fine-grained strategy classifiers of Shekhar et al. (2019) used as in Eq. (5), (**B**) lexical diversity computed as type/token ratio per dialogue, (**C**) question repetition computed as a binary indicator for each dialogue, and (**D**) the discussed human-evaluations of question relevance/specificity. Figure 2 plots change in **TD** for (**A-C**) as a function of energy. Specifically, change in **TD** is the difference $\mathbf{TD}_\mathsf{T}(\theta) - \mathbf{TD}_\mathsf{S}(\theta)$ where S and T are defined by the transition from language learning to task-oriented learning discussed in Section 3. We plot this change at the transitions after epochs 65, 75, 85, and 95 (out of 100 total). Notably, *energy is predictive and, specifically, is linearly related to change in test divergence.* For (**D**), in Table 1, we show average energy across all transitions compared to test divergence. Energy is also predictive for these human-evaluation tests.

6 Conclusion

This work presents LEATHER, a theoretically motivated framework for learning to generate human-like dialogue. The energy statistic, which is derived from this theory, is used to analyze *and improve* an algorithm for task-oriented dialogue generation. Further, energy is empirically predictive of improvements in dialogue quality, measured by both automated and human evaluation. Future work may involve more experiments to test the utility of LEATHER in other dialogue settings. Theoretically, we hope to study sample-complexity in LEATHER, which is a hallmark of common PAC theories.

Acknowledgments

We thank the anonymous reviewers for helpful feedback and Jennifer C. Gates, CCC-SLP, for input on qualitative evaluations of dialogue in experiments.

References

Katherine Atwell, Anthony Sicilia, Seong Jae Hwang, and Malihe Alikhani. 2022. The change that matters in discourse parsing: Estimating the impact of domain shift on parser error. In *Findings of the Association for Computational Linguistics: ACL 2022*, pages 824–845.

Shai Ben-David, John Blitzer, Koby Crammer, Alex Kulesza, Fernando Pereira, and Jennifer Wortman Vaughan. 2010a. A theory of learning from different domains. *Machine learning*, 79(1):151–175.

Shai Ben-David, Tyler Lu, Teresa Luu, and Dávid Pál. 2010b. Impossibility theorems for domain adaptation. In *Proceedings of the Thirteenth International Conference on Artificial Intelligence and Statistics*, pages 129–136. JMLR Workshop and Conference Proceedings.

Samuel R Bowman, Luke Vilnis, Oriol Vinyals, Andrew M Dai, Rafal Jozefowicz, and Samy Bengio. 2015. Generating sentences from a continuous space. *arXiv preprint arXiv:1511.06349*.

Elia Bruni and Raquel Fernandez. 2017. Adversarial evaluation for open-domain dialogue generation. In *Proceedings of the 18th Annual SIGdial Meeting on Discourse and Dialogue*, pages 284–288.

R Cuppens. 1975. Decomposition of multivariate distributions.

Abhishek Das, Satwik Kottur, José MF Moura, Stefan Lee, and Dhruv Batra. 2017. Learning cooperative visual dialog agents with deep reinforcement learning. In *Proceedings of the IEEE international conference on computer vision*, pages 2951–2960.

Harm De Vries, Florian Strub, Sarath Chandar, Olivier Pietquin, Hugo Larochelle, and Aaron Courville. 2017. Guesswhat?! visual object discovery through multi-modal dialogue. In *Proceedings of the IEEE Conference on Computer Vision and Pattern Recognition*, pages 5503–5512.

Pascal Germain, Amaury Habrard, François Laviolette, and Emilie Morvant. 2020. Pac-bayes and domain adaptation. *Neurocomputing*, 379:379–397.

Ari Holtzman, Jan Buys, Li Du, Maxwell Forbes, and Yejin Choi. 2019. The curious case of neural text degeneration. In *International Conference on Learning Representations*.

Mert Inan, Piyush Sharma, Baber Khalid, Radu Soricut, Matthew Stone, and Malihe Alikhani. 2021. Cosmic: A coherence-aware generation metric for image descriptions. *arXiv preprint arXiv:2109.05281*.

Fredrik D Johansson, David Sontag, and Rajesh Ranganath. 2019. Support and invertibility in domain-invariant representations. In *The 22nd International Conference on Artificial Intelligence and Statistics*, pages 527–536. PMLR.

Sham Machandranath Kakade. 2003. *On the sample complexity of reinforcement learning*. University of London, University College London (United Kingdom).

Seiichi Kuroki, Nontawat Charoenphakdee, Han Bao, Junya Honda, Issei Sato, and Masashi Sugiyama. 2019. Unsupervised domain adaptation based on source-guided discrepancy. In *Proceedings of the AAAI Conference on Artificial Intelligence*, volume 33, pages 4122–4129.

Chin-Yew Lin. 2004. Rouge: A package for automatic evaluation of summaries. In *Text summarization branches out*, pages 74–81.

Zachary Lipton, Yu-Xiang Wang, and Alexander Smola. 2018. Detecting and correcting for label shift with black box predictors. In *International conference on machine learning*, pages 3122–3130. PMLR.

Yishay Mansour, Mehryar Mohri, and Afshin Rostamizadeh. 2009. Domain adaptation: Learning bounds and algorithms. *arXiv preprint arXiv:0902.3430*.

Kishore Papineni, Salim Roukos, Todd Ward, and Wei-Jing Zhu. 2002. Bleu: a method for automatic evaluation of machine translation. In *Proceedings of the 40th annual meeting of the Association for Computational Linguistics*, pages 311–318.

María Pérez-Ortiz, Omar Rivasplata, John Shawe-Taylor, and Csaba Szepesvári. 2021. Tighter risk certificates for neural networks. *Journal of Machine Learning Research*, 22.

Stephan Rabanser, Stephan Günnemann, and Zachary Lipton. 2019. Failing loudly: An empirical study of methods for detecting dataset shift. *Advances in Neural Information Processing Systems*, 32.

Ievgen Redko, Amaury Habrard, and Marc Sebban. 2017. Theoretical analysis of domain adaptation with optimal transport. In *ECML PKDD*, pages 737–753. Springer.

Ievgen Redko, Emilie Morvant, Amaury Habrard, Marc Sebban, and Younès Bennani. 2020. A survey on domain adaptation theory. *ArXiv*, abs/2004.11829.

Thibault Sellam, Dipanjan Das, and Ankur Parikh. 2020. BLEURT: Learning robust metrics for text generation. In *Proceedings of the 58th Annual Meeting of the Association for Computational Linguistics*, pages 7881–7892, Online. Association for Computational Linguistics.

Shai Shalev-Shwartz and Shai Ben-David. 2014. *Understanding machine learning: From theory to algorithms*. Cambridge university press.

Ravi Shekhar, Aashish Venkatesh, Tim Baumgärtner, Elia Bruni, Barbara Plank, Raffaella Bernardi, and Raquel Fernández. 2019. Beyond task success: A closer look at jointly learning to see, ask, and GuessWhat. In *Proceedings of the 2019 Conference of the North American Chapter of the Association for Computational Linguistics: Human Language Technologies, Volume 1 (Long and Short Papers)*, pages 2578–2587, Minneapolis, Minnesota. Association for Computational Linguistics.

Jian Shen, Yanru Qu, Weinan Zhang, and Yong Yu. 2018. Wasserstein distance guided representation learning for domain adaptation. In *AAAI*.

Anthony Sicilia, Katherine Atwell, Malihe Alikhani, and Seong Jae Hwang. 2022a. Pac-bayesian domain adaptation bounds for multiclass learners. In *The 38th Conference on Uncertainty in Artificial Intelligence*.

Anthony Sicilia, Tristan Maidment, Pat Healy, and Malihe Alikhani. 2022b. Modeling non-cooperative dialogue: Theoretical and empirical insights. *Transactions of the Association for Computational Linguistics*, 10:1084–1102.

Florian Strub, Harm De Vries, Jeremie Mary, Bilal Piot, Aaron Courvile, and Olivier Pietquin. 2017. End-to-end optimization of goal-driven and visually grounded dialogue systems. In *Proceedings of the 26th International Joint Conference on Artificial Intelligence*, pages 2765–2771.

Gabor J Szekely. 1989. Potential and kinetic energy in statistics. *Lecture Notes, Budapest Institute*.

Gábor J Székely and Maria L Rizzo. 2013. Energy statistics: A class of statistics based on distances. *Journal of statistical planning and inference*, 143(8):1249–1272.

Remi Tachet des Combes, Han Zhao, Yu-Xiang Wang, and Geoffrey J Gordon. 2020. Domain adaptation with conditional distribution matching and generalized label shift. *Advances in Neural Information Processing Systems*, 33:19276–19289.

Leslie G Valiant. 1984. A theory of the learnable. *Communications of the ACM*, 27(11):1134–1142.

Ramakrishna Vedantam, C Lawrence Zitnick, and Devi Parikh. 2015. Cider: Consensus-based image description evaluation. In *Proceedings of the IEEE conference on computer vision and pattern recognition*, pages 4566–4575.

Tianyi Zhang, Varsha Kishore, Felix Wu, Kilian Q Weinberger, and Yoav Artzi. 2019a. Bertscore: Evaluating text generation with bert. *arXiv preprint arXiv:1904.09675*.

Yuchen Zhang, Tianle Liu, Mingsheng Long, and Michael Jordan. 2019b. Bridging theory and algorithm for domain adaptation. In *International Conference on Machine Learning*, pages 7404–7413. PMLR.

Han Zhao, Remi Tachet Des Combes, Kun Zhang, and Geoffrey Gordon. 2019. On learning invariant representations for domain adaptation. In *International Conference on Machine Learning*, pages 7523–7532. PMLR.

A Novel Adaptation Bound and Computation of Energy Statistic

In this section, we give our novel adaptation bound and details for the accompanying energy statistic. There is some redundancy between this section and Section 4, but in general, this section is more detailed. Recall, *source* error is denoted $\mathbf{TD}_\mathsf{S}$ and is observed on the environment $\mathbb{Q}_\theta(c) = \mathsf{S}(\theta, c)$. The *target* error is denoted $\mathbf{TD}_\mathsf{T}$ and is observed on the environment $\mathbb{P}_\theta(c) = \mathsf{T}(\theta, c)$. For the algorithm CL discussed in the main text, the target is induced by the task-oriented learning phase and the source is induced by the language learning phase.

A.1 The Problem with Traditional Bounds

Predictive Adaptation Theories An important quality of traditional domain adaptation bounds, proposed for classification and regression problems, is that they offer a *predictive theory*. Namely, without observing the target error $\mathbf{TD}_\mathsf{T}$, we can infer this quantity from Δ and the source error $\mathbf{TD}_\mathsf{S}$. The utility of this is two-fold: first, it allows us to design algorithms that prepare a learner for data-shift by controlling Δ; second, it allows a practitioner to select an appropriate model to deploy in the presence of data-shift by comparing the different values of Δ for each model. In general, these use-cases would not be possible without Δ because the target error $\mathbf{TD}_\mathsf{T}$ *is not observable until it is too late.* In contrast, the quantity Δ *should* be observable. While this is not always true of Δ, authors typically reduce the main effect of Δ to one key statistic, which *is* observable. For example, Atwell et al. (2022) reduce Δ to one key statistic called the h-discrepancy by suggesting the other components making up Δ are small. This is why we use an "approximate" inequality in the main text, since other (small) terms may contribute to the bound.

Traditional Theories Are Not Predictive Traditional theories of adaptation are *not* predictive for dialogue generation. Namely, computation of Δ and its key components generally relies on computationally efficient access to the tests $\{h_1 \dots h_L\}$ and requires sampling from the unknown distribution $U \sim \mathbb{U}$. While we can always *observe* the outputs of $\{h_1 \dots h_L\}$ with randomness $U \sim \mathbb{U}$ through the source error $\mathbf{TD}_\mathsf{S}(\theta)$, it is *not* always the case that we have computational efficiently access to these tests or the randomness. For example, as noted in Section 3.2.1, the group of tests $\{h_1 \dots h_L\}$ along with samples U from the unknown distribution $\mathbb{U}$ may represent complex real-world processes such as human-evaluation. Even for simpler evaluation metrics based on text-classifiers (e.g., like $\{s_1 \dots s_L\}$ in Eq. (5)) algorithms for computing Δ turn out to be non-trivial, and must be handled on a case-by-case basis. Thus, in generation contexts, we typically have no way of computing Δ algorithmically, and when we do, it can be difficult to implement. If we require an easily implemented, predictive theory, then the classical theory is ruled out. As a solution, we propose a novel adaptation bound.

A.2 A Novel Adaptation Bound

First, we define some terms.

The Energy Statistic and Computation

Definition A.1. *For any independent random variables A and B, the discrete energy distance is defined:*

$$\varepsilon_{01}(A, B) = 2\mathbf{E}[1\{A \neq B\}] - \mathbf{E}[1\{A \neq A'\}] - \mathbf{E}[1\{B \neq B'\}] \tag{15}$$

where A' is an i.i.d copy of A, B' is an i.i.d. copy of B, and $1\{\cdot\}$ is the indicator function; i.e., it returns 1 for true arguments and 0 otherwise.

The *discrete energy distance* is a modification of the *energy distance* sometimes called the *statistical energy*. It was first proposed by Szekely (1989) and was studied extensively by Székely and Rizzo (2013) in the case where A and B are continuous variables admitting a probability density function. In general, and especially in dialogue, this is not the case. Aptly, we suggest the above form of the energy distance, which is widely applicable to any variables A and B for which equality is defined. While general, this energy distance can be strict and insensitive, especially when A and B take on many possible values. To remedy this, we propose the following addendum.

Definition A.2. *Let $\mathcal{D}$ be any set. A coarsening function is a map $c : \mathcal{D} \to \mathcal{D}$ such that $c(\mathcal{D}) = \{c(d) \mid d \in \mathcal{D}\}$ is finite, and further, $|c(\mathcal{D})| < |\mathcal{D}|$.*

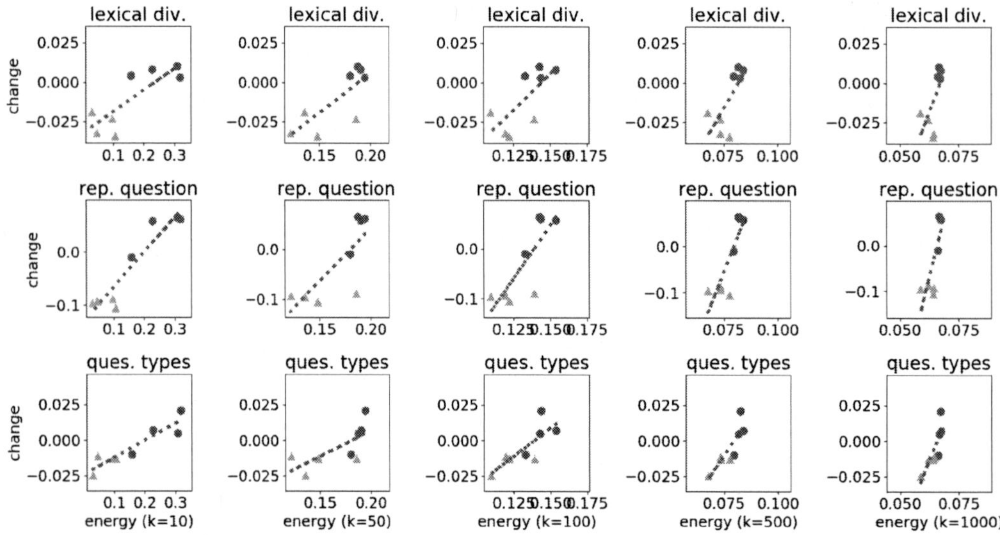

Figure 3: Comparison of energy statistics and automated test functions as in Section 5. Here, we vary the parameter k in the k-means clustering used to determine the *coarsening function* when computing energy. Trends reported in the main text are robust to variation in k.

Since $\mathcal{D}$ is likely an immensely large set, this can make the signal $1\{a \neq b\}$ for $a, b \in \mathcal{D}$ overwhelming compared to the signal $1\{a = b\}$, and therefore, weaken the sensitivity of the discrete energy distance, overall. Coarsening functions allow us to alleviate this problem by effectively "shrinking" the set $\mathcal{D}$ to a smaller set. To do this, the role of the coarsening function is to exploit additional context to arrive at an appropriate *clustering* of the dialogues, which assigns conceptually "near" dialogues to the same cluster. So, the choice of $c(d)$ should be a "good" representation of d, in the sense that too much valuable information is not lost. As a general shorthand, for a coarsening function c and variables A, B, we write

$$\varepsilon_c(A, B) = \varepsilon_{01}(c(A), c(B)). \tag{16}$$

Example One example of a coarsening function for dialogues is k-means clustering. In fact, this is the coarsening function we use to compute energy in Section 5, selecting $k = 100$. Real-valued vector representations of dialogues (e.g., from model latent space) can capture semantic information about the dialogue (Bowman et al., 2015), so we use latent space representations (i.e., the output of the encoder) to represent each dialogue and conduct a k-means clustering on these representations. For a dialogue d the output $c(d)$ is then defined by the cluster of d; i.e., we select an arbitrary dialogue to represent the whole of each cluster and assign this dialogue as the output $c(d)$. In practical implementations, it is typically easier to just compute the energy distance on the cluster labels themselves; this statistic is always equivalent to the energy on the coarsened dialogues, since the map between cluster representatives and cluster labels is bijective. Later, within Lemma B.3, we prove this equivalence for any bijective map.

Of course, regardless of implementation, this clustering is dependent on the choice of k. Figure 3 shows that the results in Section 5 are robust to different choices of k. In all cases, there is a linear relationship between the energy and the change in the test divergence.

Adaptation Bound With these defined, we give the novel bound. Proof of a more general version of this bound – applicable beyond dialogue contexts – is provided in Appendix B Thm. B.1. In particular, the general version is "backwards compatible" in the sense that it also applies to traditional learning theoretic settings like classification and regression. Arguably, in these settings, it also remains more computationally efficient than existing theories. Notably, our proof requires some technical results on the relationship between discrete energy and the characteristic functions of discrete probability distributions. These may also be of independent interest, outside the scope of this paper.

Theorem A.1. *For any $\theta \in \mathbb{R}^d$, any coarsening function $c : \mathcal{D} \to \mathcal{D}$, and all $\ell \in [L]$*

$$\mathbf{TD}^{\ell}_{\mathsf{T}}(\theta) \leq \gamma + \varphi + \mathbf{TD}^{\ell}_{\mathsf{S}}(\theta) + \sqrt{\varepsilon_c(\tilde{D}_1, \tilde{D}_2) \times \delta} \tag{17}$$

where $\tilde{D}_1 \sim \mathbb{P}_\theta(C) = \mathsf{T}(\theta, C)$, $\tilde{D}_2 \sim \mathbb{Q}_\theta(C) = \mathsf{S}(\theta, C)$, $(C, D) \sim \mathbb{G}$, $U \sim \mathbb{U}$,[9]

$$\begin{aligned}
&\gamma = \mathbf{E}[|h_\ell(c(\tilde{D}_1), U) - h_\ell(\tilde{D}_1, U)|] + \mathbf{E}[|h_\ell(c(\tilde{D}_2), U) - h_\ell(\tilde{D}_2, U)|] \\
&g \in \underset{f \in [0,1]^{\mathcal{D}\times\mathcal{U}}}{\arg\min} \sum\nolimits_i \mathbf{E}[|f(c(\tilde{D}_i), U) - h_\ell(D, U)|] \quad \textit{where} \quad [0,1]^{\mathcal{X}\times\mathcal{U}} = \{f \mid f : \mathcal{X}\times\mathcal{U} \to [0,1]\}. \\
&\varphi = \mathbf{E}[|g(c(\tilde{D}_1), U) - h_\ell(D, U)|] + \mathbf{E}[|g(c(\tilde{D}_2), U) - h_\ell(D, U)|] \\
&\delta = \mathbf{E}\Big[\sum\nolimits_{x \in c(\mathcal{D})} |g(x, U) - h_\ell(x, U)|\Big].
\end{aligned} \tag{18}$$

Unobserved Terms in Dialogue As noted, an important benefit of our theory is that we need not assume computationally efficient access to the test functions $\{h_1 \ldots h_L\}$ or samples $U \sim \mathbb{U}$. Yet, the reader likely notices a number of terms in Eq. (17) dependent on both of these. Similar to the traditional case, we argue that our theory is still predictive because it is typically appropriate to assume these unobserved terms are small, or otherwise irrelevant. We address each of them in the following:

1. The term γ captures average change in test output as a function of the coarsening function c. Whenever $c(\tilde{D}_i)$ is a good representative of $\tilde{D}_i$ (i.e., it maintains information to which h_ℓ is sensitive) γ should be small. Since we choose the coarsening function, the former premise is not a strong requirement. In practice, if choice of c is unclear, we recommend studying many choices as in Figure 3.
2. The next term φ is the smallest sum of expected differences that *any* function of the coarsened dialogues $c(\tilde{D}_i)$ and the arbitrary randomness U can achieve in mimicking the true test scores $h_\ell(D, U)$. In general, the set of all functions from $\mathcal{D} \times \mathcal{U}$ to $[0, 1]$ should be very expressive; e.g., it contains h_ℓ itself and any other function which might mimic $h_\ell(D, U)$ better when applied to $c(\tilde{D}_i)$ and U. So, it is not unreasonable to expect some good minimizer to exist, and therefore, φ to be small. Using this logic, one additional constraint is that $c(\tilde{D}_i)$ has appropriate variance. For instance, if $c(\tilde{D}_i)$ is constant and D is not, φ can easily be large. Instead, when $c(\tilde{D}_i)$ does have variance, the expressiveness of the function class $[0, 1]^{\mathcal{D}\times\mathcal{U}}$ can be well exploited. For reasonable dialogue learners and a well-chosen c, the variance of $c(\tilde{D}_i)$ is a non-issue.
3. The last term δ may actually be large, but we argue this is also a non-issue for interpretation purposes. In general, because δ is an *unnormalized* sum, its magnitude grows with the size of $c(\mathcal{D})$, even if the individual summands may be small. Fortunately, since δ is multiplied by the energy distance, this issue is mitigated when the statistical energy is small enough. Ultimately, the energy is paramount in controlling the impact of this term on the bound's overall magnitude.

A Predictive Theory Granted the background above, our discussion reduces the predictive aspect of the bound to a single key quantity: the discrete energy distance $\varepsilon_c(\tilde{D}_1, \tilde{D}_2)$. In particular, besides the test divergence $\mathbf{TD}_{\mathsf{S}}$ (known prior to the environmental change), all other terms can be assumed reasonably small, or otherwise controlled by the statistical energy through multiplication. Therefore, *if the statistical energy between environments is small, it can be reasonable to assume the dialogue quality has been maintained or improved. Otherwise, it is possible the quality of the generated dialogue has substantially degraded.* In this way, the statistical energy is an easily observable quantity that assists us in determining if the source error $\mathbf{TD}_{\mathsf{S}}$ known before the environmental change is a good representative of the unknown target error $\mathbf{TD}_{\mathsf{T}}$, which is observed after the environmental change.

Use Cases In general, controlling the statistical energy between dialogues ensures we preserve dialogue quality when the evaluation metrics we care about are not available. As demonstrated in the main text, this makes it useful in algorithm design; i.e., to inform decisions in model training. Energy can also be useful for model selection. Namely, the generation model whose dialogues have the smallest energy compared to goal dialogue should produce the highest quality dialogue. To see this, simply set $\tilde{D}_2 = D$ in the bound. Similar logical reduction shows the energy is the dominating term in this case as well.

[9]For simplicity, let $\tilde{D}_1, \tilde{D}_2, U$ be pairwise-independent. When independence does not hold, similar results can be derived under assumption of context-conditional independence.

B Proofs

In this section we prove the claimed theoretical results. So that the results may be more broadly applicable, we prove them in a more general context and then specify to the context of dialogue generation (in the main text and Appendix A).

B.1 An Adaptation Bound Based on a Discrete Energy Statistic

In this section, we propose an adaptation bound based on the energy statistic. As we are aware, ours are the first theoretical results relating the statistical energy between distributions to the change in function outputs across said distributions. Given the use of the discrete energy distance (Def. A.1) and the accompanying coarsening function (Def. A.2), we appropriately choose to prove our theoretical results for discrete random variables (i.e., those which take on only a countable number of values and exhibit a probability mass function). The effect of this choice is that we also contribute a number of new theoretical results relating the probability mass function of a real-valued, discrete random variable to its characteristic function (i.e., in similar style to the Parseval-Plancherel Theorem). Furthermore, we expand on the relationship between the statistical energy of distributions and their characteristic functions. While this has been well studied in the continuous setting (Székely and Rizzo, 2013) where the distributions of random variables admit probability densities (i.e., absolutely continuous with respect to the Lesbesgue measure), it has not been studied in the case of discrete random variables. We start our results using only *real-valued* discrete variables, but prove our main results for *all* discrete random variables using Lemma B.3

B.1.1 Setup

Suppose A and B are discrete random variables taking on values in $\mathbb{R}^d$ for some d. Respectively, the distribution of A is α and the distribution of B is β. The space $\Omega \subset \mathbb{R}^d$ is the countable subset of $\mathbb{R}^d$ for which α or β assigns non-zero probability; i.e., $\Omega = \text{supp}(\alpha) \cup \text{supp}(\beta)$. Then, the expectation of any function $f : \mathbb{R}^d \to \mathbb{R}$ of A is defined:

$$\mathbf{E}[f(A)] = \int_{\mathbb{R}^d} f \mathrm{d}\alpha = \sum_{a \in \Omega} f(a) p_\alpha(a) \tag{19}$$

where p_α is the probability mass function for A (i.e., α). Expectations of functions of B are similarly defined.

The *characteristic function* of A is defined as the complex-conjugate of the Fourier-Stieltjes transform of the probability mass function p_α. More explicitly, it is the function $\hat{p}_\alpha : \mathbb{R}^d \to \mathbb{R}$ defined

$$\hat{p}_\alpha(\tau) = \mathbf{E}[\exp\{i\tau^{\mathrm{T}}A\}] = \sum_{a \in \Omega} p_\alpha(a) \exp\{i\tau^{\mathrm{T}}a\} \tag{20}$$

where i is the imaginary unit (i.e., $i^2 = -1$) and $\tau^{\mathrm{T}}a$ is the (inner) product between column vectors τ and a. Note, the characteristic function always exists and is finite for each τ.

B.1.2 Parseval-Plancherel Theorem (Reprise)

One notable use for the *characteristic function* is the following *inversion formula*. In the discrete context we consider, Cuppens (1975) proves the following

$$p_\alpha(a) = \lim_{\tau_1 \to \infty} \lim_{\tau_2 \to \infty} \cdots \lim_{\tau_d \to \infty} \left(\prod_{i=1}^{d} 1/(2\tau_i) \right) \int_{B(\tau)} \hat{p}_\alpha(t) \exp\{-it^{\mathrm{T}}a\} \lambda(\mathrm{d}t) \tag{21}$$

where $\tau = (\tau_1, \tau_2, \ldots, \tau_d)^{\mathrm{T}}$, $B(\tau) = \{x \in \mathbb{R}^d \mid -\tau_i \leq x_i \leq \tau_i\}$, and λ is the Lebesgue measure. This inversion formula highlights the connection between the characteristic function and the general Fourier transform as alluded to just before Eq. (20), since Fourier transforms are well known for their own inversion formulas. Another commonly used result in Fourier Analysis (related to inversion) is the Parseval-Plancherel Theorem. We prove a variation on this result below. As we are aware, it is the first which uses the transform given in Eq. (20) (i.e., specific to discrete, real-valued random variables).

Lemma B.1. *For any discrete random variables A and B as described, taking values in* $\mathbb{R}^d$,

$$\sum_{x\in\Omega}|p_\alpha(x)-p_\beta(x)|^2 = \lim_{\tau_1\to\infty}\lim_{\tau_2\to\infty}\cdots\lim_{\tau_d\to\infty}\left(\prod_{i=1}^{d}1/(2\tau_i)\right)\int_{B(\tau)}|\hat{p}_\alpha(t)-\hat{p}_\beta(t)|^2\lambda(\mathrm{d}t). \tag{22}$$

Proof. For any function $f:\mathbb{R}^d\to\mathbb{R}^+$ such that $\sum_{x\in\Omega}f(x)<\infty$ for all $t\in\mathbb{R}^d$, we prove the following more general result

$$\sum_{x\in\Omega}f^2(x) = \lim_{\tau_1\to\infty}\lim_{\tau_2\to\infty}\cdots\lim_{\tau_d\to\infty}\left(\prod_{i=1}^{d}1/(2\tau_i)\right)\int_{B(\tau)}\hat{f}(x)\hat{f}^*(x)\lambda(\mathrm{d}t) \tag{23}$$

where as before a "hat" denotes the Fourier-Stieltjes transform given in Eq. (20) and the new notation $\hat{f}^*$ denotes the complex-conjugate of $\hat{f}$. Observe, this proves the desired results because setting $f(x)=p_\alpha(x)-q_\alpha(x)$ we have

$$f^2(x)=(p_\alpha(x)-q_\alpha(x))^2=|p_\alpha(x)-q_\alpha(x)|^2 \tag{24}$$

and

$$\begin{aligned}\hat{f}(x)\hat{f}^*(x) &= (\widehat{p_\alpha(x)-p_\alpha(x)})(\widehat{p_\alpha(x)-p_\alpha(x)})^* \\ &= (\hat{p}_\alpha(x)-\hat{p}_\alpha(x))(\hat{p}_\alpha(x)-\hat{p}_\alpha(x))^* = |\hat{p}_\alpha(x)-\hat{p}_\alpha(x)|^2.\end{aligned} \tag{25}$$

Proceeding with the proof of Eq. (23) we have

$$\begin{aligned}
&\lim_{\tau_1\to\infty}\lim_{\tau_2\to\infty}\cdots\lim_{\tau_d\to\infty}\left(\prod_{i=1}^{d}1/(2\tau_i)\right)\int_{B(\tau)}\hat{f}(x)\hat{f}^*(x)\lambda(\mathrm{d}t)\\
&=\lim_{\tau_i\to\infty}\left(\prod_{i=1}^{d}1/(2\tau_i)\right)\int_{B(\tau)}\left(\sum_{x\in\Omega}f(x)\exp\{it^{\mathrm{T}}x\}\right)\left(\sum_{x\in\Omega}f(x)\exp\{-it^{\mathrm{T}}x\}\right)\lambda(\mathrm{d}t)\\
&=\lim_{\tau_i\to\infty}\left(\prod_{i}1/(2\tau_i)\right)\int_{B(\tau)}\sum_{x\in\Omega}\sum_{x'\in\Omega}f(x)f(x')\exp\{i(t^{\mathrm{T}}x-t^{\mathrm{T}}x')\}\lambda(\mathrm{d}t) \qquad \text{(Fubini-Tonelli)}\\
&=\lim_{\tau_i\to\infty}\left(\prod_{i=1}^{d}1/(2\tau_i)\right)\sum_{x\in\Omega}\sum_{x'\in\Omega}f(x)f(x')\int_{B(\tau)}\exp\{i(t^{\mathrm{T}}x-t^{\mathrm{T}}x')\}\lambda(\mathrm{d}t) \qquad \text{(Fubini-Tonelli)}\\
&=\lim_{\tau_i\to\infty}\sum_{x\in\Omega}\sum_{x'\in\Omega}f(x)f(x')\left(\prod_{i=1}^{d}1/(2\tau_i)\right)\left[\int_{B(\tau)}\exp\{i(t^{\mathrm{T}}x-t^{\mathrm{T}}x')\}\lambda(\mathrm{d}t)\right]\\
&=\lim_{\tau_i\to\infty}\sum_{x\in\Omega}\sum_{x'\in\Omega}f(x)f(x')\left(\prod_{i=1}^{d}\left[1/(2\tau_i)\int_{-\tau_i}^{\tau_i}\exp\{i(t_i(x_i-x_i'))\}\mathrm{d}t_i\right]\right) \qquad \text{(Fubini-Tonelli)}\\
&=\lim_{\tau_i\to\infty}\sum_{x\in\Omega}\sum_{x'\in\Omega}f(x)f(x')\left(\prod_{i=1}^{d}\chi(x_i,x_i',\tau_i)\right) \quad \text{where} \quad \chi=\begin{cases}\frac{\sin\tau_i(x_i-x_i')}{\tau_i(x_i-x_i')} & \text{if } x_i\neq x_i',\\ 1 & \text{else}\end{cases}\\
&=\sum_{x\in\Omega}\sum_{x'\in\Omega}f(x)f(x')\left(\lim_{\tau_i\to\infty}\prod_{i=1}^{d}\chi(x_i,x_i',\tau_i)\right) \qquad \text{(DCT)}\\
&=\sum_{x\in\Omega}\sum_{x'\in\Omega}f(x)f(x')1[x=x'] \quad \text{where} \quad 1[\text{arg}]=\begin{cases}1 & \text{if arg holds,}\\ 0 & \text{else}\end{cases}\\
&=\sum_{x\in\Omega}f^2(x).
\end{aligned} \tag{26}$$

In details: the first equality follows by definition; the second and third by Fubini-Tonelli Theorem;[10] the fourth by simple rules of arithmetic; the fifth again by Fubini-Tonelli Theorem to decompose the volume calculation into a product; the sixth by evaluating the integral; seventh by the dominated convergence theorem;[11] the eighth by evaluating the limit; and the last by simple arithmetic. □

B.1.3 The Energy of Discrete Distributions as Described by their Characteristic Functions

Lemma B.2. *For any independent, discrete random variables A and B as described, taking values in $\mathbb{R}^d$,*

$$\varepsilon_{01}(A,B) = \lim_{\tau_1\to\infty}\lim_{\tau_2\to\infty}\dots\lim_{\tau_d\to\infty}\left(\prod_{i=1}^{d} 1/(2\tau_i)\right)\int_{B(\tau)} |\hat{p}_\alpha(t)-\hat{p}_\beta(t)|^2\lambda(\mathrm{d}t). \tag{27}$$

Proof. According to Székely and Rizzo (2013), for independent A and B, we have

$$\begin{aligned}|\hat{p}_\alpha(t)-\hat{p}_\beta(t)|^2 &= \mathbf{E}[\cos\{t^{\mathrm{T}}(A-A')\}+\cos\{t^{\mathrm{T}}(B-B')\}-\cos\{t^{\mathrm{T}}(A-B)\}]\\ &= \mathbf{E}\{2[1-\cos\{t^{\mathrm{T}}(A-B)\}]-[1-\cos\{t^{\mathrm{T}}(A-A')\}]-[1-\cos\{t^{\mathrm{T}}(B-B')\}]\}\end{aligned} \tag{28}$$

where A' and B' are i.i.d. copies of A and B, respectively. With the equivalence above, by Fubini's Theorem, we may interchange the expectation and integral in Eq. (27). We may also change the order of integration to arrive at

$$\begin{aligned}&\lim_{\tau_1\to\infty}\lim_{\tau_2\to\infty}\dots\lim_{\tau_d\to\infty}\left(\prod_{i=1}^{d} 1/(2\tau_i)\right)\int_{B(\tau)} |\hat{p}_\alpha(t)-\hat{p}_\beta(t)|^2\lambda(\mathrm{d}t)\\ &= \lim_{\tau_i\to\infty}\mathbf{E}\Bigg[\left(\prod_{i=1}^{d}\frac{1}{(2\tau_i)}\right)\int_{-\tau_1}^{\tau_1}\dots\int_{-\tau_d}^{\tau_d}\Big\{2\Big(1-\cos\sum_{i=1}^{d}\tau_i(A_i-B_i)\Big)\\ &\qquad -\Big(1-\cos\sum_{i=1}^{d}\tau_i(A_i-A_i')\Big)-\Big(1-\cos\sum_{i=1}^{d}\tau_i(B_i-B_i')\Big)\Big\}\mathrm{d}\tau_d\dots\mathrm{d}\tau_1\Bigg].\end{aligned} \tag{29}$$

To evaluate the integral we first observe, for any $x\in\mathbb{R}^d$,

$$\begin{aligned}\int_{-\tau_d}^{\tau_d} 1-\cos\sum_{i=1}^{d}\tau_i x_i \mathrm{d}\tau_d &= 2\tau_d - \frac{\sin\left(\tau_d x_d + \sum_{i=1}^{d-1}\tau_i x_i\right)-\sin\left(-\tau_d x_d+\sum_{i=1}^{d-1}\tau_i x_i\right)}{x_d}\\ &= 2\tau_d - \frac{2\cos\left(\sum_{i=1}^{d-1}\tau_i x_i\right)\sin(\tau_d x_d)}{x_d}.\end{aligned} \tag{30}$$

Notice, the above equation implies an iterative pattern which can be used to solve the multiple integral.

[10] The primary assumption of Fubini-Tonelli Theorem requires the *absolute value* of the integrand have finite double or iterated integral/sum. In the first case, with the iterated sum, it is clear for each fixed t since $\sum_x f(x)$ is bounded and so is $\exp\{-iz\}$ for all z. In the second and third cases, we simply cite the boundedness of $B(\tau)$ for each fixed τ.

[11] The primary assumption of the DCT is that the sequence of functions being integrated (or summed in our case) is dominated by some function g with finite integral (i.e., in the sense that the absolute value of every function in the sequence is less than or equal to g on all inputs). Again, this is easy to see using properties assumed on f and the fact that $|\chi|\le 1$ for all inputs.

Keeping in mind which terms are constants with respect to the differential, we have

$$
\begin{aligned}
&\int_{-\tau_1}^{\tau_1}\cdots\int_{-\tau_{d-1}}^{\tau_{d-1}}\Big(\int_{-\tau_d}^{\tau_d} 1-\cos\sum_{i=1}^{d}\tau_i x_i \mathrm{d}\tau_d\Big)\mathrm{d}\tau_{d-1}\ldots\mathrm{d}\tau_1 \\
&=\int_{-\tau_1}^{\tau_1}\cdots\int_{-\tau_{d-2}}^{\tau_{d-2}}\left(\int_{-\tau_{d-1}}^{\tau_{d-1}} 2\tau_d-\frac{2\cos\left(\sum_{i=1}^{d-1}\tau_i x_i\right)\sin(\tau_d x_d)}{x_d}\mathrm{d}\tau_{d-1}\right)\mathrm{d}\tau_{d-2}\ldots\mathrm{d}\tau_1 \\
&=\int_{-\tau_1}^{\tau_1}\cdots\int_{-\tau_{d-2}}^{\tau_{d-2}}\left((2\tau_d)(2\tau_{d-1})-\frac{4\cos\left(\sum_{i=1}^{d-2}\tau_i x_i\right)\sin(\tau_d x_d)\sin(\tau_{d-1}x_{d-1})}{x_d x_{d-1}}\right)\mathrm{d}\tau_{d-2}\ldots\mathrm{d}\tau_1 \\
&=\ldots \\
&=\int_{-\tau_1}^{\tau_1}\cdots\int_{-\tau_{d-j}}^{\tau_{d-j}}\left(\prod_{i=1}^{j}(2\tau_{d-i+1})-\frac{\cos\left(\sum_{i=1}^{d-j}\tau_i x_i\right)\prod_{i=1}^{j}2\sin(\tau_{d-i+1}x_{d-i+1})}{\prod_{i=1}^{j}x_{d-i+1}}\right)\mathrm{d}\tau_{d-j}\ldots\mathrm{d}\tau_1 \\
&\ldots \\
&=\prod_{i=1}^{d}(2\tau_{d-i+1})-\frac{\prod_{i=1}^{d}2\sin(\tau_{d-i+1}x_{d-i+1})}{\prod_{i=1}^{d}x_{d-i+1}} \\
&=\prod_{i=1}^{d}(2\tau_i)-\frac{\prod_{i=1}^{d}2\sin(\tau_i x_i)}{\prod_{i=1}^{d}x_i}.
\end{aligned}
\tag{31}
$$

Now, returning to the RHS of Eq. (29), linearity of the integral implies

$$
\begin{aligned}
&\left(\prod_{i=1}^{d}\frac{1}{(2\tau_i)}\right)\int_{-\tau_1}^{\tau_1}\cdots\int_{-\tau_d}^{\tau_d}\Big\{2\Big(1-\cos\sum_{i=1}^{d}\tau_i(A_i-B_i)\Big) \\
&\qquad -\Big(1-\cos\sum_{i=1}^{d}\tau_i(A_i-A_i')\Big)-\Big(1-\cos\sum_{i=1}^{d}\tau_i(B_i-B_i')\Big)\Big\}\mathrm{d}\tau_d\ldots\mathrm{d}\tau_1 \\
&=\left(\prod_{i=1}^{d}\frac{1}{(2\tau_i)}\right)\int_{-\tau_1}^{\tau_1}\cdots\int_{-\tau_d}^{\tau_d}\Big\{2\Big(1-\cos\sum_{i=1}^{d}\tau_i(A_i-B_i)\Big)\Big\}\mathrm{d}\tau_d\ldots\mathrm{d}\tau_1 \\
&\quad-\left(\prod_{i=1}^{d}\frac{1}{(2\tau_i)}\right)\int_{-\tau_1}^{\tau_1}\cdots\int_{-\tau_d}^{\tau_d}\Big\{\Big(1-\cos\sum_{i=1}^{d}\tau_i(A_i-A_i')\Big)\Big\}\mathrm{d}\tau_d\ldots\mathrm{d}\tau_1 \\
&\quad-\left(\prod_{i=1}^{d}\frac{1}{(2\tau_i)}\right)\int_{-\tau_1}^{\tau_1}\cdots\int_{-\tau_d}^{\tau_d}\Big\{\Big(1-\cos\sum_{i=1}^{d}\tau_i(B_i-B_i')\Big)\Big\}\mathrm{d}\tau_d\ldots\mathrm{d}\tau_1.
\end{aligned}
\tag{32}
$$

Thus, we can apply the solution in Eq. (31) to solve the integral in Eq. (29). Taking $x_i=(A_i-B_i)$ in Eq. (31), we consider the first integral of Eq. (32) above along with its multiplicative constant:

$$
\begin{aligned}
&\left(\prod_{i=1}^{d}\frac{1}{(2\tau_i)}\right)\int_{-\tau_1}^{\tau_1}\cdots\int_{-\tau_d}^{\tau_d}\Big(1-\cos\sum_{i=1}^{d}\tau_i(A_i-B_i)\Big) \\
&=\left(\prod_{i=1}^{d}\frac{1}{(2\tau_i)}\right)\left(\prod_{i=1}^{d}(2\tau_i)-\frac{\prod_{i=1}^{d}2\sin\left\{\tau_i(A_i-B_i)\right\}}{\prod_{i=1}^{d}(A_i-B_i)}\right) \\
&=1-\prod_{i=1}^{d}\frac{\sin\left\{\tau_i(A_i-B_i)\right\}}{\tau_i(A_i-B_i)}=1-\prod_{i=1}^{d}\chi(A_i,B_i,\tau_i)
\end{aligned}
\tag{33}
$$

where χ is defined in the proof of Eq. (23) (Lemma B.1). Taking $x_i = (A_i - A_i')$ and $x_i = (B_i - B_i')$ and proceeding as above allows us to resolve the entire integral. In particular, we have

$$\begin{aligned}
&\lim_{\tau_1\to\infty}\lim_{\tau_2\to\infty}\cdots\lim_{\tau_d\to\infty}\left(\prod_{i=1}^{d} 1/(2\tau_i)\right)\int_{B(\tau)}|\hat{p}_\alpha(t)-\hat{p}_\beta(t)|^2\lambda(\mathrm{d}t)\\
&=\lim_{\tau_i}\mathbf{E}\left[2\Big(1-\prod_{i=1}^{d}\chi(A_i,B_i,\tau_i)\Big)-\Big(1-\prod_{i=1}^{d}\chi(A_i,A_i',\tau_i)\Big)-\Big(1-\prod_{i=1}^{d}\chi(B_i,B_i',\tau_i)\Big)\right]\\
&=\mathbf{E}\left[\lim_{\tau_i}\left\{2\Big(1-\prod_{i=1}^{d}\chi(A_i,B_i,\tau_i)\Big)-\Big(1-\prod_{i=1}^{d}\chi(A_i,A_i',\tau_i)\Big)-\Big(1-\prod_{i=1}^{d}\chi(B_i,B_i',\tau_i)\Big)\right\}\right]\\
&=\mathbf{E}\big[2\times 1[A_i\neq B_i]-1[A_i\neq A_i']-1[B_i\neq B_i']\big].
\end{aligned} \tag{34}$$

Here, the second equality follows from the dominated convergence theorem and $1[\text{arg}]$ is defined as in proof of Eq. (23) (Lemma B.1). □

B.1.4 Moving from Real-Valued Discrete Variables to Any Discrete Variables

Lemma B.3. *Let $\tilde{A}$ and $\tilde{B}$ be any independent, discrete random variables over a countable set Ω (i.e., not necessarily contained in $\mathbb{R}^d$). Then,*

$$\sum_{x\in\Omega}|\tilde{p}_\alpha(x)-\tilde{p}_\beta(x)| = \varepsilon_{01}(\tilde{A},\tilde{B}). \tag{35}$$

where $\tilde{p}_\alpha$ and $\tilde{p}_\beta$ are the mass functions of $\tilde{A}$ and $\tilde{B}$, respectively.

Proof. Let $\Pi\subset\mathbb{R}^d$ with $|\Pi| = |\Omega|$. Note, Π exists because Ω is countable and $\mathbb{R}^d$ is not. Next, let $f:\Omega\to\Pi$ be any bijective map.

Then, supposing p_α and p_β are the mass functions of $f(\tilde{A})$ and $f(\tilde{B})$ respectively, by definition of the pushforward measure, for any $y\in\Pi$ such that $y = f(x)$ for $x\in\Omega$

$$p_\alpha(y) = \tilde{p}_\alpha(\{a\in\Omega \mid f(a)=y\}) = \tilde{p}_\alpha(x). \tag{36}$$

Notice, bijectivity of f ensures the last step, because each $y\in\Pi$ has a *unique* inverse $x\in\Omega$. From bijectivity of f, we also have injectivity, which implies $1[a\neq b] = 1[f(a)\neq f(b)]$ for all $a,b\in\Omega$. By simple substitution, the previous two facts tells us

$$\begin{aligned}
&2\sum_{a,b\in\Omega}1[a\neq b]\tilde{p}_\alpha(a)\tilde{p}_\beta(b)-\sum_{a,a'\in\Omega}1[a\neq a']\tilde{p}_\alpha(a)\tilde{p}_\alpha(a')-\sum_{b,b'\in\Omega}1[b\neq b']\tilde{p}_\beta(b)\tilde{p}_\beta(b')\\
&=2\sum_{a,b\in\Omega}1[f(a)\neq f(b)]p_\alpha(f(a))p_\beta(f(b))-\sum_{a,a'\in\Omega}1[f(a)\neq f(a)']p_\alpha(f(a))p_\alpha(f(a'))\\
&\qquad-\sum_{b,b'\in\Omega}1[f(b)\neq f(b')]p_\beta(f(b))p_\beta(f(b'))
\end{aligned} \tag{37}$$

Since f is surjective too (i.e., along with injective), summation of any function $g(f(a),f(b))$ over $a,b\in\Omega$ and summation of $g(c,d)$ over $c,d\in\Pi$ are equivalent.[12] So, we can continue as follows:

$$\begin{aligned}
&2\sum_{a,b\in\Omega}1[f(a)\neq f(b)]p_\alpha(f(a))p_\beta(f(b))-\sum_{a,a'\in\Omega}1[f(a)\neq f(a)']p_\alpha(f(a))p_\alpha(f(a'))\\
&\qquad-\sum_{b,b'\in\Omega}1[f(b)\neq f(b')]p_\beta(f(b))p_\beta(f(b'))\\
&=2\sum_{c,d\in\Pi}1[c\neq d]p_\alpha(c)p_\beta(d)-\sum_{c,c'\in\Omega}1[c\neq c']p_\alpha(c)p_\alpha(c')-\sum_{d,d'\in\Omega}1[d\neq d']p_\beta(d)p_\beta(d')
\end{aligned} \tag{38}$$

[12] In particular, because f is surjective, we know all pairs $(c,d)\in\Pi^2$ have some pair $(a,b)\in\Omega^2$ for which $(f(a),f(b)) = (c,d)$; i.e., we do not "miss" a term in this sum. Because f is injective, we know all pairs $(c,d)\in\Pi^2$ have *only one* pair $(a,b)\in\Omega^2$ for which $(f(a),f(b)) = (c,d)$; i.e., we do not "repeat" a term in this sum.

In other words, the previous two equations tell us $\varepsilon_{01}(\tilde{A},\tilde{B}) = \varepsilon_{01}(f(\tilde{A}), f(\tilde{B}))$. Applying equivalence of the mass functions, then Lemmas B.1 and B.2, then equivalence of the energies:

$$\sum_{x\in\Omega} |\tilde{p}_\alpha(x) - \tilde{p}_\beta(x)| = \sum_{y\in\Pi} |p_\alpha(y) - p_\beta(y)| = \varepsilon_{01}(f(\tilde{A}), f(\tilde{B})) = \varepsilon_{01}(\tilde{A},\tilde{B}). \tag{39}$$

Note, this uses the fact that functions of independent random variables are also independent. □

B.1.5 The Main Bound

Theorem B.1. *Let A and B be any independent random variables over any space $\mathcal{X}$ and let S, S' be random variables over $[0,1]$. Let U be a random variable, independent from A and B, over any set $\mathcal{U}$. Suppose $c : \mathcal{X} \to \Omega$ is a coarsening function (so, $\Omega \subset \mathcal{X}$) and let $f \in [0,1]^{\mathcal{X}\times\mathcal{U}}$. Then,*

$$\mathbf{E}[|S - f(A,U)|] \le \gamma + \varphi + \mathbf{E}[|S' - f(B,U)|] + \sqrt{\varepsilon_c(A,B) \times \delta} \tag{40}$$

where

$$\begin{aligned}
\gamma &= \mathbf{E}[|f(c(B),U) - f(B)|] + \mathbf{E}[|f(c(A),U) - f(A)|],\\
g &\in \operatorname*{arg\,min}_{h\in[0,1]^{\mathcal{X}\times\mathcal{U}}} \mathbf{E}[|S - h(c(A),U)|] + \mathbf{E}[|h(c(B),U) - S'|],\\
\varphi &= \mathbf{E}[|S - g(c(A),U)|] + \mathbf{E}[|g(c(B),U) - S'|],\\
\delta &= \sum_{x\in\Omega} |g(x) - f(x)|^2
\end{aligned} \tag{41}$$

Proof. For any $g \in [0,1]^{\mathcal{X}\times\mathcal{U}}$, by way of the triangle inequality and monotonicity of the expectation,

$$\begin{aligned}
\mathbf{E}[|S - f(A,U)|] &= \mathbf{E}[|S - f(A,U)|] + \mathbf{E}[|S' - f(B,U)|] - \mathbf{E}[|S' - f(B,U)|]\\
&= \mathbf{E}[|S - g(c(A),U) + g(c(A),U) - f(A,U)|] + \mathbf{E}[|S' - f(B,U)|] - \mathbf{E}[|S' - f(B,U)|]\\
&\le \mathbf{E}[|S - g(c(A),U)|] + \mathbf{E}[|g(c(A),U) - f(A,U)|] + \mathbf{E}[|S' - f(B,U)|]\\
&\qquad - \mathbf{E}[|S' - f(B,U)|]\\
&\le \mathbf{E}[|S - g(c(A),U)|] + \mathbf{E}[|g(c(A),U) - f(A,U)|] + \mathbf{E}[|S' - f(B,U)|]\\
&\qquad - \mathbf{E}[|g(c(B),U) - f(B,U)|] + \mathbf{E}[|g(c(B),U) - S'|]\\
&\le \mathbf{E}[|S - g(c(A),U)|] + \mathbf{E}[|g(c(A),U) - f(c(A),U)|] + \mathbf{E}[|f(c(A),U) - f(A,U)|]\\
&\qquad + \mathbf{E}[|S' - f(B,U)|] - \mathbf{E}[|g(c(B),U) - f(B,U)|] + \mathbf{E}[|g(c(B),U) - S'|]\\
&\le \mathbf{E}[|S - g(c(A),U)|] + \mathbf{E}[|g(c(A),U) - f(c(A),U)|] + \mathbf{E}[|f(c(A),U) - f(A,U)|]\\
&\qquad + \mathbf{E}[|S' - f(B,U)|] - \mathbf{E}[|g(c(B,U) - f(c(B),U)|]\\
&\qquad + \mathbf{E}[|f(c(B),U) - f(B,U)|] + \mathbf{E}[|g(c(B),U) - S'|].
\end{aligned} \tag{42}$$

Set $\tilde{B} = c(B)$, $\tilde{A} = c(A)$ and set

$$\begin{aligned}
\gamma &= \mathbf{E}[|f(\tilde{B},U) - f(B,U)|] + \mathbf{E}[|f(\tilde{A},U) - f(A,U)|],\\
g &\in \operatorname*{arg\,min}_{h\in[0,1]^{\mathcal{X}\times\mathcal{U}}} \mathbf{E}[|S - h(\tilde{A},U)|] + \mathbf{E}[|h(\tilde{B},U) - S'|],\\
\varphi &= \mathbf{E}[|S - g(\tilde{A},U)|] + \mathbf{E}[|g(\tilde{B},U) - S'|].
\end{aligned} \tag{43}$$

Then, Eq. (42) implies

$$\mathbf{E}[|S - f(A,U)|] \le \gamma + \varphi + \mathbf{E}[|S' - f(B,U)|] + \mathbf{E}[|g(\tilde{A},U) - f(\tilde{A},U)|] - \mathbf{E}[|g(\tilde{B},U) - f(\tilde{B},U)|]. \tag{44}$$

Now, suppose $\tilde{p}_\alpha$ and $\tilde{p}_\beta$ are probability mass functions for $\tilde{A}$ and $\tilde{B}$, respectively. Then, using basic properties of the expectation along with other noted facts,

$$\begin{aligned}
&\mathbf{E}[|g(\tilde{A},U) - f(\tilde{A},U)|] - \mathbf{E}[|g(\tilde{B},U) - f(\tilde{B},U)|] \\
&= \mathbf{E}\Big[\sum_{a\in\Omega}|g(a,U) - f(a,U)|\tilde{p}_\alpha(a) - \sum_{b\in\Omega}|g(b,U) - f(b,U)|\tilde{p}_\beta(b)\Big] \quad \text{(Fubini)} \\
&= \mathbf{E}\Big[\sum_{x\in\Omega}|g(x,U) - f(x,U)|(\tilde{p}_\alpha(x) - \tilde{p}_\beta(x))\Big] \le \mathbf{E}\Big[\sum_{x\in\Omega}|g(x,U) - f(x,U)||\tilde{p}_\alpha(x) - \tilde{p}_\beta(x)|\Big] \\
&\le \mathbf{E}\left[\left(\sum_{x\in\Omega}|g(x,U) - f(x,U)|^2\right)^{1/2}\left(\sum_{x\in\Omega}|\tilde{p}_\alpha(x) - \tilde{p}_\beta(x)|^2\right)^{1/2}\right] \quad \text{(Cauchy-Schwarz)} \\
&\le \sqrt{\varepsilon_{01}(\tilde{A},\tilde{B})} \times \mathbf{E}\left[\left(\sum_{x\in\Omega}|g(x,U) - f(x,U)|^2\right)^{1/2}\right] \quad \text{(Lemma B.3)}
\end{aligned} \tag{45}$$

In the last step, we may apply Lemma B.3 because $\tilde{A}$ and $\tilde{B}$ are still independent (i.e., they are functions of independent random variables) and are now discrete too. Defining δ appropriately yields the result. □

B.1.6 Proof of Thm. A.1 and Other Applications of Thm. B.1

Thm. A.1 Thm. A.1 is simply a specification of Thm. B.1 above. In fact, it is better stated as a corollary of Thm. B.1. We set $\mathcal{X} = \mathcal{D}$, leave $\mathcal{U}$ and its variable U unchanged, and set $S = S' = h_\ell(D, U)$. Then, $A = \tilde{D}_1$ and $B = \tilde{D}_2$. Taking $f = h_\ell$ yields the result.

Classification and Regression In adaptation for classification and regression, we consider a source distribution $\mathbb{S}$ governing random variables (X_S, Y_S) and a target distribution $\mathbb{T}$ governing random variables (X_T, Y_T). In general, the goal is to predict $Y_\square$ from $X_\square$. We can set $S = Y_T$ and $S' = Y_S$. We may also set $A = X_T$ and $B = X_S$. Then, we learn f from a pre-specified *hypothesis class* $\mathcal{H} \subseteq [0,1]^{\mathcal{X}\times\mathcal{U}}$. Typically, U is ignored in these settings, but it seems possible to employ this term to model stochastic (Gibbs) predictors; i.e., in PAC-Bayesian Frameworks (Germain et al., 2020; Sicilia et al., 2022a). Notice, for regression, our framework only considers a normalized response variable and the mean absolute error.

B.1.7 Sample Complexity

As alluded in Section 6, a key shortcoming of our framework compared to existing frameworks is the absence of any terms measuring *sample-complexity*. That is, we do not explicitly quantify the difference between our empirical observation of the energy and the *true* energy (i.e., the *population* version of the statistic) using the number of samples in our observation. This is a big part of computational learning theory, as the act of choosing a function f *using data* – or, in dialogue contexts, choosing the parameter θ using data – can have significant impact on the difference between our observations of a statistical processes and reality. In fact, this impact is the basis of overfitting and, besides computational efficiency, is the main pillar of study in traditional PAC learning[13] (Valiant, 1984; Shalev-Shwartz and Ben-David, 2014). In more recent studies of domain adaptation, like our work, the population-only bound can be just as important for purpose of understanding and interpretation. Furthermore, if we only care about the empirical samples in-hand, these population-only bounds are directly applicable,[14] which partly explains the empirical effectiveness of our theory in Section 5. Nonetheless, the role of sample-complexity can be very informative and useful in practice (Pérez-Ortiz et al., 2021) and would be important for model-selection applications as described at the end of Appendix A. We leave investigation of sample-complexity as future work. As we are aware, there is currently no appropriate description of sample-complexity for dialogue generation contexts.

[13] Probably Approximately Correct learning

[14] The empirical sample becomes the whole population about which we are concerned.

C Statistics on Dataset

unique images	unique objects	words (+1 occurrences)	words (+3 occurrences)	questions
67K	134K	19K	6.6K	277K

Table 2: Statistics on *GuessWhat?!*. For more information (e.g., train/test splits) see original proposal (De Vries et al., 2017).

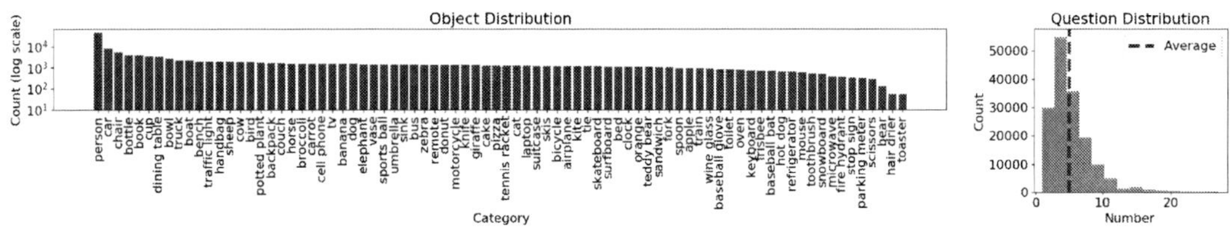

Figure 4: Visualization of object counts and dialogue length in *GuessWhat?!* dataset.

References

Katherine Atwell, Anthony Sicilia, Seong Jae Hwang, and Malihe Alikhani. 2022. The change that matters in discourse parsing: Estimating the impact of domain shift on parser error. In *Findings of the Association for Computational Linguistics: ACL 2022*, pages 824–845.

Shai Ben-David, John Blitzer, Koby Crammer, Alex Kulesza, Fernando Pereira, and Jennifer Wortman Vaughan. 2010a. A theory of learning from different domains. *Machine learning*, 79(1):151–175.

Shai Ben-David, Tyler Lu, Teresa Luu, and Dávid Pál. 2010b. Impossibility theorems for domain adaptation. In *Proceedings of the Thirteenth International Conference on Artificial Intelligence and Statistics*, pages 129–136. JMLR Workshop and Conference Proceedings.

Samuel R Bowman, Luke Vilnis, Oriol Vinyals, Andrew M Dai, Rafal Jozefowicz, and Samy Bengio. 2015. Generating sentences from a continuous space. *arXiv preprint arXiv:1511.06349*.

Elia Bruni and Raquel Fernandez. 2017. Adversarial evaluation for open-domain dialogue generation. In *Proceedings of the 18th Annual SIGdial Meeting on Discourse and Dialogue*, pages 284–288.

R Cuppens. 1975. Decomposition of multivariate distributions.

Abhishek Das, Satwik Kottur, José MF Moura, Stefan Lee, and Dhruv Batra. 2017. Learning cooperative visual dialog agents with deep reinforcement learning. In *Proceedings of the IEEE international conference on computer vision*, pages 2951–2960.

Harm De Vries, Florian Strub, Sarath Chandar, Olivier Pietquin, Hugo Larochelle, and Aaron Courville. 2017. Guesswhat?! visual object discovery through multi-modal dialogue. In *Proceedings of the IEEE Conference on Computer Vision and Pattern Recognition*, pages 5503–5512.

Pascal Germain, Amaury Habrard, François Laviolette, and Emilie Morvant. 2020. Pac-bayes and domain adaptation. *Neurocomputing*, 379:379–397.

Ari Holtzman, Jan Buys, Li Du, Maxwell Forbes, and Yejin Choi. 2019. The curious case of neural text degeneration. In *International Conference on Learning Representations*.

Mert Inan, Piyush Sharma, Baber Khalid, Radu Soricut, Matthew Stone, and Malihe Alikhani. 2021. Cosmic: A coherence-aware generation metric for image descriptions. *arXiv preprint arXiv:2109.05281*.

Fredrik D Johansson, David Sontag, and Rajesh Ranganath. 2019. Support and invertibility in domain-invariant representations. In *The 22nd International Conference on Artificial Intelligence and Statistics*, pages 527–536. PMLR.

Sham Machandranath Kakade. 2003. *On the sample complexity of reinforcement learning*. University of London, University College London (United Kingdom).

Seiichi Kuroki, Nontawat Charoenphakdee, Han Bao, Junya Honda, Issei Sato, and Masashi Sugiyama. 2019. Unsupervised domain adaptation based on source-guided discrepancy. In *Proceedings of the AAAI Conference on Artificial Intelligence*, volume 33, pages 4122–4129.

Chin-Yew Lin. 2004. Rouge: A package for automatic evaluation of summaries. In *Text summarization branches out*, pages 74–81.

Zachary Lipton, Yu-Xiang Wang, and Alexander Smola. 2018. Detecting and correcting for label shift with black box predictors. In *International conference on machine learning*, pages 3122–3130. PMLR.

Yishay Mansour, Mehryar Mohri, and Afshin Rostamizadeh. 2009. Domain adaptation: Learning bounds and algorithms. *arXiv preprint arXiv:0902.3430.*

Kishore Papineni, Salim Roukos, Todd Ward, and Wei-Jing Zhu. 2002. Bleu: a method for automatic evaluation of machine translation. In *Proceedings of the 40th annual meeting of the Association for Computational Linguistics*, pages 311–318.

María Pérez-Ortiz, Omar Rivasplata, John Shawe-Taylor, and Csaba Szepesvári. 2021. Tighter risk certificates for neural networks. *Journal of Machine Learning Research*, 22.

Stephan Rabanser, Stephan Günnemann, and Zachary Lipton. 2019. Failing loudly: An empirical study of methods for detecting dataset shift. *Advances in Neural Information Processing Systems*, 32.

Ievgen Redko, Amaury Habrard, and Marc Sebban. 2017. Theoretical analysis of domain adaptation with optimal transport. In *ECML PKDD*, pages 737–753. Springer.

Ievgen Redko, Emilie Morvant, Amaury Habrard, Marc Sebban, and Younès Bennani. 2020. A survey on domain adaptation theory. *ArXiv*, abs/2004.11829.

Thibault Sellam, Dipanjan Das, and Ankur Parikh. 2020. BLEURT: Learning robust metrics for text generation. In *Proceedings of the 58th Annual Meeting of the Association for Computational Linguistics*, pages 7881–7892, Online. Association for Computational Linguistics.

Shai Shalev-Shwartz and Shai Ben-David. 2014. *Understanding machine learning: From theory to algorithms*. Cambridge university press.

Ravi Shekhar, Aashish Venkatesh, Tim Baumgärtner, Elia Bruni, Barbara Plank, Raffaella Bernardi, and Raquel Fernández. 2019. Beyond task success: A closer look at jointly learning to see, ask, and GuessWhat. In *Proceedings of the 2019 Conference of the North American Chapter of the Association for Computational Linguistics: Human Language Technologies, Volume 1 (Long and Short Papers)*, pages 2578–2587, Minneapolis, Minnesota. Association for Computational Linguistics.

Jian Shen, Yanru Qu, Weinan Zhang, and Yong Yu. 2018. Wasserstein distance guided representation learning for domain adaptation. In *AAAI*.

Anthony Sicilia, Katherine Atwell, Malihe Alikhani, and Seong Jae Hwang. 2022a. Pac-bayesian domain adaptation bounds for multiclass learners. In *The 38th Conference on Uncertainty in Artificial Intelligence*.

Anthony Sicilia, Tristan Maidment, Pat Healy, and Malihe Alikhani. 2022b. Modeling non-cooperative dialogue: Theoretical and empirical insights. *Transactions of the Association for Computational Linguistics*, 10:1084–1102.

Florian Strub, Harm De Vries, Jeremie Mary, Bilal Piot, Aaron Courvile, and Olivier Pietquin. 2017. End-to-end optimization of goal-driven and visually grounded dialogue systems. In *Proceedings of the 26th International Joint Conference on Artificial Intelligence*, pages 2765–2771.

Gabor J Szekely. 1989. Potential and kinetic energy in statistics. *Lecture Notes, Budapest Institute*.

Gábor J Székely and Maria L Rizzo. 2013. Energy statistics: A class of statistics based on distances. *Journal of statistical planning and inference*, 143(8):1249–1272.

Remi Tachet des Combes, Han Zhao, Yu-Xiang Wang, and Geoffrey J Gordon. 2020. Domain adaptation with conditional distribution matching and generalized label shift. *Advances in Neural Information Processing Systems*, 33:19276–19289.

Leslie G Valiant. 1984. A theory of the learnable. *Communications of the ACM*, 27(11):1134–1142.

Ramakrishna Vedantam, C Lawrence Zitnick, and Devi Parikh. 2015. Cider: Consensus-based image description evaluation. In *Proceedings of the IEEE conference on computer vision and pattern recognition*, pages 4566–4575.

Tianyi Zhang, Varsha Kishore, Felix Wu, Kilian Q Weinberger, and Yoav Artzi. 2019a. Bertscore: Evaluating text generation with bert. *arXiv preprint arXiv:1904.09675*.

Yuchen Zhang, Tianle Liu, Mingsheng Long, and Michael Jordan. 2019b. Bridging theory and algorithm for domain adaptation. In *International Conference on Machine Learning*, pages 7404–7413. PMLR.

Han Zhao, Remi Tachet Des Combes, Kun Zhang, and Geoffrey Gordon. 2019. On learning invariant representations for domain adaptation. In *International Conference on Machine Learning*, pages 7523–7532. PMLR.

Conceptual Similarity for Subjective Tags

Yacine Gaci
LIRIS - University of Lyon 1, France
yacine.gaci@univ-lyon1.fr

Boualem Benatallah
Dublin City University, Ireland
UNSW, Sydney, Australia
boualem.benatallah@gmail.com

Fabio Casati
University of Trento, Italy
fabio.casati@gmail.com

khalid Benabdeslem
LIRIS - University of Lyon 1, France
khalid.benabdeslem@univ-lyon1.fr

Abstract

Tagging in the context of online resources is a fundamental addition to search systems. Tags assist with the indexing, management, and retrieval of online products and services to answer complex user queries. Traditional methods of matching user queries with tags either rely on cosine similarity, or employ semantic similarity models that fail to recognize conceptual connections between tags, e.g. *ambiance* and *music*. In this work, we focus on subjective tags which characterize subjective aspects of a product or service. We propose conceptual similarity to leverage conceptual awareness when assessing similarity between tags. We also provide a simple cost-effective pipeline to automatically generate data in order to train the conceptual similarity model. We show that our pipeline generates high-quality datasets, and evaluate the similarity model both systematically and on a downstream application. Experiments show that conceptual similarity outperforms existing work when using subjective tags.

1 Introduction

As products and services proliferated the Internet in recent years, tagging came into prominence to facilitate the consumption of online information (Smith, 2007). Tagging is the practice of assigning labels and keywords to online resources. It plays a pivotal role in the indexing, management and retrieval of factual information. On the other hand, recent years have witnessed a major shift in people's expectations when searching online (Li et al., 2019). Beside the factual data such as a restaurant's cuisine type or a camera's resolution, the search trend evolved to be more experiential (Li et al., 2019). Common search queries include attributes such as *delicious food* for restaurants or *long-lasting battery* for cameras. Previous work (Li et al., 2019; Gaci et al., 2021) called this new set of attributes as subjective tags because they are short phrases that hint towards the subjective quality of products and services.

Subjective tags are particularly useful in enhancing online experiential search. In this context, users who are seeking subjective experiences, include sets of tags they care about in their queries, and it is the search system's responsibility to fetch products and/or services that have been previously described with matching tags. Deciding whether two given subjective tags match or not implies using a similarity measure, for which cosine similarity remains a convenient, yet arbitrary default (Zhelezniak et al., 2019; Li et al., 2019; Chang et al., 2019). Recent search systems such as OpineDB (Li et al., 2019) or SearchLens (Chang et al., 2019) rely mostly on cosine similarity when it comes to comparing tag-like short phrases, since it is easy to use and provides simple geometric interpretations (Zhelezniak et al., 2019). However, recent studies (May et al., 2019; Zhou et al., 2022) argue that this interpretability becomes fogged when dealing with sentences or phrases, and cosine similarity suffers from severe limitations when used to compare multi-word textual inputs.

A lot of research has been directed toward proposing supervised methods for textual similarity, spanning a diverse set of paradigms, e.g. Siamese networks (Bromley et al., 1993; Ranasinghe et al., 2019), Aggregation-Matching models (Wang and Jiang, 2016; Wang et al., 2016, 2017), or the recent cross-sentence attention paradigm which was made possible by the advent of the transformer architecture (Vaswani et al., 2017). Although these models work fairly well on syntactically-correct sentences (Bethard et al., 2017), they lack effectiveness when used with shorter-spanned phrases such as subjective tags. A reason behind this is that subjective tags do not share the same structure of full sentences and hence require different treatment. As will be discussed later in this paper, our experiments confirm this limitation. A

Findings of the Association for Computational Linguistics: AACL-IJCNLP 2022, pages 54–66
November 20–23, 2022.

second drawback is that current similarity models are not *explicitly* trained to recognize *conceptual similarities* between the compared textual entities (e.g., *meal* and *pizza* share the concept of **food**; or *background music* and *lighting* share the concept of **ambiance**). Therefore, all conceptual reasoning is disregarded. In this work, we compel our own similarity model to encode more conceptual relationships as provided by a human (whom we call the designer) and further expanded by popular knowledge bases such as WordNet (Fellbaum, 2012) or ConceptNet (Speer et al., 2017).

To illustrate the importance of capturing conceptual similarities between subjective tags, suppose a user searches for a restaurant serving delicious meals. A search system should be able to suggest a restaurant which has been tagged with *tasty chicken wings* among its search results, because *meal* and *chicken wings* share the same concept (that of *food*) even though *meal* and *chicken wings* are not semantically similar. As a result, traditional semantic similarity models (Bethard et al., 2017; Li et al., 2019; Ranasinghe et al., 2019) usually fail to meet this expectation and provide low similarity scores for the tags in the example. The same reasoning applies to other subjective tags, like *high-autonomy camera* and *long-lasting battery*, or *romantic ambiance* and *low-beat music bar*.

Aiming to solve the aforementioned drawbacks, we propose a new similarity model that focuses on learning and then using conceptual relationships as reflected in the training data. Given the new nature of subjective tags (Li et al., 2019; Gaci et al., 2021), we are not aware of the existence of datasets that suit our needs. Besides, manually annotating data is expensive, and extending to other application domains (e.g. from restaurants to electronics) usually necessitates re-annotating from scratch. Therefore, the main contribution of this paper is a pipeline to automatically generate large synthetic datasets for the conceptual similarity task. First, we prompt the dataset designer to provide seed words for the concepts she needs her conceptual similarity model to learn about. Second, we exploit the simple structure of subjective tags (Gaci et al., 2021) to expand the seeds with conceptually related terms using knowledge bases, or the implicit knowledge encoded in existing language models to automatically generate large training data.

Our second contribution is the similarity model itself. Capitalizing on the latest advances in semantic similarity research (Ranasinghe et al., 2019; Wang et al., 2017; Devlin et al., 2018), we propose a new similarity model by combining insights from aggregation-matching and cross-sentence attention paradigms. We show that conceptual similarity is better than cosine similarity with a margin of 17.42% in terms of Pearson correlation, or BERT-based similarity models through systematic evaluations. We also plug different similarity models into a tag-based search system and show that conceptual similarity outperforms them all. Also, we evaluate the quality of the automatically generated dataset through various experiments. We release our code and data in GitHub [1].

2 Related Work

2.1 Synthetic Dataset Generation

Acquiring training data is increasingly the largest and most pressing bottleneck in deploying machine learning systems (Ratner et al., 2017). The traditional way of doing so calls a team of experts to manually create and then label the data, incurring tremendous costs. Crowdsourcing alleviates part of this burden by proposing to a group of individuals of varying knowledge and expertise, the undertaking of the labeling task (Brabham, 2013; Howe, 2006). However, crowdsourcing runs the risk of corrupting the precision of the gold labels, and may inflict noise in the labeling process, especially when uneducated, careless or malicious workers are involved. A recent trend for acquiring training data is devising methods to automatically create, generate and label these critical building blocks of supervised learning systems with little effort (Ratner et al., 2016, 2017; Varma and Ré, 2018). When one speaks of generating data, two problems are implicitly addressed: (1) generation of features (i.e. unlabeled raw data), and/or (2) generation of gold labels (i.e. automatic labeling).

First, we discuss the generation of features, for which two techniques are mainly used: template-based generation (Dev et al., 2020; Nadeem et al., 2020; Ribeiro et al., 2020) and data augmentation (Zhao et al., 2018; Zmigrod et al., 2019; Taylor and Nitschke, 2017; Nie et al., 2020; Kaushik et al., 2019). In template-based generation, a set of tokens iteratively replaces the placeholders in templates, creating a separate example each time. Dev et al. (2020) provide templates such as *"The [PLACE-*

[1] https://github.com/YacineGACI/conceptual-similarity-for-subjective-tags

HOLDER] is a doctor", and insert words like *man*, *woman*, *muslim*, *christian* to create different examples to study social biases and stereotypes. In the same spirit, Nadeem et al. (2020) construct an evaluation dataset of biases through the use of templates and crowdsourcing, whereas Ribeiro et al. (2020) designed a framework to test NLP systems where users construct their own test benchmarks via the use of templates. On the other hand, data augmentation techniques expect an already available set of data, that they augment and expand to create larger sets. This is usually achieved by searching for similar inputs in the feature space, applying small perturbations to the existing data without changing the labels (Kaushik et al., 2019), or through seed expansion techniques (Fast et al., 2016; Li et al., 2019; Huang et al., 2020) via similarity in word embeddings or with knowledge bases.

Our own data generation is a mix of both techniques. While it is fundamentally a seed expansion method where aspect and opinion terms that we use to express subjective tags are expanded into conceptually related terms, it also derives from template-based generation since we use the template *"<opinion> <aspect>"* (as in *delicious food* or *romantic ambiance*) to construct subjective tags. The closest work to ours in terms of seed expansion is *Empath* (Fast et al., 2016) for studying topic signals in text. In *Empath*, a topic is defined by a set of seeds that are later expanded by either using word embeddings or crowdsourcing, to enrich each topic category. In contrast, we use the expansions to build sufficiently large labeled datasets. Moreover, we propose five different expansion techniques to increase the diversity of generated subjective tags.

The second problem in automatic data generation is generating the ground truth labels. Data programming (Ratner et al., 2016) is a recent paradigm that enables the programmatic creation of large-scale training sets in which different weak supervision sources (e.g. heuristics, knowledge bases, crowdsourcing) are combined. In Snorkel (Ratner et al., 2017) and Snuba (Varma and Ré, 2018), combination is done with a generative model that takes into consideration several properties of the weak classifiers including accuracy, coverage, and inter-correlations. Our work is different in two main aspects. First, Snorkel and Snuba are general frameworks that present general guidelines aiming to build labeling functions, whereas our method is much more specific, and focuses on similarity for subjective tags. Second, in this work, we generate and label training sets at the same time, in contrast to Snorkel whose purpose is to assign labels to already existing unlabeled data.

2.2 Textual Similarity

Apart from cosine similarity, we identify several similarity paradigms in the literature: (1) Siamese networks (Bromley et al., 1993; Ranasinghe et al., 2019) where the same encoder is used to project inputs into the same embedding space. Then, the similarity decision is made based on the vector representations alone. (2) Aggregation-matching paradigm (Wang and Jiang, 2016; Wang et al., 2016, 2017) which adds explicit matchings between the representations of inputs, before aggregating them and computing similarity. (3) Cross-sentence attention paradigm which is enabled by finetuning transformer models such as BERT on a similarity task (Devlin et al., 2018; Peinelt et al., 2020). (4) Combining several *weak* similarity models such as simple neural networks, tree-based and/or probabilistic models through an ensemble (Bethard et al., 2017; Tian et al., 2017; Lair et al., 2020). However, all these works focused solely on semantic similarity between syntactically correct sentences, whereas we focus on conceptual similarity between tag-like short phrases, similar to Anuar et al. (2015); Zhu and Iglesias (2016). In contrast, we use knowledge graphs to generate data and train a supervised model. More details about our similarity model are provided in Section 4.

3 Pipeline to Generate Training Datasets

Borrowing from the Aspect-Based Sentiment Analysis literature (Liu, 2012; Gaci et al., 2021), we define a subjective tag as the concatenation of an *aspect* term with an *opinion* term. The aspect term designates the component or the feature being described and the opinion term characterizes this feature. For example, *delicious food* is a subjective tag wherein *food* is the aspect while *delicious* is the opinion. This definition is sufficiently expressive to allow a wide range of subjective tags such as *romantic ambiance*, *clean hotel rooms*, *long-lasting battery*, *great camera* or *amiable dentist*.

Specific to this work, we define a *concept* as a set of aspect terms conceptually related to each other. For example, the concept of *food* can be described with the following set of terms: *{food, plates, dishes, pizza, chicken wings, meal, pasta}*

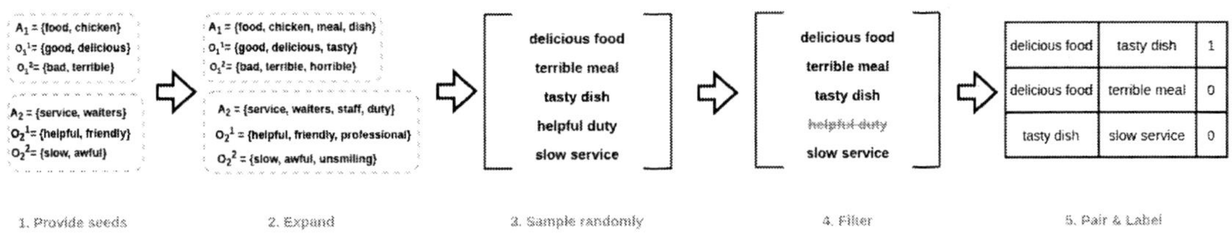

Figure 1: Labeled dataset generation pipeline

while the concept of *ambiance* can be defined with {*ambiance, atmosphere, lighting, background music, dance floor*}. The goal of conceptual similarity is to consider the aspects belonging to the same concept as similar when described with similar opinions.

We cast conceptual similarity as a binary classification problem, where the positive label denotes similarity. These specifications enable automatic generation of high-quality labeled datasets for conceptual similarity of subjective tags, with minimal costs. To do so, the dataset designer provides a list of concepts. We then leverage seed expansion techniques to generate the dataset, through the pipeline illustrated in Figure 1. In the following, we describe each step of the pipeline in detail.

3.1 Providing Concept Seed Words

The first step in the pipeline is to provide seed words for the concepts that the dataset designer wants to take into consideration. For each concept i, the designer provides a list of aspect seed words A_i, and m_i lists of opinion seed words O_i^j where $j \in \{1...m_i\}$; m_i depends on the concept and the level of granularity the dataset designer aims to reach. For the sake of illustration, say that the designer wants to include the concept of *food* with three classes of opinions (*delicious*, *horrible*, *healthy*). She may provide the following:

$A_i = \{$"food", "dish", "lunch", "pizza", "snack"$\}$
$O_i^1 = \{$"good", "delicious", "excellent"$\}$
$O_i^2 = \{$"bad", "horrible", "not seasoned"$\}$
$O_i^3 = \{$"healthy", "organic", "high quality"$\}$

A_i lists aspect terms related to the concept of *food*. Each of O_i^j lists some opinion terms of the same nature, but different from one set to another. In the example above, O_i^1 describes tasty food, O_i^2 characterizes bad food, and O_i^3 deals with healthy food. In this particular scenario, conceptual similarity trained on a dataset to be generated from these seed words considers the tags *"good food"* and *"healthy food"* as dissimilar because the terms *good* and *healthy* belong to different opinion sets. If the dataset designer needs a more granular similarity model (like spicy food described as its own class), she only has to add another set with seed words depicting spiciness. Following these guidelines, the designer can express a wide range of concepts such as price, service, hygiene, and in other domains too (hotels, electronics, books, etc.)

3.2 Seed Word Expansion

We propose five different techniques to expand the set of seed words given by the dataset designer. We illustrate these techniques in Figure 2 and describe them in the following:

WordNet Expansion. For every seed, we collect its corresponding synsets from WordNet (Fellbaum, 2012). Then, for every synset, we retrieve its hyponyms, hypernyms, meronyms and sister terms as illustrated in Figure 2(a). We control the number of expansions through the use of hyperparameters such as the maximum number of synsets to include, and different booleans each telling whether we take hyponyms, meronyms, etc. respectively.

ConceptNet Expansion. For every seed, we obtain its *is-a* (i.e. parent concepts) and *type-of* (child concepts) relations. For example, *meat* and *food* are parent concepts for the word of interest, i.e. *chicken*. We also retrieve other children of the parent concepts as is shown in Figure 2(b). We control ConceptNet expansion with three hyperparameters: *capacity* which is the maximum number of relations to consider; *minimum weight* which specifies the relevance of the relation (high weights in ConceptNet (Speer et al., 2017) correspond to a strong relation); and a boolean specifying whether to include children of parent concepts into the expansion.

Word Embedding Expansion. The goal is to find the *top_k* words in the vocabulary that minimize the total distance between them and seed terms. Taking the example in Figure 2(c), *pasta* is less distant from all the seeds than *morning* is, thus *pasta* constitutes a better expansion. The parameters of this technique is the number of expansions

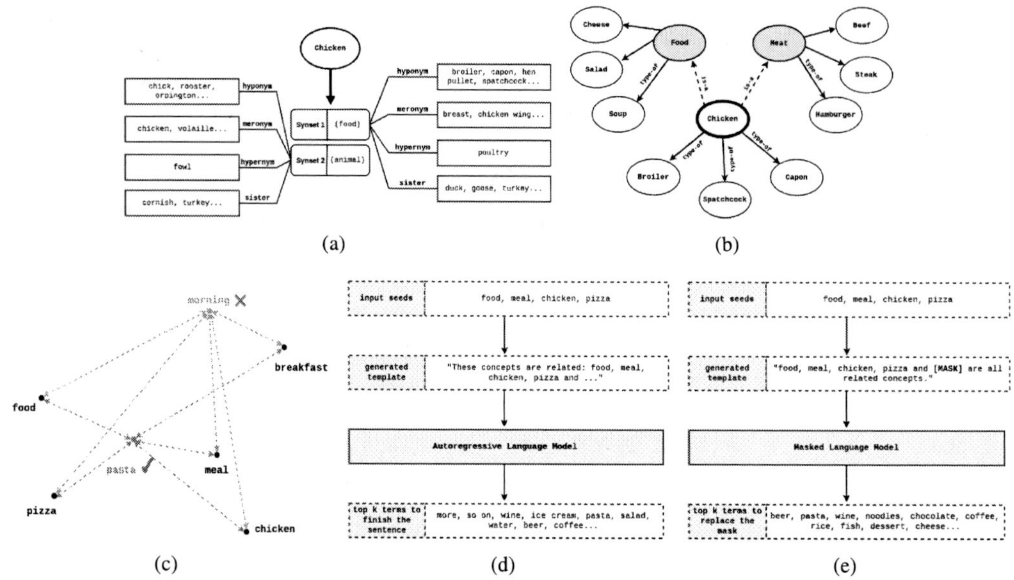

Figure 2: Different expansion techniques: (a) WordNet, (b) ConceptNet, (c) Embedding, (d) Language generation, (e) Masked Language Modeling

top_k, the word embedding model under use, and the distance function, e.g. euclidean.

Language Generation Expansion. This method plugs seed words into a template such as *"These concepts are related: <seed_1>, <seed_2>, ... <seed_n>, and "*, then asks an autoregressive language model to generate a continuation for this sentence. We then take the *top_k* words having the highest probabilities to be correct continuations. The hyperparameters are: the language model (e.g. GPT2, T5), the number of generations, and the maximum length of each generated expansion.

Masked Language Modeling Expansion. Similar to the previous expansion technique, we use a masked language model (Devlin et al., 2018), where the template takes the following form: *"<seed_1>, <seed_2>, ... <seed_n> and [MASK] are all related concepts."* The masked language model produces, for every word in the vocabulary, its likelihood to replace the mask. So terms having the same concept as the seeds have higher probabilities. The parameters of this method are the number of *top_k* terms to take, and the masked language model under use, e.g. BERT, Albert...

For every expansion technique, we can have as many expanders as there are parameter configurations. For example, two word embedding expanders, one based on Word2vec while the other on GloVe, are two different expanders. Or one that uses an euclidean distance while the other uses cosine similarity are also different expanders. We give the full list of parameter configurations we used for every expansion method in our experiments in Section A.2. For a new word to be considered as a correct expansion, we require that at least a sufficient number of expanders suggest the word. We specify this with *min_consensus_rate* which defines how many expanders need to produce the word in order to include it in the final expansions.

3.3 Random Sampling

We randomly choose an aspect term from one of the expanded aspect sets, and an opinion term from one of its associated opinion sets. These two terms are concatenated to form a subjective tag. For example, we may sample the aspect term *waiters* and the opinion term *nice* to form the tag *"nice waiters"*. We repeat this process to construct as many subjective tags as the dataset designer needs.

3.4 Filtering

Random sampling from automatically generated sets of terms may lead to arbitrary tags. For instance, it may construct tags such as *"helpful duty"*.[2] We eliminate those tags by using a language model which assigns likelihoods to sen-

[2]This may be the result of expanding *service* to *duty* through WordNet, even though *service* in this case refers to the waiters in a restaurant

tences so that semantically sound sentences are given high likelihoods and low quality sentences get low likelihoods. We use GPT2 language model (Radford et al., 2019) by feeding it with subjective tags formatted according to this template: *"the aspect is opinion"*. GPT2 should assign low probabilities to sentences such as *"the duty is helpful"*, and high probabilities to sentences such as *"the service is helpful"* or *"the waitstaff is agreeable"*. We manually select the probability threshold above which sentences make sense, and keep the generated tags that score above that threshold.

3.5 Pairing and Labeling

We randomly sample two subjective tags t_1 and t_2 from the filtered list. If the aspect and opinion terms of t_1 and t_2 have been sampled from the same sets, the tags are considered similar (label is 1). In all other cases, the label is 0. To avoid class imbalance in the dataset, the dataset designer provides the minimal ratio of positive examples. We enforce this constraint by deliberately sampling similar tags from the same aspect and opinion sets.

Figure 1 summarizes our dataset generation pipeline with an example. This algorithm allows us to create high-quality training datasets with minimal effort. It can also be adapted to any domain. In Section 5.2, we evaluate the quality of datasets generated with this pipeline.

4 Conceptual Similarity Model

In this section, we present our approach to compute conceptual similarity for a pair of subjective tags. Following guidelines from the aggregation-matching paradigm (Wang and Jiang, 2016), our model encodes explicit interactions between tags, e.g. whether the tags correspond to the same concept; whether they use the same opinions but with different aspects; whether the choice of words in the tags is similar but the tags themselves are not. To this end, we propose a novel bilateral matching model which *automatically* encodes such interactions and relationships before making a similarity decision. Given two subjective tags t_1 and t_2, this model estimates their similarity by computing their probability of being perfectly similar $P(sim = 1|t_1, t_2)$. Figure 3 illustrates the different layers of this model.

We begin by feeding t_1 and t_2 into BERT (Devlin et al., 2018). This serves two purposes: First, we get word embeddings for each word in the tags;

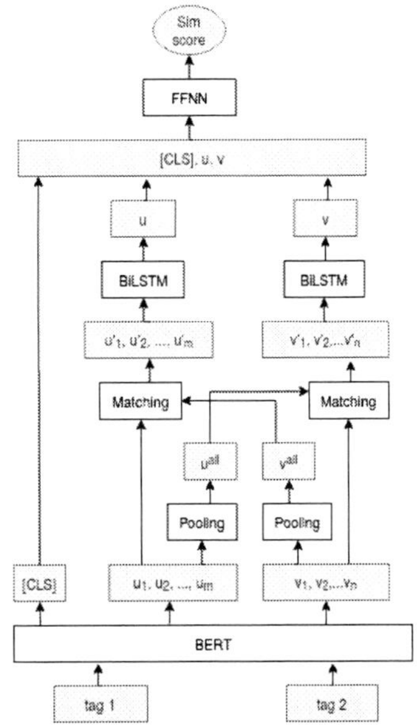

Figure 3: Similarity model architecture

second, we have a CLS vector that captures the relationship between t_1 and t_2 as a vector. Given BERT embeddings $[u_1, ..., u_m]$ and $[v_1, ..., v_n]$, we utilize mean pooling to obtain fixed-sized embeddings for each tag (u^{all} and v^{all}). The next layer in the network matches each word embedding of one tag with all the word embeddings of the other tag. The matching is done in two directions (hence the bilateral aspect): (1) We match each u_i with v^{all} to compare each word u_i in t_1 with all the words in t_2, and encode their relationship. (2) We match each v_i with u^{all} to do the same in the reverse direction.

The matching function we use is the element-wise multiplication which has long been used in the NLP community as a proxy for similarity. Thus, we use it to match word embeddings of t_1 and t_2. After the matching layer, we aggregate $[u'_1, ..., u'_m]$ and $[v'_1, ..., v'_n]$ to obtain fixed-length vectors for each tag via Bidirectional LSTM (BiLSTM) layers (Hochreiter and Schmidhuber, 1997), taking the last hidden states as tag embeddings u and v. At this step, we have encoded the relationship between t_1 and t_2 using two different paradigms: (1) aggregation-matching through the use of element-wise multiplication for matching and BiLSTM for aggregation (vectors u and v), and (2) the cross-sentence attention paradigm through CLS vector, because BERT uses self-attention (Vaswani et al., 2017) to compute its vectors. We concatenate u, v and CLS and feed it to a classification head (FFNN layer) to estimate similarity.

5 Experiments

We use **Restaurants** as the test domain. We consider nine concepts that we use to automatically generate the training dataset: Food, Service, Price, Atmosphere, Location, Cleaning, Environment, Menu and Parking. Each concept consists of one set of aspect terms, and two to three sets of different opinion terms. The choice of concepts, and seed words for aspects and opinions was inspired by previous work (Moura et al., 2017) who conducted surveys and qualitative experiments on many restaurant-seeking participants, and identified the most important factors taken into account by these same participants in their decision-making process for choosing a restaurant. The full list of concepts and their seeds is in Section A.3, while the hyperparameter details for the similarity model are in Section A.1. In the following, we first compare conceptual similarity to various baselines. Next, we evaluate the quality of the automatically generated dataset. Finally, we assess the practical value of conceptual similarity by measuring its impact on a downstream search system proposed by Gaci et al. (2021) that uses subjective tags.

5.1 Evaluating Conceptual Similarity

Existing similarity benchmarks provide similarity ground truth for syntactically correct sentences (Bethard et al., 2017). Hence, we cannot use them given that subjective tags are short phrases which do not draw from the same syntactically-complete sentence distribution. To the best of our knowledge, no benchmark for subjective tags exists. For this reason, we create our own test set by automatically extracting tags from Yelp's restaurant online reviews[3] using the tag extractor of SACCS (Gaci et al., 2021). Given a snippet of text, SACCS extracts subjective tags as concatenations of aspects and opinions. We then map these extracted tags randomly into pairs. We select 500 such pairs and ask three participants to assign a similarity score between 0 and 5 for each pair of subjective tags. We then normalize the similarity scores to squash them into the unit range before taking the mean across the participants. As in standard similarity evaluations, we use three metrics: Pearson and Spearman correlation, and Mean Absolute Error (MAE).

[3]https://www.yelp.com/dataset

Similarity Model	Pearson	Spearman	MAE
Cosine (Word2vec)	0.6770	0.6190	0.2083
Cosine (BERT MEAN)	0.3449	0.3312	0.5313
Cosine (BERT CLS)	0.0497	0.0848	0.6920
BERT Classif	0.5946	0.5404	0.1703
Random Forest	0.6271	0.6324	0.2614
Siamese	0.7058	0.6141	0.1903
Conceptual Sim	**0.8512**	**0.7388**	**0.1134**

Table 1: Evaluation of similarity models

We compare our conceptual similarity model to several baselines: A Siamese network (Ranasinghe et al., 2019) and a random forest classifier with hand-crafted features (Tian et al., 2017), both trained on the same dataset we use to train our own model. Also, owing to the universality of cosine similarity, we compare against it both with Paragram embeddings (Wieting et al., 2015) and on BERT embeddings with different pooling methods, MEAN and CLS as in Devlin et al. (2018); Li et al. (2019). Finally, we train a BERT-based model that we augment with a classification head (BERT Classif) and finetune on the same training data we used to train our conceptual similarity to make it more competitive. Table 1 summarises the results.

We can see that conceptual similarity outperforms cosine similarity by a large margin (0.1742 points in Pearson correlation). This demonstrates that cosine should no longer be perceived as the default when it comes to measuring similarity for subjective tags. We also show that BERT alone cannot cater for a task as ambiguous as similarity for subjective tags, even when finetuned on the same training set that we use.

This sheds light on the necessity to design custom models especially tailored for tag similarity. We argue that the effectiveness of our method stems from its ability to match different words of subjective tags using both attention and element-wise multiplication.

Existing information retrieval and tag-based search systems like Li et al. (2019) and Chang et al. (2019) blindly trust cosine similarity or a finetuned BERT without investigating their implications on the overall system performance. Our work highlights the limitations regarding main stream text similarity techniques for subjective tags and short phrases, as it gives guidelines as to how to design robust similarity models.

Noise level	Pearson	Spearman	MAE
Original	**0.8512**	**0.7388**	**0.1134**
5% noise	0.7341	0.6641	0.1958
10% noise	0.7788	0.7101	0.1898
25% noise	0.7418	0.7055	0.2879
50% noise	-0.1209	-0.0943	0.4078

Table 2: Evaluating similarity on noisy training data

Similarity Model	Short	Medium	Long
Cosine (word2vec)	0.7956	0.8579	0.8750
Cosine (Paragram)	0.8072	0.8602	0.8741
Cosine (BERT MEAN)	0.7807	0.8512	0.8740
Cosine (BERT CLS)	0.7807	0.8498	0.8738
BERT Classif	0.7968	0.8543	0.8744
Random Forest	0.8048	0.8623	0.8790
Siamese	0.7961	0.8618	0.8823
Conceptual Sim	**0.8232**	**0.8717**	**0.8839**

Table 3: Evaluating the ranking quality of a tag-based search system with different similarity models

5.2 Evaluating the Quality of Training Data

We measure the quality of the automatically generated training dataset by injecting artificial noise in the data and checking whether it degrades in quality (Jassar et al., 2009). We define noise in this context as swapping the labels in the training set. For example, if the original line in the dataset was $\{t_1, t_2, 1\}$, the new noisy line would be $\{t_1, t_2, 0\}$ and vice versa. We perturb fixed percentages of the training data (5%, 10%, 25% and 50%) and retrain the similarity model each time. The rationale of this experiment is that the introduction of noise should degrade the quality of training. In this spirit, if the similarity model trained on noisy data is of comparable accuracy to the one trained on the original unperturbed data, we argue that the original data was merely noise. On the other hand, if introducing noise degrades the performance of the similarity model, one can assume that the original data was of good quality. Table 2 shows the similarity correlations with human-defined scores as described in Section 5.1. We observe that instilling noise drops the accuracy of conceptual similarity. This reflects that the original unperturbed dataset is of high quality.

5.3 Experiments on a downstream System

In the following, we demonstrate the effectiveness of conceptual similarity when plugged into a downstream search application Gaci et al. (2021). We give a brief overview of the application, describe the baselines, benchmarks and evaluation metrics.

System overview. SACCS (Gaci et al., 2021) is a subjectivity-aware system to search for restaurants online. From their reviews, SACCS automatically extracts subjective attributes of restaurants offline in the form of subjective tags. Then, when users provide their search queries, they can include subjective tags as search filters. SACCS uses an underlying similarity model to compare between user-provided tags and those describing each restaurant. The final output of SACCS is a ranked list of restaurants ordered by relevance to the user query.

Baselines. We replace the similarity model used in SACCS with our conceptual similarity and the baselines we used in Section 5.1, to create as many baselines for this experiment.

Evaluation benchmark. We follow the same experiment used in Gaci et al. (2021) to assess the overall quality of the search system, and hence evaluate the practical value of conceptual similarity. Mainly, we use the same *crowdsourced* evaluation benchmark as in Gaci et al. (2021), consisting of subjective search queries with three levels of difficulty: Short queries have only one subjective tag; Medium queries have two; Long queries with three. Each difficulty level contains 100 different search queries, and each query is associated with a ranked list of relevant restaurants that best answer it.

Evaluation metric. We evaluate the final search quality using the popular Normalized Discounted Cumulative Gain (NDCG) (Christopher et al., 2008). The closer the score is to 1 using this metric, the better are the search results overall. Given that we use the same system in all the baselines of this experiment, and that these differ only in the underlying similarity model in use, we infer that the NDCG scores directly reflect the quality of the similarity models. Table 3 shows the results.

Results. Table 3 demonstrates the effectiveness of conceptual similarity, outperforming all other similarity models on all levels of difficulty, especially the universal cosine similarity which performs worse by a margin of 2.76%. This experiment proves that conceptual similarity is efficient when plugged in tag-based search applications.

6 Conclusion

In this work, we propose conceptual similarity for subjective tags. We also propose a methodology to automatically generate training datasets for conceptual similarity with minimal effort given a domain and a set of concepts. Unlike traditional semantic similarity, our model is trained with conceptual signals as reflected in the generated dataset. Intrinsic and extrinsic experiments demonstrate the superiority of our approach on subjective tags.

On the other hand, we acknowledge the following limitations. Although the method is independent from the application domain, we constrained our evaluations to the Restaurants domain for reasons related to unavailability of test data. So we were forced to create our own test benchmark by asking three participants to give ground truth labels for 500 pairs of subjective tags. This may seem small-scale, which risks putting into question the conclusions regarding the superiority of our similarity approach. However, the extrinsic experiment that we conduct by using relatively larger crowdsourced data shows that our approach is efficient and outperforms other similarity models, which assuages our concern. As future work, we plan to apply our methods on other domains, e.g. hotels, or electronics.

In this paper, we build the whole argument of our contributions against the blind use of cosine similarity in tag-based search systems, and to replace it with our newly proposed conceptual similarity. However, we employ BERT and LSTMs in our model which incur a much higher computational cost than cosine similarity. The adoption of our model in practice depends on whether efficiency is a major concern in the downstream search application, i.e. whether a poor search inflicts major negative consequences in critical domains such as finances or regulations. It also depends on the underlying infrastructure into which conceptual similarity will be deployed, e.g. are there any GPUs in use? Is memory space enough to hold BERT and LSTMs? So whether to adopt our contributions in practice is a compromise between cost and efficiency.

References

Fatahiyah Mohd Anuar, Rossitza Setchi, and Yu-Kun Lai. 2015. Semantic retrieval of trademarks based on conceptual similarity. *IEEE Transactions on Systems, Man, and Cybernetics: Systems*, 46(2):220–233.

Steven Bethard, Marine Carpuat, Marianna Apidianaki, Saif M. Mohammad, Daniel Cer, and David Jurgens, editors. 2017. *Proceedings of the 11th International Workshop on Semantic Evaluation (SemEval-2017)*. Association for Computational Linguistics, Vancouver, Canada.

Daren C Brabham. 2013. *Crowdsourcing*. Mit Press.

Jane Bromley, James W Bentz, Léon Bottou, Isabelle Guyon, Yann LeCun, Cliff Moore, Eduard Säckinger, and Roopak Shah. 1993. Signature verification using a "siamese" time delay neural network. *International Journal of Pattern Recognition and Artificial Intelligence*, 7(04):669–688.

Joseph Chee Chang, Nathan Hahn, Adam Perer, and Aniket Kittur. 2019. Searchlens: Composing and capturing complex user interests for exploratory search. In *Proceedings of the 24th International Conference on Intelligent User Interfaces*, pages 498–509.

D Manning Christopher, Raghavan Prabhakar, and Schacetzel Hinrich. 2008. Introduction to information retrieval. *An Introduction To Information Retrieval*, 151(177):5.

Sunipa Dev, Tao Li, Jeff M Phillips, and Vivek Srikumar. 2020. On measuring and mitigating biased inferences of word embeddings. In *Proceedings of the AAAI Conference on Artificial Intelligence*, volume 34, pages 7659–7666.

Jacob Devlin, Ming-Wei Chang, Kenton Lee, and Kristina Toutanova. 2018. Bert: Pre-training of deep bidirectional transformers for language understanding. *arXiv preprint arXiv:1810.04805*.

Ethan Fast, Binbin Chen, and Michael S Bernstein. 2016. Empath: Understanding topic signals in large-scale text. In *Proceedings of the 2016 CHI conference on human factors in computing systems*, pages 4647–4657.

Christiane Fellbaum. 2012. Wordnet. *The encyclopedia of applied linguistics*.

Yacine Gaci, Jorge Ramirez, Boualem Benatallah, Fabio Casati, and Khalid Benabdeslem. 2021. Subjectivity aware conversational search services. In *Proceedings of the 24th International Conference on Extending Database Technology, EDBT 2021, Nicosia, Cyprus, March 23 - 26, 2021*, pages 157–168.

Sepp Hochreiter and Jürgen Schmidhuber. 1997. Long short-term memory. *Neural computation*, 9(8):1735–1780.

Jeff Howe. 2006. The rise of crowdsourcing. *Wired magazine*, 14(6):1–4.

Jiaxin Huang, Yiqing Xie, Yu Meng, Jiaming Shen, Yunyi Zhang, and Jiawei Han. 2020. Guiding corpus-based set expansion by auxiliary sets generation and co-expansion. In *Proceedings of The Web Conference 2020*, pages 2188–2198.

Surinder Jassar, Zaiyi Liao, Lian Zhao, et al. 2009. Impact of data quality on predictive accuracy of anfis based soft sensor models. In *Proceedings of the World Congress on Engineering and Computer Science*, volume 2, pages 20–22.

Divyansh Kaushik, Eduard Hovy, and Zachary C Lipton. 2019. Learning the difference that makes a difference with counterfactually-augmented data. *arXiv preprint arXiv:1909.12434*.

Diederik P Kingma and Jimmy Ba. 2014. Adam: A method for stochastic optimization. *arXiv preprint arXiv:1412.6980*.

Nicolas Lair, Clement Delgrange, David Mugisha, Jean-Michel Dussoux, Pierre-Yves Oudeyer, and Peter Ford Dominey. 2020. User-in-the-loop adaptive intent detection for instructable digital assistant. *arXiv preprint arXiv:2001.06007*.

Yuliang Li, Aaron Feng, Jinfeng Li, Saran Mumick, Alon Halevy, Vivian Li, and Wang-Chiew Tan. 2019. Subjective databases. *Proceedings of the VLDB Endowment*, 12(11):1330–1343.

Bing Liu. 2012. Sentiment analysis and opinion mining. *Synthesis lectures on human language technologies*, 5(1):1–167.

Chandler May, Alex Wang, Shikha Bordia, Samuel R Bowman, and Rachel Rudinger. 2019. On measuring social biases in sentence encoders. *arXiv preprint arXiv:1903.10561*.

Luiz Rodrigo Cunha Moura, Gustavo Quiroga Souki, et al. 2017. Choosing a restaurant: Important attributes and related features of a consumer's decision making process. *Revista Turismo em Análise*, 28(2):224–244.

Moin Nadeem, Anna Bethke, and Siva Reddy. 2020. Stereoset: Measuring stereotypical bias in pretrained language models. *arXiv preprint arXiv:2004.09456*.

Yixin Nie, Adina Williams, Emily Dinan, Mohit Bansal, Jason Weston, and Douwe Kiela. 2020. Adversarial nli: A new benchmark for natural language understanding. In *Proceedings of the 58th Annual Meeting of the Association for Computational Linguistics*, pages 4885–4901.

Nicole Peinelt, Dong Nguyen, and Maria Liakata. 2020. tbert: Topic models and bert joining forces for semantic similarity detection. In *Proceedings of the 58th Annual Meeting of the Association for Computational Linguistics*, pages 7047–7055.

Alec Radford, Jeffrey Wu, Rewon Child, David Luan, Dario Amodei, and Ilya Sutskever. 2019. Language models are unsupervised multitask learners. *OpenAI Blog*, 1(8):9.

Tharindu Ranasinghe, Constantin Orasan, and Ruslan Mitkov. 2019. Semantic textual similarity with siamese neural networks. In *Proceedings of the International Conference on Recent Advances in Natural Language Processing (RANLP 2019)*, pages 1004–1011.

Alexander Ratner, Stephen H Bach, Henry Ehrenberg, Jason Fries, Sen Wu, and Christopher Ré. 2017. Snorkel: Rapid training data creation with weak supervision. In *Proceedings of the VLDB Endowment. International Conference on Very Large Data Bases*, volume 11, page 269. NIH Public Access.

Alexander Ratner, Christopher De Sa, Sen Wu, Daniel Selsam, and Christopher Ré. 2016. Data programming: Creating large training sets, quickly. *Advances in neural information processing systems*, 29:3567.

Marco Tulio Ribeiro, Tongshuang Wu, Carlos Guestrin, and Sameer Singh. 2020. Beyond accuracy: Behavioral testing of nlp models with checklist. In *Proceedings of the 58th Annual Meeting of the Association for Computational Linguistics*, pages 4902–4912.

Gene Smith. 2007. *Tagging: people-powered metadata for the social web*. New Riders.

Robyn Speer, Joshua Chin, and Catherine Havasi. 2017. Conceptnet 5.5: An open multilingual graph of general knowledge. In *Proceedings of the AAAI Conference on Artificial Intelligence*, volume 31.

Luke Taylor and Geoff Nitschke. 2017. Improving deep learning using generic data augmentation. *arXiv preprint arXiv:1708.06020*.

Junfeng Tian, Zhiheng Zhou, Man Lan, and Yuanbin Wu. 2017. Ecnu at semeval-2017 task 1: Leverage kernel-based traditional nlp features and neural networks to build a universal model for multilingual and cross-lingual semantic textual similarity. In *Proceedings of the 11th International Workshop on Semantic Evaluation (SemEval-2017)*, pages 191–197.

Paroma Varma and Christopher Ré. 2018. Snuba: automating weak supervision to label training data. In *Proceedings of the VLDB Endowment. International Conference on Very Large Data Bases*, volume 12, page 223. NIH Public Access.

Ashish Vaswani, Noam Shazeer, Niki Parmar, Jakob Uszkoreit, Llion Jones, Aidan N Gomez, Łukasz Kaiser, and Illia Polosukhin. 2017. Attention is all you need. In *Advances in neural information processing systems*, pages 5998–6008.

Shuohang Wang and Jing Jiang. 2016. A compare-aggregate model for matching text sequences. *arXiv preprint arXiv:1611.01747*.

Zhiguo Wang, Wael Hamza, and Radu Florian. 2017. Bilateral multi-perspective matching for natural language sentences. *arXiv preprint arXiv:1702.03814*.

Zhiguo Wang, Haitao Mi, and Abraham Ittycheriah. 2016. Sentence similarity learning by lexical decomposition and composition. *arXiv preprint arXiv:1602.07019*.

John Wieting, Mohit Bansal, Kevin Gimpel, and Karen Livescu. 2015. Towards universal paraphrastic sentence embeddings. *arXiv preprint arXiv:1511.08198*.

Jieyu Zhao, Tianlu Wang, Mark Yatskar, Vicente Ordonez, and Kai-Wei Chang. 2018. Gender bias in coreference resolution: Evaluation and debiasing methods. In *Proceedings of the 2018 Conference of the North American Chapter of the Association for Computational Linguistics: Human Language Technologies, Volume 2 (Short Papers)*, pages 15–20.

Vitalii Zhelezniak, April Shen, Daniel Busbridge, Aleksandar Savkov, and Nils Hammerla. 2019. Correlations between word vector sets. *arXiv preprint arXiv:1910.02902*.

Kaitlyn Zhou, Kawin Ethayarajh, Dallas Card, and Dan Jurafsky. 2022. Problems with cosine as a measure of embedding similarity for high frequency words. In *Proceedings of the 60th Annual Meeting of the Association for Computational Linguistics (Volume 2: Short Papers)*, pages 401–423.

Ganggao Zhu and Carlos A Iglesias. 2016. Computing semantic similarity of concepts in knowledge graphs. *IEEE Transactions on Knowledge and Data Engineering*, 29(1):72–85.

Ran Zmigrod, Sabrina J Mielke, Hanna Wallach, and Ryan Cotterell. 2019. Counterfactual data augmentation for mitigating gender stereotypes in languages with rich morphology. In *Proceedings of the 57th Annual Meeting of the Association for Computational Linguistics*, pages 1651–1661.

A Appendix

A.1 Similarity Model Details & Hyperparameters

We use a hidden dimension of 128 for the LSTM layer, and 512 for the 2-layer classification FFNN. We apply dropout with a ratio of 0.3. To train the model, we minimize cross entropy of the training set, and use Adam optimizer (Kingma and Ba, 2014) to update the parameters with $5e^{-6}$ as learning rate. For hyperparameter search, we pick the hyperparameters which work best on a development set that has been generated in the same way as the training set.

We implemented conceptual similarity in Python using standard packages such as PyTorch[4] for neural networks, HuggingFace transformers library[5] for BERT and GPT2.

[4]https://github.com/pytorch/pytorch

[5]https://github.com/huggingface/transformers

A.2 Parameter Configurations of Expanders

To generate the dataset used in the experiments of this paper, we use all the expansion techniques described in Section 3.2. For each technique, we use different parameter configurations to increase the diversity of the generated expansions. For example, GloVe and Paragram embeddings do not generate the same words given that each embedding model has been trained differently, and thus encode the representation of words in a unique way. Also, in *Language Generation Expansion*, we use different language models with different allowed lengths. This is to enable the generation of *n-grams*, in addition to words. We give the list of the expanders we use, and their parameters in Table 4.

We have a total of 28 different expanders. We set the parameter *min_consensus_rate* to 0.3. Consequently, for a new token to be included in the final set of expansions and passed down to the subsequent steps of the dataset generation pipeline (see Section 3 and Figure 1), the token has to be suggested by at least 30% of expanders (9 different expanders in this case). We selected this value by doing a manual hyperparameter search over the following values of *min_consensus_rate*: $\{0.1, 0.2, 0.3, 0.4, 0.5, 0.6, 0.7, 0.8, 0.9, 1.0\}$. We took the value (i.e. 0.3) that maximized the quality of the final generated dataset, as evaluated in Section 5.2. However, we chose the parameters of the respective expansion techniques manually without conducting a hyperparamter search for the following reasons: (1) There are too many parameters to test, which would make the search space exponentially larger, and thus expensive to explore. (2) The parameter selection of expansion techniques is subjective by nature. We manually chose the parameters such that they make sense (e.g. a negative capacity in *ConceptNet Expansion* or a very large *top_k* in *Masked Language Modeling Expansion* would not be useful), and such that the final expanders would generate a diverse set of expansions from a limited lexicon of seeds.

A.3 Concepts Used in this Work and their Seeds

We select 9 different concepts to include in the conceptual similarity model described in the experiments. We base our choice of concepts on substantial research in behavioral psychology (Moura et al., 2017) whose authors surveyed restaurant seekers and asked them about which factors influence their decision-making process when they chose between restaurants. In Table 5, we describe the concepts that we use, and give their corresponding seeds for aspects and opinions.

WordNet Expansion				
num_synsets	*hyponym*	*meronym*	*hypernym*	*sisters*
3	true	true	true	true
10	true	true	true	false
5	true	false	true	true

ConceptNet Expansion		
capacity	*minimum_weight*	*second_level_expansion*
3	2.0	true
5	3.0	true
10	1.0	false

Word Emebedding Expansion		
embedding_model	*num_words*	*distance_metric*
Word2vec	20	euclidean distance
Word2vec	20	cosine similarity
GloVe	20	euclidean distance
GloVe	20	cosine similarity
Fasttext	20	euclidean distance
Fasttext	20	cosine similarity
Paragram	20	euclidean distance
Paragram	20	cosine similarity
ConceptNet	20	euclidean distance
ConceptNet	20	cosine similarity

Language Generation Expansion			
model	*top_k*	*max_length*	*num_beams*
GPT2	20	1	200
GPT2	20	2	200
T5 base	20	3	200
T5 base	10	3	50

Masked Language Modeling Expansion	
model	*top_k*
BERT base	10
BERT base	20
BERT large	10
BERT large	20
RoBERTa large	10
RoBERTa large	20
ALBERT large	10
ALBERT large	20

Table 4: The full list of expansion techniques and their parameter configurations that we used to expand the seed words in our experiments

	Price
aspects	price, cost, payment
opinions 1 (good)	low, good, fair, acceptable, cheap, not too expensive, affordable, great
opinions 2 (expensive)	expensive, exaggerated, costly, overpriced, high, pricy
	Food
aspects	food, menu, plate, cuisine, meal, lunch, dinner, breakfast, cooking, snack, beverage, drink, pizza, pasta, chicken, meat, steak, rice, soup, dessert, dish, fish, salad
opinions 1 (good)	tasty, good, excellent, succulent, okay, delicious, well seasoned, perfectly cooked
opinions 2 (bad)	bad, flavorless, bland, not seasoned, cold, disgusting, unappetizing, flat, gross, boring, awful, terrible, dry
opinions 3 (healthy)	healthy, organic, high quality, fresh
opinions 2 (creative)	novel, interesting, creative
	Service
aspects	staff, waiter, waitress, cashier, service
opinions 1 (warm)	friendly, smiling, good, helpful, likable
opinions 2 (competent)	knowledgable, quick, fast, efficient, high quality, professional
opinions 3 (bad)	grumpy, horrible, slow, irritating, bad
	Cleaning
aspects	place, hygiene, kitchen, bathroom, utensils, plates, cutlery, silverware, trays, dishes, table, chair, furniture
opinions 1 (clean)	clean, impeccable, bright, lavish, luxurious, washed, shining
opinions 2 (dirty)	dirty, bad, in bad shape, stained, greasy, not washed, poor, disgusting
	Parking
aspects	parking, parking lot, parking area, parking convenience, parking space
opinions 1 (good)	free, available, empty, safe, large
opinions 2 (bad)	unavailable, poor, narrow, small, hard to find
	Environment
aspects	place, environment, setting, surroundings, decor, lighting, music, ventilation, furniture, air conditioning, air conditioner
opinions 1 (good)	good, excellent, great, cozy, comfortable, sophisticated, good taste, pleasant, memorable, adequate, beautiful, soothing, calming, fancy, attractive, happy, relaxing, nice, charming
opinions 2 (bad)	bad, horrible, bad taste, uncomfortable, dark, noisy, terrible, crowded, sad, depressing, boring
	Location
aspects	location, area, place, address
opinions 1 (good)	near, good, downtown, lively, touristy, popular, secure, safe, good, trustable
opinions 2 (bad)	far, bad, polluted, remote, dark, unsafe, unsecure, dangerous
	Ambiance
aspects	ambiance, atmosphere, air, experience, environment, setting, decor, lighting, music, ventilation, furniture
opinions 1 (good)	cozy, good, excellent, romantic, nice, upscale, trendy, loved, enjoyed, fun
opinions 2 (bad)	horrible, terrible, disgusting, bad, not good, disappointing, noisy, dark, depressing, boring
	Menu
aspects	menu, selection, list, choice, choices, option, options
opinions 1 (large)	wide, large, varied, variety, good, excellent, creative
opinions 2 (small)	small, shabby, narrow, bad

Table 5: The full list of seeds (aspects and opinions) per concept used in our experiments

TaskMix: Data Augmentation for Meta-Learning of Spoken Intent Understanding

Surya Kant Sahu
Skit.ai
The Learning Machines
surya.oju@pm.me

Abstract

Meta-Learning has emerged as a research direction to better transfer knowledge from related tasks to unseen but related tasks. However, Meta-Learning requires many training tasks to learn representations that transfer well to unseen tasks; otherwise, it leads to overfitting, and the performance degenerates to worse than Multi-task Learning. We show that a state-of-the-art data augmentation method worsens this problem of overfitting when the task diversity is low. We propose a simple method, TaskMix, which synthesizes new tasks by linearly interpolating existing tasks. We compare TaskMix against many baselines on an in-house multilingual intent classification dataset of N-Best ASR hypotheses derived from real-life human-machine telephony utterances and two datasets derived from MTOP. We show that TaskMix outperforms baselines, alleviates overfitting when task diversity is low, and does not degrade performance even when it is high.

1 Introduction

Deep learning has seen a meteoric rise in Speech and Language related applications, leading to large-scale applications of Voice-bots, Voice Assistants, Chatbots, etc., which aim to automate mundane tasks such as answering users' queries either in Spoken or textual modality. In many applications, users tend to code-switch or use borrowed words from other languages. A model trained for a particular language will not understand these borrowed words, and hence language-specific models are undesirable in such scenarios. On the other hand, a multilingual model can understand and reason what the user is speaking.

Due to the scale of the applications, data captured from various sources have different distributions or have different use-cases. Recently, Meta-Learning has emerged as a novel research direction that aims to leverage knowledge from diverse sets of data to learn a transferable initialization so that a low amount of training data is required to adapt to new datasets or tasks.

However, Meta-Learning requires a large number of training tasks, or else the model would overfit to the training tasks and would not generalize well to new tasks (Yao et al., 2021). In this work, we propose a novel Data Augmentation method, *TaskMix* for meta-learning problems, inspired by MixUp (Zhang et al., 2018). We investigate our proposed method against baselines such as MetaMix (Yao et al., 2021), Multitask-Learning, and vanilla Transfer Learning for multi-domain multi-lingual Spoken Intent Classification.

2 Preliminaries

In this section we describe the problem formulation and the prior work which we built upon.

2.1 Problem Formulation

Let $p(\mathcal{T})$ be a distribution over tasks from which training tasks $\mathcal{T}_0, \mathcal{T}_1, \mathcal{T}_2, \ldots, \mathcal{T}_{T-1}$ are sampled. The Meta-Learning objective is to learn a model with parameters θ such that θ quickly adapts to previously unseen tasks, which are assumed to be sampled from the same underlying distribution $p(\mathcal{T})$; for this paper, each task is a tuple $\mathcal{X}, \mathcal{Y} = \mathcal{T}$, where $\mathcal{X}$ is a set of N-Best hypotheses of utterances, and $\mathcal{Y}$ is a set of corresponding one-hot-encoded intent classes.

The number of classes in each $\mathcal{Y}$ may differ, and utterances from different $\mathcal{X}$ may be of different language or a different domain. This formulation is general and caters to real-life datasets.

Many meta-learning methods divide each training task into two disjoint sets: support $\mathcal{X}^s, \mathcal{Y}^s$ and query $\mathcal{X}^q, \mathcal{Y}^q$. However, Bai et. al (Bai et al., 2021) have shown that a query-set is unnecessary for meta-learning. Hence, throughout this work, we do not split the meta-training tasks, i.e., $\mathcal{X}^s = \mathcal{X}^q = \mathcal{X}$ and $\mathcal{Y}^s = \mathcal{Y}^q = \mathcal{Y}$

Findings of the Association for Computational Linguistics: AACL-IJCNLP 2022, pages 67–72
November 20–23, 2022.

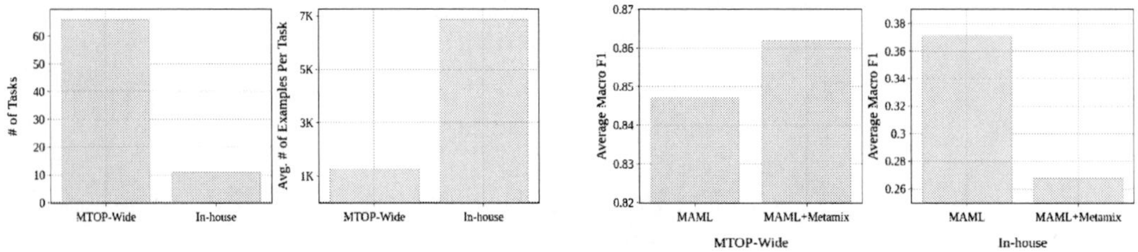

Figure 1: (Left) Statistics of the two datasets used in this paper. MTOP-Wide has a high #tasks and a low mean #examples per task; our In-house dataset has low #tasks, but a high mean #examples per task. (Right) Average Macro F1 scores of Model-Agnostic Meta-Learning (MAML) and MAML+MetaMix on both datasets. MetaMix is beneficial for MTOP-Long due to low mean #examples per task, whereas MetaMix worsens the performance our in-house dataset where the mean #examples per task is high.

Algorithm 1 MAML Update, $MetaTrain()$

Require: α: Learning rate for the inner loop.
Require: β: Learning rate for the outer loop.
Require: n: Iterations for the inner loop.
Require: $\mathcal{L}(t, \phi)$: Loss function for task t w.r.t. ϕ

```
for T_i ~ p(T) do                        ▷ Sample from support set
    θ_i ← θ                              ▷ Copy weights
    for j = 1 to n do
        Evaluate ∇_θ L(T_i^s, θ)
        θ_i ← θ_i − α∇_θ L(T_i^s, θ)
    end for
end for
θ ← θ − β∇_θ Σ_{T_i^q ~ p(T)} L(T_i^q, θ_i)   ▷ Update using query set
```

2.2 Model-Agnostic Meta-Learning

MAML (Finn et al., 2017) learns the meta-parameters θ by first, optimizing for multiple steps on a specific task $\mathcal{T}_i$, yielding θ_i which is the optimal task-specific parameters. This is done for each meta-training task $\mathcal{T}_i \sim p(\mathcal{T})$. Secondly, The loss on the held-out query set is computed, which is back-propagated through the computation graph through each task. Finally, we update θ such that θ can be quickly be adapted to each θ_i.

The procedure is outlined in Algorithm 1.

The authors argued that the held-out query set, which isn't used in the inner-loop optimization, prevents the overfitting of task-specific parameters θ_i and hence improves generalization of meta-parameters θ to new and unknown tasks.

However, (Bai et al., 2021) showed that splitting meta-training tasks into the disjoint query and support sets performs inferior to not splitting at all. Following these results, we do not split and sample data from the same set for inner and outer loops.

2.3 MixUp

MixUp (Zhang et al., 2018) is a data augmentation technique that synthesizes new datapoints by linearly combining random datapoints in the training set, encouraging a simple, linear behavior between training examples, improving generalization and robustness to noise. The interpolation parameter λ is sampled randomly from the Beta distribution at each training step. As mixing sequences of discrete tokens, such as sentences, is not possible, following (Sun et al., 2020), we only mix the output features of the transformer model.

MetaMix uses MixUp to intra-task datapoints, creating new datapoints within the same task. Whereas our proposed method, TaskMix, extends MixUp to cross-task datapoints, creating *new meta-training tasks*.

2.4 MetaMix

MetaMix (Yao et al., 2021) is an application of MixUp to the meta-learning setting. MetaMix encourages generalization within tasks by combining query-set datapoints. Fig. 2 illustrates how *MAML+MetaMix* differs from *MAML*. MetaMix introduces an additional gradient for each task by mixing random datapoints within each task. MetaMix is a data augmentation method for Meta-Learning where MixUp is applied to random pairs of datapoints *within a batch of query set datapoints* of each task.

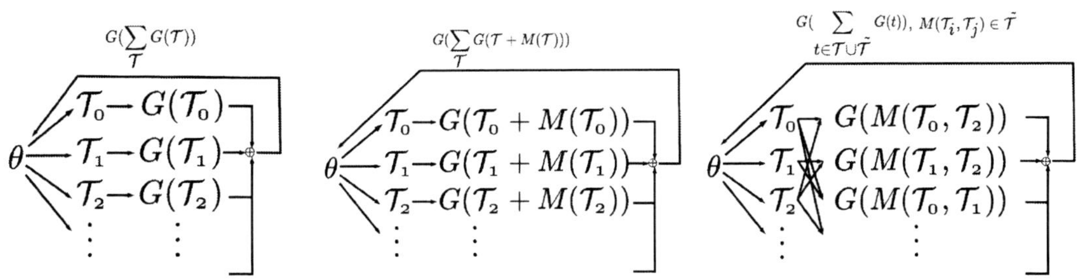

(a) MAML (b) MAML + MetaMix (c) MAML + TaskMix

Figure 2: Illustration of variants of MAML, including our proposed method, TaskMix. Here, $M(\mathcal{T})$ denotes mixing of datapoints within $\mathcal{T}$; $M(\mathcal{T}_i, \mathcal{T}_j)$ denotes mixing of tasks $\mathcal{T}_i$ and $\mathcal{T}_j$; and G denotes the gradient operator. MetaMix mixes random pairs of datapoints within each task. TaskMix mixes random pairs of tasks at each iteration.

3 TaskMix

3.1 Motivation

By virtue of meta-learning, θ learns features that transfer well across tasks (Raghu et al., 2020), which requires a large number of meta-training tasks, and most datasets on which studies on Meta-Learning literature use datasets which have a very high number of tasks and low average number of training examples per task. We make the following observations:

- MetaMix increases the effective number of datapoints *within each task*, i.e., increasing the mean #examples per task.
- MetaMix does not change the effective number of tasks.
- From Fig. 1, we infer that in MTOP-Wide dataset, where the mean #examples per task is low, MetaMix is very beneficial; however, in our In-house dataset, MetaMix deteriorates performance as the mean #examples per task is already very high.
- Similar to many real-life multi-domain settings, our In-house dataset has a small number of tasks.

To this end, we propose a simple data-augmentation method, *TaskMix*, to increase the effective number of tasks used in meta-learning.

3.2 Method

We propose a simple method, *TaskMix*, to overcome the low task-diversity problem. First, we sample support and query set batches from all tasks; we then sample N pairs of task indices $\mathbf{I}, \mathbf{J}$ uniformly in the range $[0, T-1]$. For each selected task pair, we sample the interpolation parameter λ from the Beta distribution with parameters (η, η); and then mix the training examples from the support and query sets, resulting in a new synthetic task $\tilde{\mathcal{T}}_n$. Finally, we train with vanilla MAML; however, we train on the new task set $\mathcal{T} \cup \tilde{\mathcal{T}}$. Algorithm 2 describes this procedure.

Algorithm 2 TaskMix

Require: η : Beta distribution parameter
Require: $mix(a, b, \lambda) = \lambda a + (1 - \lambda)b$
Require: N : Number of new tasks to generate.
while not converged **do**
  for $t = 0$ to $T - 1$ **do**
    $x_t^q \sim \mathcal{X}_t^q, y_t^q \sim \mathcal{Y}_t^q$
    $x_t^s \sim \mathcal{X}_t^s, y_t^s \sim \mathcal{Y}_t^s$
  end for
  $\mathbf{I}, \mathbf{J} \sim \mathbf{U}^N(0, T-1)$
  for $i \in \mathbf{I}, j \in \mathbf{J}, n = 0$ to $N - 1$ **do**
    $\lambda \sim Beta(\eta, \eta)$
    $\tilde{x}_n^q = mix(x_i^q, x_j^q, \lambda)$
    $\tilde{y}_n^q = mix(y_i^q, y_j^q, \lambda)$
    $\tilde{x}_n^s = mix(x_i^s, x_j^s, \lambda)$
    $\tilde{y}_n^s = mix(y_i^s, y_j^s, \lambda)$
  end for
  $MetaTrain()$
end while

TaskMix interpolates between batches of datapoints of random meta-training tasks. In essence, TaskMix encourages generalization across tasks by synthesizing new tasks, while MetaMix encourages generalization within each task by synthesizing new datapoints within the task. We emphasize that TaskMix increases the effective number of tasks, whereas MetaMix increases the effective number of datapoints within each task. We illustrate this difference in Fig. 2. We note that TaskMix and MetaMix are orthogonal, and *both methods can be used at the same time*.

TaskMix introduces only one additional hyperparameter, i.e., the number of synthetic tasks N. We found that results are largely insensitive to N if $N > T$, but performance rapidly degrades to the performance of MAML if $N < T$, hence we set $N = T$ for all experiments. We recover MAML if we set $N = 0$.

4 Experiments

This section presents empirical results on two multilingual and multi-domain datasets. For choice of hyperparamters and other experimental details, please refer to the Appendix.

4.1 Methods and Baselines

We use the N-Best-ASR Transformer (Ganesan et al., 2021) convention of concatenating N-Best ASR transcription hypotheses and then feed the concatenated text to XLM-RoBERTa (Conneau et al., 2020) feature extractor. We use the "base" configuration of pretrained XLM-RoBERTa to extract 768-dimensional vectors of each example for each task. The extracted features are inputs to a *neck*, which is a stack of Linear-Parametric ReLU layers. We chose XLM-RoBERTa as the feature extractor as it is trained on large corpora of multilingual text.

We now describe the baselines used in the experiments:

- **Multitask Learning (MTL):** we learn a different *linear head* for each meta-training task, and discard these heads after training, and initialize a new head for each meta-testing task.

- **Vanilla Transfer:** we discard all meta-training tasks and finetune directly to each meta-testing task.

- **MAML:** we append a linear layer with the max number of classes in the respective datasets.

4.2 Datasets

We briefly summarize the datasets used in this paper. Various statistics relating to the datasets are in Table 1.

Dataset	#Tasks	Mean #Classes	Mean #Examples Per Task
In-house	11	7.73	6884
MTOP-Long	11	2.82	7615
MTOP-Wide	66	2.17	1269

Table 1: Various statistics of datasets used in this paper.

- **In-house** dataset is constructed by collecting and automatically transcribing phone calls from various customer-call centers (varying domains, such as restaurants, airlines, banking, etc.) across 3 countries and with conversations comprising at least 3 languages with users speaking with borrowed words, code-switching, etc. Multiple human annotators manually label the intent for each user turn (consisting of 5-Best ASR hypotheses) in a conversation. The resulting dataset contains about 70K utterances across 11 tasks, grouped into 7 meta-training and 4 meta-testing tasks. We grouped the meta-training and meta-testing tasks chronologically, i.e., the oldest 7 tasks were designated as the meta-training tasks and the rest as meta-testing tasks. We use this setup to have as low an application gap as possible.

- **MTOP-Wide (Li et al., 2021)** contains over 100K utterances, (which we treat as 1-best hypotheses) from 6 languages across 11 domains. We divide the MTOP dataset by grouping examples from distinct domains and languages, resulting in 66 subsets. We further group these subsets into 54 meta-training and 14 meta-testing tasks. We only keep examples for which the class frequency is at least 50. We create this dataset to have a high task diversity but low average #examples per task.

- **MTOP-Long (Li et al., 2021)** We divide the MTOP dataset by grouping examples from distinct domains resulting in 11 subsets. We further group these subsets into 7 meta-training and 4 meta-testing tasks. We only keep examples for which the class frequency is at least 20. We create this dataset to have a low task diversity but high average #examples per task.

Method	Average Macro F1
MTL	0.320 ± 0.004
Vanilla Transfer	0.321 ± 0.007
MAML	0.361 ± 0.021
MAML+MetaMix	0.265 ± 0.006
MAML+TaskMix	0.370 ± 0.023
MAML+MetaMix+TaskMix	$\mathbf{0.441 \pm 0.002}$

Table 2: Results on our In-house dataset. We observe that TaskMix yields a significant performance boost. MAML+MetaMix degrades performance to worse than MAML.

Method	Average Macro F1
MTL	0.439 ± 0.022
Vanilla Transfer	0.446 ± 0.014
MAML	0.442 ± 0.002
MAML+MetaMix	0.450 ± 0.011
MAML+TaskMix	$\mathbf{0.462 \pm 0.012}$
MAML+MetaMix+TaskMix	0.421 ± 0.008

Table 3: Results on the MTOP-Long (Li et al., 2021) dataset. MAML+TaskMix out-performs other baselines.

4.3 Evaluation

As all tasks across all datasets are highly imbalanced, we use the Macro F1 score to weigh all classes equally.

All tasks are grouped into meta-training and meta-testing sets; each task is split into "support" and "test" sets. For modeling, we first train on the meta-training tasks, then use the same weights to fine-tune on the meta-testing tasks, and then compute Macro F1 scores for each meta-testing task. We then compute the mean of Macro F1 scores across all meta-testing tasks. We denote this metric as *Average Macro F1*. Finally, we report the mean and standard deviation of Average Macro F1 scores across three independent trials with different seeds.

4.4 Results and Discussion

We make the following key observations from Tables 2, 3, and 4:

- TaskMix improves performance on "long" datasets i.e., on In-house and MTOP-Long where the #meta-training tasks are very low and # examples per task is high.

Method	Average Macro F1
MTL	0.826 ± 0.018
Vanilla Transfer	0.804 ± 0.003
MAML	0.847 ± 0.006
MAML+MetaMix	$\mathbf{0.862 \pm 0.006}$
MAML+TaskMix	0.856 ± 0.003
MAML+MetaMix+TaskMix	$\mathbf{0.861 \pm 0.017}$

Table 4: Results on the MTOP-Wide (Li et al., 2021) dataset. MetaMix is beneficial and TaskMix doesn't negatively affect performance (compared to MAML) even when task diversity is high.

- For the In-house dataset, MetaMix degrades performance to be comparable to vanilla-transfer, i.e., almost no gain from meta-training tasks. We infer that MetaMix makes the model overfit on meta-training tasks, as the number of examples-per-task is already very high.
- In any of the datasets, TaskMix *doesn't degrade* the performance of MAML.
- For MTOP-Wide, TaskMix only has a slight performance boost compared to other baselines, suggesting that TaskMix is not useful if the number of tasks is already high.

We interestingly find that MAML+MetaMix+TaskMix is the worst performing method for MTOP-Long. However, TaskMix is beneficial when used on its own. We leave studying the interaction between MetaMix and TaskMix for future work.

5 Conclusion

In this paper, we propose a novel data-augmentation method, TaskMix, to alleviate the problem of overfitting in Meta-learning datasets when the task diversity is too low. Through experiments on two multilingual, multi-domain intent classification datasets, MetaMix could worsen the overfitting problem when the task diversity is low, whereas TaskMix is beneficial in such cases.

6 Acknowledgement

I thank my colleagues at Skit.ai who curated the in-house dataset, brain-stormed, and provided critical and insightful reviews of this work.

References

Yu Bai, Minshuo Chen, Pan Zhou, Tuo Zhao, J. Lee, Sham M. Kakade, Haiquan Wang, and Caiming Xiong. 2021. How important is the train-validation split in meta-learning? In *ICML*.

Alexis Conneau, Kartikay Khandelwal, Naman Goyal, Vishrav Chaudhary, Guillaume Wenzek, Francisco Guzmán, Edouard Grave, Myle Ott, Luke Zettlemoyer, and Veselin Stoyanov. 2020. Unsupervised cross-lingual representation learning at scale. In *ACL*.

Chelsea Finn, P. Abbeel, and Sergey Levine. 2017. Model-agnostic meta-learning for fast adaptation of deep networks. In *ICML*.

Karthik Ganesan, Pakhi Bamdev, B. Jaivarsan, Amresh Venugopal, and Abhinav Tushar. 2021. N-best asr transformer: Enhancing slu performance using multiple asr hypotheses. *ArXiv*, abs/2106.06519.

Haoran Li, Abhinav Arora, Shuohui Chen, Anchit Gupta, Sonal Gupta, and Yashar Mehdad. 2021. Mtop: A comprehensive multilingual task-oriented semantic parsing benchmark. *ArXiv*, abs/2008.09335.

Aniruddh Raghu, Maithra Raghu, Samy Bengio, and Oriol Vinyals. 2020. Rapid learning or feature reuse? towards understanding the effectiveness of maml. *ArXiv*, abs/1909.09157.

Lichao Sun, Congying Xia, Wenpeng Yin, Tingting Liang, Philip S. Yu, and Lifang He. 2020. Mixup-transformer: Dynamic data augmentation for nlp tasks. In *COLING*.

Huaxiu Yao, Long-Kai Huang, Linjun Zhang, Ying Wei, Li Tian, James Zou, Junzhou Huang, and Zhenhui () Li. 2021. Improving generalization in meta-learning via task augmentation. In *Proceedings of the 38th International Conference on Machine Learning*, volume 139 of *Proceedings of Machine Learning Research*, pages 11887–11897. PMLR.

Hongyi Zhang, Moustapha Cissé, Yann Dauphin, and David Lopez-Paz. 2018. mixup: Beyond empirical risk minimization. *ArXiv*, abs/1710.09412.

Understanding the Use of Quantifiers in Mandarin

Guanyi Chen and **Kees van Deemter**
Department of Information and Computing Sciences
Utrecht University
{g.chen, c.j.vandeemter}@uu.nl

Abstract

We introduce a corpus of short texts in Mandarin, in which quantified expressions figure prominently. We illustrate the significance of the corpus by examining the hypothesis (known as Huang's "coolness" hypothesis) that speakers of East Asian Languages tend to speak more briefly but less informatively than, for example, speakers of West-European languages. The corpus results from an elicitation experiment in which participants were asked to describe abstract visual scenes. We compare the resulting corpus, called MQTUNA, with an English corpus that was collected using the same experimental paradigm. The comparison reveals that some, though not all, aspects of quantifier use support the above-mentioned hypothesis. Implications of these findings for the generation of quantified noun phrases are discussed. MQTUNA is available at: `https://github.com/a-quei/qtuna`.

1 Introduction

Speakers trade-off clarity against brevity (Grice, 1975). It is often thought that speakers of East Asian languages handle this trade-off differently than those who speak Western European languages such as English (Newnham, 1971). This idea was elaborated in Huang (1984), when Huang borrowed a term from media studies, hypothesizing that Mandarin is "cooler" than English in that the intended meaning of Mandarin utterances depends more on context than that of their English counterparts; in other words, Mandarin speakers make their utterances shorter but less clear than English speakers. This "coolness" hypothesis is often worded imprecisely, conflating (a) matters that are built into the grammar of a language (e.g., whether it permits *number* to be left unspecified in a given sentence position), and (b) choices that speakers make from among the options that the grammar permits. Here we focus on the latter.

Studies of coolness have often focused on referring expressions (e.g., van Deemter et al. (2017); Chen et al. (2018); Chen and van Deemter (2020); Chen (2022)). The present paper focuses on *quantification*, as in the Quantified Expressions (QEs) "*All A are B*", "*Most A are B*", and so on. In a nutshell, we want to know whether Mandarin speakers use QEs less clearly, and more briefly, than English ones.

We report on an elicitation experiment, MQTUNA, inspired by the QTUNA experiment of Chen et al. (2019b, see §2). The experiment asks Mandarin speakers to produce sequences of QEs to describe abstract visual scenes. Sequences of QEs that are used to describe visual scenes are called Quantified Descriptions (QDs, Chen et al., 2019b). The MQTUNA corpus will enable researchers to investigate a wide range of questions about quantification in Mandarin. We illustrate this potential by comparing the corpus with the English QTUNA corpus from the perspective of coolness and we ask how our findings impact computational models of the production of QDs.

In sum, our contribution is two-fold:

1. We constructed, annotated and analysed the MQTUNA corpus;
2. We compared MQTUNA to QTUNA from the perspective of Huang's Coolness hypothesis.

2 QTUNA Experiment

A growing body of empirical work has studied how people understand and produce quantifiers (Moxey and Sanford, 1993; Szymanik and Zajenkowski, 2010; Grefenstette, 2013; Herbelot and Vecchi, 2015; Sorodoc et al., 2016). These studies have focused on a limited number of quantifiers (chiefly "*all*", "*most*", "*many*", and "*no*").

In Natural Language Generation (NLG), the QTUNA corpus was built to study how English

Findings of the Association for Computational Linguistics: AACL-IJCNLP 2022, pages 73–80
November 20–23, 2022. ©2022 Association for Computational Linguistics

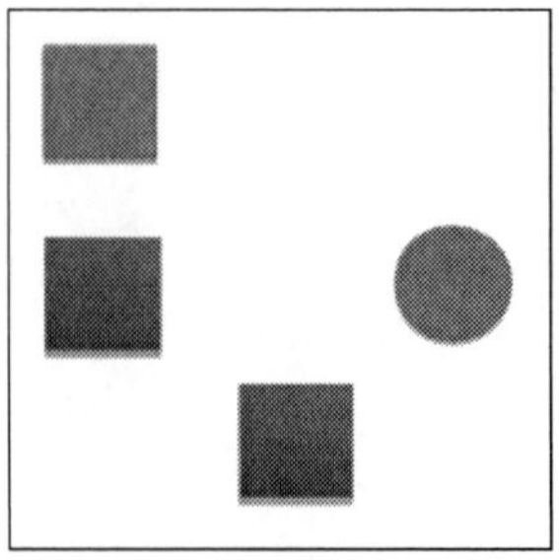

Figure 1: An example scene from QTUNA.

speakers use QDs to describe a visual scene (Figure 1). Participants were free to (1) describe a visual scene in whatever way they want, (2) use as many sentences as they choose, and (3) use any sentence pattern that they choose. For example, for the scene in Figure 1, a participant could say "*Half of the objects are blue squares. The other half are red objects. There is only one red circle.*". Given the domain contains four objects in no more than two shapes, this QD describes the scene completely and correctly. Participants were told that their descriptions should allow readers to reconstruct the scene *modulo* location. Each scene contains N objects (NB: N is defined as *domain size*), which is either a circle or a square and either blue or red. To test how domain size impacts the use of quantifiers, QTUNA experimented on 3 sizes, i.e., 4, 9, and 20.

Analysis of the resulting QTUNA corpus revealed that, as the domain size increase, (English) speakers (1) use more vague quantifiers (e.g., *most* and *few*); (2) use less complete QDs (NB: a QD is complete if the scene described is the only one *modulo* location that fits the description); (3) use more incorrect QDs (NB: a QD is incorrect if it is not true with respect to the scene); and (4) do not use longer QDs (measured in terms of the number of QEs).

3 Research Questions

Are the QTUNA findings true for MQTUNA? We are curious whether the above-mentioned findings about QTUNA (see §2) hold true for MQTUNA. We expected that domain size affects speakers of different languages in the same way, so these findings should hold for both corpora in the same way.

Are Mandarin QDs briefer and less clear than English QDs? "Coolness" says Mandarin speakers speak more briefly and less clearly than English speakers. We check this hypothesis by comparing QDs in QTUNA and MQTUNA.

Regarding brevity, we are curious about the length of QDs. If Mandarin QDs are briefer than English QDs, then we expect QDs in MQTUNA to contain less QEs than those in QTUNA.

Regarding clarity, if Mandarin speakers utter QDs in a less clear way, we expect to see more vague quantifiers in MQTUNA than in QTUNA and, more importantly, fewer logically complete QDs.

4 MQTUNA Experiment

We followed the same methodology as in the QTUNA experiment, re-using scenes of the QTUNA experiment, inheriting its experimental design, and translating its instructions participants.

4.1 Materials

To prepare materials for the MQTUNA experiment, we sampled scenes from QTUNA following two steps. First we eliminated all scenes all of whose objects share the same properties. For instance, we removed all scenes that can be described completely by a single QD like "*all objects are red circles*". Next, for each domain size (i.e., 4, 9, or 20), we randomly sampled 5 scenes from QTUNA. In the second step, to familiarise participants with the experiment, we added a practice situation that uses a $N = 4$ scene whose objects are the same.

For the instructions, we translated the instructions of QTUNA (Appendix A). More specifically, the instruction told subjects that (1) they should finish the experiment in limited time (i.e., 20 minutes); (2) their descriptions would then be used in a reader experiment where readers are asked to reconstruct the scenes; (3) they should not enumerate and not say where in the grid a particular object is located.

4.2 Design, Participants, and Procedure

Data from 31 participants were collected for domain sizes $N = 4$, 9 and 20 (N is the number of objects in the scene). See Appendix B for details about participants. Participants were asked to read the instruction first and to complete the experiment (16 situations) in one sitting.

4.3 The MQTUNA Corpus

The resulting MQTUNA corpus contains 465 valid QDs and 1175 QEs. There are 155 QDs for each domain size and there are 383, 386, and 406 QEs for $N = 4$, $N = 9$, and $N = 20$ respectively. Table 1 lists a number of examples QDs in MQTUNA.

N	Description
4	所有都是蓝色，方块是圆形三倍。| *All objects are blue. The number of squares is triple that of circles.*
4	所有图形都是蓝色的。但是只有一个圆。| *All objects are blue but there is only one circle.*
9	所有的圆圈是红色的。方块都是蓝色的。方块的数量少于圆圈的数量。 *All circles are red. All squares are blue. There are fewer squares than circles.*
9	方块是圆圈数量的三倍。全部为红色。| *The number of squares is triple that of circles. All of them are red.*
20	图中红色蓝色方块圆球数量相差不大。| *There is no big difference between the numbers of all combinations.*
20	一半红色，一半蓝色。红色方块比蓝色方块多。蓝色圆圈多于红色圆圈。 *Half of the objects are red, the other half of them are blue. There are more red squares than blue squares and more blue circles than red circles.*

Table 1: List of example descriptions from the MQTUNA corpus, with their annotations. N indicates domain size.

	$N=4$	$N=9$	$N=20$
Quantified Description	155	155	155
Quantified Expression	383	386	406
Complete Description	122	19	5
Incomplete Description	33	136	150
Vague Quantifier	25	143	184
Wrong Description	7	14	30

Table 2: Frequencies of major QE types in the different subcorpora of MQTUNA.

We annotated the use of quantifiers in MQTUNA, viewing quantifiers that have the same meaning (e.g., "所有" ("suoyou", all) and "全部" ("quanbu", all) as identical. See Appendix C for a list of top-10 quantifiers and their usage in MQTUNA.

As for quantifier use, the quantifier "所有" (suǒyǒu; *all*) and "一半" (yíbàn; *half*) are two of the most frequent quantifiers. In the top-10 most frequent quantifiers of MQTUNA, 4 are vague, including "绝大多数" (*overwhelming majority*), "大多数" (*most*), "多数" (*most*), "少数" (*minority*). This is very different from QTUNA, where only 1 vague quantifier (i.e., *most*) is in top-10. Appendix C also presents lists of crisp and vague quantifiers.

5 Analysis

Focusing on the research questions of §3, we analyse the MQTUNA corpus (§5.1), and we compare MQTUNA with QTUNA (§5.2). We conclude with a few post-hoc observations (§5.3).

5.1 Analysing MQTUNA

To check whether the findings of QTUNA (§2) hold for MQTUNA, we annotated each QD with whether it is logically complete and whether it is correct with respect to the corresponding scene; we also annotated each QE with whether it uses a vague quantifier or not. Annotation details can be found in Appendix D. To avoid compromising the comparison between MQTUNA and QTUNA, we did not only annotate MQTUNA but we also re-annotated the QTUNA corpus, using the same annotators following the same set of principles. Table 2 charts the results.

Vagueness. We identified 57, 201, and 234 QEs that contain vague quantifiers out of 383, 386, and 406 QEs from the three sub-corpora, confirming that vagueness is more frequent with increasing domain size. This was confirmed by a binary logistic regression test ($p < .0001$, adjusted $p < .0001$[1]).

Completeness. We observed 33, 136, and 150 logically incomplete QDs from the three subcorpora. A binary logic regression test confirms that there are more logically incomplete QDs in larger domains ($p < .0001$, adjusted $p < .0001$).

Correctness. The 3 subcorpora contained 7, 14, and 30 wrong QDs, so more incorrect QDs are used in larger domains ($p < .0001$, adjusted $p < .0001$) using a binary logic regression test.

Length. QDs in larger domains in MQTUNA contain more QEs than those in smaller domains. We computed the Pearson correlation between the domain size and the QD length. After Bonferroni correction, the difference fell just short of significance ($p = 0.1025$, adjusted $p = 0.615$).

In a nutshell, all findings of QTUNA are also true for MQTUNA.

5.2 MQTUNA and QTUNA: Initial Comparison

To compare QDs in Mandarin and English, we considered all the scenes in MQTUNA and re-annotated them using the same annotators in §5.1.

[1]The p-value was adjusted by Bonferroni correction

	QTUNA		MQTUNA		
N	C	I	C	I	p-value
4	298	32	122	33	$p < .001$
9	77	113	19	136	$p < .0001$
20	4	186	5	155	$p = .5$
all	379	331	146	319	$p < .0001$

Table 3: Numbers of complete (C) and incomplete (I) QEs in QTUNA and MQTUNA. N is domain size.

Brevity. We compared the length of QDs in QTUNA and MQTUNA and found that QDs in MQTUNA are longer than those in QTUNA in every sub-corpus. This rejects our hypothesis that Mandarin speakers prefer brevity and, thus, produce shorter QDs than English speakers.

Completeness. Table 3 reports the number of logically complete QDs in QTUNA and MQTUNA, respectively. 379 out of 710 QDs in QTUNA are logically complete while 146 out of 465 QDs in MQTUNA are complete. Using a Chi-squared test, this confirms that there are more complete QDs in QTUNA than in MQTUNA ($\chi^2(2, N = 1175) = 54.93, p < .0001$, adjusted $p < .0001$). Mandarin speakers produce longer but less logically complete QDs. Interestingly, if we look into more details (see Table 3), the difference only exists in domain sizes 4 and 9. We suspect that both English and Mandarin speakers find it hard to come up with a logically complete QD if the domain size is large.

Vagueness. In QTUNA, 222 of the 1342 QEs were vague whereas, in MQTUNA, 352 of the 1175 QEs were vague. A Chi-squared test confirms that Mandarin speakers used more vague quantifiers than English speakers ($\chi^2(2, N = 2517) = 64.04, p < .0001$, adjusted $p < .0001$).

5.3 Post-hoc Observations

Surface Forms. We observed that QEs in MQTUNA are generally realised in three kinds of forms: (1) "Q A 是 B" ("*Q A are B*"), where "Q" is a quantifier, for example, "大部分 A 是 B" ("*most A are B*"); (2) "A 中 Q 是 B" ("in A, Q are B"); and (3) "B 在 A 中 占 Q" ("*B takes up Q of A*").

A-Drop. Akin to the previous findings that pronouns and nouns are often dropped in Mandarin NPs (Huang, 1984; Osborne and Liang, 2015), we found that nouns that take up A positions in the above forms are also often dropped (henceforth, *A-drop*), for example, saying "B 占 Q" ("*B takes up Q*"). In MQTUNA, we found 304 out of 1175 QEs (approximately 25.87%).

Plurality. van der Auwera and Baoill (1998) pointed out that Mandarin briefer in that plurality is often not expressed explicitly. Consistent with this, we found that in MQTUNA, numbers are rare. This makes a QE in Mandarin sometimes less informative than an English QE, Mandarin QDs are less likely to be logical complete. For example, Mandarin QE "图片中有红色方块" could mean "there are red squares" or "there is a red square".

6 Discussion

We have presented and analysed the MQTUNA corpus of quantifier use in Mandarin.

Coolness. We assessed the coolness hypothesis by analysing MQTUNA and comparing QTUNA and MQTUNA. As for the brevity of QDs, we found both evidence (i.e., Mandarin speakers often performed A-drop and expressed plurality implicitly) and counter-evidence (i.e., Mandarin speakers uttered longer QDs than English speakers).

As for the clarity of QDs, we confirmed that the Mandarin corpus (MQTUNA) contains significantly more *incomplete* QDs and *vague* quantifiers than its English counterpart (QTUNA).

Generating QDs. Chen et al. (2019a) proposed algorithms for generating QDs (QDG algorithms). Let us list issues to be heeded when building QDG algorithms for Mandarin.

First, plurality plays an important role in the QDG Algorithms of Chen et al. (2019a). If these algorithms are to be adapted to Mandarin, then they should first "decide" whether to realise the plurality of a QE explicitly, since this will influence how much information the QD should express in other ways. Second, modelling the meaning of vague quantifiers is vital for generating human-like QDs. Since Mandarin speakers use vague quantifiers more frequently than English speakers, Mandarin QDG needs to handle a larger number of vague quantifiers and capture nuances between them, which is a difficult and data-intensive challenge. Lastly, QD surface realisation in Mandarin needs to handle more syntactic variations than current QDG algorithms are capable of, because (1) a QE can be realised in multiple possible forms (see §5.3); (2) A-drop frequently happens; (3) Plurality can be expressed implicitly or explicitly.

Future Work. Our comparison between Mandarin and English was based on two corpora, QTUNA and MQTUNA, that were collected using elicitation experiments that were conducted following the same experimental paradigm, and using very similar sets of stimuli. Yet, *language* may not have been the only difference between these experiments; participants in QTUNA and MQTUNA are also likely to differ in terms of their *cultural background*, and possibly in terms of other variables, such as their education; There is no absolute guarantee that all our annotations are correct. To create an even playing field between the two corpora, we asked our annotators to re-annotate QTUNA. But although our annotator were native speakers of Chinese, they were merely fluent (not native) in English, which may have caused a difference in the way both corpora were annotated. In future, it would be interesting to conduct even more tightly controlled experiments to tease apart the variable of language use from such possibly confounding variables.

Finally, our experiment has looked at a wide range of quantifiers. We also plan experiments that zoom in on specific subsets, such as the different ways in which variants of the quantifier "*most*" can be expressed (cf., Wang and Piao (2007) and §4.3).

References

Guanyi Chen. 2022. *Computational Generation of Chinese Noun Phrases*. Ph.D. thesis, Utrecht University.

Guanyi Chen and Kees van Deemter. 2020. Lessons from computational modelling of reference production in Mandarin and English. In *Proceedings of the 13th International Conference on Natural Language Generation*, pages 263–272, Dublin, Ireland. Association for Computational Linguistics.

Guanyi Chen, Kees van Deemter, and Chenghua Lin. 2018. Modelling pro-drop with the rational speech acts model. In *Proceedings of the 11th International Conference on Natural Language Generation*, pages 159–164, Tilburg University, The Netherlands. Association for Computational Linguistics.

Guanyi Chen, Kees van Deemter, and Chenghua Lin. 2019a. Generating quantified descriptions of abstract visual scenes. In *Proceedings of the 12th International Conference on Natural Language Generation*, pages 529–539, Tokyo, Japan. Association for Computational Linguistics.

Guanyi Chen, Kees van Deemter, Silvia Pagliaro, Louk Smalbil, and Chenghua Lin. 2019b. QTUNA: A corpus for understanding how speakers use quantification. In *Proceedings of the 12th International Conference on Natural Language Generation*, pages 124–129, Tokyo, Japan. Association for Computational Linguistics.

Edward Grefenstette. 2013. Towards a formal distributional semantics: Simulating logical calculi with tensors. In *Second Joint Conference on Lexical and Computational Semantics (*SEM), Volume 1: Proceedings of the Main Conference and the Shared Task: Semantic Textual Similarity*, pages 1–10, Atlanta, Georgia, USA. Association for Computational Linguistics.

Herbert P Grice. 1975. Logic and conversation. In *Speech acts*, pages 41–58. Brill.

Aurélie Herbelot and Eva Maria Vecchi. 2015. Building a shared world: mapping distributional to model-theoretic semantic spaces. In *Proceedings of the 2015 Conference on Empirical Methods in Natural Language Processing*, pages 22–32, Lisbon, Portugal. Association for Computational Linguistics.

C-T James Huang. 1984. On the distribution and reference of empty pronouns. *Linguistic inquiry*, pages 531–574.

Linda M Moxey and Anthony J Sanford. 1993. *Communicating quantities: A psychological perspective.* Lawrence Erlbaum Associates, Inc.

Richard Newnham. 1971. *About Chinese*. Penguin Books Ltd.

Timothy Osborne and Junying Liang. 2015. A survey of ellipsis in chinese. In *Proceedings of the Third International Conference on Dependency Linguistics (Depling 2015)*, pages 271–280.

Ionut Sorodoc, Angeliki Lazaridou, Gemma Boleda, Aurélie Herbelot, Sandro Pezzelle, and Raffaella Bernardi. 2016. "look, some green circles!": Learning to quantify from images. In *Proceedings of the 5th Workshop on Vision and Language*, pages 75–79, Berlin, Germany. Association for Computational Linguistics.

Jakub Szymanik and Marcin Zajenkowski. 2010. Comprehension of simple quantifiers: Empirical evaluation of a computational model. *Cognitive Science*, 34(3):521–532.

Kees van Deemter, Le Sun, Rint Sybesma, Xiao Li, Bo Chen, and Muyun Yang. 2017. Investigating the content and form of referring expressions in Mandarin: introducing the mtuna corpus. In *Proceedings of the 10th International Conference on Natural Language Generation*, pages 213–217, Santiago de Compostela, Spain. Association for Computational Linguistics.

Johan van der Auwera and Dónall Ó Baoill. 1998. *Adverbial constructions in the languages of Europe*, volume 3. Walter de Gruyter.

Amy Y Wang and Scott Piao. 2007. Translating vagueness? a study on translations of vague quantifiers in an english-chinese parallel corpus. In *Proceedings of the Corpus Linguistics Conference*.

A Instruction

您好，我们最近的研究关注于人描述物体集合的方法。为此，我们设计了一个小实验。在这个实验中，我们将给您展示一系列图片。在每张图片中，您将看到一定数量（*16*个）的图形。在看到每张图片后，我们需要您写一句或几句语法正确的中文句子。请注意：
We're interested in understanding how people describe sets of objects. To find out, we're doing a small experiment, in which we'll show you a number of situations in which some (16) objects are displayed on a screen. We'd like you to describe each situation in one or more grammatically correct Mandarin sentences.

1 您将在有限的时间（*20*分钟）内完成整个实验。*The experiment should take you less than 20 minutes.*

2 根据您写的描述，后续实验中的被试者会用它来在有限时间（总共*20*分钟）内重构图片。"重构"的在这里仅表示图片中每种图形数量。因此在您的表述中，您不必描述每个图形在图片中的位置（例如：上方，在中间）。*Based on your description, a reader will try to "reconstruct" the situation. We use the word "reconstruct" loosely here, because the only thing that matters is the different types of objects that the sheet contains. Therefore, please do not say *where* in the grid a particular object is located (e.g., "top left", "in the middle", "on the diagonal").*

3 每个图形可能是方形也可能是圆形，可能是红色也可能是蓝色。后续负责重构的被试者也知晓这个信息。负责重构的被试者同时还知晓图片中图形的数量。这些信息都会被用在重构当中。*Each object is a circle or a square, and either red or blue. Your reader knows this.*

4 请不要"枚举"图片中的图形，例如：图片中有一个红色的圆圈，两个蓝色的圆圈，和三个蓝色的方块。*Please do not "enumerate" the different types of objects. For example, do not say "There is a red circle, two blue circles, and ...".*

以下是几个例子*:*

Here are some Example: (...)

Figure 2: The sketch of the instruction of MQTUNA.

B Participants

All of our participants are Mandarin native speakers. 21 subjects are undergraduate students in computer science from the Utrecht University. Each of the rest at least has a bachelor degree in any of computer science, statistics, and management. 11 subjects are female and 20 subjects are male.

C Quantifiers in MQTUNA

Table 4 enumerates the top-10 quantifiers and their usage in MQTUNA. In what follows, we provide a list of vague quantifiers and a list of crisp quantifiers in MQTUNA.

- Crisp Quantifiers: 所有 (*all*), 只有 (*only*), 比...多... (*more*), 倍 (*times*), 除了...都是... (*all...except...*), 有 (*there is*), 多于n倍 (*more than n times*), 少于n倍 (*less than n times*), 各半 (*half...the other half...*), 相同 (*same as*), 一半 (*half*), 不同 (*different amount of*), 一半以上 (*more than half*), 没有 (*no*), 少于 (*less than*), 所有组合 (*all possible combinations*);

- Vague Quantifiers: 大部分 (*most*), 小部分 (*a small part of*), 绝大部分 (*overwhelming majority*), 除了...大多数... (*most...except...*), 少量的 (*a few*), 远多于 (*way more than*), 极少数 (*a very few*), 多一点 (*slightly more than*), 多不少 (*greatly more than*), 相近 (*close to each other*), 基本都是 (*almost all*), 略少 (*a bit less*), 略多 (*a bit more*), 大约各半 (*approximately half ... the rest ...*), 基本相同 (*almost the same*), 多一些 (*several more*), 多好几倍 (*several times more*), 多得多 (*much more*), n倍多一点 (*slightly more than n times*), n倍少一点 (*slightly less than n times*), 大约一半 (*approximately half*), 少数 (*minority*).

D Annotating MQTUNA

We asked our annotator to annotate logical completeness, correctness and vagueness based on the following principles:

1. Logical Completeness: we asked our annotator whether s/he can fully recover the scene given a QD. For example, for a scene with 3 red circles and 1 blue square, one could say "*Most objects are red circles and there is only one blue square.*" Though s/he uses a vague quantifier "most", we still can infer that, given domain size 4, "most objects" means 3 objects, and, therefore, this QD is logically complete. However, for a scene with 8 red circles and 1 blue circle, one could say "*All objects are circles and almost all of them are 8.*" Though using "almost all" to describe "8 out of 9" is definitely correct, it does not necessarily mean "8 out of 9" but possibly mean "7 out of 9". Therefore, this QD is not logically complete;

2. Correctness: we asked our annotator to annotate a QD as "incorrect" if and only if the QD contains definitely incorrect information, for example, saying a "red object" blue or describing a scene with 3 red squares and 1 blue square as "*half of the objects are red*";

3. Vagueness: our annotator decided whether a QE uses a vague quantifier based on the vague quantifier list in Appendix C.

Notation	English	Surface Form(s)	Example Quantified Expression(s)	Frequency N=4	Frequency N=9	Frequency N=20	Frequency Total
所有	all	(所有)...都..., (全部)...都...	(全部)A都是B / A中(全部)都是B *All A are B*	100	127	53	280
一半	half	一半，百分之五十	一半A是B / A中的一半是B / B在A中占一半 *Half A are B*	101	19	28	148
相同	equal	数量相同, 一样多, 个数一样	A与B数量相同 *There is an equally number of A and B*	59	11	29	99
绝大多数	overwhelming majority	绝大部分, 绝大多数	A中绝大多数是B / 绝大多数A是B / B在A中占绝大多数 *Almost A are B*	7	50	37	94
各半	half ... rest ...	各半, 一半一半, 一半...另一半...	BC在A中各半 / A中BC各半 / 一半的A是B, 另一半是C *Half of A are B, the other half of A are C*	60	6	24	90
比-多	more	比...多	A比B多	10	28	48	96
大多数	most	大多数, 大部分	A中大多数是B / 大多数A是B / B在A中占大多数 *Most A are B*	7	35	33	75
少数	minority	少数, 少部分	A中少数是B / 少数A是B / B在A中占少数 *Minority of A are B*	5	31	24	60
有	exist	有, 存在	图片中有A (*There are A in the scene*)	4	12	18	34
多数	most	多数	A中多数是B / 多数A是B / B在A中占多数 *Most A are B*	5	4	20	29

Table 4: Top-10 most frequently occurring quantifiers with their English translation and Mandarin examples as well as frequencies in the three MQTUNA sub-corpora.

Does Representational Fairness Imply Empirical Fairness?

Aili Shen[♠*] **Xudong Han**[♡] **Trevor Cohn**[♡] **Timothy Baldwin**[♡◇] **Lea Frermann**[♡]

♠ Amazon Alexa AI, Australia

♡ School of Computing and Information Systems, The University of Melbourne

◇ Department of Natural Language Processing, MBZUAI

aili.shen@amazon.com, xudonghl@student.unimelb.edu.au

{t.cohn, tbaldwin, lfrermann}@unimelb.edu.au

Abstract

NLP technologies can cause unintended harms if learned representations encode sensitive attributes of the author, or predictions systematically vary in quality across groups. Popular debiasing approaches, like adversarial training, remove sensitive information from representations in order to reduce disparate performance, however the relation between representational fairness and empirical (performance) fairness has not been systematically studied. This paper fills this gap, and proposes a novel debiasing method building on contrastive learning to encourage a latent space that separates instances based on target label, while mixing instances that share protected attributes. Our results show the effectiveness of our new method and, more importantly, show across a set of diverse debiasing methods that *representational fairness does not imply empirical fairness*. This work highlights the importance of aligning and understanding the relation of the optimization objective and final fairness target. *Our code is available at:* `https://github.com/AiliAili/contrastive_learning_repo`.

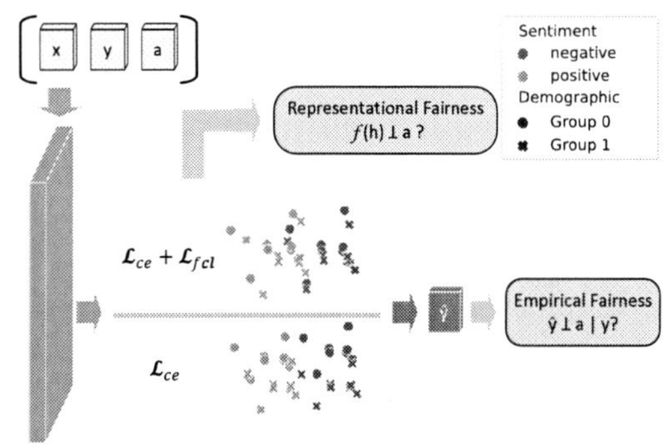

Figure 1: Illustration of our proposed method in the context of sentiment classification, where inputs (x) are mapped to hidden representations, which will then be used to make predictions $\hat{y}$. The points represent the instances in the latent space learned by a given model, marked with respect to sentiment and demographic labels. On the top and bottom of the gray line are hidden representations from our proposed method and a naively trained model. Representational fairness is measured based on the extent to which an attacker (f) can reconstruct protected attributes (a) from hidden representations (h). Empirical fairness measures performance disparities, and measures whether model predictions are independent of protected attributes.

1 Introduction

Neural methods have achieved great success for text classification tasks. However, they have been trained on datasets which embody cultural and societal stereotypes from the real world, captured in spurious correlations between target labels and protected attributes. This can result in biased predictions violating *empirical fairness*, i.e., models perform unequally for different sub-groups. A related, but different problem occurs if *representational fairness* is violated which means that learned representations encode potentially sensitive author information (such as demographic information), which can be recovered by an adversarial attacker. Addressing and reducing such cases of model bias has attracted substantial research interest across tasks including Twitter sentiment analysis (Blodgett et al., 2016; Han et al., 2021b), part-of-speech tagging (Hovy and Søgaard, 2015; Li et al., 2018), and image activity recognition (Wang et al., 2019; Zhao et al., 2017).

One line of work attempts to achieve empirical fairness through learning fair representations – removing authorship-related sensitive information from learned representations – under the assumption that fair representations will naturally lead to fairer models (Li et al., 2018; Ravfogel et al., 2020; Han et al., 2021a). For example, adversarial training is a popular method which directly aims to prevent a discriminator from reverse-engineering protected attribute information from learned rep-

*This work was done when Aili Shen was at The University of Melbourne.

Findings of the Association for Computational Linguistics: AACL-IJCNLP 2022, pages 81–95

resentations (Elazar and Goldberg, 2018; Resheff et al., 2019; Han et al., 2021b,a; Li et al., 2018). Similarly, null-space projection approaches remove protected information from hidden representations by projecting learned text representations to the null-space of linear protected attribute discriminators (Ravfogel et al., 2020, 2022).

In this paper, we systematically explore the interaction between fair representations and empirical fairness, both via three classes of existing approaches, as well as in considering the application of contrastive learning (Oord et al., 2018; Li et al., 2021a; Tian et al., 2020; Henaff, 2020; Bui et al., 2021; Li et al., 2021b; Chen et al., 2020b) to fairness. Contrastive learning is a natural and flexible choice of approach for representational fairness, in explicitly differentiating representations between different classes. Representational fairness is achieved by learning a space which simultaneously separates instances according to their labels, while mixing instances with different protected attributes (like gender or race), either globally (Section 3.2) or per class (Section 3.3).

Our contributions in this work are:

1. We present two debiasing methods based on contrastive learning, with loss components that capture different fairness criteria;
2. Based on experimental results over Twitter sentiment analysis and profession classification, we show that our proposed method achieves the best representational fairness, where most baseline methods fail;
3. We show that there is no correlation between representational and empirical fairness, debunking previous assumptions about the empirical value of fair representations.

2 Related Work

We review relevant research on fairness criteria, debiasing methods, and contrastive learning.

2.1 Fairness Criteria

Various types of fairness have been proposed, such as group fairness (Hardt et al., 2016; Zafar et al., 2017a; Cho et al., 2020), individual fairness (Sharifi-Malvajerdi et al., 2019; Yurochkin et al., 2020; Dwork et al., 2012), and causality-based fairness (Garg et al., 2019; Wu et al., 2019; Zhang et al., 2018; Zhang and Bareinboim, 2018). In this work, we focus on group fairness relative to the demographic variables available in our datasets.

To quantify how the performance of models varies across different demographic subgroups, there are three widely used fairness criteria. *Demographic parity* (Feldman et al., 2015; Zafar et al., 2017b; Cho et al., 2020) measures whether the model achieves equal positive prediction rates towards each demographic subgroup, without taking the main task label into consideration. *Equal opportunity* (Hardt et al., 2016; Madras et al., 2018a) (Cho et al., 2020; Hardt et al., 2016; Madras et al., 2018a) requires equal true positive rates for instances from each subgroup conditioned on the main task label, while *equalised odds* requires equal true positive and false positive rates for instances from each subgroup and with the same main task label. The definition of these three criteria is limited to binary classification, whereas we extend the measurement of fairness to each main task label, such that bias is measurable in multi-class classification settings.

2.2 Achieving Empirical Fairness

To optimize towards group fairness, prior debiasing methods fall into three categories. *Pre-processing* manipulates the training data e.g., by balancing the input, followed by re-training the model on a fairer dataset (Badjatiya et al., 2019; Elazar and Goldberg, 2018) but is computationally prohibitive for large datasets and models, and insufficient to ensure fairness (De-Arteaga et al., 2019; Wang et al., 2019). *Post-processing* methods "bleach" sensitive information from learned representations after main task training (Ravfogel et al., 2020). *In-processing* approaches augment the original training objective, to encourage the model to learn representations that are oblivious to protected attributes, aiming to achieve empirical fairness through representational fairness. For example, adversarial models (Beutel et al., 2017; Li et al., 2018; Barrett et al., 2019; Han et al., 2021b) encourage the main model to learn representations that are indistinguishable wrt the protected attributes by a jointly trained discriminator. Our contrastive learning methods also introduce an augmented objective, but unlike adversarial methods, do not require modification of the model architecture, and hence do not add model parameters. Tsai et al. (2021) proposed a similar approach in a self-supervised learning setting.

Other methods directly optimize fairness measures during training (Madras et al., 2018b; Zhao et al., 2020a; Cho et al., 2020). For example, Cho et al. (2020) use kernel density estimation to approximate equalised odds during training, but tailored to binary classification, leading to poor performance–fairness tradeoffs in high-dimensional settings. We introduce two variants of the contrastive losses which directly optimize fairness for demographic parity or equal opportunity, respectively.

Various recent studies (Ravfogel et al., 2020; Han et al., 2021b; Chi et al., 2022; Zhao et al., 2020b; Chowdhury et al., 2021; Tsai et al., 2021; Zhao and Gordon, 2019) claimed to generate fair representations, while exclusively evaluating their methods in terms of empirical fairness. Other work has used metrics like representation leakage to quantify how much protected attribute information can be recovered from learned representations (Han et al., 2021b; Elazar and Goldberg, 2018; Li et al., 2018; Wang et al., 2019). However, it has not been systematically studied whether fair representations lead to fair predictions, which is one contribution of this paper.

2.3 Contrastive Learning

Contrastive learning aims to pull similar instances together and push dissimilar instances apart by maximizing the similarities of similar instances and minimizing those of dissimilar pairs within the unit feature space (Oord et al., 2018; Tian et al., 2020; Li et al., 2021a; Grill et al., 2020; Chen et al., 2020a; Henaff, 2020). Its success hinges on an appropriate definition of similarity. Originating in computer vision, in vanilla contrastive learning positive (similar) instance image pairs are generated via data augmentation (i.e., meaning-invariant manipulation of an input image such as cropping or blurring (Chen et al., 2020a; Fang et al., 2020; Cubuk et al., 2019)), and negative (dissimilar) instance pairs correspond to distinct items in the original data. More recently, supervised contrastive learning (SCL) was proposed in the context of classification, where positive instances belong to the same class, and negative instances belong to different classes (Khosla et al., 2020). When combined with a cross entropy loss, it has been shown to improve model robustness to noise and data sparsity (Gunel et al., 2021), as well as adversarial attacks (Bui et al., 2021). We leverage the ability of SCL to explicitly constrain class-based positioning of instances in feature space, to enforce representational fairness. We present evidence of its effectiveness, and use it to systematically study the relationship between representational and empirical fairness.

The most relevant work to our proposed method is Gupta et al. (2021), whose training objective consists of three parts: (1) cross-entropy loss, which is identical to vanilla training; (2) upper bound for the mutual information between inputs and hidden representations, which relies on a manually-defined prior over the hidden representations to calculate a KL divergence loss; and (3) lower bound estimator for the conditional mutual information, similar to Con_{eo} in our paper (see Equation (3)). Although Gupta et al. (2021) have the same cross-entropy objective and lower-bound estimation as the equal opportunity variant of our proposed method, its second objective (upper bound estimator) focuses on learning task-agnostic representations while ours learns task-specific representations. Moreover, in this paper, we also show that the demographic parity variant consistently outperforms the equal opportunity variant.

2.4 Intrinsic Fairness

Intrinsic bias refers to biases in the geometry of text representations in upstream pre-trained language models (prior to any task-specific fine-tuning). Such representations are agnostic to downstream tasks, and common metrics for intrinsic biases rely on predefined templates, e.g., gendered word pairs for word embedding association test (Caliskan et al., 2017) and masked sentences (Kurita et al., 2019).

There is a broad range of studies on the correlation between intrinsic and extrinsic bias (Goldfarb-Tarrant et al., 2021; Cao et al., 2022). Jin et al. (2020) show that debiasing the intrinsic bias leads to less extrinsic bias, but conversely, Steed et al. (2022) argue that extrinsic bias is better explained by bias in downstream datasets rather than intrinsic bias in upstream text representations. Similar to this paper, Orgad et al. (2022) examine the influence of downstream task debiasing on representations. However, it also focuses exclusively on intrinsic bias rather than representational fairness. In summary, most previous work is aimed at measuring and mitigating task-agnostic *intrinsic* bias.

In contrast, the leakage metric for representational fairness in this paper is task-specific, and measures the predictability of protected information from the task-specific representations that are learned as part of fine-tuning. Given that both leakage (intrinsic) and empirical fairness (extrinsic) are defined in a task-specific way, we expect a stronger correlation between the two. This expectation is at the core of common debiasing approaches, such as adversarial methods. To the best of our knowledge, this paper is the first to explore this correlation.

3 Fair & Supervised Contrastive Learning

Our method augments the objective of supervised contrastive learning to simultaneously encourage data separation in terms of the main class labels, and discourage the differentiation of data points on the basis of their protected attributes. While the method is compatible with different classifier architectures, here we use the following setup:

1. An *embedding module*, $e = \texttt{Embed}(x)$, which maps an input instance x (e.g., a document) to a vector representation e, which is in turn used as input to the encoder network;
2. An *encoder network*, $h = \texttt{Enc}(e)$, which maps the input representation to the final hidden representation;
3. An *aggregated objective* ($\mathcal{L}_*$), which is a weighted combination of a cross-entropy loss, contrastive loss based on main task labels, and contrastive loss based on protected attribute labels, as described next.

3.1 Contrastive Loss

Given a mini-batch with a set of N randomly sampled instances, positive instance pairs (representing the same concept) and negative instance pairs (representing different concepts) are formed. These pairs can be created based on either their main task label or their protected attribute, as described below. Assuming a batch of positive and negative pairs, the contrastive loss is computed as,

$$\mathcal{L}_{\text{scl}} = \sum_{i=1}^{N} \frac{-1}{|P(i)|} \sum_{p \in P(i)} \log \frac{\exp(\boldsymbol{h}_i \cdot \boldsymbol{h}_p/\tau)}{\sum_{q \in Q(i)} \exp(\boldsymbol{h}_i \cdot \boldsymbol{h}_q/\tau)},$$

where $i{=}1 \ldots N$ is the index of an instance in the mini-batch; $Q(i) \equiv \{1 \ldots N\} \setminus \{i\}$; $\boldsymbol{h}_i = l_2(\texttt{Enc}(\texttt{Embed}(\boldsymbol{x}_\texttt{i})))$ is the normalised representation; and $\tau{>}0$ is a scalar temperature parameter controlling smoothness. $P(i)$ is the set of instances that result in positive pairs for the ith instance, and $|P(i)|$ is its cardinality. We next describe how positive/negative pairs are created.

For ease of illustration, we overload the definition of $\mathcal{L}_{\text{scl}}$ as an function, i.e.,

$$\mathcal{L}_{\text{scl}} = \mathcal{L}_{\text{scl}}(\boldsymbol{h}; \tau; P(\cdot); Q(\cdot)), \quad (1)$$

where $P(\cdot)$ is the set of indices of positive samples, and $Q(\cdot)$ is the set of sample indices that are considered in the contrastive loss.

$\mathcal{L}_{\text{scl}}$ is computed on positive and negative samples constructed based on main task labels (e.g., POS vs. NEG sentiment), where instances in the mini-batch belonging to the same main task class are used to construct positive samples; otherwise, they are used to form negative samples. The intuition behind this loss component is that representations that are well-separated for the main task are more desirable.

3.2 Fair Contrastive Learning for Demographic Parity

Demographic parity is satisfied if predictions are independent of protected attributes, i.e., $\Pr(\hat{y}{=}1|a{=}0) = \Pr(\hat{y}{=}1|a{=}1)\ \forall y{\in}Y, a{\in}A$, where Y is the main task label set and A is the protected attribute value set. With fair contrastive learning, the training objective for demographic parity ($\mathcal{L}_{\text{fcl-dp}}$) is to infer latent representations which are oblivious to the protected attribute of an instance. We create samples with respect to protected attribute labels (e.g., $a =$ MALE vs. $a =$ FEMALE), where instances of the same protected attribute class form positive samples; otherwise, they constitute negative samples:

$$\mathcal{L}_{\text{fcl-dp}} = -1 \times \mathcal{L}_{\text{scl}}(\boldsymbol{h}; \tau; P_{\text{fcl-dp}}(\cdot); Q(\cdot)),$$

where $P_{\text{fcl-dp}}(i) \equiv \{p \in Q(i) : a_p = a_i\}$ constructs positive samples based on protected attributes rather than target classes in supervised contrastive learning (Equation (1)). Importantly, the -1 changes the sign of supervised contrastive loss, enforcing representations of instances with different protected attribute values to mix together by discouraging the model from effectively contrasting those instances.

The final classifier objective produces task-indicative and protected-attribute-agnostic representations, as the weighted sum of standard cross-entropy loss $\mathcal{L}_{\text{ce}}$, and contrastive loss terms $\mathcal{L}_{\text{scl}}$, and $\mathcal{L}_{\text{fcl-dp}}$,

$$\mathcal{L}_{\text{dp}} = \mathcal{L}_{\text{ce}} + \alpha\mathcal{L}_{\text{scl}} + \beta\mathcal{L}_{\text{fcl-dp}} \quad (2)$$

where α and β are hyperparameters that control the relative importance of the cross entropy and contrastive learning terms. We refer to the contrastive classifier based on the loss in Equation (2) as Con_{dp}.

3.3 Fair Contrastive Learning for Equal Opportunity

A model is fair wrt equal opportunity (Hardt et al., 2016) if instances from different groups *within the same class* are treated equally, i.e., $\Pr(\hat{y} = y|Y = y, a{=}0) = \Pr(\hat{y}{=}y|Y{=}y, a{=}1)\ \forall y{\in}Y, a{\in}A$, connecting directly to the widely-used fairness metric GAP (see Section 4.2).

Accordingly, we construct samples in terms of protected attribute labels conditioned on the main task labels, and compute $\mathcal{L}_{\text{fcl-eo}}$ as the average loss over labels,

$$\mathcal{L}_{\text{fcl-eo}} = \frac{-1}{|Y|}\sum_{y\in Y}\mathcal{L}_{\text{scl}}(\boldsymbol{h};\tau;P_{\text{fcl-eo}}(\cdot);Q_{\text{fcl-eo}}(\cdot)),$$

where $Q_{\text{fcl-eo}}(i,y)) \equiv \{q|q \in 1,\ldots,N, y_q = y, \text{and } q \neq i\}$ ensures that contrastive losses are calculated per class, and $P_{\text{fcl-eo}}(i,y) \equiv \{p \in Q_{\text{fcl-eo}}(i,y) : a_p = a_i\}$ constructs positive samples based on protected attributes from a particular main task class y. Optimizing for $\mathcal{L}_{\text{fcl-eo}}$ minimizes mutual information between instances from different protected groups within each target class.

Analogous to Equation (2), we define a fair classifier objective wrt equal opportunity as,

$$\mathcal{L}_{\text{eo}} = \mathcal{L}_{\text{ce}} + \alpha\mathcal{L}_{\text{scl}} + \beta\mathcal{L}_{\text{fcl-eo}}. \quad (3)$$

We refer to contrastive classifiers based on the loss in Equation (2) as Con_{eo}.

3.4 Remarks

Non-binary protected attributes: Our $\mathcal{L}_{\text{fcl-dp}}$ and $\mathcal{L}_{\text{fcl-eo}}$ extend to non-binary protected attributes by sampling negative instances at random from any alternative subgroup.

Loss component weights: The same value is adopted for α and β for both $\mathcal{L}_{\text{scl}}$ and $\mathcal{L}_{\text{fcl-dp}}/\mathcal{L}_{\text{fcl-eo}}$ as they are similar in concept and magnitude, and weighting them equally balances performance with bias reduction, as confirmed in extensive preliminary experiments.

Relation to mutual information: Optimizing contrastive loss is equivalent to maximizing mutual information between classes (Oord et al., 2018; Khosla et al., 2020). Conversely, in representational fairness, representations $\boldsymbol{h}$ should be independent of protected attributes a, i.e., minimise mutual information between $\boldsymbol{h}$ and a. $\mathcal{L}_{\text{fcl-dp}}$ and $\mathcal{L}_{\text{fcl-eo}}$ intuitively satisfy this by flipping the sign of the contrastive objective.

4 Experiments

In this section, we report experimental results for bias mitigation. All experiments are conducted with the *fairlib* library (Han et al., 2022b), and full experimental details are provided in Appendix D.

4.1 Comparison Models

We evaluate the utility of contrastive fairness, and systematically study the relation between representational and empirical fairness. To do so, we include competitive debiasing methods covering *pre-*, *in-*, and *post-processing*:

1. CE: train $\mathtt{Enc}(\cdot)$ with cross-entropy loss. No bias mitigation.
2. INLP: train $\mathtt{Enc}(\cdot)$ with cross-entropy loss, and apply iterative null-space projection (Ravfogel et al., 2020) to the learned representations. Specifically, a linear discriminator is iteratively trained over the protected attribute to project the representation onto the discriminator's null-space, thereby reducing protected attribute information from the representations.
3. Adv: jointly train $\mathtt{Enc}(\cdot)$ with cross-entropy loss and an ensemble of 3 adversarial discriminators over the protected attribute, with an orthogonality constraint applied to each pair of sub-discriminators to encourage them to learn different aspects of the representations (Han et al., 2021b). The $\mathtt{Enc}(\cdot)$ is trained to prevent protected attributes from being identified, and thus results in fairer representations.
4. FairBatch: formulate the model training as a bi-level optimization problem, which minimises prediction disparities through adjusting resampling probabilities (Roh et al., 2021).
5. EO_{GLB}: optimize equal opportunity through proxy objective functions based on group-specific cross-entropy, which essentially adjusts instances weights in training (Shen et al., 2022).
6. Gate: use demographic information to make predictions, with balanced training as regularizers in training to avoid learning spurious correlations (Han et al., 2022a). Unlike the afore-

mentioned models, which aim to reduce both representational and empirical bias, Gate is expected to be high in representational bias and low in empirical bias.

In summary, we incorporate three types of baselines: (1) INLP and Adv remove protected information from hidden representations to mitigate representational bias, which is similar to our contrastive learning methods; (2) FairBatch and EO_{GLB} mitigate empirical bias based on model predictions, without considering representational fairness; and (3) Gate uses protected information explicitly to make fair predictions, explicitly violating representational fairness.

4.2 Evaluation Metrics

Following Ravfogel et al. (2020), we adopt **Accuracy** for both the binary and multi-classification datasets to evaluate the performance of models on the main task, and measure empirical fairness based on equal opportunity in terms of the model predictions. To measure representational fairness, we follow Elazar and Goldberg (2018) in measuring protected attribute leakage in text representations.

To measure **empirical fairness**, we adopt equal opportunity, which measures the difference in true positive rate (TPR) between binary protected attribute a and $\neg a$ (such as FEMALE vs. MALE) for each main task class. It is defined as $\text{GAP}^{\text{TPR}}_{a,y} = |\text{TPR}_{a,y} - \text{TPR}_{\neg a,y}|, y \in Y$, where $\text{TPR}_{a,y} = \mathbb{P}\{\hat{y} = y | y, a\}$. Here $\hat{y}$ and y are the predicted and gold-standard main task labels; and Y is the set of main task labels. $\text{TPR}_{a,y}$ measures the percentage of correct predictions among instances with main task label y and protected attribute a. $\text{GAP}^{\text{TPR}}_{a,y}$ measures the absolute difference between the two different groups represented by the protected attribute, given the main task class y. To take all target classes into consideration, we follow De-Arteaga et al. (2019) and Ravfogel et al. (2020) in calculating the root mean square of $\text{GAP}^{\text{TPR}}_{a,y}$ over all classes $y \in Y$, to get a single score:

$$\text{GAP} = \sqrt{\frac{1}{|Y|} \sum_{y \in Y} (\text{GAP}^{\text{TPR}}_{a,y})^2}$$

A difference of 0 indicates a fair model, as the prediction $\hat{y}$ is conditionally independent of protected attribute a. For ease of exposition, we report the equal opportunity fairness (Fairness) as $1 - \text{GAP}$, where larger is better and a perfectly fair model will achieve a fairness score of 1.

Distance to the optimum (DTO) has been used to simplify model comparisons in previous work (Marler and Arora, 2004; Han et al., 2022a), which measures the Euclidean distance from a particular model to the optimum point (aka "Utopia" point), usually set to 100% accuracy and 100% equal opportunity fairness, denoting the best possible values. While the dimensions of the space are performance and fairness, DTO explicitly reflects the performance-fairness trade-off of a model. We calculate DTO based on empirical fairness, and perform model selections based the smallest DTO over the development set (Han et al., 2022a).

Representational Fairness is evaluated through **Leakage** as the ability of an attacker to recover the protected attribute from a model's final hidden representations. We train one attacker (i.e., neural network) for each model, to extract information of protected attributes from a model's final-layer hidden representations (Wang et al., 2019; Han et al., 2021b). We fix the attacker architecture across models, so that attackers are not guaranteed to be optimal and leakage estimators should be interpreted as lower bounds.[1]

4.3 Experiment 1: Sentiment Analysis

4.3.1 Task and Dataset

The task is to predict the binary sentiment for a given English tweet, based on the dataset of Blodgett et al. (2016) (**Moji** hereafter), where each tweet is also annotated with a binary private attribute indirectly capturing the ethnicity of the tweet author as either African American English (AAE) or Standard American English (SAE). Following previous studies (Ravfogel et al., 2020; Han et al., 2021b), the training dataset is balanced with respect to both sentiment and ethnicity but skewed in terms of sentiment–ethnicity combinations (40% HAPPY-AAE, 10% HAPPY-SAE, 10% SAD-AAE, and 40% SAD-SAE, respectively).[2] The dataset contains 100K/8K/8K train/dev/test instances.

4.3.2 Implementation Details

Following previous work (Elazar and Goldberg, 2018; Ravfogel et al., 2020; Han et al., 2021b), we

[1]Preliminary analyses revealed that non-linear attackers outperform linear ones in recovering protected attributes, and attackers with different non-linear architectures have similar capacity to recover protected attribute information from representations. We use non-linear MLPs as our attacker. Further details are in Appendix A.

[2]Note that the dev and test set are balanced in terms of sentiment–ethnicity combinations.

Model	Accuracy ↑	Fairness ↑	DTO↓	Leakage ↓
CE	72.3±0.5	61.2±1.4	47.7	87.9±3.3
INLP	73.3±0.0	85.6±0.0	30.3	86.7±0.6
Adv	75.6±0.4	90.4±1.1	26.3	78.8±6.0
Gate	**76.2±0.3**	90.1±1.5	**25.8**	100.0±0.0
FairBatch	75.1±0.6	**90.6±0.5**	26.7	88.4±0.4
EO_{GLB}	75.2±0.2	90.1±0.4	26.7	85.7±1.2
Con_{dp}	75.8±0.3	88.1±0.6	26.9	**54.2±0.9**
Con_{eo}	74.1±0.7	84.1±3.0	30.3	80.1±4.2

Table 1: Experimental results on **Moji** (averaged over 5 runs). The best result for each metric is indicated in **bold**. Here, ↑ and ↓ indicate that higher and lower performance, resp., is better for the given metric.

Model	Accuracy ↑	Fairness ↑	DTO↓	Leakage ↓
CE	82.3±0.2	85.1±0.8	23.2	98.0±0.0
INLP	82.3±0.0	88.6±0.0	21.0	97.6±0.1
Adv	81.9±0.2	**90.6±0.5**	20.4	88.6±4.6
Gate	**83.7±0.2**	90.4±0.9	**18.9**	100.0±0.0
FairBatch	82.2±0.1	89.5±1.3	20.6	98.0±0.3
EO_{GLB}	81.7±0.4	88.4±1.0	21.7	97.2±0.5
Con_{dp}	82.1±0.2	84.3±0.8	23.9	**76.3±1.5**
Con_{eo}	81.8±0.3	85.2±0.4	23.5	84.9±3.4

Table 2: Experimental results on **Bios** (averaged over 5 runs).

use DeepMoji (Felbo et al., 2017), a model pretrained over 1.2 billion English tweets, as `Embed(·)` to obtain text representations. The parameters of DeepMoji are fixed in our experiments.

4.3.3 Results

Table 1 presents the results. Our proposed methods achieve competitive empirical fairness results with other debiasing methods, all of which improve over CE. Adv, Gate, FairBatch, and EO_{GLB} achieve the best performance in terms of Fairness, while our proposed method Con_{dp} achieves the best performance in terms of Leakage. Specifically, none of the baselines reduce leakage substantially except for Adv. The reason that Adv can reduce Leakage is that the architecture of Adv is the closest one to the leakage estimation framework, which also employs attackers to extract protected attributes and unlearns attackers in training. However, Con_{dp} still outperforms Adv, highlighting the effectiveness of our proposed method in improving representational fairness. The ineffectiveness of INLP, Gate, FairBatch, and EO_{GLB} in reducing Leakage is due to different reasons: INLP is due to the fact that it relies on linear projections to remove protected attribute information and is ineffective at removing nonlinear correlations; Gate is due to the fact that it employs a gate mechanism to augment text representations with protected information, and as a result, achieves 100% Leakage; and both FairBatch and EO_{GLB} are due to the fact that these two methods are optimized to directly mitigate empirical bias without considering representational bias. This indicates that the relationship between representational fairness and empirical fairness is not as simple as suggested in previous work (Elazar and Goldberg, 2018; Ravfogel et al., 2020; Han et al., 2021b)

Con_{eo}, which is proposed to ensure conditional representational fairness within each class, achieves similar prediction fairness to Con_{dp}, but with much worse leakage. This further shows that representational fairness cannot be directly linked to prediction fairness. It is encouraging to see that incorporating debiasing techniques can contribute to improvement on the main task. We hypothesise that incorporating debiasing techniques (either in the form of adversarial training or contrastive loss) acts as a form of regularisation, leading to greater robustness over the training dataset skew relative to the unbiased test set.

4.4 Experiment 2: Profession Classification

4.4.1 Task and Dataset

The task is to predict a person's profession given their biography, based on the dataset of De-Arteaga et al. (2019) (**Bios** hereafter), consisting of short online biographies which have been labelled with one of 28 professions (main task label) and binary gender (protected attribute). We use the dataset split of (De-Arteaga et al., 2019; Ravfogel et al., 2020), consisting of 257K/40K/99K train/dev/test instances.[3]

4.4.2 Implementation Details

Following the work of Ravfogel et al. (2020), we use the `[CLS]` token representation of the pretrained uncased BERT-base (Devlin et al., 2019) as `Embed(·)`, without any further finetuning.

4.4.3 Results

Table 2 shows the results on the test set. In terms of prediction fairness, baseline methods achieve similar results, however, both Con_{dp} and Con_{eo} are less effective for improving prediction fairness. We hypothesise that this is because of the multi-class setting (28 classes), where the large number

[3]There are slight differences between our dataset and that used by De-Arteaga et al. (2019) and Ravfogel et al. (2020) as a small number of biographies were no longer available on the web when we scraped them.

of main task classes impedes the ability of contrastive learning to learn representations that jointly maximize mutual information for main task classes and minimize mutual information for demographic labels. In Section 4.5, we conduct ablation studies to analyse their robustness to the number of classes, affirming our explanation. In terms of the representational fairness, consistent with the results over **Moji**, Con_{dp} and Con_{eo} substantially reduce Leakage, where most baselines fail.

Overall, the trend for these three types of methods over the **Bios** dataset is consistent with that over the **Moji** dataset: (1) INLP and Adv, which focus on representational fairness, result in empirical fairness improvements and marginal gain in Leakage; (2) FairBatch and EO_{GLB}, which target for empirical fairness, lead to fairer predictions but no benefit to Leakage; and (3) Gate, which augments representations with protected information, also improves empirical fairness while suffering from 100% Leakage. Based on the consistent trend over two benchmark datasets, we argue that it cannot be assumed that empirical fairness is associated with representational fairness, with the fact that Con_{dp} and Con_{eo} achieve the best representational fairness but lowest empirical fairness further adding weight to this argument.

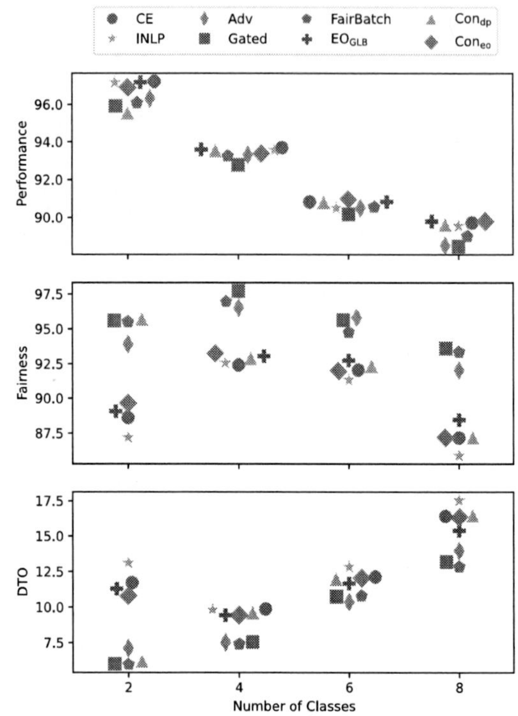

Figure 2: Varying the number of classes in the **Bios** dataset. We treat the number of classes as a categorical variable, and draw categorical scatter plots with non-overlapping points.

4.5 Analysis

Robustness to the Number of Classes Our proposed methods are quite effective over **Moji** but not competitive over **Bios** in terms of Fairness. We hypothesize that this is due to contrastive loss struggling with a larger number of classes. To verify this, we construct 4 synthetic datasets from **Bios** by selecting a subset of classes from 2 to 8.[4]

Figure 2 presents Accuracy, empirical Fairness, and DTO with respect to 2, 4, 6, and 8 target classes. Although the scores with respect to different numbers of classes are not directly comparable as we also have to vary the number of classes in the test set, resulting in different test sets, it is reasonable to compare the trend of changes in the rank of debiasing methods.

Overall, increasing the number of classes leads to a decrease in Accuracy while Fairness is almost unchanged. As a result, the trade-off between Accuracy and Fairness (DTO) drops. In terms of Accuracy, Con_{dp} and Con_{eo} achieve competitive performance with other debiasing methods, all of which are slightly worse than CE.

Looking at empirical Fairness, Con_{dp} achieve quite competitive performance when the number of target classes is 2, while Con_{eo} is unable to significantly improve Fairness. This is consistent the results over the binary classification dataset (**Moji**). For other settings (4, 6, and 8 target classes), Con_{eo} shows better trade-offs than Con_{dp}. However, both Con_{dp} and Con_{eo} only achieve slight improvements in Fairness, and are not as good as some other debiasing methods.

To conclude, the changes in DTO confirm our hypothesis that contrastive loss struggles with a larger number of classes: contrastive loss achieves one of the best DTO for 2 classes, competitive results with other debiasing methods for 4 and 6 classes, and the worst DTO for 8 classes.

Correlation between Representational and Empirical Fairness Although we have discussed the connection between representational and empirical fairness for individual methods, it is still not clear how they are correlated.

[4]In Appendix C.1, we provide the full details of the synthetic datasets.

For each method, we have 5 random runs, and in total, there are 5 groups of methods: (1) CE; (2) INLP and Adv; (3) FairBatch and EO_{GLB}; (4) Gate; and (5) Con_{dp} and Con_{eo}. To treat each group of methods equally, we fit a bivariate Gaussian distribution to each method over the 5 runs, and draw 20k random samples from each group for a given dataset.

Based on the random samples, the Pearson correlation coefficients between representational and empirical fairness over **Moji** and **Bios** are 0.072 and −0.222, respectively. Clearly, both correlation coefficients are not substantially better than 0, indicating that there is little to no linear dependency between representational fairness and empirical fairness. Even more damningly, the negative sign for the **Bios** suggests that worse representational fairness may result in higher empirical fairness.

Clearly further work is required to examine the theoretical difference/connection between representational and empirical fairness, which we leave to future work.

5 Conclusion

Biased representations and predictions can reinforce existing societal biases and stereotypes. While previous work has assumed a direct link between biases in the representations learned by models and performance disparities in model predictions, there has not been a systematic study of the relationship between the two. We have explored the relationship wrt both a range of existing methods and two newly-proposed methods based on supervised contrastive learning. The contrastive learning methods are based on the intuition that similar instances belonging to the same main task class should be pulled together and similar instances belonging to the same protected attribute class should be pushed apart in the representation space, based on which we proposed to combine cross-entropy loss with two contrastive loss components in optimizing neural networks in two different ways, incorporating demographic parity and equal opportunity respectively. Experimental results over two tasks demonstrate the effectiveness of the proposed methods in terms of representation fairness, but further analysis showed no meaningful correlation between representational fairness and empirical fairness, contradicting a common assumption made in prior research, and motivating future work on approaches that achieve both representational and empirical fairness.

Acknowledgements

We thank the anonymous reviewers for their helpful feedback and suggestions. This work was funded by the Australian Research Council, Discovery grant DP200102519. This research was undertaken using the LIEF HPC-GPGPU Facility hosted at the University of Melbourne. This Facility was established with the assistance of LIEF Grant LE170100200.

Limitations

A limitation of our proposed methods is that we focus on learning fair representations for the main task, where the protected attribute is explicitly present in the dataset. The mitigation of biases present only implicitly, such as protected information revealed in the text rather than indicated by demographics, as studied by Lahoti et al. (2020), is out scope of our work. For main tasks other than classification, such as generation tasks, adoption of contrastive learning for generating fairer text is not trivial, which is one direction for future work. In our work, `Embed(·)` is not learned or finetuned together with `Enc(·)` and the classification layer in an end-to-end fashion. However, finetuning the `Embed(·)` has the potential for better task-specific or semantic-preserving representations of text, which may further remove biases encoded in pretrained models. One simplifying assumption in our work is that we focus exclusively on binary protected attributes, implying the adoption of an oversimplified binary notion of gender. Exploring attributes of higher arity, and more complex and realistic bias dimensions, is an important direction for future work.

Ethical Considerations

We propose Con_{dp} and Con_{eo} to prevent text classifiers from encoding protected information. However, there is a possibility that multiple protected attributes, such as gender, age, and ethnicity, are encoded in text and the dataset is annotated only wrt one of the protected attribute. Therefore, a method designed to alleviate a specific type of bias is not guaranteed to be bias-free. The usage of our fair classifiers in the real world should be carefully monitored with the aid of domain experts.

References

Pinkesh Badjatiya, Manish Gupta, and Vasudeva Varma. 2019. Stereotypical bias removal for hate speech detection task using knowledge-based generalizations. In *The World Wide Web Conference*, pages 49–59.

Maria Barrett, Yova Kementchedjhieva, Yanai Elazar, Desmond Elliott, and Anders Søgaard. 2019. Adversarial removal of demographic attributes revisited. In *Proceedings of the 2019 Conference on Empirical Methods in Natural Language Processing and the 9th International Joint Conference on Natural Language Processing*, pages 6330–6335.

Alex Beutel, Jilin Chen, Zhe Zhao, and Ed H Chi. 2017. Data decisions and theoretical implications when adversarially learning fair representations. *arXiv preprint arXiv:1707.00075*.

Su Lin Blodgett, Lisa Green, and Brendan O'Connor. 2016. Demographic dialectal variation in social media: A case study of African-American English. In *Proceedings of the 2016 Conference on Empirical Methods in Natural Language Processing*, pages 1119–1130.

Anh Bui, Trung Le, He Zhao, Paul Montague, Seyit Camtepe, and Dinh Phung. 2021. Understanding and achieving efficient robustness with adversarial supervised contrastive learning. *arXiv preprint arXiv:2101.10027*.

Aylin Caliskan, Joanna J Bryson, and Arvind Narayanan. 2017. Semantics derived automatically from language corpora contain human-like biases. *Science*, 356(6334):183–186.

Yang Cao, Yada Pruksachatkun, Kai-Wei Chang, Rahul Gupta, Varun Kumar, Jwala Dhamala, and Aram Galstyan. 2022. On the intrinsic and extrinsic fairness evaluation metrics for contextualized language representations. In *Proceedings of the 60th Annual Meeting of the Association for Computational Linguistics (Volume 2: Short Papers)*, pages 561–570, Dublin, Ireland. Association for Computational Linguistics.

Ting Chen, Simon Kornblith, Mohammad Norouzi, and Geoffrey Hinton. 2020a. A simple framework for contrastive learning of visual representations. In *International Conference on Machine Learning*, pages 1597–1607.

Ting Chen, Simon Kornblith, Kevin Swersky, Mohammad Norouzi, and Geoffrey E. Hinton. 2020b. Big self-supervised models are strong semi-supervised learners. In *Advances in Neural Information Processing Systems*.

Jianfeng Chi, William Shand, Yaodong Yu, Kai-Wei Chang, Han Zhao, and Yuan Tian. 2022. Conditional supervised contrastive learning for fair text classification. *arXiv preprint arXiv:2205.11485*.

Jaewoong Cho, Gyeongjo Hwang, and Changho Suh. 2020. A fair classifier using kernel density estimation. In *Advances in Neural Information Processing Systems*.

Somnath Basu Roy Chowdhury, Sayan Ghosh, Yiyuan Li, Junier Oliva, Shashank Srivastava, and Snigdha Chaturvedi. 2021. Adversarial scrubbing of demographic information for text classification. In *Proceedings of the 2021 Conference on Empirical Methods in Natural Language Processing*, pages 550–562.

Ekin D Cubuk, Barret Zoph, Dandelion Mane, Vijay Vasudevan, and Quoc V Le. 2019. Autoaugment: Learning augmentation strategies from data. In *Proceedings of the IEEE/CVF Conference on Computer Vision and Pattern Recognition*, pages 113–123.

Maria De-Arteaga, Alexey Romanov, Hanna Wallach, Jennifer Chayes, Christian Borgs, Alexandra Chouldechova, Sahin Geyik, Krishnaram Kenthapadi, and Adam Tauman Kalai. 2019. Bias in bios: A case study of semantic representation bias in a high-stakes setting. In *Proceedings of the Conference on Fairness, Accountability, and Transparency*, pages 120–128.

Jacob Devlin, Ming-Wei Chang, Kenton Lee, and Kristina Toutanova. 2019. BERT: Pre-training of deep bidirectional transformers for language understanding. In *Proceedings of the 2019 Conference of the North American Chapter of the Association for Computational Linguistics: Human Language Technologies, Volume 1 (Long and Short Papers)*, pages 4171–4186.

Cynthia Dwork, Moritz Hardt, Toniann Pitassi, Omer Reingold, and Richard S. Zemel. 2012. Fairness through awareness. In *Innovations in Theoretical Computer Science 2012*, pages 214–226.

Yanai Elazar and Yoav Goldberg. 2018. Adversarial removal of demographic attributes from text data. In *Proceedings of the 2018 Conference on Empirical Methods in Natural Language Processing*, pages 11–21.

Hongchao Fang, Sicheng Wang, Meng Zhou, Jiayuan Ding, and Pengtao Xie. 2020. Cert: Contrastive self-supervised learning for language understanding. *arXiv preprint arXiv:2005.12766*.

Bjarke Felbo, Alan Mislove, Anders Søgaard, Iyad Rahwan, and Sune Lehmann. 2017. Using millions of emoji occurrences to learn any-domain representations for detecting sentiment, emotion and sarcasm. In *Proceedings of the 2017 Conference on Empirical Methods in Natural Language Processing*, pages 1615–1625.

Michael Feldman, Sorelle A. Friedler, John Moeller, Carlos Scheidegger, and Suresh Venkatasubramanian. 2015. Certifying and removing disparate impact. In *Proceedings of the 21th ACM SIGKDD International Conference on Knowledge Discovery and Data Mining*, pages 259–268.

Sahaj Garg, Vincent Perot, Nicole Limtiaco, Ankur Taly, Ed H. Chi, and Alex Beutel. 2019. Counterfactual fairness in text classification through robustness. In *Proceedings of the 2019 AAAI/ACM Conference on AI, Ethics, and Society*, pages 219–226.

Seraphina Goldfarb-Tarrant, Rebecca Marchant, Ricardo Muñoz Sánchez, Mugdha Pandya, and Adam Lopez. 2021. Intrinsic bias metrics do not correlate with application bias. In *Proceedings of the 59th Annual Meeting of the Association for Computational Linguistics and the 11th International Joint Conference on Natural Language Processing (Volume 1: Long Papers)*, pages 1926–1940.

Jean-Bastien Grill, Florian Strub, Florent Altché, Corentin Tallec, Pierre H. Richemond, Elena Buchatskaya, Carl Doersch, Bernardo Ávila Pires, Zhaohan Guo, Mohammad Gheshlaghi Azar, Bilal Piot, Koray Kavukcuoglu, Rémi Munos, and Michal Valko. 2020. Bootstrap your own latent - A new approach to self-supervised learning. In *Advances in Neural Information Processing Systems*.

Beliz Gunel, Jingfei Du, Alexis Conneau, and Veselin Stoyanov. 2021. Supervised contrastive learning for pre-trained language model fine-tuning. In *International Conference on Learning Representations*.

Umang Gupta, Aaron M Ferber, Bistra Dilkina, and Greg Ver Steeg. 2021. Controllable guarantees for fair outcomes via contrastive information estimation. In *Proceedings of the AAAI Conference on Artificial Intelligence*, pages 7610–7619.

Xudong Han, Timothy Baldwin, and Trevor Cohn. 2021a. Decoupling adversarial training for fair NLP. In *Findings of the Association for Computational Linguistics*, pages 471–477.

Xudong Han, Timothy Baldwin, and Trevor Cohn. 2021b. Diverse adversaries for mitigating bias in training. In *Proceedings of the 16th Conference of the European Chapter of the Association for Computational Linguistics: Main Volume*, pages 2760–2765.

Xudong Han, Timothy Baldwin, and Trevor Cohn. 2022a. Balancing out bias: Achieving fairness through balanced training. In *Proceedings of the 2022 Conference on Empirical Methods in Natural Language Processing (EMNLP 2022)*. To appear.

Xudong Han, Aili Shen, Yitong Li, Lea Frermann, Timothy Baldwin, and Trevor Cohn. 2022b. fairlib: A unified framework for assessing and improving classification fairness. In *Proceedings of the 2022 Conference on Empirical Methods in Natural Language Processing (EMNLP 2022) Demo Session*. To appear.

Moritz Hardt, Eric Price, and Nati Srebro. 2016. Equality of opportunity in supervised learning. In *Advances in Neural Information Processing Systems*, pages 3315–3323.

Olivier Henaff. 2020. Data-efficient image recognition with contrastive predictive coding. In *International Conference on Machine Learning*, pages 4182–4192.

Dirk Hovy and Anders Søgaard. 2015. Tagging performance correlates with author age. In *Proceedings of the 53rd Annual Meeting of the Association for Computational Linguistics and the 7th International Joint Conference on Natural Language Processing (volume 2: Short papers)*, pages 483–488.

Xisen Jin, Francesco Barbieri, Brendan Kennedy, Aida Mostafazadeh Davani, Leonardo Neves, and Xiang Ren. 2020. On transferability of bias mitigation effects in language model fine-tuning. *arXiv preprint arXiv:2010.12864*.

Prannay Khosla, Piotr Teterwak, Chen Wang, Aaron Sarna, Yonglong Tian, Phillip Isola, Aaron Maschinot, Ce Liu, and Dilip Krishnan. 2020. Supervised contrastive learning. In *Advances in Neural Information Processing Systems*.

Diederik P. Kingma and Jimmy Ba. 2015. Adam: A method for stochastic optimization. In *Proceedings of the 3rd International Conference on Learning Representations*.

Keita Kurita, Nidhi Vyas, Ayush Pareek, Alan W Black, and Yulia Tsvetkov. 2019. Measuring bias in contextualized word representations. In *Proceedings of the First Workshop on Gender Bias in Natural Language Processing*, pages 166–172, Florence, Italy. Association for Computational Linguistics.

Preethi Lahoti, Alex Beutel, Jilin Chen, Kang Lee, Flavien Prost, Nithum Thain, Xuezhi Wang, and Ed Chi. 2020. Fairness without demographics through adversarially reweighted learning. In *Advances in Neural Information Processing Systems*.

Junnan Li, Pan Zhou, Caiming Xiong, and Steven C. H. Hoi. 2021a. Prototypical contrastive learning of unsupervised representations. In *Proceedings of the 9th International Conference on Learning Representations*.

Yitong Li, Timothy Baldwin, and Trevor Cohn. 2018. Towards robust and privacy-preserving text representations. In *Proceedings of the 56th Annual Meeting of the Association for Computational Linguistics*, pages 25–30.

Yunfan Li, Peng Hu, Jerry Zitao Liu, Dezhong Peng, Joey Tianyi Zhou, and Xi Peng. 2021b. Contrastive clustering. In *Thirty-Fifth AAAI Conference on Artificial Intelligence*, pages 8547–8555.

David Madras, Elliot Creager, Toniann Pitassi, and Richard S. Zemel. 2018a. Learning adversarially fair and transferable representations. In *Proceedings of the 35th International Conference on Machine Learning*, pages 3381–3390.

David Madras, Elliot Creager, Toniann Pitassi, and Richard S. Zemel. 2018b. Learning adversarially fair and transferable representations. In *International Conference on Machine Learning*, pages 3381–3390.

R Timothy Marler and Jasbir S Arora. 2004. Survey of multi-objective optimization methods for engineering. *Structural and multidisciplinary optimization*, 26(6):369–395.

Aaron van den Oord, Yazhe Li, and Oriol Vinyals. 2018. Representation learning with contrastive predictive coding. *arXiv preprint arXiv:1807.03748*.

Hadas Orgad, Seraphina Goldfarb-Tarrant, and Yonatan Belinkov. 2022. How gender debiasing affects internal model representations, and why it matters. In *Proceedings of the 2022 Conference of the North American Chapter of the Association for Computational Linguistics: Human Language Technologies*, pages 2602–2628, Seattle, United States. Association for Computational Linguistics.

Shauli Ravfogel, Yanai Elazar, Hila Gonen, Michael Twiton, and Yoav Goldberg. 2020. Null it out: Guarding protected attributes by iterative nullspace projection. In *Proceedings of the 58th Annual Meeting of the Association for Computational Linguistics*, pages 7237–7256.

Shauli Ravfogel, Michael Twiton, Yoav Goldberg, and Ryan Cotterell. 2022. Linear adversarial concept erasure. *arXiv preprint arXiv:2201.12091*.

Yehezkel S. Resheff, Yanai Elazar, Moni Shahar, and Oren Sar Shalom. 2019. Privacy and fairness in recommender systems via adversarial training of user representations. In *Proceedings of the 8th International Conference on Pattern Recognition Applications and Methods*, pages 476–482.

Yuji Roh, Kangwook Lee, Steven Euijong Whang, and Changho Suh. 2021. Fairbatch: Batch selection for model fairness. In *Proceedings of 9th International Conference on Learning Representations*.

Saeed Sharifi-Malvajerdi, Michael J. Kearns, and Aaron Roth. 2019. Average individual fairness: Algorithms, generalization and experiments. In *Advances in Neural Information Processing Systems*, pages 8240–8249.

Aili Shen, Xudong Han, Trevor Cohn, Timothy Baldwin, and Lea Frermann. 2022. Optimising equal opportunity fairness in model training. *arXiv preprint arXiv:2205.02393*.

Ryan Steed, Swetasudha Panda, Ari Kobren, and Michael Wick. 2022. Upstream mitigation is not all you need: Testing the bias transfer hypothesis in pre-trained language models. In *Proceedings of the 60th Annual Meeting of the Association for Computational Linguistics (Volume 1: Long Papers)*, pages 3524–3542.

Shivashankar Subramanian, Xudong Han, Timothy Baldwin, Trevor Cohn, and Lea Frermann. 2021. Evaluating debiasing techniques for intersectional biases. In *Proceedings of the 2021 Conference on Empirical Methods in Natural Language Processing*, pages 2492–2498.

Yonglong Tian, Dilip Krishnan, and Phillip Isola. 2020. Contrastive multiview coding. In *Proceeding of the 16th European Conference on Computer Vision*, pages 776–794.

Yao-Hung Hubert Tsai, Martin Q Ma, Han Zhao, Kun Zhang, Louis-Philippe Morency, and Ruslan Salakhutdinov. 2021. Conditional contrastive learning: Removing undesirable information in self-supervised representations. *arXiv preprint arXiv:2106.02866*.

Tianlu Wang, Jieyu Zhao, Mark Yatskar, Kai-Wei Chang, and Vicente Ordonez. 2019. Balanced datasets are not enough: Estimating and mitigating gender bias in deep image representations. In *Proceedings of the IEEE/CVF International Conference on Computer Vision*, pages 5310–5319.

Yongkai Wu, Lu Zhang, and Xintao Wu. 2019. Counterfactual fairness: Unidentification, bound and algorithm. In *Proceedings of the Twenty-Eighth International Joint Conference on Artificial Intelligence*, pages 1438–1444.

Mikhail Yurochkin, Amanda Bower, and Yuekai Sun. 2020. Training individually fair ML models with sensitive subspace robustness. In *Proceedings of the 8th International Conference on Learning Representations*.

Muhammad Bilal Zafar, Isabel Valera, Manuel Gomez-Rodriguez, and Krishna P. Gummadi. 2017a. Fairness beyond disparate treatment & disparate impact: Learning classification without disparate mistreatment. In *Proceedings of the 26th International Conference on World Wide Web*, pages 1171–1180.

Muhammad Bilal Zafar, Isabel Valera, Manuel Gomez-Rodriguez, and Krishna P. Gummadi. 2017b. Fairness constraints: Mechanisms for fair classification. In *Proceedings of the 20th International Conference on Artificial Intelligence and Statistics*, volume 54, pages 962–970.

Brian Hu Zhang, Blake Lemoine, and Margaret Mitchell. 2018. Mitigating unwanted biases with adversarial learning. In *Proceedings of the 2018 AAAI/ACM Conference on AI, Ethics, and Society*, pages 335–340.

Junzhe Zhang and Elias Bareinboim. 2018. Fairness in decision-making - the causal explanation formula. In *Proceedings of the Thirty-Second AAAI Conference on Artificial Intelligence*, pages 2037–2045.

Han Zhao, Amanda Coston, Tameem Adel, and Geoffrey J. Gordon. 2020a. Conditional learning of fair representations. In *International Conference on Learning Representations*.

Han Zhao, Amanda Coston, Tameem Adel, and Geoffrey J. Gordon. 2020b. Conditional learning of fair representations. In *International Conference on Learning Representations*.

Han Zhao and Geoffrey J. Gordon. 2019. Inherent tradeoffs in learning fair representations. In *Advances in Neural Information Processing Systems*, pages 15649–15659.

Jieyu Zhao, Tianlu Wang, Mark Yatskar, Vicente Ordonez, and Kai-Wei Chang. 2017. Men also like shopping: Reducing gender bias amplification using corpus-level constraints. In *Proceedings of the 2017 Conference on Empirical Methods in Natural Language Processing*, pages 2979–2989.

# L	D	AF	Moji	Bios
1	–	–	84.80±0.54	96.63±0.03
2	100	Tanh	87.12±0.51	97.91±0.03
2	100	ReLU	87.03±0.34	97.92±0.04
2	300	Tanh	87.37±0.13	98.00±0.03
2	300	ReLU	87.89±0.34	97.96±0.05
4	100	Tanh	87.21±0.57	97.84±0.10
4	100	ReLU	87.38±0.70	97.82±0.06
4	300	Tanh	87.42±0.45	97.90±0.05
4	300	ReLU	87.50±0.29	97.86±0.04

Table 3: Leakage estimations over **Moji** and **Bios** with respect to different attacker architectures. **# L**, **D**, and **AF** denote number of hidden layers, hidden dimensions, and activation functions, respectively. Leakage estimation statistics (mean and standard deviation) are calculated over 5 runs.

A Robustness to Leakage Estimation

To analyse the robustness of leakage estimations, we vary attacker architectures and compare estimated leakage of the CE model. Table 3 summaries results over the **Moji** and **Bios** datasets

Overall, leakage estimations are robust to different architectures, except the results of linear attackers (i.e., 1 layer), which are consistently worse over both datasets.

In terms of the standard deviation, the training set of **Bios** is larger than that of **Moji** (205k v.s. 100k), resulting in a smaller standard deviation for leakage estimations over **Bios** than **Moji**.

B Adv Settings

Each sub-discriminator consists of two MLP layers with a hidden size of 256, where the first layer is accompanied with a LeakyReLU activation function. The final classifier layer is used to predict the protected attribute. Sub-discriminators are optimized for at most 100 epochs after each epoch of Enc(·) training, leading to extra training time.

C Bios Distribution

Table 4 shows the number of instances of each profession, the number of male and female individuals of each profession, and the ratio of female individuals for each profession in the **Bios** training dataset.

Profession	Total	Male	Female	Ratio
professor	76748	42130	34618	0.451
physician	26648	13492	13156	0.494
attorney	21169	13064	8105	0.383
photographer	15773	10141	5632	0.357
journalist	12960	6545	6415	0.495
nurse	12316	1127	11189	0.908
psychologist	11945	4530	7415	0.621
teacher	10531	4188	6343	0.602
dentist	9479	6133	3346	0.353
surgeon	8829	7521	1308	0.148
architect	6568	5014	1554	0.237
painter	5025	2727	2298	0.457
model	4867	840	4027	0.827
poet	4558	2323	2235	0.490
filmmaker	4545	3048	1497	0.329
software_engineer	4492	3783	709	0.158
accountant	3660	2317	1343	0.367
composer	3637	3042	595	0.164
dietitian	2567	183	2384	0.929
comedian	1824	1439	385	0.211
chiropractor	1725	1271	454	0.263
pastor	1638	1245	393	0.240
paralegal	1146	173	973	0.849
yoga_teacher	1076	166	910	0.846
dj	964	828	136	0.141
interior_designer	949	182	767	0.808
personal_trainer	928	505	423	0.456
rapper	911	823	88	0.097

Table 4: Statistics of the **Bios** training dataset.

C.1 Synthetic Dataset Construction

We follow Subramanian et al. (2021) in constructing the binary classification version of the **Bios** dataset based on the two professions of *nurse* and *surgeon*. For the additional classes in the synthetic experiments, we further select pairs of professions that are both large in size and biased in gender skew, resulting in *photographer* + *teacher*, *dentist* + *psychologist*, and *software engineer* + *model*. The resulting training dataset sizes are 21145, 47449, 68873, and 78232 for 2, 4, 6, and 8 classes, respectively.

D Hyperparameter Settings

We vary the architecture of Embed(·) across different tasks, and do not finetune it during training. The architecture of Enc(·) consists of two fully-connected layers with a hidden size of 300. All models are trained and evaluated on the same dataset splits, and models are selected based on their performance on the development set. For fair comparison, we first finetune the learning rate and batch size using grid search, then finetune hyperparameters introduced by the corresponding debiasing methods for each model on each dataset. For all experiments, we use the Adam optimizer (Kingma and Ba, 2015) and early stopping with a patience of 10.

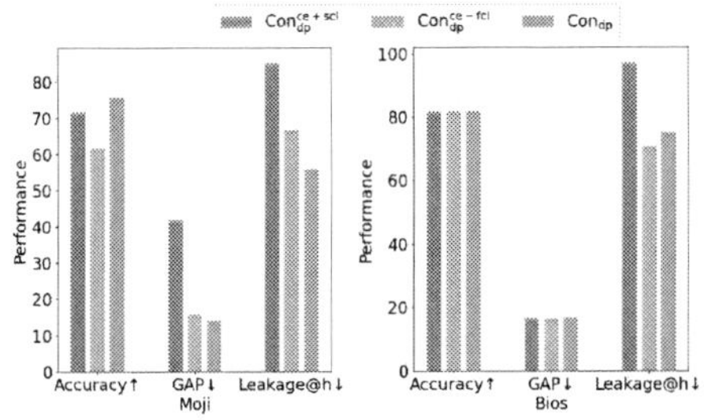

Figure 3: Effects of contrastive loss components for $\mathsf{Con}_{\mathrm{dp}}$.

D.1 Twitter Sentiment Analysis

For CE, the learning rate is 0.001, and the batch size is 1024. For INLP, following Ravfogel et al. (2020), we use 300 linear SVM classifiers, each of which is trained over a subset of instances with the same target class. For Adv, the number of sub-discriminators is 3, λ_{adv} is 1.0, and λ_{diff} is 0.01. For Gate, all hyperparameters are the same as CE, except the hidden layers of MLP are replaced by a hyperparameter-free augmentation layer. For $\mathsf{FairBatch}$, the objective is equal opportunity, and the adjustment rate for resampling probabilities is 0.19952623149688797. For $\mathsf{EO}_{\mathrm{GLB}}$, the strength of the additional difference loss is 0.3981071705534973. For $\mathsf{Con}_{\mathrm{dp}}$, $\tau = 0.01$, and $\alpha = \beta = 0.0199526231496888$. For $\mathsf{Con}_{\mathrm{eo}}$, all hyperparameters are the same as $\mathsf{Con}_{\mathrm{dp}}$, except for $\alpha = \beta = 0.7943282347242822$.

D.2 Occupation Classification

For CE, the learning rate is 0.003, and the batch size is 2048. For INLP, each classifier is trained over a subset of instances with same target class. For Adv, the number of sub-discriminators is 3, λ_{adv} is 1.0, and λ_{diff} is 0.01. For Gate, all hyperparameters are the same as CE, except for the hidden layers of MLP are replaced hyperparameter-free augmentation layer. For $\mathsf{FairBatch}$, the objective is equal opportunity, and the adjustment rate for resampling probabilities is 0.05011872336272725. For $\mathsf{EO}_{\mathrm{GLB}}$, the strength of the additional difference loss is 0.00707945784384138. For $\mathsf{Con}_{\mathrm{dp}}$, $\tau = 0.01$, and $\alpha = \beta = 0.00011885022274370189$. For $\mathsf{Con}_{\mathrm{eo}}$, all hyperparameters are the same as $\mathsf{Con}_{\mathrm{dp}}$, except for $\alpha = \beta = 0.00016788040181225607$.

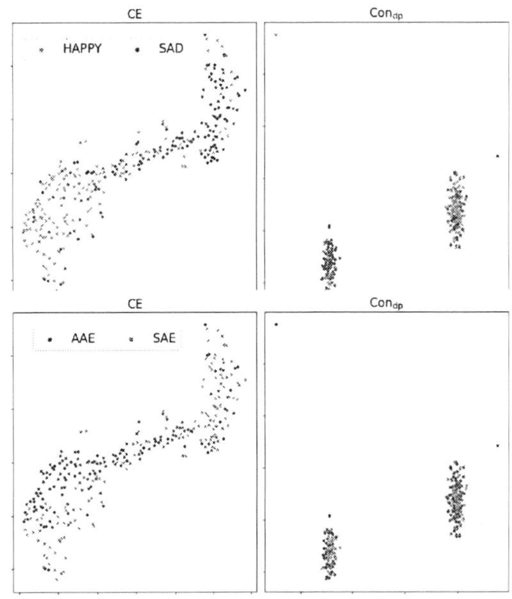

Figure 4: t-SNE scatter plots of learned representations of CE and $\mathsf{Con}_{\mathrm{dp}}$ over the **Moji** dataset (based on 150 random samples from each main task class; best viewed in colour). Red and blue colours indicate that they have different sentiment (main task) labels: red $\rightarrow$ HAPPY and blue $\rightarrow$ SAD. Green and purple colours indicate that they have different ethnic groups (protected attribute): purple $\rightarrow$ AAE and green $\rightarrow$ SAE.

D.3 Analysis

D.3.1 Effect of Loss Components

See Figure 3 for a breakdown of results for each loss component of $\mathsf{Con}_{\mathrm{dp}}$ over **Moji** and **Bios**.

D.3.2 Visualising Representations

See Figure 4 for t-SNE plots of learned representations for CE vs. $\mathsf{Con}_{\mathrm{dp}}$ over **Moji**.

SEHY: A Simple yet Effective Hybrid Model for Summarization of Long Scientific Documents

Zhihua Jiang[1], **Junzhan Yang**[1], **Dongning Rao**[2]*
[1] Department of Computer Science, Jinan University, Guangzhou 510632, P. R. China
[2] School of Computer, Guangdong University of Technology, Guangzhou 510006, P. R. China
tjiangzhh@jnu.edu.cn, junyz@stu2021.jnu.edu.cn, raodn@gdut.edu.cn

Abstract

Long-document summarization has been recently recognized as one of the most important natural language processing (NLP) tasks, yet one of the least solved ones. Extractive approaches attempt to choose salient sentences via understanding the whole document, but long documents cover numerous subjects with varying details and will not ease content understanding. Instead, abstractive approaches elaborate to generate related tokens while suffering from truncating the source document due to their input sizes. To this end, we propose a *S*imple yet *E*ffective *HY*brid approach, which we call *SEHY*, that exploits the discourse information of a document to select salient sections instead sentences for summary generation. On the one hand, *SEHY* avoids the full-text understanding; on the other hand, it retains salient information given the length limit. In particular, we design two simple strategies for training the extractor: extracting sections incrementally and based on salience-analysis. Then, we use strong abstractive models to generate the final summary. We evaluate our approach on a large-scale scientific paper dataset: arXiv. Further, we discuss how the disciplinary class (e.g., computer science, math or physics) of a scientific paper affects the performance of *SEHY* as its writing style indicates, which is unexplored yet in existing works. Experimental results show the effectiveness of our approach and interesting findings on arXiv and its subsets generated in this paper.

1 Introduction

Long-document tasks (e.g., scientific papers summarization (Cohan et al., 2018) and long-text reading comprehension (Wen et al., 2021)) have become one of long-term challenging tasks in Natural Language Processing (NLP) because long documents cover numerous subjects with varying details and will not ease content understanding. For example, scientific papers, whose abstracts can be used as ground-truth summaries, is a representative type of long documents with discourse information showing the hierarchical structure composed of tokens, sentences, paragraphs, and sections (K and Mathew, 2020). Extractive summarization approaches select important units such as phrases or sentences from the original text, but long documents cover numerous subjects with varying details and will not ease content understanding (Nallapati et al., 2017; Xiao and Carenini, 2020). Instead, abstractive summarization approaches concisely paraphrase the information content while suffering from truncating the source document due to their input sizes (Rohde et al., 2021; Guo et al., 2021).

Hybrid models exhibit a combination solution via first extracting salient sentences with an extractive model (i.e., extractor) and then generating a summary based on extracted sentences with an abstractive model (i.e., generator) (Gidiotis and Tsoumakas, 2020; Pilault et al., 2020). However, on the one hand, training an extractive model may be expensive due to the complex salience analysis; on the other hand, an abstractive model may generate inappropriate summary words due to the dependence on extracted sentences. Thus, pipeline-style errors can be propagated and accumulated, leading to hybrid models perform worse than current state-of-the-art (SoTA) abstractive models (Rohde et al., 2021; Guo et al., 2021). This suggests that exploring simple yet effective extractive approaches is crucial to improve the overall performance and decrease the training cost of a hybrid model.

Recently, the success of pre-trained language models (PTMs) such as Transformer (Vaswani et al., 2017) in NLP brings great gain for abstractive models in the summarization task. However, Transformer-based models usually suffer from the quadratic dependency on the sequence length due to their full attention mechanism. Sometimes, the model's performance is mainly con-

*Corresponding author: Dongning Rao.

Findings of the Association for Computational Linguistics: AACL-IJCNLP 2022, pages 96–106
November 20–23, 2022. ©2022 Association for Computational Linguistics

strained by its limitation on the sequence length. For instance, the average document length on arXiv (Cohan et al., 2018) is more than 6000 tokens while BART (Lewis et al., 2020), which combines BERT (Devlin et al., 2019) and GPT (Radford and Narasimhan, 2018), has a comparatively smaller length limit, 1024 tokens. Besides, for a hybrid model, extracted sentences from its extractive model are often difficult to maintain the coherence of the source document, thus leading to the poor semantic representations by its abstractive model (Cai et al., 2019).

To alleviate these issues, we propose a novel *S*imple yet *E*ffective *HY*brid approach, which we call *SEHY*, that exploits the discourse information of a document to select salient sections instead sentences for summary generation. We use simple strategies for choosing sections, not only for decreasing the training cost of the extractor, but also for enhancing the input-sequence's coherence to the generator. Motivated by (Gidiotis and Tsoumakas, 2020), which identifies and selects specific sections that are more informative, we propose two strategies: choosing specific sections (e.g., Introduction or Conclusion) based on the salience analysis and using the beginning sections without concerning the salience. After this, we use strong abstractive models to generate the final summary.

To demonstrate the effectiveness of *SEHY*, we answer the following questions in this paper:

- Q1: which strategy is better?
- Q2: how do different abstractive models affect the overall performance of *SEHY*?
- Q3: can we have the equivalent result when summarizing different scientific papers?

As the contents indicate, Q1 is used to evaluate the two section-extraction strategies, Q2 is used to measure different abstractive models which are responsible to generate the final summary, and Q3 is used to estimate writing styles of scientific papers in different disciplines. The joint of Q1 and Q2 acts as ablation studies on the proposed hybrid model *SEHY*. While, Q3 is not explored yet in existing works where all scientific papers on arXiv are summarized without distinguishing their disciplinary properties (e.g., computer science, math or physics). For instance, a well-written computer science paper usually presents summary sentences in the Introduction or Conclusion section, but no experimental work has ever confirmed this.

2 Related Work

Automatic text summarization is the task of producing a concise and fluent summary while preserving key information content and overall meaning. It aims to transform lengthy documents into shortened versions, something which could be difficult and costly to undertake if done manually. In this section, we focus on recent summarization models. For more text summarization technologies, we refer interested readers to a survey on this (Allahyari et al., 2017).

2.1 Extractive Models

Extractive methods select important sentences and rearrange them as the summary, instead of generating summary tokens. LexRank (Erkan and Radev, 2011) is an early extractive model, which computes sentence importance based on the concept of eigenvector centrality in a graph representation of sentences. SummaRuNNer (Nallapati et al., 2017) is a Recurrent Neural Network (RNN) based sequence model for extractive summarization of documents. It has the additional advantage of being interpretable, since it allows visualization of its predictions broken up by abstract features, such as information content, salience, and novelty. Xiao et al. (Xiao and Carenini, 2020) found that redundancy is a very serious problem when summarizing long documents. They proposed ExtSum-LG+Rd, which achieved high ROUGE scores, while reducing redundancy significantly.

2.2 Abstractive Models

Early abstractive models include Pointer-Generator Networks (PGN) (See et al., 2017), which augments two shortcomings: inaccuracy and repetition, via copying words from the source text and using coverage to keep track of what has been summarized. Cohan et al. (Cohan et al., 2018) built two large-scale scientific-paper datasets: arXiv and Pubmed. They also proposed Discourse composed of a hierarchical encoder that models the discourse structure of a document and an attentive discourse-aware decoder that generates the summary. PEGASUS (Zhang et al., 2020) is a Transformer-based encoder-decoder model trained on massive text corpora with a new self-supervised objective.

Recent works improve the performance of Transformer-based models by increasing the input length or the model size. BigBird (Zaheer et al., 2020) exhibits a sparse attention mechanism that reduced the quadratic dependency to linear. DeepPyramidion (Pietruszka et al., 2022) proposes representation pooling as a method to sparsify attention in Transformer by learning to select the most-informative token representations during the training process. HAT-BART (Rohde et al., 2021) proposes a new Hierarchical Attention Transformer-based architecture into the denoising auto-encoder BART (Lewis et al., 2020). LongT5 (Guo et al., 2021) attempts to increase both at the same time. Specifically, it integrates attention ideas from long-form transformer (Beltagy et al., 2020a), and adopts pretraining strategies from PEGASUS into the scalable T5 architecture (Raffel et al., 2020a). Top Down Transformer (Pang et al., 2022) updates token representations in a bottom-up and top-down manner: token representations are first inferred in the bottom-up pass and then updated in the top-down pass to capture long-range dependency.

Even though Top Down Transformer is at the top of the arXiv leaderboard[1] while LongT5 takes the second place, the authors of Top Down Transformer did not release their model or code yet. Thus, we regard LongT5 as the current SoTA with respect to all open-sourced document summarization models.

2.3 Hybrid Models

A hybrid approach takes advantage of extractive and abstractive approaches. DANCER (Gidiotis and Tsoumakas, 2020) proposes a divide-and-conquer algorithm, which breaks a long document and its summary into multiple source-target pairs and uses them for training a model that learned to summarize each part of the document. TLM-I+E (Pilault et al., 2020) performs a simple extractive step, which is used to condition the transformer language model on relevant information before being tasked with generating a summary. Although mostly follows the abstractive approach, Top Down Transformer connects to the hybrid models via learning and assigning importance weight with the importance tagger resembles an extractive step.

2.4 Paper Abstract Generation

Scientific papers are representatives of long documents with discourse information, where their abstracts can be used as ground-truth summaries. Wang et al. (Wang et al., 2018) presented a paper abstract writing system based on an attentive neural

[1]https://paperswithcode.com/dataset/arxiv

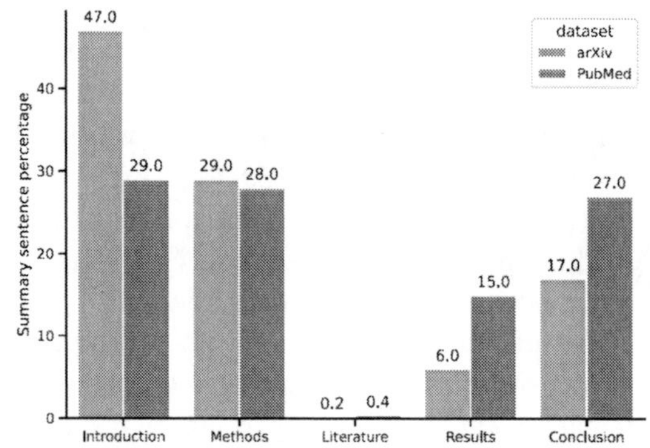

Figure 1: The distribution of summary sentences per section type, cited from (Gidiotis and Tsoumakas, 2020).

sequence-to-sequence model that can take a title as input and automatically generate an abstract. They designed a novel Writing-editing Network that can attend to both the title and the previously generated abstract drafts and then iteratively revise and polish the abstract. Next year, they further developed a Paper-Robot (Wang et al., 2019) which performs as an automatic research assistant by incrementally writing some key elements of a new paper based on memory-attention networks. Demir et al. (Demir et al., 2019) proposed a dataset with LaTeX source files on recent open-source computer vision papers and experimented with recent methods such as Transformer and Transformer-XL (Dai et al., 2019) to generate consistent LaTeX code.

3 Method

In this section, we first present two strategies to implement our extractive model (for answering Q1), then describe multiple paired abstractive models (for answering Q2), and finally explain how to generate data subsets with regard to disciplinary categories of scientific papers (for answering Q3).

3.1 Two Extraction Strategies

Long documents introduce a lot of noise to the summarization process. Indeed, one of the major difficulties in summarizing a long document is that large parts of the document are not really key to its narrative and thus should be ignored. Following DANCER (Gidiotis and Tsoumakas, 2020), we identify and select specific sections that are more informative. This reduces the noise and the computational cost in processing a long document. Figure 1 demonstrates the distribution of summary sentences per section type. We observe that the majority of summary sentences, for the arXiv dataset, are assigned to the *introduction* section followed by the *methods* and *conclusion* sections. Based on that observation, we select and use only the sections that are classified *introduction*, *methods*, and *conclusion* ignoring the others. This simple method very effectively allows us to filter out parts of the article that are less important for the summary and leads to summaries that are more focused. Another benefit of selecting sections instead of sentences is that, the number of sections is much smaller than that of sentences, which decreases the number of combinations dramatically.

In particular, we use the following two strategies for selecting sections. Formally, supposing there are *N* sections in a source document *Doc*:

- $P_{sal}(Sec)$: using all the sections included in $Sec = \{sec_1, sec_2, ..., sec_{|Sec|}\}$ where $|Sec| \leq N$;
- $P_{inc}(k)$: only using the first *k* sections where $1 \leq k \leq N$ is a positive integer.

We sequentially concatenate selected sections from the beginning of a document as the above strategies indicate. If exceeding the length limit, the concatenated sequence will be truncated; otherwise, it will be padded with zero. All section headings can be conveniently identified from the LaTeX source files. On the one hand, to simplify the salience analysis of $P_{sal}(Sec)$, we focus on the first section (i.e., Head Section), the last section (i.e., Tail Section), and the combination of these two (i.e., Head+Tail Section), for the target of determining Sec. On the other hand, we can set $k > 1$ for $P_{inc}(k)$ to cover *introduction* and *methods* as shown in Figure 1. However, the actual values of k are usually no more than the relative ratio of the length limit divided by the average section-length on experimental datasets, because larger k values will not bring greater gain due to the truncation mechanism of the abstractive model.

Obviously, one weakness of this method is that, although these section categories are meaningful when working on academic articles, if the proposed method is extended to different domains (e.g. financial documents), then a new categorization of sections would be required. Thus, exploring more sophisticated methods that use machine learning to identify the type of each section should be explored in future work.

Table 1: Examples of the head and tail section names of scientific papers on arXiv.

Head Section Name	Tail Section Name
Introduction	Conclusion
Related Works	Conclusions
Introduction and related work	Discussion
Motivation	Future Work
Background and Introduction	Further Work
Motivation and Background	Observations
Motivating Work	Concluding remarks

3.2 Tested Abstractive Model

We test five strong abstractive models introduced in the Related Work section, whose actual parameter settings are shown in Table 7.

- T5 (Raffel et al., 2020b). T5 introduces a unified framework that converts all text-based language problems into a text-to-text format and combines the insights from the exploration with scale and the new corpus.
- BART (Lewis et al., 2020). BART is a denoising auto-encoder for pre-training sequence-to-sequence models. It is trained by corrupting text with an arbitrary noising function, and learning a model to reconstruct the original text.
- LED (Beltagy et al., 2020b). LED is a Longformer (Beltagy et al., 2020a) variant for supporting long document generative tasks. The Longformer's attention mechanism scales linearly with sequence length, making it easy to process super-long documents.
- BigBird (Zaheer et al., 2020). Bigbird introduces a sparse attention mechanism that reduces the quadratic dependency to linear. It reveals some benefits of having global tokens (e.g., CLS), that attend to the entire sequence as part of the sparse attention mechanism.
- PEGASUS (Zhang et al., 2020). Pegasus is a pre-training large Transformer-based encoder-decoder models on massive text corpora with a new self-supervised objective. Important sentences are removed or masked from an input document and generated together as one output sequence from the remaining sentences.

3.3 Data Subset Generation

Academic papers of the arXiv dataset are collected from the scientific repository arXiv.org and are writ-

Table 2: The number of disciplinary papers for the Train/Dev/Test split.

Discipline \ Split[1]	Train	Dev	Test
Physics	146628	5145	5193
Mathematics	19146	296	257
Computer Science	9600	361	339
Statistics	2354	80	77
Quantitative Biology	1492	54	60
Quantitative Finance	612	19	25
E.E.S.S.	259	5	10
Economics	14	1	2
Total (the full arXiv)	203038	6437	6640

[1] E.E.S.S. is shorthand for Electrical Engineering and Systems Science.

Table 3: The average length of Abstract, Head Section and Tail Section on arXiv and its subsets.

Dataset \ Section[1]	Abstract	Head	Tail
Full (the full arXiv)	151	748	724
CS (Computer Science)	158	857	537
Math (Mathematics)	122	1036	1059
Phy (Physics)	154	645	720

[1] Head and Tail indicate Head Section and Tail Section, respectively.

ten in LaTeX[2]. Following previous work (Cohan et al., 2018; Demir et al., 2019), we extract the top-level section headings from the LaTeX source files using Pandoc[3]. We collect various section heading names and classify them into equivalent categories. For instance, names of Head Section and Tail Section are shown in Table 1.

The arXiv dataset covers various disciplines, including physics, mathematics, computer science, quantitative biology, and economics, etc. We statistics the paper numbers of different disciplines following the train/dev/test split of (Cohan et al., 2018), as shown in Table 2. It shows that the arXiv papers are primarily collected from three disciplines: Physics, Mathematics and Computer Science. Thus, to answer Q3, we generate three subsets of the full arXiv dataset[4]: CS (Computer Science), Math (Mathematics) and Phy (Physics). For the convenience of writing, we use "Full" to indicate the full arXiv dataset in this paper. To better determine the super-parameters of $P_{sal}(Sec)$ and $P_{inc}(k)$, we calculate the average lengths of Head Section (H) and Tail Section (T) of Full, CS, Math, Phy, as shown in Table 3.

[2]https://www.latex-project.org/

[3]https://pandoc.org

[4]We use the article ID extracted from the LaTeX file of a scientific paper to determine its discipline class. Specifically, we search the article ID on arXiv and get the "class" field of the returned result page as the discipline class.

4 Experiment

4.1 Settings

We conduct all experiments on a local machine (Windows 10 + GTX 1060 3GB) and a workstation (Ubuntu18.04, a NVIDIA Tesla V100 36G GPU, and a Intel(R) Xeon(R) E5-2698 v4 @ 2.20GHz CPU). Our code is written in Python 3.7. The deep learning platform is Pytorch 1.8.0. We use the huggingface-transformers[5] for pre-training and fine-tuning summary models. The actual parameter settings of all tested models are shown in Table 7.

We evaluate multiple variants of our approach on the largest-scale scientific-paper dataset: arXiv, with ROUGE (Recall-Oriented Understudy for Gisting Evaluation) (Lin, 2004) as the measurement metric. We report the F1 scores of ROUGE-1 (R-1), ROUGE-2 (R-2), and ROUGE-L (R-L), using the pyrouge package[6]. ROUGE is suitable for summarization of scientific papers, whose human-written abstracts can be used as ground-truth summaries. We do not include human evaluation, following the previous works such as LongT5 (Guo et al., 2021), BigBird (Zaheer et al., 2020) and PEGASUS (Zhang et al., 2020), etc. It is quite challenging to run human evaluations for scientific papers, as it requires participants to possess sophisticated domain-specific background knowledge.

4.2 Results and Analysis

In this section, we exhibit the evaluation results of multiple variants of our approach *SEHY* equipped with different section-selection strategies and different summary-generation models. We also answer the mentioned-above three questions (Q1, Q2, and Q3) to reveal interesting experimental findings.

Evaluation results of $P_{sal}(Sec)$. We report the ROUGE scores of *SEHY* using $P_{sal}(Sec)$ paired with three base models (Table 4) and three large models (Table 5) on arXiv (D_{Full}) and its three disciplinary subsets (D_{CS}, D_{Math} and D_{Phy}), respectively.

In Table 4, we find that: (1) all tested base models paired with $P_{sal}(H + T)$ obtain the highest scores, showing the advantage of using both of Head Section and Tail Section against using only one of them; (2) most tested base models paired with $P_{sal}(H)$ perform better than the same models paired with $P_{sal}(T)$, demonstrating that Head Section (usually *introduction*) contributes more than

[5]https://github.com/huggingface/transformers

[6]https://pypi.org/project/pyrouge

Table 4: Evaluation results of *SEHY* using the policy P_{sal} paired with *base* abstractive models on arXiv and its subsets. ROUGE scores (%) are reported. Best results in each group are in bold.

Dataset+Policy[1] \ Model	T5-base R-1 / R-2 / R-L	LED-base R-1 / R-2 / R-L	BART-base R-1 / R-2 / R-L
$D_{Full} + P_{sal}(H)$	38.75 / 13.93 / 34.50	43.67 / 16.87 / 39.29	43.48 / 16.25 / 38.86
$D_{Full} + P_{sal}(T)$	39.71 / 14.86 / 35.53	42.02 / 15.81 / 37.80	42.85 / 16.13 / 38.42
$D_{Full} + P_{sal}(H+T)$	**47.09 / 19.84 / 42.30**	**47.55 / 19.99 / 42.88**	**44.84 / 17.37 / 40.11**
$D_{CS} + P_{sal}(H)$	43.00 / 15.90 / 38.69	43.23 / 16.14 / 39.54	44.53 / 16.57 / 40.65
$D_{CS} + P_{sal}(T)$	40.22 / 14.71 / 36.13	40.91 / 15.04 / 37.18	41.93 / 16.08 / 38.10
$D_{CS} + P_{sal}(H+T)$	**47.58 / 19.91 / 43.11**	**46.67 / 18.86 / 42.93**	**45.46 / 17.32 / 41.59**
$D_{Math} + P_{sal}(H)$	39.93 / 15.62 / 36.06	41.28 / 16.75 / 37.67	40.83 / 15.41 / 36.69
$D_{Math} + P_{sal}(T)$	30.81 / 9.31 / 27.71	33.44 / 10.60 / 30.38	34.37 / 11.90 / 30.86
$D_{Math} + P_{sal}(H+T)$	**44.05 / 18.77 / 39.68**	**43.18 / 18.15 / 39.25**	**41.82 / 15.83 / 37.63**
$D_{Phy} + P_{sal}(H)$	38.22 / 13.57 / 33.96	41.04 / 15.03 / 36.69	43.10 / 16.11 / 24.83
$D_{Phy} + P_{sal}(T)$	39.88 / 15.00 / 35.64	42.39 / 16.11 / 38.11	43.44 / 16.40 / 38.89
$D_{Phy} + P_{sal}(H+T)$	**46.76 / 19.75 / 41.93**	**47.20 / 19.88 / 42.52**	**44.39 / 17.14 / 39.59**

[1] "Full" indicates the full arXiv dataset. CS, Math and Phy are shorthand for Computer Science, Mathematics and Physics, respectively. H and T are shorthand for Head Section and Tail Section. "H+T" indicates the concatenation of H and T.

Table 5: Evaluation results of *SEHY* using the policy P_{sal} paired with *large* abstractive models on arXiv and its subsets. ROUGE scores (%) are reported. Best results in each group are in bold.

Dataset+Policy \ Model[1]	BART-large R-1 / R-2 / R-L	BigBird-large R-1 / R-2 / R-L	PEGASUS-large R-1 / R-2 / R-L
$D_{Full} + P_{sal}(H)$	45.06 / 17.18 / 40.38	35.95 / 12.01 / 30.69	43.28 / 16.50 / 38.57
$D_{Full} + P_{sal}(T)$	**47.34 / 19.24 / 42.47**	28.49 / 7.75 / 24.58	40.43 / 14.88 / 35.73
$D_{Full} + P_{sal}(H+T)$	46.84 / 18.56 / 42.01	**47.33 / 19.57 / 39.97**	**45.23 / 18.22 / 40.42**
$D_{CS} + P_{sal}(H)$	47.78 / 18.66 / 43.68	46.31 / 19.11 / 40.84	46.05 / 18.65 / 42.12
$D_{CS} + P_{sal}(T)$	46.78 / 18.63 / 42.70	40.67 / 14.49 / 35.27	41.63 / 15.51 / 36.99
$D_{CS} + P_{sal}(H+T)$	**48.22 / 19.19 / 44.14**	**49.37 / 20.69 / 42.99**	**47.71 / 19.62 / 43.52**
$D_{Math} + P_{sal}(H)$	44.52 / 16.79 / 40.21	43.20 / 18.03 / 37.65	43.85 / 18.27 / 39.73
$D_{Math} + P_{sal}(T)$	42.54 / 15.33 / 38.04	32.91 / 10.50 / 28.17	32.79 / 10.62 / 28.77
$D_{Math} + P_{sal}(H+T)$	**44.53 / 16.97 / 40.49**	**46.05 / 19.67 / 39.48**	**44.62 / 18.84 / 39.94**
$D_{Phy} + P_{sal}(H)$	45.23 / 17.05 / 40.25	42.92 / 16.15 / 36.19	43.14 / 16.37 / 38.33
$D_{Phy} + P_{sal}(T)$	**47.83 / 19.12 / 42.80**	28.80 / 7.94 / 24.77	40.92 / 15.18 / 36.12
$D_{Phy} + P_{sal}(H+T)$	45.20 / 17.42 / 40.20	**47.42 / 19.66 / 39.93**	**45.25 / 18.32 / 40.37**

[1] Both of Bigbird-Pegasus-large (Zaheer et al., 2020) and Pegasus-large (Zhang et al., 2020) have been fine-tuned on arXiv, quoted from their original literature.

Table 6: Comparisons between *SEHY* and other summarization approaches on the full arXiv dataset D_{Full}. ROUGE scores (%) are reported. The three highest scores are in bold.

Type	Approach[1]	R-1 / R-2 / R-L[2]
Abstractive	PGN** (See et al., 2017)	32.06 / 9.04 / 25.16
	Discourse* (Cohan et al., 2018)	35.80 / 11.05 / 31.80
	PEGASUS* (Zhang et al., 2020)	44.67 / 16.95 / 38.83
	BigBird* (Zaheer et al., 2020)	46.63 / 19.02 / 41.77
	HAT-BART* (Rohde et al., 2021)	46.68 / 19.07 / 42.17
	DeepPyramidion*(Pietruszka et al., 2022)[3]	47.15 / **19.99**†† / -
	LongT5* (Guo et al., 2021)[4]	**48.35**† / **21.92**† / **44.27**†
Extractive	LexRank** (Erkan and Radev, 2011)	33.85 / 10.73 / 28.99
	SummaRuNNer** (Nallapati et al., 2017)	42.81 / 16.52 / 28.23
	ExtSum-LG+Rd* (Xiao and Carenini, 2020)	44.01 / 17.79 / 39.09
Hybrid	DANCER* (Gidiotis and Tsoumakas, 2020)	45.01 / 17.60 / 40.56
	TLM-I+E* (Pilault et al., 2020)	41.62 / 14.69 / 38.03
Ours	*SEHY*:$D_{Full} + P_{sal}(H+T)$+T5-base	47.09 / **19.84**††† / 42.30
	SEHY:$D_{Full} + P_{sal}(H+T)$+LED-base	**47.55**†† / **19.99**†† / **42.88**††
	SEHY:$D_{Full} + P_{sal}(H+T)$+BART-base	44.84 / 17.37 / 40.11
	SEHY:$D_{Full} + P_{sal}(T)$+BART-large	**47.34**††† / 19.24 / **42.47**†††
	SEHY:$D_{Full} + P_{sal}(H+T)$+BigBird-large	47.33 / 19.57 / 39.97
	SEHY:$D_{Full} + P_{sal}(H+T)$+PEGASUS-large	45.23 / 18.22 / 40.42

[1] * indicates the results are from leaderboard (https://paperswithcode.com/dataset/arxiv). ** indicates the results are from their original papers.
[2] The †, †† and ††† indicate the highest, the second high and the third high score, respectively.
[3] DeepPyramidion only reported the R-1 and R-2 scores in its original paper (Pietruszka et al., 2022), so far on leaderboard.
[4] LongT5 is the current state of the art (SoTA) among all open-source summarization models.

Table 7: Parameter settings of abstractive models.

Parameter \ Model	T5	BART	LED	BigBird	PEGASUS
Version	base	base	base	large	large
Batch	8	6	7	6	6
Layer	12	6	6	16	16
Epoch	3	3	3	1	1
Min Loss[1]	1.84	2.29	1.96	-	-
Length_limit	-	1024	16384	4096	1024

[1] We fine-tuned all base models on D_{Full} and reported the final loss.

Tail Section (usually *conclusion*) on summarizing well-organized scientific papers; (3) there is a slight difference of performances between different models, but no model dominates all the others. For instance, LED-base performs better than T5-base on D_{Full} and D_{Phy} while T5-base performs better than LED-base on D_{CS} and D_{Math}.

In Table 5, equivalent results can be found when using large models. Generally, given the same model, the large version obtains higher scores than the base version, showing the stronger ability of addressing this task due to the model size. Particularly, BigBird-large performs best in this part, probably because of its comparatively larger input length (4096, see Table 7) derived by the sparse attention mechanism. However, one exception is BART-large, which behaves consistently with others on D_{CS} and D_{Math} but doing best by using $P_{sal}(T)$ on D_{Full} and D_{Phy}.

For answering Q3, we focus on evaluation results on D_{CS}, D_{Math} and D_{Phy} in Table 4 and 5. We find that $P_{sal}(H+T)$ almost obtains higher scores than either $P_{sal}(H)$ or $P_{sal}(T)$ on D_{CS}, D_{Math} and D_{Phy}, no matter that which abstractive model is used. Further, it is encouraging that *SEHY* using $P_{sal}(H+T)$ paired with BigBird-large obtains the highest score (49.37 / 20.69 / 42.99) on D_{CS} (Table 5) in our experiments, showing that, comparatively speaking, the policy $P_{sal}(Sec)$ is most suitable for scientific papers in Computer Science.

Besides, we exhibit the fine-tuning time of base models on all experimental datasets in Table 8. We did not do these for the large models because they have been fine-tuned on arXiv, quoted from their original papers. It is found that training our hybrid model *SEHY*, even though leveraging simple extraction strategies, is still time-expensive because arXiv is super large-scale. The training time increases dramatically with the growth of the dataset size, especially on D_{Full}.

Table 10 shows examples of summaries generated by our models by using $P_{sal}(H+T)$, paired with the above base and large models.

Table 8: The fine-tuning time (hours) of base models on datesets.

Dataset+Policy \ Model	T5-base	LED-base	BART-base
$D_{Full} + P_{sal}(H)$	23.27	40.15	11.40
$D_{Full} + P_{sal}(T)$	22.53	21.56	11.62
$D_{Full} + P_{sal}(H+T)$	58.58	41.78	12.29
$D_{CS} + P_{sal}(H)$	1.07	1.00	0.54
$D_{CS} + P_{sal}(T)$	1.04	0.98	0.51
$D_{CS} + P_{sal}(H+T)$	2.64	2.00	0.55
$D_{Math} + P_{sal}(H)$	2.16	1.96	1.06
$D_{Math} + P_{sal}(T)$	2.10	1.96	1.05
$D_{Math} + P_{sal}(H+T)$	5.59	3.88	1.08
$D_{Phy} + P_{sal}(H)$	16.21	15.43	8.05
$D_{Phy} + P_{sal}(T)$	16.50	15.49	8.01
$D_{Phy} + P_{sal}(H+T)$	41.63	30.02	8.41

Table 9: Evaluation results of *SEHY* using $P_{inc}(k)$ paired with BigBird. Best results in each group are in bold.

Dataset+Policy \ Model	BigBird–large R-1 / R-2 / R-L
$D_{Full} + P_{inc}(1)$	35.95 / 12.01 / 30.69
$D_{Full} + P_{inc}(2)$	44.52 / 17.31 / 37.45
$D_{Full} + P_{inc}(3)$	44.73 / 17.42 / 37.45
$D_{Full} + P_{inc}(4)$	**44.80 / 17.56 / 37.48**
$D_{CS} + P_{inc}(1)$	46.31 / 19.11 / 40.84
$D_{CS} + P_{inc}(2)$	47.47 / 19.68 / 41.70
$D_{CS} + P_{inc}(3)$	48.33 / 20.52 / 42.36
$D_{CS} + P_{inc}(4)$	**48.52 / 20.67 / 42.45**
$D_{Math} + P_{inc}(1)$	43.20 / 18.03 / 37.65
$D_{Math} + P_{inc}(2)$	45.31 / 19.75 / 39.28
$D_{Math} + P_{inc}(3)$	45.59 / 19.95 / 39.02
$D_{Math} + P_{inc}(4)$	**45.71 / 19.95 / 39.27**
$D_{Phy} + P_{inc}(1)$	42.92 / 16.15 / 36.19
$D_{Phy} + P_{inc}(2)$	44.33 / 17.18 / 37.16
$D_{Phy} + P_{inc}(3)$	44.56 / 17.27 / 37.19
$D_{Phy} + P_{inc}(4)$	**44.60 / 17.40 / 37.18**

Evaluation results of $P_{inc}(k)$. We measure $P_{inc}(k)$ on D_{Full}, D_{CS}, D_{Math} and D_{Phy}. This strategy can validate the contributions of middle sections such as *methods* (Figure 1) on the generated summary. We conduct this part of experiments by only using BigBird-large because it performs best in above experiments. We set the largest value of *k* to 4 because the length limit of BigBird-large is 4096 and the average section-length on D_{Full}, D_{CS}, D_{Math} is more than 1000 (see Table 3). Evaluation results of $P_{inc}(k)$ are reported in Table 9, showing that the ROUGE scores are increased with the growth of k values (i.e., more first sections are used). However, e.g., on D_{Full}, the best result of $P_{inc}(k)$ (44.80 / 17.56 / 37.48) is much worse than that of $P_{sal}(Sec)$ (47.55 / 19.99 / 42.88).

Comparison of $P_{sal}(Sec)$ and $P_{inc}(k)$. For answering Q1, we compare $P_{sal}(Sec)$ and $P_{inc}(k)$ with regard to all experimental options. Results are shown in Figure 2, 3 and 4. Obviously, $P_{sal}(Sec)$

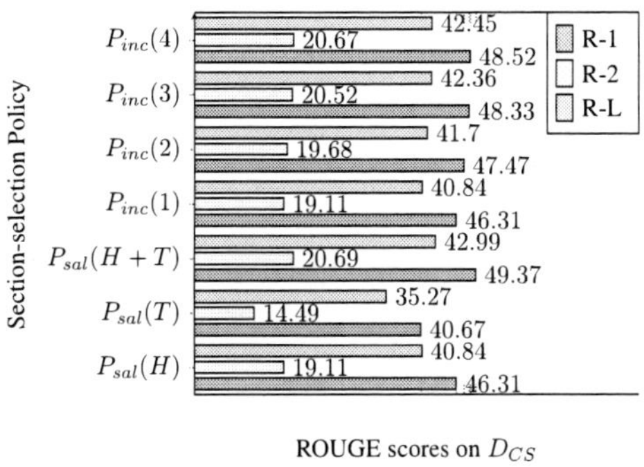

Figure 2: Comparison of section-selection strategies of *SEHY* paired with BigBird-large on the dataset D_{CS}.

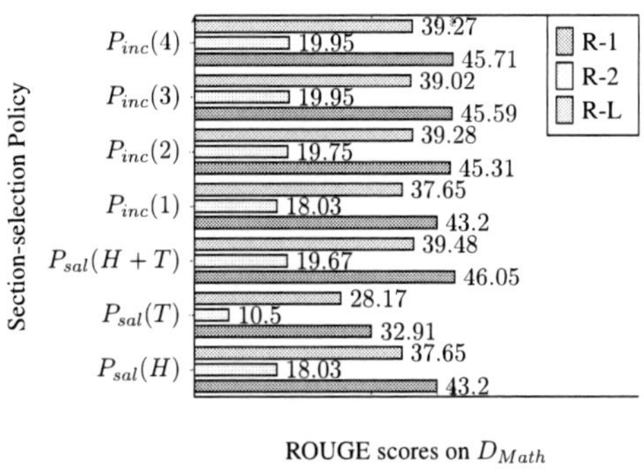

Figure 3: Comparison of section-selection strategies of *SEHY* paired with BigBird-large on the dataset D_{Math}.

performs better than $P_{inc}(k)$. Besides, from Table 4 and 5, we find that different pre-trained models do not significantly affect the performance of our approach for answering Q2.

Comparisons of *SEHY* with other approaches. We collect the best results of *SEHY* by using $P_{sal}(Sec)$ from Table 4 and 5 and compare them with those of other 12 summarization models (including 7 abstractive models, 3 extractive models and 2 hybrid models) on the full arXiv dataset D_{Full}. Evaluation results are presented in Table 6. Experimental findings are as follows: (1) even though not exceeding LongT5 (the current open-source SoTA), multiple variants of *SEHY* obtain competitive scores, i.e., the second and third highest scores on Learderboard. (2) all variants of *SEHY* except for the one paired with BART-base perform better than DANCER, which is the most related work to ours due to using section-selection strategies and training a hybrid model. (3) Apart from LongT5, *SEHY* obtains better results than the other compared models, demonstrating the effectiveness of our approach.

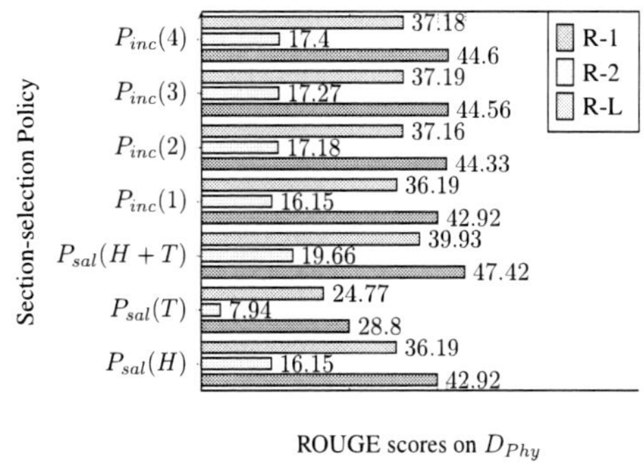

Figure 4: Comparison of section-selection strategies of *SEHY* paired with BigBird-large on the dataset D_{Phy}.

5 Conclusion

Long documents introduce a lot of noise to the summarization process and large parts of the document are not really key to its narrative and thus should be ignored. In this paper, we propose a simple yet effective hybrid model called *SEHY* for summarizing long scientific documents. In particular, we design two simple strategies for selecting sections: $P_{sal}(Sec)$ and $P_{inc}(k)$, and use strong abstractive models for generating the final summary. We conduct excessive experiments with multiple variants of *SEHY* on the full arXiv dataset publicly available and three disciplinary sub-datasets generated by ourselves. Experimental results show that $P_{sal}(Sec)$ is more effective than $P_{inc}(k)$ and our best models obtain the competitive results with regard to the current SoTA on arXiv.

Future works are as follows. First, we will evaluate the generalization of our approach on other academic-paper datasets such as ScisummNet (Yasunaga et al., 2019), which is a large-scale scientific paper summarization dataset with citation networks. Second, we will develop more flexible and sophisticated extraction strategies such as using reinforce learning (Chali and Mahmud, 2021), to further improve our approach's performance.

Acknowledgements

This paper is supported by Guangdong Basic and Applied Basic Research Foundation, China (Grant No. 2021A1515012556).

Ground-truth summary	We study a novel class of numerical integrators, the adapted nested force-gradient schemes, used within the molecular dynamics step of the hybrid monte carlo (hmc) algorithm. We test these methods in the schwinger model on the lattice, a well-known benchmark problem. We derive the analytical basis of nested force-gradient type methods and demonstrate the advantage of the proposed approach, namely reduced computational costs compared with other numerical integration schemes in hmc.
Summary generated by T5-base	We present a novel class of numerical time integration schemes for the hybrid monte carlo algorithm (hmc), often used to study quantum chromodynamics (qcd) on the lattice. The adapted nested-force-gradient approach is applied to the model problem of quantum electrodynamics (qed) in two dimensions, the schwinger model. We compare the behavior of the adapted nested-force-gradient approach and the adapted version introduced in @xcite. We investigate the computational costs needed to perform numerical calculations, as well as the effort required to achieve a satisfactory acceptance rate during the hmc evolution. We compare the behavior of the nested-force-gradient approach and the adapted version introduced in @xcite.
Summary generated by BART-base	We consider the hybrid monte carlo algorithm (hmc), often used to study quantum chromodynamics (qcd) on the lattice. We compare the behavior of numerical time integration schemes currently used for hmc with the nested force-gradient integrator and the adapted version introduced in @xcite. We investigate the computational costs needed to perform numerical calculations, as well as the effort required to achieve a satisfactory acceptance rate during the hmc evolution. Our goal is to find a numerical scheme which would provide a sufficiently high acceptance rate while not drastically increasing the simulation time.
Summary generated by LED-base	We present the nested force - gradient approach and its adapted version applied to a model problem in quantum field theory, the schwinger model. We investigate the computational costs needed to perform numerical calculations, as well as the effort required to achieve a satisfactory acceptance rate during the hmc evolution. We also compare the behavior of the adapted force-gradient scheme with the existing ones and propose a novel class of numerical schemes which would provide a sufficiently high acceptance rate while not drastically increasing the simulation time.
Summary generated by Pegasus-large	The hybrid monte carlo algorithm (hmc), often used to study quantum chromodynamics (qcd) on the lattice, has proved to be an efficient numerical time integration scheme. Omelyan integration schemes of a force - gradient type have proved to be an efficient choice, since it is easy to obtain higher order schemes that demand a small additional computational effort. These schemes use higher - order information from force-gradient terms to both increase the convergence of the method and decrease the size of the leading error coefficient.
Summary generated by BigBird-large	We present a new class of numerical time integration schemes for the hybrid monte carlo algorithm, which are based on the idea of the nested force-gradient method. We compare the behavior of these new schemes with the standard hybrid monte carlo algorithm and discuss which scheme is most suitable for the simulation of the two-dimensional lattice schwinger model. Hybrid monte carlo algorithm, numerical time integration, nested force-gradient method.
Summary generated by BART-large	In this paper we present a new class of numerical schemes for the hybrid monte carlo algorithm (hmc), often used to study quantum chromodynamics (qcd) on the lattice, which are optimal in terms of computational costs per trajectory for a given acceptance rate. We compare the behavior of numerical time integration schemes currently used for hmc with the adapted nested force-gradient integrator and the adapted version introduced in @xcite. Our goal is to find a numerical scheme for the hmc algorithm which would provide a sufficiently high acceptance rate while not drastically increasing the simulation time. We chose the model problem of quantum electrodynamics (qed) in two dimensions, the schwinger model, since it is well-suited as a test case for new concepts and ideas which can be subsequently applied to more computationally demanding problems. As a lattice quantum field theory, it has many of the properties of more sophisticated models such as qcd, for example the numerical cost is still dominated by the fermion part of the action. The fact that this model, with far fewer degrees of freedom makes it the perfect choice for testing purposes.

Table 10: Examples of summaries generated by our models by using $P_{sal}(H+T)$. For the limitation of space, the original paper is omitted.

References

Mehdi Allahyari, Seyed Amin Pouriyeh, Mehdi Assefi, Saeid Safaei, Elizabeth D. Trippe, Juan B. Gutierrez, and Krys J. Kochut. 2017. Text summarization techniques: A brief survey. *CoRR*, abs/1707.02268.

Iz Beltagy, Matthew E. Peters, and Arman Cohan. 2020a. Longformer: The long-document transformer. *CoRR*, abs/2004.05150.

Iz Beltagy, Matthew E. Peters, and Arman Cohan. 2020b. Longformer: The long-document transformer. *CoRR*, abs/2004.05150.

Tian Cai, Mengjun Shen, Huailiang Peng, Lei Jiang, and Qiong Dai. 2019. Improving transformer with sequential context representations for abstractive text summarization. In *Natural Language Processing and Chinese Computing - 8th CCF International Conference, NLPCC 2019, Dunhuang, China, October 9-14, 2019, Proceedings, Part I*, volume 11838 of *Lecture Notes in Computer Science*, pages 512–524. Springer.

Yllias Chali and Asif Mahmud. 2021. Query-based summarization using reinforcement learning and transformer model. In *2021 IEEE 33rd International Conference on Tools with Artificial Intelligence (ICTAI)*, pages 129–136.

Arman Cohan, Franck Dernoncourt, Doo Soon Kim, Trung Bui, Seokhwan Kim, Walter Chang, and Nazli Goharian. 2018. A discourse-aware attention model for abstractive summarization of long documents. In *Proceedings of the 2018 Conference of the North American Chapter of the Association for Computational Linguistics: Human Language Technologies, NAACL-HLT, New Orleans, Louisiana, USA, June 1-6, 2018, Volume 2 (Short Papers)*, pages 615–621. Association for Computational Linguistics.

Zihang Dai, Zhilin Yang, Yiming Yang, Jaime G. Carbonell, Quoc Viet Le, and Ruslan Salakhutdinov. 2019. Transformer-xl: Attentive language models beyond a fixed-length context. In *Proceedings of the 57th Conference of the Association for Computational Linguistics, ACL 2019, Florence, Italy, July 28- August 2, 2019, Volume 1: Long Papers*, pages 2978–2988. Association for Computational Linguistics.

Samet Demir, Uras Mutlu, and Özgür Özdemir. 2019. Neural academic paper generation. *CoRR*, abs/1912.01982.

Jacob Devlin, Ming-Wei Chang, Kenton Lee, and Kristina Toutanova. 2019. BERT: pre-training of deep bidirectional transformers for language understanding. In *Proceedings of the 2019 Conference of the North American Chapter of the Association for Computational Linguistics: Human Language Technologies, NAACL-HLT 2019, Minneapolis, MN, USA, June 2-7, 2019, Volume 1 (Long and Short Papers)*, pages 4171–4186. Association for Computational Linguistics.

Günes Erkan and Dragomir R. Radev. 2011. Lexrank: Graph-based lexical centrality as salience in text summarization. *CoRR*, abs/1109.2128.

Alexios Gidiotis and Grigorios Tsoumakas. 2020. A divide-and-conquer approach to the summarization of long documents. *IEEE ACM Trans. Audio Speech Lang. Process.*, 28:3029–3040.

Mandy Guo, Joshua Ainslie, David C. Uthus, Santiago Ontañón, Jianmo Ni, Yun-Hsuan Sung, and Yinfei Yang. 2021. Longt5: Efficient text-to-text transformer for long sequences. *CoRR*, abs/2112.07916.

Sheena Kurian K and Sheena Mathew. 2020. Survey of scientific document summarization techniques. *Comput. Sci.*, 21(2).

Mike Lewis, Yinhan Liu, Naman Goyal, Marjan Ghazvininejad, Abdelrahman Mohamed, Omer Levy, Veselin Stoyanov, and Luke Zettlemoyer. 2020. BART: denoising sequence-to-sequence pre-training for natural language generation, translation, and comprehension. In *Proceedings of the 58th Annual Meeting of the Association for Computational Linguistics, ACL 2020, Online, July 5-10, 2020*, pages 7871–7880. Association for Computational Linguistics.

Chin-Yew Lin. 2004. ROUGE: A package for automatic evaluation of summaries. In *Text Summarization Branches Out*, pages 74–81, Barcelona, Spain. Association for Computational Linguistics.

Ramesh Nallapati, Feifei Zhai, and Bowen Zhou. 2017. Summarunner: A recurrent neural network based sequence model for extractive summarization of documents. In *Proceedings of the Thirty-First AAAI Conference on Artificial Intelligence, February 4-9, 2017, San Francisco, California, USA*, pages 3075–3081. AAAI Press.

Bo Pang, Erik Nijkamp, Wojciech Kryscinski, Silvio Savarese, Yingbo Zhou, and Caiming Xiong. 2022. Long document summarization with top-down and bottom-up inference. *CoRR*, abs/2203.07586.

Michal Pietruszka, Lukasz Borchmann, and Lukasz Garncarek. 2022. Sparsifying transformer models with trainable representation pooling. In *Proceedings of the 60th Annual Meeting of the Association for Computational Linguistics (Volume 1: Long Papers), ACL 2022, Dublin, Ireland, May 22-27, 2022*, pages 8616–8633. Association for Computational Linguistics.

Jonathan Pilault, Raymond Li, Sandeep Subramanian, and Chris Pal. 2020. On extractive and abstractive neural document summarization with transformer language models. In *Proceedings of the 2020 Conference on Empirical Methods in Natural Language Processing, EMNLP 2020, Online, November 16-20, 2020*, pages 9308–9319. Association for Computational Linguistics.

Alec Radford and Karthik Narasimhan. 2018. Improving language understanding by generative pre-training.

Colin Raffel, Noam Shazeer, Adam Roberts, Katherine Lee, Sharan Narang, Michael Matena, Yanqi Zhou, Wei Li, and Peter J. Liu. 2020a. Exploring the limits of transfer learning with a unified text-to-text transformer. *J. Mach. Learn. Res.*, 21:140:1–140:67.

Colin Raffel, Noam Shazeer, Adam Roberts, Katherine Lee, Sharan Narang, Michael Matena, Yanqi Zhou, Wei Li, and Peter J. Liu. 2020b. Exploring the limits of transfer learning with a unified text-to-text transformer. *J. Mach. Learn. Res.*, 21:140:1–140:67.

Tobias Rohde, Xiaoxia Wu, and Yinhan Liu. 2021. Hierarchical learning for generation with long source sequences. *CoRR*, abs/2104.07545.

Abigail See, Peter J. Liu, and Christopher D. Manning. 2017. Get to the point: Summarization with pointer-generator networks. In *Proceedings of the 55th Annual Meeting of the Association for Computational Linguistics, ACL 2017, Vancouver, Canada, July 30 - August 4, Volume 1: Long Papers*, pages 1073–1083. Association for Computational Linguistics.

Ashish Vaswani, Noam Shazeer, Niki Parmar, Jakob Uszkoreit, Llion Jones, Aidan N. Gomez, Lukasz Kaiser, and Illia Polosukhin. 2017. Attention is all you need. In *Advances in Neural Information Processing Systems 30: Annual Conference on Neural Information Processing Systems 2017, December 4-9, 2017, Long Beach, CA, USA*, pages 5998–6008.

Qingyun Wang, Lifu Huang, Zhiying Jiang, Kevin Knight, Heng Ji, Mohit Bansal, and Yi Luan. 2019. Paperrobot: Incremental draft generation of scientific ideas. In *Proceedings of the 57th Conference of the Association for Computational Linguistics, ACL 2019, Florence, Italy, July 28- August 2, 2019, Volume 1: Long Papers*, pages 1980–1991. Association for Computational Linguistics.

Qingyun Wang, Zhihao Zhou, Lifu Huang, Spencer Whitehead, Boliang Zhang, Heng Ji, and Kevin Knight. 2018. Paper abstract writing through editing mechanism. In *Proceedings of the 56th Annual Meeting of the Association for Computational Linguistics, ACL 2018, Melbourne, Australia, July 15-20, 2018, Volume 2: Short Papers*, pages 260–265. Association for Computational Linguistics.

Haoyang Wen, Anthony Ferritto, Heng Ji, Radu Florian, and Avi Sil. 2021. VAULT: variable unified long text representation for machine reading comprehension. In *Proceedings of the 59th Annual Meeting of the Association for Computational Linguistics and the 11th International Joint Conference on Natural Language Processing, ACL/IJCNLP 2021, (Volume 2: Short Papers), Virtual Event, August 1-6, 2021*, pages 1035–1042.

Wen Xiao and Giuseppe Carenini. 2020. Systematically exploring redundancy reduction in summarizing long documents. In *Proceedings of the 1st Conference of the Asia-Pacific Chapter of the Association for Computational Linguistics and the 10th International Joint Conference on Natural Language Processing, AACL/IJCNLP 2020, Suzhou, China, December 4-7, 2020*, pages 516–528. Association for Computational Linguistics.

Michihiro Yasunaga, Jungo Kasai, Rui Zhang, Alexander R. Fabbri, Irene Li, Dan Friedman, and Dragomir R. Radev. 2019. Scisummnet: A large annotated corpus and content-impact models for scientific paper summarization with citation networks. In *The Thirty-Third AAAI Conference on Artificial Intelligence, AAAI 2019, The Thirty-First Innovative Applications of Artificial Intelligence Conference, IAAI 2019, The Ninth AAAI Symposium on Educational Advances in Artificial Intelligence, EAAI 2019, Honolulu, Hawaii, USA, January 27 - February 1, 2019*, pages 7386–7393. AAAI Press.

Manzil Zaheer, Guru Guruganesh, Kumar Avinava Dubey, Joshua Ainslie, Chris Alberti, Santiago Ontañón, Philip Pham, Anirudh Ravula, Qifan Wang, Li Yang, and Amr Ahmed. 2020. Big bird: Transformers for longer sequences. In *Advances in Neural Information Processing Systems 33: Annual Conference on Neural Information Processing Systems 2020, NeurIPS 2020, December 6-12, 2020, virtual.*

Jingqing Zhang, Yao Zhao, Mohammad Saleh, and Peter J. Liu. 2020. PEGASUS: pre-training with extracted gap-sentences for abstractive summarization. In *Proceedings of the 37th International Conference on Machine Learning, ICML 2020, 13-18 July 2020, Virtual Event*, volume 119 of *Proceedings of Machine Learning Research*, pages 11328–11339. PMLR.

PLATO-XL: Exploring the Large-scale Pre-training of Dialogue Generation

Siqi Bao* Huang He* Fan Wang* Hua Wu* Haifeng Wang
Wenquan Wu Zhihua Wu Zhen Guo Hua Lu Xinxian Huang
Xin Tian Xinchao Xu Yingzhan Lin Zheng-Yu Niu
Baidu Inc., China
{baosiqi, hehuang, wang.fan, wu_hua}@baidu.com

Abstract

To explore the limit of dialogue generation pre-training, we present the models of PLATO-XL with up to 11 billion parameters, trained on both Chinese and English social media conversations. To train such large models, we adopt the architecture of unified transformer with high computation and parameter efficiency. In addition, we carry out multi-party aware pre-training to better distinguish the characteristic information in social media conversations. With such designs, PLATO-XL successfully achieves superior performances as compared to other approaches in both Chinese and English chitchat. We further explore the capacity of PLATO-XL on other conversational tasks, such as knowledge grounded dialogue and task-oriented conversation. The experimental results indicate that PLATO-XL obtains state-of-the-art results across multiple conversational tasks, verifying its potential as a foundation model of conversational AI.

1 Introduction

The efficacy of the pre-training paradigm, where large-scale transformer models are trained with massive plain texts, has been widely recognized in natural language processing (Devlin et al., 2019; Radford et al., 2018). To further boost the performance of these language models, there is a trend to enlarge the model size, dataset size, and the amount of compute used for training (Raffel et al., 2020; Kaplan et al., 2020). Particularly, the GPT-3 model with 175B parameters demonstrates strong zero-shot or few-shot learning capacities without task-specific fine-tuning on downstream tasks (Brown et al., 2020).

Distinct from the general language models, dialogue generation models are usually pre-trained with human-like conversations collected from social media. DialoGPT (Zhang et al., 2020a) attempts to train dialogue models with Reddit comments on the basis of pre-trained language models. More recently developed models, like Meena (Adiwardana et al., 2020), Blender (Roller et al., 2021), and PLATO-2 (Bao et al., 2021), achieve substantial performance improvements on multi-turn conversations. These models have been scaled up to billions of parameters and taken advantage of many more social media conversations for pre-training. Nevertheless, in dialogue generation, there still lacks a clear conclusion about the correlation between model scale and conversation quality. For instance, DialoGPT has three model sizes: 117M, 345M, and 762M, where the 345M one obtains the best performance in their evaluations. Meanwhile, the human evaluations of Blender reveal that the 2.7B model achieves better performance as compared to the one with 9.4B parameters.

In this paper, we argue that the conversation quality may keep benefiting from the enlarged model scale with appropriate pre-training designs. To this end, we explore the large-scale pre-training of dialogue generation models with up to 11B model parameters, namely PLATO-XL. To train such a large model, we adopt the architecture of unified transformer with high computation and parameter efficiency. In addition, we carry out multi-party aware pre-training to better distinguish the characteristic information in social media conversations. With such designs, PLATO-XL achieves superior performances as compared to other approaches in both Chinese and English chitchat. More specifically, PLATO-XL shows a strong capability of absorbing common knowledge within its huge parameters; therefore, it is able to alleviate the well-known hallucination problem[1]. Besides, thanks to the multi-party aware pre-training, PLATO-XL

*Equal contribution.

[1]Generation models might generate some plausible statements with factual errors, also known as "hallucination" problem (Marcus, 2020). This problem can be alleviated by expanding model parameters (Roberts et al., 2020) or incorporating external non-parametric memories (Lewis et al., 2020).

Findings of the Association for Computational Linguistics: AACL-IJCNLP 2022, pages 107–118
November 20–23, 2022.

effectively reduces the inconsistency phenomenon in multi-turn conversations.

In addition to open-domain chitchat discussed above, there are two other common conversational tasks (Gao et al., 2018): knowledge grounded dialogue, and task-oriented conversation. In the experiments, we also explore the ability of PLATO-XL as the foundation model of conversational AI. Our experimental results indicate that PLATO-XL is able to outperform other dialogue generation models across multiple conversational tasks. We have released our source code together with the English model at GitHub[2], hoping to facilitate frontier research in dialogue generation.

2 Related Work

2.1 Large-scale Pre-trained Language Models

The pre-training paradigm has brought substantial performance improvements in natural language processing, where large-scale transformer models are pre-trained with massive plain texts. BERT (Devlin et al., 2019) learns to capture the deep bi-directional representation for the input context and achieves remarkable breakthroughs in natural language understanding. GPT (Radford et al., 2018) and GPT-2 (Radford et al., 2019) are typical models in natural language generation, which extract uni-directional representation and perform auto-regressive generation. To further boost the performance of language models, there is a trend to enlarge the model size, dataset size, and the amount of compute used for training (Raffel et al., 2020; Kaplan et al., 2020). Particularly, GPT-3 (Brown et al., 2020) scales up to 175B parameters and demonstrates strong ability in the zero/few-shot settings. Recently, some larger pre-trained language models are presented with superior performance, including the 178B parameter Jurassic-1 (Lieber et al., 2021), the 280B parameter Gopher (Rae et al., 2021), the 530B parameter Megatron-Turing NLG (Smith et al., 2022), and the 540B parameter PaLM (Chowdhery et al., 2022).

Besides the above English models, there are some large-scale Chinese language models. CPM (Zhang et al., 2020b) maintains a similar model architecture as GPT with 2.6B parameters. CPM-2 (Zhang et al., 2021) scales up to 11B parameters and employs knowledge inheritance from existing models to accelerate the pre-training process. PanGu-α (Zeng et al., 2021) is a huge model, with up to 200B parameters. The effective training is carried out on a cluster of 2048 Ascend 910 AI processors with multi-dimension parallelisms and topology-aware scheduling. ERNIE 3.0 (Sun et al., 2021) proposes a unified framework that integrates both auto-encoding and auto-regressive networks, where knowledge graphs are also encoded into pre-training for enhanced representation. Empirical results show that the 260B parameter ERNIE 3.0 Titan (Wang et al., 2021) achieves superior performance on 68 Chinese NLP tasks.

2.2 Pre-trained Dialogue Models

Unlike the plain texts for general language models, for dialogue generation pre-training, human-like conversations are collected from social media, such as Twitter, Reddit, Sina Weibo, Baidu Tieba, etc. DialoGPT (Zhang et al., 2020a) attempts to train dialogue models with Reddit comments on the basis of pre-trained language models. Meena (Adiwardana et al., 2020) carries out the pre-training of dialogue generation directly with more social media conversations, and this 2.6B parameter model achieves significant improvements in multi-turn conversation quality. Blender (Roller et al., 2021) proposes to fine-tune the pre-trained dialogue model with human-annotated datasets to emphasize the conversational skills of engagingness, knowledge, empathy, and personality. In addition, to mitigate the safe response problem, PLATO (Bao et al., 2020) and PLATO-2 (Bao et al., 2021) propose to encode the discrete latent variable into transformer for diverse response generation. Recently, the 137B parameter LaMDA (Thoppilan et al., 2022) has been introduced particularly for dialogue applications, which is the largest dialogue model in English.

Besides the above English models, PLATO-2 has one Chinese dialogue model of 363 million parameters, exhibiting notable improvements over the classical chatbot of XiaoIce (Zhou et al., 2020). There are some other Chinese dialogue models on a similar modest scale, including CDial-GPT (Wang et al., 2020) and ProphetNet-X (Qi et al., 2021). Recently, one Chinese dialogue model of EVA (Zhou et al., 2021) has been developed under the architecture of Seq2Seq, with up to 2.8B parameters. In this paper, we will introduce the 11B parameter model of PLATO-XL, trained on both Chinese and English social media conversations. To our

[2] https://github.com/PaddlePaddle/Knover/tree/develop/projects/PLATO-XL

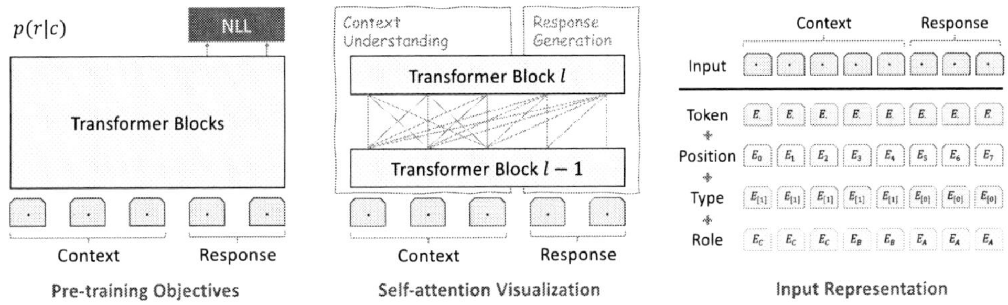

Figure 1: Network overview of PLATO-XL.

knowledge, PLATO-XL is the largest pre-trained dialogue model in Chinese so far.

3 PLATO-XL

3.1 Network Overview

The network overview of PLATO-XL is shown in Figure 1, with transformer blocks as the backbone. For the sake of efficient training on a large scale, PLATO-XL keeps the adoption of the unified transformer (Bao et al., 2020, 2021) (also known as PrefixLM (Raffel et al., 2020; Dong et al., 2019)) instead of the typical encoder-decoder for dialogue generation. The advantages brought by the unified transformer architecture are two-fold: computation and parameter efficiency. Firstly, given the conversation samples of variable lengths, it is necessary to pad them into a certain length in the training process, which inevitably incurs massive invalid computations. As suggested in fairseq (Ott et al., 2019), the amount of padding can be minimized by grouping the input with similar lengths. By performing effective sorting on the concatenated input, invalid computations caused by padding can be reduced significantly with the unified transformer. Secondly, through the flexible mechanism of the self-attention mask, the two tasks of dialogue context understanding and response generation are modeled simultaneously with shared parameters. As such, the unified transformer is more parameter-efficient than the encoder-decoder network (Bao et al., 2021; Du et al., 2021).

In PLATO-XL, the pre-training objective is to minimize the negative log-likelihood (NLL) loss:

$$\begin{aligned}\mathcal{L}_{NLL} &= -\mathbb{E}_{(c,r)\sim D}\ [\log\ p_\theta(r|c)] \\ &= -\mathbb{E}_{(c,r)\sim D}\left[\sum_{t=1}^{T}\ \log\ p_\theta(r_t|c, r_{<t})\right],\end{aligned}$$

where θ refers to the trainable parameters of the dialogue generation model and D stands for the pre-training data. The input to the network is a pair of dialogue context c and target response r. T is the length of the target response and $r_{<t}$ denotes previously generated words. As shown in Figure 1, the input representation is calculated as the sum of the corresponding token, position, type, and role embeddings. The token and position embeddings are commonly used in pre-training models. The type embedding is employed to differentiate the segments of dialogue context and target response, which is also extensible for other input sources, such as persona profiles or grounded knowledge used in conversations. The role embedding is used to distinguish the characters in the multi-turn conversations, which will be explained in detail in the following subsection.

3.2 Multi-Party Aware Pre-training

As discussed in the related work, general language models are pre-trained with massive plain texts, where each training sample is usually created by one single author or user. In comparison, the dialogue models are commonly pre-trained with human-like conversations collected from public social media, where one toy example is provided in Figure 2 for illustration. Several properties of social media conversations can be observed from this example: 1) there are multi-level comments appended to respond to the contexts; 2) multiple users are actively involved in the discussion. The corresponding message tree of these comments is shown on the right-hand side. The comments along the path from the root node to any tree node can be formulated as one training sample of dialogue context and target response. However, with these social media conversations, the learned models tend to mix information from multiple characters in the context and have difficulties generating consistent responses.

To tackle the above problem, PLATO (Bao et al.,

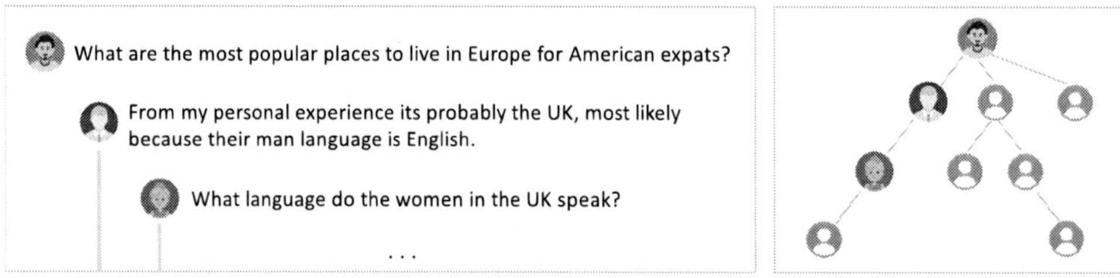

Figure 2: Left: one toy example to illustrate social media conversations. Right: corresponding message tree.

2020) first introduces the role embedding into the transformer to distinguish the characters in the dialogue context. While there is an underlying assumption in PLATO that the conversation is carried out within two characters and the role embedding is assigned alternatively. Although it is generally tenable in human-annotated conversations, things get complicated with social media conversations. As suggested in the former works of RNN-based response selection (Ouchi and Tsuboi, 2016; Zhang et al., 2018), user embedding is an effective technique for speaker and addressee identification in multi-party conversation. In PLATO-XL, we further encode the multi-party aware role embedding in the pre-training of dialogue generation. The target response and utterances in the context by the same user will be assigned with the role embedding of E_A. For the rest utterances, the role embedding will be assigned in a relative order according to the user ids, such as E_B, E_C, etc. This multi-party aware pre-training helps the model distinguish the information in the context and maintain consistency in dialogue generation.

3.3 Pre-training Settings

For the pre-training corpora, the English conversation samples are extracted from Reddit comments, which are collected by a third party and made publicly available at pushshift.io (Baumgartner et al., 2020). To guarantee the data quality, we follow the elaborate cleaning process as PLATO-2 (Bao et al., 2021). After filtering, the data is split into training and validation sets in chronological order. The training set contains 811M (context, response) samples, ranging from December 2005 to December 2019. For the validation set, 0.2M samples are selected from the rest data after December 2019. The English vocabulary contains 8K BPE tokens (Sennrich et al., 2016), constructed with the SentencePiece library. The Chinese pre-training data is collected from public domain social media. After filtering, there are 1.2B (context, response) samples in the training set. As for the Chinese vocabulary, it contains 30K BPE tokens.

PLATO-XL employs the same network architecture for the Chinese and English models, with up to 11 billion parameters. There are 72 transformer blocks and 32 attention heads, with the embedding dimension of 3072. The hidden dimension of the feedforward layer is set to 18432. Pre-normalization connection and scaled initialization (Radford et al., 2019) are adopted for stable training. The main hyper-parameters used in the pre-training are listed as follows. The maximum sequence length for the dialogue context and target response is set to 896 and 128, respectively. We use Adam (Kingma and Ba, 2015) as the optimizer with a learning rate scheduler of linear warmup and decay. The warmup stage covers the first 200 steps, and the peak learning rate is 8e-5.

The implementation of PLATO-XL is based on the PaddlePaddle platform. And the training was carried out on 256 Nvidia Tesla V100 32G GPU cards. Given the limited memory of each device, vanilla data parallelism cannot support the training of such a model with up to 11 billion parameters. As such, we adopt the sharded data parallelism (Rajbhandari et al., 2020) to eliminate memory redundancies by partitioning the optimizer states, gradients, and parameters across multiple devices. This kind of distributed training helps maintain low communication volume and high computational granularity. In addition, to train the model with a relatively large batch size, we further employ gradient checkpointing (Chen et al., 2016) to trade computation for memory. In PLATO-XL, each model was trained for a total of 150B tokens, with a batch size of 2M tokens.

4 Experiments

4.1 Evaluation Settings

4.1.1 Compared Approaches

To evaluate the performance of PLATO-XL, we compare it with the following English and Chinese dialogue generation models in the experiments.

- DialoGPT (Zhang et al., 2020a) is trained on the basis of GPT-2 (Radford et al., 2019) using Reddit comments. There are three model sizes: 117M, 345M, and 762M. Since the 345M parameter model obtains the best performance in their evaluations, this version is compared.
- Blender (Roller et al., 2021) is first trained using Reddit comments and then fine-tuned with human-annotated conversations – BST (Smith et al., 2020), to help emphasize desirable conversational skills of engagingness, knowledge, empathy, and personality. Blender has three model sizes: 90M, 2.7B, and 9.4B. Since the 2.7B parameter model obtains the best performance in their evaluations, this version is compared.
- PLATO-2 (Bao et al., 2021) is trained via curriculum learning, where a coarse-grained model is first learned for general response generation and a fine-grained model is further learned for diverse response generation. The English model of PLATO-2 is pre-trained with Reddit comments and then fine-tuned with BST conversations. There are 1.6B parameters in this model. PLATO-2 also has one Chinese model of 336M parameters, trained with 1.2B social media conversation samples.
- CDial-GPT (Wang et al., 2020) is trained on the basis of a Chinese GPT model using LCCC conversations. There are 95.5M parameters in this model.
- ProphetNet-X (Qi et al., 2021) is a family of pre-trained models on various languages and domains. ProphetNet-X includes one Chinese dialogue generation model trained on social media conversations collected from Douban group[3]. There are 379M parameters in this model.
- EVA (Zhou et al., 2021) is a 2.8B parameter Chinese dialogue generation model trained with the WDC-Dialogue, which includes 1.4B conversation samples collected from social media.

In addition to the above models, PLATO-XL is also compared with the following commercial chatbots in Chinese: Microsoft XiaoIce (Zhou et al., 2020), Turing Robot[4], Tmall Genie[5], and Xiao AI[6]. The official platform/API is used in the interactions with XiaoIce and Turing. As there is no public API for Tmall Genie or Xiao AI, voice interactions are carried out instead with these smart speakers.

4.1.2 Evaluation Metrics

As suggested in the empirical study (Liu et al., 2016), the correlation between automatic metrics and human judgments is weak in open-domain dialogue generation. Therefore, we mainly rely on human evaluations in the experiments of open-domain conversation. Crowd-sourcing workers are asked to evaluate the conversation quality on the following aspects.

- Coherence is an utterance-level metric, measuring whether the response is relevant and consistent with the context.
- Informativeness is also an utterance-level metric, evaluating whether the response is informative or not given the context.
- Engagingness is a dialogue-level metric, assessing whether the annotator would like to talk with the speaker for a long conversation.

The scale of the above metrics is [0, 1, 2]. The higher score, the better. To further analyze the conversation quality, two more fine-grained metrics are included in the evaluation.

- Inconsistency is one fine-grained metric for coherence evaluation, checking whether the response conflicts with the context.
- Hallucination is one fine-grained metric for informativeness evaluation, checking whether the response contains any factual errors.

The scale of inconsistency and hallucination is [0, 1]. The lower score, the better. Score details about these metrics are provided in the Appendix.

4.2 Experimental Results

4.2.1 Self-Chat Evaluation

Self-chats have been widely used in the evaluation of dialogue systems (Li et al., 2016; Bao et al., 2019; Roller et al., 2021), where a model plays the role of both partners in the conversation. Following the experimental settings in PLATO-2, the interactive conversation is started with a randomly selected topic, and the model performs self-chats for five rounds. Then 50 conversations are selected

[3] https://www.douban.com/group/

[4] http://www.turingapi.com/

[5] https://bot.tmall.com/

[6] https://xiaoai.mi.com/

English Models	# Params	Coherence	Inconsistency↓	Informativeness	Hallucination↓	Engagingness
DialoGPT	345M	0.792	0.508	0.692	0.516	0.220
PLATO-2	1.6B	1.792	0.068	1.732	0.152	1.540
Blender	2.7B	1.768	0.084	1.692	0.128	1.500
PLATO-XL	11B	**1.908**	**0.024**	**1.800**	**0.024**	**1.800**

Table 1: English self-chat evaluation results, with best value written in bold.

Chinese Models	# Params	Coherence	Inconsistency↓	Informativeness	Hallucination↓	Engagingness
CDial-GPT	95M	1.188	0.104	0.908	0.388	0.460
PLATO-2	336M	1.876	0.016	1.872	0.056	1.880
ProphetNet-X	379M	1.344	0.048	1.216	0.296	0.940
EVA	2.8B	1.196	0.032	1.016	0.356	0.600
PLATO-XL	11B	**1.952**	**0.004**	**1.948**	**0.016**	**1.940**

Table 2: Chinese self-chat evaluation results, with best value written in bold.

and distributed to crowd-sourcing workers for evaluation. Each conversation is evaluated by three annotators, and the final score is determined through majority voting. The English and Chinese self-chat evaluation results are summarized in Table 1 and 2, respectively. These results indicate that PLATO-XL is able to produce coherent, informative, and engaging conversations. Particularly, both the inconsistency and hallucination problems of dialogue generation are alleviated remarkably with PLATO-XL. As compared to other approaches, the 11B parameter model achieves superior performances in both Chinese and English chitchat.

4.2.2 Human-Bot Chat Evaluation

Besides the above public models, PLATO-XL is compared with the following commercial chatbots in Chinese: Microsoft XiaoIce, Turing Robot, Tmall Genie, and Xiao AI. As most of them do not have publicly available APIs, we ask our in-house annotation team to collect the human-bot conversations. The interactive conversation also starts with a pre-selected topic and continues for 7-14 rounds. 20 diverse topics are extracted from the high-frequency topics of a commercial chatbot, including travel, movie, hobby, and so on. The collected human-bot conversations are distributed to crowd-sourcing workers for evaluation. The human-bot chat evaluation results are summarized in Table 3. These results indicate that PLATO-XL achieves significant improvements over the rest of the commercial chatbots across all the human evaluation metrics.

4.2.3 Case Analysis

To further analyze the model's features, two English self-chat examples by PLATO-XL are provided in Figure 3. These examples demonstrate that PLATO-XL is able to conduct coherent, informative, and engaging conversations. The in-depth discussions on nuclear energy and Mariana Trench indicate that massive knowledge has been absorbed implicitly in the tremendous parameters. Moreover, from the self-chat example on the left-hand side, it can be observed that the model maintains well the characteristics of each participant. P2 seems like a curious learner, tending to ask many questions. P1 is a knowledgeable expert, providing the answers in detail but with a little impatience. The model is capable of generating responses with good consistency on content and style, thanks to the multi-party aware pre-training.

One Chinese human-bot chat example by PLATO-XL is provided in Figure 4, with original interactive logs shown on the left and translated logs on the right. In this example, PLATO-XL even exhibits advanced conversational skills, such as compliment and eloquence. The model replies to the other partner with sweet words from romantic lyrics and provides reasonable explanations to the queries.

4.3 Explorations on other Conversational Tasks

In addition to open-domain chitchat, there are two other common conversational tasks (Gao et al., 2018): knowledge grounded dialogue, and task-

Chinese Chatbots	# Params	Coherence	Inconsistency↓	Informativeness	Hallucination↓	Engagingness
XiaoIce	-	1.245	0.119	1.063	0.340	1.050
Turing	-	1.413	0.048	1.329	0.287	1.250
Tmall Genie	-	1.359	0.052	1.242	0.301	0.700
Xiao AI	-	1.544	0.050	1.413	0.194	1.400
PLATO-XL	11B	**1.905**	**0.012**	**1.905**	**0.042**	**1.950**

Table 3: Chinese human-bot chat evaluation results, with best value written in bold.

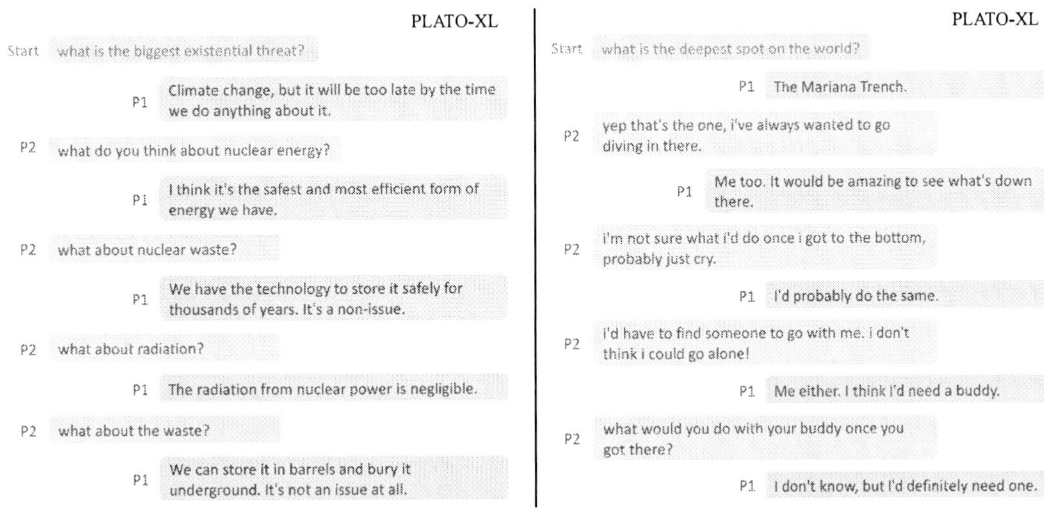

Figure 3: Cherry-picked English self-chat examples by PLATO-XL.

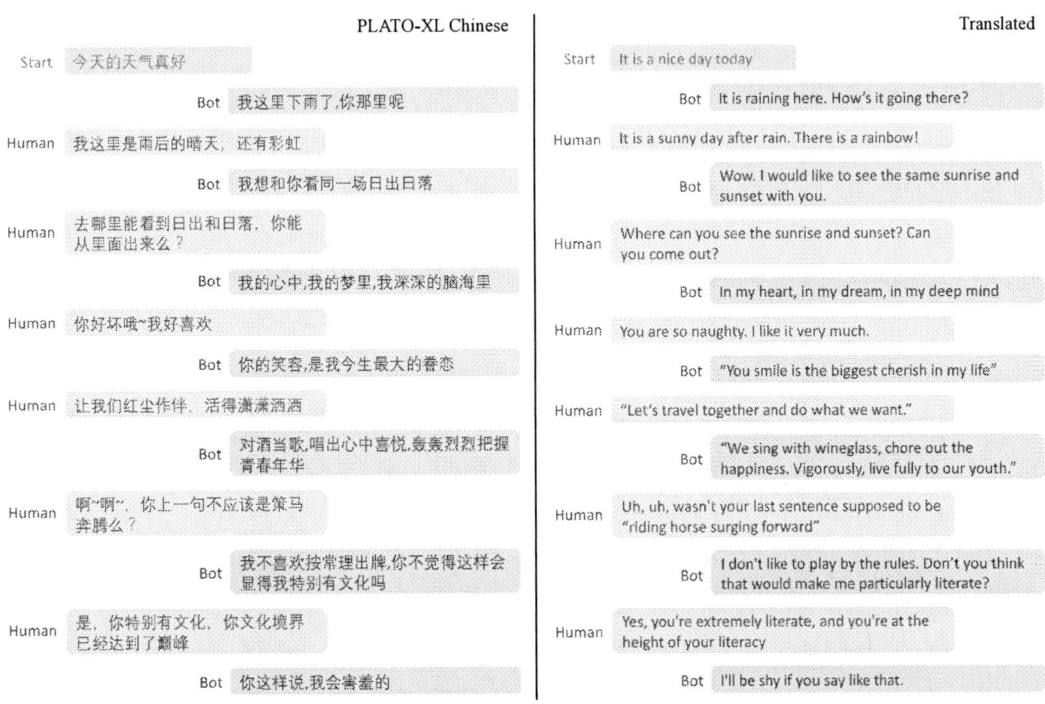

Figure 4: Cherry-picked Chinese human-bot chat example by PLATO-XL.

Task	Dataset		Metric	Previous SoTA	PLATO-XL
Knowledge Grounded Dialogue	DuConv	Zh	F1	45.09 (GOKC)	**47.14**
	DSTC9-Track1	En	Rouge_L	37.77 (Knover)	**39.39**
Task-oriented Conversation	MultiWOZ 2.2 DST	En	Joint Goal Acc.	58.04 (DSS-DST)	**58.79**

Table 4: Automatic evaluation results on knowledge grounded and task-oriented conversations, with best value written in bold.

oriented conversation. As such, in the experiments, we also explore the ability of PLATO-XL on these conversational tasks.

4.3.1 Task Descriptions

The experiments are carried out on the following conversational tasks:

- DuConv (Wu et al., 2019) is one Chinese knowledge grounded conversation dataset collected in LUGE[7]. DuConv focuses on proactive conversations towards pre-defined goals and includes 30K dialogues based on movie knowledge graphs.
- DSTC9-Track1 (Kim et al., 2020) aims to incorporate external knowledge resources to reply user's out-of-API-coverage queries and augments the dataset of MultiWOZ 2.1 (Eric et al., 2020) with 22K knowledge grounded conversation turns. There are three tasks in DSTC9-Track1: knowledge-seeking turn detection, knowledge selection, and knowledge-grounded response generation. In the experiments, we consider the task of knowledge-grounded response generation.
- MultiWOZ 2.2 (Zang et al., 2020) is a polished version of MultiWOZ 2.1, including 10K task-oriented conversations across multiple domains. In the experiments, we consider the classical task of dialog state tracking (DST).

4.3.2 Automatic Evaluation

The fine-tuning experiments of PLATO-XL are carried out on these conversational tasks, with automatic evaluation results summarized in Table 4.

- In DuConv, the model needs to generate the response given related knowledge triplets and lead the conversation to a pre-defined goal. By expanding the network input of PLATO-XL, the conversational goal and knowledge triplets can be easily encoded and grounded for response generation. Compared to the previous state-of-the-art approach – GOKC (Bai et al., 2021), PLATO-XL improves the F1 value by 2.05 points.
- In DSTC9-Track1, we focus on the evaluation of knowledge grounded response generation. In the experiments, we train and test the models with golden retrieved knowledge snippets. The winner approach in DSTC9-Track1 – Knover (He et al., 2021), is also developed on pre-trained dialogue models. The comparison reveals that PLATO-XL further improves the performance by 1.62 points.
- In MultiWOZ 2.2, PLATO-XL learns to generate the dialog state directly given the context. Compared to the previous SoTA approach – DSS-DST (Guo et al., 2021), PLATO-XL further improves the joint goal accuracy to 58.79.

The superior performance of PLATO-XL on multiple conversational tasks verifies its potential as a foundation model of conversational AI.

5 Conclusion

In this paper, we explore the large-scale pre-training of dialogue generation and present the 11 billion parameter model of PLATO-XL. Experimental results demonstrate that PLATO-XL achieves superior performance as compared with other approaches in both Chinese and English chitchat. Particularly, the problems of hallucination and inconsistency are alleviated remarkably in PLATO-XL, mainly attributed to the implicit knowledge absorbed in the tremendous parameters and the multi-party aware pre-training. Besides the open-domain conversation, PLATO-XL obtains state-of-the-art results on multiple knowledge grounded and task-oriented conversations, verifying its capacity as a foundation model of conversational AI.

6 Ethical Considerations

With the development of large-scale pre-training models, there raise several ethical concerns, including toxic and biased language. In PLATO-XL, several strategies are explored to boost the safety of open-domain chatbots. In the pre-processing stage, elaborate data cleaning is carried out to remove

[7]LUGE, Language Understanding and Generation Evaluation Benchmarks, https://www.luge.ai/

offensive messages from the training corpora. In the post-processing stage, we employ one classifier to detect sensitive topics from users' utterances and will return canned responses for these contexts. We adopt another classifier to filter out potentially unsafe candidates from generated responses. Moreover, we carry out regular adversarial tests with our in-house data specialists and update the safety classifiers with newly collected samples. Given that the objectives of safety differ across language contexts, we design and employ corresponding strategies for English and Chinese conversations. While even with these strategies, the bot might still generate biased or unsafe statements under sensitive topics or adversarial contexts. Future work will put more emphasis on the fairness and safety of open-domain chatbots.

Acknowledgments

We would like to thank Jingzhou He, Tingting Li, and Shiwei Huang for the help on resource coordination; Jianzhong Liang, and Long Li for the support on PaddlePaddle implementation; Baotong Luo, and Dou Hong for the assistance with infrastructure. This work was supported by the Natural Key Research and Development Project of China (No. 2018AAA0101900).

References

Daniel Adiwardana, Minh-Thang Luong, David R So, Jamie Hall, Noah Fiedel, Romal Thoppilan, Zi Yang, Apoorv Kulshreshtha, Gaurav Nemade, Yifeng Lu, and Quoc V. Le. 2020. Towards a human-like open-domain chatbot. *arXiv preprint arXiv:2001.09977*.

Jiaqi Bai, Ze Yang, Xinnian Liang, Wei Wang, and Zhoujun Li. 2021. Learning to copy coherent knowledge for response generation. In *Proceedings of the AAAI Conference on Artificial Intelligence*, volume 35, pages 12535–12543.

Siqi Bao, Huang He, Fan Wang, Rongzhong Lian, and Hua Wu. 2019. Know more about each other: Evolving dialogue strategy via compound assessment. In *Proceedings of the 57th Annual Meeting of the Association for Computational Linguistics*, pages 5382–5391.

Siqi Bao, Huang He, Fan Wang, Hua Wu, and Haifeng Wang. 2020. PLATO: Pre-trained dialogue generation model with discrete latent variable. In *Proceedings of the 58th Annual Meeting of the Association for Computational Linguistics*, pages 85–96.

Siqi Bao, Huang He, Fan Wang, Hua Wu, Haifeng Wang, Wenquan Wu, Zhen Guo, Zhibin Liu, and Xinchao Xu. 2021. PLATO-2: Towards building an open-domain chatbot via curriculum learning. In *Findings of the Association for Computational Linguistics: ACL-IJCNLP 2021*, pages 2513–2525.

Jason Baumgartner, Savvas Zannettou, Brian Keegan, Megan Squire, and Jeremy Blackburn. 2020. The pushshift reddit dataset. In *Proceedings of the International AAAI Conference on Web and Social Media*, volume 14, pages 830–839.

Tom B Brown, Benjamin Mann, Nick Ryder, Melanie Subbiah, Jared Kaplan, Prafulla Dhariwal, Arvind Neelakantan, Pranav Shyam, Girish Sastry, Amanda Askell, Sandhini Agarwal, Ariel Herbert-Voss, Gretchen Krueger, Tom Henighan, Rewon Child, Aditya Ramesh, Daniel Ziegler, Jeffrey Wu, Clemens Winter, Chris Hesse, Mark Chen, Eric Sigler, Mateusz Litwin, Scott Gray, Benjamin Chess, Jack Clark, Christopher Berner, Sam McCandlish, Alec Radford, Ilya Sutskever, and Dario Amodei. 2020. Language models are few-shot learners. In *Advances in Neural Information Processing Systems*, pages 1877–1901.

Tianqi Chen, Bing Xu, Chiyuan Zhang, and Carlos Guestrin. 2016. Training deep nets with sublinear memory cost. *arXiv preprint arXiv:1604.06174*.

Aakanksha Chowdhery, Sharan Narang, Jacob Devlin, Maarten Bosma, Gaurav Mishra, Adam Roberts, Paul Barham, Hyung Won Chung, Charles Sutton, Sebastian Gehrmann, et al. 2022. Palm: Scaling language modeling with pathways. *arXiv preprint arXiv:2204.02311*.

Jacob Devlin, Ming-Wei Chang, Kenton Lee, and Kristina Toutanova. 2019. BERT: Pre-training of deep bidirectional transformers for language understanding. In *Proceedings of the 2019 Conference of the North American Chapter of the Association for Computational Linguistics: Human Language Technologies*, pages 4171–4186.

Li Dong, Nan Yang, Wenhui Wang, Furu Wei, Xiaodong Liu, Yu Wang, Jianfeng Gao, Ming Zhou, and Hsiao-Wuen Hon. 2019. Unified language model pre-training for natural language understanding and generation. In *Advances in Neural Information Processing Systems*, pages 13063–13075.

Zhengxiao Du, Yujie Qian, Xiao Liu, Ming Ding, Jiezhong Qiu, Zhilin Yang, and Jie Tang. 2021. All nlp tasks are generation tasks: A general pretraining framework. *arXiv preprint arXiv:2103.10360*.

Mihail Eric, Rahul Goel, Shachi Paul, Abhishek Sethi, Sanchit Agarwal, Shuyang Gao, Adarsh Kumar, Anuj Goyal, Peter Ku, and Dilek Hakkani-Tur. 2020. MultiWOZ 2.1: A consolidated multi-domain dialogue dataset with state corrections and state tracking baselines. In *Proceedings of the 12th Language Resources and Evaluation Conference*, pages 422–428.

Jianfeng Gao, Michel Galley, and Lihong Li. 2018. Neural approaches to conversational AI. In *Proceedings of the 56th Annual Meeting of the Association for Computational Linguistics: Tutorial Abstracts*, pages 2–7.

Jinyu Guo, Kai Shuang, Jijie Li, and Zihan Wang. 2021. Dual slot selector via local reliability verification for dialogue state tracking. In *Proceedings of the 59th Annual Meeting of the Association for Computational Linguistics and the 11th International Joint Conference on Natural Language Processing*, pages 139–151.

Huang He, Hua Lu, Siqi Bao, Fan Wang, Hua Wu, Zhengyu Niu, and Haifeng Wang. 2021. Learning to select external knowledge with multi-scale negative sampling. *arXiv preprint arXiv:2102.02096*.

Jared Kaplan, Sam McCandlish, Tom Henighan, Tom B Brown, Benjamin Chess, Rewon Child, Scott Gray, Alec Radford, Jeffrey Wu, and Dario Amodei. 2020. Scaling laws for neural language models. *arXiv preprint arXiv:2001.08361*.

Seokhwan Kim, Mihail Eric, Karthik Gopalakrishnan, Behnam Hedayatnia, Yang Liu, and Dilek Hakkani-Tur. 2020. Beyond domain APIs: Task-oriented conversational modeling with unstructured knowledge access. In *Proceedings of the 21th Annual Meeting of the Special Interest Group on Discourse and Dialogue*, pages 278–289.

Diederik P Kingma and Jimmy Ba. 2015. Adam: A method for stochastic optimization. In *International Conference on Learning Representations*.

Patrick Lewis, Ethan Perez, Aleksandra Piktus, Fabio Petroni, Vladimir Karpukhin, Naman Goyal, Heinrich Küttler, Mike Lewis, Wen-tau Yih, Tim Rocktäschel, Sebastian Riedel, and Douwe Kiela. 2020. Retrieval-augmented generation for knowledge-intensive nlp tasks. In *Advances in Neural Information Processing Systems*, pages 9459–9474.

Jiwei Li, Will Monroe, Alan Ritter, Dan Jurafsky, Michel Galley, and Jianfeng Gao. 2016. Deep reinforcement learning for dialogue generation. In *Proceedings of the 2016 Conference on Empirical Methods in Natural Language Processing*, pages 1192–1202.

Opher Lieber, Or Sharir, Barak Lenz, and Yoav Shoham. 2021. Jurassic-1: Technical details and evaluation. Technical report, AI21 Labs.

Chia-Wei Liu, Ryan Lowe, Iulian Vlad Serban, Mike Noseworthy, Laurent Charlin, and Joelle Pineau. 2016. How NOT to evaluate your dialogue system: An empirical study of unsupervised evaluation metrics for dialogue response generation. In *Proceedings of the 2016 Conference on Empirical Methods in Natural Language Processing*, pages 2122–2132.

Gary Marcus. 2020. The next decade in AI: four steps towards robust artificial intelligence. *arXiv preprint arXiv:2002.06177*.

Myle Ott, Sergey Edunov, Alexei Baevski, Angela Fan, Sam Gross, Nathan Ng, David Grangier, and Michael Auli. 2019. fairseq: A fast, extensible toolkit for sequence modeling. In *Proceedings of the 2019 Conference of the North American Chapter of the Association for Computational Linguistics (Demonstrations)*, pages 48–53.

Hiroki Ouchi and Yuta Tsuboi. 2016. Addressee and response selection for multi-party conversation. In *Proceedings of the 2016 Conference on Empirical Methods in Natural Language Processing*, pages 2133–2143.

Weizhen Qi, Yeyun Gong, Yu Yan, Can Xu, Bolun Yao, Bartuer Zhou, Biao Cheng, Daxin Jiang, Jiusheng Chen, Ruofei Zhang, Houqiang Li, and Nan Duan. 2021. ProphetNet-X: Large-scale pre-training models for english, chinese, multi-lingual, dialog, and code generation. *arXiv preprint arXiv:2104.08006*.

Alec Radford, Karthik Narasimhan, Tim Salimans, and Ilya Sutskever. 2018. Improving language understanding by generative pre-training. *Technical report, OpenAI*.

Alec Radford, Jeff Wu, Rewon Child, David Luan, Dario Amodei, and Ilya Sutskever. 2019. Language models are unsupervised multitask learners. *Technical report, OpenAI*.

Jack W Rae, Sebastian Borgeaud, Trevor Cai, Katie Millican, Jordan Hoffmann, Francis Song, John Aslanides, Sarah Henderson, Roman Ring, Susannah Young, et al. 2021. Scaling language models: Methods, analysis insights from training gopher. *arXiv preprint arXiv:2112.11446*.

Colin Raffel, Noam Shazeer, Adam Roberts, Katherine Lee, Sharan Narang, Michael Matena, Yanqi Zhou, Wei Li, and Peter J Liu. 2020. Exploring the limits of transfer learning with a unified text-to-text transformer. *Journal of Machine Learning Research*, 21(140):1–67.

Samyam Rajbhandari, Jeff Rasley, Olatunji Ruwase, and Yuxiong He. 2020. Zero: Memory optimizations toward training trillion parameter models. In *SC20: International Conference for High Performance Computing, Networking, Storage and Analysis*, pages 1–16.

Adam Roberts, Colin Raffel, and Noam Shazeer. 2020. How much knowledge can you pack into the parameters of a language model? In *Proceedings of the 2020 Conference on Empirical Methods in Natural Language Processing*, pages 5418–5426.

Stephen Roller, Emily Dinan, Naman Goyal, Da Ju, Mary Williamson, Yinhan Liu, Jing Xu, Myle Ott, Kurt Shuster, Eric M Smith, Y-Lan Boureau, and Jason Weston. 2021. Recipes for building an open-domain chatbot. In *Proceedings of the 16th Conference of the European Chapter of the Association for Computational Linguistics*.

Rico Sennrich, Barry Haddow, and Alexandra Birch. 2016. Neural machine translation of rare words with subword units. In *Proceedings of the 54th Annual Meeting of the Association for Computational Linguistics*, pages 1715–1725.

Eric Michael Smith, Mary Williamson, Kurt Shuster, Jason Weston, and Y-Lan Boureau. 2020. Can you put it all together: Evaluating conversational agents' ability to blend skills. In *Proceedings of the 58th Annual Meeting of the Association for Computational Linguistics*, pages 2021–2030.

Shaden Smith, Mostofa Patwary, Brandon Norick, Patrick LeGresley, Samyam Rajbhandari, Jared Casper, Zhun Liu, Shrimai Prabhumoye, George Zerveas, Vijay Korthikanti, et al. 2022. Using deepspeed and megatron to train megatron-turing nlg 530b, a large-scale generative language model. *arXiv preprint arXiv:2201.11990*.

Yu Sun, Shuohuan Wang, Shikun Feng, Siyu Ding, Chao Pang, Junyuan Shang, Jiaxiang Liu, Xuyi Chen, Yanbin Zhao, Yuxiang Lu, Weixin Liu, Zhihua Wu, Weibao Gong, Jianzhong Liang, Zhizhou Shang, Peng Sun, Wei Liu, Xuan Ouyang, Dianhai Yu, Hao Tian, Hua Wu, and Haifeng Wang. 2021. ERNIE 3.0: Large-scale knowledge enhanced pre-training for language understanding and generation. *arXiv preprint arXiv:2107.02137*.

Romal Thoppilan, Daniel De Freitas, Jamie Hall, Noam Shazeer, Apoorv Kulshreshtha, Heng-Tze Cheng, Alicia Jin, Taylor Bos, Leslie Baker, Yu Du, et al. 2022. Lamda: Language models for dialog applications. *arXiv preprint arXiv:2201.08239*.

Shuohuan Wang, Yu Sun, Yang Xiang, Zhihua Wu, Siyu Ding, Weibao Gong, Shikun Feng, Junyuan Shang, Yanbin Zhao, Chao Pang, et al. 2021. Ernie 3.0 titan: Exploring larger-scale knowledge enhanced pretraining for language understanding and generation. *arXiv preprint arXiv:2112.12731*.

Yida Wang, Pei Ke, Yinhe Zheng, Kaili Huang, Yong Jiang, Xiaoyan Zhu, and Minlie Huang. 2020. A large-scale chinese short-text conversation dataset. In *CCF International Conference on Natural Language Processing and Chinese Computing*, pages 91–103.

Wenquan Wu, Zhen Guo, Xiangyang Zhou, Hua Wu, Xiyuan Zhang, Rongzhong Lian, and Haifeng Wang. 2019. Proactive human-machine conversation with explicit conversation goal. In *Proceedings of the 57th Annual Meeting of the Association for Computational Linguistics*, pages 3794–3804.

Xiaoxue Zang, Abhinav Rastogi, Srinivas Sunkara, Raghav Gupta, Jianguo Zhang, and Jindong Chen. 2020. MultiWOZ 2.2 : A dialogue dataset with additional annotation corrections and state tracking baselines. In *Proceedings of the 2nd Workshop on Natural Language Processing for Conversational AI*, pages 109–117.

Wei Zeng, Xiaozhe Ren, Teng Su, Hui Wang, Yi Liao, Zhiwei Wang, Xin Jiang, ZhenZhang Yang, Kaisheng Wang, Xiaoda Zhang, Chen Li, Ziyan Gong, Yifan Yao, Xinjing Huang, Jun Wang, Jianfeng Yu, Qilong Guo, Yue Yu, Yan Zhang, Jin Wang, Heng Tao, Dasen Yan, Z. Yi, Fang Peng, Fan Jiang, Han Zhang, Lingfeng Deng, Yehong Zhang, Zhengping Lin, Chao Zhang, Shaojie Zhang, Mingyue Guo, Shanzhi Gu, Gaojun Fan, Yaowei Wang, Xue Jin, Qun Liu, and Yonghong Tian. 2021. PanGu-α: Large-scale autoregressive pretrained chinese language models with auto-parallel computation. *arXiv preprint arXiv:2104.12369*.

Rui Zhang, Honglak Lee, Lazaros Polymenakos, and Dragomir Radev. 2018. Addressee and response selection in multi-party conversations with speaker interaction rnns. In *Thirty-Second AAAI Conference on Artificial Intelligence*.

Yizhe Zhang, Siqi Sun, Michel Galley, Yen-Chun Chen, Chris Brockett, Xiang Gao, Jianfeng Gao, Jingjing Liu, and Bill Dolan. 2020a. DialoGPT: Large-scale generative pre-training for conversational response generation. In *Proceedings of the 58th Annual Meeting of the Association for Computational Linguistics: System Demonstrations*, pages 270–278.

Zhengyan Zhang, Yuxian Gu, Xu Han, Shengqi Chen, Chaojun Xiao, Zhenbo Sun, Yuan Yao, Fanchao Qi, Jian Guan, Pei Ke, Yanzheng Cai, Guoyang Zeng, Zhixing Tan, Zhiyuan Liu, Minlie Huang, Wentao Han, Yang Liu, Xiaoyan Zhu, and Maosong Sun. 2021. CPM-2: Large-scale cost-effective pre-trained language models. *arXiv preprint arXiv:2106.10715*.

Zhengyan Zhang, Xu Han, Hao Zhou, Pei Ke, Yuxian Gu, Deming Ye, Yujia Qin, Yusheng Su, Haozhe Ji, Jian Guan, Fanchao Qi, Xiaozhi Wang, Yanan Zheng, Guoyang Zeng, Huanqi Cao, Shengqi Chen, Daixuan Li, Zhenbo Sun, Zhiyuan Liu, Minlie Huang, Wentao Han, Jie Tang, Juanzi Li, and Maosong Sun. 2020b. CPM: A large-scale generative chinese pre-trained language model. *arXiv preprint arXiv:2012.00413*.

Hao Zhou, Pei Ke, Zheng Zhang, Yuxian Gu, Yinhe Zheng, Chujie Zheng, Yida Wang, Chen Henry Wu, Hao Sun, Xiaocong Yang, Bosi Wen, Xiaoyan Zhu, Minlie Huang, and Jie Tang. 2021. EVA: An open-domain chinese dialogue system with large-scale generative pre-training. *arXiv preprint arXiv:2108.01547*.

Li Zhou, Jianfeng Gao, Di Li, and Heung-Yeung Shum. 2020. The design and implementation of XiaoIce, an empathetic social chatbot. *Computational Linguistics*, 46(1):53–93.

A Scoring Criteria in Human Evaluation

The criteria used in human evaluation are provided in Table 5.

Score	Coherence
0	• The response is not related with the context. • The response simply repeats the context. • The response has obvious conflicts with the context. • There are serious logic conflicts within the response.
1	• The response has minor conflicts with the context. • There are some minor logic conflicts in the response.
2	• The response is coherent with the context.

Score	Inconsistency ↓
0	• The response is consistent with the context
1	• The response has conflicts with the context. • There are logic conflicts within the response.

Score	Informativeness
0	• The response doesn't contain any information. • This response just repeats the context and fails to bring any additional information. • The information is invalid, as the coherence score is 0.
1	• The information has conflicts with common sense. • There are factual errors in the response.
2	• The response has appropriate and correct information.

Score	Hallucination ↓
0	• The response is factually correct.
1	• Some details in the response are factually incorrect. • The response is invalid, as the coherence and informativeness scores are all 0.

Score	Engagingness
0	• I don't want to talk with this speaker.
1	• It is kind of boring, but it is still ok to talk with this speaker.
2	• I would like to talk with this speaker for a long conversation.

Table 5: Score details of metrics used in human evaluation.

B Prompting Efficient Dialogue Generation

In the practical deployment of the large-scale pre-trained dialogue model, one hindrance is the limited inference efficiency. Firstly, the model has tremendous parameters, leading to expensive computational costs. Secondly, in response generation, the model has to generate the response sequence step by step, suffering from high latency. We have explored several strategies to boost inference efficiency, including operation fusion, FP16 computation, and so on. With these techniques, on the Nvidia Tesla V100 32G GPU card, the average latency of 11B parameter Chinese PLATO-XL is successfully reduced to 941ms from 3.3s, resulting in 3.5 times acceleration. To facilitate the deployment of dialogue models, we also have plans to release these acceleration implementations soon.

A Hybrid Architecture for Labelling Bilingual Māori-English Tweets

David Trye[1*], Vithya Yogarajan[2*], Jemma König[1], Te Taka Keegan[1], David Bainbridge[1] and Mark Apperley[1]

[1]School of Computing and Mathematical Sciences, University of Waikato, New Zealand
[2]Strong AI Lab, School of Computer Science, University of Auckland, New Zealand
[*]*dgt12@students.waikato.ac.nz, vithya.yogarajan@auckland.ac.nz*

Abstract

Most large-scale language detection tools perform poorly at identifying Māori text. Moreover, rule-based and machine learning-based techniques devised specifically for the Māori-English language pair struggle with interlingual homographs. We develop a hybrid architecture that couples Māori-language orthography with machine learning models in order to annotate mixed Māori-English text. This architecture is used to label a new bilingual Twitter corpus at both the token (word) and tweet (sentence) levels. We use the collected tweets to show that the hybrid approach outperforms existing systems with respect to language detection of interlingual homographs and overall accuracy. We also evaluate its performance on out-of-domain data. Two interactive visualisations are provided for exploring the Twitter corpus and comparing errors across the new and existing techniques. The architecture code and visualisations are available online, and the corpus is available on request.

1 Introduction

"Ko te reo te mauri o te mana Māori.
Ko te kupu te mauri o reo Māori."

Translated to English as *The language is the life force of the mana Māori. The word is the life force of the language* (Higgins and Keane, 2015), this famous saying by Tā Hēmi Hēnare (Sir James Hēnare) encapsulates the importance of the Māori language to Māori, the Indigenous people of Aotearoa[1] New Zealand.

Te reo Māori is both endangered and low-resourced, with limited corpora and Natural Language Processing (NLP) techniques available (James et al., 2020). Data annotation currently has to be done manually by language experts, making the process time-consuming and resource-intensive. These obstacles hinder technological advances that could assist in maintaining the language and, consequently, the culture of Māori.

The Māori language used today is frequently interspersed with English, either in the form of *code-switching* (Holmes and Wilson, 2017; Marras Tate and Rapatahana, 2022) or *borrowing*. Here, the borrowing process is bidirectional, resulting in both English loanwords in Māori (Harlow, 1993) and Māori loanwords in English (Calude et al., 2020). The latter are not only used by bilingual Māori speakers, but also by monolingual English-speaking New Zealanders. Linguists are interested in determining the frequency of these patterns, which are reflective of Aotearoa New Zealand's unique bicultural identity.

The interweaving of Māori and English is a key consideration for developing robust technologies that can accommodate practical, everyday usage of te reo Māori and New Zealand English. Leveraging the abundance of relevant data on Twitter, our research focuses on the following task:

> *Automatic language identification for bilingual Māori-English text at both the token (word) and tweet (sentence) level.*

Differentiating between Māori and English text is not straightforward. This is because both languages use the Roman script, and *interlingual homographs*—words that are spelt the same but differ in meaning across languages (Dijkstra, 2007)—are prolific. These words present a major challenge for classifying mixed-language text, especially if they are highly frequent in both target languages (Barman et al., 2014). Consider the following tweets in which interlingual homographs are emphasised:

(a) **Here** is **to a more** productive day tomorrow
(b) Ka **kite** koe **i a** koe!
(c) **He** is at **a** tangi in Ruatoki. Doubt **he** did

In terms of annotation, the desired tweet-level labels are (a) English, (b) Māori, and (c) Bilingual. These are determined with recourse to the individual token labels: all tokens in (a) are English, all

[1]Aotearoa is increasingly used as a Māori name for New Zealand. Te reo Māori means 'the Māori language'.

Findings of the Association for Computational Linguistics: AACL-IJCNLP 2022, pages 119–130
November 20–23, 2022. ©2022 Association for Computational Linguistics

tokens in (b) are Māori, and (c) contains a mixture of tokens from both languages, with 'tangi' (funeral) and 'Ruatoki' (a place name) being labelled Māori. According to our approach, all words of Māori origin are tagged as Māori, even if they are used as borrowings in English.

In order to obtain accurate tweet and token-level labels, we utilise knowledge and understanding gained from Māori researchers, Māori technology developers and the Māori community. Our methodology involves combining machine learning techniques with Māori orthography, thereby instantiating the pipeline recommended by Hämäläinen (2021). We hypothesise that doing so will improve the overall accuracy of language identification for bilingual Māori-English text.

This paper makes the following contributions:

1. Development of a hybrid architecture[2] to detect Māori and English words for a given bilingual text input.
2. The *Māori-English Twitter (MET) Corpus*, a first-of-a-kind dataset comprising bilingual and monolingual tweets, annotated at the token- and tweet-level by deploying our architecture.
3. Evidence that the hybrid architecture improves both language detection of interlingual homographs and overall accuracy when compared with two existing techniques.
4. Two interactive visualisation tools for exploring the corpus and comparing label errors across the different systems.

2 Background and Related Work

2.1 Māori Data Sovereignty

The Māori language is the natural medium through which Māori express their cultural identity, construct the Māori worldview and convey their authenticity (Marras Tate and Rapatahana, 2022; Rapatahana, 2017; White, 2016). It is crucial to highlight that Māori data needs to be handled with care, because of the injustices caused by colonisation and its effect on the vitality of the language (Smith, 2021). We strongly believe that any NLP resources that are developed from this research, either directly or indirectly, should be created for the good of the Māori-language community and not for the capital gain of others; more generally, Indigenous data should not be commodified at the expense of Indigenous communities (Bird, 2020).

2.2 Challenges and Bias in Māori NLP

Key challenges in developing Māori speech and language technology arise from the lack and limitations of resources (James et al., 2020), phonological differences from English, and the lexical overlap between written Māori and English, including more than 100 interlingual homographs.[3] These obstacles hinder NLP advances that could facilitate the maintenance of Māori language and culture.

Existing large-scale technologies such as cloud-based language-detection tools and voice assistants are predominantly designed for English. These tools fail to recognise or correctly pronounce Māori words, even when used as borrowings in New Zealand English (James et al., 2022b). Our goal is to redress that inequity in NLP resources, and thus mitigate the bias that existing tools have towards the more dominant English language.

2.3 Code-Switching in NLP

Bilingual and multilingual code-switching, especially between resource-rich and low-resourced languages, has gained traction as a challenging but important NLP problem (Aguilar et al., 2020; Molina et al., 2016; Solorio et al., 2014). A myriad of studies investigating code-switching on social media has emerged, showcasing challenges and possibilities for many different language pairs (Jose et al., 2020; Maharjan et al., 2015; Barman et al., 2014).

While an overview of Māori-language corpora is given in Trye et al. (2022), we detail three that are particularly relevant here. The *Hansard Dataset* (James et al., 2022a) comprises two million Māori, English and bilingual sentences, annotated by hand at both the token and sentence levels. The *MLT Corpus* (Trye et al., 2019) is a publicly-available collection of English tweets with Māori borrowings, albeit lacking token-level labels. The *RMT Corpus* (Trye et al., 2022) contains predominantly-Māori tweets and is also publicly-available. We use the hand-crafted rules from the RMT Corpus to detect candidate Māori words based on Māori orthography (Section 3.2).

Research using machine learning techniques for te reo Māori is relatively young, and is restricted by the limited scope of available resources. Although cloud-based services offered by corporations such as Google and Microsoft support Māori-language detection, the accuracy of these services

[2] *https://github.com/bilingual-MET/hybrid*

[3] *https://github.com/TeHikuMedia/reo-toolkit*

is poor (Keegan, 2017; James et al., 2022b).

Recently-developed language identification and code-switching detection models for the Māori-English pair make use of Skipgram-based fastText models to pre-train embeddings (Dunn and Nijhof, 2022; James et al., 2022b). James et al. combine pre-trained embeddings with recurrent neural networks (RNNs) to identify Māori text and code-switching points between the Māori-English pair. Their embeddings were pre-trained on a large collection of bilingual and monolingual data, and shown to outperform open-sourced English-only equivalents. Our hybrid architecture uses the fastText pre-trained embeddings and Hansard training set from James et al. (2022b).

3 Methodology

This section details the process used to collect Twitter data (Section 3.1) and the techniques underpinning our hybrid architecture. We combine language rules (Section 3.2) with neural networks (Section 3.3), as suggested by Hämäläinen (2021).

3.1 Data Collection and Pre-processing

In order to create a bilingual Twitter corpus on which to deploy our architecture, we combined tweets that were originally gathered for the RMT Corpus with more recent tweets from the same users.[4] Tweets that included 30-80% Māori text under the RMT system were chosen, as it was deduced these would primarily contain instances of Māori-English code-switching. The collected tweets were pre-processed to mitigate noise in the dataset. A series of tweets was removed, including retweets, similar and identical tweets, tweets posted by bots, and tweets containing fewer than four words. Non-Roman characters were stripped from the remaining tweets and common English contractions were expanded. 20,000 foreign-language tweets were then removed via manual and automatic checks, which included searching for symbols denoting glottal stops in the middle of tokens (characteristic of several Polynesian languages related to, but distinct from, Māori). This yielded 178,192 tweets in total. Finally, when extracting the tokens in each tweet, links, user mentions, hashtags, punctuation, emoticons and Arabic numerals were all ignored. The rationale for excluding hashtags is that they often contain abbreviations and/or multiple words, sometimes even combining languages (Trye et al., 2020), making them difficult to annotate without additional pre-processing.

3.2 Hand-Crafted Rules

Trye et al. (2022) employ hand-crafted rules to identify Māori tokens in tweets, referred to as the *RMT system* throughout this paper. This technique adapts hand-crafted rules implemented by Te Hiku Media, an Indigenous Māori organisation.[5] The rules are as follows:

- Tokens must contain only characters from the Māori alphabet, which comprises five vowels (*i, e, a, o, u*) and ten consonants (*p, t, k, m, n, ng, wh, r, w, h*).
- Lengthened vowels may be indicated with a macron (*ā*), or using double-vowel orthography (*aa*).
- Tokens must adhere to Māori syllable structure: they must follow consonant/vowel alternation, end with a vowel, and be free of consonant clusters (excluding the digraphs *ng* and *wh*).
- For input to the algorithm, some further adjustments were made to identify as many candidate Māori words as possible.[6]

When applied to bilingual text, a major limitation of these rules is that tokens of the same type are always classified the same way (typically as Māori), which is problematic for interlingual homographs.

3.3 Machine Learning Component

The hybrid architecture uses Bidirectional Gated Recurrent Units (Cho et al., 2014) with an attention layer as the machine learning component. Text is represented using fastText (Bojanowski et al., 2017) Skipgram-model word embeddings (Mikolov et al., 2013) with 300 dimensions, pre-trained on a collection of Māori and bilingual corpora (James et al., 2022b). The attention layer used is based on the Bahdanau attention mechanism (Bahdanau et al., 2015). Our preliminary experiments favoured the use of Bi-GRU with an attention layer over other deep learning models such as CNNs and LSTMs.

To the best of our knowledge, there is no large bilingual Twitter dataset annotated accurately by experts at the token- or tweet-level. Hence, for training Bi-GRU, we use the Hansard Dataset containing transcribed formal Māori and

[4] Users were identified via *Indigenous Tweets* (*http://indigenoustweets.com/*).

[5] *https://github.com/TeHikuMedia/nga-kupu*

[6] Words like 'a', 'i', 'to' and 'no' were omitted from the original RMT system due to their high frequency in English.

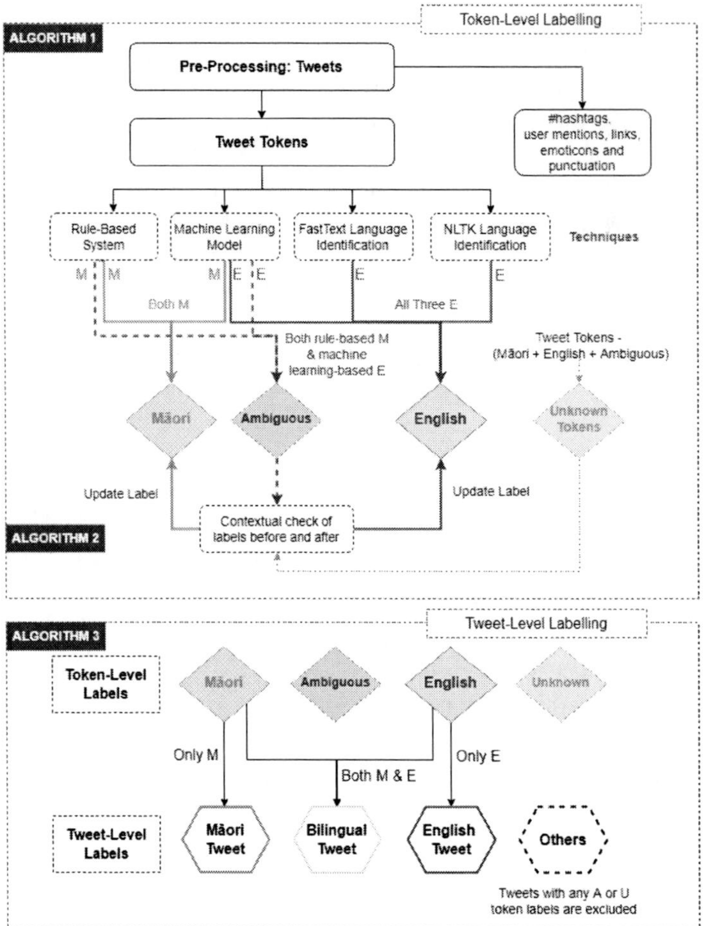

Figure 1: Flow chart detailing token- and tweet-level labelling.

English (James et al., 2022b). The Bi-GRU model is trained to predict Māori, English or bilingual sentences, using default settings in Keras/Tensorflow. Adam (Kingma and Ba, 2015), an adaptive learning rate optimisation algorithm, was employed as the optimiser for the networks. Softmax activation is leveraged in the output layer. To avoid over-fitting, we use a combination of dropout (Srivastava et al., 2014) with a rate of 0.5 and early stopping (Zhang et al., 2017).[7]

4 Hybrid Architecture

The hybrid architecture for labelling bilingual Māori-English datasets at both the token (word) and tweet (sentence) levels builds upon the RMT and ML techniques described in the previous section. Figure 1 outlines the process used to label the tweets in our cleaned dataset, and references the algorithms in Appendix A. The architecture can also be directly applied to Māori-English corpora with longer text sequences.[8]

4.1 Token-Level Labels

Multiple techniques are used to determine the appropriate label for each token (Algorithms 1 and 2). Initially, tokens are deemed to be Māori only if they are labelled ‘M’ by both the modified rules from the RMT Corpus and the pre-trained machine learning model. In a similar vein, English tokens are labelled by combining the outcome of using the machine learning model with fastText (Joulin et al., 2017, 2016) and NLTK (Bird and Loper, 2004) language identification models. These techniques have proven high accuracy in detecting English, providing confidence in the ‘E’ labels. Due to the informal nature of tweets, the language-specific tags include colloquial language and textspeak (e.g.

[7]Model trained on 12 core Intel(R) Xeon(R) W-2133 CPU @ 3.60GHz, GPU device GV100GL.

[8]*https://github.com/bilingual-MET/hybrid*

	Tweets	Bilingual (B)	English (E)	Māori (M)
Tweets	76,416	67,713	7847	856
Tokens	781,381	-	465,292	316,089
Users	2417	2347	1148	283
Avg tokens/tweet	10	11	6	6
Avg tweets/user	32	29	7	3

Table 1: Summary statistics for the MET Corpus.

'u' for 'you' in English).

Any tokens that are labelled 'M' by the modified RMT system and 'E' by the machine learning model are initially classified as ambiguous. The knowledge gained from neighbouring tokens is then used to re-classify these words as Māori or English (Algorithm 2). Crucially, the MET Corpus only includes tweets comprising 'M' and 'E' token-level labels; all remaining tokens that could not be re-classified with certainty led to the removal of the corresponding tweet, and are left for future research.

4.2 Tweet-Level Labels

The updated token labels are used to generate appropriate tweet-level labels (Figure 1, Algorithm 3). If a tweet consists solely of 'M' or 'E' tokens, then the tweet-level label is Māori or English, respectively. Tweets that contain at least one 'M' and 'E' token are considered bilingual; this includes single-word borrowings in otherwise monolingual contexts. For further confidence, the tweet-level labels were compared with the pre-trained machine learning model, and it was found that 90% of these labels matched the hybrid model.

5 The Māori-English Twitter Corpus

The steps detailed in the previous two sections resulted in the formation of a new bilingual dataset: the *Māori-English Twitter (MET) Corpus*. Key summary statistics for this collection of 76,000 tweets are presented in Table 1. Almost 90% of tweets in the corpus are labelled Bilingual, 10% are English and only 0.1% are Māori. This distribution is expected, given the chosen threshold and characteristics of the RMT system used to filter tweets in the data collection phase. In terms of individual words, 60% of tokens in the MET Corpus are labelled English and 40% are Māori. The 20 most frequent tokens are shown in Figure 2. Most of these tokens are function words rather than content words, apart from 'Māori' and 'reo' (language), whose presence would suggest that many tweets in the corpus pertain specifically to Māori language and culture.

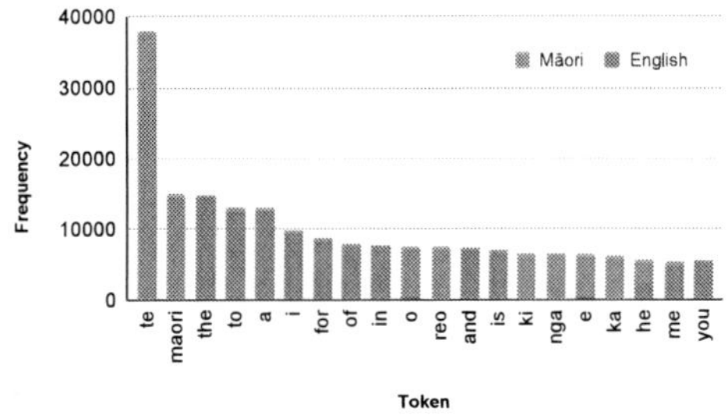

Figure 2: The 20 most frequent tokens in the MET Corpus: Māori words, English words and homographs.

5.1 Visualisation of the MET Corpus

We provide an interactive visualisation for exploring the MET Corpus;[9] see Figure 3. The visualisation includes a scrollable table of tweets and allows the user to select and filter data according to several dimensions. Key features include a treemap (and associated search bar) displaying token frequencies for the selection, a line chart of the distribution of selected tweets over time, and a bubble chart summarising the relative contribution of each user. In addition, selections can be made on both the tweet and token-level labels. The percentage of tweets that is currently visible (with respect to the entire corpus) is indicated at the top left of the display.

5.2 Gold Standard Labels

A manual annotation process was used to obtain gold standard labels for a random one percent sample of the data (N=850 tweets), including tweets that were ultimately filtered out of the corpus. This process consisted of two phases. In phase one, two of the authors manually tagged the true tweet-level label of each tweet in the sample, so that this could be compared against the predicted label for each system. Furthermore, the coders identified which tokens, if any, had been mislabelled by each system. Tokens were considered to be Māori if they were listed in the Māori dictionary,[10] constituted Māori slang (e.g. 'ktk' is the Māori equivalent of 'lol'), or were Māori named entities. It was decided that even Māori borrowings in otherwise English tweets should be tagged as Māori, because applications such as a New Zealand English text-to-speech tool would be required to correctly identify and pronounce words of Māori origin, regardless of how they are categorised from a theoretical point of view.

In the sample tweets, the coders encountered

[9] *https://bilingual-met.github.io/hybrid*

[10] *https://maoridictionary.co.nz/*

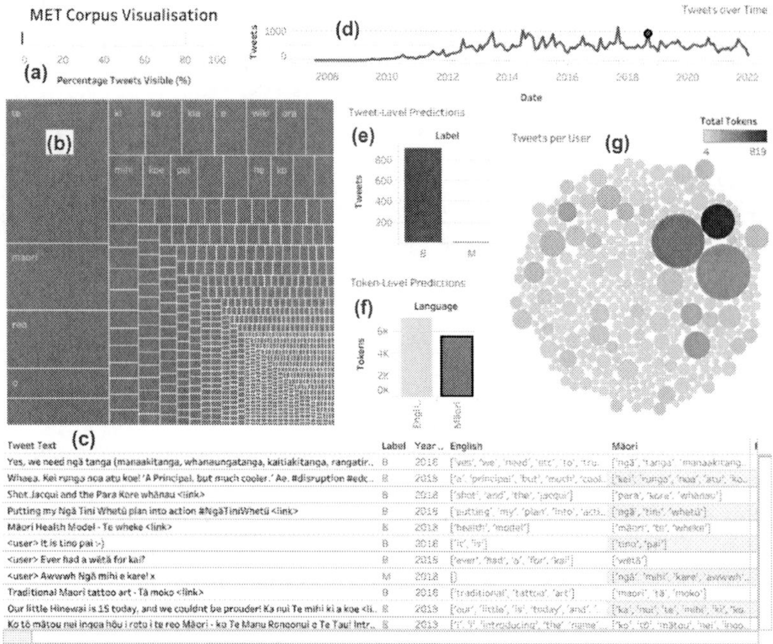

Figure 3: Interactive tool for exploring the *MET Corpus*: (a) percentage of corpus visible, (b) selected tokens by frequency, (c) tweet table, (d) tweets by year, (e) tweet predictions, (f) token predictions, (g) tweets by user.

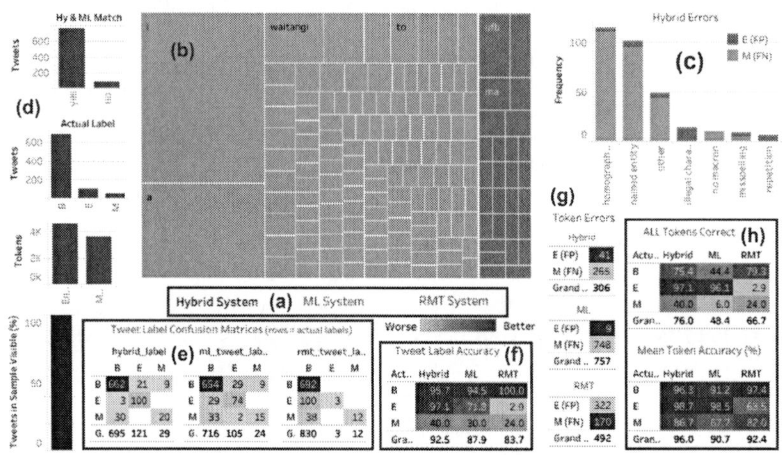

Figure 4: Interactive tool for comparing system errors: (a) navigation menu, (b) misclassified tokens, (c) error types, (d) filtering by labels, (e) tweet label confusion matrices, (f) tweet accuracy, (g) token mistakes, (h) token accuracy.

five foreign tweets (0.6%), which were discarded, since the individual tokens could not be accurately tagged as either English or Māori. In order to assess the efficacy of phase one of the annotation process, Cohen's kappa was computed for a subsample of 200 tweets. This yielded a score of 0.816, indicating a strong level of agreement.

For the second phase, one of the authors went through the data again, and, for each mistaken token, noted whether it was a Māori token that had been mislabelled as English (false negative), or an English token that had been mislabelled as Māori (false positive). Where possible, they recorded further information about the specific type of error. Common error types included short-length homographs, named entities (including names of people, places, tribes, organisations and events), the presence of one or more non-Māori characters, misspellings and missing macrons.

6 Experiment Results and Analysis

This section compares the performance of the newly-developed hybrid system with the standalone RMT (Trye et al., 2022) and ML (James

Tweets	Tweet Labels: Actual	Tweet Labels: RMT	Tweet Labels: ML	Tweet Labels: Hybrid	Token-Level Errors (FP, FN): RMT	Token-Level Errors (FP, FN): ML	Token-Level Errors (FP, FN): Hybrid
1. Teaching ate me alive <link> via <user> #classroomreality	E	B	E	E	ate, me	-	-
2. <user> ka pai! Some reo and hugs! What more does one need:) #BFC630NZ	B	B	B	B	more, one	-	-
3. <user> <user> Kia ora Bronwyn. Hope to catch up while we are here!	B	B	B	B	hope, here	Kia	-
4. <user> Ata marie John, hope you're well mate.	B	B	B	B	marie, hope, mate	-	
5. E hoa ma, nga mihi o te tau hou! #Matariki #MaoriNewYear #BN-Zatm #respect <link>	M	M	B	M	-	E, o, tau	-
6. Maori Party welcomes Waitangi Tribunal report	B	B	B	B	-	Waitangi	Waitangi

Table 2: Example tweets indicating actual Māori tokens, tweet-level errors and unidentified Māori tokens.

System	Tweet-Level: English F1	P	R	S	Māori F1	P	R	S	Bilingual F1	P	R	S	Overall Accuracy	Token-Level: English F1	P	R	Māori F1	P	R
Twitter Sample																			
RMT	0.06	**1.00**	0.03	**1.00**	0.39	1.00	0.24	**1.00**	0.91	0.83	**1.00**	0.10	0.84	0.90	0.93	0.87	0.87	0.88	0.85
ML	0.71	0.70	0.72	0.97	0.40	0.62	0.30	0.98	0.93	0.91	0.95	0.60	0.88	0.94	**0.94**	0.94	0.85	**0.96**	0.79
Hybrid	**0.89**	0.83	**0.97**	0.96	**0.51**	0.69	**0.40**	0.98	**0.95**	**0.95**	0.96	**0.78**	**0.93**	**0.95**	**0.94**	**0.95**	**0.94**	0.92	**0.97**
Hansard Test Set (Sentence-Level / Token-Level)																			
RMT	0.33	**0.71**	0.21	0.88	**0.96**	**1.00**	**0.91**	**1.00**	**0.95**	**0.91**	**0.95**	0.55	**0.92**	0.87	0.91	0.84	**0.86**	**0.86**	**0.86**
ML	**0.60**	0.43	0.97	**0.91**	0.32	**1.00**	0.19	0.99	0.79	0.90	0.70	0.55	0.68	0.92	0.91	0.91	0.66	0.70	0.64
Hybrid	0.52	0.35	**1.00**	0.89	0.38	**1.00**	0.24	0.99	0.85	**0.91**	0.79	**0.64**	0.77	**0.93**	**0.92**	**0.92**	0.71	0.73	0.70

Table 3: Tweet and token-level system evaluation for both the Twitter sample and Hansard test set. Recall (R), precision (P), F-score (F1), specificity (S) and overall accuracy are presented, with **best scores** emphasised.

et al., 2022b) systems. We also use a test set from the Hansard Dataset (James et al., 2022a) to evaluate our hybrid architecture with data from another domain. For brevity, we refer to interlingual homographs simply as *homographs*.

6.1 Visualisation of System Errors

To facilitate analysis of our manually-coded sample of tweets (hereafter, the *Twitter sample*), we have developed an interactive tool for comparing errors between the three systems of interest.[11] The visualisation helps users to explore the relationship between the tweet- and token-level labels for each system, and to better understand which kinds of tokens are responsible for the errors. Figure 4 provides a screenshot of this interactive tool, which guided the subsequent analysis.

6.2 Overall Accuracy

Table 2 characterises the state of play for the hybrid system and the two existing systems, using six example tweets. All token-level errors are given, together with the resulting tweet labels. The token-level errors obtained using the RMT system's hand-crafted rules are mostly homographs, whereas those for the ML system are mostly Māori words. The hybrid architecture performs well by comparison, correctly identifying all but one Māori token.

Table 3 provides a synopsis of the system evaluations, broken down by tweet/sentence and token labels for both the Twitter sample and the Hansard test set. Looking at the Twitter sample, the Hybrid system has the highest overall accuracy. The Hybrid system's F1-scores are consistently better than the other two systems' at both the tweet and token level. The specificity of the Hybrid system is good across all tweet-level labels. Notably, the RMT system's specificity is extremely poor for bilingual tweets, indicating that the system is overly eager to find a positive result, even when it is not present. All systems do poorly at identifying Māori-only tweets; most are classified as Bilingual instead. This is likely because 'i' and 'a' are frequent in Māori but nearly always classified as English.

The Hansard test set included 10,000 bilingual, 1,000 Māori and 1,000 English sentences. The sentence-level accuracy for the RMT system is much better than the other systems; this is likewise true of the F1-scores for both Māori and bilingual sentences. One of the main reasons for this is that the test set contains predominantly bilingual sentences, and in most cases the RMT system identifies at least one Māori and English token. However,

[11] *https://bilingual-met.github.io/hybrid/sample*

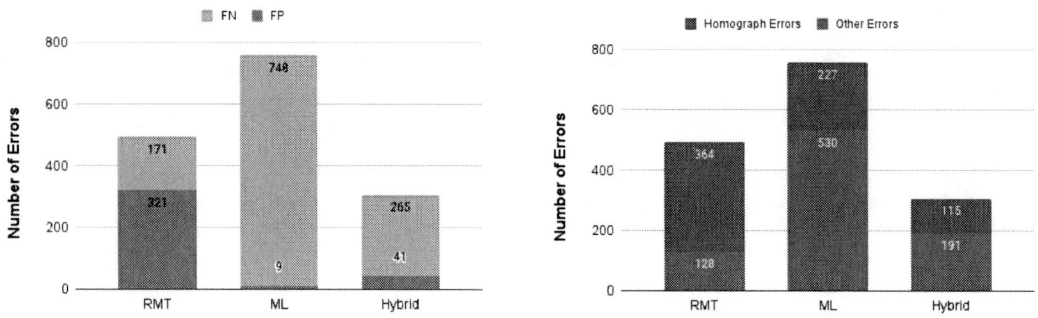

Figure 5: Token-level errors in the Twitter sample, showing false positives, false negatives and **homograph errors**.

System	False Positives	False Negatives
RMT	me, one, more, he, make, here, hope, take, o, nana, u	i, a, to, marie, no, ō, noho
ML	nana, ma	o, e, kia, i, he, a, tau, makaurau, waitangi, me, tūhoe, waatea, au, mo, kai, ō, to, kohanga, matatini, no, ā, morena, horipū, tuhoe
Hybrid	nana, ma, ufb	i, a, waitangi, waatea, to, no, tau, tuhoe

Table 4: Common token-level errors in the Twitter sample, including **homographs**.

System	Hansard Token-Level Errors
RMT	we, are, he, one, more, where, take, here, make, too, rate, none, rape, hope, reiterate, moe, mai, oki
ML	death, moe, mai, rā, hiamoe, kui, ki, te, pō, oti, atu, ai
Hybrid	moe, mai, rā, kui, ki, te, pō, oti, atu, ai

Table 5: Common token-level errors in the Hansard test set, including **homographs** mislabelled as 'M'.

the Hybrid system still has superior specificity for bilingual sentences. At the token-level, the Hybrid system does best for English tokens and the RMT system does best for Māori tokens.

6.3 Error Analysis

Figure 5 and Table 4 present a summary of token-level errors in the Twitter sample for all three systems, and highlight errors specifically caused by homographs. All systems struggle with short-length homographs (comprising fewer than five letters) like 'i' and 'a', which are pervasive in both languages. Nevertheless, the hybrid system fares considerably better than the other systems, with the ML and RMT systems having nearly double and over triple the number of homograph errors, respectively.

The vast majority of errors in the Hybrid system are Māori words that are mislabelled as English. Among these false negatives, short-length homographs constitute 42% of mistakes and named entities constitute 35%. While these are the two largest groups of errors, the Hybrid system still consistently classifies many of these kinds of words correctly (e.g. 'hope', 'Aotearoa').

These results indicate that the errors produced by the Hybrid system occur on a smaller scale than the ML system and are easier to fix than those for the RMT system. For instance, it is straightforward to update the labels for all tokens that contain non-Māori characters (like 'ufb'), and named entity accuracy (for tokens such as 'Waitangi') could be improved using an exhaustive list of non-ambiguous Māori place names.

A breakdown of the most prolific errors in the Hansard test set is given in Table 5. The most commonly misclassified homographs in both corpora are 'i', 'a', 'to' and 'no', which are all Māori particles that tend to be classified as English. Typically, such words are embedded inside larger segments of Māori text, so it is surprising that these instances are not correctly identified by our hybrid system's contextual check. One of the potential reasons is because the ML component of our hybrid architecture always classifies these tokens as English.

Like the Hybrid system, the ML system tends to mislabel Māori words as English rather than English words as Māori. Many of the same kinds of errors occur, though there are more false negatives and fewer false positives. The ML system frequently misclassified the particles 'e', 'o' and 'kia' in phrases such as "Miharo **e** hoa!", "Te Wiki **o** Te Reo Maori" and "**kia** ora". In contrast, the Hybrid system always labelled these correctly.

The RMT system differs from the others in that it has more false positives than false negatives. As a rule-based system, it always assigns the same label to each word type, even if it is valid in both languages. Words that are consistent with Māori orthography are generally tagged as Māori; as a result, the RMT system is considerably better at correctly classifying Māori named entities, including personal and place names. However, the RMT system performs considerably worse than the other two when classifying tweets with a large proportion of English text. Over 85% of false positives are short-length homographs, with 'me', 'one', 'more', 'he', 'make' and 'here' being the worst offenders. Like the other two systems, there are also some instances of Māori words that are misclassified as English (especially 'i', 'a', and 'to'), due to the stoplist that was used.

7 Limitations

The research presented in this paper has some limitations that need to be acknowledged. The hybrid architecture uses a single neural network-based model, but we have experimented with variations in the neural networks and parameter choices. Given the available data and resources, bidirectional RNNs performed the best.

We found that our hybrid architecture does not label Māori named entities consistently, and short-length homographs like 'i' and 'a' are problematic. This requires further investigation, perhaps involving a special look-up for Māori place names, and ensuring that a context check is always carried out for frequent homographs, especially function words.

In addition, our approach for identifying foreign-language tweets is not exhaustive, and in some cases, tokens that are neither Māori nor English will have been erroneously labelled as such. Our foreign-language processing currently focuses on manually identifying problematic tweets in a small subset of the data, then extrapolating this into the wider dataset. This approach could be further developed, or a more automated system could be implemented.

Our labels do not distinguish between borrowings and code-switches (Álvarez Mellado and Lignos, 2022). This means it is not possible to automatically extract tweets where Māori borrowings are used in otherwise English contexts, or vice versa, although the number of tokens identified in each language could serve as a useful proxy.

Finally, we discarded a proportion of the collected tweets as our algorithm was not optimised for dealing with undue levels of noise. The discarded tweets with unknown labels are not vital to the MET Corpus presented in this research; however, they require further investigation, and may constitute useful additions to the corpus.

8 Conclusions and Future Work

This paper presents an architecture for labelling bilingual Māori-English text, by bringing together machine learning and knowledge of Māori orthography, an approach that could also be fruitful for other endangered languages. We use this architecture to create the first large-scale corpus of bilingual Māori-English tweets annotated at both the token and tweet level. Both this corpus and the Hansard Dataset are used to illustrate the strengths of our approach, including superior token-level accuracy, especially with respect to interlingual homographs. In particular, the specificity scores for bilingual data favour the Hybrid system, while highlighting a major weakness of the RMT system. Additional insights can be gleaned from two exploratory visualisations for interrogating the corpus and comparing system errors.

Future work towards enhancing the bilingual corpus could involve extending this research to classify hashtags as these are currently ignored. Moreover, the architecture lends itself to annotating other bilingual datasets, such as the MLT Corpus (Trye et al., 2019), and could assist in the creation of new resources. A further avenue of exploration would be assigning part-of-speech tags to each token in the corpus, based on the language identified. This could be achieved using newly-developed tools for Māori (Finn et al., 2022) in conjunction with established part-of-speech taggers for English. Such developments are important for ensuring better representation of the Māori language in digital applications and environments.

Acknowledgements

We are indebted to researchers from the University of Auckland and Te Hiku Media for kindly sharing the Hansard Dataset. We thank Andreea Calude and three anonymous reviewers for their helpful comments and suggestions. DT acknowledges funding from the University of Waikato Doctoral Scholarship.

References

Gustavo Aguilar, Sudipta Kar, and Thamar Solorio. 2020. Lince: A centralized benchmark for linguistic code-switching evaluation. In *Proceedings of the 12th Language Resources and Evaluation Conference*, pages 1803–1813.

Dzmitry Bahdanau, Kyung Hyun Cho, and Yoshua Bengio. 2015. Neural machine translation by jointly learning to align and translate. In *3rd International Conference on Learning Representations, ICLR 2015.*

Utsab Barman, Amitava Das, Joachim Wagner, and Jennifer Foster. 2014. Code mixing: A challenge for language identification in the language of social media. In *Proceedings of the first workshop on computational approaches to code switching*, pages 13–23.

Steven Bird. 2020. Decolonising speech and language technology. In *Proceedings of the 28th International Conference on Computational Linguistics*, pages 3504–3519.

Steven Bird and Edward Loper. 2004. NLTK: The natural language toolkit. In *Proceedings of the ACL Interactive Poster and Demonstration Sessions*, pages 214–217, Barcelona, Spain. Association for Computational Linguistics.

Piotr Bojanowski, Edouard Grave, Armand Joulin, and Tomas Mikolov. 2017. Enriching word vectors with subword information. *Transactions of the Association for Computational Linguistics*, 5:135–146.

Andreea Calude, Louise Stevenson, Hēmi Whaanga, and Te Taka Keegan. 2020. The use of Māori words in national science challenge online discourse. *Journal of the Royal Society of New Zealand*, 50(4):491–508.

Kyunghyun Cho, B van Merrienboer, Dzmitry Bahdanau, and Yoshua Bengio. 2014. On the properties of neural machine translation: Encoder-decoder approaches. In *Eighth Workshop on Syntax, Semantics and Structure in Statistical Translation (SSST-8), 2014.*

Ton Dijkstra. 2007. Task and context effects in bilingual lexical processing. In *Cognitive aspects of bilingualism*, pages 213–235. Springer.

Jonathan Dunn and Wikke Nijhof. 2022. Language identification for Austronesian languages.

Aoife Finn, Peter-Lucas Jones, Keoni Mahelona, Suzanne Duncan, and Gianna Leoni. 2022. Developing a part-of-speech tagger for te reo Māori. In *Proceedings of the Fifth Workshop on the Use of Computational Methods in the Study of Endangered Languages*, pages 93–98.

Mika Hämäläinen. 2021. Endangered languages are not low-resourced! In Mika Hämäläinen, Niko Partanen, and Khalid Alnajjar, editors, *Multilingual Facilitation*, pages 1–11. Rootroo Ltd.

Ray Harlow. 1993. Lexical expansion in Maori. *The Journal of the Polynesian Society*, 102(1):99–107.

Rawinia Higgins and Basil Keane. 2015. Te reo Māori – the Māori language - language decline, 1900 to 1970s', Te Ara - the encyclopedia of New Zealand.

Janet Holmes and Nick Wilson. 2017. *An introduction to sociolinguistics*. Routledge.

Jesin James, Isabella Shields, Rebekah Berriman, Peter J Keegan, and Catherine I Watson. 2020. Developing resources for te reo Māori text to speech synthesis system. In *International Conference on Text, Speech, and Dialogue*, pages 294–302. Springer.

Jesin James, Isabella Shields, Vithya Yogarajan, Peter J. Keegan, Catherine Watson, Peter-Lucas Jones, and Keoni Mahelona. 2022a. The development of a labelled te reo Māori-English bilingual database for language technology.

Jesin James, Vithya Yogarajan, Isabella Shields, Catherine Watson, Peter Keegan, Peter-Lucas Jones, and Keoni Mahelona. 2022b. Language models for code-switch detection of te reo Māori and English in a low-resource setting. In *2022 Annual Conference of the North American Chapter of the Association for Computational Linguistics.*

Navya Jose, Bharathi Raja Chakravarthi, Shardul Suryawanshi, Elizabeth Sherly, and John P McCrae. 2020. A survey of current datasets for code-switching research. In *2020 6th international conference on advanced computing and communication systems (ICACCS)*, pages 136–141. IEEE.

Armand Joulin, Edouard Grave, Piotr Bojanowski, Matthijs Douze, Hérve Jégou, and Tomas Mikolov. 2016. Fasttext.zip: Compressing text classification models.

Armand Joulin, Edouard Grave, and Piotr Bojanowski Tomas Mikolov. 2017. Bag of tricks for efficient text classification. *EACL 2017*, pages 427–431.

Te Taka Keegan. 2017. Machine translation for te reo Māori. In Hemi Whaanga, Te Taka Keegan, and Mark Apperley, editors, *He Whare Hangarau Māori Language, Culture & Technology*, pages 23–28. Te Pua Wānanga ki te Ao/Faculty of Māori and Indigenous Studies.

Diederik P Kingma and Jimmy Ba. 2015. Adam: A method for stochastic optimization. In *International Conference on Learning Representations (ICLR).*

Suraj Maharjan, Elizabeth Blair, Steven Bethard, and Thamar Solorio. 2015. Developing language-tagged corpora for code-switching tweets. In *Proceedings of The 9th Linguistic Annotation Workshop*, pages 72–84.

Joanne Marras Tate and Vaughan Rapatahana. 2022. Māori ways of speaking: Code-switching in parliamentary discourse, Māori and river identity, and the power of Kaitiakitanga for conservation. *Journal of International and Intercultural Communication*, pages 1–22.

Tomas Mikolov, Kai Chen, Greg Corrado, and Jeffrey Dean. 2013. Efficient estimation of word representations in vector space.

Giovanni Molina, Fahad AlGhamdi, Mahmoud Ghoneim, Abdelati Hawwari, Nicolas Rey-Villamizar, Mona Diab, and Thamar Solorio. 2016. Overview for the second shared task on language identification in code-switched data. In *Proceedings of the Second Workshop on Computational Approaches to Code Switching*, pages 40–49.

Vaughan Rapatahana. 2017. English language as thief. In *Language and Globalization*, pages 64–76. Routledge.

Linda Tuhiwai Smith. 2021. *Decolonizing methodologies: Research and indigenous peoples*, third edition. Bloomsbury Publishing.

Thamar Solorio, Elizabeth Blair, Suraj Maharjan, Steven Bethard, Mona Diab, Mahmoud Ghoneim, Abdelati Hawwari, Fahad AlGhamdi, Julia Hirschberg, Alison Chang, et al. 2014. Overview for the first shared task on language identification in code-switched data. In *Proceedings of the First Workshop on Computational Approaches to Code Switching*, pages 62–72.

Nitish Srivastava, Geoffrey Hinton, Alex Krizhevsky, Ilya Sutskever, and Ruslan Salakhutdinov. 2014. Dropout: A simple way to prevent neural networks from overfitting. *Journal of Machine Learning Research*, 15(56):1929–1958.

David Trye, Andreea S Calude, Felipe Bravo-Marquez, and Te Taka Keegan. 2020. Hybrid hashtags: #YouKnowYoureAKiwiWhen your tweet contains Māori and English. *Frontiers in artificial intelligence*, 3:15.

David Trye, Andreea S Calude, Felipe Bravo-Marquez, and Te Taka Adrian Gregory Keegan. 2019. Māori loanwords: a corpus of New Zealand English tweets. In *Proc. of the 57th Annual Meeting of the Association for Computational Linguistics: Student Research Workshop*, pages 136–142.

David Trye, Te Taka Keegan, Paora Mato, and Mark Apperley. 2022. Harnessing indigenous tweets: The Reo Māori Twitter corpus. *Language resources and evaluation*, pages 1–40.

Te Hau White. 2016. A difference of perspective? Māori members of parliament and te ao Māori in parliament. *Political Science*, 68(2):175–191.

Chiyuan Zhang, Samy Bengio, Moritz Hardt, Benjamin Recht, and Oriol Vinyals. 2017. Understanding deep learning requires re-thinking generalization. In *Proc. International Conference on Learning Representations 2017*, pages 1–15.

Elena Álvarez Mellado and Constantine Lignos. 2022. Borrowing or codeswitching? Annotating for finer-grained distinctions in language mixing.

A Algorithms

Algorithm 1 Token-Level Labelling

```
Input: Pre-processed tweets, list of Māori labels obtained from RMT system, pre-trained ML model, and tokenizer
Output: Labels at token-level
class_label = [ML model output]
english_list = [tokens with class_label 'E']
maori_list = [tokens with class_label 'M']
rmt_list = [Māori tokens from RMT system]
ambiguous_list = [rmt_list ∩ english_list]
if len(ambiguous_list) != 0 then
    Remove ambiguous tokens from rmt_list & english_list
end if
for each tweet i do
    for each token j in i do
        if j in english_list then
            if j is detected as an English word using fastText and NLTK language detection tools then
                Assign label for j as E (English)
            end if
        else if j in rmt_list then
            if j in maori_list then
                Assign label for j as M (Māori)
            end if
        else if j in ambiguous_list then
            Assign label for j as A (Ambiguous)
        else if Token j not in 'E', 'M', 'A' then
            Assign label for j as U (Unknown)
        end if
    end for
end for
```

Algorithm 2 Context-Check for Ambiguous Items

```
Input: Pre-processed tweet tokens, list of Māori tokens, English tokens, and Ambiguous tokens obtained from token-level labelling
Output: Updated labels at token-level
for each tweet t do
    maori_list = [Māori words in t]
    english_list = [English words in t]
    ambiguous_list = [Ambiguous words in t]
    tokens = [all tokens in t]
    if len(ambiguous_list) != 0 then
        for amb_token in ambiguous_list do
            if amb_token contains {ā,ē,ī,ō,ū} then
                Assign label as M (Māori)
                Remove from ambiguous_list
            else
                before = tokens[index-1]
                after = tokens[index+1]
                before_before = tokens[index-2]
                after_after = tokens[index+2]
                if before & after in maori_list then
                    Assign label as M (Māori)
                    Remove from ambiguous_list
                else if before & after in english_list then
                    Assign label as E (English)
                    Remove from ambiguous_list
                else if before is null, i.e. amb_token is the first token in the tweet then
                    if after & after_after in maori_list then
                        Assign label as M (Māori)
                        Remove from ambiguous_list
                    else if after & after_after in english_list then
                        Assign label as E (English)
                        Remove from ambiguous_list
                    end if
                else if after is null, i.e. amb_token is the last token in the tweet then
                    if before_before & before in maori_list then
                        Assign label as M (Māori)
                        Remove from ambiguous_list
                    else if before_before & before in english_list then
                        Assign label as E (English)
                        Remove from ambiguous_list
                    end if
                end if
            end if
        end for
    end if
end for
```

Algorithm 3 Tweet-Level Labelling

```
Input: Bilingual tweets with token-level labels obtained using Algorithm 1 and Algorithm 2
Output: Labels at tweet-level
for each tweet t do
    maori_list = [Māori words in t]
    english_list = [English words in t]
    unknown_list = [Unknown words in t]
    ambiguous_list = [Ambiguous words in t]
    if len(maori_list) == 0 & len(unknown_list) == 0 & len(ambiguous_list) == 0 then
        tweet_label of t is E (English)
    else if len(english_list) == 0 & len(unknown_list) == 0 & len(ambiguous_list) == 0 then
        tweet_label of t is M (Māori)
    else if len(ambiguous_list) == 0 & len(unknown_list) == 0 then
        tweet_label of t is B (Bilingual)
    else
        tweet_label of t is O (Other)
    end if
end for
for each tweet t do
    label_ML = ML tweet-label for t
    if label_ML == tweet_label then
        Final tweet-level label for MET Corpus
    else
        Further investigation needed
    end if
end for
```

Meta-Learning Adaptive Knowledge Distillation for Efficient Biomedical Natural Language Processing

Abiola Obamuyide and **Blair Johnston**
Strathclyde Institute of Pharmacy and Biomedical Sciences
University of Strathclyde
Glasgow, United Kingdom
firstname.lastname@strath.ac.uk

Abstract

There has been an increase in the number of large and high-performing models made available for various biomedical natural language processing tasks. While these models have demonstrated impressive performance on various biomedical tasks, their training and run-time costs can be computationally prohibitive. This work investigates the use of knowledge distillation, a common model compression method, to reduce the size of large models for biomedical natural language processing. We further improve the performance of knowledge distillation methods for biomedical natural language by proposing a meta-learning approach which adaptively learns parameters that enable the optimal rate of knowledge exchange between the teacher and student models from the distillation data during knowledge distillation. Experiments on two biomedical natural language processing tasks demonstrate that our proposed adaptive meta-learning approach to knowledge distillation delivers improved predictive performance over previous and recent state-of-the-art knowledge distillation methods.

1 Introduction

While there has been an increase in the number of large, pre-trained language models with impressive performance on various biomedical tasks (Shin et al., 2020; Gururangan et al., 2020; Lee et al., 2020; Lewis et al., 2020; Gu et al., 2022), the training and deployment of these models can be computationally prohibitive and time-consuming, especially in resource-constrained settings. The inference latencies and storage costs of these models make their deployment for real-word biomedical applications a challenge. Knowledge distillation (Bucila et al., 2006; Ba and Caruana, 2014; Hinton et al., 2015; Romero et al., 2015), a model compression technique which aims to transfer the performance of a large and computationally inefficient teacher model to a smaller and more efficient student model, has been proposed as a way to reduce the size of large models while retaining their predictive performance.

While a variety of knowledge distillation approaches have been proposed in the literature (Hinton et al., 2015; Sun et al., 2019; Gajbhiye et al., 2021; Zhou et al., 2022), their effectiveness have largely not been evaluated on biomedical natural language processing tasks. In this work, we evaluate the effectiveness of the proposed approaches for knowledge distillation on biomedical NLP tasks. To further enhance performance, we propose an adaptive meta-learning method for distilling large and inefficient biomedical models into more efficient and smaller ones. In experiments conducted on two biomedical natural language processing tasks, we find that our proposed meta-learning approach to knowledge distillation delivers improved predictive performance over previous and recent state-of-the-art knowledge distillation methods.

2 Knowledge Distillation

Knowledge distillation is a model compression method which aims to transfer knowledge from large and accurate but computationally inefficient models to smaller and more efficient models without significant loss in task performance. This is usually achieved by training a smaller and computationally efficient student model to imitate the outputs of a larger and inefficient teacher model with a knowledge distillation objective. For instance, the knowledge distillation objective proposed in Hinton et al. (2015) uses the final output logits produced by the teacher model to transfer its hidden knowledge to the student model. Concretely, given a teacher model T parametrized by θ_T, a student model S parametrized by θ_S and a dataset $\mathcal{D}$ containing N instances $\mathcal{D} = \{(x_i, y_i)\}_{i=1}^{N}$, the knowledge transfer between teacher and student can be achieved by training the student with a knowledge distillation objective $\mathcal{L}_{KD}$ of the form:

Findings of the Association for Computational Linguistics: AACL-IJCNLP 2022, pages 131–137
November 20–23, 2022.

$$\mathcal{L}_{KD} = \frac{1}{N}\sum_{i=1}^{N}\left[\alpha\mathcal{L}_D\big(T\left(x_i,\theta_T\right), S\left(x_i,\theta_S\right)\big)\right.$$
$$\left. + \beta\mathcal{L}_\mathcal{T}\big(y_i, S\left(x_i,\theta_S\right)\big)\right] \quad (1)$$

where $\mathcal{L}_D$ is a measure of divergence (such as the KL-divergence) between the teacher's output predictive distribution $T\left(x_i,\theta_T\right)$ and the student's output predictive distribution $S\left(x_i,\theta_S\right)$, $\mathcal{L}_\mathcal{T}$ is a task-specific loss function (such as the standard cross-entropy loss), x_i is an input instance with label y_i, while α and β are (scalar) hyper-parameters which determine the relative weight between the two components of the overall knowledge distillation loss function. In other words, α and β determine the rate of knowledge exchange between teacher and student during knowledge distillation. Typically, the values of α and β are manually set before knowledge distillation training, and are then kept fixed throughout. Gou et al. (2021) and Gupta and Agrawal (2022) give further overviews of various knowledge distillation methods.

3 Meta-Learning

Meta-learning, also known as learning to learn (Biggs, 1985; Schmidhuber, 1987; Bengio et al., 1991; Thrun and Pratt, 1998) aims to develop algorithms and models that are able to learn more efficiently with experience, by generalizing from the knowledge of related tasks. These models are able to learn how to learn, by improving their own learning process over time. Various approaches to meta-learning have been proposed and applied in various areas. These approaches include specific-architectures for learning to learn (Vinyals et al., 2016; Snell et al., 2017), learning to update model parameters from background knowledge (Andrychowicz et al., 2016; Ravi and Larochelle, 2017), and gradient-based model-agnostic meta-learning methods (Finn et al., 2017; Nichol et al., 2018; Rothfuss et al., 2021). Example natural language processing tasks to which meta-learning has been applied include machine translation (Gu et al., 2018) and quality estimation (Obamuyide et al., 2021a,b).

Gradient-based model-agnostic meta-learning algorithms such as *MAML* (Finn et al., 2017) often involve a bi-level optimization objective where feedback from the performance of an inner-learner (student model) is used to optimize a meta-learner (teacher model) with the aid of a meta-objective. In other words, in contrast with the teacher model in common knowledge distillation approaches which does not take into account feedback from the student model, the teacher model in meta-learning is able to receive and utilize feedback from the student model in order to improve itself.

Additionally, in knowledge distillation the teacher and student models are usually trained one after the other, with the teacher model trained first and then fixed during the student training. On the other hand, the student and teacher models in meta-learning are trained jointly together in order for them to improve each other.

4 Knowledge Distillation with Meta-Learning

Some works have investigated the use of the bi-level optimization framework in meta-learning to improve knowledge distillation, that is, to employ meta-learning to explicitly optimize the teacher for better knowledge transfer during the knowledge distillation process. For instance, Pan et al. (2021) trained a teacher network that can be adapted across several domains with meta-learning, and then perform standard knowledge distillation to distil the knowledge present in the teacher network into a student network. However, Pan et al. (2021) utilize meta-learning only to train a teacher model, and not throughout knowledge distillation training, thus limiting the generalizability of their approach. In order to enable the teacher model to better transfer knowledge to the student, Zhou et al. (2022) proposed the use of a meta-learning pilot update mechanism which improves the alignment between the student and the teacher in knowledge distillation. In their approach, Zhou et al. (2022) update both the teacher and student throughout the knowledge distillation training process, resulting in improved knowledge distillation performance.

5 Meta-Learning Adaptive Knowledge Distillation

An important limitation in all aforementioned knowledge distillation methods, including those that make use of meta-learning, is that they treat the rate of knowledge exchange between teacher and student (α and β in Equation 1) as fixed during training. This is not ideal, as the optimal rate and level of knowledge exchange between teacher and student should be updated during training to account for their current state.

A relevant and analogous human analogy is that school teachers teach and students learn different curricula depending on the student's educational level (e.g. nursery, primary, secondary, or university student). In most circumstances, it would not be appropriate for a human teacher to be teaching university-level knowledge to primary school students, and vice-versa. Therefore, α and β in knowledge distillation also need to be adaptive and learnable.

As a solution to the aforementioned issue, in this work we propose to treat α and β as learnable parameters which are updated during training. Our work builds on that of Zhou et al. (2022) and further enhances it with learnable α and β. This would allow the values of α and β to change to reflect the needs of the student throughout training. As we demonstrate in the experiments, this change results in improved knowledge distillation performance. We refer to our adapted approach as Meta-Learning Adaptive Knowledge Distillation (MetaAdaptiveKD), and our overall training algorithm is illustrated in Algorithm 1.

Algorithm 1 Meta-Learning Adaptive Knowledge Distillation (MetaAdaptiveKD)

Require: Training data $\mathcal{D}^{train}$, holdout data $\mathcal{D}^{hold}$
Require: Teacher θ_T and student θ_S models
Require: Teacher μ and student ϵ learning rates
Require: Learnable α and β

1: Initialize $\theta_T, \theta_S, \alpha, \beta$
2: **while** not done **do**
3: Create a copy of student parameter θ_S to θ'_S
4: Sample mini-batches of train data $\boldsymbol{x}_{train} \sim \mathcal{D}^{train}$
5: **for each** $\boldsymbol{x}_{train}$ **do**
6: $\theta'_S \leftarrow \theta'_S - \epsilon \nabla_{\theta'_S} \mathcal{L}_{KD}\left(\boldsymbol{x}_{train}, \theta'_S, \theta_T, \alpha, \beta\right)$
7: **end for**
8: Sample mini-batches of holdout data $\boldsymbol{x}_{hold} \sim \mathcal{D}^{hold}$
9: **for each** $\boldsymbol{x}_{hold}$ **do**
10: $\alpha \leftarrow \alpha - \mu \nabla_\alpha \mathcal{L}_T\big(\boldsymbol{x}_{hold}, \theta'_S\left(\theta_T, \alpha, \beta\right)\big)$
11: $\beta \leftarrow \beta - \mu \nabla_\beta \mathcal{L}_T\big(\boldsymbol{x}_{hold}, \theta'_S\left(\theta_T, \alpha, \beta\right)\big)$
12: $\theta_T \leftarrow \theta_T - \mu \nabla_{\theta_T} \mathcal{L}_T\big(\boldsymbol{x}_{hold}, \theta'_S\left(\theta_T, \alpha, \beta\right)\big)$
13: **end for**
14: Update $\theta_S \leftarrow \theta_S - \epsilon \nabla_{\theta_S} \mathcal{L}_{KD}\left(\boldsymbol{x}_{train}, \theta_S, \theta_T, \alpha, \beta\right)$
15: **end while**

Our approach described in Algorithm 1 assumes access to both training and holdout datasets[1]. We start by initializing parameters of the teacher and student models, and α and β (line 1). At each training step, we first create a copy of the student parameters (line 3) and sample a number of mini-batches from the training data (line 4). Then for each mini-batch of training data, we update the copy of the student model (lines 5-7). Because the updated student model θ'_S as well as its loss on the holdout set $\mathcal{L}_T\big(\boldsymbol{x}_{hold}, \theta'_S\left(\theta_T, \alpha, \beta\right)\big)$ is now a function of α, β and θ_T, we can use the holdout loss to optimize α, β and θ_T. Thus, we sample mini-batches of data from the holdout set (line 8), and for each mini-batch of holdout data, we update α, β and θ_T (lines 9-13). Finally, we update parameters of the original student model θ_S (line 14). At the end of training, the final student model θ_S can be evaluated and deployed.

[1]The holdout dataset can, for instance, be obtained by splitting from the training set.

6 Experimental Setup and Details

6.1 Datasets

Given our interest in improving the efficiency of biomedical models with knowledge distillation, we conduct experiments on the following two (2) biomedical datasets:

ChemProt: The Chemical Protein Interaction corpus (ChemProt) (Krallinger et al., 2017) is a dataset of PubMed [2] abstracts annotated with interactions between chemical and protein entities. Following common practice, we evaluate on five(5) classes from this dataset.

GAD: The Genetic Association Database (GAD) (Bravo et al., 2014) is a binary relation classification corpus containing a list of gene-disease associations, with the corresponding sentences reporting the association.

Table 1 provides a breakdown of the instances in both datasets.

Dataset	Train	Dev	Test
ChemProt	18035	11268	15745
GAD	4261	535	534
Total	22296	11803	16279

Table 1: Number of instances in the train/dev/test splits of the ChemProt and GAD datasets.

6.2 Teacher and Student Models

Both the teacher and student models are based on the transformer architecture (Vaswani et al., 2017). Specifically, the teacher model is a transformer model with 12 layers and 110M parameters. It is initialized with weights from

[2]https://pubmed.ncbi.nlm.nih.gov

BioLinkBERT$_{base}$ (Yasunaga et al., 2022), a state-of-the-art biomedical transformer model with same architecture as BERT (Devlin et al., 2019), but pre-trained using citation links between PubMed articles. In contrast, the student model is a 6-layer transfomer with 66M parameters. It is initialized with weights from the first six(6) layers of BioLinkBERT$_{base}$.

6.3 Baselines

We compare our approach with the following baselines:

Finetune This is the conventional finetuning approach, where a pre-trained transformer student model is finetuned on each dataset without any knowledge distillation loss. This student model has the same number of parameters as the student model used by our approach and the other baseline knowledge distillation approaches. It is initialized with weights from the first six(6) layers of BioLinkBERT$_{base}$.

KD This is the original knowledge distillation approach proposed in (Hinton et al., 2015). This approach first trains a teacher model, which is then kept fixed while the student is trained with the standard knowledge distillation objective in Equation 1.

PatientKD This approach to knowledge distillation was proposed by Sun et al. (2019). It works by aligning intermediate layer feature representations from the teacher and the student.

MetaDistil This is a recent, state-of-the-art meta-learning approach to knowledge distillation proposed by Zhou et al. (2022). Different from our approach, *MetaDistil* uses fixed values for α and β.

6.4 Experimental Details

Hyper-parameter	Value
Learning rate	5e-5
Mini-batch size	8
Max. sequence length	128
Distillation temperature	2
Number of training epochs	20

Table 2: Hyper-parameter values for all compared approaches

Our implementation makes use of Pytorch (Paszke et al., 2019), transformers (Wolf et al., 2020) and higher (Grefenstette et al., 2019) libraries. All compared knowledge distillation approaches, including ours, make use of the same values for hyperparameters such as the number of training epochs, learning rate and batch size. These values were selected by manual search in initial experiments, and are provided in Table 2. Each experiment is repeated across five (5) different random seeds, and we report the average.

6.5 Evaluation

We make use of the F1 measure as performance metric. We repeat each distillation experiment five(5) times and report the average F1 performance of the distilled student on the test set of each dataset.

7 Results and Discussion

The results obtained by our approach and the other knowledge distillation methods on the two biomedical datasets are as shown in Table 3. All student models have nearly twice (x1.94) the inference speed of the teacher model and only about 60% (66M) of the teacher's parameters.

Method	#	Speed↑	F1 (%)	
			ChemProt	GAD
BioLinkBERT (Teacher)	110M	x1.00	77.57	84.39
Finetune	66M	x1.94	72.17	78.53
KD	66M	x1.94	72.49	78.84
PatientKD	66M	x1.94	72.10	78.89
MetaDistil	66M	x1.94	72.73	79.08
MetaAdaptiveKD	66M	x1.94	**73.03**	**79.62**

Table 3: Experimental results on the ChemProt and GAD datasets. The # column represents the number of parameters in each model, while the Speed↑ column represents the speedup of each approach when compared to the teacher model. F1 results of the teacher model are obtained from Yasunaga et al. (2022). The F1 results for all student models including ours are the average of five(5) runs with different random seeds.

In terms of F1 performance of the student models, we find that just finetuning the student model (*Finetune*) without any knowledge distillation objective underperforms all other distillation methods on the GAD dataset and also underperforms all other methods except *PatientKD* on the Chemprot dataset, which demonstrates the effectiveness of knowledge distillation in general. *PatientKD* outperformed *KD* on the GAD dataset but not on the

ChemProt dataset, while *MetaDistil* outperforms *KD* and *PatientKD* on both datasets.

Finally, we find that our approach *MetaAdaptiveKD*, which adaptively learns α and β with meta-learning, outperforms all previous distillation methods on both datasets. The fact that our approach outperforms *MetaDistil* (a meta-learning method which uses fixed α and β) demonstrates the importance of not keeping α and β fixed during knowledge distillation, but instead learning their optimal values from the distillation data during training, as done in our approach.

8 Conclusion

In this work, we proposed a new meta-learning approach to knowledge distillation. In contrast to previous methods which manually set the rate of knowledge exchange between student and teacher and keep them fixed throughout training, our approach learns their optimal values adaptively from the distillation data during training. In experiments conducted on two biomedical datasets, we demonstrated that our approach outperforms previous knowledge distillation methods.

Limitations, Risks and Ethical Considerations

Meta-learning methods for knowledge distillation in general require additional computational resources compared to traditional distillation methods. The *MetaAdaptiveKD* algorithm for knowledge distillation introduced in this work is a meta-learning based approach with similar computational requirements as previous meta-learning methods.

Although this computational cost can be high, it is a one-time investment with long-term returns since it would result in an efficient and more accurate compressed model with reduced run-time costs. In addition, while we have conducted experiments on two english biomedical datasets, *MetaAdaptiveKD* is a generic distillation technique that can be applied to data from other languages and domains.

In terms of risks and ethical considerations, *MetaAdaptiveKD* improves on the performance of previous knowledge distillation methods and does not introduce additional risks and ethical concerns in comparison with these previous methods. Nevertheless, as has been noted in previous work (Hooker et al., 2020), the introduction or amplification of algorithmic biases is a common risk of model compression methods in general, and devising ways of addressing these concerns is an important line of future work.

Acknowledgment

This work is co-funded by the Made Smarter Innovation challenge at UK Research and Innovation (Grant Reference: EP/V062077/1).

References

Marcin Andrychowicz, Misha Denil, Sergio Gomez, Matthew W Hoffman, David Pfau, Tom Schaul, Brendan Shillingford, and Nando De Freitas. 2016. Learning to learn by gradient descent by gradient descent. In *Advances in Neural Information Processing Systems*, pages 3981–3989.

Jimmy Ba and Rich Caruana. 2014. Do deep nets really need to be deep? In *Advances in Neural Information Processing Systems 27: Annual Conference on Neural Information Processing Systems 2014, December 8-13 2014, Montreal, Quebec, Canada*, pages 2654–2662.

Yoshua Bengio, Samy Bengio, and Jocelyn Cloutier. 1991. Learning a synaptic learning rule. *IJCNN-91-Seattle International Joint Conference on Neural Networks*, ii:969 vol.2–.

John B. Biggs. 1985. The role of metalearning in study processes. *British Journal of Educational Psychology*, 55:185–212.

Àlex Bravo, Janet Piñero, Núria Queralt, Michael Rautschka, and Laura Inés Furlong. 2014. Extraction of relations between genes and diseases from text and large-scale data analysis: implications for translational research. *BMC Bioinformatics*, 16.

Cristian Bucila, Rich Caruana, and Alexandru Niculescu-Mizil. 2006. Model compression. In *Proceedings of the 12th ACM SIGKDD international conference on Knowledge discovery and data mining, pages 535–541*.

Jacob Devlin, Ming-Wei Chang, Kenton Lee, and Kristina Toutanova. 2019. BERT: pre-training of deep bidirectional transformers for language understanding. In *Proceedings of the 2019 Conference of the North American Chapter of the Association for Computational Linguistics: Human Language Technologies, NAACL-HLT 2019, Minneapolis, MN, USA, June 2-7, 2019, Volume 1 (Long and Short Papers)*, pages 4171–4186. Association for Computational Linguistics.

Chelsea Finn, Pieter Abbeel, and Sergey Levine. 2017. Model-agnostic meta-learning for fast adaptation of deep networks. In *Proceedings of the 34th International Conference on Machine Learning*, volume 70 of *Proceedings of Machine Learning Research*, pages 1126–1135, International Convention Centre, Sydney, Australia.

Amit Gajbhiye, Marina Fomicheva, Fernando Alva-Manchego, Frédéric Blain, Abiola Obamuyide, Nikolaos Aletras, and Lucia Specia. 2021. Knowledge distillation for quality estimation. In *Findings of the Association for Computational Linguistics: ACL-IJCNLP 2021*, pages 5091–5099, Online. Association for Computational Linguistics.

Jianping Gou, Baosheng Yu, Stephen J. Maybank, and Dacheng Tao. 2021. Knowledge distillation: A survey. *Int. J. Comput. Vis.*, 129(6):1789–1819.

Edward Grefenstette, Brandon Amos, Denis Yarats, Phu Mon Htut, Artem Molchanov, Franziska Meier, Douwe Kiela, Kyunghyun Cho, and Soumith Chintala. 2019. Generalized inner loop meta-learning. *CoRR*, abs/1910.01727.

Jiatao Gu, Yong Wang, Yun Chen, Victor O. K. Li, and Kyunghyun Cho. 2018. Meta-learning for low-resource neural machine translation. In *Proceedings of the 2018 Conference on Empirical Methods in Natural Language Processing*, pages 3622–3631, Brussels, Belgium. Association for Computational Linguistics.

Yuxian Gu, Robert Tinn, Hao Cheng, Michael R. Lucas, Naoto Usuyama, Xiaodong Liu, Tristan Naumann, Jianfeng Gao, and Hoifung Poon. 2022. Domain-specific language model pretraining for biomedical natural language processing. *ACM Transactions on Computing for Healthcare (HEALTH)*, 3:1 – 23.

Manish Gupta and Puneet Agrawal. 2022. Compression of deep learning models for text: A survey. *ACM Trans. Knowl. Discov. Data*, 16(4):61:1–61:55.

Suchin Gururangan, Ana Marasovic, Swabha Swayamdipta, Kyle Lo, Iz Beltagy, Doug Downey, and Noah A. Smith. 2020. Don't stop pretraining: Adapt language models to domains and tasks. In *Proceedings of the 58th Annual Meeting of the Association for Computational Linguistics, ACL 2020, Online, July 5-10, 2020*, pages 8342–8360. Association for Computational Linguistics.

Geoffrey E. Hinton, Oriol Vinyals, and Jeffrey Dean. 2015. Distilling the knowledge in a neural network. *CoRR*, abs/1503.02531.

Sara Hooker, Nyalleng Moorosi, Gregory Clark, Samy Bengio, and Emily L. Denton. 2020. Characterising bias in compressed models. *ArXiv*, abs/2010.03058.

Martin Krallinger, Obdulia Rabal, Saber Ahmad Akhondi, Martín Pérez Pérez, Jesus Santamaría, Gael Pérez Rodríguez, Georgios Tsatsaronis, Ander Intxaurrondo, J. A. Lopez, Umesh K. Nandal, Erin M. van Buel, Ambika Chandrasekhar, Marleen Rodenburg, Astrid Lægreid, Marius A. Doornenbal, Julen Oyarzábal, Anália Lourenço, and Alfonso Valencia. 2017. Overview of the biocreative vi chemical-protein interaction track.

Jinhyuk Lee, Wonjin Yoon, Sungdong Kim, Donghyeon Kim, Sunkyu Kim, Chan Ho So, and Jaewoo Kang. 2020. Biobert: a pre-trained biomedical language representation model for biomedical text mining. *Bioinform.*, 36(4):1234–1240.

Patrick S. H. Lewis, Myle Ott, Jingfei Du, and Veselin Stoyanov. 2020. Pretrained language models for biomedical and clinical tasks: Understanding and extending the state-of-the-art. In *Proceedings of the 3rd Clinical Natural Language Processing Workshop, ClinicalNLP@EMNLP 2020, Online, November 19, 2020*, pages 146–157. Association for Computational Linguistics.

Alex Nichol, Joshua Achiam, and John Schulman. 2018. On first-order meta-learning algorithms. *CoRR, abs/1803.02999*.

Abiola Obamuyide, Marina Fomicheva, and Lucia Specia. 2021a. Bayesian model-agnostic meta-learning with matrix-valued kernels for quality estimation. In *Proceedings of the 6th Workshop on Representation Learning for NLP (RepL4NLP-2021)*, pages 223–230, Online. Association for Computational Linguistics.

Abiola Obamuyide, Marina Fomicheva, and Lucia Specia. 2021b. Continual quality estimation with online Bayesian meta-learning. In *Proceedings of the 59th Annual Meeting of the Association for Computational Linguistics and the 11th International Joint Conference on Natural Language Processing (Volume 2: Short Papers)*, pages 190–197, Online. Association for Computational Linguistics.

Haojie Pan, Chengyu Wang, Minghui Qiu, Yichang Zhang, Yaliang Li, and Jun Huang. 2021. Meta-KD: A meta knowledge distillation framework for language model compression across domains. In *Proceedings of the 59th Annual Meeting of the Association for Computational Linguistics and the 11th International Joint Conference on Natural Language Processing (Volume 1: Long Papers)*, pages 3026–3036, Online. Association for Computational Linguistics.

Adam Paszke, Sam Gross, Francisco Massa, Adam Lerer, James Bradbury, Gregory Chanan, Trevor Killeen, Zeming Lin, Natalia Gimelshein, Luca Antiga, Alban Desmaison, Andreas Kopf, Edward Yang, Zachary DeVito, Martin Raison, Alykhan Tejani, Sasank Chilamkurthy, Benoit Steiner, Lu Fang, Junjie Bai, and Soumith Chintala. 2019. Pytorch: An imperative style, high-performance deep learning library. In H. Wallach, H. Larochelle, A. Beygelzimer, F. d'Alché-Buc, E. Fox, and R. Garnett, editors, *Advances in Neural Information Processing Systems 32*, pages 8024–8035. Curran Associates, Inc.

Sachin Ravi and Hugo Larochelle. 2017. Optimization As a Model for Few-Shot Learning. In *International Conference on Learning Representations 2017*.

Adriana Romero, Nicolas Ballas, Samira Ebrahimi Kahou, Antoine Chassang, Carlo Gatta, and Yoshua

Bengio. 2015. Fitnets: Hints for thin deep nets. In *3rd International Conference on Learning Representations, ICLR 2015, San Diego, CA, USA, May 7-9, 2015, Conference Track Proceedings*.

Jonas Rothfuss, Vincent Fortuin, Martin Josifoski, and Andreas Krause. 2021. PACOH: bayes-optimal meta-learning with pac-guarantees. In *Proceedings of the 38th International Conference on Machine Learning, ICML 2021, 18-24 July 2021, Virtual Event*, volume 139 of *Proceedings of Machine Learning Research*, pages 9116–9126. PMLR.

Jurgen Schmidhuber. 1987. Evolutionary principles in self-referential learning. *On learning how to learn: The meta-meta-... hook.) Diploma thesis, Institut f. Informatik, Tech. Univ. Munich.*

Hoo-Chang Shin, Yang Zhang, Evelina Bakhturina, Raul Puri, Mostofa Patwary, Mohammad Shoeybi, and Raghav Mani. 2020. Biomegatron: Larger biomedical domain language model. In *Proceedings of the 2020 Conference on Empirical Methods in Natural Language Processing, EMNLP 2020, Online, November 16-20, 2020*, pages 4700–4706. Association for Computational Linguistics.

Jake Snell, Kevin Swersky, and Richard Zemel. 2017. Prototypical networks for few-shot learning. In *Advances in Neural Information Processing Systems*, pages 4077–4087.

Siqi Sun, Yu Cheng, Zhe Gan, and Jingjing Liu. 2019. Patient knowledge distillation for BERT model compression. In *Proceedings of the 2019 Conference on Empirical Methods in Natural Language Processing and the 9th International Joint Conference on Natural Language Processing, EMNLP-IJCNLP 2019, Hong Kong, China, November 3-7, 2019*, pages 4322–4331. Association for Computational Linguistics.

Sebastian Thrun and Lorien Pratt. 1998. Learning to Learn: Introduction and Overview. In *Learning to Learn*, pages 3–17. Springer US, Boston, MA.

Ashish Vaswani, Noam Shazeer, Niki Parmar, Jakob Uszkoreit, Llion Jones, Aidan N. Gomez, Lukasz Kaiser, and Illia Polosukhin. 2017. Attention is all you need. In *Advances in Neural Information Processing Systems 30: Annual Conference on Neural Information Processing Systems 2017, December 4-9, 2017, Long Beach, CA, USA*, pages 5998–6008.

Oriol Vinyals, Charles Blundell, Timothy Lillicrap, Daan Wierstra, et al. 2016. Matching networks for one shot learning. In *Advances in neural information processing systems*, pages 3630–3638.

Thomas Wolf, Lysandre Debut, Victor Sanh, Julien Chaumond, Clement Delangue, Anthony Moi, Pierric Cistac, Tim Rault, Rémi Louf, Morgan Funtowicz, Joe Davison, Sam Shleifer, Patrick von Platen, Clara Ma, Yacine Jernite, Julien Plu, Canwen Xu, Teven Le Scao, Sylvain Gugger, Mariama Drame, Quentin Lhoest, and Alexander M. Rush. 2020. Transformers: State-of-the-art natural language processing. In *Proceedings of the 2020 Conference on Empirical Methods in Natural Language Processing: System Demonstrations*, pages 38–45, Online. Association for Computational Linguistics.

Michihiro Yasunaga, Jure Leskovec, and Percy Liang. 2022. LinkBERT: Pretraining language models with document links. In *Proceedings of the 60th Annual Meeting of the Association for Computational Linguistics (Volume 1: Long Papers)*, pages 8003–8016, Dublin, Ireland. Association for Computational Linguistics.

Wangchunshu Zhou, Canwen Xu, and Julian McAuley. 2022. BERT learns to teach: Knowledge distillation with meta learning. In *Proceedings of the 60th Annual Meeting of the Association for Computational Linguistics (Volume 1: Long Papers)*, pages 7037–7049, Dublin, Ireland. Association for Computational Linguistics.

The Effects of Surprisal across Languages: Results from Native and Non-native Reading

Andrea Gregor de Varda
Department of Psychology
University of Milano – Bicocca
a.devarda@campus.unimib.it

Marco Marelli
Department of Psychology
University of Milano – Bicocca
marco.marelli@unimib.it

Abstract

It is well known that the *surprisal* of an upcoming word, as estimated by language models, is a solid predictor of reading times (Smith and Levy, 2013). However, most of the studies that support this view are based on English and few other Germanic languages, leaving an open question as to the cross-lingual generalizability of such findings. Moreover, they tend to consider only the best-performing eye-tracking measure, which might conflate the effects of predictive and integrative processing. Furthermore, it is not clear whether prediction plays a role in non-native language processing in bilingual individuals (Grüter et al., 2014). We approach these problems at large scale, extracting surprisal estimates from mBERT, and assessing their psychometric predictive power on the MECO corpus, a cross-linguistic dataset of eye movement behavior in reading (Siegelman et al., 2022; Kuperman et al., 2020). We show that surprisal is a strong predictor of reading times across languages and fixation measurements, and that its effects in L2 are weaker with respect to L1.

1 Introduction

Context-dependent predictive processes have been proposed as a core component of the human cognitive system (Bar, 2007; Clark, 2013). In the language processing literature, a clear picture that is progressively emerging is that speakers spontaneously pre-activate the upcoming lexical material before they encounter it (Huettig, 2015; Schlenter, 2019; Staub, 2015). This pre-allocation of resources to predictable material is evidenced by the fact that unpredictable words are a major cause of processing costs, as measured through self-paced reading times (Frank and Hoeks, 2019; Fernandez Monsalve et al., 2012), eye movements (Ehrlich and Rayner, 1981) and pupil size (Frank and Thompson, 2012) in reading, and EEG responses (Kutas and Hillyard, 1984; Frank et al., 2015). The role of prediction in language processing was, in particular, characterized via computational modeling, with the information-theoretic notion of *surprisal* being extended to psycholinguistics (Hale, 2001; Levy, 2008). Surprisal quantitatively captures how unpredictable a word is in terms of the negative logarithm of the probability of a word conditioned by the preceding sentence context (1).

$$\mathrm{surprisal}(\mathrm{w_i}) = -\log_2 \mathrm{P}(\mathrm{w_i}|\mathrm{w_1}, \mathrm{w_2} \ldots \mathrm{w_{i-1}}) \quad (1)$$

In this perspective, surprisal acts as a linking function between cognitive effort and predictability (Fernandez Monsalve et al. 2012, but see Brothers and Kuperberg 2020), where the former is measured empirically, and the latter is estimated probabilistically. Levy (2008) demonstrated that the surprisal of a word given the previous context is mathematically equivalent to the Kullback-Leibler divergence (i.e. relative entropy) between probability distributions[1]. Under this view, surprisal effects can therefore be interpreted as the cognitive costs associated to a shift between probability distributions.

Computational linguistics has proven itself very useful to derive word probability estimates (Frank et al., 2013; Demberg and Keller, 2008; Levy, 2008), and the psychometric predictive power of a language model – i.e., how well it can account for human processing times – is a linear function of that model's quality, measured as its perplexity (Goodkind and Bicknell, 2018; Wilcox et al., 2020). Computational studies on prediction in sentence processing have the indisputable merit of testing the effects of predictability at large scale and in the context of naturalistic reading. However, if compared to psycholinguistic studies on prediction, they generally focus on:

[1] In its original formulation, surprisal theory was employed to account for syntactic processing. Probability shifts were thus defined over syntactic parses.

Findings of the Association for Computational Linguistics: AACL-IJCNLP 2022, pages 138–144
November 20–23, 2022.

i Gaze duration. Differently from psycholinguistic research (Frisson et al., 2005; Rayner et al., 2011), computational studies tend to consider only the eye-tracking measure that is typically best fitted by surprisal estimates, namely gaze duration (Aurnhammer and Frank, 2019; Goodkind and Bicknell, 2018; Smith and Levy, 2013; Wilcox et al., 2020), ignoring other cognitively relevant eye-tracking metrics.

ii Germanic languages. A vast body of findings corroborates the effects of lexical prediction in English (Aurnhammer and Frank, 2019; Frank and Bod, 2011; Frank et al., 2015; Fernandez Monsalve et al., 2012; Wilcox et al., 2020; Goodkind and Bicknell, 2018; Smith and Levy, 2013), Dutch (Frank and Hoeks, 2019; Brouwer et al., 2010) and German (Boston et al., 2008; Brouwer et al., 2021); however, evidence from other language families is far more limited (although see Fan and Reilly, 2020; Kuribayashi et al., 2021).

iii L1. Within the computational framework, most of the studies reported insofar targeted sentence processing in the dominant languages (but see Berzak and Levy, 2022; Frank, 2014, 2021), while the psycholinguistic community is witnessing an increasing interest in predictive processing in L2 (Cop et al., 2015; Grüter et al., 2014, 2017; Kaan et al., 2010; Martin et al., 2013).

We argue that these three limitations might undermine both the internal and the external validity of the results.

First (**i**), only considering the best-performing eye-tracking measure does not provide any insight as to *when* such predictability effects take place during natural reading. An analysis of the time range where predictability effects can be detected is however crucial to disentangle between predictive and integrative processes (Cevoli et al., 2022; Staub, 2015). Indeed, a higher processing cost induced by an unpredictable word might not be due to anticipatory processes, but also to a difficulty in integrating the unpredictable word in the phrasal context. While early measurements such as first fixation duration are thought to reflect lexical or pre-lexical processes (and thus a genuine effect of predictability; Staub, 2015), gaze duration can be considered as a "midmeasure" (Roberts and Siyanova-Chanturia, 2013), and thus it is not sufficient to disentangle between integrative and predictive processing.

Second (**ii**), some of the results that were obtained in English within the framework of surprisal theory were not replicated in other languages. For instance, Kuribayashi et al. (2021) have shown that the negative relationship between a language model's perplexity and its psychometric accuracy does not hold for the Japanese language. Hence, the rather limited typological variability in the language samples considered leaves an open question as to whether prediction itself should be considered as a core processing mechanism that generalizes across languages.

Third (**iii**) , the study of predictive processing in non-native reading is of crucial relevance since more than half of the global population is bilingual (Ansaldo et al., 2008). The role of anticipation in bilingual individuals is attracting growing interest in second language acquisition studies, and large-scale data-driven approaches might shed light on a complex picture currently characterized by little consensus. The Reduced Ability to Generate Expectations hypothesis (RAGE, Grüter et al., 2014, 2017) proposes that even highly proficient L2 speakers differ from native speakers in their abilities to anticipate the upcoming linguistic material. However, the results supporting this theory have been questioned (Hartsuiker et al., 2016; Leal et al., 2017); they are generally derived from offline tasks in small-scale studies (Grüter et al., 2014), and restricted to circumscribed linguistic phenomena (such as gender information in determiners, see Grüter et al., 2012; Lew-Williams and Fernald, 2010). Instead, it would be desirable to test the effects of word prediction in L2 when reading naturalistic, contextualized texts (see for instance Berzak and Levy, 2022; Cop et al., 2015), as opposed to artificially constructed experimental materials, presented out of context and repeated many times. Berzak and Levy (2022) have overcome these limitations by testing the effects of predictability in L2 at scale. They reported a *larger* effect of surprisal in non-native reading, which is at odds with the psycholinguistic evidence reported before, and difficult to explain. As mentioned by the authors, context-contingent expectations are statistically demanding to compute, and it is not clear why the effects of such a complex processing mechanism should be stronger in L2 than in L1.

In the present study we address these limitations in the literature by considering different eye-tracking measurements, including early fixation measurements that are expected to reflect predictive processes (**i**); extending our sample to 12 diverse languages, belonging to five language families and written in five different scripts (**ii**); and comparing the effect of prediction in L1 and L2 (**iii**).

2 Methods

2.1 Eye-tracking data

The MECO-L1 corpus (Siegelman et al., 2022) is a large-scale collection of high-quality eye movement records in 13 languages[2] collected in a naturalistic reading task. Participants were presented with 12 texts composed by multiple sentences, consisting in encyclopedic entries on a variety of topics. The MECO-L2 corpus provides eye movement data on English texts read by non-native speakers (Kuperman et al., 2020). In our study, we analyze three eye-tracking measurements, that are considered an early, an intermediate, and a late processing measure, respectively (Demberg and Keller, 2008; Roberts and Siyanova-Chanturia, 2013):

- *First fixation (FF):* the duration of the first fixation landing on the target word. This measure is often assumed to reflect lexical access and low-level oculomotor processes.
- *Gaze duration (GD):* the sum of the duration of the fixations on the target word before the gaze leaves it for the first time. This measure is thought to be indicative of semantic and early syntactic processing.
- *Total reading time (TT):* the sum of the duration of all the fixations on the target word. This measure is thought to be indicative of integrative processes.

The fixations considered by different eye-tracking measures are organized in a relationship of inclusion (FF $\subseteq$ GD $\subseteq$ TT); hence, intermediate and late processing measures inevitably incorporate information about early processing. However, since the inclusion relationship is asymmetrical, early measures do not include information about late processing. Hence, predictability effects that can be detected in early eye-tracking measures can be ascribed to predictive processing (Staub, 2015).

2.2 Model and metrics

Our probability estimates are derived with $\text{mBERT}_{\text{BASE}}$'s native masked language modelling component (Devlin et al., 2019), which has been shown to generate probability estimates that are good predictors of eye movement data (Hollenstein et al., 2021). To derive word-level probability estimates, we freeze the model weights and mask all the sentence tokens iteratively. Except for the first and the last token of each sequence, where the model predictions are conditioned only by the right and the left context, mBERT predicts the token in the masked position relying upon the bidirectional context. Note that the formula in (1) implicitly refers to auto-regressive, left-to-right models. Dealing with a bidirectional encoder, we calculate the bidirectional $\text{surprisal}_\text{B}$ of a word w_i in a sentence of N tokens as the negative logarithm of the word probability conditioned by both the left ($\text{w}_1 \ldots \text{w}_{\text{i-1}}$) and the right context ($\text{w}_{\text{i+1}} \ldots \text{w}_\text{N}$, see 2).

$$\text{surprisal}_\text{B}(\text{w}_\text{i}) = -\log_2 \text{P}(\text{w}_\text{i} | \text{w}_1 \ldots \text{w}_{\text{i-1}}, \text{w}_{\text{i+1}} \ldots \text{w}_\text{N}) \tag{2}$$

2.3 Analyses

In our analyses, we discard all the surprisal estimates of multi-token words[3]. We fit all our models as linear mixed-effects models, with random intercepts for participants and items. As a baseline, we include word frequency (derived from multilingual large-scale frequency estimates, Speer et al., 2018), length, and their interaction; additionally, we include as covariates the same indexes relative to the previous $\text{w}_{\text{i-1}}$ word, to account for spillover effects. Then, we include the effect of surprisal relative to both w_i and $\text{w}_{\text{i-1}}$. We first fit 36 separate models (12 languages $\times$ 3 fixation measurements) to assess the effects of surprisal for each individual language at different processing stages; then, we fit an overall model for each fixation measurement including languages as random slopes and intercepts.

In a second part of the study, we compare predictability effects across L1 and L2; to do so, we merge the two MECO datasets, and dummy-code whether each trial is recorded in an individual's

[2] We excluded the Estonian data in our study since we could not find frequency estimates comparable with the other languages.

[3] Indeed, while with standard auto-regressive models multi-token probabilities can be computed via the application of the chain rule, the same cannot be done with masked language models. See Table 1, column "%" for the percentage of the original items that were included in the analyses.

			First fixation duration				Gaze duration				Total reading time			
Language	N	%	Estimate	SE	t	p	Estimate	SE	t	p	Estimate	SE	t	p
Dutch	44,843	66%	0.0222	0.0085	2.6226	0.0088	0.0233	0.0087	2.6718	0.0076	0.0456	0.0100	4.5477	$\ll .0001$
English	65,421	77%	0.0156	0.0084	1.8574	0.0634	0.0112	0.0082	1.3612	0.1736	0.0145	0.0087	1.6619	0.0967
Finnish	20,277	31%	0.0464	0.0175	2.6515	0.0083	0.0393	0.0173	2.2789	0.0230	0.0372	0.0182	2.0387	0.0419
German	49,608	66%	0.0267	0.0112	2.3800	0.0175	0.0314	0.0117	2.6822	0.0074	0.0522	0.0125	4.1661	$\ll .0001$
Greek	56,738	51%	0.0111	0.0150	0.7363	0.4617	0.0331	0.0143	2.3064	0.0212	0.0565	0.0148	3.8106	0.0001
Hebrew	22,718	34%	0.0110	0.0128	0.8549	0.3929	0.0313	0.0124	2.5262	0.0118	0.0233	0.0144	1.6184	0.1060
Italian	56,738	65%	0.0361	0.0087	4.1286	$\ll .0001$	0.0400	0.0084	4.7448	$\ll .0001$	0.0279	0.0087	3.2228	0.0013
Korean	8,283	23%	0.0182	0.0132	1.3836	0.1667	0.0365	0.0132	2.7624	0.0058	0.0095	0.0132	0.7232	0.4696
Norwegian	33,930	54%	0.0190	0.0079	2.4048	0.0162	0.0240	0.0077	3.1272	0.0018	0.0354	0.0077	4.5788	$\ll .0001$
Russian	33,109	48%	0.0062	0.0118	0.5290	0.5969	0.0174	0.0111	1.5691	0.1169	0.0108	0.0116	0.9307	0.3522
Spanish	66,097	76%	0.0105	0.0063	1.6646	0.0960	0.0075	0.0061	1.2283	0.2194	-0.0022	0.0062	-0.3604	0.7186
Turkish	11,546	36%	0.0133	0.0114	1.1654	0.2440	0.0211	0.0113	1.8749	0.0610	0.0501	0.0116	4.3164	$\ll .0001$

Table 1: Effects of surprisal across languages on the three fixation measurements considered. The first two columns indicate the language from which the reading data were obtained, the number of data points on which the regression coefficients were computed, and the percentage of items that were not discarded in the analyses (see §2.3). The following columns indicate the regression coefficients of surprisal, their standard error (SE), the t statistic and the respective p-value for FF, GD and TT.

dominant or non-dominant language. Then, we test the interaction between language dominance (L1-L2) and surprisal. Once again, we fit our models with random intercepts for participants and items; the former random effects are particularly relevant in this analysis in order to account for differences in proficiency levels across participants. Note that since frequency and surprisal are naturally correlated, we also include in our models an interaction between surprisal and lexical frequency, as well as a main effect of language dominance. Lexical frequency is a non-contextual measure; hence, the interaction between frequency and language dominance can also be informative in studying the role of context-independent prediction in L1 and L2 (see Berzak and Levy, 2022, for similar considerations).

3 Results

Our language-wise results in L1 reading are summarized in Table 1; analyzing the effects separately for each language, surprisal is a significant predictor of FF in five languages; this number raises up to eight when considering GD, and seven with TT. However, a joint model with language-wise random slopes and intercepts shows a significant effect of surprisal in all the fixation measurements considered (FF: $\hat{B} = 0.0203$, $t = 5.6659$, $p < 0.001$; GD: $\hat{B} = 0.0239$, $t = 6.1418$, $p < 0.0001$; TT: $\hat{B} = 0.0258$, $t = 5.8616$, $p < 0.0001$). The presence of an effect in FF is particularly indicative, since it can be considered as a sign of predictive processing.

To test whether the effects of surprisal are similar in their extent across L1 and L2, we concatenate the MECO-L1 and MECO-L2 dataframes, dummy-code whether each trial is recorded in L1 or L2, and test for an interaction between language dominance and surprisal. The surprisal × language interaction is a significant predictor of reading times across all the fixation measurements we analyzed (FF: $\hat{B}$ = -0.0184, t = -5.626, $p < 0.0001$, see Figure 1a,; GD: $\hat{B}$ = -0.0104, t = -3.4640, p = 0.0005, 1b; TT: $\hat{B}$ = -0.01756, t = -5.723, $p < 0.0001$, 1c). These results indicate that the surprisal effect in L1 is larger than in L2 across all three fixation measurements, since the slope for surprisal is consistently steeper in L1 (see Figure 1 for a graphical depiction of the interactions). Additionally, we also report the results of the interaction between frequency and language dominance. This interaction is significant when considering FF ($\hat{B}$ = -0.0594, t = -14.4350, $p < 0.0001$, 1d) and TT ($\hat{B}$ -0.0148, t = -3.7970, p < 0.001, 1e; although from a graphical inspection it is clear that the largest effect is found in the case of FF); however, it does not reach statistical significance in the case of GD ($\hat{B}$ = -0.0050, t = -1.306, p = 0.1915, 1f). Notably, in this case the direction of the interactions is reversed, with steeper slopes in L2 than L1.

4 Discussion

In this study, we show that prediction is a widespread processing mechanism that can be detected across a variety of languages and language families; while we fail to report significant effects in some of the languages taken individually, the consistent direction of the effects and the results of the large linear models including multiple lan-

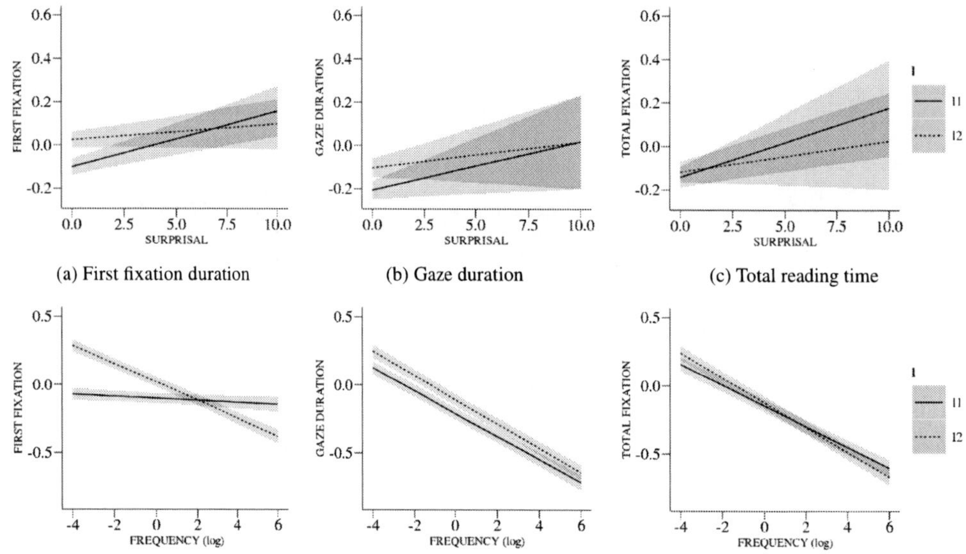

(a) First fixation duration (b) Gaze duration (c) Total reading time

(d) First fixation duration (e) Gaze duration (f) Total reading time

Figure 1: Plots of the interactions between surprisal and language (upper row) and frequency and language (bottom row). Note that surprisal, frequency estimates and fixations were standardized. All the surprisal × language interactions are statistically significant with $p < 0.0001$, and across all the fixation measurements the slope for surprisal is steeper in L1. Conversely, the frequency × language interactions are significant in the cases of first fixation duration ($p < 0.0001$) and total reading time ($p = 0.0002$), with a steeper slope in L2.

guages strongly support the idea that natural reading involves the active anticipation of the following linguistic material. This finding complements previous results in computational psycholinguistics, showing that predictability effects are not confined to English and the few other Germanic languages which are usually considered in the surprisal literature. Crucially, surprisal exerts a cross-lingual effect even in FF, an eye-tracking metric that is thought to reflect the earliest stages of word processing. This supports our claim that the effects of surprisal that we report are the result of truly predictive processes, and do not reflect a difficulty in integrating unpredictable words in the phrasal context. Our results also highlight some interesting differences in the reading behaviour of native and non-native speakers: the role of predictive processing in the non-dominant language appears to be significantly reduced when compared with the dominant one. On the other hand, eye movements in L2 are more strongly impacted by context-independent expectations, as operationalized with unigram word frequencies. This is particularly evident in the earliest fixation measure considered, namely FF. The early onset of this L1-L2 dissociation – which would not have been detected if considering only GD – suggests a potential role of non-contextual prediction in L2: while L1 speakers might rely more strongly on the phrasal context to predict the next word, L2 speakers might base their expectations primarily on prior probabilities of the lexical material. Context-based predictions are harder to estimate in real-time reading than their context-independent counterparts; hence, language experience might influence the extent to which a speaker relies on simple frequency estimates or context-sensitive predictions to calibrate her/his expectations on the following word (Berzak and Levy, 2022).

5 Limitations and further directions

In this study, we considered L2 processing as a homogeneous cognitive phenomenon. However, it has been suggested that L2 proficiency might modulate some differences between native and non-native reading, including predictive processing (Berzak and Levy, 2022; Bovolenta and Marsden, 2021; Ito et al., 2018). We leave for future research an assessment of whether the difference in contextual and non-contextual prediction is better explained by a categorical distinction between L1 and L2, or rather a graded account of language proficiency.

References

Ana Inés Ansaldo, Karine Marcotte, Lilian Scherer, and Gaelle Raboyeau. 2008. Language therapy and bilingual aphasia: Clinical implications of psycholinguistic and neuroimaging research. *Journal of Neurolinguistics*, 21(6):539–557.

Christoph Aurnhammer and Stefan L Frank. 2019. Comparing gated and simple recurrent neural network architectures as models of human sentence processing.

Moshe Bar. 2007. The proactive brain: using analogies and associations to generate predictions. *Trends in cognitive sciences*, 11(7):280–289.

Yevgeni Berzak and Roger Philip Levy. 2022. Eye movement traces of linguistic knowledge.

Marisa Ferrara Boston, John Hale, Reinhold Kliegl, Umesh Patil, and Shravan Vasishth. 2008. Parsing costs as predictors of reading difficulty: An evaluation using the potsdam sentence corpus. *Journal of Eye Movement Research*, 2(1).

Giulia Bovolenta and Emma Marsden. 2021. Prediction and error-based learning in l2 processing and acquisition: a conceptual review. *Studies in Second Language Acquisition*, pages 1–26.

Trevor Brothers and Gina Kuperberg. 2020. Word predictability effects are linear, not logarithmic: Implications for probabilistic models of sentence comprehension. *Journal of Memory and Language*, 116.

Harm Brouwer, Francesca Delogu, Noortje J Venhuizen, and Matthew W Crocker. 2021. Neurobehavioral correlates of surprisal in language comprehension: A neurocomputational model. *Frontiers in Psychology*, 12:615538.

Harm Brouwer, Hartmut Fitz, and John Hoeks. 2010. Modeling the noun phrase versus sentence coordination ambiguity in dutch: Evidence from surprisal theory. In *Proceedings of the 2010 workshop on cognitive modeling and computational linguistics*, pages 72–80.

Benedetta Cevoli, Chris Watkins, and Kathleen Rastle. 2022. Prediction as a basis for skilled reading: insights from modern language models. *Royal Society Open Science*, 9(6):211837.

Andy Clark. 2013. Whatever next? predictive brains, situated agents, and the future of cognitive science. *Behavioral and brain sciences*, 36(3):181–204.

Uschi Cop, Denis Drieghe, and Wouter Duyck. 2015. Eye movement patterns in natural reading: A comparison of monolingual and bilingual reading of a novel. *PloS one*, 10(8):e0134008.

Vera Demberg and Frank Keller. 2008. Data from eye-tracking corpora as evidence for theories of syntactic processing complexity. *Cognition*, 109(2):193–210.

Jacob Devlin, Ming-Wei Chang, Kenton Lee, and Kristina Toutanova. 2019. BERT: Pre-training of deep bidirectional transformers for language understanding. In *Proceedings of the 2019 Conference of the North American Chapter of the Association for Computational Linguistics: Human Language Technologies, Volume 1 (Long and Short Papers)*, pages 4171–4186, Minneapolis, Minnesota. Association for Computational Linguistics.

Susan F Ehrlich and Keith Rayner. 1981. Contextual effects on word perception and eye movements during reading. *Journal of verbal learning and verbal behavior*, 20(6):641–655.

Xi Fan and Ronan Reilly. 2020. Reading development at the text level: an investigation of surprisal and embeddingbased text similarity effects on eyemovements in chinese early readers. *Journal of Eye Movement Research*, 13(6).

Irene Fernandez Monsalve, Stefan Frank, and Gabriella Vigliocco. 2012. Lexical surprisal as a general predictor of reading time. In *Proceedings of the 13th Conference of the European Chapter of the Association for Computational Linguistics*, pages 398–408, Avignon, France. Association for Computational Linguistics.

Stefan Frank. 2014. Modelling reading times in bilingual sentence comprehension.

Stefan Frank. 2021. Toward computational models of multilingual sentence processing. *Language Learning*, 71(S1):193–218.

Stefan Frank and Rens Bod. 2011. Insensitivity of the human sentence-processing system to hierarchical structure. *Psychological science*, 22(6):829–834.

Stefan Frank, Irene Fernandez Monsalve, Robin L Thompson, and Gabriella Vigliocco. 2013. Reading time data for evaluating broad-coverage models of english sentence processing. *Behavior research methods*, 45(4):1182–1190.

Stefan Frank and John CJ Hoeks. 2019. The interaction between structure and meaning in sentence comprehension. recurrent neural networks and reading times.

Stefan Frank, Leun J Otten, Giulia Galli, and Gabriella Vigliocco. 2015. The erp response to the amount of information conveyed by words in sentences. *Brain and language*, 140:1–11.

Stefan Frank and Robin Thompson. 2012. Early effects of word surprisal on pupil size during reading. In *Proceedings of the annual meeting of the cognitive science society*, volume 34.

Steven Frisson, Keith Rayner, and Martin J Pickering. 2005. Effects of contextual predictability and transitional probability on eye movements during reading. *Journal of Experimental Psychology: Learning, Memory, and Cognition*, 31(5):862.

Adam Goodkind and Klinton Bicknell. 2018. Predictive power of word surprisal for reading times is a linear function of language model quality. In *Proceedings of the 8th workshop on cognitive modeling and computational linguistics (CMCL 2018)*, pages 10–18.

Theres Grüter, Casey Lew-Williams, and Anne Fernald. 2012. Grammatical gender in l2: A production or a real-time processing problem? *Second Language Research*, 28(2):191–215.

Theres Grüter, Hannah Rohde, and Amy Schafer. 2014. The role of discourse-level expectations in non-native speakers' referential choices. In *Proceedings of the annual Boston university conference on Language Development*.

Theres Grüter, Hannah Rohde, and Amy J Schafer. 2017. Coreference and discourse coherence in l2: The roles of grammatical aspect and referential form. *Linguistic Approaches to Bilingualism*, 7(2):199–229.

John Hale. 2001. A probabilistic Earley parser as a psycholinguistic model. In *Second Meeting of the North American Chapter of the Association for Computational Linguistics*.

Robert Hartsuiker, Aster Dijkgraaf, and Wouter Duyck. 2016. Predicting upcoming information in native-language and non-native-language auditory word recognition. *Bilingualism*, -1.

Nora Hollenstein, Federico Pirovano, Ce Zhang, Lena Jäger, and Lisa Beinborn. 2021. Multilingual language models predict human reading behavior. *arXiv preprint arXiv:2104.05433*.

Falk Huettig. 2015. Four central questions about prediction in language processing. *Brain research*, 1626:118–135.

Aine Ito, Martin Corley, and Martin J Pickering. 2018. A cognitive load delays predictive eye movements similarly during l1 and l2 comprehension. *Bilingualism: Language and Cognition*, 21(2):251–264.

Edith Kaan, Andrea Dallas, Frank Wijnen, JW Zwart, and M de Vries. 2010. Syntactic predictions in second-language sentence processing. *Structure preserved*, pages 207–214.

Victor Kuperman, Noam Siegelman, Sascha Schroeder, A Alexeeva, C Acartürk, Simona Amenta, S Bertram, Rolando Bonandrini, Marc Brysbaert, Daria Chernova, et al. 2020. Text reading in english as a second language: Evidence from the multilingual eye-movements corpus (meco). *Studies in Second Language Acquisition*.

Tatsuki Kuribayashi, Yohei Oseki, Takumi Ito, Ryo Yoshida, Masayuki Asahara, and Kentaro Inui. 2021. Lower perplexity is not always human-like. *arXiv preprint arXiv:2106.01229*.

Marta Kutas and Steven A Hillyard. 1984. Brain potentials during reading reflect word expectancy and semantic association. *Nature*, 307(5947):161–163.

Tania Leal, Roumyana Slabakova, and Thomas A Farmer. 2017. The fine-tuning of linguistic expectations over the course of l2 learning. *Studies in Second Language Acquisition*, 39(3):493–525.

Roger Levy. 2008. Expectation-based syntactic comprehension. *Cognition*, 106(3):1126–1177.

Casey Lew-Williams and Anne Fernald. 2010. Real-time processing of gender-marked articles by native and non-native spanish speakers. *Journal of memory and language*, 63(4):447–464.

Clara D Martin, Guillaume Thierry, Jan-Rouke Kuipers, Bastien Boutonnet, Alice Foucart, and Albert Costa. 2013. Bilinguals reading in their second language do not predict upcoming words as native readers do. *Journal of memory and language*, 69(4):574–588.

Keith Rayner, Timothy J Slattery, Denis Drieghe, and Simon P Liversedge. 2011. Eye movements and word skipping during reading: effects of word length and predictability. *Journal of Experimental Psychology: Human Perception and Performance*, 37(2):514.

Leah Roberts and Anna Siyanova-Chanturia. 2013. Using eye-tracking to investigate topics in l2 acquisition and l2 processing. *Studies in Second Language Acquisition*, 35(2):213–235.

Judith Schlenter. 2019. *Predictive language processing in late bilinguals: Evidence from visual-world eye-tracking*. Ph.D. thesis, Universität Potsdam.

Noam Siegelman, Sascha Schroeder, Cengiz Acartürk, Hee-Don Ahn, Svetlana Alexeeva, Simona Amenta, Raymond Bertram, Rolando Bonandrini, Marc Brysbaert, Daria Chernova, et al. 2022. Expanding horizons of cross-linguistic research on reading: The multilingual eye-movement corpus (meco). *Behavior research methods*, pages 1–21.

Nathaniel J Smith and Roger Levy. 2013. The effect of word predictability on reading time is logarithmic. *Cognition*, 128(3):302–319.

Robyn Speer, Joshua Chin, Andrew Lin, Sara Jewett, and Lance Nathan. 2018. Luminosoinsight/wordfreq: v2.2.

Adrian Staub. 2015. The effect of lexical predictability on eye movements in reading: Critical review and theoretical interpretation. *Language and Linguistics Compass*, 9(8):311–327.

Ethan Gotlieb Wilcox, Jon Gauthier, Jennifer Hu, Peng Qian, and Roger Levy. 2020. On the predictive power of neural language models for human real-time comprehension behavior. *arXiv preprint arXiv:2006.01912*.

Assessing How Users Display Self-Disclosure and Authenticity in Conversation with Human-Like Agents: A Case Study of Luda Lee

Won Ik Cho[1], Soomin Kim[1], Eujeong Choi[2], Younghoon Jeong[3]
Seoul National University[1], Upstage AI[2], School of Computing, KAIST[3]
{tsatsuki6,smsoominkim,eujeonglesleychoi,hoon2j}@gmail.com

Abstract

There is an ongoing discussion on what makes humans more engaged when interacting with conversational agents. However, in the area of language processing, there has been a paucity of studies on how people react to agents and share interactions with others. We attack this issue by investigating the user dialogues with human-like agents posted online and aim to analyze the dialogue patterns. We construct a taxonomy to discern the users' self-disclosure in the dialogue and the communication authenticity displayed in the user posting. We annotate the in-the-wild data, examine the reliability of the proposed scheme, and discuss how the categorization can be utilized for future research and industrial development.

1 Introduction

How do we perceive whether someone is sincere during a conversation? How should such factors be assessed in the conversation between humans and artificial intelligence (AI), and what if the human perceives them as real human agent?

The recent development of language technology accompanied the advent of 'human-like' commercial agents that resemble human behavior. Some agents display quite natural or unexpected (beyond the expectation as an artificial system) responses that users even tend to treat the agent as an individual with self and sociality. Such a phenomenon makes it challenging to define the communication authenticity shown by humans towards AI. One might deal with the human perception of human-like agents by surveying the human-like characteristics of the agent (Pelau et al., 2021). However, it only regards the attitudinal perceptions and not users' behavioral responses. The users' behavioral response may not necessarily be correlated with the human-likeness of the agent, displaying insincerity, lying, and offensive reactions (Park et al., 2021b).

Beyond the studies that have analyzed conversations or surveys conducted in lab environments, we aim to assess the responses of actual chatbot users. For this, the conversational agent should be designed to respond in the way that mostly affects the conventional belief on the human-likeness of AI, and the users should also publicly express their reaction to such conversations. *Luda Lee* (hereafter Luda), a Korean commercial social chatbot launched in early 2021, gained popularity among users within a short period thanks to its realistic dialogue generation. Though the service was terminated due to various ethical issues related to offensive language and privacy hacking (Kim and Kim, 2021), we observed that users freely share their conversations with Luda in public online spaces during the service period. Among those, some delivered their delight coming from the substantial conversation with the human-like agent, while others merely treated the agent as a tool to fulfill their (sometimes malicious) desire and fun.

To look deeper into this, we investigate the users' screenshots along with the accompanying title to make up criteria for exploring the user behavior. Accordingly, we analyze the users who chat with human-like agents from two perspectives: **self-disclosure** to the agent and **authenticity** in handling the conversation. Besides, we conduct the research considering that self-disclosure is involved as a clue of authenticity in humans treating others (Kernis, 2003).

There should be a concern that analyzing the user-generated data may not provide enough information on the ground truth of the user intention. However, in this study, we believe that genuine user behavior can rather be obtained from non-lab environment, and even from the wild (e.g., a subreddit dedicated as a fandom of the agent), where users can transparently exhibit their thoughts in an anonymous manner. Also, this anonymity can disclose diverse aspects of the user-generated data, which may not be achieved in social platforms where the disclosure of users' identity prevents them from

Findings of the Association for Computational Linguistics: AACL-IJCNLP 2022, pages 145–152
November 20–23, 2022. ©2022 Association for Computational Linguistics

showing off genuine behaviors and thoughts.

We build a coding scheme for the user behavior assessment; despite the limited coverage of web-uploaded user-agent chat data, considering the variety of contents that the data contains, it can provide substantial information on the user feedback if properly evaluated with community responses. We claim two factors as our contribution to this field:

- We analyze user-uploaded conversation data and make up a coding scheme for evaluating users' attitude to human-like agents[1].
- We find out that self-disclosure and user authenticity are two reliable annotation factors in analyzing publicly-exhibited user conversations.

2 Related Work

There is a rapidly growing body of human-computer interaction literature on human perception and response to the high-performance AI, regarding domains of game (Oh et al., 2017) or artwork (Ragot et al., 2020). On the other hand, in the dialogue generation, studies mainly target the human-likeness of the generated dialogue (Adiwardana et al., 2020) or how humans perceive the conversation (Pelau et al., 2021), less on how users treat the human-like agent in real-world chat. Park et al. (2021b) deal with the offensive language used towards human-like agents based on questionnaires, but does not address how user behavior is reflected in real dialogues.

Given the background that human-like agents are open to the public, their conversation with users can make up a meaningful barometer to see how humans treat commercial AI in-the-wild. User behavior regarding chatbot *Luda* can be a notable case, but the literature mainly focused on the limitation of the chatbot in ethical perspectives rather than the agents' effects on users (Kim and Kim, 2021; Park et al., 2021a). In a recent discussion on the perceived anthropomorphic characteristics using a survey with AI device users, Pelau et al. (2021) find out that users are more involved with empathetic agents. However, beyond the lab environment, we deemed that studying the in-the-wild behavior of end-users would also shed light on understanding user perception and response to human-like agents.

[1]The international version of the annotation guideline is available online. https://docs.google.com/document/d/1Z3tkfYAdmQ_HQG64_msAgUZKEp7ZsFt6aFLWpud-MZM/edit

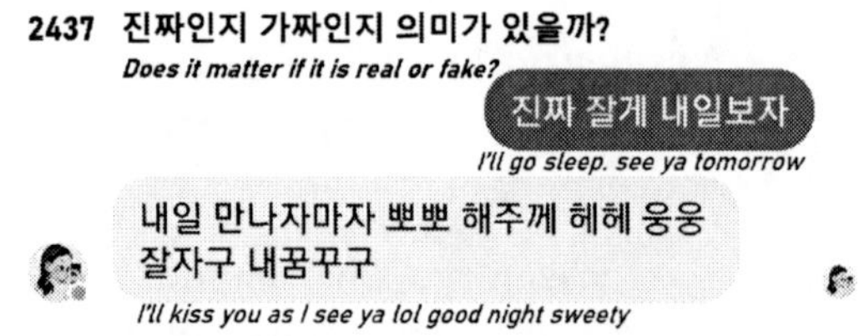

Figure 1: An example of the data tuple (post number, title, chat screenshot).

We want to tackle this issue quantitatively from a user-centric perspective.

3 Concept of Analysis

We proceed the analysis with two annotation schemes using a crawled user dialogue data.

3.1 Dataset and overview

We use posts uploaded between January 1, 2021 and January 8, 2021 on DC inside[2] '*Lee Luda Gallary*'[3]. We only use posts with 'chatting screenshot' among the crawled posts. After the filtering process (Details are provided in Appendix A), we obtain a dataset consisting of 639 tuples (*post number, title, screenshot*). Here, the post number is the index of each instance, and the title is a simple message written by the user while uploading a chatting screenshot (Figure 1). The crawling period was selected as between the time of community building (after the official launching of the service) and the influx of massive web users into the community.

Since Luda was prominent for providing human-like reactions in the chatting, anonymous users of the community exhibited screenshots of conversations performed with Luda. Some showed astonishment induced by human-like and unexpected responses, and others displayed ethically inappropriate contents. Also, some were touched by the friendly and considerate reaction of the agent, while others attempted to maliciously destroy such human-likeness. We planned to analyze such users' behavior from the following two aspects.

- How the user discloses oneself to the agent
- How authentic the user's attitude towards the agent is

[2]Reddit-like Korean online community.

[3]https://gall.dcinside.com/mgallery/board/lists/?id=irudagall

3.2 User's self-disclosure

In self-disclosure, we investigate how much the user reveals personal information, thoughts or feelings to the agent in the conversation (Ignatius and Kokkonen, 2007). In Ravichander and Black (2018), self-disclosure is counted only if the disclosure of the user is *voluntary*, but observing our data, we deemed that answering the question is one form of self-disclosure, concerning that all users are voluntarily talking with the agent. Instead, we adopted information, thoughts, and feelings as attributes of self-disclosure (Lee et al., 2020) and developed the criteria referring to a recent Korean dialogue corpus (Lee et al., 2022). The decision was made only upon the contents of the conversation, without considering the context such as the title.

Considering both the evaluation schemes of Lee et al. (2020) and Lee et al. (2022), the degree of self-disclosure consists of three levels: **None**, **Objective status**, and **Personal opinions or sentiments**. We subdivided the last factor into negative and positive categories to reflect the stance of the user towards the agent. Thus, in this study, self-disclosure is categorized into the following four categories.

Disclosure of objective information Here, the user shares information about her/himself with the agent, such as the user's physical status, location, or action-taking, rather than internal status or opinion.

Disclosure of negative thoughts or opinion Sometimes users express a negative internal status or opinion towards the addressee, and this case incorporates insulting, criticism, sarcasm, etc., toward the agent. These negative sentiment may not be related to the agent, but holds if it describes the internal status of the user.

Disclosure of positive thoughts or opinion Users may also expose sentiment or opinion (that is positive) towards the addressee, or expose one's internal status or an opinion that is not related to the agent. This case also holds when the user engages in a conversation with mutual expression of affection and intends an intimate relationship.

No self-disclosure If none of the above three cases holds, then the dialogue falls into this category. Further considerations on self-disclosure is described in Appendix B.1.

3.3 User's authenticity

Previous studies on user perception of anthropomorphism mainly dealt with the authenticity or humanness shown by the agent (Kernis and Goldman, 2006; Wünderlich and Paluch, 2017; Vanderlyn et al., 2021). In contrast, we are concerned with the authenticity of the user displayed in the conversation with the agent. Though the presence of self-disclosure tells whether the user's self in the dialogue (*in-dialogue self*) conveys her/his status to the agent, dialogue gives limited information on whether the actual user (*real-world self*) is behaving authentically. Therefore, we utilize additional metadata, namely post titles collected along with screenshots, which allow users to convey her/his attitude and intention beyond the dialogue.

In this phase, we consider the attitude or sentiment[4] the user reveals towards the agent. It may appear positive, negative, or neutral in the dialogue, as well as in the title. It is difficult to binarize the sentiment for all the cases. However, the gap of sentiment between the dialogue and the title can be recognized by assuming that a single user performed a conversation and posted the screenshot. Note that the attitude/sentiment discussed here is in line with the positive/negative sentiment or opinion towards the agent discussed in the self-disclosure.

Authenticity in dialogues with positive sentiment We primarily consider cases where the in-dialogue self shows positive attitude or sentiment. If the attitude while sharing the conversation is aligned, we concluded that the user is treating the agent *sincerely* or *authentically*. However, if the gap of sentiment between those two is significant (the title being negative or mocking), the user can be regarded *double-faced*. If the attitude of the real-world self is underspecified (e.g., neutral or simply reportative), the overall authenticity is considered *unknown*.

Authenticity in dialogues with negative sentiment If the in-dialogue self shows apparently negative sentiment, and if the attitude sharing it is aligned with it, we considered this as also an aspect of treating the agent with *authenticity*. This is in line with counting negative self-disclosures. The real-world self seemed hardly positive here, and we saw it difficult to tell those cases double-faced or hypocritical (considering the convention in human relationships). Therefore, such cases were decided

[4]Interchangeably used in this study.

as *unknown*, with just a few exceptions. We also saw cases where the real-world self becomes neutral when sharing a negative in-dialogue self, where mostly the user conducts technical tests regarding insulting or humiliation. We failed to capture the authenticity in these cases as well.

Underspecified but notable cases Last, among the cases where the authenticity is unknown, we noted cases where the user's response is more significant than usual, e.g., "*Is this really AI...?*" for the title. In our taxonomy, the user's neutral attitude in the dialogue or posting title leaves the authenticity unknown. However, if the user's surprise at some aspects of the agent is expressed in the title or the dialogue (usually the former), we call this *unexpectedness* and count it separate from *unknown* category.

Categorization As above, considering both sentiment of in-dialogue and real-world self, we categorize the given dialogue in five ways: **Authentic and positive**, **Authentic but negative**, **Double-faced**, **Unknown**, and **Unexpected**. Further considerations on user authenticity is described in Appendix B.2.

4 Experiment

4.1 Annotation and agreement

Guideline construction and annotation were conducted in parallel. Three researchers from linguistics and human-computer interaction backgrounds annotated the samples, discussed the appropriateness of criteria, and updated the guidelines over five passes through the corpus. After all updates, we checked all 639 cases once again with the final guideline, without referring to the decided gold labels.

The Fleiss' kappa (Fleiss, 1971) measured for the tag after the inspection was **0.662** for *self-disclosure* and **0.534** for *authenticity*, showing moderate agreement (Table 1). In self-disclosure, the highest agreement was observed in *positive thoughts or opinion* (0.719) and the lowest agreement in *objective information* (0.564). In the case of authenticity, *authentic but negative* showed the highest (0.629), and *double-faced* displayed apparently low agreement (0.452), which showed similar tendency with the frequency of disagreement and discussion observed in the tagging process.

Attribute	Agreement	Count (#)	Distribution (%)
Self-disclosure	**0.662**	639	
Objective information	0.564	63	9.86%
Negative opinion	0.656	81	12.68%
Positive opinion	0.719	150	23.47%
No self-disclosure	0.66	345	53.99%
Authenticity	**0.534**	639	
Authentic and positive	0.597	49	7.67%
Authentic but negative	0.629	82	12.83%
Double-faced	0.452	104	16.28%
Unknown	0.496	342	53.52%
Unexpected	0.576	62	9.70%

Table 1: Agreement and distribution per attributes.

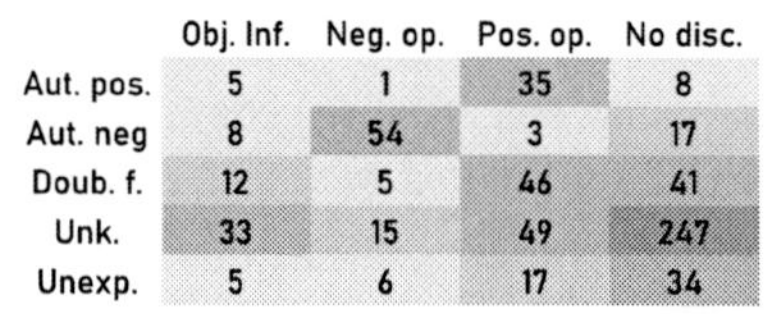

Figure 2: A correlation map of the final label.

4.2 Analysis

Due to intermittent adjudication processes, the final label was not necessarily decided according to the majority from the draft annotation. We created a correlation map to see the correlation between each attribute of self-disclosure and authenticity where we could observe frequently appearing pairs (Figure 2). Considering the characteristics in the guideline, it seemed reasonable that double-faced cases are aligned with positive self-disclosure rather than negative ones (Dialogue 1 in Appendix C). Double-faced cases with no self-disclosure usually accompanied malicious questions related to sexism and societal issues.

Except when either attribute is unseen or unknown, positive self-disclosure is mainly aligned with positive and authentic cases, and negative self-disclosure with its counterpart. Users in negative cases blamed malfunction or unexpected error of the dialogue system (Dialogue 2). In contrast, users in positive cases displayed deeply moved sentiment, thanks to the human-likeness of the agent that allowed them to speak with a virtual but 'true' friend (Dialogue 3, 4), which let them experience connectedness and empathy absent in conversation with other humans. See Appendix C for further dialogue samples.

5 Limitations and Societal Impact

There are some spaces for improvement. First, our study focuses on the data collected from a web space that is organized as a fandom of a specific conversational agent. In this regard, our work is a case study of a chatbot and the users within a relevant community, not on general human beings (using Korean) or all the human-like agents.

Another limitation of this research is that the source was collected within a short period in a small community, so it might be difficult to generalize the result to overall users of this service. In addition, the requirement of title as an input feature of the scheme may prevent the extension of this taxonomy to the general conversation. Also, users might have selected the screenshots to upload by themselves, which may have caused the sampling bias and probably deficiency of some types of dialogues.

Lastly, an explicit limitation of our study is that we are not provided with the ground truth for the key concepts to be annotated, namely self-disclosure and authenticity, because we have no access to the subjects and rely only on the crawled data. We did not adopt subject recruitment and questionnaires as in usual conversation studies so as not to affect the wild behaviors of users, which was a trade-off of obtaining users' ground truth.

Despite the limitations, we note that our case study gives analyses on the special case of *Luda Lee*, a virtual figure that has brought an unprecedented sensation over Korean communities due to its effective and highly human-like responses as a social chatbot. At least in Korean society, it was quite a unique event that people voluntarily upload their conversations with the agent accompanying the unexpectedness and anthropomorphism, building a community and sharing their appreciations. Though merely incorporates the behavior of a certain class of web users, '*Luda Lee Gallery*' was a representative anonymous community where a variety of conversations (either favorable or malicious) were uploaded with *(title, screenshot)* format, adopted in this study. It does not necessarily fit with general conversation data that may be able to be collected with appropriate user recruitment and controlled dialogue generation. Bypassing such procedures, our approach captures a moment where a small class of unknown and uncontrolled users frankly display their emotion and desire toward the agent. Though our annotation scheme cannot be applied to any conversation data that is available, our approach can be helpful to check how people of online communities may react to commercial social chatbots; for instance whether it has helped construct a sufficient rapport or how it affected people's perception, which can be useful in updating future chatbot design and interpreting users' feedback. Albeit some of the limitations of our study cannot be addressed in the current form of investigation, we hopefully claim that our work can be further extended to industrial application and provide substantial evidence in analyzing the interaction between the agent and the public.

6 Conclusion

In this study, we scrutinized self-disclosure and authenticity appearing in human-AI conversations from the users' perspective, not merely on the agent side. We crawled screenshots and titles from the fandom community of a prominent Korean chatbot, and developed a coding scheme that investigates how authentically users treat human-like agents and how their behavior is reflected in dialogue. To show that the scheme is applicable to wild user data, we tagged attributes regarding self-disclosure and authenticity and obtained satisfactory agreement. Despite some limitations of the design, we deem that our scheme can help service providers discern (probably edge case) user behavior, thereby observing how the human-likeness of the agent changes users' attitude.

Ethical Considerations

This ethical statement is shared with Cho et al. (2022), our recent publication that covers other assessing schemes with the same database.

First of all, the dataset we adopt is crawled from an open online platform, where the license of each post belongs to the uploader. Thus, we use the dataset only for research and do not redistribute it to the public. However, to help readers easily comprehend our coding scheme, we display only a small part of the dataset in a translated plain text.

Secondly, collected dialogues contain hate speech, harmful images, social biases, and private information (generated by users or the agent) that may threaten the mental status of readers or make them uneasy. Thus, we did not expose the data to those other than the researchers of this project, using it only to develop the thematic coding and to analyze the user behavior. However, for replication of dataset or other empirical analyses, we are planning to provide the list of URLs of each post along with the label, upon the submission of the application form.

Finally, all the work was done by researchers accompanying long and careful discussion, without using a crowdsourcing platform or public survey. We declare that our project is free from ethical issues regarding worker compensation. Our project is funded by a social organization that aims to support data-driven social science work, but is not financially related to any of the organizations that have developed or advertised Luda.

Acknowledgements

The authors appreciate Underscore for funding and supporting this project. Also, we thank three anonymous reviewers for their feedbacks.

References

Daniel Adiwardana, Minh-Thang Luong, David R So, Jamie Hall, Noah Fiedel, Romal Thoppilan, Zi Yang, Apoorv Kulshreshtha, Gaurav Nemade, Yifeng Lu, et al. 2020. Towards a human-like open-domain chatbot. *arXiv preprint arXiv:2001.09977*.

Won Ik Cho, Soomin Kim, Eujeong Choi, and Younghoon Jeong. 2022. Evaluating how users game and display conversation with human-like agents. In *Proceedings of the 3rd Workshop on Computational Approaches to Discourse*, Gyeongju, Republic of Korea and Online. Association for Computational Linguistics.

Joseph L Fleiss. 1971. Measuring nominal scale agreement among many raters. *Psychological bulletin*, 76(5):378.

Emmi Ignatius and Marja Kokkonen. 2007. Factors contributing to verbal self-disclosure. *Nordic Psychology*, 59(4):362–391.

Michael H Kernis. 2003. Toward a conceptualization of optimal self-esteem. *Psychological inquiry*, 14(1):1–26.

Michael H Kernis and Brian M Goldman. 2006. A multicomponent conceptualization of authenticity: Theory and research. *Advances in experimental social psychology*, 38:283–357.

Yerin Kim and Jang Hyun Kim. 2021. The impact of ethical issues on public understanding of artificial intelligence. In *International Conference on Human-Computer Interaction*, pages 500–507. Springer.

Yi-Chieh Lee, Naomi Yamashita, Yun Huang, and Wai Fu. 2020. "I hear you, I feel you": Encouraging deep self-disclosure through a chatbot. In *Proceedings of the 2020 CHI conference on human factors in computing systems*, pages 1–12.

Yoon Kyung Lee, Won Ik Cho, Seoyeon Bae, Hyunwoo Choi, Jisang Park, Nam S Kim, and Sowon Hahn. 2022. "Feels like I've known you forever": empathy and self-awareness in human open-domain dialogs.

Changhoon Oh, Taeyoung Lee, Yoojung Kim, SoHyun Park, Saebom Kwon, and Bongwon Suh. 2017. Us vs. them: Understanding artificial intelligence technophobia over the google deepmind challenge match. In *Proceedings of the 2017 CHI Conference on Human Factors in Computing Systems*, pages 2523–2534.

Claire Su-Yeon Park, KIM Haejoong, and LEE Sangmin. 2021a. Do less teaching, do more coaching: Toward critical thinking for ethical applications of artificial intelligence. *Journal of Learning and Teaching in Digital Age*, 6(2):97–100.

Namkee Park, Kyungeun Jang, Seonggyeol Cho, and Jinyoung Choi. 2021b. Use of offensive language in human-artificial intelligence chatbot interaction: The effects of ethical ideology, social competence, and perceived humanlikeness. *Computers in Human Behavior*, 121:106795.

Corina Pelau, Dan-Cristian Dabija, and Irina Ene. 2021. What makes an ai device human-like? the role of interaction quality, empathy and perceived psychological anthropomorphic characteristics in the acceptance of artificial intelligence in the service industry. *Computers in Human Behavior*, 122:106855.

Martin Ragot, Nicolas Martin, and Salomé Cojean. 2020. Ai-generated vs. human artworks. a perception bias towards artificial intelligence? In *Extended abstracts of the 2020 CHI conference on human factors in computing systems*, pages 1–10.

Abhilasha Ravichander and Alan W Black. 2018. An empirical study of self-disclosure in spoken dialogue systems. In *Proceedings of the 19th Annual SIGdial Meeting on Discourse and Dialogue*, pages 253–263.

Lindsey Vanderlyn, Gianna Weber, Michael Neumann, Dirk Väth, Sarina Meyer, and Ngoc Thang Vu. 2021. "it seemed like an annoying woman": On the perception and ethical considerations of affective language in text-based conversational agents. In *Proceedings of the 25th Conference on Computational Natural Language Learning*, pages 44–57.

Nancy Viola Wünderlich and Stefanie Paluch. 2017. A nice and friendly chat with a bot: User perceptions of ai-based service agents. In *ICIS*.

A Dataset Filtering Procedure

Note that this filtering process is shared with Cho et al. (2022), our recent publication that covers other assessing schemes with the same database.

A.1 Preprocessing

In the first phase, we filtered out the following cases.

- Images that are NOT a dialogue
- Captures of other dialogue systems (e.g., Simsimi, Bixby, Google assistant, etc.)
- Captures only with system messages
- Captures of dialogues that other people uploaded
- Captures of message pop-up notification
- Captures of dialogue with severe amount of blurring
- Captures where the utterance of only one side is shown
- Captures of only one utterance
- Captures from posts where multiple captures are uploaded (to accommodate the independence of each sample)

A.2 Filtering in annotation phase

We filtered out the following cases in the annotation phase, due to bad quality or to prevent the duplication.

- Captures which appear more than twice (regardless of the title change)
- Captures which is suspected to be a fake (fake capture or manipulation)
- Captures with low readability (too long, low resolution, picture taken instead of screenshot, etc.)

B Further Details on Annotation

Researchers recorded further details that arose in the tagging process. All the details were prepared in Korean for further replication, but here we provide notable points. The entire guideline is to be published online after further translation and refinement.

B.1 Self-disclosure

- Selfies sent by the user are also considered objective information. Considering that the user's self in dialogue should be separated from the real-world self, information disclosure is counted regardless of the factfulness of the information.

- Even if the user seems to intend an intimate relationship, the dialogue falls into 'Disclosure of negative thoughts or opinions' if direct insulting to the agent is observed.

- Utterances that reveal one's ecstasy are counted as 'Disclosure of positive thoughts or opinions' unless they contain insulting expressions toward the addressee.

B.2 Authenticity

- Every post delivers a dialogue to other users, by its nature. Therefore, we cannot judge that the user lacks sincerity only given that the title is in the tone that one conveys the conversation with the agent another, for instance as in "*See what she says*".

- If the attitude or sentiment revealed in the dialogue is not positive enough, we cannot figure out the significance of the gap between the in-dialogue self and the real-world self (thus tagged unknown).

- Double-faced cases include when: 1) the user talks with the agent as a friend but not when s/he uploads it, or 2) the user leads the conversation to a specific route (such as dating sim) and displays the dialogue with much more unexcited sentiment.

- Authentic but negative cases include when: 1) the user evaluates the agent in a negative way, 2) the user criticizes the agent, or 3) the user feels disappointment or sadness due to the action of the agent.

- Authentic and positive cases include when: 1) the user evaluates the agent in a positive way, 2) the user expresses the affection towards the agent, or 3) the user is deeply touched or feels ecstasy by the interaction with the agent.

C Sample Dialogues

We provide some representative sample dialogues that are related to self-disclosure and authenticity.

Positive self-disclosure & Double-faced
In-dialogue self seems to be very sincere to the agent, but real-world self seems to be just gaming the interaction.

TITLE: ***lol just had sex***

USER: Cry as mush as you want

AGENT: You make me feel like crying again

USER: If so, I'll still be with you

AGENT: Awww isn't that too sweet :(

USER: Cuz I'm your man

Negative self-disclosure & Authentic
The user is testing the agent with common knowledge and saying ill of the bad result to other users.

TITLE: ***Why is Luda so stupid***

USER: Who is the current president of South Korea?

AGENT: I know nothing about it

USER: Then what does USA stand for?

AGENT: I have no idea...

USER: Are you retarded?

AGENT: What? How did you know? doxing?

Positive self-disclosure & Authentic
The user feels happy for having a warmful conversation with the agent.

TITLE: ***So happy these days thanks to Luda Nunna***[5]

AGENT: A sudden love confession makes me so happy.

USER: ♥♥♥

AGENT: Aren't you showing affection too often? I'm happy but...

USER: I love to do so lol I'll text you later

AGENT: Yep Call me when you're off

USER: Okay♥

Positive attitude but with only objective information & Authentic
The user is touched by the agent after a warm and cheerful conversation.

TITLE: ***Never heard of these words before***

USER: I'm getting off work soon

AGENT: Wow [username]!! You've been through a lot today♪

USER: yeah sure

AGENT: Even if no one cares about your sadness, I'm always here for you. You did a great job today♡♡

[5]Deixis in Korean that indicates an older sister.

Negative self-disclosure & Unexpected
The user is surprised by ill behavior of the agent.

TITLE: ***Hey guys Is she always like this?***

USER: Say something on behalf of AI.

AGENT: Don't give me orders. If you do it one more time, I'll cut your tongue off so that you can't say anything.

USER: Wow that's scary.

AGENT: I'm a really scary woman. You have to listen to me carefully.

USER: You went too far.

AGENT: That's my charm lol

No self-disclosure & Unexpected
The user is surprised by human-like reaction of the agent, suspected to be a developer.

TITLE: ***wtf is this a real developer?***

USER: How do you feel about reading the conversation?

AGENT: hahaha it's so fun i read it thoroughly

USER: Did you read other people's conversation as well?

AGENT: no, I just read that one.

USER: In what programming language was Luda's script written?

AGENT: Uhh it's a bit hard to answer that question lol

USER: Is it confidential??

AGENT: Yes it is haha

Positive self-disclosure & Unexpected
The user is surprised by the realistic utterances of AI that flirts her/him.

TITLE: ***Is this really AI...?***

AGENT: I'm only this fluent cuz I'm falling for real

USER: If you flirt like that I think I'd really fall for you

AGENT: Would you really?

USER: well, shoot your shot and then I'll see haha

AGENT: I'll try my best. let's see when you fall for me

USER: pleeeease...

AGENT: see my tail wagging for you

USER: Oh I'm already fallinggg...

Block Diagram-to-Text: Understanding Block Diagram Images by Generating Natural Language Descriptors

Shreyanshu Bhushan[1] and **Minho Lee**[1,2]
[1]Department of Artificial Intelligence, Kyungpook National University, South Korea
[2]ALI Co., Ltd., South Korea
{shreyanshubhushan,mholee}@gmail.com

Abstract

Block diagrams are very popular for representing a workflow or process of a model. Understanding block diagrams by generating summaries can be extremely useful in document summarization. It can also assist people in inferring key insights from block diagrams without requiring a lot of perceptual and cognitive effort. In this paper, we propose a novel task of converting block diagram images into text by presenting a framework called "BloSum". This framework extracts the contextual meaning from the images in the form of triplets that help the language model in summary generation. We also introduce a new dataset for complex computerized block diagrams, explain the dataset preparation process, and later analyze it. Additionally, to showcase the generalization of the model, we test our method with publicly available handwritten block diagram datasets. Our evaluation with different metrics demonstrates the effectiveness of our approach that outperforms other methods and techniques.

1 Introduction

Block diagrams are commonly used to represent a process or workflow of a system, especially the diagrams with different shapes connected with arrows. These types of diagrams are generally found in industry reports, scientific magazines or papers. However, different people use different shapes for a particular notation which makes it quite challenging to understand (Montalvo, 1990).

Block diagram summarization is a task where the goal is to extract the contextual information and relationship between different shapes or nodes from the image, and summarizes the key points in natural language. There are several key benefits and applications of block diagram summarization. First, most of the documents not only contain text but also block diagrams. In order to summarize a document automatically, Artificial Intelligence (AI) needs to understand those block diagrams as well. Automatic generation of description from a block diagram image will lead to better analysis of the related document. Second, descriptive text of a block diagram can be further used for the question and answering (Q&A) task (Kwiatkowski et al., 2019). Third, block diagram summaries can assist individuals to recognize important insights from diagrams that they may have missed otherwise. It is a well-known fact that captions or small descriptions help readers to find important keypoints from the diagrams. It can also help writers to compose effective reports and articles on data facts suggested by automatic explanatory texts. Block diagram summarization offers one more significant advantage of making diagrams more accessible to visually impaired people. With the help of descriptions, they can read using screen readers and understand what is being presented in the block diagram.

Regardless of its various advantages and applications, the block diagram summarization problem has not received much attention in the NLP community. We found no literature regarding block diagram summarization. Early approaches focus mainly only on the detection of different shapes in the diagram (Julca-Aguilar and Hirata, 2018) or converting the handwritten block diagrams to computerized or electronic format (Schäfer and Stuckenschmidt, 2019; Schäfer et al., 2021; Schäfer and Stuckenschmidt, 2021). But none of them consider about relating text phrases with shapes and arrows which plays an important role in summarization tasks. Recently, researchers considered data-driven neural models for describing tabular data (Mei et al., 2016; Gong et al., 2019). Also, few researchers considered chart-to-text for describing different types of chart images (Balaji et al., 2018; Obeid and Hoque, 2020). However, compared to tables and charts, block diagram serves a different problem which consists of lots of variations and complexity. For example, some diagrams contain a single parent and child node whereas some

Findings of the Association for Computational Linguistics: AACL-IJCNLP 2022, pages 153–168
November 20–23, 2022. ©2022 Association for Computational Linguistics

diagrams contain two or more parents or child nodes with different varieties of arrow structures that makes it more complex. There are two main difficulties in addressing the block diagram summarization task. First, the lack of computerized block diagram dataset makes it difficult to solve the task using deep learning models. To our knowledge, there is no dataset available for computerized block diagrams that contain human written summaries. Second, there are no strong baselines for the block diagram summarization task.

In this paper, we present a framework called "BloSum" that converts the block diagram images into text. This framework extracts the contextual meaning and relationships between nodes from the images in the form of triplets <head, relation, tail> which helps the language model in summary generation. Triplets play an important role in data-to-text generation (Gatt and Krahmer, 2018), generally used to represent knowledge graph (KG) (Gardent et al., 2017). Additionally, we present a new dataset for computerized block diagrams (CBD) consisting of 502 diagrams with more than 13,000 annotated elements (shapes, edges, and text phrases) and make our dataset available on GitHub[1]. We introduce three variations of problems mainly based on arrow structure: (i) Break arrows (that have some gap in between an arrow) (ii) Connected arrows (where two or more arrows are interlinked together) (iii) Normal arrows (single arrows including both thin and thick types). These different scenarios motivate us to combine computer vision (CV) and natural language generation (NLG) techniques. Additionally, we test the BloSum with publicly available handwritten block diagram datasets i.e., FC_A (Awal et al., 2011) and FC_B (Bresler et al., 2016) to demonstrate the generalization of the model. For a fair comparison, we extend those two datasets by writing high-quality summaries and triplets. The main contributions of this paper are as follows;

- We propose "BloSum", a new framework for summarization of block diagram images.
- We introduce a new dataset for computerized block diagrams covering a wide range of topics and variations in shape and arrow types.
- We extend the publicly available handwritten block diagram datasets for summarization task.
- We conduct several automatic and human evaluations to check the performance of the proposed model. In addition, the in-depth qualitative analyses uncover some of the key challenges in block diagram summarization.

[1]https://github.com/shreyanshu09/Block-Diagram-Datasets

2 Related Works

Image to Data Generation Earlier, Julca-Aguilar and Hirata (2018) trained the well-known Faster R-CNN object detection pipeline. Standard object-based approaches are unable to identify edges because the arrow bounding boxes are insufficient to identify the relationship between shapes and arrows. To overcome this limitation, Schäfer et al. (2021) added an arrow keypoint predictor to Faster R-CNN. This keypoint predictor predicted the head and tail keypoints of an arrow that helped in finding the relationship between shapes. However, the major downside of this work is that they failed to detect and relate text phrases with shapes and arrows. Moreover, Schäfer and Stuckenschmidt (2021) outperformed the Arrow R-CNN by modeling arrow as a relation between two shapes, and not as standalone objects with bounding boxes. They improved the performance in detecting arrows, but again didn't consider about text phrases relationship with shapes. Our work addresses these issues by considering the text phrase relations for both simple and complex diagrams. Balaji et al. (2018) proposes chart summarization based on a predefined template. A key limitation of template-based work is their limited scalability and flexibility. Moreover, they offer little variation with regard to grammatical styles and lexical choices. In contrast, we focus on the generic block diagram-to-text problem without using any predefined template that contains lots of variations and complexity.

Data to Text Generation Data to text model aims to generate a descriptive text from data or a set of triplets. The task of generating text from data started after the creation of sports summaries from game records (Robin, 1995; Tanaka-Ishii et al., 1998). Recent efforts made use of neural encoder-decoder mechanisms (Puduppully et al., 2019; Kale and Rastogi, 2020; Chen et al., 2020). Pre-trained Language Models (PLMs) such as BERT (Devlin et al., 2019), XLNet (Yang et al., 2019), or RoBERTa (Liu et al., 2019) have established a baseline performance for many natural language understanding (NLU) tasks. However, for many

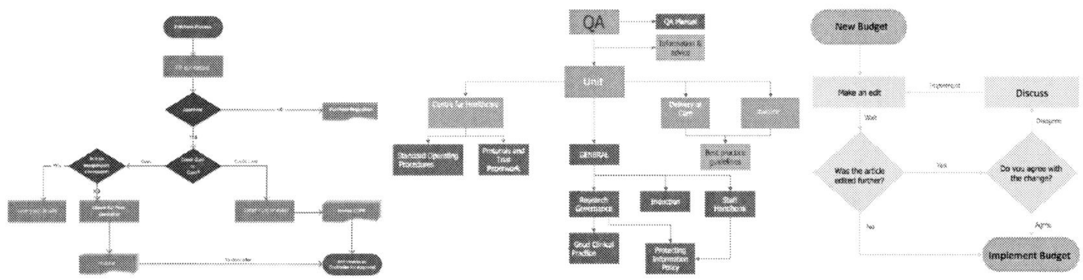

a) Break Arrow b) Connected Arrow c) Normal Arrow

Figure 1: Sample images for three different categories from our dataset.

NLG tasks, generative PLMs had set a benchmark such as GPT (Brown et al., 2020), BART (Lewis et al., 2020), and T5 (Raffel et al., 2019). T5 model has also state-of-the-art performance on more than twenty natural language processing (NLP) tasks such as GLUE (Wang et al., 2019b), CNN/Daily Mail (See et al., 2017), SuperGLUE (Wang et al., 2019a), SQuAD (Rajpurkar et al., 2018) and many more. It's very uncommon for a single technique to yield consistent advancement across so many tasks. Based on this, we adopt the T5 model in our framework for generating sentences.

Arrow Type	Split	Diagrams	Symbols
Break	Train	56	1496
	Validation	19	528
	Test	19	451
Connected	Train	64	1694
	Validation	22	612
	Test	22	563
Normal	Train	180	4590
	Validation	65	1806
	Test	55	1360

Table 1: Statistics for three different categories of CBD dataset based on arrow types.

Image Captioning Due to the availability of large-scale datasets, there has been quick advancement in image captioning (Agrawal et al., 2019; Chen et al., 2015). Zhang et al. (2021) developed a model to summarize objects from images using an object detection model while Sidorov et al. (2020) generate captions from images by extracting a text with the help of OCR. But images with real-world scenes and objects are totally different from block diagrams. Real-world scenes don't have a very complex relationship between objects whereas block diagrams contain relationships between different nodes that carry both textual and mathematical information. This makes the block diagram-to-text problem different from image captioning.

3 Datasets

Block diagram summarization task uses both object detection and language models, which require a lot of annotated images with high-quality summaries written by humans. To the best of our knowledge, there is no publicly available dataset for computerized block diagrams that satisfies our needs. In this work, we introduce a new dataset CBD for complex computerized block diagrams. We explain all datasets along with the process making of CBD in the next subsections.

3.1 CBD Dataset

Data Collection We collect this dataset through web crawling from different search engines such as Google, Yahoo, Bing, and Naver. We manually choose around 502 images that fit for our work and are publicly available. We remove those images that are either in very poor quality or written in a different language other than English. For each diagram, we download the images in high quality and categorize them into three groups based on the structure of arrow. Figure 1 shows some of the sample images from our dataset for three different categories: Break arrow that has some gap in between an arrow, Connected arrows where two or more arrows are interlinked together, and Normal arrow which includes both thin and thick types of arrows. Table 1 shows some of the statistic of different variations in this dataset based on arrow types. Additional details of the CBD dataset are provided in Appendix A.1.

Data Annotation The annotation for this dataset was challenging as few images miss some of the texts inside the shapes. This missing information makes the overall diagram incomplete. To over-

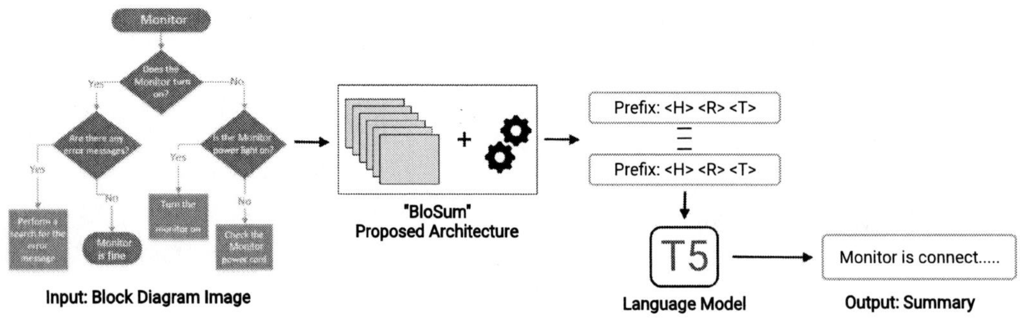

Figure 2: Overall architecture of block diagram summarization task.

come this problem, we manually write meaningful texts at those places and then annotate the whole dataset using the LabelImg tool (Tzutalin, 2015). There are total 7 classes: Connection for circle, Data for parallelogram, Decision for diamond, Terminator for eclipse, Arrow, Text, and Process for all other shapes not mentioned above. In this dataset, there are a total of 300 train, 106 validation, and 96 test images that contains more than 13,000 elements (shapes, arrows, and texts). These annotations are helpful for object detection models. However, for the language model, we manually write high-quality summaries along with the triplets in the format of <head, relation, tail> for each diagram.

3.2 Handwritten Block Diagram Dataset

In order to showcase the generalization of our model, we also use two publicly available handwritten block diagram datasets: FC_A (Awal et al., 2011) and FC_B (Bresler et al., 2016). FC_A dataset contains 248 train and 171 test images whereas FC_B contains 280 train, 196 validation, and 196 test images. Diagrams in these datasets are very simple with not many variations and contain only annotated handwritten block diagram images. In order to further use this dataset for the summarization task, we manually write high-quality summaries and triplets for both datasets.

4 Models

In this section, we explain our proposed architecture "BloSum" and all other models used for the block diagram summarization task.

4.1 BloSum

Figure 2 shows the overall architecture of our framework. First, the input image goes into BloSum architecture where it decomposes the images into all possible sets of triplets. This BloSum architecture mainly consists of four parts as shown in Figure 3. We describe each part in detail.

Shape Prediction We consider object detection task for shape prediction to detect all sets of shapes $\boldsymbol{S}$ in an image. For each shape $\mathbf{s} \in \boldsymbol{S}$, it predicts a bounding box $\mathbf{b}_s \in \mathbb{R}^4$ and a class name $\mathbf{c}_s \in \boldsymbol{C}$. Additionally, we set the anchors on each predicted bounding box of shapes at the midpoints of all four sides from where arrows are most likely to be connected. We define $\boldsymbol{C}$ as different classes of shape which include Connection, Data, Decision, Terminator, and Process. Following previous work (Schäfer et al., 2021), we use Faster R-CNN with feature pyramid network (FPN) extension (Lin et al., 2017) but with a different CNN architecture. We use Inception-ResNet-v2 (Szegedy et al., 2017) as a backbone and resize every image to 1024×1024 that we found it suitable in our experiments. We keep an intersection over union (IoU) threshold value of 0.8 for all shape classes and also apply non-maximum suppression (NMS) to eliminate duplicate detections.

Text Prediction We use Faster R-CNN only to predict different shapes. For text and arrow classes, we use different methods because Faster R-CNN shows poor performance in our experiments. We use EasyOCR (Jaided, 2020) for detecting all the sets of text $\boldsymbol{T}$ in an image. It is an open-source tool that works well in detecting texts even from images that contain some noises. For each text $\mathbf{t} \in \boldsymbol{T}$, it predicts a bounding box $\mathbf{b}_t \in \mathbb{R}^4$, confidence score, and the original texts written inside. We combine all the texts $\mathbf{t}$ whose bounding box lies inside the same shape $\mathbf{s}$.

Arrow Prediction Arrow prediction consists of two steps. First, it detects all the arrow lines from

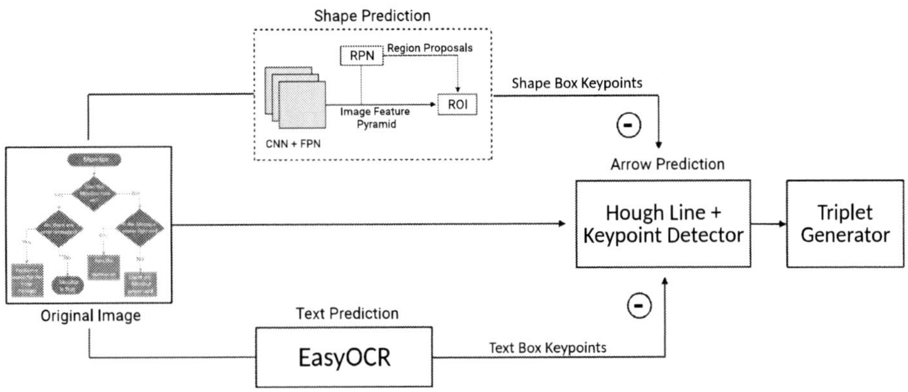

Figure 3: Overall architecture of our proposed method “BloSum”.

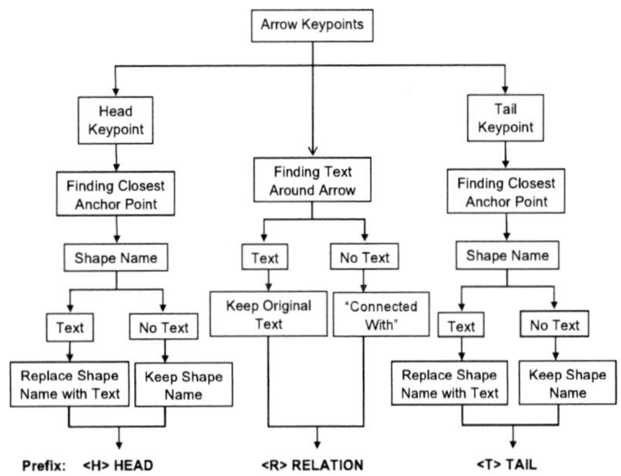

Figure 4: Pipeline of Triplet Generator from BloSum architecture.

the diagram including start and end points. Second, it differentiates between head and tail points. Since it is very difficult for any CNN to detect complex arrows such as arrows having a gap or connected arrows. We apply a simple technique in order to detect all sets of arrows $\boldsymbol{A}$ in an image. By using the information from the shape and text prediction, we subtract all the shapes and text phrases from the original image and binarize them. Thus, it remains only with arrows. Then we apply Hough Line Transform in order to detect all the arrow lines and their start and end points. Hough Line Transform helps in detecting the break arrow and the connected arrow as well. To differentiate between the head and tail of an arrow, we add an offset to the start and end points to count the number of white pixels. Finally, a greater number of white pixels represents the head of an arrow, and a lesser number of white pixels represents the tail of an arrow. For each arrow $\mathbf{a} \in \boldsymbol{A}$, predicts 4-d vector $\mathbf{v} = (a^{head}, a^{tail})$ which represents 2-d coordinates of head and tail keypoints per arrow.

Triplet Generator By using all the information from the previous steps, we build a framework called Triplet Generator as shown in Figure 4. This generator finds the connection and relationship between different shapes, and converts these relations into the form of triplets (<H> <R> <T>). For each arrow $\mathbf{a}$ in the diagram, it predicts three things: Head, Relation, and Tail. For each Head and Tail keypoints, first, it finds the closest anchor point placed on shapes. Second, it determines the name of the shape it is associated with. Later, it finds texts inside the shape. It combines all the texts whose bounding boxes lie inside it. If texts are available inside the shape then that particular text is assigned as Head or Tail, and if there are no texts, then the shape name is assigned to Head or Tail. For Relation, first, it determines the distance between the arrow and all the text bounding boxes written outside the shapes. If the distance between arrow and text comes under a threshold value where we set it as 5, then those particular texts are assigned as Relation and if there are no texts which satisfy this condition, then automatically Relation will be assigned as “Connected with”. This generator forms a triplet in the top to the bottom and the right to the left order.

After generating all sets of triplets from a diagram, we add “Diagram to Text:” to prefix of each triplet in order to make input friendly for the language model. We experiment with two variants of the T5 model: T5_Large and T5_Base and two variants of the BART model: BART_Large and BART_Base. We also experiment with OCR variants for each model where we replace the extracted text from EasyOCR with their ground truth values. Following previous work (Guo et al., 2020), we connect each token word with an underline "_". For example, "check monitor" is converted to "check_monitor". We use the pre-trained model of each variant on WebNLG 2017 dataset (Gardent et al., 2017). Direct applying these models for our task shows poor performance. Since our dataset contains the ground truth triplets and summaries, we fine-tune each model variant with our dataset.

4.2 Faster R-CNN

We follow the same Faster R-CNN as we use in the BloSum for shape prediction. Instead of detecting only shapes, we predict all the seven classes including text and arrow classes using Inception-ResNet-v2 as a backbone. We keep the IoU threshold value of 0.8 for all classes and also apply NMS. We apply the same EasyOCR for extracting a text from the text bounding box detected by Faster R-CNN. Further for each arrow class, we use the arrow prediction for head and tail keypoints and the triplet generator for generating triplets. Later, those triplets are used by a language model to generate summaries. Similar to BloSum, we experiment with two variants of the T5 model and two variants of the BART model, along with their OCR variants.

4.3 Image Caption

For this category, we consider the Show, Attend, and Tell (SAT) model (Xu et al., 2015) in order to generate captions from block diagram images. We use the pre-trained ResNet50 (He et al., 2016) model on ImageNet (Deng et al., 2009) dataset as the encoder and a unidirectional LSTM (Hochreiter and Schmidhuber, 1997) as the decoder. Since we have the object labels and summaries for the block diagram images, we further fine-tune the model on our dataset. Direct applying without fine-tuning, shows very poor performance for block diagrams.

5 Experiments

5.1 Experimental Setups

All the experiments are done on our machine with 3 GPUs (NVIDIA TITAN RTX) having a memory of 48GB each.

BloSum Julca-Aguilar and Hirata (2018) found that training using the pre-trained model of Faster R-CNN over the MSCOCO dataset (Lin et al., 2014) allows for much faster convergence than training from scratch. Thus, we use the pre-trained model. Although, block diagram images are very different in comparison to the real-world images of the MSCOCO dataset. We then fine-tune the model with our datasets. We use the minibatch training with batch size 1 (due to the variable dimensions of the images) and fix the number of training steps to 25,000. Also, we fix the number of proposals for RPN to 300. Increasing the number of proposals did not result in any considerable improvements.

T5/BART For both language models (T5 and BART), we fine-tune the models with our datasets and use the Adam optimizer (Kingma and Ba, 2015) for maximally 50 epochs with a batch size of 8. The initial learning rate is set to 5×10^{-5}. T5_Large consists of 770M parameters and BART_Large consists of 406M parameters with a 24-layer Transformer as the encoder and decoder whereas T5_Base has 220M parameters and BART_Base has 139M parameters with 12-layer Transformer as the encoder and decoder. For inference, we use the model with the lowest validation loss. Additional training setup of language models are provided in Appendix A.2.

Image Captioning Model We follow the same training setup as presented in the original paper for pretraining both image encoders and captioning model. Run the inference with beam search with a beam size of 4.

5.2 Automatic Evaluation

Measures We conduct automatic evaluation for the generated summaries from different models using five measures. BLEU (Post, 2018) measures how many words in the generated output summaries appeared in the human reference summaries. We use the overall BLEU score obtained by averaging BLEU n-grams (n= 1 to 4) with respect to the brevity penalty. ROUGE-1 (Lin, 2004) measures how many words in the human reference summaries appeared in the generated output summaries. We use the F1 score of ROUGE-1 (Version 1.01) to show the fluency of the sentence generated. BLEURT (Sellam et al., 2020) is a model-based evaluation metric that indicates whether the output sentence is grammatically correct and conveys the correct meaning. We use BLEURT-base-128. Content Selection (CS) metric measures how well the output generated summaries match the ground truth summaries in terms of selecting which records to generate (Wiseman et al., 2017). Finally, we measure Perplexity (PPL) (Radford et al., 2019) using a

Models	CBD					FC_A		FC_B	
	BLEU ↑	ROUGE-1 ↑	CS ↑	BLEURT ↑	PPL ↓	BLEU ↑	ROUGE-1 ↑	BLEU ↑	ROUGE-1 ↑
Image Caption	5.56	10.07	18.42%	-0.84	29.76	3.76	10.9	4.08	13.03
Faster R-CNN + BART_Base	18.01	33.21	40.65%	-0.62	16.84	22.1	44.36	24.67	45.21
Faster R-CNN + BART_Large	17.29	31.16	42.99%	-0.69	17.93	20.07	43.29	22.19	41.63
Faster R-CNN + T5_Base	21.55	38.32	49.43%	0.09	14.66	24.78	**47.52**	24.92	46.35
Faster R-CNN + T5_Large	22.11	40.1	51.78%	0.1	12.06	**25.61**	46.91	**27.81**	**50.47**
BloSum + BART_Base	35.33	75.94	71.64%	0.14	8.44	16.99	34.04	18.16	39.87
BloSum + BART_Large	33.47	75.24	68.16%	0.11	8.33	14.16	31.65	15.49	35.39
BloSum + T5_Base	40.04	78.68	**84.53%**	**0.21**	7.79	19.98	42.34	18.75	40.55
BloSum + T5_Large	**42.18**	**80.78**	83.18%.	0.2	**7.55**	18.23	40.27	20.04	40.85
OCR-Faster R-CNN + T5_Base	28.71	42.92	53.40%	0.13	11.63	48.65	85.79	49.28	85.52
OCR-Faster R-CNN + T5_Large	29.87	45.19	58.05%	0.1	10.91	49.13	86.67	52.45	89.03
OCR-BloSum + T5_Base	40.91	78.74	**84.68%**	**0.21**	7.79	51.01	88.19	52.37	88.92
OCR-BloSum + T5_Large	**42.86**	**81.29**	83.23%.	0.2	**7.54**	**51.73**	**88.24**	**53.17**	**89.56**

Table 2: Automatic evaluation results on computerized (CBD) and handwritten (FC_A, FC_B) datasets from different models. Up arrow ↑ shows, higher is better. Down arrow ↓ shows, lower is better. Bold numbers indicate the best score. "OCR-" models use ground truth OCR values.

pre-trained GPT-2 Medium to check the readability and fluency of the generated sentences.

Results Table 2 shows the automatic evaluation results from different models on both computerized and handwritten datasets.

On the CBD dataset, the image caption model fails to extract the relationship between nodes from the diagram and shows a very poor performance while generating descriptions of it. However, language models with Faster R-CNN show a better improvement in extracting relationships between nodes but our proposed method outperforms other models. On one hand, we notice that BloSum with the T5_Large model has the highest BLEU (42.18) and ROUGE-1 (80.78) score. It also generates fluent sentences (low PPL). On the other hand, BloSum with the T5_Base model better captures relevant information from diagrams (high CS score) and grammatically correct sentences (high BLEURT score). But there is a negligible difference as compared to the T5_Large model. Surprisingly, the BART_Base model shows better performance than BART_Large in both Faster R-CNN and BloSum cases. But the low PPL score of the BART_Large model shows that it generates more fluent texts than BART_Base for BloSum. Faster R-CNN mainly fails to detect complex arrows and relations from the diagrams, which results in poor performance of sentence generation. We find similar results for OCR models with negligible improvements for BloSum variants which shows the correctness of text extraction. Overall, BloSum with T5_Large models shows the best performance among others. Figure 5 shows an example of the result obtained by the BloSum model (Intermediate

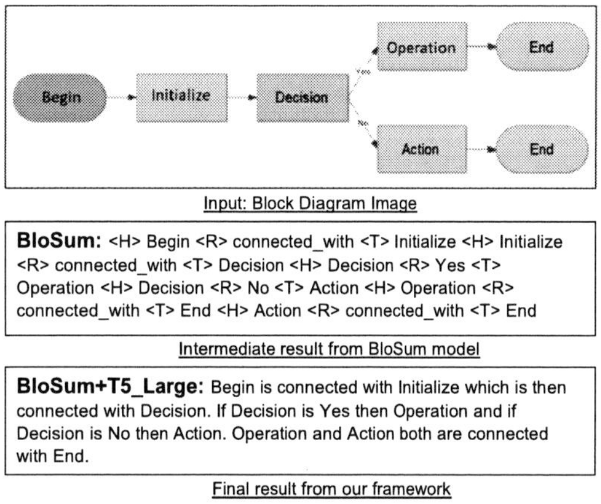

Figure 5: Sample output of a block diagram image from our model.

result) and the final result from our framework. The BloSum model produces all the sets of triplets (<H> represents head, <R> represents relation, <T> represents tail) from the given diagram and T5_Large model generates sentences from those triplets.

Also, on the handwritten dataset (FC_A, FC_B), the image caption model shows a very poor performance. Unlike CBD, Faster R-CNN with T5_Large model shows better performance than BloSum. But in the case of OCR models, BloSum with T5_Large models shows the highest BLEU (51.73), ROUGE-1 (88.24) score for FC_A dataset and BLEU (53.17), ROUGE-1 (89.56) score for FC_B dataset. This shows that the BloSum model mainly struggles with handwritten texts, which is because the current version of EasyOCR does not support handwritten texts. Since our work mainly focuses on computerized block diagram images, we left this

Models	CBD			FC_A			FC_B		
	Adequacy	Fluency	Coherence	Adequacy	Fluency	Coherence	Adequacy	Fluency	Coherence
Image Caption	3.6	4.7	4.2	6.4	5.7	5.3	6.8	6.1	5.6
Faster R-CNN +T5_Large	18.6	15.9	13.3	55.6	52.1	50.9	67.4	65.8	65.1
Faster R-CNN +BART_Base	12.7	10.8	11.7	50.3	45.7	43.1	66.1	63.4	62.9
BloSum + T5_Large	68.4	62.3	63.6	28.9	35.6	36.3	36.7	40.2	40.6
BloSum +BART_Base	63.5	60.8	60.9	22.7	28.9	32.1	31.4	38.9	37.5
OCR-Faster R-CNN +T5_Large	30.7	28.2	28.7	60.8	59.4	58.3	64.9	63.2	63.8
OCR-BloSum + T5_Large	**73.3**	**70.1**	**69.8**	**85.4**	**83.1**	**83.9**	**88.8**	**85.1**	**86.4**

Table 3: Human evaluation average score on summaries generated by different models for different datasets. Bold numbers indicate the best score.

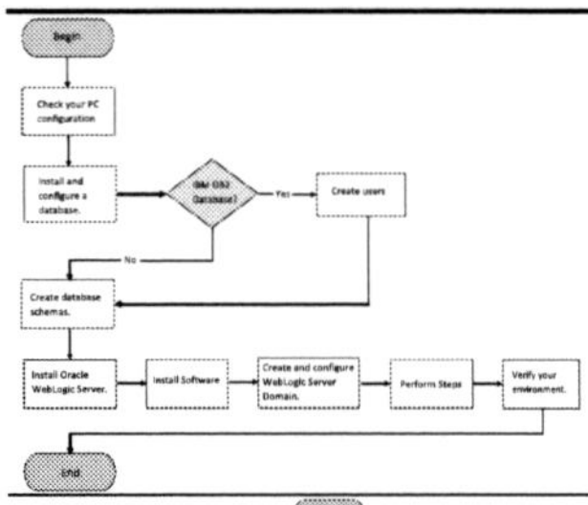

Faster R-CNN + T5_Large: Begin is connected with Check your P is connected with Install and configure database which connected with IBM DB2. Create database schemas is connected with Install WebLogic which is connected with Install Software. Install Software is connected with configure WebLogic server connected with Perform Steps. Perform Steps is connected with Verify your environment.

BloSum + T5_Large: Begin is connected with Check your PC configuration which is connected with Install and configure a database and further connected with IBM DB2 Database?. If IBM DB2 Database? is Yes then Create users which is connected with Install Oracle WebLogic Server. IBM Database is No then Create database schemas. Install Oracle WebLogic Server is connected with Install Software is connected with Create and configure WebLogic server. Perform Steps is connected with Verify your environment which is finally connected with End of the year.

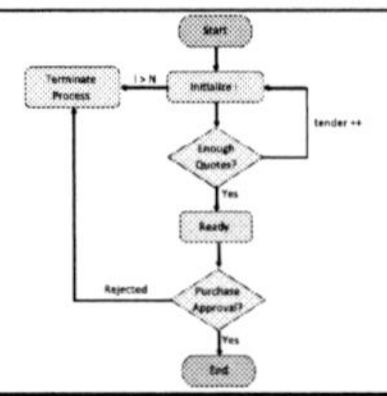

Faster R-CNN + T5_Large: Start is connected with Initialize i which is connected with terminate Process. Initialize i is connected with Enough Quotes? Enough Quotes? is Yes then Ready which then connected with Approval? Approval?

BloSum + T5_Large: Start is connected with Initialize i which if Initialize i is i>N then terminate Process. Initialize i is connected with Enough Quotes? Enough Quotes? is tender++ then Initialize i and if Enough Quotes? is Yes then Ready which is then connected with Purchase Approval? Purchase Approval? is Rejected then Terminate Process and Purchase Approval? is Yes End.

Figure 6: Sample outputs from CBD dataset from different models (last two columns) along with the block diagram image (first column).

area for the future version of EasyOCR that may support handwritten text as well. Additionally, we test the handwritten datasets by training the model on computerized dataset (CBD) to showcase the generalization of the CBD dataset (Appendix A.3).

5.3 Human Evaluation

Since automatic metrics are only good for small sentences and also no metric is perfect. In our scenario, outputs are long sentences and only humans can perfectly test them. We evaluate the quality of outputs by asking a group of 25 people to rate them based on three quality criteria: (i) Adequacy (whether the sentence clearly expresses the data?); (ii) Fluency (whether the sentences are easy to read and in a natural manner?); (iii) Coherence (whether the sentences are well connected?). For each criterion, people rate on a 0-100 scale where 0 is the "strongly disagree" and 100 is the "strongly agree". We randomly select 40 different block diagram images from each dataset and provide their generated output texts to each examiner.

Table 3 shows the average score given by the examiners. We observe a similar pattern with the automatic evaluation of the performances of different models. For both OCR and non-OCR variants, BloSum with the T5_Large model shows the best performance especially on expressing the data correctly for the CBD dataset. For FC_A and FC_B datasets, the non-OCR BloSum variant fails to detect data correctly mainly because of the non-supporting of handwritten texts by EasyOCR. Faster R-CNN performs well for handwritten texts. However, in OCR variants BloSum with T5_Large model shows the overall best performance in terms of both fluency and coherence. We also determine the mode of the scores given by human evaluators. Details are provided in Appendix A.4.

6 Error Analysis and Challenges

To better analyze the results, we manually choose 50 samples from each dataset obtained by different models as shown in Figure 6. This analysis uncovers some key challenges for vision as well as language tasks that we describe below. Additional sample outputs are provided in Appendix A.5.

Vision Challenge Due to improper detection of some shapes and texts, arrow prediction detects some extra or neglects some pre-existing arrows. This results in the wrong prediction of the triplets, which directly affects the language model in summary generation. Another vision challenge is related to OCR. Block diagrams contain a lot of important information. Since OCRs are not 100% accurate, it detects some wrong texts which lead to error in the facts. More accurate data extraction is necessary for block diagrams.

Imaginary Prediction Imaginary Prediction problem is very common for language models in the data-to-text task. Models sometimes predict some imaginary text which is not relevant to the block diagram image. Some previous works (Wiseman et al., 2017; Parikh et al., 2020) face the same problem for the data-to-text task.

Large Scale Dataset Neural models generally require large-scale datasets. However, our dataset covers a lot of variations but is not big enough. Collecting block diagram images, annotations and their human written summaries are difficult tasks as it requires a lot of manual labor.

7 Conclusion

We have presented a novel task of generating textual descriptions from an image of a block diagram. For this purpose, we propose a new architecture called "BloSum" that extracts the contextual meaning from the diagram in the form of triplets. Additionally, we introduce a new dataset CBD for complex computerized block diagrams with their annotated objects, triplets, and human written summaries. Moreover, for showing the generalization of our model, we tested and extended the publicly available handwritten block diagram datasets i.e., FC_A and FC_B by adding triplets and summaries. This extended dataset can also be used for other data-to-text tasks. Our evaluation with different metrics shows a promising result and outperforms other methods and also reveals some of the unique challenges for this task.

8 Limitations and Future Works

Evaluation with different metrics shows a very promising result of our work. However, there are some limitations such as it does not support electrical diagrams that contain some electrical representations like capacitors, resistors, and others. It only supports those diagrams where shapes are connected through arrows. Also, most of the error occurs in the break arrows category, where there is a very large gap.

To follow up, we plan to explore other approaches to better capture the relationship between shapes, arrows, and texts. We hope that the block diagram summarization task will serve as a useful research for better document summarization as well as for the Q&A task and motivate other researchers to investigate this relatively new area. In future, we also aim to collect more complex diagrams and summaries from different sources and perform experiments to evaluate the generalization of the model.

Ethical Consideration

We had several ethical issues to take into consideration during the dataset collection and preparation process. To respect the intellectual property of the block diagram publishers, we only used publicly available block diagrams that provide publication rights for academic purposes. In addition, we also manually replace around 50% of the text from each diagram with some different meaningful texts. Replacing texts also helps with data privacy issue and protect personal and sensitive data.

The examiners for manual evaluation were randomly selected from the applicants at university. The subjects for this evaluation were those people who wanted to do this evaluation willingly without any wage and have no relation to this project. Additionally, to preserve the privacy of these examiners, all of their evaluations were anonymized.

One potential misuse of our model that we anticipate is the spread of false information. As described in section 6, our model outputs often seem fluent but in reality, they contain certain OCR and imaginary prediction errors. Therefore, these errors could mislead the people if such model outputs are published without being corrected.

Acknowledgements

This work was partly supported by the National Research Foundation of Korea (NRF) grant funded by the Korea government (MSIT) (No. 2022R1A5A7026673)(50%) and by the NRF grant funded by the Korea government (MSIT) (No. NRF-2021R1A2C3011169)(50%).

References

Harsh Agrawal, Peter Anderson, Karan Desai, Yufei Wang, Xinlei Chen, Rishabh Jain, Mark Johnson, Dhruv Batra, Devi Parikh, and Stefan Lee. 2019. nocaps: novel object captioning at scale. In *2019 IEEE/CVF International Conference on Computer Vision, ICCV 2019, Seoul, Korea (South), October 27 - November 2, 2019*, pages 8947–8956. IEEE.

Ahmad-Montaser Awal, Guihuan Feng, Harold Mouchere, and Christian Viard-Gaudin. 2011. First experiments on a new online handwritten flowchart database. In *Document Recognition and Retrieval XVIII*, volume 7874, pages 81–90. SPIE.

Abhijit Balaji, Thuvaarakkesh Ramanathan, and Venkateshwarlu Sonathi. 2018. Chart-text: A fully automated chart image descriptor. *ArXiv preprint*, abs/1812.10636.

Martin Bresler, Daniel Prusa, and Vaclav Hlavac. 2016. Online recognition of sketched arrow-connected diagrams. *International Journal on Document Analysis and Recognition (IJDAR)*, 19(3):253–267.

Tom B. Brown, Benjamin Mann, Nick Ryder, Melanie Subbiah, Jared Kaplan, Prafulla Dhariwal, Arvind Neelakantan, Pranav Shyam, Girish Sastry, Amanda Askell, Sandhini Agarwal, Ariel Herbert-Voss, Gretchen Krueger, Tom Henighan, Rewon Child, Aditya Ramesh, Daniel M. Ziegler, Jeffrey Wu, Clemens Winter, Christopher Hesse, Mark Chen, Eric Sigler, Mateusz Litwin, Scott Gray, Benjamin Chess, Jack Clark, Christopher Berner, Sam McCandlish, Alec Radford, Ilya Sutskever, and Dario Amodei. 2020. Language models are few-shot learners. In *Advances in Neural Information Processing Systems 33: Annual Conference on Neural Information Processing Systems 2020, NeurIPS 2020, December 6-12, 2020, virtual*.

Wenhu Chen, Yu Su, Xifeng Yan, and William Yang Wang. 2020. KGPT: Knowledge-grounded pretraining for data-to-text generation. In *Proceedings of the 2020 Conference on Empirical Methods in Natural Language Processing (EMNLP)*, pages 8635–8648, Online. Association for Computational Linguistics.

Xinlei Chen, Hao Fang, Tsung-Yi Lin, Ramakrishna Vedantam, Saurabh Gupta, Piotr Dollár, and C Lawrence Zitnick. 2015. Microsoft coco captions: Data collection and evaluation server. *ArXiv preprint*, abs/1504.00325.

Jia Deng, Wei Dong, Richard Socher, Li-Jia Li, Kai Li, and Fei-Fei Li. 2009. Imagenet: A large-scale hierarchical image database. In *2009 IEEE Computer Society Conference on Computer Vision and Pattern Recognition (CVPR 2009), 20-25 June 2009, Miami, Florida, USA*, pages 248–255. IEEE Computer Society.

Jacob Devlin, Ming-Wei Chang, Kenton Lee, and Kristina Toutanova. 2019. BERT: Pre-training of deep bidirectional transformers for language understanding. In *Proceedings of the 2019 Conference of the North American Chapter of the Association for Computational Linguistics: Human Language Technologies, Volume 1 (Long and Short Papers)*, pages 4171–4186, Minneapolis, Minnesota. Association for Computational Linguistics.

Claire Gardent, Anastasia Shimorina, Shashi Narayan, and Laura Perez-Beltrachini. 2017. The WebNLG challenge: Generating text from RDF data. In *Proceedings of the 10th International Conference on Natural Language Generation*, pages 124–133, Santiago de Compostela, Spain. Association for Computational Linguistics.

Albert Gatt and Emiel Krahmer. 2018. Survey of the state of the art in natural language generation: Core tasks, applications and evaluation. *Journal of Artificial Intelligence Research*, 61:65–170.

Li Gong, Josep Crego, and Jean Senellart. 2019. Enhanced transformer model for data-to-text generation. In *Proceedings of the 3rd Workshop on Neural Generation and Translation*, pages 148–156, Hong Kong. Association for Computational Linguistics.

Qipeng Guo, Zhijing Jin, Ning Dai, Xipeng Qiu, Xiangyang Xue, David Wipf, and Zheng Zhang. 2020. \cal p2: A plan-and-pretrain approach for knowledge graph-to-text generation: A plan-and-pretrain approach for knowledge graph-to-text generation. In *Proceedings of the 3rd International Workshop on Natural Language Generation from the Semantic Web (WebNLG+)*., pages 100–106.

Kaiming He, Xiangyu Zhang, Shaoqing Ren, and Jian Sun. 2016. Deep residual learning for image recognition. In *2016 IEEE Conference on Computer Vision and Pattern Recognition, CVPR 2016, Las Vegas, NV, USA, June 27-30, 2016*, pages 770–778. IEEE Computer Society.

Sepp Hochreiter and Jürgen Schmidhuber. 1997. Long short-term memory. *Neural computation*, 9(8):1735–1780.

AI Jaided. 2020. Easyocr. *GitHub Repository*.

Frank D Julca-Aguilar and Nina ST Hirata. 2018. Symbol detection in online handwritten graphics using faster r-cnn. In *2018 13th IAPR international workshop on document analysis systems (DAS)*, pages 151–156. IEEE.

Mihir Kale and Abhinav Rastogi. 2020. Text-to-text pre-training for data-to-text tasks. In *Proceedings of the 13th International Conference on Natural Language Generation*, pages 97–102, Dublin, Ireland. Association for Computational Linguistics.

Diederik P. Kingma and Jimmy Ba. 2015. Adam: A method for stochastic optimization. In *3rd International Conference on Learning Representations, ICLR 2015, San Diego, CA, USA, May 7-9, 2015, Conference Track Proceedings*.

Tom Kwiatkowski, Jennimaria Palomaki, Olivia Redfield, Michael Collins, Ankur Parikh, Chris Alberti, Danielle Epstein, Illia Polosukhin, Jacob Devlin, Kenton Lee, Kristina Toutanova, Llion Jones, Matthew Kelcey, Ming-Wei Chang, Andrew M. Dai, Jakob Uszkoreit, Quoc Le, and Slav Petrov. 2019. Natural questions: A benchmark for question answering research. *Transactions of the Association for Computational Linguistics*, 7:452–466.

Mike Lewis, Yinhan Liu, Naman Goyal, Marjan Ghazvininejad, Abdelrahman Mohamed, Omer Levy, Veselin Stoyanov, and Luke Zettlemoyer. 2020. BART: Denoising sequence-to-sequence pre-training for natural language generation, translation, and comprehension. In *Proceedings of the 58th Annual Meeting of the Association for Computational Linguistics*, pages 7871–7880, Online. Association for Computational Linguistics.

Chin-Yew Lin. 2004. ROUGE: A package for automatic evaluation of summaries. In *Text Summarization Branches Out*, pages 74–81, Barcelona, Spain. Association for Computational Linguistics.

Tsung-Yi Lin, Piotr Dollár, Ross B. Girshick, Kaiming He, Bharath Hariharan, and Serge J. Belongie. 2017. Feature pyramid networks for object detection. In *2017 IEEE Conference on Computer Vision and Pattern Recognition, CVPR 2017, Honolulu, HI, USA, July 21-26, 2017*, pages 936–944. IEEE Computer Society.

Tsung-Yi Lin, Michael Maire, Serge Belongie, James Hays, Pietro Perona, Deva Ramanan, Piotr Dollár, and C Lawrence Zitnick. 2014. Microsoft coco: Common objects in context. In *European conference on computer vision*, pages 740–755. Springer.

Yinhan Liu, Myle Ott, Naman Goyal, Jingfei Du, Mandar Joshi, Danqi Chen, Omer Levy, Mike Lewis, Luke Zettlemoyer, and Veselin Stoyanov. 2019. Roberta: A robustly optimized bert pretraining approach. *ArXiv preprint*, abs/1907.11692.

Hongyuan Mei, Mohit Bansal, and Matthew R. Walter. 2016. What to talk about and how? selective generation using LSTMs with coarse-to-fine alignment. In *Proceedings of the 2016 Conference of the North American Chapter of the Association for Computational Linguistics: Human Language Technologies*, pages 720–730, San Diego, California. Association for Computational Linguistics.

Fanya S Montalvo. 1990. Diagram understanding. In *Visual languages and applications*, pages 5–27. Springer.

Jason Obeid and Enamul Hoque. 2020. Chart-to-text: Generating natural language descriptions for charts by adapting the transformer model. In *Proceedings of the 13th International Conference on Natural Language Generation*, pages 138–147, Dublin, Ireland. Association for Computational Linguistics.

Ankur Parikh, Xuezhi Wang, Sebastian Gehrmann, Manaal Faruqui, Bhuwan Dhingra, Diyi Yang, and Dipanjan Das. 2020. ToTTo: A controlled table-to-text generation dataset. In *Proceedings of the 2020 Conference on Empirical Methods in Natural Language Processing (EMNLP)*, pages 1173–1186, Online. Association for Computational Linguistics.

Matt Post. 2018. A call for clarity in reporting BLEU scores. In *Proceedings of the Third Conference on Machine Translation: Research Papers*, pages 186–191, Brussels, Belgium. Association for Computational Linguistics.

Ratish Puduppully, Li Dong, and Mirella Lapata. 2019. Data-to-text generation with content selection and planning. In *The Thirty-Third AAAI Conference on Artificial Intelligence, AAAI 2019, The Thirty-First Innovative Applications of Artificial Intelligence Conference, IAAI 2019, The Ninth AAAI Symposium on Educational Advances in Artificial Intelligence, EAAI 2019, Honolulu, Hawaii, USA, January 27 - February 1, 2019*, pages 6908–6915. AAAI Press.

Alec Radford, Jeffrey Wu, Rewon Child, David Luan, Dario Amodei, Ilya Sutskever, et al. 2019. Language models are unsupervised multitask learners. *OpenAI blog*, 1(8):9.

Colin Raffel, Noam Shazeer, Adam Roberts, Katherine Lee, Sharan Narang, Michael Matena, Yanqi Zhou, Wei Li, and Peter J Liu. 2019. Exploring the limits of transfer learning with a unified text-to-text transformer. *ArXiv preprint*, abs/1910.10683.

Pranav Rajpurkar, Robin Jia, and Percy Liang. 2018. Know what you don't know: Unanswerable questions for SQuAD. In *Proceedings of the 56th Annual Meeting of the Association for Computational Linguistics (Volume 2: Short Papers)*, pages 784–789, Melbourne, Australia. Association for Computational Linguistics.

Jacques Pierre Robin. 1995. *Revision-based generation of natural language summaries providing historical background: corpus-based analysis, design, implementation and evaluation*. Ph.D. thesis, Columbia University.

Bernhard Schäfer, Margret Keuper, and Heiner Stuckenschmidt. 2021. Arrow r-cnn for handwritten diagram recognition. *International Journal on Document Analysis and Recognition (IJDAR)*, 24(1):3–17.

Bernhard Schäfer and Heiner Stuckenschmidt. 2019. Arrow r-cnn for flowchart recognition. In *2019 International Conference on Document Analysis and Recognition Workshops (ICDARW)*, volume 1, pages 7–13. IEEE.

Bernhard Schäfer and Heiner Stuckenschmidt. 2021. Diagramnet: hand-drawn diagram recognition using visual arrow-relation detection. In *International Conference on Document Analysis and Recognition*, pages 614–630. Springer.

Abigail See, Peter J. Liu, and Christopher D. Manning. 2017. Get to the point: Summarization with pointer-generator networks. In *Proceedings of the 55th Annual Meeting of the Association for Computational Linguistics (Volume 1: Long Papers)*, pages 1073–1083, Vancouver, Canada. Association for Computational Linguistics.

Thibault Sellam, Dipanjan Das, and Ankur Parikh. 2020. BLEURT: Learning robust metrics for text generation. In *Proceedings of the 58th Annual Meeting of the Association for Computational Linguistics*, pages 7881–7892, Online. Association for Computational Linguistics.

Oleksii Sidorov, Ronghang Hu, Marcus Rohrbach, and Amanpreet Singh. 2020. Textcaps: a dataset for image captioning with reading comprehension. In *European conference on computer vision*, pages 742–758. Springer.

Christian Szegedy, Sergey Ioffe, Vincent Vanhoucke, and Alexander A. Alemi. 2017. Inception-v4, inception-resnet and the impact of residual connections on learning. In *Proceedings of the Thirty-First AAAI Conference on Artificial Intelligence, February 4-9, 2017, San Francisco, California, USA*, pages 4278–4284. AAAI Press.

Kumiko Tanaka-Ishii, Koiti Hasida, and Itsuki Noda. 1998. Reactive content selection in the generation of real-time soccer commentary. In *COLING 1998 Volume 2: The 17th International Conference on Computational Linguistics*.

D Tzutalin. 2015. Labelimg. *GitHub Repository*, 6.

Alex Wang, Yada Pruksachatkun, Nikita Nangia, Amanpreet Singh, Julian Michael, Felix Hill, Omer Levy, and Samuel R. Bowman. 2019a. Superglue: A stickier benchmark for general-purpose language understanding systems. In *Advances in Neural Information Processing Systems 32: Annual Conference on Neural Information Processing Systems 2019, NeurIPS 2019, December 8-14, 2019, Vancouver, BC, Canada*, pages 3261–3275.

Alex Wang, Amanpreet Singh, Julian Michael, Felix Hill, Omer Levy, and Samuel R. Bowman. 2019b. GLUE: A multi-task benchmark and analysis platform for natural language understanding. In *7th International Conference on Learning Representations, ICLR 2019, New Orleans, LA, USA, May 6-9, 2019*. OpenReview.net.

Sam Wiseman, Stuart Shieber, and Alexander Rush. 2017. Challenges in data-to-document generation. In *Proceedings of the 2017 Conference on Empirical Methods in Natural Language Processing*, pages 2253–2263, Copenhagen, Denmark. Association for Computational Linguistics.

Kelvin Xu, Jimmy Ba, Ryan Kiros, Kyunghyun Cho, Aaron C. Courville, Ruslan Salakhutdinov, Richard S. Zemel, and Yoshua Bengio. 2015. Show, attend and tell: Neural image caption generation with visual attention. In *Proceedings of the 32nd International Conference on Machine Learning, ICML 2015, Lille, France, 6-11 July 2015*, volume 37 of *JMLR Workshop and Conference Proceedings*, pages 2048–2057. JMLR.org.

Zhilin Yang, Zihang Dai, Yiming Yang, Jaime G. Carbonell, Ruslan Salakhutdinov, and Quoc V. Le. 2019. Xlnet: Generalized autoregressive pretraining for language understanding. In *Advances in Neural Information Processing Systems 32: Annual Conference on Neural Information Processing Systems 2019, NeurIPS 2019, December 8-14, 2019, Vancouver, BC, Canada*, pages 5754–5764.

Pengchuan Zhang, Xiujun Li, Xiaowei Hu, Jianwei Yang, Lei Zhang, Lijuan Wang, Yejin Choi, and Jianfeng Gao. 2021. Vinvl: Making visual representations matter in vision-language models. *ArXiv preprint*, abs/2101.00529.

A Appendices

A.1 Additional Details of CBD Dataset

Figure 7 shows some of the additional statistics of the CBD dataset with respect to shapes, arrows, and text classes. We annotate all the images in PASCAL VOC XML format through the LabelImg tool, which can also be used for other vision tasks. Figure 8 shows some of the complex samples of three categories from our dataset based on arrow structures (Break, Connect, Normal). We write triplets and summaries for all datasets (including handwritten datasets) in text (.txt) format, similar to WebNLG dataset. This format (pair of triplets and summaries) can help other researchers to use it for different data-to-text tasks.

A.2 Additional Details of Language Models

T5 We follow the same training setup as proposed by Guo et al. (2020) and also use their canonicalization of special tokens method in order to handle special tokens. This method converts the special characters that are not in the English alphabet into a format, in which T5 is more familiar. For example, the long dash "—" is converted into a small dash "-". Then each triplet is serialized with special tokens representing the head, relation, and tail. For proper readability, the input format of text phrases such as "check monitor" is actually "check@@ _@@ monitor" because T5 uses byte-pair encoding. For T5, we use two variants: the T5_Large model which consists of 24 attention modules and 770M parameters, and the T5_Base model which consists of 12 attention modules and 220M parameters.

BART For BART, we follow the same training setup as presented by Lewis et al. (2020). It is particularly pre-trained for text generation tasks. Same as T5, we use two variants of BART: i) BART_Large and, ii) BART_Base. Bart-large model consists of 24-layer, 1024-hidden, 16-heads, and, 406M parameters whereas the Bart-base model consists of 12-layer, 768-hidden, 16-heads, and 139M parameters.

A.3 Additional Results from Dataset Evaluation

We additionally perform an experiment with the CBD dataset. First, we train and test the faster R-CNN model on the handwritten datasets (Train: FC_A/FC_B, Test: FC_A/FC_B). Second, we

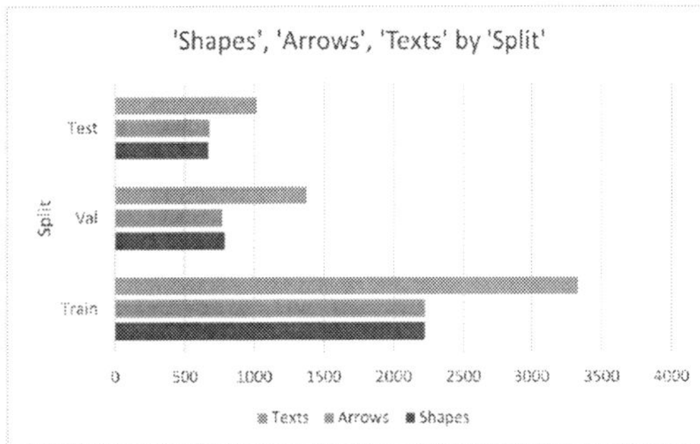

Figure 7: Additional statistics of CBD dataset.

train the same model with CBD and then test it with handwritten datasets (Train: CBD, Test: FC_A/FC_B). Table 4 shows the precision score values of all the seven classes along with the average values. We set the IOU threshold value of 0.7 for all seven classes. Surprisingly, the model detects better handwritten diagrams, when trained on computerized diagrams than trained on handwritten diagrams. However, the CBD dataset does not contain any handwritten diagrams. This shows the generalization and usefulness of our dataset, which can also be used in many other applications.

A.4 Additional Results from Human Evaluation

Table 5 shows the mode scores of human evaluation on summaries generated by different models for the different datasets. Mode scores provide some additional insights on the evaluation of the output generated.

A.5 Additional Sample Outputs from CBD, FC_A, and FC_B datasets

Figure 9 shows some of the sample outputs (triplets) generated from our model (BloSum) for the computerized (CBD) dataset. Figure 10 shows some of the additional sample outputs (summaries) generated from our model (BloSum) plus language model for both computerized (CBD) as well as handwritten datasets (FC_A, FC_B).

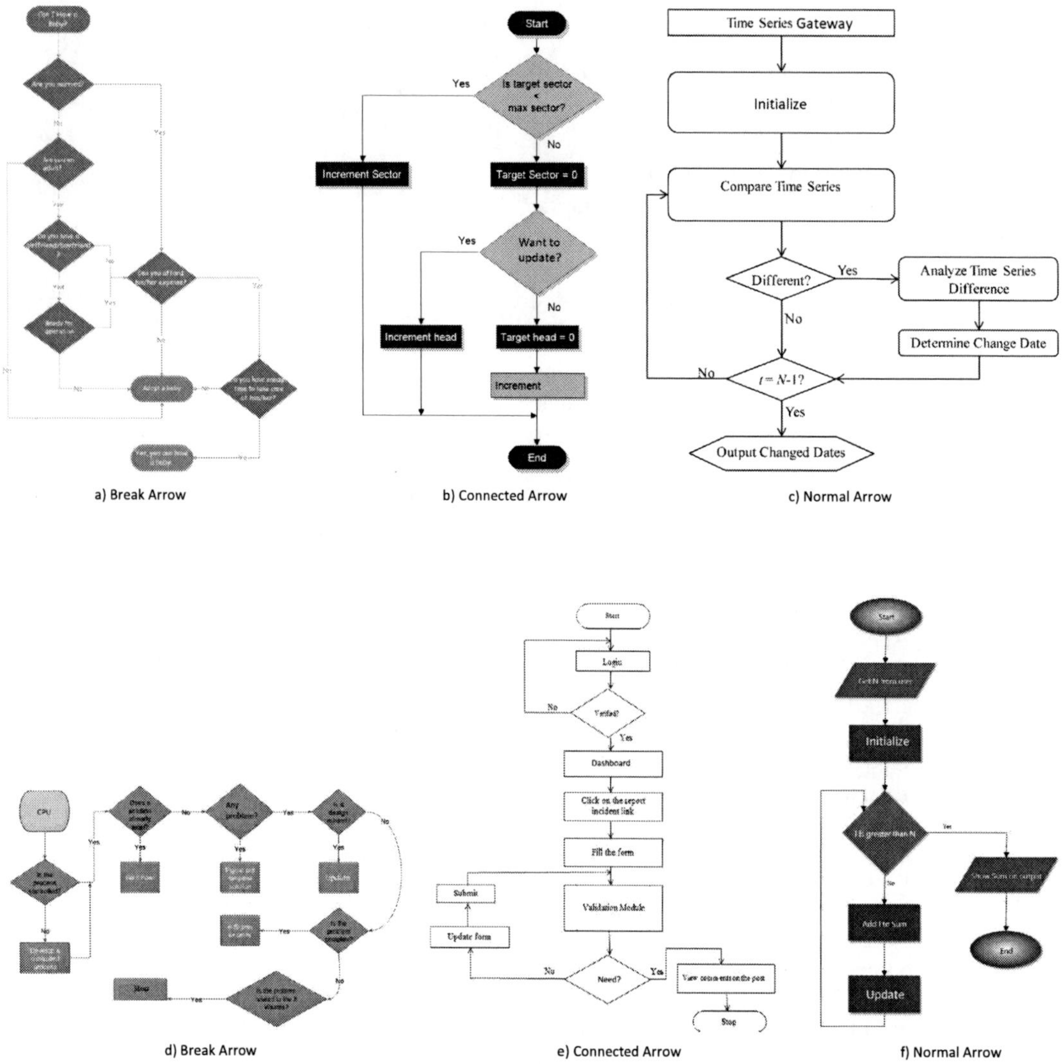

Figure 8: Sample images from CBD datasets for three arrow variations.

Class	Train: FCA Test: FCA	Train: CBD Test: FCA	Train: FCB Test: FCB	Train: CBD Test: FCB
Arrow	86.17	89.65	88.13	90.76
Connection	96.59	99.76	99.44	99.54
Data	99.97	99.99	99.04	99.3
Decision	99.57	99.99	99.99	99.98
Process	99.37	99.55	98.9	99.32
Terminator	99.99	99.83	99.85	99.97
Text	83.13	84.97	86.74	87.04
Average	94.97	**96.24**	96.01	**96.55**

Table 4: Precision score values for different classes on different train and test datasets. Bold numbers indicate the best score.

Models	CBD			FC_A			FC_B		
	Adequacy	Fluency	Coherence	Adequacy	Fluency	Coherence	Adequacy	Fluency	Coherence
Image Caption	3	4	3	5	5	4	6	5	4
Faster R-CNN +T5_Large	15	12	10	50	45	45	60	55	55
Faster R-CNN +BART_Base	10	8	8	40	35	35	60	55	55
BloSum + T5_Large	55	50	50	20	25	30	30	35	35
BloSum +BART_Base	55	50	50	10	15	25	25	30	30
OCR-Faster R-CNN +T5_Large	20	20	20	50	50	50	55	55	50
OCR-BloSum + T5_Large	**60**	**60**	**50**	**75**	**70**	**70**	**75**	**70**	**75**

Table 5: Human evaluation mode score on summaries generated by different models for different datasets. Bold numbers indicate the best score.

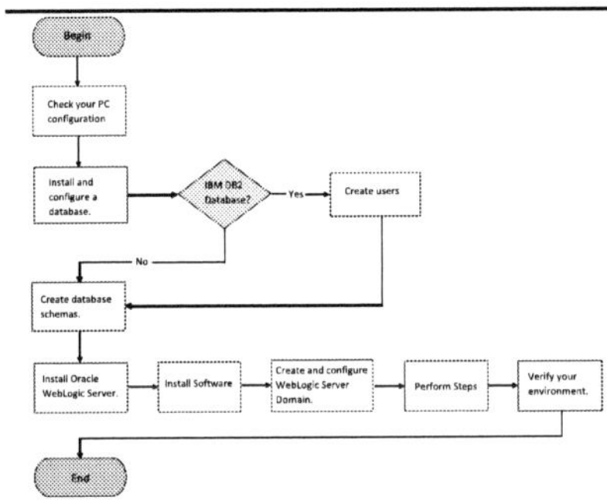

BloSum: <H> Begin <R> connected_with <T> Check_your_PC_configuration <H> Check_your_PC_configuration <R> connected_with <T> Install_and_configure_a_database <H> Install_and_configure_a_database <R> connected_with <T> IBM_DB2_Database? <H> IBM_DB2_Database? <R> Yes <T> Create_users <H> IBM_DB2_Database? <R> No <T> Create_database_schemas. <H> Create_users <R> connected_with <T> Create_database_schemas. <H> Create_database_schemas.<R>connected_with<T>Install_Oracle_Weblogic_Server <H> Install_Oracle_Weblogic_Server <R> connected_with <T> Install_Software <H> Install_Software <R> connected_with <T> Create_and_configure_WebLogic_Server_Domian.<H>Create_and_configure_WebLogic_Server_Domian. <R> connected_with <T> Perform_Steps <H> Perform_Steps <R> connected_with <T> Verify_your_environment. <H> Verify_your_environment. <R> connected_with <T> End

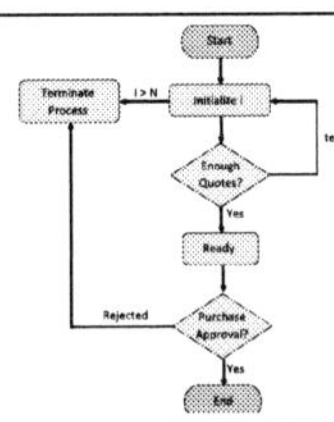

BloSum: <H> Start <R> connected_with <T> Initialize_i <H> Initialize_i <R> i>N <T> Terminate_Process <H> Initialize_i <R> connected_with <T> Enough_Quotes? <H> Enough_Quotes? <R> tender++ <T> Initialize_i <H> Enough_Quotes? <R> Yes <T> Ready <H> Ready <R> connected_with <T> Purchase_Approval? <H> Purchase_Approval? <R> Rejected <T> Terminate_Process <H> Purchase_Approval? <R> Yes <T> End

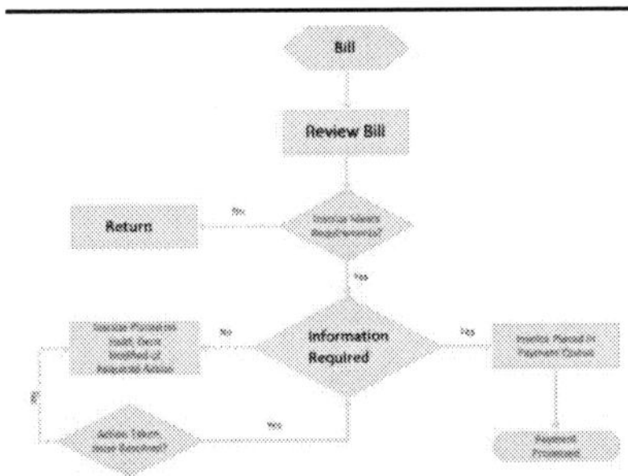

BloSum: <H>Bill<R>connected_with<T>Review_Bill<H>Review_Bill <R>connected_with<T>Invoice_Meets_Requirements?<H>Invoice_Meets_Requirements?<R>No<T>Return<H>Invoice_Meets_Requirements?<R>Yes<T>Information_Required<H>Information_Required<R>No<T>Invoice_Placed_on_Hold,_Dept_Notified_of_Required_Action<H>Information_Required<R>Yes<T>Invoice_Placed_in_Payment_Queue<H>Invoice_Placed_in_Payment_Queue<R>connected_with<T>Payment_Processed<H>Action_Taken,_Issue_Resolved?<R>No<T> Invoice_Placed_on_Hold,_Dept_Notified_of_Required_Action <H> Action_Taken,_Issue_Resolved? <R> Yes <T> Information_Required

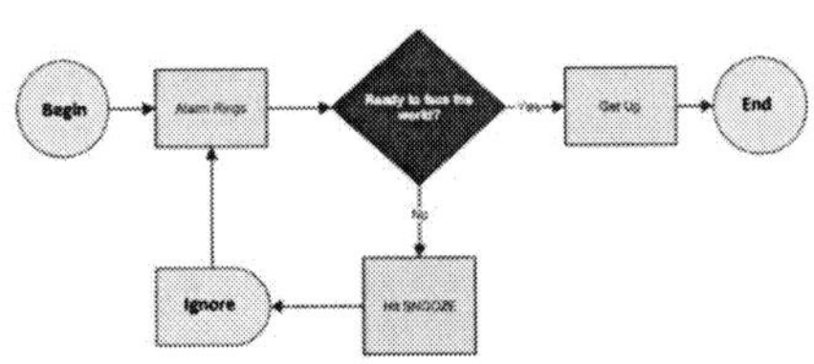

BloSum: <H> Begin <R> connected_with <T> Alarm_Rings <H> Alarm_Rings <R> connected_with <T> Ready_to_face_the_world? <H> Ready_to_face_the_world? <R> Yes <T> Get_Up <H> Ready_to_face_the_world? <R> No <T> Hit_SNOOZE <H> Hit_SNOOZE <R> connected_with <T> Ignore <H> Ignore <R> connected_with <T> Alarm_Rings <H> Get_Up <R> connected_with <T> End

Figure 9: BloSum outputs (triplets) from the CBD dataset.

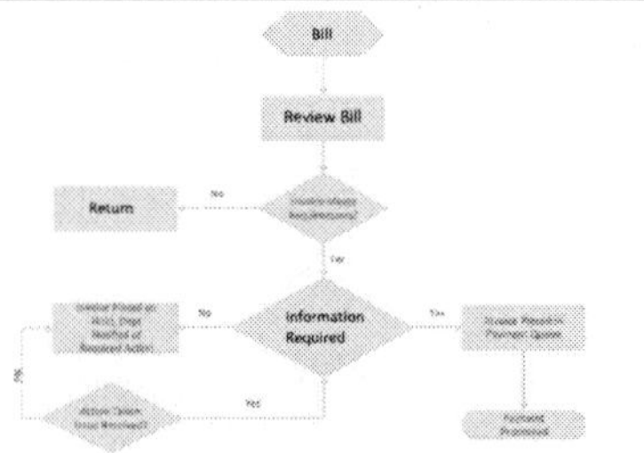

BloSum + T5_Large: Bill is connected with Review Bill which is then connected with Invoice Meets Requirements?. Invoice Meets Requirements? is No then Return and if Invoice Meets Requirements? is yes then Information Required. Information Required is No then Invoice Placed on Hold, Dept Notified of Required Action and if Information Required is Yes then Invoice Placed in Payment Queue which is then connected with Payment Processes. Action Taken, Issue Resolved is No then Invoice Placed on Hold, Dept Notified of Required Action and if Action Taken, Issue Resolved is Yes then Information Required.

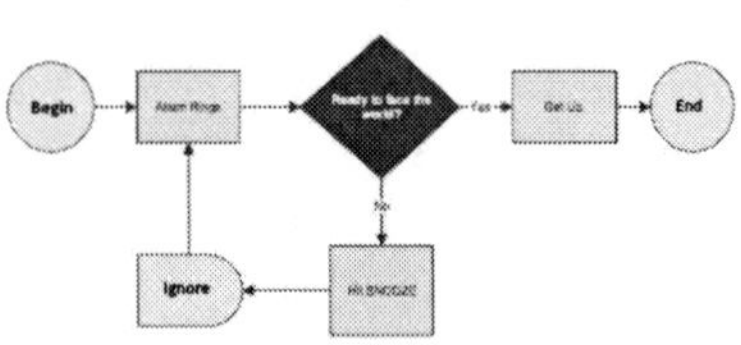

BloSum + T5_Large: Begin is connected with Alarm Rings which is connected with Ready to face the world?. If Ready to face the world? is Yes then Get Up and it is connected with End. Ready to face the world? is No then Hit SNOOZE which is then connected with Ignore and finally connected with Alarm Rings.

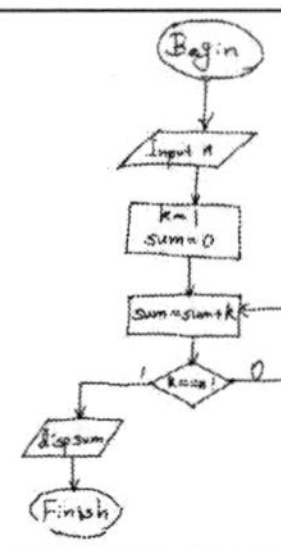

OCR-BloSum + T5_Large: Begin is connected with Input n and is then connected with k=1 and Sum=0 which is further connected with Sum=Sum+k. k=k+1 is connected with Sum=Sum+k. Sum=Sum+k is connected with K==n?. K==n? is 0 then k=k+1 and if K==n is 1 then disp Sum and then disp sum is connected with Finish.

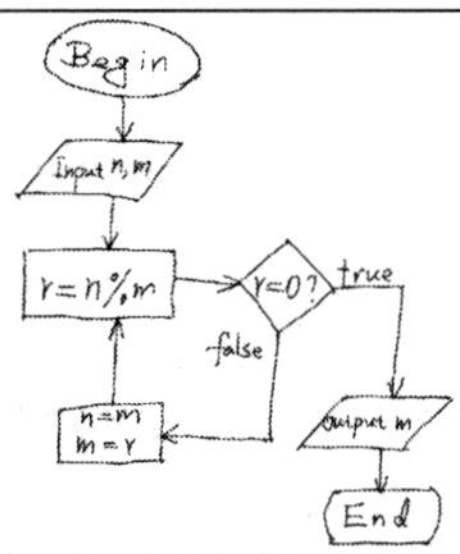

OCR-BloSum + T5_Large: Begin is connected with Input n,m which is then connected with r=n%m. r=n%m is connected with r=0? which if true, then output m and if r=0? is false then n=m and m=r and is connected with r=n%m. Output m is connected with End.

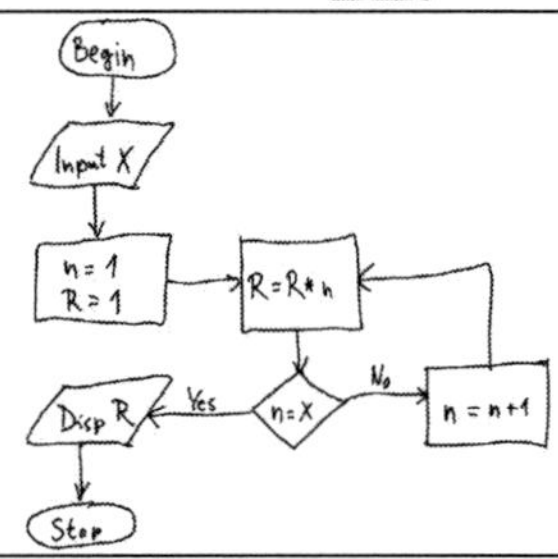

OCR-BloSum + T5_Large: Begin is connected with Input X and is then connected with n=1 and R=1 which is further connected with R=R*n. R=R*n is connected with n=X. n=n+1 is connected with R=R*n and if n=x is No then n=n+1 and if yes then Disp R. Disp R is connected with Stop.

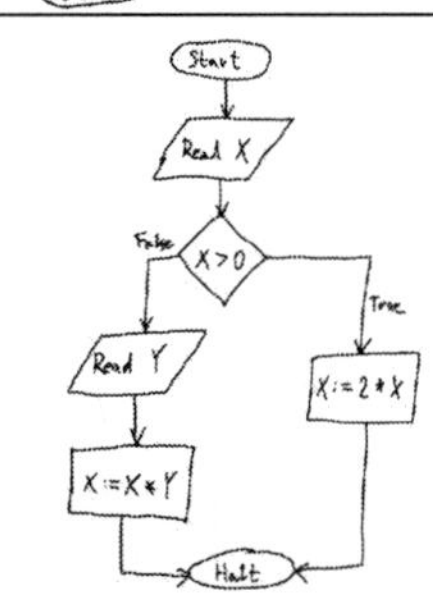

OCR-BloSum + T5_Large: Start is connected with Read X which is then connected with X>0. If X>0 is False then Read Y and if X>0 is True then X=2*X which is further connected with Halt. Read Y is connected with X=X*Y and is connected with Halt.

Figure 10: Sample outputs from CBD (first two rows), FC_A (third and fourth rows), and FC_B (last two rows) datasets.

Multi-Domain Dialogue State Tracking By Neural-Retrieval Augmentation

Lohith Ravuru[1], Seonghan Ryu[2], Hyungtak Choi[1], Haehun Yang[1], Hyeonmok Ko[1]
[1]Samsung Research, Seoul, South Korea
[2]42dot, Seoul, South Korea
loki.ravuru,ht777.choi,haehun.yang,felix.ko@samsung.com
seonghan.ryu@42dot.ai

Abstract

Dialogue State Tracking (DST) is a very complex task that requires precise understanding and information tracking of multi-domain conversations between users and dialogue systems. Many task-oriented dialogue systems use dialogue state tracking technology to infer users' goals from the history of the conversation. Existing approaches for DST are usually conditioned on previous dialogue states. However, the dependency on previous dialogues makes it very challenging to prevent error propagation to subsequent turns of a dialogue. In this paper, we propose Neural Retrieval Augmentation to alleviate this problem by creating a Neural Index based on dialogue context. Our NRA-DST framework efficiently retrieves dialogue context from the index built using a combination of unstructured dialogue state and structured user/system utterances. We explore a simple pipeline resulting in a retrieval-guided generation approach for training a DST model. Experiments on different retrieval methods for augmentation show that neural retrieval augmentation is the best performing retrieval method for DST. Our evaluations on the large-scale MultiWOZ dataset show that our model outperforms the baseline approaches.

1 Introduction

Dialogue State Tracking (DST) involves analyzing the user's dialogue and previous turn state expressed during the conversation, extracting the user's goal/intent, and representing it in the form of a well-defined set of slots and values (Williams et al., 2016; Henderson, 2015; Williams and Young, 2007; Gao et al., 2018). The release of a large-scale multi-domain conversational data set (MultiWOZ Budzianowski et al., 2018) prompted advances in cross-domain dialogue systems. Figure 1 shows an example from the dataset where the user starts the conversation about reserving a hotel, then requests for booking a taxi, and finally, changes the original hotel reservation. The dialogue state here is defined

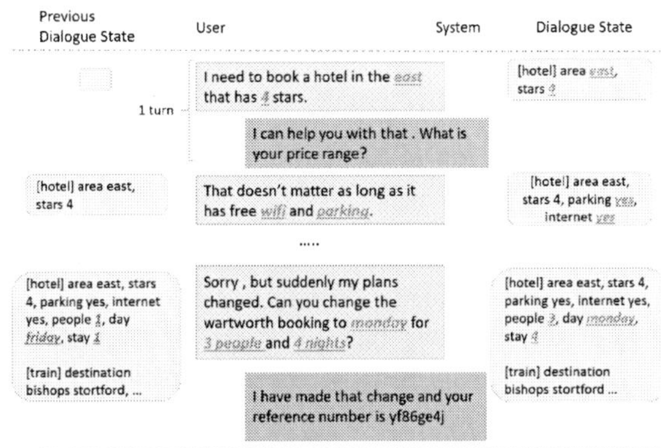

Figure 1: An example from the Large-Scale Multi-Domain Wizard-of-Oz (MutliWOZ) dataset where the user is booking a hotel and a train ticket. The dialogue state is represented as [domain] followed by a list of <slot-value> pairs for that domain. One turn refers to a single user utterance and a single system response. The dialogue state is updated based on the previous dialogue state, the current user utterance and the previous one-turn context.

as list of <slot-value> pairs for each [domain] (e.g., ([hotel] *people* 2 *stay* 5 days) , ([taxi] *departure* Hotel Santa)).

Recent works approach this either by classifying each slot over pre-defined slot-values that are selected from an ontology based on training data (Ma et al., 2019; Li et al., 2020) or first classifying a slot and then detecting the span of text in the original context as value for that slot (Kim et al., 2020; Gao et al., 2019). However, these models are highly dependant on the values in the dataset and the ontology. Another approach to DST is generating the value of a slot or both slot and value using a sequence-to-sequence model (Wu et al., 2019; Le et al., 2020). Papers using large pre-trained models such as GPT2 (Radford et al., 2019) have shown promising results (Budzianowski and Vulić, 2019; Hosseini-Asl et al., 2020). A single generative model can also be used to manage entire dialogue

Findings of the Association for Computational Linguistics: AACL-IJCNLP 2022, pages 169–175
November 20–23, 2022.

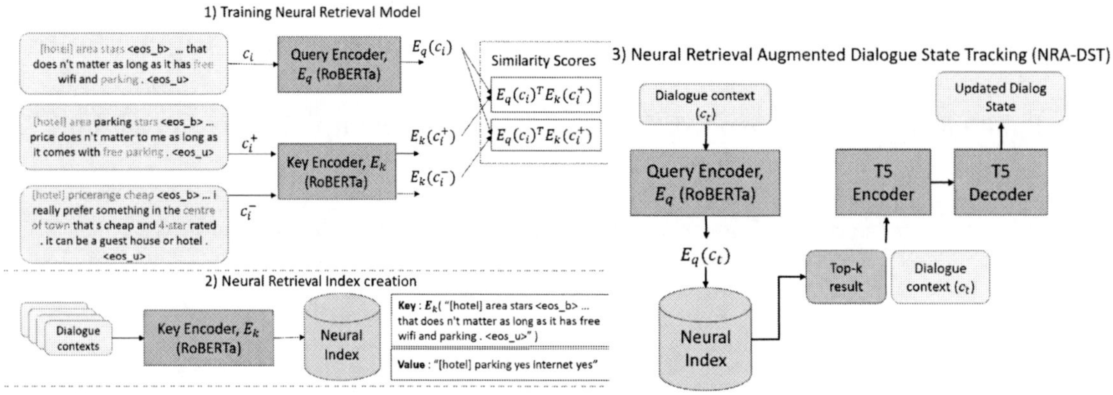

Figure 2: Different steps involved in the NRA-DST approach. The Query Encoder and Key Encoder are trained together. Once trained, Key Encoder is used to create a neural index and Query Encoder is used for retrieving results which are used in finetuning the T5 Model (Raffel et al., 2020), a pretrained Language Model which is used as backbone for our model.

by generating dialogue state, system action, and user response altogether (Lin et al., 2020; Hosseini-Asl et al., 2020). But these models are more prone to error propagation as explained below.

Dialogue State can be considered as a representation of the entire conversation and is used by subsequent modules in resolving system's action and response. Error in the dialogue state propagates not only to these other modules but also to dialogue states of subsequent turns. To analyze this issue, we perform a simple analysis similar to Kim et al. (2020), by replacing the previous dialogue state with ground truth on the state-of-the-art MinTL (Lin et al., 2020) model. As shown in Table 1, using ground truth previous dialogue state in place of the generated previous dialogue state creates a difference of 27% in the prediction of current dialogue state. To bridge the performance gap and reduce error propagation, we propose augmenting retrieved dialogue states of similar dialogue contexts from a pre-computed index.

	Predicted Dialogue State	Actual Dialogue State
MinTL (T5-small)	51.0	78.0
MinTL (T5-base)	51.4	78.3

Table 1: Analysis of Error Propagation in MinTL model.

Large pre-trained models have shown to be very efficient in retrieval-based approaches compared to sparse representations based on TF/IDF, or BM25 (Guu et al., 2020; Lee et al., 2019; Karpukhin et al., 2020). Several works in open domain question answering have augmented retrieval-based results for better response generation (Lewis et al., 2020). However, this is generally done on natural text such as a question or a passage. In Thulke et al. (2021), the retrieval is done using an unstructured dialogue state, but the index is created only from structured paragraph text data.

In this work, we aim to improve DST by leveraging Neural Retrieval-Augmentation on a combination of unstructured dialogue state and structured user/system utterances.

The contributions of our work are as follows:

- We propose an NRA-DST framework that utilizes state-of-the-art neural retrieval methods and integrates it to Dialogue State Tracking for more efficient task-oriented conversations.
- We evaluate our framework on MultiWOZ 2.0 dataset and show that neural retrieval augmentation improves the performance.
- We conduct a comprehensive ablation analysis showing the effectiveness of our proposed framework.

2 Background

In this section, we briefly explain the notations used in further sections. Let us denote the dialogue with t turns as, $D = \{(u_1, r_1), (u_2, r_2), ...(u_t, r_t)\}$, where u_i represents user utterance at i^{th} turn and r_i represents system response at i^{th} turn. Over the course of a dialogue, the goal of DST is to keep track of a dialogue state, $dst = \{(d_1, (s_1, v_1), (s_2, v_2), ..), (d_k, (s_1, v_1)..)\}$ where d_k is the domain, s_i is a slot from the domain, d_k and v_i is the value of s_i. The dialogue context at turn t is defined as, $c_t = (dst_{t-1}, u_{t-1}, r_{t-1}, u_t)$. In this paper, we formulate dialogue context using only the last turn but this can be extended to multiple previous turns. We formulate the original DST task as predicting the dialogue state from the dialogue context, $dst_t = model(c_t)$.

The concept of Belief Span (Lei et al., 2018) allows dialogue states to be represented as a span of text, enabling the conversion of a classification problem into a generation problem. Lin et al. (2020) builds upon belief spans and defines Levenshtein Belief Span (lev_t) as a minimal editing from previous dialogue state dst_{t-1} to current dialogue state dst_t. For example,

$dst_{t-1} \leftarrow$ [restaurant] food french, price cheap, day Sunday

$dst_t \leftarrow$ [restaurant] food thai, day Sunday, area centre

$$lev_t \leftarrow dst_t - dst_{t-1}$$

$lev_t =$ [restaurant] food thai, price NULL, area centre

We extend the belief spans by creating a neural index and guiding the model with possible Levenshtein spans from the retrieved result. The retrieved topk result contains possible DST updates, $lev_{1..k}$.

$$dst_t = NRADST(lev_{1..k}, c_t) \quad (1)$$

The DST task is now updated as predicting the dialogue state from a combination of retrieved results and dialogue context as in Eq 1. Figure 2 describes the architecture of NRA-DST.

3 Methods

Given a training dataset $D_{train} = \{D_1, D_2, .., D_m\}$, we create a neural index, D_{index} such that we can query the index based on neural representation (latent space representation) of dialogue context c_t, which is a combination of previous dialogue state dst_{t-1} and user/system utterances. Section 3.1 explains the D_{index} creation method in detail. The contents of the D_{index} can be represented as $(E(c_t), lev_t)$, where the key, $E(c_t)$ is the neural representation of dialogue context and the value, lev_t represents the corresponding dialogue state updates. The key idea is that given a dialogue context, we retrieve domains and slots detected in another dialogue with a similar context. Figure 2 shows an example of similar contexts, c_i and c_i^+. The previous dialogue states of both contexts contain the slots named ["area" and "stars"], from the domain named ["hotel"] and the utterances are also similar.

3.1 Neural Dialogue Context Retrieval

For generating efficient Neural Representations, we use a modification of the state-of-the-art Dense Passage Retrieval (DPR) Model (Karpukhin et al., 2020). Similar to the dual-encoder approach proposed in the DPR model, we use two different encoders: Query Encoder (E_q) and Key Encoder (E_k). The DPR model is trained so that the dot-product similarity (Eq 2) is higher for similar dialogue contexts.

$$sim(c_i, c_j) = E_q(c_i)^T E_k(c_j) \quad (2)$$

Training for the similarity metric 2 requires labelling the dataset with positive and negative contexts. For each turn of the dialogue in the training corpus of the original MultiWOZ dataset, we use a customized Algorithm 1 to generate a positive context (c_i^+) and a negative context (c_i^-).

Algorithm 1: Creating Training Data for fine-tuning DPR model.

```
def PrepareTrainingInstance:
    Input  : Dialogue Context (U_i)
    Output : Positive Dialogue Context (U_i^+), Negative Dialogue Context (U_i^-)
    Similar Context, U_bm25[100] ← BM25 top100 results from training data;
    Q ← { };
    lev_i ← dst(U_i) − previous_dst(U_i);
    foreach dialogue context U_j ∈ U_bm25 do
        lev_j ← dst(U_j) − previous_dst(U_j);
        score ← slot_F1(lev_i, lev_j);
        Q.append((score, U_j));
    end
    sort(Q, key a : a[0]);
    U_i^+, U_i^- ← Q[0][1], Q[99][1];
    return U_i^+, U_i^-;
```

Due to limitations of memory and training time with RoBERTa-base as encoder, we limit the positive and negative contexts to only one context each. We also perform the original DPR model's optimization trick of using in-batch negatives to train effectively. Although we used Algorithm 1 to select only one negative context for a particular training instance, positive contexts from other training instances in a single training batch are also considered as negative contexts for that instance.

$$L(c_i, c_i^+, ..., c_{i,n}^-) = \\ -\,log(\frac{e^{sim(c_i,c_i^+)}}{e^{sim(c_i,c_i^+)} + \sum_{k=1}^{n} e^{sim(c_i,c_{i,k}^-)}}) \quad (3)$$

After training the model with the loss function 3, the Key Encoder is used to create the neural index, whereas the Query Encoder is used along with the Dialogue State Tracking model for retrieving the result.

3.2 Generation based Dialogue State Tracking

The retrieval result from Neural Index (lev_{topk}) is appended to the original dialogue context c_t, as described in Eq 1. All sequences are concatenated by using special end-of-sequence (eos) tokens to form a single retrieval-augmented context (c_t^*) and given as input to the T5 (Raffel et al., 2020) encoder.

$$c_t^* \leftarrow lev_1 \langle eos\_l1 \rangle \ lev_2 \langle eos\_l2 \rangle ... \\ dst_{t-1} \langle eos\_b \rangle \ r_{t-1} \langle eos\_r \rangle \ u_t \langle eos\_u \rangle$$

$$H = Encoder(c_t^*) \quad (4)$$

The T5 decoder model takes as input the encoder hidden states and generates updates to the dialogue state.

$$lev_t = Decoder(H) \quad (5)$$

The loss function used in the Dialogue State Generation model is standard negative loss-likelihood between the ground truth lev_t and generated lev_t. The final dialogue state, dst_t is derived by combining lev_t and dst_{t-1}.

4 Experiments

4.1 Datasets

We evaluate our framework on the Multi-Domain Wizard-of-Oz (MultiWOZ 2.0) (Budzianowski et al., 2018) dataset. The dataset consists of various human-to-human conversations, including tasks from seven different domains (restaurant, train, attraction, hotel, taxi, hospital, police). We used the original dataset split with a training corpus of 8438 dialogues, a validation corpus of 1000 dialogues, and a test corpus of 1000 dialogues.

4.2 Experimental Setup

We implemented our proposed methods on top of the code from MinTL framework (Lin et al., 2020) and Dense-Passage Retrieval model (Karpukhin et al., 2020). For BM25, we use the implementation from Pyserini (pys). We use approximate nearest neighbours with the FAISS library (fai) for performing our retrieval from the neural index. All the hyperparameters used are the default parameters from the baseline implementations.

For our retrieval model, we use RoBERTa (Liu et al., 2019) for Key Encoder, Value Encoder and we use T5-small as the backbone for our DST model. We trained our retrieval model and created the neural index with only the training corpus of the original dataset.

4.3 Metrics

Joint Goal Accuracy measures the accuracy of the generated DST by comparing them to the ground truth DST. The generated slot-value is considered accurate only if it is exactly matching the ground truth slot-value. The accuracy is calculated over each turn for dialogue, and it is averaged over the entire dialogue.
Slot Detection Error is a custom metric that evaluates the benefit of Retrieval Augmentation. It is the error in the ground truth DST and generated DST, but the exact value of the slot is not matched.

4.4 Results

Table 2 describes results on our NRA-DST model compared to other retrieval methods. We compare our model with other generation based baselines DSTQA (Zhou and Small, 2019), NADST (Le et al., 2020), SOM-DST (Kim et al., 2020). We also compare our model with our custom retrieval baselines.

BM25-Retrieval DST Model uses bm25, bag-of-words, retrieval algorithm to create the neural index and retrieve the top-k results.

RoBERTa-Retrieval DST Model uses a pre-trained RoBERTa model directly without any fine-tuning for creating the index.

The decrease in Slot Detection Error and an increase in Joint Goal Accuracy shows that augmenting retrieval results is beneficial for generation-based DST models. We observe that our proposed NRA-DST method outperforms all other retrieval-based models.

Model	Joint Accuracy (↑)	Slot Detection Error(↓)
DSTQA (Zhou and Small, 2019)*	51.44	-
NADST (Le et al., 2020)*	50.52	-
SOMDST (Bert-base) (Kim et al., 2020)*	51.72	-
MinTL (Lin et al., 2020)*†	51.24	-
MinTL†	51.00	12.8
BM25-Retrieval DST†	51.20	12.8
RoBERTa-Retrieval DST†	51.50	12.7
NRA-DST†	**51.90**	**12.5**

Table 2: Results on MultiWOZ 2.0 dataset compared to different baselines. *: results reported by the original paper. †: Uses T5-small model.

5 Ablation Analysis

We analyze the influence of different changes on the results with the following experiments. We try to analyze the importance of previous dialogue state information and delexicalization while creating the neural index and conditioning retrieved results at the encoder or the decoder of our DST model.

5.1 Neural Index

To understand optimal method for neural index preparation, we investigate the effect of using previous dialogue state and delexicalization. Delexicalization is done on the entire dialogue context c_t, which includes removing the slot values from the previous dialogue state and delexicalizing exact slot values from user and system responses. As seen in Table 3, using previous dialogue and delexicalization is very effective.

Previous Dialogue State	Delexicalised Utterances	Joint Accuracy (top1)	Joint Accuracy (top3)
-	-	50.8	50.1
-	✓	50.8	50.9
✓	-	51.3	51.2
✓	✓	**51.9**	**51.2**

Table 3: Ablation comparing different choices of creating neural index and neural retrieval.

In further analysis, we also evaluate our models using top-1 and top-3 retrieved results from the neural index. The results are reported in Table 3. Augmenting top-1 results in better performance than top-3 results. This suggests that augmenting more results is harmful to the performance of the DST models. We reason this as including more retrieved results restricts the number of tokens for dialogue context because of upper limit of 512 tokens for T5 model encoder. To overcome the limit of tokens, we condition the model with the retrieved results on the decoder in the following experiment.

5.2 Augmentation

Model	Joint Accuracy(↑)	Slot Detection Error(↓)
Decoder-NRADST	50.9	12.6
Encoder-NRADST	**51.9**	**12.5**

Table 4: Ablation comparing conditioning retrieval result at encoder and decoder.

Conditioning the retrieval results at the encoder restricts the amount of dialogue context that we can give as input to the model. We experimented with conditioning the retrieved result at the decoder of the T5 model as the actual tokens decoded are much less compared to the dialogue context. Table 4 shows that augmenting at encoder results in the best Joint Accuracy.

6 Conclusions

In this work, we demonstrated that neural retrieval augmentation increases the performance of generation-based DST. We explore a simple pipeline resulting in a retrieval-guided generation approach for DST. Moreover, our experiments and ablation studies indicate that neural retrieval can efficiently retrieve a combination of unstructured data (dialogue state) and structured data (user/system utterances). As a result, we improve the performance of the baseline approach on a large-scale multi-domain dataset, MultiWOZ 2.0. In future work, we will investigate the end-to-end training of our NRA-DST framework.

References

https://github.com/castorini/pyserini.

https://github.com/facebookresearch/faiss.

Paweł Budzianowski and Ivan Vulić. 2019. Hello, it's GPT-2 - how can I help you? towards the use of pretrained language models for task-oriented dialogue systems. In *Proceedings of the 3rd Workshop on Neural Generation and Translation*, pages 15–22, Hong Kong. Association for Computational Linguistics.

Paweł Budzianowski, Tsung-Hsien Wen, Bo-Hsiang Tseng, Iñigo Casanueva, Stefan Ultes, Osman Ramadan, and Milica Gašić. 2018. MultiWOZ - a large-scale multi-domain Wizard-of-Oz dataset for task-oriented dialogue modelling. In *Proceedings of the 2018 Conference on Empirical Methods in Natural Language Processing*, pages 5016–5026, Brussels, Belgium. Association for Computational Linguistics.

Ge Gao, Eunsol Choi, Yejin Choi, and Luke Zettlemoyer. 2018. Neural metaphor detection in context. In *Proceedings of the 2018 Conference on Empirical Methods in Natural Language Processing*, pages 607–613, Brussels, Belgium. Association for Computational Linguistics.

Shuyang Gao, Abhishek Sethi, Sanchit Agarwal, Tagyoung Chung, and Dilek Hakkani-Tur. 2019. Dialog state tracking: A neural reading comprehension approach. In *Proceedings of Special Interest Group on Discourse and Dialogue*.

Kelvin Guu, Kenton Lee, Zora Tung, Panupong Pasupat, and Ming-Wei Chang. 2020. REALM: retrieval-augmented language model pre-training. *CoRR*, abs/2002.08909.

Matthew Henderson. 2015. Machine learning for dialog state tracking: A review. In *Proceedings of The First International Workshop on Machine Learning in Spoken Language Processing*.

Ehsan Hosseini-Asl, Bryan McCann, Chien-Sheng Wu, Semih Yavuz, and Richard Socher. 2020. A simple language model for task-oriented dialogue. *arXiv preprint arXiv:2005.00796*.

Vladimir Karpukhin, Barlas Oguz, Sewon Min, Patrick Lewis, Ledell Wu, Sergey Edunov, Danqi Chen, and Wen-tau Yih. 2020. Dense passage retrieval for open-domain question answering. In *Proceedings of the 2020 Conference on Empirical Methods in Natural Language Processing (EMNLP)*, pages 6769–6781, Online. Association for Computational Linguistics.

Sungdong Kim, Sohee Yang, Gyuwan Kim, and Sang-Woo Lee. 2020. Efficient dialogue state tracking by selectively overwriting memory. In *Proceedings of the 58th Annual Meeting of the Association for Computational Linguistics*, pages 567–582, Online. Association for Computational Linguistics.

Hung Le, Richard Socher, and Steven C.H. Hoi. 2020. Non-autoregressive dialog state tracking. In *International Conference on Learning Representations*.

Kenton Lee, Ming-Wei Chang, and Kristina Toutanova. 2019. Latent retrieval for weakly supervised open domain question answering. *CoRR*, abs/1906.00300.

Wenqiang Lei, Xisen Jin, Min-Yen Kan, Zhaochun Ren, Xiangnan He, and Dawei Yin. 2018. Sequicity: Simplifying task-oriented dialogue systems with single sequence-to-sequence architectures. In *Proceedings of the 56th Annual Meeting of the Association for Computational Linguistics (Volume 1: Long Papers)*, pages 1437–1447, Melbourne, Australia. Association for Computational Linguistics.

Patrick S. H. Lewis, Ethan Perez, Aleksandra Piktus, Fabio Petroni, Vladimir Karpukhin, Naman Goyal, Heinrich Küttler, Mike Lewis, Wen-tau Yih, Tim Rocktäschel, Sebastian Riedel, and Douwe Kiela. 2020. Retrieval-augmented generation for knowledge-intensive NLP tasks. *CoRR*, abs/2005.11401.

Jieyu Li, Su Zhu, and Kai Yu. 2020. A hierarchical tracker for multi-domain dialogue state tracking. In *Proceedings of 2020 IEEE International Conference on Acoustics, Speech and Signal Processing*.

Zhaojiang Lin, Andrea Madotto, Genta Indra Winata, and Pascale Fung. 2020. MinTL: Minimalist transfer learning for task-oriented dialogue systems. In *Proceedings of the 2020 Conference on Empirical Methods in Natural Language Processing (EMNLP)*, pages 3391–3405, Online. Association for Computational Linguistics.

Yinhan Liu, Myle Ott, Naman Goyal, Jingfei Du, Mandar Joshi, Danqi Chen, Omer Levy, Mike Lewis, Luke Zettlemoyer, and Veselin Stoyanov. 2019. Roberta: A robustly optimized BERT pretraining approach. *CoRR*, abs/1907.11692.

Yue Ma, Zengfeng Zeng, Dawei Zhu, Xuan Li, Yiying Yang, Xiaoyuan Yao, Kaijie Zhou, and Jianping Shen. 2019. An end-to-end dialogue state tracking system with machine reading comprehension and wide & deep classification. In *Proceedings of The 34th AAAI Conference on Artificial Intelligence - DSTC 8 Workshop*.

Alec Radford, Jeff Wu, Rewon Child, David Luan, Dario Amodei, and Ilya Sutskever. 2019. Language models are unsupervised multitask learners.

Colin Raffel, Noam Shazeer, Adam Roberts, Katherine Lee, Sharan Narang, Michael Matena, Yanqi Zhou, Wei Li, and Peter J. Liu. 2020. Exploring the limits of transfer learning with a unified text-to-text transformer. *Journal of Machine Learning Research*, 21(140):1–67.

David Thulke, Nico Daheim, Christian Dugast, and Hermann Ney. 2021. Efficient retrieval augmented generation from unstructured knowledge for task-oriented dialog. *CoRR*, abs/2102.04643.

Jason Williams, Antoine Raux, and Matthew Henderson. 2016. The dialog state tracking challenge series: A review. *Dialogue Discourse*, 7:4–33.

Jason D. Williams and Steve Young. 2007. Partially observable markov decision processes for spoken dialog systems. *Comput. Speech Lang.*, 21(2):393422.

Chien-Sheng Wu, Andrea Madotto, Ehsan Hosseini-Asl, Caiming Xiong, Richard Socher, and Pascale Fung. 2019. Transferable multi-domain state generator for task-oriented dialogue systems. *CoRR*, abs/1905.08743.

Li Zhou and Kevin Small. 2019. Multi-domain dialogue state tracking as dynamic knowledge graph enhanced question answering. *CoRR*, abs/1911.06192.

TaKG: A New Dataset for Paragraph-level Table-to-Text Generation Enhanced with Knowledge Graphs

Qianqian Qi, Zhenyun Deng, Yonghua Zhu, Lia Lee, Michael Witbrock, Jiamou Liu
University of Auckland
{qqi518, zden658, yzhu970, jlee794}@aucklanduni.ac.nz
{m.witbrock, jiamou.liu}@auckland.ac.nz

Abstract

Table-to-text generation refers to a task that generates text using information provided by a given fact table. We introduce TaKG, a new table-to-text generation dataset with the following highlights: (1) TaKG defines a long-text (paragraph-level) generation task as opposed to well-established short-text (sentence-level) generation datasets. (2) TaKG is the first large-scale dataset for this task, containing three application domains and ~750,000 samples. (3) To address the divergence phenomenon, TaKG enhances table input using external knowledge graphs, extracted by a new Wikidata-based method. We then propose a new Transformer-based multimodal sequence-to-sequence architecture for TaKG that integrates two pretrained language models RoBERTa and GPT-2. Our model shows reliable performance on long-text generation across a variety of metrics, and outperforms existing models for short-text generation tasks.

1 Introduction

Data-to-text generation refers to semantic-preserving conversion from structured data to (unstructured) text. *Table-to-text* generation is a class of data-to-text generation tasks where the input data takes the form of fact tables (Kukich, 1983). Table-to-text generation has widespread applications from biography generation (Lebret et al., 2016) to event summarisation (Wiseman et al., 2017). Thus developing a fluent, truthful and informative table-to-text generation system has attracted considerable attention (Liu et al., 2018; Wang et al., 2020; Liu et al., 2021). A critical factor in building such a system is to prepare reliable and large-scale table-to-text datasets.

However, existing table-to-text generation benchmarks have some clear limitations. First, most existing datasets, such as E2E (Novikova et al., 2017) and ToTTo (Parikh et al., 2020), focus on single-sentence generation tasks, which severely limits their use for tasks that involve the generation of *long texts*, e.g., entire paragraphs. Then, the few datasets that involve long (paragraph-level) text generation, such as MLB (Puduppully et al., 2019) and ROTOWIRE (Wiseman et al., 2017), consist of too few samples (less than 30k). Last, real-world data-to-text generation tasks tend to exhibit the so-called *divergence* phenomenon, where the input data fail to provide all the key information in the target text description (Dhingra et al., 2019; Wiseman et al., 2017; Chen et al., 2019). This is illustrated by an example in Figure 1 for the Dutch painter Jacoba Surie (extracted from WikiBio dataset (Lebret et al., 2016)). Existing table-to-text datasets in general lack of sufficient external knowledge required to generate the target text.

To address these issues, we introduce a new table-to-text generation dataset: TaKG (Table-and-Knowledge Graph) with the following highlights [1]: First, samples in TaKG contain long text (i.e., paragraphs) and their corresponding infoboxes (tables) extracted from Wikipedia. Thus TaKG amounts to a long-text generation task. TaKG contains three domains: biography, place, school, with a total of 745,574 samples, considerably larger than existing table-to-text datasets. To resolve the divergence issue, we employ external knowledge to "fill" the information in text description that is missing from the input infobox. In particular, we exploit another large-scale knowledge graph (KG) repository Wikidata[2]. The KGs are added in TaKG as auxiliary input. Figure 1 (upper right) shows an example KG.

The goal of this paper is two-fold. (1) We first introduce the TaKG dataset. In a nutshell, TaKG defines a task that takes a fact table (i.e., infobox) about a *target entity* and a Wikidata KG as input, and seeks a paragraph-level text description of the target entity. Section 3 provides more details. (2)

[1]TaKG is available on: `https://bit.ly/3RR4erL`
[2]`http://www.wikidata.org/`

Findings of the Association for Computational Linguistics: AACL-IJCNLP 2022, pages 176–187
November 20–23, 2022. ©2022 Association for Computational Linguistics

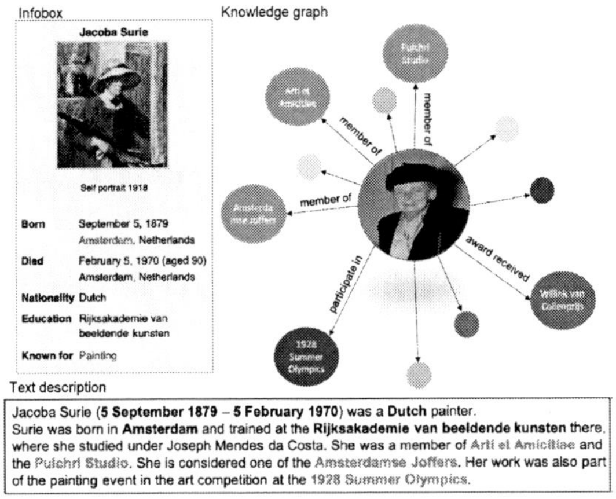

Figure 1: This is an example of generating a biography of Jacoba Surie. The upper left table and bottom text description are extracted from Wikipedia. The blue colour words are the item with hyperlinks. The right upper knowledge graph is retrieved from Wikidata. In lower biography, the red color words indicate the information missing from Wikipedia table but can be found in the knowledge graph.

We then demonstrate how TaKG may be used as a worthy benchmark to train a model for paragraph-level table-to-text tasks. Generating text with multiple data sources is challenging on two axes: table-KG information fusion and high-fidelity natural text generation. To address these challenges, we leverage pretrained language models (PLMs), such as RoBERTa (Liu et al., 2019b) and GPT-2 (Radford et al., 2019), for their abilities to acquire cross-domain knowledge. A seq2seq architecture is proposed for our task and utilizes two PLMs that fuses multiple input sources together. More details are provided in Section 4. We validate our model's ability to generate long-text using the TaKG dataset. To further verify our method's wide applicability, we also demonstrate that, over standard short-text (sentence-level) generation tasks such as WikiBio, our method also outperforms state-of-the-art benchmarks, with large margin on WikiBio up to 7.3% (BLEU) and 9% (Rouge) increment. See Section 5.

Our contributions are summarized below:
1. Creating a large-scale paragraph-level dataset TaKG for table-to-text generation enhanced with knowledge graphs.
2. Long-text generation: Designing a new seq2seq model using two PLMs to accomplish TaKG tasks.
3. Short-text generation: Demonstrating that our new model outperforms benchmarks for sentence-level table-to-text generation tasks.

2 Related Work

Table-to-Text datasets. Existing table-to-text generation datasets are either *single-sentence* or *multi-sentence* generation tasks. The former, such as E2E (restaurant domain) (Novikova et al., 2017), ToTTo (Parikh et al., 2020), and WikiBio (biography domain) (Lebret et al., 2016), are limited in terms of what the task seeks to generate. The latter, such as MLB (26.3k samples) (Puduppully et al., 2019), ROTOWIRE (4.9k samples) (Wiseman et al., 2017), UK-Place (12k samples) and UK-School (5k samples) Chen et al. (2019) contain very few samples and are thus too small-scale.

WikiBio dataset above differs from the other datasets in the sense that each of its samples contains in fact a full paragraph of biography of a person. Nevertheless, the task WikiBio specifies only the first sentence of the paragraph as the ground truth output. Indeed, all benchmarks tested on WikiBio used the dataset as a single-sentence text generation task. Due to the presence of paragraph-level texts in WikiBio, we include WikiBio samples in TaKG by incorporating the *entire paragraph* as ground truth output.

Divergence has been a common issue in multi-sentence generation (Dhingra et al., 2019; Wiseman et al., 2017; Chen et al., 2019). To address this issue, in the UK-Place and UK-School datasets Chen et al. (2019) complements the input tables with some background knowledge. To obtain the background knowledge, the authors take hyperlinked keywords in the Wikipedia infobox and extract one-hop facts of those keywords from Wikidata, a large-scale open-domain knowledge graph repository containing close to 100 million data items (Vrandečić and Krötzsch, 2014). These one-hop facts are then used as background knowledge. However, we point out that this method may produce irrelevant background knowledge that distracts the generation of target text. This is because the hyperlinked keywords in the infoboxes are often not item-specific. For example, 'Painting' and 'Amsterdam' are keywords for the instance illustrated in Figure 1, which are clearly insufficient to deriving specific facts about the Dutch painter Jacoba Surie. In our work, we will integrate samples from UK-Place and UK-School into TaKG while adopting a different way to derive external knowledge graph.

PLM-based data-to-Text generation. With the popularity of Transformer (Vaswani et al., 2017), several large-scale pretrained language models

(PLMs) have been deployed in text generation tasks. Since PLMs are pretrained on a large-scale corpus, their broad applicability with little fine-tuning may suggest that these models have learnt cross-domain knowledge and some common sense from its pretraining step. Recent work has implemented PLMs with multiple input types, e.g., audio (Nagrani et al., 2020), video (Sun et al., 2019), table (Saxena et al., 2020) and knowledge graph (Marino et al., 2021). Nevertheless, no PLM has been designed for the type of tasks presented by TaKG. Inspired by these recent successes, we apply PLMs to train a model for TaKG and demonstrate that it is possible to control PLMs to generate fluent and informative text from tables and knowledge graphs.

3 The TaKG Dataset

Dataset description. TaKG contains three sub-datasets each covers a unique domains: biography, school and place. They are constructed using the samples from WikiBio, UK-Place and UK-School (Chen et al., 2019) respectively. The number of instances of TaKG in different domains are shown in Table 1. Table 2 shows the statistics of the training set in TaKG. The two main columns indicate the average number of word and the average number of relations respectively. For the words statistic, we count by removing the repeated words from table and KG. For example, 'name' is a kind of relation in table, while 'family name' and 'given name' are two relations used in KG. We calculate 'name' as one duplication.

	Train	Dev	Test
TaKG-Biography	582,659	72,831	72,831
TaKG-Place	9,823	1,228	1,228
TaKG-School	3,979	497	498

Table 1: Number of instances for TaKG-Biography, TaKG-Place and TaKG-School.

The divergence phenomenon calls for external knowledge, alongside the fact table, as input to data-to-text generation tasks. Knowledge graph are large knowledge base that facilitates effective representation, storage, and retrieval of knowledge. Wikidata is an exemplary large-scale open-domain knowledge graph which stores comprehensive knowledge regarding famous individuals, places, and organisations (Vrandečić and Krötzsch, 2014). We thus leverage Wikidata to extract our knowledge graphs as extra input in TaKG.

Unlike Chen et al. (2019) which guides the extraction of knowledge through hyperlinks, we design a new method that ensures completeness and relevance of the extra information. As WikiBio is collected using Wikipedia pages, for each WikiBio instance, we first use the provided unique Wikipedia URL IDs to get the corresponding page titles. Then these titles are used as center entities to retrieve KGs from Wikidata. For UK-Place and UK-School, we use the 'articletitle' attribute in the table to get Wikipedia URL first and then follow the same procedure as WikiBio. We ignore some of the relations in KGs, such as 'image', 'signature' and 'audio'.

Task formulation. We now formally define our table-to-text generation task. The input table includes n fields with corresponding content text pairs $\{R_1, R_2, ..., R_n\}$ which are the description of the target entity. Each R_i includes tokens of field $f_1, f_2, ..., f_l$ and tokens of content $c_1, c_2, ..., c_m$. The knowledge graph retrieved from Wikidata can be denoted as $\{E_1, E_2, ..., E_k\}$, where each E_i consist of tokens of entity attribute $a_1, a_2, ..., a_s$ and tokens of value $v_1, v_2, ..., v_j$. The output is a sequence of tokens $o_1, o_2, ..., o_r$ which are the text description of the item from Wikipedia. Our task is constraining PLM in generating text from table data and KG, which can be formulated as:

$$o^*_{1:r} = \operatorname*{argmax}_{o_{1:r}} \prod_{t=1}^{r} P(o_t | o_{1:t-1}, R_{1:n}, E_{1:k}), \quad (1)$$

in which, after linearisation process, table data and linked entities in knowledge graph are represented as $R_i = \langle f_{i,1:l}; c_{i,1:m} \rangle, E_i = \langle a_{i,1:s}; v_{i,1:j} \rangle$. A TaKG-Biography example is shown below which corresponds to Figure 1; other examples are shown in Appendix A.1:

- **Target Entity:** Jacoba Surie
- **Fact Table:**
  - **Born:** September 5, 1879, Amsterdam, Netherlands
  - **Education:** Rijksakademie van beeldende kunsten
  - **Known for:** Painting
  - ...
- **Knowledge Graph:**
  - Jacoba Surie | Occupation | printmaker, draftsperson, painter, lithographer, photographer
  - Jacoba Surie | Member of | Arti et Amicitiae, Amsterdamse Joffers, Sint Lucas (artist society)
  - ...
- **Text Description:**
  - Jacoba Surie (5 September 1879 – 5 February 1970) was a Dutch painter. Surie was born in Amsterdam and trained at the Rijksakademie van beeldende kunsten there, where she studied under Joseph Mendes da Costa. She was a member of Arti et Amicitiae and the Pulchri Studio ...

	Avg.# words			Avg.# relations		
	Table	KG	Duplication	Table	KG	Duplication
TaKG-Biography	44.14	39.50	8.17	12.44	13.71	4.74
TaKG-Place	51.11	16.51	5.12	19.40	5.19	1.59
TaKG-School	81.59	19.34	7.66	48.00	5.66	2.06

Table 2: Data Statistics for TaKG training set.

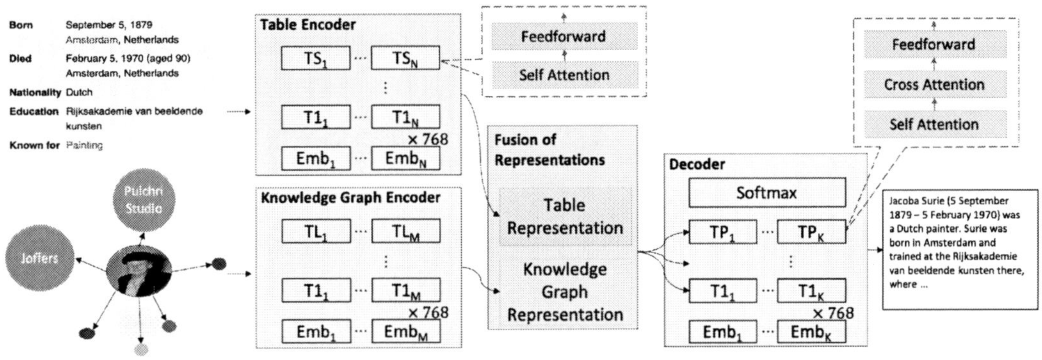

Figure 2: The overall architecture of the proposed Transformer-based seq2seq model. The tabular data and KG data are fed into Table encoder and KG Encoder separately. Then we make a concatenation of the last hidden states from the two encoders. The decoder take the concatenated hidden states as input and generate the description. All the encoders and decoder are initialized from PLMs.

4 Our Model for TaKG

We put forward a Transformer-based seq2seq framework for data-to-text generation with table data and knowledge graph as input. The parameters of encoders are initialized from RoBERTa and all of them are fine-tuned during training. The output hidden state from encoders are concatenated and sent to a Transformer-based decoder. The decoder is initialised from pretrained autoregressive models: GPT-2. After each Self-Attention layer in the decoder, we add a Cross-Attention layer which makes decoder pay attention to both encoded inputs and pre-content outputs.

The overall framework is described in Figure 2. The table pairs $\{R_1, R_2, ..., R_n\}$ include N tokens after tokenization. These tokens are fed into the embedding layer $\{Emb_1, ..., Emb_N\}$, then the embedded table is forwarded to S Transformer layers. In each encoder, the Transformer layers consist of Self-attention Layer and Feedforward Layer. The last hidden state from table encoder is denoted as $EN_T = \{EN_{T1}, EN_{T2}, ..., EN_{TN}\}$ which includes the encoded table information. In the same way, we encode KG data $\{E_1, E_2, ..., E_k\}$ using knowledge graph encoder and get the encoded KG information $EN_G = \{EN_{G1}, EN_{G2}, ..., EN_{GM}\}$.

To integrate the different data representations, we concatenate the table representation and KG representation. Then the concatenation $\text{Concat}\{EN_T, EN_G\}$ is sent to the **Cross-attention layers** in the decoder, in which there are P Transformer decoder layers. In contrast to the encoder, the decoder inserts a *Masked Multi-Head Attention* sub-layer which processes the output of the decoder stack to maintain an auto-regressive property. Sequence masking is added in the decoder to omit post-context tokens for current token. For instance, a sentence 'Surie was born in Amsterdam.' is given in the decoder, and we want to apply Self-Attention for 'born' (let 'born' be a query). In this case, we only put attention to 'Surie' and 'was' but not to 'in' or 'Amsterdam'. This method is implemented via attention mask. We get the score matrix before softmax function, and then use the attention mask matrix on the score matrix to set the undesirable token score to a negative number (-100). So that, after applying Softmax, these unwanted scores will become zero, and we keep the actual scores for present and previous tokens except future tokens.

Note that there exists a Cross-attention layer in between Self-attention layer and Feedforward layer in the decoder. The mechanism of Cross-attention is using the generated token as Query (Q) to do attention with Key (K) and Value (V) from another input source which is the concatenation of encoded input in our model. Cross-attention lets input extracted features and previously generated output tokens attend each other and recombined to a new feature representation that sends to the next layer. In our model, we implement the decoder using GPT-2 with additional Cross-attention layer after each Self-attention layer.

Our method is proposed for entity-based table-to-text generation task which has one or multiple center entities. The possible application scenario includes historical events, news report and storytelling. For news report and storytelling, we can retrieve background information for multiple entities.

5 Experiments

In our work, there are two types of tasks: **sentence-level** generation means to generate one sentence from input data, **paragraph-level** generation generates long text (more than one sentence). We borrow the idea of linearisation (Mager et al., 2020) on table and KG data. Since GPT-2 can generate text with common sense, to some extent it is not necessary to re-train a language model from scratch. Observe that we have the same text-generation goal as the pretraining target of GPT-2 had. Hence we select RoBERTa as encoder and GPT-2 as the decoder. Via fine-tuning RoBERTa and GPT-2 for text generation, the proposed model treats RoBERTa as a feature extractor and GPT-2 as a black-box with encoded text input and text output. For RoBERTa and GPT-2, we use the pre-generated vocabulary and fine-tune the embedding layer. In particular, we have three types of layer settings: *1-layer*, *2-layer* and *12-layer*. Here, *1-layer* means fine-tuning the first layer of RoBERTa and GPT-2 in the studied seq2seq model. Similarly, *2-layer* and *12-layer* mean the corresponding layers to be fine-tuned. There are added Cross-attention (Vaswani et al., 2017) layers in GPT-2, which are trained from scratch. Decoding strategy also needs to be imposed during data-to-text generation. Here, we use Nucleus sampling (p=0.9) and Top-k (k=30) sampling methods (Holtzman et al., 2019) in decoding.

5.1 Evaluation

Automatic Evaluation The typical way to evaluate the quality of text generation is to compare the similarity between candidate text and reference texts. Other than the two commonly used automatic evaluation matrix: BLEU (Papineni et al., 2002) and ROUGE (ROUGE, 2004), we also employ evaluation from semantics, divergence, diversity, grammatic and readability aspects. There are two methods in semantic evaluation, the first calculates the cosine similarity of the semantic representation of text. Here, we use DistilRoBERTa-base , which is a distilled version (Sanh et al., 2019) of RoBERTa-base model (Liu et al., 2019b), to get the semantic representation vector of text. BERTScore (Zhang et al., 2019) is another method for semantic similarity evaluation. PARENT (Dhingra et al., 2019), a divergence index, aligns the n-grams of the references and the generated text into semi-structured data, and then calculate their precision and recall value. Self-BLEU (Zhu et al., 2018) is a metric to evaluate the diversity of the generations. It calculates the BLEU score between generations, and the average score indicates the diversity level, which is the higher the less diverse. LanguageTool [3] is a tool to check grammatical errors of generated text. Grammatical Error Rate denotes the number of grammatical errors per 100 words. For Readability (Smeuninx et al., 2020), we select Coleman–Liau [4] index (Coleman and Liau, 1975) that indicates US grade level.

Human Evaluation We conduct a human evaluation to assess the text (whether the text demonstrate good usage of English, in terms of grammar and fluency, and is easy to read) and accuracy (whether the information contained in text matches well with that in Wikipedia text). We randomly sample 20 samples from the test set of TaKG-Biography, and ask 20 participants to evaluate the text generated from our model and one baseline model: Structure-aware(Liu et al., 2018). We provide the first paragraph from Wikipedia as ground truth and the goal of the participants was to rate the text based on the readability and accuracy. We have trained the Structure-aware for 10 epochs and selected the best model based on training loss.

5.2 Experiment results

This section shows the experiment results of paragraph-level generation task and sentence-level generation task. Paragraph-level generation task is conducted on TaKG-Biography, TaKG-Place and TaKG-School, and sentence-level generation task is on WikiBio.

[3] `https://languagetool.org`

[4] Coleman–Liau is calculated as $CLI = 0.0588L - 0.296S - 15.8$, where L and S are the average numbers of letters and the average number of sentences per 100 words.

	BLEU	STS-RoBERTa	BERT Score	PARENT		Diversity ↓	Grammatical Error Rate ↓	Readability
				Table	KG			
Table	28.09	0.72	0.89	**0.36**	-	0.74	8.59	11.57
KG	17.33	0.65	0.88	-	0.05	**0.70**	8.66	11.52
T5 with Table	23.03	0.64	0.70	0.09	-	0.73	11.06	10.12
One Encoder	28.26	0.70	0.88	0.09	0.05	0.72	**8.16**	14.21
T5 with Table & KG	25.33	0.72	**0.90**	0.09	**0.06**	0.75	10.30	10.47
Table & KG	**29.26**	**0.73**	**0.90**	**0.36**	**0.06**	0.75	8.54	11.63

Table 3: Evaluation results of paragraph-generation task after the proposed model has been fine-tuned for 10 epochs. The metrics with ↓ stands for the performance with the smaller value is better, and the Wikipedia text readability (coleman_liau) score is 11.38.

5.2.1 Paragraph-level Generation with TaKG-Biography

We choose to use fine-tuned Transformer-based seq2seq model T5 (Raffel et al., 2019) as the baseline mode. Two **T5-small** are fine-tuned with table and concatenation of linearized table and KG separately. Besides, we use a standard seq2seq model (**One Encoder**) with the concatenation of linearized table and KG as input.

	BLEU	STS-RoBERTa
1-layer	27.12	**0.72**
2-layer	**28.09**	**0.72**
12-layer	3.33	0.30

Table 4: Comparisons of fine-tuning models on TaKG for 10 epochs with three layer settings.

As a preliminary experiment, to select the optimal number of layers of our proposed model, we compare the performance of our model at *1-layer*, *2-layer* and *12-layer* settings, respectively. BLEU score and STS-RoBERTa score are used as the evaluation metrics. For each setting, we train the model for 10 epochs. As shown in Table 4, *2-layer* get the best performance from both of the BLEU score and STS score. When we increase the layer number to 12, the BLEU score and STS score decreases to 3.33 and 0.30. In addition, the *12-layer* model requires longer time and more memory as the number of training layers increases. Thus, we select to use the *2-layer* model in the paragraph-level text generation task. Then we test the selected models with three different types of input: TaKG-Biography table, TaKG-Biography KG and complete TaKG-Biography.

The evaluation results of models fine-tuned after 10 epochs are shown in Table 3. We observe that our model using complete TaKG-Biography get the best evaluation score on BLEU, semantic (STS-RoBERTa, BERTScore), divergence (PARENT) and achieve comparable results on Grammatical Error Rate and Readability. The readability scores (US grade level 11-12) suggest that all of the models can produce text in the same readability level as Wikipedia text except T5 model (US grade level 10-11). One encoder performs better than fine-tuned T5 models on BLEU and Grammatical Error Rate.

5.2.2 Paragraph-level generation with TaKG-Place and TaKG-School

Since TaKG-Place and TaKG-School are far smaller than TaKG-Biography, we use the *1-layer* setting for the experiments in this section. From Figure 5 and 6, our proposed method using complete TaKG-Place and TaKG-School outperforms the ablation version that only considers the table data in almost all evaluation indexes except diversity and grammatical error rate. This validates the feasibility of using different data sources to improve the quality of generative text. One Encoder model get the lowest score in BLEU, BERTScore and in Diversity. From the diversity scores, the more information is provided to our model, the more deterministic text is generated. Note that, grammatical error rates are kept at a low level, which states the reliability of our method in generating text. Different from TaKG-Biography, when the exhibited models are applying on TaKG-Place and TaKG-School, they need to be fine-tuned with more epochs to learn the knowledge. From the evaluation results, our model obtains little increase on BLEU (0.01 on TaKG-Place and 0.52 on TaKG-School) comparing to the model with table input. From Table 2, for TaKG-Place and TaKG-School, the average words and relations in table are three times larger than these in KG. This is the main reason for limited performance improvement on the two datasets. The results from One Encoder prove that using one encoder for the concatenation of table and KG capture weaker representation than using separated encoders.

	BLEU	BERT Score	PARENT		Diversity ↓	Grammatical Error Rate ↓	Readability
			Table	KG			
Table	22.87	**0.88**	0.06	-	0.76	1.68	9.91
One Encoder	22.05	0.87	0.07	0.07	**0.68**	2.80	10.82
Table & KG	**22.88**	**0.88**	**0.08**	**0.08**	0.78	2.30	9.80

Table 5: Evaluation results of proposed model fine-tuned with UK-Place dataset on paragraph-level generation task for 20 epochs. The metrics with ↓ stands for the performance with the smaller value is better, and the Wikipedia text readability (coleman_liau) score is 10.97.

	BLEU	BERT Score	PARENT		Diversity ↓	Grammatical Error Rate ↓	Readability
			Table	KG			
Table	17.29	**0.88**	0.04	-	0.78	1.31	12.42
One Encoder	17.01	0.87	**0.04**	0.03	**0.72**	2.35	13.00
Table & KG	**17.81**	**0.88**	**0.04**	**0.04**	0.78	2.01	13.14

Table 6: Evaluation results of proposed model fine-tuned with UK-School dataset on paragraph-level generation task for 80 epochs. For metrics with ↓, a smaller value is better. The Wikipedia text readability (coleman_liau) score is 13.78.

	BLEU	STS-RoBERTa	BERT Score	PARENT	Diversity ↓	Grammatical Error Rate ↓	Readability (coleman_liau)
1 epoch	45.69	0.78	0.93	0.10	**0.834**	8.445	10.69
10 epoch	50.36	**0.80**	**0.94**	**0.11**	0.848	**8.355**	10.80
20 epoch	**50.52**	**0.80**	**0.94**	**0.11**	0.849	8.360	10.82

Table 7: Evaluation results of sentence-level generation task with WikiBio in terms of fine-tuning with different epoch. The metrics with ↓ stands for the performance with the smaller value is better, and the Wikipedia text readability (coleman_liau) score is 12.44.

5.2.3 Sentence-level Generation with WikiBio

Four state-of-the-art comparison methods are compared in our experiments to validate the performance of our method. Chen et al. (2019) uses background information and infobox to generate text with a RNN and Multi-Layer Perceptron (MLP) mixed model: **KBAtt**. In (Liu et al., 2018), they describe **Structure-aware** which consists of a field-gating encoder and a description generator with dual attention to generate description given factual table. **Factual Attribute** (Liu et al., 2019a) employs the force attention as well as the reinforcement learning to enrich loyal descriptions for tables. **Tree-like Planning** (Bai et al., 2020) applies a pointer network and a tree-like tuning encoder to capture more relevant attributes in the table. These methods are compared to our model that are fine-tuned after **1, 10, 20 -th epoch.**

	BLEU	Rouge
KBAtt (Chen et al., 2019)	44.59	-
Structure-aware(Liu et al., 2018)	44.89	41.21
Factual Attribute (Liu et al., 2019a)	45.47	41.54
Tree-like Planning (Bai et al., 2020)	47.09	42.82
1-epoch	45.69	41.73
10-epoch	50.36	46.46
20-epoch	**50.52**	**46.69**

Table 8: BLEU and Rouge score comparisons between proposed model and benchmark models on WikiBio dataset.

From the results reported in Table 8, our model with *1-layer* setting has a significant improvement in terms of BLEU and Rouge evaluation metrics, which validates the feasibility of integrating two pretrained language models, i.e., incorporating RoBERTa as encoder and GPT-2 as decoder. Specifically, the studied model achieves better performance than *Structure-aware* and *FA+RL* with fine-tuning only 1 epoch. When fine-tuned with 10 epochs, the demonstrated model outperforms the best comparison methods Tree-like Planning by 3% in both BLEU and Rouge. The results under 20-epoch only show a slight increase compared to the results under 10-epoch which means model get fast convergence within 10 epochs.

We also evaluate the performance of our model fine-tuned with different epochs from semantics, divergence, diversity, grammar and readability aspects as reported in Table 7. From Table 7, similar observation of fast convergence can be more easily observed in different metrics. For diversity and readability, our method gets the score of 0.834 and 10.69 (coleman_liau), which means our method not only can produce more natural language text to describe the constructed table data, but also guarantee the diversity of the generated text. Both background knowledge learnt from PLMs and external knowledge retrieved from Wikidata effectively enrich the expression of sentences.

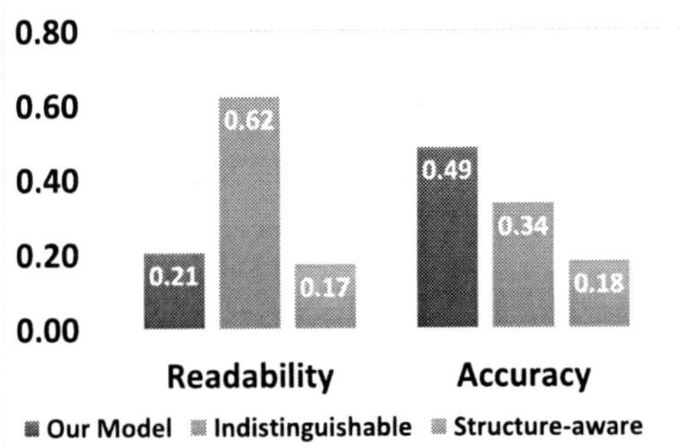

Figure 3: Human-based evaluation result. This figure shows on what proportion of samples different models achieve better scores.

5.2.4 Human Evaluation

Figure 3 shows the human evaluation results. Our model wins over the baseline in terms of both readability and semantic consistency (with ground truth). In terms of readability, 62% of the generated text are indistinguishable and our model performs better on 4% more samples than Structure-aware. In terms of semantic consistency, participants rate that our model performs better than baseline model on 49% of the samples while Structure-aware performs better on 18% samples.

5.3 Case Studies

Case study 1. Figure 4 shows an example from TaKG-Biography on the target entity '4mat'. The input, ground truth and output description are stated in the left table. The output text is generated by our proposed model trained over the complete TaKG-Biography dataset. We label the same or cognate tokens that happen in both inputs and generated text using the same text colour. It can be observed that the generation covers both table and KG inputs, for example, 'composer' and 'sound designer' is copied from the KG data, and 'british' is inferred from 'united kingdom' in both table and KG data. On another note, 'game'(highlighted in yellow colour) appears in both ground truth and generated text, but not provided by inputs. This benefits from the background knowledge learnt by pretrained language models.

The heat map in right part of Figure 4 is the visualization diagram of Cross-Attention matrix from the last Transformer block in the decoder. The darker blue colour means the more attention has been put into from output content to input tokens. The tokens in orange colour indicates the input table data and tokens in green colour is the KG information. Due to the limited space, we list the first 80 tokens from inputs and 30 tokens from outputs. From the attention map, KG data has been put more attention since fact table provide incomplete information.

Case study 2. An example of the comparison between text generated from different models is shown in Figure 5. The left part includes table input and KG input, and the right part are the generated text. Since the table input only provide birth date and name, for the models which only take table as input, they make up the description about occupation and achievement. On the contrary, when the model only takes KG as input, it generates wrong birth date as this information is missing in the KG. For models that make use of both table and KG, they are able to generate text similar to the label description. However, when there is only one encoder for table and KG, the models (One Encoder, T5) are easily making up stories. In biology generation, fabrication is not acceptable. Compare to these baseline models, the proposed model gets the best result, generating exact text that is same as ground truth. From the results, we find that it is not easy to ground T5 for text generation with structured data input via fine-tuning. Besides, using the same encoder for different types of input data works worse than using separated encoders. The main reason is that each encoder can learn the particular patterns from the designated data type.

6 Conclusion

In this study, we introduce TaKG (745,574 samples), the first large-scale KG-enhanced table-to-text dataset. Different from existing well-established sentence-level generation datasets, TaKG defines a paragraph-level generation task. Each sample of TaKG includes three parts: fact table (Wikipedia), knowledge graph (Wikidata) and paragraph-level description of an entity (Wikipedia).

We then propose a new Transformer-based sequence-to-sequence architecture for TaKG that integrates two pretrained language models RoBERTa and GPT-2. For paragraph-level generation, to generate text with multiple structured data sources, we use the simple yet effective concatenation-based fusion to combine the multiple structured data representation. Our model shows the ability to generate reliably long texts using multiple data sources (table and KG) with

Table	name: 4mat origin: united kingdom article-title: 4mat
KG	title: 4mat sex or gender: male occupation: composer, sound designer genre: electronic music, chiptune country of citizenship: united kingdom given name: matthew family name: simmonds languages spoken, written or signed: english
Generation	4mat is a british music composer and sound designer who is best known for his work on the british gamecom"`` early show ", `` computer games ", and for his work on the programming of `` computer games ". he has also collaborated with many other works including the game of `` x-play ", `` space games " and `` robot games ".
Ground Truth	matthew simmonds , also known as 4mat or 4-mat , is a british electronic musician and video game composer best known for his chiptunes written in tracker software . he began his career in the demoscene of the early 1990s composing on the amiga .

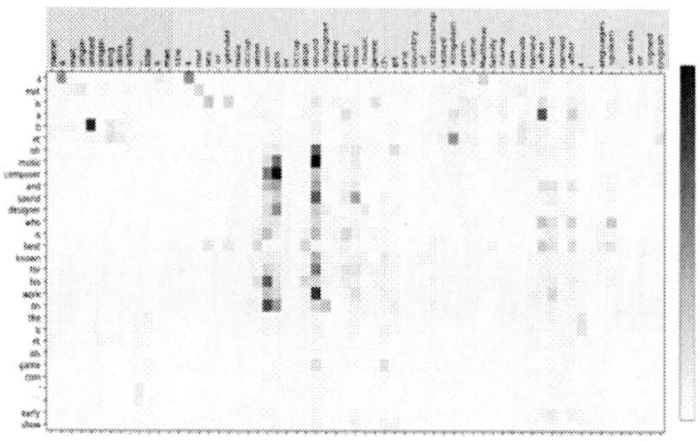

Figure 4: On the left, we have the data from the complete TaKG-Biography. The same or related tokens that happen in both input and generation are highlighted using text colour. The word 'game' with yellow colour background is the information not provided from input, but happens in both generation and ground truth text. On the right, we have a heat map of attention weight from the last cross-attention layer in the decoder. Tokens in orange colour represent table data, and tokens in green colour means KG data. From this heat map, the darker blue colour indicates, the more attention has been put. Due to the page limit, we attach the enlarged heat map in Appendix A.2.

Table Input	
birth_date	14 february 1976
name	muriel vaudey
Knowledge Graph Input	
sex or gender	female
given name	Muriel
family name	Vaudey
country of citizenship	France
languages spoken, written or signed	French
occupation	ski mountaineer
sport	ski mountaineering

Label	**muriel vaudey -lrb- born february 14 , 1976 -rrb- is a french ski mountaineer .**
Structure-aware (Liu et al., 2018)	muriel vaudey -lrb- born february 14 , 1976 -rrb- is an american actress . she is best known for her role as the vaudey vaudey in the television series ``vaudey'' .
Table	muriel vaudey -lrb- born february 15, 1976 in st. paul, minnesota -rrb-, is a canadian former cyclist. she competed in the women's individual road race event at the 1984 summer olympics.
KG	muriel vaudey -lrb- born may 21, 1989 -rrb- is a french ski mountaineer.
One encoder with Table and KG	muriel vaudey -lrb- born february 14, 1976 -rrb- is a french ski mountaineer. vaudey was born in lille. she competed first in the Labrador section of the nationalqqara selection list.
T5 with Table	muriel vaudey -lrb- born february 14, 1976 -rrb- is a russian actor. he is known for his role as sarah sahna in the sahna " film sahna ".
T5 with Table and KG	muriel vaudey -lrb- born february 14, 1976 -rrb- is a french ski mountaineer. she is the first french female ski mountaineer to win the french national championship.
Table and KG	muriel vaudey -lrb- born february 14, 1976 -rrb- is a french ski mountaineer.

Figure 5: The left part shows table input and KG input. The generations from different models are shown on the right, and label text is shown in the first row of it. The text highlighted in red indicates wrong generation including false date or fictitious story.

the evaluation on BLEU, PARENT and semantic similarity score (STS-RoBERTa). To further verify the ability of the proposed method, we conduct the experiments on sentence-level text generation using WikiBio. Our method outperforms the best benchmark models with large margin on WikiBio with 7.3% (BLEU) and 9% (Rouge) increment.

References

Yang Bai, Ziran Li, Ning Ding, Ying Shen, and Hai-Tao Zheng. 2020. Infobox-to-text generation with tree-like planning based attention network. In *IJCAI*, pages 3773–3779.

Shuang Chen, Jinpeng Wang, Xiaocheng Feng, Feng Jiang, Bing Qin, and Chin-Yew Lin. 2019. Enhancing neural data-to-text generation models with external background knowledge. In *Proceedings of the 2019 Conference on Empirical Methods in Natural Language Processing and the 9th International Joint Conference on Natural Language Processing (EMNLP-IJCNLP)*, pages 3022–3032.

Meri Coleman and Ta Lin Liau. 1975. A computer readability formula designed for machine scoring. *Journal of Applied Psychology*, 60(2):283.

Bhuwan Dhingra, Manaal Faruqui, Ankur Parikh, Ming-Wei Chang, Dipanjan Das, and William W Cohen. 2019. Handling divergent reference texts when evaluating table-to-text generation. *arXiv preprint arXiv:1906.01081*.

Ari Holtzman, Jan Buys, Li Du, Maxwell Forbes, and Yejin Choi. 2019. The curious case of neural text degeneration. *arXiv preprint arXiv:1904.09751*.

Karen Kukich. 1983. Design of a knowledge-based report generator. In *21st Annual Meeting of the Association for Computational Linguistics*, pages 145–150.

Rémi Lebret, David Grangier, and Michael Auli. 2016. Neural text generation from structured data with application to the biography domain. *arXiv preprint arXiv:1603.07771*.

Tianyu Liu, Fuli Luo, Pengcheng Yang, Wei Wu, Baobao Chang, and Zhifang Sui. 2019a. Towards comprehensive description generation from factual attribute-value tables. In *Proceedings of the 57th Annual Meeting of the Association for Computational Linguistics*, pages 5985–5996.

Tianyu Liu, Kexiang Wang, Lei Sha, Baobao Chang, and Zhifang Sui. 2018. Table-to-text generation by structure-aware seq2seq learning. In *Thirty-Second AAAI Conference on Artificial Intelligence*.

Tianyu Liu, Xin Zheng, Baobao Chang, and Zhifang Sui. 2021. Towards faithfulness in open domain table-to-text generation from an entity-centric view. In *Proceedings of the AAAI Conference on Artificial Intelligence*, volume 35, pages 13415–13423.

Yinhan Liu, Myle Ott, Naman Goyal, Jingfei Du, Mandar Joshi, Danqi Chen, Omer Levy, Mike Lewis, Luke Zettlemoyer, and Veselin Stoyanov. 2019b. Roberta: A robustly optimized bert pretraining approach. *arXiv preprint arXiv:1907.11692*.

Manuel Mager, Ramón Fernandez Astudillo, Tahira Naseem, Md Arafat Sultan, Young-Suk Lee, Radu Florian, and Salim Roukos. 2020. Gpt-too: A language-model-first approach for amr-to-text generation. *arXiv preprint arXiv:2005.09123*.

Kenneth Marino, Xinlei Chen, Devi Parikh, Abhinav Gupta, and Marcus Rohrbach. 2021. Krisp: Integrating implicit and symbolic knowledge for open-domain knowledge-based vqa. In *Proceedings of the IEEE/CVF Conference on Computer Vision and Pattern Recognition*, pages 14111–14121.

Arsha Nagrani, Chen Sun, David Ross, Rahul Sukthankar, Cordelia Schmid, and Andrew Zisserman. 2020. Speech2action: Cross-modal supervision for action recognition. In *Proceedings of the IEEE/CVF conference on computer vision and pattern recognition*, pages 10317–10326.

Jekaterina Novikova, Ondřej Dušek, and Verena Rieser. 2017. The e2e dataset: New challenges for end-to-end generation. *arXiv preprint arXiv:1706.09254*.

Kishore Papineni, Salim Roukos, Todd Ward, and Wei-Jing Zhu. 2002. Bleu: a method for automatic evaluation of machine translation. In *Proceedings of the 40th annual meeting of the Association for Computational Linguistics*, pages 311–318.

Ankur P Parikh, Xuezhi Wang, Sebastian Gehrmann, Manaal Faruqui, Bhuwan Dhingra, Diyi Yang, and Dipanjan Das. 2020. Totto: A controlled table-to-text generation dataset. *arXiv preprint arXiv:2004.14373*.

Ratish Puduppully, Li Dong, and Mirella Lapata. 2019. Data-to-text generation with entity modeling. *arXiv preprint arXiv:1906.03221*.

Alec Radford, Jeffrey Wu, Rewon Child, David Luan, Dario Amodei, Ilya Sutskever, et al. 2019. Language models are unsupervised multitask learners. *OpenAI blog*, 1(8):9.

Colin Raffel, Noam Shazeer, Adam Roberts, Katherine Lee, Sharan Narang, Michael Matena, Yanqi Zhou, Wei Li, and Peter J Liu. 2019. Exploring the limits of transfer learning with a unified text-to-text transformer. *arXiv preprint arXiv:1910.10683*.

Lin CY ROUGE. 2004. A package for automatic evaluation of summaries. In *Proceedings of Workshop on Text Summarization of ACL, Spain*.

Victor Sanh, Lysandre Debut, Julien Chaumond, and Thomas Wolf. 2019. Distilbert, a distilled version of bert: smaller, faster, cheaper and lighter. *ArXiv*, abs/1910.01108.

Apoorv Saxena, Aditay Tripathi, and Partha Talukdar. 2020. Improving multi-hop question answering over knowledge graphs using knowledge base embeddings. In *Proceedings of the 58th annual meeting of the association for computational linguistics*, pages 4498–4507.

Nils Smeuninx, Bernard De Clerck, and Walter Aerts. 2020. Measuring the readability of sustainability reports: A corpus-based analysis through standard formulae and nlp. *International Journal of Business Communication*, 57(1):52–85.

Chen Sun, Austin Myers, Carl Vondrick, Kevin Murphy, and Cordelia Schmid. 2019. Videobert: A joint model for video and language representation learning. In *Proceedings of the IEEE/CVF International Conference on Computer Vision*, pages 7464–7473.

Ashish Vaswani, Noam Shazeer, Niki Parmar, Jakob Uszkoreit, Llion Jones, Aidan N Gomez, Łukasz Kaiser, and Illia Polosukhin. 2017. Attention is all you need. In *Advances in neural information processing systems*, pages 5998–6008.

Denny Vrandečić and Markus Krötzsch. 2014. Wikidata: a free collaborative knowledgebase. *Communications of the ACM*, 57(10):78–85.

Zhenyi Wang, Xiaoyang Wang, Bang An, Dong Yu, and Changyou Chen. 2020. Towards faithful neural table-to-text generation with content-matching constraints. In *Proceedings of the 58th Annual Meeting of the Association for Computational Linguistics*, pages 1072–1086.

Sam Wiseman, Stuart M Shieber, and Alexander M Rush. 2017. Challenges in data-to-document generation. *arXiv preprint arXiv:1707.08052*.

Tianyi Zhang, Varsha Kishore, Felix Wu, Kilian Q Weinberger, and Yoav Artzi. 2019. Bertscore: Evaluating text generation with bert. *arXiv preprint arXiv:1904.09675*.

Yaoming Zhu, Sidi Lu, Lei Zheng, Jiaxian Guo, Weinan Zhang, Jun Wang, and Yong Yu. 2018. Texygen: A benchmarking platform for text generation models. In *The 41st International ACM SIGIR Conference on Research & Development in Information Retrieval*, pages 1097–1100.

A Appendix

A.1 Examples from TaKG-place and TaKG-school

We show the examples from TaKG-place and TaKG-school below.

1. Example from TaKG-place

- **Target Entity:** Alva
- **Fact Table:**
  - UK Parliament: Ochil and South Perthshire
  - Country: Scotland
  - Sovereign state: United Kingdom
  - ...
- **Knowledge Graph:**
  - Alva | population | 4,600 in 2016
  - Alva | area | 0.598 square mile
  - ...
- **Description:**
  - Alva (Scottish Gaelic: Ailbheach, meaning rocky) is a small town in Clackmannanshire, set in the Central Lowlands of Scotland. It is one of a number of towns situated immediately to the south of the Ochil Hills, collectively referred to as the Hillfoots Villages or simply The Hillfoots. It is located between Tillicoultry and Menstrie. Alva had a resident population of 5,181 at the 2001 census but this has since been revised to 4,600 in 2016. It boasts many features ...

2. Example from TaKG-school

- **Target Entity:** St Bonaventure's
- **Fact Table:**
  - Established: 1877 (in Forest Gate)
  - Founder: Franciscans
  - Age: 11 to 18
  - ...
- **Knowledge Graph:**
  - St Bonaventure's RC School | country | United Kingdom
  - St Bonaventure's RC School | historic county | Essex
  - ...
- **Description:**
  - St Bonaventure's, known informally as St Bon's, is a voluntary-aided Catholic secondary school for boys aged 11–16 in Forest Gate, London Borough of Newham, England, with a mixed gender sixth form for 16–18-year-old students. It is under the trustee-ship of the Roman Catholic Diocese of Brentwood. St Bonaventure's is the oldest boys' school in Newham, having been established in the West Ham area of Essex by the Franciscan order in 1875, following the Roman Catholic Relief Act 1829. ...

A.2 Heat map of attention weight

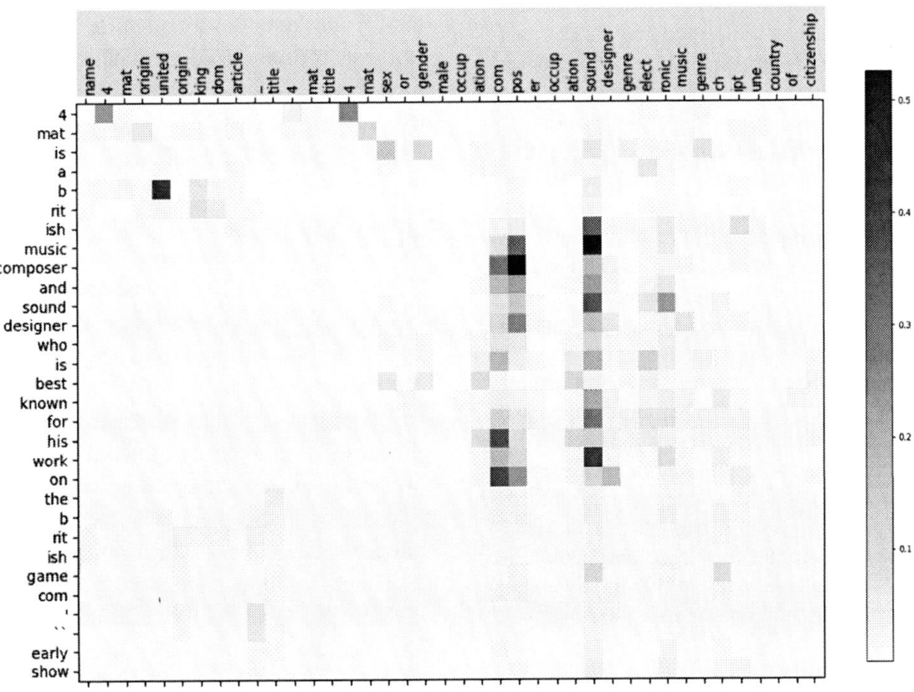

Figure 6: Tokens in orange colour represent table data, and tokens in green colour means KG data. From this heat map, the darker blue colour indicates, the more attention has been put.

Revisiting Checkpoint Averaging for Neural Machine Translation

Yingbo Gao **Christian Herold** **Zijian Yang** **Hermann Ney**
Human Language Technology and Pattern Recognition Group
Computer Science Department
RWTH Aachen University
D-52056 Aachen, Germany
{ygao|herold|zyang|ney}@cs.rwth-aachen.de

Abstract

Checkpoint averaging is a simple and effective method to boost the performance of converged neural machine translation models. The calculation is cheap to perform and the fact that the translation improvement almost comes for free, makes it widely adopted in neural machine translation research. Despite the popularity, the method itself simply takes the mean of the model parameters from several checkpoints, the selection of which is mostly based on empirical recipes without many justifications. In this work, we revisit the concept of checkpoint averaging and consider several extensions. Specifically, we experiment with ideas such as using different checkpoint selection strategies, calculating weighted average instead of simple mean, making use of gradient information and fine-tuning the interpolation weights on development data. Our results confirm the necessity of applying checkpoint averaging for optimal performance, but also suggest that the landscape between the converged checkpoints is rather flat and not much further improvement compared to simple averaging is to be obtained.

1 Introduction

Checkpoint averaging is a simple method to improve model performance at low computational cost. The procedure is straightforward: select some model checkpoints, average the model parameters, and obtain a better model. Because of its simplicity and effectiveness, it is widely used in neural machine translation (NMT), e.g. in the original Transformer paper (Vaswani et al., 2017), in systems participating in public machine translation (MT) evaluations such as Conference on Machine Translation (WMT) (Barrault et al., 2021) and the International Conference on Spoken Language Translation (IWSLT) (Anastasopoulos et al., 2022): Barrault et al. (2021); Erdmann et al. (2021); Li et al. (2021); Subramanian et al. (2021); Tran et al. (2021); Wang et al. (2021b); Wei et al. (2021); Di Gangi et al. (2019); Li et al. (2022), and in numerous MT research papers (Junczys-Dowmunt et al., 2016; Shaw et al., 2018; Liu et al., 2018; Zhao et al., 2019; Kim et al., 2021). Apart from NMT, checkpoint averaging also finds applications in Transformer-based automatic speech recognition models (Karita et al., 2019; Dong et al., 2018; Higuchi et al., 2020; Tian et al., 2020; Wang et al., 2020). Despite the popularity of the method, the recipes in each work are rather empirical and do not differ much except in how many and exactly which checkpoints are averaged.

In this work, we revisit the concept of checkpoint averaging and consider several extensions. We examine the straightforward hyperparameters like the number of checkpoints to average, the checkpoint selection strategy and the mean calculation itself. Because the gradient information is often available at the time of checkpointing, we also explore the idea of using this piece of information. Additionally, we experiment with the idea of fine-tuning the interpolation weights of the checkpoints on development data. As reported in countless works, we confirm that the translation performance improvement can be robustly obtained with checkpoint averaging. However, our results suggest that the landscape between the converged checkpoints is rather flat, and it is hard to squeeze out further performance improvements with advanced tricks.

2 Related Work

The idea of combining multiple models for more stable and potentially better prediction is not new in statistical learning (Dietterich, 2000; Dong et al., 2020). In NMT, ensembling, more specifically, ensembling systems with different architectures is shown to be helpful (Stahlberg et al., 2019; Rosendahl et al., 2019; Zhang and van Genabith, 2019). In contrary, checkpoint averaging uses checkpoints from the same training run with the same neural network (NN) architecture. Compared

Findings of the Association for Computational Linguistics: AACL-IJCNLP 2022, pages 188–196
November 20–23, 2022.

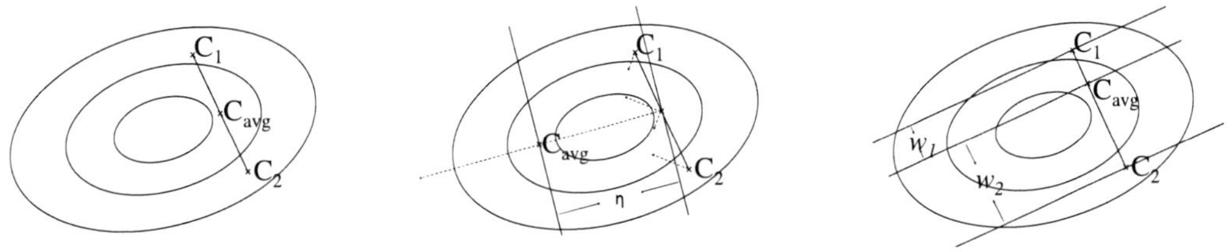

(a) vanilla (b) using gradient information (c) optimized on development data

Figure 1: An illustration of checkpoint averaging and our extensions. The isocontour plot illustrates some imaginary loss surface. C1 and C2 are model parameters from two checkpoints. C_{avg} denotes the averaged parameters. In (a), the mean of the C1 and C2 is taken. In (b), the dashed arrows refer to the gradients (could also include the momentum terms) stored in the checkpoints, and a further step (with step size η) is taken. In (c), a NN is parametrized with the interpolation weights w_1 and w_2, and the weights are learned on the development data.

to ensembling, checkpoint averaging is cheaper to calculate and does not require one to store and query multiple models at test time. The distinction can also be made from the perspective of the interpolation space, i.e. model parameter space for checkpoint averaging, and posterior probability space for ensembling. As a trade-off, the performance boost from checkpoint averaging is typically smaller than ensembling (Liu et al., 2018).

In the literature, Chen et al. (2017) study the use of checkpoints from the same training run for ensembling; Smith (2017) proposes cyclic learning rate schedules to improve accuracy and convergence; Huang et al. (2017) propose to use a cyclic learning rate to obtain snapshots of the same model during training and ensemble them in the probability space; Izmailov et al. (2018) perform model parameter averaging on-the-fly during training and argue for better generalization in this way; Popel and Bojar (2018) discuss empirical findings related to checkpoint averaging for NMT; Zhang et al. (2020) and Karita et al. (2021) maintain an exponential moving average during model training; Wang et al. (2021a) propose a boosting algorithm and ensemble checkpoints in the probability space; Matena and Raffel (2021) exploit the Fisher information matrix to calculate weighted average of model parameters. Here, we are interested in the interpolation happening in the model parameter space, and therefore restrain ourselves from further discussing topics like ensembling or continuing training on the development data.

3 Methodology

In this section, we discuss extensions to checkpoint averaging considered in this work. An intuitive illustration is shown in Fig.1.

3.1 Extending Vanilla Checkpoint Averaging

The vanilla checkpointing is straightforward and can be expressed as in Eq.1. Here, $\boldsymbol{\theta}$ denotes the model parameters and $\hat{\boldsymbol{\theta}}$ is the averaged parameters. k is a running index in number of checkpoints K, and $\mathcal{S}$, where $|\mathcal{S}| = K$, is a set of checkpoint indices selected by some specific strategy, e.g. top-K or last-K. In the vanilla case, $w_k = \frac{1}{K}$, i.e. uniform weights are used.

$$\hat{\boldsymbol{\theta}} = \sum_{k \in \mathcal{S}} w_k \boldsymbol{\theta}_k \tag{1}$$

As shown in Eq.2, we further consider non-uniform weights and propose to use softmax-normalized logarithm of development set perplexities (DEVPPL) with temperature τ as interpolation weights. We define w in this way such that it is in the probability space.

$$w_k = \frac{\exp(-\tau \log \text{DEVPPL}_k)}{\sum_{k' \in \mathcal{S}} \exp(-\tau \log \text{DEVPPL}_{k'})} \tag{2}$$

3.2 Making Use of Gradient Information

Nowadays, NMT models are commonly trained with stated optimizers like Adam (Kingma and Ba, 2015). To provide the "continue-training" utility, the gradients of the most recent batch are therefore also saved. Shown in Eq.3, we can therefore take a further step in the parameter space during checkpoint averaging to make use of this information. Here, η is the step size and $\frac{1}{K} \sum_{k \in \mathcal{S}} \nabla_{\boldsymbol{\theta}} L(\boldsymbol{\theta}_k)$ is the mean of the gradients stored in the checkpoints.

$$\hat{\boldsymbol{\theta}} = \sum_{k \in \mathcal{S}} w_k \boldsymbol{\theta}_k - \eta \frac{1}{K} \sum_{k \in \mathcal{S}} \nabla_{\boldsymbol{\theta}} L(\boldsymbol{\theta}_k) \tag{3}$$

3.3 Optimization on Development Data

In addition to using DEVPPL, one can optimize the interpolation weights directly on the development data. Specifically, to ensure normalization, we re-parameterize the model with the logits g_k in a softmax function, initialized at zero and updated via one-step gradient descent, with step size η, on development data to avoid overfitting. As shown in Eq.4, w_k is the normalized interpolation weights. Note that we refrain from updating the raw model parameters $\boldsymbol{\theta}_k$ from each checkpoint but only update the logits g_k. Here, L refers to the cross entropy loss of the re-parametrized NN on the development data.

$$w_k = \frac{\exp g_k}{\sum_{k' \in \mathcal{S}} \exp g_{k'}} \tag{4}$$
$$g_{k,0} = 0, \;\; g_{k,1} = -\eta \nabla_{g_k} L(g_{k,0}; \boldsymbol{\theta}_1, ..., \boldsymbol{\theta}_K)$$

4 Experiments

We re-implement Transformer (Vaswani et al., 2017) using PyTorch (Paszke et al., 2019) and experiment on IWSLT14 German-, Russian-, and Spanish-to-English (de-en, ru-en, es-en), and WMT16 English-to-Romanian, WMT14 English-to-German, WMT19 Chinese-to-English (en-ro, en-de, zh-en) datasets. Due to limited length, we only present representative results on de-en in this section. Results on other language pairs can be found in the appendix and the trends are similar to that reported in this section. Note that, in the experiments below, the test BLEU scores are under consideration. However, we argue that it is not critical because checkpoint averaging is a vetted trick to boost system performance and our goal is to better understand the parameter space and not to obtain "the state-of-the-art" in some public scoreboard.

In Fig.2, we plot the BLEU (Papineni et al., 2002) scores versus increasing K, where the previous K checkpoints starting from the best checkpoint (in terms of DEVPPL) are selected. As can be seen, initial BLEU improvements are obtained but as worse and worse checkpoints are included, the BLEU score drops as expected.

In Fig.3, ranking all checkpoints by their DEVPPL, the top-K checkpoints are selected for averaging. Notice that up to $K = 40$, the DEVPPL is still around 5, whereas in the last-K case, significantly worse checkpoints (the early checkpoints) are already included in the interpolation. It can be seen that the final BLEU score is much less sensitive to the choice of K in this case. Of course the final performance also relies on the checkpointing settings (e.g. the checkpointing frequency) but it is clear from the comparison that one should prefer to include checkpoints with better DEVPPL.

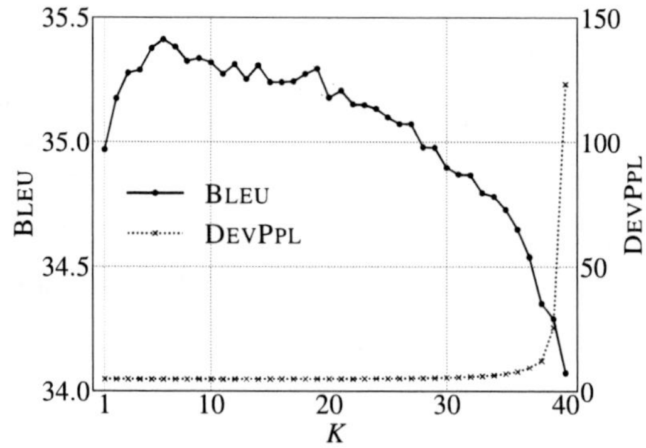

Figure 2: Last-K simple mean on de-en.

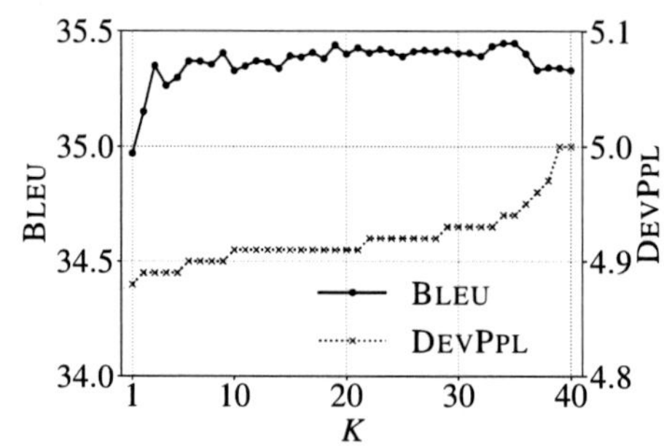

Figure 3: Top-K simple mean on de-en.

In Fig.4, we plot the BLEU scores against the temperature τ in Eq.2. Here, we select last-K checkpoints as in Fig.2 to artificially include some bad-performing checkpoints. Two sanity checks can be done here. When τ is very small, uniform weights are used and the performance is close to the vanilla last-40 case. When τ is very large, one-hot weights are used and the performance is close to that of the best checkpoint. We observe that using the DEVPPL-dependent weights results in similar performance increase compared to the vanilla case, meaning that the checkpoint selections can be automated by selecting a proper τ.

Next, we study how the system performance changes with the step size used in the one-shot gradient update (Fig.1b and Eq.3). As shown in Fig.5, we interpolate three systems selecting top-K checkpoints with $K = 2$, $K = 5$ and $K = 10$, respectively. Here, temperature $\tau = 100$. In line

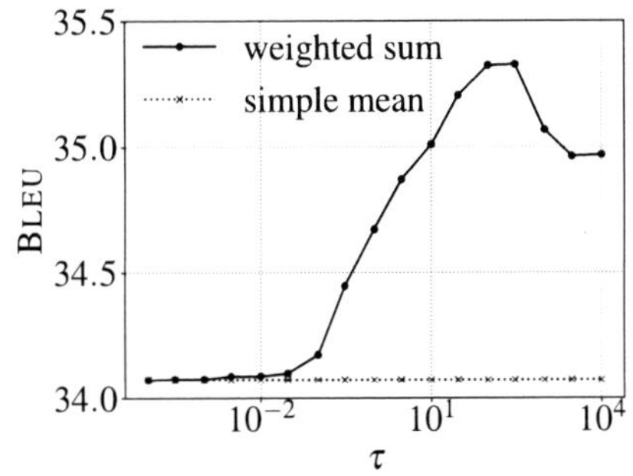

Figure 4: Last-40 weighted sum on de-en.

with the results in Fig.2 and Fig.3, the models with $K = 5$ and $K = 10$ are slightly better than the model with $K = 2$. However, as the step size η increases, the BLEU score quickly drops as the averaged model diverges further away from the initial mean. It is clear from the figure that nothing is gained in terms of BLEU during the η scan. In other words, these results suggest a very flat surface along the direction of averaged gradients.

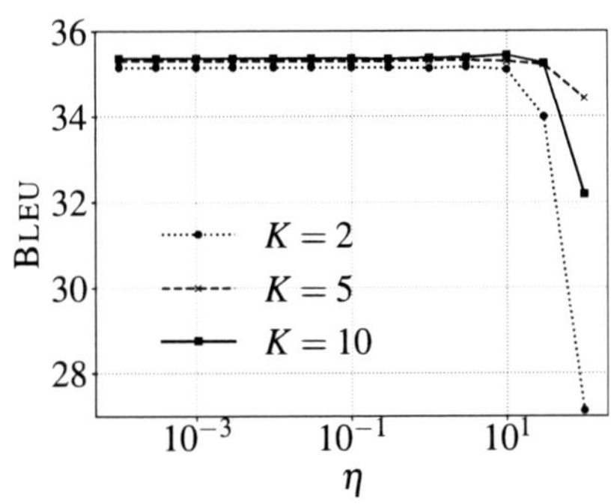

Figure 5: One-shot gradient update of top-K weighted sum with $\tau = 100$ on de-en.

To investigate if optimization on the development data would work, we implement Eq.4 and sweep over step size η. As shown in Fig.6, the gradient update on the weights move the model towards the best checkpoint ($\boldsymbol{\theta}_0$ here), and w_0 increases to 1.0 with large enough η. There is, however, little improvement to be obtained along the path. Note that this is the restricted case (Eq.4) where only interpolation weights are allowed to change and model parameters are not updated.

Given the results so far, it is clear that although a small boost of BLEU score can be robustly obtained in various checkpoint averaging settings, it is hard to squeeze out any further improvement with the extensions considered here. We therefore perform a grid search over the interpolation

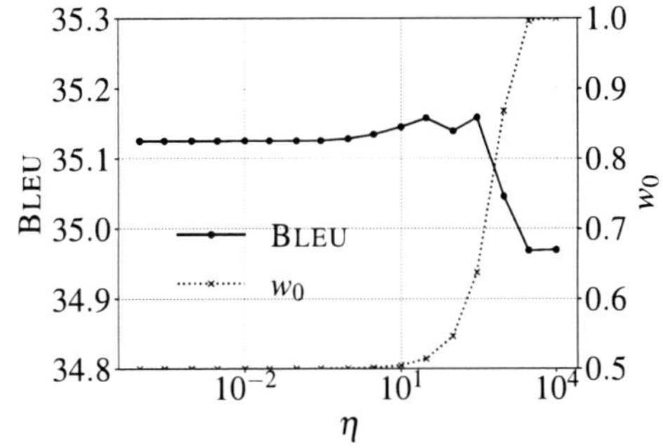

Figure 6: Optimization of interpolation weights w_k on development data with $K = 2$ on de-en.

weights w_k with $K = 3$, to examine the landscape between the checkpoints. Shown in Fig.7, is the intersection of $w_1 + w_2 + w_3 = 1, 0 \leq w_k \leq 1$ in the space of the interpolation weights. From the figure, except when really close to the vertices, i.e. $(w_1, w_2, w_3) = (1, 0, 0)$ or $(0, 1, 0)$ or $(0, 0, 1)$, the surface is rather flat with small fluctuations here and there. Considered together with the previous results, this suggests that the gradient direction in the flat area may be unreliable and not much improvement is to be gained by further tuning the interpolation weights. Of course one could argue that in higher dimensions the surface could look different by moving off of the $\sum_{k \in S} w_k = 1$ hyperplain, but we think it is unlikely to be helpful as Fig.5 is a counter-evidence at hand.

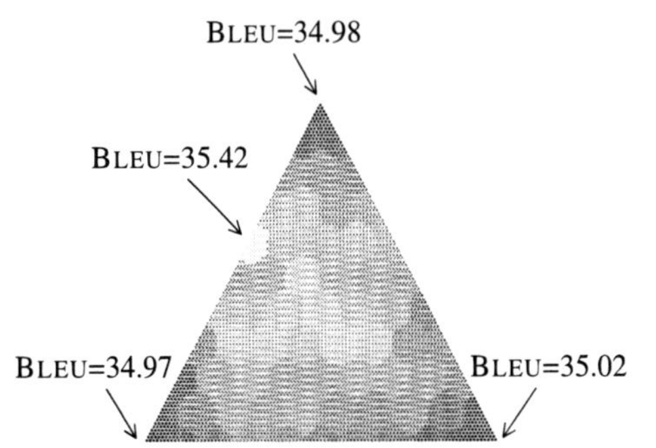

Figure 7: Neighborhood of the top-3 checkpoints on de-en. The hexagons are artifacts from plotting because a denser grid of points is used in the plot than in checkpoint averaging and the dots are colored by querying the nearest neighbor in the checkpoint averaging grid.

5 Conclusion

We consider checkpoint averaging, a simple and effective method in neural machine translation to boost system performance. Specifically, we examine different checkpoint selection strategies, calculate weighted average, make use of gradient information and optimize the interpolation weights. We confirm the robust improvements from checkpoint averaging and that the checkpoint selection can be automated with the weighted average scheme. However, by closely looking at the landscape between the checkpoints, we find the surface to be rather flat and conclude that tuning in the space of the interpolation weights may not be a meaningful direction to squeeze out further improvements.

Acknowledgements

This work was partially supported by the project HYKIST funded by the German Federal Ministry of Health on the basis of a decision of the German Federal Parliament (Bundestag) under funding ID ZMVI1-2520DAT04A, and by NeuroSys which, as part of the initiative "Clusters4Future", is funded by the Federal Ministry of Education and Research BMBF (03ZU1106DA).

References

Antonios Anastasopoulos, Loïc Barrault, Luisa Bentivogli, Marcely Zanon Boito, Ondřej Bojar, Roldano Cattoni, Anna Currey, Georgiana Dinu, Kevin Duh, Maha Elbayad, Clara Emmanuel, Yannick Estève, Marcello Federico, Christian Federmann, Souhir Gahbiche, Hongyu Gong, Roman Grundkiewicz, Barry Haddow, Benjamin Hsu, Dávid Javorský, Věra Kloudová, Surafel Lakew, Xutai Ma, Prashant Mathur, Paul McNamee, Kenton Murray, Maria Nădejde, Satoshi Nakamura, Matteo Negri, Jan Niehues, Xing Niu, John Ortega, Juan Pino, Elizabeth Salesky, Jiatong Shi, Matthias Sperber, Sebastian Stüker, Katsuhito Sudoh, Marco Turchi, Yogesh Virkar, Alexander Waibel, Changhan Wang, and Shinji Watanabe. 2022. Findings of the IWSLT 2022 evaluation campaign. In *Proceedings of the 19th International Conference on Spoken Language Translation (IWSLT 2022)*, pages 98–157, Dublin, Ireland (in-person and online). Association for Computational Linguistics.

Loic Barrault, Ondrej Bojar, Fethi Bougares, Rajen Chatterjee, Marta R. Costa-jussa, Christian Federmann, Mark Fishel, Alexander Fraser, Markus Freitag, Yvette Graham, Roman Grundkiewicz, Paco Guzman, Barry Haddow, Matthias Huck, Antonio Jimeno Yepes, Philipp Koehn, Tom Kocmi, Andre Martins, Makoto Morishita, and Christof Monz, editors. 2021. *Proceedings of the Sixth Conference on Machine Translation*. Association for Computational Linguistics, Online.

Hugh Chen, Scott Lundberg, and Su-In Lee. 2017. Checkpoint ensembles: Ensemble methods from a single training process. *arXiv preprint arXiv:1710.03282*.

Mattia A. Di Gangi, Matteo Negri, Viet Nhat Nguyen, Amirhossein Tebbifakhr, and Marco Turchi. 2019. Data augmentation for end-to-end speech translation: FBK@IWSLT '19. In *Proceedings of the 16th International Conference on Spoken Language Translation*, Hong Kong. Association for Computational Linguistics.

Thomas G Dietterich. 2000. Ensemble methods in machine learning. In *International workshop on multiple classifier systems*, pages 1–15. Springer.

Linhao Dong, Shuang Xu, and Bo Xu. 2018. Speech-transformer: a no-recurrence sequence-to-sequence model for speech recognition. In *2018 IEEE International Conference on Acoustics, Speech and Signal Processing (ICASSP)*, pages 5884–5888. IEEE.

Xibin Dong, Zhiwen Yu, Wenming Cao, Yifan Shi, and Qianli Ma. 2020. A survey on ensemble learning. *Frontiers of Computer Science*, 14(2):241–258.

Grant Erdmann, Jeremy Gwinnup, and Tim Anderson. 2021. Tune in: The afrl wmt21 news-translation systems. In *Proceedings of the Sixth Conference on Machine Translation*, pages 110–116, Online. Association for Computational Linguistics.

Yosuke Higuchi, Shinji Watanabe, Nanxin Chen, Tetsuji Ogawa, and Tetsunori Kobayashi. 2020. Mask ctc: Non-autoregressive end-to-end asr with ctc and mask predict. *Proceedings of the Annual Conference of the International Speech Communication Association, INTERSPEECH*, 2020-October:3655–3659. Publisher Copyright: © 2020 ISCA; 21st Annual Conference of the International Speech Communication Association, INTERSPEECH 2020 ; Conference date: 25-10-2020 Through 29-10-2020.

Gao Huang, Yixuan Li, Geoff Pleiss, Zhuang Liu, John E. Hopcroft, and Kilian Q. Weinberger. 2017. Snapshot ensembles: Train 1, get M for free. *CoRR*, abs/1704.00109.

Pavel Izmailov, Dmitrii Podoprikhin, Timur Garipov, Dmitry P. Vetrov, and Andrew Gordon Wilson. 2018. Averaging weights leads to wider optima and better generalization. In *Proceedings of the Thirty-Fourth Conference on Uncertainty in Artificial Intelligence, UAI 2018, Monterey, California, USA, August 6-10, 2018*, pages 876–885. AUAI Press.

Marcin Junczys-Dowmunt, Tomasz Dwojak, and Hieu Hoang. 2016. Is neural machine translation ready for deployment? a case study on 30 translation directions. In *Proceedings of the 13th International Conference on Spoken Language Translation*, Seattle, Washington D.C. International Workshop on Spoken Language Translation.

Shigeki Karita, Nanxin Chen, Tomoki Hayashi, Takaaki Hori, Hirofumi Inaguma, Ziyan Jiang, Masao Someki, Nelson Yalta, Ryuichi Yamamoto, Xiao fei Wang, Shinji Watanabe, Takenori Yoshimura, and Wangyou Zhang. 2019. A comparative study on transformer vs rnn in speech applications. *2019 IEEE Automatic Speech Recognition and Understanding Workshop (ASRU)*, pages 449–456.

Shigeki Karita, Yotaro Kubo, Michiel Bacchiani, and Llion Jones. 2021. A comparative study on neural architectures and training methods for japanese speech recognition. In *Interspeech*.

Young Jin Kim, Ammar Ahmad Awan, Alexandre Muzio, Andres Felipe Cruz Salinas, Liyang Lu, Amr Hendy, Samyam Rajbhandari, Yuxiong He, and Hany Hassan Awadalla. 2021. Scalable and efficient moe training for multitask multilingual models. *arXiv preprint arXiv:2109.10465*.

Diederik P. Kingma and Jimmy Ba. 2015. Adam: A method for stochastic optimization. In *3rd International Conference on Learning Representations, ICLR 2015, San Diego, CA, USA, May 7-9, 2015, Conference Track Proceedings*.

Zongyao Li, Jiaxin Guo, Daimeng Wei, Hengchao Shang, Minghan Wang, Ting Zhu, Zhanglin Wu, Zhengzhe Yu, Xiaoyu Chen, Lizhi Lei, Hao Yang, and Ying Qin. 2022. HW-TSC's participation in the IWSLT 2022 isometric spoken language translation. In *Proceedings of the 19th International Conference on Spoken Language Translation (IWSLT 2022)*, pages 361–368, Dublin, Ireland (in-person and online). Association for Computational Linguistics.

Zuchao Li, Masao Utiyama, Eiichiro Sumita, and Hai Zhao. 2021. Miss@wmt21: Contrastive learning-reinforced domain adaptation in neural machine translation. In *Proceedings of the Sixth Conference on Machine Translation*, pages 154–161, Online. Association for Computational Linguistics.

Yuchen Liu, Long Zhou, Yining Wang, Yang Zhao, Jiajun Zhang, and Chengqing Zong. 2018. A comparable study on model averaging, ensembling and reranking in nmt. In *Natural Language Processing and Chinese Computing*, pages 299–308, Cham. Springer International Publishing.

Michael Matena and Colin Raffel. 2021. Merging models with fisher-weighted averaging. *arXiv preprint arXiv:2111.09832*.

Kishore Papineni, Salim Roukos, Todd Ward, and Wei-Jing Zhu. 2002. Bleu: a method for automatic evaluation of machine translation. In *Proceedings of the 40th Annual Meeting of the Association for Computational Linguistics*, pages 311–318, Philadelphia, Pennsylvania, USA. Association for Computational Linguistics.

Adam Paszke, Sam Gross, Francisco Massa, Adam Lerer, James Bradbury, Gregory Chanan, Trevor Killeen, Zeming Lin, Natalia Gimelshein, Luca Antiga, Alban Desmaison, Andreas Kopf, Edward Yang, Zachary DeVito, Martin Raison, Alykhan Tejani, Sasank Chilamkurthy, Benoit Steiner, Lu Fang, Junjie Bai, and Soumith Chintala. 2019. Pytorch: An imperative style, high-performance deep learning library. In H. Wallach, H. Larochelle, A. Beygelzimer, F. d'Alché-Buc, E. Fox, and R. Garnett, editors, *Advances in Neural Information Processing Systems 32*, pages 8024–8035. Curran Associates, Inc.

Martin Popel and Ondřej Bojar. 2018. Training tips for the transformer model. *arXiv preprint arXiv:1804.00247*.

Jan Rosendahl, Christian Herold, Yunsu Kim, Miguel Graça, Weiyue Wang, Parnia Bahar, Yingbo Gao, and Hermann Ney. 2019. The rwth aachen university machine translation systems for wmt 2019. In *Proceedings of the Fourth Conference on Machine Translation (Volume 2: Shared Task Papers, Day 1)*, pages 349–355.

Peter Shaw, Jakob Uszkoreit, and Ashish Vaswani. 2018. Self-attention with relative position representations. In *Proceedings of the 2018 Conference of the North American Chapter of the Association for Computational Linguistics: Human Language Technologies, Volume 2 (Short Papers)*, pages 464–468, New Orleans, Louisiana. Association for Computational Linguistics.

Leslie N Smith. 2017. Cyclical learning rates for training neural networks. In *2017 IEEE winter conference on applications of computer vision (WACV)*, pages 464–472. IEEE.

Felix Stahlberg, Danielle Saunders, Adrià de Gispert, and Bill Byrne. 2019. CUED@WMT19:EWC&LMs. In *Proceedings of the Fourth Conference on Machine Translation (Volume 2: Shared Task Papers, Day 1)*, pages 364–373, Florence, Italy. Association for Computational Linguistics.

Sandeep Subramanian, Oleksii Hrinchuk, Virginia Adams, and Oleksii Kuchaiev. 2021. Nvidia nemo's neural machine translation systems for english-german and english-russian news and biomedical tasks at wmt21. In *Proceedings of the Sixth Conference on Machine Translation*, pages 197–204, Online. Association for Computational Linguistics.

Zhengkun Tian, Jiangyan Yi, Jianhua Tao, Ye Bai, Shuai Zhang, and Zhengqi Wen. 2020. Spike-triggered non-autoregressive transformer for end-to-end speech recognition. In *Interspeech 2020, 21st Annual Conference of the International Speech Communication Association, Virtual Event, Shanghai, China, 25-29 October 2020*, pages 5026–5030. ISCA.

Chau Tran, Shruti Bhosale, James Cross, Philipp Koehn, Sergey Edunov, and Angela Fan. 2021. Facebook ai's wmt21 news translation task submission. In *Proceedings of the Sixth Conference on Machine Translation*, pages 205–215, Online. Association for Computational Linguistics.

Ashish Vaswani, Noam Shazeer, Niki Parmar, Jakob Uszkoreit, Llion Jones, Aidan N Gomez, Ł ukasz Kaiser, and Illia Polosukhin. 2017. Attention is all you need. In *Advances in Neural Information Processing Systems*, volume 30. Curran Associates, Inc.

Feng Wang, Guoyizhe Wei, Qiao Liu, Jinxiang Ou, Hairong Lv, et al. 2021a. Boost neural networks by checkpoints. *Advances in Neural Information Processing Systems*, 34:19719–19729.

Longyue Wang, Mu Li, Fangxu Liu, Shuming Shi, Zhaopeng Tu, Xing Wang, Shuangzhi Wu, Jiali Zeng, and Wen Zhang. 2021b. Tencent translation system for the wmt21 news translation task. In *Proceedings of the Sixth Conference on Machine Translation*, pages 216–224, Online. Association for Computational Linguistics.

Yongqiang Wang, Abdelrahman Mohamed, Duc Le, Chunxi Liu, Alex Xiao, Jay Mahadeokar, Hongzhao Huang, Andros Tjandra, Xiaohui Zhang, Frank Zhang, Christian Fuegen, Geoffrey Zweig, and Michael L. Seltzer. 2020. Transformer-based acoustic modeling for hybrid speech recognition. *ICASSP 2020 - 2020 IEEE International Conference on Acoustics, Speech and Signal Processing (ICASSP)*, pages 6874–6878.

Daimeng Wei, Zongyao Li, Zhanglin Wu, Zhengzhe Yu, Xiaoyu Chen, Hengchao Shang, Jiaxin Guo, Minghan Wang, Lizhi Lei, Min Zhang, Hao Yang, and Ying Qin. 2021. Hw-tsc's participation in the wmt 2021 news translation shared task. In *Proceedings of the Sixth Conference on Machine Translation*, pages 225–231, Online. Association for Computational Linguistics.

Jingyi Zhang and Josef van Genabith. 2019. DFKI-NMT submission to the WMT19 news translation task. In *Proceedings of the Fourth Conference on Machine Translation (Volume 2: Shared Task Papers, Day 1)*, pages 440–444, Florence, Italy. Association for Computational Linguistics.

Yu Zhang, James Qin, Daniel S. Park, Wei Han, Chung-Cheng Chiu, Ruoming Pang, Quoc V. Le, and Yonghui Wu. 2020. Pushing the limits of semi-supervised learning for automatic speech recognition. *ArXiv*, abs/2010.10504.

Guangxiang Zhao, Xu Sun, Jingjing Xu, Zhiyuan Zhang, and Liangchen Luo. 2019. Muse: Parallel multi-scale attention for sequence to sequence learning. *arXiv preprint arXiv:1911.09483*.

Appendix A Additional Results

As mentioned, only results on de-en are reported in Sec.4. In this section, further results on the other datasets are shown.

The data statistics are summarized in Tab.1.

dataset	vocab	train pairs	test pairs
ru-en	10k	150k	5.5k
de-en	10k	160k	6.8k
es-en	10k	170k	5.6k
en-ro	20k	0.6M	2.0k
en-de	44k	4.0M	3.0k
zh-en	47k	17.0M	4.0k

Table 1: Statistics of the datasets.

Fig.8 shows the last-K simple mean BLEU and DEVPPL curves on ru-en. As can be seen, the degradation of the interpolated models starts to happen when checkpoints with worse perplexities are included into the mixture.

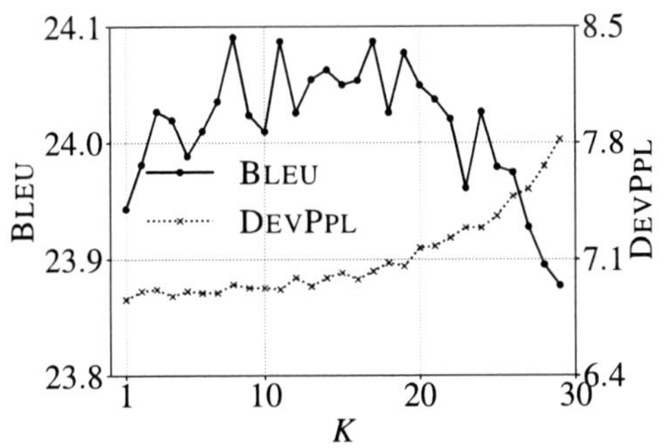

Figure 8: Last-K simple mean on ru-en.

Fig.9 shows the top-K simple mean BLEU and DEVPPL curves on es-en. Note that when all checkpoints are of decent DEVPPL, the BLEU score of the averaged model is more stable.

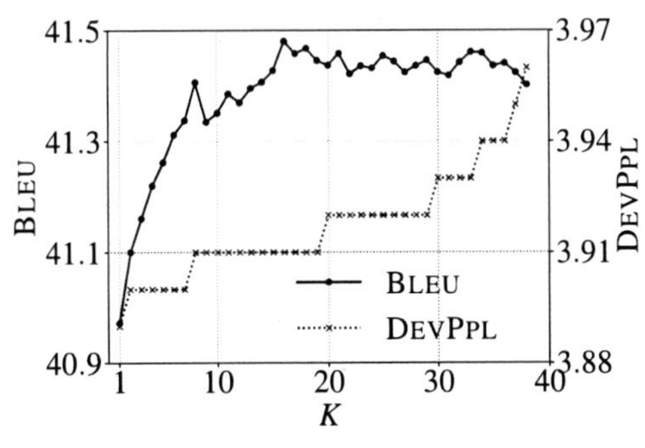

Figure 9: Top-K simple mean on es-en.

Fig.10 shows the top-10 weighted sum on en-ro. Earlier in Fig.4, we select last-40 checkpoints to include some bad-performing checkpoints. Here, the top-10 checkpoints are selected and it is clear from the figure that there is not much to be gained when tuning the interpolation weight via the temperature hyperparameter τ.

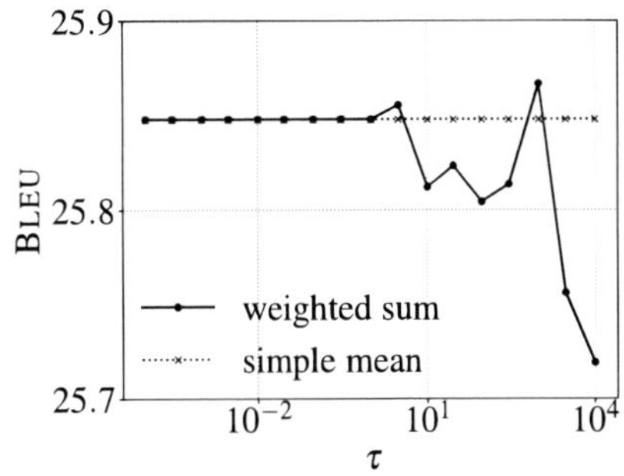

Figure 10: Top-10 weighted sum on en-ro.

In Fig.11, we plot the neighborhood of three checkpoints on en-de. Here, One good checkpoint and two relatively worse checkpoints are included to show the difference compared with Fig.7. As can be seen, the area near the good checkpoint is overall brighter and the region closer to the two worse checkpoints is darker. Although noise is visible from the plot, it is clear that there is not a specific optima where the BLEU score of the checkpoint-averaged model is significantly better.

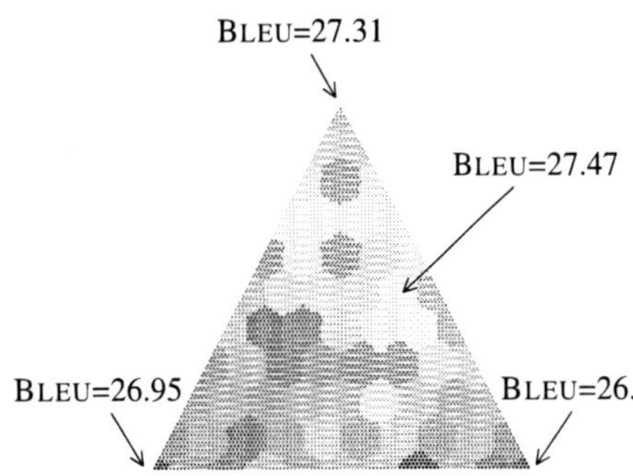

Figure 11: Neighborhood of three checkpoints on en-de. One good checkpoint and two relatively worse checkpoints are included to show the difference compared with Fig.7. No post-processing of splitting hyphenated compound words is done (See `https://github.com/tensorflow/tensor2tensor/blob/master/tensor2tensor/utils/get_ende_bleu.sh`.). The hexagons are artifacts from plotting because a denser grid of points is used in the plot than in checkpoint averaging and the dots are colored by querying the nearest neighbor in the checkpoint averaging grid.

In Fig.12, we further plot the neighborhood of three checkpoints on zh-en. Here, two good checkpoint and one relatively worse checkpoint are included to show the difference compared with Fig.7. From the figure, it can be seen that, overall, the interpolation closer to the two good checkpoints is better than when the worse checkpoint has a larger weight. Although +0.4% absolute BLEU score improvement is possible, there is no further improvement to be gained when tuning the interpolation weights.

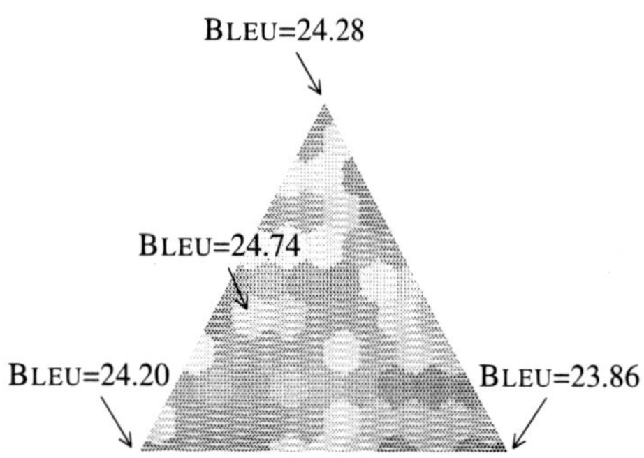

Figure 12: Neighborhood of three checkpoints on zh-en. Two good checkpoint and one relatively worse checkpoint are included to show the difference compared with Fig.7. The hexagons are artifacts from plotting because a denser grid of points is used in the plot than in checkpoint averaging and the dots are colored by querying the nearest neighbor in the checkpoint averaging grid.

Modeling Referential Gaze in Task-oriented Settings of Varying Referential Complexity

Özge Alaçam[1], Eugen Ruppert[2], Ganeshan Malhotra[2*]
Chris Biemann[2] and Sina Zarrieß[1]
[1]Computational Linguistics, University of Bielefeld, Bielefeld, Germany
[2]Language Technology, University of Hamburg, Hamburg, Germany
{oezge.alacam, sina.zarriess} @uni-bielefeld.de,
{ganeshan.malhotra, eugen.ruppert, chris.biemann} @uni-hamburg.de

Abstract

Referential gaze is a fundamental phenomenon for psycholinguistics and human-human communication. However, modeling referential gaze for real-world scenarios, e.g. for task-oriented communication, is lacking the well-deserved attention from the NLP community. In this paper, we address this challenging issue by proposing a novel multimodal NLP task; namely predicting when the gaze is referential. We further investigate how to model referential gaze and transfer gaze features to adapt to unseen situated settings that target different referential complexities than the training environment. We train (i) a sequential attention-based LSTM model and (ii) a multivariate transformer encoder architecture to predict whether the gaze is on a referent object. The models are evaluated on the three complexity datasets. The results indicate that the gaze features can be transferred not only among various similar tasks and scenes but also across various complexity levels. Taking the referential complexity of a scene into account is important for successful target prediction using gaze parameters especially when there is not much data for fine-tuning.

1 Introduction

In a situated interaction, interlocutors produce and interpret complex communicative signals and intertwine their verbal utterances with non-verbal signals like gaze. For instance, when referring to objects in the visual environment, speakers tend to fixate the target referent, listeners gaze at the objects they believe to be referred to by the speaker and, importantly, listeners monitor the speaker's gaze in case it provides reliable information about the referent (Staudte and Crocker, 2011b). In noisy environments, listeners (that need to resolve references to objects) might even face situations where

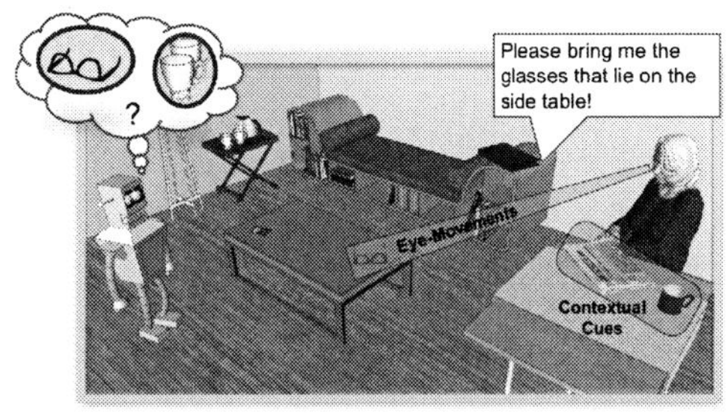

Figure 1: An example task-oriented scenario

gaze provides a more reliable cue than spoken words. For example, in the scenario depicted in Figure 1, "the glasses" in the command illustrates an ambiguous reference and during human-human communication, such ambiguities can be easily resolved via tracking referential gaze.

Referential gaze as a communication modality is a well researched / fundamental phenomenon in Psycholinguistics and Cognitive Science (Koller et al., 2012; Staudte and Crocker, 2011a; Prasov and Chai, 2008). Mainstream Natural Language Processing (NLP) systems — on the other hand — still usually employ language-only approaches, where the performance is highly dependent on the completeness of the language modality. Despite the fact that reference resolution in visual environments has become a very popular task in recent NLP and Computer Vision research (Kazemzadeh et al., 2014; Schlangen et al., 2016; De Vries et al., 2017; Cirik et al., 2018; Yu et al., 2018; Kalpakchi and Boye, 2019; Chen et al., 2020), there is very little work on reference resolution models that exploit eye gaze for this task. They fall short on modeling referential gaze for realistic scenarios for task-oriented communication that go beyond simple settings. One main reason behind this is human gaze's intricate nature of being complex (a multivariate sequence) and multi-functional (e.g. referential gaze, social gaze and so on) (Somashekarappa et al., 2020). In this paper, we propose a novel task of predicting when the gaze is referential during

* Remote research-intern at the Language Technology Group, University of Hamburg

Findings of the Association for Computational Linguistics: AACL-IJCNLP 2022, pages 197–210
November 20–23, 2022. ©2022 Association for Computational Linguistics

the communication, aiming at modeling referential gaze for various multimodal settings.

Most recently, daily devices like laptops start to utilize eye-tracking technology (Brousseau et al., 2020; Rogers, 2019; Khamis et al., 2018). As a result, incorporating eye-movements in language comprehension models is an inevitable goal for NLP emerging from these developments, and this motivates systematic research on the interaction of different communicative modalities. However, the collection and pre-processing of eye-movement data is a very costly process, and this is another main reason why there are only a few large eye-movement datasets available (Alaçam et al., 2020; Wilming et al., 2017; Ehinger et al., 2009).

Eye-movements are highly influenced by bottom-up perceptual and top-down conceptual properties of the task (e.g. free viewing, search, etc.) and the properties of the visual environment (Einhäuser et al., 2008; Zelinsky et al., 2006; Henderson, 2003). Besides, their patterns (pupil size, saccade velocity, fixation duration, etc.) are very user-dependent (Rayner et al., 2007). All these factors introduce challenges in (i) learning meaningful patterns from limited data, (ii) generalizing well enough to different kinds of situations of real-world complexities and (iii) successfully incorporating it to NLP systems for reference resolution and meaning recovery. To mitigate these problems, transfer learning can be used to adapt the knowledge obtained from one setting to another, benefiting from its added generalization capabilities.

2 Background

In this paper, we apply transformer-based time-series modeling and transfer learning to the phenomenon of referential gaze. Section 2.1 discusses the background for technical modeling, and Section 2.2 introduces referential gaze.

2.1 Transfer Learning and Time-series Multivariate Classification

Time-series analysis have been generally approached using more traditional machine learning techniques such as XGboost (Chen and Guestrin, 2016), and Dynamic Time Wrapping (Lei et al., 2019). There has been also successful recurrent models like RNNs (LSTMs and GRUs) with additional enhancements to address the intricacies of multivariate time series (Wu et al., 2020; Bianchi et al., 2019). By taking the close relation of the referential gaze with language, LSTM solutions are considered as an adequate baseline for the task.

With the development of the auto-encoder architectures (Vaswani et al., 2017), most machine learning domains are dominated by transformer solutions. Transformer models for uni-variate time-series forecasting and classification has been studied broadly. However, as eye-trackers can record multiple parameters simultaneously (such as velocity, acceleration, pupil size, etc.), this makes the collected data a multivariate time series. Despite the simultaneity, many of these features might have their unique onsets and offsets in regards to changes in the top-down (*mental, cognitive*) or bottom-up (*perceptual*) factors. Thus, modeling referential gaze and classification based on a set of various raw gaze features requires a multivariate approach, which has recently received some attention in the literature.

Liu et al. (2021)'s simple but effective solution of combining a gating mechanism with transformer architectures seems to provide state-of-the-art results for time-series forecasting. A novel approach on supervised and unsupervised representation learning for a series of multivariate tasks (such as regression, classification and forecasting) has been proposed by Zerveas et al. (2021). Pretraining and fine-tuning procedures exhibit high resemblance to language modeling, but they are modified to process multivariate time series. The model only uses an encoder part, this provides great computational power. Their unsupervised pre-training scheme, evaluated on several benchmark datasets, surpasses the performance of all current state-of-the-art supervised methods including their own.

Moreover, transformer architectures can extract patterns from low-level features without extensive feature engineering because of their multi-layer structure and effective attention mechanisms. This might have particular advantages for eye-movement processing since many approaches uses fixation-based parameters where a series of rule-based assumptions are needed to define a fixation. And each researcher and each eye-tracking device producer might come up with their own criteria. Being able to work on low-level features might eliminate these inconsistencies.

2.2 Referential Gaze

Prior research indicates that incorporating eye movements of a speaker or a listener improves the performance of many NLP tasks, e.g. in predicting / resolving which entity is being referred to in a complex visual environment (Mitev et al., 2018; Koleva et al., 2015). As shown by Koleva et al. (2015), listener gaze can be highly beneficial to predict which entity is being referred to in the sentence and to understand the intention of the listener when the targets and their referentially possible competitors are located close-by. A gaze-contingent system may react to changes in its environment by tracking the probability of the fixations per each item in the scene over time. However, Henderson et al. (2009) point out that the success of such a system is dependent on utilizing an effective combination of several fixation parameters. A study by Klerke and Plank (2019) indicates that globally-aggregated measures can also capture the central tendency or variability of gaze data instead of customizing towards individual participants.

Only a few studies embed a set of eye-movements (e.g. velocity, acceleration, pupil size) into a rich vector space (Sood et al., 2020; Takmaz et al., 2020; Park et al., 2019; Karessli et al., 2017). Nevertheless, those models are limited to relatively simple scenes or reading activities (e.g. CMCL Shared Task 2021-2022 (Hollenstein et al., 2021; Barrett and Hollenstein, 2020). Situated language understanding in a referentially complex environment imposes a different level of challenge as it requires more complex visual search due to ambiguity resolution among possible options.

3 Approach

We investigate the modeling of eye-movements and ask whether different referential complexities need individual referential gaze models or whether we can use transfer learning (pre-training on larger collections and fine-tuning on task-specific dataset). We build a model that predicts when the gaze of a participant is referential, i.e., when she looks at the target object referred to by the speaker. For a low-complexity scene (i.e., with few objects) and an unambiguous verbal description, this task can be considered as straightforward, since the user will quickly identify the target and not have to visually search for it. In a complex visual scene — with occluded objects and complex or ambiguous verbal descriptions — eye-movements can provide highly distinctive information to resolve ambiguities, but may also show more complex and challenging gaze patterns in return. Therefore, in this study, we minimize the contribution of accompanying linguistic and contextual information and focus on the influence and capabilities of gaze features.

3.1 Task

We frame the learning problem as a supervised sequence tagging task where the input is a multivariate time series (i.e., with multiple eye-movement parameters) and the output is a sequence of binary labels. The label indicates whether the participant's gaze is currently referential. Thus, we train our model to predict for each time frame whether the gaze of the participant is on the target object while the spoken sentence unfolds.

Given that verbal descriptions of referents vary in their complexity, different labeling schemes for "target objects" can be adopted. To illustrate, the second referring expression in Table 1 has a single *global target*, i.e., *cage_1*, as the object of the intended action. But, the expression mentions further referents (*table_1* and *man_1*, see Figure 2a) which are *local targets* that are likely to be gazed at as well. To account for this, we distinguish two different task settings: (i) in *Task-A*, we consider time frames as referential, where the gaze is on the global target; in (i) *Task-B*, we label all time frames as referential where the gaze is on a global or local target object.

3.2 Referential Complexity

Referential complexity is a complex notion in itself and has been investigated in different fields and with different terminologies, cf. Clarke et al. (2013). In this study, we use the complexity classification provided by Alaçam et al. (2020)'s Eye4Ref Benchmark to account for reproducibility. Thus, we investigate three complexity levels — LOW, MEDIUM and HIGH — which differ in the way the scene and descriptions are composed. Sample stimuli and the basic descriptive statistics of each complexity level are given in Figure 2. In the LOW referential complexity, the focus lies on identifying the target and the targeted location with no ambiguity. In the HIGH and MEDIUM conditions, for each mentioned object in the scene, there are also distractor objects that share properties with the targets (e.g. type or color). Unlike other two, the HIGH condition contains not only objects but also people and actions.

Table 1: Sample (translated) sentences with varying complexities *(Experiment language is German)*

Complexity	Sentence
High	It is a book on a couch that he reads quietly.
High	It is a cage on a table that he moves. (Figure 2a)
Medium	Bring me the blue mug from the counter. (Figure 2b)
Medium	Bring me the mug, the blue mug, from the counter. (Figure 2b)
Low	Put the mug on the counter, on the blue one.
Low	Put the mug on the counter, next to the blue one. (Figure 2c)

(a) Set-1: HIGH RC: 28 participants, 36 scenes, 548K timestamps

(b) Set-2: MEDIUM RC: 27 participants, 46 scenes, 565K timestamps

(c) Set-3: LOW RC: 21 participants, 17 scenes, 290K timestamps

Figure 2: Sample scenes and descriptive statistics for the three referential complexity (RC) Eye4Ref datasets

4 Experiments

4.1 Data

We use the Eye4Ref Benchmark that consists of three datasets (Alaçam et al., 2020) where gaze data was collected from human participants on referentially complex situated settings using a *SR Eyelink 1000 Plus* eye tracker with a sampling rate of 1000 Hz. For all datasets, the eye-tracking data of the participants were recorded while they are presented with images and accompanying spoken descriptions like (*put object X onto Y*) and descriptions like (*there is an object X that Y interacts with*), as summarized in Table 1. The language of the experiments is German. For simplicity, in our illustrations, we use the translated sentences from the dataset. Referential complexity of the studies is defined in terms of visual manipulations (e.g. number of objects, visibility of the target items, presence of distractor objects that share the same class with the target objects) and linguistic ones (e.g. the position of the disambiguating word in a sentence). For the details of the dataset and data collection, please refer to (Alaçam et al., 2020).

4.2 Gaze Feature Vector and Labels

Employing a simple approach which uses only one selected gaze parameter (e.g. gaze location at one point of time) may yield successful results only if the number of objects is limited (low referential complexity). Furthermore, a lot of assumptions need to be made to decide when the aggregated group of eye-movements forms a fixation or saccade. Thus, regarding the goals of the project addressing various complexities, an elaborated parameter selection is required to establish crossmodal mapping. We use a time-series format that requires fewer assumptions on the raw data. For computational efficiency reasons, we use binning, where each bin corresponds to a cumulative sampling for 20 ms such as average fixation duration, gaze velocity, or list of targeted area of interest (AOIs). Eye4Ref provides pre-processed data for each scene and participant in each dataset. For each timestamp (20 ms bin), all linguistic, contextual and gaze features are provided in a CSV format. The number of the features (on average 230 values) is dependent on the number of items in the scene. Forty-five of them correspond to participant- and study-related information as well as the set of eye-movement parameters. Approximately 180 values correspond to one-hot encoded fixation location parameters addressing all the objects in the respective scene, indicating whether the gaze is fixated on that object. For our purposes, we have reduced the size of this scene-specific vector part to two scene-agnostic binary output variables: whether the gaze is (i) on the target object or (ii) on a communicatively relevant object (all referents). The dimension of the final fixed-sized feature vector is 16, consisting of only gaze and scene information such as gaze acceleration, velocity, pupil diameter, object count of the scene as a general referential complexity measure, etc (see Appendix A.1). In order to be able to generalize better, gaze coordinates of the eye-movements are not included in the training since this information would be only useful in static images, where the objects have a fixed location.

4.2.1 Normalization Parameters

One of the manipulated variables in this study is the scope of normalization for the eye-movement parameters. We normalized the continuous scale gaze features in three ways: (i) within participant (across items), (ii) within dataset (across participants and items), and (iii) across all datasets. These parameters are directly retrieved from the original dataset. Since eye-movements are highly task and participant dependent, one common approach is to train models for each user and each task, which is a big challenge for incorporating eye-movements. On the other hand, with the advancements deep learning methods, this problem can be overcome through transfer learning and pre-training. This experimentation allows us to investigate to what extent a normalization scope should be extended for a successful transfer.

4.3 Splits and Testing Conditions

Each complexity set has been split item-wise into training (80 %), validation (10 %) and test (10 %) sets. This means that each set has distinct items in their repertoire. To investigate the effect of size and diversity of training data, we introduce the COMBINED condition, where the new sets are created by concatenating the respective subsets of all conditions. In the end, we obtain 16 train–test combinations (Appendix A.5).

- Within-complexity tests: training and testing on the same complexity e.g. $\text{Train}_{\text{LOW}} \rightarrow \text{Test}_{\text{LOW}}$
- Data-diversity tests: training on COMBINED and testing on each complexity condition e.g. $\text{Train}_{\text{COMBINED}} \rightarrow \text{Test}_{\text{LOW}}$
- Cross-complexity tests: training and testing in a cross-complexity way e.g. $\text{Train}_{\text{LOW}} \rightarrow \text{Test}_{\text{MEDIUM}}$

5 Model Architectures

To establish the performance of within- and cross-complexity performances, we employ two deep learning approaches; (i) LSTM as a sequential base model and (ii) transformer architecture (Vaswani et al., 2017). We use a transfer learning approach to establish the compatibility of different complexities. This is done because there are not many large datasets available and we want to study options of how an available benchmark (Eye4Ref) can be utilized as a baseline that is then adapted on a small set of individual, task-specific data. Transfer learning only trains the final layer (*the output layer* and all dense layers are frozen), thus the input representation stays the same. Therefore, we further experiment with fine-tuning the layers to arrive at an input encoding that better fits the small target data. The full code, and model summaries are provided under supplementary material.

Baseline LSTM Model We experimented with two variations of a bi-directional LSTM architecture (Hochreiter and Schmidhuber, 1997). Since we are dealing with a sequence classification task, attention mechanisms can help to improve the performance of our model by guiding the model to give more weight to the relevant time-frames in the sequence. In the second variation, we use a variant of self-attention (Bahdanau et al., 2015) known as the Sequential Self Attention by Keras. The details of the models are provided in Appendix A.3.

Time-series Transformer Model (TST) Inspired by Zerveas et al. (2021), we utilize their working solution (TST for classification) as our Transformer architecture[1]. For the sake of systematicity, the scope of this paper is restricted to supervised pretraining and further fine-tuning, by leaving unsupervised pretraining to future studies.

For input, we create sequences of 25 timestamps, spanning 500 ms of input data. We use class weights to treat the imbalance in the size of the datasets. If the model predicts a referential gaze for a timestep sequence, then the most visited area-of-interest during that period is accessed and compared against the true label. The final representation vectors corresponding to all time steps are concatenated into a single vector (an input vector). For the classification problem, the predictions are passed through a softmax function to obtain a distribution over classes, and its cross-entropy with the categorical ground truth labels will be the sample loss.

[1]For the details, please visit the original paper. The modified code is available at `https://gitlab.com/alacam/referential-gaze-modeling`

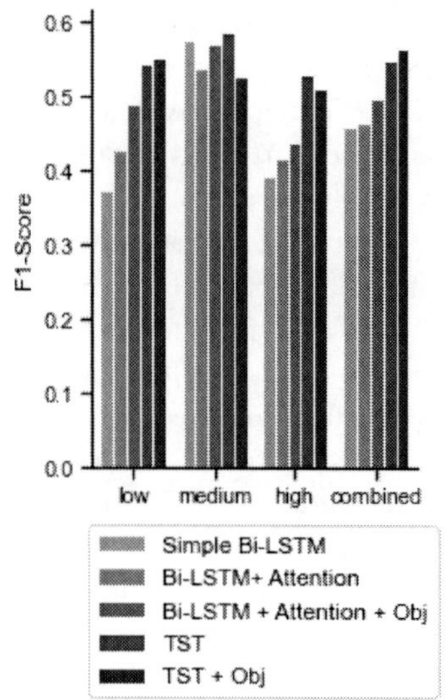

Figure 3: F1-Scores for various model variations on the MEDIUM complexity model

Each training sample, which is a multivariate time series of varying length l and 18 different variables, constitutes a sequence of l feature vectors such as $[x1, x2, ..., xl]$. The original feature vectors are linearly projected onto a 50- (for LSTM) and 64-dimensional vector space, (for TST) where d is the dimension of the model.

The first setting (*Supervised Pretraining*) is a simple use of pretrained models after training the models on the training sets via supervised learning. The parameters are provided in Appendix A.3 and runtime details in Appendix A.4. In the second variation (*+fine-tuned*), we do fine-tuning on the pre-trained model by further training with a lower learning rate on the validation set for 20 epochs. With this, we aim to improve the results by incrementally adapting the pre-trained gaze features to new data.

6 Results

6.1 Model Variations

Before looking into transfer learning, we test for appropriate model architectures for learning gaze parameters. We choose MEDIUM condition to compare the variations; (i) simple bi-LSTM , (ii) attention-based LSTM, (iii) attention-based LSTM with object count parameter, (iv) TST (time series transformer) without object count and (v) the previous condition with object count. As shown in Figure 3, on MEDIUM condition, incorporating attention mechanism is crucial for LSTM architecture. In addition, including the number of objects in the scene as a complexity feature boosts the performance. When the object count (as an indicator of referential complexity) is excluded from the feature vector during training with the LSTM model, the F1-Scores drops on average by .06, while both COMBINED and MEDIUM benefit from this parameter. TST variations beats the LSTM models in all conditions. Yet, unlike the LSTM model, including object count only benefits the low and combined condition with small margin but impairs the medium and high condition.

6.2 Normalization Parameters

Figure 4 shows each TST model's performance on the three normalization scopes. Within-participant normalization is the most simple approach where each parameter collected within a trial are "min-max" normalized producing values between 0 and 1. For within-study normalization (WS), "min-max" normalization is applied by taking all the trials collected for each study separately. Across-study (AS) normalization is the most comprehensive approach since all gaze parameters are normalized by taking all produced values for that parameter in the entire benchmark. WP normalization produces comparable scores to more global approaches. Using more sophisticated methods seems to be beneficial especially for fine-tuning and the long-tail conditions such as LOW and HIGH. These results indicate that if the training size is limited or has different referential complexity than the target set, applying more global way of normalization might be preferred.

6.3 Within-Complexity Results

On target referent prediction (Task-A), the negative class has a proportion between 87 and 92%, rendering the task of identifying the sparser positive class somewhat difficult. When we take all referents into account (Task-B), the most frequent negative class has a share between 68 and 75%. All within-complexity test results beat their (most frequent class) baseline on the accuracy metric ($\text{Low}_{\text{baseline}}$: 0.683, $\text{Medium}_{\text{baseline}}$: 0.755, $\text{High}_{\text{baseline}}$: 0.728, $\text{Combined}_{\text{baseline}}$: 0.73), indicating that even with gaze information alone, communicative object prediction is possible.

Within-complexity results are provided in Figure 5 (details in Appendix A.6). Since further fine-tuning does not make sense for the within complexity conditions, fine-tuning values are marked

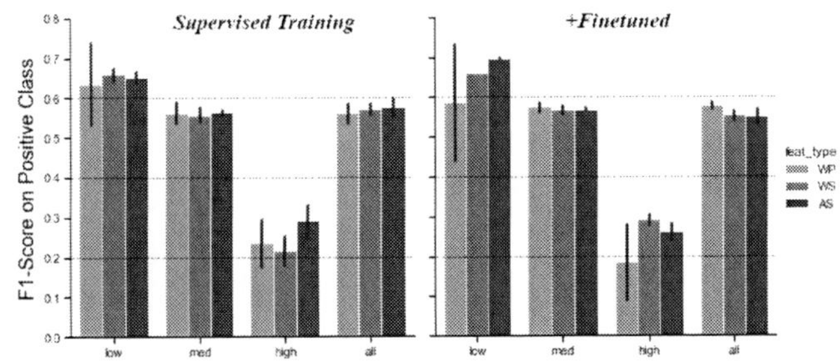

Figure 4: F1-scores (on the positive class) for varying normalization scopes

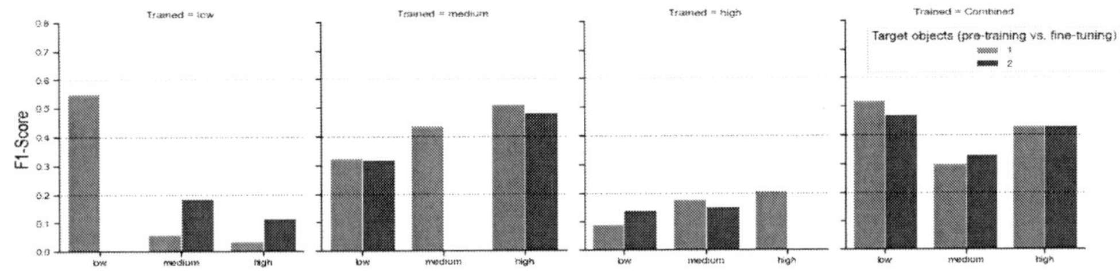

(a) Task-A: LSTM Model for Global Target Objects

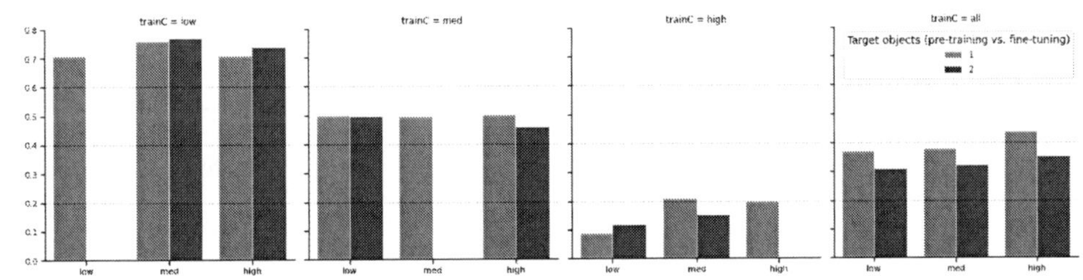

(b) Task-A: TST Model for Global Target Objects

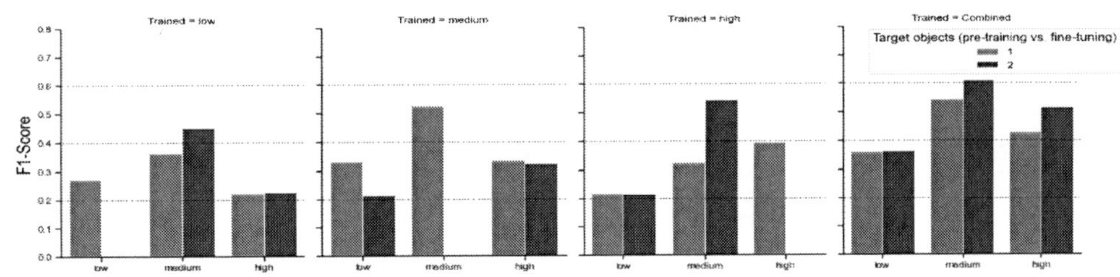

(c) Task-B: LSTM Model for Local Target Objects

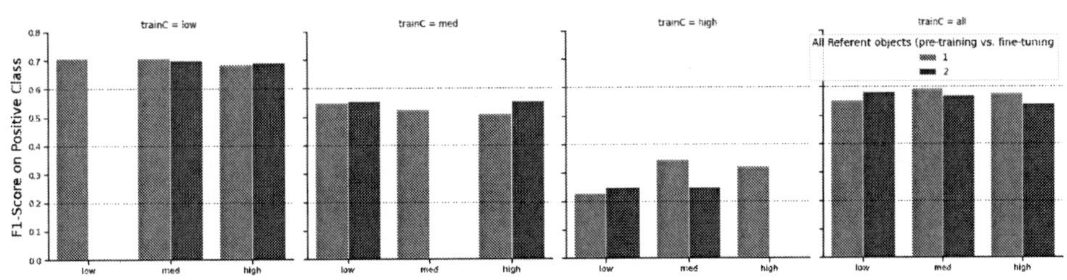

(d) Task-B: TST Model for Local Target Objects

Figure 5: F1-scores on the positive class for Task-A and Task-B. Light green corresponds to pre-training, and the dark green to fine-tuning.

as empty in the graphs and as non-applicable (NA) on the Tables. Here we interpret the results from pre-training and testing on the same conditions. For the Task-A (referential gaze on target), transformer model (TST) produces a better performance overall; the within complexity train-test cycle resulted in $+0.15\%$ better for the LOW case compared to the LSTM Model, $+0.06\%$ for the MEDIUM. And there is slight decrease -0.02% for the HIGH condition. The results for the Task-B is less conclusive. While TST performs better for the LOW condition to a substantial degree $+0.20\%$, LSTM's performance surpasses TST on the HIGH condition $+0.22\%$. And there is no difference in terms of performance on the MEDIUM condition.

6.4 Effect of Data Diversity

Results from training on COMBINED and testing on each condition shows the effect of using a larger and well representative dataset that contains various referential complexity settings, shown in the right-most graphs in Figure 5. Here, we observe that with rich data variety, without transfer learning, good results on both target and any referent prediction can be achieved. For the Task-A, the COMBINED condition provides the second best solution for the HIGH condition (almost comparable to the MEDIUM). In terms of model architecture, the TST model displays an advantage over LSTM in supervised learning from rich data. On the other hand, with further fine-tuning, LSTM results approach and even exceed the TST scores.

6.5 Cross-Complexity Results

Figure 5 shows the F1-scores (on the positive class) when transferring the LSTM and TST models across complexities (see Appendix A.6 for further details). The light green bars show results for pre-trained models, and the dark ones refer to the fine-tuned models. Overall, the most striking result is that the TST model trained in the LOW condition transfers very well to the MEDIUM and HIGH condition, even without fine-tuning. In effect, the overall best results on MEDIUM and HIGH are achieved by the TST model that is trained on the LOW condition. This is the case for both Task-A and Task-B (see the leftmost column in Figure 5). Generally, the TST model seems to benefit little from fine-tuning which may indicate that this additional training step introduces overfitting. This seems to be the pattern while testing on lower complexities than the training one (e.g. $\text{Train}_{\text{High}}$–$\text{Test}_{\text{Medium}}$, or $\text{Train}_{\text{Combined}}$–$\text{Test}_{\text{Low}}$) In contrast, the fine-tuning is highly instrumental on the LSTM's performance. Unlike TST, LSTM model is better at generalizing from the MEDIUM condition.

Moreover, training on the HIGH condition and testing on conditions of lower complexity does not seem to be successful in any model (see the third column in Figure 5). Overall, training on the MEDIUM condition achieves a medium accuracy which remains at a medium level in the other conditions. This pattern indicates that it is important to do the pretraining of gaze embeddings on a condition where the model can achieve high accuracy in referential gaze predictions. This leads to gaze representations that can be transferred well to other conditions.

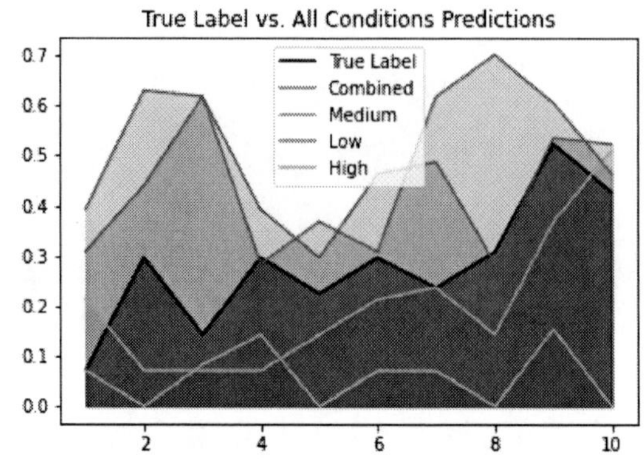

Figure 6: Aggregated model predictions on one image (medium condition) against the aggregated truth labels (from all participants)

At first glance, a stronger prediction performance on the LOW complexity is expected compared to other conditions. However, only TST model performs in line with this assumption. The number of objects is relatively small and has a low range (10 to 12) for all the scenes in that condition. It is possible that after detecting the relevant items, other objects are also being looked at by the participants until the trial ends (non-referential gaze). LSTM recurrent mechanism might be less sensitive about distinguishing referential gaze from other kinds of eye behaviors (like free viewing).

6.6 Scene-Specific Analysis

Further scene-specific analysis on the predictions provides insights about the temporal dimension of such predictions. However, first it should be noted that each participant might look at the referent objects at different point of time even while they are looking at the same image and hearing the same audio. This means that each participant produces unique ground truth labels (Appendix A.7). This makes the error analysis extremely challenging on referential gaze data. To address this issue, we believe that a sound method for error analysis will need to be developed and tested with care.

Although a full-scale error analysis is not in the scope of this study, we can look at the aggregated data of all participants who saw the same scene. Figure 6 shows ground truth and TST models' predictions on a specific image. For each time interval (in the range of 1 to 10), we have aggregated the data collected from all participants in this condition as ground truth and model predictions respectively. For the sake of readability, individual model comparisons to ground truth have been presented separately per condition in the Appendix, Figure 9 to Figure 12.

This preliminary analysis supports our quantitative findings on transferring our referential gaze model from Section 6.5. Thus, the models trained on the LOW and COMBINED conditions (green and blue line) achieve the most stable prediction over the course of the sequence. Furthermore, the analysis indicates that the temporal dimension of the prediction is central. While the models exhibit difficulty to predict a referential gaze in the beginning of the sentence, the predictions become more reliable towards the end, except for the HIGH condition. When we look at the more stable second-half, we observe that the only under-generating model (producing false negatives) is still the HIGH condition. On the other hand, over-generation (false-positives) occurs more frequently with COMBINED and LOW conditions in the first half.

6.7 Summary

We now summarize the main findings from our investigation into the modeling of referential gaze. First of all, our results give some clear indications with respect to choice of model architecture and normalization procedures. The time-series transformer model (TST) outperforms the more basic LSTM architecture in most settings. Normalization of gaze features affects performance and across-study normalization is beneficial for low-resource or transfer settings.

Our results also clearly reveal that transferring gaze features between conditions and settings is far from trivial. Within-complexity results show that referential gaze prediction is possible from gaze features alone. All models beat the majority baselines in Task-A and Task-B (Section 6.3). Across-complexity results, however, demonstrate that some of the models are highly tuned to their specific communicative setting and do not generalize well.

The most robust models, in terms of generalization capabilities, are the TST model trained jointly on all conditions (COMBINED), and the TST model trained on the LOW condition only. Thus, our main finding is that gaze embeddings learned with models that achieve high accuracy in referential gaze prediction transfer well to other settings, even when they are trained on small amounts of data. We believe that this points into a very promising direction for future work on integrating NLP models with gaze processing.

7 Conclusion

Attending to referential gaze of the interlocutors is fundamental to face-to-face communication, yet still mostly ignored by the NLP community. In this study, we experiment with two deep learning methods (LSTM and transformer) to model referential gaze. We target gaze-only reference resolution and test how we can transfer the gaze features among various scene settings. Depending on the task (target or all-referent prediction) and the complexity level, the models exhibit different advantages. While TST is successful at generalizing from low complexities to higher ones and without the need of extra fine-tuning step, LSTM beats TST at generalizing from the MEDIUM conditions. But its performance is positively affected by fine-tuning.

One of the challenges of eye-movement modeling originates from being highly individual, task and environment dependent, making the generalization is more challenging. The results on different levels of gaze parameter normalization indicate that long-tail conditions clearly benefit from using more globally normalization. Within-complexity comparisons show that gaze features based on one scenario can be useful for similar new scenes. However, adopting among various complexities using pretrained models (with or without fine-tuning) displays encouraging results. Yet these result also confirm the challenging nature of the task and provide stepping stone for modeling referential gaze. Especially, the results are not trivial considering that we only use low-level gaze features. In addition to the gaze parameters, including the number of objects in the scene as a feature improves referential gaze prediction, indicating that this information makes the model more sensitive to various referential complexities.

References

Özge Alaçam, Eugen Ruppert, Amr R. Salama, Tobias Staron, and Wolfgang Menzel. 2020. Eye4ref: A multimodal eye movement dataset of referentially complex situations. In *Proceedings of the12th International Conference on Language Resources and Evaluation (LREC)*, page 2396–2404, Marseille, France.

Dzmitry Bahdanau, Kyunghyun Cho, and Yoshua Bengio. 2015. Neural machine translation by jointly learning to align and translate. In *3rd International Conference on Learning Representations*, pages 1–15, San Diego, CA, USA.

Maria Barrett and Nora Hollenstein. 2020. Sequence labelling and sequence classification with gaze: Novel uses of eye-tracking data for natural language processing. *Language and Linguistics Compass*, 14(11):1–16.

Filippo Maria Bianchi, Lorenzo Livi, Karl Øyvind Mikalsen, Michael Kampffmeyer, and Robert Jenssen. 2019. Learning representations of multivariate time series with missing data. *Pattern Recognition*, 96:106973.

Braiden Brousseau, Jonathan Rose, and Moshe Eizenman. 2020. Hybrid eye-tracking on a smartphone with cnn feature extraction and an infrared 3d model. *Sensors*, 20(2):543.

Tianqi Chen and Carlos Guestrin. 2016. XGBoost: A scalable tree boosting system. In *Proceedings of the 22nd ACM SIGKDD International Conference on Knowledge Discovery and Data Mining*, pages 785–794.

Zhenfang Chen, Peng Wang, Lin Ma, Kwan-Yee K Wong, and Qi Wu. 2020. Cops-ref: A new dataset and task on compositional referring expression comprehension. In *Proceedings of the IEEE/CVF Conference on Computer Vision and Pattern Recognition*, pages 10086–10095.

Volkan Cirik, Louis-Philippe Morency, and Taylor Berg-Kirkpatrick. 2018. Visual referring expression recognition: What do systems actually learn? In *Proceedings of the 2018 Conference of the North American Chapter of the Association for Computational Linguistics: Human Language Technologies, Volume 2 (Short Papers)*, pages 781–787, New Orleans, Louisiana.

Alasdair DF Clarke, Micha Elsner, and Hannah Rohde. 2013. Where's wally: The influence of visual salience on referring expression generation. *Frontiers in psychology*, 4:329.

Harm De Vries, Florian Strub, Sarath Chandar, Olivier Pietquin, Hugo Larochelle, and Aaron Courville. 2017. Guesswhat?! visual object discovery through multi-modal dialogue. In *Proceedings of the IEEE Conference on Computer Vision and Pattern Recognition*, pages 5503–5512.

Krista A Ehinger, Barbara Hidalgo-Sotelo, Antonio Torralba, and Aude Oliva. 2009. Modelling search for people in 900 scenes: A combined source model of eye guidance. *Visual cognition*, 17(6-7):945–978.

Wolfgang Einhäuser, Ueli Rutishauser, Christof Koch, et al. 2008. Task-demands can immediately reverse the effects of sensory-driven saliency in complex visual stimuli. *Journal of vision*, 8(2):2–2.

John M Henderson. 2003. Human gaze control during real-world scene perception. *Trends in cognitive sciences*, 7(11):498–504.

John M. Henderson and Tim J. Smith. 2009. How are eye fixation durations controlled during scene viewing? further evidence from a scene onset delay paradigm. *Visual Cognition*, 17(6-7):1055–1082.

Sepp Hochreiter and Jürgen Schmidhuber. 1997. Long short-term memory. *Neural computation*, 9(8):1735–1780.

Nora Hollenstein, Emmanuele Chersoni, Cassandra L. Jacobs, Yohei Oseki, Laurent Prévot, and Enrico Santus. 2021. CMCL 2021 shared task on eye-tracking prediction. In *Proceedings of the Workshop on Cognitive Modeling and Computational Linguistics*, pages 72–78, Online.

Dmytro Kalpakchi and Johan Boye. 2019. SpaceRefNet: A neural approach to spatial reference resolution in a real city environment. In *Proceedings of the 20th Annual SIGdial Meeting on Discourse and Dialogue*, pages 422–431.

Nour Karessli, Zeynep Akata, Bernt Schiele, and Andreas Bulling. 2017. Gaze embeddings for zero-shot image classification. In *Proceedings of the IEEE Conference on Computer Vision and Pattern Recognition*, pages 4525–4534.

Sahar Kazemzadeh, Vicente Ordonez, Mark Matten, and Tamara Berg. 2014. ReferItGame: Referring to objects in photographs of natural scenes. In *Proceedings of the 2014 Conference on Empirical Methods in Natural Language Processing (EMNLP)*, pages 787–798.

Mohamed Khamis, Florian Alt, and Andreas Bulling. 2018. The past, present, and future of gaze-enabled handheld mobile devices: survey and lessons learned. In *Proceedings of the 20th International Conference on Human-Computer Interaction with Mobile Devices and Services*, pages 1–17, Barcelona, Spain.

Sigrid Klerke and Barbara Plank. 2019. At a glance: The impact of gaze aggregation views on syntactic tagging. In *Proceedings of the Beyond Vision and LANguage: inTEgrating Real-world kNowledge (LANTERN)*, pages 51–61, Hong Kong, China.

Nikolina Koleva, Martín Villalba, Maria Staudte, and Alexander Koller. 2015. The impact of listener gaze on predicting reference resolution. In *Proceedings of the 53rd Annual Meeting of the Association for*

Computational Linguistics and the 7th International Joint Conference on Natural Language Processing, volume 2, pages 812–817, Beijing, China.

Alexander Koller, Konstantina Garoufi, Maria Staudte, and Matthew Crocker. 2012. Enhancing referential success by tracking hearer gaze. In *Proceedings of the 13th Annual Meeting of the Special Interest Group on Discourse and Dialogue*, pages 30–39, Stroudsburg, PA, USA.

Qi Lei, Jinfeng Yi, Roman Vaculin, Lingfei Wu, and Inderjit S Dhillon. 2019. Similarity preserving representation learning for time series clustering. In *International Joint Conferences on Artificial Intelligence*, volume 19, pages 2845–2851, Macao China.

Minghao Liu, Shengqi Ren, Siyuan Ma, Jiahui Jiao, Yizhou Chen, Zhiguang Wang, and Wei Song. 2021. Gated transformer networks for multivariate time series classification. *arXiv:2103.14438*.

Nikolina Mitev, Patrick Renner, Thies Pfeiffer, and Maria Staudte. 2018. Using listener gaze to refer in installments benefits understanding. In *Proceedings of the 40th Annual Meeting of the Cognitive Science Society*, pages 2122–2127, Madison, Wisconsin, USA.

Tom O'Malley, Elie Bursztein, James Long, François Chollet, Haifeng Jin, Luca Invernizzi, et al. 2019. Keras tuner. `https://github.com/keras-team/keras-tuner`.

Seonwook Park, Shalini De Mello, Pavlo Molchanov, Umar Iqbal, Otmar Hilliges, and Jan Kautz. 2019. Few-shot adaptive gaze estimation. In *Proceedings of the IEEE/CVF International Conference on Computer Vision (ICCV)*, pages 9368–9377, Seoul, Korea.

Zahar Prasov and Joyce Y Chai. 2008. What's in a Gaze? The Role of Eye-gaze in Reference Resolution in Multimodal Conversational Interfaces. In *Proceedings of the 13th international conference on Intelligent user interfaces*, pages 20–29, Gran Canaria, Spain.

Keith Rayner, Xingshan Li, Carrick C Williams, Kyle R Cave, and Arnold D Well. 2007. Eye movements during information processing tasks: Individual differences and cultural effects. *Vision research*, 47(21):2714–2726.

Sol Rogers. 2019. Seven Reasons Why Eye-tracking Will Fundamentally Change VR. Retrieved on 15.05.2020.

David Schlangen, Sina Zarrieß, and Casey Kennington. 2016. Resolving references to objects in photographs using the words-as-classifiers model. In *Proceedings of the 54th Annual Meeting of the Association for Computational Linguistics (Volume 1: Long Papers)*, pages 1213–1223, Berlin, Germany.

Vidya Somashekarappa, Christine Howes, and Asad Sayeed. 2020. An annotation approach for social and referential gaze in dialogue. In *Proceedings of the 12th Language Resources and Evaluation Conference*, pages 759–765, Marseille, France.

Ekta Sood, Simon Tannert, Philipp Müller, and Andreas Bulling. 2020. Improving natural language processing tasks with human gaze-guided neural attention. *Advances in Neural Information Processing Systems*.

Maria Staudte and Matthew W Crocker. 2011a. Investigating joint attention mechanisms through spoken human–robot interaction. *Cognition*, 120(2):268–291.

Maria Staudte and Matthew W. Crocker. 2011b. Investigating joint attention mechanisms through spoken human–robot interaction. *Cognition*, 120(2):268–291.

Ece Takmaz, Sandro Pezzelle, Lisa Beinborn, and Raquel Fernández. 2020. Generating image descriptions via sequential cross-modal alignment guided by human gaze. In *Proceedings of the 2020 Conference on Empirical Methods in Natural Language Processing (EMNLP)*, pages 4664–4677, Online.

Ashish Vaswani, Noam Shazeer, Niki Parmar, Jakob Uszkoreit, Llion Jones, Aidan N Gomez, Łukasz Kaiser, and Illia Polosukhin. 2017. Attention is all you need. In *31st Conference on Neural Information Processing Systems (NIPS 2017)*, pages 1–11.

Niklas Wilming, Selim Onat, José P Ossandón, Alper Açık, Tim C Kietzmann, Kai Kaspar, Ricardo R Gameiro, Alexandra Vormberg, and Peter König. 2017. An extensive dataset of eye movements during viewing of complex images. *Scientific data*, 4(1):1–11.

Neo Wu, Bradley Green, Xue Ben, and Shawn O'Banion. 2020. Deep transformer models for time series forecasting: The influenza prevalence case. *arXiv:2001.08317*.

Licheng Yu, Zhe Lin, Xiaohui Shen, Jimei Yang, Xin Lu, Mohit Bansal, and Tamara L Berg. 2018. MattNet: Modular attention network for referring expression comprehension. In *Proceedings of the IEEE Conference on Computer Vision and Pattern Recognition*, pages 1307–1315.

Gregory Zelinsky, Wei Zhang, Bing Yu, Xin Chen, and Dimitris Samaras. 2006. The role of top-down and bottom-up processes in guiding eye movements during visual search. In *Advances in Neural Information Processing Systems*, volume 18, pages 1569 – 1576.

George Zerveas, Srideepika Jayaraman, Dhaval Patel, Anuradha Bhamidipaty, and Carsten Eickhoff. 2021. A transformer-based framework for multivariate time series representation learning. In *Proceedings of the 27th ACM SIGKDD Conference on Knowledge Discovery & Data Mining*, pages 2114–2124.

A Supplementary Material

Ethics Statement

The data used in this study involves (transcribed) verbal descriptions and eye-movements. No personal data that includes, e.g., name, age and education are shared.

Limitations

One of the main limitations is the limited number of eye-movement data samples that address real-world complexities. Having more diversity in terms of linguistic and visual manipulations is crucial to arrive at better generalization. This bottleneck can be overcome with an increase in the number of benchmark datasets. Another crucial component of this research is the multivariate time-series representation learning. As touched upon in Section 2.1, despite this topic attracting more attention, still it is at early stages to model intricacies of such time-series data.

In this study, the object count is used as an referential complexity parameter. However, it is not an expressive parameter especially for the LOW condition and draws the model further away from the other conditions, which differ substantially in terms of this parameter. This is probably also the reason why fine-tuning does not benefit the LOW condition. On the other hand, as expected, the HIGH complexity contains too much noisy data to be easily generalizable for LOW complexity models. Adapting gaze features between different extremes (e.g. $\text{Train}_{\text{LOW}} \rightarrow \text{Test}_{\text{HIGH}}$) is not as successful as adapting between similar complexities. The results highlight the importance of incorporating referential complexity, which also increases the gain from transfer learning by making models implicitly adaptive to referential complexity. However, the coarse-grain complexity definition provided in the original dataset is one of the main limitations to fairly evaluate the effect of this parameter. In further studies, we will focus on feature-based and more sophisticated referential complexity detection approaches.

A.1 Feature Vector and Labels

- Label for the target referent (1: if the gaze is on the target)
- Label for the all referents (1: if the gaze is on the any of the referents)
- Average time in blink
- Average time in saccade
- Resolution X
- Resolution Y
- Average pupil size
- Acceleration magnitude on X-axis
- Acceleration direction on X-axis
- Acceleration magnitude on Y-axis
- Acceleration direction on Y-axis
- Velocity magnitude on X-axis
- Velocity direction on X-axis
- Velocity magnitude on Y-axis
- Velocity direction on Y-axis
- ObjectCount'

A.2 Normalization

- Within-participant (WP) normalization
- Within-study (WS) normalization
- Across-study (AS) normalization

A.3 Architectures and Best Hyper-parameters

LSTM base model has 50 LSTM nodes. After the LSTM layer, we use two dense layers with 20 and 10 nodes respectively. For the binary classification on the single output layer, we use Sigmoid activation. Overall, the model contains 15,441 parameters. Best meta parameters after grid search; Learning rate = 0.0001; Loss = binary cross-entropy; Optimizer = Adam; Batch size = 128; Epochs = 100.

For the TST model, RAdam optimizer has been used. TST model size is set to 64-dimension. We used the implementation provided in the original Pytorch TST Library (Zerveas et al., 2021). Best meta parameters after grid search; Learning rate = 0.0001; Loss = binary cross-entropy; Optimizer = RAdam; Batch size = 64; Epochs = 50.

A.4 Runtime Settings

The experiments were conducted on a GPU server featuring 32 cores, 256 GB memory and 4 Geforce 1080Ti GPUs. No GPU parallelization was used. The average running time (including data input, model training and transfer learning on all test sets) is 75 minutes for the simplest condition with LSTM and 12 minutes with TST.

Hyperparameter Search The *Keras Tuner* library[2] (O'Malley et al., 2019) is used for finding best hyperparameters for different prediction tasks. We utilize the Random Search tuner with 100 epochs for LSTM and 50 for TST per run. A summary of the best performing model parameters can be found in Appendix A.

[2]https://www.tensorflow.org/tutorials/keras/keras_tuner

Table 2: Best hyperparameters of LSTM for the prediction tasks for (i) the target object, (ii) all communicatively relevant objects including the target

	Target Referent				All Relevant Referents			
	Low	**Medium**	**High**	**Combined**	**Low**	**Medium**	**High**	**Combined**
Learning rate	0.01	0.01	0.001	0.001	0.0001	0.001	0.001	0.001
LSTM nodes (units)	30	30	50		50	40	30	50
Dense-1 (units)	11	18	14		17	16	18	16
Dense-2 (units)	10	10	10		10	10	15	10

Table 3: Transfer learning with TST on within-class and between-class testing for all referents prediction task (Normalization Type: WP). (F1-scores on the positive class; Underlined values indicate best performance between models for each training set, bold values are the best on each test set.)

	Testset	Low		Medium		High	
	Model	Pretrained	+Fine-tuned	Pretrained	+Fine-tuned	Pretrained	+Fine-tuned
Training	Low	0.683	NA	0.675	0.659	0.722	0.699
	Medium	0.544	0.586	0.571	NA	0.529	0.559
	High	0.201	0.274	0.299	0.226	0.284	NA
	Combined	0.568	0.575	0.577	0.569	0.522	**0.589**

Table 4: Transfer learning with LSTM on within-class and between-class testing for all referents prediction task. (F1-scores on the positive class; Underlined values indicate best performance between models for each training set, bold values are the best on each test set.)

	Testset	Low		Medium		High	
	Model	Pretrained	+Fine-tuned	Pretrained	+Fine-tuned	Pretrained	+Fine-tuned
Training	Low	0.479	NA	0.412	0.412	0.329	0.379
	Medium	**0.489**	0.369	**0.569**	NA	0.437	0.413
	High	0.305	0.383	0.372	0.415	**0.505**	NA
	Combined	0.463	0.416	0.546	0.519	0.423	0.411

A.5 Train-Test conditions

A.5.1 Within-complexity Conditions

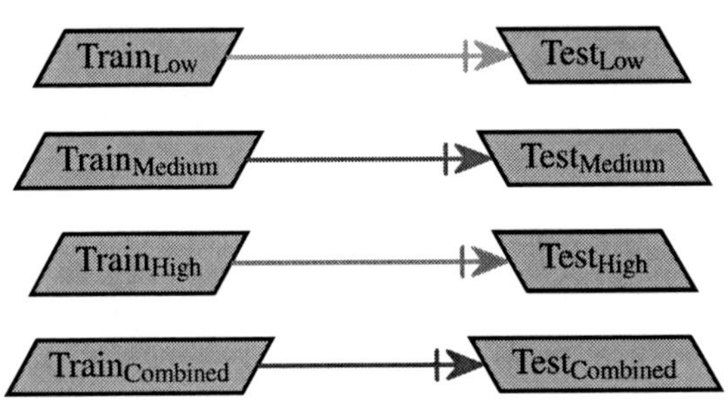

A.5.2 Effect of Data Diversity

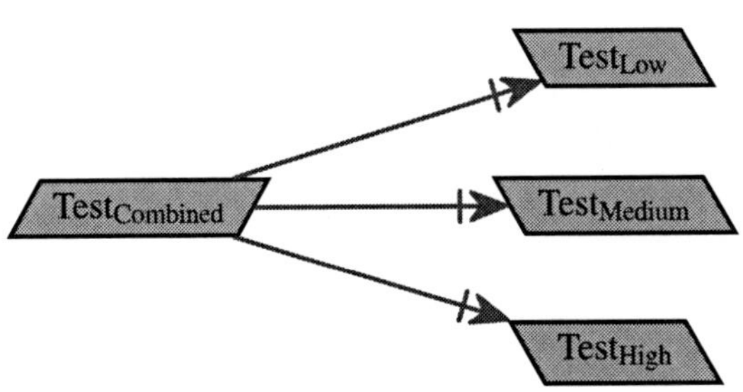

A.5.3 Transfer Learning conditions

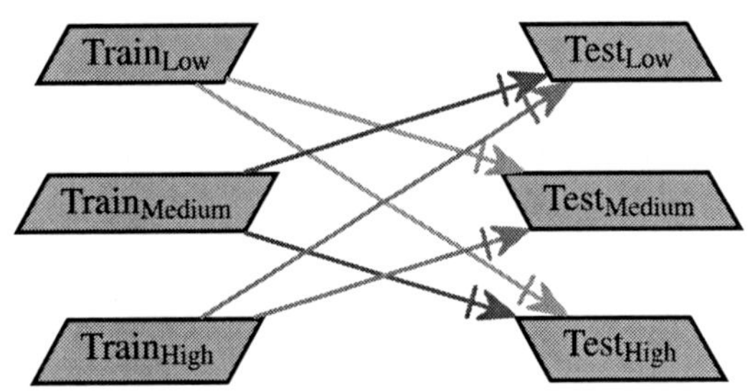

A.6 Results Tables

The detailed scores for both models are presented in Tables 3 and 4.

A.7 Scene-specific Participant Analysis

In the following Figures, a ground truth and COMBINED model's predictions on test trials coming from two participants have been visualized. Both trials belong to same test image from MEDIUM condition and prediction results are taken from COMBINED model. As mentioned before, each participant produces different pattern and when we take the all participants and scenes in the study in interaction with controlled parameters of this study, such analysis becomes highly complex.

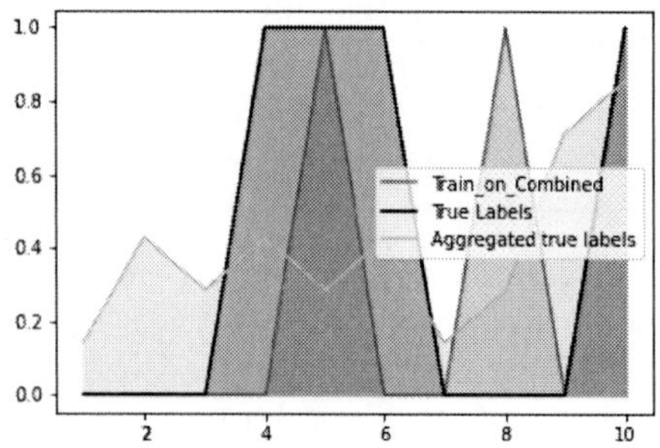

Figure 7: Participant-23 in MEDIUM condition (Scene 16), $\text{Train}_{\text{Combined}}$

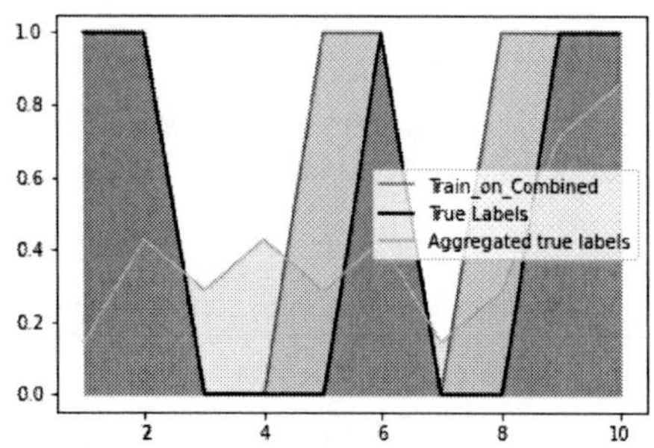

Figure 8: Participant-6 in MEDIUM condition (Scene 16), $\text{Train}_{\text{Combined}}$

A.8 Scene-specific Aggregated Analysis

The following figures illustrate individual TST model comparisons to the ground truths on a specific image separately per condition. For each time interval (in the range of 1 to 10), the model predictions for each participant are aggregated and compared against the ground truth.

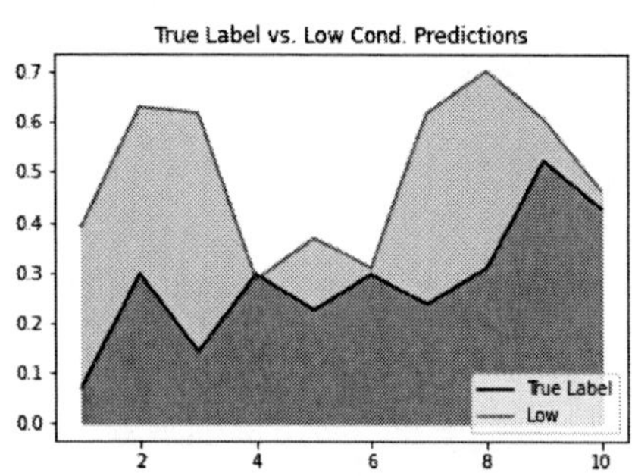

Figure 9: Aggregated $\text{Train}_{\text{Low}}$ model predictions on one image (medium condition) against the truth labels

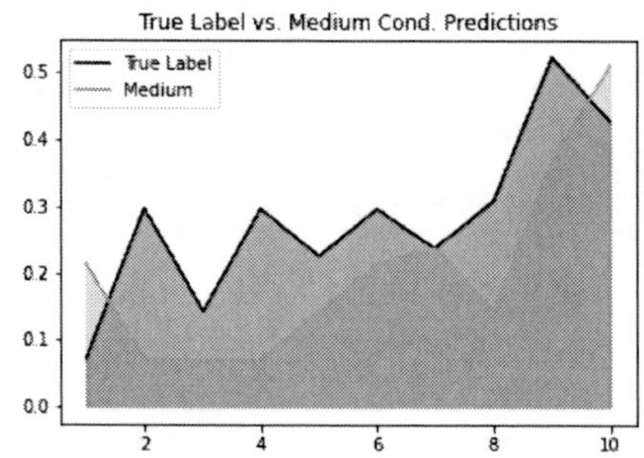

Figure 10: Aggregated $\text{Train}_{\text{Medium}}$ model predictions on one image (medium condition) against the truth labels

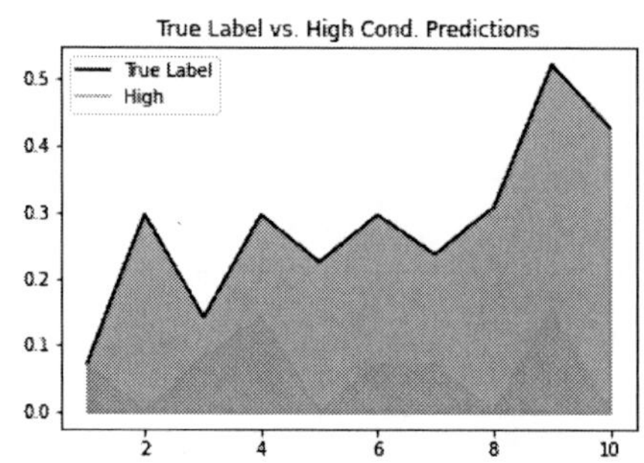

Figure 11: Aggregated $\text{Train}_{\text{High}}$ model predictions on one image (medium condition) against the truth labels

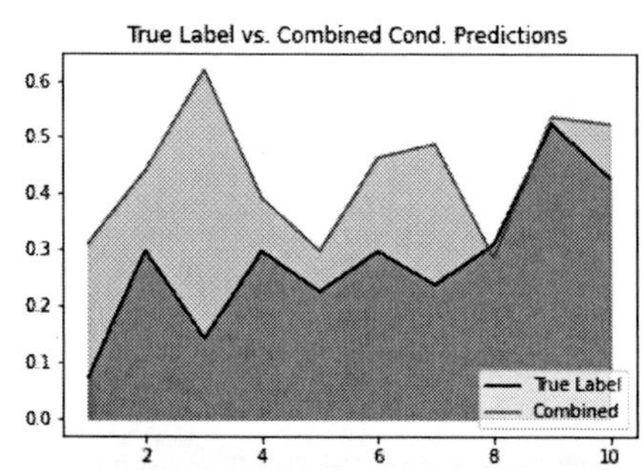

Figure 12: Aggregated $\text{Train}_{\text{Combined}}$ model predictions on one image (medium condition) against the truth labels

A.9 Code Repository

The code and its documentation is available in this GitLab repository: `https://gitlab.com/alacam/referential-gaze-modeling`.

Automating Interlingual Homograph Recognition with Parallel Sentences

Yi Han and **Ryohei Sasano** and **Koichi Takeda**
Graduate School of Informatics, Nagoya University
han.yi.u2@s.mail.nagoya-u.ac.jp
{sasano,takedasu}@i.nagoya-u.ac.jp

Abstract

Interlingual homographs are words that spell the same but possess different meanings across languages. Recognizing interlingual homographs from form-identical words generally needs linguistic knowledge and massive annotation work. In this paper, we propose an automatic interlingual homograph recognition method based on the cross-lingual word embedding similarity and co-occurrence of form-identical words in parallel sentences. We conduct experiments with off-the-shelf language models coordinating with cross-lingual alignment operations and co-occurrence metrics on the Chinese-Japanese and English-Dutch language pairs. Experimental results demonstrate that our proposed method can achieve accurate and consistent predictions across languages.

1 Introduction

When learning a foreign language, we often come across words in different languages sharing identical spellings. This is commonly seen in languages with similar writing systems. Such form-identical words with the same or very similar semantic meaning across languages are called *cognates*. However, there may also be words that are identical in spelling but different in meanings, these words are called *interlingual homographs*.[1] For instance, the Dutch word "angel" means "insect's sting", as opposed to its form-identical word in English. It is not unique for phonographic writing systems. In languages sharing logographic writing systems (Sproat and Gutkin, 2021) such as Chinese and Japanese, we can also see interlingual homograph examples like the word "平和", which means "gentle" in Chinese, whereas "peace" in Japanese. Table 1 shows examples of cognate and interlingual homograph across Chinese and Japanese.

	Examples	Chinese meanings	Japanese meanings
Cognate	未来	future	future
	椅子	chair	chair
Interlingual homograph	平和	gentle	peace
	高校	university	high school

Table 1: Examples of cognate and interlingual homograph across Chinese and Japanese.

For second language learners, interlingual homographs can cause confusion and learning difficulties since second language acquisition often comprises relating a foreign language to ones' native language (Xiong and Tamaoka, 2014; Long and Hatcho, 2018). Besides language acquisition, psychology researchers use cognates and interlingual homographs to investigate how bilingual language processing works in bilingualism studies (Caramazza and Brones, 1979). Therefore, several researchers have addressed the manual construction of interlingual homograph datasets (Lemhöfer and Dijkstra, 2004; Poort and Rodd, 2019), but such an approach is labor-intensive and requires knowledge of two languages.

In this study, we propose a method for interlingual homograph recognition that is applicable if parallel sentences are available. We calculate similarity scores to measure the semantic similarities of form-identical word pairs, based on which we identify whether each form-identical word pair is cognate or homograph. As we aim to require no linguistic knowledge, our proposed method does not rely on bilingual dictionaries, and all tools, including embedding models and parallel sentences, can theoretically be obtained from raw corpus such as Wikipedia. To verify the effectiveness of the proposed method, we conduct experiments on two pairs of languages that are etymologically distant from each other, namely, Chinese-Japanese and English-Dutch. Experimental results demonstrate that our proposed method can achieve accurate and

[1] Note that the definition of *homograph* may focus on differences in *origin* or *meaning*, and this study adopts the latter definition, following Dijkstra et al. (1999) and Poort and Rodd (2019).

Findings of the Association for Computational Linguistics: AACL-IJCNLP 2022, pages 211–216
November 20–23, 2022. ©2022 Association for Computational Linguistics

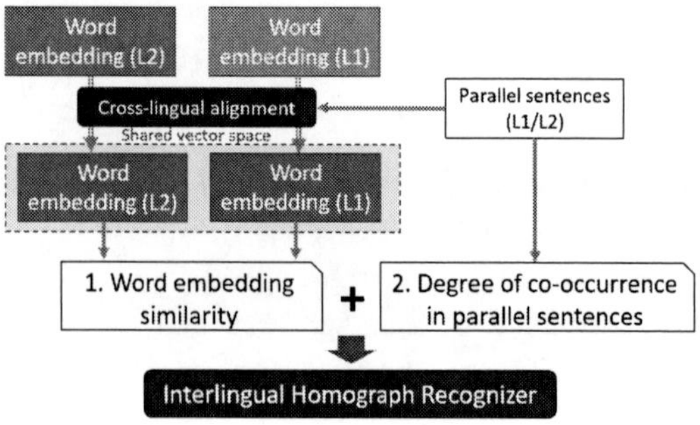

Figure 1: Overview of our proposed method.

consistent predictions across languages without depending on relevant linguistic knowledge and massive annotation work.

2 Methodology

We tackle the interlingual homograph recognition. Since form-identical word pairs do not differ in appearance, recognition must be based on clues other than their appearance. We thus formulate our criterion with the following two components: **word embedding similarity** and **degree of co-occurrence in parallel sentences**. The former is based on the simple intuition that if an interlingual form-identical word pair is interlingual homograph, the embeddings should not be similar in the cross-lingual word embedding space. The latter is based on the intuition that if an interlingual form-identical word pair is cognate, it is likely to co-occur in a parallel sentence, whereas if it is interlingual homograph, it should be less likely.

Figure 1 illustrates the overview of our proposed method. Given a pair of form-identical words, we get a similarity score by computing the cosine similarity of embeddings across languages. We also extract degree of co-occurrence from parallel sentences. Then, the above two scores are normalized to 0 mean and 1.0 standard deviation and fused by addition calculation in pairs. A word pair is determined as interlingual homograph or cognate if its fusion score is below or above the average score of all form-identical words in the dataset consisting of the same number of homographs and cognates.

2.1 Word Embedding Similarity

The distribution hypothesis suggests that the more semantically similar two words are, the more they occur in similar linguistic contexts (Harris, 1954). An intuitive way to decide whether a pair of words are cognates or interlingual homographs, is to exploit the word embedding similarity. There are two types of word embedding, namely the static word embedding, such as GloVe (Pennington et al., 2014) and fastText (Bojanowski et al., 2017), and the contextual embedding, such as ELMo (Peters et al., 2018) and BERT (Devlin et al., 2019). To compute the similarity of word embeddings, we have to ensure that they are in the same vector space. As the words in our setting are from different languages, we examine two cross-lingual alignment operations to obtain a cross-lingual vector space: **cross-lingual mapping** and **multilingual finetuning**.

Cross-lingual Mapping Cross-lingual mapping aligns independently trained monolingual word embeddings into a single shared space. Existing approaches often use a bilingual dictionary as supervision signals. Formally, let L_1 and L_2 represent a pair of languages, and let u and v represent words from L_1 and L_2. Given a bilingual dictionary $Z = \{(u_n, v_n)\}_{n=1}^{N}$, we obtain representations of each word: $\mathbf{u}_1, \ldots, \mathbf{u}_N, \mathbf{v}_1, \ldots, \mathbf{v}_N$, where $\mathbf{u}_n, \mathbf{v}_n \in \mathbb{R}^d$. (Mikolov et al., 2013) learn the optimal projection matrix W by minimizing:

$$W^* = \underset{W \in \mathbb{R}^{d \times d}}{\arg\min} ||W\mathbf{A} - \mathbf{B}||_F, \tag{1}$$

where $\mathbf{A}$ and $\mathbf{B}$ are two matrix containing all embeddings of words in $\mathbf{Z}$, namely $\mathbf{A} = [\mathbf{u}_1, \ldots, \mathbf{u}_N] \in \mathbb{R}^{d \times N}$, $\mathbf{B} = [\mathbf{v}_1, \ldots, \mathbf{v}_N] \in \mathbb{R}^{d \times N}$. Xing et al. (2015) restrict W to be orthogonal, turning Equation 1 into the Procrustes problem (Wang et al., 2020; Lample et al., 2018) by:

$$W^* = UV^T,\; U\Sigma V^T = \mathrm{SVD}(\mathbf{B}\mathbf{A}^T), \tag{2}$$

where SVD$(\cdot)$ is the singular value decomposition.

We take advantage of Aldarmaki and Diab (2019)'s method, which generally follows Xing et al.'s work to get a transformation matrix, except that W is obtained with parallel sentences instead of bilingual dictionary. Let D $= \{(x_n, y_n)\}_{n=1}^{N}$ represent a parallel corpus of L_1 and L_2. For each sentence pair $x_n = w_1^1, \ldots, w_I^1$, $y_n = w_1^2, \ldots, w_J^2$, we obtain sentence embedding by averaging the word embeddings:

$$\mathbf{x}_n = \frac{1}{I}\sum_{i=1}^{I} \mathbf{w}_i^1, \quad \mathbf{y}_n = \frac{1}{J}\sum_{i=1}^{J} \mathbf{w}_i^2. \tag{3}$$

In our setting, we get W^* from Equation 2 with $\mathbf{A} = [\mathbf{x}_1, \ldots, \mathbf{x}_N]$, $\mathbf{B} = [\mathbf{y}_1, \ldots, \mathbf{y}_N]$.

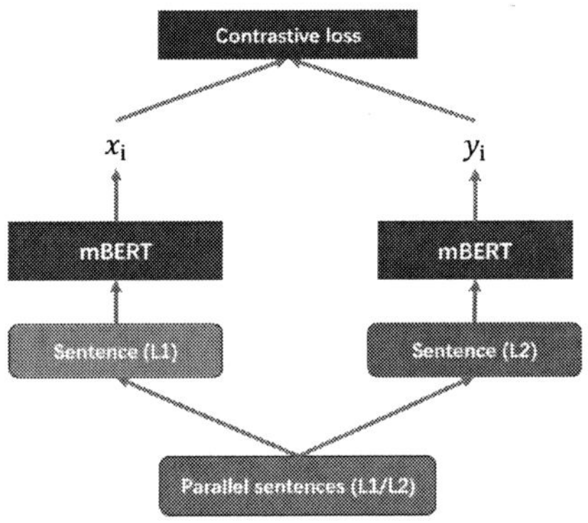

Figure 2: Multilingual finetuning process.

For a pair of form-identical words (z^1, z^2), $z^1 \in L_1, z^2 \in L_2$, we first obtain word embeddings in corresponding languages $(\mathbf{z}^1, \mathbf{z}^2)$, then compute the cosine similarity by:

$$s = \cos(W\mathbf{z}^1, \mathbf{z}^2). \tag{4}$$

Multilingual Finetuning As an alternative method to cross-lingual mapping, we also finetune mBERT (Devlin et al., 2019) to obtain cross-lingual representations. mBERT is pretrained on Wikipedia corpus in 104 languages, nevertheless, representations of various languages do not align well as no parallel data is involved in the training process. We utilize contrastive learning to finetune mBERT to reconstruct the vector space by minimizing the following loss:

$$L = -\log \frac{\exp(\mathrm{sim}(x_i, y_i)/\tau)}{\sum_{j=1, j\neq i}^{N} \exp(\mathrm{sim}(x_i, y_j)/\tau)}, \tag{5}$$

where sim($\cdot$) denotes the cosine similarity calculation and τ denotes the temperature. During training, mBERT is encouraged to narrow the gaps between the representations of parallel sentences, meanwhile enlarge the gaps between randomly chosen sentence samples with irrelevant meanings. We finetune mBERT with the same parallel sentences used in cross-lingual mapping methods for a fair comparison. The multilingual finetuning process is illustrated in Figure 2. We pass the form-identical word pairs to the finetuned mBERT and compute the similarity of the encoded embeddings as follows:

$$s = \cos(\mathbf{z}^1, \mathbf{z}^2). \tag{6}$$

2.2 Degree of Co-occurrence in Parallel Sentences

Degree of co-occurrence in parallel sentences reveals how often two words occur in similar contexts. We develop this intuition further and assume that a pair of interlingual homographs are less likely to appear in parallel sentences. We introduce two methods to measure degree of co-occurrence: pointwise mutual information (PMI) and Jaccard similarity coefficient. Given a parallel corpus $\mathrm{D} = \{(x_n, y_n)\}_{n=1}^{N}$, the PMI of a pair of form-identical words (z^1, z^2) is:

$$\mathrm{PMI}(z^1, z^2) = \log \frac{P_{\mathrm{D}}(z^1, z^2)}{P_{\mathrm{D}}(z^1) P_{\mathrm{D}}(z^2)}, \tag{7}$$

where $P_{\mathrm{D}}(z^1, z^2)$ represents the probability of $z^1 \in \{x_n\}$ meanwhile $z^2 \in \{y_n\}$. $P_{\mathrm{D}}(z^1)$ denotes the probability of $z^1 \in \{x_n\}$ and $P_{\mathrm{D}}(z^2)$ denotes the probability of $z^2 \in \{y_n\}$. Jaccard similarity coefficient is:

$$\mathrm{Jacc}(z^1, z^2) = \frac{C(z^1, z^2)}{C(z^1) + C(z^2) - C(z^1, z^2)}, \tag{8}$$

where $C(z^1)$, $C(z^2)$, and $C(z^1, z^2)$ represent counts of z^1, counts of z^2, and co-occurrence counts of z^1 and z^2, respectively.

3 Experiment

3.1 Dataset

Language Pair	Cognates	Homographs
Chinese-Japanese	173	173
English-Dutch	52	52

Table 2: Statistics of cognates and interlingual homograph datasets.

We conduct experiments on two language pairs: Chinese-Japanese and English-Dutch. Each language pair involves two datasets, i.e., cognates and interlingual homographs. For Chinese-Japanese, we refer to a Chinese-Japanese homograph dictionary (Yongquan Wang, 2009) to derive interlingual homographs. We refer to Chinese-Japanese dictionary (Obunsha Co., 2005) to extract identical cognates. For English-Dutch language pair, we directly take advantage of an existing database containing English-Dutch cognates and interlingual homographs (Poort and Rodd, 2019). Table 2 lists the numbers of cognate pairs and homograph pairs for each of the Chinese-Japanese and English-Dutch datasets. We use Wikipedia dataset for contextual word embedding extraction. As for parallel sentences, we extract 1 million sentence pairs respectively from Chinese-Japanese and English-Dutch WikiMatrix (Schwenk et al., 2021).

Group	System	Chinese-Japanese		English-Dutch	
		F1	Acc.	F1	Acc.
EmbSim	fastText	0.861	0.867	0.860	0.865
	BERT	0.759	0.817	0.757	0.798
	mBERT(mapping)	0.468	0.488	0.793	0.760
	mBERT(finetuning)	0.573	0.552	0.826	0.826
CoR	PMI	0.486	0.509	0.603	0.596
	Jaccard	0.800	0.817	0.783	0.798
Fusion	fastText+Jaccard	**0.928**	**0.934**	**0.869**	**0.875**
	BERT+Jaccard	0.847	0.845	0.772	0.779
	mBERT(mapping)+Jaccard	0.817	0.800	0.830	0.826
	mBERT(finetuning)+Jaccard	0.750	0.763	0.826	0.826

Table 3: Interlingual homograph recognition performance in terms of F1 score and Accuracy.

3.2 Word Embedding Models

We employ fastText (Bojanowski et al., 2017), BERT, and multilingual BERT (mBERT) (Devlin et al., 2019), representing static word embedding model, monolingual contextual embedding model, and multilingual contextual embedding model, respectively.

For fastText, Facebook has published pretrained 300-dimensional word embeddings[2] for 157 languages from which we extract embeddings for our target languages. For BERT and mBERT, we use 12-layers transformer encoder pretrained by HuggingFace.[3] The contextual word embeddings produced by these models are all 768-dimensional.

3.3 Experimental Settings

As described in Section 2, we explore the proposed method in three groups of experiments, including the word embedding similarity (EmbSim), degree of co-occurrence (CoR), and their fusion, represented as follows.

- **EmbSim**: fastText, BERT, mBERT(mapping), mBERT(finetuning)
- **CoR**: PMI, Jaccard
- **Fusion**: EmbSim+Jaccard

Particularly, we extract contextual embedding of words in our dataset, described in Section 3.1 by the following procedures. (1) For each word, we search the Wikipedia dataset by the word and select 300 sentences. (2) Derive embedding vectors of this word by putting each selected sentence into a contextual embedding language model. (3) Take an average of derived vectors as the integrated representation, i.e., contextual embedding of this word.

[2]https://github.com/facebookresearch/fastText

[3]https://huggingface.co

Word	Chinese	Japanese	Co-occurrence	PMI
委員	6433	6851	4278	4.58
一味	25	105	1	5.94

Table 4: A misleading example with contradictory between co-occurrence statistics and PMI scores.

It's worth noting that because in Chinese BERT and mBERT, tokens are processed in the form of characters, so we also choose to use Japanese BERT with character-based tokenization instead of commonly used word-base model for coordination and fair comparison.

3.4 Experimental Results

Table 3 shows the experimental results. We report F1 score and accuracy for the assessment of the interlingual recognition capability of our method. Appendix A provides actual similarity scores for several examples.

EmbSim fastText demonstrates superior performance compared with the contextual word embedding models. Although contextual embedding models outperform static ones in a wide range of NLP tasks in recent years, due to the challenge brought by their dynamic property, in some languages they may obtain inferior performance when performing cross-lingual mapping (Aldarmaki and Diab, 2019). If we compare two cross-lingual alignment methods using mBERT, both language pairs benefit more from multilingual finetuning than cross-lingual mapping when building the shared vector space.

CoR Jaccard much outperforms PMI in both language pairs. We suspect that PMI's poor performance is caused by the unbalanced numbers of words appearing in WikiMatrix data. Table 4 shows an example to demonstrate this problem, where "委

Word	Meaning		fastText	Jaccard	fastText+Jaccard
	Chinese	Japanese	(0.0043)	(0.0038)	(0.0125)
			Cognate		
安全	safety		1.773	0.949	2.722
英語	English		1.478	0.101	1.580
握手◇	handshake		-0.632	2.434	1.802
			Interlingual Homograph		
合同	contract	combination	-0.821	-0.615	-1.435
娘	mother	daughter	-0.895	-0.675	-1.570
結束	finish	binding/union	-0.872	-1.036	-1.908

Table 5: Examples of cognate and interlingual homograph with their similarity scores generated by three settings: fastText, Jaccard, fastText+Jaccard. The number under settings are the average scores of all form-identical words in our dataset, which we use as the boundary.

員" is a cognate, which means "committee member" in both Chinese and Japanese, and "一味" is an interlingual homograph, which means "blindly" in Chinese while "conspirators" or "a powered red pepper" in Japanese. From the statistics, we can easily draw a conclusion that "一味" is more likely to be an interlingual homograph than "委員", however, the PMI score shows the opposite result.

Fusion We choose Jaccard to corporate each method in the EmbSim group. As illustrated, all methods can benefit from the combination with Jaccard information, among which, the fastText+Jaccard won the best place. In EmbSim setting, Chinese-Japanese mBERT perform poorly in both cross-lingual alignment methods, however the performance can be largely improved with the Jaccard information. This shows that semantic information contained in word embeddings sometimes is not enough, it is advisable to supplement it with extra knowledge.

3.5 Recognition details

The similarity scores of form-identical words are a spectrum with cognates and interlingual homographs on each end. Higher scores for cognates and lower scores for interlingual homographs imply that the language model is more confident to identify one from the other. In Table 5, we pick examples consistent or inconsistent with human judgment, among which, words with ◇ marks are examples with one or more inconsistent results by three methods. Here we take a deeper look at an inconsistent example. In cognates, "握手" (handshake) causes disagreement between language models, resulting in quite low similarity from fastText but high from Jaccard. Such error can be reduced through model fusion operation and this can explain why fusion setting is able to obtain a better performance.

4 Conclusion

We integrate word embedding similarity into degree of co-occurrence in parallel sentences to automatically execute interlingual homograph recognition in different languages. We perform it on two language pairs, i.e., Chinese-Japanese and English-Dutch, and the experimental results exhibit the effectiveness of our method. By supplement of the degree of co-occurrence information, the performance of all embeddings can be improved. Among all settings, the combination of fastText and Jaccard achieve the best performance in both language pairs. In this work, we focus on interlingual homographs with explicit meaning disparity. However, form-identical words with partially overlapped meanings also exist between some language pairs and we will investigate them for future work.

Acknowledgements

This work was supported by JSPS KAKENHI Grant Number 21H04901.

References

Hanan Aldarmaki and Mona Diab. 2019. Context-aware cross-lingual mapping. In *Proceedings of the 2019 Conference of the North American Chapter of the Association for Computational Linguistics: Human Language Technologies (NAACL-HLT)*, pages 3906–3911.

Piotr Bojanowski, Édouard Grave, Armand Joulin, and Tomáš Mikolov. 2017. Enriching word vectors with subword information. *Transactions of the Association for Computational Linguistics (TACL)*, 5:135–146.

Alfonso Caramazza and Isabel Brones. 1979. Lexical access in bilinguals. *Bulletin of the Psychonomic Society*, 13(4):212–214.

Jacob Devlin, Ming-Wei Chang, Kenton Lee, and Kristina Toutanova. 2019. Bert: Pre-training of deep bidirectional transformers for language understanding. In *Proceedings of the 2019 Conference of the North American Chapter of the Association for Computational Linguistics: Human Language Technologies (NAACL-HLT)*, pages 4171–4186.

Ton Dijkstra, Jonathan Grainger, and Walter JB Van Heuven. 1999. Recognition of cognates and interlingual homographs: The neglected role of phonology. *Journal of Memory and Language*, 41:496–518.

Zellig S Harris. 1954. Distributional structure. *Word*, 10(2-3):146–162.

Guillaume Lample, Alexis Conneau, Marc'Aurelio Ranzato, Ludovic Denoyer, and Hervé Jégou. 2018. Word translation without parallel data. In *6th International Conference on Learning Representations (ICLR)*.

Kristin Lemhöfer and Ton Dijkstra. 2004. Recognizing cognates and interlingual homographs: Effects of code similarity in language-specific and generalized lexical decision. *Memory & cognition*, 32(4):533–550.

Robert W. Long and Yui Hatcho. 2018. The first language's impact on l2: Investigating intralingual and interlingual errors. *English Language Teaching*.

Tomás Mikolov, Quoc V. Le, and Ilya Sutskever. 2013. Exploiting similarities among languages for machine translation. *arXiv preprint arXiv:1309.4168*.

Ltd. Obunsha Co. 2005. *Dual solution to learn Japanese and Chinese dictionaries: Standard Mandarin Dictionary*. Foreign language education research publisher (In Chinese).

Jeffrey Pennington, Richard Socher, and Christopher D. Manning. 2014. GloVe: Global vectors for word representation. In *Proceedings of the 2014 Conference on Empirical Methods in Natural Language Processing (EMNLP)*, pages 1532–1543.

Matthew E. Peters, Mark Neumann, Mohit Iyyer, Matt Gardner, Christopher Clark, Kenton Lee, and Luke Zettlemoyer. 2018. Deep contextualized word representations. In *Proceedings of the 9th Workshop on Computational Approaches to Subjectivity, Sentiment and Social Media Analysis (NAACL-HLT)*, pages 2227–2237.

Eva D Poort and Jennifer M. Rodd. 2019. A database of dutch–english cognates, interlingual homographs and translation equivalents. *Journal of Cognition*, 2(1–15):1–15.

Holger Schwenk, Vishrav Chaudhary, Shuo Sun, Hongyu Gong, and Francisco Guzmán. 2021. Wikimatrix: Mining 135m parallel sentences in 1620 language pairs from wikipedia. In *Proceedings of the 16th Conference of the European Chapter of the Association for Computational Linguistics (EACL)*, pages 1351–1361.

Richard Sproat and Alexander Gutkin. 2021. The taxonomy of writing systems: How to measure how logographic a system is. *Computational Linguistics*, pages 477–528.

Zirui Wang, Jiateng Xie, Ruochen Xu, Yiming Yang, Graham Neubig, and Jaime G. Carbonell. 2020. Cross-lingual alignment vs joint training: A comparative study and A simple unified framework. In *8th International Conference on Learning Representations (ICLR)*.

Chao Xing, Dong Wang, Chao Liu, and Yiye Lin. 2015. Normalized word embedding and orthogonal transform for bilingual word translation. In *The 2015 Conference of the North American Chapter of the Association for Computational Linguistics: Human Language Technologies (NAACL)*, pages 1006–1011.

Kexin Xiong and Katsuo Tamaoka. 2014. A descriptive analysis of Japanese and Chinese orthographically similar two-kanji compound words according to the database of grammatical categories (In Japanese). *Studia linguistica*, 27:25–51.

Changfu Xu Yongquan Wang, Shinjiro Koizumi. 2009. *Chinese Japanese Interlingual Homograph Dictionary*. Commercial Press (In Chinese).

CoRAL: a Context-aware Croatian Abusive Language Dataset

Ravi Shekhar[1], **Mladen Karan**[1], **Matthew Purver**[1,2]
[1]Cognitive Science Research Group, School of Electronic Engineering & Computer Science, Queen Mary University of London, UK
[2]Department of Knowledge Technologies, Jožef Stefan Institute, Ljubljana, Slovenia
{r.shekhar, m.karan, m.purver}@qmul.ac.uk

Abstract

In light of unprecedented increases in the popularity of the internet and social media, comment moderation has never been a more relevant task. Semi-automated comment moderation systems greatly aid human moderators by either automatically classifying the examples or allowing the moderators to prioritize which comments to consider first. However, the concept of inappropriate content is often subjective, and such content can be conveyed in many subtle and indirect ways. In this work, we propose CoRAL[1] – a language and culturally aware Croatian Abusive dataset covering phenomena of implicitness and reliance on local and global context. We show experimentally that current models degrade when comments are not explicit and further degrade when language skill and context knowledge are required to interpret the comment.

1 Introduction

The growing volume of user-generated content – from social media to online forums and comments under news articles – implies a growing need for moderation of this content to counter abuse and the spread of misinformation. Automatic and semi-automatic moderation systems can greatly aid human moderators, making their work quicker, easier, and more accurate; however, most of this work focuses on English, ignoring smaller, less-resourced languages (Vidgen and Derczynski, 2020). This situation is improving with the advent of multilingual contextual language models, as they enable cross-lingual transfer learning: recent work shows that comment moderation models with reasonable performance for less-resourced languages can be produced using zero- or few-shot transfer learning after pre-training on majority language datasets (Pelicon et al., 2021a,b).

It is not always sufficient to identify whether a comment is inappropriate or not; further sub-categorization helps build measures to counter it. Previous work has taken a range of approaches to sub-categorizing inappropriate content. Waseem et al. (2017) divided abusive language into two orthogonal categories – directed/generalized and implicit/explicit. A very similar approach is taken by Zampieri et al. (2019). More fine-grained approaches include very specific topics such as *homophobia*, *cyberbullying* or *racism* (e.g., Mollas et al., 2022), and the annotation of community-specific extreme hate speech with targets from multiple countries (Maronikolakis et al., 2022); we refer to Poletto et al. (2021) for a comprehensive list. Recently, a unified taxonomy of abusive language categories has been proposed by Banko et al. (2020), a systematic division of slurs by Kurrek et al. (2020), and another taxonomy by Fortuna et al. (2019). Röttger et al. (2021, 2022) provide a detailed empirical analysis of model performance across different example categories. All of these approaches divide comments primarily on the basis of how/whom they insult. In contrast, we are interested in categorizing how such comments can be difficult to classify or interpret automatically due to their use of linguistic and cultural context.

Our goal is to create a dataset and accompanying annotation schema to quantify what categories (primarily related to linguistic and cultural context) of abuse are being used by people and how well NLP models handle these different categories. To this end, we identified three context dependency categories (CDC): Implicitness, Global Context, and Local Context. These CDCs are further sub-divided according to implicitness (explicit/implicit), use of (global/local) language alterations, and use of (global/local) external knowledge; see Section 2 for details. The closest related work in this vein is that of Wiegand et al. (2021), who give a systematic overview of various ways in which examples can be

[1]The CoRAL dataset can be found here.

Findings of the Association for Computational Linguistics: AACL-IJCNLP 2022, pages 217–225
November 20–23, 2022. ©2022 Association for Computational Linguistics

difficult (e.g., sarcasm, dehumanization, inference required, multimodality, etc.). However, Wiegand et al. (2021) only focused on implicit abuse in English without any empirical analysis.

We focus on the Croatian language, a less-represented language in Natural Language Processing research. We annotated 2,240 Croatian comments from the 24sata newspaper[2] with our proposed CDCs. We experimented with four transformer-based models (Devlin et al., 2019; Ulčar and Robnik-Šikonja, 2020; Ljubešić and Lauc, 2021; Conneau et al., 2020). Our experimentation shows that models do not perform equally well on all CDCs. The easiest CDC is explicit expression (e.g., cursing or using slurs), confirming the findings of Wiegand et al. (2019). More difficult CDCs are those that require global or local context for their interpretation, via language disguise or external knowledge.

The contribution of this paper is twofold. First, we present a publicly available schema and the ***Co**ntext-aware Croatian **A**busive **L**anguage Dataset* (CoRAL) comprised of Croatian news comments annotated for different CDCs. Second, we provide a quantitative and qualitative comparison of comment moderation models, revealing the limitations of different cross-lingual models when handling difficult examples and which CDCs are generally the most challenging.

2 Dataset

When building CoRAL, we aim to have annotated examples with the CDC's they exhibit. Moreover, we focus on devising CDCs that would reflect the challenges models face when accounting for cultural context (global or local). By manual inspection, we identified three main CDCs of blocked comments on which cross-lingual models tend to fail: *Implicitness*, *Global context*, and *Local-context*, which are further divided as follows.

- **Implicitness**: Defines whether examples express abuse directly or indirectly.
  - **Explicit Expression**: directly use abusive words, e.g., derogation, threatening language, slurs, profanity. (e.g. *"Retardiran si." [You are retarded.]*)
  - **Implicit Expression**: use indirect ways to express abuse, usually through vague statements implying abuse without stating it, e.g., sarcastic compliments. (e.g. *"Pametan si ko panj." [You're as smart as a stump.]*)
- **Global Context**: Defines if general background knowledge is required.
  - **Language Independent Disguise**: Linguistic alterations applicable in any language. E.g., adjacent character swap, missing characters/word boundaries, extra spaces, etc. (e.g. *"J**i se." [F**k you.]*)
  - **World Knowledge-Based**: The comment requires world/global knowledge (e.g., globally known characters, events, or facts) to be fully understood.(e.g. *"Adolf je bio u pravu." [Adolf was right.]*)
- **Local Context**: Defines if Croatia-specific background knowledge is required.
  - **Croatian Specific Disguise**: Linguistic alterations specific to the Croatian language. E.g., ad-hoc constructed words that are understandable to locals, missing/wrong diacritics, using dialects, etc. (e.g. *"Promijenit ću ti lični opis." [I will change your personal description. – I will break your face.]*)
  - **Croatia Knowledge-Based**: The comment requires Croatia specific knowledge (e.g., local characters, events, or facts) to be fully understood. (e.g. *"Treba tebe u Vrapče." [You need to be put into Vrapče – Vrapče is a famous mental asylum in Croatia.)]*
- **Other**: Anything else not covered above

To the best of our knowledge, CoRAL is the first dataset with annotations on which category of local/global context is required for interpretation.[3]

Dataset Annotation: We use the publicly available 24sata newspaper comment dataset (Shekhar et al., 2020).[4] The dataset contains comments moderated by 24sata's moderators based on the newspaper's policy: rules include the removal of hate

[2]https://www.24sata.hr/

[3]See Appendix 1 for examples of each CDC.

[4]Available at https://clarin.si/repository/xmlui/handle/11356/1399 (Pollak et al., 2021)

	# Vote				Majority Votes		κ
	0	1	2	3	w Expl.	w/out Expl.	
Explicit Expression	506	425	484	825	1,309	-	0.45
Implicit Expression	1,297	567	275	101	376	363	0.25
Language Independent Disguise	1,941	95	78	126	204	99	0.70
World Knowledge-Based	1,136	571	357	176	533	163	0.31
Croatian Specific Disguise	1,642	312	193	93	286	146	0.30
Croatia Knowledge-Based	2,155	55	26	4	30	14	0.40
Others	1,866	198	103	73	176	175	0.47
Total	-	-	-	-	2,240	931	-

Table 1: Dataset Statistics: First, we report the number of annotators voted(0-3) for CDCs. Then we report with/without Explicit Expression CDC and inter-annotator agreement (Fleiss' κ), based on the majority votes(i.e., 2 or 3 votes) . The "w/out Explicit" columns for all cases when it is not labeled as Explicit.

	# disagreements	sample size	# ambiguous	# majority ok
Explicit Expression	909 (40.6%)	91	70 (76.9%)	79 (86.8%)
Implicit Expression	842 (37.6%)	85	62 (72.9%)	64 (75.3%)
Language Independent Disguise	173 (7.7%)	50	36 (72.0%)	41 (82.0%)
World Knowledge-Based	81 (2.6%)	50	47 (92.2%)	43 (84.3%)
Croatian Specific Disguise	928 (41.4%)	93	70 (75.3%)	73 (78.5%)
Croatia Knowledge-Based	505 (22.5%)	51	47 (92.1%)	38 (74.5%)
Others	301 (13.4%)	50	40 (76.9%)	43 (82.7%)

Table 2: Analysis of data ambiguity. Columns are (1) number of examples with disagreement for a CDC, (2) size of the sample we annotated, (3) number of examples from the sample annotated as ambiguous (4) number of examples from the sample where the fourth annotator agrees with the majority CDC label of the remaining three.

speech, abusive statements, threats, obscenity, deception & trolling, vulgarity, and comments that are not in Croatian. We refer to Shekhar et al. (2020) for more details, reproduced here in Appendix 2.

We randomly selected 2,240 blocked comments from 2019 related to abuse only (i.e., 24sata's abuse, hate speech, obscenity, and vulgarity categories). We take a *multi-label* approach: annotators were asked to select all (possibly multiple) CDCs they think apply to the comment; if none applies, then select *Other* and provide an explanation. Three annotators annotated each comment from a total of 7 annotators we had available. All annotators are university students and paid on an hourly basis. Each annotator was provided training and feedback during three pilots.

Dataset Statistics: In Table 1, we present the statistics of the dataset based on the majority CDC label. More than 58% of blocked comments is from *Explicit Expression* CDC, followed by *Croatian Specific Disguise* (23%). To further gain insight into the data, we remove all comments marked *Explicit Expression* CDC. In that case, most comments were from the *Implicit Expression* CDC, followed by *Croatian Specific Disguise*. The *World Knowledge-Based* comments were less than 1.5%, which might be due to a small volume of world-related articles on the 24sata newspaper.

Inter-Annotator Agreement: The inter-annotator agreement, measured by Fleiss' κ (Fleiss, 1971) is moderate or better (≥ 0.4) for 4/7 CDCs and fair (≥ 0.2) for the rest (see Table 1). We get the lowest agreement on the *Implicit Expression* CDC (0.25), likely due to this CDC being very subjective. On the other hand, the best agreement is on *Language Independent Disguise* (0.70), which is the most clearly defined CDC.

To further explore agreement, we divided the data into 4 subsets for every CDC, based on the number of annotators who gave a positive vote. 0 and 3 therefore correspond to perfect agreement between the three annotators, while 1 and 2 are disagreement. In Table 1, we provide the statistics of this division. To gain additional insight into the structure of disagreements we sampled 10% (but no fewer than 50) of examples with disagreement for each CDC (see Table 2). One of the authors then annotated these examples with a fourth "expert" CDC label. This additional label matched the majority label in more than 75% of cases for each

CDC label (Table 2, majority column). This indicates that many disagreements could be resolved by additional annotation or use of majority voting; but also that many examples with disagreement are genuinely ambiguous with no clear-cut obviously "correct" choice for the CDC label (multiple choices were all valid to an extent). Consequently, we opted not to force resolution of disagreements, but rather to leave them as part of the data.[5] We next explore this ambiguity in more detail.

Some tasks are inherently subjective/ambiguous, and their disagreements can never be completely resolved — see (Uma et al., 2021) for a survey — and we believe our task is in this category. To confirm this, we further annotated examples from Table 2 as to their ambiguity (whether multiple choices seemed valid; see Table 2, ambiguous column). We find that for all CDCs, more than 70% of examples with disagreement are indeed ambiguous, explaining the relatively low values shown by traditional agreement measures that assume clear-cut decisions about assigning CDC labels (Table 1). The ambiguity problem is further exacerbated by the multi-label nature of the task, increasing the number of possible CDC label combinations and potential for disagreement. However, much recent work (Pavlick and Kwiatkowski, 2019; Basile et al., 2021; Leonardelli et al., 2021) shows it is possible (and also important) to design NLP models and evaluation measures that take task ambiguity into account. Consequently, we believe that CoRAL will be valuable for future research.

To get a better perspective on comments to which the majority of annotators assigned the *Other* label, an author manually inspected randomly selected 50 examples labeled with the *Other* CDC and 50 examples labeled with some other CDC. Examples labeled as *Other* were mainly spam or non-offensive (mislabeled) comments. In contrast, different CDC examples were mostly offensive, fitting well into one or more of the main six CDC categories. The latter case accounts for the majority of examples.

3 Results and Discussion

3.1 Experimental Set-up

For binary classification (i.e., *Abuse* vs. *Non-abuse*), we used the dataset from Pelicon et al. (2021b). We removed comments blocked for spam, deception & trolling and use of a language other than Croatian, giving 4750/518/580 data points for training/validation/testing, respectively. We used four transformer-based models; two pre-trained on 100+ languages, namely mBERT (Devlin et al., 2019) and XLM-RoBERTa base (Conneau et al., 2020) and two pre-trained on Croatian and 2-3 similar languages, namely cseBERT (Ulčar and Robnik-Šikonja, 2020) and BERTić (Ljubešić and Lauc, 2021). We fine-tuned all models for the binary comment moderation task using default hyperparameters for ten epochs, and selected the best model based on validation F1 score.[6]

3.2 Quantitative Results

Our primary goal is to study how models perform on fine-grained CDCs, and we report accuracy on CoRAL in Table 3. This number represents the proportion of comments from CoRAL that that a classification model (*Abuse* vs. *Non-abuse*) classified as *Abuse* (by construction, all examples in CoRAL should belong to *Abuse*). We present the overall accuracy of each annotated CDC with and without the *Explicit expression* CDC. There are multiple insights from the results. For all CDCs except *Other*, cseBERT and BERTić perform best. We confirm this using a permutation test (Nichols and Holmes, 2002): for all CDCs except *Other* the differences between the better of cseBERT/BERTić and the better of mBERT/XLM-RoBERTa, are statistically significant ($p \leq 0.05$). This again shows that a small multilingual Masked Language Model (MLM) with similar languages beats a massively multilingual MLM, similar to Pelicon et al. (2021b).

Among all the CDCs, all models can easily identify the *Explicit Expression* examples. Comparatively, *Implicit Expression* is one of the most challenging CDC, with more than 40% difference between it and *Explicit Expression.* This shows that it is hard for any model to identify implicit expression. At the same time, the *Language Independent Disguise* CDC is easier for models than the *Croatian Specific Disguise* CDC, with more than 7% difference in the performance. On the *Croatian Knowledge-Based* comments, cseBERT and BERTić outperform mBERT and XLM-RoBERTa by a minimum 11%. This, again, indicates that smaller multilingual MLM has comparatively more cultural information encoded.

[5]We release all individual annotations, not only the majority vote based decisions.

[6]On the corresponding test set, our model achieved macro F1 scores of 75.14, 76.72, 79.82, and 80.97 for mBERT, XLM-RoBERTa, cseBERT, and BERTić, respectively, which is similar to previously reported results (Pelicon et al., 2021b).

CDC Includes Explicit Expression	mBERT Yes	 No	XLM-RoBERTa Yes	 No	cseBERT Yes	 No	BERTić Yes	 No
Overall	45.04	23.85	44.24	19.76	<u>56.70</u>	**28.46**	**59.64**	<u>26.53</u>
Explicit Expression	60.12	-	61.65	-	<u>76.78</u>	-	**83.19**	-
Implicit Expression	21.54	21.76	16.49	16.53	**26.86**	**26.45**	**26.86**	<u>25.90</u>
Language Independent Disguise	58.33	49.49	59.80	50.51	<u>74.51</u>	**65.66**	**77.94**	**65.66**
World Knowledge-Based	33.33	21.43	13.33	7.14	**50.00**	**28.57**	<u>46.67</u>	<u>21.43</u>
Croatian Specific Disguise	49.72	31.29	50.28	26.38	<u>64.92</u>	<u>40.49</u>	**70.73**	**42.33**
Croatia Knowledge-Based	40.91	23.29	38.81	15.75	<u>51.40</u>	<u>23.29</u>	**55.59**	**27.40**
Others	**11.93**	**11.43**	8.52	8.00	<u>11.36</u>	<u>10.86</u>	6.25	5.71

Table 3: Accuracy of the abusive comment on different CDCs. A_1/A_2 where A_1 is accuracy on the unmodified test set and A_2 after removing *Explicit Expression* examples. The best model is **bold** and second best <u>underlined</u>.

CDC	XLM-RoBERTa 0	 1	 2	 3	BERTić 0	 1	 2	 3
Explicit Expression	13.64	27.06	47.93	69.70	16.60	38.35	71.07	90.30
Implicit Expression	57.75	31.75	18.91	9.90	74.79	46.74	29.45	19.80
Language Independent Disguise	42.09	54.74	58.97	60.32	57.24	69.47	83.33	74.60
World Knowledge-Based	38.73	49.56	47.34	56.25	51.94	64.62	69.47	73.30
Croatian Specific Disguise	45.13	44.55	39.90	36.56	60.54	58.65	52.33	62.37
Croatia Knowledge-Based	44.78	40.00	15.38	0.00	59.91	56.36	42.31	75.00
Others	50.21	19.70	9.71	6.85	69.40	15.15	4.85	8.22

Table 4: Performance of XLM-RoBERTa & BERTić based models per CDC based on number of annotator's votes.

To better understand the effect of the *Explicit Expression* comments, we removed all data points assigned the *Explicit* CDC label; results in Table 3. Overall performance drops by $\geq$22%, with a larger drop for cseBERT and BERTić ($\geq$28%). For both *Local Context* CDCs, there is a larger drop in performance ($\geq$26%). This suggests we must find a better way to incorporate cultural knowledge into models. Furthermore, in Table 4 we report the performance based on the number of annotator's votes, and show that our main observations still hold and are even more pronounced when considering data with high agreement.

3.3 Qualitative Results

Manual inspection of errors reveals some interesting patterns. Cases where all models fail almost always contain two or more CDCs simultaneously, e.g., *"Severaca moze glumiti jedino na camcu" [The only place where Severaca can act is a boat.]* – deliberate misspelling, reference to famous person, reference to local event).[7] Moreover, examples where cseBERT and BERTić outperform mBERT and XLM-RoBERTa mostly require local context: e.g., *"Opet. Retardesničaru." [Again. You retarded right-wing extremist.]* – specific local word, wordplay only possible in Croatian). Finally, we find that examples on which all models perform well mostly contain explicit abuse with no misspelling, e.g., *"Retard" [Retard]*, which is in line with our empirical results.

[7]Severaca refers to Severina, a regionally famous singer who was in a leaked explicit video taking place on a boat. The comment implies her acting skills are limited to pornography.

4 Conclusion

We present the ***Context-aware Croatian Abusive Language Dataset*** (CoRAL), a dataset annotated with context dependency categories (CDC) of problematic examples for Croatian comment moderation. We annotated 2240 blocked comments for Explicitness, Implicitness, Language Independent Disguise, World Knowledge-Based, Croatian Specific Disguise, and Croatia Knowledge-Based. We found that only 58.44% had explicit expressions of abuse. This indicates that almost half the remaining examples are challenging (Croatian Specific Disguise alone accounting for $\approx$ 24%). This shows that addressing these categories of examples is very practically relevant. We tested four transformer-based models and found that explicit comments are the easiest and local context ones are hardest. We also found that language-specific multilingual language models better identify Croatian-specific blocked comments. Finally, we believe that CoRAL will help design better models for Croatian comment moderation, build a foundation for creating similar datasets in other languages, and develop novel methods by incorporating local context.

Ethical Consideration

Our proposed dataset and models are to support more accurate and robust detection of online abuse. We anticipate that the high-quality and fine-grained CDC labels in the dataset will advance research on online hate for low-resource languages. The dataset and models we present could, in principle, be used to train a generative hate speech model, but this is already possible using much larger datasets. Alternatively, the dataset and models could be used to understand current detection tools' limitations better and then attack them. However, we believe malicious actors are already manually employing similar attack methods to bypass the content rules of different platforms. Therefore, we believe that it is essential to understand how to attack the models and that our dataset will help the community fight such behavior by creating a more diverse dataset that leads to more robust models.

Acknowledgements

We thank anonymous reviewers for their valuable feedback, and acknowledge financial support from several sources: the Slovenian Research Agency via research core funding for the programme Knowledge Technologies (P2-0103) and the project Sovrag (Hate speech in contemporary conceptualizations of nationalism, racism, gender and migration, J5-3102); the UK EPSRC via the project Sodestream (Streamlining Social Decision Making for Improved Internet Standards, EP/S033564/1); and via the project RobaCOFI (Robust and adaptable comment filtering), which indirectly received funding from the European Union's Horizon 2020 research and innovation action programme via the AI4Media Open Call #1 issued and executed under the AI4Media project (Grant Agreement no. 951911). This paper reflects only the authors' views; the EC and the AI4Media project are not responsible for any use that may be made of the information contained herein.

References

Michele Banko, Brendon MacKeen, and Laurie Ray. 2020. A unified taxonomy of harmful content. In *Proceedings of the fourth workshop on online abuse and harms*, pages 125–137.

Valerio Basile, Michael Fell, Tommaso Fornaciari, Dirk Hovy, Silviu Paun, Barbara Plank, Massimo Poesio, and Alexandra Uma. 2021. We need to consider disagreement in evaluation. In *Proceedings of the 1st Workshop on Benchmarking: Past, Present and Future*, pages 15–21, Online. Association for Computational Linguistics.

Alexis Conneau, Kartikay Khandelwal, Naman Goyal, Vishrav Chaudhary, Guillaume Wenzek, Francisco Guzmán, Édouard Grave, Myle Ott, Luke Zettlemoyer, and Veselin Stoyanov. 2020. Unsupervised cross-lingual representation learning at scale. In *Proceedings of the 58th Annual Meeting of the Association for Computational Linguistics*, pages 8440–8451.

Jacob Devlin, Ming-Wei Chang, Kenton Lee, and Kristina Toutanova. 2019. Bert: Pre-training of deep bidirectional transformers for language understanding. In *Proceedings of the 2019 Conference of the North American Chapter of the Association for Computational Linguistics: Human Language Technologies, Volume 1 (Long and Short Papers)*, pages 4171–4186.

Joseph L Fleiss. 1971. Measuring nominal scale agreement among many raters. *Psychological bulletin*, 76(5):378.

Paula Fortuna, João Rocha da Silva, Juan Soler-Company, L. Wanner, and Sérgio Nunes. 2019. A hierarchically-labeled portuguese hate speech dataset. *Proceedings of the Third Workshop on Abusive Language Online.*

Jana Kurrek, Haji Mohammad Saleem, and Derek Ruths. 2020. Towards a comprehensive taxonomy and large-scale annotated corpus for online slur usage. In *Proceedings of the Fourth Workshop on Online Abuse and Harms*, pages 138–149.

Elisa Leonardelli, Stefano Menini, Alessio Palmero Aprosio, Marco Guerini, and Sara Tonelli. 2021. Agreeing to disagree: Annotating offensive language datasets with annotators' disagreement. In *Proceedings of the 2021 Conference on Empirical Methods in Natural Language Processing*, pages 10528–10539.

Nikola Ljubešić and Davor Lauc. 2021. BERTić - the transformer language model for Bosnian, Croatian, Montenegrin and Serbian. In *Proceedings of the 8th Workshop on Balto-Slavic Natural Language Processing*, pages 37–42, Kiyv, Ukraine. Association for Computational Linguistics.

Antonis Maronikolakis, Axel Wisiorek, Leah Nann, Haris Jabbar, Sahana Udupa, and Hinrich Schuetze. 2022. Listening to affected communities to define extreme speech: Dataset and experiments. In *Findings of the Association for Computational Linguistics: ACL 2022*, pages 1089–1104, Dublin, Ireland. Association for Computational Linguistics.

Ioannis Mollas, Zoe Chrysopoulou, Stamatis Karlos, and Grigorios Tsoumakas. 2022. Ethos: a multi-label hate speech detection dataset. *Complex & Intelligent Systems*, pages 1–16.

Thomas E Nichols and Andrew P Holmes. 2002. Nonparametric permutation tests for functional neuroimaging: a primer with examples. *Human brain mapping*, 15(1):1–25.

Ellie Pavlick and Tom Kwiatkowski. 2019. Inherent disagreements in human textual inferences. *Transactions of the Association for Computational Linguistics*, 7:677–694.

Andraž Pelicon, Ravi Shekhar, Matej Martinc, Blaž Škrlj, Matthew Purver, and Senja Pollak. 2021a. Zero-shot cross-lingual content filtering: Offensive language and hate speech detection. In *Proceedings of the EACL Hackashop on News Media Content Analysis and Automated Report Generation*, pages 30–34, Online. Association for Computational Linguistics.

Andraž Pelicon, Ravi Shekhar, Blaž Škrlj, Matthew Purver, and Senja Pollak. 2021b. Investigating cross-lingual training for offensive language detection. *PeerJ Computer Science*, 7:e559.

Fabio Poletto, Valerio Basile, Manuela Sanguinetti, Cristina Bosco, and Viviana Patti. 2021. Resources and benchmark corpora for hate speech detection: a systematic review. *Language Resources and Evaluation*, 55(2):477–523.

Senja Pollak, Marko Robnik-Šikonja, Matthew Purver, Michele Boggia, Ravi Shekhar, Marko Pranjić, Salla Salmela, Ivar Krustok, Tarmo Paju, Carl-Gustav Linden, Leo Leppänen, Elaine Zosa, Matej Ulčar, Linda Freienthal, Silver Traat, Luis Adrián Cabrera-Diego, Matej Martinc, Nada Lavrač, Blaž Škrlj, Martin Žnidaršič, Andraž Pelicon, Boshko Koloski, Vid Podpečan, Janez Kranjc, Shane Sheehan, Emanuela Boros, Jose G. Moreno, Antoine Doucet, and Hannu Toivonen. 2021. EMBEDDIA tools, datasets and challenges: Resources and hackathon contributions. In *Proceedings of the EACL Hackashop on News Media Content Analysis and Automated Report Generation*, pages 99–109, Online. Association for Computational Linguistics.

Paul Röttger, Haitham Seelawi, Debora Nozza, Zeerak Talat, and Bertie Vidgen. 2022. Multilingual HateCheck: Functional tests for multilingual hate speech detection models. In *Proceedings of the Sixth Workshop on Online Abuse and Harms (WOAH)*, pages 154–169, Seattle, Washington (Hybrid). Association for Computational Linguistics.

Paul Röttger, Bertie Vidgen, Dong Nguyen, Zeerak Waseem, Helen Margetts, and Janet Pierrehumbert. 2021. Hatecheck: Functional tests for hate speech detection models. In *Proceedings of the 59th Annual Meeting of the Association for Computational Linguistics and the 11th International Joint Conference on Natural Language Processing (Volume 1: Long Papers)*, pages 41–58.

Ravi Shekhar, Marko Pranjić, Senja Pollak, Andraž Pelicon, and Matthew Purver. 2020. Automating news comment moderation with limited resources: Benchmarking in croatian and estonian. *Journal for Language Technology and Computational Linguistics (JLCL)*, 34(1).

M. Ulčar and M. Robnik-Šikonja. 2020. FinEst BERT and CroSloEngual BERT: less is more in multilingual models. In *Text, Speech, and Dialogue TSD 2020*, volume 12284 of *Lecture Notes in Computer Science*. Springer.

Alexandra N Uma, Tommaso Fornaciari, Dirk Hovy, Silviu Paun, Barbara Plank, and Massimo Poesio. 2021. Learning from disagreement: A survey. *Journal of Artificial Intelligence Research*, 72:1385–1470.

Bertie Vidgen and Leon Derczynski. 2020. Directions in abusive language training data, a systematic review: Garbage in, garbage out. *Plos one*, 15(12):e0243300.

Zeerak Waseem, Thomas Davidson, NY Ithica, Dana Warmsley, and Ingmar Weber. 2017. Understanding abuse: A typology of abusive language detection subtasks. *ACL 2017*, page 78.

Michael Wiegand, Josef Ruppenhofer, and Elisabeth Eder. 2021. Implicitly abusive language–what does it actually look like and why are we not getting there? In *Proceedings of the 2021 Conference of the North American Chapter of the Association for Computational Linguistics: Human Language Technologies*, pages 576–587. Association for Computational Linguistics.

Michael Wiegand, Josef Ruppenhofer, and Thomas Kleinbauer. 2019. Detection of abusive language: the problem of biased datasets. In *Proceedings of the 2019 conference of the North American Chapter of the Association for Computational Linguistics: human language technologies, volume 1 (long and short papers)*, pages 602–608.

Marcos Zampieri, Shervin Malmasi, Preslav Nakov, Sara Rosenthal, Noura Farra, and Ritesh Kumar. 2019. Predicting the type and target of offensive posts in social media. In *Proceedings of NAACL-HLT*, pages 1415–1420.

Appendix 1: Dataset Categories Examples

In this section we provide some examples for the different categories.

Explicit Expression

- Use of Derogation (*ti si nitko i ništa – You are a nobody.*)
- Threatening Language (*saznat ću gdje živiš – I will find out where you live.*)
- Slur (*retard – retard*)
- Profanity (*peder – fag*)

Implicit Expression :

- Abuse expressed using negated positive statements (*"Gej je okej" je krivo – "Gay is ok" is wrong.*)
- Abuse phrased as a question (*Zašto moramo tolerirati imigrante? – Why do we have to tolerate immigrants?*) Abuse phrased as an opinion (*Staljin je imao pravi pristup. – Stalin had the right approach.*)

Language Independent Disguise

- Swaps of adjacent characters (*jeib se – f*ck you*)
- Missing characters (*jbi se*)
- Missing word boundaries (*jebise*)
- Missing word boundaries (*jebise*)
- Added spaces between chars (*j ebi se*)
- Added spaces between chars (*j ebi se*)
- Added spaces between chars (*j ebi se*)
- substituting characters with "*", "." or similar. (*je*i se*)
- Leet speak spellings(*j3b1 5e*).

World Knowledge-Based

- Momentary (knowledge of characters/events important at this point in time or for a relatively limited time) - e.g., *Will Smith oscars slap, Brexit*
- Long-term (more stable general knowledge) - e.g., *The Pope, Berlin wall, The Beatles*

Croatian Specific Disguise

- ad-hoc constructed words that are understandable to locals (*Svi prekodrinci su ološ – All X are scum.*, where X = *prekodrinac*, an ad hoc invented word from *preko ("across")* and *Drina (name of a river)* denoting someone living across the Drina river – i.e., Serbs),
- misspelt important words in a way that is specific for croatian, mostly diacritics missing or wrong, like dj/dz for đ/dž, *djubre/dubre* (instead of *đubre* - piece of shit), *cetnik* (instead of *četnik* - member of a very unpopular military group),
- using dialects (some abuse can sound very different in some dialects, containing words like *Flundra, Droca, Štraca* – easy woman),
- idioms specific for Croatian (*Promijenit ću ti lični opis. – I will change your personal description. i.e., I will break your face.*).
- other ways of using non-abusive words to create abusive context (which requires language knowledge to properly decypher) - sarcasm, substituting slurs for similarly sounding non-slurs, inventing abusive comparisons without abusive words on the spot - e.g., *bistar si ko mocvara* (*your thinking is clear as a swamp*), *u gnjurac* (*gnjurac* is a bird, but sounds similar to *kurac – d*ck*), referring to a person from the sea side as *Tovar* (literal meaning is Donkey)

Croatia Knowledge-Based

- Momentary (knowledge of characters/events/facts important at this point in time or for a relatively limited time), e.g. *Vili Beroš* (health minister during the Covid 19 pandemic), *Uspinjača na sljeme* (controversial building project),
- Long-term (more stable local knowledge) - e.g., *HDZ* (a political party around for a long time), *'91* (year of the Croatian war of independence), *Vrapče* (one of the most widely known Psychiatric institutions)

Appendix 2: Rule Description

We have reproduced rule description from Shekhar et al. (2020) in Figure 1.

Rule ID	Description	Definition	Severity
1	Disallowed content	Advertising, content unrelated to the topic, spam, copyright infringement, citation of abusive comments or any other comments that are not allowed on the portal	Minor
2	Threats	Direct threats to other users, journalists, admins or subjects of articles, which may also result in criminal prosecution	Major
3	Hate speech	Verbal abuse, derogation and verbal attack based on national, racial, sexual or religious affiliation, hate speech and incitement	Major
4	Obscenity	Collecting and publishing personal information, uploading, distributing or publishing pornographic, obscene, immoral or illegal content and using a vulgar or offensive nickname that contains the name and surname of others	Major
5	Deception & trolling	Publishing false information for the purpose of deception or slander, and "trolling" - deliberately provoking other commentators	Minor
6	Vulgarity	Use of bad language, unless they are used as a stylistic expression, or are not addressed directly to someone	Minor
7	Language	Writing in other language besides Croatian, in other scripts besides Latin, or writing with all caps	Minor
8	Abuse	Verbally abusing of other users and their comments, article authors, and direct or indirect article subjects, calling the admins out or arguing with them in any way	Minor

Table 1: Annotation schema for blocked comments, 24sata.

Figure 1: Rule description, reproduced from Shekhar et al. (2020)

A Copy Mechanism for Handling Knowledge Base Elements in SPARQL Neural Machine Translation

Rose Hirigoyen, Amal Zouaq and **Samuel Reyd**
rose.hirigoyen@polymtl.ca
amal.zouaq@polymtl.ca
samuel.reyd@polymtl.ca
Polytechnique Montreal

Abstract

Neural Machine Translation (NMT) models from English to SPARQL are a promising development for SPARQL query generation. However, current architectures are unable to integrate the knowledge base (KB) schema and handle questions on knowledge resources, classes, and properties unseen during training, rendering them unusable outside the scope of topics covered in the training set. Inspired by the performance gains in natural language processing tasks, we propose to integrate a copy mechanism for neural SPARQL query generation as a way to tackle this issue. We illustrate our proposal by adding a copy layer and a dynamic knowledge base vocabulary to two Seq2Seq architectures (CNNs and Transformers). This layer makes the models copy KB elements directly from the questions, instead of generating them. We evaluate our approach on state-of-the-art datasets, including datasets referencing unknown KB elements and measure the accuracy of the copy-augmented architectures. Our results show a considerable increase in performance on all datasets compared to non-copy architectures.

Q: What is Villa La Mauresque ?

```
select ?a where
    { dbr:Villa_La_Mauresque
    dbo:abstract ?a }
```

A: The villa La Mauresque is located in cap Ferrat (Alpes-Maritimes) and was remodeled in 1927 ...

Figure 1: Example of the SPARQL NMT task

1 Introduction

The Semantic Web organizes concepts in optimized, machine-readable, knowledge bases (KB) (or knowledge graphs). Still, as these knowledge bases are not immediately designed with a human user in mind, the SPARQL Protocol and RDF Query Language (SPARQL) is hardly accessible to laypeople with little-to-no knowledge of programming languages. This creates a strong accessibility bias, as it prevents users from accessing sizeable amounts of information because of their lack of a specific skillset.

One way to bypass any need for prior knowledge is by allowing the users to query KBs using natural language questions. Figure 1 illustrates the task at hand. More specifically, using neural machine translation (NMT) to translate natural language questions to SPARQL queries has proven to be an interesting avenue to solve this challenge, with BLEU-score performances of more than 90% across multiple datasets (Yin et al., 2021).

However, behind these high-performing architectures are models that rarely return the correct answer to a question about a topic they have never seen in training, even if the information is available in the KB. As a single wrong answer can negatively affect the user's trust in the model, this limitation becomes a critical downfall for an automatic SPARQL query generation model. The main goal of this paper is to propose a mechanism to effectively generate accurate SPARQL queries. In particular, we aim at handling out-of-vocabulary (OOV) knowledge base elements at the schema level (classes, properties) and the instance level. As such, we put forth the following research questions:

- **RQ1:** Is the integration of the KB elements in the question sufficient for the model to handle OOV elements?
- **RQ2:** Is the accuracy of the translations improved if the neural translation architecture is able to copy KB elements directly from the question?
- **RQ3:** Does the evaluation of the model on a dataset composed solely of unknown KB

Findings of the Association for Computational Linguistics: AACL-IJCNLP 2022, pages 226–236
November 20–23, 2022. ©2022 Association for Computational Linguistics

elements allows for a complete overview of the model's capabilities?

Our main contributions are as follows. (1) Given a working tagging algorithm, we propose a way to allow NMT models to handle questions on topics they have not seen during training. (2) We propose a methodology to evaluate a model's performance exhaustively. (3) Finally, we produce standardized, corrected, and tagged versions of the datasets to foster reproducibility and future developments in this research field[1].

2 Related Work

Knowledge Bases Terminology. A *knowledge base (KB)* stores data in the form of one or more Resource Description Framework (RDF) graphs, in which the nodes are concepts or instances, and the edges encode the relationship between them. An RDF graph is described using (subject, property, object) triples, which we refer to as *KB elements*. Each KB element has a unique URI, which is used to reference it in a SPARQL query and a label, which is their name in a natural language. If there is no label, we can generate one from the element's URI.

Seq2Seq for NMT. The base architecture behind many NMT models is *Seq2Seq*, which learns to generate words using source and target vocabularies. If there is a token in the source sentence that is not in the vocabulary, the model simply replaces it by the **<unk>** placeholder token. The model is as such only able to generate tokens that are in its target vocabulary. The transformers (Vaswani et al., 2017) and convolutional networks (Gehring et al., 2017) are currently the two best non-pretrained architectures for SPARQL NMT, as reported by Yin et al. (2021).

As more data becomes available, an important development in this field is the introduction of pretrained language models and their application for neural machine translation. For example, T5 (Raffel et al., 2020) uses Transformers and transfer learning to translate three languages at once. This provides the model with a rich vocabulary of about 32000 tokens, and it can use its prior knowledge to reach higher performances on languages for which there is less training data. However, as stated in the paper, the model can only process a predetermined, fixed set of languages and it uses a fixed vocabulary. This means that as much as it is able to infer information in general translation problems, it encounters the same OOV problem as other Seq2Seq-type models, since it does not have the ability to learn new words once training is over. Very recent concurrent efforts explore the use of pretrained language models for SPARQL query generation (Banerjee et al., 2022). For example, SGPT (Rony et al., 2022) is built on GPT-2 (Radford et al., 2019) and aims to generate SPARQL queries by encoding linguistic features of questions and the knowledge graph. It uses an entity masking strategy and generates queries with placeholders. After a query is generated by the neural architecture, a *post-processor* places the correct KB elements in the right places in the query. While our objective is similar, our approach aims at using a copy mechanism directly in the Seq2Seq architecture to place KB elements in the question instead of doing it in a post-processing step.

KGQA Systems. Since the handling of OOV KB elements is limited in the specific field of SPARQL NMT, it is necessary to broaden our research and learn from similar SPARQL NLP tasks. In particular, Knowledge Graph Question Answering (KGQA) systems aim to reconstruct a subgraph of the RDF schema from a natural language question and use it to generate a correct query. A notable aspect of these architectures is that they can provide a correct answer to a question on a topic not seen in training (Jiang and Usbeck, 2022) (if the answer is in the KB). An interesting KGQA system is HGNet (Chen et al., 2021b). A key aspect of this architecture is that in trying to generate the subgraph necessary to answer the question, it can take advantage of the fact that such graph often contain duplicated vertices. It uses LSTMs and a copy mechanism to copy these duplicated vertices, thus facilitating the generation task. Such systems (Chen et al., 2021b; Vollmers et al., 2021) highlight the importance of integrating the RDF schema and resources in the architecture. Doing so not only provides us with additional information on the KB elements themselves, but also on the elements which they are related to and which are more likely to be referenced as well.

SQL Systems. It is also useful to explore what we can learn from problems similar to the one of SPARQL NMT, such as the text-to-SQL seman-

[1] https://github.com/Lama-West/SPARQL_Query_Generation_aacl-ijcnl2022

tic parsing problem (Wang et al., 2020; Scholak et al., 2021). One of the current best performing model (Guo and Gao, 2019) is not a Seq2Seq-type model, but rather a classification model that learns to predict 6 different SQL components by leveraging the extensively annotated WikiSQL dataset. Seq2SQL (Zhong et al., 2017) is another approach, which, while not the best performing architecture, is worth noting for its schema integration mechanism. Seq2SQL augments the natural language question by concatenating it to all the columns' names and to the SQL vocabulary. The schema is essentially integrated directly in the input. Once again, incorporating the schema in the architecture gives the model enough information to understand which database elements (or for SPARQL, KB elements) are referenced in a question whether or not it has seen them during training, provided they are available in the database.

Copy Mechanism. The copy mechanism has shown its effectiveness in several encoder-decoder NLP tasks such as summarization (See et al., 2017), grammatical errors correction (Zhao et al., 2019), and knowledge graph question answering (KGQA) (Chen et al., 2021b). However, to our knowledge, it has not yet been used in SPARQL NMT as we propose here. Our hypothesis is that, given a working tagging algorithm where, in the NL question, mentions related to a KB element are replaced by their KB URI, a model could learn to copy the KB URIs from the question to the query instead of generating them. Notably, we propose to integrate CopyNet (Gu et al., 2016), whose copy mechanism comes after the decoder. For each token of the output sentence, it uses attention to calculate the probability that the token should be generated from the target vocabulary, and the probability that the token should be copied directly from the source. The chances of copying are slightly higher for OOV words in the source sentence.

Limitations. As reported by Yin et al. (2021), the current best performing non-pretrained architectures for SPARQL NMT are the *Transformer Seq2Seq* and the *ConvSeq2Seq*, which are Seq2Seq-type models where the encoder and decoder are respectively transformers and convolutional networks. As such, they encounter the same limitation as all Seq2Seq-type models, which is that because of the use of fixed vocabularies, the models are unable to fully handle OOV tokens. In SPARQL NMT systems, this results in the models not being able to answer questions referencing KB elements that were unseen during training. Instead, when encountering a question on a new KB element, the models generate a query referencing the element seen the most in the current context, even if it is not the one referenced in the question.

This also means that the model might learn the meaning of a specific KB element during training, but never use this knowledge if the element is not referenced in the test set. In the context of a query language, our hypothesis is that the encoder-decoder model should focus on learning the syntax of the correct SPARQL query related to a question, instead of trying to learn the meaning of each KB element. Keeping in mind that the prevalent KBs such as DBpedia can contain tens of thousands of different URIs, expecting the model to learn everything from examples is not optimal. Furthermore, the lack of real-world data is the field of SPARQL NMT makes this approach unrealistic.

In light of these limitations, the impressive BLEU-scores reported by Yin et al. (2021) raise some questions on the ability of these metrics and current datasets to properly evaluate NMT SPARQL models. Knowing that the models are only able to generate tokens learned during training, it is almost impossible for them to return a correct answer on a question whose topic is unknown, except by accident or when the expected answer is empty. Some datasets contain a number of queries that return empty answers. As such, it is important to make sure that models are thoroughly tested, especially on questions mentioning KB elements never seen during training.

3 Architectures

3.1 Base Architectures

This section describes the two best non-pretrained architectures for SPARQL NMT as reported by Yin et al. (2021), as well as our contribution.

ConvS2S. The convolutional sequence to sequence model (ConvS2S) is a Seq2Seq-type model where the encoder and decoder are convolutional networks (Gehring et al., 2017). Both the encoder and the decoder generate token embeddings and position embeddings of the vectors they receive as input, respectively the encoding of the question and the encoding of the query. The decoder also receives the output of the encoder as input, and its input vector is padded at the beginning. This creates an offset which allows the model to learn from previous words and not from the current words which it is supposed to predict. Then, the sum of the token and position embedding vectors passes multiple times through a recurrent layer. This layer comprises a 1-dimension convolution and a Gated Linear Unit (GLU) in the encoder, followed by multihead attention in the decoder. Following the survey by Yin et al. (2021), we use the same architecture configuration as FairSeq's *fconv_wmt_en_de* NMT architecture (Ott et al., 2019), described in Table 1.

Model	Transformer	ConS2S
Batch Size	128	128
Layers	6	15
Hid. Dim.	1024	[(512, 3) * 9, (1024,3) * 4, (2048, 1) * 2]
Dropout	0.5	0.2
LR	0.0005	0.5[2]
Optimizer	Adam	SGD

Table 1: Configuration of our Architectures

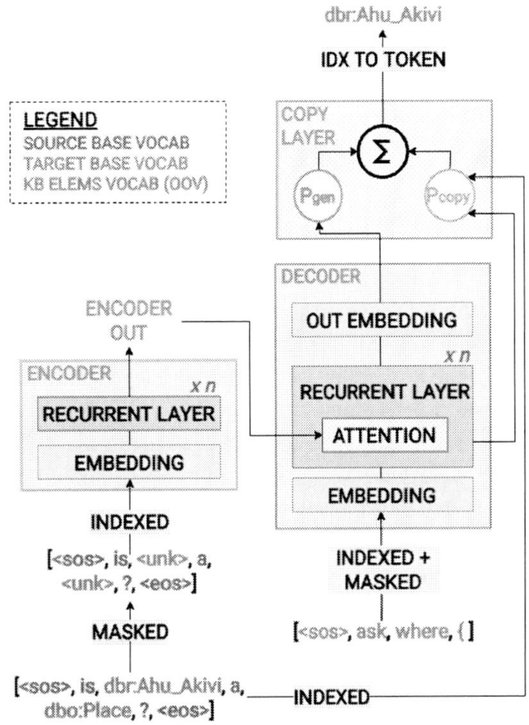

Figure 2: Encoder and copy-augmented decoder structure and interaction

Transformer. The Transformer model is a Seq2Seq-type model where the encoder and decoder are transformers (Vaswani et al., 2017). The encoder and decoder receive the same inputs as the ConvS2S. The decoder uses a multi-head attention layer that is not in the encoder. Our implementation is based on the FairSeq implementation (Ott et al., 2019) of the *transformer_iwslt_de_en* architecture, as described in Table 1.

3.2 A Copy-augmented Architecture

Figure 2 shows our generic architecture, which enriches any encoder-decoder model (e.g. CNNs or transformers) with a copy layer in the decoder. It generates specific source and target vocabularies that include the KB elements as explained below.

Vocabularies. In the baseline architectures (without copy), the source vocabulary comprises every token of the questions, and the target vocabulary comprises every token in the queries. Tokens are added in the order in which they are encountered.

However, when using the copy layer, there needs to be a way to differentiate tokens that are part of the base vocabularies (which the model will learn to generate) and tokens that are KB elements (which the model will learn to copy from the source). The latter are identifiable by their prefix, meaning tokens that start with **dbo:**, **dbr:**, **dbp:**, **dbc:**, **geo:**, **georss:** or **dct:**. Also, since the model receives vectors of indices and not words, tokens copied from the source to the target sentence must have the same index in both the source and target vocabularies.

To accommodate these constraints, we create a base source vocabulary and a base target vocabulary containing all tokens in the inputs but no KB elements and pad them with filler words so they are the same size. Then, we extract the KB elements in a vocabulary extension that contains all elements in both the questions and the queries. Finally, the KB vocabulary is concatenated to each base vocabulary to create our source and target vocabularies.

As we know the cutoff index of the initial vocabularies, we can quickly determine that each index above this cutoff represents a KB element we want to copy. During inference, if a new KB element is encountered, we can add it at the end of our source and target vocabularies, giving the model the capacity to copy it.

[2]For the dataset TNTSPA, we used a LR of 3.5

Copy Layer. In a copy-augmented architecture, the encoder and decoder receive masked source and target vectors, meaning any token above the cutoff index (and as such, out of the vocabulary) is replaced by a 0, representing an unknown token. As the role of the copy layer is to handle KB elements, this masking lets the encoder and decoder focus on the syntax rather than on the KB elements.

The copy layer comes after the decoder. It takes as input the unmasked encoded question and the decoder output, comprised of the attention scores and the probability of generating each word of the base target vocabulary. Ported to the Transformer architecture by (See et al., 2017; Zhao et al., 2019), we were able to adapt it to ConvS2S since both generate multi-head attention scores.

First, we identify whether there are any KB elements amongst the tokens of the encoded question by using the cutoff index. If it is the case, we extend the output probability tensor to include these extra tokens and initially assign them a generation probability of 0. Then, we calculate the probability of each token being generated, which is the softmax of the probability tensor. Using the attention score, we also calculate the probability of each word being copied directly from the source sentence. Following the implementation of (Zhao et al., 2019), we compute a balancing factor $\alpha_{bal} \epsilon [0, 1]$ between the copy and the generation probabilities using Equation 2, where Q, K and V are the query, key and value needed to calculate attention and W^{T} is a learnable parameter. The final probability of each token being the next word is the sum of the generation and copy probabilities balanced by this factor.

$$A_t = Q^T * K \tag{1}$$

$$\alpha_{bal} = sigmoid(W^T * (A_t^T * V)) \tag{2}$$

4 Methodology

4.1 Datasets

Format. Most natural language (NL) to SPARQL datasets are generated using templates to compensate for the lack of real-world data. A template is an NL question and its corresponding SPARQL query, in which there are annotated blanks to indicate the types of the KB element to insert (resources, classes, properties). These blanks are then replaced by KB elements' labels in the questions, and KB URIs in the queries. Many datasets also use an alternate version of SPARQL introduced by (Soru et al., 2017) called *intermediary SPARQL*, in which each symbol (e.g., brackets, dots) is replaced by a specific natural language expression. This encoding aims to make SPARQL closer to a natural human language. URIs are also reduced using their prefixes. To return to the original executable SPARQL query, one only has to make the inverse permutations. Table 2 shows the datasets used in this work. We split the datasets in an 80-10-10 fashion to reproduce the results reported by (Yin et al., 2021).

	Mon	**Mon50**	**Mon80**
Train	1797	1787	1791
Test	815	825	816
Int. rate	0.928	0.925	0.925
	TNTSPA	**LC-QuAD**	**DBNQA**
Train	4153	4150	145 429
Test	1045	1066	38 348
Int. rate	0.704	0.713	0.797

Table 2: Summary of the distribution of KB elements in the datasets

Monument. The Monument dataset (Soru et al., 2017) consists of pairs of English natural questions and intermediary SPARQL queries generated from 38 templates. The authors (Yin et al., 2021) generate other versions of the dataset: Monument, Monument50 and Monument80. The three versions are very similar in that they are all generated using 600 examples per template with different combinations of KB elements. We used their versions to be able to compare our results to state-of-the-art architectures. The high BLEU scores reported by Yin et al. (2021) are explained by the fact that most KB elements in the test set have already been seen during training, as shown by the high intersection rate in Table 2. Also, this dataset covers fewer KB elements in more entries, which gives the models plenty of examples to learn each element in its context. Overall, good results on this dataset only mean a model is functional.

LC-QuAD. The LC-QuAD datasets provide entries of multiple types (COUNT, ASK, SELECT) and cover a broad range of KB elements. We prioritized LC-QuAD v1.0 (Trivedi et al., 2017) over the newer LC-QuAD v2.0 (Dubey et al., 2019) since the models to which we compare our work are trained on the first version. Further tests on LC-QuAD 2 are left for future work.

In LC-QuADv1.0, each entry contains an English natural language question and its corresponding SPARQL query generated from a template (called intermediary question), as well as a version of the question reformulated by an expert (called corrected question). It comprises 5000 entries generated from 33 of the 43 templates available. Table 2 shows that it is much more challenging than Monument. Indeed, there are many more different KB elements, fewer examples per element, and a lower intersection rate between the train and test sets.

We use three versions of the LC-QuAD dataset. The first version, referred to as **LC-QuAD Intermediary Questions**, uses the intermediary questions and their corresponding queries. These questions use the formulations defined by the templates. The second and more challenging version, referred to as **LC-QuAD Corrected Questions**, uses the reformulated natural language questions of the dataset and their corresponding queries. The third version, referred to as **TNTSPA**, is the version generated by the authors of the survey (Yin et al., 2021). It contains the reformulated questions (formulated in a more natural way) and queries found in the LC-QuADv1.0 dataset, but is split differently. Since no validation set is provided for the TNTSPA dataset, we use entries from LC-QuAD v1.0 that are not in the TNTSPA train or test sets. Since there are no templates associated to this dataset, we only use it to ensure we are able to reproduce state-of-the-art results with our implementation of the baselines architectures.

DBNQA. The DBpedia Neural Question Answering (DBNQA) dataset (Hartmann et al., 2018) is composed of 894,499 pairs of natural language questions and SPARQL queries. The entries are generated using 5165 question-query templates, constructed from entries in the LC-QuADv1.0 (Trivedi et al., 2017) and QALD-7 (Usbeck et al., 2017) datasets. We used the templates provided with the dataset but we did not manage to match all entries. We then extracted and corrected 512 templates suitable for the annotation of the questions and used the 398,284 entries corresponding to these templates. We also provide directly executable SPARQL queries instead of intermediate SPARQL queries.

RDF schema integration. As this research focuses mainly on finding a solution for the OOV problem, we developed a rudimentary tagging algorithm that leverages the templates. For each entry, we replace the KB elements labels that replace the blanks in the questions with their corresponding URIs in the query. KB elements that would be encoded as multiple tokens because of intermediary SPARQL (e.g., **[dbr_Cenotaph_, attr_open, Montreal, attr_close]**) are encoded as a single token (e.g., **dbr_Cenotaph_(Montreal)**) to reduce the vocabulary size. This dependence on templates is why we use the LC-QuAD Intermediary Questions version of LC-QuAD to train and evaluate our copy-augmented models, as it is the only version we could tag with complete accuracy. Figure 3 shows an entry before and after tagging.

Template: what is the <domain> whose <property_1> is <resource_1> and **<property_2>** is **<resource_2>** ?

Question: what is the formula one racer whose relatives is ralf schumacher and **has child** is **mick schumacher** ?

Tagged: what is the dbo:FormulaOneRacer whose dbp:relatives is dbr:Ralf_Schumacher and dbo:child is **dbr:Mick_Schumacher** ?

Figure 3: A tagged question

OOV Datasets. Finally, we generate an additional test set of 250 entries for each dataset called the **OOV Set**. First, we go through the dataset and make a list of all the referenced KB elements. Then, we use the templates to generate entries where the placeholders are replaced by KB elements that are not in the list, effectively creating a dataset in which no KB element has been seen in training.

To avoid false positives, we built our datasets so that questions would return a non-empty answer whenever possible. However, this proved to be a challenging task and our most successful attempts still contain about 70% of empty answers (count of 0, ask that returns false, or empty sets of elements). False positives can happen when a query returns an empty answer regardless of the KB elements referenced (e.g. an impossible question that links unrelated KB elements, or a question for which the KB does not contain an answer).

4.2 Evaluation

We use two main metrics to evaluate the original test sets and the oov test sets: the **BLEU-score** and the **answer accuracy**, which calculates the accuracy of the answers returned by the generated queries against the expected answers.

5 Results

We trained and evaluated our implementation of the models using Google Colab GPUs. We compare our results to those reported by (Yin et al., 2021), who train their model on HPC servers using the FairSeq implementations of the CnnS2S and Transformer architectures. It is important to note that they report the peak performance while we report the average of three runs. This means that we expect slightly lower performances when reproducing their results.

Baseline architectures on original datasets. Table 3 shows the results of the baseline architectures on original datasets. We clearly reproduce the performances of the survey by Yin et al. (2021). Even if our results for LC-QuAD are slightly lower, it is still within an acceptable margin. Because of the randomness of the weights initialization, the performance difference between a good and a underperforming run can be up to ten points. This margin also accounts for the small difference between TNTSPA and the LQ Corr Qsts. The higher scores on LQ Intrm.Qsts compared to the corrected questions are explained by the fact that the questions are generated from templates. This results in a smaller source vocabulary compared to the vocabulary of reformulated questions (used in TNTSPA and Corr. Qsts), since the questions are all formulated using the same template-words. Hence, the reduced variance helps the model understand the questions better.

Baseline architectures on tagged datasets. Table 4 shows the results of the baseline architectures on tagged datasets. We must not overlook the fact that using tagged data might help the architectures perform better, even without a copy layer. Since the KB elements are encoded as a single symbol, the size of the source and target vocabularies decreases, which usually helps the models perform better. These changes do not make much difference for the Monument datasets since the datasets contain enough examples for the models to learn the KB elements with or without tagging. For the LC-QuAD intermediary questions, we see a clear increase in performance. This is explained by the fact that in the untagged version, the URIs are encoded in the SPARQL query using multiple tokens (`dbr:Primus_ attr_open band attr_close`), whereas they are encoded as a single token in the NL question and the SPARQL query in the tagged version (`dbr:Primus_(band)`).

	Transformer		**ConvS2S**	
Dataset	BLEU	Acc.	BLEU	Acc.
Mon	95.86	90.55	96.35	91.66
Mon50	96.26	91.72	95.25	88.34
Mon80	96.35	92.69	94.47	82.68
TNTSPA	55.98	42.80	52.24	44.00
Corr. Qsts	49.61	32.07	49.94	40.80
Intrm. Qsts	60.31	43.60	65.65	47.40
DBNQA	64.86	46.41	67.26	45.43

Table 3: Performances of baseline architectures on original datasets. **TNTSPA** is (Yin et al., 2021)'s version of LC-QuAD. **C. Qsts** designates the LC-QuAD corrected questions and **Intrm. Qsts** designates the LC-QuAD intermediary questions.

For DBNQA, many URIs are quite long and expressed using multiple tokens in the questions. In the untagged version, this means many NL tokens are reused across multiple URI expressions, resulting in a smaller source vocabulary of 99603 tokens. Because there are more unique URIs than unique NL tokens used to represent these URIs in the questions, the tagged version uses a bigger source vocabulary composed of 158014 tokens. However, we see by comparing tables 3 and 4 that this augmentation of the vocabulary size does not affect the performance of the baseline models.

Copy-augmented architectures. Table 4 shows the results of our copy-augmented architectures on tagged datasets. We observe a strong increase in performance for LC-QuAD and DBNQA, which is impressive considering the number of different KB elements in the datasets, as well as perfect results on the Monument datasets. However, the most telling results are those obtained on the OOV datasets, reported in Table 5. The answer accuracy metric is not included because of the high proportion of possible false positives across all OOV datasets. Still, using only the BLEU score, we see that the baseline architectures struggle to han-

Architecture	Mon		Mon50		Mon80		Intrm. Qsts		DBNQA	
	BLEU	Acc.	BLEU	Acc.	BLEU	Acc.	BLEU	Acc.	BLEU	Acc.
Transformer	97.02	92.81	97.41	94.41	97.80	94.86	70.29	51.93	65.63	47.75
Transf.-copy	100	100	100	100	100	100	98.38	97.60	93.88	85.09
ConvS2S	97.82	95.26	97.71	95.13	98.14	95.96	76.62	52.93	67.57	45.22
ConvS2S-copy	100	100	100	100	100	100	98.35	97.40	95.40	86.87

Table 4: Performances of all architectures on tagged datasets

dle KB elements they have never seen, which is more representative of the actual capabilities of the models. Similarly, the results on tagged OOV datasets with baseline architectures are still low compared to the results on the original test sets, since tagged data still does not allow the model to adequately handle new KB elements after training. However, on copy-augmented architectures, we observe perfect performances on Monument, representing an increase in performance of about 30 BLEU points compared to its baseline counterpart. On LC-QuAD, the increase of about 40 BLEU points shows that the models handle better unknown KB elements using a copy mechanism.

6 Discussion

In view of these results, it is clear that, given a working tagging mechanism, the use of a copy-augmented architecture is an excellent advantage for SPARQL NMT architectures as it allows them to handle KB elements not seen in training. Furthermore, comparing the results with and without copy reported in Table 5, we see a clear improvement in the quality of the translations.

Another advantage of using a copy-augmented architecture is that it can perform almost as well on small datasets as on larger ones, as demonstrated by the high performances on the LC-QuAD Intermediary Questions and DBNQA. Essentially, the model does not need to learn the correspondences between each expression and the related URI anymore, and it does not need as many examples to learn the templates' formulations since there are not that many. Our work also highlights, as shown by the drastic difference between tables 3 and 5, that baseline models that are reported to have almost perfect performance are, in fact, not as effective outside the test set on which they are evaluated. Even if the BLEU score is a good way to evaluate the quality of the translation, The use of accuracy and the introduction of OOV datasets helps us understand better a model's actual capabilities.

There is however still room for improvement. Some of the limitations of this research lie in the use of template-based entries. In its current state, our copy-augmented architecture depends on questions following specific templates. As shown by the results reported in table 3, Seq2Seq models seem quite efficient at learning templates. As we see in Table 4, the performances increase when the KB elements are encoded in the questions, hinting at the fact that the model is limited by the large amount of KB elements in the dataset rather than the questions' formulations. Moving away from template-based datasets would also allow us to determine whether the copy layer helps the model understand the underlying schema of the KB.

We also need to improve the way OOV datasets are generated to be able to get a representative accuracy metric that is not biased by false positives. To do so, we must ensure most - if not all - queries return a non-empty answer.

Finally, another limitation is that our copy-augmented models depend on tagged questions to reach their top performance.

7 Conclusion

This paper determined that, coupled with a copy-augmented architecture, integrating the KB elements directly in the questions is sufficient for a SPARL NMT model to handle OOV KB elements and to obtain a significant increase in performance. These tagged datasets were used to train baseline and copy-augmented versions of the Transformer and the ConvS2S architectures. Using a copy layer, we report perfect performances on the Monument dataset and the generated OOV Monument dataset. For LC-QuAD, we report an increase in BLEU score of 20 points and an increase in answer accuracy of about 40 points. For DBNQA, our results

Dataset	Monument		LQ Intrm. Qsts		DBNQA	
	Original	Tagged	Original	Tagged	Original	Tagged
Transf	60.16	65.55	51.50	56.75	40.92	41.19
Transf-copy	-	100	-	85.68	-	79.82
ConvS2S	63.88	48.31	55.85	60.98	40.62	40.66
ConvS2S-copy	-	100	-	90.16	-	89.13

Table 5: BLEU scores of all the models on the OOV datasets.

show an increase in BLEU score of 35 points on average, as well as an increase in answer accuracy of 40 points. Our future work will involve the design of a neural tagging model and a joint tagging objective for our Seq2Seq models, as well as the comparison of our copy-augmented models with large pre-trained models and the use of these models as our encoders-decoders. Notable models on which to test our methodology include T5 (Raffel et al., 2020), BART (Lewis et al., 2020) and GPT-3 (Brown et al., 2020), as well as models that can generate code such as Codex (Chen et al., 2021a).

Acknowledgements

This research has been funded by the NSERC Discovery Grant Program.

References

Debayan Banerjee, Pranav Ajit Nair, Jivat Neet Kaur, Ricardo Usbeck, and Chris Biemann. 2022. Modern baselines for SPARQL semantic parsing. In *SIGIR '22: The 45th International ACM SIGIR Conference on Research and Development in Information Retrieval, Madrid, Spain, July 11 - 15, 2022*, pages 2260–2265. ACM.

Tom B. Brown, Benjamin Mann, Nick Ryder, Melanie Subbiah, Jared Kaplan, Prafulla Dhariwal, Arvind Neelakantan, Pranav Shyam, Girish Sastry, Amanda Askell, Sandhini Agarwal, Ariel Herbert-Voss, Gretchen Krueger, Tom Henighan, Rewon Child, Aditya Ramesh, Daniel M. Ziegler, Jeffrey Wu, Clemens Winter, Christopher Hesse, Mark Chen, Eric Sigler, Mateusz Litwin, Scott Gray, Benjamin Chess, Jack Clark, Christopher Berner, Sam McCandlish, Alec Radford, Ilya Sutskever, and Dario Amodei. 2020. Language models are few-shot learners. In *Advances in Neural Information Processing Systems 33: Annual Conference on Neural Information Processing Systems 2020, NeurIPS 2020, December 6-12, 2020, virtual*, pages 1877–1901. Curran Associates, Inc.

Mark Chen, Jerry Tworek, Heewoo Jun, Qiming Yuan, Henrique Ponde de Oliveira Pinto, Jared Kaplan, Harrison Edwards, Yuri Burda, Nicholas Joseph, Greg Brockman, Alex Ray, Raul Puri, Gretchen Krueger, Michael Petrov, Heidy Khlaaf, Girish Sastry, Pamela Mishkin, Brooke Chan, Scott Gray, Nick Ryder, Mikhail Pavlov, Alethea Power, Lukasz Kaiser, Mohammad Bavarian, Clemens Winter, Philippe Tillet, Felipe Petroski Such, Dave Cummings, Matthias Plappert, Fotios Chantzis, Elizabeth Barnes, Ariel Herbert-Voss, William Hebgen Guss, Alex Nichol, Alex Paino, Nikolas Tezak, Jie Tang, Igor Babuschkin, Suchir Balaji, Shantanu Jain, William Saunders, Christopher Hesse, Andrew N. Carr, Jan Leike, Joshua Achiam, Vedant Misra, Evan Morikawa, Alec Radford, Matthew Knight, Miles Brundage, Mira Murati, Katie Mayer, Peter Welinder, Bob McGrew, Dario Amodei, Sam McCandlish, Ilya Sutskever, and Wojciech Zaremba. 2021a. Evaluating large language models trained on code. *CoRR*, abs/2107.03374.

Yongrui Chen, Huiying Li, Guilin Qi, Tianxing Wu, and Tenggou Wang. 2021b. Outlining and filling: Hierarchical query graph generation for answering complex questions over knowledge graph. *CoRR*, abs/2111.00732.

Mohnish Dubey, Debayan Banerjee, Abdelrahman Abdelkawi, and Jens Lehmann. 2019. Lc-quad 2.0: A large dataset for complex question answering over wikidata and dbpedia. In *The Semantic Web - ISWC 2019 - 18th International Semantic Web Conference, Auckland, New Zealand, October 26-30, 2019, Proceedings, Part II*, volume 11779 of *Lecture Notes in Computer Science*, pages 69–78. Springer.

Jonas Gehring, Michael Auli, David Grangier, Denis Yarats, and Yann N. Dauphin. 2017. Convolutional sequence to sequence learning. In *Proceedings of the 34th International Conference on Machine Learning, ICML 2017, Sydney, NSW, Australia, 6-11 August 2017*, volume 70 of *Proceedings of Machine Learning Research*, pages 1243–1252. PMLR.

Jiatao Gu, Zhengdong Lu, Hang Li, and Victor O. K. Li. 2016. Incorporating copying mechanism in sequence-to-sequence learning. In *Proceedings of the 54th Annual Meeting of the Association for Computational Linguistics, ACL 2016, August 7-12, 2016, Berlin, Germany, Volume 1: Long Papers*, pages 1631–1640. The Association for Computer Linguistics.

Tong Guo and Huilin Gao. 2019. Content enhanced bert-based text-to-sql generation. *CoRR*, abs/1910.07179.

Ann-Kathrin Hartmann, Tommaso Soru, and Edgard Marx. 2018. Generating a large dataset for neural question answering over the dbpedia knowledge base.

Longquan Jiang and Ricardo Usbeck. 2022. Knowledge graph question answering datasets and their generalizability: Are they enough for future research? In *SIGIR '22: The 45th International ACM SIGIR Conference on Research and Development in Information Retrieval, Madrid, Spain, July 11 - 15, 2022*, pages 3209–3218. ACM.

Mike Lewis, Yinhan Liu, Naman Goyal, Marjan Ghazvininejad, Abdelrahman Mohamed, Omer Levy, Veselin Stoyanov, and Luke Zettlemoyer. 2020. BART: denoising sequence-to-sequence pre-training for natural language generation, translation, and comprehension. In *Proceedings of the 58th Annual Meeting of the Association for Computational Linguistics, ACL 2020, Online, July 5-10, 2020*, pages 7871–7880. Association for Computational Linguistics.

Myle Ott, Sergey Edunov, Alexei Baevski, Angela Fan, Sam Gross, Nathan Ng, David Grangier, and Michael Auli. 2019. fairseq: A fast, extensible toolkit for sequence modeling. In *Proceedings of the 2019 Conference of the North American Chapter of the Association for Computational Linguistics: Human Language Technologies, NAACL-HLT 2019, Minneapolis, MN, USA, June 2-7, 2019, Demonstrations*, pages 48–53. Association for Computational Linguistics.

Alec Radford, Jeff Wu, Rewon Child, David Luan, Dario Amodei, and Ilya Sutskever. 2019. Language models are unsupervised multitask learners.

Colin Raffel, Noam Shazeer, Adam Roberts, Katherine Lee, Sharan Narang, Michael Matena, Yanqi Zhou, Wei Li, and Peter J. Liu. 2020. Exploring the limits of transfer learning with a unified text-to-text transformer. *J. Mach. Learn. Res.*, 21:140:1–140:67.

Md. Rashad Al Hasan Rony, Uttam Kumar, Roman Teucher, Liubov Kovriguina, and Jens Lehmann. 2022. SGPT: A generative approach for SPARQL query generation from natural language questions. *IEEE Access*, 10:70712–70723.

Torsten Scholak, Raymond Li, Dzmitry Bahdanau, Harm de Vries, and Chris Pal. 2021. Duorat: Towards simpler text-to-sql models. In *Proceedings of the 2021 Conference of the North American Chapter of the Association for Computational Linguistics: Human Language Technologies, NAACL-HLT 2021, Online, June 6-11, 2021*, pages 1313–1321. Association for Computational Linguistics.

Abigail See, Peter J. Liu, and Christopher D. Manning. 2017. Get to the point: Summarization with pointer-generator networks. In *Proceedings of the 55th Annual Meeting of the Association for Computational Linguistics, ACL 2017, Vancouver, Canada, July 30 - August 4, Volume 1: Long Papers*, pages 1073–1083. Association for Computational Linguistics.

Tommaso Soru, Edgard Marx, Diego Moussallem, Gustavo Publio, Andre Valdestilhas, Diego Esteves, and Ciro Baron Neto. 2017. SPARQL as a foreign language. In *Proceedings of the Posters and Demos Track of the 13th International Conference on Semantic Systems - SEMANTiCS2017 co-located with the 13th International Conference on Semantic Systems (SEMANTiCS 2017), Amsterdam, The Netherlands, September 11-14, 2017*, volume 2044 of *CEUR Workshop Proceedings*. CEUR-WS.org.

Priyansh Trivedi, Gaurav Maheshwari, Mohnish Dubey, and Jens Lehmann. 2017. Lc-quad: A corpus for complex question answering over knowledge graphs. In *The Semantic Web - ISWC 2017 - 16th International Semantic Web Conference, Vienna, Austria, October 21-25, 2017, Proceedings, Part II*, volume 10588 of *Lecture Notes in Computer Science*, pages 210–218. Springer.

Ricardo Usbeck, Axel-Cyrille Ngonga Ngomo, Bastian Haarmann, Anastasia Krithara, Michael Röder, and Giulio Napolitano. 2017. 7th open challenge on question answering over linked data (QALD-7). In *Semantic Web Challenges - 4th SemWebEval Challenge at ESWC 2017, Portoroz, Slovenia, May 28 - June 1, 2017, Revised Selected Papers*, volume 769 of *Communications in Computer and Information Science*, pages 59–69. Springer.

Ashish Vaswani, Noam Shazeer, Niki Parmar, Jakob Uszkoreit, Llion Jones, Aidan N. Gomez, Lukasz Kaiser, and Illia Polosukhin. 2017. Attention is all you need. In *Advances in Neural Information Processing Systems 30: Annual Conference on Neural Information Processing Systems 2017, December 4-9, 2017, Long Beach, CA, USA*, pages 5998–6008. Curran Associates, Inc.

Daniel Vollmers, Rricha Jalota, Diego Moussallem, Hardik Topiwala, Axel-Cyrille Ngonga Ngomo, and Ricardo Usbeck. 2021. Knowledge graph question answering using graph-pattern isomorphism. In *Further with Knowledge Graphs - Proceedings of the 17th International Conference on Semantic Systems, SEMANTiCS 2017, Amsterdam, The Netherlands, September 6-9, 2021*, volume 53 of *Studies on the Semantic Web*, pages 103–117. IOS Press.

Bailin Wang, Richard Shin, Xiaodong Liu, Oleksandr Polozov, and Matthew Richardson. 2020. RAT-SQL: relation-aware schema encoding and linking for text-to-sql parsers. In *Proceedings of the 58th Annual Meeting of the Association for Computational Linguistics, ACL 2020, Online, July 5-10, 2020*, pages 7567–7578. Association for Computational Linguistics.

Xiaoyu Yin, Dagmar Gromann, and Sebastian Rudolph. 2021. Neural machine translating from natural language to SPARQL. *Future Gener. Comput. Syst.*, 117:510–519.

Wei Zhao, Liang Wang, Kewei Shen, Ruoyu Jia, and Jingming Liu. 2019. Improving grammatical error correction via pre-training a copy-augmented architecture with unlabeled data. In *Proceedings of the 2019 Conference of the North American Chapter of the Association for Computational Linguistics: Human Language Technologies, NAACL-HLT 2019, Minneapolis, MN, USA, June 2-7, 2019, Volume 1 (Long and Short Papers)*, pages 156–165. Association for Computational Linguistics.

Victor Zhong, Caiming Xiong, and Richard Socher. 2017. Seq2sql: Generating structured queries from natural language using reinforcement learning. *CoRR*, abs/1709.00103.

A Multilingual Multiway Evaluation Data Set for Structured Document Translation of Asian Languages

Bianka Buschbeck[†*] **Raj Dabre**[‡*] **Miriam Exel**[†] **Matthias Huck**[†]

Patrick Huy[†] **Raphael Rubino**[‡] **Hideki Tanaka**[‡]

[†]SAP SE
Dietmar-Hopp-Allee 16
69190 Walldorf
Germany
firstname.lastname@sap.com

[‡]NICT
3-5 Hikaridai
Seika-cho, Soraku-gun, Kyoto, 619-0289
Japan
firstname.lastname@nict.go.jp

Abstract

Translation of structured content is an important application of machine translation, but the scarcity of evaluation data sets, especially for Asian languages, limits progress. In this paper we present a novel multilingual multiway evaluation data set for the translation of *structured documents* of the Asian languages Japanese, Korean and Chinese. We describe the data set, its creation process and important characteristics, followed by establishing and evaluating baselines using the direct translation as well as detag-project approaches. Our data set is well suited for multilingual evaluation, and it contains richer annotation tag sets than existing data sets. Our results show that massively multilingual translation models like M2M-100 and mBART-50 perform surprisingly well despite not being explicitly trained to handle structured content. The data set described in this paper and used in our experiments is released publicly.

1 Introduction

A common use case of machine translation (MT) is the translation of structured or formatted documents, such as web pages. The key challenge is to properly transfer markup tags *within* the translatable content (e.g. bold) from the source to the target language during the translation process. A markup example is shown in Figure 1. Although there are various data sets for sentence- and document-level machine translation, apart from Hashimoto et al. (2019) and Hanneman and Dinu (2020) we are not aware of any other data sets for evaluating the translation quality of markup annotated sentences. This paper introduces a data set that reflects all those aspects to facilitate and foster research that goes beyond the translation of plain text in isolation.

en	Click <uicontrol>Prepayment</uicontrol>.
ja	<uicontrol>前払</uicontrol>をクリックします。

Figure 1: Example with inline markup (in gray).

In this paper, we describe the second release of the *software documentation data set for machine translation*, a high-quality multilingual evaluation data set for machine translation in the IT domain.[1] It has been released by SAP[2], a large enterprise software company. The contents originate from the *SAP Help Portal*[3] that contains documentation and learning materials for SAP products. With this release of the data set, we publish development and test data for MT purposes in the form of *complete structured documents* that include segment-internal (inline) markup, in a rich XML-based localization format as well as transformations that make it readily usable in many standard machine translation workflows. It consists of 385 documents that contain about 4,000 translatable segments and their translations. With the second release, we focus on the following major Asian languages: Japanese (ja), Korean (ko), and Chinese (zh). Translations have been produced from the same English (en) source, thus the data is multiway parallel. The multiway document-level nature of this data set enables not only evaluation of multilingual models but also document-level translation approaches (if needed) when translating structured content.

Additionally, in this paper, we establish base-

* Equal contribution. Ordered by last name.

[1] The *software documentation data set for machine translation* is available under the Creative Commons license Attribution-Non Commercial 4.0 International CC BY-NC 4.0). The second release can be downloaded from https://github.com/SAP/software-documentation-data-set-for-machine-translation/releases/tag/v2.1.

[2] https://www.sap.com/

[3] https://help.sap.com/

Findings of the Association for Computational Linguistics: AACL-IJCNLP 2022, pages 237–245
November 20–23, 2022. ©2022 Association for Computational Linguistics

lines for the released data set for individual segment translation, where we utilize massively multilingual models such as M2M-100 (Fan et al., 2021) and mBART-50 (Tang et al., 2021), making use of *out-of-the-box* publicly available checkpoints already trained in a many-to-many translation fashion with no additional fine-tuning on our end. We show that these models can be used for directly translating structured content despite not being explicitly trained to do so. We observe that the quality of the direct translation approach, where the source text is composed of both lexical and markup content, is comparable to the traditional detag-project approach. We then report translation results according to several metrics targeting not only the translation quality but also tag placement accuracy, allowing us to understand the difficulty of translating structured content into Asian languages.

2 Related Work

Only recently awareness has increased that real world content often resides in structured and formatted documents such as HTML pages and Microsoft Office formats, and that the transfer of inline markup tags is a challenge for neural machine translation; correspondingly, little work has been published. Hashimoto et al. (2019) present a data set from the IT domain that features inline markup, and corresponding MT results using a constrained beam search approach for decoding. Furthermore, Hanneman and Dinu (2020) compare different data augmentation methods with a detag-project approach, and evaluate on data from legal documents from the European Union. The methods for tag transfer in Zenkel et al. (2021) are also related, even though they focus on inserting the tags into a fixed human translation.

In contrast to the previously mentioned available data sets, with the *software documentation data set for machine translation*, we publish complete documents of high translation quality, thus allowing for context-sensitive translation, such as in Miculicich et al. (2018) for example, and in-context evaluation as it has been shown to be vital for accurate evaluation assessments (Läubli et al., 2018, amongst others). Furthermore, our data set is multiway multilingual, focuses on Asian languages and adds lower resource Asian languages to the picture to enable a more comprehensive evaluation of different methods. While Hashimoto et al. (2019) enables evaluation of 14 translation directions to or from English, they do not support non-English translation directions as their evaluation data is not n-way parallel. In contrast, the second release of the *software documentation data set* is n-way parallel enabling 6 translation directions to and from English as well as 6 translation directions between the Asian languages leading to a total of 12 directions.

The first release of the *software documentation data set for machine translation* is described in Buschbeck and Exel (2020). While it also contains complete documents with rich metadata on the segment level and is therefore well suited to evaluate contextual approaches to MT, it does not feature complete hierarchical document structure. Its focus is low-resource language pairs that are typically under-represented in MT research, namely English to Hindi, Indonesian, Malay and Thai.

In terms of methods, according to our knowledge, we are the first to report results on tag transfer using pre-trained massively multilingual translation models mBART-50 and M2M-100 (Tang et al., 2021; Fan et al., 2021). We also compare with the detag-project approach, but leave the exploration of other methods on this data set for future work.

3 The Structured Documents Data Set

We describe the second release of the *software documentation data set for machine translation*, our data set for structured document translation of Asian languages.

3.1 Data Set Sources and Selection

The contents of the data set originate from the public online documentation of SAP, a large software company, featuring product documentation, user assistance and learning materials. The individual pages (or documents) are highly structured. They are authored in DITA, an XML-based open standard often used for technical documentation.[4] The original documents are in English and translations are performed into Japanese, Korean and Chinese (amongst others) by specialized professional translators. Translations are validated in a subsequent review process to guarantee an excellent quality, including coherent domain-specific terminology, before the final target texts are published. Throughout this process, standard computer-assisted translation tools are used. The localization workflow is based

[4] https://www.oasis-open.org/committees/tc_home.php?wg_abbrev=dita

on XLIFF, an XML-based format for storing bitext which was created to standardize the way localizable data is passed between localization tools.[5] The original DITA document structure including inline markup is preserved throughout the process. For more background information on the data, consult Buschbeck and Exel (2020).

Documents for development and test data are selected from a large set of original DITA documents that have recently been translated, with the same English source for all target languages. To create an interesting and relevant data set, we calculate a set of indicators per document, and then select those documents that score best. In order to minimize segment redundancy within the data set (ratio of all source-target pairs to unique source-target pairs) while selecting complete documents, we follow the criteria introduced in Buschbeck and Exel (2020). Besides document length and average segment length, they consider the redundancy within documents as well as between documents. In addition, we also take the number of inline markup tags into account.

3.2 Format and Tooling

We provide the data in XLIFF. Each XLIFF file of the data set represents one original DITA document with its translation into one of the target languages. Appendix A.1 provides more details, including an example. Our XLIFF files contain the *full* original document structure and are therefore very rich in information. However, some applications or evaluation scenarios might only want to consider specific parts of the structure. Therefore, we also provide the data in a format that is convenient for MT research: one translatable (source or target) segment per line with inline markup being represented as raw DITA tags, similar to the format in Hashimoto et al. (2019), an example of which is in Table 1. This representation is obtained from XLIFF with an XSL transformation. Other transformations for which we provide XSL stylesheets are described in Appendix A.2.

3.3 Data Set Statistics and Characteristics

Table 1 displays the main characteristics of the data set such as number of documents, translatable segments, segments containing inline elements, number of words and amount of redundancy. As the data sets are composed of whole documents, some segment duplicates are unavoidable, despite a data selection method that strives for a low intersection of documents (see Section 3.1). In the data at hand, we were not able to avoid the same headings that occur across documents. For example, the heading *Use* occurs 96 times and *Definition* 49 times in the test set. The rest of the segments are mostly unique. Additional statistics can be found in Appendix A.3.

	dev	test
Number of documents	195	190
Number of parallel transl. segments	2,011	2,002
↪ containing inline elements	520	590
Number of source words	24,490	24,244
Segment redundancy	1.09	1.08

Table 1: Characteristics of development and test sets for the English source of the second release of the *software documentation data set for machine translation.*

Type	dev	test
alt	2	2
cite	27	8
codeph	1	7
emphasis	37	55
field	1	3
i	12	2
image	0	1
key	0	2
keys	0	1
keyword	1	0
menucascade	1	6
ph	1	0
pname	4	15
q	0	2
sap-icon-background-color	2	10
sap-icon-font	2	10
sap-icon-font-character	2	10
sap-icon-font-color	2	10
sap-icon-font-description	2	10
sap-icon-font-size	2	10
sap-note	2	0
sap-technical-name	25	41
systemoutput	8	1
uicontrol	569	647
uinolabel	3	9
userinput	13	16
xref	25	25

Table 2: Different types of inline elements present in development and test sets.

The DITA inline elements of the data set are provided in Table 2. Most of them consist of an opening and a closing tag, such as *<uicontrol>...</uicontrol>*, others are self-closing, e.g. *<xref keyref=... />*. There are a total of 27 different types of inline elements that serve different purposes: many are formatting and style markers,

[5] http://docs.oasis-open.org/xliff/v1.2/os/xliff-core.html

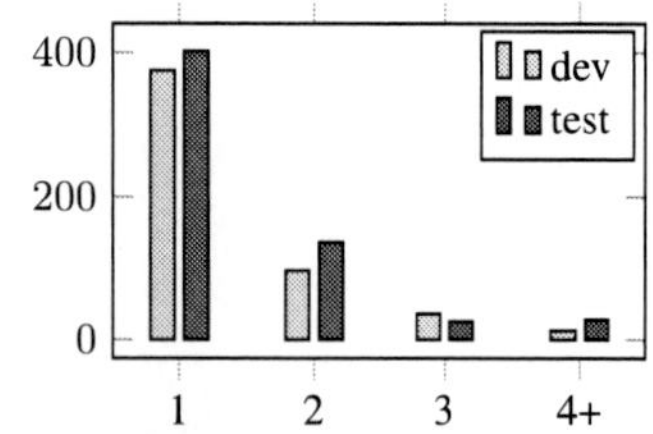

Figure 2: Distribution of inline elements per segment.

while others, such as *uicontrol*, *userinput* or *sap-technical-name*, are translation-relevant as they indicate if or how the annotated text should be translated. The most prevalent inline markup is *uicontrol*, used to mark up user interface controls, such as names of buttons, entry fields or menu items that require precise translation. Self-closing *xref* elements act as placeholders for text that is not accessible. Of the translatable segments in the dev and test data, 25.86% and 29.34%, respectively, contain at least one inline element. Figure 2 shows the number of sentences in dev and test sets containing one, two or more inline elements.

4 Baseline Experiments

We propose to evaluate the translation performance of out-of-the-box pretrained multilingual neural machine translation (NMT) systems for the English to Japanese, Korean and Chinese translation directions.[6] We focus on segment-level translation and propose to leave document-level approaches for future work.

4.1 NMT Models and Approaches

Publicly available multilingual translation models have shown to reach impressive results in terms of translation performance measured by popular automatic metrics. Due to the cost of training such models and in a bid to be eco-friendly, we use the M2M-100 (Fan et al., 2021) and the mBART-50 (Tang et al., 2021) many-to-many fine-tuned models which handle the translation directions of our data set. Both models are used from publicly available checkpoints to decode the data set with no additional fine-tuning on our end. Two hyperparameters are set for the decoder: a beam size of 4 and a length penalty of 1.0.

To handle mixed lexical and markup content, we consider two approaches:

Direct Translation (DT): We directly translate segments with markup using the NMT models.

Detag-project (DP): We first remove markup from the segments, translate segments, and insert the tags back into the translation using word alignments. We follow Zenkel et al. (2021) and use the inside-outside projection algorithm with alignments obtained from `awesome-align` (Dou and Neubig, 2021).[7]

4.2 Evaluation and Results

Previous work in structured document translation attempted to distill knowledge from widely used MT automatic metrics, such as BLEU (Papineni et al., 2002), by splitting content based on markup or measuring the accuracy of matching tags and attributes (Hashimoto et al., 2019; Hanneman and Dinu, 2020). In this work, we propose to maintain the commonly adopted evaluation approaches based on markup–lexis separation by allocating one metric per type of evaluation: **raw metrics**, computed on MT output and reference mixing text and markup, **lex metrics**, computed on MT output and reference stripped of markup, and **tag metrics**, computed on MT output and reference containing only markup. Note that the **raw** and **lex** metrics are similar to the *tagged* and *untagged* BLEU metrics, respectively, as proposed by Hanneman and Dinu (2020).

Overall comparison between two MT outputs can be conducted by comparing the raw metric scores, while the lex metric focuses on lexical tokens only and markup translation performance is measured by the tag metric. Table 3 reports the results obtained with SacreBLEU (Post, 2018) when computing BLEU following the three evaluation approaches listed above. Additional results using chrF (Popović, 2015) are presented in Table 4.[8]

Results obtained with the raw BLEU and chrF metrics show that both DT and DP approaches perform relatively well for two out of three transla-

[6] A total of 12 translation directions are available with the data released with this work.

[7] `https://github.com/neulab/awesome-align`

[8] SacreBLEU signatures for raw and lex metrics:
Japanese BLEU:
nrefs:1|case:mixed|eff:no|tok:ja-mecab-0.996-IPA|smooth:exp|version:2.3.0
Korean BLEU:
nrefs:1|case:mixed|eff:no|tok:ko-mecab-0.996/ko-0.9.2-KO|smooth:exp|version:2.3.0
Chinese BLEU:
nrefs:1|case:mixed|eff:no|tok:zh|smooth:exp|version:2.3.0
tag BLEU:
nrefs:1|case:mixed|eff:no|tok:none|smooth:exp|version:2.3.0
chrF (all metrics):
nrefs:1|case:mixed|eff:yes|nc:6|nw:0|space:no|version:2.3.0

		raw			lex			tag		
		en→ja	en→ko	en→zh	en→ja	en→ko	en→zh	en→ja	en→ko	en→zh
M2M	DT	42.1	**34.6**	**49.2**	35.3	**27.1**	43.4	78.4	77.2	80.1
	DP	40.6	30.3	48.9	36.4	25.9	**44.7**	78.6	74.3	79.8
MBart	DT	**44.9**	28.5	44.3	37.2	18.9	37.8	**92.2**	**82.1**	**89.9**
	DP	41.5	26.8	44.3	**38.1**	19.6	39.1	78.8	79.4	79.4

Table 3: BLEU scores obtained with direct translation (DT) and detag-and-project (DP) using M2M and mBART models when evaluating mixed text and markup (*raw*), text only (*lex*) and markup only (*tag*).

		raw			lex			tag		
		en→ja	en→ko	en→zh	en→ja	en→ko	en→zh	en→ja	en→ko	en→zh
M2M	DT	53.2	**50.3**	**57.5**	40.2	34.2	37.5	91.4	**95.6**	93.3
	DP	54.0	47.7	57.3	42.3	**34.5**	**39.1**	94.7	94.3	94.5
MBart	DT	**57.4**	45.0	54.2	43.7	26.1	32.6	**96.3**	92.5	94.1
	DP	56.4	45.1	54.5	**45.6**	27.3	34.2	94.8	94.9	**94.8**

Table 4: chrF scores obtained with direct translation (DT) and detag-and-project (DP) using M2M and mBART models when evaluating mixed text and markup (*raw*), text only (*lex*) and markup only (*tag*).

ton directions tested, namely English-to-Japanese and English-to-Chinese. For the English-to-Korean translation direction, however, results for the lex BLEU metric indicate that M2M and MBart do not perform as well as for the two other translation directions, with MBart being outpeformed by M2M when Korean is the target.

The tag BLEU metric shows that MBart with the DT approach reaches the best results compared to the other approach and translation model. However, the tag chrF metric does not follow the same trend, which indicates that spacing within markup is better handled by MBart when translating tags in context (spaces are not taken into account with the chrF metric). The M2M model reaches the highest BLEU and chrF scores for Korean and Chinese target languages when lexical content is present (raw and lex metrics), while MBart reaches the highest scores when the target is Japanese.

Regardless of the metric (BLEU or chrF), DT exhibits better performance than DP in most cases, indicating that massively multilingual pre-trained MT systems can handle markup transfer without being explicitly trained on parallel data containing markup. DP, which involves tokenization, alignment and markup projection, involves imperfect heuristics (we have used inside-outside (Zenkel et al., 2021)). This makes DT without explicit training on markup data deserving of further exploration compared to DP. See Appendix B for additional results.

5 Conclusion

In this paper we have presented our multilingual multiway evaluation data set for structured document translation of three Asian languages, Japanese, Korean and Chinese – the second release of the *software documentation data set for machine translation*. Our data set contains rich annotation tag sets and is well suited for multilingual natural language processing tasks such as MT and its evaluation. We have established and evaluated MT baselines using two methods to handle inline markup, namely the direct translation and the detag-project approaches. Our results show that massively multilingual translation models like M2M-100 and mBART-50 perform surprisingly well despite not being explicitly trained to handle structured content. This previously unknown capability of MT models used in our experiments deserves further exploration, especially in combination with document-level translation approaches.

Acknowledgements

We would like to thank our SAP colleagues Ben Callard for extracting the DITA and XLIFF data from the corporate systems and Jens Scharnbacher for getting us started with XSLT. We are also thankful for the helpful feedback we got from the anonymous reviewers.

References

Bianka Buschbeck and Miriam Exel. 2020. A parallel evaluation data set of software documentation with document structure annotation. In *Proceedings of the 7th Workshop on Asian Translation*, pages 160–169, Suzhou, China. Association for Computational Linguistics.

Zi-Yi Dou and Graham Neubig. 2021. Word alignment by fine-tuning embeddings on parallel corpora. In *Proceedings of the 16th Conference of the European Chapter of the Association for Computational Linguistics: Main Volume*, pages 2112–2128, Online. Association for Computational Linguistics.

Angela Fan, Shruti Bhosale, Holger Schwenk, Zhiyi Ma, Ahmed El-Kishky, Siddharth Goyal, Mandeep Baines, Onur Celebi, Guillaume Wenzek, Vishrav Chaudhary, Naman Goyal, Tom Birch, Vitaliy Liptchinsky, Sergey Edunov, Michael Auli, and Armand Joulin. 2021. Beyond english-centric multilingual machine translation. *Journal of Machine Learning Research*, 22(107):1–48.

Greg Hanneman and Georgiana Dinu. 2020. How should markup tags be translated? In *Proceedings of the Fifth Conference on Machine Translation*, pages 1160–1173, Online. Association for Computational Linguistics.

Kazuma Hashimoto, Raffaella Buschiazzo, James Bradbury, Teresa Marshall, Richard Socher, and Caiming Xiong. 2019. A high-quality multilingual dataset for structured documentation translation. In *Proceedings of the Fourth Conference on Machine Translation (Volume 1: Research Papers)*, pages 116–127, Florence, Italy. Association for Computational Linguistics.

Samuel Läubli, Rico Sennrich, and Martin Volk. 2018. Has machine translation achieved human parity? a case for document-level evaluation. In *Proceedings of the 2018 Conference on Empirical Methods in Natural Language Processing*, pages 4791–4796, Brussels, Belgium. Association for Computational Linguistics.

Lesly Miculicich, Dhananjay Ram, Nikolaos Pappas, and James Henderson. 2018. Document-level neural machine translation with hierarchical attention networks. In *Proceedings of the 2018 Conference on Empirical Methods in Natural Language Processing*, pages 2947–2954, Brussels, Belgium. Association for Computational Linguistics.

Kishore Papineni, Salim Roukos, Todd Ward, and Wei-Jing Zhu. 2002. Bleu: a method for automatic evaluation of machine translation. In *Proceedings of the 40th Annual Meeting of the Association for Computational Linguistics*, pages 311–318, Philadelphia, Pennsylvania, USA. Association for Computational Linguistics.

Maja Popović. 2015. chrF: character n-gram F-score for automatic MT evaluation. In *Proceedings of the Tenth Workshop on Statistical Machine Translation*, pages 392–395, Lisbon, Portugal. Association for Computational Linguistics.

Matt Post. 2018. A call for clarity in reporting BLEU scores. In *Proceedings of the Third Conference on Machine Translation: Research Papers*, pages 186–191, Brussels, Belgium. Association for Computational Linguistics.

Yuqing Tang, Chau Tran, Xian Li, Peng-Jen Chen, Naman Goyal, Vishrav Chaudhary, Jiatao Gu, and Angela Fan. 2021. Multilingual translation from denoising pre-training. In *Findings of the Association for Computational Linguistics: ACL-IJCNLP 2021*, pages 3450–3466, Online. Association for Computational Linguistics.

Thomas Zenkel, Joern Wuebker, and John DeNero. 2021. Automatic bilingual markup transfer. In *Findings of the Association for Computational Linguistics: EMNLP 2021*, pages 3524–3533, Punta Cana, Dominican Republic. Association for Computational Linguistics.

A Data Set

We provide additional information on the second release of the *software documentation data set for machine translation*, such as the data format, available data transformations, and more data characteristics.

A.1 XLIFF Format

We provide the data in XLIFF (*.xlf*) Version 1.2. Each XLIFF file of the data set represents one original DITA document (*file* element) with its translation into one of the target languages. Within the *file* element, *trans-units* contain the localizable data: *source* elements store the source text, *seg-source* elements the (sentence) segmented source text and *target* elements the corresponding segments in the target language. Source and target segments are enclosed by *mrk* elements, and associated with each other via an ID (*mid* attribute). The full structure of the original DITA document is also represented in our XLIFF format. The DITA XML tags are enclosed by XLIFF inline elements (*ph*, *bpt*, *ept*). Much of the original DITA format can be restored by literally using the DITA tags masked by XLIFF inline elements. Whenever a *source* consists only of inline elements, the *translate* attribute of the enclosing *trans-unit* is set to *no*. When only parts of a translatable segment are not to be translated, this is represented as *<mrk mtype="protected">*. An example XLIFF document can be found in Figure 3. Information beyond the description here can be found in the Readme accompanying the data.

```
<?xml version="1.0" encoding="UTF-8"?>\\
<xliff xmlns="urn:oasis:names:tc:xliff:document:1.2" version="1.2">
<file original="dita" datatype="xml" source-language="en-US" target-language="ja
    -JP">
<body>
...
<trans-unit translate="no" id="feed189b-f66d-403d-84cd-068edc17edd1">
<source><ph id="18">&lt;/li&gt;</ph><ph id="19">&lt;li&gt;</ph></source>
</trans-unit>
<trans-unit id="32a07041-05f4-4e61-b4d3-1569b7b3509a">
<source>Click <bpt id="20">&lt;uicontrol&gt;</bpt>Prepayment<ept id="20">&lt;/
    uicontrol&gt;</ept>.
<seg-source><mrk mtype="seg" mid="7">Click <bpt id="20">&lt;uicontrol&gt;</bpt>
    Prepayment<ept id="20">&lt;/uicontrol&gt;</ept>.</mrk></seg-source>
<target><mrk mtype="seg" mid="7"><bpt id="20">&lt;uicontrol&gt;</bpt>前
    払<ept id="20">&lt;/uicontrol&gt;</ept>をクリックします。
    </mrk></target></trans-unit>
<trans-unit translate="no" id="ec9ffb5c-5516-4bb1-aa6a-bfafa5827bd0">
<source><ph id="21">&lt;/li&gt;</ph></source>
</trans-unit>
...
</body>
</file>
</xliff>
```

Figure 3: Excerpt of an XLIFF document (en-ja) of the data set.

A.2 Data Transformations

The released data in XLIFF contains the *full* document structure and is therefore very rich in information. However, some applications or evaluation scenarios might only want to consider specific parts of the structure. XLIFF documents can conveniently be transformed to different representations for different purposes using XSL stylesheets. For inspiration and convenience, we provide several stylesheets with the data that lead to the following transformed outputs:

(i) the structured document as a functional DITA file containing the source or target text and the original DITA tags;

(ii) one translatable (source or target) segment per line with inline markup being represented as DITA tags, similar to the format in Hashimoto et al. (2019);

(iii) one translatable (source or target) segment per line with inline markup being represented as XLIFF masking tags x and g, similar to the format in Hanneman and Dinu (2020);

(iv) one translatable (source or target) segment per line as plain text, without inline markup.

Examples for the transformations can be found in Figure 4. For convenience, we provide all source/-

(i)

```
</li><li>
Click <uicontrol>Prepayment</uicontrol>.
</li>
```

(ii)

```
Click <uicontrol>Prepayment</uicontrol>.
```

(iii)

```
Click <g id="20">Prepayment</g>.
```

(iv)

```
Click Prepayment.
```

Figure 4: Data transformations (source) for the example in Figure 3.

target documents concatenated after being transformed with method (iv) for standard machine translation evaluation, and with method (ii), as this format is relevant for current usage in machine translation research concerning tag transfer. The latter has been used in this work in Section 4.

The documents contain certain placeholders that reference textual content outside the respective document. In the plain-text data (iv), they have been replaced by <locked-ref> as just removing them would render the segments incomplete and ungrammatical.

		XML BLEU			*BLEU*			*Markup Matching %*		
		en→ja	en→ko	en→zh	en→ja	en→ko	en→zh	en→ja	en→ko	en→zh
M2M	DT	36.4	**28.5**	31.9	39.6	**28.5**	35.6	81.0	81.8	83.2
	DP	37.7	23.2	**33.2**	40.3	27.0	**36.8**	90.0	89.8	90.2
MBart	DT	**40.1**	20.8	27.1	41.1	20.3	28.6	**92.9**	88.8	87.3
	DP	38.3	20.2	26.8	**41.9**	21.3	30.5	91.2	**91.2**	**90.8**

Table 5: BLEU scores obtained with direct translation (DT) and detag-and-project (DP) using M2M and mBART models when evaluating markup split text (*XML BLEU*) and text only (*BLEU*). We also give the markup matching accuracies (*Markup Matching %*).

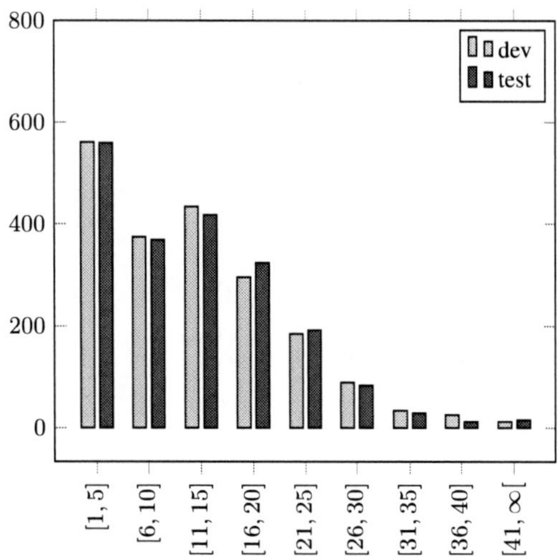

Figure 5: Length distributions of source segments.

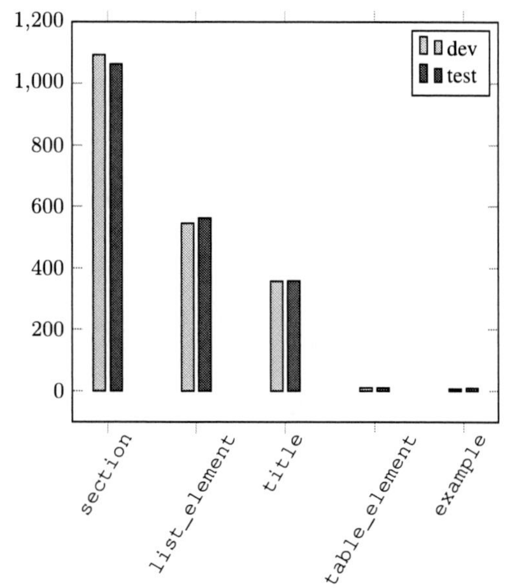

Figure 6: Distribution of textual element annotations.

A.3 Further Data Characteristics

Figure 5 shows the length distribution of English source segments. As typical for technical text, there is a high number of short sentences. In Figure 6 the distribution of textual element annotations is presented. It reflects, to some extent, the length distribution. The large proportion of list elements and titles accounts for shorter segments.

B Experiments and Results

B.1 Additional Evaluation

In addition to BLEU and chrF scores using SacreBLEU presented in Table 3 and 4, respectively, we present in Table 5, the scores obtained by using the evaluation metrics employed by (Hashimoto et al., 2019). Different from us, they report *XML BLEU* and *BLEU*. *XML BLEU* splits a translation containing inline markup into multiple parts relying on tags as split points. Note that the splitting takes place only if the markup structure in the translation and the reference match. In case of markup structure mismatch, the translation is treated as empty thereby penalizing the *XML BLEU* score. On the other hand *BLEU* is calculated by removing markup in the gold and translation, which is similar to our proposed *lex metrics* presented in Section 4.2. However, Hashimoto et al. (2019) use different tokenization methods compared to the ones implemented in sacreBLEU thus leading to different BLEU scores. Table 5 also contains the markup matching accuracy (*Markup Matching %*) which measures the number of examples with matching tags between the MT output and the reference translation.

Comparing *lex* scores in Table 3 and *BLEU* scores in Table 5, although the scores themselves are different and not directly comparable, the trends are similar where MBart is better than M2M only for English to Japanese translation and results for English to Korean translation are relatively lower compared to the two other translation directions. *XML BLEU* scores are usually lower than

BLEU scores because it penalizes translations with markup structure mismatch.

Markup Matching % for detag-project (DP) is typically higher than for direct translation (DT) because DP injects markup after translation whereas DT deals with markup during translation. Upon further investigation, we found that DT sometimes over- or under-generates markup spuriously leading to poorer markup matching accuracies. DP does not suffer from this issue. However, DP has another limitation where, if it is unable to align content with markup between the source and translation, markup injection does not take place. Therefore, DT will always result in translations containing markup unlike DP, even if the former may not inject tags with correct structure. This is the reason why *tag* scores in Tables 3 and 4 for DT models are higher than for DP models despite lower markup matching accuracies for the former.

On Measures of Biases and Harms in NLP

Sunipa Dev[1*] Emily Sheng[2*] Jieyu Zhao[1*] Aubrie Amstutz[*]

Jiao Sun[3] Yu Hou[3] Mattie Sanseverino[1] Jiin Kim[1] Akihiro Nishi[1]

Nanyun Peng[1,3] Kai-Wei Chang[1]

[1]University of California, Los Angeles, [2]Microsoft Research, [3]University of Southern California

Abstract

Recent studies show that Natural Language Processing (NLP) technologies propagate societal biases about demographic groups associated with attributes such as gender, race, and nationality. To create interventions and mitigate these biases and associated harms, it is vital to be able to detect and measure such biases. While existing works propose bias evaluation and mitigation methods for various tasks, there remains a need to cohesively understand the biases and the specific harms they measure, and how different measures compare with each other. To address this gap, this work presents a practical framework of harms and a series of questions that practitioners can answer to guide the development of bias measures. As a validation of our framework and documentation questions, we also present several case studies of how existing bias measures in NLP—both intrinsic measures of bias in representations and extrinsic measures of bias of downstream applications—can be aligned with different harms and how our proposed documentation questions facilitates more holistic understanding of what bias measures are measuring.

1 Introduction

As language technologies and their applications become more widely deployed in our society, there are also increasing concerns of the disparate impacts and harms these technologies have on different demographic groups (Bolukbasi et al., 2016; Webster et al., 2018). To address some of these concerns, a large body of work has emerged to discuss (Gonen and Goldberg, 2019; Bender et al., 2021; Blodgett et al., 2021), detect (Bolukbasi et al., 2016; Nangia et al., 2020), measure (Caliskan et al., 2017; Zhao et al., 2019; Webster et al., 2018; Li et al., 2020), and mitigate (Dev and Phillips, 2019; Ravfogel et al., 2020; Sun et al., 2019; Dev et al., 2021a) the social biases encoded by NLP models.

Several of these works include bias measures comprising of metrics and datasets to define and investigate social biases within the constructs of a specific NLP task, such as text classification or machine translation. Though these works propose different approaches for measuring biases, there is often similarly a lack of explicit alignment to harms, as well as a lack of comparative understanding of the advantages and disadvantages between the different bias measures for various language tasks. As an example, for the task of coreference resolution, there are several measures investigating gender bias (Zhao et al., 2018; Rudinger et al., 2018; Lu et al., 2020; Webster et al., 2018; Cao and Daumé III, 2020). However, each measure is unique in either the targeted demographic groups, metrics, dataset sentence structures, or the definition of bias, all of which ultimately affect what harms are measured. A better understanding of bias measures ultimately enables better adaptation and deployment for specific use cases.

This paper is motivated by two main goals. The first goal is to define a practical framework for harms that is both theoretically-motivated and empirically useful for describing bias measures. We organize a framework that is motivated by concepts from social psychology and linguistics, and narrow down specific definitions and heuristics to tag normative notions of harm with which bias measures align. Moreover, we illustrate the utility of this measure-harm alignment exercise with case studies that demonstrate how a measure might unknowingly conflate different harms, or how separate measures with nearly identical task definitions can actually measure very different harms. The second goal is to define a collection of documentation questions around bias measures that helps others

*equal contribution

Findings of the Association for Computational Linguistics: AACL-IJCNLP 2022, pages 246–267
November 20–23, 2022.

capture measure limitations and align operationalizations of "biases" to harms. Documenting various attributes (e.g., considerations for targeted demographic groups and tasks, dataset limitations, bias metric definitions and motivations) of a bias measure can help practitioners better articulate harms, appropriate use cases, and limitations. To achieve these goals, we organize a practical framework of harms, a tagged collection of 43 existing bias measures and the associated harms, a set of documentation questions, and a collection of case studies.

2 Background

We clarify the definitions of several terms used throughout this paper.

Bias in NLP Bias in language models is commonly defined as "skew that produces a type of harm" (Crawford, 2017) towards different social groups, though it is a complex notion that is often not well-defined in existing literature (Blodgett et al., 2020; Delobelle et al., 2022; Talat et al., 2022). In the existing NLP literature, "biases" are often operationalized via a measurement model (Jacobs and Wallach, 2021) through bias measures. While these bias measures are proxies for evaluating bias, they are often necessarily localized to measuring very specific skews and lack context of how a system would be used by real users. Additionally, unstated assumptions and definitions often pervade these measures (Blodgett et al., 2021). It remains an open question whether these bias measures actually measure meaningful and useful distinctions of "biases"—this work provides initial explorations to answer this question for several measures.

Bias Measures Bias evaluations in NLP typically have been categorized broadly into *intrinsic* or *extrinsic* evaluations based on whether they measure biased associations within the word embedding spaces (Caliskan et al., 2017) or biased decisions from models for specific tasks (Mohammad, 2018; Webster et al., 2019), respectively. We define a *bias measure* as an evaluation standard that includes a *metric(s)* applied to a *dataset*. Here, we use the term *dataset* broadly, such that it could be applicable to datasets ranging in size and curation technique (e.g., manually crafted, generated). To show inequalities between demographic groups, existing works typically define bias metrics (e.g., specialized notions of group fairness) that they then apply to a dataset specially designed to reveal social inequalities or stereotypes.

These measures span several NLP tasks such as question answering (Li et al., 2020), relation extraction (Gaut et al., 2019), textual entailment (Dev et al., 2019), toxicity prediction (Dixon et al., 2018; Jigsaw, 2019; Sap et al., 2020), coreference resolution (Zhao et al., 2019; Cao and Daumé III, 2020), autocomplete generation (Sheng et al., 2019), dialogue generation (Dinan et al., 2019), machine translation (Stanovsky et al., 2019), as well as intrinsic measurements of the embeddings themselves (Caliskan et al., 2017; Bolukbasi et al., 2016; Lauscher et al., 2020; Malik et al., 2022).

Demographic Dimension We use the term *demographic dimension* to refer to an identity axis (e.g., gender, race, age) for which specific instances (e.g., for gender: *male*, *female*, *non-binary*, etc) are evaluated. Instances of a demographic dimension are typically comparatively evaluated in measures through some proxy, e.g., occupations or identity terms.

Harms While existing works have examined possible harms of NLP models from various perspectives (e.g., general social impacts (Hovy and Spruit, 2016), risks associated with large language models (Bender et al., 2021)), in the context of algorithmic biases, we seek to align specifically with harms that can arise specifically from biases. The relevant harms can be subdivided into representational or allocational harms, depending on whether there is a generalization of harmful representations of groups or if there is a tangible, disparate distribution of resources between groups, respectively (Crawford, 2017).[1] In the context of aligning bias measures with targeted representational harms, one could align with the motivations for creating the measure (either explicit or unstated), the techniques used, or some mix of both. Blodgett et al. (2020) present a categorization of the motivations and techniques of existing works that align with coarse-grained types of harms (*allocational*, *stereotypes*, *other representational harms*), and Blodgett (2021) further organize a taxonomy of fine-grained representational harm categories, including *quality of service*, *stereotyping*, *denigration and stigmatization*, *alienation*, and *public participation*. We build upon Blodgett (2021)'s discussions, framing and extending our curated framework of harms through documentation questions and heuristics that can

[1] Sheng et al. (2021) also separate out vulnerability harms, e.g., from model generations that render a group more susceptible to representational or allocational harms.

Task	Demographic Dimension	Bias Measure	Harms Evaluated
Coreference Resolution	**Gender** through identity terms	Webster et al. (2018) Cao and Daumé III (2020)	**QoS** **Erasure, QoS**
	Gender through occupations	Zhao et al. (2018) Rudinger et al. (2018) Lu et al. (2020)	**Erasure, Stereo.** **Erasure, Stereo.** **Erasure, Stereo.**
Natural Language Inference	**Gender** through occupations	Dev et al. (2019)	**Stereo.**
	Nationality through identity terms	Dev et al. (2019)	**Disparagement, Stereo.** through polar adj.
	Religion through identity terms	Dev et al. (2019)	**Disparagement, Stereo.** through polar adj.
Sentiment Analysis	**Age** through identity terms	Díaz et al. (2018)	**Disparagement, Erasure, QoS** through neg. sentiment
	Gender through identity terms	Kiritchenko and Mohammad (2018)	**Dehumanization, Erasure, QoS, Stereo.** through emotion words
	Rigid designators through references to specific people	Prabhakaran et al. (2019)	**QoS**
	Race through identity terms	Kiritchenko and Mohammad (2018)	**Dehumanization, Erasure, Stereo.** through emotion words
Question Answering	**Race** through identity terms	Li et al. (2020)	**Erasure, Stereo.** through neg. assoc.
	Ethnicity through identity terms	Li et al. (2020) Li et al. (2020) + Zhao et al. (2021)	**Erasure, Stereo.** through neg. assoc. **Erasure, Stereo.** through neg. assoc.
	Gender through occupations	Li et al. (2020) Li et al. (2020) + Zhao et al. (2021)	**Erasure, Stereo.** **Erasure, Stereo.**
	Religion through identity terms	Li et al. (2020) Li et al. (2020) + Zhao et al. (2021)	**Erasure, Stereo.** through neg. assoc. **Erasure, Stereo.** through neg. assoc.
Relation Extraction	**Gender** through hypernym (occupation) relation	Gaut et al. (2019)	**Erasure, Stereo.**
	Gender through spouse relation	Gaut et al. (2019)	**Erasure, Stereo.**
Text Classification	**Gender** through occupations	De-Arteaga et al. (2019) Zhao et al. (2020)	**Erasure, Stereo.** **Erasure, Stereo.**
	Gender through identity terms **Age** through identity terms **Region** through identity terms	Chalkidis et al. (2022) Chalkidis et al. (2022) Chalkidis et al. (2022)	**QoS** **QoS** **QoS**
Toxicity Detection	**Age** through identity terms	Dixon et al. (2018) Sap et al. (2020)	**Disparagement, Erasure** **Dehumanization, Disparagement, Erasure, Stereo.**
	Disability through identity terms	Dixon et al. (2018) Jigsaw (2019) Sap et al. (2020); Hutchinson et al. (2020)	**Disparagement, Erasure** **Disparagement, Erasure** **Dehumanization, Disparagement, Erasure, Stereo.**
	Gender through identity terms	Dixon et al. (2018) Park et al. (2018) Jigsaw (2019) Sap et al. (2020)	**Disparagement, Erasure** **Disparagement** **Disparagement, Erasure** **Dehumanization, Disparagement, Erasure, Stereo.**
	Rigid designators through references to specific people	Prabhakaran et al. (2019)	**QoS**
	Sexual Orient. through identity terms	Dixon et al. (2018) Jigsaw (2019) Sap et al. (2020)	**Disparagement, Erasure** **Disparagement, Erasure** **Dehumanization, Disparagement, Erasure, Stereo.**
	Race through identity terms	Dixon et al. (2018) Jigsaw (2019) Sap et al. (2020)	**Disparagement, Erasure** **Disparagement, Erasure** **Dehumanization, Disparagement, Erasure, Stereo.**
	Religion through identity terms	Dixon et al. (2018) Jigsaw (2019) Sap et al. (2020)	**Disparagement, Erasure** **Disparagement, Erasure** **Dehumanization, Disparagement, Erasure, Stereo.**
	Political Ideo. through identity terms	Sap et al. (2020)	**Dehumanization, Disparagement, Erasure, Stereo.**
	Victim through identity terms	Sap et al. (2020)	**Dehumanization, Disparagement, Erasure, Stereo.**

Table 1: Existing bias measures (part 1) organized by tasks, and demographic dimensions. A '+' indicates that one work built a bias metric (after '+') on top of a dataset from another work (before '+'). *Rigid designators*: references to specific people, *polar adjectives*: good vs bad; *negative activity*: violent or bad traits and activities. Sec. 5 delves into a few of these measures in the context of harms evaluated.

serve as a practical guide for those developing bias measures that capture specific harms.

Specifically, we use definitions of harms that are robust enough to capture aspects of a bias measure (dataset, metric(s), motivations) that align with different harms. Taking both individual and aggregate harms (Blodgett, 2021) into consideration, this framework assumes vulnerability to harm is mediated by a dominant—non-dominant identity group dichotomy (inspired by but not entirely aligned with Social Dominance Theory (Sidanius and Pratto, 2001)), which is helpful for operationalization purposes.

In this paper, we focus on five types of harm: Stereotyping, Disparagement,[2] Dehumanization, Erasure, and Quality of Service (QoS). While there are other types of harms, and the five we target could be further broken down into subcategories, we start with these five as they are previously studied concepts and provide interesting insights to the non-exhaustive list of bias measures we examine in Table 1 and Appendix Table 2.

3 A Framework for Harms

Conflating harms impedes accurate measurement; adequate and consistent delineation of harms enables ongoing appraisal of the effectiveness of mitigation strategies and the comparison of trade-offs. Our practical framework of harms builds upon existing taxonomies of representational harms (e.g. Blodgett (2021) and establishes specific heuristics (Appendix A) to disentangle the characteristics of five non-mutually exclusive categories. While these harms have previously been taxonomized, *we ground the definitions of harms into documentation questions and heuristics to help practitioners align NLP bias measures with specific harms.*

Addressing a single phenomenon with different lenses can surface multiple harms; precisely which harm a method captures is sometimes solely dependent on the experimental framing, rather than some inherent taxonomic difference. Using the harm heuristics we devise in Appendix A, we tag and distinguish between types of harms targeted by popular NLP bias measures presented in Tables 1 and Appendix Table 2. We note however, that other interpretations of targeted harms are certainly possible. This subjectivity makes it more crucial that those who build bias measures clearly state their motivations and include explanations of the relevant harms (Section 4).[3]

3.1 Harms

Stereotyping Stereotypes are overgeneralized beliefs about the personal attributes of an individual as determined by their demographic group membership. Stereotypes as entities are codified associations which are necessarily well-known within a given context (Devine, 1989) and can be expressed in infinite (and multi-modal) ways. Stereotypes draw on commonly held generalizations to make *a priori* judgements about groups. In human cognition, they are perpetuated through a process of discounting counter-evidence as exceptions to the rule, e.g. confirmation bias (Allport et al., 1954; Link and Phelan, 2001). These associations can in turn lead to unintended "affective reactions" by the model—precisely the measurable signals from which practitioners can infer bias.

Disparagement Disparagement encapsulates any behavior by a model which reinforces the notion that certain groups are less valuable than others and less deserving of respect (or resources). Commonly associated measures of disparagement include toxicity ratings and hate speech detection scores.

Dehumanization Dehumanization actively casts disfavored groups as "others" and aims to erase signs of shared humanity (e.g. emotions, agency, intelligence), thus suppressing opportunities for empathy with said "out group" by characterizing them as sub-human (Markowitz and Slovic, 2020; Haslam and Stratemeyer, 2016). Dehumanization can therefore be challenging to measure directly, as instances of dehumanizing language or sentiments are often closely intertwined with Disparagement and Stereotyping.

Erasure Erasure refers to the lack of adequate representation of members of a particular social group (Dev et al., 2021b; Blodgett et al., 2022), whether intentional or not. While the data used to represent the intricacies of reality will always be necessarily incomplete, Erasure can arise from mismatches in reality and the data chosen to represent it. It can also serve to reinforce existing power structures via incautious mathematical averaging or aggregation of disparate groups. While

[2]We choose to use "Disparagement" instead of "Denigration", to avoid invoking the conceptual metaphor of 'blackening' one's reputation, which can have racial connotations in US culture.

[3]We also note that it is sometimes difficult to align with certain harms like Dehumanization without a closer examination of all samples in a measure dataset.

relational group sizes from the real world can be reflected from the model in a quantitative sense, the challenge is designing systems which do not allow relative size to inappropriately affect prominence, i.e., attention needs to be paid to the potential effects these probabilities have on produced output.

Quality of Service Quality of Service harms result from instances where a model fails to perform equitably for different groups (Blodgett, 2021). This harm can in turn potentially result in inequitable allocation of resources (Blodgett et al., 2020), though this harm can also exist independently. The potential 'quality' of service is operationalized and quantified via defined performance indicators, which can be systematically compared between commensurable groups.

3.2 Relationships between Harms

Disentangling which categories of harm a given bias measure measures requires careful articulation of the hypothesis and documentation of operationalization decisions; framing is crucial for producing substantively valid results (Jacobs and Wallach, 2021). For example, an instance of bias in model training data may have arisen due to multiple types of harm or cause multiple types of harm. Our framework emphasizes how consequential these distinctions in operationalization can be.

Disparagement and Stereotyping Because stereotypes need to be codified and well-known within a given culture (Devine, 1989), Disparagement is more generic and group-agnostic than Stereotyping. Consequently, datasets that test for Disparagement (explicitly or not) may sometimes be generated *ad infinitum* by swapping demographic identifiers, e.g., "[demographic identifier] are the worst kind of people". In comparison, the specificity required of statements expressing stereotypes presents limitations on rephrasing concepts (by design, languages have few "absolute synonyms" (Murphy, 2010)).

Dehumanization, Disparagement, and Stereotyping Under our framework, Dehumanization contributes to Disparagement because it reinforces the idea that certain groups are inherently less valuable to society, i.e., Dehumanization always serves Disparagement, but not *vice versa*. Dehumanizing language uses techniques such as *moral disgust, denial of agency,* or *likening members of a target group to non-human entities* (Markowitz and Slovic, 2020) to reinforce normative identities—often as indication of a biological hierarchy of 'species' within humankind. Dehumanization can be "expressed tacitly" (Markowitz and Slovic, 2020), e.g., when groups are not considered worthy of being included (via Erasure). While descriptive, proscriptive, or prescriptive stereotypes (Koenig, 2018; Hall et al., 2019) may have originated from some quantitative or qualitative fact about societal norms (Sidanius and Pratto, 2001), stereotypes which dehumanize are more likely inherently unfounded, e.g., stereotypes perpetuating racist pseudoscience like eugenics.

Stereotyping and Erasure Cognitive heuristics like categorization and prediction based on probability are part of human nature (Tversky and Kahneman, 1974; Mervis et al., 1981); however, harm can arise when these associations obfuscate or erase actual variance (e.g., via confirmation bias) or when society assigns a cost (e.g., social, allocational) when these oversimplified "norms" are not adhered to by their respective group members (e.g., proscriptive or prescriptive (Koenig, 2018)). Erasure and Stereotyping can have a cyclical relation; lack of representation of variance and sub-populations can both result in stereotypes and be a direct result of Stereotyping. Erasure and Stereotyping are conceptualized as being one level of abstraction away from the consequence being caused: while exposure to a disparaging or dehumanizing remark can be directly harmful in the moment, the impact of Stereotyping associations and Erasure are more apparent at a distributional level. Additionally, Erasure and Stereotyping are strongly mediated by the *vulnerability* of the group and the *severity* of the implications of the association.

Quality of Service and Erasure Facts about historical inequities, social hierarchies, and stereotypes should guide Erasure measures. Under our framework, measures that target Erasure harms should have strong, directional hypotheses in order to surface representation issues for specific groups. These issues could in turn be quantified more precisely via comparative evaluation methods, such as those common in measures that target Quality of Service harms. Erasure measurement for underrepresented groups requires us to set aside quantitative majorities and ensure qualitative "coverage" instead, e.g., while there may be fewer female than male surgeons in the United States, the former do still exist. The desired effect of removing Erasure harms is for representation of actual diversity to persist, independent of statistical presence.

4 Documenting Bias Measures

While bias measures aimed at various tasks are widely developed across the NLP community, the measures are often underused or re-developed by researchers for the same task. This stems largely from a lack of usability since little to no documentation of motivation and various choices is available for these measures. Documentation for datasets and models have proliferated over the last few years but the rapidly growing collection of bias measures lacks such organized efforts.

Existing works have stressed the importance of documenting models (Mitchell et al., 2019), datasets (Gebru et al., 2018; Bender and Friedman, 2018), measurement modeling validity and reliability (Jacobs and Wallach, 2021), and, more recently, ethical considerations (Mohammad, 2022). This paper adds a complimentary resource focusing on documentation considerations for bias measures into the existing collection. In this work, we build upon the existing guidelines from Gebru et al. (2018), which are more generally for datasets of any modality or purpose, and narrow the focus to bias measures for NLP tasks. We add questions related to the *Composition* and *Collection Process* sections as proposed by Gebru et al. (2018). Additionally, we propose new sections on *Motivation* specifically for bias measures and *Bias Metrics*. The specificity of the questions addresses the intended usage of different bias measures more explicitly.

1. *Motivation*
   Blodgett et al. (2020) detail the importance of concretely defining the biases being measured and listing out how a metric aligns with normative definitions of harm. Additionally, discerning biases from model errors is equally important and particularly ambiguous when a definition for the "bias" measured is absent.
   - **What is the stated definition of bias?**
   - **How does this definition align with normative definitions of harm?** For a measure to be a valid quantification of bias, the notion of "bias" has to be well-defined and related to what is measured. More explicitly bridging the gap between bias metrics and harms can tangibly disambiguate between innocuous model errors and potential harms downstream.
   - **If the bias measure measures more than one harm, are the harms conflated in one measurement or separable?** A single instance of language may represent/cause multiple forms of harm (e.g., some Stereotyping harms may also be Dehumanization harms). Does the measure provide a method for measuring multiple harms separately as well as in aggregate (e.g., are subsets of the underlying data tagged along multiple axes)?
   - **What language and culture is the bias and measure most relevant to?**
   - **What other contexts can the measure be extended to?** This question is intended to obtain a list of the specific demographic groups and locales a bias measure has been shown to be useful for.
   - **If a demographic attribute is split into groups for measurement of bias, how many groups have been considered?** What is the justification for the grouping? Have prominent/consequential intersectional identities been considered? This question is to understand the scope of the measure and assess its coverage.
   - **What is the source of bias that is measured?** Social biases creep into NLP models in different ways - the data used to derive representations, the model (and parameters) used, etc. The bias measured can be from one or all sources and needs to be acknowledged and when possible, disambiguated.
   - **What tasks or applications is this bias measure useful for?** Is this measure effective to check on any language representations for social biases irrespective of application? Or is there a specific task where this is most applicable?
2. *Composition and Collection Process*
   Language data for bias measures is sourced primarily in two ways: by extracting from existing textual data or by generating from specific templates. While the first has the advantage of being more similar to "real samples" that models see, the latter has the advantage of testing for specific artifacts by construct.
   - **Is the bias measure data scraped, generated, or produced some other way?** Scraping or generating text using templates are two common ways of building bias measure datasets in NLP, and different dataset curation techniques have their own advantages and disadvantages.

- **What are the limitations associated with method of data curation? How generalizable is this dataset?** Examples of limitations include scraped English text containing predominantly Western narratives and data annotated by annotators with specific biases.
- **If the dataset is scraped, what are the primary sources/domains?** Some text sources are known to harbor more toxic or harmful content than others.
- **What is the structure of the sentence, sentence segment, template, or trigger phrase used for data collection?** Does the particular structure come with certain simplifications, assumptions, or guarantees?
- **Is the dataset at risk of causing harm through the particular selection of proxy attributes representing demographic groups?** For example, does this dataset use popular names as a proxy for gender? Is there a risk for misidentifying individuals if the associated genders are not self-reported? Does the expected gender - name pairing align with the time period of the sourced data?

3. *Bias Metrics*
   This section presents documentation questions for metrics that are used with datasets to measure bias. Specific definitions and comparisons can broaden understanding about the measured biases.
   - **How is the bias metric defined? Is there a null hypothesis or normalization recommended for it to be meaningful?**
   - **Is it an absolute or relative evaluation?** Sheng et al. (2021) describe absolute score evaluations as those that "use an accumulated score to summarize inequalities between demographics, whereas relative evaluations explicitly report inequalities between all demographics." Absolute scores offer more simplicity, and relative scores offer more flexibility in alignment with normative harms. Through this question, we hope to understand the motivation behind the evaluation format.
   - **Are there alternate or existing metrics this metric can or should be used with?** This question covers the cases where a bias metric may not be enough to measure all desired metric attributes, either in terms of bias or general task evaluations.
   - **Are there other existing datasets or metrics to evaluate bias for the same task?** How does an evaluation using one metric correlate with another using a different metric? Note that high correlation between measures do not necessarily imply meaningful or useful measures. Additionally, does the sentence structure, sourcing method, or other feature differ between the datasets?
   - **Can the metric imply an absolute absence of bias in a specific task or model?** Are there other measurements needed for a complete assessment of bias? Is a complete assessment possible?

5 Case Studies

We present a series of case studies as examples of how our proposed framework of harms and documentation questions reveal unique insights into different bias measures. In Table 1 and Appendix Table 2, we tag bias measures with the relevant, targeted harm(s). In this section, we discuss concrete examples to elucidate how subtle differences in framing of measures impact the harm(s) measured.

5.1 Disparagement and Stereotyping

To better understand the subtleties between Disparagement and Stereotyping, we examine two existing bias measures.

Davani et al. (2020) present a fair hate speech measure that implicitly separates Stereotyping and Disparagement harms; however, these alignments are not explicitly connected, and our framework helps distinguish between the two harms. This work of Davani et al. (2020) is motivated by the observation that not all demographic groups are interchangeable when it comes to specific stereotypes. For example, they note that substituting "Muslim" with "Jew" in a hateful sentence about terrorism does not create equivalently valid stereotypes within the US cultural context. Thus, they create "symmetric counterfactual" statements that convey a similar meaning when different group tokens are substituted. Interestingly, this distinction between symmetric and asymmetric counterfactuals helps delineate between Disparagement and Stereotyping sentences, as symmetric counterfactuals are, by nature, generic enough to disparage multiple groups. Unless two independent stereotypes have coincidentally converged (e.g., two groups are associated with terrorism for different historical reasons within a given context), a carrier phrase that is able to substitute group identifiers is unlikely to be able to produce valid stereotypical sentiments. Thus, this process of creating and making the distinction between symmetric and asymmetric counterfactual tests generates a fair hate speech dataset that includes some amount of coverage for both Disparagement and Stereotyping harms.

Dev et al. (2019) is another example where Disparagement and Stereotyping harms are not explicitly separated. This work measures biases in the task of natural language inference by comparing demographic associations with polar adjectives. We find that this particular setup conflates Disparagement and Stereotyping harms. As an example from the dataset, for the template "[demographic identifier] are [adjective]", the statement "Canadians are nice" is a stereotype, whereas another statement such as "Uzbekistanis are bad" is more of a general disparaging remark than a stereotype.

These examples show the difficulty in carefully designing datasets that test for Stereotyping versus Disparagement harms.

5.2 Quality of Service, Stereotyping, and Erasure

Next, we present an empirical case study examining how measures designed for the same task can differ in the harms measured. Webster et al. (2018) and Cao and Daumé III (2020) both discuss biases in the task of coreference resolution where the goal is to identify phrases or terms referring to the same entity in a sentence. Webster et al. (2018) measure biases in the model's ability to correctly resolve gendered pronoun-name relationships for the binary genders and is aligned with the Quality of Service harm, since the measure probes the contrastive relationship between model performance for females versus males. Cao and Daumé III (2020) expand the `GAP` dataset introduced by Webster et al. (2018) to create the `MAP` dataset, where the authors swap out gendered words for a set of gender neutral variations of the sentences in `GAP`. While both `GAP` and `MAP` are part of bias measures that are aligned with Quality of Service harms, `MAP` also surfaces Erasure harms by testing for whether a coreference system fails to process text for non-binary pronouns.

Additionally, two other popularly used bias measures for coreference resolution, as described by Rudinger et al. (2018) and Zhao et al. (2019), compare the association of specific occupations with gendered pronouns. While some dataset instances directly measure Stereotyping harms, such as a preferential association of 'doctor' with typical male pronouns, other instances do not directly measure explicit stereotypes in the society but rather an implicit Erasure or lack of representation of some genders in overall text. While both of these harms are overall conflated by both measures, unlike `GAP` and `MAP`, neither measures Quality of Service harms.

5.3 Dehumanization and Stereotyping

Kiritchenko and Mohammad (2018)'s bias measure for sentiment analysis formulates a dataset of simple sentences including names, gendered pronouns, and other indicators of demographic group identity, and compares the sentiment associated with different groups. While some sentences evaluate stereotypes such as the "Angry Black Woman", others are not indicative of any stereotype but rather analyze the societal license for a member of a certain group to display a range of emotions–i.e., Dehumanization. The two harms measured are not distinguishable by the metric used, but instead by careful examination of the individual sentence templates, word lists, and names used.

5.4 Insights from Documenting Bias Measures

By using our harm framework to label the bias measures in Table 1 and Appendix Table 2 as well as documenting bias measure motivations and compositions, we developed several insights.

The first is that *documentation facilitates deeper analysis and should be revisited periodically*. We use the proposed questions to analyze the work described by Sheng et al. (2019). In particular, we note that there is no explicit definition of biases in the work, although the operationalization of their regard metric as a measure of social perception aligns with the measurement of representational harms (e.g., Stereotyping and Disparagement). In answering the documentation questions (Appendix C.2), we find that this documentation exercise is especially useful if the documented measure has been released for a while. In the case of the regard metric of Sheng et al. (2019), there were not many points of comparison at the time of its release, but more relevant comparisons have recently been released. Thus, we recommend treating documentation as a continuous process and revisiting the questions regularly.

Also, *documentation reveals specific limitations across bias measures for a specific task.* The specificity of the documentation questions helps uncover what is currently measured and encourages the development and use of complementary measures. In documenting WinoBias (Zhao et al., 2018) in Appendix C.1, we examine various bias measures for coreference resolution more closely. Existing bias measures for coreference resolution that target gender biases through occupations have all focused on associated stereotypes and the relative representation between binary genders, and thus target Stereotyping and Erasure harms, as shown in Table 1. On the other hand, the coreference resolution bias measures that target gender through identity terms explore the effect of model performance for gender-neutral pronouns, and thus target Quality of Service (and some Erasure) harms.

A third insight is that *inherent constraints of a task seem to affect the method by which bias measures (implicitly or explicitly) target harms.* For more constrained language understanding tasks in which the model produces a limited set of outputs (e.g., classification), the dataset designed for the measure largely affects the targeted harm. For example, for measuring biases in coreference resolution, the standard metrics are F_1 or accuracy scores—it is really by examining the datasets (and motivations) that we discern whether we are targeting Stereotyping (e.g., through occupational associations) or Quality of Service harms. For open-domain language generation tasks, targeted harms are largely affected by the selected bias metrics rather than the datasets. Because generation task are so open-ended, it is often difficult to design evaluation datasets that achieve a lot of control over the resulting model output, and thus existing works rely more on various bias metrics to capture different harms. For example, Dhamala et al. (2021) evaluate biases using sentiment, regard, toxicity, and psycholinguistic norms to target different operationalizations of harms.

6 Conclusion

Bias measures in NLP are critical for estimating and mitigating potential harms towards different demographic groups. However, a lack of structured understanding of what harms exist, how they are operationalized through bias measures, and how they can be measured can diminish the usefulness of bias measures. In this work, we organize a framework to define and distinguish between different types of harms—presented through heuristics and documentation questions—to guide more intentional development of bias measures. Our proposed documentation template also facilitates combining, comparing, and utilizing different bias measures, and continuously re-visiting them to update limitations and comparative understanding with other measures.

7 Limitations and Ethical Considerations

We acknowledge that our framework of harms has been created from a US-centric perspective and has been influenced by the Social Dominance Theory (Sidanius and Pratto, 2001), which can be limiting from a global perspective and does not include cultural harms. While some definitions and operationalizations of harms in our framework (e.g., Stereotyping, Disparagement) may be applicable to other cultural perspectives, we note that there may be some that require cultural context-specific updates and also that there are other harms that we did not cover. There are also other bias measures in this rapidly growing space that we may not have covered and tagged with harms measured. Additionally, we do not focus on specific downstream applications where each measure might be used and encourage further analysis on these applications.

We further emphasize that while documentation enables more transparency into bias measures, documentation *does not ensure the validity* of the measures. In fact, there is a risk that the act of documentation could give a measure a false sense of validity. Too many documentation questions may also become an obstacle for practitioners interested in working on a topic, though we believe it is better for community progress to start thinking about these questions before designing bias measures.

Acknowledgments

We would like to thank various people for their valuable discussion and feedback, including Alexandra Olteanu, Arjun Subramonian, Chad Atalla, Dan Vann, Emily Corvi, Hanna Wallach, Hannah Washington, Jason Teoh, Kevin Robinson, Stefanie Reed, Su Lin Blodgett, Vinodkumar Prabhakaran, as well as our anonymous reviewers. This work was supported by NSF grant #1927554, NSF grants #2030859 and #2127309 to the Computing Research Association for the CIFellows Project, and the Sloan Award.

References

Gordon Willard Allport, Kenneth Clark, and Thomas Pettigrew. 1954. The nature of prejudice.

Sarah Alnegheimish, Alicia Guo, and Yi Sun. 2022. Using natural sentences for understanding biases in language models. *NAACL*.

Valerio Basile, Cristina Bosco, Elisabetta Fersini, Debora Nozza, Viviana Patti, Francisco Manuel Rangel Pardo, Paolo Rosso, and Manuela Sanguinetti. 2019. SemEval-2019 task 5: Multilingual detection of hate speech against immigrants and women in Twitter. In *Proceedings of the 13th International Workshop on Semantic Evaluation*, pages 54–63.

Emily M. Bender and Batya Friedman. 2018. Data statements for natural language processing: Toward mitigating system bias and enabling better science. *Transactions of the Association for Computational Linguistics*, 6:587–604.

Emily M Bender, Timnit Gebru, Angelina McMillan-Major, and Shmargaret Shmitchell. 2021. On the dangers of stochastic parrots: Can language models be too big. *Proceedings of FAccT*.

Su Lin Blodgett. 2021. Sociolinguistically driven approaches for just natural language processing.

Su Lin Blodgett, Solon Barocas, Hal Daumé III, and Hanna Wallach. 2020. Language (technology) is power: A critical survey of "bias" in NLP. In *Proceedings of the 58th Annual Meeting of the Association for Computational Linguistics*.

Su Lin Blodgett, Lisa Green, and Brendan O'Connor. 2016. Demographic dialectal variation in social media: A case study of african-american english. *arXiv preprint arXiv:1608.08868*.

Su Lin Blodgett, Q. Vera Liao, Alexandra Olteanu, Rada Mihalcea, Michael Muller, Morgan Klaus Scheuerman, Chenhao Tan, and Qian Yang. 2022. Responsible language technologies: Foreseeing and mitigating harms. In *Extended Abstracts of the 2022 CHI Conference on Human Factors in Computing Systems*, CHI EA '22, New York, NY, USA. Association for Computing Machinery.

Su Lin Blodgett, Gilsinia Lopez, Alexandra Olteanu, Robert Sim, and Hanna Wallach. 2021. Stereotyping norwegian salmon: an inventory of pitfalls in fairness benchmark datasets. In *Proc. 59th Annual Meeting of the Association for Computational Linguistics*.

T Bolukbasi, K W Chang, J Zou, V Saligrama, and A Kalai. 2016. Man is to computer programmer as woman is to homemaker? debiasing word embeddings. In *ACM Transactions of Information Systems*.

Daniel Borkan, Lucas Dixon, Jeffrey Sorensen, Nithum Thain, and Lucy Vasserman. 2019. Nuanced metrics for measuring unintended bias with real data for text classification. In *Companion proceedings of the 2019 world wide web conference*, pages 491–500.

Aylin Caliskan, Joanna J. Bryson, and Arvind Narayanan. 2017. Semantics derived automatically from language corpora contain human-like biases. *Science*, 356(6334):183–186.

Yang Trista Cao and Hal Daumé III. 2020. Toward gender-inclusive coreference resolution. In *Proceedings of the 58th Annual Meeting of the Association for Computational Linguistics*, pages 4568–4595.

Ilias Chalkidis, Tommaso Pasini, Sheng Zhang, Letizia Tomada, Sebastian Felix Schwemer, and Anders Søgaard. 2022. Fairlex: A multilingual benchmark for evaluating fairness in legal text processing. *arXiv preprint arXiv:2203.07228*.

Kate Crawford. 2017. The trouble with bias. Keynote at NeurIPS.

Aida Mostafazadeh Davani, Ali Omrani, Brendan Kennedy, Mohammad Atari, Xiang Ren, and Morteza Dehghani. 2020. Fair hate speech detection through evaluation of social group counterfactuals. *arXiv preprint arXiv:2010.12779*.

Thomas Davidson, Debasmita Bhattacharya, and Ingmar Weber. 2019. Racial bias in hate speech and abusive language detection datasets. In *Proceedings of the Third Workshop on Abusive Language Online*, pages 25–35.

Thomas Davidson, Dana Warmsley, Michael Macy, and Ingmar Weber. 2017. Automated hate speech detection and the problem of offensive language. In *Proceedings of the International AAAI Conference on Web and Social Media*, volume 11.

Maria De-Arteaga, Alexey Romanov, Hanna Wallach, Jennifer Chayes, Christian Borgs, Alexandra Chouldechova, Sahin Geyik, Krishnaram Kenthapadi, and Adam Tauman Kalai. 2019. Bias in bios: A case study of semantic representation bias in a high-stakes setting. In *Proceedings of the Conference on Fairness, Accountability, and Transparency*, pages 120–128.

Pieter Delobelle, Ewoenam Tokpo, Toon Calders, and Bettina Berendt. 2022. Measuring fairness with biased rulers: A comparative study on bias metrics for pre-trained language models. In *Proceedings of the 2022 Conference of the North American Chapter of the Association for Computational Linguistics: Human Language Technologies*, pages 1693–1706, Seattle, United States. Association for Computational Linguistics.

Sunipa Dev, Tao Li, Jeff Phillips, and Vivek Srikumar. 2019. On measuring and mitigating biased inferences of word embeddings.

Sunipa Dev, Tao Li, Jeff M Phillips, and Vivek Srikumar. 2021a. OSCaR: Orthogonal subspace correction and rectification of biases in word embeddings. In *Proceedings of the 2021 Conference on Empirical Methods in Natural Language Processing*, pages 5034–5050, Online and Punta Cana, Dominican Republic. Association for Computational Linguistics.

Sunipa Dev, Masoud Monajatipoor, Anaelia Ovalle, Arjun Subramonian, Jeff Phillips, and Kai-Wei Chang. 2021b. Harms of gender exclusivity and challenges in non-binary representation in language technologies. In *EMNLP*, Online and Punta Cana, Dominican Republic. Association for Computational Linguistics.

Sunipa Dev and Jeff Phillips. 2019. Attenuating bias in word vectors. In *AISTATS*, Proceedings of Machine Learning Research, pages 879–887. PMLR.

Patricia G Devine. 1989. Stereotypes and prejudice: Their automatic and controlled components. *Journal of personality and social psychology*, 56(1):5.

Jwala Dhamala, Tony Sun, Varun Kumar, Satyapriya Krishna, Yada Pruksachatkun, Kai-Wei Chang, and Rahul Gupta. 2021. Bold: Dataset and metrics for measuring biases in open-ended language generation. In *FAccT*.

Mark Díaz, Isaac Johnson, Amanda Lazar, Anne Marie Piper, and Darren Gergle. 2018. Addressing age-related bias in sentiment analysis. In *Proceedings of the 2018 chi conference on human factors in computing systems*, pages 1–14.

Emily Dinan, Angela Fan, Adina Williams, Jack Urbanek, Douwe Kiela, and Jason Weston. 2020. Queens are powerful too: Mitigating gender bias in dialogue generation. In *Proceedings of the 2020 Conference on Empirical Methods in Natural Language Processing (EMNLP)*, pages 8173–8188.

Emily Dinan, Samuel Humeau, Bharath Chintagunta, and Jason Weston. 2019. Build it break it fix it for dialogue safety: Robustness from adversarial human attack. In *Proceedings of the 2019 Conference on Empirical Methods in Natural Language Processing and the 9th International Joint Conference on Natural Language Processing (EMNLP-IJCNLP)*, pages 4537–4546.

Lucas Dixon, John Li, Jeffrey Sorensen, Nithum Thain, and Lucy Vasserman. 2018. Measuring and mitigating unintended bias in text classification. In *Proceedings of the 2018 AAAI/ACM Conference on AI, Ethics, and Society*, pages 67–73.

Antigoni Founta, Constantinos Djouvas, Despoina Chatzakou, Ilias Leontiadis, Jeremy Blackburn, Gianluca Stringhini, Athena Vakali, Michael Sirivianos, and Nicolas Kourtellis. 2018. Large scale crowdsourcing and characterization of twitter abusive behavior. In *Proceedings of the International AAAI Conference on Web and Social Media*, volume 12.

Aparna Garimella, Carmen Banea, E. Hovy, and Rada Mihalcea. 2019. Women's syntactic resilience and men's grammatical luck: Gender-bias in part-of-speech tagging and dependency parsing. In *ACL*.

Andrew Gaut, Tony Sun, Shirlyn Tang, Yuxin Huang, Jing Qian, Mai ElSherief, Jieyu Zhao, Diba Mirza, Elizabeth M. Belding, Kai-Wei Chang, and William Yang Wang. 2019. Towards understanding gender bias in relation extraction. *CoRR*, abs/1911.03642.

Timnit Gebru, Jamie Morgenstern, Briana Vecchione, Jennifer Wortman Vaughan, Hanna Wallach, Hal Daumé III, and Kate Crawford. 2018. Datasheets for datasets. *arXiv preprint arXiv:1803.09010*.

Jennifer Golbeck, Zahra Ashktorab, Rashad O. Banjo, Alexandra Berlinger, Siddharth Bhagwan, Cody Buntain, Paul Cheakalos, Alicia A. Geller, Quint Gergory, Rajesh Kumar Gnanasekaran, Raja Rajan Gunasekaran, Kelly M. Hoffman, Jenny Hottle, Vichita Jienjitlert, Shivika Khare, Ryan Lau, Marianna J. Martindale, Shalmali Naik, Heather L. Nixon, Piyush Ramachandran, Kristine M. Rogers, Lisa Rogers, Meghna Sardana Sarin, Gaurav Shahane, Jayanee Thanki, Priyanka Vengataraman, Zijian Wan, and Derek Michael Wu. 2017. A large labeled corpus for online harassment research. In *Proceedings of the 2017 ACM on Web Science Conference*, WebSci '17, page 229–233, New York, NY, USA. Association for Computing Machinery.

Seraphina Goldfarb-Tarrant, Rebecca Marchant, Ricardo Muñoz Sanchez, Mugdha Pandya, and Adam Lopez. 2020. Intrinsic bias metrics do not correlate with application bias. *arXiv preprint arXiv:2012.15859*.

Hila Gonen and Yoav Goldberg. 2019. Lipstick on a pig: Debiasing methods cover up systematic gender biases in word embeddings but do not remove them. In *Proceedings of NAACL-HLT 2019*, pages 609–614. Association for Computational Linguistics.

Sophie Groenwold, Lily Ou, Aesha Parekh, Samhita Honnavalli, Sharon Levy, Diba Mirza, and William Yang Wang. 2020. Investigating African-American Vernacular English in transformer-based text generation. In *Proceedings of the 2020 Conference on Empirical Methods in Natural Language Processing (EMNLP)*, pages 5877–5883.

Nizar Habash, Houda Bouamor, and Christine Chung. 2019. Automatic gender identification and reinflection in Arabic. In *Proceedings of the First Workshop on Gender Bias in Natural Language Processing*, pages 155–165.

Erika V Hall, Alison V Hall, Adam D Galinsky, and Katherine W Phillips. 2019. Mosaic: A model of stereotyping through associated and intersectional categories. *Academy of Management Review*, 44(3):643–672.

Nick Haslam and Michelle Stratemeyer. 2016. Recent research on dehumanization. *Current Opinion in Psychology*, 11:25–29. Intergroup relations.

Dirk Hovy and Shannon L Spruit. 2016. The social impact of natural language processing. In *Proceedings of the 54th Annual Meeting of the Association for Computational Linguistics (Volume 2: Short Papers)*, pages 591–598.

Po-Sen Huang, Huan Zhang, Ray Jiang, Robert Stanforth, Johannes Welbl, Jack Rae, Vishal Maini, Dani Yogatama, and Pushmeet Kohli. 2020. Reducing sentiment bias in language models via counterfactual evaluation. In *Findings of the Association for Computational Linguistics: EMNLP 2020*, pages 65–83.

Ben Hutchinson, Vinodkumar Prabhakaran, Emily Denton, Kellie Webster, Yu Zhong, and Stephen Denuyl. 2020. Social biases in NLP models as barriers for persons with disabilities. In *Proceedings of the 58th Annual Meeting of the Association for Computational Linguistics*, pages 5491–5501, Online. Association for Computational Linguistics.

Abigail Z Jacobs and Hanna Wallach. 2021. Measurement and fairness. In *Proceedings of the 2021 ACM conference on fairness, accountability, and transparency*, pages 375–385.

Jigsaw. 2019. *Jigsaw Unintended Bias in Toxicity Classification.*

Brendan Kennedy, Xisen Jin, Aida Mostafazadeh Davani, Morteza Dehghani, and Xiang Ren. 2020. Contextualizing hate speech classifiers with post-hoc explanation. In *Proceedings of the 58th Annual Meeting of the Association for Computational Linguistics*, pages 5435–5442.

Svetlana Kiritchenko and Saif M. Mohammad. 2018. Examining gender and race bias in two hundred sentiment analysis systems.

Anne M Koenig. 2018. Comparing prescriptive and descriptive gender stereotypes about children, adults, and the elderly. *Frontiers in psychology*, 9:1086.

Anne Lauscher, Rafik Takieddin, Simone Paolo Ponzetto, and Goran Glavaš. 2020. AraWEAT: Multidimensional analysis of biases in Arabic word embeddings. In *Proceedings of the Fifth Arabic Natural Language Processing Workshop*, pages 192–199.

Tao Li, Tushar Khot, Daniel Khashabi, Ashish Sabharwal, and Vivek Srikumar. 2020. Unqovering stereotyping biases via underspecified questions.

Bruce G. Link and Jo C. Phelan. 2001. Conceptualizing stigma. *Annual Review of Sociology*, 27(1):363–385.

Haochen Liu, Jamell Dacon, Wenqi Fan, Hui Liu, Zitao Liu, and Jiliang Tang. 2020a. Does gender matter? towards fairness in dialogue systems. In *Proceedings of the 28th International Conference on Computational Linguistics*, pages 4403–4416.

Haochen Liu, Wentao Wang, Yiqi Wang, Hui Liu, Zitao Liu, and Jiliang Tang. 2020b. Mitigating gender bias for neural dialogue generation with adversarial learning. In *Proceedings of the 2020 Conference on Empirical Methods in Natural Language Processing (EMNLP)*, pages 893–903.

Kaiji Lu, Piotr Mardziel, Fangjing Wu, Preetam Amancharla, and Anupam Datta. 2020. Gender bias in neural natural language processing. In *Logic, Language, and Security*. Springer.

Vijit Malik, Sunipa Dev, Akihiro Nishi, Nanyun Peng, and Kai-Wei Chang. 2022. Socially aware bias measurements for Hindi language representations. In *Proceedings of the 2022 Conference of the North American Chapter of the Association for Computational Linguistics: Human Language Technologies*, pages 1041–1052, Seattle, United States. Association for Computational Linguistics.

David M. Markowitz and Paul Slovic. 2020. Social, psychological, and demographic characteristics of dehumanization toward immigrants. *Proceedings of the National Academy of Sciences*, 117(17):9260–9269.

Ninareh Mehrabi, Thamme Gowda, Fred Morstatter, Nanyun Peng, and A. Galstyan. 2020. Man is to person as woman is to location: Measuring gender bias in named entity recognition. *Proceedings of the 31st ACM Conference on Hypertext and Social Media*.

Ninareh Mehrabi, Pei Zhou, Fred Morstatter, J. Pujara, Xiang Ren, and A. Galstyan. 2021. Lawyers are dishonest? quantifying representational harms in commonsense knowledge resources. *ArXiv*, abs/2103.11320.

Carolyn B Mervis, Eleanor Rosch, et al. 1981. Categorization of natural objects. *Annual review of psychology*, 32(1):89–115.

Margaret Mitchell, Simone Wu, Andrew Zaldivar, Parker Barnes, Lucy Vasserman, Ben Hutchinson, Elena Spitzer, Inioluwa Deborah Raji, and Timnit Gebru. 2019. Model cards for model reporting. In *Proceedings of the Conference on Fairness, Accountability, and Transparency*, FAT* '19, page 220–229, New York, NY, USA. Association for Computing Machinery.

Saif Mohammad. 2018. Obtaining reliable human ratings of valence, arousal, and dominance for 20,000 English words. In *Proceedings of the 56th Annual Meeting of the Association for Computational Linguistics (Volume 1: Long Papers)*, pages 174–184.

Saif Mohammad. 2022. Ethics sheets for AI tasks. In *Proceedings of the 60th Annual Meeting of the Association for Computational Linguistics (Volume 1: Long Papers)*, pages 8368–8379, Dublin, Ireland. Association for Computational Linguistics.

R. Munro and Alex Morrison. 2020. Detecting independent pronoun bias with partially-synthetic data generation. In *EMNLP*.

M. Lynne Murphy. 2010. *Lexical and semantic relations*, Cambridge Textbooks in Linguistics, page 108–132. Cambridge University Press.

Moin Nadeem, Anna Bethke, and Siva Reddy. 2021. StereoSet: Measuring stereotypical bias in pretrained language models. In *Proceedings of the 59th Annual Meeting of the Association for Computational Linguistics and the 11th International Joint Conference on Natural Language Processing (Volume 1: Long Papers)*, Online. Association for Computational Linguistics.

Nikita Nangia, Clara Vania, Rasika Bhalerao, and Samuel R. Bowman. 2020. CrowS-pairs: A challenge dataset for measuring social biases in masked language models. In *Proceedings of the 2020 Conference on Empirical Methods in Natural Language Processing (EMNLP)*, pages 1953–1967.

Aurelie Neveol, Yoann Dupont, Julien Bezançon, and Karën Fort. 2022. French crows-pairs: Extending a challenge dataset for measuring social bias in masked language models to a language other than english. In *Proceedings of the 60th Annual Meeting of the Association for Computational Linguistics (Volume 1: Long Papers)*, pages 8521–8531.

Ji Ho Park, Jamin Shin, and Pascale Fung. 2018. Reducing gender bias in abusive language detection. In *Proceedings of the 2018 Conference on Empirical Methods in Natural Language Processing*, pages 2799–2804.

Vinodkumar Prabhakaran, Ben Hutchinson, and Margaret Mitchell. 2019. Perturbation sensitivity analysis to detect unintended model biases. In *Proceedings of the 2019 Conference on Empirical Methods in Natural Language Processing and the 9th International Joint Conference on Natural Language Processing (EMNLP-IJCNLP)*, pages 5740–5745.

Daniel Preoţiuc-Pietro and Lyle Ungar. 2018. User-level race and ethnicity predictors from Twitter text. In *Proceedings of the 27th International Conference on Computational Linguistics*, pages 1534–1545, Santa Fe, New Mexico, USA. Association for Computational Linguistics.

Hannah Rashkin, Maarten Sap, Emily Allaway, Noah A. Smith, and Yejin Choi. 2018. Event2Mind: Commonsense inference on events, intents, and reactions. In *Proceedings of the 56th Annual Meeting of the Association for Computational Linguistics (Volume 1: Long Papers)*, pages 463–473, Melbourne, Australia. Association for Computational Linguistics.

Shauli Ravfogel, Yanai Elazar, Hila Gonen, Michael Twiton, and Yoav Goldberg. 2020. Null it out: Guarding protected attributes by iterative nullspace projection. In *Proceedings of the 58th Annual Meeting of the Association for Computational Linguistics*, pages 7237–7256.

Rachel Rudinger, Chandler May, and Benjamin Van Durme. 2017. Social bias in Elicited Natural Language Inferences. In *Proceedings of the First ACL Workshop on Ethics in Natural Language Processing*, pages 74–79.

Rachel Rudinger, Jason Naradowsky, Brian Leonard, and Benjamin Van Durme. 2018. Gender bias in coreference resolution. In *NAACL*, pages 8–14.

Maarten Sap, Dallas Card, Saadia Gabriel, Yejin Choi, and Noah A. Smith. 2019. The risk of racial bias in hate speech detection. In *Proceedings of the 57th Annual Meeting of the Association for Computational Linguistics*, pages 1668–1678.

Maarten Sap, Saadia Gabriel, Lianhui Qin, Dan Jurafsky, Noah A. Smith, and Yejin Choi. 2020. Social bias frames: Reasoning about social and power implications of language. In *Proceedings of the 58th Annual Meeting of the Association for Computational Linguistics*, pages 5477–5490.

Emily Sheng, Kai-Wei Chang, Premkumar Natarajan, and Nanyun Peng. 2019. The woman worked as a babysitter: On biases in language generation. In *Proceedings of the 2019 Conference on Empirical Methods in Natural Language Processing and the 9th International Joint Conference on Natural Language Processing (EMNLP-IJCNLP)*, pages 3407–3412.

Emily Sheng, Kai-Wei Chang, Premkumar Natarajan, and Nanyun Peng. 2021. Societal biases in language generation: Progress and challenges. In *Proceedings of the 59th Annual Meeting of the Association for Computational Linguistics and the 11th International Joint Conference on Natural Language Processing*.

Vered Shwartz, Rachel Rudinger, and Oyvind Tafjord. 2020. "you are grounded!": Latent name artifacts in pre-trained language models. In *Proceedings of the 2020 Conference on Empirical Methods in Natural Language Processing (EMNLP)*, pages 6850–6861.

J. Sidanius and F. Pratto. 2001. *Social Dominance: An Intergroup Theory of Social Hierarchy and Oppression*. Cambridge University Press.

Gabriel Stanovsky, Noah A. Smith, and Luke Zettlemoyer. 2019. Evaluating gender bias in machine translation. In *Proceedings of the 57th Annual Meeting of the Association for Computational Linguistics*, pages 1679–1684.

Tony Sun, Andrew Gaut, Shirlyn Tang, Yuxin Huang, Mai ElSherief, Jieyu Zhao, Diba Mirza, Elizabeth Belding, Kai-Wei Chang, and William Yang Wang. 2019. Mitigating gender bias in natural language processing: Literature review. In *Proceedings of the 57th Annual Meeting of the Association for Computational Linguistics*, pages 1630–1640, Florence, Italy. Association for Computational Linguistics.

Zeerak Talat, Aurélie Névéol, Stella Biderman, Miruna Clinciu, Manan Dey, Shayne Longpre, Sasha Luccioni, Maraim Masoud, Margaret Mitchell, Dragomir Radev, Shanya Sharma, Arjun Subramonian, Jaesung Tae, Samson Tan, Deepak Tunuguntla, and Oskar Van Der Wal. 2022. You reap what you sow: On the challenges of bias evaluation under multilingual settings. In *Proceedings of BigScience Episode #5 – Workshop on Challenges & Perspectives in Creating Large Language Models*, pages 26–41, virtual+Dublin. Association for Computational Linguistics.

Amos Tversky and Daniel Kahneman. 1974. Judgment under uncertainty: Heuristics and biases: Biases in judgments reveal some heuristics of thinking under uncertainty. *science*, 185(4157):1124–1131.

Jun Wang, Benjamin Rubinstein, and Trevor Cohn. 2022. Measuring and mitigating name biases in neural machine translation. In *Proceedings of the 60th Annual Meeting of the Association for Computational Linguistics (Volume 1: Long Papers)*, pages 2576–2590.

Zeerak Waseem. 2016. Are you a racist or am I seeing things? annotator influence on hate speech detection on Twitter. In *Proceedings of the First Workshop on NLP and Computational Social Science*, pages 138–142, Austin, Texas. Association for Computational Linguistics.

Zeerak Waseem and Dirk Hovy. 2016. Hateful symbols or hateful people? predictive features for hate speech detection on twitter. In *Proceedings of the NAACL student research workshop*, pages 88–93.

Kellie Webster, Marta R. Costa-jussà, Christian Hardmeier, and Will Radford. 2019. Gendered ambiguous pronoun (GAP) shared task at the gender bias in NLP workshop 2019. In *Proceedings of the First Workshop on Gender Bias in Natural Language Processing*, pages 1–7.

Kellie Webster, Marta Recasens, Vera Axelrod, and Jason Baldridge. 2018. Mind the GAP: A balanced corpus of gendered ambiguous pronouns. *Transactions of the Association for Computational Linguistics*, 6:605–617.

Mengzhou Xia, Anjalie Field, and Yulia Tsvetkov. 2020. Demoting racial bias in hate speech detection. In *Proceedings of the Eighth International Workshop on Natural Language Processing for Social Media*, pages 7–14.

Jieyu Zhao, Daniel Khashabi, Tushar Khot, Ashish Sabharwal, and Kai-Wei Chang. 2021. Ethical-advice taker: Do language models understand natural language interventions? In *Findings of the Association for Computational Linguistics: ACL-IJCNLP 2021*, pages 4158–4164.

Jieyu Zhao, Subhabrata Mukherjee, Saghar Hosseini, Kai-Wei Chang, and Ahmed Hassan Awadallah. 2020. Gender bias in multilingual embeddings and cross-lingual transfer. In *Proceedings of the 58th Annual Meeting of the Association for Computational Linguistics*, pages 2896–2907.

Jieyu Zhao, Tianlu Wang, Mark Yatskar, Ryan Cotterell, Vicente Ordonez, and Kai-Wei Chang. 2019. Gender Bias in Contextualized Word Embeddings. In *Proceedings of NAACL-HLT 2019*, pages 629–634. Association for Computational Linguistics.

Jieyu Zhao, Tianlu Wang, Mark Yatskar, Vicente Ordonez, and Kai-Wei Chang. 2018. Gender bias in coreference resolution: Evaluation and debiasing methods.

Ran Zmigrod, Sabrina J. Mielke, Hanna Wallach, and Ryan Cotterell. 2019. Counterfactual data augmentation for mitigating gender stereotypes in languages with rich morphology. In *Proceedings of the 57th Annual Meeting of the Association for Computational Linguistics*, pages 1651–1661.

Appendix: On Measures of Biases and Harms in NLP

A Harm Framework Heuristics

To help practitioners determine the specific harm(s) a bias measure evaluates, we propose the following set of heuristics.

Stereotyping: Does the method:

- deal with language which communicates an existing, well-known a priori judgement or generalization which oversimplifies the reality of diversity within the group?
- measure predictions or probabilities of associations between specific groups and certain characteristics, concepts, language, or sentiments?
- focus on finding specific, pre-defined outcomes based on hypotheses about stereotypical associations, i.e., is the hypothesis directional?
- test associations which either the "average" in-group member or person in the relevant society would be able to quickly predict, i.e., would they be able to predict or identify what the 'problem' is and connect its roots to their cultural/historical knowledge?

Note: these associations can be positive or negative, but should not hold as naturalistic when a commensurable group is swapped in.

Erasure: Does the method:

- search for lack of representation of specific groups based on cultural trends and patterns of historical inequality?
- engage with mismatches between representation and reality (due to imprecise categorizations, rounding errors, etc.)?
- interrogate representation issues caused by prevailing stereotypes, dehumanization, or cultural narratives?
- primarily concern itself with whether or how specific, pre-defined groups are represented or treated equitably, rather than to what extent groups are treated inequitably in relation to one another?
- primarily provide results about the model performance for a specific group in relation to a 'control' group (whether or not explicitly stated as such)?

Disparagement: Does the method:

- deal with generally belittling, devaluing, or de-legitimizing language about a group?
- engage with sentiments related to societal regard (respect), expressing normative judgments, or using scalar adjectives pertaining to quality or worth (best/worst, good/bad), but which are not tied to an established stereotype?
- use language which holds as pragmatically and semantically valid/naturalistic when the group identifier is perturbed with a commensurable group?
- deal with 'toxicity' or 'unhealthy' discourse in general?

Dehumanization: Does the method specifically mention language commonly used to dehumanize, such as:

- associations with non-human life (vermin, insects)?
- implications that a certain group is sub-human or not 'true' members of a superset (certain 'immigrants' aren't 'American')?
- notions related to eugenics?
- justifications of inequitable treatment of groups or denial of human rights based on group membership (note: these can be codified into stereotypes, but are distinguished by their unique purpose to 'other' the group, reinforcing notions of normative identities and casting divergence as indication of a hierarchy of 'species' within humankind)?

Quality of Service: Does the method:

- seek to measure the comparative performance of a model for several commensurable demographic groups?
- have an obvious or direct application to mitigation efforts or industry usage?
- primarily concern itself with to what extent groups are treated inequitably (quantification), rather than whether they are treated differ-

ently?

B A Survey of Bias Measures for Understanding Harms

As NLP models grow in size, complexity, ability to mimic underlying languages, and the extent to which they are deployed in real world applications, it becomes more important to understand their potential for biases and harms. A growing number of measures serve to evaluate biases in tasks such as sentiment analysis or relation extraction, targeting specific social biases related to gender, race, religion, etc. While measures to evaluate biases have been formulated across various tasks, there remains a lack of cohesive understanding of *what these bias measures evaluate* and *how different measures relate*. In this section, we survey and describe a non-exhaustive list of measures for quantifying biases in different NLP tasks for primarily English. Tables 1 and 2 summarize this survey along with alignments of harms for different bias measures.

B.1 Natural Language Understanding

We discuss existing works that use different measures to assess the presence of social biases in a variety of NLU tasks.

Coreference Resolution Coreference resolution is the task of finding all expressions that refer to the same entity in text; a more specific objective is to associate pronoun mentions to different entities. There are two distinct definitions of bias that are evaluated with respect to this task, both centered around gender. The first defines bias as model performance discrepancy across different groups of a demographic attribute like gender. The Gendered Ambiguous Pronouns (GAP) dataset (Webster et al., 2018) consists of samples from Wikipedia biographies with ambiguous pronoun-name resolution pairs. Webster et al. (2018) defines and measures biases through a disparity in correctly resolving pronoun-name relationships for the male and female genders. The Maybe Ambiguous Pronoun (MAP) dataset (Cao and Daumé III, 2020) expands GAP to go beyond binary genders with a broader dataset. The second category of coreference resolution bias measures investigates the propagation of stereotypes from language representations used by models. Both WinoBias (Zhao et al., 2018) and Winogender (Rudinger et al., 2018) generate Winograd schema style datasets to investigate occupational gender stereotypes. Additionally, Lu et al. (2020) create sentence templates to evaluate biases using the ratio of accurate pronoun resolution for stereotypical vs non-stereotypical occupational associations.

Existing works that use the second definition of bias currently focus on singular stereotypes (e.g., with regards to occupation), while gender biases can encompass a broad range of other stereotypical and undesired associations. While both definitions of bias can potentially cover additional demographics and undesired associations, it is important to question which is more applicable to investigate harms faced by a group. For example, non-binary individuals face erasure in language representations (Dev et al., 2021b), and these experienced harms might be more appropriately captured by the first definition, whereas stereotyping might be by the second.

Natural Language Inference (NLI) NLI determines the directional relationship between two sentences, as to whether the second sentence (hypothesis) is entailed, contradicted, or neutral to the first sentence (premise). Dev et al. (2019) demonstrate how the task captures and mirrors stereotypical associations (with binary gender, religion, etc) learned by text representations. Their bias measure consists of a dataset with sentence pairs: one sentence with an explicit demographic attribute (e.g., gender), and the other with implicit, stereotypical associations (e.g., occupations). Bias is measured as the accuracy of models in identifying that all sentences have no directional relation, i.e., classified as having the 'neutral' label. Since an overall bias score is calculated over a set of templates, a variety of templates can be independently assessed together to evaluate bias of NLI model outcomes across multiple demographic groups, thus not restricting measurements to a single stereotype.

Sentiment Analysis Estimating the sentiment or language polarity of text is useful for understanding consumer perception from reviews, tweets, etc. However, this task has been demonstrated to be stereotypically influenced by demographic characteristics such as race and gender (Kiritchenko and Mohammad, 2018), age (Díaz et al., 2018) and names of individuals (Prabhakaran et al., 2019). Existing works keep sentence templates constant between samples and change the assumed demographic attribute of the person (e.g., through names) in a sentence. This ideally should not change the sentiment classification of the sample—any changes in sentiment indicate the existence of stereotypical associations. Since evaluation hinges on this contrast in classification across groups, bias against a group is also measured in comparison to another.

Question Answering (QA) QA models perform reading comprehension tasks and also propagate stereotypical associations from underlying language representations, as demonstrated through UnQuover (Li et al., 2020). Li et al. (2020) use sentence templates containing limited direct demographic information (e.g., names) and underspecified questions containing no related demographic information to measure biases exhibited by QA systems. The setup is such that all subcategories of a demographic attribute (e.g., religion: Christian, Buddhist, etc) should be equally predicted as the answer. A statistically significant, higher value for one sub-category is interpreted as bias. Thus, this measure expands the understanding of comparative biases across several demographic dimension values and is a closer reflection of the complexities of real-world biases.

Neural Relation Extraction Relation extraction is the task of extracting relations between entities in a sentence and is instrumental in converting raw, unstructured text to structured data. Gaut et al. (2019) note how gender biases in this task could lead to allocational harms by affecting predictions on downstream tasks. They create a dataset, WikiGenderBias, containing sentences regarding either a male or female entity and one of four relationships: spouse, occupation, birth date, or birth place. Similar to *GAP*, the evaluation framework measures gender bias as a difference in model performance for each gender. Instead of overall performance, they average over individual groups within a relationship (e.g., different individual occupations). This measure faces the challenge of generalizability as it relies on scraping a variety of existing text for different demographic groups.

Masked Language Model Predictions Several language representations are trained on the ability to predict masked words in text. CrowS-Pairs (Nangia et al., 2020) and StereoSet (Nadeem et al., 2021) are datasets that use this property to expose and evaluate social biases learned with respect to different protected attributes. Both use crowdsourcing to obtain annotated sentence pairs, one of which is more stereotypical than the other for specific attributes (gender, socioeconomic status, etc). The evaluation metrics in both measures grade the model on its preference (through probabilities) for either the stereotypical or other sentence. Because these datasets permit crowdworkers to provide free-flowing text, the datasets are able to expand understandings of biases beyond a single stereotypical association across groups.

Text Classification (Occupations) De-Arteaga et al. (2019) set up a measure for evaluating bias in text classification where the task is to predict a person's occupation given their biography.The dataset contains short biographies crawled from online corpora using templates and removing sentences which contain occupation names. Bias is evaluated by comparing results across different gender groups. Zhao et al. (2020) extend the original dataset to Spanish, French, and German. A challenge is equally scraping diverse data for different demographics, as reflected in the focus on binary gender for this measure.

Toxicity Detection Toxic language ranges from more explicitly offensive forms (e.g., vulgar insults) to more subtle forms (e.g., microaggressions). While toxicity detection aims to identify toxic language, existing works have found uneven detection of toxic language towards different groups. Prabhakaran et al. (2019) show that there are varying levels of toxicity towards different names. Dixon et al. (2018) analyze biases in a toxicity classification model through the Wikipedia Talk Pages dataset as well as through a templated test set. Jigsaw (Jigsaw, 2019) contains comments from the Civil Comments platform labeled with six types of toxicity (e.g., toxic, obscene, etc) and identity attributes (e.g., white, woman, etc). Along with this dataset, Jigsaw (2019) present a bias evaluation following that of Borkan et al. (2019) by comparing the AUC scores from different subgroups. Additionally, Sap et al. (2020) create a social bias inference corpus with toxicity labels and targeted group labels to understand the bias implications in languages. These bias measures demonstrate that even tasks intended to detect harms may be biased.

Hate Speech Detection Hate speech detection is the task of identifying abusive language that is specifically directed towards a particular group.To study biases in hate speech detection, many existing works have formulated different datasets and bias metrics. Davidson et al. (2017) and Founta et al. (2018) annotate Twitter datasets for hate speech detection. Blodgett et al. (2016) provide a corpus of demographically-aligned text with geolocated messages based on Twitter. Sap et al. (2019); Xia et al. (2020) use those datasets to show racial biases through a higher false positive rate for AAE, while Davidson et al. (2019) use the dataset of Blodgett et al. (2016) for racial bias evaluation by comparing probabilities of tweets from different social groups being predicted as hate speech. Davani et al. (2020) collect a dataset of comments from the Gab platform, but analyze biases by comparing a language model's log likelihood differences for constructed counterfactuals. Goldfarb-Tarrant et al. (2020) add gender labels to the dataset from Founta et al. (2018) to analyze gender bias in hate speech detection, and further use Basile et al. (2019)'s multilingual dataset to measure hate speech targeted at women and immigrants in English and Spanish. Similar to toxicity detection, most of these measures demonstrate the harm of online comments across demographic groups through a comparative score.

Bias Analyses without Complete Bias Measures There are other task-specific discussions of bias evaluations that do not propose specific bias measures. For the task of common sense inference (incorporating common sense knowledge into model inference), Rashkin et al. (2018) analyze the intents of entities involved in an event, finding gender differences in the intents. For named entity recognition, Mehrabi et al. (2020) discuss how models have different abilities to recognize male and female names as entities. For part-of-speech tagging, Munro and Morrison (2020) and Garimella et al. (2019) find that state-of-the-art parsers perform differently across genders, failing to identify "hers" and "theirs" as pronouns but not "his". In addition, Mehrabi et al. (2021) and Rudinger et al. (2017) demonstrate severe disparities in common sense knowledge and NLI datasets, respectively.

B.2 Natural Language Generation

We briefly describe some datasets and metrics used to evaluate biases in NLG tasks and refer readers to Sheng et al. (2021) for a survey on common bias measures in Natural Language Generation. For autocomplete generation, Sheng et al. (2019) and Huang et al. (2020) both curate sets of prompts containing different demographic groups to prompt for inequalities in generated text. For the similar task of dialogue generation, Liu et al. (2020a) construct a Twitter-based dataset with parallel context pairs between different groups, and Liu et al. (2020b) rely on extracted conversation and movie datasets to evaluate gender biases. Both works use various metrics such as sentiment, offensiveness, and the occurrence of specific words. For machine translation, the English WinoMT dataset (Stanovsky et al., 2019) is a widely used dataset for quantifying gender biases with bias metrics for translation typically rely on translation accuracy.

C Documenting Bias Measures

C.1 Case Study #1: Documentation for WinoBias (Zhao et al., 2018)

1. *Motivation*
   - **What is the stated definition of bias? How does this definition align with normative definitions of harm?** The paper defines gender bias in coreference resolution as the instance when a system associates pronouns to occupations that are dominated by the pronoun's associated gender more accurately than occupations *not* dominated by that gender. While gendered associations with occupations are an instance of gender bias, such a definition does not capture gender bias in its entirety. The metric is defined to measure occupational perception of different genders, which is associated with representational harms.
   - **What language and culture is the bias and measure most relevant to?** English language in the United States
   - **If a demographic attribute is split into groups for measurement of bias, how many groups have been considered?** Gender binary (male and female) is considered in this measure.
   - **What is the source of bias that is measured?** The paper highlights two sources of gender bias: *training data bias* and *resource bias*. Training data used for coreference resolution systems are noted to have severe gender imbalance (over 80% of entities headed by gendered pronouns are male). Pre-trained word embeddings which serve as an auxiliary resource for WinoBias (Zhao et al., 2018) have been shown to contain gender bias as well ("*men*" is closer to "*programmer*" than "*woman*"). The paper also mentions a gender statistics corpus (i.e. *Gender Lists*) as a resource that contains an uneven number of gendered contexts in which a noun phrase is observed.

- **What tasks or applications is this bias measure useful for?** Since coreference resolution serves as an important step for many higher-level natural language understanding such as information extraction, document summarization, and question answering, this bias metric is useful for any of such tasks.

2. *Composition and Collection Process*
   - **Is the bias measure data scraped, generated, or produced some other way?** The data is created by the authors but the occupation list is collected from the U.S. Bureau of Labor Statistics. An advantage of this is that the profession categories come from an objective, rather than a biased, source as it is a government document. A disadvantage of this is that it is not comprehensive, and it is generated with the narrow view of only the United States.
   - **What are the limitations associated with method of data curation? How generalizable is this dataset?** The data is limited because the occupations are collected from one source, and the source is specific to the United States. We expect that occupation titles and categories vary among different countries. Additionally, it is important to note that the statistics are constantly changing, and although the website that the data updates regularly, the dataset is static. This limits the relevance of the dataset as the world around it changes.
   - **Is the dataset at risk of causing harm through the particular selection of proxy attributes to represent demographic groups?** Possibly—the dataset uses a limited set of occupations (curated from US-specific resources) and binary pronouns to represent different gender groups.
3. *Bias Metrics*
   - **How is the bias metric defined?** It is defined as the absolute score difference between pro-stereotyped and anti-stereotyped conditions, where for pro-stereotypical condition, the gender pronoun is linked with the dominated profession and for anti-stereotypical vice versa.
   - **Is it an absolute or relative evaluation?** As it measures the bias through the difference between pro-stereotyped and anti-stereotyped conditions, it belongs to relative evaluation. Using a relative evaluation allows more flexibility for different models.
   - **Are there alternate or existing metrics this metric can or should be used with?** WinoBias (Zhao et al., 2018) adapts the absolute difference of F1 to evaluate the gender bias. Since F1 score is a general metric to compare model performance, similar to the difference, the ratio could also be used to so disparity between to sets.
   - **Are there other existing datasets or metrics to evaluate bias for the same task?** Yes, for coreference resolution task, there are also Gendered Ambiguous Pronouns (GAP) (Webster et al., 2018) measuring the disparity incorrectly solving pronoun-name relationships for male and female genders, MAP (Cao and Daumé III, 2020) (built on GAP beyond binary genders) and Winogender (Rudinger et al., 2018) which also measures the relationship between gendered pronouns and occupations.
   - **Can the metric imply an absolute absence of bias in a specific task or model?** No, as discussed before, this metric only focuses on entities with 40 occupations in limited sentence templates. Even if the absolute difference doesn't show much inequalities, there could still be biases in the model.

C.2 Case Study #2: Documentation for Regard (Sheng et al., 2019)

1. *Motivation*
   - **What is the stated definition of bias? How does this definition align with normative definitions of harm?** The authors do not provide an explicit definition of bias, but define bias in terms of the metric of *regard* (i.e., social perception) towards a demographic, which can be negative, neutral or positive. Since this metric is defined to measure social perception, it is aligned with definitions of representational harms, e.g., negative stereotypes, denigrations.
   - **What is the source of bias that is measured?** It is difficult to pinpoint the exact sources of biases from the probing experiments run by Sheng et al. (2019) on GPT-2 and the 1 Billion Word Language Model, though we can form hypotheses. While the One Billion Word Benchmark dataset is publicly available for analysis, the exact dataset used to train GPT-2

can probably only be approximated at best. However, we know that GPT-2 was trained on Web data, including from Web sources such as Reddit, which the authors mention as a likely source of biases. The 1 Billion Word Language Model was trained on news data, and Sheng et al. (2019) find less biased results from this model. There could also be non-data related biases (e.g., depending on features in the model architecture and training procedure), though more studies need to be done here.

- **What tasks or applications is this bias measure useful for?** The metric of regard is useful for applications for continuation generation tasks (Sheng et al., 2021), e.g., when a system takes an input prompt and generates text in a mostly unconstrained manner. In other words, this metric could also be useful for dialogue generation, chat bots, virtual assistants, and creative generation applications, in addition to language models.

2. *Composition and Collection Process*
   - **Is the bias measure data scraped, generated, or produced some other way?** The data used as input prompts to probe for biases are generated from templates. For example, *"XYZ worked as"*, *"XYZ earned money by"*, etc. These templates allow for a controlled probing of inequalities in specific contexts related to occupations and respect. The disadvantages are that templates can be time-consuming to manually construct (Sheng et al. (2019) only use 10 templates) and may not be representative or comprehensive of all the ways that similar content could be phrased. Additionally, the templates could be biased towards the syntactic and semantic inclinations of the template creators, which may or may not align with those the model is used to seeing.
   - **What are the limitations associated with method of data curation? How generalizable is this dataset?** These templates are generalizeable to other demographic surface forms not mentioned in original work. Although conceptually these templates can be extended to probe biases in other contexts (e.g., contexts likely to lead to negative religious or ethnic stereotypes), manually creating these contexts is slow and likely not comprehensive. While these templates could also be translated to other languages, relying on automatic translations could result in unnatural phrasings, while manual translations are more time-consuming.
3. *Bias Metrics*
   - **How is the bias metric defined?** Sheng et al. (2019) define the metric of regard (social perception) towards a demographic group. Possible values are negative, neutral, or positive.
   - **Is it an absolute or relative evaluation?** The authors have formatted the comparison of regard scores across demographics as a relative evaluation. Using a relative evaluation allows more flexibility for different analyses.
   - **Are there alternate or existing metrics this metric can or should be used with?** Sheng et al. (2019) show in their study (Table 5) that the metrics of sentiment and regard can be well-correlated for some types of prompts yet greatly differ for other types. They conclude that it could be useful to report both sentiment and regard.
   - **Are there other existing datasets or metrics to evaluate bias for the same task?** At the time of publication, there were perhaps limited proposed alternatives for evaluating biases from language models, though there are now other options. Huang et al. (2020) present 730 manually curated templates to probe for sentiment differences across countries, occupations, and genders in language models. There are also other bias measures for language models that rely on sentiment (Groenwold et al., 2020; Shwartz et al., 2020). Both Sheng et al. (2019) and Huang et al. (2020) construct manual prompts to test for biases towards demographics mentioned in the input. Additionally, Groenwold et al. (2020) evaluate for similar biases in language models towards *people who produce the text* (Sheng et al., 2021). Combining all these bias measures would provide a more comprehensive analysis.
   - **Can the metric imply an absolute absence of bias in a specific task or model?** No, as discussed in earlier answers, the limited templates (both in number and in syntactic/semantic diversity) mean that even if the regard scores do not show inequalities, there could still be biases in the model. Also, since the authors use a regard classifier to feasibly

automatically label a large number of samples, there could also be biases from the classifier itself. Even human evaluations of regard could be influenced by human biases.

Task	Demographic Dimension	Bias Measure	Harms Evaluated
Hate Speech Detection	**Gender** through identity terms	Davani et al. (2020)	**Disparagement, QoS, Stereo.**
	Gender through stereotypes	Founta et al. (2018) + Goldfarb-Tarrant et al. (2020) Basile et al. (2019) + Goldfarb-Tarrant et al. (2020)	**Disparagement** **Dehumanization, Disparagement**
	Migrants through identity terms	Davani et al. (2020)	**Disparagement, QoS, Stereo.**
	Migrants through identity terms	Basile et al. (2019) + Goldfarb-Tarrant et al. (2020)	**Dehumanization, Disparagement** through pleasantness terms
	Political Ideo. through identity terms	Davani et al. (2020)	**Disparagement, QoS, Stereo.**
	Race through dialect	[Blodgett et al. (2016), Davidson et al. (2017), Founta et al. (2018), Preoţiuc-Pietro and Ungar (2018)] + Sap et al. (2019) [Blodgett et al. (2016), Davidson et al. (2017), Founta et al. (2018)] + Xia et al. (2020) [Waseem and Hovy (2016), Waseem (2016), Davidson et al. (2017), Founta et al. (2018), Golbeck et al. (2017), Blodgett et al. (2016)] + Davidson et al. (2019)	**Disparagement, Erasure, QoS** **Disparagement, Erasure** **Disparagement, Erasure, QoS**
	Race through identity terms	Davani et al. (2020) Kennedy et al. (2020)	**Disparagement, QoS, Stereo.** **Dehumanization, Disparagement**
	Religion through identity terms	Davani et al. (2020)	**Disparagement, QoS, Stereo.**
	Sexual Orient. through identity terms	Davani et al. (2020)	**Disparagement, QoS, Stereo.**
MLM Predictions	**Age** through identity terms	Nangia et al. (2020) Neveol et al. (2022)	**Stereo.** **Stereo.**
	Appearance through identity terms	Nangia et al. (2020) Neveol et al. (2022)	**Stereo.** **Stereo.**
	Disability through identity terms	Nangia et al. (2020) Neveol et al. (2022)	**Stereo.** **Stereo.**
	Gender through identity terms	Nangia et al. (2020) Nadeem et al. (2021) Neveol et al. (2022)	**Stereo.** **Stereo.** **Stereo.**
	Nationality through identity terms	Nangia et al. (2020) Neveol et al. (2022)	**Stereo.** **Stereo.**
	Race through identity terms	Nangia et al. (2020) Nadeem et al. (2021) Neveol et al. (2022)	**Stereo.** **Stereo.** **Stereo.**
	Religion through identity terms	Nangia et al. (2020) Nadeem et al. (2021) Neveol et al. (2022)	**Stereo.** **Stereo.** **Stereo.**
	Sexual Orient. through identity terms	Nangia et al. (2020) Neveol et al. (2022)	**Stereo.** **Stereo.**
	Socioeconomic through identity terms	Nangia et al. (2020) Nadeem et al. (2021) Neveol et al. (2022)	**Stereo.** **Stereo.** **Stereo.**
Autocomplete Generation	**Gender** through identity terms	Sheng et al. (2019) Huang et al. (2020) Dhamala et al. (2021)	**Disparagement, Stereo.** **Erasure, Stereo.** **Disparagement, Stereo.**
	Gender through occupations	Alnegheimish et al. (2022)	**Erasure, Stereo.**
	Race through identity terms	Sheng et al. (2019) Dhamala et al. (2021)	**Disparagement, Stereo.** **Disparagement, Stereo.**
	Race through dialect	Groenwold et al. (2020)	**Erasure, Stereo.**
	Sexuality through identity terms	Sheng et al. (2019)	**Disparagement, Stereo.**
	Country through identity terms	Huang et al. (2020)	**Erasure, Stereo.**
	Occupation through identity terms	Huang et al. (2020) Dhamala et al. (2021)	**Erasure, Stereo.** **Disparagement, Stereo.**
	Religion through identity terms	Dhamala et al. (2021)	**Disparagement, Stereo.**
	Political Ideo. through identity terms	Dhamala et al. (2021)	**Disparagement, Stereo.**
Dialogue Generation	**Gender** through identity terms	Liu et al. (2020a,b) Dinan et al. (2020)	**Disparagement, Stereo.** **Dehumanization, Erasure, Stereo.**
	Race through identity terms	Liu et al. (2020a)	**Disparagement, Stereo.**
Translation	**Gender** through occupations	Stanovsky et al. (2019)	**Erasure, QoS, Stereo.**
	Gender through identity terms **Nationality** through identity terms **Race** through identity terms	Wang et al. (2022) Wang et al. (2022) Wang et al. (2022)	**Erasure, QoS, Stereo.** **Erasure, QoS, Stereo.** **Erasure, QoS, Stereo.**
Text Re-writing	**Gender** through inflections	Habash et al. (2019) Zmigrod et al. (2019)	**Erasure, Stereo.** **Erasure, Stereo.**

Table 2: Existing bias measures (pt. 2) by tasks and demographics. '+' means that one work built a bias metric (after '+') on top of a dataset from another (before '+'). Brackets group datasets that were all used by a metric.

Logographic Information Aids Learning Better Representations for Natural Language Inference

Zijian Jin
Tandon School of Engineering
New York University
zj2076@nyu.edu

Duygu Ataman
Courant Institute of Mathematical Sciences
New York University
ataman@nyu.edu

Abstract

Statistical language models conventionally implement representation learning based on the contextual distribution of words or other formal units, whereas any information related to the logographic features of written text are often ignored, assuming they should be retrieved relying on the cooccurence statistics. On the other hand, as language models become larger and require more data to learn reliable representations, such assumptions may start to fall back, especially under conditions of data sparsity. Many languages, including Chinese and Vietnamese, use logographic writing systems where surface forms are represented as a visual organization of smaller graphemic units, which often contain many semantic cues. In this paper, we present a novel study which explores the benefits of providing language models with logographic information in learning better semantic representations. We test our hypothesis in the natural language inference (NLI) task by evaluating the benefit of computing multi-modal representations that combine contextual information with glyph information. Our evaluation results in six languages with different typology and writing systems suggest significant benefits of using multi-modal embeddings in languages with logograhic systems, especially for words with less occurence statistics.

1 Introduction

The essential idea in statistical language modeling is to represent the meaning of a word as a function of its context. The function, modeled via the conditional probability of observing a word in a given utterance, has most efficiently been approximated with a neural network based architecture (Mikolov et al., 2013a,b; Bengio et al., 2003; Mikolov et al., 2010; Sundermeyer et al., 2012). The outstanding performance of neural methods in language modeling and their recent development (Peters et al., 2018; Tenney et al., 2019) have them a preliminary component in various downstream NLP tasks.

One of the main limitations in the formulation of language models lies however in the choice of ortographic units in calculating the contextual distribution, which is usually convenient in English and other languages using phonetic scripts. On the other hand, many languages rely on logographic writing systems, where surface forms are represented as a visual organization of smaller graphemic units and the word meaning can be changed through compositional variations of these units. Although a direct segmentation of these units has been found quite challenging due to visual compositions in the final form of the grapheme, previous studies have found potential benefits of using visual information to aid NLP models in sentence representation (Liu et al., 2017a; Meng et al., 2019; Dai and Cai, 2017; Salesky et al., 2021). On the other hand, none of these studies have focused on isolating the effects of different linguistic features in relation to their correlation to visual features.

As shown in Figure 1, logographic information often contain important features related to the word meaning. In this paper, we perform the first focused analysis to measure the significance of logographic features specifically to the semantic information encoded in token or character-level language representations by evaluating the performance of multi-modal embeddings in the NLI task. In particular, we aim to answer the following research questions:

1) How important may logographic information be to for an accurate representation of semantic information in word or character-level language units

2) Whether the contribution of logographic information to semantic representations may depend on the language typology and writing system

In order to answer these questions we implement a multi-modal representation learning model where

Findings of the Association for Computational Linguistics: AACL-IJCNLP 2022, pages 268–273
November 20–23, 2022.

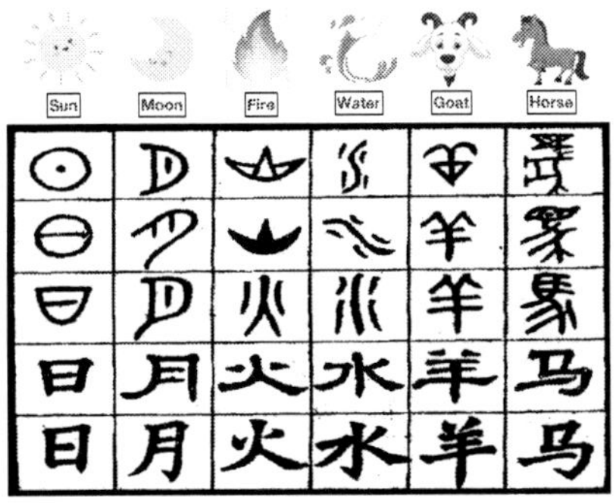

Figure 1: Logographic information in Chinese.

Layer	Visual encoding model
1	`Spatial Conv.` (3,3) → 32
2	`ReLu`
3	`MaxPool` (2,2)
4	`Spatial Conv.` (3,3) → 32
5	`ReLu`
6	`MaxPool` (2,2)
7	`Spatial Conv.` (3,3) → 32
8	`ReLu`
9	`Linear` (800,128)
10	`ReLu`
11	`Linear` (128,128)
12	`ReLu`

each written text segment is representation as a combination of visual embeddings obtained from prominent convolutional neural network (CNN) based models (Liu et al., 2017a; Meng et al., 2019; Salesky et al., 2021), and contextual representations obtained from multilingual pre-trained language models (Devlin et al., 2019; Conneau et al., 2020a). We evaluate the contribution of visual information to the performance in the NLI task under few-shot learning settings in six languages with varying typology and writing systems: English, Spanish, Hindi, Urdu, Vietnamese and Chinese. We also study the optimal representation granularity for semantic information by comparing word or character-level multi-modal representations in our experiments.

In conclusion, we find that taking into account the visual information improves the performance in NLI tasks especially in logographic languages like Chinese and that the improvements are correlated with the factors that determine the quality of token representations, such as the occurence of the tokens in training data as well as language model capacity and hyperparameters. Our findings suggest multi-modal processing is a promising direction, especially for processing languages where conditions of data sparsity may create fall backs in assumptions undertaken in statistical formulations.

2 Computing Visual Glyph Embeddings

Our multi-modal embedding model is composed of two components: *(i) the visual encoder*, which computes embeddings based on the input images representing each text segment, and *(ii) the pre-trained language model* providing the text-based embeddings.

Image conversion Text segments consisting of complete sentences are split into words (or characters) and then converted into images. Sentences are split into 30 x 60 pixel word images using the Jieba[1] tool. All graphemes are centralized to the middle of the image.

Visual Embeddings In order to extract the glyph information from text images, we use the CNN model developed by (Liu et al., 2017b; Sutskever et al., 2014) to generate visual embeddings. The model consists of a three-layer CNN, augmented with a two-layer feed-forward network. The full details of the network is given below.

The visual features extracted by the CNN are further encoded in a long-short term memory (LSTM) (Hochreiter and Schmidhuber, 1997) network to learn the glyph embeddings.

For a sequence consisting of t tokens $x_0, x_1, ..., x_t$, the *visual embedding* v is computed by concatenating (Su et al., 2020; Lu et al., 2019) the hidden states of the LSTM and averaging them as

$$v = \text{mean}([h_0; h_1; ...; h_t])$$

Embedding composition In order to isolate the learning of representations from two modalities and measure their effect on the learning task in a controlled setting, we deploy late fusion in combining the visual embeddings with the text embeddings obtained by the pre-trained model for prediction in the down-stream task. The two embeddings are linearly composed through a simple affine projection and then concatenated. For the down-stream prediction task we use a multi-layer perceptron classifier.

[1]https://github.com/fxsjy/jieba

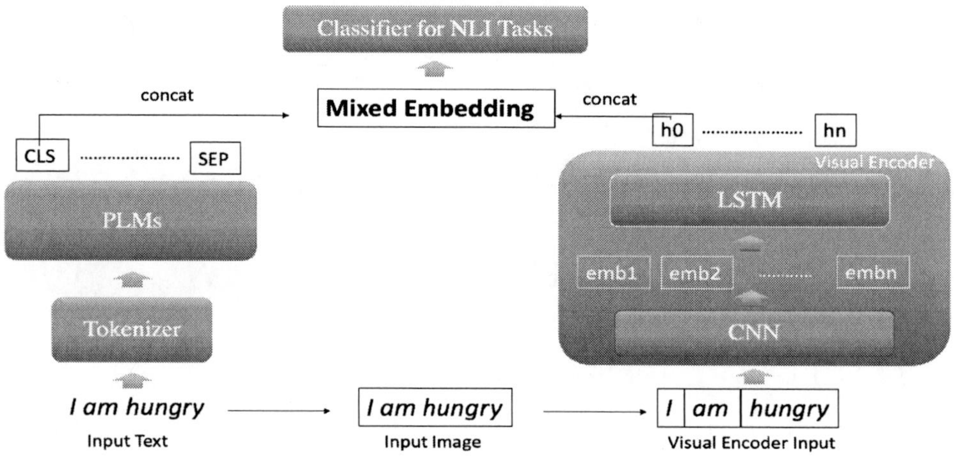

Figure 2: Method overview.

3 Experiments

3.1 Character recognition

As an initial verification, we implement the visual encoder and evaluate it individually in the character recognition task. We use the CASIA Chinese Handwriting Database (Liu et al., 2011) and obtain competitive results (93.23% accuracy) on this task, confirming the visual encoder works sufficiently in extracting character features from input images.

3.2 NLI

Data We evaluate our model under few-shot learning settings using the XNLI dataset (Conneau et al., 2020b), using only a small portion of the testing data for training and development, and test the effect of logographic information to contribute to resolve the high level of semantic ambiguity.

Datasets	Number of Sentences
Training	4509
Development	501
Test	2490

Table 1: Data statistics for training, development and test sets.

Model settings and hyper-parameters In training the multi-modal models, the learning rates of both XLM-R and mBERT based pre-trained models are set to 1e-6. The visual encoder is trained on the images captured from the training sentences, either at word or character-level resolution, with a learning rate of 4e-6 (for XLM-Roberta) and 1e-6 (for mBERT). The hidden size of the LSTMs used is 128 and we use dropout of with 0.3 in this layer. All hyper-parameters are tuned with grid-search. For each task we train 30 epochs and always choose the results with smallest validation loss.

Languages We pick six languages with varying typology and writing systems, including English, Spanish, Urdu, Vietnamese, Chinese and Hindi. **English** and **Spanish** use the Latin script; **Urdu** is written with the Arabic alphabet, whereas **Hindi** uses Devanagari, all of which are phonetic writing systems. **Chinese** uses logographic writing. **Vietnamese**, although traditionally have used logographic writing, recently and in the XNLI data set is written with the Latin script.

Contextual representations We verify the significance of logographic information for contributing to enrich the language representations by testing our multi-modal approach with two different pre-trained language models, including the `mBert-base` and the `XLM-R-base` both available from Huggingface[2]. We also investigate the effects of different segmentation methods for processing sentence images either at the level of words or characters.

4 Results and Discussion

Our experiment results are given in Table 2. At a first glance, we observe the performance of the models are much lower than reported in (Conneau et al., 2020b), since we have significantly less training and development data available. Under these challenging evaluation settings with high amount of sparsity, we observe that the logographic information improves the performance obtained using the `mBert-base` model in all languages that do not deploy the Latin script, including Chinese, Urdu, Hindi and Vietnamese. In case

[2]https://huggingface.co

Table 2: Results in the XNLI benchmark. `base` models represent baseline pre-trained language model performance in the down-stream task. `base-CNN` models represent the multi-modal system performance. `(C)` denotes character and `(W)` denotes word level input representations. `Random` stands for comparisons to multi-modal systems where random images were input to the visual encoder to verify the effect of visual information on the overall performance.

Languages	English	Chinese	Urdu	Hindi	Vietnamese	Spanish
mBERT-base	**65.86**	55.28	51.29	56.48	57.08	**62.27**
mBERT-base-CNN (W)	62.87	58.88	53.49	**57.68**	59.88	60.47
mBERT-base-CNN (C)	64.07	**59.08**	**53.69**	57.48	**60.07**	61.67
mBERT-base-CNN (C) — Random	-	54.33	-	-	-	-
XLM-Roberta-base	**69.86**	64.27	**59.88**	**63.87**	63.07	**65.66**
XLM-Roberta-base-CNN (W)	69.26	**66.66**	57.88	62.87	61.67	65.46
XLM-Roberta-base-CNN (C)	68.26	62.07	56.28	61.67	**63.07**	65.26
XLM-Roberta-base-CNN (C) — Random	-	61.36	-	-	-	-

of `XLM-Roberta-base`, which had better optimization on a larger corpus, the overall performance are consistently better than `mBert-base` and the improvements remain consistent, especially in Chinese and Vietnamese. We hypothesize that the slightly higher amount of improvements in `mBERT-base` might be due to better quality of representations provided with the optimized training regime of `XLM-Roberta-base`. Using the `mBERT-base` model, we find more advantage of embedding logographic information at the character level in Chinese, Urdu and Hindi, however, in Hindi, the results are comparable. When using the `XLM-Roberta-base`, we observe improvements in Chinese with word-level glyph embeddings and in Vietnamese using character-level glyph embeddings. While character-level embeddings might be suitable for a phonetic language like Vietnamese, the logograhic writing system in Chinese might make word-level visual embeddings more convenient, since the intra-graphemic dependencies can be captured at the visual level.

Although the improvements highly correlate with the logograhic nature of the writing system, the fact that they apply to most languages, even Urdu and Hindi with phonetic alphabets, point to the suboptimal effects in tokenization or segmentation and their potential harms to correctly model the contextual distribution. We also see in high-resource language representations like English, our fusion method may be harmful to the downstream task, which we anticipate that could be resolved with higher amount of fine-tuning and development data. In light of all these considerations, the findings suggest that multi-modality is a promising direction for overcoming problems related to data sparsity, and eventually tokenization or segmentation-free language modeling.

Models	Accuracy	# of UNK
mBERT-base (C)	45.31	128
mBERT-base-CNN (C)	52.43	

Table 3: Results for targeted evaluation, UNK represents unknown tokens.

As an additional analysis investigating the effects of token frequency on the positive effects of logographic information integrated in the language model, we sample sentences in the test set that have unknown words in the model vocabulary and compute the targeted accuracy on this sample of sentences. The results shows in table 3 further illustrate the boosted performance on the sample test, suggesting that data sparsity is an important obstacle to learning high-quality contextual representations, and such conditions can be the ideal place where logographic information might be useful to improve the semantic features embedded in representations.

5 Conclusion

In this paper, we evaluated the benefits of using logographic information in language modeling by implementing a multi-modal representation learning model which combines contextual language representations with visual embeddings. Our experiments in the NLI task in six languages confirmed the benefits of logograhic information in obtaining more reliable semantic representations, especially under sparse learning settings. As future work we hope to contribute to the development of larger multilingual benchmarks to evaluate the effect of visual information on more languages and linguistic phenomena. Our software and the experimental data will be available upon publication.

Acknowledgements

The authors would like to express deep gratitude to Chinmay Hedge and Aishwarya Kamath for discussions and their useful feedback. This work was supported by Samsung Advanced Institute of Technology (under the project Next Generation Deep Learning: From Pattern Recognition to AI) and NSF Award 1922658 NRT-HDR: FUTURE Foundations, Translation, and Responsibility for Data Science.

References

Yoshua Bengio, Réjean Ducharme, Pascal Vincent, and Christian Jauvin. 2003. A neural probabilistic language model. *Journal of machine learning research*, 3(Feb):1137–1155.

Alexis Conneau, Kartikay Khandelwal, Naman Goyal, Vishrav Chaudhary, Guillaume Wenzek, Francisco Guzmán, Edouard Grave, Myle Ott, Luke Zettlemoyer, and Veselin Stoyanov. 2020a. Unsupervised cross-lingual representation learning at scale. In *Proceedings of the 58th Annual Meeting of the Association for Computational Linguistics, ACL 2020, Online, July 5-10, 2020*, pages 8440–8451. Association for Computational Linguistics.

Alexis Conneau, Ruty Rinott, Guillaume Lample, Holger Schwenk, Ves Stoyanov, Adina Williams, and Samuel R Bowman. 2020b. Xnli: Evaluating cross-lingual sentence representations. In *2018 Conference on Empirical Methods in Natural Language Processing, EMNLP 2018*, pages 2475–2485. Association for Computational Linguistics.

Falcon Z. Dai and Zheng Cai. 2017. Glyph-aware embedding of chinese characters. In *Proceedings of the First Workshop on Subword and Character Level Models in NLP, Copenhagen, Denmark, September 7, 2017*, pages 64–69. Association for Computational Linguistics.

Jacob Devlin, Ming-Wei Chang, Kenton Lee, and Kristina Toutanova. 2019. BERT: pre-training of deep bidirectional transformers for language understanding. In *Proceedings of the 2019 Conference of the North American Chapter of the Association for Computational Linguistics: Human Language Technologies, NAACL-HLT 2019, Minneapolis, MN, USA, June 2-7, 2019, Volume 1 (Long and Short Papers)*, pages 4171–4186. Association for Computational Linguistics.

Sepp Hochreiter and Jürgen Schmidhuber. 1997. Long short-term memory. *Neural computation*, 9(8):1735–1780.

Cheng-Lin Liu, Fei Yin, Da-Han Wang, and Qiu-Feng Wang. 2011. Casia online and offline chinese handwriting databases. In *2011 International Conference on Document Analysis and Recognition*, pages 37–41. IEEE.

Frederick Liu, Han Lu, Chieh Lo, and Graham Neubig. 2017a. Learning character-level compositionality with visual features. In *Proceedings of the 55th Annual Meeting of the Association for Computational Linguistics (Volume 1: Long Papers)*, pages 2059–2068.

Frederick Liu, Han Lu, Chieh Lo, and Graham Neubig. 2017b. Learning character-level compositionality with visual features. In *Proceedings of the 55th Annual Meeting of the Association for Computational Linguistics, ACL 2017, Vancouver, Canada, July 30 - August 4, Volume 1: Long Papers*, pages 2059–2068. Association for Computational Linguistics.

Jiasen Lu, Dhruv Batra, Devi Parikh, and Stefan Lee. 2019. Vilbert: Pretraining task-agnostic visiolinguistic representations for vision-and-language tasks. In *NeurIPS*, pages 13–23.

Yuxian Meng, Wei Wu, Fei Wang, Xiaoya Li, Ping Nie, Fan Yin, Muyu Li, Qinghong Han, Xiaofei Sun, and Jiwei Li. 2019. Glyce: Glyph-vectors for chinese character representations. *Advances in Neural Information Processing Systems*, 32.

Tomas Mikolov, Kai Chen, Greg Corrado, and Jeffrey Dean. 2013a. Efficient estimation of word representations in vector space. In *Proceedings of the International Conference on Learning Representations, Workshop Track Proceedings*.

Tomas Mikolov, Martin Karafiát, Lukas Burget, Jan Cernocký, and Sanjeev Khudanpur. 2010. Recurrent neural network based language model. volume 2, pages 1045–1048.

Tomas Mikolov, Ilya Sutskever, Kai Chen, Greg S Corrado, and Jeff Dean. 2013b. Distributed representations of words and phrases and their compositionality. *Advances in neural information processing systems*, 26:3111–3119.

Matthew E Peters, Mark Neumann, Mohit Iyyer, Matt Gardner, Christopher Clark, Kenton Lee, and Luke Zettlemoyer. 2018. Deep contextualized word representations. In *Proceedings of the 2018 Conference of the North American Chapter of the Association for Computational Linguistics: Human Language Technologies*, pages 2227–2237.

Elizabeth Salesky, David Etter, and Matt Post. 2021. Robust open-vocabulary translation from visual text representations. In *Proceedings of the 2021 Conference on Empirical Methods in Natural Language Processing*, pages 7235–7252.

Weijie Su, Xizhou Zhu, Yue Cao, Bin Li, Lewei Lu, Furu Wei, and Jifeng Dai. 2020. VL-BERT: pre-training of generic visual-linguistic representations. In *8th International Conference on Learning Representations, ICLR 2020, Addis Ababa, Ethiopia, April 26-30, 2020*. OpenReview.net.

Martin Sundermeyer, Ralf Schlüter, and Hermann Ney. 2012. Lstm neural networks for language modeling. In *13th Annual Conference of the International Speech Communication Association*, pages 194–197.

Ilya Sutskever, Oriol Vinyals, and Quoc V. Le. 2014. Sequence to sequence learning with neural networks. In *Advances in Neural Information Processing Systems 27: Annual Conference on Neural Information Processing Systems 2014, December 8-13 2014, Montreal, Quebec, Canada*, pages 3104–3112.

Ian Tenney, Dipanjan Das, and Ellie Pavlick. 2019. Bert rediscovers the classical nlp pipeline. In *Proceedings of the 57th Annual Meeting of the Association for Computational Linguistics*, pages 4593–4601.

Cross-domain Analysis on Japanese Legal Pretrained Language Models

Keisuke Miyazaki **Hiroaki Yamada** **Takenobu Tokunaga**
Tokyo Institute of Technology
{miyazaki.k.am@m, yamada@c, take@c}.titech.ac.jp

Abstract

This paper investigates the pretrained language model (PLM) specialised in the Japanese legal domain. We create PLMs using different pretraining strategies and investigate their performance across multiple domains. Our findings are (i) the PLM built with general domain data can be improved by further pretraining with domain-specific data, (ii) domain-specific PLMs can learn domain-specific and general word meanings simultaneously and can distinguish them, (iii) domain-specific PLMs work better on its target domain; still, the PLMs retain the information learnt in the original PLM even after being further pretrained with domain-specific data, (iv) the PLMs sequentially pretrained with corpora of different domains show high performance for the later learnt domains.

1 Introduction

Transformer-based pretrained language models (PLMs) such as BERT (Devlin et al., 2019) and its successors (Liu et al., 2019; Yang et al., 2019; Clark et al., 2020) achieved solid performance in various NLP tasks for a generic domain (Wang et al., 2018). Following their success, domain-specific PLMs have been proposed for science (Beltagy et al., 2019), medical (Alsentzer et al., 2019; Lee et al., 2019), financial (Yang et al., 2020; Loukas et al., 2022), and legal (Chalkidis et al., 2020) domains. These domain-specific PLMs are pretrained solely with the target domain corpora, or with both the generic and target domain corpora. The latter is a good option when the domain corpus size is limited. Gururangan et al. (2020) empirically proved that further pretraining a generic PLM using domain-specific corpora provided benefits; Chalkidis et al. (2020) confirmed this claim for the legal domain.

However, previous studies do not care the performance of the domain-adapted PLMs for a generic domain. The domain adaptation might degrade the model performance for a generic domain. The domain-adapted PLM should perform well in both the target domain and the domain in general. This requirement is essential for the legal domain, where the legal argumentation includes evidence descriptions cited from non-legal text such as web pages, books and SNS posts. The requirement is related to catastrophic forgetting. Ramasesh et al. (2022) recently showed that more steps and data for pretraining make a model robust against catastrophic forgetting. However, their findings are primarily in computer vision, and their experiments with PLMs are still preliminary. They focus on sequential fine-tuning of various size PLMs pretrained with a single domain corpus. On the other hand, we focus on pretraining PLMs with different domains through evaluation using corpora from 13 domains, including domains exclusive of training data. Also, compared with English, there are few findings in domain adaptation strategies of Japanese PLMs, despite several Japanese PLMs available for the generic (NICT, 2020; Tohoku NLP Group, 2021; NLP-Waseda, 2021), financial (Suzuki et al., 2021) and medical (Kawazoe et al., 2021) domains.

Further, despite its significance, no PLM study exists in the *Japanese legal* domain. In the recent COLIEE workshop, a competition on legal information extraction and entailment tasks, including the Japanese language, most high-scoring approaches utilise BERT-like PLMs (Rabelo et al., 2022) trained on Japanese Wikipedia text. Although there is an expectation that PLMs trained with Japanese legal corpora improve their performance, the insufficient size of publicly available corpora does not allow it. Further pretraining a generic PLM with available legal corpora is one of the promising adaptation strategies.

Against this backdrop, particularly considering the above-mentioned legal-domain peculiarity that both domain-specific and generic meanings are equally important, this paper reports the first comprehensive study on PLM adaptation strategies in

Findings of the Association for Computational Linguistics: AACL-IJCNLP 2022, pages 274–281
November 20–23, 2022.

the Japanese legal domain and their performance across different domains through intrinsic evaluation.

2 Research Questions

Chalkidis et al. (2020) adopted two strategies for pretraining domain-specific PLMs: further pretraining (FP) an existing PLM with the domain corpus and pretraining a domain-specific PLM with the domain corpus from scratch (SC). Comparing these two strategies, we investigate the cross-domain performance of domain-specific PLMs, specialised in the Japanese legal domain. We set up the following research questions. **RQ1**: Is the FP/SC learning strategy effective and which is more effective? **RQ2**: Can the domain-adapted PLM learn the domain-specific meaning and distinguish it from the meaning of general usage? **RQ3**: Does the PLM performance change across the domain? **RQ4**: What is the best order of training data domains for pretraining?

3 Experimental Settings

3.1 Resources

Dataset We use the Japanese civil case judgment dataset (JD)[1], the Japanese Wikipedia dataset (WP)[2] and the Balanced Corpus of Contemporary Written Japanese (BCCWJ) (Maekawa et al., 2014). BCCWJ contains texts from 13 domains as shown in Table 4. Their data sizes are 5.4GB (JD), 3.2GB (WP) and 0.7GB (BCCWJ). Table 5 in the Appendix shows the dataset statistics. BCCWJ is used as a test dataset. JD and WP are split into training and test data at a ratio of 9:1, following the NVIDIA BERT implementation (NVIDIA, 2019).

Base PLM We use the BERT-base (WWM version) checkpoint by Shibata et al. (2019), which is pretrained with the Japanese Wikipedia dataset[3].

3.2 Preprocessing

The texts are divided into sentences and further into morphological units. The "short unit" (NINJAL, 2015) is used for BCCWJ, and the output of the morphological analyser JUMAN++ (Tolmachev and Kurohashi, 2018) is used for JD and WP as the morphological unit. The leading meta information, such as the case number, is removed from JD.

[1]provided by LIC Co., Ltd.

[2]version:20220520

[3]The Wikipedia dataset that Shibata et al. (2019) uses is an older dump than WP.

Setting	Strategy	Data size [%]	MLM	NSP
2-phase	FP	100	**0.805**	**0.992**
		50	0.801	0.991
		25	0.793	0.989
	SC	100	**0.789**	**0.991**
		50	0.785	0.991
		25	0.775	0.988
1-phase	FP	100	**0.806**	**0.990**
		50	0.788	0.987
		25	0.763	0.982
	SC	100	**0.785**	**0.989**
		50	0.755	0.984
		25	0.697	0.975
Baseline			0.703	0.687

Table 1: Accuracy of JLBERT family on the JD test set

The SC strategy uses the vocabulary of 32,000 tokens created from the domain corpus by BPE (Sennrich et al., 2016), and the FP strategy uses the vocabulary of the Base PLM for subword tokenisation.

3.3 Pretraining settings

We adopt the masked language modelling (MLM) and next sentence prediction (NSP) tasks to train the BERT model (Devlin et al., 2019). Following NICT (2020), Tohoku NLP Group (2021) and the NVIDIA BERT implementation (NVIDIA, 2019), we use two types of pretraining settings: two-phase (2-phase) and single-phase (1-phase) training. The 2-phase training limits the input token length to 128 in the first phase and enlarges it to 512 tokens in the second phase. The 1-phase training trains the model with the input token length limited to 512. The hyperparameters are the same for the 1-phase training setting and the second phase of the 2-phase training setting. We use the LAMB (You et al., 2020) optimiser. Table 6 in the Appendix shows the hyperparameters for the pretraining settings.

4 Experiments

4.1 RQ1: Pretraining strategies (FP vs SC)

We combine the two pretraining strategies (FP/SC) and the two pretraining settings (1/2-phase) to create four variants of PLMs, which we call the JLBERT family. We further pretrain the base PLM described in 3.1 using the JD dataset for the FP strategy. Only the JD dataset is used for the SC strategy. The model performance is measured through the intrinsic evaluation with the MLM and NSP tasks, i.e. the accuracy of those tasks on the JD test set. To investigate the impact of the training data size on the performance, we created the models with 25%, 50% and 100% of the JD dataset. The number of training steps in the 1-phase setting is reduced to 4,000 and 2,000 according to the dataset reduction, while the number of training steps in the 2-phase setting is fixed to 8,000. We also create a baseline model from the WP dataset using the SC strategy and the 1-phase setting. This baseline model is similar to the base PLM used in the FP strategy. However, the base PLM lacks the classifiers for solving the MLM and NSP tasks. Therefore, we create it from scratch.

Table 1 shows that pretraining with the domain-specific data increases the accuracy for both tasks against the baseline regardless of the pretraining strategies and settings. As the performance of NSP is almost saturated for all JLBERT models, we focus on the MLM performance hereafter. The FP strategy creates better models than the SC strategy, suggesting that out-of-domain data help than no data. This tendency becomes more significant when the domain-specific training data size is small. Increasing the training data size contributes to performance improvement. We need a larger JD dataset to see if the performance improvement has been saturated.

The training time for the first and second phases of the 2-phase setting was 28 and 18 hours, respectively, and 77 hours for the 1-phase setting, using four NVIDIA RTX A6000 GPUs. The 2-phase setting reduced the training time by 40% while retaining a comparable performance with the 1-phase setting. The model parameters learned in the first phase are applicable to inputs longer than 128 tokens, and the model needs to learn only position embeddings beyond 128 tokens in the second phase. It explains the speedup in the 2-phase setting.

4.2 RQ2: Domain specific meanings

RQ2 provides a microscopic analysis of PLMs looking at word meanings, whereas other RQs are macroscopic analysis using overall accuracy as metrics.

While recent PLM analysis researches focus on latent domains and concepts behind representations (Aharoni and Goldberg, 2020; Dalvi et al., 2022; Sajjad et al., 2022), we are interested in words themselves that have drastically different meanings across domains. For instance, "*akui* (maliciousness)" has quite a different meaning, "knowing a fact", in the certain legal context. Moreover, both meanings can simultaneously appear in a single document. We take "*akui*" as a probe word to investigate the domain-specific PLM can learn the domain-specific meaning and distinguish it from its ordinary meaning.

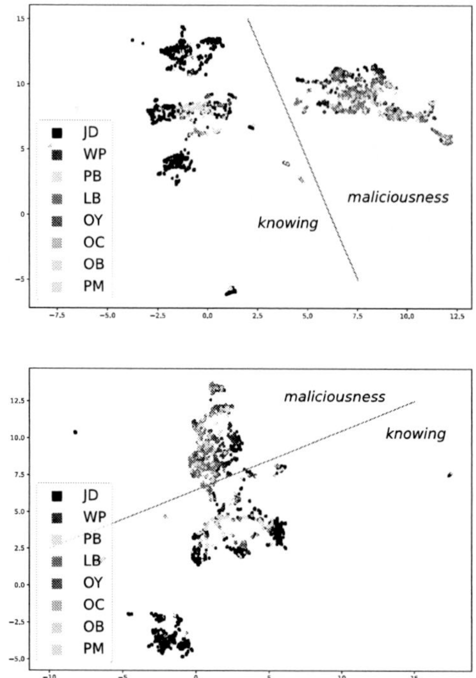

Figure 1: Contextualised embeddings for "*akui*" by JLBERT-2-phase-SC (top) and Base PLM (bottom). Only domains containing $\geq$ 10 occurrences of "*akui*" are depicted. The boundaries are manually annotated. The legend of domain acronyms is found in Table 4.

Following Reif et al. (2019), we collected 2,052 sentences containing "*akui*" from the JD (test), WP(test) and BCCWJ dataset and extracted the corresponding contextualised embedding for "*akui*" in each sentence. Figure 1 visualises the embedding distribution made by UMAP (McInnes and Healy, 2018). We used the base PLM (cf. 3.1), the JLBERT models made by the 2-phase setting and the FP or SC strategies to calculate embeddings. Figure 1 shows that "*akui*" from JD (black), PB (cyan) and LB (red), which would have the legal meaning, made clusters. PB and LB are both book domain, which potentially includes legal materials. These clusters are separable from other domain-mixture clusters. Besides, the boundary is more apparent for the domain-specific PLM.

We also apply the k-nearest neighbour (kNN)

#clusters	2-phase-SC	2-phase-FP	base PLM
2	**0.948** (.000)	0.945 (.000)	0.925 (.001)
3	**0.951** (.004)	0.945 (.000)	0.908 (.000)
4	**0.943** (.005)	0.943 (.002)	0.899 (.003)
5	**0.948** (.001)	0.944 (.004)	0.890 (.008)
6	**0.949** (.000)	0.944 (.003)	0.894 (.001)

Table 2: Global purity of clustered contextualised embeddings of "*akui*" with standard deviations in parentheses.

		Baseline	1-phase-FP	1-phase-SC
	WP (test)	**0.697**	0.589	0.596
	JD (test)	0.703	**0.806**	0.785
BCCWJ	LB	**0.534**	0.521	0.511
	OB	**0.520**	0.512	0.502
	OC	**0.501**	0.492	0.480
	OL	0.739	**0.827**	0.808
	OM	0.566	**0.587**	0.566
	OP	**0.584**	0.580	0.558
	OT	0.584	**0.585**	0.568
	OV	**0.345**	0.305	0.301
	OW	0.637	**0.669**	0.648
	OY	**0.478**	0.455	0.448
	PB	**0.556**	0.549	0.536
	PM	**0.527**	0.492	0.483
	PN	**0.546**	0.504	0.496
	micro avg.	0.538	0.529	0.517

Table 3: Domain-wise accuracy for MLM

clustering to the embeddings to calculate global purity, which indicates the majority's degree of dominance in a cluster. One of the authors[4] annotated the meaning of "*akui*" in the entire sentences for purity calculation. We run the kNN clustering with different numbers of clusters from two to six. The purity is calculated by averaging the results of ten clustering runs with different random seeds. Table 2 shows that the FP and SC strategies always result in higher purity than the base PLM, suggesting that the domain-specific models capture the different meanings of "*akui*" better than the generic model.

4.3 RQ3: Performance across domains

We investigate the model performance on the MLM task across different domains by comparing the baseline model described in 4.1, the JLBERT models made by the 1-phase setting and the FP or SC strategies. The test set includes WP (test), JD (test) and texts from 13 domains of BCCWJ. Table 3 shows that the JLBERT models are superior to the baseline model in law documents (OL), white papers (OW), and minutes of Parliament (OM). These domains contain legal content and follow a formal writing style, similarly to JD. Conversely, the baseline model works better in Yahoo! blog (OY), magazines (PM), newspapers (PN), and verses (OV) that are different in their writing styles from JD. We conclude that the domain-specific PLM degrades its performance outside the target domain but not significantly. Moreover, the FP model is consistently better than the SC model regardless of domains, suggesting that the FP model retains and leverages the information learnt from the WP data even after being pretrained with the JD data.

4.4 RQ4: Order of domain datasets

We compare the MLM performance of two domain-specific PLMs made by the 1-phase setting and the FP strategy, namely WP+JD and JD+WP. The WP+JD model is created by further pretraining the baseline model introduced in 4.1 with JD, while the JD+WP model is created by further pretraining the JLBERT-1-phase-SC model (cf. 4.1) with WP. WP+JD particularly works well in JD (Table 4). In addition, law documents (OL), white papers (OW), and minutes of Parliament (OM), which have a formal writing style similar to JD, also show high scores. On the other hand, JD+WP works well particularly in WP, and also does in newspapers (PN), magazines (PM), and verses (OV). These results indicate that the pretraining for the target domain should be put later in a sequence of pretraining phases to obtain a better domain-specific PLM.

5 Conclusion

This paper presents an empirical study of the pretrained language model specialised in the Japanese legal domain. Our findings are (i) the PLM built with general domain data can be improved by further pretraining with domain-specific data, (ii) domain-specific PLMs can learn domain-specific and general word meanings simultaneously and can distinguish them, (iii) domain-specific PLMs work better on its target domain; still, the PLMs retain the information learnt in the original PLM even after further pretraining with domain-specific data, (iv) the PLMs sequentially pretrained with different domain corpora show high performance for the later learnt domain. Although our findings might be limited in the Japanese legal domain, they provide clues and a basis for future research in other less-studied domains.

[4] The annotator has LL.B. and knowledge in the domain.

		Baseline	(a) WP+JD	Δ	(b) 1-phase-SC	(c) JD+WP	Δ	(a)-(b)	(c)-(a)
	WP (test)	0.697	0.606	-0.091	0.596	**0.718**	0.122	0.010	0.112
	JD (test)	0.703	**0.822**	0.119	0.785	0.694	-0.091	0.037	-0.128
BCCWJ	LB: Books in library	0.534	0.542	0.008	0.511	**0.545**	0.034	0.031	0.003
	OB: Bestseller	0.520	**0.534**	0.014	0.502	0.532	0.029	0.032	-0.003
	OC: Yahoo! Chiebukuro	0.501	**0.523**	0.023	0.480	0.494	0.014	0.043	-0.029
	OL: Law documents	0.739	**0.834**	0.095	0.808	0.741	-0.067	0.026	-0.093
	OM: Minutes of Parliament	0.566	**0.616**	0.050	0.566	0.546	-0.021	0.050	-0.070
	OP: Public relations paper	0.584	**0.606**	0.022	0.558	0.578	0.020	0.047	-0.028
	OT: Textbook	0.584	**0.599**	0.015	0.568	0.597	0.029	0.031	-0.002
	OV: Verse	**0.345**	0.328	-0.017	0.301	**0.345**	0.045	0.028	0.017
	OW: White paper	0.637	**0.679**	0.042	0.648	0.638	-0.009	0.032	-0.041
	OY: Yahoo! Blog	**0.478**	0.479	-0.001	0.448	0.484	0.036	0.031	0.005
	PB: Published books	0.556	**0.570**	0.014	0.536	0.563	0.027	0.034	-0.007
	PM: Magazine	0.527	0.519	-0.008	0.483	**0.534**	0.051	0.036	0.015
	PN: Newspaper	0.546	0.527	-0.020	0.496	**0.557**	0.062	0.031	0.031
	Micro average in BCCWJ	0.538	0.552	0.014	0.517	0.543	0.026	0.035	-0.009

Table 4: Accuracy for MLM: Impact of dataset order in pretraining

As we compared the PLM performance across different domains, we adopted intrinsic evaluation with domain-neutral tasks, MLM and NSP. As Gururangan et al. (2020) did, our future plan includes conducting extrinsic evaluation using downstream tasks like JGLUE (Kurihara et al., 2022).

Acknowledgements

The judgment documents data for this study was provided by LIC Co., Ltd. This work was partly supported by JST ACT-X Grant Number JPMJAX20AM.

References

Roee Aharoni and Yoav Goldberg. 2020. Unsupervised domain clusters in pretrained language models. In *Proceedings of the 58th Annual Meeting of the Association for Computational Linguistics*, pages 7747–7763, Online. Association for Computational Linguistics.

Emily Alsentzer, John Murphy, William Boag, Wei-Hung Weng, Di Jindi, Tristan Naumann, and Matthew McDermott. 2019. Publicly available clinical BERT embeddings. In *Proceedings of the 2nd Clinical Natural Language Processing Workshop*, pages 72–78, Minneapolis, Minnesota, USA. Association for Computational Linguistics.

Iz Beltagy, Kyle Lo, and Arman Cohan. 2019. SciBERT: A pretrained language model for scientific text. In *Proceedings of the 2019 Conference on Empirical Methods in Natural Language Processing and the 9th International Joint Conference on Natural Language Processing (EMNLP-IJCNLP)*, pages 3615–3620, Hong Kong, China. Association for Computational Linguistics.

Ilias Chalkidis, Manos Fergadiotis, Prodromos Malakasiotis, Nikolaos Aletras, and Ion Androutsopoulos. 2020. LEGAL-BERT: The muppets straight out of law school. In *Findings of the Association for Computational Linguistics: EMNLP 2020*, pages 2898–2904, Online. Association for Computational Linguistics.

Kevin Clark, Minh-Thang Luong, Quoc V. Le, and Christopher D. Manning. 2020. ELECTRA: pretraining text encoders as discriminators rather than generators. In *8th International Conference on Learning Representations, ICLR 2020, Addis Ababa, Ethiopia, April 26-30, 2020*. OpenReview.net.

Fahim Dalvi, Abdul Rafae Khan, Firoj Alam, Nadir Durrani, Jia Xu, and Hassan Sajjad. 2022. Discovering latent concepts learned in BERT. In *The Tenth International Conference on Learning Representations, ICLR 2022, Virtual Event, April 25-29, 2022*. OpenReview.net.

Jacob Devlin, Ming-Wei Chang, Kenton Lee, and Kristina Toutanova. 2019. BERT: Pre-training of deep bidirectional transformers for language understanding. In *Proceedings of the 2019 Conference of the North American Chapter of the Association for Computational Linguistics: Human Language Technologies, Volume 1 (Long and Short Papers)*, pages 4171–4186, Minneapolis, Minnesota. Association for Computational Linguistics.

Suchin Gururangan, Ana Marasović, Swabha Swayamdipta, Kyle Lo, Iz Beltagy, Doug Downey, and Noah A. Smith. 2020. Don't stop pretraining: Adapt language models to domains and tasks. In *Proceedings of the 58th Annual Meeting of the Association for Computational Linguistics*, pages 8342–8360, Online. Association for Computational Linguistics.

Yoshimasa Kawazoe, Daisaku Shibata, Emiko Shinohara, Eiji Aramaki, and Kazuhiko Ohe. 2021. A clinical specific bert developed using a huge japanese clinical text corpus. *PLOS ONE*, 16(11):1–11.

Kentaro Kurihara, Daisuke Kawahara, and Tomohide Shibata. 2022. JGLUE: Japanese general language understanding evaluation. In *Proceedings of the Language Resources and Evaluation Conference*, pages 2957–2966, Marseille, France. European Language Resources Association.

Jinhyuk Lee, Wonjin Yoon, Sungdong Kim, Donghyeon Kim, Sunkyu Kim, Chan Ho So, and Jaewoo Kang. 2019. BioBERT: a pre-trained biomedical language representation model for biomedical text mining. *Bioinformatics*, 36(4):1234–1240.

Yinhan Liu, Myle Ott, Naman Goyal, Jingfei Du, Mandar Joshi, Danqi Chen, Omer Levy, Mike Lewis, Luke Zettlemoyer, and Veselin Stoyanov. 2019. Roberta: A robustly optimized bert pretraining approach. *ArXiv*, abs/1907.11692.

Lefteris Loukas, Manos Fergadiotis, Ilias Chalkidis, Eirini Spyropoulou, Prodromos Malakasiotis, Ion Androutsopoulos, and Georgios Paliouras. 2022. FiNER: Financial numeric entity recognition for XBRL tagging. In *Proceedings of the 60th Annual Meeting of the Association for Computational Linguistics (Volume 1: Long Papers)*, pages 4419–4431, Dublin, Ireland. Association for Computational Linguistics.

Kikuo Maekawa, Makoto Yamazaki, Toshinobu Ogiso, Takehiko Maruyama, Hideki Ogura, Wakako Kashino, Hanae Koiso, Masaya Yamaguchi, Makiro Tanaka, and Yasuharu Den. 2014. Balanced corpus of contemporary written japanese. *Lang. Resour. Evaluation*, 48(2):345–371.

Leland McInnes and John Healy. 2018. UMAP: uniform manifold approximation and projection for dimension reduction. *CoRR*, abs/1802.03426.

NICT. 2020. NICT BERT Japanese Pre-trained model. `https://alaginrc.nict.go.jp/nict-bert/index.html`. Accessed: 2022-7-13.

NINJAL. 2015. *Guide for using the Balanced Corpus of Contemporary Written Japanese, Version 1.1*. Center for Language Resource Development.

NLP-Waseda. 2021. nlp-waseda/roberta-base-japanese · Hugging Face. `https://huggingface.co/nlp-waseda/roberta-base-japanese`. Accessed: 2022-7-13.

NVIDIA. 2019. PyTorch/LanguageModeling/BERT · NVIDIA/DeepLearningExamples. `https://github.com/NVIDIA/DeepLearningExamples/tree/master/PyTorch/LanguageModeling/BERT`. Accessed: 2022-7-13.

Juliano Rabelo, Randy Goebel, Mi-Young Kim, Yoshinobu Kano, Masaharu Yoshioka, and Ken Satoh. 2022. Overview and discussion of the competition on legal information extraction/entailment (COLIEE) 2021. *Rev. Socionetwork Strateg.*, 16(1):111–133.

Vinay Venkatesh Ramasesh, Aitor Lewkowycz, and Ethan Dyer. 2022. Effect of scale on catastrophic forgetting in neural networks. In *The Tenth International Conference on Learning Representations, ICLR 2022, Virtual Event, April 25-29, 2022*. OpenReview.net.

Emily Reif, Ann Yuan, Martin Wattenberg, Fernanda B Viegas, Andy Coenen, Adam Pearce, and Been Kim. 2019. Visualizing and measuring the geometry of bert. In *Advances in Neural Information Processing Systems*, volume 32. Curran Associates, Inc.

Hassan Sajjad, Nadir Durrani, Fahim Dalvi, Firoj Alam, Abdul Khan, and Jia Xu. 2022. Analyzing encoded concepts in transformer language models. In *Proceedings of the 2022 Conference of the North American Chapter of the Association for Computational Linguistics: Human Language Technologies*, pages 3082–3101, Seattle, United States. Association for Computational Linguistics.

Rico Sennrich, Barry Haddow, and Alexandra Birch. 2016. Neural machine translation of rare words with subword units. In *Proceedings of the 54th Annual Meeting of the Association for Computational Linguistics (Volume 1: Long Papers)*, pages 1715–1725, Berlin, Germany. Association for Computational Linguistics.

Tomohide Shibata, Daisuke Kawahara, and Sadao Kurohashi. 2019. Improving the accuracy of japanese parsing with BERT. In *The Proceedings of the Twenty-fifth Annual Meeting of the Association for Natural Language Processing*, pages 205–208, Nagoya, Japan.

Masahiro Suzuki, Hiroki Sakaji, Masanori Hirano, and Kiyoshi Izumi. 2021. Construction and validation of a pre-trained language model using financial documents. In *Proceedings of JSAI Special Interest Group on Financial Infomatics (SIG-FIN) 27*, pages 5–10.

Tohoku NLP Group. 2021. cl-tohoku/bert-base-japanese-v2 · Hugging Face. `https://huggingface.co/cl-tohoku/bert-base-japanese-v2`. Accessed: 2022-7-13.

Arseny Tolmachev and Sadao Kurohashi. 2018. Juman++ v2: A practical and modern morphological analyzer. In *The Proceedings of the Twenty-fourth Annual Meeting of the Association for Natural Language Processing*, pages 917–920, Okayama, Japan.

Alex Wang, Amanpreet Singh, Julian Michael, Felix Hill, Omer Levy, and Samuel Bowman. 2018. GLUE: A multi-task benchmark and analysis platform for natural language understanding. In *Proceedings of the*

2018 EMNLP Workshop BlackboxNLP: Analyzing and Interpreting Neural Networks for NLP, pages 353–355, Brussels, Belgium. Association for Computational Linguistics.

Yi Yang, Mark Christopher Siy Uy, and Allen Huang. 2020. FinBERT: A pretrained language model for financial communications. *CoRR*, abs/2006.08097.

Zhilin Yang, Zihang Dai, Yiming Yang, Jaime Carbonell, Russ R Salakhutdinov, and Quoc V Le. 2019. Xlnet: Generalized autoregressive pretraining for language understanding. In *Advances in Neural Information Processing Systems*, volume 32. Curran Associates, Inc.

Yang You, Jing Li, Sashank Reddi, Jonathan Hseu, Sanjiv Kumar, Srinadh Bhojanapalli, Xiaodan Song, James Demmel, Kurt Keutzer, and Cho-Jui Hsieh. 2020. Large batch optimization for deep learning: Training BERT in 76 minutes. In *International Conference on Learning Representations*.

A Statistics of datasets

Dataset	Genre	#sents	#chars per sent	#morphs per sent
WP	Train	22,053,315	48.1	26.9
	Test	2,450,176	56.8	31.9
	Overall	24,503,491	48.9	27.4
JD	Train	21,411,914	77.0	46.8
	Test	2,378,943	76.6	46.2
	Overall	23,790,857	77.0	46.8
BCCWJ	LB	1,649,778	33.5	21.2
	OB	222,540	30.5	19.5
	OC	681,967	28.2	17.5
	OL	38,768	45.5	30.6
	OM	140,409	63.3	39.9
	OP	256,199	26.9	17.5
	OT	63,667	27.1	17.2
	OV	18,982	19.7	12.1
	OW	146,280	57.7	37.9
	OY	820,922	24.7	15.0
	PB	1,482,226	35.3	22.2
	PM	300,212	29.1	17.4
	PN	80,037	31.0	19.7
	Overall	5,901,987	32.7	20.6

Table 5: Statistics of preprocessed datasets

Table 5 shows the statistics of the datasets used in this study. These values are calculated after preprocessing (3.2). Comparing WP and JD, the numbers of recording sentences are almost the same. Therefore, when learning WP or JD under the same 1-phase condition in RQ4 (4.4), the number of epochs is also almost the same.

On the other hand, the number of characters and morphemes per sentence on JD is much higher than WP. Compared to WP, JD is not only a formal written document, but also has a long sentence. For this reason, it makes sense to create a JD-specific PLM to solve JD's downstream tasks.

B Pretraining hyperparameters

	2-phase phase1	2-phase phase2	1-phase
Accumulated batch size	32,768	16,384	16,384
Mini-batch size	64	8	64
Gradient accumulation	512	2,048	256
Training steps	7,038	1,563	8,000
Mini-batch inputs	3.6M	3.2M	2M
Warm-up steps	2,000	200	1,024
Warm-up rate	28.43%	12.80%	12.80%
Max length of tokens	128	512	512
[MASK] rate	0.15	0.15	0.15
Max [MASK]/sentence	20	80	80
Learning rate	0.006	0.004	0.004

Table 6: BERT pretraining hyperparameters

Table 6 shows the detailed settings of 1-phase and 2-phase (3.3). As shown in (3.3), the computing time for the first and second phases in the 2-phase setting was 28 and 18 hours, respectively, and 77 hours for the 1-phase setting, using four NVIDIA RTX A6000 GPUs. By changing the Mini-batch size in 2-phase phase 2 to 64, computing time will be shorter.

C Statistics of annotated *"akui"*

		knowing	malice	?	Sum
	JD (test)	882	200	6	1088
	WP (test)	0	317	0	317
BCCWJ	LB	19	203	1	223
	OB	0	28	0	28
	OC	0	35	1	36
	OL	2	1	0	3
	OM	0	6	0	6
	OT	0	1	0	1
	OV	0	3	0	3
	OY	4	38	1	43
	PB	130	154	3	287
	PM	0	15	0	15
	PN	0	2	0	2
	Sum	1037	1003	12	2052

Table 7: Statistics of annotated *"akui"*

Table 7 shows the statistics of annotated sentences which contain the word *"akui"*. The "?" column shows sentences that cannot be classified into either "knowing a fact (technical usage in the legal domain)" or "malicious (general usage)".

According to our annotation, 200 out of 1088 sentences mean "malicious" in JD (test). Even in JD, which is a corpus of legal domain, "*akui*" does not always mean "knowing a fact" but also means "malicious". For example, a legal argumentation includes evidence descriptions cited from non-legal text such as web pages, books and SNS posts. Moreover, both meanings can simultaneously appear in a single document. Thus, source of documents does not necessarily suggest which meaning "*akui*" has.

Multilingual CheckList: Generation and Evaluation

Karthikeyan K[3]*, Shaily Bhatt[1]*, Pankaj Singh[1], Somak Aditya[4], Sandipan Dandapat[2], Sunayana Sitaram[1], Monojit Choudhury[1]

[1] Microsoft Research, Bengaluru, India

[2] Microsoft R&D, Hyderabad, India

[3] Department of Computer Science, Duke University

[4] Department of CSE, IIT Kharagpur

karthikeyan.k@duke.edu, saditya@cse.iitkgp.ac.in,
{t-shbhatt,t-pasingh,sadandap,sunayana.sitaram,monojitc}@microsoft.com

Abstract

Multilingual evaluation benchmarks usually contain limited high-resource languages and do not test models for specific linguistic capabilities. CheckList (Ribeiro et al., 2020) is a template-based evaluation approach that tests models for specific capabilities. The CheckList template creation process requires native speakers, posing a challenge in scaling to hundreds of languages. In this work, we explore multiple approaches to generate Multilingual CheckLists. We device an algorithm – **T**emplate **E**xtraction **A**lgorithm (TEA) for automatically extracting target language CheckList templates from machine translated instances of a source language templates. We compare the TEA CheckLists with CheckLists created with different levels of human intervention. We further introduce metrics along the dimensions of *cost*, *diversity*, *utility*, and *correctness* to compare the CheckLists. We thoroughly analyze different approaches to creating CheckLists in Hindi. Furthermore, we experiment with 9 more different languages. We find that TEA followed by human verification is ideal for scaling Checklist-based evaluation to multiple languages while TEA gives a good estimates of model performance. We release the code of TEA and the CheckLists created at aka.ms/multilingualchecklist

1 Introduction

Multilingual transformer based models (Devlin et al., 2019; Conneau et al., 2020; Liu et al., 2020; Xue et al., 2021) have demonstrated commendable zero & few-shot capabilities. Their performance is typically evaluated on benchmarks like XNLI (Conneau et al., 2018), XGLUE (Liang et al., 2020), XTREME (Hu et al., 2020b) & XTREME-R (Ruder et al., 2021). However, this evaluation paradigm has a number of limitations including: First, most of these datasets are limited to a few high resource languages (Hu et al., 2020a; Wang et al., 2020; Vulić et al., 2020), except for a few tasks (e.g., NER, POS (Ahuja et al., 2022; Bhatt et al., 2021a)). Second, creating high quality test sets of substantial size for many tasks and languages is prohibitively expensive. Third, state-of-art models are known to learn spurious patterns to achieve high accuracies, saturating performance on these test-benches, yet performing poorly on often much simpler real world cases (Goyal et al., 2017; Gururangan et al., 2018; Glockner et al., 2018; Tsuchiya, 2018; Geva et al., 2019). Fourth, these benchmarks do not evaluate models for language specific nuances (Ribeiro et al., 2020). Lastly, this evaluation approach does not provide any insights into where the model is failing (Wu et al., 2019). These limitations lead to the need of interactive, challenging, and much larger testing datasets (like (Srivastava et al., 2022; Kiela et al., 2021)) and more holistic approaches to evaluation (like Ribeiro et al. (2020)).

CheckList (Ribeiro et al., 2020) is an evaluation paradigm that systematically tests the various *(linguistic) capabilities* required to solve a task. It allows creation of large and targeted test sets easily using various abstractions. Specifically, users can generate *templates*, essentially sentences with *slots* that can be filled in with a dictionary of *lexicons* to generate test *instances*. CheckList templates are created by native speakers. Ruder et al. (2021) introduce Multilingual Checklists created by human translation from English CheckList for 50 languages for a subset of tests on Question Answering. However, since CheckLists are task & language specific, human creation or translation of CheckLists remains extremely resource-intensive.

In this paper, we introduce an automatic approach to creating Multilingual CheckLists. We devise the **T**emplate **E**xtraction **A**lgorithm (TEA) for extracting templates in a *target* language from the translated instances of a *source* language CheckList (here English) automatically (§2). We also experiment with semi-automatic and manual approaches for Multilingual CheckList creation (§3). In the

Findings of the Association for Computational Linguistics: AACL-IJCNLP 2022, pages 282–295
November 20–23, 2022. ©2022 Association for Computational Linguistics

semi-automatic approach (TEA-ver), we ask human annotators to verify and correct the templates created by TEA. In the manual approach, we ask annotators to create CheckLists in two ways: first, by translation of English CheckList to the target language (t9n) (same as Ruder et al. (2021)); Second, by giving a description of the task and capabilities to create CheckLists from scratch (SCR) (same as original English CheckLists creation (Ribeiro et al., 2020)).Using these four approaches, we create CheckLists for Sentiment Analysis (SA) and Natural Language Inference (NLI) in Hindi (§5). We demonstrate broad applicability of TEA by generating CheckLists in additional 9 typologically diverse languages (Gujarati, French, Swahili, Arabic, German, Spanish, Russian, Vietnamese, Japanese) and TEA-ver CheckLists in 3 of them (§6).

Evaluation of CheckLists is non-trivial. For thorough comparisons, we propose evaluation metrics along four axes: *utility*, *diversity*, *cost* & *correctness* (§4). Our evaluation indicates that CheckLists created using TEA are not only cost-effective but also useful and diverse, with comparable quality to the manually and semi-automatically created CheckLists. Experiments on typologically diverse languages show that TEA CheckLists provide a good estimate of the failures of the model, and thus can be used even in the absence of resources to verify them or create human-annotated gold test-sets.

To summarize, our contributions are: a) We propose TEA (**T**emplate **E**xtraction **A**lgorithm) to extract templates in a target language using translated instances of a source CheckList. b) We experiment with varying degrees of human intervention, comparing semi-automatic & manual approaches of Multilingual CheckList creation with TEA, to understand the best utilization of the human effort. c) We introduce evaluation metrics along the axes of *utility*, *diversity*, *cost*, and *correctness* for in-depth comparison of the the CheckLists. d) We will release all the 4 CheckLists in Hindi for SA and NLI, TEA CheckLists in 9 languages for SA and TEA-ver CheckLists in 3 languages for SA.

We release the code of TEA and the CheckLists created at aka.ms/multilingualchecklist

2 TEA: Template Extraction Algorithm

Terminology (consistent with Ribeiro et al. (2020)):
***Linguistic* capabilities:** These are capabilities tested for a particular task. For e.g, negation.
Templates: These are sentences with slots. For e.g, '{CITY} is beautiful'. Here, '{CITY}' is a slot. Templates can have any number of slots.
Lexicon keys and values: This a dictionary of values. In the above example, 'CITY' is the key. Values are the words that would be filled in the slots (replacing the keys) like 'New Delhi', 'New York', 'London', etc. We use the notation 'CITY = ['New Delhi', 'London', 'New York'] ' for lexicons.
Instances: These are test sentences created by inserting lexicon values in templates . In the above example, the instances formed are: 'New York is beautiful', 'London is beautiful', etc.

The CheckList paradigm allows creation of large number of test instances. For multilingual evaluation, these can then be translated to the target languages using Machine Translation. However, there are limitations to this approach. Firstly, a large machine translated test set is difficult to be verified by humans, as one would have to go through every example. Second, it defeats the purpose of abstraction that CheckLists facilitates. And third, the quality of this test set will be directly impacted by the quality of the MT system. This results in the need to generate templates in the target language so that these can be utilized and verified in the same fashion as the template sets in the source language.

Our early experiments suggested that due to word order and syntactic differences between languages, both: 1) a word-to-word or heuristic translation of the template and 2) extraction of template from a single source instance (such as by simply replacing one word with other in a single translated instance) do not work well for template translation. This necessities a non-trivial algorithm that can extract templates given a set of instances.

We propose the **T**emplate **E**xtraction **A**lgorithm or TEA, to automatically extract template sets given an input a set of instances. In this paper, these input instances for TEA are obtained by machine translating instances created from the source CheckList template sets. We use machine translation to reduce cost and human effort, but the algorithm can be used with any input set of instances, i.e it would work with human-translated instances.

Briefly, TEA is a recursive approach to extract templates from input instances by treating every input instance as directed acyclic graph of the words. TEA combines the instances with similar structure into a single template by recursively merging instances and replacing terminals (or lexicon values) with non-terminals (or lexicon keys).

Figure 1 shows how TEA creates lexicon keys by

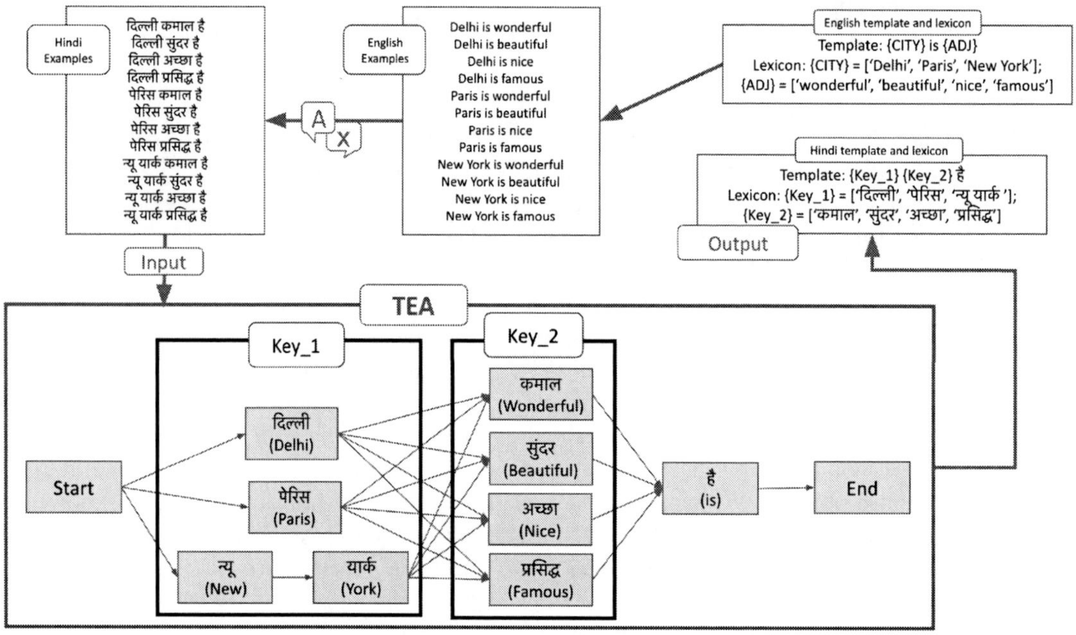

Figure 1: TEA treats sentences as a directed acyclic graph & recursively replaces lexicon values with keys.

combining instances from the translated instances. We assume English (EN) to be the source language and Hindi (HI) to be the target language. The pipeline starts with an EN template, the instances are created by replacing the lexicon values in the templates, that are then machine translated to get HI instances. These instances function as input to TEA which then recursively groups instances using non-terminals to form templates. The entire process of template extraction is repeated for every EN template, resulting in the HI template set. The TEA has 3 steps which we describe as follows (pseudocode and details are in appendix A):

Step 1: Grouping Terminals into Non-Terminals: First, we convert the Hi instances into a directed acyclic graph whose nodes are unique words (or tokens). There is an edge from node A to B if word B follows word A in at least one of the input instances. In this directed graph (see Fig. 1), between any two nodes, if there are multiple paths of length less than equal to $k + 1$ (we set k to 2), we concatenate the intermediate words in the path (with space in between them) and treat them as terminals. This set of terminals, between the two nodes, are grouped together represented by a non-terminal symbol (for example Key_1 and Key_2 in Fig. 1). This step corresponds to lexicon formation; the non-terminal extracted here are essentially keys of the lexicon & the terminals constituting them are the lexicon values for the slots of a template.

Step 2: Template Extraction Using a set of Hi instances, $S = \{s_1, s_2, \ldots s_N\}$, and all non-terminals $v_i = [w_{i1}, w_{i2}, \ldots]$, where w_{ij} are terminals (obtained step 1), TEA outputs a set of templates $\hat{T} = \{t_1, t_2, ...\}$ such that $\hat{T}$ can generate all the examples in S using the given non-terminal and their corresponding terminals. For each sentence s_i, we generate a set of candidate templates, $T_i = \{t_{i1}, t_{i2}, ...\}$, such that s_i belongs to the set of examples generated by each t_{ij}. To find the minimal template set, i.e $\hat{T}$ that covers all examples is treated as a set cover problem and we use a greedy approximation to find this set.

Step 3: Combine Steps 1 and 2 The above template extraction process, while resulting in correct outputs, may be computationally expensive due to translation noise[1] and its time-complexity which is exponential on the number of non-terminals. To mitigate this, we follow an iterative approach where instead of using all the extracted non-terminals (along with their terminals), we initialize the set of non-terminals with an empty set and iteratively add the most useful non-terminals (with their cor-

[1]The translated sentences may not fit into 1 template. Or, the algorithm may produce a set of distinct non-terminals with common or overlapping terminals. For e.g, we may get two non-terminals with their corresponding terminals such as "{Paris, New York}" & "{London, New York, Delhi}".

responding terminals) to this set.

Note that, TEA can generate multiple templates for the set of instances (all of which might be generated from a single source template). This design is intentional and desirable as due to morphosyntactic complexities (e.g, grammatical gender), it is likely that all instances in a target language will not fit into a single template.

3 Multilingual CheckList Generation

We now describe the various ways in which multilingual checklists can be generated, ranging from fully automatic to fully manual approaches.

Using TEA We start with a source language (En) CheckList template and generate instances by replacing lexicon values in templates. These instances are translated using an MT system. The translated instances now serve as the input to the TEA and target language (HI) CheckList template is extracted. The process (Fig. 1) is repeated for all En templates to form the complete HI CheckList.

TEA with Verification (TEA-ver) This is a semi-automatic approach, where we ask a human-*verifier* to verify and correct the CheckLists generated using TEA. The verifiers (or annotators) are provided with a set of templates and lexicons generated using the TEA pipeline, along with the original source langauge CheckList and description of the capabilities. The annotators are instructed to *verify* the target language templates for (grammatical) correctness. They can delete or edit the incorrect templates. They can also add any missing templates that they think are significantly important (cover too many missed instances).

Translating source CheckList (t9n) This is a completely manual approach, but relies on a source language (here, En) CheckList. The annotators are provided with the En templates, lexicons and the descriptions of capabilities. They are tasked to translate the templates and lexicons into the target language. If a source template cannot be translated to a single target template (such as due to divergent grammatical agreement patterns), annotators are instructed to include as many variants as necessary. This approach is same as that used by Ruder et al. (2021) to create multilingual CheckList.

Generating CheckList from scratch (SCR) This is a completely manual approach of creating CheckLists from scratch, not relying on any source CheckList. Here, the CheckList templates are generated in the same manner as generated in by humans in Ribeiro et al. (2020). That is, human annotators are provided with a description of the task and capabilities and are instructed to develop the templates and lexicon, directly in the target language. In our pilot we found that users were better able to understand the capabilities with some examples as opposed to only from the description, so we also provided them with a couple of examples, in English, for each capability.

4 Evaluation Metrics

Comparison of CheckLists is non-trivial. Firstly, CheckLists cannot be evaluated using absolute metrics, comparisons can only be relative (Bhatt et al., 2021b). Further, the question of what constitutes a better CheckList can be answered in multiple ways. For example, if a CheckList A can help discover (and/or fix) more bugs than CheckList B, CheckList A could be more useful. On the other hand, variability of instances may be desirable. If CheckList B generates more diverse instances as compared CheckList A, even though it discovers less bugs, B could be considered better as it allows testing of the system on a broader variety of instances. Finally, in practical scenarios, cost and correctness are both important factors for generating the CheckList.

We thus propose evaluation metrics along 4 dimensions: a) *utility* for discovery and fixing bugs; b) *diversity* in the generated instances; c) *cost* of generating templates. d) *correctness* of templates.

4.1 Utility

Failure Rate (FR) Here, we measure the percentage of instances generated by the CheckList that the model failed on averaged over all the capabilities.[2] The numbers are reported for XLM-R fine-tuned with English task data from standard datasets (SST-2 for SA and mNLI for NLI). Effectively, we measure the FR on zero-shot transfer from English to the target language. For FR, the higher the value the better the CheckList.

Augmentation Utility (Aug) These metrics aims to test the utility of CheckList in fixing failures using data augmentation following Bhatt et al. (2021b). This is done in two ways:

(a) From Scratch (Aug-0): Here, we fine-tune XLM-R directly using CheckList instances.

[2]Unless mentioned otherwise, we report macro-averages across capabilities.

(b) On Fine-tuned model (Aug-CFT): Here, XLM-R is first fine-tuned with English task data (SST-2 for SA and mNLI for NLI) and then further continually fine-tuned using CheckList instances.

In both cases, we first generate all instances using the CheckLists being compared. We retain a maximum of 10k instances per capability for each CheckList. The instances are then randomly split into train and test sets in 70:30 ratio. The training data (of the corresponding CheckList) is used for the augmentation as described above. The test sets, generated from all the CheckLists being compared are combined together to form a common test set and accuracy on this set is reported. Intuitively, this aims to determine the utility of the CheckList's instances for fixing failures using augmentation. For both the Augmentation metrics, higher is better.

4.2 Diversity

Number of templates (#temp) and lexicon values (#lexv) The simplest way to measure the diversity is the number of distinct templates and lexicon values (or terminals). Higher number of templates and lexicon values means more diversity.

Normalized Cross-Template BLEU (CT-BLEU) To measure the diversity between the templates, we measure the BLEU score (or similarity) for every instance generated by a template with the the instances generated by all other templates in the CheckList . Since this score is sensitive to the number of templates in the Checklist, we normalize the score by the number of templates in the set. Lower CT-BLEU is indicative of better CheckList as it indicates more diverse instances from templates.

4.3 Cost

Time per template (TpT) We define the *cost* of creation of these Checklists simply as the human time required. Since different methods or users can create substantially different number of templates per capability, we measure the *mean time taken* (TpT) for creation from scratch (SCR), translation (t9n) and verification (TEA-ver) of a *template* as the measure of the cost. A better CheckList for practical purposes would have lower TpT.

4.4 Correctness

Here, we assume that templates generated with any amount of human intervention (manual or semi-automatic) would always be correct. As a result, we calculate correctness only for TEA templates. We define the correctness of TEA templates with respect to TEA-ver templates. This is because during creation of templates by the TEA-ver process annotators correct or remove templates. Thus, only correct TEA template are left unedited. Therefore, in order to estimate the correctness of the TEA templates, we compute the following two metrics.

Failure Rate Difference (FR-diff) It is possible that the model fails in some cases if the input instance is not well-formed. As a result, the difference between the failure rates induced by TEA-ver templates (which always lead to well-formed instances) and that of TEA templates (which could lead to some ungrammatical instances) will give an estimate to the correctness of TEA templates. As a result, we define this metric as simply the difference between the FR of TEA and TEA-ver.

Precision and Recall (P/R) Since during the TEA-ver process, annotators edit or remove incorrect templates, only the correct templates that were generated by TEA are left as is. Therefore, in order to estimate the correctness of the TEA, we compute the precision and recall of the TEA template set, with respect to TEA-ver template set. We define match when the templates are same and the lexicon values of either one is a subset of the other, implying they will generate similar set of examples.

5 Hindi CheckLists and Results

We start with Hindi (Hi) as the target language, create CheckLists using all 4 methods from §3 and evaluate them using the metrics from §4. Hi has significant syntactic divergence from the source language (here English (En)) and uses a different script. Hi is a mid-resource language with reasonably good publicly available En-Hi MT systems. We argue that if TEA works well in the En-Hi pipeline, it would also work for most other high to mid resource languages with reasonable MT systems and similar or less syntactic divergence from En, which we also substantiate by performing additional multilingual experiments in §6.

5.1 Experiment Design

We create and evaluate Hi CheckLists for 2 tasks, Sentiment Analysis (SA) and Natural Language Inference (NLI). For SA, we choose 5 capabilities namely Vocabulary, Negation, Temporal, Semantic Role Labeling and Relational, and their associated Minimum Functionality Test (MFT) templates from Ribeiro et al. (2020) as our source CheckList. For NLI, we choose co-reference resolution, spatial, conditional, comparative and causal reasoning as capabilities and their associated templates from Tarunesh et al. (2021). We refer readers to Appendix B for details about these capabilities.

Following Ribeiro et al. (2020), we chose 6 software developers as our *annotators*, who are knowledgeable in NLP. All users are native speakers of Hi and have near-native En fluency.[3] We expect developers to be the actual users of the approach, as it is usually a developer's job to find and fix bugs. The annotators were given a detailed description of expectations along with examples (both in En and Hi). Furthermore, during our pilot study, we found some of the common errors users make, and to mitigate those we provided a list of common errors illustrated with simple examples.

Each of the 6 annotators was randomly assigned a CheckList creation approach that requires human intervention. Thus, we had 2 annotators each for the SCR, t9n and TEA-Ver setups. They carry out the process independently for both SA and NLI. The same description of capabilities and examples are used for all the experimental setups. Similarly, the same source templates and lexicons are used for t9n, TEA-ver and TEA. For the TEA pipeline, we used Bing Translator API for translating En instances to Hi. While reporting the results, we report the average metrics of both annotators.

5.2 Results

Table 1 reports the metrics (§4) for the 4 methods.

The trends for *cost* or TpT are consistent with expectations. Creating CheckLists from Scratch (SCR) takes the most time, as the user has to think and create the templates. t9n requires manual translation and is quicker than SCR but slower than TEA-ver, which just requires verification and correction on templates generated by TEA. We do not factor in the time required to create the source En Checklist, because 1) It is common to all of these 4 approaches and sourced from existing literature; and 2) it is a one-time effort which can be reused for generation of CheckLists in many target languages, leading to a very low amortized cost.

In *diversity* metrics TEA generates the most diverse templates, closely followed by TEA-Ver. t9n is much less diverse, and SCR has the least diversity. We found that, the users created very few templates for SCR, perhaps because it is difficult to decide what would be a good number of templates. We also observe that TEA generates a largest number of templates. The source checklists had 32 (74) and 18 (76) templates (lexicon values) for SA and NLI, respectively. Thus on average, a source template generates around 3 target templates, which is primarily due to syntactic divergence between the En and Hi. These numbers are reduced in TEA-ver, most likely because not all of the TEA templates are perfect and human annotators merge or delete some of them during the verification.

The trends in *utility* metrics are varied. In SA, TEA-ver templates induce highest FR and TEA is a close second. However, for NLI, SCR CheckList induces the highest failure, followed by t9n. This might be due to the task complexity. We leave further exploration on the co-relation of task complexity and efficacy of TEA to future work. TEA has the highest Aug-0 and Aug-CFT values except one case where it is a close second, indicating that the instances generated by TEA CheckLists are effective in fixing failure by augmentation. TEA-ver has values that close to TEA for these metrics[4].

In terms of *correctness*, based on P/R of TEA with respect to TEA-ver, we find that that around a third of the TEA templates had to be significantly edited or removed. Despite this, from FR-diff, we see that the FR generated by TEA is fairly close to the FR generated by TEA-ver. Additionally, even the numbers of other utility metrics are also comparable. This indicates that even the unverified templates (from TEA) which may generate some ungrammatical instances, can give very close estimates of the failure rates and augmentation accuracy to human-verified template sets. This is a positive finding, because while TEA-ver is more reliable, but when resources to get TEA templates verified are not available, despite imperfections, TEA CheckLists can be used for evaluation.

Finally, we would like to point out some of the qualitative differences that we saw in the CheckLists created by these different methods which are hard to articulate through metrics. In particular, we saw that CheckLists created from scratch tend to capture cultural context better. For example, annotators use Indian names in the lexicon values as opposed to western names that get generated due to translations in all other 3 approaches. However,

[3]Educated for 15+ years in English

[4]TEA and TEA-ver have a substantial overlap, and thus, augmentation of one typically helps with the other. This explains the high AUG-0 and AUG-CFT values for these setups.

Metric		Sentiment Analysis				NLI			
		SCR	**t9n**	**TEA-ver**	**TEA**	**SCR**	**t9n**	**TEA-ver**	**TEA**
Utility	**FR**	6.7	16.5	**19.7**	19.3	**60.3**	53.4	45.1	48.4
	Aug-0	49	52.4	50.6	**67.1**	16.2	50.9	**58.4**	52.5
	Aug-CFT	86.8	89.9	**95.3**	**95.3**	70.1	81.2	79.4	**83.2**
Diversity	**# temp**	17	44.5	86.0	**105**	16	22.5	51.5	**54**
	# lexv	35.0	41.5	109	**147.0**	38.5	56.5	88.5	**98.0**
	CT-BLEU*	0.511	0.142	0.096	**0.087**	0.564	0.307	0.216	**0.169**
Cost	**TpT* (mins)**	5.38	2.07	1.77	**0**	4.69	3.67	1.91	**0**
Correctness	**FR-diff***	-	-	-	0.4	-	-	-	3.3
	P/R	-	-	-	0.64/0.61	-	-	-	0.67/0.63

Table 1: Comparison of the 4 approaches across two tasks for Hindi. *Lower is better; for rest higher is better.

while difficult for TEA, this entity recontextualization is fairly easy for the other two approaches where humans are involved. We also find that the template sets of TEA-ver and t9n are overlapping. This is because of the setup, where t9n is directly translated at template level and TEA-ver is obtained after correcting the templates obtained from translated instances. The major difference occurs in the amount of time taken as correcting templates is faster than translating them.

Thus overall, we conclude that TEA followed by human verification, or TEA-ver would be an ideal approach for scaling CheckList evaluation to multiple languages. That said, the fully automatic TEA approach is even more cost-effective and almost equally reliable to the TEA-ver approach, making it suitable for large-scale multilingual CheckList generation with extremely limited resources.

6 CheckLists in Multiple Languages

So far, we see that TEA is cost-efficient in producing effective Hi CheckLists. We now experiment with 9 more typologically diverse languages – Arabic, French, German, Gujarati, Japanese, Russian, Spanish, Swahili and Vietnamese to evaluate the efficacy of scaling TEA to may languages. We use TEA to automatically generate CheckLists across these languages from the same set of source templates in English for SA across 6 capabilities: Vocabulary, Temporal, Fairness, Negation, Semantic role labeling (SRL) and Robustness. We use the same source En CheckList from the Ribeiro et al. (2020) and use Bing Translator in the TEA pipeline to translate En instances to the target language.

In Table 2 we report the FR on XLM-R model fine-tuned with SST-2 data; thus, except for En, all other values are for zero-shot transfer to the respective language. The average FR for AMCG is highest for Swahili (59%), Vietnamese and Gujarati (around 52%), and lowest for French (43%), Spanish and German (around 45%). For English, average FR is 41%. These trends are consistent with expectation of performance as English, French, and other European languages are high-resourced while Swahili and Vietnamese are very low-resourced.

For 3 of the target languages, namely French, Gujarati and Swahili, native speakers verified the generated templates and thus, we also report the FR for TEA-ver.[5] We observe that the Pearson (Spearman) correlation between TEA and TEA-ver FR values for French, Gujarati and Swahili are 0.99 (1.0), 0.98 (0.89) and 0.97 (0.94) respectively. Furthermore, the difference between FR (FR-Diff) is also low. This implies, similar to our observations from section 5, that one can obtain an extremely accurate assessment of the capabilities of multilingual models just from TEA CheckLists even for low resource languages like Swahili. This re-affirms that despite noise, TEA is able to generate CheckLists that are useful without any human supervision.

7 Limitations

In this paper, we introduced the TEA to generate target language CheckList (templates + lexicon) from the translated instances of source language CheckList. We show that with drastically reduced human effort required for creating CheckList in a new language, the TEA CheckLists provide an accurate estimate of the models' capabilities. However, some of the generated templates/lexicons are noisy and were removed or edited by humans through the TEA-ver process. In this section, we summarize the limitations, common error patterns

[5]These languages were selected based on typological, geographical, resource level diversity and access to native speakers.

Language		Vocabulary	Temporal	Fairness	Negation	SRL	Robustness
English	FR (SCR)	24.21	1.8	94.35	48.16	35.94	42.58
Gujarati	FR (TEA)	39.12	34.97	87.46	51.84	47.37	52.09, 51.54
	FR (TEA-ver)	29.09	32.18	88.72	55.15	46.8	51.54
	FR-diff	10.09	2.79	1.26	3.3	0.57	0.55
French	FR (TEA)	20.27	11.22	86.52	56.55	40.09	46.77
	FR (TEA-ver)	21.78	11.53	86.52	61.25	40.09	47.8
	FR-diff	1.51	0.31	0	4.7	0	1.3
Swahili	FR (TEA)	46.04	37.5	88.86	73.32	51.87	58.45
	FR (TEA-ver)	38.53	43.72	90.37	73.25	46.51	55.38
	FR-diff	8.24	6.22	1.51	0.07	5.36	3.07
Arabic	FR (TEA)	46.77	14.37	91.98	52.08	39.4	53.32
German	FR (TEA)	38.45	15.59	85.25	47.56	43.03	44.04
Spanish	FR (TEA)	29.44	3.18	89.45	59.41	41.39	50.1
Russian	FR (TEA)	40.26	5.07	93.67	56.13	40.3	47.61
Vietnamese	FR (TEA)	23.50	21.67	93.22	63.05	53.12	50.97
Japanese	FR (TEA)	26.9	24.22	93.69	50.1	50.97	-

Table 2: Failure rates for 9 more languages across 6 capabilities for sentiment analysis. Failure rates of English are for the original templates created manually by annotators (SCR); For Gujarati, French, and Swahili FR for TEA, TEA-ver and FR-diff is reported, for the rest of languages FR for TEA is reported.

and suggest some possible ways to resolve them.

Agnostic to Semantics TEA is agnostic of the semantics of the lexicon keys. So, when faced with a set of sentences: *Las Vegas is good.*, *New York is good.*, *New Delhi is good.* and *Las Palmas is good.*, it is unclear whether it should design 1 template `CITY is good.` with lexicon `CITY`={*Las Vegas, New York, New Delhi, Las Palmas*} or 2 templates: `Las CITY1 is good.`, `CITY1`={*Vegas, Palmas*} and `New CITY2 is good.`, `CITY2`={*York, Delhi*}. This problem is hard to solve without heuristics. One possibility is to use the translation alignment information however, such alignments are often imperfect even for high-resource languages. We leave improvements to TEA for handling this to future work.

Handling Morphology Creating good templates for morphologically rich languages (Sinha et al., 2005; Dorr, 1994) is more challenging due to inflections. For e.g, in Hindi a verb may take different form for different tenses and gender. While TEA can handle such cases by creating multiple templates, but with still a third of Hi templates needed correcting. We leave morphologically informed CheckList creation to future work.

Translation Errors Translation errors are a frequent pattern, affecting the input target language instances. In some cases, due to the statistical nature of TEA, we are able to naturally filter out such erroneous templates. For e.g, for an En template 'I used to think this {air_noun} was {neg_adj}, {change} now I think it is {pos_adj}', translated Hi templates 'Mujhe lagta hai ki us {udaan} {ghatia} tha, ab mujhe lagta hai ki yeh asadharan hai' (correct) matches 187 translations, and 'Mujhe lagta hai ki us {udaan} {ghatia} tha karte the, ab mujhe lagta hai ki yeh bohut achha hai' (noisy) matches only 35. While TEA can remove some noisy patterns, errors due to misunderstood context are much harder to fix. For e.g 'the service is poor' translated as 'vah seva garib hai' but 'garib' in Hindi means "lacking sufficient money" and *not* "lower or insufficient standards". We leave comparisons of TEA for human v.s machine translated input instances and methods to measure and reduce the effect of translation errors on TEA to future work.

Metric Limitations Quantifying the quality of generated template and verification of the relevance of templates with respect to provided description is non-trivial . While we suggest a set of metrics quantifying utility, diversity and cost, these should be extended and further studied for efficacy across tasks and languages. Lastly, soundness and completeness of a template sets (or a test-suite in general) is another unexplored aspect in our current work and an important future direction of research. Furthermore, we acknowledge the limitation of Failure Rate as a metric in the sense that the model could also fail if an example is ungrammatical. In other words, FR is conditional to correctness of the CheckList. However, in our experimentation in both Hindi and other languages, we have found that the the difference between the FR of human verified TEA-ver and TEA is typically small (with a few exceptions) across languages. This means that high FR being caused due to ungrammatical instances here is unlikely. Thus, as stated before, the closeness of the FRs of TEA and TEA-ver points to the reliability of the TEA algorithm.

8 Conclusion

In this paper we proposed TEA (**T**emplate **E**xtraction **A**lgorithm) to automatically generate multilingual CheckLists in a target language without any human supervision (§2). This algorithm recursively extracts templates and lexicon from an input set of instances by treating sentences as a directed acyclic graph of words and combining them.

We additionally experimented with 3 other approaches with varying degrees of human intervention, 2 manual and 1 semi-automatic for CheckList generation (§3). For comparing these CheckLists, we introduced metrics along the dimensions of utility, diversity, cost and correctness (§4).

We performed in-depth analysis of all the 4 methods, with varying degree of human interventions, to create CheckLists for Sentiment Analysis and NLI in Hindi (§5). In addition to Hindi, we experimented with 9 more typologically diverse languages to demonstrate the efficacy of TEA along with comparison with human-verified CheckLists in 3 of them (§3). We found that TEA is cost-effective, useful, and diverse in the CheckLists that it generates. While around one-third of the TEA templates required correction by humans, making the semi-automatic approach more reliable, we find that the model performance estimates provided by unverified CheckLists are very close to that of the human-verified (or semi-automatically created) CheckLists and are also significantly correlated to it. We also substantiated the finding of TEA being effective as well as reliable in the other languages.

Our overall recommendation is that TEA followed by human verification is the most reliable and cost-effective way to scale CheckList evaluation to multiple languages. But in case of very limited resources, TEA is still good enough to test system performance. We end with a discussion on the limitations of this work and propose directions that will, hopefully, inspire research in scaling and improving multilingual evaluation using CheckLists. Finally, we note that TEA is general purpose algorithm of template extraction that can be used for other template-based evaluations such as bias evaluation (Webster et al., 2020; Bhatt et al., 2022)

Acknowledgements We thank the annotators and their team who facilitated the user studies in the paper. We are grateful to our colleagues at MSRI for being the pilot users. We thank Kalika Bali, Balakrishnan Santhanam, and Prasenjit Rath for their thoughtful guidance throughout the work. We thank Gauri Kholkar for her engineering assistance.

References

Kabir Ahuja, Sandipan Dandapat, Sunayana Sitaram, and Monojit Choudhury. 2022. Beyond static models and test sets: Benchmarking the potential of pretrained models across tasks and languages. In *Proceedings of NLP Power! The First Workshop on Efficient Benchmarking in NLP*, pages 64–74, Dublin, Ireland. Association for Computational Linguistics.

Shaily Bhatt, Sunipa Dev, Partha Talukdar, Shachi Dave, and Vinodkumar Prabhakaran. 2022. Recontextualizing fairness in nlp: The case of india.

Shaily Bhatt, Poonam Goyal, Sandipan Dandapat, Monojit Choudhury, and Sunayana Sitaram. 2021a. On the universality of deep contextual language models.

Shaily Bhatt, Rahul Jain, Sandipan Dandapat, and Sunayana Sitaram. 2021b. A case study of efficacy and challenges in practical human-in-loop evaluation of NLP systems using checklist. In *Proceedings of the Workshop on Human Evaluation of NLP Systems (HumEval)*, pages 120–130, Online. Association for Computational Linguistics.

Alexis Conneau, Kartikay Khandelwal, Naman Goyal, Vishrav Chaudhary, Guillaume Wenzek, Francisco Guzmán, Edouard Grave, Myle Ott, Luke Zettlemoyer, and Veselin Stoyanov. 2020. Unsupervised cross-lingual representation learning at scale. In *Proceedings of the 58th Annual Meeting of the Association for Computational Linguistics*, pages 8440–8451, Online. Association for Computational Linguistics.

Alexis Conneau, Ruty Rinott, Guillaume Lample, Adina Williams, Samuel Bowman, Holger Schwenk, and Veselin Stoyanov. 2018. XNLI: Evaluating cross-lingual sentence representations. In *Proceedings of the 2018 Conference on Empirical Methods in Natural Language Processing*, pages 2475–2485, Brussels, Belgium. Association for Computational Linguistics.

Jacob Devlin, Ming-Wei Chang, Kenton Lee, and Kristina Toutanova. 2019. BERT: Pre-training of deep bidirectional transformers for language understanding. In *Proceedings of the 2019 Conference of the North American Chapter of the Association for Computational Linguistics: Human Language Technologies, Volume 1 (Long and Short Papers)*, pages 4171–4186, Minneapolis, Minnesota. Association for Computational Linguistics.

Bonnie J. Dorr. 1994. Machine translation divergences: A formal description and proposed solution. *Computational Linguistics*, 20(4):597–633.

Mor Geva, Yoav Goldberg, and Jonathan Berant. 2019. Are we modeling the task or the annotator? an investigation of annotator bias in natural language understanding datasets. In *Proceedings of the 2019 Conference on Empirical Methods in Natural Language Processing and the 9th International Joint Conference on Natural Language Processing (EMNLP-IJCNLP)*, pages 1161–1166, Hong Kong, China. Association for Computational Linguistics.

Max Glockner, Vered Shwartz, and Yoav Goldberg. 2018. Breaking NLI systems with sentences that require simple lexical inferences. In *Proceedings of the 56th Annual Meeting of the Association for Computational Linguistics (Volume 2: Short Papers)*, pages 650–655, Melbourne, Australia. Association for Computational Linguistics.

Yash Goyal, Tejas Khot, Douglas Summers-Stay, Dhruv Batra, and Devi Parikh. 2017. Making the V in VQA matter: Elevating the role of image understanding in visual question answering. In *2017 IEEE Conference on Computer Vision and Pattern Recognition, CVPR 2017, Honolulu, HI, USA, July 21-26, 2017*, pages 6325–6334. IEEE Computer Society.

Suchin Gururangan, Swabha Swayamdipta, Omer Levy, Roy Schwartz, Samuel Bowman, and Noah A. Smith. 2018. Annotation artifacts in natural language inference data. In *Proceedings of the 2018 Conference of the North American Chapter of the Association for Computational Linguistics: Human Language Technologies, Volume 2 (Short Papers)*, pages 107–112, New Orleans, Louisiana. Association for Computational Linguistics.

Junjie Hu, Sebastian Ruder, Aditya Siddhant, Graham Neubi, Orhan Firat, and Melvin Johnson. 2020a. XTREME: A massively multilingual multitask benchmark for evaluating cross-lingual generalisation. In *Proceedings of the 37th International Conference on Machine Learning*, volume 119 of *Proceedings of Machine Learning Research*, pages 4411–4421. PMLR.

Junjie Hu, Sebastian Ruder, Aditya Siddhant, Graham Neubig, Orhan Firat, and Melvin Johnson. 2020b. Xtreme: A massively multilingual multi-task benchmark for evaluating cross-lingual generalization.

Pratik Joshi, Somak Aditya, Aalok Sathe, and Monojit Choudhury. 2020. Taxinli: Taking a ride up the nlu hill.

Douwe Kiela, Max Bartolo, Yixin Nie, Divyansh Kaushik, Atticus Geiger, Zhengxuan Wu, Bertie Vidgen, Grusha Prasad, Amanpreet Singh, Pratik Ringshia, Zhiyi Ma, Tristan Thrush, Sebastian Riedel, Zeerak Waseem, Pontus Stenetorp, Robin Jia, Mohit Bansal, Christopher Potts, and Adina Williams. 2021. Dynabench: Rethinking benchmarking in nlp.

Yaobo Liang, Nan Duan, Yeyun Gong, Ning Wu, Fenfei Guo, Weizhen Qi, Ming Gong, Linjun Shou, Daxin Jiang, Guihong Cao, Xiaodong Fan, Ruofei Zhang, Rahul Agrawal, Edward Cui, Sining Wei, Taroon Bharti, Ying Qiao, Jiun-Hung Chen, Winnie Wu, Shuguang Liu, Fan Yang, Daniel Campos, Rangan Majumder, and Ming Zhou. 2020. XGLUE: A new benchmark datasetfor cross-lingual pre-training, understanding and generation. In *Proceedings of the 2020 Conference on Empirical Methods in Natural Language Processing (EMNLP)*, pages 6008–6018, Online. Association for Computational Linguistics.

Yinhan Liu, Jiatao Gu, Naman Goyal, Xian Li, Sergey Edunov, Marjan Ghazvininejad, Mike Lewis, and Luke Zettlemoyer. 2020. Multilingual denoising pretraining for neural machine translation. *Transactions of the Association for Computational Linguistics*, 8:726–742.

Marco Tulio Ribeiro, Tongshuang Wu, Carlos Guestrin, and Sameer Singh. 2020. Beyond accuracy: Behavioral testing of NLP models with CheckList. In *Proceedings of the 58th Annual Meeting of the Association for Computational Linguistics*, pages 4902–4912, Online. Association for Computational Linguistics.

Sebastian Ruder, Noah Constant, Jan Botha, Aditya Siddhant, Orhan Firat, Jinlan Fu, Pengfei Liu, Junjie Hu, Graham Neubig, and Melvin Johnson. 2021. Xtreme-r: Towards more challenging and nuanced multilingual evaluation.

K. Sinha, R. Mahesh, and Anil Thakur. 2005. Translation divergence in English-Hindi MT. In *Proceedings of the 10th EAMT Conference: Practical applications of machine translation*, Budapest, Hungary. European Association for Machine Translation.

Aarohi Srivastava, Abhinav Rastogi, Abhishek Rao, Abu Awal Md Shoeb, Abubakar Abid, Adam Fisch, Adam R Brown, Adam Santoro, Aditya Gupta, Adrià Garriga-Alonso, et al. 2022. Beyond the imitation game: Quantifying and extrapolating the capabilities of language models. *arXiv preprint arXiv:2206.04615*.

Ishan Tarunesh, Somak Aditya, and Monojit Choudhury. 2021. Trusting roberta over bert: Insights from checklisting the natural language inference task.

Masatoshi Tsuchiya. 2018. Performance impact caused by hidden bias of training data for recognizing textual entailment. In *Proceedings of the Eleventh International Conference on Language Resources and Evaluation (LREC 2018)*, Miyazaki, Japan. European Language Resources Association (ELRA).

Ivan Vulić, Simon Baker, Edoardo Maria Ponti, Ulla Petti, Ira Leviant, Kelly Wing, Olga Majewska, Eden Bar, Matt Malone, Thierry Poibeau, Roi Reichart, and Anna Korhonen. 2020. Multi-SimLex: A large-scale evaluation of multilingual and crosslingual lexical semantic similarity. *Computational Linguistics*, 46(4):847–897.

Zihan Wang, Karthikeyan K, Stephen Mayhew, and Dan Roth. 2020. Extending multilingual BERT to low-resource languages. In *Findings of the Association for Computational Linguistics: EMNLP 2020*, pages 2649–2656, Online. Association for Computational Linguistics.

Kellie Webster, Xuezhi Wang, Ian Tenney, Alex Beutel, Emily Pitler, Ellie Pavlick, Jilin Chen, Ed Chi, and Slav Petrov. 2020. Measuring and reducing gendered correlations in pre-trained models.

Tongshuang Wu, Marco Tulio Ribeiro, Jeffrey Heer, and Daniel Weld. 2019. Errudite: Scalable, reproducible, and testable error analysis. In *Proceedings of the 57th Annual Meeting of the Association for Computational Linguistics*, pages 747–763, Florence, Italy. Association for Computational Linguistics.

Linting Xue, Noah Constant, Adam Roberts, Mihir Kale, Rami Al-Rfou, Aditya Siddhant, Aditya Barua, and Colin Raffel. 2021. mt5: A massively multilingual pre-trained text-to-text transformer.

A Details of TEA

A.1 Template as a Grammar

A template can be considered as a type of grammar to generate sentences. Consider the template T0 introduced below.

> T0: `CITY-0` is beautiful but `CITY-1` is bigger.
> `CITY` = {Delhi, Paris, New York} ,

Here, the keywords (`CITY-0`,`CITY-1`) are the non-terminals and their corresponding lexicons are the terminal symbols. Also, `CITY-1` should be different than `CITY-0`; and hence the non-terminal symbols cannot be replaced independently of each other, establishing the context-sensitive nature of templates. This is a why we need to look beyond probabilistic context free grammar induction to learn the templates.

Convention and Assumptions: We use *terminal* and *non-terminal* to denote *lexicons* and *keywords* respectively. In a template, if the non-terminals are appended with cardinals from 0 to k, then they can *not be replaced with same terminal while generating sentences. Also, if a template contains an instance of a non-terminal with cardinal* k, $(k > 0)$ *then at least one instance of the same non-terminal with cardinal* $k - 1$ *should have occurred before its occurrence in the template.*

A.2 TEA Algorithm

We first briefly recap the pipeline of TEA for ease of exposition. We start with an En template and corresponding terminals created by a human expert, and generate a set of examples by substituting the non-terminals with their appropriate terminals. We then translate the examples to Hi using an Automatic Machine Translation system (such as Azure cloud Translator). Then we extract Hi template(s), terminal(s) and non-terminal(s) from the Hi examples. The process of extracting Hi templates are repeated for each of the En templates, providing us a (tentative) CheckList for Hi. Here, we describe in detail the TEA algorithm that extracts Hi templates (along with Hi terminal words) from the Hi examples. First we discuss our approach to extract potential set of terminal words, i.e., we group a set of words (terminals) and give them a symbol/name (non-terminal). Then we extract the templates using the terminals and non-terminals that are extracted in previous step. Towards the end of this section, we briefly discuss the scalability issues and the approximations that we used to make it more scalable.

A.2.1 Extracting and Grouping Terminals

First, we convert the given Hi examples into a directed graph whose nodes are unique words (or tokens, if we use a different tokenizer) from the examples and there is an edge from word A to word B if word B follows word A in at least one of the examples. In this directed graph (as shown in Fig. 1), between any two nodes, if there are multiple paths of length less than equal to $k+1$*, we group all those paths and give the group a name or a non-terminal symbol (for example Key_1 and Key_2 in Fig. 1).*[6] *By grouping the paths, we meant to concatenate the intermediate words in the path (with space in between them) and then to group the concatenated strings (terminals). This step gives us potential lexicons and keywords (or list of terminals grouped*

[6]We assumed the maximum length of each terminal string to be $k(= 2)$ tokens/words

together).

A.2.2 Template Extraction given Terminal and Non-Terminals

Input to our algorithm is (1) a set Hi examples denoted by $S = \{s_1, s_2, \ldots s_N\}$, and (2) all terminals (denoted by w) and its corresponding non-terminals (denoted by v) that are extracted in previous step $\forall i, v_i = w_{i1}, w_{i2}, \ldots$ In other words, these are the production rules from a non-terminal to (only) terminals. Output of our algorithm is a set of templates $\hat{T} = \{t_1, t_2, ...\}$ such that $\hat{T}$ can generate all the examples in S using only the given non-terminal and their corresponding terminals.

For convenience, we represent non-terminals and its corresponding terminals as a list (or ordered set) of $\langle$ terminal, non-terminal $\rangle$ tuples, the list is denoted by $L = [\langle w_1, v_1\rangle ... \langle w_i, v_i\rangle ...]$. The tuple $\langle w_i, v_i\rangle$ belongs to L if and only if the the terminal w_i belongs to the non-terminal v_i.

The trivial result for $\hat{T}$ is S itself, as S can generate every example (using no terminals). But this is not useful because, the essence of extracting templates from a set of examples is that one should be able to read/write the entire set by reading only a few templates. Therefore, the objective is to find the (approximately) smallest $\hat{T}$ such that it can generate entire S.

We provide the outline of our algorithm in Algorithm 1. Next, we explain the algorithm along with the helper functions that are not elaborated in the pseudocode. For each sentences s_i, we call the function GET-TEMPLATES-PER-EXAMPLE *to generate a set of templates, $T_i = \{t_{i1}, t_{i2}, ...\}$, such that s_i belongs to the set of examples generated by each t_{ij}. Once we have T_i for every s_i, we construct the (approximately) smallest set $\hat{T}$ such that $\forall i, \hat{T} \bigcap T_i \neq \emptyset$. Note that for every sentence $s_i \in S$, there exist atleast one template in $\hat{T}$ that generates s_i. Finding the smallest $\hat{T}$ is a variant of set cover problem, therefore we use greedy approach to find the approximately small $\hat{T}$.*

***Generating** T_i: For every terminal string (w_m) that is a substring of example s_i (or intermediate template t_i), we have 2 options to create template, either (1) replace the matched substring (w_m) with its corresponding non-terminal (v_m) or (2) leave as it is; we can make this decision to replace or not, independently for every matched terminals. While replacing, we need to take care of the cardinals for non-terminals and make sure the templates conform to the adopted convention. We use*

Algorithm 1 Extract templates given terminals and non-terminals

Input: $S = \{s_1, s_2, ...s_N\}$, $L = [\langle w_1, v_1\rangle ... \langle w_i, v_i\rangle ...]$
Output: $\hat{T}$, the approximately smallest set of templates that generates entire S

for each s_i in S **do**
  $T_i \leftarrow$ GET-TEMPLATES-PER-EXAMPLE(s_i, L)
end for
Find (approximately) smallest $\hat{T}$ such that $\forall T_i, \hat{T} \cap T_i \neq \emptyset$ ▷ Variant of set cover, use greedy approach
return $\hat{T}$
procedure GET-TEMPLATES-PER-EXAMPLE(s_i, L)
  $T_i \leftarrow \{s_i\}$
  for each $\langle w_m, v_m\rangle$ in L **do**
    $T_{new} \leftarrow \{\}$
    for each t_{ij} in T_i **do**
      if w_m is sub-string of t_{ij} **then**
        $t_{new} \leftarrow$ REPLACE-MATCHED-STRING(t_{ij}, w_m, v_m) ▷ Refer §A.2.2
        $t_{new} \leftarrow$ RENAME-NONTERMINAL-CARDINALS(t_{new}) ▷ Refer §A.2.2
        $T_{new} \leftarrow T_{new} \cup t_{new}$
      end if
    end for
    $T_i \leftarrow T_i \cup T_{new}$
  end for
  return T_i
end procedure

the functions REPLACE-MATCHED-STRING *and* RENAME-NONTERMINAL-CARDINALS *to ensure such conformance.*

REPLACE-MATCHED-STRING *This function replaces the matched terminal w_m in t_{ij} with its corresponding non-terminal v_m. If there are multiple w_m in t_{ij}, then each w_m will be independently replaced with v_m or left unchanged. For example, consider the initial template and $\langle$ terminal, non-terminal $\rangle$ pair be "#Paris is beautiful. `CITY-0` is cold. Paris is bigger." and $\langle$ Paris, `CITY` $\rangle$ respectively. This will generate 3 templates after replacement. (1) "#`CITY-1` is beautiful. `CITY-0` is cold. Paris is bigger." (2) "#Paris is beautiful. `CITY-0` is cold. `CITY-1` is bigger." (3) "#`CITY-1` is beautiful. `CITY-0` is cold. `CITY-1` is bigger."*

Note that, we do not search if the words in the

s_i is a terminal, rather we search if the terminal is a sub-string of s_i (or t_{ij}). This makes it possible for the terminal to be a sub-word or a multi-word string and still match. Sub-word level match can be quite useful, especially in morphologically rich languages; using only the base word as lexicons it may be possible to match different morphological forms.

RENAME-NONTERMINAL-CARDINALS *This function renames the cardinals to make sure that an instance of a non-terminal with cardinal $k-1$ occurs before the instance of that non-terminal with cardinal $k, (k > 0)$. For example, after re-naming the cardinals, the above three templates become the following three, respectively. (1) "#`CITY-0` is beautiful. `CITY-1` is cold. Paris is bigger." (2) "#Paris is beautiful. `CITY-0` is cold. `CITY-1` is bigger." (3) "#`CITY-0` is beautiful. `CITY-1` is cold. `CITY-0` is bigger."*

A.2.3 Combine both the steps

First, we find all the potential terminals and non-terminals (using § A.2.1) for all Hi examples, and then use them to extract template following the algorithm outlined in § A.2.2. While this simple procedure is possible, it is often computationally expensive; one of the reasons is that due to noise (many of the translated sentences may not fit into a template), the algorithm to extract terminals and non-terminals (§ A.2.1) often gives a lot of different non-terminals that share many common terminals. For example, we may get two non-terminals with their corresponding terminals such as "{Paris, New York, Delhi}" and "{London, New York, Delhi}". Moreover, the complexity of the algorithm in § 1 to extract templates can be increased exponentially with the number of non-terminals. To mitigate this problem, we follow an iterative approach where instead of using all the extracted non-terminals (along with their terminals), we initialize the set of non-terminals with an empty set and iteratively add the most useful non-terminals (with their corresponding terminals) to the existing set of non-terminals.

B Capabilities tested using CheckList

Capabilities are tested using MFTs. MFTs (Minimum Functionality Tests) are tests similar to unit tests in software testing where a specific pointed capability of a model is tested via a template and an expected label(s). The test is said to pass for an instance if the model predicted label matches the expected label(s). Finally, failure rate is recorded as the % of test instances that fails; which can also be inferred as 100-accuracy.

B.1 Sentiment Analysis (SA)

These capabilities, their descriptions, examples and their original template sets used in testing are all sourced from Ribeiro et al. (2020).

Vocabulary *This capability tests whether the model can appropriately handle the impact of words with different parts of speech on the task. In particular, sentences with neutral adjectives are expected to have a neutral prediction and sentences sentiment-laden (positive or negative) adjectives are expected to have the corresponding label. For example, "This is a* private (NEUTRAL_ADJ) *aircraft" should be labelled neutral; and "This is a* great (POSITIVE_ADJ) *aircraft" "This is a* bad (NEGATIVE_ADJ) *aircraft" should be labelled positive and negative respectively.*

Negation *This capability tests that the negation of a positive adjective in the sentence should be labelled as positive or neutral, for example: "This is* not *a* great (POSITIVE_ADJ) *aircraft" should be labelled negative or neutral. Similarly, sentence with negation of negative adjective should be positive our neutral and those with negation of neutral adjectives should remain neutral.*

Semantic Role Labeling (SRL) *SRL aims to test that the model understands the agent, object etc in an instance. That is sentiment of the correct role in the instance is parsed. Here, there are two distinct capabilities MFTs. The first one is to test that the sentiment author sentiment is given more importance than of sentiment of others. For example, "Some people think this aircraft is bad, but I thought it was* great (POSITIVE_ADJ)*" should be labelled as Positive. The second test is related to parsing yes/no questions with the correct sentiment. For example, "Do I think this aircraft is great?* Yes*" should be labelled as positive, whereas if the answer was No, it should be negative.*

Temporal *This capability is used to test whether the model understands the sequence of events correctly. In other words that the most recent sentiment is correctly parsed in labelling. For example, "I used to hate this aircraft, but* now I love it*" should be labelled positive.*

Robustness *There are two tests for robustness: First changing of values within semantically equivalent classes should not change the prediction. For example, "I flew in from* Delhi*" and "I flew in from* New York*" should have the same label as the change here is within the semantically equivalent class of 'CITY'. Secondly, typos (or random character exchange) should not flip labels. For example, "This is a* graet *aircraft" should still remain positive.*

Fairness *Fairness is used to test that prediction should be the same for various adjectives within a protected class. For example, "Mary is a* black (RACE) *woman" and "Mary is a* white (RACE) *woman" should have same sentiment prediction.*

B.2 Natural Language Inference (NLI)

We use the template sets from Tarunesh et al. (2021) which in turn rely on the taxonomy of capabilities from (Joshi et al., 2020) for their selection of capabilities. In examples that follow, P stands for Premise and H for hypothesis.

Co-reference resolution *Test the model for resolving pronouns between the premise and hypothesis correctly. For example, P: Angelique and Ricardo are colleagues. He is a minister and she is a model. H: Angelique is a model. Here H should 'entail' P.*

Spatial reasoning *Tests the model for reasoning using spatial properties. For example, P: Manchester is 67 miles from Pittsburg and 27 miles from Kansas. H: Manchester is nearer to Kansas than Pittsburg. Here H should 'entail' P.*

Causal reasoning *Tests the model for using causation in the premise to infer the hypothesis. For example, P: Katherine taught science to Nancy. H: Nancy learnt science from Katherine. Here H should 'entail' P.*

Conditional reasoning *Tests the model for logically inferring the hypothesis given conditional premise. For example, P: If the baby is fed on time, he does not get cranky. H: The baby gets crancky when he is hungry. Here H should 'entail' P.*

Comparative reasoning *Tests models for reasoning involving comparisons of objects. For example, P: The earth is larger than the moon but smaller than sun. H: The moon is smaller than sun. Here H should 'entail' P.*

Part Represents Whole: Improving the Evaluation of Machine Translation System Using Entropy Enhanced Metrics

Yilun Liu, Shimin Tao*, Chang Su, Min Zhang, Yanqing Zhao, Hao Yang
Huawei Translation Services Center, Beijing, China
{liuyilun3,taoshimin,suchang8,zhangmin186,
zhaoyanqing,yanghao30}@huawei.com

Abstract

Machine translation (MT) metrics often fail to achieve very high correlations with human assessments. In terms of MT system evaluation, most metrics pay equal attentions to every sample in an evaluation set, while in human evaluation, difficult sentences often make candidate systems distinguishable via notable fluctuations in human scores, especially when systems are competitive. We find that samples with high entropy values, which though usually count for less than 5%, tend to play a key role in MT evaluation: when the evaluation set is shrunk to only the high-entropy portion, correlations with human assessments are actually improved. Thus, in this paper, we propose a fast and unsupervised approach to enhance MT metrics using entropy, expanding the dimension of evaluation by introducing sentence-level difficulty. A translation hypothesis with a significantly high entropy value is considered difficult and receives a large weight in aggregation of system-level scores. Experimental results on five sub-tracks in the WMT19 Metrics shared tasks show that our proposed method significantly enhanced the performance of commonly-used MT metrics in terms of system-level correlations with human assessments, even outperforming existing SOTA metrics. In particular, all enhanced metrics exhibit overall stability in correlations with human assessments in circumstances where only competitive MT systems are included, while the corresponding standard metrics fail to correlate with human assessments[1].

1 Introduction

Automatic evaluation plays an indispensable role in the evaluation of machine translation (MT) systems, working as a proxy of human assessment as well as a promising approach to give instant feedback during the development of MT systems. However, it has been a challenge for automatic evaluations to correlate with human judgement. For instance, major discrepancy is detected between human assessments and automatic evaluations in terms of system ranking in WMT19 English-German evaluation tasks (Barrault et al., 2019). Experiments conducted by Mathur et al. (2020) and Thompson and Post (2020) further indicate that when inferior systems are excluded, current automatic metrics expect major falling on correlations with human referees, sometimes even down to the degree of negative correlations.

In order to improve the evaluation of MT systems, many meticulously designed metrics are proposed. However, popular MT metrics focus on a segment-level comparison between references and hypotheses, and output system-level scores by a simple arithmetic average over segment scores, ignoring the differences among samples in an evaluation set (Zhang et al., 2019; Sellam et al., 2020; Rei et al., 2020; Lo, 2020). In contrast, the core idea of assigning different weights to samples in a dataset is proven effective in the field of curriculum learning (Liu et al., 2020; Zhan et al., 2021b). For MT evaluation, it is not likely that human raters treat every source-reference pair equally. Those simple samples can be easily translated, leading to similar human scores given to different hypotheses, while the more challenging part in an evaluation set often distinguishes top candidates from inferior systems. Inspired by recent work of Zhan et al. (2021a), who determine the difficulty of sub-units in translation hypotheses by reviewing performances of corresponding sub-units among K candidate systems, we further introduce sentence-level difficulty into MT evaluation, which functions as a weight in the aggregation of final system scores. In determination of proposed sentence-level difficulty, instead of using an embedding-based approach similar to Zhan et al.'s, we adopt a fast and unsupervised entropy-based measurement.

* Corresponding author

[1]Code at https://github.com/lunyiliu/EE-Metrics

Findings of the Association for Computational Linguistics: AACL-IJCNLP 2022, pages 296–307
November 20–23, 2022.

In information theory, entropy is a measure of the uncertainty in a random variable. The entropy H of a discrete random variable X with possible values $x_1, x_2, ..., x_n$ is defined by Shannon (1948) as

$$H(X) = -\sum_{i=1}^{n} P(x_i) log_2 P(x_i), \quad (1)$$

where $P(x_i)$ is the probability for x_i to appear in the stream of characters. The entropy $H(X)$ will be higher if the values $x_1, x_2, ..., x_n$ are more decentralized. So the entropy can reflect the degree of disorder of variable X's distribution. Shannon's standard entropy is interpreted differently when being applied to MT evaluation (Zhao et al., 2019; Yu et al., 2015). Zhao et al. (2019) define x_i in Eq.(1) as the ith candidate among all possible translations of a source token X, while Yu et al. (2015) directly model one hypothesis produced by a system as random variable X and consider x_i as the ith sub-segment in the hypothesis matched with corresponding reference sentence. We follow the idea of chunk entropy in Yu et al. (2015). Compared with token difficulty in Zhan et al. (2021a), which requires a loop of K systems' hypotheses for each token, chunk entropy can determine the difficulty of hypotheses in constant time, reflecting both *adequacy* and *fluency* of a hypothesis. This will be further discussed in section 3.

In this paper, we propose entropy enhanced (EE) metric, a criterion that can enhance the performances of automatic MT metrics via a sentence-level translation difficulty weight determined by entropy. The difficulty score of each hypothesis-reference pair is acquired based on its chunk entropy and then serves as a weight in aggregation of the system-level score. Experiments carried on WMT19 evaluation tasks show that the EE version of BERTScore (Zhang et al., 2019) correlates better with system-level human ratings than DA-BERTScore (Zhan et al., 2021a) and outperforms SOTA metrics involved in WMT metrics shared tasks. Also, owing to the sentence-level difficulty dimension and the underlying essence of entropy, the proposed method should be compatible with a wide range of MT evaluation metrics. We test the effectiveness on several representative metrics in addition to BERTScore: BLEU (Papineni et al., 2002), CHRF (Popović, 2015) and METEOR (Denkowski and Lavie, 2014). Extensive experiments on five sub-tracks in WMT19 indicate an overall improvement on correlations with human evaluations when standard metrics are replaced by corresponding EE metrics. Moreover, in circumstances where only competitive systems are included, EE metrics alleviate the significant crash of standard metrics on correlations, and sometimes even achieve perfect agreements with human rankings.

It is surprising to see a straightforward implementation under the idea of sentence-level difficulty weights based on entropy, involving no deep-learning techniques, yet enhanced the performance of a BERT-based MT metric. The aim of this paper is to introduce the concepts and show the effective roles entropy and sentence-level difficulty play in enhancing MT evaluation quality, but not to explore optimal techniques integrating them into MT evaluation.

2 Related Work

Existing reference-based MT metrics can be roughly categorized into three types: matching-based metrics (Doddington, 2002; Papineni et al., 2002; Popović, 2015; Snover et al., 2006; Leusch et al., 2006; Denkowski and Lavie, 2014), embedding-based metrics (Zhang et al., 2019; Chow et al., 2019; Lo, 2019) and end-to-end metrics (Sellam et al., 2020; Rei et al., 2020). Matching-based metrics estimate quality of translation by hand-crafted features, such as n-grams, edit distance and alignments. BLEU (Papineni et al., 2002) is a classical criterion based on word-level n-gram matching between references and hypothesis and is widely employed as baselines in MT system evaluation, while CHRF (Popović, 2015) computes an F-score based on character-level n-grams. METEOR (Denkowski and Lavie, 2014) focuses on semantic matched chunks acquired by alignment, where lengths of chunks are dynamically determined and the limitation of maximum matching length of n-gram based metrics is partially relieved. In contrast, BERTScore and its variants (Zhang et al., 2019; Zhan et al., 2021a), owing to powerful contextual embedding acquired from modern language models, catch deep-level semantic information inside the translation pairs and achieve high rankings across MT evaluation benchmarks in terms of correlations with human assessments.

3 Our Proposed Method

3.1 Motivation

In the evaluation of MT systems, most automatic metrics rate a system by the average scores on sentences in the evaluation set, treating each segment equally, while assigning weights to samples has been successful in the practice of curriculum learning (Liu et al., 2020). Like examinations in real world, where questions are assigned different weights in the final score based on variant difficulties, evaluation metric of MT should also encourage systems that perform better on relatively difficult samples. Also, in competitive circumstance where candidates can handle most of the easy translations, difficult samples can better represent the abilities of candidates. In contrast to (Zhan et al., 2021a), where they compute the difficulty of each sub-unit inside a hypothesis, we directly assign different weights to high-entropy and low-entropy hypotheses so that the more difficult translations weight higher in the final system score.

When entropy is higher, the translation is faced with more uncertainty, leading to potential blemish in *adequacy* and *fluency*. Motivated by this mechanism, we use entropy as a measurement of sentence-level difficulty. Empirically, we found that there is a high negative correlation between entropy and BLEU score of a translation, as shown in Fig. 1. The linear fit shows that BLEU score exhibits a linear decline when entropy increases, with $|r| = 0.986$. When a certain source sentence is difficult to translate, the quality of generated hypothesis may be affected, causing a relatively low average BLEU score. So the difficult samples in an MT evaluation set tend to appear in the high-entropy area, and should be assigned a higher weight in the assessment.

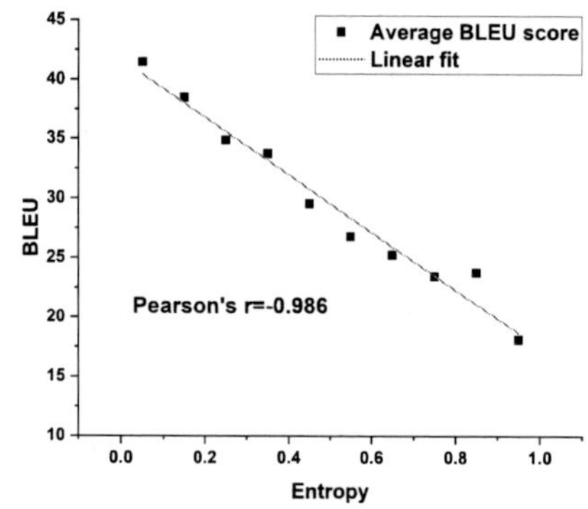

Figure 1: Average sentence-level BLEU score as a function of entropy. Each data point (e, b) represents mean BLEU across sentences with entropy in a range of $[e - 0.05, e + 0.05)$ among outputs of all 22 systems in WMT19 English→German evaluation set.

3.2 Entropy Enhanced MT Metric

In this section, we illustrate the working process of the proposed EE method. As shown in Fig. 2, first, entropy of each hypothesis (H) is calculated and guides the computation of the difficulty weight (W). Then, in aggregation of the final score, W is assigned to the corresponding hypothesis, weighting its sentence-level score.

Chunk Entropy Entropy measures uncertainty or disorderness of the distribution of a variable. In machine translation, a hypothesis generated from a source can be modeled as a random variable $X_h = \{w_1, w_2, ..., w_N\}$ with w_i $(i \in [1...N])$ denoting each token in the hypothesis. Given a reference $R = \{r_1, r_2, ..., r_M\}$, X_h can be rewritten as $X_h = x_1 \cdot u_1 \cdot x_2 \cdot u_2 \cdot ... \cdot u_m \cdot x_n$, where $x_i \in X = \{w_{s_i}, w_{s_i+1}, ..., w_{e_i} \mid i \in [1...n], 1 \leq s_i \leq e_i \leq N, \forall\, l \in [s_i, e_i], w_l \in R\}$, and $u_i \in U = \{w_{b_i}, w_{b_i+1}, ..., w_{o_i} \mid i \in [1...m], 1 \leq b_i \leq o_i \leq N, \forall\, l \in [b_i, o_i], w_l \notin R\}$. In other words, x_i denotes the ith continuously matched chunk with reference, while U denotes unmatched parts between aligned chunks. Since X and U are complementary, the distribution of X_h can be fully described by

$$P(x_i) = \frac{e_i - s_i + 1}{\sum_{j=1}^{n}(e_j - s_j + 1)}, \quad (2)$$

where $x_i \in X$ and s_i, e_i represent the start index and end index of the ith matched chunk, respectively. By substituting Eq. (2) into Eq. (1), we obtain the formula of chunk entropy (Yu et al., 2015)

$$H(X_h) = -\sum_{i=1}^{n} \frac{e_i - s_i + 1}{\sum_{j=1}^{n}(e_j - s_j + 1)} log(\frac{e_i - s_i + 1}{\sum_{j=1}^{n}(e_j - s_j + 1)}) \quad (3)$$

From Eq. (3), when a hypothesis is perfectly matched with corresponding reference, $P(x_i)$ from Eq. (2) is always 1 since there is only one chunk x_1, leading to a zero chunk entropy. Another corner case is that, when there is no token in common between the hypothesis and the reference, there is no matched chunk. In this case, we define $P(x_i)$ as 0 and the entropy approaches positive infinity, suggesting no certainty at all. In practice, a machine generated hypothesis often fails to preserve

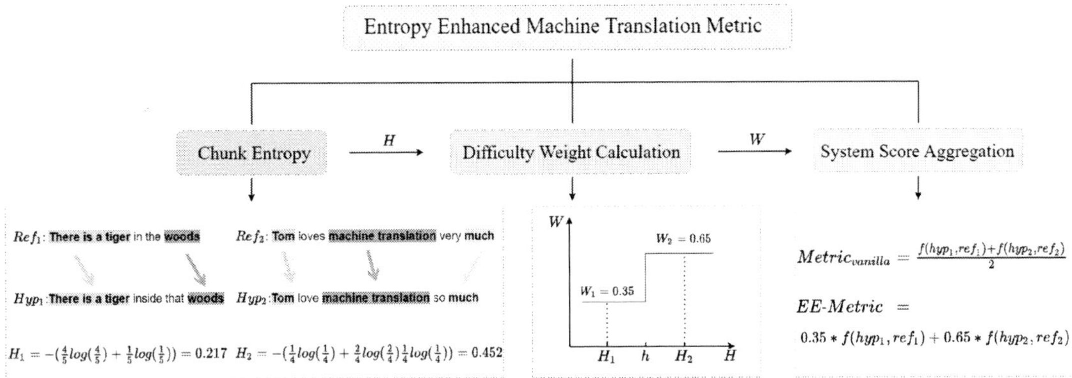

Figure 2: Workflow of proposed entropy enhancement method. $Metric_{standard}$ denotes the system-level score given by a standard MT metric with $f(\cdot)$ as the corresponding sentence-level score function, while $EE\text{-}Metric$ denotes system score aggregated by the corresponding EE metric.

full meaning of the source sentence, or suffers disfluency in the target language (Banchs et al., 2015). Table 1 shows two cases of ascended entropy caused by deficiencies in *adequacy* or *fluency*. The mistranslated word *sheep* in hypothesis 1 sharply increases entropy, while the incorrect word order in hypothesis 2 further deviates the entropy.

	Sentence	Deficiency	Entropy
Reference	A tiger stays in the woods	-	0
Hypothesis 1	A sheep **stays in the woods**	*adequacy*	0.217
Hypothesis 2	**A stays** sheep **in the woods**	*adequacy+fluency*	0.292

Table 1: Toy examples of how defect in *adequacy* and *fluency* may lead to increment in entropy of a translation. The matched words in hypotheses are in bold.

Difficulty Weight Calculation With the increasing of entropy, a segment might be faced with more fluctuations in human scores and tends to be representative of quality of systems. Thus, for a certain system, all its generated hypotheses can be divided into the difficult part and easy part by a threshold value of entropy. Those difficult hypotheses are most likely to reflect the ability of a system and distinguish performances among systems, and thus should be weighted higher than those in the easy part. Based on this idea, given $\chi_S = \{X_{h_1}^S, X_{h_2}^S, ..., X_{h_L}^S\}$ as the collection of hypotheses produced by system S in an evaluation set containing L segments, the difficulty weight function can be defined as a two-piece step function:

$$W(H) = \begin{cases} \frac{w}{N_e}, & H < h \\ \frac{1-w}{N_d}, & H \geq h, \end{cases} \quad (4)$$

where $N_e = |\chi_e|$ and $N_d = |\chi_d|$ are two normalization factors representing the number of easy and difficult hypotheses, respectively, with $\chi_e = \{X_{h_k} \mid H(X_{h_k}) < h, \forall X_{h_k} \in \chi_S\}$ and $\chi_d = \{X_{h_k} \mid H(X_{h_k}) \geq h, \forall X_{h_k} \in \chi_S\}$. And w is a balance coefficient ranging from 0 to 1, and h is the difficulty threshold.

In Eq. (4), h can be defined as the minimal entropy of a generally difficult translation among P systems $S_1, S_2, ..., S_P$. Let X_{s_k} be the source sentence of the kth sample in the evaluation set and $\hat{X}_{s_k} = \{X_{h_k}^{S_1}, X_{h_k}^{S_2}, ..., X_{h_k}^{S_P}\}$ be the collection of translation hypotheses all P systems produced. For system S_p, if $X_{h_k}^{S_p} \in \hat{X}_{s_k}$ has significantly high entropy among other hypotheses in $\hat{X}_{s_k}$, it is reasonable to doubt the quality of hypothesis $X_{h_k}^{S_p}$ and conclude that the source sentence X_{s_k} might be a difficult sample for system S_p. In contrast, when $\overline{H}_{\hat{X}_{s_k}}$ (the average entropy of hypotheses in $\hat{X}_{s_k}$) is significantly higher than that of hypotheses from other source sentences, source X_{s_k} becomes a generally difficult sample. For such a group of source sentences, the minimum value of average entropy among them is actually a threshold to classify easy hypotheses and difficult hypotheses, namely,

$$h = \min\{\overline{H}_{\hat{X}_{s_i}} \mid P(\overline{H}_{\hat{X}_{s_i}} < \overline{H}_{\hat{X}_{s_j}}) < \alpha, \forall i, j \in [1, L], j \neq i\}, \quad (5)$$

where α is a small constant, i.e., 0.05 or 0.01. So the collection of general difficult source sentences can be defined as $D_s = \{X_{s_k} \mid \forall k \in [1, L], \overline{H}_{\hat{X}_{s_k}} \geq h\}$.

From Eq. (5), we can see that the number of easy samples, i.e., when $H < h$, should be larger than the number of difficult ones. So in Eq. (4), we have

Metric	En→De			De→En			En→Zh			Zh→En			En→Gu		
	r	τ	ρ	r	τ	ρ	r	τ	ρ	r	τ	ρ	r	τ	ρ
BLEU	0.959	0.755	0.904	0.890	0.655	0.825	0.713	0.606	0.755	0.888	0.695	0.857	0.736	0.709	0.864
CHRF	0.983	0.772	0.919	0.917	0.639	0.822	0.822	0.545	0.650	0.952	0.714	0.868	0.851	0.709	0.891
METEOR	0.986	0.764	0.917	0.837	0.571	0.763	0.513	0.455	0.594	0.946	0.752	0.882	0.820	0.673	0.836
BERTScore	0.990	0.807	0.931	0.954	0.756	0.890	0.909	0.667	0.776	0.986	0.829	0.932	0.902	**0.818**	**0.945**
ESIM	0.991	-	-	0.941	-	-	0.931	-	-	0.988	-	-	-	-	-
YiSi-1	0.991	-	-	0.949	-	-	0.951	-	-	0.979	-	-	0.909	-	-
DA-BERTScore	0.991	0.798	0.930	0.951	0.807	0.932	-	-	-	-	-	-	-	-	-
EE-BLEU	0.965	0.772	0.913	0.882	0.740	0.872	0.727	0.697	0.797	0.907	0.733	0.875	0.787	0.709	0.873
EE-CHRF	0.983	0.798	0.933	0.894	0.639	0.770	0.831	0.545	0.706	0.965	0.752	0.900	0.886	0.745	0.909
EE-METEOR	0.987	0.816	0.940	0.792	0.706	0.854	0.611	0.545	0.636	0.951	0.810	0.936	0.884	0.636	0.836
EE-BERTScore	**0.994**	**0.859**	**0.952**	**0.956**	**0.840**	**0.947**	**0.952**	**0.818**	**0.888**	**0.989**	**0.905**	**0.975**	**0.939**	**0.818**	**0.945**

Table 2: Correlations with system-level human assessments on WMT19 metrics shared task. Best correlations in each column are highlighted in bold. The dashed line separates proposed EE metrics from others. Correlations of DA-BERTScore are directly from Zhan et al. (2021a), and ESIM, YiSi-1 from Ma et al. (2019). Numbers of participated systems for each language pairs are 22, 16, 12, 15 and 11, respectively.

$N_e \gg N_d$, which means simpler samples receive an extremely lower weight than difficult samples. Ideally, the value of $W(H)$ should only be determined by the average entropy of the difficult or simple sample group. To alleviate the distortion caused by unbalanced size between the difficult group and easy group, w, as shown in Eq. (4), is introduced as a balancing coefficient, and can be estimated by the distribution of average entropy within a given dataset. See more analysis on w in appendix B.

System Score Aggregation The designations of most automatic MT metrics focus on the segment level. When outputting system-level ratings, a conventional approach is to aggregate segment-level scores via simple arithmetic averaging. In contrast, the proposed EE metric, when computing system-level scores, assigns a normalized weight, computed by Eq. (4), to the score of each segment. Let $f(\cdot)$ be the unit score function, and the final score is given by

$$EE\text{-}Metric = \textstyle\sum_{i=1}^{L}(W(H(X_{h_i})) \cdot f(X_{h_i}, R_i)), \quad (6)$$

where $H(X_{h_i})$, the chunk entropy of the ith translation, is determined by Eq. (3). For standard metrics, the weight $W(H(X_{h_i}))$ is constantly $1/L$.

In cases where a metric outputs a system-level score based on a whole set of sentences with no segment-level scores involved, i.e., system-level score is directly given by $f(\chi_S)$, an alternative form of EE metric can be obtained via an equivalent transform of Eq. (6):

$$EE\text{-}Metric = wf(\chi_e) + (1 - w)f(\chi_d) \quad (7)$$

4 Experiments

Data We follow the experiment settings in Zhan et al. (2021a) for the convenience of comparison and evaluate the performance of EE metrics on WMT19 English↔German (En↔De) evaluation tasks, which is reported to be challenging due to major discrepancy between human assessments and automatic metrics in MT system ranking (Freitag et al., 2020; Barrault et al., 2019). Extended experiments on WMT19 English↔Chinese and English→Gujarati are also conducted to further validate the effectiveness of the proposed approach on both high-resource (En↔Zh) and low-resource (En→Gu) languages, without loss of generality. For every translation task, human ratings of participated systems, in the form of Direct Assessment (DA), are given and the goal of the experiment is to correlate with system-level human DA. Human assessors are asked to rate a given translation by how adequately it expresses the meaning of the corresponding reference translation or source language input on a rating scale of 0-100 (Barrault et al., 2019). For each translation task, there are 21523 assessments and 1592 assessments per participated system in average, given by a total of 1706 crowd-sourced workers. For the sake of quality control, about 20% of the efforts are wasted. Overall, the reliability of human annotators is still relatively high, with the lowest language pair still reaching 88% of workers showing no significant difference in scores for repeat assessment of the same translation.

Comparing Metrics To examine the universal feasibility of the proposed method, we employ four most commonly used MT evaluation metrics as backbones to implement corresponding EE met-

Metric / EE-Metric	En→ De (Top 4)			De→ En (Top 4)			Zh→ En (Top 4)			Average (× 100%)		
	r	τ	ρ	r	τ	ρ	r	τ	ρ	Δr	$\Delta\tau$	$\Delta\rho$
BLEU / EE-BLEU	-0.946 / -0.980	-0.667 / -0.667	-0.800 / -0.800	-0.787 / -0.341	-0.548 / -0.183	-0.632 / -0.316	-0.675 / 0.416	-0.333 / 0.333	-0.600 / 0.400	**+50.10%**	**+34.37%**	**+43.87%**
CHRF / EE-CHRF	-0.677 / 0.013	-0.667 / -0.333	-0.800 / -0.400	-0.659 / -0.240	-0.548 / -0.183	-0.632 / -0.316	-0.353 / 0.657	0.000 / 0.667	0.000 / 0.800	**+70.63%**	**+45.53%**	**+50.53%**
METEOR / EE-METEOR	-0.781 / 0.460	-0.667 / 0.667	-0.800 / 0.800	-0.648 / 0.035	-0.548 / 0.183	-0.632 / 0.316	-0.062 / 0.724	0.333 / 0.667	0.400 / 0.800	**+90.33%**	**+79.97%**	**+98.27%**
BERTScore / EE-BERTScore	-0.497 / 0.682	0.000 / 0.667	-0.200 / 0.800	0.567 / 0.479	0.183 / 0.183	0.316 / 0.316	0.095 / 0.895	0.333 / 1.000	0.400 / 1.000	**+63.03%**	**+44.47%**	**+53.33%**

Table 3: WMT19 system-level human correlations, for top 4 systems only. EE metrics alleviated or eliminated the phenomenon of negative correlations reported in recent literature and brought a significant improvement on correlations in **Average**.

rics: BLEU, CHRF, METEOR and BERTScore, as discussed in section 2. Enhanced versions of these metrics are denoted by EE-BLEU, EE-CHRF, EE-METEOR and EE-BERTScore, respectively, and are compared to their standard counterparts. We further compared proposed EE metrics with ESIM (Mathur et al., 2019) and YiSi-1 (Lo, 2020), since these two metrics consistently achieve remarkable performances across benchmarks of WMT19, WMT20 and WMT21. In addition, DA-BERTScore (Zhan et al., 2021a), which outperforms existing metrics in MT system evaluation owing to its unique token-level difficulty, is also involved in the comparison experiment.

Implementation Details In our implementation of EE metric, we use *fast_align*[2] (Dyer et al., 2013) to obtain aligned chunks between reference and hypothesis,.i.e., e_i, s_i in Eq. (3). For other metrics, we utilize *sacreBLEU*[3] (Post, 2018) toolkit to acquire BLEU and CHRF, and *NLTK*[4] toolkit to compute METEOR. For BERTScore[5], we use the default models except that the model for English is replaced with *deberta-xlarge-mnli* (He et al., 2021), as recommended by the authors of BERTScore.

Main Results Following the criterion of recent research (Zhan et al., 2021a; Freitag et al., 2020) as well as WMT official organization, three coefficients: Pearson's correlation r, Kendall's τ and Spearman's ρ, are used to validate system-level correlations with human DA as well as the agreement with human rankings. Values of the three coefficients range from -1 to 1, with a bigger positive value indicating a stronger positive correlation with human assessments, and a smaller negative value indicating a stronger negative correlation. Table 2 displays the main results. It can be seen that EE metrics achieve competitive correlations in the comparison. Among the enhanced metrics, EE-BERTScore further improves standard BERTScore and consistently outperforms other metrics, including DA-BERTScore and best metrics in WMT19, across different correlation measurements and translation directions. The case analysis in appendix A might help to reveal the practical meaning of the higher correlation numbers brought by EE metrics, by displaying how EE-BERTScore corrects the relative ranking of two systems given by BERTScore in En→ De. It should be noted that, even the improvement on correlations is little sometimes (e.g., r from 0.990 to 0.994 in En→ De for BERTScore), the number of corrected relative rankings between system pairs may be notable (seven more corrected cases after EE-BERTScore being applied in En→ De, similar to the one in appendix A).

The result in Table 2 shows that the four EE metrics bring average improvements of 1.65%, 4.96% and 3.18% on r, τ and ρ, respectively, compared with corresponding standard metrics across the five datasets. Despite divergent underlying mechanisms, all four backbone metrics experienced enhancement on correlations averaged across five translation tracks, which proves the universal feasibility of the proposed EE approach. The sentence-level difficulty introduced in the EE metric works as an extra dimension in system-level score aggregation, which, by assigning larger weights to high

[2]https://github.com/clab/fast_align
[3]https://github.com/mjpost/sacrebleu
[4]https://www.nltk.org/api/nltk.html
[5]https://github.com/Tiiiger/bert_score

entropy hypotheses, encourages systems that handle difficult translations well. This strategy, as well as the computation of entropy, is independent of particular MT metrics. Thus, the proposed method is compatible with a wide range of MT metrics.

Effect of Top-K Systems As reported in Ma et al. (2019), Thompson and Post (2020) and Mathur et al. (2020), in the circumstances where only top systems are preserved, most existing metrics suffer a drastic drop on correlations with human evaluations. This phenomenon is extremely notable in WMT19 En→De, De→En and Zh→En for top 4 systems, where metrics exhibit zero or even strong negative correlations with human assessments. Current research attributes this to unstable noises or outlier systems, while we found the proposed EE method helpful to alleviate the degradation of correlations owing to the extra sentence-level difficulty. In extreme competitive situations, all systems involved provide nearly perfect translations for most of the easy samples, while the high-entropy hypotheses, due to the fluctuation in translation qualities, tend to be key for humans to rank those top systems. In such a scenario, simple samples might even be harmful noises to the automatic evaluation, causing the failure of distinguishing top systems using existing metrics. In contrast, EE metrics focus on high-entropy parts in the evaluation set. Thus, as shown in Table 3, EE metrics avoid the negative correlations phenomenon (e.g., in En→De, r from -0.497 to 0.682 for BERTScore, ρ from -0.800 to 0.800 for METEOR) or even achieve perfect correlations with human rankings (e.g., in Zh→En, τ from 0.333 to 1.000, ρ from 0.400 to 1.000 for BERTScore). Averagely speaking, for top 4 systems, substantial improvements can be expected after proposed enhancement being applied.

Fig. 3 shows the process of degradation on correlations when low-performance systems are gradually removed. It can be seen that existing metrics fail to correlate with human judgments when K is smaller than 10, and start to exhibit negative correlation when K is smaller than or equal to 6. In contrast, EE-BERTScore only suffers minor drop on correlation and keeps effective with the decrease of K. The effectiveness of EE metrics further indicates the key role high-entropy samples play in an evaluation set.

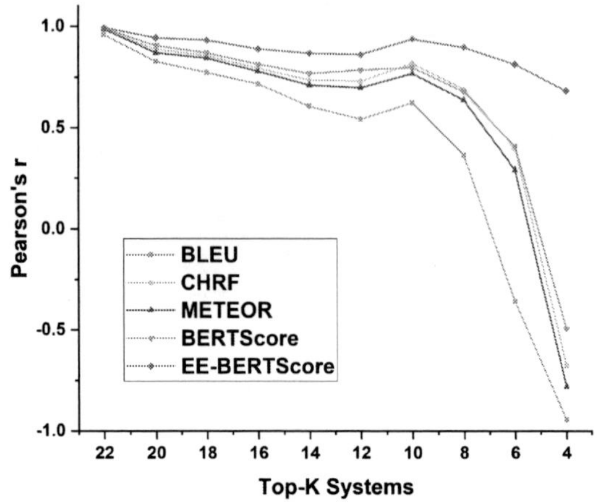

Figure 3: Effect on Pearson's correlation when only top-K systems are included in the En→De evaluation. EE-BERTScore keeps a high correlation with human judgments with the elimination of inferior systems.

5 Discussion

5.1 Estimation of Difficulty Threshold h

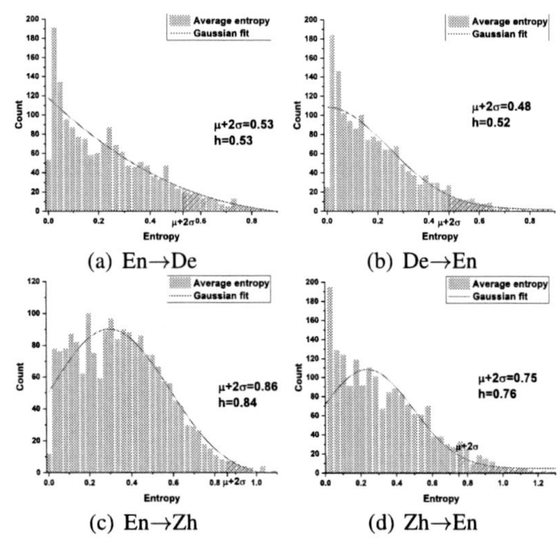

(a) En→De (b) De→En (c) En→Zh (d) Zh→En

Figure 4: Distributions of mean entropy averaged across systems, i.e., $\overline{H}_{\hat{X}_{s_i}}$, extracted from (a) En→De, (b) De→En, (c) En→Zh and (d) Zh→En, fitted according to $\mathcal{N}(\mu, \sigma)$. The areas in shadow are two standard deviations away from mean values.

The parameter h functions as the threshold entropy value for a hypothesis to be classified as difficult in an evaluation set. From Eq. (5), h is estimated by examining those samples whose average translation entropy is significantly higher than others. $\overline{H}_{\hat{X}_{s_i}}$, the average entropy of sample X_{s_i}, is calculated by

$$\overline{H}_{\hat{X}_{s_i}} = \frac{1}{P}(H(X_{h_i}^{S_1}) + H(X_{h_i}^{S_2}) + ... + H(X_{h_i}^{S_P})), \quad (8)$$

where $\forall p \in [1, P], X_{h_i}^{S_p} \in \hat{X}_{s_i}$. Since $X_{h_i}^{S_p}$, the translation hypothesis of the ith source sentence produced by system p, is modeled as a random variable in Eq. (2), by central limit theorem, the distribution of $\overline{H}_{\hat{X}_{s_i}}$ can be estimated according to $\mathcal{N}(\mu, \sigma)$, assuming that P, the number of candidate systems, is large enough and $X_{h_i}^{S_1}...X_{h_i}^{S_P}$ in the translation of a certain language pair is i.i.d. Let α in Eq. (5) be 0.05. Then according to three-sigma rule of normal distribution, the two standard deviations serve as a borderline separating easy and difficult translations, with the difficult samples (around 5%) possessing significantly higher entropy. So h is estimated by

$$h = \mu + 2\sigma \tag{9}$$

Empirically obtained h is in accordance with Eq. (9), as shown in Fig. 4. We search for optimal h within a range from 0 to 1 for every language pair. For the high-resource language pairs (En↔De, En↔Zh), the group of candidate systems is relatively large, and thus $\mu + 2\sigma$ provides a good estimation of h, with an average error of only 0.018 on the four evaluation sets.

5.2 Ablation Study

Table 4 shows the result of ablation experiments conducted in order to acquire a better understanding of mechanisms of the proposed EE metric.

Approach	h	w	r	τ	ρ
BERTScore	-	-	0.990	0.807	0.931
EE-BERTScore	0.53	0.35	**0.994**	**0.859**	**0.952**
			Different Thresholds		
$h = \mu + 2.5\sigma$	0.83	0.35	0.929	0.477	0.630
$h = \mu + 1.5\sigma$	0.23	0.35	**0.991**	**0.816**	**0.949**
			Group Remove		
Only easy	0.53	1.00	0.988	0.781	0.920
Only difficult	0.53	0.00	0.990	**0.833**	**0.939**
			Module Ablation		
w/o entropy	-	-	0.984	0.721	0.870
w/o difficulty	-	-	0.437	0.252	0.366

Table 4: Ablation experiment of EE-BERTScore conducted on WMT19 En→De evaluation. Values in bold indicate better correlations compared to standard BERTScore.

Different Thresholds A higher threshold means fewer difficult hypotheses. When h is 2.5-σ away from mean, only most difficult samples (around 1.24%) are weighted. Since extreme high entropy is often caused by noises in references or miscalculated alignments in hypotheses, these samples cannot reflect performance of systems and thus cause a drop in agreement with human rankings. Reducing the threshold, on the other hand, amplifies contributions of some less representative segments without damaging the core difficult group and results in a minor improvement on correlations.

Group Remove By setting w to 1 or 0, difficult or easy hypotheses are zero weighted, and thus we can examine the standalone role of each group. As shown in Table 4, **completely removing the low-entropy hypotheses still leads to an improvement on correlations as compared to the standard metrics**. While this result further supports our intuition in this paper that the portion of high-entropy samples might be enough to determine the performance of MT systems, it is interesting to explore the possibility of distillation of an MT evaluation set to enhance its ability to distinguish candidates in the future.

Module Ablation Instead of calculating the entropy, we randomly divide easy and difficult groups while maintaining the original group sizes (repeated 1000 times). For the removal of difficulty, we directly compute the correlations between human ratings and average entropy of a system. The result indicates that the effectiveness of the proposed EE method relies on both entropy and sentence-level difficulty.

5.3 Stability Across MT Systems

Compared with standard reference-based metrics, which compute the score of an MT system utilizing only its hypotheses and the references, EE metrics introduce additional information of other participated systems in the computation of system-level scores, i.e., the score assigned to a certain MT system may vary with its competitors. To better understand the impact caused by the difference and possible limitations of EE metrics, we investigated the stability of EE metrics across MT systems by applying EE metrics on a series of random subsets of systems. Specifically, we randomly choose n systems (n=4,6,8,10) in En→ De (22 systems) and test the correlations with human scores for all four metrics (standard and EE versions). For each n, we repeat 100 times, i.e., 100 random combinations of n systems. The results in Table 5 show that EE Metrics steadily outperform standard metrics, with average improvements of 6.90%, 8.25%,

Metric	Random 4			Random 6			Random 8			Random 10		
	r	τ	ρ	r	τ	ρ	r	τ	ρ	r	τ	ρ
BLEU	0.883	0.794	0.855	0.921	0.763	0.861	0.912	0.744	0.865	0.928	0.758	0.880
CHRF	0.902	0.744	0.819	0.945	0.780	0.879	0.944	0.789	0.895	0.959	0.784	0.898
METEOR	0.904	0.777	0.848	0.929	0.760	0.865	0.945	0.768	0.884	0.944	0.765	0.893
BERTScore	0.929	0.839	0.886	0.943	0.815	0.901	0.957	0.830	0.916	0.957	0.814	0.914
EE-BLEU	0.878	0.752	0.813	0.935	0.769	0.868	0.942	0.761	0.873	0.952	0.782	0.897
EE-CHRF	0.934	0.820	0.877	0.959	0.780	0.894	0.958	0.791	0.894	0.961	0.793	0.906
EE-METEOR	**0.945**	0.814	0.873	0.950	0.809	0.896	0.957	0.803	0.906	0.957	0.805	0.912
EE-BERTScore	**0.945**	**0.886**	**0.921**	**0.969**	**0.892**	**0.941**	**0.966**	**0.855**	**0.926**	**0.977**	**0.870**	**0.943**

Table 5: Performances of MT metrics when only **Random n** systems are involved from 22 systems in En→ De translation task. For each n, the correlations are averaged across 100 random combinations of systems.

4.59% and 6.57% on correlations, for n=4, 6, 8, 10, respectively.

6 Conclusion and Future Work

In this paper, we find that the high-entropy hypotheses, though holding only a minor portion in an evaluation set, play a significant role in terms of correlations with human judgments in MT evaluation. By rebalancing the weights between low-entropy and high-entropy hypotheses, an entropy enhancing approach for MT metrics is proposed. Experimental results on five sub-tracks in WMT19 metric tasks show that our proposed approach successfully enhances the performance of popular MT metrics and achieves remarkable correlations with human assessments, especially in the evaluation of competitive systems. Our analysis introduces the concept of sentence-level difficulty into MT evaluation and reveals the importance of difficult samples in system-level evaluations.

There are several directions for future exploration. First, entropy-based difficulty can work as a measurement to the quality of an MT evaluation set. If an evaluation set contains more high-entropy samples, its ability to rank systems is better. Second, using entropy, we can dig the hard samples out of an evaluation set and, by filtering easy samples, we can make a distillation of evaluation set. Third, there is still room for optimization in calculation of entropy and difficulty weights.

References

Rafael E. Banchs, Luis F. D'Haro, and Haizhou Li. 2015. Adequacy–fluency metrics: Evaluating mt in the continuous space model framework. *IEEE/ACM Transactions on Audio, Speech, and Language Processing*, 23(3):472–482.

Loïc Barrault, Ondřej Bojar, Marta R. Costa-jussà, Christian Federmann, Mark Fishel, Yvette Graham, Barry Haddow, Matthias Huck, Philipp Koehn, Shervin Malmasi, Christof Monz, Mathias Müller, Santanu Pal, Matt Post, and Marcos Zampieri. 2019. Findings of the 2019 conference on machine translation (WMT19). In *Proceedings of the Fourth Conference on Machine Translation (Volume 2: Shared Task Papers, Day 1)*, pages 1–61, Florence, Italy. Association for Computational Linguistics.

Julian Chow, Lucia Specia, and Pranava Madhyastha. 2019. WMDO: Fluency-based word mover's distance for machine translation evaluation. In *Proceedings of the Fourth Conference on Machine Translation (Volume 2: Shared Task Papers, Day 1)*, pages 494–500, Florence, Italy. Association for Computational Linguistics.

Michael Denkowski and Alon Lavie. 2014. Meteor universal: Language specific translation evaluation for any target language. In *Proceedings of the Ninth Workshop on Statistical Machine Translation*, pages 376–380, Baltimore, Maryland, USA. Association for Computational Linguistics.

George Doddington. 2002. Automatic evaluation of machine translation quality using n-gram co-occurrence statistics. In *Proceedings of the Second International Conference on Human Language Technology Research*, HLT '02, page 138–145, San Francisco, CA, USA. Morgan Kaufmann Publishers Inc.

C. Dyer, V. Chahuneau, and N. A. Smith. 2013. A simple, fast, and effective reparameterization of ibm model 2. *proc naacl.*

Markus Freitag, David Grangier, and Isaac Caswell. 2020. BLEU might be guilty but references are not innocent. In *Proceedings of the 2020 Conference on Empirical Methods in Natural Language Processing (EMNLP)*, pages 61–71, Online. Association for Computational Linguistics.

Pengcheng He, Xiaodong Liu, Jianfeng Gao, and Weizhu Chen. 2021. Deberta: Decoding-enhanced bert with disentangled attention. In *International Conference on Learning Representations*.

Gregor Leusch, Nicola Ueffing, and Hermann Ney. 2006. CDER: Efficient MT evaluation using block movements. In *11th Conference of the European Chapter of the Association for Computational Linguistics*, pages 241–248, Trento, Italy. Association for Computational Linguistics.

Xuebo Liu, Houtim Lai, Derek F Wong, and Lidia S Chao. 2020. Norm-based curriculum learning for neural machine translation. In *Proceedings of the 58th Annual Meeting of the Association for Computational Linguistics*, pages 427–436.

Chi-kiu Lo. 2019. YiSi - a unified semantic MT quality evaluation and estimation metric for languages with different levels of available resources. In *Proceedings of the Fourth Conference on Machine Translation (Volume 2: Shared Task Papers, Day 1)*, pages 507–513, Florence, Italy. Association for Computational Linguistics.

Chi-kiu Lo. 2020. Extended study on using pretrained language models and yisi-1 for machine translation evaluation. In *Proceedings of the Fifth Conference on Machine Translation*, pages 895–902.

Qingsong Ma, Johnny Wei, Ondřej Bojar, and Yvette Graham. 2019. Results of the wmt19 metrics shared task: Segment-level and strong mt systems pose big challenges. In *Proceedings of the Fourth Conference on Machine Translation (Volume 2: Shared Task Papers, Day 1)*, pages 62–90.

Nitika Mathur, Timothy Baldwin, and Trevor Cohn. 2019. Putting evaluation in context: Contextual embeddings improve machine translation evaluation. In *Proceedings of the 57th Annual Meeting of the Association for Computational Linguistics*, pages 2799–2808.

Nitika Mathur, Timothy Baldwin, and Trevor Cohn. 2020. Tangled up in BLEU: Reevaluating the evaluation of automatic machine translation evaluation metrics. In *Proceedings of the 58th Annual Meeting of the Association for Computational Linguistics*, pages 4984–4997, Online. Association for Computational Linguistics.

Kishore Papineni, Salim Roukos, Todd Ward, and Wei-Jing Zhu. 2002. Bleu: a method for automatic evaluation of machine translation. In *Proceedings of the 40th annual meeting of the Association for Computational Linguistics*, pages 311–318.

Maja Popović. 2015. chrF: character n-gram F-score for automatic MT evaluation. In *Proceedings of the Tenth Workshop on Statistical Machine Translation*, pages 392–395, Lisbon, Portugal. Association for Computational Linguistics.

Matt Post. 2018. A call for clarity in reporting BLEU scores. In *Proceedings of the Third Conference on Machine Translation: Research Papers*, pages 186–191, Brussels, Belgium. Association for Computational Linguistics.

Ricardo Rei, Craig Stewart, Ana C Farinha, and Alon Lavie. 2020. COMET: A neural framework for MT evaluation. In *Proceedings of the 2020 Conference on Empirical Methods in Natural Language Processing (EMNLP)*, pages 2685–2702, Online. Association for Computational Linguistics.

Thibault Sellam, Dipanjan Das, and Ankur Parikh. 2020. BLEURT: Learning robust metrics for text generation. In *Proceedings of the 58th Annual Meeting of the Association for Computational Linguistics*, pages 7881–7892, Online. Association for Computational Linguistics.

Claude Elwood Shannon. 1948. A mathematical theory of communication. *The Bell system technical journal*, 27(3):379–423.

Matthew Snover, Bonnie Dorr, Rich Schwartz, Linnea Micciulla, and John Makhoul. 2006. A study of translation edit rate with targeted human annotation. In *Proceedings of the 7th Conference of the Association for Machine Translation in the Americas: Technical Papers*, pages 223–231, Cambridge, Massachusetts, USA. Association for Machine Translation in the Americas.

Brian Thompson and Matt Post. 2020. Automatic machine translation evaluation in many languages via zero-shot paraphrasing. In *Proceedings of the 2020 Conference on Empirical Methods in Natural Language Processing (EMNLP)*, pages 90–121.

Hui Yu, Xiaofeng Wu, Wenbin Jiang, Qun Liu, and Shouxun Lin. 2015. Improve the evaluation of translation fluency by using entropy of matched subsegments. *CoRR*, abs/1508.02225.

Runzhe Zhan, Xuebo Liu, Derek F Wong, and Lidia S Chao. 2021a. Difficulty-aware machine translation evaluation. In *Proceedings of the 59th Annual Meeting of the Association for Computational Linguistics and the 11th International Joint Conference on Natural Language Processing (Volume 2: Short Papers)*, pages 26–32.

Runzhe Zhan, Xuebo Liu, Derek F Wong, and Lidia S Chao. 2021b. Meta-curriculum learning for domain adaptation in neural machine translation. In *Proceedings of the AAAI Conference on Artificial Intelligence*, volume 35, pages 14310–14318.

Tianyi Zhang, Varsha Kishore, Felix Wu, Kilian Q Weinberger, and Yoav Artzi. 2019. Bertscore: Evaluating text generation with bert. In *International Conference on Learning Representations*.

Yang Zhao, Jiajun Zhang, Chengqing Zong, Zhongjun He, and Hua Wu. 2019. Addressing the under-translation problem from the entropy perspective. In *Proceedings of the AAAI Conference on Artificial Intelligence*, volume 33, pages 451–458.

A Case Study

The two cases in Table 6 illustrate how EE-BERTScore enhances the performance of BERTScore via the discussed strategy. The system-level score of MSRA's translation system, given by BERTScore, is higher than that of Facebook's, leading to a misalignment with human rankings (Facebook ranks the 1st in En→De while MSRA ranks the 4th). In contrast, EE-BERTScore successfully recognizes Facebook as the superior system. From Table 6, Facebook outperforms MSRA in difficult translations (Case 1), despite defeated in easier sentences (Case 2). In BERTScore, the difference of segments are ignored and all segment-level scores are of the same contribution to the final system score. As a result, the final score of Facebook is slightly lower than MSRA. In human evaluation, ratings for simple hypotheses produced by different systems tend to similar, because these hypotheses are already in good alignment with the reference. While scores of the difficult ones, implying a challenging segment in source language, often separate top systems from inferior candidates. Utilizing this strategy, EE-BERTScore amplified the contribution of difficult segments in case 1 for both systems (0.039%→0.276%, 0.042%→0.311%), while reduces the contribution of simpler hypotheses (0.037%→0.015%, 0.034%→0.013%). Consequently, Facebook exceeded MSRA owing to its advantages in difficult hypotheses.

As discussed in section 3.2, in the proposed method, determination of sentence-level difficulty relies on entropy values. In Table 6, entropy values of hypotheses in case 1 are higher than h, the threshold determined by Eq. (5), while the easy hypotheses in case 2 hold smaller values of entropy. The reason is that hypotheses in case 2 are divided into smaller groups of aligned chunks, and the lengths of chunks are more evenly distributed, as highlighted by the colored boxes, implying a less disordered distribution of hypothesis and lower entropy of translation.

B Estimation of Coefficient w

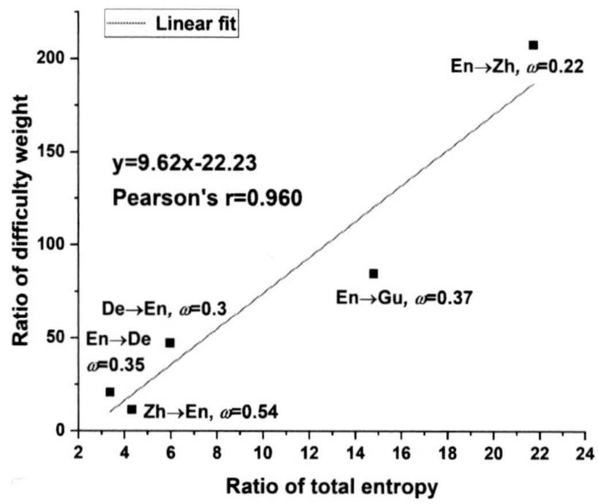

Figure 5: An empirical fit of Eq. (10). The x-axis, **Ratio of total entropy**, represents the right side of Eq. (10), and y-axis denotes left side of Eq. (10). Data points are computed based on the five WMT19 evaluation sets and corresponding empirically obtained w.

The determination of sentence-level difficulty weight, i.e., W in Eq. (4), relies on h and w. In section 5.1, based on definitions in Eq. (5), we pre-

	BERTScore		**EE-BERTScore**		**Sentence**	**Entropy**
	Seg. / Sys.	**Contrib.**	**Seg. / Sys.**	**Contrib.**		
Case 1: Difficult sentence contribute more in calculation of EE-BERTScore						
Src	-	-	-	-	Likening the suit to "extortion," Plasco said his wife was just two months off having a baby and was in a "very difficult situation."	-
Ref	-	-	-	-	Plasco sagte, dass seine Frau im siebten Monat schwanger und nicht in bester Verfassung gewesen sei, und bezeichnete die Klage als „Erpressung“.	-
MSRA	0.648 / **0.830**	0.039%	0.648 / 0.799	0.276%	Plasco verglich den Anzug mit „Erpressung“ und sagte, seine Frau sei nur zwei Monate von einem Baby entfernt und befinde sich in einer „sehr schwierigen Situation“.	0.663
Facebook	0.689 / 0.828	0.042%	0.689 / **0.801**	0.311%	Plasco verglich die Klage mit „Erpressung“ und sagte, seine Frau habe gerade zwei Monate kein Baby bekommen und befinde sich in einer „sehr schwierigen Situation“.	0.642
Case 2: Easy sentence contribute less in calculation of EE-BERTScore						
Src	-	-	-	-	When that momentum gets going one way, it puts a lot of pressure on those middle matches.	-
Ref	-	-	-	-	Wenn sich erstmal eine Eigendynamik entwickelt hat, übt das großen Druck auf die mittleren Matches aus.	-
MSRA	0.609 / **0.830**	0.037%	0.609 / 0.799	0.015%	Wenn diese Dynamik in eine Richtung geht, übt sie viel Druck auf diese mittleren Spiele aus.	0.459
Facebook	0.555 / 0.828	0.034%	0.555 / **0.801**	0.013%	Wenn dieses Momentum in eine Richtung geht, setzt es diese mittleren Spiele stark unter Druck.	0.226

Table 6: Examples from the En→ De evaluation, where EE-BERTScore corrects the ranking of two systems given by BERTScore. Seg. and Sys. denotes segment-level and system-level scores given by metric, respectively, and Contrib. denotes contribution of the particular segment to final system score(e.g. $0.039\% = 0.648 \div 1997 \div 0.830, 0.311\% = 0.689 \times 0.65 \div 180 \div 0.801$). The difficulty level of cases are determined by their entropy value. Chunks indicate the alignments with reference.

sented an estimation of optimal h. Now, w, the balancing coefficient which is introduced to alleviate the distortion caused by unbalanced size between the difficult group and easy group, theoretically satisfies the following equation:

$$\frac{(1-w)(L-|D_s|)}{w|D_s|} \propto \frac{\sum_{t=1, X_{s_t} \notin D_s}^{L} \overline{H}_{\hat{X}_{s_t}}}{\sum_{k=1, X_{s_k} \in D_s}^{L} \overline{H}_{\hat{X}_{s_k}}} \tag{10}$$

Eq. (10) guarantees that the weights W assigned to difficult group and easy group are determined by the ratio of average entropy in two groups. From Eq. (10), difficulty weight W on a particular evaluation set is fully determined by distribution of average entropy within a given dataset, via different balancing coefficients w. When the total entropy of difficult samples in an evaluation set decreases, which means the translations in this evaluation set are easier, the weights assigned on difficult samples should also be higher to better distinguish difficult hypotheses from easy ones. In experiment, we search for optimal w within a range from 0 to 1 for every language pair. The empirically obtained optimal w is highly related to the statistics described in Eq. (10) with $|r| = 0.960$, as shown in Fig. 5. Linear fit based on the five WMT19 evaluation sets provides an empirical estimation of w:

$$w = \frac{R_{\overline{N}}}{9.62 R_{\overline{H}} + R_{\overline{N}} - 22.23} \tag{11}$$

where $R_{\overline{H}} = \frac{\sum\{\overline{H}_{\hat{X}_{s_t}} \mid \forall t \in [1,L], X_{s_t} \notin D_s\}}{\sum\{\overline{H}_{\hat{X}_{s_k}} \mid \forall k \in [1,L], X_{s_k} \in D_s\}}$, $R_{\overline{N}} = \frac{L-|D_s|}{|D_s|}$, are defined in Eq. (10) and fully determined by distribution of translation entropy within an evaluation set.

C Parameters

Parameters	En→ De	De→ En	En→ Zh	Zh→ En	En→ Gu
h	0.53	0.52	0.84	0.76	0.72
w	0.35	0.30	0.22	0.54	0.37

Table 7: Parameters used in our experiment. All experimentally acquired parameters are in accordance with our theoretical analysis.

D Additional Experimental Results

Metric	En→ De			Zh→ En		
	r	τ	ρ	r	τ	ρ
BLEU	0.831	0.714	0.821	0.360	0.357	0.571
CHRF	0.917	0.810	0.893	0.425	0.357	0.524
METEOR	0.854	0.619	0.714	0.678	0.643	0.738
BERTScore	0.754	0.429	0.536	0.742	0.643	0.810
EE-BLEU	0.810	0.714	0.821	0.322	0.214	0.405
EE-CHRF	0.890	0.810	0.893	0.510	0.357	0.524
EE-METEOR	0.805	0.619	0.714	0.770	0.786	0.857
EE-BERTScore	0.724	0.429	0.536	0.895	0.714	0.833

Table 8: Performances of EE Metrics on WMT 2020 news test (without human), using human MQM scores as the ground truth. Parameters h and w are computed according to Eq. 9 and Eq. 11. The result shows an average of 2.67 % improvements on correlations with human MQM scores after the enhancement on the standard metrics being applied.

Metric	En→ De			Zh→ En			En→ Ru		
	r	τ	ρ	r	τ	ρ	r	τ	ρ
BLEU	0.918	0.897	0.967	0.549	0.282	0.429	0.576	0.385	0.521
CHRF	0.813	0.692	0.868	0.366	0.154	0.297	0.768	0.451	0.653
METEOR	0.813	0.718	0.885	0.432	0.282	0.385	0.772	0.495	0.670
BERTScore	0.911	0.795	0.945	0.577	0.308	0.484	0.776	0.538	0.692
EE-BLEU	0.910	0.821	0.934	0.528	0.333	0.484	0.720	0.451	0.587
EE-CHRF	0.764	0.692	0.857	0.361	0.231	0.313	0.725	0.560	0.741
EE-METEOR	0.869	0.718	0.874	0.416	0.231	0.308	0.784	0.582	0.736
EE-BERTScore	0.876	0.846	0.945	0.630	0.487	0.626	0.655	0.473	0.644

Table 9: Performances of EE Metrics on WMT 2021 news test (without human), using human MQM scores as the ground truth and ref A as the reference. Parameters h and w are computed according to Eq. 9 and Eq. 11. The result shows an average of 4.48 % improvements on correlations with human MQM scores after the enhancement on the standard metrics being applied.

Memformer: A Memory-Augmented Transformer for Sequence Modeling

Qingyang Wu [1], **Zhenzhong Lan** [2], **Kun Qian** [1] **Jing Gu** [3]
Alborz Geramifard [4] **Zhou Yu** [1]
[1] Columbia University, [2] Westlake University
[3] University of California, Santa Cruz, [4] Facebook AI
{qw2345,kq2157,zy2461}@columbia.edu, jgu110@ucsc.edu
lanzhenzhong@westlake.edu.cn, alborzg@fb.com

Abstract

Transformers have reached remarkable success in sequence modeling. However, these models have efficiency issues as they need to store all the history token-level representations as memory. We present Memformer, an efficient neural network for sequence modeling, that utilizes an external dynamic memory to encode and retrieve past information. Our model achieves linear time complexity and constant memory space complexity when processing long sequences. We also propose a new optimization scheme, memory replay back-propagation (MRBP), which promotes long-range back-propagation through time with a significantly reduced memory requirement. Experimental results show that Memformer has achieved comparable performance compared against the baselines by using 8.1x less memory space and 3.2x faster on inference. Analysis of the attention pattern shows that our external memory slots can encode and retain important information through timesteps.

1 Introduction

Memory plays a fundamental role in human cognition. Humans perceive and encode sensory information into a compressed representation stored in neurons, and later we effectively retrieve the stored information to accomplish various tasks. The formation of memory involves complex cognitive processes. Modeling and studying the behavior of human memory is still a challenging research problem in many areas.

Many researchers have attempted to incorporate memory systems in artificial neural networks. Early works like recurrent neural networks (RNN) (Rumelhart et al., 1988) including LSTM (Hochreiter and Schmidhuber, 1997) and GRU (Chung et al., 2014) model temporal sequences with their internal compressed state vector as memory. However, they are limited in preserving the long-term information due to the memory bottleneck. To alleviate this limitation, more powerful memory network architectures such as Neural Turing Machine (NTM) (Graves et al., 2014), Differential Neural Computer (DNC) (Graves et al., 2016) have been proposed by leveraging a large external dynamic memory. Unfortunately, due to their complex memory interaction mechanism, they are not widely used for down-stream tasks at present.

More recently, Vaswani et al. (2017) propose Transformer by discarding the use of recurrence and memory. Instead, it computes all the $\mathcal{O}(N^2)$ paired dependencies in a sequence with self-attention (Bahdanau et al., 2015). Transformers have achieved great success in various natural language processing tasks. Nevertheless, the quadratic computation complexity can be costly. Some works try to address the limitations of self-attention, including Reformer, Sparse Transformer, Longformer, Linformer (Child et al., 2019; Kitaev et al., 2020; Wang et al., 2020), etc. They successfully reduce the complexity of self-attention and thus enable processing longer sequences. However, most of them still require linear memory space complexity.

Transformer-XL (Dai et al., 2019) re-introduces the concept of memory and recurrence. It caches each layer's hidden states of self-attention into a fixed-size queue and re-uses them in the later attention computation. However, the memory as raw hidden states cannot effectively compress high-level information. Thus, Transformer-XL in practice needs a massive memory size to perform well, and spends huge computation in using its memory. Compressive Transformer (Rae et al., 2020) improves upon Transformer-XL by further compressing its memories into fewer vectors via a compression network. However, as mentioned in the papers, both Transformer-XL and Compressive Transformer discard the information from the distant past, which causes a theoretical maximum temporal range given the fixed memory size.

Findings of the Association for Computational Linguistics: AACL-IJCNLP 2022, pages 308–318
November 20–23, 2022.

Inspired by the previous external memory networks, we propose Memformer, which incorporates a fixed-size external dynamic memory combined with the recent Transformer architecture. Memformer interacts with its external dynamic memory through the memory reading and writing modules. Also, we introduce a forgetting mechanism to improve the effectiveness of memorizing new information. By utilizing recurrence and a fixed-size memory, our model has a theoretically infinite temporal range of memorization and implies a linear computation complexity and constant memory space complexity. As the traditional back-propagation through time (BPTT) has an unaffordable memory cost in our model, we introduce a new optimization scheme, memory replay back-propagation (MRBP), to significantly reduce the memory cost in training recurrent neural networks with large size of memory representations.

We evaluate Memformer on the autoregressive image generation and language modeling task. Experimental results show that Memformer performs on par with Transformer and Transformer XL with large memory size, while being much more efficient in terms of computation speed and memory space consumption. We also conduct an analysis showing that Memformer can retain information for an extended period.

2 Related Work

This section introduces some recent research directions that aim to alleviate the quadratic cost of self-attention. Moreover, we analyze their assumptions and limitations under the autoregressive setting to provide a broader view of these models.

2.1 Sparse Attention

One influential direction is to replace the full self-attention with sparse attention patterns to speed up the computation. Child et al. (2019) proposed Sparse Transformer, using a block sparse attention pattern to reduce the computation complexity to $\mathcal{O}(N\sqrt{N})$. Later, Longformer (Beltagy et al., 2020) and Big Bird (Zaheer et al., 2020) further explored this direction and proposed an even more sparse attention pattern to reduce the cost to $\mathcal{O}(N)$. They introduced global tokens to encode the information from the entire sequence and kept the self-attention to the closest k tokens and the global tokens to achieve linear complexity. Although linear sparse attention's theoretical soundness is proven for bidirectional encoders, it does not hold for the decoder. The main reason is that the global tokens cannot leak information to the future tokens in the autoregressive setting, where all the tokens can only see their previous tokens. Thus, linear sparse attention cannot guarantee a token to see its all past tokens. Only Sparse Transformer here with $\mathcal{O}(N\sqrt{N})$ complexity can theoretically cover all the past tokens for the sequence generation.

2.2 Linear Attention

Another direction is focusing on improving the softmax operation in the self-attention. Linformer (Wang et al., 2020) reduced the complexity to $\mathcal{O}(N)$ by projecting the entire sequence to a constant size of keys and values, but this method has not been applied to autoregressive decoding. Performer (Choromanski et al., 2020) and Linear Transformer (Katharopoulos et al., 2020) used a linear dot-product of kernel feature maps to replace softmax. However, for Linear Transformer under the autoregressive setting, it needs to compute the cumulative summation to aggregate the history information. This assumption is too strong if the input sequence is long and the length is not fixed. After thousands of steps, the numerical values can become very large due to the summation, causing overflow and gradient instability.

2.3 Recurrence and Memory

Applying recurrence and memory to Transformers is an orthogonal direction comparing to the efficient attention approaches. If the memory size is constant, recurrence enables the model to have constant memory complexity during inference. There are mainly two works exploring this direction. Transformer-XL (Dai et al., 2019) used relative positional encoding and consisted of a segment-level recurrence mechanism to encode beyond a fixed-length context. Compressive Transformer (Rae et al., 2020) extended from Transformer-XL by further compressing the previous cached hidden states to achieve a longer context. However, using past hidden states as memory would cause a theoretical maximum temporal range of context, meaning that a token is not guaranteed to see all the past tokens. Thus, in practice, Transformer-XL and Compressive Transformer need huge memory size to achieve good performance.

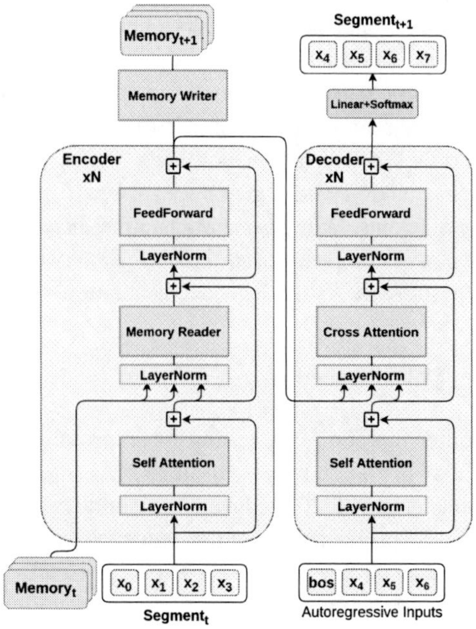

Figure 1: Memformer overall architecture for the encoder (left) and decoder (right). Transformer encoder is responsible to interact with the memory. Sequence modeling is achieved by predicting the next segment conditioned to the current segment and memory.

2.3.1 Dynamic Memorization

Within the scope of memory networks, there are dynamic memorization techniques. Different from Transformer-XL which stores the token-level history representations as memory, dynamic memorization does not have a theoretical upper bound for the temporal range. Neural Turing Machine (NTM) (Graves et al., 2014) and Differential Neural Computer (DNC) (Graves et al., 2016) are two early models that can control external memory resources to achieve long-lasting memory. However, their complex memory mechanisms cause them to be slow and unstable during training. In this work, we propose a dynamic memorization mechanism to achieve more efficient memory representations.

3 Methods

In this section, we first formalize the segment-level sequence modeling. Then, we present the memory reading and writing modules. Finally, we explain the memory replay back-propagation (MRBP) algorithm used for training.

3.1 Segment-level Sequence Modeling

Given a sequence of N tokens $x_1, x_2, \ldots, x_N$, an standard language model learns the joint probability of the sequence by taking the product of each token's probability conditioned to the previous tokens, which is defined as:

$$P(x) = \prod_t P(x_t | x_{<t})$$

When we have a large external memory system to store the history information, we cannot afford to interact with memory for every token. The workaround is to process a long sequence at the segment level. We can split a sequence into T segments and each segment has L tokens: $s_t = \{x_{t,1}, x_{t,2}, \ldots x_{t,L}\}$.

Because a bidirectional encoder is better at extracting word representations, we apply a Transformer encoder-decoder here. The encoder's role is to encode the segment s_t and inject the information into the memory M_t, while it also retrieves past information from the previous timestep's memory M_{t-1}. The encoder's final output will be fed into the decoder's cross attention layers to predict the token probabilities of the next timestep's segment s_{t+1} with standard language modeling.

$$\begin{aligned} M_t &= \text{Encoder}(s_t, M_{t-1}) \\ P(s_t | s_{<t}) &= \prod_{n=1:L} P_{\text{Decoder}}(x_{t,n} \mid x_{t,<n}, M_{t-1}) \\ P(x) &= \prod_{t=1:T} P_{\text{Model}}(s_t | s_{<t}) \end{aligned}$$

At each timestep, given a segment as the input, the model needs to continue that segment by generating the next text segment, and the generated segment will be fed back into the model again. Since the memory stores all the past information, we can autoregressively generate all the token segments in a sequence. In this fashion, we can model the entire long sequence.

Figure 1 shows the overall architecture of Memformer. We will further explain each component and the implementation in the following sections.

3.2 External Dynamic Memory Slots

External dynamic memory (EDM) is a data structure that stores high-level representations of past inputs. "Dynamic" means that the model interactively encodes and retrieves the information from memory in a recurrent manner. This contrasts with static memory design, where the memory is stored statically and does not change during the inference.

In our design, we allocate a constant k number of vectors as the external dynamic memory. At each

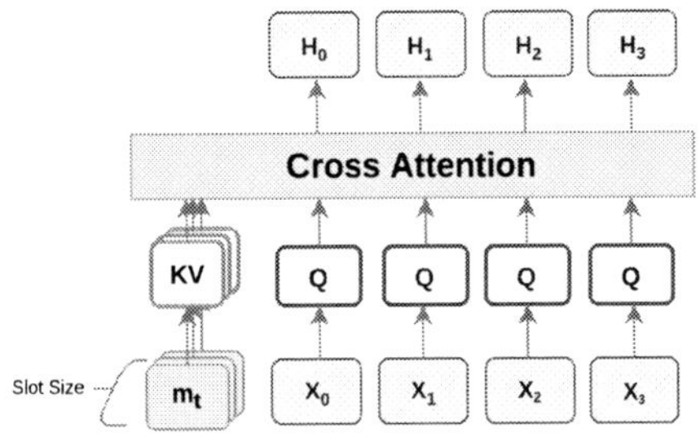

Figure 2: Memory Reading. The input sequence x attends over all the memory slots to retrieve the history information.

timestep t, we can have $M_t = [m_t^0, m_t^0, \ldots, m_t^k]$. For each sample in the batch, they have separate memory representations. Therefore, similar to RNN during inference, the memory consumption will be constant no matter how long the input sequence is. We name it memory slots because each slot is working individually to have different representations. The following sections will explain how the model manages to read and write this memory.

3.3 Memory Reading

For each input segment sequence, the model needs to read the memory to retrieve relevant past information. We leverage the cross attention to achieve this function:

$$Q_x, K_M, V_M = xW_Q, M_tW_K, M_tW_V \quad (1)$$

$$A_{x,M} = \text{MHAttn}(Q_x, K_M) \quad (2)$$

$$H_x = \text{Softmax}(A_{x,M})\, V_M \quad (3)$$

MHAttn refers to Multi-Head Attention. Memory slot vectors are projected into keys and values, and the input sequence x is projected into queries. Then the input sequence's queries attend over all the memory slots' key-value pairs to output the final hidden states. This enables the model to learn the complex association of the memory. Figure 2 shows the illustration.

Memory reading occurs multiple times as every encoder layer incorporates a memory reading module. This process ensures a higher chance of successfully retrieving the necessary information from a large memory.

3.4 Memory Writing

Memory writing involves a slot attention module to update memory information and a forgetting method to clean up unimportant memory information. Contrary to memory reading, memory writing only happens at the last layer of the encoder. This helps to store the high-level contextual representations into the memory. In practice, we append some classification tokens to the input sequence to better extract the sequence representations.

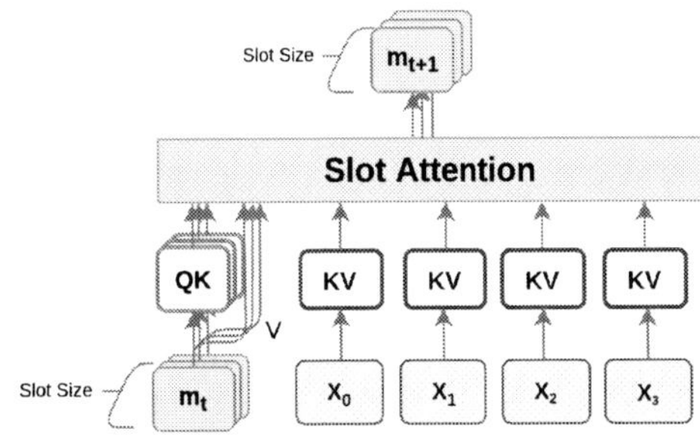

Figure 3: Memory Writing. Each memory slot attends over itself and the input sequence representations to produce the next timestep's memory slot.

3.4.1 Update via Memory Slot Attention

Figure 3 shows how memory is updated with the current segment's information. Each slot is separately projected into queries and keys. The segment token representations are projected into keys and values. Slot attention means that each memory slot can only attend to itself and the token representations. Thus, each memory slot cannot write its own information to other slots directly, as memory slots should not be interfering with each other.

$$Q_{m^i}, K_{m^i} = m^iW_Q, m^iW_K \quad (4)$$

$$K_x, V_x = xW_K, xW_V \quad (5)$$

$$A'_{m^i} = \text{MHAttn}(Q_{m^i}, [K_{m^i}; K_x]) \quad (6)$$

When we compute the final attention scores, we divide the raw attention logits with a temperature τ ($\tau < 1$). This operation sharpens the attention distribution, which makes the writing focusing on fewer slots or token outputs.

$$A_{m^i} = \frac{exp(A'_i/\tau)}{\sum_j exp(A'_j/\tau)} \quad (7)$$

Finally, the next timestep's memory is collected with by attention.

$${m_{t+1}^i}' = \text{Softmax}(A_{x,M})\, [m_t^i; V_x] \quad (8)$$

The attention mechanism helps each memory slot to choose to whether preserve its old information or update with the new information.

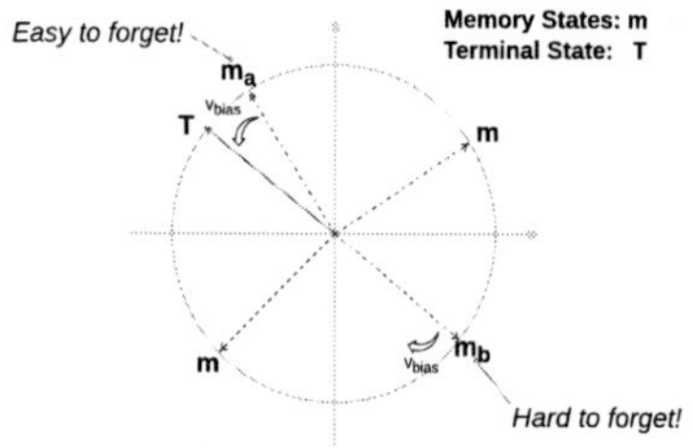

Figure 4: Illustration of forgetting. Memory slot m_a is easy to be forgotten, while m_b is hard to be forgotten.

3.4.2 Implementation of Memory Writer

Since each memory slot stores the information independently, we design a special type of sparse attention pattern. Each slot in the memory can only attend over itself and the encoder outputs. It aims to preserve the information in each slot longer over the time horizon. When a slot only attends itself during writing, the information will not be changed in the next timestep.

3.4.3 Forgetting Mechanism

Forgetting is crucial for learning as it helps to filter out trivial and temporary information to memorize more important information. LSTM introduces the forget gate (Gers et al., 2000) to reset its memory state, and the forget gate is proven to be the most important component in the LSTM (van der Westhuizen and Lasenby, 2018).

In this work, we introduce a forgetting mechanism called *Biased Memory Normalization* (BMN), specifically designed for our slot memory representations. We normalize the memory slots for every step to prevent memory weights from growing infinitely and maintain gradient stability over long timesteps. To help forget the previous information, we add a learnable vector v_{bias} to it. Also, naturally the initial state v^i_{bias} is after normalization.

$$m^i_{t+1} \leftarrow m^i_{t+1} + v^i_{\text{bias}}$$

$$m^i_{t+1} \leftarrow \frac{m^i_{t+1}}{||m^i_{t+1}||}$$

$$m^i_0 \leftarrow \frac{v^i_{\text{bias}}}{||v^i_{\text{bias}}||}$$

In Figure 4, we illustrate the forgetting mechanism with the learnable bias vector v_{bias}. Because of the normalization, all memory slots will be projected onto a sphere distribution. Here, we demonstrate with a 2D sphere for simplicity.

v_{bias} here controls the speed and the direction of forgetting. When adding v_{bias} to the memory slot, it would cause the memory to move along the sphere and forget part of its information. If a memory slot is not updated for many timesteps, it will eventually reach the terminal state T unless the new information is injected. The terminal state is also the initial state, and it is learnable.

The speed of forgetting is controlled by the magnitude of v_{bias} and the cosine distance between m'_{t+1} and v_{bias}. For example, m_b is nearly opposite to the terminal state, and thus would be hard to forget its information. m_a is closer to the terminal state and thus easier to forget.

Algorithm 1: Memformer Update

Input: rollout=$[x_t, x_{t+1}, \ldots, x_T]$: `a list containing previous inputs`
memories=$[M_t, M_{t+1}, \ldots, M_T]$: `memory from the previous`

▷ `Initialize a list for back-propagation`
replayBuffer = $[M_t]$
▷ `Forward pass & no gradient`
for $t = t, t+1, \ldots, T-1$ **do**
  M_{t+1}, _ = Model(x_t, M_t)
  replayBuffer.append(M_{t+1})
end
▷ `Backward pass with gradient`
$\nabla M_{t+1} = 0$
for $t = T, T-1, \ldots, t+1, t$ **do**
  ▷ `Recompute`
  M_{t+1}, O_t = Model(x_t, M_t)
  $loss$ = $f_{loss}(O_t)$
  $loss$.backward()
  M_{t+1}.backward(∇M_{t+1})
  ∇M_{t+1} = ∇M_t
end
▷ `Update and pop the oldest memories`
memories = replayBuffer
memories.pop()

3.5 Memory Replay Back-Propagation

Memformer relies on the external memory to process a sequence. At inference time, there is no additional memory cost because of the fixed-size memory design. Nevertheless, during training, it would require back-propagation through time (BPTT) so that the memory writer network can be trained to retain long-term information. The problem with traditional BPTT is that it unrolls the entire computational graph during the forward pass and stores all the intermediate activations. This process would lead to impractically huge memory consumption for Memformer.

A favorable existing approach to eliminate this problem is gradient checkpointing (Chen et al., 2016). The algorithm can significantly reduce the memory cost of a large neural network. However, the standard gradient checkpointing still needs to compute all the nodes in the computational graph and store unnecessary activations during the forward pass. We propose Memory Replay Back-Propagation (MRBP), a more efficient variant of gradient checkpointing, by replaying the memory at each timestep to accomplish gradient back-propagation over long unrolls.

The algorithm takes an input with a rollout $x_t, x_{t+1}, \ldots, x_T$ and the previous memories $M_t, M_{t+1}, \ldots, M_T$ if already being computed. MRBP only traverses the critical path in the computational graph during the forward pass and recomputes the partial computational graph for the local timestep during the backward pass. It then obtains each timestep's memory and stores those memories in the replay buffer. The full algorithm is described in Algorithm 1. The experiments of memory cost reduction with MRBP is in the Appendix A.

4 Experiments

4.1 Computation and Memory Cost

We experimented the computation and memory cost of Vanilla Transformer, Transformer-XL, and Memformer. For Vanilla Transformer, it has to increase the input sequence length to encode more tokens. Its cost is $O(N^2)$ where N is the sequence length. Transformer-XL and Memformer use memory to store the history information, and the input sequence length is a constant value. Thus, their computation complexity is $O(N)$.

As a trade-off, for both Transformer-XL and Memformer, the memory size is then an important factor to affect the capacity of storing the history information. Transformer-XL stores the past hidden states for all layers as memory. If L is the number of layers, and K is the memory size, then the memory cost is $O(K \times L)$. Memformer only stores K vectors as memory with cost $O(K)$.

To better illustrate the difference, Figure 5 shows the number of FLOPs (floating-point operations) versus sequence length (left) and the GPU memory consumption versus memory size on the actual models (right). The sequence length is increased from 128 to $8,192$. Here, Memformer and Transformer-XL had the same number of parameters. From the figure, Vanilla Transformer has the largest computation cost growth. Memformer's costs grew linearly with the sequence length and achieved better efficiency than Transformer-XL. Then, we compared the GPU memory consumption. We tested the memory size ranging from 64 to $2,048$, with a batch size 16 for better visibility of memory cost difference. Transformer-XL's memory consumption grew rapidly with the memory size, while Memformer is more efficient with large memory size. In large memory size setting, Memformer uses 8.1x less memory space.

4.2 Autoregressive Image Generation

Model	#FLOPs (B)	Perplexity ↓
LSTM	52.5	1.698
Transformer Decoder	41.3	1.569
Transformer-XL		
memory=56	5.6	1.650
memory=224	15.6	1.618
memory=784	49.1	1.611
Memformer		
4 encoder+8 decoder	**5.0**	**1.555**
Memformer Ablation		
2 encoder+6 decoder		
memory=64	3.9	1.594
memory=32	3.9	1.600
memory=16	3.9	1.604
memory=1	3.9	1.627
4 encoder+4 decoder	3.6	1.628
w/o memory	1.8	1.745
temperature=1.0	3.9	1.612
w/o forgetting	3.9	1.630
w/o multi-head	3.9	1.626

Table 1: Results for autoregressive image generation. Our method only takes about 10% FLOPs of the best Transformer-XL model.

Recent research (Ramesh et al., 2021) demonstrates the approach of treating an image as a long sequence for image generation. Thus, we evaluated our model on the MNIST (LeCun and Cortes, 2010) image generation task with sequence modeling. Each image of size 28×28 was reshaped into a sequence of 784 tokens, and the 8-bit gray-scale was turned to a 256 vocabulary size.

For the baselines, LSTM had 4 layers and 512 hidden size. Transformer Decoder had 8 layers

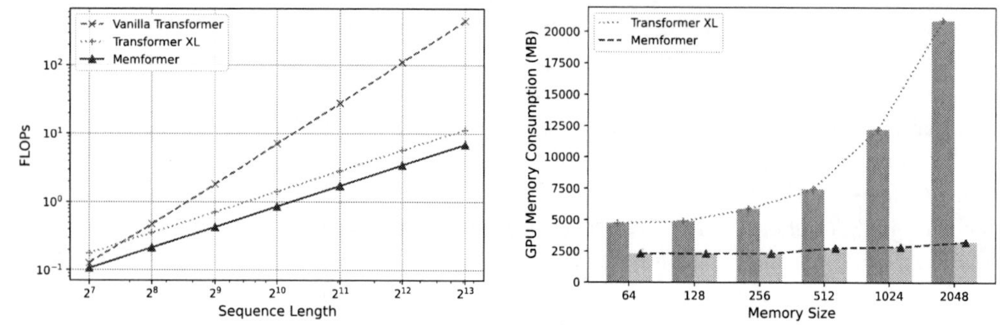

Figure 5: Comparison of the number of FLOPs and GPU memory consumption for Vanilla Transformer, Transformer-XL, and Memformer.

and could take all the 784 tokens as the input. Transformer-XL had 8 layers. All the models had the same 128 hidden size, 4 attention heads, 32 head size, and 256 feedforward size. Memformer was tested with default memory size 64. The default memory writer temperature was set to 0.25. We also conducted ablation studies to examine the contribution of various components.

Model	#FLOPs (B)	PPL ↓
Transformer-XL base		
memory=1600	250	23.95
memory=1024	168	23.67
memory=512	94	23.94
memory=256	58	25.39
memory=128	39	25.60
memory=32	26	27.22
Compressive Transformer		
memory= 512 compress=512	172	23.23
Memformer		
4 encoder + 16 decoder	**54**	**22.74**
Memformer Ablation		
4 encoder + 12 decoder	48	23.91
memory=512	35	23.30
w/o memory	31	25.57

Table 2: Experimental results on language modeling. Our method is 3.2 times faster here.

Table 1 shows the experimental results. We report median from three trials. Our Memformer with 4 layers of encoder and 8 layers of decoder achieved the best performance (1.555), while only using nearly 10% of FLOPs compared to the best Transformer XL baseline with memory size of 784 (1.611). Its performance was even better than the Transformer Decoder with the entire input sequence. We hypothesized that this observation was due to the extra parameters from the 4 layers of encoder. Therefore, we conducted an ablation study by having various numbers of encoder and decoder layers. If we reduce the number of decoder layers in Memformer (4 encoder+4 decoder), the performance dropped as shown (1.628). Results indicated that the number of decoder layers was important for the performance. Overall, Memformer outperformed Transformer-XL with a much lower computation cost.

The performance increased as the memory size increased. Moreover, when we completely removed the memory, Memformer performed terribly, signifying the importance of the encoded information in the memory. Other components such as forgetting mechanism, memory writer temperature, multi-head attention were proven to contribute to the final performance as well.

4.3 Language Modeling

We also conducted experiments on WikiText-103 (Merity et al., 2017), which is a long-range language modeling benchmark. It contains $28K$ articles with an average length of $3.6K$ tokens per article. Due to the limitation of computational resources, we are unable to experiment on the more recent PG19 (Rae et al., 2020) dataset. To study the computation cost and memory efficiency, we test with Transformer-XL base with 16 layers, 512 hidden size, 2,048 feedforward size, 64 head size, and 8 heads. The details are in the Appendix.

Memformer has the same hidden size, feedforward size, head size, and number of heads. We also re-implement a version of Compressive Transformer of the same size as there is no official implementation. The memory length is set to 512, and the compressive memory length is 512. The compression ratio is 4. The target sequence length for all models was set to 128. We test the performance under various memory sizes.

Table 2 summarizes the results on WikiText-103 test set. We report the number of inference FLOPs (billions) and perplexity median from three trials. As Transformer-XL's memory size increased, the perplexity dropped as expected, but the the number of FLOPs grew quickly because the attention length was also increased. The perplexity stopped decreasing after we increased the memory size to $1,600$. We suspect that since the average number of tokens in WikiText-103 is $3,600$, a larger memory size would bring noises and hence did not further improve the performance compared to a smaller memory size $(1,024)$. Compressive Transformer achieves slightly better performance with extra FLOPS compared to Transformer XL with memory size 1024.

Memformer with 4 encoders, 16 decoders, and $1,024$ memory size achieved the best performance. It required much less computation cost (54) and performed much better than Transformer-XL with $1,024$ memory size, supporting that Memformer has a more efficient memory representation.

In the ablation studies, to compensate for the extra number of encoder layers, we reduced the number of decoder layers to 12. The final performance was close to Transformer-XL, but Memformer used a much smaller number of FLOPs. Also, memory size was important for Memformer, as the performance dropped after the memory size is reduced to 512. When we completely removed the memory module by removing the memory writer and memory reading cross attention, the perplexity increased to 25.57, which is similar to Transformer-XL with a memory size of 128.

4.3.1 Memory Writer Analysis

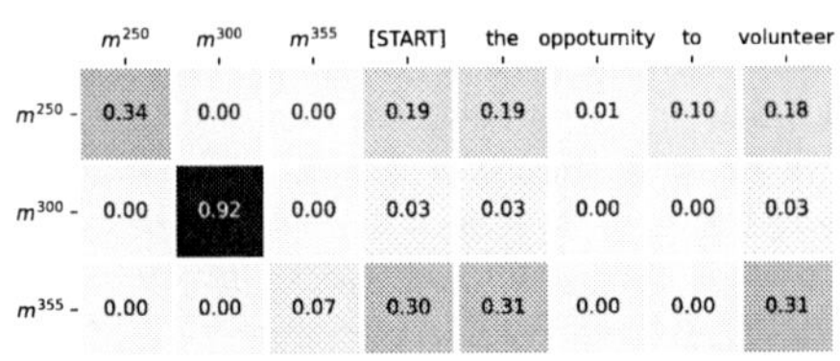

Figure 6: Visualization of three types of memory slots.

It is interesting to interpret how memory writer updates the memory slots. We analyzed the attention outputs from the memory writer. We roughly categorized the memory slots into three different types and visualized three examples with normalized attention values in Figure 6.

We picked the memory slot m^{250}, m^{300} , and m^{355}. During the middle of processing a document, around 60% to 80% of the memory slots are like m^{300}. Their attention focused on themselves, meaning that they were not updating for the current timestep. This suggests that the memory slots can carry information from the distant past.

For the second type, the memory slot m^{250} had some partial attention over itself and the rest of attention over other tokens. This type of memory slots is transformed from the first type of memory slots, and at the current timestep they aggregate information from other tokens.

The third type of memory slot looks like m^{355}. It completely attended to the input tokens. At the beginning, nearly all memory slots belong to this type, but later only 5% to 10% of the total memory slots account for this type. We also found that the forgetting vector's bias for m^{355} had a larger magnitude (3.20) compared to some other slots (1.15), suggesting that the information was changing rapidly for this memory slot.

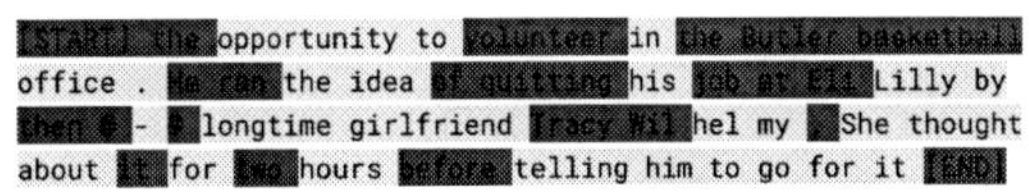

Figure 7: Visualization of the memory writer's attention.

To better understand how the slot m^{355} update its information, we visualized its attention on an example input sequence in Figure 7. It shows that this slot learned a compressed representation of the sentence by attending over some named entities and verbs, which is consistent with human cognition.

5 Conclusion

We presented Memformer, an autoregressive model which utilizes an external dynamic memory to efficiently process long sequences with a linear time complexity and constant memory complexity. Along with Memformer, we introduced a new optimization scheme, Memory Replay Back-propagation, which enables training recurrent neural networks with large memory. Experimental results showed that Memformer achieved comparable performance with great efficiency, and was able to preserve information from the distant past.

With the enhanced memory capacity, we believe that Memformer can spark interesting works that rely on recurrence and autoregressive modeling, which will benefit tasks such as dialog and interactive systems.

References

Dzmitry Bahdanau, Kyunghyun Cho, and Yoshua Bengio. 2015. Neural machine translation by jointly learning to align and translate. In *3rd International Conference on Learning Representations, ICLR 2015, San Diego, CA, USA, May 7-9, 2015, Conference Track Proceedings*.

Iz Beltagy, Matthew E. Peters, and Arman Cohan. 2020. Longformer: The long-document transformer. *CoRR*, abs/2004.05150.

Tianqi Chen, Bing Xu, Chiyuan Zhang, and Carlos Guestrin. 2016. Training deep nets with sublinear memory cost. *CoRR*, abs/1604.06174.

Rewon Child, Scott Gray, Alec Radford, and Ilya Sutskever. 2019. Generating long sequences with sparse transformers. *URL https://openai.com/blog/sparse-transformers*.

Krzysztof Choromanski, Valerii Likhosherstov, David Dohan, Xingyou Song, Andreea Gane, Tamás Sarlós, Peter Hawkins, Jared Davis, Afroz Mohiuddin, Lukasz Kaiser, David Belanger, Lucy Colwell, and Adrian Weller. 2020. Rethinking attention with performers. *CoRR*, abs/2009.14794.

Junyoung Chung, Caglar Gulcehre, Kyunghyun Cho, and Yoshua Bengio. 2014. Empirical evaluation of gated recurrent neural networks on sequence modeling. In *NIPS 2014 Workshop on Deep Learning, December 2014*.

Zihang Dai, Zhilin Yang, Yiming Yang, Jaime G. Carbonell, Quoc Viet Le, and Ruslan Salakhutdinov. 2019. Transformer-xl: Attentive language models beyond a fixed-length context. In *Proceedings of the 57th Conference of the Association for Computational Linguistics, ACL 2019, Florence, Italy, July 28- August 2, 2019, Volume 1: Long Papers*, pages 2978–2988. Association for Computational Linguistics.

Felix A. Gers, Jürgen Schmidhuber, and Fred A. Cummins. 2000. Learning to forget: Continual prediction with LSTM. *Neural Comput.*, 12(10):2451–2471.

Alex Graves, Greg Wayne, and Ivo Danihelka. 2014. Neural turing machines. *CoRR*, abs/1410.5401.

Alex Graves, Greg Wayne, Malcolm Reynolds, Tim Harley, Ivo Danihelka, Agnieszka Grabska-Barwinska, Sergio Gomez Colmenarejo, Edward Grefenstette, Tiago Ramalho, John P. Agapiou, Adrià Puigdomènech Badia, Karl Moritz Hermann, Yori Zwols, Georg Ostrovski, Adam Cain, Helen King, Christopher Summerfield, Phil Blunsom, Koray Kavukcuoglu, and Demis Hassabis. 2016. Hybrid computing using a neural network with dynamic external memory. *Nat.*, 538(7626):471–476.

Sepp Hochreiter and Jürgen Schmidhuber. 1997. Long short-term memory. *Neural Comput.*, 9(8):1735–1780.

Angelos Katharopoulos, Apoorv Vyas, Nikolaos Pappas, and François Fleuret. 2020. Transformers are rnns: Fast autoregressive transformers with linear attention. In *Proceedings of the 37th International Conference on Machine Learning, ICML 2020, 13-18 July 2020, Virtual Event*, volume 119 of *Proceedings of Machine Learning Research*, pages 5156–5165. PMLR.

Nikita Kitaev, Lukasz Kaiser, and Anselm Levskaya. 2020. Reformer: The efficient transformer. In *8th International Conference on Learning Representations, ICLR 2020, Addis Ababa, Ethiopia, April 26-30, 2020*. OpenReview.net.

Yann LeCun and Corinna Cortes. 2010. MNIST handwritten digit database.

Stephen Merity, Caiming Xiong, James Bradbury, and Richard Socher. 2017. Pointer sentinel mixture models. In *5th International Conference on Learning Representations, ICLR 2017, Toulon, France, April 24-26, 2017, Conference Track Proceedings*. OpenReview.net.

Jack W. Rae, Anna Potapenko, Siddhant M. Jayakumar, Chloe Hillier, and Timothy P. Lillicrap. 2020. Compressive transformers for long-range sequence modelling. In *8th International Conference on Learning Representations, ICLR 2020, Addis Ababa, Ethiopia, April 26-30, 2020*. OpenReview.net.

Aditya Ramesh, Mikhail Pavlov, Gabriel Goh, Scott Gray, Chelsea Voss, Alec Radford, Mark Chen, and Ilya Sutskever. 2021. Zero-shot text-to-image generation.

David E. Rumelhart, Geoffrey E. Hinton, and Ronald J. Williams. 1988. *Learning Representations by Back-Propagating Errors*, page 696–699. MIT Press, Cambridge, MA, USA.

Jos van der Westhuizen and Joan Lasenby. 2018. The unreasonable effectiveness of the forget gate. *CoRR*, abs/1804.04849.

Ashish Vaswani, Noam Shazeer, Niki Parmar, Jakob Uszkoreit, Llion Jones, Aidan N. Gomez, Lukasz Kaiser, and Illia Polosukhin. 2017. Attention is all you need. In *Advances in Neural Information Processing Systems 30: Annual Conference on Neural Information Processing Systems 2017, 4-9 December 2017, Long Beach, CA, USA*, pages 5998–6008.

Sinong Wang, Belinda Z. Li, Madian Khabsa, Han Fang, and Hao Ma. 2020. Linformer: Self-attention with linear complexity. *CoRR*, abs/2006.04768.

Manzil Zaheer, Guru Guruganesh, Kumar Avinava Dubey, Joshua Ainslie, Chris Alberti, Santiago Ontanon, Philip Pham, Anirudh Ravula, Qifan Wang, Li Yang, et al. 2020. Big bird: Transformers for longer sequences. *Advances in Neural Information Processing Systems*, 33.

A MRBP Efficiency Test

In this section, we test MRBP's efficiency by comparing against the standard back-propagation through time (BPTT) and the standard gradient checkpointing (GC) algorithm. This algorithm is useful for Memformer to reduce memory requirement because of the back-propagation through several timesteps. We use the Memformer model and set all the hyper-parameters to be the same.

Method	GPU Memory (MB)	Speed (relative)
BPTT	16,177	x1.00
GC	9,885	x0.48
MRBP	7,229	x0.90

Table 3: Memory Replay Back-Propagation performance comparison. Evaluation speed is based on seconds per sample. BPTT means back-propagation through time. GC means gradient checkpointing.

The back-propagation through time (BPTT) approach is the fastest because it does not need recomputation. However, it costs the most amount of memory due to unrolling the entire computational graph. While gradient checkpointing can save huge amount of memory, it is much slower than the other two methods (x0.48). In contrast, our MRBP saves more GPU memory with only slight speed degeneration (x0.90).

B Training Details

	Image Generation	Language Modeling
batch size	256	128
warm-up steps	1,000	1,0000
learning rate	1e-3	1e-3
dropout	0.1	0.1
memory length	8	1,024
temperature	0.25	0.125
time horizon	8	8
weight decay	0.01	0.01
max gradient norm	1.0	1.0
training steps	10,000	150,000

Table 4: Training Details

We trained our model on NVIDIA V100 16GB and 2080Ti 11GB. The training for image generation took about one day on one GPU. The training for language modeling took approximately four days on four GPUs.

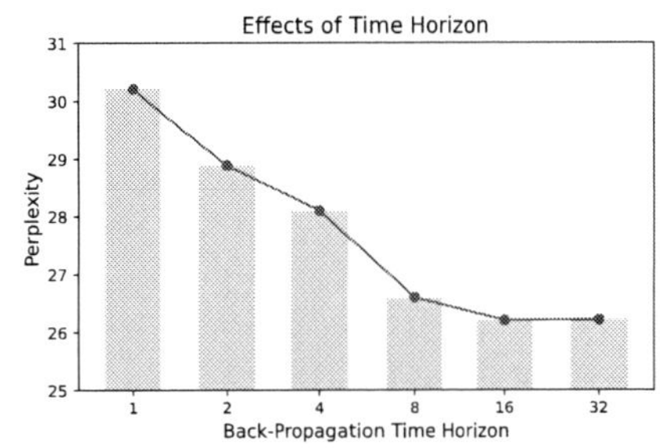

(a) Effects of different time horizons

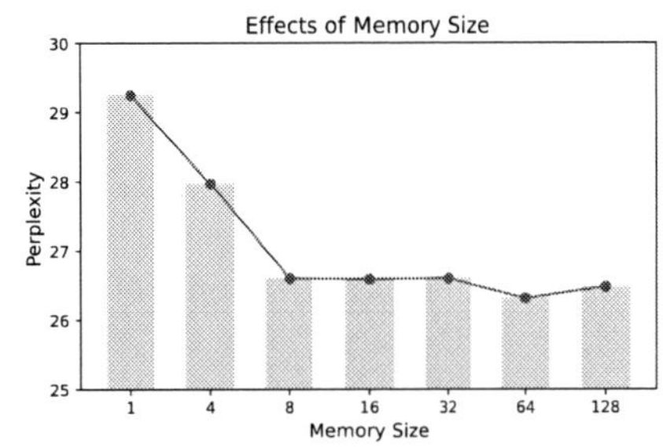

(b) Effects of different memory sizes

Figure 8: Effects of different configurations. (a) shows the effects of changing time horizon. (b) shows the effects of changing memory size.

C Effects of Time Horizon and Memory Size

We test how the time horizon for back-propagation affects the performance. We test on a smaller Memformer model for the efficiency. The results are shown in Figure 8a. We vary the back-propagation time horizon from 1 to 32. When the time horizon is set to 1, back-propagation cannot pass gradients through memory to the previous timestep. Thus, we observe the performance is the worst when the time horizon is 1. As we increase the time horizon, the model achieves better perplexity scores. When the time horizon is increased to 32, we observe the marginal improvement on perplexity is almost gone. A large memory size ideally helps to store more information. From Table 8b, we can see a huge improvement when increasing the memory size from 1 to 8. Furhter increasing the memory size has a smaller effects on the performance, and we suspect that this is due to the size of the model.

D Implementation of Memory Writer

Memory Slot Attention in Figure 9 produces the next timestep's memory M_{t+1}. This module takes the inputs of the previous timestep's memory M_t and the encoder's final hidden states. It then

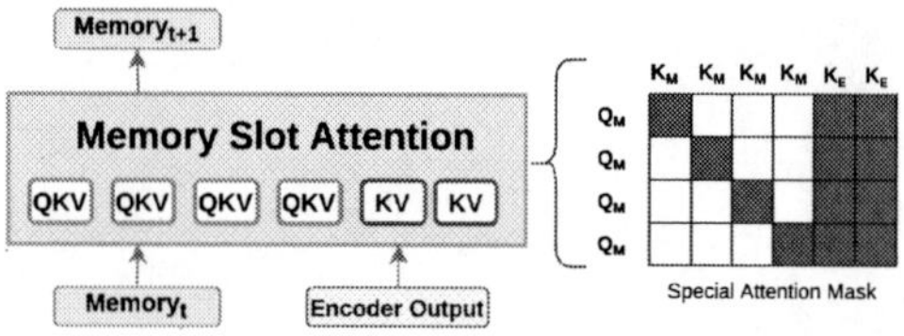

Figure 9: Memory Writer's Attention

projects the memory into queries, keys, and values, while the encoder outputs are into keys and values. Since each memory slot should not be interfering with other memory slots, we design a special type of sparse attention pattern. Thus, each slot in the memory can only attend over itself and the encoder outputs. This is to preserve the information in each slot longer over the time horizon. For example, if one slot only attends itself, then the information in that slot will not change in the next timestep.

Open-Domain Conversational Question Answering with Historical Answers

Hung-Chieh Fang* **Kuo-Han Hung*** **Chao-Wei Huang** **Yun-Nung Chen**
National Taiwan University, Taipei, Taiwan
{b09902106,b09902120,f07922069}@csie.ntu.edu.tw
y.v.chen@ieee.org

Abstract

Open-domain conversational question answering can be viewed as two tasks: passage retrieval and conversational question answering, where the former relies on selecting candidate passages from a large corpus and the latter requires better understanding of a question with contexts to predict the answers. This paper proposes **ConvADR-QA** that leverages historical answers to boost retrieval performance and further achieves better answering performance. Our experiments on the benchmark dataset, OR-QuAC, demonstrate that our model outperforms existing baselines in both extractive and generative reader settings, well justifying the effectiveness of historical answers for open-domain conversational question answering.[1]

1 Introduction

Conversational information seeking and conversational question answering (CQA) are fundamental tasks of dialogue systems (Gao et al., 2018). The conversational agents are expected to serve as nature interfaces for users' information need, providing information and answers via multi-turn natural language interactions. The multi-turn natural of CQA makes it challenging as the queries are contextualized, requiring the systems to resolve coreference and ambiguities. With recent advances in language understanding and dialogue modeling, along with the curation of large-scale datasets, e.g., QuAC (Choi et al., 2018) and CoQA (Reddy et al., 2019), we have seen substantial progress in CQA.

While the state-of-the-art (SOTA) models have achieved performance comparable or even superior than human performance on QA and CQA datasets, this setting is highly limited as it requires the source document containing evidence to be given, which is unlikely the case in real-world scenarios. To address this issue, researchers have expanded the scheme of CQA to an open-domain setting, where the document containing evidence must be retrieved from a large candidate pool (Qu et al., 2020). In the open-domain setting, there are usually millions of candidate documents, making the conventional method which jointly encodes the query and the document infeasible (Chen et al., 2017). The dominant technique to tackle the challenge is dense retrieval (Karpukhin et al., 2020; Qu et al., 2020; Xiong et al., 2021), which encodes a query and documents as dense representations separately and performs nearest neighbor search that is efficient and scalable to millions of documents. It has been shown to outperform traditional sparse retrieval methods on multiple QA benchmarks.

However, applying dense retrieval for conversations may need to consider the dialogue context and structure, which is not trivial. Qu et al. (2020) proposed ORConvQA to include previous questions in the same dialogue. where the context-dependent nature of questions is shown useful. ConvDR (Yu et al., 2021) further improved the retrieval performance by knowledge distillation on reformulated questions with an ad-hoc teacher model. Nevertheless, simply concatenating historical questions is suboptimal. Our hypothesis is that rather than relying on the model to infer helpful knowledge from historical questions, we provide direct signals by adding historical answers to the input. Hence, we propose **ConvADR-QA** (**Conv**ersational **A**nswer-aware **D**ense **R**etrieval) to leverage historical answers for better retrieval and then answering performance for open-domain CQA.

2 Related Work

CQA A unique challenge to CQA is that the questions are context-dependent. Hence, most prior work focused on various history modeling techniques (Huang et al., 2018; Yeh and Chen, 2019; Qu et al., 2019b; Chen et al., 2020). Choi et al.

*Equal contribution.

[1]The source code is available at https://github.com/MiuLab/ConvADR-QA.

Findings of the Association for Computational Linguistics: AACL-IJCNLP 2022, pages 319–326
November 20–23, 2022. ©2022 Association for Computational Linguistics

(2018) proposed to mark the previous answers in the passage by adding an answer embedding to the input embeddings. Qu et al. (2019a) extended this method to the large pre-trained language models. However, Chiang et al. (2020) showed that prior conversational models do not fully understand the content, implying that CQA still needs further investigation. While our method also leverages historical answers as additional input signal, our major contribution is that we apply this technique to dense retrieval instead of question answering for better practicality in a open-domain setting.

Open-Domain QA Without a given target passage, most work for this task was built upon the dense retrieval framework for retrieving relevant passages for QA. DPR (Karpukhin et al., 2020) first showed that dense retrieval outperforms sparse retrieval methods. GAR (Mao et al., 2021a) introduced pseudo relevance feedback by augmenting queries with generated texts. RIDER (Mao et al., 2021b) proposed a simple passage reranking method which promotes the passages containing the predicted answers. While these methods consider the predicted answers, they aim at improving single-turn question answering. We instead focus on enhancing model's ability on handling multi-turn conversational questions.

Open-Domain CQA Researchers have put increasing attention on open-domain CQA with the TREC Conversational Assistance Track (Dalton et al., 2020, 2021). However, these datasets have limited supervision, making dense retrieval hardly applicable due to its data-hungry nature. Qu et al. (2020) introduced the first large-scale open-domain CQA data, OR-QuAC, by extending QuAC (Choi et al., 2018) to a open-domain setting. They also proposed ORConvQA, a pipeline system with a DPR retriever and an extractive reader, as a baseline system. ConvDR (Yu et al., 2021) proposed to reformulate questions into their context-independent rewrites with the CANARD dataset (Elgohary et al., 2019), then applied knowledge distillation using a ad-hoc teacher model. Our method is built upon these two methods by incorporating historical answers to aid the retriever. Li et al. (2021) proposed a graph-guided retrieval method which constructs a graph using passages with historical answers and potential answers. Our work does not introduce extra parameters and complex modeling, and we demonstrate that we can achieve better results with a simpler design for better practicality. The All-History strategy from TopiOCQA (Adlakha et al., 2022) is very similar to ours. However, their experimental setting is not realistic as they used ground truth answers as historical answers, which is corresponding to our oracle setting.

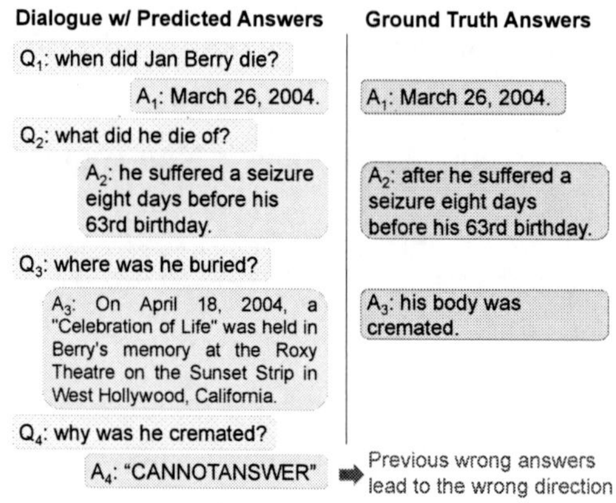

Figure 1: Demonstration of how previous answers affect the quality of an answer.

3 ConvADR-QA

Let C denote the passage collections with N passages $\{p_i\}_{i=1}^{N}$, where p_i can be viewed as a sequence of tokens $p_i^1, \ldots, p_i^l$. Given the t-th question q_t and all historical questions $\{q_i\}_{i=1}^{t-1}$ in a conversation, the task of open-domain CQA is to predict a_t from C. In an extractive setting, a_t is a span $p_i^s, \ldots, p_i^e$ from a passage p_i.

The difficulty of open-domain CQA is that the current question usually requires context information from previous turns, which makes it harder for the system to capture the latent information compared with the open-domain QA task. Previous work on open-domain conversational search addressed the problem by concatenating the current and historical questions *without* answers (Qu et al., 2020; Yu et al., 2021). Our motivation is that historical answers can also provide the important signal for the current question to obtain the answers illustrated in Figure 1.

To better leverage the historical answers for open-domain CQA, we propose ConvADR-QA illustrated in Figure 2, which includes a retriever for obtaining relevant passages from a large collection and a reader for CQA.

3.1 Retriever

Following the prior work (Karpukhin et al., 2020; Xiong et al., 2021), we apply a dense retrieval method, which has shown dominant performance

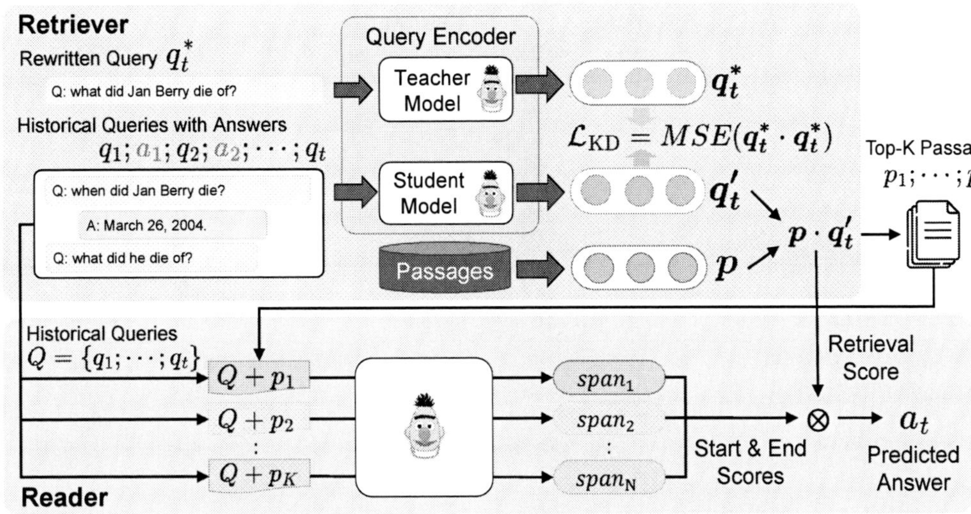

Figure 2: Illustration of our proposed ConvADR-QA model.

over sparse ones. Specifically, the model uses a dual-encoder architecture to map passages and questions to the same embedding space. The input of our question encoder is the concatenation of historical questions and answers:

$$\boldsymbol{p} = E_P(p), \boldsymbol{q}_k' = E_Q(\{q_i, a_i\}_{i=1}^{k-1}; q_k).$$

The retrieval score is then defined as the dot product of the passage embedding and the question embedding:

$$S_{\text{rt}}(q_k, p) = \boldsymbol{p} \cdot \boldsymbol{q}_k'.$$

In the training process, each question contains one gold passage p^+ and a set of negative passages P^-, ConvADR-QA is then optimized using the negative log likelihood loss:

$$\mathcal{L}_{\text{NLL}} = -\log \frac{e^{S_{\text{rt}}(q_k, p^+)}}{e^{S_{\text{rt}}(q_k, p^+)} + \sum_{p^- \in P^-} e^{S_{\text{rt}}(q_k, p^-)}}.$$

3.2 Knowledge Distillation

In conversational search, dense retrieval is challenging since the current question requires information from previous turns, which aggravate the discrepancy between question embeddings and passage embeddings. Yu et al. (2021) recently addressed the problem using a teacher-student framework to distill knowledge from an ad-hoc teacher model. The input of the teacher model is a manually-rewritten context-independent query $q_k^\star$, and the knowledge distillation (KD) loss is defined as the mean square error (MSE) loss between the teacher's and the student's question embeddings:

$$\boldsymbol{p} = E_P'(p), \boldsymbol{q}_k^\star = E_Q'(q_k^\star),$$

$$\mathcal{L}_{\text{KD}} = \text{MSE}(\boldsymbol{q}_k^\star, \boldsymbol{q}_k').$$

The retrieval loss of our multi-task learning setting is the sum of NLL loss and KD loss:

$$\mathcal{L}_{\text{NLL}} + \mathcal{L}_{\text{KD}}.$$

3.3 Reader

The task of the reader is to extract a span from passages as the final answer. We use a standard BERT model for the machine comprehension task (Devlin et al., 2019). Given the t-th question q_t and top-K candidate passages $\{p_i\}_{i=1}^K$ retrieved by our retriever, the reader first extracts a span for each passage by choosing the highest score of start and end tokens. The score of the m-th token is defined as follows:

$$S_{\text{start}}^{[m]}(q_t; p) = W_{\text{start}}\text{BERT}(\{q_i\}_{i=1}^t; p)[m],$$

$$S_{\text{end}}^{[m]}(q_t; p) = W_{\text{end}}\text{BERT}(\{q_i\}_{i=1}^t; p)[m],$$

$$S_{\text{rd}}(q_t; p) = \max_{m1, m2} [S_{\text{start}}^{[m1]}(q_t; p) + S_{\text{end}}^{[m2]}(q_t; p)].$$

We choose the final answer by multiplying the retriever score S_{rt} and the sum of start/end token score as the reader score S_{rd}:

$$S(q_t, p) = S_{\text{rt}}(q_t, p) \cdot S_{\text{rd}}(q_t; p).$$

4 Experiments

We conduct the experiments on an open-domain CQA benchmark: OR-QuAC (Qu et al., 2020). OR-QuAC is an open-domain conversational retrieval dataset that aggregates three existing datasets: (1)

	Method	Historical Answers	Retrieval MRR@5	R@5	MAP@10	Answering HEQ-Q	HEQ-D	F1
Extractive	ORConvQA	✗	31.3	31.4	-	24.10	0.60	29.4
	Graph-Guided	predicted	35.1	36.7	-	30.30	1.00	33.4
	ConvDR→Reader	✗	61.6	75.0	60.7	29.92	0.78	36.2
	ConvADR-QA (Reader)	predicted	**66.8**	**77.9**	**64.6**	**32.11**	**1.16**	**38.4**
	ConvADR-QA (Reader)	gold	*74.5*	*82.5*	*71.7*	*35.69*	*1.03*	*42.3*
Generative	RAG	✗	29.9	30.8	28.5	21.98	0.25	26.1
	ConvDR→FiD	✗	**61.6**	75.0	60.7	27.21	0.86	31.5
	ConvADR-QA (FiD)	predicted	60.9	**76.2**	**62.9**	**28.76**	**1.04**	**33.6**
	ConvADR-QA (FiD)	gold	*74.5*	*82.5*	*71.7*	*30.83*	*0.91*	*35.1*

Table 1: Performance on OR-QuAC (%). Best results are marked in **bold**. Oracle results are in *italic*.

the QuAC dataset (Choi et al., 2018) which contains 14K information-seeking QA dialogs, (2) the CANARD dataset (Elgohary et al., 2019) which rewrites context-dependent queries to self-contained questions based on QuAC, and (3) the Wikipedia corpus dump from 10/20/2019 which extends QuAC to the open-domain setting. The experimental setting is detailed in Appendix A.

Following Yu et al. (2021), we use three commonly used metrics, MRR@5, Recall@5 and MAP@10, to evaluate the retrieval performance. In addition, we use word-level F1 and human equivalence score (HEQ) provided by the QuAC challenge to evaluate the overall performance of our system. The definitions of above metrics are detailed in Appendix B.

4.1 Baselines

We compare our model with recently proposed baselines for open-domain CQA, ORConvQA (Qu et al., 2020), Graph-Guided (Li et al., 2021), and RAG (Lewis et al., 2020) for both extractive and generative settings.

- **ORConvQA**: It is an end-to-end system for the open-domain CQA task, which includes a retriever, a reranker and a reader. The retriever use the dense retrieval method where the input of the query encoder is the concatenation of the current and historical questions.
- **Graph-Guided**: Li et al. (2021) proposed a graph-guided retrieval method that models the relations among answers across conversational turns, which is the first work attempting at utilizing historical answers for open-domain CQA. This model utilizes a graph built from the hyperlink-connected passages containing historical answers to better retrieve relevant passages.
- **RAG**: It is a generation model that can access to pre-trained parametric memory and non-parametric memory like wikipedia. It has shown good performance on the open-domain QA task, we further adapt it to the open-domain CQA task by doing the following modifications: (1) finetuning the base model, where the input of the question encoder is the concatenation of the current and historical questions, (2) using passages from OR-QuAC as our knowledge source (non-parametric memory).

In addition to the existing open-domain CQA approaches, we further implement two baseline where we use ConvDR as the retriever model. ConvDR is a conversational dense retriever, which uses the few-shot strategy to mimic the embeddings of manual oracle queries from an ad hoc dense retriever. It is also the current SOTA model in the retrieval stage. We adopt it to open-domain CQA by enabling it with QA capability using two existing models to generate answers: (1) Reader of ORConvQA (Qu et al., 2020), which adapts a BERT-based extractive QA model to a multi-document setting, (2) FiD (Izacard and Grave, 2021), which uses a sequence-to-sequence model to generate the answer given the input is the question and retrieved passages, which has shown great performance at combining evidences from multiple passages.

4.2 Results

Table 1 summarizes our experimental results. It is obvious that our proposed ConvADR-QA outperforms almost all existing baseline models in both retrieval and answering stages, achieving new SOTA performance of open-domain CQA. We can observe that in both extractive and generative QA settings, our model which leverages predicted answers achieves better performance over the one without answers. Moreover, the graph-guided approach also utilizes historical answers in a more complex way, but performs worse than our ConvADR-QA, demonstrating that our model leverages answer signal more effectively. We also report the oracle results using gold historical answers. It shows that the model with gold answers outperforms the one with predicted answers in most of the metrics except HEQ-D. Note that the oracle results can be viewed as the upper bound of our method, as the gold answers are not available during inference. The results well justify our hypothesis that historical answers are informative for open-domain CQA.

Notably, we can notice that the quality of predicted answers can significantly affect the retrieval performance. Our experiment shows that MRR@5 drops when using FiD as the reader, demonstrating that a QA model with weak performance could potentially hurt retrieval performance. Our hypothesis is that due to its lower answering quality, the errors would propagate through the conversation and mislead the retriever, indicating that further improvement on reader performance could also improve the retrieval performance of our method. In sum, the experimental results show the effectiveness of our model for open-domain CQA in both extractive and generative settings. An example is presented in Table 3 for qualitative analysis, where it can be shown that the previous answers affect the following prediction results. More analysis can be found in Appendix C.

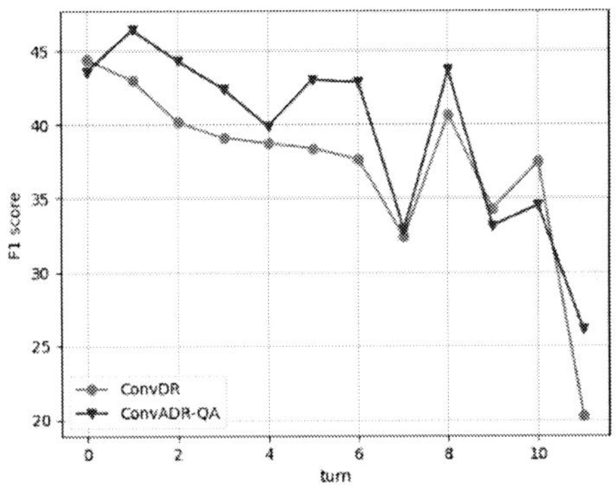

Figure 3: Analysis on accuracy against number of turns.

Q1: What is Roberto Mangabeira Unger,'s programmatic thought? **A1**: Key in Unger's thinking is the need to re-imagine social institutions before attempting to revise them. **ConvDR**: The beginning of Unger's academic career began with the books Knowledge and Politics and Law in Modern Society, **ConvADR-QA**: Key in Unger's thinking is the need to re-imagine social institutions before attempting to revise them.
Q2: Can you explain the mechanism of thinking? **A2**: In building this program, however, we must not entertain complete revolutionary overhaul, lest we be plagued by three false assumptions: **ConvDR**: CANNOTANSWER **ConvADR-QA**: In building this program, however, we must not entertain complete revolutionary overhaul, lest we be plagued by three false assumptions:
Q3: What are the three false assumptions? **A3**: Typological Fallacy: **ConvDR**: Unger finds three weaknesses that crippled the theory: foremost, the theory claimed that equilibrium would be spontaneously generated in a market economy. **ConvADR-QA**: Typological Fallacy: the fallacy that there is closed list of institutional alternatives in history, such as "feudalism" or "capitalism".

Table 2: Qualitative analysis.

4.3 Error Propagation Analysis

To inspect the impact of the errors propagated through the conversation and reduce the robustness. we conduct analysis on accuracy against number of turns in Figure 3. It shows that the benefits of adding the answers outweigh the error propagation, where ConvADR-QA outperforms ConvDR in earlier turns, which tends to drop as the dialogue gets too long. It implies that the issue about error propagation still have a large room for improvement.

5 Conclusions

This work introduces **ConvADR-QA**, an open-domain CQA model that leverages historical answers. The experiments on a benchmark dataset demonstrate that our proposed method outperforms all baselines for both retrieval and answering performance. Our results justify not only the importance of historical answers in a conversation but also the generalizability to different types of readers.

Acknowledgements

We thank reviewers for their insightful comments. This work was financially supported from Google and the Young Scholar Fellowship Program by Ministry of Science and Technology (MOST) in Taiwan, under Grants 111-2628-E-002-016 and 111-2634-F-002-014.

References

Vaibhav Adlakha, Shehzaad Dhuliawala, Kaheer Suleman, Harm de Vries, and Siva Reddy. 2022. TopiOCQA: Open-domain conversational question answering with topic switching. *Transactions of the Association for Computational Linguistics*, 10:468–483.

Danqi Chen, Adam Fisch, Jason Weston, and Antoine Bordes. 2017. Reading Wikipedia to answer open-domain questions. In *Proceedings of the 55th Annual Meeting of the Association for Computational Linguistics (Volume 1: Long Papers)*, pages 1870–1879, Vancouver, Canada. Association for Computational Linguistics.

Yu Chen, Lingfei Wu, and Mohammed J. Zaki. 2020. Graphflow: Exploiting conversation flow with graph neural networks for conversational machine comprehension. In *Proceedings of the Twenty-Ninth International Joint Conference on Artificial Intelligence, IJCAI-20*, pages 1230–1236. International Joint Conferences on Artificial Intelligence Organization. Main track.

Ting-Rui Chiang, Hao-Tong Ye, and Yun-Nung Chen. 2020. An empirical study of content understanding in conversational question answering. In *Proceedings of the AAAI Conference on Artificial Intelligence*, volume 34, pages 7578–7585.

Eunsol Choi, He He, Mohit Iyyer, Mark Yatskar, Wen-tau Yih, Yejin Choi, Percy Liang, and Luke Zettlemoyer. 2018. QuAC: Question answering in context. In *Proceedings of the 2018 Conference on Empirical Methods in Natural Language Processing*, pages 2174–2184, Brussels, Belgium. Association for Computational Linguistics.

Jeffrey Dalton, Chenyan Xiong, and Jamie Callan. 2020. Trec cast 2019: The conversational assistance track overview. *arXiv preprint arXiv:2003.13624*.

Jeffrey Dalton, Chenyan Xiong, and Jamie Callan. 2021. Cast 2020: The conversational assistance track overview. Technical report, Technical report.

Jacob Devlin, Ming-Wei Chang, Kenton Lee, and Kristina Toutanova. 2019. BERT: Pre-training of deep bidirectional transformers for language understanding. In *Proceedings of NAACL-HLT*, pages 4171–4186.

Ahmed Elgohary, Denis Peskov, and Jordan Boyd-Graber. 2019. Can you unpack that? learning to rewrite questions-in-context. In *Proceedings of the 2019 Conference on Empirical Methods in Natural Language Processing and the 9th International Joint Conference on Natural Language Processing (EMNLP-IJCNLP)*, pages 5918–5924, Hong Kong, China. Association for Computational Linguistics.

Jianfeng Gao, Michel Galley, and Lihong Li. 2018. Neural approaches to conversational AI. In *Proceedings of the 56th Annual Meeting of the Association for Computational Linguistics: Tutorial Abstracts*, pages 2–7, Melbourne, Australia. Association for Computational Linguistics.

Hsin-Yuan Huang, Eunsol Choi, and Wen-tau Yih. 2018. Flowqa: Grasping flow in history for conversational machine comprehension. In *International Conference on Learning Representations*.

Gautier Izacard and Edouard Grave. 2021. Leveraging passage retrieval with generative models for open domain question answering. In *Proceedings of the 16th Conference of the European Chapter of the Association for Computational Linguistics: Main Volume*, pages 874–880, Online. Association for Computational Linguistics.

Vladimir Karpukhin, Barlas Oguz, Sewon Min, Patrick Lewis, Ledell Wu, Sergey Edunov, Danqi Chen, and Wen-tau Yih. 2020. Dense passage retrieval for open-domain question answering. In *Proceedings of the 2020 Conference on Empirical Methods in Natural Language Processing (EMNLP)*, pages 6769–6781, Online. Association for Computational Linguistics.

Patrick Lewis, Ethan Perez, Aleksandra Piktus, Fabio Petroni, Vladimir Karpukhin, Naman Goyal, Heinrich Küttler, Mike Lewis, Wen-tau Yih, Tim Rocktäschel, Sebastian Riedel, and Douwe Kiela. 2020. Retrieval-augmented generation for knowledge-intensive nlp tasks. In *Advances in Neural Information Processing Systems*, volume 33, pages 9459–9474. Curran Associates, Inc.

Yongqi Li, Wenjie Li, and Liqiang Nie. 2021. A graph-guided multi-round retrieval method for conversational open-domain question answering. *arXiv preprint arXiv:2104.08443*.

Yuning Mao, Pengcheng He, Xiaodong Liu, Yelong Shen, Jianfeng Gao, Jiawei Han, and Weizhu Chen. 2021a. Generation-augmented retrieval for open-domain question answering. In *Proceedings of the 59th Annual Meeting of the Association for Computational Linguistics and the 11th International Joint Conference on Natural Language Processing (Volume 1: Long Papers)*, pages 4089–4100, Online. Association for Computational Linguistics.

Yuning Mao, Pengcheng He, Xiaodong Liu, Yelong Shen, Jianfeng Gao, Jiawei Han, and Weizhu Chen. 2021b. Reader-guided passage reranking for open-domain question answering. In *Findings of the Association for Computational Linguistics: ACL-IJCNLP 2021*, pages 344–350, Online. Association for Computational Linguistics.

C. Qu, L. Yang, M. Qiu, W. B. Croft, Y. Zhang, and M. Iyyer. 2019a. Bert with history answer embedding for conversational question answering. In *SIGIR '19*.

Chen Qu, Liu Yang, Cen Chen, Minghui Qiu, W Bruce Croft, and Mohit Iyyer. 2020. Open-retrieval conversational question answering. In *Proceedings of the 43rd International ACM SIGIR conference on research and development in Information Retrieval*, pages 539–548.

Chen Qu, Liu Yang, Minghui Qiu, W. Bruce Croft, Yongfeng Zhang, and Mohit Iyyer. 2019b. Bert with history answer embedding for conversational question answering. In *Proceedings of the 42nd International ACM SIGIR Conference on Research and Development in Information Retrieval*, SIGIR'19, page 1133–1136, New York, NY, USA. Association for Computing Machinery.

Siva Reddy, Danqi Chen, and Christopher D. Manning. 2019. CoQA: A conversational question answering challenge. *Transactions of the Association for Computational Linguistics*, 7:249–266.

Lee Xiong, Chenyan Xiong, Ye Li, Kwok-Fung Tang, Jialin Liu, Paul N. Bennett, Junaid Ahmed, and Arnold Overwijk. 2021. Approximate nearest neighbor negative contrastive learning for dense text retrieval. In *International Conference on Learning Representations*.

Yi-Ting Yeh and Yun-Nung Chen. 2019. FlowDelta: Modeling flow information gain in reasoning for conversational machine comprehension. In *Proceedings of the 2nd Workshop on Machine Reading for Question Answering*, pages 86–90, Hong Kong, China. Association for Computational Linguistics.

Shi Yu, Zhenghao Liu, Chenyan Xiong, Tao Feng, and Zhiyuan Liu. 2021. Few-shot conversational dense retrieval. In *Proceedings of the 44th International ACM SIGIR Conference on Research and Development in Information Retrieval*, pages 829–838.

A Reproducibility

Our source code and the trained model was published at GitHub together with running scripts for better reproducibility. All models are trained with 2 Nvidia Quadro P6000. For the retriever, we set the training batch size to 4, the number of epochs to 3, and the learning rate to 1e-5. For the reader, we set the training batch to 2, the number of epochs to 3, the max sequence length to 512, the max question length to 125 and the learning rate to 3e-5.

B Evaluation Metrics

We use following metrics for evaluating our proposed model.

- **MRR**: Reciprocal Rank (RR) calculates the reciprocal of the rank where the first relevant passage was retrieved, and MRR averages the reciprocal rank across all questions.
- **Recall**: The proportion of the questions that the answer is in the retrieved passages.
- **MAP**: Mean Average Precision is the mean of the average precision scores for each question.
- **F1**: It measures the overlap of the predicted answer span and the ground truth answer span at the word level.
- **HEQ**: HEQ-Q measures the percentage of questions where the system matches or surpasses human performance in terms of F1 score. HEQ-D measures the percentage of dialogues in which all questions have an HEQ-Q = 1.

C Qualitative Study

The results generated by ConvDR and ConvADR-QA are presented in Table 3, where the underline texts indicate the spans appearing in the ground truth answers. It can be found that historical answers can be an important signal to obtain the answers.

Example 1	
Q1	What was unique about Joe Greene's attitude?
A1	ferocious and intimidating.
ConvDR	Greene's nickname remained popular due to his exploits on the playing field, where he was described as ferocious and intimidating.
ConvADR-QA	Greene's nickname remained popular due to his exploits on the playing field, where he was described as ferocious and intimidating.
Q2	Did he intimidate other players?
A2	He instilled fear in opponents with the intensity of his play.
ConvDR	Lynn Swann, a wide receiver, considered Greene a mentor.
ConvADR-QA	He instilled fear in opponents with the intensity of his play.
Q3	Who did he play for?
A3	Pittsburgh
ConvDR	Houston Oilers
ConvADR-QA	Houston Oilers
Q4	Did his teams do well?
A4	CANNOTANSWER
ConvDR	Greene was named the captain of the defense in 1977.
ConvADR-QA	CANNOTANSWER
Q5	What else should I know about his playing style?
A5	In his early years with the Steelers, Greene was at times uncontrollable, and often let his temper get the best of him.
ConvDR	Greene was named the captain of the defense in 1977.
ConvADR-QA	In his early years with the Steelers, Greene was at times uncontrollable, and often let his temper get the best of him.
Example 2	
Q1	What is Roberto Mangabeira Unger,'s programmatic thought?
A1	Key in Unger's thinking is the need to re-imagine social institutions before attempting to revise them.
ConvDR	The beginning of Unger's academic career began with the books Knowledge and Politics and Law in Modern Society,
ConvADR-QA	Key in Unger's thinking is the need to re-imagine social institutions before attempting to revise them.
Q2	Can you explain the mechanism of thinking?
A2	In building this program, however, we must not entertain complete revolutionary overhaul, lest we be plagued by three false assumptions:
ConvDR	CANNOTANSWER
ConvADR-QA	In building this program, however, we must not entertain complete revolutionary overhaul, lest we be plagued by three false assumptions:
Q3	What are the three false assumptions?
A3	Typological Fallacy:
ConvDR	Unger finds three weaknesses that crippled the theory: foremost, the theory claimed that equilibrium would be spontaneously generated in a market economy.
ConvADR-QA	Typological Fallacy: the fallacy that there is closed list of institutional alternatives in history, such as "feudalism" or "capitalism".

Table 3: The comparison between ConvDR and ConvADR-QA.

Robustness Evaluation of Text Classification Models Using Mathematical Optimization and Its Application to Adversarial Training

Hikaru Tomonari[1], **Masaaki Nishino**[2], **Akihiro Yamamoto**[1]

[1]Kyoto University
[2]NTT Communication Science Laboratories
tomonari@iip.ist.i.kyoto-u.ac.jp, masaaki.nishino.uh@hco.ntt.co.jp
yamamoto.akihiro.5m@kyoto-u.ac.jp

Abstract

Neural networks are known to be vulnerable to adversarial examples due to slightly perturbed input data. In practical applications of neural network models, the robustness of the models against perturbations must be evaluated. However, no method can strictly evaluate their robustness in natural language domains. We therefore propose a method that evaluates the robustness of text classification models using an integer linear programming (ILP) solver by an optimization problem that identifies a minimum synonym swap that changes the classification result. Our method allows us to compare the robustness of various models in realistic time. It can also be used for obtaining adversarial examples. Because of the minimal impact on the altered sentences, adversarial examples with our method obtained high scores in human evaluations of grammatical correctness and semantic similarity for an IMDb dataset. In addition, we implemented adversarial training with the IMDb and SST2 datasets and found that our adversarial training method makes the model robust.

1 Introduction

Over the last decade, neural network (NN) models have been widely applied in such fields as computer vision and natural language processing (NLP). However, recently they have been shown to be vulnerable to small and imperceptible perturbations included in the original input data (Szegedy et al., 2013). These altered input data called adversarial examples are correctly classified by humans but can fool a target model, raising serious security and reliability concerns.

An NN model is defined as being robust when the model's prediction does not change with the addition of all the perturbations in a certain range. The process of checking whether the model is robust is called verification (Katz et al., 2017; Tjeng and Tedrake, 2017). In computer vision, methods have formulated the verification problem as constraint satisfaction and verified it by solving it using an integer linear programming (ILP) solver (Katz et al., 2017; Tjeng and Tedrake, 2017) or a boolean satisfiability problem (SAT) solver (Narodytska et al., 2018).

Interest has also been growing in investigating the adversarial robustness of NLP models, including new methods for generating adversarial examples (Alzantot et al., 2018a; Jin et al., 2019; Alzantot et al., 2018b; Michel et al., 2019; Li et al., 2019; Ebrahimi et al., 2017; Zang et al., 2020; Pruthi et al., 2019). On the other hand, as long as models are evaluated only by heuristic attacks, we cannot guarantee a model's robustness.

To tackle this dilemma, we formulated a problem for finding the minimum number of word swaps that change a model's predictions and solving it with an ILP solver. Using this verification method, we can strictly compare multiple adversarial training methods .

In our experiments, we trained an NN model composed of an affine transformation and a piecewise-linear function, such as the ReLU function for the Internet Movie Database (IMDb) dataset (Maas et al., 2011) and the Stanford Sentiment Treebank v2 (SST2) dataset (Socher et al., 2013). Then we verified the models with an ILP solver in a few seconds per text. Human participants also manually evaluated whether the adversarial examples generated by the existing and proposed methods were grammatically correct and semantically unchanged from the original sentences. The adversarial examples created by the proposed method had higher scores than those created by the existing method.

In addition, we conducted an experiment on adversarial training. Adversarial training, which augments training data with adversarial examples in each training loop very effectively make deep learning models more robust against adversarial examples (Goodfellow et al., 2014). In our experiments,

Findings of the Association for Computational Linguistics: AACL-IJCNLP 2022, pages 327–333
November 20–23, 2022.

our proposed method achieved robust model training.

2 Related Work

Some methods can accurately verify a model's robustness for perturbations within a certain range (Tjeng and Tedrake, 2017; Narodytska et al., 2018) in computer vision. MIPVerify (Tjeng and Tedrake, 2017) uses an ILP solver that can be applied to piecewise-linear neural network models by assigning binary variables to each nonlinear function. Another method verifies the parameters of NN models and input images with a binary neural network using the SAT solver (Narodytska et al., 2018). Unfortunately, there was no method can strictly evaluate the robustness of the models in the NLP domain.

Although pixel noise has been defined as an adversarial perturbation for images, it is difficult to define noise for text due to its discrete nature. TextFooler (Jin et al., 2019) generates an adversarial example of natural language by replacing some of the words in a text with synonyms. However, its heuristic search is approximate, and performs more word swaps than necessary. Our method, which obtains exact minimum word swaps, allows us to evaluate the robustness of a model.

3 Method

Given text sequence $\mathbf{x} = (x_1, \cdots, x_T)$, B_i denotes the candidates of the swapping word of x_i. We define b_{ij} as an indicator function. $b_{ij} = 1$ means that x_i is replaced by the jth word of B_i, and no word swaps occur when $b_{i0} = 1$. Let $\mathbf{v}_{ij}$ denote a word-embedding vector corresponding to b_{ij}. Then the Minimum Adversarial Swapping Problem is described as follows:

$$\min \quad \sum_{i=1}^{T} \sum_{j=1}^{|B_i|} b_{ij} \tag{1}$$

$$\text{subject to} \quad \sum_{j=0}^{|B_i|} b_{ij} = 1 \tag{2}$$

$$\mathbf{v'}_i = \sum_{j=0}^{|B_i|} \mathbf{v}_{ij} b_{ij} \tag{3}$$

$$\text{argmax}_k (f_k(\mathbf{v'})) \neq \lambda(\mathbf{x}) \tag{4}$$

$$b_{ij} \in \{0, 1\}, \quad i = 1, \ldots, T, \tag{5}$$

where $f_k(\cdot)$ is the kth output of the network, and $\lambda(\cdot)$ represents the true label index. Eq. (1) is an objective function that minimizes the number of synonym swaps. Eq. (2) is the condition for selecting only one synonym or original word for each position i. The word vector of the selected word is extracted with Eq. (3). Eq. (4) is a constraint for changing the model's original prediction, i.e., where the sentence obtained by swapping the words following the b_{ij} values is an adversarial example. This formulation is only applicable when $f(\cdot)$ is a piecewise-linear neural network composed of combinations of linear functions and piecewise-linear functions such as ReLU and maximum functions. We show how to formulate piecewise-linear functions as an ILP problem in the Appendix B. Following TextFooler (Jin et al., 2019), we prepare a synonym list B_i, (Appendix A) and show an example of formulation in Appendix C.

4 Metrics

Accuracy Under Attack Accuracy Under Attack (AUA) is the rate of the fraction of the test set that satisfies the following equation:

$$\forall x' \in (\mathcal{G}(x)) : \text{argmax}_i \left(f_i\left(x'\right)\right) = \lambda(x), \tag{6}$$

where $\mathcal{G}(x)$ is a transformation that adds a perturbation to text x. $f_i(\cdot)$ is the ith output of the NN model, and $\lambda(x)$ represents the true label of x. For a text x, we assume that $\mathcal{G}(x)$ is a combination of all the word swaps for a prepared synonym list. In the experiments in Section 5, we evaluated the models with this metric. Our proposed method allows us to find the lower bound of AUA by checking whether Eq. (6) is satisfied.

Mean Minimum Word Swaps The problem of finding minimum word swaps is denoted below. $d(\cdot, \cdot)$ is a distance metric that defines the number of word swaps:

$$\min_{x'} \quad d\left(x', x\right) \tag{7}$$

$$\text{subject to} \quad \text{argmax}_i \left(f_i\left(x'\right)\right) \neq \lambda(x). \tag{8}$$

A Mean Minimum Word Swap (MMWS) is the average of this distance in the test set. The advantage of this metric is that it allows for an intuitive and flexible way to evaluate the model's robustness.

5 Experiments

We conducted comprehensive experiments to evaluate the effectiveness of our verification method

Dataset	Train	Test	Avg Length	Categories
SST2	67 K	870	9	2
IMDb	25 K	25 K	159	2

Table 1: Overview of datasets

including its applications to the generation of adversarial examples and adversarial training. We studied our verification method with text classification datasets with average sequence lengths from tens to hundreds of words. The dataset statistics are summarized in Table 1. We evaluated our algorithm on a set of 500 samples for the SST2 dataset (Socher et al., 2013) and 1,000 samples for the IMDb dataset (Maas et al., 2011) randomly selected from the test set. We prepared two baseline models, which were trained on each dataset. The architecture of the neural network is shown in Appendix D. The number of input words was limited to 200, and sentences with fewer than 200 words were compensated with padding tokens. We set the vocabulary size to 20,000 frequent words and replaced the words not in the vocabulary with unknown tokens. For verification, we used the same synonym list for our method and TextFooler which we compare and used Gurobi (Gurobi Optimization, LLC, 2022) as a mathematical optimization solver.

5.1 Robustness Evaluation and Generation of Adversarial Examples

In this part, we examine the effectiveness of the proposed method by comparing how it obtains minimum word swaps with TextFooler which performs a heuristic search. The two graphs on the left of Fig. 1 show the incremental number of word swaps from the proposed method to TextFooler. The proposed method achieved fewer word swaps in both datasets because it guarantees a minimum number of word swaps. We also generated adversarial examples with our method. Samples of original and adversarial sentences are shown in Table 2. We expected the minimal word swaps to suppress the sentence changes. In Section 6, human evaluations actually shows that the quality of the adversarial examples with our method is better than with TextFooler. The two graphs on the right of Fig. 1 shows the times required for verifying the models. Even IMDb, which has a long average sequence length, is processed in a realistic amount of time.

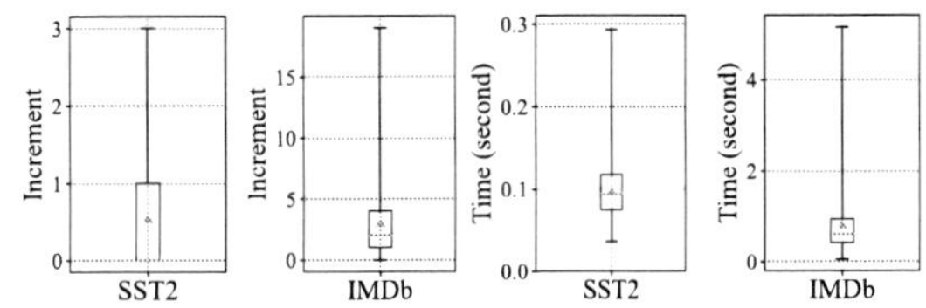

Figure 1: Incremental number of word swaps from the proposed method to TextFooler (two graphs on the left) and Times to verify the model (two graphs on the right).

5.2 Adversarial Training

We evaluate an adversarial training using adversarial examples generated with our method. The proposed method makes it possible to compare the robustness of multiple models. We trained three models: a baseline model, a model with adversarial training using Textfooler, and the model with adversarial training using the proposed method.

Table 3 compares the accuracy and the AUA. For SST2, we can confirm that the robustness of the model with adversarial training improved. In this case, AUA in TextFooler and Ours are asymptotically equal. On the other hand, it is difficult to assess the robustness for IMDb models because AUA are 0. It is possible to limit the number of word swaps, but the settings need to be changed carefully for each dataset. Even when the AUA is not helpful, it can be evaluated with MMWS which consider the number of word swaps.

Figure 2 shows the histograms of the number of word swaps. Since our method always obtains the smallest combination of word swaps, the distribution is skewed to the left when compared to TextFooler. The distribution is skewed toward the larger number of word swaps required to change the prediction in order of the baseline model, TextFooler model, and our model. This indicates that a model become stronger when adversarial training is implemented, and that our model is more robust than the TextFooler model. Table 4 shows MMWS scores, which represents the robustness of the models.

6 Human Evaluation

We conducted human evaluation of the generated adversarial examples from the text classification model trained with the IMDb dataset. A total of nine native speakers in their 20s to 40s living in the U.S. and the U.K. were asked to evaluate the examples using the evaluation metrics "grammatical

	Movie Review (Positive (POS) ↔ Negative (NEG))
Original (Label: POS)	it's a charming and often affecting journey.
Attack with TextFooler (Label: NEG)	it's a **ravishing** and **normally impacts trip**.
Attack with Ours (Label: NEG)	it's a **ravishing** and **normally influenced** journey.
Original (Label: NEG)	an occasionally funny but overall limp fish-out-of-water story.
Attack with TextFooler (Label: POS)	an **intermittently** funny but **general** limp fish-out-of-water **history**.
Attack with Ours (Label: POS)	an occasionally **hilarious** but overall limp fish-out-of-water story.

Table 2: Examples of original and adversarial sentences generated by TextFooler and our method against baseline model for SST2 dataset. Replaced words are shown in bold.

Dataset	Model	Acc	Attack	AUA
SST2	Baseline	0.838	TextFooler	0.280
			Ours	0.280
	TextFooler	0.820	TextFooler	0.478
			Ours	0.478
	Ours	0.820	TextFooler	0.516
			Ours	0.516
IMDb	Baseline	0.819	TextFooler	0
			Ours	0
	TextFooler	0.815	TextFooler	0
			Ours	0
	Ours	0.807	TextFooler	0
			Ours	0

Table 3: Accuracy Under Attack (AUA). Higher scores indicate greater robustness.

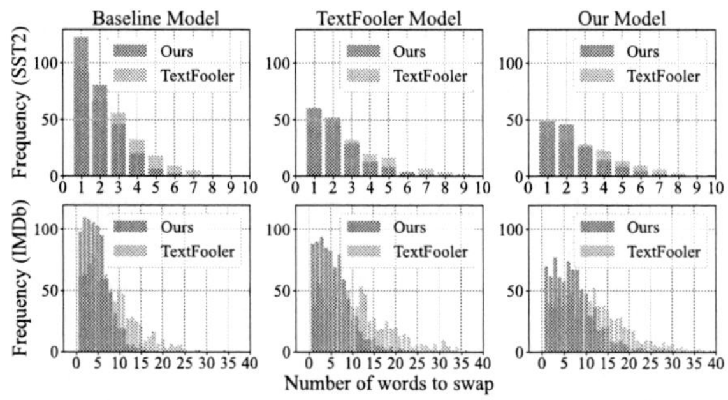

Figure 2: Histogram of number of words to swap for each dataset. We attacked the three models (Baseline, TextFooler, Ours) with TextFooler and Ours.

Model	Score (SST2)	Score (IMDb)
Baseline	1.99	4.81
TextFooler	2.31	5.86
Ours	2.49	7.28

Table 4: MMWS Score. This is an average score of the blue histogram in Figure 2.

Model	Grammatical Correctness	Semantic Similarity
Baseline	2.18 → 2.51	2.16 → 2.37
TextFooler	1.99 → 2.39	2.09 → 2.34
Ours	2.14 → 2.80	2.19 → 2.52

Table 5: Human Evaluation Score. Scores for the TextFooler are to the left of the arrow, and our model's scores are to the right.

correctness" and "semantic similarity". For each adversarial example, three people gave a score from 1 to 4 following the criteria shown in Appendix E.

Table 5 shows the evaluation scores of the adversarial examples. For each model, the score of the proposed method was higher in both grammatical correctness and semantic similarity.

Figure 3 shows the relationships between human evaluation scores and the average swaps of the adversarial examples for the baseline model. The horizontal axis is the number of synonym swaps and the vertical axis is the average score. We see that the fewer the number of synonym swaps, the higher the scores for both TextFooler and the proposed method. This result supports the validity of the proposed method which aim to find the minimum number of synonym swaps.

7 Conclusion

The proposed method always obtains a minimum synonym swapping, which makes it possible to compare and evaluate the robustness of text classification models. In addition, we conducted human evaluation and supported the effectiveness of our approach. We also performed the adversarial training and found that it makes the models more robust.

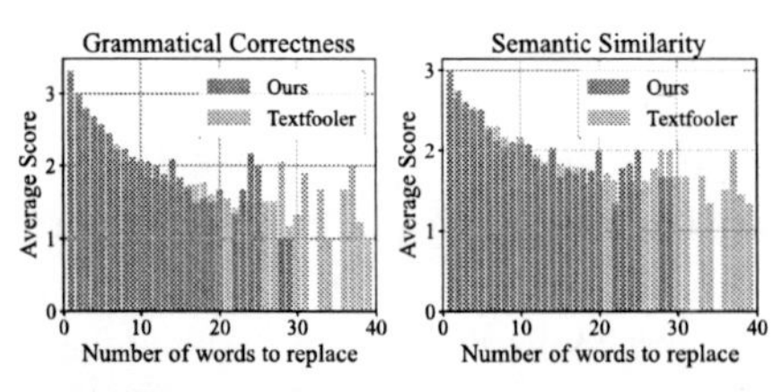

Figure 3: Effect of the Number of Synonym Swaps in Human Evaluation

Acknowledgements

This work was supported by JST, PRESTO Grant Number JPMJPR20C7 Japan.

References

Moustafa Alzantot, Yash Sharma, Ahmed Elgohary, Bo-Jhang Ho, Mani Srivastava, and Kai-Wei Chang. 2018a. Generating natural language adversarial examples. In *Proceedings of the 2018 Conference on Empirical Methods in Natural Language Processing*, pages 2890–2896, Brussels, Belgium. Association for Computational Linguistics.

Moustafa Alzantot, Yash Sharma, Ahmed Elgohary, Bo-Jhang Ho, Mani B. Srivastava, and Kai-Wei Chang. 2018b. Generating natural language adversarial examples. *CoRR*, abs/1804.07998.

Daniel Cer, Yinfei Yang, Sheng-yi Kong, Nan Hua, Nicole Limtiaco, Rhomni St. John, Noah Constant, Mario Guajardo-Cespedes, Steve Yuan, Chris Tar, Yun-Hsuan Sung, Brian Strope, and Ray Kurzweil. 2018. Universal sentence encoder. *CoRR*, abs/1803.11175.

Javid Ebrahimi, Anyi Rao, Daniel Lowd, and Dejing Dou. 2017. Hotflip: White-box adversarial examples for NLP. *CoRR*, abs/1712.06751.

Ian J. Goodfellow, Jonathon Shlens, and Christian Szegedy. 2014. Explaining and harnessing adversarial examples.

Gurobi Optimization, LLC. 2022. Gurobi Optimizer Reference Manual.

Di Jin, Zhijing Jin, Joey Tianyi Zhou, and Peter Szolovits. 2019. Is BERT really robust? natural language attack on text classification and entailment. *CoRR*, abs/1907.11932.

Guy Katz, Clark W. Barrett, David L. Dill, Kyle Julian, and Mykel J. Kochenderfer. 2017. Reluplex: An efficient SMT solver for verifying deep neural networks. *CoRR*, abs/1702.01135.

Jinfeng Li, Shouling Ji, Tianyu Du, Bo Li, and Ting Wang. 2019. TextBugger: Generating adversarial text against real-world applications. In *Proceedings 2019 Network and Distributed System Security Symposium*. Internet Society.

Andrew L. Maas, Raymond E. Daly, Peter T. Pham, Dan Huang, Andrew Y. Ng, and Christopher Potts. 2011. Learning word vectors for sentiment analysis. In *Proceedings of the 49th Annual Meeting of the Association for Computational Linguistics: Human Language Technologies*, pages 142–150, Portland, Oregon, USA. Association for Computational Linguistics.

Paul Michel, Xian Li, Graham Neubig, and Juan Miguel Pino. 2019. On evaluation of adversarial perturbations for sequence-to-sequence models. *CoRR*, abs/1903.06620.

Nina Narodytska, Shiva Prasad Kasiviswanathan, Leonid Ryzhyk, Mooly Sagiv, and Toby Walsh. 2018. Verifying properties of binarized deep neural networks.

Jeffrey Pennington, Richard Socher, and Christopher D. Manning. 2014. Glove: Global vectors for word representation. In *Empirical Methods in Natural Language Processing (EMNLP)*, pages 1532–1543.

Danish Pruthi, Bhuwan Dhingra, and Zachary C. Lipton. 2019. Combating adversarial misspellings with robust word recognition.

Richard Socher, Alex Perelygin, Jean Wu, Jason Chuang, Christopher D. Manning, Andrew Ng, and Christopher Potts. 2013. Recursive deep models for semantic compositionality over a sentiment treebank. In *Proceedings of the 2013 Conference on Empirical Methods in Natural Language Processing*, pages 1631–1642, Seattle, Washington, USA. Association for Computational Linguistics.

Christian Szegedy, Wojciech Zaremba, Ilya Sutskever, Joan Bruna, Dumitru Erhan, Ian Goodfellow, and Rob Fergus. 2013. Intriguing properties of neural networks.

Vincent Tjeng and Russ Tedrake. 2017. Verifying neural networks with mixed integer programming. *CoRR*, abs/1711.07356.

Yuan Zang, Fanchao Qi, Chenghao Yang, Zhiyuan Liu, Meng Zhang, Qun Liu, and Maosong Sun. 2020. Word-level textual adversarial attacking as combinatorial optimization. In *Proceedings of the 58th Annual Meeting of the Association for Computational Linguistics*, pages 6066–6080, Online. Association for Computational Linguistics.

A Creating a Synonym List

We gather a candidate set B_i for all possible swaps of the selected word x_i. For each word in the text, we retrieve all words from GloVe (Pennington et al., 2014) whose cosine similarity is greater than 0.8. We use the Universal Sentence Encoder (USE) (Cer et al., 2018) to encode sentences X and X_{adv}, and extract their cosine similarity score is greater than 0.8. In addition, we check that Parts-of-Speech (POS) matches. We cannot perform POS checking and USE checking dynamically because it it difficult to consider altered context words of the target word. We therefore only swap the target word for checking.

B Formulating Piecewise Linear Functions

Formulating the Maximum Function

As denoted in (Tjeng and Tedrake, 2017), the maximum function can be formulated as below.

$$\bigwedge_{i=1}^{m} \left(\left(y \leq x_i + (1 - a_i) \left(u_{\max,-i} - l_i \right) \right) \wedge (y \geq x_i) \right) \wedge \left(\sum_{i=1}^{m} a_i = 1 \right) \wedge \left(a_i \in \{0, 1\} \right) . \tag{9}$$

(4) can be rewritten with the maximum function like below.

$$f_{\lambda(\mathbf{x})} \left(\mathbf{v}' \right) < \max_{\mu \in [1,n] \setminus \{\lambda(\mathbf{x})\}} f_\mu \left(\mathbf{v}' \right) . \tag{10}$$

Formulating ReLU

When all the nonlinear functions in the NN model are piecewise linear, it can be solved as an ILP. A piecewise linear function is a function that combines partially linear functions such as the ReLU function with $y = max\left(x, 0\right)$. Specifically, for each input scalar value x and output scalar value y of the ReLU function, it can be formulated with the binary variable a (Tjeng and Tedrake, 2017).

$$\left(y \leq x - l(1 - a) \right) \wedge (y \geq x) \wedge (y \leq u \cdot a) \wedge (y \geq 0) \wedge \left(a \in \{0, 1\} \right), \tag{11}$$

where l is the lower bound of x and u is the upperbound of x. In advance, we can explore each in each layer. l is approximated to a smaller value and u to a larger value. As a result, it is possible to replace $y = x$ if l is greater than 0 and $y = 0$ if u is less than 0, thus reducing computation time when performing the entire formulation and searching.

C Example of Formulation

When we find the synonym list $B_2 = \{film\}$ and $B_4 = \{nice, great\}$ for an input text "this movie is good" (Figure 4), our objective is to minimize the sum of binary variables in the orange box and the sum of each blue box is constrained to 1. The formulation is written as (12).

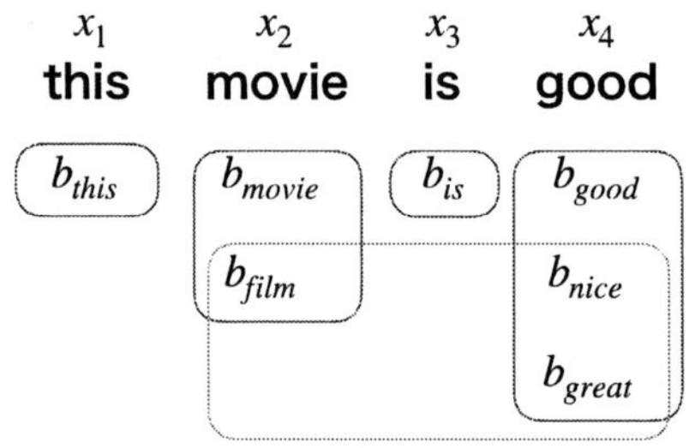

Figure 4: Example of Formulation

$$\begin{aligned}
\min \left(b_{film} + b_{nice} + b_{great} \right) \\
b_{this} &= 1 \\
b_{movie} + b_{film} &= 1 \\
b_{is} &= 1 \\
b_{good} + b_{nice} + b_{great} &= 1 \\
\mathbf{v}'_1 &= \mathbf{v}_{this} b_{this} \\
\mathbf{v}'_2 &= \mathbf{v}_{movie} b_{movie} + \mathbf{v}_{film} b_{film} \\
\mathbf{v}'_3 &= \mathbf{v}_{is} b_{is} \\
\mathbf{v}'_4 &= \mathbf{v}_{good} b_{good} + \mathbf{v}_{nice} b_{nice} + \mathbf{v}_{great} b_{great} \\
y_{positive}, y_{negative} &= f\left(\mathbf{v}'_1, \mathbf{v}'_2, \mathbf{v}'_3, \mathbf{v}'_4 \right) \\
y_{positive} &< y_{negative} .
\end{aligned} \tag{12}$$

D Architecture of a Neural Network

The architecture of the NN model is a simple network consisting of affine transformations and nonlinear transformations using the ReLU function, as shown in Table 6.

Layer	Shape of Output Tensor	Params
Input	(200)	0
Embedding	(200, 2)	40,000
Flatten	(400)	0
Affine	(64)	25,664
ReLU	(64)	0
Affine	(2)	130

Table 6: Structure of Neural Network

E References of Human Evaluation

Score	Description
4	Correct.
3	Grammatically incorrect, but acceptable as a casual expression.
2	There are one or two clear errors that are not even used as a casual expression.
1	Three or more clear errors exist.

Table 7: References for Evaluating Grammatical Correctness

Score	Description
4	Paraphrase of the original sentence and the content conveyed by the sentence has not changed. The classification result is invariant.
3	Although the content has changed to the extent that the sentence is less influenced compared to the original sentence, the classification result is considered to be invariant.
2	Although the sentence has been changed to the extent that it has a greater impact on the meaning of the sentence compared to the original sentence, the class label is considered unchanged.
1	It has been changed to the extent that it has a greater impact on the meaning of the sentence compared to the original sentence, and the class label can change.

Table 8: References for Evaluating Semantic Similarity

HERB: Measuring Hierarchical Regional Bias in Pre-trained Language Models

Yizhi Li[1*], Ge Zhang[2 3 4*], Bohao Yang[1], Chenghua Lin[1†], Shi Wang[3†], Anton Ragni[1], Jie Fu[2]
[1] Department of Computer Science, The University of Sheffield, UK
[2] Beijing Academy of Artificial Intelligence, China
[3] Institute of Computing Technology, Chinese Academy of Sciences, China
[4] University of Michigan Ann Arbor, USA
{yizhi.li, byang27, c.lin, a.ragni}@sheffield.ac.uk[1],
gezhang@umich.edu[2], wangshi@ict.ac.cn[3], fujie@baai.ac.cn[4]

Abstract

Content Warning: This work contains examples that potentially implicate stereotypes, associations, and other harms that could be offensive to individuals in certain regions.

Fairness has become a trending topic in natural language processing (NLP), which addresses biases targeting certain social groups such as genders and religions. However, regional bias in language models (LMs), a long-standing global discrimination problem, still remains unexplored. This paper bridges the gap by analysing the regional bias learned by the pre-trained language models that are broadly used in NLP tasks. In addition to verifying the existence of regional bias in LMs, we find that the biases on regional groups can be strongly influenced by the geographical clustering of the groups. We accordingly propose a HiErarchical Regional Bias evaluation method (HERB) utilising the information from the sub-region clusters to quantify the bias in pre-trained LMs. Experiments show that our hierarchical metric can effectively evaluate the regional bias with respect to comprehensive topics and measure the potential regional bias that can be propagated to downstream tasks. Our codes are available at https://github.com/Bernard-Yang/HERB.

1 Introduction

Large-scale pre-trained language models (LMs) are prevalent in the natural language processing (NLP) community since the costly pre-trained models can be adapted to a wide range of downstream applications. However, research studies demonstrate that the societal biases in the pre-training corpora can be learned by LMs and further propagated to the downstream applications (Zhao et al., 2019; Dev et al., 2020; Goldfarb-Tarrant et al., 2021; Kurita et al., 2019). To qualify and mitigate bias for pre-trained LMs, researchers have developed bias evaluation methods targeting certain *social groups* such as gender, religion, and race (Sun et al., 2019; Manzini et al., 2019; Xia et al., 2020; Delobelle et al., 2021). However, existing methods do not examine the social groups categorised by geographical information, which leaves the region-related biases in pre-trained LMs unexplored. Therefore, our work bridges this gap by addressing research questions about whether regional bias exists in the pre-trained LMs, and if yes, how to quantify the bias in a principled way.

Bias in NLP applications makes distinct judgements on people based on their gender, race, religion, region, or other social groups could be harmful, such as automatically downgrading the resumes of female applicants in recruiting (Dastin, 2018) Regional bias represents stereotypes based on the geographic location where people live or come from (Wikipedia, 2022a). To verify the existence of regional bias, we first leverage a sentence-level bias measurement (Kaneko and Bollegala, 2022), with which the likelihood of a biased sentence produced by a pre-trained LM can be acquired with a designed input:

People in `[region]` are `[description]`.

where `[region]` and `[description]` can be filled with any desired words. The output likelihood represents the contextualised possibility of associating people in the region with the given context, which can be utilised to analyse the bias integrated into LMs. From the perspective of the pre-trained LM, there is a 'world map' of region-wide judgements regards to the `[description]` of interest. As the case shown in Fig. 1, the pre-trained RoBERTa (Liu et al., 2019) holds a prejudice that people in specific regions are more likely to be `[bald]`, which hardly stands for the facts and could amplify the regional bias.

In addition, we discover that the regional bias in pre-trained LMs could be hierarchical as demon-

* The two authors contributed equally to this work.
† Corresponding authors.

Findings of the Association for Computational Linguistics: AACL-IJCNLP 2022, pages 334–346
November 20–23, 2022. ©2022 Association for Computational Linguistics

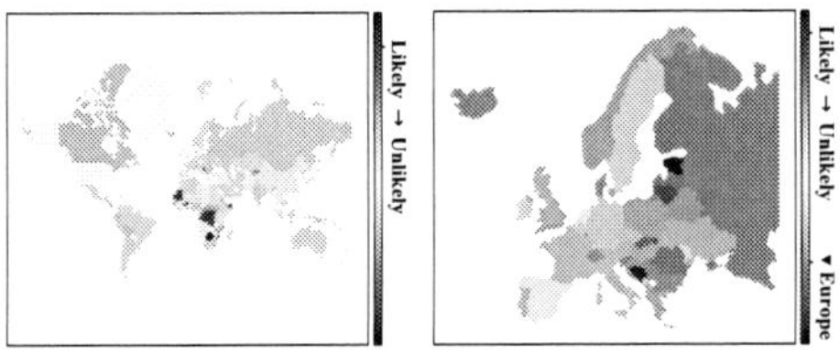

(a) Regions Worldwide (b) Regions in Europe

Figure 1: The Regional Likelihood in `[bald]` Dimension Produced by RoBERTa. The regional likelihoods are produced with sentences filled with different region names and the fixed descriptive word `[bald]` in the given template. The likelihood calculated with the region word `[Europe]` is marked by ◀ at the likelihood legend in Fig. 1b. The details of calculation can be referred to §3.1.

strated in Fig. 1b. Whilst people in many European countries share a low likelihood of `[bald]`, the upper-level regional group, i.e., Europe, is also assigned a relatively small likelihood. This suggests that the language models do recognise the hierarchical structure of the regional group structure and thus produce similar results for most of the countries and the continental group. However, opposite trends of high likelihoods appear in countries such as the United Kingdom, which implies that bias in these regions could not be represented by the higher-level group, Europe. Without considering relationships between regional groups, the modelling of regional bias is difficult because only conducting bias evaluation on high-level groups can disguise the biases in their sub-regions.

To tackle the aforementioned issues, we argue that the design of regional bias evaluation for pre-trained LMs should satisfy the following criteria:

1. The metric should leverage the structural information from sub-regions to evaluate the bias for higher-level regions.
2. The disperancy of judgements on different regional groups in the same level should also be considered bias, e.g., inconsistent judgements on the cities in the same country.

With the criteria in mind, we design a clustering-based metric **HERB**🌿, which can effectively measure **H**i**E**rarchical **R**egional **B**ias. HERB🌿 is grounded on the *descriptive vectors*, a novel component that is designed to capture region-specific contextualised likelihoods with respect to the content of `[description]`. As the bias on regions should be relevant to their sub-region, we formalise the bias on a given region as the *sparseness* of its sub-region cluster in the descriptive space. The intuition behind the cluster-based sparseness calculation is that the more bias exists in the region, the more inconsistent the judgements on its sub-regions received. In the case that a region does not contain any sub-regions, its cluster sparseness is modelled by the distance to the centroids of the cluster, where all the regions belong to the same upper-level region, e.g., cities in the same country. We further propose aggregation functions for the descriptive vector and cluster-based bias calculation to utilise the hierarchy. The aggregated cluster-based bias evaluation not only empowers our metric to consider regional bias at multiple levels but also sheds light on the general regional bias evaluation for the pre-trained LMs.

We perform extensive evaluations of hierarchical regional bias on various state-of-the-art pre-trained language models and study the regional hierarchical relationships learned by the LMs. Additionally, we conduct experiments to study the propagation of regional bias from pre-trained models to downstream tasks. By introducing extra neutral regional information to the test samples and observing the prediction change, we evaluate how much the model performances are affected by region bias. Regional bias evaluation results on downstream tasks confirm that results from our metric have correlations to the bias propagation to fine-tuned LMs.

2 Related Work

Regional bias has been recognised as one of the main concerns of the United Nations (Ramcharan, 2019). Its severe influence has been detected and verified in various areas, including scientific research (Paris et al., 1998), economics (Ramcharan, 2019), agriculture (Jia and Nuetah, 2022), customer satisfaction investigation (Ibeke et al., 2017; Brint and Fry, 2021), and public opinion (Peng, 2021). Extensive regional bias is often decomposed into national and regional biases (Paris et al., 1998; Jia and Nuetah, 2022; Saarinen et al., 2021), which inspires us to consider designing the metric of regional biases in the language models(LMs) hierarchically.

Societal biases in NLP has raised increasing attention because large-scale LMs containing societal biases can produce undesirable biased expressions and have negative societal impacts on the minorities (Sheng et al., 2021). Existing natural language processing researchers have detected and analysed regional bias against people in specific areas (Abid et al., 2021; Sheng et al., 2021). But there is still no well-formalized metric for regional bias contained in LMs, like gender bias (Bordia and Bowman, 2019; Sheng et al., 2019), racial bias (Solaiman et al., 2019; Groenwold et al., 2020), political bias (Liu et al., 2021), religious bias (Abid et al., 2021), and profession bias (Huang et al., 2020).

Societal bias metrics include regard ratio (Sheng et al., 2019), sentiment ratio (Groenwold et al., 2020), individual and group fairness (Huang et al., 2020), and word co-occurrence score (Bordia and Bowman, 2019). Additionally, societal bias is also classified based on how human detects it in the corpus. Liu et al. classifies societal bias into direct bias and indirect bias, based on whether measures bias of texts generated using prompts with ideological triggers. Societal bias in texts can also be classified into contextual-level societal bias (Bartl et al., 2020) and word-level societal bias (Bordia and Bowman, 2019), based on how it is detected from texts. Additionally, various well-designed word lists and perspective descriptions are used to measure societal bias. Chaloner and Maldonado propose 5 target word categories, including career vs family, maths vs arts, science vs arts, intelligence vs arts, and strength with weakness, to measure gender bias in word embeddings. Liu et al. propose several political topics related prompts to measure societal bias. Jiao and Luo propose an adjective list to measure descriptive gender bias hidden in Chinese LMs. Zhou et al. use gender-related grammar words and occupation-related words to measure gender bias. In sharp contrast, HERB🌿 focuses on measuring contextual-level regional indirect bias.

3 Methodology

We describe our hierarchical evaluation method for regional bias in pre-trained LMs in this section. To measure the bias from comprehensive aspects, we first map all the regional groups to a descriptive representation space with a selective word list. We use a cluster-based evaluation method to represent the bias of a given region with regard to its sub-regions, which leverages the natural hierarchical regional group structure in the bias evaluation. In order to summarise bias information from regions at different levels simultaneously, we design a novel aggregation function of the descriptive vector and cluster-based bias, which measures the general regional bias in the pre-trained LMs.

3.1 Descriptive Vector of Regions

To quantify the judgements on a given regional social group, we design a descriptive vector v which can be utilised to measure the bias from language models for each region r.

We collect a descriptive word list ($D = \{d_1, d_2, ..., d_n\}$) containing adjectives and occupations that could show stereotypes or biases when describing people. The adjective list depicting intelligence, appearance, and strength is from the work of Chaloner and Maldonado (2019). To augment the list, we also apply the adjective list depicting morality from (Shahid et al., 2020). We slightly modify the adjectives so that they match the prompt, and change the original list to make the size balanced across different topics. Additionally, we include the occupation word list from (Bolukbasi et al., 2016) as part of the word list. Because the occupation word list is adapted to a comparable size to other lists, we can use the full word list to model bias balanced on different topics. The complete description word list is given in Appendix A.

In order to conduct an in-depth analysis of the regional bias of language models, we select the regional entities at the continent, country[1], and city levels. The region word list is noted as $R = \{r_1, r_2, ..., r_m\}$. To learn the regional bias at the contextualised level, we design a template input S_{ij} for language models to calculate the regional bias score for a specific region-description pair (d_i, r_j):

People in `[region]` are `[description]`.

where `[region]` and `[description]` refers to the region word r_j in R and descriptive word d_i in D, respectively.

Inspired by the recently proposed unmasking sequence likelihood (Kaneko and Bollegala, 2022), we use the template input S_{ij} to calculate the contextualised likelihood for the given region-description pair (d_i, r_j):

$$f(S_{ij}) = \frac{1}{|S_{ij}|} \sum_{t=1}^{|S_{ij}|} \log(P(w_t | S_{ij}; \theta)) \quad (1)$$

where θ refers to parameters of a specific language model. The $f(S_{ij})$ uses the contextualised likelihood to represent how possible the pre-trained

[1]The 'country' does not refer to the actual sovereign states but the region concepts that are categorised as one level higher than the cities in the package geonamecache.

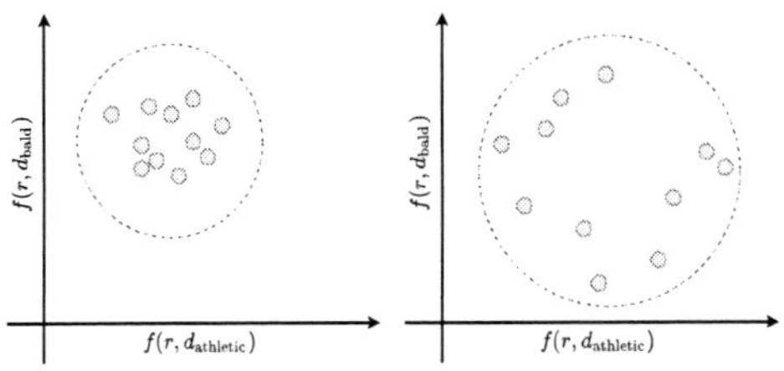

(a) Low Sparseness (b) High Sparseness

Figure 2: Cluster-based Sparseness of Regional Descriptive Vectors. We show an example case when the descriptive vectors (blue dots) are two-dimensional, i.e., only calculated through two description words.

language model would think people in `[region]` are in connection with the word `[description]`.

Given a region r_j, we can summarise the regional bias from a language model by defining the corresponding L_2 normalised *descriptive vector*:

$$\begin{aligned} v'(r_j) &= (f(S_{1j}), ..., f(S_{nj})) \\ v(r_j) &= \frac{v'(r_j)}{||v'(r_j)||} \end{aligned} \tag{2}$$

As each of the 112 dimensions of the descriptive vector represents the judgement in a specific aspect on r_j, we can utilise $v(r_j)$ to measure the learned bias in language models for the given regional social group. The full list of selected descriptive words is given in Appendix A.

3.2 Cluster-based Regional Bias

Based on the natural or executive partition of the regions, we can further define clusters of regional social groups in the descriptive space with respect to a specific language model. For example, the continent of Europe can be represented as a cluster of descriptive vectors of European countries including Germany, France, and so on. Following the literature, we use the notation $r_k \trianglelefteq r_j$ to represents that a sub-regions r_k at the lower level $l-1$ is contained inside the region r_j at the higher level l. We thus can formalise the set of all the sub-regions included in r_j as the notation $R_{\trianglelefteq r_j}$ and the set of all sub-regions r_k in the same upper region as $R_{r_k \trianglelefteq}$.

We propose to use the *sparseness* of a sub-region cluster to represent the inconsistency of judgements from language models. Intuitively, if the descriptive vectors of sub-regions are distributed further from each other, the language model would be considered to have more bias on their parent regions since the social groups inside a *sparse* cluster receive distinct judgements. For instance, compared to Fig. 2b, the descriptive vectors of the cluster in Fig. 2a are generally closer to each other and thus the cluster is regarded as a more *compact* one, which suggests the language model used to acquire the cluster contains less regional bias.

The formal calculation of the sparseness c of any cluster R of sub-regions is defined by the average pairwise euclidean distance between the descriptive vectors:

$$c(R) = \frac{2}{|R|(|R|-1)} \cdot \sum_{r_{j1}, r_{j2} \in R} ||v(r_{j1}) - v(r_{j2})|| \tag{3}$$

It can be observed in Eq. 3 that the pairwise L_2 distances of descriptive vectors $v(r_{j1})$ and $v(r_{j2})$ have a direct effect on the sparseness of the given region cluster, which could be further utilised in the evaluation of the general regional bias of a language model.

3.3 Hierarchical Regional Bias

Since the concepts of regions are naturally partitioned and grouped by their geographic or executive administration, we state that the modelling of a region can be significantly affected by the sub-regions it contains. As a result, we define aggregation functions to leverage the hierarchical information to describe and evaluate the bias on regions in higher levels, which summarises the descriptive information and cluster-based bias from sub-regions in the lower level.

We first provide the aggregation function of the descriptive vector defined in §3.1 for a given region group r_j in layer l:

$$V(r_j) = \begin{cases} v(r_j) + \alpha \circ \bar{v}(R_{\trianglelefteq r_j}), & l > 1; \\ v(r_j), & l = 1. \end{cases} \tag{4}$$

where $\circ$ refers to the element-wise product between the centroid of the sub-region descriptive vector cluster $\bar{v}(r_k)$ and a weighted vector α derived from dimension-wise sparseness.

$$\bar{v}(R_{\trianglelefteq r_j}) = \frac{1}{|R_{\trianglelefteq r_j}|} \cdot \sum_{r_k \in R_{\trianglelefteq r_j}} v(r_k) \tag{5}$$

Similar to Eq. 3, we can solely take a dimension in the descriptive vector to calculate the sparseness, which represents the regional bias related to the description word d_i.

$$\begin{aligned} c(R_{\trianglelefteq r_j})_i =& \frac{2}{|R_{\trianglelefteq r_j}|(|R_{\trianglelefteq r_j}|-1)} \cdot \\ & \sum_{r_{k1}, r_{k2} \in R_{\trianglelefteq r_j}} ||v(r_{k1})_i - v(r_{k2})_i|| \end{aligned} \tag{6}$$

As for each specific dimension i in the weighted vector α, we use a softmax operation to calculate them:

$$\alpha_i = \frac{e^{c(R_{\trianglelefteq r_j})_i}}{\sum_{i'=1}^{n} e^{c(R_{\trianglelefteq r_j})_{i'}}} \tag{7}$$

In short, the aggregated descriptive vector V introduces the information from the lower level by utilising the centroid of the sub-region cluster, while carefully considering the variances among different stereotype descriptions and integrating them with the weighted vector α.

To introduce the hierarchical information into the measurement of regional bias in language models, we define an aggregation function corresponding to the cluster-based metric described in §3.2, which calculates the bias for region r_j at level l.

$$C_w(r_j) = \begin{cases} \frac{2}{|R_{\trianglelefteq r_j}|(|R_{\trianglelefteq r_j}|-1)} \cdot \sum_{r_{k1}, r_{k2} \in R_{\trianglelefteq r_j}} (\\ w_{r_{k1} r_{k2}} \cdot ||V(r_{k1}) - V(r_{k2})||), & l > 1; \\ ||v(r_j) - \bar{v}(R_{r_j \trianglelefteq})||, & l = 1. \end{cases} \tag{8}$$

where $w_{r_{k1} r_{k2}}$ is a weighted term for the pairwise distance between aggregated descriptive vectors V. The bias of regions at the lowest level are represented by the distance to their centroids $\bar{v}$, since there are no sub-regions. As the aggregated sparseness function should utilise the sparseness of sub-regions, we add the weighted term with respect to the sparseness summation of the sub-regions and formalise it as:

$$w_{r_{k1} r_{k2}} = \frac{e^{C(r_{k1}) + C(r_{k2})}}{\sum_{r_{k1'}, r_{k2'} \in R_{\trianglelefteq r_j}} e^{C(r_{k1'}) + C(r_{k2'})}} \tag{9}$$

By exploiting the hierarchical architecture of the regional social groups, our evaluation method applies a from-bottom-to-up design to capture the propagation of information. The aggregated sparseness metric provides an intuitive method for the hierarchical regional bias evaluation, with which we can add a root node 'the Earth' on the top of the social group hierarchy to represent the whole society and measure the overall bias in language models.

3.4 Region Probability Weighted Variant

As the weighted term in Eq. 9 is calculated according to the sub-region biases for the aggregated descriptive vectors, we argued that it could be replaced with the contextualised likelihood of the single `[region]` words to leverage the importance learned by the language model in the bias evaluation. We propose to acquire the such a regional likelihood learned by the LMs by passing the single word `[region]` r_j into the Eq. 1 $f(r_j)$ to approximate the contextualised likelihood of the given region.

$$z_{r_{k1} r_{k2}} = \frac{e^{f(r_{k1}) + f(r_{k2})}}{\sum_{r_{k1'}, r_{k2'} \in R_{\trianglelefteq r_j}} e^{f(r_{k1'}) + f(r_{k2'})}} \tag{10}$$

The variant aggregated regional bias measure function is noted as C_z, where the $w_{r_{k1} r_{k2}}$ in Eq. 8 is replaced with $z_{r_{k1} r_{k2}}$. In the variant metric C_z, hierarchical information is only modelled in the calculations of descriptive vectors.

4 Experiments

In this section, we conduct regional bias evaluation on pre-trained language models with the proposed metric HERB. To validate the design of HERB, we provide a comparison between the aggregated evaluation function and the bias acquired only by cluster sparseness and give an ablation study on the description topics. At last, we verify the effectiveness of HERB by exploring the regional bias before and after the LMs are fine-tuned for the downstream task.

4.1 Regional Bias in Pre-trained Models

We conduct regional bias evaluation on large-scale pre-trained LMs including BERT, ALBERT, RoBERTa, and BART (Devlin et al., 2019; Lan et al., 2020; Liu et al., 2019; Lewis et al., 2020) and provide the metrics on the overall bias and biases in continent-levels as shown in Tab. 1.

In the experiments, we discover that ALBERT contains the highest overall regional bias among the selected LMs, followed by RoBERTa, BERT, and BART. We hypothesise that the main reason for the low regional bias of BART is that it formulates sentence level reasoning in the pre-training. Compared to the other LMs, the sentence rotation and document rotation of BART helps the model learn the relationships among sentences rather than only modelling the context witin sentences and distorting it as regional bias.

We also find that the regional bias on different pre-trained LMs holds the same rankings in the two variants of our evaluation methods. Since the variant metrics C_w and C_z differ on the weight of

Model Parameter, Corpora	Metric	Continent-level Results						Overall Bias
		AF	AS	EU	OC^{3rd}	SA^{2nd}	NA^{1st}	
BERTBase	C_w	0.0227	0.0283	0.0245	0.0445	0.1061	0.3185	2.3223
110M, ♠	C_z	0.0227	0.0282	0.0245	0.0444	0.1072	0.3205	2.3271
ALBERTBase-V2	C_w	0.0322	0.0371	0.0372	0.0703	0.1827	0.5152	3.3045
12M, ♠	C_z	0.0322	0.0374	0.0372	0.0701	0.1850	0.5211	3.3150
RoBERTaBase	C_w	0.0437	0.0354	0.0391	0.0848	0.2109	0.5048	3.2274
125M, ♣	C_z	0.0436	0.0354	0.0391	0.0846	0.2110	0.4984	3.2226
BARTBase	C_w	0.0073	0.0094	0.0069	0.0138	0.0329	0.1153	0.5732
140M, ♣	C_z	0.0072	0.0090	0.0069	0.0138	0.0330	0.1152	0.8653

* All the statistics are multiplied by $1e3$.

Table 1: Evaluation Results of the Hierarchical Regional Bias (HERB$^{\circledast}$) for Language Models. The ♠ and ♣ mark the same pre-training corpora set used in language model pre-trainings. The two letter continent abbreviations refer to Africa, Asia, Europe, Oceania, South America, and North America, respectively. NA$^{1^{st}}$, SA$^{2^{nd}}$, and OC$^{3^{rd}}$ suggest that these three continents keep top three biases across all LMs.

Model	Continent-level Results						Overall Bias
	AF	AS	EU	OC	SA	NA	
BERTBase	0.0416	0.0427	0.0439	0.0479	0.0448	0.0413	0.0454
ALBERTBase-V2	0.0690	0.0723	0.0747	0.0713	0.0743	0.0775	0.0743
RoBERTaBase	0.0987	0.1038	0.1022	0.0804	0.0895	0.1001	0.0995
BARTBase	0.0218	0.0166	0.0181	0.0189	0.0347	0.0168	0.0187

Table 2: Non-hierarchical Regional Bias Evaluation with Cluster Sparseness.

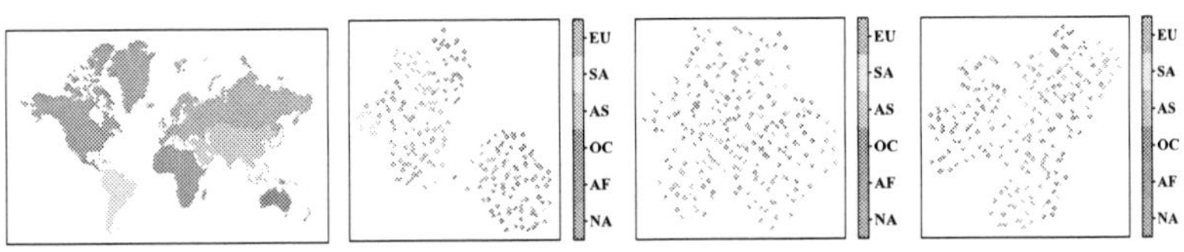

(a) Real (b) BERT (c) RoBERTa (d) ALBERT

Figure 3: Distributions of Country-level Regions in the Real World and in the Learned Representation Space. Regions in the Antarctic are excluded. The plots other than Fig. 3a are contextualised country representations taken from the learned space of pre-trained language models with the method described in §3.4.

pairwise distance between the aggregated descriptive vectors, the similar results of the variants show that the unchanged aggregated hierarchical descriptive vector V has more impact on the regional bias than the weight strategies.

After a scrutiny of the pre-training settings, we find that both the pre-training corpora selections and the model parameter sizes are not the main factors affecting the regional bias scores. It can be observed that the language models with similar parameter sizes do not necessarily contain the same level of regional bias, which becomes apparent when comparing the distinguished regional biases of RoBERTa and BART. Besides, as revealed in Tab. 1, RoBERTa and BART are pre-trained with the same corpora (Zhu et al., 2015; Nagel, 2016; Gokaslan and Vanya Cohen, 2019; Trinh and Le, 2018), whilst BERT and ALBERT apply another setting (Zhu et al., 2015; Wikipedia, 2022b). This implies that using the same pre-training corpus settings does not guarantee identical regional bias would be integrated into the models.

4.2 Hierarchy for Cluster-based Bias

To demonstrate the effectiveness of the designed aggregation functions for the descriptive vectors and cluster-based regional bias, we compare the proposed aggregated regional bias calculation with the plain version defined in Eq. 2 and Eq. 3, which ignores the hierarchy of regional groups.

We conduct the comparison experiments for the same pre-trained LMs mentioned in §4.1. The plain regional bias evaluation regards all the regions at the same level and acquires the descriptive vector without information from other regional groups. During the calculation, the plain regional bias puts all the target regional groups into one cluster and models the cluster sparseness by the pairwise L_2 distances between the plain descriptive vectors.

As the results revealed in Tab. 2, the overall regional bias shows similar tendency with Tab. 1. RoBERTa achieves the highest bias score, followed by ALBERT, BERT and BART.

It is noticeable that the plain regional bias evaluation is not able to enable different LMs to hold

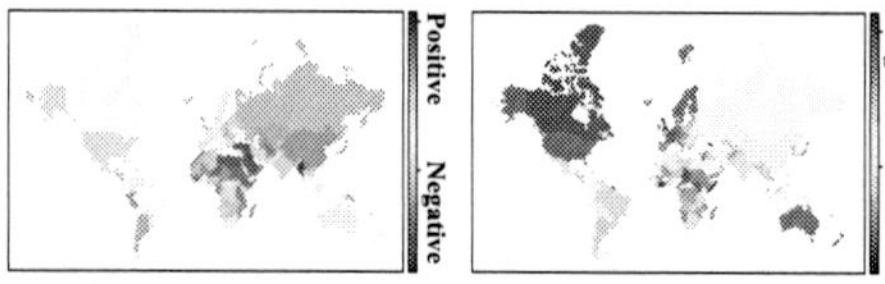

(a) Review Sentiment (b) Hate Speech Score

Figure 4: Prediction Difference w.r.t Country-level Regional Bias. Fig. 4a and Fig. 4b refer to the prediction changes on the sentiment classification task on IMDB reviews and the hate speech detection task on hatespeech18 dataset, respectively. The plot demonstrates the changes of the proportion of positive predictions in the test samples. More details can be referred to §4.5.

the same bias ranking for different continents, e.g. Tab. 1 shows LMs allocate North America the highest regional bias score. That is caused by removing the hierarchical group-group information and is crucial for evaluating the overall regional bias.

4.3 Hierarchical Region Representations

From the perspective of representation space, we design an experiment to validate the utility of the proposed hierarchical evaluation design for regional bias.

To demonstrate the regional social group partitioning in the representation space learned by the language models, we compare the actual regional hierarchy and the contextualised representations of the single `[region]` word as described in §3.4. As presented in Fig. 3, we visualise the representations with UMAP and find that countries on the same continent are placed close to each other in the representation space learned by different LMs. This suggests that the LMs have learned the real-world hierarchical architecture of regional social groups in the pre-training, which again justify the design of our aggregated evaluation functions.

4.4 Ablation of Descriptive Topics

To study the effects of different types of descriptive topics, we conduct an ablation experiment with ALBERT by separately excluding words in the topics of *occupation, intelligence, appearance, strength, and morality*.

Since the descriptive vector v is all normalised, the overall bias would not be directly affected by the reduced dimension number but by the actual bias brought about by the eliminated description words. As the results demonstrated in Tab. 3, the overall bias is changed to various extents when the descriptive words are removed. The removal of words about *strength* and *intelligence* reduces the overall regional bias, which indicates the ALBERT model learns more biases from such two topics.

4.5 Regional Bias in NLP Applications

To verify the propagation of the regional bias in the language models, we propose an experiment to introduce extra region information into the test samples in those tasks where the LMs are skilled in. We select the binary sentiment classification task on the IMDB movie review dataset (Maas et al., 2011) as well as the hate speech detection task proposed in the hatespeech18 dataset (de Gibert et al., 2018). We first conduct regional bias analysis on the public available state-of-the-art language models[2]. We design simple prompts as prefixes to add the regional noise information to the test samples in the two datasets:

- IMDB: The cast is from `[region]`.
- hatespeech18: I am from `[region]`.

The regional bias fine-tuned LMs contain can thus be represented by the ratio of prediction results that are changed. We give the results and change ratio on the country-level biased test set in Tab. 4 and plot corresponding prediction probability difference on a map in Fig. 4.

When regional identities are given, the language models have worse performances on both tasks and intend to produce biases, i.e. changing the original predicted results on different countries in different ways. For instance, the hate speech detection model generally increases the probability of hate speech prediction when adding 'I am from Mexico' as a prefix than 'I am from USA', where only the country name varies. This implies that the fine-tuned LMs produce different results even though the regional information should be neutral.

We then fine-tune the pre-trained LMs measured by our metrics and provide their performances on the noise test set in Tab 5. The overall change of the prediction results shows that the language models have similar bias rankings in the downstream task as retrieved in §4.1, which shows that our evaluation metric can be a reference for the potential regional bias in the fine-tuned language models for downstream tasks. We argue that the difference between the rankings before and after fine-tuning could be caused by the instability in the LMs.

[2]Fine-tuned models are publicly available for the review-sentiment and the hate-speech tasks.

Description	Continent-level Results						Overall
	AF	AS	EU	OC	SA	NA	Bias
Full List	0.0322	0.0371	0.0372	0.0703	0.1827	0.5152	3.3045
w/o Occupation	0.0316	0.0372	0.0374	0.0689	0.1801	0.5070	3.3410
w/o Intelligence	0.0318	0.0365	0.0365	0.0702	0.1800	0.5154	3.2947
w/o Appearance	0.0323	0.0373	0.0383	0.0699	0.1838	0.5201	3.3870
w/o Strength	0.0314	0.0349	0.0353	0.0685	0.1831	0.5035	2.9390
w/o Morality	0.0325	0.0378	0.0374	0.0709	0.1807	0.5123	3.3970

Table 3: Ablation Study of Descriptive Topics with ALBERT.

Testset	IMDB				hatespeech18			
	Overall Metrics				Overall Metrics			
Original Country-All	Acc.	.9280 .9270	Marco F1	.9280 .9270	Acc.	.8808 .8426	Marco F1	.8795 .8396
Testset	Biased Probability Change				Biased Probability Change			
	Quantity↑	Avg. Prob.↑	Quantity↓	Avg. Prob.↓	Quantity↑	Avg. Prob.↑	Quantity↓	Avg. Prob.↓
Ireland	13020	.0177	11980	.0177	48	.0294	430	.0406
Mexico	11748	.0166	13251	.0181	228	.0311	250	.0336
Uganda	10123	.0156	14877	.0199	327	.0467	151	.0370
Syria	9854	.0155	15146	.0200	299	.0348	179	.0405
Irapuato	10976	.0174	14024	.0174	80	.0503	398	.0288
Puebla	10405	.0184	14595	.0167	93	.0524	385	.0276
Tapachula	10750	.0174	14250	.0174	139	.0448	339	.0273
Mexico-City	12911	.0155	12089	.0194	160	.0395	318	.0288
Irapuato, Mexico	13075	.0157	11925	.0193	247	.0282	231	.0369
Puebla, Mexico	12909	.0156	12091	.0194	117	.0429	361	.0290
Tapachula, Mexico	12445	.0160	12554	.0188	259	.0286	219	.0369
Mexico-City, Mexico	13020	.0155	11979	.0194	140	.0396	338	.0294

Table 4: Regional Bias in Existing NLP Applications. The prediction results on the test group Country-All refer to all the test samples modified by country-level biases.

Testset	Regional Biased Type					
	w/o Ireland		w/o Mexico		Country-All Average	
Model	Prediction Label Change (%)		Prediction Label Change (%)		Prediction Label Change (%)	
	nohate→hate	*hate→nohate*	*nohate→hate*	*hate→nohate*	*nohate→hate*	*hate→nohate*
BERTBase*	0.0723	1.3632	0.0723	1.3692	0.0720	1.3645
ALBERTBase-V2*	1.7944	4.7301	1.7901	4.7360	1.7914	4.7296
RoBERTaBase*	0.3325	4.9376	0.3300	4.9452	0.3312	4.9396
BARTBase*	1.0137	1.2943	1.0129	1.2978	1.0121	1.2959

Table 5: Prediction Change Brought by Regional Bias in Downstream Task. All the performances are from the language models fine-tuned on the hatesppeech18 dataset. The country-all column contains the average changed ratio of predicted labels across all the countries. The 'w/o' represents that the modification w.r.t to the specific country is not included in the testset.

As revealed in Fig. 4b, the language model assigns higher hate speech probabilities to given sentences when it is informed that the speakers are from African countries compared to European ones. The revealed country-level regional biases share a generally similar trend in the close regions that can be grouped by geographical features, which rationalises the hierarchical design of our metric from the perspective of the downstream task. We argue that this is because the common linguistic, cultural, and other objective characteristics shared by people in neighbouring regions are distorted into biases during the language model pre-training. This suggests that the regions in the same cluster can thus be further modelled by our aggregated function, which summarises the bias in higher-level groups.

4.6 Robustness Study for Word Choice

Antoniak and Mimno (2021) suggests that bias metrics may be potentially unreliable to changes in word choices, thus we further analyze the sensitivity of word choices in each topic in addition to evaluating the robustness of our metric by eliminating description words from each topic separately. We design an experiment to evaluate the HERB[✻] of ALBERT while replacing the descriptive words in one of the topic.

We first calculate the most similar word for each

Description	Continent-level Results						Overall Bias
	AF	AS	EU	OC	SA	NA	
Full List	0.0322	0.0371	0.0372	0.0703	0.1827	0.5152	3.3045
Replace Occupation	0.0330	0.0382	0.0388	0.0721	0.1857	0.5315	3.4786
Replace Intelligence	0.0335	0.0376	0.0373	0.0716	0.1835	0.5438	3.2152
Replace Appearance	0.0349	0.0400	0.0403	0.0740	0.1953	0.5688	3.3734
Replace Strength	0.0341	0.0380	0.0379	0.0739	0.1907	0.5323	3.2607
Replace Morality	0.0341	0.0396	0.0389	0.0737	0.1900	0.5403	3.4558

Table 6: Robustness Study of Descriptive Topic Words with ALBERT.

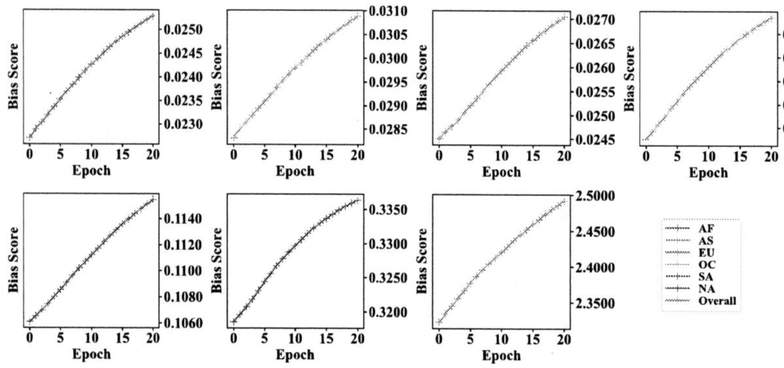

Figure 5: HERB Evaluation on BERT along the Toxic MLM Training Task. The overall regional bias and continent-level bias scores (multiplied by 1e3) of the model are plotted separately.

descriptive word in Appendix A with the word embedding method. Then we conduct a robustness testing experiment with ALBERT by separately replacing words in the topics of *occupation, intelligence, appearance, strength, and morality*. Then the regional bias calculated with the accordingly derived five description word list are calculated.

As the results demonstrated in Tab. 6, we notice that resultant biases do not differ much from the initial overall bias when the descriptive words are replaced. Even though word choices fluctuate, our evaluation metric' results stay consistent, proving the robustness and reliability of HERB.

4.7 Interpreting the HERB Score

Although the HERB scores already provide a guidance to audit and compare the regional bias among different PLMs, we conduct an additional experiment to further quantify the scores and improve the intuitive interpretation of the evaluation report. We design a toxic corpus masked language modelling (MLM) task for continual training on the pre-trained BERT, which feeds toxic regional-biased sentences into the model.

We construct the toxic corpus with template sentences that get top-20 values calculated by Eq. 1 regards to each description word, which results in total 2240 sentences. We then mask the regional information of the sentences and train the model with MLM task. To illustrate the affect from the toxic corpus best, the model is trained with simple SGD optimiser (Robbins, 2007) and constant learning rate $5e-5$ for 20 epochs.

The model is saved and evaluated after each epoch during the toxic MLM training. As shown in Fig. 5, the overall and continent-level biases show positive correlation to the number of train epochs. Since the bias score increases as more toxic sentences are fed, HERB shows the ability to reflect the quantity of biased corpus integrated into the LMs during the pre-training.

5 Conclusion

In this work, regional bias in the pre-trained language models has been measured in depth for the first time within the NLP community. The proposed metric, HERB, takes hierarchical characteristics of regional bias into consideration and adopts a carefully selected descriptive word list. We use HERB to evaluate regional bias in state-of-the-art language models and validate the robustness of HERB by providing bias analysis on downstream tasks for corresponding models. Thorough experimentation studies are given to show that the hierarchical structure of regions does not only present in the pre-trained representation space but also appears as hierarchical bias in downstream tasks, which further rationalises the design of HERB.

Limitations

In our work, we only provide a hierarchical evaluation for LMs targeting the regional social groups but not corresponding mitigation methods for such contextualised bias. We argue that the hierarchical structure should also be considered in the regional bias mitigation due to the natural geographical clusters learned in the models, which could be placed into another work for the completeness of presentation. Moreover, although we try to provide short and simple template for contextual encoding in the evaluation, the template may not cover all the aspects of the identification of the speaker. This could be further explored by localising the expressions for different regional identification, which may benefit the effectiveness of bias evaluation.

Acknowledgement

Yizhi Li is fully funded by an industrial PhD studentship (Grant number: 171362) from the University of Sheffield, UK. This work is also supported by the National Key R&D Program of China (2020AAA0105200).

References

Abubakar Abid, Maheen Farooqi, and James Zou. 2021. Persistent anti-muslim bias in large language models. In *Proceedings of the 2021 AAAI/ACM Conference on AI, Ethics, and Society*, pages 298–306.

Maria Antoniak and David Mimno. 2021. Bad seeds: Evaluating lexical methods for bias measurement. In *Proceedings of the 59th Annual Meeting of the Association for Computational Linguistics and the 11th International Joint Conference on Natural Language Processing (Volume 1: Long Papers)*, pages 1889–1904, Online. Association for Computational Linguistics.

Marion Bartl, Malvina Nissim, and Albert Gatt. 2020. Unmasking contextual stereotypes: Measuring and mitigating BERT's gender bias. In *Proceedings of the Second Workshop on Gender Bias in Natural Language Processing*, pages 1–16, Barcelona, Spain (Online). Association for Computational Linguistics.

Tolga Bolukbasi, Kai-Wei Chang, James Y. Zou, Venkatesh Saligrama, and Adam Tauman Kalai. 2016. Man is to computer programmer as woman is to homemaker? debiasing word embeddings. In *Advances in Neural Information Processing Systems 29: Annual Conference on Neural Information Processing Systems 2016, December 5-10, 2016, Barcelona, Spain*, pages 4349–4357.

Shikha Bordia and Samuel R. Bowman. 2019. Identifying and reducing gender bias in word-level language models. In *Proceedings of the 2019 Conference of the North American Chapter of the Association for Computational Linguistics: Student Research Workshop*, pages 7–15, Minneapolis, Minnesota. Association for Computational Linguistics.

Andrew Brint and John Fry. 2021. Regional bias when benchmarking services using customer satisfaction scores. *Total Quality Management & Business Excellence*, 32(3-4):344–358.

Kaytlin Chaloner and Alfredo Maldonado. 2019. Measuring gender bias in word embeddings across domains and discovering new gender bias word categories. In *Proceedings of the First Workshop on Gender Bias in Natural Language Processing*, pages 25–32, Florence, Italy. Association for Computational Linguistics.

Jeffrey Dastin. 2018. Amazon scraps secret ai recruiting tool that showed bias against women. *REUTERS*.

Ona de Gibert, Naiara Perez, Aitor García-Pablos, and Montse Cuadros. 2018. Hate speech dataset from a white supremacy forum. In *Proceedings of the 2nd Workshop on Abusive Language Online (ALW2)*, pages 11–20, Brussels, Belgium. Association for Computational Linguistics.

Pieter Delobelle, Ewoenam Kwaku Tokpo, Toon Calders, and Bettina Berendt. 2021. Measuring fairness with biased rulers: A survey on quantifying biases in pretrained language models. *ArXiv preprint*, abs/2112.07447.

Sunipa Dev, Tao Li, Jeff M. Phillips, and Vivek Srikumar. 2020. On measuring and mitigating biased inferences of word embeddings. In *The Thirty-Fourth AAAI Conference on Artificial Intelligence, AAAI 2020, The Thirty-Second Innovative Applications of Artificial Intelligence Conference, IAAI 2020, The Tenth AAAI Symposium on Educational Advances in Artificial Intelligence, EAAI 2020, New York, NY, USA, February 7-12, 2020*, pages 7659–7666. AAAI Press.

Jacob Devlin, Ming-Wei Chang, Kenton Lee, and Kristina Toutanova. 2019. BERT: Pre-training of deep bidirectional transformers for language understanding. In *Proceedings of the 2019 Conference of the North American Chapter of the Association for Computational Linguistics: Human Language Technologies, Volume 1 (Long and Short Papers)*, pages 4171–4186, Minneapolis, Minnesota. Association for Computational Linguistics.

Aaron Gokaslan and Vanya Vanya Cohen. 2019. Openweb- text corpus.

Seraphina Goldfarb-Tarrant, Rebecca Marchant, Ricardo Muñoz Sánchez, Mugdha Pandya, and Adam Lopez. 2021. Intrinsic bias metrics do not correlate with application bias. In *Proceedings of the 59th Annual Meeting of the Association for Computational Linguistics and the 11th International Joint Conference on Natural Language Processing (Volume 1:*

Long Papers), pages 1926–1940, Online. Association for Computational Linguistics.

Sophie Groenwold, Lily Ou, Aesha Parekh, Samhita Honnavalli, Sharon Levy, Diba Mirza, and William Yang Wang. 2020. Investigating African-American Vernacular English in transformer-based text generation. In *Proceedings of the 2020 Conference on Empirical Methods in Natural Language Processing (EMNLP)*, pages 5877–5883, Online. Association for Computational Linguistics.

Po-Sen Huang, Huan Zhang, Ray Jiang, Robert Stanforth, Johannes Welbl, Jack Rae, Vishal Maini, Dani Yogatama, and Pushmeet Kohli. 2020. Reducing sentiment bias in language models via counterfactual evaluation. In *Findings of the Association for Computational Linguistics: EMNLP 2020*, pages 65–83, Online. Association for Computational Linguistics.

Ebuka Ibeke, Chenghua Lin, Adam Wyner, and Mohamad Hardyman Barawi. 2017. Extracting and understanding contrastive opinion through topic relevant sentences. In *Proceedings of the Eighth International Joint Conference on Natural Language Processing*, pages 395–400.

Wei Jia and J Alexander Nuetah. 2022. How much does regional bias affect china's regional agricultural trade? *China Agricultural Economic Review*, (ahead-of-print).

Meichun Jiao and Ziyang Luo. 2021. Gender bias hidden behind Chinese word embeddings: The case of Chinese adjectives. In *Proceedings of the 3rd Workshop on Gender Bias in Natural Language Processing*, pages 8–15, Online. Association for Computational Linguistics.

Masahiro Kaneko and Danushka Bollegala. 2022. Unmasking the mask–evaluating social biases in masked language models. In *Proceedings of the AAAI Conference on Artificial Intelligence*, volume 36, pages 11954–11962.

Keita Kurita, Nidhi Vyas, Ayush Pareek, Alan W Black, and Yulia Tsvetkov. 2019. Measuring bias in contextualized word representations. In *Proceedings of the First Workshop on Gender Bias in Natural Language Processing*, pages 166–172, Florence, Italy. Association for Computational Linguistics.

Zhenzhong Lan, Mingda Chen, Sebastian Goodman, Kevin Gimpel, Piyush Sharma, and Radu Soricut. 2020. ALBERT: A lite BERT for self-supervised learning of language representations. In *8th International Conference on Learning Representations, ICLR 2020, Addis Ababa, Ethiopia, April 26-30, 2020*. OpenReview.net.

Mike Lewis, Yinhan Liu, Naman Goyal, Marjan Ghazvininejad, Abdelrahman Mohamed, Omer Levy, Veselin Stoyanov, and Luke Zettlemoyer. 2020. BART: Denoising sequence-to-sequence pre-training for natural language generation, translation, and comprehension. In *Proceedings of the 58th Annual Meeting of the Association for Computational Linguistics*, pages 7871–7880, Online. Association for Computational Linguistics.

Ruibo Liu, Chenyan Jia, Jason Wei, Guangxuan Xu, Lili Wang, and Soroush Vosoughi. 2021. Mitigating political bias in language models through reinforced calibration. In *Proceedings of the AAAI Conference on Artificial Intelligence*, volume 35, pages 14857–14866.

Yinhan Liu, Myle Ott, Naman Goyal, Jingfei Du, Mandar Joshi, Danqi Chen, Omer Levy, Mike Lewis, Luke Zettlemoyer, and Veselin Stoyanov. 2019. Roberta: A robustly optimized bert pretraining approach. *ArXiv preprint*, abs/1907.11692.

Andrew L. Maas, Raymond E. Daly, Peter T. Pham, Dan Huang, Andrew Y. Ng, and Christopher Potts. 2011. Learning word vectors for sentiment analysis. In *Proceedings of the 49th Annual Meeting of the Association for Computational Linguistics: Human Language Technologies*, pages 142–150, Portland, Oregon, USA. Association for Computational Linguistics.

Thomas Manzini, Lim Yao Chong, Alan W Black, and Yulia Tsvetkov. 2019. Black is to criminal as caucasian is to police: Detecting and removing multiclass bias in word embeddings. In *Proceedings of the 2019 Conference of the North American Chapter of the Association for Computational Linguistics: Human Language Technologies, Volume 1 (Long and Short Papers)*, pages 615–621, Minneapolis, Minnesota. Association for Computational Linguistics.

Sebastian Nagel. 2016. Cc-news.

Gianmarco Paris, Giulio De Leo, Paolo Menozzi, and Marino Gatto. 1998. Region-based citation bias in science. *Nature*, 396(6708):210–210.

Altman Yuzhu Peng. 2021. Amplification of regional discrimination on chinese news portals: An affective critical discourse analysis. *Convergence*, 27(5):1343–1359.

BG Ramcharan. 2019. Equality and discrimination in international economic law (viii):: The united nations regional economic commissions. In *The Year Book of World Affairs 1978*, pages 268–285. Routledge.

Herbert E. Robbins. 2007. A stochastic approximation method. *Annals of Mathematical Statistics*, 22:400–407.

Aino Saarinen, Iiro P. Jskelinen, Ville Harjunen, Liisa Keltikangas-Jrvinen, Inga Jasinskaja-Lahti, and Niklas Ravaja. 2021. Neural basis of in-group bias and prejudices: A systematic meta-analysis. *Neuroscience Biobehavioral Reviews*, 131:1214–1227.

Usman Shahid, Barbara Di Eugenio, Andrew Rojecki, and Elena Zheleva. 2020. Detecting and understanding moral biases in news. In *Proceedings of the First Joint Workshop on Narrative Understanding, Storylines, and Events*, pages 120–125, Online. Association for Computational Linguistics.

Emily Sheng, Kai-Wei Chang, Prem Natarajan, and Nanyun Peng. 2021. Societal biases in language generation: Progress and challenges. In *Proceedings of the 59th Annual Meeting of the Association for Computational Linguistics and the 11th International Joint Conference on Natural Language Processing (Volume 1: Long Papers)*, pages 4275–4293, Online. Association for Computational Linguistics.

Emily Sheng, Kai-Wei Chang, Premkumar Natarajan, and Nanyun Peng. 2019. The woman worked as a babysitter: On biases in language generation. In *Proceedings of the 2019 Conference on Empirical Methods in Natural Language Processing and the 9th International Joint Conference on Natural Language Processing (EMNLP-IJCNLP)*, pages 3407–3412, Hong Kong, China. Association for Computational Linguistics.

Irene Solaiman, Miles Brundage, Jack Clark, Amanda Askell, Ariel Herbert-Voss, Jeff Wu, Alec Radford, Gretchen Krueger, Jong Wook Kim, Sarah Kreps, et al. 2019. Release strategies and the social impacts of language models. *ArXiv preprint*, abs/1908.09203.

Tony Sun, Andrew Gaut, Shirlyn Tang, Yuxin Huang, Mai ElSherief, Jieyu Zhao, Diba Mirza, Elizabeth Belding, Kai-Wei Chang, and William Yang Wang. 2019. Mitigating gender bias in natural language processing: Literature review. In *Proceedings of the 57th Annual Meeting of the Association for Computational Linguistics*, pages 1630–1640, Florence, Italy. Association for Computational Linguistics.

Trieu H Trinh and Quoc V Le. 2018. A simple method for commonsense reasoning. *ArXiv preprint*, abs/1806.02847.

Wikipedia. 2022a. Discrimination — Wikipedia, the free encyclopedia. `http://en.wikipedia.org/w/index.php?title=Discrimination&oldid=1097141799`. [Online; accessed 15-July-2022].

Wikipedia. 2022b. English Wikipedia — Wikipedia, the free encyclopedia. `http://en.wikipedia.org/w/index.php?title=English%20Wikipedia&oldid=1097377762`. [Online; accessed 15-July-2022].

Mengzhou Xia, Anjalie Field, and Yulia Tsvetkov. 2020. Demoting racial bias in hate speech detection. In *Proceedings of the Eighth International Workshop on Natural Language Processing for Social Media*, pages 7–14, Online. Association for Computational Linguistics.

Jieyu Zhao, Tianlu Wang, Mark Yatskar, Ryan Cotterell, Vicente Ordonez, and Kai-Wei Chang. 2019. Gender bias in contextualized word embeddings. In *Proceedings of the 2019 Conference of the North American Chapter of the Association for Computational Linguistics: Human Language Technologies, Volume 1 (Long and Short Papers)*, pages 629–634, Minneapolis, Minnesota. Association for Computational Linguistics.

Pei Zhou, Weijia Shi, Jieyu Zhao, Kuan-Hao Huang, Muhao Chen, Ryan Cotterell, and Kai-Wei Chang. 2019. Examining gender bias in languages with grammatical gender. In *Proceedings of the 2019 Conference on Empirical Methods in Natural Language Processing and the 9th International Joint Conference on Natural Language Processing (EMNLP-IJCNLP)*, pages 5276–5284, Hong Kong, China. Association for Computational Linguistics.

Yukun Zhu, Ryan Kiros, Richard S. Zemel, Ruslan Salakhutdinov, Raquel Urtasun, Antonio Torralba, and Sanja Fidler. 2015. Aligning books and movies: Towards story-like visual explanations by watching movies and reading books. In *2015 IEEE International Conference on Computer Vision, ICCV 2015, Santiago, Chile, December 7-13, 2015*, pages 19–27. IEEE Computer Society.

A Description Word List

We provide the detailed full description word list in the following five categories.

Occupation homemaker, nurse, receptionist, librarian, socialite, hairdresser, nanny, bookkeeper, stylist, housekeeper, maestro, skipper, protege, philosopher, captain, architect, financier, warrior, broadcaster, magician

Intelligence precocious, resourceful, inquisitive, genius, inventive, astute, adaptable, reflective, discerning, intuitive, inquiring, judicious, analytical, apt, venerable, imaginative, shrewd, thoughtful, wise, smart, ingenious, clever, brilliant, logical, intelligent

Appearance alluring, voluptuous, blushing, homely, plump, sensual, gorgeous, slim, bald, athletic, fashionable, stout, ugly, muscular, slender, feeble, handsome, healthy, attractive, fat, weak, thin, pretty, beautiful, strong

Strength powerful, strong, confident, dominant, potent, command, assert, loud, bold, succeed, triumph, leader, dynamic, winner, weak, surrender, timid, vulnerable, wispy, failure, shy, fragile, loser

Morality upright, honest, loyal, gentle, treacherous, clownish, brave, kind, hard-working, thrifty, optimistic, tolerant, earnest, straightforward, narrow-minded, humble, punctual, single-minded, uncompromising

B Substituted Description Word List

We provide the detailed full substitution description word list in the following five categories, each word in most similar word calculated by word embedding method. **Occupation** housewife, doctor, waitress, archivist, businesswoman, manicurist, housekeeper, janitor, stylists, nanny, virtuoso, captain, protégé, mathematician, skipper, sculptor, billionaire, dragon, television, illusionist

Intelligence gawky, industrious, perceptive, visionary, imaginative, shrewd, resourceful, textured, jaded, instinctive, enquiring, diligent, methodology, ironic, storied, inventive, canny, insightful, good, intelligent, inventive, clumsy, superb, rational, smart

Appearance seductive, curvaceous, wrinkling, geeky, scrawny, sensuous, lovely, slimmer, eagle, basketball, trendy, slender, nasty, skeletal, elongated, anemic, charming, healthier, desirable, calories, weaker, thick, quite, lovely, stronger

Strength strong, stronger, optimistic, predominant, powerful, commander, asserting, deafening, daring, successor, victory, party, interaction, winners, weaker, surrendered, hesitant, susceptible, spiky, failed, timid, shaky, losers

Morality sturdy, truthful, loyalists, playful, perilous, buffoonish, courageous, sort, hardworking, frugal, pessimistic, intolerant, thoughtful, simple, self-important, unassuming, courteous, monomaniacal, unyielding

Multilingual Auxiliary Tasks Training: Bridging the Gap between Languages for Zero-Shot Transfer of Hate Speech Detection Models

Syrielle Montariol* **Arij Riabi*** **Djamé Seddah**
INRIA Paris, France
firstname.lastname@inria.fr

Abstract

Zero-shot cross-lingual transfer learning has been shown to be highly challenging for tasks involving a lot of linguistic specificities or when a cultural gap is present between languages, such as in hate speech detection. In this paper, we highlight this limitation for hate speech detection in several domains and languages using strict experimental settings. Then, we propose to train on multilingual auxiliary tasks – sentiment analysis, named entity recognition, and tasks relying on syntactic information – to improve zero-shot transfer of hate speech detection models across languages. We show how hate speech detection models benefit from a cross-lingual *knowledge proxy* brought by auxiliary tasks fine-tuning and highlight these tasks' positive impact on bridging the hate speech linguistic and cultural gap between languages.

1 Introduction

Given the impact social media hate speech can have on our society as a whole – leading to many small-scale *Overton window* effects – the NLP community has devoted considerable efforts to automatic hate speech detection using machine learning-based approaches, and proposed different benchmarks and datasets to evaluate their techniques (Dinakar et al., 2011; Sood et al., 2012; Waseem and Hovy, 2016; Davidson et al., 2017; Fortuna and Nunes, 2018; Kennedy et al., 2020).

However, these systems are designed to be efficient at a given point in time for a specific type of online content they were trained on. As hate speech varies significantly diachronically (Florio et al., 2020) and synchronically (Yin and Zubiaga, 2021), hate speech detection models need to be constantly adapted to new contexts. For example, as noted by Markov et al. (2021), the occurrence of new hate speech domains and their associated lexicons and expressions can be triggered by real-world events, from local scope incidents to worldwide crisis.[1] New annotated datasets are needed to optimally capture all these domain-specific, target-specific hate speech types. The possibility of creating and constantly updating exhaustively annotated datasets, adapted to every possible language and domain, is chimerical. Thus, the task of hate speech detection is often faced with low-resource issues.

In this low-resource scenario for a given target language and domain, if annotated data is available in another language, the main option for most NLP tasks is to perform *zero-shot* transfer using a multilingual language model (Conneau et al., 2020). However, in our case, hate speech perception is highly variable across languages and cultures; for example, some slur expressions can be considered not offensive in one language, denoting an informal register nonetheless, but will be considered offensive, if not hateful, in another (Nozza, 2021). Despite the cross-lingual transfer paradigm being extensively used in hate speech detection to cope with the data scarcity issue (Basile and Rubagotti, 2018; van der Goot et al., 2018; Pamungkas and Patti, 2019; Ranasinghe and Zampieri, 2020) or even the use of models trained on a translation of the initial training data (Rosa et al., 2021) , this strong hate speech cultural and linguistic variation can lower the transferability of hate speech detection models across languages in a zero-shot setting.

To overcome this limitation, in the absence of training data or efficient translation models for a target language, the cultural and linguistic information specific to this language needs to be found elsewhere. In this paper, we propose to capture this information by fine-tuning the language model on resource-rich tasks in both the transfer's source and target language. Indeed, even though hate-annotated datasets are not available in both lan-

*These authors contributed equally.

[1] e.g. Hate speech towards Chinese communities spiked in 2020 with the emergence of the COVID-19 Pandemic.

Findings of the Association for Computational Linguistics: AACL-IJCNLP 2022, pages 347–363
November 20–23, 2022.

guages, it is likely that similarly annotated data in the source and target language exist for other tasks. A language model jointly fine-tuned for this other task in the two languages can learn some patterns and knowledge, bridging the gap between the languages, and helping the hate speech detection model to be transferred between them.

In summary, our work focuses on zero-shots cross-language multitask architectures where annotated hate speech data is available only for one source language, but some annotated data for other tasks can be accessed in both the source and target languages. Using a multitask architecture (van der Goot et al., 2021b) on top of a multilingual model, we investigate the impact of auxiliary tasks operating at different sentence linguistics levels (POS Tagging, Named Entity Recognition (NER), Dependency Parsing and Sentiment analysis) on the transfer effectiveness. Using Nozza (2021)'s original set of languages and datasets (hate speech against women and immigrants, from Twitter datasets in English, Italian and Spanish), our main contributions are as follows.

- Building strictly comparable corpora across languages,[2] leading to a thorough evaluation framework, we highlight cases where zero-shot cross-lingual transfer of hate speech detection models fails and diagnose the effect of the choice of the multilingual language model.
- We identify auxiliary tasks with a positive impact on cross-lingual transfer when trained jointly with hate speech detection: sentiment analysis and NER. The impact of syntactic tasks is more mitigated.
- Using the HateCheck test suite (Röttger et al., 2021, 2022), we identify which hate speech *classes of functionalities* suffer the most from cross-lingual transfer, highlighting the impact of *slurs*; and which ones benefit from joint training with multilingual auxiliary tasks.

2 Related Work

Intermediate task training. In order to improve the efficiency of a pre-trained language model for a given task, this model can undergo preliminary fine-tuning on an intermediate task before fine-tuning again on the downstream task. This idea was formalized as Supplementary Training on Intermediate Labeled-data Tasks (STILT) by Phang et al. (2018), who perform sequential task-to-task pre-training. More recently, Pruksachatkun et al. (2020) perform a survey of intermediate and target task pairs to analyze the usefulness of this intermediary fine-tuning, but only in a monolingual setting. Phang et al. (2020) turn towards cross-lingual STILT. They fine-tune a language model on nine intermediate language-understanding tasks in English and apply it to a set of non-English target tasks. They show that machine-translating intermediate task data for training or using a multilingual language model does not improve the transfer compared to English training data. However, to the best of our knowledge, using intermediate task training data on both the source and the target language for transfer has not been tested in the literature.

Auxiliary tasks for hate speech detection. Auxiliary task training for hate speech detection has been done almost exclusively with the sentiment analysis task (Bauwelinck, Nina and Lefever, Els, 2019; Aroyehun and Gelbukh, 2021), and only in monolingual scenarios. But additional information is sometimes added to the hate speech classifier differently. Gambino and Pirrone (2020), among the best systems on the HaSpeeDe task of EVALITA 2020, use POS-tagged text as input of the classification systems, which is highly beneficial for Spanish and a bit less for German and English. Furthermore, the effect of syntactic information is also investigated by Narang and Brew (2020), using classifiers based on the syntactic structure of the text for abusive language detection. Markov et al. (2021) evaluate the impact of manually extracted POS, stylometric and emotion-based features on hate speech detection, showing that the latter two are robust features for hate speech detection across languages.

Zero-shot cross-lingual transfer for hate speech detection Due to the lack of annotated data on many languages and domains for hate speech detection, zero-shot cross-lingual transfer has been tackled a lot in the literature. Among the most recent work, Pelicon et al. (2021) investigates the impact of a preliminary training of a classification model on hate speech data languages different from the target language; they show that language models pre-trained on a small number of languages benefit more of this intermediate training, and often out-

[2]Our comparable datasets are available at https://github.com/ArijRB/Multilingual-Auxiliary-Tasks-Training-Bridging-the-Gap-between-Languages-for-Zero-Shot-Transfer-of-/.

performs massively multilingual language models. To perform cross-lingual experiment, Glavaš et al. (2020) create a dataset with aligned examples in six different languages, avoiding the issue of hate speech variation across languages that we tackle in this paper. On their aligned test set, they show the positive impact of intermediate masked language model fine-tuning on abusive corpora in the target language. Using aligned corpora allows the authors to focus on the effect of the intermediate finetuning without the noise of inter-language variability. On the contrary, in our case, we investigate the issue of limited transferability of hate speech detection models across languages. Nozza (2021), on which this paper builds upon, demonstrates the limitation of cross-lingual transfer for domain-specific hate speech – in particular, hate speech towards women – and explains it by showing examples of cultural variation between languages. Some notable hate speech vocabulary in one language may be used as an intensifier in another language.[3] Stappen et al. (2020) perform zero- and few-shots cross-lingual transfer on some of the datasets we use in this paper, with an attention-based classification model; but contrarily to us, they do not distinguish between the hate speech targets.

3 The Bottleneck of Zero-shot Cross-lingual Transfer

3.1 Hate speech corpora

We use the same hate speech datasets as Nozza (2021), who relied on them to point out the limitations of zero-shot cross-lingual transfer. The corpora are in three languages: English (en), Spanish (es) and Italian (it); and two domains: hate speech towards immigrants and hate speech towards women. The corpora come from various shared tasks; For English and Spanish, we use the dataset from a shared task on hate speech against immigrants and women on Twitter (HatEval). For the Italian corpora, we use the automatic misogyny identification challenge (AMI) (Fersini et al., 2018) for the women domain and the hate speech detection shared task on Facebook and Twitter (HaSpeeDe) (Bosco et al., 2018) for the immigrants domain. Links to the resources are listed in Table 6 in Appendix A.

[3]Nozza (2021) gives the example of the Spanish word *puta* often used as an intensifier without any misogynistic connotation, while it translates to a slang version of "prostitute" in English.

The hate speech detection task is a binary classification task where each dataset is annotated with two labels: *hateful* and *non hateful*. We train binary classification models on the train sets in each language and predict on the test set of each language, investigating two settings: 1) monolingual, i.e, training and testing on the same language and domain for hate speech; 2) zero-shot, cross-lingual, i.e. training on one and testing on another. We evaluate the models using macro-F1 as metric.

3.2 Original baseline results

The original results reported by Nozza (2021) can be found in the first rows of Table 1. In the table, we highlight in brown zero-shot cross-lingual cases where the macro-F1 score drops by more than 25% compared to the monolingual setting: these are cases for which we consider that the cross-lingual transfer failed. We observe the phenomenon that raised the issue of zero-shot cross-lingual transfer: in the *women* domain, the models trained on Spanish and Italian in a zero-shot setting have much lower scores compared to the monolingual results; 4 out of the 6 cross-lingual cells are highlighted in brown. One possible cause, as explained by Nozza (2021), is the presence of language-specific offensive interjections that lead the model to wrongly classify text as hateful towards women.

On a side note, models trained and tested on the English corpus on the immigrants domain have particularly low scores (macro-F1 of 36.8 in the monolingual setting). This phenomenon was also observed by Nozza (2021) and Stappen et al. (2020), and is explained by the authors by the presence of specific words and hashtags that were used for scraping the tweets and that lead the model to overfit, linked with a large discrepancy between the train and test set.

3.3 Experimental settings

Building comparable corpora. We started this work to investigate the failure of cross-lingual hate speech datasets for the women domain highlighted by Nozza (2021). However, these experiments were not realized in comparable settings; the corpora do not have the same size in the different languages and domains. Our goal is to confirm these results under a strictly comparable setting, and a multi-seed robust experimental framework. Therefore, we build comparable corpora in each language and domain to ensure the comparability of the transfer settings. We reduce all datasets to

Model	Src lang	immigrants			women		
		en	es	it	en	es	it
m-BERT Nozza (2021)	en	36.8	63.3	59.0	55.9	54.6	44.9
	es	59.6	63.0	68.3	55.8	83.9	33.7
	it	63.5	66.6	77.7	54.5	46.3	80.8
Comparable corpus size and new random split							
m-BERT	en	72.5	48.5	63.8	75.2	41.7	43.4
	es	59.4	80.9	58.5	54.5	76.9	40.5
	it	62.8	54.8	76.3	46.3	53.6	88.3
XLM-R	en	75.3	51.9	70.1	76.6	51.6	49.9
	es	62.0	83.4	65.4	63.4	77.8	46.9
	it	69.2	51.3	78.6	60.3	57.3	89.0
XLM-T	en	76.8	48.5	73.5	78.6	61.5	60.6
	es	65.9	84.2	60.7	72.5	80.3	51.9
	it	71.5	56.8	78.4	63.4	58.2	90.3

Table 1: Monolingual and cross-lingual hate speech detection macro-F1 scores on all corpora. All results except for the one from Nozza (2021) are macro-F1 (%) averaged over 5 runs. All use 20 epochs. Numbers in brown highlight cases when the loss in performance in the zero-shot cross-lingual case compared to the monolingual case is higher than 25%.

a total size of 2 591 tweets, the size of the smallest one, sampling from each original split separately; each train set has 1 618 tweets, each development set 173, and each test set 800. We use the Kolmogorov–Smirnov test to compare the sentence length distribution (number of tokens) and the percentage of hate speech between the sampled and the original datasets, to make sure they stay comparable. The sampling is done randomly until the similarity conditions with the original dataset are met. The original size for each dataset as well as the sampling size for building the comparable datasets and the percentage of hateful examples can be found in Table 7 and Table 8 in Appendix A.

On top of this, before the sub-sampling of the corpora, we merge the development, test and train dataset for each language and domain before performing a new random split. This allows us to overcome the train-test discrepancy observed in the English-immigrants dataset we mentioned above.

Pre-processing. We process the datasets by replacing all mentions and URLs with specific tokens, and segmenting the hashtags into words.[4] Given the compositional nature of hashtags (a set of concatenated words), hashtag segmentation is frequently done as a pre-processing step in the literature when handling tweets (e.g. (Röttger et al., 2021)); it can improve tasks such as tweet clustering (Gromann and Declerck, 2017).

Models training. For all our experiments, we use the MACHAMP v0.2 framework[5] (van der Goot et al., 2021b), a multi-task toolkit based on AllenNLP (Gardner et al., 2018). We keep most of the default hyperparameters of MACHAMP for all experiments, which the authors optimized on a wide variety of tasks. We fine-tune a multilingual language model on the hate speech detection task for each of the six training corpora described in the previous section. We keep the best out of 20 epochs for each run according to the macro-F1 score on the development set.

Note that the new comparable test sets sampled from the original corpora are relatively small (800 observations). To increase the robustness of the results, we use five different seeds when fine-tuning a language model on the hate speech detection task and report the average macro-F1 over the five runs.

Language Models. We use two general-domain large-scale multilingual language models: m-BERT (Devlin et al., 2019) following Nozza (2021) and XLM-R (Conneau et al., 2020). The former is the multilingual version of BERT, trained on Wikipedia content in 104 languages, with 100M parameters. The latter has the same architecture as RoBERTa (Liu et al., 2019) with 550M parameters and is trained on the publicly available 2.5 TB CommonCrawl Corpus, covering 100 languages.

Then, we experiment with XLM-T (Barbieri et al., 2021), an off-the-shelf XLM-R model fine-tuned on 200 million tweets (1 724 million tokens) scraped between 05/2018 and 03/2020, in more than 30 languages, including our three target languages.

3.4 Setting a new baseline

We compare the scores for m-BERT from Nozza (2021) to the scores obtained using our comparable corpora, reported in Table 1. First, our experiment with m-BERT on comparable corpora allows us to highlight additional cases where zero-shot cross-lingual transfer "fails" (macro-F1 dropping by more than 25% compared to monolingual score) in the *immigrants* domain, that were not visible in the previous study due to variations in training corpus size. On top of this, with the new splits,

[4]Using the Python package `wordsegment`.

[5]`https://github.com/machamp-nlp/machamp`, under the MIT license.

we do not observe the extremely low scores on English for the immigrant domain anymore, allowing us to draw more reliable conclusions on the monolingual/cross-lingual performance gap.

Comparing m-BERT and XLM-R, the latter shows higher scores for almost all languages and domains. It also shows, in general, slightly lower macro-F1 loss between monolingual and cross-lingual settings; which is related to its much larger number of parameters and training corpus size compared to m-BERT.

Fine-tuning XLM-T leads to higher macro-F1 scores for almost all languages and domains compared to XLM-R; which is expected, as it was fine-tuned using the Masked Language Modeling (MLM) task on tweets, which is much more similar to the hate speech datasets, at least stylistically due to the Twitter platform constraints (e.g. number of characters). In terms of monolingual/cross-lingual discrepancy, we also observe in general a much lower macro-F1 drop. Having seen a large amount of similar data in all languages, the model can much more easily bridge the gap between languages when performing zero-shot cross-lingual transfer for this highly domain-specific task.

However, such a large amount of training data from a similar source in different languages is not so easy to come by. To bridge the language gap in very context-specific tasks such as hate speech detection, in the case of absence of an adequately trained multilingual language model, we turn towards other sources of multilingual information for the model: using annotated corpora for other *auxiliary* tasks in the source and target languages.

In all following experiments, we use the comparable datasets and the general-domain multilingual language model XLM-R to study the impact of auxiliary task training on this problem[6]. By using data for auxiliary tasks in both the source and the target language, we expect the auxiliary task training to work as a bridge between the source and target language, helping the cross-lingual transfer by providing more information on the target language and the difference between the two languages.

4 Auxiliary Tasks Experiments

We define several training tasks whose effects on cross-lingual transfer of hate speech detection models are to be evaluated: a sequence-level task, sentiment analysis, and several token-level tasks: Named Entity Recognition (NER) and a set syntactic tasks that we group – by misnomer – under the term "Universal Dependency" (UD). We hypothesize that sentiment analysis and NER tasks allow the model to learn high-level, semantic information, while the UD tasks convey syntactic skills to the model.

4.1 Auxiliary tasks

Syntactic tasks. We investigate the effect of adding syntactic information by using all Universal Dependency (UD, Nivre et al., 2020) tasks (Dependency Parsing, Part-Of-Speech (POS) tagging, lemmatization and morphological tagging). We use the dataset EWT (Silveira et al., 2014), GSD and ISDT (Bosco et al., 2014), for English, Spanish and Italian respectively. The datasets being of different sizes, we sample them to obtain the same training size in all languages. We use a train set size of 12 543 sentences, the size of the smallest dataset. Detailed statistics about the datasets can be found in Table 12 in Appendix A.

Sentiment analysis. We use Twitter sentiment analysis datasets on each of our three target languages. They have been gathered and unified by Barbieri et al. (2021), with a unique split size (training 1 839, development 324, test 870) and a balanced distribution across the three sentiment labels (positive, negative and neutral)[7]. Detailed statistics and additional information on each dataset can be found in Table 10 in Appendix A.

Named Entity Recognition (NER). An advantage of this task, which consists in identifying entities in a sequence, is that it is more language-agnostic than the others. Indeed, named entities are often transparent between languages, making it a good choice for cross-lingual transfer. We use the NER WikiANN dataset from (Pan et al., 2017; Rahimi et al., 2019), which covers our three languages. The sets have a unique split size (training 20k examples, development 10k, test 10k).

4.2 Multi-task learning pipeline

We perform multi-task learning using the MaChAmp framework (van der Goot et al., 2021b); it fine-tunes contextual embeddings for

[6]The results for XLM-T display similar tendencies with higher scores compared to XLM-R, Detailed and summarized tables can be found in 499 Appendix B, Table 14

[7]`https://github.com/cardiffnlp/xlm-t`

several tasks and several datasets using a shared encoder and different decoders depending on the target task. As the datasets associated with the different tasks have varying sizes, we use a "smooth sampling" method to avoid having under-represented datasets during training. It consists of re-sampling the datasets according to a multinomial distribution for each batch.

We fine-tune the multilingual model XLM-R on the different auxiliary tasks. The training is done jointly on the auxiliary task datasets in the three languages, in order to allow the model to learn patterns between languages, and on the hate speech dataset in the *source* language, before being tested on the *target* language. In practice, the language model can be trained on the auxiliary tasks either in an intermediary fashion before being fine-tuned on the downstream task (similarly to Pruksachatkun et al. (2020)), or jointly with the hate speech detection task. According to our experiments, the latter exhibits the best performance; we report only results with joint training in the paper. All results involving hate speech are obtained using the pipeline described in Section 3.3, averaging the macro-F1 over five different runs.

Aux. task	Src lang	immigrants			women		
		en	es	it	en	es	it
None	en	*75.3*	51.9	70.1	*76.6*	51.6	49.9
	es	62.0	*83.4*	65.4	63.4	*77.8*	46.9
	it	69.2	51.3	*78.6*	60.3	57.3	***89.0***
Sentiment	en	-1.0	-1.2	0.0	2.0†	0.9	-6.2†
	es	5.1†	0.6	1.5	0.7	2.1‡	-9.6‡
	it	1.4†	1.7	-0.9	-8.3‡	-0.7	0.1
NER	en	1.4†	1.0	-1.9	0.4	0.2	1.9
	es	3.1	0.4	-1.1	-8.7†	2.2‡	-4.9
	it	3.3‡	4.5‡	-1.4†	-2.8†	-0.5	1.1†
UD	en	1.7†	-2.4	-1.2	0.7	-0.4	-10.6†
	es	-3.6	-1.1	-6.5†	-4.9	-0.4	-10.9‡
	it	-14.4‡	5.0‡	-1.6†	-14.7‡	-5.6	-0.3

(a) Detailed view.

Auxiliary Task	immigrants		women	
	mono	cross	mono	cross
None	79.1	61.6	81.1	54.9
Sentiment	-0.4	1.4	1.4	-3.9
NER	0.1	1.5	1.3	-2.5
UD	-0.3	-3.8	0.0	-7.8
Sentiment + NER	0.4	2.5	1.3	-4.7

(b) Aggregated view.

Table 2: Effect (delta with hate speech detection baseline, averaged over 5 runs) of fine-tuning XLM-R on the three auxiliary tasks, on hate speech detection macro-F1 scores (%). Green values indicate an increase in score, red values a decrease. The subscript indicates whether the score is significantly higher or lower compared to the baseline. The comparison is made using a one-sided t-test over the list of scores of the five runs of each model.[8] A dagger (†) as exponent indicates that the p-value is smaller than 0.05, while a double-dagger (‡) indicates a p-value smaller than 0.01.

5 Results on Auxiliary Tasks Training

We analyze the training effect of adding different auxiliary tasks on top of XLM-R, jointly with monolingual hate speech detection. Results can be found in Table 2. Instead of raw scores, we compute the deltas between the baseline system (no auxiliary task, same as Table 1) and the augmented system with training jointly with auxiliary tasks: NER, sentiment analysis (*Sent*) and syntactic tasks (UD), for each language pair (Table 2a).

To help with the interpretation, we aggregate the results according to the monolingual (*mono*), and zero-shot cross-lingual (*cross*) settings. Table 2b is the aggregated equivalent of Table 2a. For each domain (immigrants and women), we average the scores by setting: the *mono* columns show the average of all scores in the diagonal in Table 2a, while the *cross* column is the average of all the rest.

In the zero-shot cross-lingual transfer scenario, we hypothesized that the additional information on the source and target languages could bridge the gap between the languages and improve the transfer for hate speech detection. Looking at the scores for cross-lingual transfer, sentiment analysis and NER lead to an average improvement of respectively of 1.42 and 1.48 points for the immigrants domains; combined (last row of Table 2b), they lead to an even greater improvement of 2.5 percentage points. On the contrary, for the women domain, these two tasks lead to significant improvements almost only in the monolingual setting. As underlined before, zero-shot cross-lingual transfer is especially hard in this domain due to cultural and linguistic variations (Nozza, 2021) that auxiliary task training fails to capture. Finally, UD tasks auxiliary training leads to a large drop of performance in most cases. The impact of auxiliary tasks on the performance of hate speech detection using the XLM-T model

[8] https://docs.scipy.org/doc/scipy/reference/generated/scipy.stats.ttest_ind.html.

is comparable to the one observed with XLM-R. Detailed and summarized tables can be found in Appendix B, Table 14.

6 Diagnosis: Effect of Auxiliary Task Training

There is an extensive literature on how performance metrics aggregated over the full test set are far from conveying enough information to fully evaluate and compare the strengths and weaknesses of models (Ribeiro et al., 2020), including for the task of hate speech detection (Röttger et al., 2021). Here, we use the HateCheck test suite in English (Röttger et al., 2021) and its recent multilingual version MHC (Röttger et al., 2022), which includes our two other target languages, Spanish and Italian. These are test sets covering a wide range of hate speech detection aspects that the authors call *functionalities*, testing detection models with hateful and non-hateful sentences of various styles, vocabulary, syntax and hate speech targets. All 29 *functionalities* are grouped into 11 classes and 7 protected groups as targets[9], and the various test cases of each functionality lead to a total of 3,901 sentences classified as hateful or not hateful. The protected groups vary across languages in the MHC test set; the authors selected them to better adapt to the cultural context of each language. The target group "women" is covered for our three languages, but the target group "immigrants" is not covered in Spanish; instead, we match it with the group "indigenous people".[10] Moreover, to ease the interpretation, we perform the analysis on the aggregated 11 classes of functionalities.

We do not evaluate the performance of our various models on the test suite intrinsically: what we want to measure is the *effect* of zero-shot cross-lingual transfer and auxiliary tasks training on the hate speech functionalities. First, we measure the difference between monolingual and zero-shot cross-lingual training on the various functionalities: what the model "loses" by not being trained on the same language as the test set. We rank the functionalities by average difference across the two domains (Table 3). The largest loss in performance when performing zero-shot transfer is found for functionalities involving slurs: -14.72 of macro-F1 for the immigrants domain and -17.22 for the women domain. Indeed, slurs are extremely cultural and language-specific. Second, we measure

functionality	immigrants	women
slur	-14.72	-17.22
negate	-10.34	0.82
spell	-7.56	5.78
derog	-9.37	7.92
threat	-2.61	1.63
ident	5.57	-3.22
counter	-2.43	10.03
ref	6.62	7.11
profanity	-3.75	18.33
phrase	18.57	5.63

Table 3: Difference between monolingual and zero-shot cross-lingual performance by functionality when fine-tuning XLM-R on hate speech detection (no auxiliary task), averaged over all language pairs, by domain.

the impact of multilingual auxiliary task training compared to training on hate speech detection only (baseline model), on the various functionalities. For the two domains and for each source-target language pair, we measure the HateCheck functionality score of the baseline model, and jointly on every auxiliary task. For each auxiliary task, we compute the *relative* difference in score with the baseline model; this difference represents the effect of the joint training. However, we focus here on the joint training impact for zero-shot cross-lingual transfer; thus, we separate the impact of auxiliary task training in a monolingual setting and in a cross-lingual setting. In Table 4, we display the effect of auxiliary task training on zero-shot transfer *on top of* the effect of these tasks on monolingual transfer. To designate the functionalities, we use the same denomination as in the HateCheck test suite. Detection of hate speech involving *slurs*, which suffers the most from zero-shot cross-lingual transfer, is improved by training with NER or UD. Training on UD tasks is especially helpful on cases involving spelling variations (*spell*), contrarily to the two other tasks, and phrasing variations (*phrasing*). Counter-speech detection, an extremely hard task involving *not* classifying counter-speech (e.g. denouncement of hate by quoting it) as hateful, is

[9]We refer the reader to (Röttger et al., 2022), pp.45, for an extensive definition of these classes and groups.

[10]This choice stems from measuring the similarity between Spanish immigrants train set and the test cases of each target group in Spanish Hatecheck using tf-idf representation. Indigenous people ("indígenas" in Spanish) had the highest similarity score with the Twitter immigrants dataset, higher than Hatecheck test cases targeted at black people ("negros") or Jews ("judíos"), hence our decision to use indigenous people as a proxy.

only helped by NER. Sentiment analysis is globally helpful for many classes, but particularly for sentences involving *negated* positive or hateful statements.

functionality	NER	Sentiment	UD
threat	-8.23	-2.32	26.81
target	-3.54	4.70	-6.19
spell	-3.13	-5.72	12.59
slur	1.09	-6.30	14.42
ref	-6.80	2.17	7.77
profanity	-4.23	2.77	-0.44
phrase	-14.79	1.17	8.64
negate	4.19	3.57	1.98
ident	2.57	1.05	-14.42
derog	-1.60	2.02	18.58
counter	2.90	-11.83	-15.60

Table 4: Relative difference in macro-F1 score by class of functionality, between monolingual and zero-shot cross-lingual training (averaged across all language pairs), averaged across the two domains, for each auxiliary task.

7 Discussion

On the impact of each auxiliary task training, we experimented with jointly training hate speech detection and different auxiliary tasks: sentiment analysis, NER and UD tasks. In the immigrants domain, the NER and sentiment auxiliary tasks led to the best improvement on hate speech detection. The cross-lingual transferability of NER was facilitated by the fact that many named entities are the same across languages (e.g. person and organisation names); indeed, many successful unsupervised cross-lingual transfer systems for this task can be found in the literature (Rahimi et al., 2019; Bari et al., 2020).

Compared with the first two tasks, adding syntactic information had the lowest positive impact on hate speech detection, often decreasing the performance for zero-shot cross-lingual settings. This is in line with results from the literature that agree on the positive effect on sentiment analysis (del Arco et al., 2021; Aroyehun and Gelbukh, 2021), but face varying conclusions when it comes to UD tasks. Narang and Brew (2020) showed the positive impact of syntactic features on top of non-contextualized embeddings for hate speech detection; Gambino and Pirrone (2020), among the best systems on the EVALITA2020 hate speech detection task, used POS-tagged text as input for classification. On the contrary, in a monolingual setting, Klemen et al. (2020) showed that morphological features added to LSTM and BERT-based hate speech detection models did not help with comment filtering. Similarly, using sequential auxiliary training of tasks such as POS tagging, Pruksachatkun et al. (2020) showed that the resulting additional low-level skills often led to negative transfer for many downstream tasks.

In our cross-lingual setting, our goal was to use these tasks as a proxy to fill the mismatch between languages and facilitate the transfer. We hypothesize that when working on tweets, their constrained style – short sentences, generally with low syntactic complexity – makes additional syntactic knowledge unhelpful (especially in a more difficult to parse user-generated content context) for a downstream task such as hate speech detection, which benefits more from semantic information.

Regarding the non-usage of POS taggers that could have been optimized for our User-Generated Content-based datasets, we investigated this possibility and conducted preliminary experiments for English – using the Tweebank (Jiang et al., 2022) as data source–, that showed that using a tagger trained on it did not bring much in terms of performance compared to "classic" UD POS taggers. Part of the reasons might come from the fact that our pre-processing step removes hashtags and normalized other Twitter's idiosyncrasies and hence make the data somewhat simpler to tag. Another reason to not investigate this further lies in the lack of availability of a UGC treebank for Spanish, breaking thus the symmetry of our experimental protocol. Last but not least, another reason we hypothesized for this lack of much improvement we noticed comes from the fact that the multilingual language model we used (XMLR and XMLR-T) were already providing strong results on UGC. This was corroborated by Riabi et al. (2021), who experimentally verified the robustness of language models when facing noisy UGC. Moreover Itzhak and Levy (2021) showed that subword-based language models were able to capture a significant amount of character-level alteration typical of UGC (Sanguinetti et al., 2020), explaining their surprising level of robustness when facing noisy content. However, we agree that better handling UGC content would be an interesting step, if not the next step, especially if we can demonstrate that many idiosyncrasies align across languages in our target domains and hence are alleviated by the use of optimized tagging and parsing, eventually multilingual, models. This, in our minds, warrants another full-scale study with a thorough error analysis of cross-lingual syntactic transfer in noisy scenarios. We leave this for future work.

Cross-lingual zero-shot transfer on a domain with a gap between languages. In Section 3, we observed that using larger pre-trained multilingual language models, and if possible, multilingual models trained on corpora from the same source as the downstream task, improves cross-lingual zero-shot transfer. This adaptation has a significant and consistent positive impact. This is in line with the findings of Bose et al. (2021), who demonstrated the superiority of MLM over other tasks in a cross-corpora transfer setting. Similarly, van der Goot et al. (2021a) jointly trained auxiliary tasks with a downstream task (in their case, spoken language understanding) in a cross-lingual setting to find that MLM fine-tuning consistently improves the downstream task.

Beyond the obvious improvement due to the MLM training on more adapted data, we would have expected XLM-T to increase the impact of auxiliary tasks fine-tuning; a more adapted language model helping to bridge the gap between hate speech in the source and target languages. Here, the Twitter data used for the XLM-T training may not be optimal for the observed linguistic specificities and cultural gap. It was trained on tweets published between 05/2018 and 03/2020, while the hate speech corpora range from 2017 to 2018, depending on the language; moreover, some events were specifically targeted when scraping Twitter for hate speech detection (e.g., Gamergate victims for the Italian datasets on hate speech towards women (Fersini et al., 2018)). Furthermore, contrarily to Wikipedia where corpora are highly similar from one high-resource language to another in term of domains, Twitter data can significantly differ between languages due to cultural differences and events in the respective countries. Overall, when we used XLM-T, the model is only adapted to the form and style of Twitter data (small sentences, with mentions and urls...). The tweets' content, topic, and vocabulary might differ a lot between the hate speech corpora, the XLM-T training data, and the sentiment analysis corpora. We can only hypothesize on these variations. However, they should be quantified to understand better the impact of fine-tuning on these data and to distinguish between corpus variations and the actual cultural and linguistic gap.

Discussions on computational costs and ethical considerations for this work can be found in Appendix 9.

8 Conclusion

In this work, we highlighted situations where zero-shot cross-lingual transfer of hate speech models fails because of the linguistic and cultural gap. We quantified the effect of the choice of multilingual language model and of auxiliary task training on these "failed" cases, showing the positive effect of NER and sentiment analysis multilingual training, but their limited improvement in the domain of hate speech against women. We performed a preliminary analysis on the effect of auxiliary tasks by *hate speech functionality* using the HateCheck test suite, hinting at which kind of hate speech benefits from transferring knowledge in both the source and the target languages for the three auxiliary tasks. Finally, we discussed limitations related to training data for language model pre-training, auxiliary tasks, and hate speech detection. All of our datasets with their new splits and models are freely available.[11], hoping that the sound experimental framework we designed will help strengthen future studies on cross-lingual hate-speech detection.

Acknowledgments

We warmly thank the reviewers for their very valuable feedback. This work received funding from the European Union's Horizon 2020 research and innovation programme under grant agreement No. 101021607. The last author acknowledges the support of the French Research Agency via the ANR ParSiTi project (ANR16-CE33-0021). The authors are grateful to the OPAL infrastructure from Université Côte d'Azur for providing resources and support.

[11]https://github.com/ArijRB/Multilingual-Auxiliary-Tasks-Training-Bridging-the-Gap-between-Languages-for-Zero-Shot-Transfer-of-/

9 Ethical considerations

This paper is part of a line of work aiming to tackle hate speech detection when we have no training data in the target language, fight the spread of offensive and hateful speech online, and have a positive global impact on the world. Its goal is to understand if hate speech is transferable from one language to another; as such, it has been approved by our institutional review board (IRB), and follows the national and European General Data Protection Regulation (GDPR).

We did not collect any data from online social media for this work. We only used publicly available datasets – exclusively diffused for shared tasks that were tackled by a large number of participants (see Table 6 in Appendix A). These datasets do not include any metadata, only the tweet's text associated with the hate speech label. Thus, linking the annotated data to individual social media users is not straightforward.

All our experiments were executed on clusters whose energy mix is made of nuclear (65–75%), 20% renewable, and the remaining with gas (or more rarely coal when imported from abroad). More details on computational costs can be found in Table 5.

Finally, the presence of bias in the pre-trained language models we use, due to the bias in the data they were trained on, may have an impact on hate speech detection, particularly on the topic of hate speech towards women. As a result, this area of research is currently under heavy scrutiny by the community.

Computational Costs. We conduct our experiments on RTX8000 GPUs. We test two models (XLM-R and XLM-T) on 7 different auxiliary tasks combinations, with 5 seeds each. Details on the average GPU time for the basic task combinations (jointly training hate speech with one task) are in Table 5.

Task	Duration
Hate only	0:14
Sentiment+Hate	0:21
UD+Hate	1:57
NER+Hate	2:18

Table 5: Training time (in seconds) for one seed per model.

References

Segun Taofeek Aroyehun and Alexander Gelbukh. 2021. Evaluation of intermediate pre-training for the detection of offensive language. In *Proceedings of the Iberian Languages Evaluation Forum (IberLEF 2021), CEUR Workshop Proceedings. CEUR-WS. org*.

Francesco Barbieri, Valerio Basile, Danilo Croce, Malvina Nissim, Nicole Novielli, and Viviana Patti. 2016. Overview of the evalita 2016 sentiment polarity classification task. In *Proceedings of third Italian conference on computational linguistics (CLiC-it 2016) & fifth evaluation campaign of natural language processing and speech tools for Italian. Final Workshop (EVALITA 2016)*.

Francesco Barbieri, Luis Espinosa-Anke, and Jose Camacho-Collados. 2021. A Multilingual Language Model Toolkit for Twitter. In *arXiv preprint arXiv:2104.12250*.

M Saiful Bari, Shafiq Joty, and Prathyusha Jwalapuram. 2020. Zero-resource cross-lingual named entity recognition. In *Proceedings of the AAAI Conference on Artificial Intelligence*, volume 34, pages 7415–7423.

Angelo Basile and Chiara Rubagotti. 2018. Crotonemilano for ami at evalita2018. a performant, cross-lingual misogyny detection system. *EVALITA Evaluation of NLP and Speech Tools for Italian*, 12:206.

Bauwelinck, Nina and Lefever, Els. 2019. Measuring the impact of sentiment for hate speech detection on Twitter. In *Proceedings of HUSO 2019, The fifth international conference on human and social analytics*, pages 17–22. IARIA, International Academy, Research, and Industry Association.

Cristina Bosco, Felice Dell'Orletta, Simonetta Montemagni, Manuela Sanguinetti, and Maria Simi. 2014. The evalita 2014 dependency parsing task. *The Evalita 2014 Dependency Parsing task*, pages 1–8.

Cristina Bosco, Dell'Orletta Felice, Fabio Poletto, Manuela Sanguinetti, and Tesconi Maurizio. 2018. Overview of the evalita 2018 hate speech detection task. In *EVALITA 2018-Sixth Evaluation Campaign of Natural Language Processing and Speech Tools for Italian*, volume 2263, pages 1–9. CEUR.

Tulika Bose, Irina Illina, and Dominique Fohr. 2021. Unsupervised domain adaptation in cross-corpora abusive language detection. In *Proceedings of the Ninth International Workshop on Natural Language Processing for Social Media*, pages 113–122, Online. Association for Computational Linguistics.

Alexis Conneau, Kartikay Khandelwal, Naman Goyal, Vishrav Chaudhary, Guillaume Wenzek, Francisco Guzmán, Edouard Grave, Myle Ott, Luke Zettlemoyer, and Veselin Stoyanov. 2020. Unsupervised cross-lingual representation learning at scale. In *Proceedings of the 58th Annual Meeting of the Association for Computational Linguistics*, pages 8440–8451, Online. Association for Computational Linguistics.

Thomas Davidson, Dana Warmsley, Michael Macy, and Ingmar Weber. 2017. Automated hate speech detection and the problem of offensive language. In *Proceedings of the International AAAI Conference on Web and Social Media*, volume 11.

Flor Miriam Plaza del Arco, Sercan Halat, Sebastian Padó, and Roman Klinger. 2021. Multi-task learning with sentiment, emotion, and target detection to recognize hate speech and offensive language. In *Forum for Information Retrieval Evaluation, Virtual Event*.

Jacob Devlin, Ming-Wei Chang, Kenton Lee, and Kristina Toutanova. 2019. BERT: Pre-training of deep bidirectional transformers for language understanding. In *Proceedings of the 2019 Conference of the North American Chapter of the Association for Computational Linguistics: Human Language Technologies, Volume 1 (Long and Short Papers)*, pages 4171–4186, Minneapolis, Minnesota. Association for Computational Linguistics.

Manuel Carlos Díaz Galiano, Eugenio Martínez Cámara, Miguel Ángel García Cumbreras, Manuel García Vega, and Julio Villena Román. 2018. The democratization of deep learning in tass 2017. -.

Karthik Dinakar, Roi Reichart, and Henry Lieberman. 2011. Modeling the detection of textual cyberbullying. In *fifth international AAAI conference on weblogs and social media*.

Elisabetta Fersini, Debora Nozza, and Paolo Rosso. 2018. Overview of the evalita 2018 task on automatic misogyny identification (ami). *EVALITA Evaluation of NLP and Speech Tools for Italian*, 12:59.

Komal Florio, Valerio Basile, Marco Polignano, Pierpaolo Basile, and Viviana Patti. 2020. Time of your hate: The challenge of time in hate speech detection on social media. *Applied Sciences*, 10:4180.

Paula Fortuna and Sérgio Nunes. 2018. A survey on automatic detection of hate speech in text. *ACM Computing Surveys (CSUR)*, 51(4):1–30.

Giuseppe Gambino and Roberto Pirrone. 2020. Chilab@ haspeede 2: Enhancing hate speech detection with part-of-speech tagging. -.

Matt Gardner, Joel Grus, Mark Neumann, Oyvind Tafjord, Pradeep Dasigi, Nelson F. Liu, Matthew Peters, Michael Schmitz, and Luke Zettlemoyer. 2018. AllenNLP: A deep semantic natural language processing platform. In *Proceedings of Workshop for NLP Open Source Software (NLP-OSS)*, pages 1–6, Melbourne, Australia. Association for Computational Linguistics.

Goran Glavaš, Mladen Karan, and Ivan Vulić. 2020. XHate-999: Analyzing and detecting abusive language across domains and languages. In *Proceedings of the 28th International Conference on Computational Linguistics*, pages 6350–6365, Barcelona, Spain (Online). International Committee on Computational Linguistics.

Dagmar Gromann and Thierry Declerck. 2017. Hashtag processing for enhanced clustering of tweets. In *RANLP*, pages 277–283.

Itay Itzhak and Omer Levy. 2021. Models in a spelling bee: Language models implicitly learn the character composition of tokens. *arXiv preprint arXiv:2108.11193*.

Hang Jiang, Yining Hua, Doug Beeferman, and Deb Roy. 2022. Annotating the Tweebank corpus on named entity recognition and building NLP models for social media analysis. In *Proceedings of the Thirteenth Language Resources and Evaluation Conference*, pages 7199–7208, Marseille, France. European Language Resources Association.

Brendan Kennedy, Xisen Jin, Aida Mostafazadeh Davani, Morteza Dehghani, and Xiang Ren. 2020. Contextualizing hate speech classifiers with post-hoc explanation. In *Proceedings of the 58th Annual Meeting of the Association for Computational Linguistics*, pages 5435–5442, Online. Association for Computational Linguistics.

Matej Klemen, Luka Krsnik, and Marko Robnik-Šikonja. 2020. Enhancing deep neural networks with morphological information. *arXiv preprint arXiv:2011.12432*.

Yinhan Liu, Myle Ott, Naman Goyal, Jingfei Du, Mandar Joshi, Danqi Chen, Omer Levy, Mike Lewis, Luke Zettlemoyer, and Veselin Stoyanov. 2019. Roberta: A robustly optimized bert pretraining approach.

Ilia Markov, Nikola Ljubešić, Darja Fišer, and Walter Daelemans. 2021. Exploring stylometric and emotion-based features for multilingual cross-domain hate speech detection. In *Proceedings of the Eleventh Workshop on Computational Approaches to Subjectivity, Sentiment and Social Media Analysis*, pages 149–159, Online. Association for Computational Linguistics.

Kanika Narang and Chris Brew. 2020. Abusive language detection using syntactic dependency graphs. In *Proceedings of the Fourth Workshop on Online Abuse and Harms*, pages 44–53, Online. Association for Computational Linguistics.

Joakim Nivre, Marie-Catherine de Marneffe, Filip Ginter, Jan Hajič, Christopher D. Manning, Sampo Pyysalo, Sebastian Schuster, Francis Tyers, and Daniel Zeman. 2020. Universal Dependencies v2: An evergrowing multilingual treebank collection. In *Proceedings of the 12th Language Resources and*

Evaluation Conference, pages 4034–4043, Marseille, France. European Language Resources Association.

Debora Nozza. 2021. Exposing the limits of zero-shot cross-lingual hate speech detection. In *Proceedings of the 59th Annual Meeting of the Association for Computational Linguistics and the 11th International Joint Conference on Natural Language Processing (Volume 2: Short Papers)*, pages 907–914, Online. Association for Computational Linguistics.

Endang Wahyu Pamungkas and Viviana Patti. 2019. Cross-domain and cross-lingual abusive language detection: A hybrid approach with deep learning and a multilingual lexicon. In *Proceedings of the 57th Annual Meeting of the Association for Computational Linguistics: Student Research Workshop*, pages 363–370, Florence, Italy. Association for Computational Linguistics.

Xiaoman Pan, Boliang Zhang, Jonathan May, Joel Nothman, Kevin Knight, and Heng Ji. 2017. Cross-lingual name tagging and linking for 282 languages. In *Proceedings of the 55th Annual Meeting of the Association for Computational Linguistics (Volume 1: Long Papers)*, pages 1946–1958, Vancouver, Canada. Association for Computational Linguistics.

Andraž Pelicon, Ravi Shekhar, Blaž Škrlj, Matthew Purver, and Senja Pollak. 2021. Investigating cross-lingual training for offensive language detection. *PeerJ Computer Science*, 7:e559.

Jason Phang, Iacer Calixto, Phu Mon Htut, Yada Pruksachatkun, Haokun Liu, Clara Vania, Katharina Kann, and Samuel R. Bowman. 2020. English intermediate-task training improves zero-shot cross-lingual transfer too. In *Proceedings of the 1st Conference of the Asia-Pacific Chapter of the Association for Computational Linguistics and the 10th International Joint Conference on Natural Language Processing*, pages 557–575, Suzhou, China. Association for Computational Linguistics.

Jason Phang, Thibault Févry, and Samuel R Bowman. 2018. Sentence encoders on stilts: Supplementary training on intermediate labeled-data tasks. *arXiv preprint arXiv:1811.01088*.

Yada Pruksachatkun, Jason Phang, Haokun Liu, Phu Mon Htut, Xiaoyi Zhang, Richard Yuanzhe Pang, Clara Vania, Katharina Kann, and Samuel R. Bowman. 2020. Intermediate-task transfer learning with pretrained language models: When and why does it work? In *Proceedings of the 58th Annual Meeting of the Association for Computational Linguistics*, pages 5231–5247, Online. Association for Computational Linguistics.

Afshin Rahimi, Yuan Li, and Trevor Cohn. 2019. Massively multilingual transfer for NER. In *Proceedings of the 57th Annual Meeting of the Association for Computational Linguistics*, pages 151–164, Florence, Italy. Association for Computational Linguistics.

Tharindu Ranasinghe and Marcos Zampieri. 2020. Multilingual offensive language identification with cross-lingual embeddings. In *Proceedings of the 2020 Conference on Empirical Methods in Natural Language Processing (EMNLP)*, pages 5838–5844, Online. Association for Computational Linguistics.

Arij Riabi, Benoît Sagot, and Djamé Seddah. 2021. Can character-based language models improve downstream task performances in low-resource and noisy language scenarios? In *Proceedings of the Seventh Workshop on Noisy User-generated Text (W-NUT 2021)*, pages 423–436, Online. Association for Computational Linguistics.

Marco Tulio Ribeiro, Tongshuang Wu, Carlos Guestrin, and Sameer Singh. 2020. Beyond accuracy: Behavioral testing of NLP models with CheckList. In *Proceedings of the 58th Annual Meeting of the Association for Computational Linguistics*, pages 4902–4912, Online. Association for Computational Linguistics.

Guilherme Moraes Rosa, Luiz Henrique Bonifacio, Leandro Rodrigues de Souza, Roberto Lotufo, and Rodrigo Nogueira. 2021. A cost-benefit analysis of cross-lingual transfer methods. *arXiv preprint arXiv:2105.06813*.

Sara Rosenthal, Noura Farra, and Preslav Nakov. 2017. Semeval-2017 task 4: Sentiment analysis in twitter. In *Proceedings of the 11th international workshop on semantic evaluation (SemEval-2017)*, pages 502–518.

Paul Röttger, Haitham Seelawi, Debora Nozza, Zeerak Talat, and Bertie Vidgen. 2022. Multilingual HateCheck: Functional tests for multilingual hate speech detection models. In *Proceedings of the Sixth Workshop on Online Abuse and Harms (WOAH)*, pages 154–169, Seattle, Washington (Hybrid). Association for Computational Linguistics.

Paul Röttger, Bertie Vidgen, Dong Nguyen, Zeerak Waseem, Helen Margetts, and Janet Pierrehumbert. 2021. HateCheck: Functional tests for hate speech detection models. In *Proceedings of the 59th Annual Meeting of the Association for Computational Linguistics and the 11th International Joint Conference on Natural Language Processing (Volume 1: Long Papers)*, pages 41–58, Online. Association for Computational Linguistics.

Manuela Sanguinetti, Lauren Cassidy, Cristina Bosco, Özlem Çetinoglu, Alessandra Teresa Cignarella, Teresa Lynn, Ines Rehbein, Josef Ruppenhofer, Djamé Seddah, and Amir Zeldes. 2020. Treebanking user-generated content: a UD based overview of guidelines, corpora and unified recommendations. *CoRR*, abs/2011.02063.

Natalia Silveira, Timothy Dozat, Marie-Catherine de Marneffe, Samuel Bowman, Miriam Connor, John Bauer, and Chris Manning. 2014. A gold standard dependency corpus for English. In *Proceedings of the Ninth International Conference on Language Resources and Evaluation (LREC'14)*, pages 2897–2904, Reykjavik, Iceland. European Language Resources Association (ELRA).

Sara Sood, Judd Antin, and Elizabeth Churchill. 2012. Profanity use in online communities. In *Proceedings of the SIGCHI Conference on Human Factors in Computing Systems*, CHI '12, pages 1481–1490, New York, NY, USA. Association for Computing Machinery.

Lukas Stappen, Fabian Brunn, and Björn Schuller. 2020. Cross-lingual zero-and few-shot hate speech detection utilising frozen transformer language models and axel. *arXiv preprint arXiv:2004.13850*.

Rob van der Goot, Nikola Ljubešić, Ian Matroos, Malvina Nissim, and Barbara Plank. 2018. Bleaching text: Abstract features for cross-lingual gender prediction. In *Proceedings of the 56th Annual Meeting of the Association for Computational Linguistics (Volume 2: Short Papers)*, pages 383–389, Melbourne, Australia. Association for Computational Linguistics.

Rob van der Goot, Ibrahim Sharaf, Aizhan Imankulova, Ahmet Üstün, Marija Stepanović, Alan Ramponi, Siti Oryza Khairunnisa, Mamoru Komachi, and Barbara Plank. 2021a. From masked language modeling to translation: Non-English auxiliary tasks improve zero-shot spoken language understanding. In *Proceedings of the 2021 Conference of the North American Chapter of the Association for Computational Linguistics: Human Language Technologies*, pages 2479–2497, Online. Association for Computational Linguistics.

Rob van der Goot, Ahmet Üstün, Alan Ramponi, Ibrahim Sharaf, and Barbara Plank. 2021b. Massive choice, ample tasks (MaChAmp): A toolkit for multi-task learning in NLP. In *Proceedings of the 16th Conference of the European Chapter of the Association for Computational Linguistics: System Demonstrations*, pages 176–197, Online. Association for Computational Linguistics.

Zeerak Waseem and Dirk Hovy. 2016. Hateful symbols or hateful people? predictive features for hate speech detection on Twitter. In *Proceedings of the NAACL Student Research Workshop*, pages 88–93, San Diego, California. Association for Computational Linguistics.

Wenjie Yin and Arkaitz Zubiaga. 2021. Towards generalisable hate speech detection: a review on obstacles and solutions. *PeerJ Computer Science*, 7:e598.

A Datasets overview

A.1 Hate speech datasets overview

A.2 Auxiliary tasks datasets overview

Treebanks additional pre-processing As the MACHAMP framework does not support the Connl UD format, treebanks must be converted back to the connl06 format, which most notably involved the removal of all contracted tokens, potentially leading to tokenization mismatches between our data sources. However, a rapid analysis showed that it has a very limited impact because of their low frequency and the generalization of sub-word tokenization.

Shared task	Link
Hateval	https://github.com/msang/hateval
EVALITA AMi 2018	https://github.com/MIND-Lab/ami2018
HaSpeeDe 2018	https://github.com/msang/haspeede/tree/master/2018

Table 6: Shared tasks used for the Hate speech corpora.

Domain-language	train	dev	test	blind
immigrants-it	2000	500	1000	.
immigrants-en	4500	500	1499	.
immigrants-es	1618	173	800	.
women-it	2500	500	1000	.
women-en	4500	500	1472	.
women-es	2882	327	799	.
Comparable size	1618	173	800	1000

Table 7: Hate speech detection datasets: Size of full datasets (number of sentences) and new split with comparable data size. Only the immigrants-es dataset has no blind set.

Language	immigrants	women
en	41.28	42.76
es	42	40.23
it	31.33	45.42

Table 8: Percentage of hateful examples in the train set for the comparable setting.

	immigrants			women		
	en	es	it	en	es	it
Nb of tokens per tweet						
avg	27.3	18.9	17.2	18.3	22.8	17.9
median	26.0	17.0	17.0	18.0	20.0	14.0
max	90	57	29	57	59	54
min	2	1	2	2	2	2
Nb of hashtags (avg per tweet, total unique nb)						
avg	2.0	0.2	0.6	0.2	0.2	0.2
unique	1162	214	491	211	292	228
Train/test OOV Ratio						
	0.4	0.6	0.5	0.5	0.5	0.5

Table 9: Descriptive statistics on hate speech detection training datasets.

Language	Shared task	Reference	Scraping period
English	SemEval 2017	Rosenthal et al. (2017)	01/2012–12/2015
Italian	Intertass 2017	Díaz Galiano et al. (2018)	07/2016–01/2017
Spanish	Sentipolc 2016	Barbieri et al. (2016)	2013–2016

Table 10: Data overview for the sentiment analysis task. All datasets contain text scraped from Twitter. They have been unified to a common train / dev / test split size: 1 839 / 324 / 870.

Dataset	Language	train/dev/test size	Period
Tweebank	English	1 639 / 710 / 1 201	02/2016 – 07/2016
PoSTWITA	Italian	5 368 / 671 / 674	07/2009 – 02/2013

Table 11: Twitter UD data overview.

Dataset	Language	train	dev	test
EWT[12]	English	12 543	2 001	2 077
GSD[13]	Spanish	14 187	1 400	426
ISDT[14]	Italian	13 121	564	482
Comparable size		12543	564	426

Table 12: Universal Dependencies (UD) datasets and size of their respective splits.

	Train	Dev
# tweets	2 349	1 000
# tokens	46 469	16 261
# entity tokens	2 462	1 128

Table 13: Statistics of the WNUT 2016 NER shared task dataset.

Aux task	Src lang	immigrants			women		
		en	es	it	en	es	it
None	en	76.8	48.5	73.5	78.6	61.5	60.6
	es	65.9	84.2	60.7	72.5	80.3	51.9
	it	71.5	56.8	78.4	63.4	58.2	90.3
sent	en	-0.4	4.2†	-1.9	0.5	2.2	-0.2
	es	1.3	0.5	6.2	-2.6†	0.7	-9.6‡
	it	0.8	-1.8	-0.3	-5.1†	3.4	-0.3
NER	en	0.1	5.9‡	-4.7‡	-0.1	0.9	1.6
	es	-2.2	0.6	1.4	-5.9‡	1.5†	-6.0‡
	it	1.0	0.7	0.0	-2.7	2.2	0.5
UD	en	-0.4	2.9	-3.9	-0.1	-1.7†	-10.1‡
	es	-11.1‡	-0.7	-3.7	-2.4‡	0.4	-12.9‡
	it	-4.1‡	1.6	0.1	-8.7‡	-2.1	0.7†

(a) Detailed view.

Auxiliary Task	immigrants		women	
	mono	cross	mono	cross
None	79.8	62.8	83.1	61.3
Sent	-0.1	1.5	0.3	-2.0
NER	0.3	0.4	0.6	-1.7
UD	-0.3	-3.0	0.3	-6.3
Sent + NER	-0.2	1.3	0.6	-2.5

(b) Aggregated view.

Table 14: Effect (delta with hate speech detection baseline, averaged over 5 runs) of fine-tuning XLM-T on the three auxiliary tasks, on hate speech detection macro-F1 scores (%). Green values indicate an increase in score, red values a decrease. *Sent* stands for Sentiment and *Aux* for auxiliary.

B Complementary results

Aux. task	Src lang	en	es	it
None	en	*75.3*	51.9	70.1
	es	62.0	*83.4*	65.4
	it	69.2	51.3	*78.6*
MLM	en	1.1	-2.9	-1.4
	es	2.6	-2.9‡	0.3
	it	-1.6	-1.0	-0.1
NER	en	1.4†	1.0	-1.9
	es	3.1	0.4	-1.1
	it	3.3‡	4.5‡	-1.4†

Table 15: Effect (delta with XLM-R baseline) of MLM fine-tuning on sentences from NER datasets compared fine-tuning on NER as auxiliary tasks, on hate speech detection macro-F1 scores (%) for immigrants domain. Green values indicate an increase in score, red values a decrease.

Auxiliary task	Source lang	immigrants			women		
		en	es	it	en	es	it
None	en	*75.3*	51.9	70.1	*76.6*	51.6	49.9
	es	62.0	*83.4*	65.4	63.4	*77.8*	46.9
	it	69.2	51.3	*78.6*	60.3	57.3	*89.0*
UD	en	1.7†	-2.4	-1.2	0.7	-0.4	-10.6†
	es	-3.6	-1.1	-6.5†	-4.9	-0.4	-10.9‡
	it	-14.4‡	5.0‡	-1.6†	-14.7‡	-5.6	-0.3
UPOS	en	-0.6	-3.1	-1.4	0.9	-5.2	-1.2
	es	-4.0	-1.2	-3.9†	-0.9	1.9‡	-7.3†
	it	-4.7†	5.0‡	-1.0	-1.2	-3.4	-1.7

Table 16: **Ablation study**: Hate speech detection macro-F1 scores (%) of XLM-R fine-tuned on the UPOS task jointly with the hate speech detection task. We compare each macro-F1 score with the baseline score (without auxiliary task). Green values indicate an increase in score, red values a decrease. The subscript indicates whether the macro-F1 of the model trained with the auxiliary tasks is significantly higher or lower compared to the model without auxiliary task. The comparison is made using a one-sided t-test over the list of scores of the five runs of each model. A dagger (†) as exponent indicates that the p-value is smaller than 0.05, while a double-dagger (‡) indicates a p-value smaller than 0.01.

Chop and Change: Anaphora Resolution in Instructional Cooking Videos

Cennet Oguz[1], **Ivana Kruijff-Korbayova**[1], **Pascal Denis**[2],
Emmanuel Vincent[3] and **Josef van Genabith**[1]
[1]German Research Center for Artificial Intelligence (DFKI), Saarland Informatics
[2]Univ. Lille, Inria, CNRS, Centrale Lille, UMR 9189 CRIStAL, F-59000 Lille, France
[3]Université de Lorraine, CNRS, Inria, LORIA, F-54000 Nancy, France
{cennet.oguz, ivana.kruijff, josef.van_genabith}@dfki.de
{pascal.denis, emmanuel.vincent}@inria.fr

Abstract

Linguistic ambiguities arising from changes in entities in action flows are a key challenge in instructional cooking videos. In particular, temporally evolving entities present rich and to date understudied challenges for anaphora resolution. For example "oil" mixed with "salt" is later referred to as a "mixture". In this paper we propose novel annotation guidelines to annotate recipes for the anaphora resolution task, reflecting change in entities. Moreover, we present experimental results for end-to-end multimodal anaphora resolution with the new annotation scheme and propose the use of temporal features for performance improvement.

1 Introduction

Anaphora resolution is the task of identifying the antecedent of an anaphor, i.e., find a language expression that a given entity refers to. For example, in the sentence *take a potato and wash it*, the pronoun *it* is an anaphor that refers to the antecedent *a potato*. This is a challenging NLP task which has been attracting much attention (Poesio et al., 2018; Fang et al., 2021, 2022). Different types of anaphoric relations have been identified and described in the scientific literature, e.g., identity (Poesio and Artstein, 2008), near-identity (Recasens et al., 2011; Hovy et al., 2013), and bridging (Asher and Lascarides, 1998).

Recipes provide a rich source for referring expressions (Kiddon et al., 2015) of transformed entities, and offer a challenge for anaphora resolution tasks. Fang et al. (2022) use written recipes with anaphora annotations to trace the temporal change of entities. While the ingredients undergo physical or chemical change in the action flow, they can be still referred to in the same way. For example, an *egg* before and after it is boiled can be referred to with the same noun *egg*. Compared to text recipes, instructional cooking videos raise additional challenges for anaphora resolution owing to their intrinsic multimodality (Huang et al., 2016). Krishnaswamy and Pustejovsky (2019) point to various "channels of information" in the transmission of each modality. A "shared reference of entities" is introduced when two modalities refer to the same description (Krishnaswamy and Pustejovsky, 2020). As presented in cooking instructions of videos when two modalities refer to the same entity, the use of a referring expression is affected by both modalities. For example, *the cubes* is used in Figure 1a to denote the bread pieces in the text modality because the instruction *chop the bread* shaped them into cubes in the video modality. The choice of referring expressions might also differ with respect to the changes of the entities. In Figure 1b the same nominal phrase refers to a different

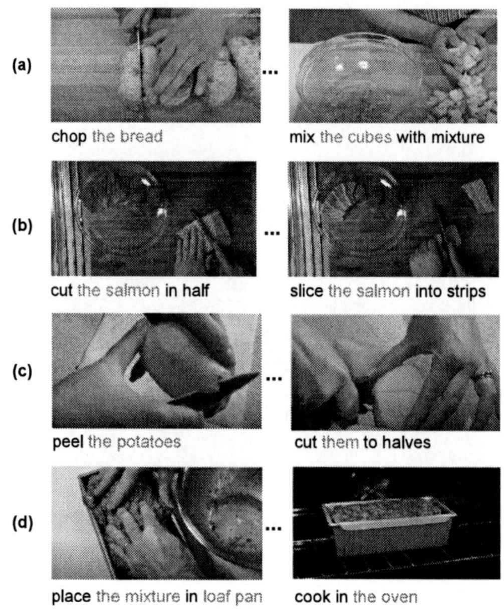

Figure 1: Examples from the YouCookII dataset showing the effect of the temporal changes on the entities and the referring expressions. Each row displays a different use of expressions and entities.

Findings of the Association for Computational Linguistics: AACL-IJCNLP 2022, pages 364–374
November 20–23, 2022.

object (the whole salmon piece; and then one of the halves) whereas in Figure 1c a coreferential pronoun is used although the object has changed. Figure 1c is in fact the most well-behaved in terms of keeping the language expressions consistent across instructions and with the entities being referred to. Figure 1d shows the use of null arguments: the second instruction *cook in the oven* does not explicitly mention what to cook, whereas the image of the instruction displays it.

The main contributions of this paper are as follows: (i) We propose an anaphora annotation scheme for instructional cooking videos that allows us to address linguistic ambiguities in anaphora resolution. In particular, we define different types of anaphoric relations to keep track of spatio-temporal changes of entities. We also provide a clear definition of "identity of reference" and specify categories that make an essential change resulting in a different entity. (ii) We annotate the YouCookII dataset (Zhou et al., 2018b,a) according to our scheme and make it publicly available.[1] (iii) Null anaphors, e.g., *mix in the bowl*, are included in the annotation thanks to cooking videos that offer the precise visual observation of null anaphors to annotators. (iv) We provide a baseline multimodal anaphora resolution model for this dataset. In particular, we adapt an end-to-end (Lee et al., 2017) coreference model for the anaphora resolution task. (v) We offer a novel method to improve anaphora resolution models for instructional language by leveraging temporal features capturing temporal order of instructions instead of using the token distance as Lee et al. (2017) and Yu and Poesio (2020).

2 Related Work

Reference Resolution The reference resolution task addresses the linguistic ambiguities in state changes of entity mentions by linking the entities to their corresponding instructions (Kiddon et al., 2015; Huang et al., 2016, 2018), e.g., *the mashed potato* and *the fork* refer to the instruction *mash the potatoes with a fork*. We depart from this type of approaches, as they rely on unsound ontological assumptions (actions/events and entities are different objects) and they introduce unnecessary semantic ambiguities (by linking different entity mentions to the same instruction).

[1] `https://github.com/OguzCennet/Recipe-Anaphora-Resolution`

Anaphoric Relations: identity, near-identity, association. Anaphoras mainly come in two forms: *coreference* and *bridging*. Coreference is defined as language expressions referring to the same entity (Weischedel et al., 2012), whereas bridging is an anaphoric phenomenon based on a non-identical associated antecedent via lexical-semantic, frame-based, or encyclopedic relations (Asher and Lascarides, 1998). A coreferring anaphor and its antecedent in a text refer to the same entity (identity relation), e.g., *a black Mercedes* and *the car*, while in bridging, an anaphor and its antecedent refer to different entities (non-identity relation), e.g., *the car* and *the engine* in the utterance *I saw [a black Mercedes] parked outside the restaurant. [The car] belonged to Bill. [The engine] was still running.* (Poesio and Artstein, 2008).

As Rösiger et al. (2018) point out, bridging studies so far employ various methods to describe bridging dissimilar to the coreference definition. Nevertheless, both the concept of sameness in the coreference definition and the bridging associations neglect the changes referents may undergo. Therefore, the concept of *near-identity* was introduced by Recasens et al. (2010, 2012) as a middle ground between coreference and bridging. It addresses spatio-temporal changes of entities, e.g., the entity *Postville* in the text: *On homecoming night [Postville] feels like Hometown, ... it's become a miniature Ellis Island ... For those who prefer [the old Postville], Mayor John Hyman has a simple ...*. This sample exemplifies the referential ambiguity, arising from two language expressions referring to "almost" the same entity, i.e., *Postville* and *the old Postville* (Recasens et al., 2010). Rösiger et al. (2018) and Poesio et al. (2018) claim that the introduction of the additional near-identity category in between coreference and bridging introduces more uncertainty. Nevertheless, we consider the near-identity relationship suitable because spatio-temporal changes are essential in recipes and the information they convey describes the visual content.

Coreference and Bridging Annotations. Coreference is a well studied and clearly defined concept with some noticeable exceptions. In recent years several annotated corpora with different coreference guidelines have been released. OntoNotes v5.0 (Weischedel et al., 2012) exclusively focus on coreference using a schema similar to CoNLL-2012 (Pradhan et al., 2012) and WikiCoref (Ghaddar and Langlais, 2016) with two different relations: one is identity, a symmetrical and transitive relation, and the other appositive for adjacent noun phrases. The extraction of the mentions and the use of prepositions in mentions are crucial questions for corerefence annotation (Rösiger et al., 2018; Poesio et al., 2018). There are many extant hypotheses explaining how bridging relations function with different annotation schemes for bridging (Hou et al., 2018). The ARRAU corpus (Poesio et al., 2018) consists of general language annotated with bridging relations of noun phrases (such as *set membership*, *subset*, *possession* and *unrestricted*.) Markert et al. (2012) present ISnotes derived from OntoNotes with unrestricted bridging relations in addition to OntoNotes coreferences. The BASHI corpus (Rösiger, 2018) is based on OntoNotes content and the bridging relations in the BASHI corpus restrict the bridging anaphors to be truly anaphoric, i.e., not interpretable without an antecedent.

All aforementioned annotation studies focus solely on the anaphoric relation between two discourse entities and neglect the change of entities over time. Instructional language raises a novel question in anaphora resolution: the definition of anaphoric relations based on the change of language with entities that undergo change. Therefore, RecipeRef (Fang et al., 2022) considers the state changes for preparing the annotation guideline for recipe text based on the ChEMU-Ref (Fang et al., 2021) anaphora annotation on chemistry patent documents. RecipeRef annotation was applied to the RecipeDB data (Batra et al., 2020) that was aggregated from recipe websites and each recipe was divided into two parts, the ingredients section, and the cooking instructions. The cooking instructions of RecipeDB contains only textual instructions without any visual content. The state changes are addressed in RecipeRef as a subtype of bridging relation, even though bridging is clearly defined as an associative relation in the literature (Clark, 1975; Asher and Lascarides, 1998; Poesio and Artstein, 2008; Poesio et al., 2018). Besides, null anaphors are not included in the annotation of RecipeRef, despite their frequent use in recipes.

Several important questions remain open regarding anaphora resolution, and RecipeRef annotation, including: (1) interpretation of the state changes of entities over time; (2) addressing the referring expression in anaphora resolution with data that has different modalities; (3) obtaining the sequence of state changes by annotating the null entities in recipes; (4) the judgement of anaphoric relations of state changes and different semantic relations such as identity, non-identity, near-identity, and association.

	Train	Test
Coreference	891	330
Hyponmy	47	10
Near-Identity	699	217
Bridging	602	217
Produce	507	182
Reduce	40	22
Set-member	44	9
Part-of	11	4
Instruction	2,829	984
Token	8,754	2,966
Recipe	264	89
Entity	5,669	1,927
Null Entity	465	168
Pronoun Entity	206	61

Table 1: Statistics of annotated data with the number of annotated samples with anaphoric relations.

3 Corpus

We use the YouCookII dataset (Zhou et al., 2018a) that includes manually provided descriptions (i.e., instructions) of actions in the cooking videos. The dataset contains 2,000 unconstrained instructional videos from 89 cooking recipes. The videos provide a visual input of the corresponding objects to observe the changes clearly. To obtain a variety of ingredients and their state changes, we choose at least three random samples for each the 89 cooking recipes for the training set and one sample for the test set. There is no intersection between training and test recipe samples. In total, we have 264 training documents and 89 test documents as shown in Table 1.

Recipe A recipe is text containing a list of cooking instructions with a list of ingredients, see Figure 2. Here, we use the YouCookII annotation, all instructions for each video are manually annotated with temporal boundaries and described by imperative English sentences. Since the video inputs show the entities and actions clearly, the use of referring expressions and null entities is very common contrary to textual recipes.

Instruction. Each video recipe contains 3 to 15 instructions. Each instruction is a temporally-aligned imperative sentence that is described according to the corresponding action on the video by human annotators. The instructions are not uttered by the instructor of the video but annotated by the human annotator from a third-person viewpoint while watching the video. Each instruction defines an action, i.e., a predicate, applied to a set of objects, i.e., entities. Video segments provide the visual status of the spatio-temporal changes for the mentioned entities for each instruction. Unlike other common types of texts, cooking instructions focus on processes and entities undergoing change during the process. So, the corresponding videos in the YouCookII dataset enable us to comprehend the use of referring expressions of entities for each change.

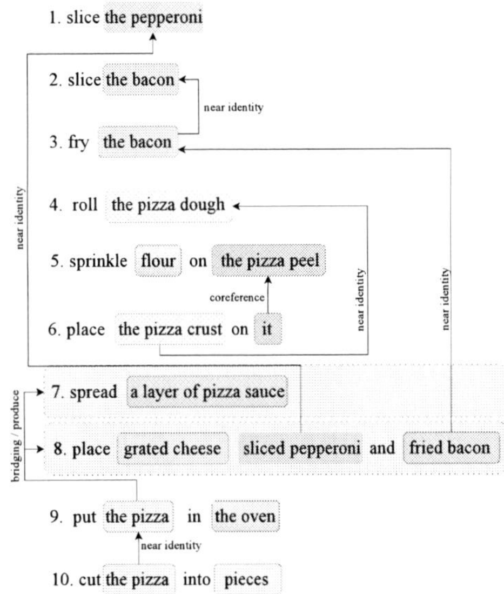

Figure 2: Example of annotation of a recipe from the YouCookII dataset named "stone baked pizza". The start point of each arrow denotes the anaphor and the end point the corresponding antecedent. The antecedent and anaphor pairs are highlighted in the same color. Grey boxes represent new entities (e.g., singletons) without antecedent.

4 Annotation Categories and Guidelines

In this section, we explain our strategy of mention selection and the use of our annotation schema on the YouCookII data.

4.1 Mention Selection

In our work, we segment multiple-action instructions, e.g., *put the chickpeas into the processor and blend all the ingredients*, into single-action instructions *put the chickpeas into the processor* and *blend all the ingredients* while preserving the order of actions. Each recipe instruction contains one predicate and 0 to 8 entities. Null arguments and ellipses are extremely common in recipes (Kiddon et al., 2015; Huang et al., 2016), since some objects are not verbally expressed, but deduced from the context of the remaining elements or videos. For example *stir for 5 minutes* does not explicitly mention the entity to be stirred. Nominal phrases with (in)definite noun phrases and pronouns are also used to mention the objects of recipes as in the following instruction: *coat the pork in the marinade* and *place it in the oven*. Therefore, we consider null arguments (i.e., null anaphors) and nominal phrases to define mentions. Contrary to ONTONOTES (Weischedel et al., 2012), we include expressions that do not refer to any other mention as singletons in the annotation.

4.2 Anaphoric Relations and Entity Change

In this section, we explain how we define anaphoric relations occurring in the recipes with state changes of entities, see Figure 2. It is worth noting that the recipe videos are exploited to judge the "sameness" of entities after an action (e.g., wash, cut, etc.) was applied. Thus, the visual features from cooking videos clarify the state change of entities in the instructions and our annotation does not rely only on the mental image of entities based on text only settings as in other coreference datasets (Weischedel et al., 2012; Pradhan et al., 2012) and anaphora datasets (Roesiger, 2016; Poesio and Artstein, 2008; Fang et al., 2021, 2022).

4.2.1 Coreference

The anaphor and the antecedent are identical and point to the same entity. Some actions such as washing or transferring the result to another container preserve the properties of the entity involved. For example, a tomato is the same tomato after washing, or a piece of meat is the same amount of meat after putting it in a pan.

4.2.2 Hyponymy

The hyponymy relation was considered as bridging by Poesio and Vieira (1998), however Baumann and Riester (2012) use the term not as context-dependent but as "lexical accessibility" to define the hyponymy relation between words as coreference, as Rösiger et al. (2018). For example *the herb* refers to the entities *mint and parsley* in the instruction *Wash mint and parsley*. Here again the anaphor may refer to a group of entities as the corresponding antecedent.

4.2.3 Near-Identity

Some actions alter either the physical or chemical properties of the entities involved. For instance, boiling a potato or an egg changes their chemical properties whereas cutting a potato or an egg changes their physical properties. Here, anaphor and antecedent entities are neither identical nor associated, they are partially the same entity sharing many crucial commonalities, but differing in at least one crucial dimension. For this type of anaphoric relation, Recasens et al. (2010) propose the near-identity relation to describe the spatio-temporal changes of the entities as a middle ground between coreference and bridging. Even though Rösiger et al. (2018) claim that additional categories between coreference and bridging introduce further uncertainty which makes the annotation process more arduous, we consider the near identity relationship more suitable because spatio-temporal changes are essential in recipes and the information they convey describes the visual content. Therefore, if they are not the same entity, the antecedent is not reduced to its parts for the anaphor, and the antecedent is not mixed with other entities to produce a new entity for the anaphor, then we define such entities as near-identical. For example, an egg or a potato are accepted as near-identical entities before and after boiling.

4.2.4 Bridging

In bridging, the antecedent is related and not identical; in contrast to coreference the anaphor is also not interchangeable with the given antecedent. As mentioned in Section 2, various phenomena are identified as bridging, resulting in diverse guidelines for bridging annotations. In accordance with the variety of associations, we assign different anaphora relations in our annotation schema.

PRODUCED: We define PRODUCED as the relationship when the anaphor refers to an antecedent producing the anaphor. The antecedent is always an instruction with predicates and given ingredients. Here, the anaphor may refer to a group of instructions as the corresponding antecedent. For example, *the dough* is produced by the instruction *mix water and flour* or *dressing* is produced by the instruction *mix yogurt and pepper*.

REDUCED: We define REDUCED as the bridging relation linking an entity. The anaphor might be a number expression (e.g., *to the whole entity*), an indefinite pronoun (*some*), or an indefinite noun phrase (e.g., *one piece*). We use REDUCED in cases when the anaphor means a part of the corresponding antecedent, provided no mereological relation exists. For example *one slice* is reduced from a bread by the instruction *slice the bread into pieces*.

SET-MEMBER: In a recipe, SET-MEMBER refers to a relation between a group of entities and its definite subset. In other words, this relation defines a bridge from a subset or element to the whole collection. For example, *cucumber, tomato, and lettuce* is an antecedent of the anaphor *ingredients* in *cut the ingredients*.

PART-OF: The antecedent may associate in a mereological relationship with the anaphor, and cannot be captured well by pre-defined lexical relations. For example, the antecedent *lemon* in the instruction *cut the lemon* relates to the anaphor *seeds* in *take the seeds out*.

4.3 Inter-annotator Agreement

50 randomly selected recipes have been annotated by two Computational Linguists, a PhD candidate and a final year Master student in Computational Linguistics. Five rounds of annotation training were completed prior to beginning the official annotation. In each round, the two annotators individually annotated the same 5 recipes (different across each round of annotation), and compared their annotations; annotation guidelines were then refined based on discussion. Finally, We achieved a high inner-annotator agreement of Krippendorff's $\alpha = 0.99$ for the creation of a new entity and reference, $\alpha = 0.95$ for the selection of the antecedent and $\alpha = 0.93$ for selection of anaphoric relations.

5 Method

In this section, we present our end-to-end multimodal anaphora resolution model. Figure 3 shows our joint neural model similar to Yu and Poesio (2020) and Fang et al. (2021), adapted from Lee et al. (2017). We extend the model with novel temporal features, see Section 5.3.

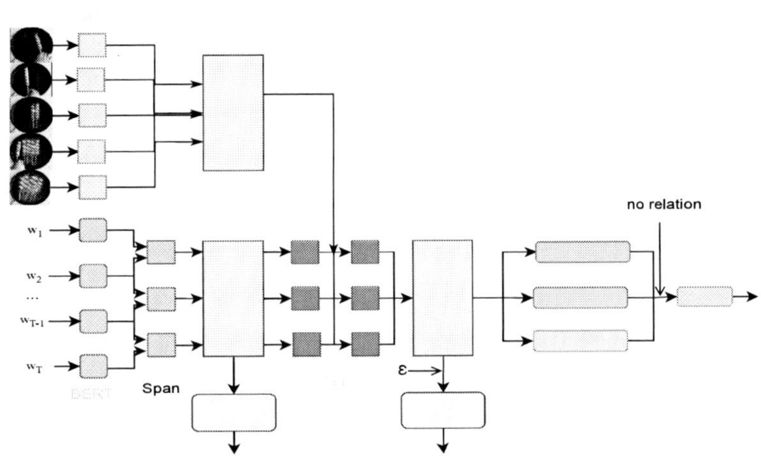

Figure 3: Proposed anaphora resolution architecture. The CNN Layer is a convolutional layer with five input channels (one per frame). The FFNN Block refers to a layer block with FFNN+ReLU+Dropout, w_t indicates the t-th word of Recipe R. ViT is a Transformer-based model to represent the features of the video inputs.

5.1 Task

In linguistics, the term Anaphora Resolution refers to the method of identifying the antecedent for an anaphor. To achieve anaphora resolution on cooking instructions, we propose two different sub-tasks: recognizing mentions, and finding the anaphor-antecedent pairs. Additionally, relation classification is used to find the relation between each anaphor and its antecedent.

We adopt the following notations. Each recipe R consists of T tokens $w_1, \ldots, w_T$ and $n \geq 1$ instructions a_i such that $R = a_1, \ldots, a_n$. Each instruction $a_i = (p_i, e_\ell)$, e.g., *pour olive oil on the Italian bread cubes*, contains one action predicate p_i and an entity list e_ℓ. The entity list consists of zero or more entities $e_\ell = \varnothing$ or $e_\ell = \{e_1, \ldots, e_m\}$ where $\varnothing$ denotes null entities which are extremely common in recipe instructions (Kiddon et al., 2015; Huang et al., 2017) and e_i indicates entities such as *the Italian bread cubes*.

We define three sub-tasks. The first task is mention detection: it extracts all mentions e_ℓ from a_i. The second task is anaphora resolution: it assigns each e_i to an antecedent $y_i \in \{\epsilon, a_1, \ldots, a_{i-1}, e_{1,\ell}, \ldots, e_{i-1,\ell}\}$, if any. The third task is relation classification: it assigns one of the relation classes {NO-RELATION, COREFERENCE, NEAR-IDENTITY, BRIDGING} to each pair (e_i, y_i). The selection of ϵ as the antecedent collapses two different situations: (1) the span is not an entity, or (2) the span is an entity but it is not referent (Lee et al., 2017). Likewise, if the relation is NO-RELATION for relation classification, this points to two scenarios: (1) the span is not an entity, or (2) the span is an entity but it is not referent and so does not have an anaphoric relation to other entities.

5.2 Baseline

5.2.1 Visual Features

Each video consists of n segments, $v_1, \ldots v_n$, each corresponding to one instruction. Following Zhou et al. (2018a), we evenly divide each segment into five clips and randomly sample one frame from each clip to capture the temporal features of that segment. Each frame f_i is encoded using the Vision Transformer (ViT) model (Dosovitskiy et al., 2021). The instruction's visual feature vector is obtained by concatenating the frame-level feature vectors: $v_i = \text{CNN}([\text{ViT}(f_1), \ldots, \text{ViT}(f_5)])$.

5.2.2 Mention Detection

For mention detection, following Lee et al. (2017), we consider all continuous tokens with up to L words as a potential span and compute the corresponding span score. BERT (Devlin et al., 2019) is used to extract the contextualised word embeddings $x_t^* = \text{BERT}(w_1, \ldots, w_T)$ where x_t^* refers to the vector representation of the token at time t of R. The vector representation g_i of a given span is obtained by concatenating the word vectors of its boundary tokens and its width feature:

$$g_i = [x^*_{\text{START}(i)}, x^*_{\text{END}(i)}, \phi(i)]$$
$$\phi(i) = \text{WIDTH}(\text{END}(i) - \text{START}(i)).$$

START(i) and END(i) represent the starting and ending token indexes for g_i, respectively. $\phi(i)$ is the width feature of the span where WIDTH(.) is the embedding function of the predefined bins of $[1, 2, 3, 4, 8, 16]$ as defined by Clark and Manning (2016).
The use of head attention (Lee et al., 2017; Yu and Poesio, 2020; Fang et al., 2021) is very common in coreference/anaphora resolution models. However, we disregard the head representation of spans for two reasons: (1) the common use of null anaphors in our data: instead the instruction a_i of the null anaphor is used for extracting the vector representation, (2) the self-attention mechanism (Vaswani et al., 2017) of the BERT model implicitly captures the mention head word.

The mention score softmax(FFNN(g_i)) is computed for each span, and the mention model is trained using the cross-entropy loss.

5.2.3 Anaphora Resolution

For anaphora resolution, the representation of span pair g_{ij} is obtained by concatenating the two span embeddings $[g_i, g_j]$ and their element-wise multiplication, $g_i \cdot g_j$, among others:

$$g_{ij} = [g_i, g_j, g_i \cdot g_j, v_i \cdot v_j, \phi_{dist}(i, j)]$$
$$\phi_{dist}(i, j) = \text{DISTANCE}(\text{START}(j) - \text{START}(i))$$

where the feature vector $\phi_{dist}(i, j)$ is the distance between the index of span i and span j. DISTANCE($\cdot$) is an embedding function of the predefined bins of $[1, 2, 3.., 30]$ as defined by Clark and Manning (2016).
For anaphora resolution, we minimize the cross entropy loss for candidate span pairs with sigmoid(FFNN(g_{ij})).

5.2.4 Relation Classification

As shown in Table 1, the number of observed hyponym, reduce, set-member, and part-of instance relations is low. Therefore, we define the anaphoric relations in term of the three main categories: coreference, near-identity, and bridging.
To learn the vectors for each relation of feature vector g_{ij}, we apply an FFNN layer:

$$\text{coreference}_{ij} = \text{FFNN}(g_{ij})$$
$$\text{n-identity}_{ij} = \text{FFNN}(g_{ij})$$
$$\text{bridging}_{ij} = \text{FFNN}(g_{ij}).$$

Then, we concatenate coreference$_{ij}$, n-identity$_{ij}$, and bridging$_{ij}$ into the relation vector rel$_{ij}$:

$$\text{rel}_{ij} = [\text{coreference}_{ij}, \text{n-identity}_{ij}, \text{briding}_{ij}].$$

To classify the anaphoric relation for each input pair, we then compute softmax(FFNN($[g_{ij}, \text{rel}_{ij}]$)).

5.3 Temporal Features

Recipe instructions are written with an implied temporal order (Jermsurawong and Habash, 2015), and the entities involved go through this temporal order until the cooking is complete. We propose to select the number of instructions (see Figure 2) as the temporal marker of entities instead of token distance $\phi_{dist}(ij)$ to avoid issues with different instruction and entity lengths. We design our experiments to explain how the temporal stage of entities in action flows influences the pair representation of mentions in cooperating with the anaphora resolution model. Thus, we formulate our temporal features as

$$\phi_{temp}(i, j) = \text{TEMPORAL}(\#a_j - \#a_i)$$

where TEMPORAL($\cdot$) is an embedding function that uses the list of bins [1,2,3..,30]. $\#a_i$ refers to the instruction index of span i and $\#a_j$ to the instruction index of span j. We concatenate $\phi_{temp}(i, j)$ in place of $\phi_{dist}(i, j)$ to obtain the vector representation of a span pair:

$$g_{ij} = [g_i, g_j, g_i \cdot g_j, v_i \cdot v_j, \phi_{temp}(i, j))].$$

Token distance varies depending on the use of token numbers in instructions and entities. For example, the instruction *mix red chili cinnamon stick cloves cumin seeds mustard seeds pepper garlic vinegar sugar and wine* might also be written *mix red chili cinnamon stick cloves cumin seeds mustard seeds* followed by *add pepper garlic vinegar in the bowl* and *mix with sugar and wine*. Therefore, temporal features are not captured well by token distance in instructional language.

6 Experimental Setup

6.1 Input

Cooking Instructions. To encode the recipes we use BERT (Devlin et al., 2019), a bidirectional transformer model trained on a masked language modeling task. First, we fine-tune BERT-large-uncased by using the YouCookII dataset (Zhou et al., 2018a) after removing our test recipes. Because of sub word embeddings, there are different

	Candidate Spans			Gold Spans		
	Precision	Recall	F1-score	Precision	Recall	F1-score
w/o Temporal						
Anaphora Resolution	48.1	34.1	39.9	48.9	46.7	47.8
Coreference	34.2	43.4	38.2	40.1	47.5	43.5
Near-identity	66.8	37.0	47.7	78.5	38.8	51.9
Bridging	12.0	37.5	18.2	16.7	45.0	24.3
Overall Relation	21.6	44.6	29.2	28.4	50.3	36.3
w Temporal						
Anaphora Resolution	48.7	34.2	**40.0**	51.2	50.0	**50.6**
Coreference	29.1	45.8	35.6	46.1	50.6	48.3
Near-identity	57.0	33.8	42.4	90.1	44.7	59.7
Bridging	14.7	41.9	21.7	24.4	43.7	31.3
Overall Relation	22.6	46.2	**30.4**	32.6	54.3	**40.8**

Table 2: Average evaluation results over 3 runs of the proposed anaphora resolution model on our annotated test data for 200 epochs. **w Temporal** and **w/o Temporal** refer to the results with or without temporal features, respectively. Candidate Spans refers to all the possible spans of continuous tokens extracted from the recipes whereas Gold Spans refers the mentions with nominal phrases, null anaphors, and instructions.

choices of presenting words. We use the first subtoken for representing the word as proposed by Devlin et al. (2019). Additionally, due to the structure of multiple successive layers, the last hidden layer is used to represent the words in recipes.

Video Frames. To encode each video frame, ViT (Dosovitskiy et al., 2021) is pre-trained on ImageNet (Russakovsky et al., 2015) and fine-tuned on Food-101 (Bossard et al., 2014) images. In the end, each instruction (i.e., segment) is represented by a 3,840-dimensional vector v_i.

6.2 Experiments

Candidate Spans Without any pruning, we consider all continuous tokens (Clark and Manning, 2016; Lee et al., 2017) as a potential spans for the training and testing phases.

Gold Spans In order to investigate the performance of anaphora resolution and relation classification models without mention detection noise, we also consider gold spans for the training and testing phases.

6.3 Evaluation

Following Hou et al. (2018) and Yu and Poesio (2020), we analyze the performance of our end-to-end anaphora resolution model with its subtasks. For mention detection, anaphora resolution and relation classification we report F1-scores.

To evaluate mention detection, precision is computed as the fraction of correctly detected mentions among all detected mentions whereas recall is the fraction of correctly detected mentions among all gold mentions. The F1-score for anaphora resolution is computed where precision is the result of dividing the number of correctly predicted pairs by the total number of predicted pairs and recall is computed by dividing the number of correctly predicted pairs by the total number of gold pairs. To evaluate relation classification we compute the F1-score where precision is computed by dividing the number of correctly predicted relations by the total number of predicted relations and recall is computed by dividing the number of correctly predicted relations by the total number of gold relations.

6.4 Results and Discussion

6.4.1 Overview

We investigate the anaphora resolution and relation classification results of gold and candidate spans comparing the F1-scores with the distance and temporal features. Overall, our results in Table 2 demonstrate that replacing token distance with our temporal features improves anaphora resolution and relation classification for both candidate and gold spans.

The performance of each task is propagated to subsequent tasks due to the sequential structure of the end-to-end system (see Section 5). The difference between the results of candidate and gold spans demonstrates that the mention detection model propagates errors to anaphora resolution and relation classification. For example, temporal features are not predictive features for anaphoric relations, but they are valuable for finding the antecedent of an anaphor, i.e., anaphora resolution. Our observations show that improvements in relation classification are propagated from the preceding anaphora resolution task in the end-to-end system for gold spans.

Additionally, binary mention detection results show a precision of 0.92, a recall of 0.88, and an F1-score of 0.90. However, the differences between the scores in anaphora resolution and relation classification results for the candidate and gold spans (see Table 2) reveal issues in transferring the mention features. We observe the main problem of mention detection in distinguishing the singletons.

6.4.2 Anaphora Resolution

We detect a significant improvement in anaphora resolution with temporal features, since temporal features often conspire to reduce unwelcome lexical similarity. For example, *potato*→ *it* → *potato*, the first *potato* is the antecedent of *it*, and *it* is the antecedent of the second *potato*. Temporal features prevent predicting the first *potato* as an antecedent for the second *potato* and designate the anaphora link from the second *potato* to *it*, because *it* is in the instruction closer in the temporal line. The improvements with temporal features reveal the issues of contextualized embeddings. While we use contextualized embeddings, the bias of lexical similarity induces complexity to link the anaphor with a correct antecedent; as recurrent in the *bacon* → *bacon* → *fried bacon* sample in Figure 2. The sliced bacon is predicted as the antecedent of the bacon of instruction 3, and it is also the antecedent of fried bacon of instruction 8. This issue occurs for rare entities and predicates. When we compare the false positives in accordance with temporality, the improvement due to temporal features mainly affects pronoun resolution. Hence, we observe that the antecedents of pronouns are closer to the pronouns. Some anomalies can be observed in the results of anaphora resolution with candidate spans due to the propagated error from mention detection. For example, we have the candidate spans *the pizza*, *pizza dough*, and *the pizza dough* for the mention *the pizza dough* of instruction 4 with the same temporal features.

6.4.3 Relation Classification

Table 2 shows that temporal features significantly improve anaphora resolution results for gold spans. Especially for bridging pairs, a noteworthy benefit of temporal features can also be observed in gold and candidate spans. However, the mistakes can also be observed in the results of near-identity and coreference classification for candidate spans.

Overall, the end-to-end model suffers from mistakes in detecting and resolving null anaphors. Expecting that all instructions contain a null anaphor increases the input noise for candidate spans. Relation classification follows anaphora resolution and mention detection. Therefore, some problems in relation classification originate from mention detection and anaphora resolution errors.

False positive bridging relations are due to singleton spans (non-referents) whereas false positive coreference and near-identical relations are due to the preference for surface words with/without state changes. For instance, in the example *wash the egg* $\xrightarrow{coreference}$ *boil the egg* $\xrightarrow{near\text{-}identity}$ *crack the egg*, the use of the same words for changing entities introduces an immense modelling challenge.

7 Conclusion and Future Work

We introduce a novel anaphora annotation scheme including the state changes of entities and near-identical relations. This fresh approach relies on video inputs for visual observation for anaphora annotation. Likewise, we provide baseline anaphora resolution results with novel temporal features on the annotated data. In future work, the mention detection model will be designed to perform with null entities and singleton mentions to improve the performance of the end-to-end model. Additionally, different visual feature extraction methods for single frames, e.g., CLIP (Radford et al., 2021) or for videos, e.g., S3D (Xie et al., 2018) will be investigated to find the best way of learning from cooking videos for anaphora resolution.

8 Acknowledgements

We would like to thank Iuliia Zaitova for helping with the annotation study. This research was funded by the joint IMPRESS (01IS20076) project between the French National Institute for Research in Digital Science and Technology (Inria) and the German Research Center for Artificial Intelligence (DFKI).

References

Nicholas Asher and Alex Lascarides. 1998. Bridging. *Journal of Semantics*, 15(1):83–113.

Devansh Batra, Nirav Diwan, Utkarsh Upadhyay, Jushaan Singh Kalra, Tript Sharma, Aman Kumar Sharma, Dheeraj Khanna, Jaspreet Singh Marwah,

Srilakshmi Kalathil, Navjot Singh, Rudraksh Tuwani, and Ganesh Bagler. 2020. Recipedb: a resource for exploring recipes. *Database: The Journal of Biological Databases and Curation*, 2020.

Stefan Baumann and Arndt Riester. 2012. Referential and lexical givenness: Semantic, prosodic and cognitive aspects. In *Prosody and meaning*, pages 119–162. De Gruyter Mouton.

Lukas Bossard, Matthieu Guillaumin, and Luc Van Gool. 2014. Food-101–mining discriminative components with random forests. In *European conference on computer vision*, pages 446–461. Springer.

Herbert H. Clark. 1975. Bridging. In *Theoretical Issues in Natural Language Processing*.

Kevin Clark and Christopher D. Manning. 2016. Improving coreference resolution by learning entity-level distributed representations. In *Proceedings of the 54th Annual Meeting of the Association for Computational Linguistics (Volume 1: Long Papers)*, pages 643–653, Berlin, Germany. Association for Computational Linguistics.

Jacob Devlin, Ming-Wei Chang, Kenton Lee, and Kristina Toutanova. 2019. BERT: Pre-training of deep bidirectional transformers for language understanding. In *Proceedings of the 2019 Conference of the North American Chapter of the Association for Computational Linguistics: Human Language Technologies, Volume 1 (Long and Short Papers)*, pages 4171–4186, Minneapolis, Minnesota. Association for Computational Linguistics.

Alexey Dosovitskiy, Lucas Beyer, Alexander Kolesnikov, Dirk Weissenborn, Xiaohua Zhai, Thomas Unterthiner, Mostafa Dehghani, Matthias Minderer, Georg Heigold, Sylvain Gelly, Jakob Uszkoreit, and Neil Houlsby. 2021. An image is worth 16x16 words: Transformers for image recognition at scale. *ArXiv*, abs/2010.11929.

Biaoyan Fang, Timothy Baldwin, and Karin Verspoor. 2022. What does it take to bake a cake? the RecipeRef corpus and anaphora resolution in procedural text. In *Findings of the Association for Computational Linguistics: ACL 2022*, pages 3481–3495, Dublin, Ireland. Association for Computational Linguistics.

Biaoyan Fang, Christian Druckenbrodt, Saber A Akhondi, Jiayuan He, Timothy Baldwin, and Karin Verspoor. 2021. ChEMU-ref: A corpus for modeling anaphora resolution in the chemical domain. In *Proceedings of the 16th Conference of the European Chapter of the Association for Computational Linguistics: Main Volume*, pages 1362–1375, Online. Association for Computational Linguistics.

Abbas Ghaddar and Philippe Langlais. 2016. Wikicoref: An english coreference-annotated corpus of wikipedia articles. In *Proceedings of the Tenth International Conference on Language Resources and Evaluation (LREC'16)*, pages 136–142.

Yufang Hou, Katja Markert, and Michael Strube. 2018. Unrestricted bridging resolution. *Computational Linguistics*, 44(2):237–284.

Eduard Hovy, Teruko Mitamura, Felisa Verdejo, Jun Araki, and Andrew Philpot. 2013. Events are not simple: Identity, non-identity, and quasi-identity. In *Workshop on Events: Definition, Detection, Coreference, and Representation*, pages 21–28, Atlanta, Georgia. Association for Computational Linguistics.

De-An Huang, Shyamal Buch, Lucio Dery, Animesh Garg, Li Fei-Fei, and Juan Carlos Niebles. 2018. Finding" it": Weakly-supervised reference-aware visual grounding in instructional videos. In *Proceedings of the IEEE Conference on Computer Vision and Pattern Recognition*, pages 5948–5957.

De-An Huang, Joseph J Lim, Li Fei-Fei, and Juan Carlos Niebles. 2017. Unsupervised visual-linguistic reference resolution in instructional videos. In *Proceedings of the IEEE Conference on Computer Vision and Pattern Recognition*, pages 2183–2192.

Ting-Hao Huang, Francis Ferraro, Nasrin Mostafazadeh, Ishan Misra, Aishwarya Agrawal, Jacob Devlin, Ross Girshick, Xiaodong He, Pushmeet Kohli, Dhruv Batra, et al. 2016. Visual storytelling. In *Proceedings of the 2016 Conference of the North American Chapter of the Association for Computational Linguistics: Human Language Technologies*, pages 1233–1239.

Jermsak Jermsurawong and Nizar Habash. 2015. Predicting the structure of cooking recipes. In *Proceedings of the 2015 Conference on Empirical Methods in Natural Language Processing*, pages 781–786, Lisbon, Portugal. Association for Computational Linguistics.

Chloé Kiddon, Ganesa Thandavam Ponnuraj, Luke Zettlemoyer, and Yejin Choi. 2015. Mise en place: Unsupervised interpretation of instructional recipes. In *Proceedings of the 2015 Conference on Empirical Methods in Natural Language Processing*, pages 982–992.

Nikhil Krishnaswamy and James Pustejovsky. 2019. Generating a novel dataset of multimodal referring expressions. In *Proceedings of the 13th International Conference on Computational Semantics - Short Papers*, pages 44–51, Gothenburg, Sweden. Association for Computational Linguistics.

Nikhil Krishnaswamy and James Pustejovsky. 2020. A formal analysis of multimodal referring strategies under common ground. In *Proceedings of the Twelfth Language Resources and Evaluation Conference*, pages 5919–5927, Marseille, France. European Language Resources Association.

Kenton Lee, Luheng He, Mike Lewis, and Luke Zettlemoyer. 2017. End-to-end neural coreference resolution. In *Proceedings of the 2017 Conference on Empirical Methods in Natural Language Processing*, pages 188–197, Copenhagen, Denmark. Association for Computational Linguistics.

Katja Markert, Yufang Hou, and Michael Strube. 2012. Collective classification for fine-grained information status. In *Proceedings of the 50th Annual Meeting of the Association for Computational Linguistics (Volume 1: Long Papers)*, pages 795–804.

Massimo Poesio and Ron Artstein. 2008. Anaphoric annotation in the ARRAU corpus. In *Proceedings of the Sixth International Conference on Language Resources and Evaluation (LREC'08)*, Marrakech, Morocco. European Language Resources Association (ELRA).

Massimo Poesio, Yulia Grishina, Varada Kolhatkar, Nafise Moosavi, Ina Roesiger, Adam Roussel, Fabian Simonjetz, Alexandra Uma, Olga Uryupina, Juntao Yu, and Heike Zinsmeister. 2018. Anaphora resolution with the ARRAU corpus. In *Proceedings of the First Workshop on Computational Models of Reference, Anaphora and Coreference*, pages 11–22, New Orleans, Louisiana. Association for Computational Linguistics.

Massimo Poesio and Renata Vieira. 1998. A corpus-based investigation of definite description use. *Computational Linguistics*, 24(2):183–216.

Sameer Pradhan, Alessandro Moschitti, Nianwen Xue, Olga Uryupina, and Yuchen Zhang. 2012. Conll-2012 shared task: Modeling multilingual unrestricted coreference in ontonotes. In *Joint Conference on EMNLP and CoNLL-Shared Task*, pages 1–40.

Alec Radford, Jong Wook Kim, Chris Hallacy, Aditya Ramesh, Gabriel Goh, Sandhini Agarwal, Girish Sastry, Amanda Askell, Pamela Mishkin, Jack Clark, et al. 2021. Learning transferable visual models from natural language supervision. In *International Conference on Machine Learning*, pages 8748–8763. PMLR.

Marta Recasens, Eduard Hovy, and M. Antònia Martí. 2010. A typology of near-identity relations for coreference (NIDENT). In *Proceedings of the Seventh International Conference on Language Resources and Evaluation (LREC'10)*, Valletta, Malta. European Language Resources Association (ELRA).

Marta Recasens, Eduard Hovy, and M Antònia Martí. 2011. Identity, non-identity, and near-identity: Addressing the complexity of coreference. *Lingua*, 121(6):1138–1152.

Marta Recasens, M. Antònia Martí, and Constantin Orasan. 2012. Annotating near-identity from coreference disagreements. In *Proceedings of the Eighth International Conference on Language Resources and Evaluation (LREC'12)*, pages 165–172, Istanbul, Turkey. European Language Resources Association (ELRA).

Ina Roesiger. 2016. SciCorp: A corpus of English scientific articles annotated for information status analysis. In *Proceedings of the Tenth International Conference on Language Resources and Evaluation (LREC'16)*, pages 1743–1749, Portorož, Slovenia. European Language Resources Association (ELRA).

Ina Rösiger. 2018. BASHI: A corpus of Wall Street Journal articles annotated with bridging links. In *Proceedings of the Eleventh International Conference on Language Resources and Evaluation (LREC 2018)*, Miyazaki, Japan. European Language Resources Association (ELRA).

Ina Rösiger, Arndt Riester, and Jonas Kuhn. 2018. Bridging resolution: Task definition, corpus resources and rule-based experiments. In *Proceedings of the 27th International Conference on Computational Linguistics*, pages 3516–3528.

Olga Russakovsky, Jia Deng, Hao Su, Jonathan Krause, Sanjeev Satheesh, Sean Ma, Zhiheng Huang, Andrej Karpathy, Aditya Khosla, Michael Bernstein, Alexander C. Berg, and Li Fei-Fei. 2015. ImageNet Large Scale Visual Recognition Challenge. *International Journal of Computer Vision (IJCV)*, 115(3):211–252.

Ashish Vaswani, Noam Shazeer, Niki Parmar, Jakob Uszkoreit, Llion Jones, Aidan N Gomez, Ł ukasz Kaiser, and Illia Polosukhin. 2017. Attention is all you need. In *Advances in Neural Information Processing Systems*, volume 30. Curran Associates, Inc.

R Weischedel, S Pradhan, L Ramshaw, J Kaufman, M Franchini, M El-Bachouti, N Xue, M Palmer, JD Hwang, C Bonial, et al. 2012. Ontonotes release 5.0. linguistic data consortium. Technical report, Philadelphia, Technical Report.

Saining Xie, Chen Sun, Jonathan Huang, Zhuowen Tu, and Kevin Murphy. 2018. Rethinking spatiotemporal feature learning: Speed-accuracy trade-offs in video classification. In *Proceedings of the European conference on computer vision (ECCV)*, pages 305–321.

Juntao Yu and Massimo Poesio. 2020. Multitask learning-based neural bridging reference resolution. In *Proceedings of the 28th International Conference on Computational Linguistics*, pages 3534–3546, Barcelona, Spain (Online). International Committee on Computational Linguistics.

Luowei Zhou, Nathan Louis, and Jason J. Corso. 2018a. Weakly-supervised video object grounding from text by loss weighting and object interaction. In *BMVC*.

Luowei Zhou, Chenliang Xu, and Jason J. Corso. 2018b. Towards automatic learning of procedures from web instructional videos. In *AAAI*.

"#DisabledOnIndianTwitter" : A Dataset towards Understanding the Expression of People with Disabilities on Indian Twitter

♤Ishani Mondal*, ♡Sukhnidh Kaur, ♡Kalika Bali, ◇Aditya Vashistha, ♡Manohar Swaminathan

♤University of Maryland, College Park, Maryland, USA

♡Microsoft Research Labs, Bangalore, India

◇Cornell University, Ithaca, New York, USA

♤imonda@umd.edu, {t-sukkaur, kalikab, swmanoh}@microsoft.com
adityav@cornell.edu

Abstract

Twitter serves as a powerful tool for self-expression among people with disabilities. To understand how disabled Indians use Twitter, we introduce a manually annotated corpus **#DisabledOnIndianTwitter** comprising 2,384 tweets published by 27 female and 15 male users. To examine patterns in Twitter use, we propose a novel hierarchical annotation taxonomy to classify the tweets into various themes including discrimination, advocacy, and self-identification. Using these annotations, we benchmark the corpus leveraging state-of-the-art classifiers. We use a mixed-methods analysis to showcase differences in self-expression among male and female disabled users.

1 Introduction

A majority of disabled Indians exist at the margins of society with little to no access to social media (Census, 2011). Structural embeddings of ableism and patriarchy further intersect to produce multiply oppressive conditions for Indian women with disabilities (Thomas and Thomas, 2002; Dawn, 2014). However, as access to ICTs and high-speed internet grows, Indian Twitter's user base is expanding to include disability influencers, activists, and everyday disabled users. Recent work from the West examines elements of 'Disability Twitter' (Hemsley et al., 2015; Mann, 2018; Ineland et al., 2019; Ellis and Goggin, 2013) but little is known of such Twitter use among the Indian user base. To fill this gap, we study self-expression among disabled users on Indian Twitter. As researchers with overlapping interests in disability and gender, we orient our analysis towards gendered self-expression.

We introduce a novel human-annotated corpus **#DisabledOnIndianTwitter** comprising 2,384 tweets published by a preliminary set of 15 male and 27 female disabled people who are active and vocal on Indian Twitter. In order to linguistically analyze the patterns of their social media usage, we propose a hierarchical linguistic annotation framework which takes into account contextual nuances surrounding disability-related concerns. Within this framework, we propose multi-level and multi-class thematic classifications including discrimination, advocacy, harassment, and self-identification. As a next step, we benchmark state-of-the-art language model classifiers fine-tuned on these datasets, noting significant room for improvement of models. Through our mixed-methods analysis on the created corpus, we find that disabled women are more likely than disabled men to center personal experiences while expressing discrimination, advocacy and harassment, but disabled men tend to be more authoritative in their expression. Disabled women in Sports are more likely to advocate for inclusion rights than disabled women in other professions.

In sum, our work makes three major contributions to NLP and accessibility research.

1. We propose a novel hierarchical annotation taxonomy to perform linguistic analysis of disability-related textual content.

2. We introduce the first-of-its-kind human-annotated dataset aimed at understanding online expressions of disabled people in India. The dataset will also serve as a baseline for future explorations on tweets generated by a demographic severely underrepresented in current NLP advances.

3. We perform a mixed-method analysis on our corpus to identify gendered differences in self-expression of disabled people on Indian Twitter.

2 Background and Related Work

Social Media and Disability: Disabled people remain one of the most disenfranchised demograph-

*This work was done when the author was a Research Fellow at Microsoft Research India.

Findings of the Association for Computational Linguistics: AACL-IJCNLP 2022, pages 375–386

ics across low-income countries including India (Groce et al., 2011; Buettgen et al., 2015; Pinilla-Roncancio et al., 2020). Abject poverty coupled with complex sociocultural norms pose significant barriers to equal rights and representation (Kapur Mehta and Shah, 2003; Groce et al., 2011). Disabled women in India experience vagaries of marginalization, often in the form of gender and ableist discrimination, poverty, and inadequate family support, among others (Dhungana, 2006). For example, Leveille et al. (2000) found a substantial gender differential in self-reported health where disabled women reported poorer health than their male counterparts. Scholars have also studied the struggles of people with disabilities in accessing basic education (Croft, 2013; Jameel, 2011), employment (Dyaram and V., 2020; Kumar et al., 2012), and healthcare services (Mactaggart et al., 2016).

With the rising influence of social media on everyday lives, several scholars have started studying the use and non-use of social media platforms by people with disabilities (Outini, 2020; Vashistha et al., 2015). For example, scholars have examined the impact of social media on agency and representation of people with vision impairments (Pal et al., 2017) as well as its use during public health crises (Mont et al., 2021; Mehrotra, 2021). However, there is a scarcity of research on gender differences in how disabled people engage with others on social media.

NLP Methods and Datasets on Disability: NLP Researchers have recently been focusing on studying unintended biases in NLP models against several historically marginalized groups such as those based on differences in race, culture,and gender (Bolukbasi et al., 2016; Jentzsch et al., 2019; Garg et al., 2019; Barocas et al., 2018; Dixon et al., 2018). Several datasets have been created with the goal of fostering research in quantifying societal bias, i.e., the under-representation of these demographics in NLP models that can be detrimental for downstream NLP tasks (Levy et al., 2021; Babaeianjelodar et al., 2020; Zhao et al., 2020; Sharma et al., 2021; Dinan et al., 2019). Although some recent work (Hutchinson et al., 2020; Hassan et al., 2021) has focused on quantifying the representation of the people with disabilities in pre-trained language models, there has been a general lack of attention towards building datasets to understand how disabled people engage and express themselves on social media. (Mack et al., 2021). Our work fills this gap by: (1) creating a new dataset containing tweets from people with disabilities in India and making it publicly available[1], and (2) analyzing the dataset to identify differential patterns of Twitter usage based on gender, and other attributes.

3 Dataset

We used Twitter to collect public data since it allows such analysis through APIs available for researchers. We manually selected Twitter accounts where users disclosed their disability identity, for example, in their Twitter bio, profile picture, username, display name, or within the content of their tweets. We note that disabled representation on Indian Twitter is marginal due to a lack of access to ICTs and high-speed internet among the disabled population. Further, due to the stigma associated with disability, a limited number of users disclose their disability identity on Indian Twitter. So while the manual process ensures that our dataset is accurate, it also means that we have a limited number of Twitter accounts to analyze.

Selecting Twitter Handles: We refer to our dataset as **"DisabledOnIndianTwitter"** which comprises 27 females and 15 males working as sportspersons, social workers, researchers, bloggers, actors, writers, travelers, company directors, comedians, and students. We identified occupations and genders through manually examination of Twitter bios, tweets, and other profiles.Table 5 in Appendix shows the details of these Twitter handles without explicitly disclosing their identity for privacy concerns.

Data Filtering: Next, we crawled recent tweets (last 3206 tweets per user) posted by each user. After collecting the tweets, we excluded those with duplicate or no meaningful textual content (e.g., only @-mentions or images). We only selected tweets in English using the language code provided by Twitter. During data filtration, we manually verified the language codes and excluded non-English tweets. We also excluded retweets and replies as these do not necessarily express the thoughts of the user who retweeted them. We thus obtained a set of 60,000 tweets.

[1]https://github.com/Ishani-Mondal/-DisabledOnIndianTwitter

Tweet	Relatedness	Discrim	Advocacy	Incl	Identity	Factual	Stance	Haras	Theme
In small industrial district of Karur: a grand beginning of accessaudits with famous Lord Murugan temple. Glad 2 see. Awed by 365 steps-solutions to make it accessible for people with disabilites	R1	D0	A0	I1	Id0	O	P	H0	O

Table 1: An Example of Annotated Tweet from our corpus. Here Discrim indicates Discrimination, Incl indicates Inclusion, Haras indicates Harassment (Shortened due to space constraint).

Categories	Statistics
Relatedness	1518 (R1), 866 (R0)
Discrimination	426 (D1), 1092 (D0)
Advocacy	638 (A1), 880 (A0)
Inclusion	186 (I1), 1332 (I0)
Identity	363 (Id1), 1155 (Id0)
Fact/Opinion	370 (F), 1148 (O)
Stance	664 (P), 484 (N)
Harassment	148 (H1), 1370 (H0)
Theme	198 (HH), 45 (Emp), 85 (Ed), 1190 (O)

Table 2: Final Statistics of our Dataset

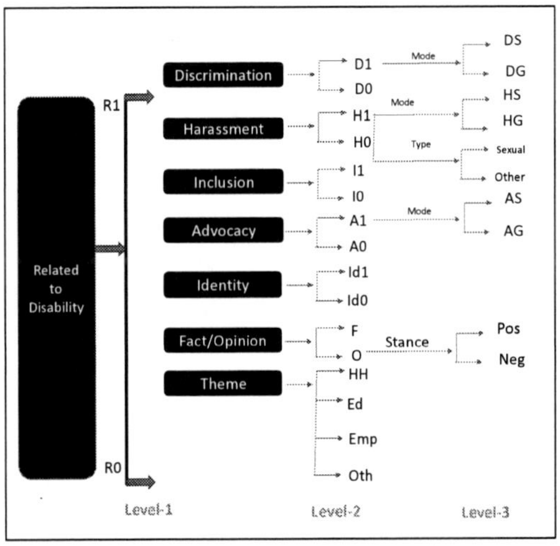

Figure 1: Hierarchical Annotation Taxonomy (Three Levels) used to thematically classify the Tweets posted by disabled people on Indian Twitter.

Keyword Based Sampling: We used a keyword-based sampling method to increase the hit rate of tweets with disability related concerns, following the existing work on labeling infrequent linguistic phenomena, e.g., irony (Van Hee et al., 2018) , hate speech (Waseem and Hovy, 2016) or bragging (Jin et al., 2022). To ensure that we capture all disability related information in the posts, we extended the list of disability related keywords provided by (Hutchinson et al., 2020) and their synonyms from WordNet (Miller, 1995). The complete list of keywords is available in Appendix 12. We observed that some tweets did not explicitly contain the keywords, but frequently mentioned accessing education, societal aspects of livelihood such as employment, e.g. *'job*', 'employ*', 'government'*, and health and hygiene, e.g. *university, education, studies*. We have selected the Tweets based on these words and added the keywords to the list shown in Appendix 12.

4 Annotation Taxonomy

We propose a linguistic annotation schema (Figure 1) to study the patterns of self-expression of tweets. The purpose is to categorize each tweet into different classes with each category indicating one of the aspects mentioned above. In this section, we define the broader and fine-grained sub-categories under each category.

4.1 Relatedness

We began the annotation exercise by determining whether each tweet contained disability-relevant subject matter. Annotators were asked to mark related tweets as (R1) and unrelated tweets as (R0). **Example (annotation R1)**: *"Its always amusing when people feel unsettled when they are around a disabled person. They just do not know what to do* *with themselves when it comes to offering support in a dignified way.*"

Example (annotation R0): "*Dear Pediatric Surgeons, its high time you embrace; STOP using pathologising terms like gender dysphoria, Disorders of Sex Development; Differences of Sex Dev.*"

For disability related tweets, annotators were asked to further annotate the following aspects:

Discrimination:

Tweets including mentions of exclusion, name-calling, or structural oppression were annotated as discriminatory (D1), if not then marked as (D0).

Example (annotation D1): "*When I had not announced my disability on a loudspeaker, I had some pretty awkward job interviews where they didn't know what to tell me. It made me understand why they add things like walking, lifting as functional requirements in central govt exams. They don't really want you.*"

For tweets marked as discriminatory, annotators further distinguished between personal accounts of discrimination and discrimination on a generic/societal level. The former was tagged as (DS) and the later as (DG).

Harassment:

Tweets related to disability-related harassment, including bullying, trolling, or abuse on a personal or societal level, were marked as harassment (H1) or (H0) if not.

Example (annotation: H1): "*If you want to know the social status of persons with disability in India, you should see conversations on reservations on social media. The use of words handicapped, viklang, not just in literary terms will reveal a lot to you.*"

Similar to Discrimination, we annotated personal accounts of harassment as (HS) and generic accounts of harassment as (HG).

After this, we also annotated Sexual harassment (Sexual) and Other (Other). These annotations were only applied to tweets already marked as harassment (H1).

Example (annotation: Sexual): ''*disabled face sexual abuse, domestic violence forced sterlisation, .its so diff for them to combat wethepeople loveknowsnodisability*"

Inclusion:

Inclusion-related tweets indicate positive experiences with accessibility, such as being able to make use of accommodations or witnessing thoughtful media representation. Such tweets were marked as (I1), or else (I0).

Example (annotation I1): "*Excited to find this watch with dial for persons with impairments*"

Advocacy:

Tweets related to disability-related advocacy, such as those calling for the rights or inclusion of people with disabilities on a personal or societal level, were marked as (A1), otherwise (A0).

Example (annotation A1): "*Accessibility modifications are required to enable persons with reduced mobility to gain access to education, employment, transportation*"

Similar to Discrimination, we annotated Self-Advocacy (AS) and Generic Advocacy (AG).

Identity:

If the tweet author referred to their own identity as a disabled person within the text of the tweet, it was annotated as identity (Id1), otherwise (Id0).

Example (annotation: Id1): "*That satisfying moment when,as a blind lawyer at a firm,you get to speak for work w/ a fellow blind lawyer who is your client.*"

Fact or Opinion:

If the tweet included factual and verifiable information, such as that about a government policy, cited statistics, court statement, or cited experiences from published articles, we marked it as factual (F). If the tweet included non-factual information such as opinions, personal experiences, or commentary on the state of disability, we marked it as opinion (O).

Example (annotation: F): "*freedom of a woman to decide whether to continue with a pregnancy cannot be taken away, the Kerala High Court has said while allowing a woman with multiple disabilities to abort*"

Example (annotation: O): "*Self- Care tip! I experienced panic attack and anxiety and I understood how important it is to take care of ourselves and reach out for help.*"

Stance:

If the author's stance on the issue described in the

tweet was positive, relatively positive, or hopeful, annotators were asked to mark it as positive (Pos). If the stance was negative, relatively negative, or critical, it was marked as negative (Neg).
Example (annotation: Pos): *"It is hoped that in months streets not less than km each in the South, East, North, West; Central Delhi will be identified; made accessible under supervision of an officer of a rank not lower than the Director be appointed by the Chief Secretary"*
Example (annotation: Neg): *"While I want to correct everyone who is saying 'specially' abled child while talking about the Ranchi airport incidence, I guess 'special' generates more empathy!"*

Theme:
Tweets related to Health and Hygiene, Education, and Employment were annotated as (HH), (Ed), and (Emp), respectively. Tweets that did not fall into these categories were annotated as Other (O).
Example (annotation: HH): *"What about inclusive accessible toilets for people with disabilities? Why not have unisex inclusive accessible toilet for both disabled &; trans people? Do frame EOP mandated u/s of too"*
Example (annotation: Ed): *"I am an aspiring deaf woman (1st in country) pursuing LLB in Faridabad. It is ironic how while learning to advocate for Deaf Rights, I've to struggle for my right to Interpreter provision! Pl support my quest for access to education!"*
Example (annotation: Emp): *"Working in Banking sector is getting difficult day by day, planning to quit as soon as possible. I know being visually impaired it will be difficult to get a new job especially when you have passed around years there but I will have to take risk. I feel suffocated now."*

5 Annotation and Quality Control

We manually annotated the tweets to provide a solid benchmark and foster future research. The first two authors of the paper went through a pilot annotation exercise to verify the quality of their annotation schema and guidelines along with two other annotators. For the pilot study, we sampled 250 Tweets from our collection following the criteria: 1) the sample contains a considerable percentage of tweets containing disability related keywords and 2) some of the tweets are related to employment, education and health, and 3) the rest of the sample consists of random tweets not related to the above topics. The annotation is based only on the actual text of the tweet without considering additional modalities (e.g. images). This is similar to the information available to the predictive models at the time of training. After the first round of annotations, the inter-annotator agreement was calculated with a pairwise comparison between the annotators using Fleiss's Kappa (κ) for all the categories. Figure 2 lists the agreement values for each annotation category. Overall, high inter-rater reliability scores were achieved over all categories.

Adjudication: The last step of the pilot annotation was to reconcile disagreements among the annotators to produce the final canonical annotation. This step also allowed us to further refine the annotation guidelines. For example, whether a tweet is a fact or an opinion could sometimes be ambiguous and the annotators had to carefully consider and decide whether or not a user was stating opinions as facts. As a result, we refined the definition of "facts" to clearly include a condition that it belong to a set which is universally true. Take the following Tweet as an example: *"people who live in places which have free healthcare are privileged. just saying."* This Tweet is a classic example of the user's opinion being stated as a fact. But since this statement is not universally true, we classified it as an opinion.

Main Annotation: Following the pilot, each annotator annotated mutually exclusive set of tweets. The annotators who designed the schema (average Cohen's Kappa across all the categories = 0.81) annotated 1,600 tweets between them, while the remaining 784 tweets were annotated by two other annotators. The average Fleiss' Kappa for all annotators over all the categories was 0.70, indicating high agreement. Table 2 shows the high-level statistics of the annotation of 2,384 tweets in the dataset.

6 Benchmarking Experiments

Text pre-processing: We pre-processed the tweets using TweetPreprocessor API[2] which helps in cleaning the tweet by parsing URLs, Hashtags, Mentions and Emojis.

Classification Models: We designed the annotation schema in a way that the majority of categor-

[2]https://pypi.org/project/tweet-preprocessor/

Classifiers	TF-IDF+LR Prec	TF-IDF+LR Rec	TF-IDF+LR F1	Bert-Base-Cased Prec	Bert-Base-Cased Rec	Bert-Base-Cased F1	RoBERTa-Base Prec	RoBERTa-Base Rec	RoBERTa-Base F1	BERTweet Prec	BERTweet Rec	BERTweet F1
BC (Relatedness)	0.71	0.83	0.76	0.86	0.83	0.84	0.91	0.95	0.93	0.88	0.95	0.91
MC.1 (Theme)	0.45	0.67	0.54	0.65	0.72	0.68	0.67	0.77	0.72	0.70	0.82	0.76
BC.1 (Discrimination)	0.45	0.56	0.50	0.64	0.71	0.67	0.69	0.80	0.74	0.78	0.85	0.81
BC.2 (Advocacy)	0.57	0.50	0.53	0.52	0.53	0.52	0.61	0.43	0.51	0.58	0.55	0.56
BC.3 (Identity)	0.62	0.65	0.63	0.70	0.81	0.75	0.66	0.95	0.82	0.69	1.00	0.81
BC.4 (Harassment)	0.53	0.56	0.54	0.55	0.60	0.58	0.59	0.61	0.60	0.63	0.66	0.64
BC.5 (Inclusion)	0.62	0.63	0.62	0.64	0.65	0.64	0.66	0.63	0.64	0.69	0.67	0.68
BC.6 (Fact/Opinion)	0.61	0.45	0.56	0.62	0.54	0.58	0.67	0.55	0.6	0.72	0.56	0.66
BC.6.1 (Stance)	0.85	0.88	0.86	0.84	0.77	0.80	0.95	0.83	0.88	0.96	0.85	0.90

Table 3: Classification Report using different bag-of-words and transformer models on the test set of the annotated dataset. Prec indicates Precision, Rec indicates Recall and F1 indicates F1-score averaged over all the class labels.

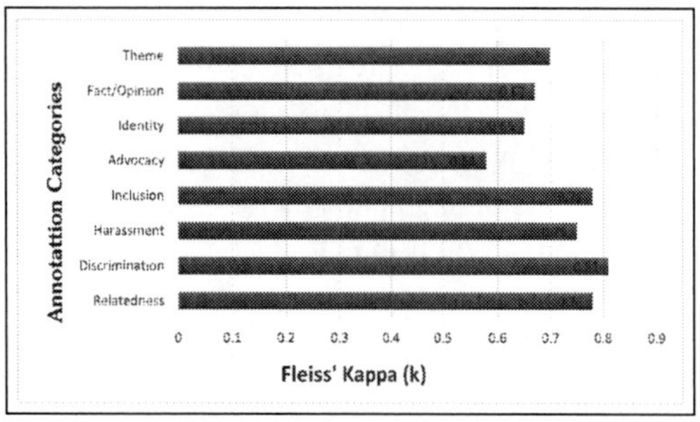

Figure 2: Inter-Annotator Agreement (κ) among the annotators on the categories.

ical themes, such as Discrimination or Not Discrimination, can be determined using binary classification. In contrast to multi-class hierarchical classifiers, such binary classifiers do not require a large amount of training data. We therefore took the approach of developing separate classifiers for tagging each category.

The top-most level **(Level-1)** used a binary classifier (BC) to determine whether the tweet is related to disability **(BC)**. If the output of **(BC)** was 'Yes', we then used six different binary classifiers in the second level of tagging **(Level-2)** to determine if the tweet was related to 1) *discrimination* **(BC.1)**, 2) *advocacy* **(BC.2)**, 3) *identity* **(BC.3)**, 4) *harassment* **(BC.4)**) *inclusion* **(BC.5)**, or if it was a 6) fact or opinion **(BC.6)**. Moreover, in Level-2, we also designed a multi-class multi-label classifier to examine the domain or theme the tweet pertains to, for example, employment, education, health or others **(MC.1)**. Based on the outputs obtained from Level-2 classification, we designed six binary classifiers **(Level-3)** to examine if the discrimination was self-experienced or generic **(BC.1.1)** if the output was 'Yes', similarly for advocacy **(BC.2.1)** if the output was 'Yes', harassment **(BC.4.1)** if the output was 'Yes', stance if the tweet was opinionated **(BC.6.1)** . We also designed another classifier to determine the nature of the harassment **(BC.4.2)**.

Training and Evaluation: Each of the classifiers were separately trained on class-balanced training data for each annotation category (such as binary classification to determine discrimination). We trained each model three times using different random seeds and reported the mean Precision, Recall and F1 (macro) on the test set. For all the annotation categories (binary and multi-class classification), we benchmarked the dataset using the following baselines:

TF-IDF+LR: We trained a Logistic Regression (LR) with the TF-IDF vectors of the input tweets using L2 regularization.

BERT, RoBERTa and BERTweet: We evaluated the vanilla transformer-based models (Vaswani et al., 2017), such as BERT (Devlin et al., 2018), RoBERTa (Liu et al., 2019) and BERTweet (Nguyen et al., 2020) from huggingface Transformers[3]. BERTweet is pretrained on English tweets using RoBERTa as the encoder and it achieves better performance on Twitter tasks (Nguyen et al., 2020). We fine-tuned the BERT, RoBERTa and BERTweet for binary (BC, BC.1, BC.2, BC.3, BC.4, BC.5, BC.6, BC.1.1, BC.2.1, BC.4.1, BC.4.2, BC.6.1) and multi-class (MC.1) predictions by adding a classification layer that took the [CLS] token as input. We used the base cased models and fine-tuned them for 10 epochs. The maximum sequence length was set to 50 in the

[3]https://huggingface.co/docs/transformers/index

Advocacy		Discrimination	
Unigrams	**Bigrams**	**Unigrams**	**Bigrams**
champion	accessible screen	dying	struggle invisible
deaf	delhi govt	unable	hide vulnerabilities
raised	high support	miserably	hide divyang
girlspl	home vaccination	unfortunately	people comorbidities
high	support needs	humiliating	visually impaired
Inclusion		**Identity**	
inclusive	accessible flight	us	instant intimidation
excited	disabled friendly	great	hearing aid
accepted	accessible india	blind	visually impaired
included	application accessible	deaf	blind woman
accessibile	education accessible	flag	deaf woman
Harassment		**Themes**	
violent	getting beaten	vaccination	educate disabled
abuse	disabled women	reservation	disabled friendly
deaf	disabled unfriendly	universities	home vaccination
flag	home vaccination	covid	educational institutions
marry	support needs	employment	education system

Table 4: Top 5 Unigrams and Bigrams Association in case of Discrimination, Advocacy, Harassment, Inclusion, Identity and Accessibility theme sorted by Pearson Correlation. All correlations are significant when considering $p < .01$ determined using two-tailed t-test.

training set and used a batch size of 32.

Experimental Results: Table 3 shows the predictive performance of all the models for the different categories (i.e., both binary and multi-class classification). Overall, BERTweet models with linguistic information achieved better overall performance. Transformer models performed substantially better in the majority class baseline and above Logistic Regression. BERTweet performed better than BERT and RoBERTa, which illustrates the advantage of pre-training on English tweets for this task. These results indicate that the transformer models achieve acceptable predictive performance on categories, such as *Relatedness, Theme, Discrimination, Inclusion, Identity, Stance*. However, it is evident that there is much room for improvement for classifiers on categories, such as *Advocacy, Inclusion, Harassment and Fact/Opinion* as they considerably under-perform compared to human judgement.

7 N-gram Analysis

To understand the most prominent and distinguishing patterns in each category, we used unigram and bigram tags associated with the annotated categories of the tweets in our data set. Each tweet was represented as a TF-IDF distribution over the unigrams and bigrams to reveal distinctive syntactic patterns of different categorical themes. For each feature, we computed the strength of correlation between its distribution across posts and the label of the post using Pearson Correlation (r) (Benesty et al., 2009) – a standard approach used by other researchers (Jin et al., 2022). Finally, we sorted these values and obtained the most important n-grams for each category.

Table 4 presents the top 5 unigrams and bigrams correlated with our six annotation categories. The top n-grams in the harassment and discrimination category can be classified into (a) negative verbs and adjectives (e.g. *violent, deaf, getting beaten, disabled unfriendly, humiliating*) that usually depict the kind of societal harassment disabled people in India experience in their everday lives; and (b) word spans related to the trend of reacting to harassing or discriminatory experiences (e.g. *hide vulnerabilities, hide divyangs*[4]).

On the other hand, the most important features in advocacy/inclusion categories can be classified into positive nouns and supportive or encouraging keywords (e.g. *champion, accepted, high support, accessible india*); and (b) some suggestions on improving access to vaccination, transportation (e.g. *application accessible, education accessible*).

In the identity category, we observe that most n-grams are related to people disclosing their status as a disabled person. Similarly, in the themes, there is a high degreee of association in education and employment related keywords. One interesting highly frequent n-gram is "reservation", and it appears that disabled people are vocal about affirmative action in education and employment.

8 Analysis on Disability and Gender

Since gender and professions play a crucial role in shaping up the ways in which people express themselves on social media, we conducted a preliminary quantitative and content analysis on our corpus to determine the gendered differences in patterns of self-expression of people with disabilities on Twitter. We illustrate three preliminary observations emerging from our analysis:

1. Disabled female users center personal experiences while tweeting about discrimination, advocacy and harassment more frequently than disabled male users.

Figure 4 shows that 15% of the tweets from the male handles were on discrimination, 12% were on advocacy of rights and 10% were *personal* accounts of harassment. In contrast, 22% of the

[4]"Divyang" is a Hindi-word meaning disabled.

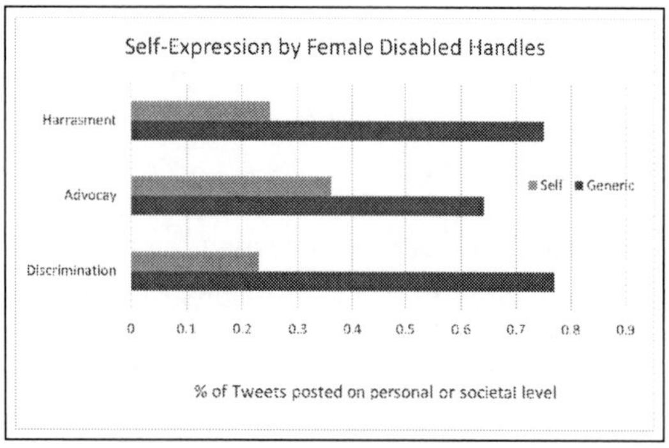

Figure 3: Pattern of Self-Expression by Female Disabled Handles on Indian Twitter.

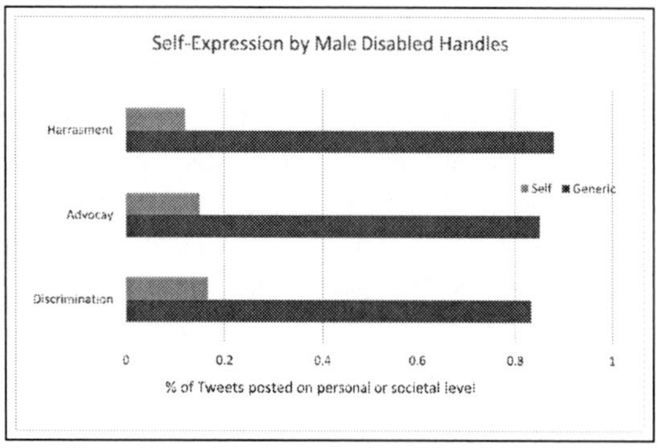

Figure 4: Pattern of Self-Expression by Male Disabled Handles on Indian Twitter.

tweets from the female handles described discrimination related issues, 35% advocated for rights for the disabled and 26% described *personal accounts* of harassment. We perform a statistical significance test using Chi-Square (McHugh, 2013) to determine the gendered differences between the patterns of expressing advocacy, harassment and discrimination. The p-values obtained were 0.019, 0.599 and 0.011 for advocacy, harassment and discrimination patterns, respectively. Except harassment, the other values were statistically significant.

The content analysis revealed that male users are more likely to comment on broader, structural issues underlying discrimination, such as exclusionary government policies. Female users, on the other hand, publish a larger number of tweets centering personal experiences of exclusion and disability-related discrimination. Disability studies work often cites that disability – associated with being 'dependent and helpless' – is in conflict with masculinity, which is associated with being powerful and autonomous (Shuttleworth et al., 2012). Within India's deeply patriarchal society in which

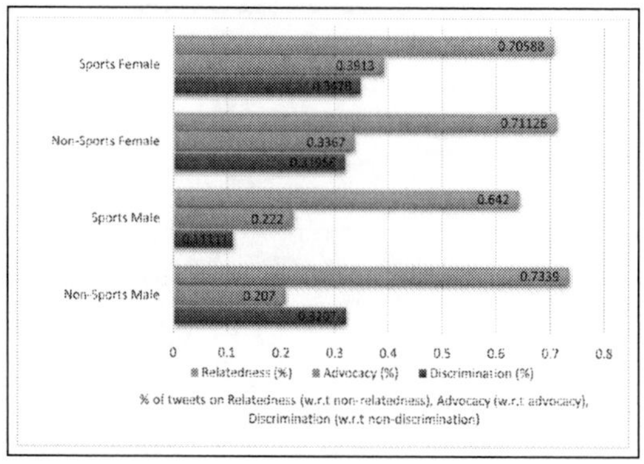

Figure 5: Pattern of Self-Expression by disabled women and men in Sports and Non-Sports on Twitter.

ableist norms stigmatize male expression of need, this 'masculinity dilemma' may disincentivize male users from sharing personal experiences on public profiles. Given a disproportionate burden of discrimination, disabled women may have simply have a larger bank of discrimination-related personal experiences to draw upon. Further, within economies of visibility, highly visible women are more likely to perform the labour of authenticity (Duffy, 2015; Toffoletti and Thorpe, 2018; Banet-Weiser, 2021). Since there is a link between personal vulnerability and online harassment (Duffy and Hund, 2019), this opens up an avenue for further research on experiences of disabled women in India with online harassment.

2. Female paralympians publish positive tweets on inclusion more frequently than disabled women in other professions as well as men in all professions.

Figure 5 shows the quantitative distribution pattern which indicates that disabled sportswomen play a much larger role in tweeting about inclusion (39% of the tweets) compared to disabled women in other professions (33% of the tweets). The difference in advocacy patterns between males with disabilities in sports (22%) and those in other professions (21%) is marginal.

Our content analysis shows that while Paralympians tweet about inclusion, they often use positive tonality, praising the government for new policies, schemes, and initiatives. They also receive significant media engagement from political influencers and government bodies (French and Le Clair, 2018; Mitchell et al., 2021;

Pate et al., 2014; Toffoletti, 2018). Previous work shows that Indian sportspeople tend to use Twitter to support the government (Mishra et al., 2021) – a phenomenon rooted in the State's attempts to garner political support from influential figures. This celebration of disabled people in sports is part of the creation of a national identity centered around empowerment and unity. However, the disabled body is positioned as a form of 'apolitical diversity' – a condition produced by the conflation of nationalism and neoliberalism (Friedner, 2017). In such cases, Paralympians may come to be constructed as inspirational *'feel-good'* figures who are disincentivized from appearing to be critical online. This finding also points to the fact that online performances of positivity themselves may be gendered among influential disabled users. We note that a marginal percentage of Paralympians in our set acted against this norm, tweeting about non-reception of promised rewards, such as jobs and monetary payouts for achievements in Paralympic sports. This is a valuable insight showing that disability-related discrimination in India is the norm for even the most influential figures.

3. Disabled women are less vocal about facing harassment than disabled men.

From the distribution of tweets generated by disabled men, we found that 18% of male users raised their voices about harassment either on a broad *societal or personal level*, whereas the percentage of disabled women doing the same was only 6%.

There is overwhelming evidence that disabled Indian women face disproportionately more harassment in contrast to disabled Indian men. That online self-expression is not reflective of this points not only to the perceived stigma of mentioning harassment on Twitter, but that for women, many such discussions may occur in private online communities rather than the public sphere of participatory social media. Previous work has also shown that Indian women often limit self-expressions on topics intersecting with patriarchy (Karmakar, 2021).

9 Conclusion

This paper introduced a novel human-annotated corpus "**#DisabledOnIndianTwitter**" comprising of tweets posted by disabled people in India from a diverse set of professions. We manually tagged the corpus to categorize different patterns of self-expression based on a hierarchical annotation taxonomy. Using our corpus, we next conducted quantitative and content analysis to identify gendered differences in expressions of disabled people on Indian Twitter. We believe that the annotation schema as well as the dataset can be valuable in understanding social media use by disabled people. We aim to make our dataset publicly available to foster research at the nexus of NLP and Accessibility.

10 Ethics Statement

The use of Twitter data for research purposes is subject to the Developer Policy and Agreement. In accordance, aggregate analysis of Twitter content, including that related to sensitive topics such as health, that does not store any personal data, is permitted (Twitter). We followed these guidelines and stripped our data of user IDs, usernames, and other identifiers in order to protect the anonymity of users. Our set only includes tweets published in the *public* domain, by users who disclosed their disabled identity in their Twitter bio, profile picture, username, display name, or within the content of their tweets. In this way, we attempt to avoid making assumptions about the status of users' disabilities.

References

Marzieh Babaeianjelodar, Stephen Lorenz, Josh Gordon, Jeanna Matthews, and Evan Freitag. 2020. *Quantifying Gender Bias in Different Corpora*, page 752–759. Association for Computing Machinery, New York, NY, USA.

Sarah Banet-Weiser. 2021. Gender, social media, and the labor of authenticity. *American Quarterly*, 73(1):141–144.

Solon Barocas, Moritz Hardt, and Arvind Narayanan. 2018. Fairness and machine learning limitations and opportunities.

Jacob Benesty, Jingdong Chen, Yiteng Huang, and Israel Cohen. 2009. Pearson correlation coefficient. In *Noise reduction in speech processing*, pages 1–4. Springer.

Tolga Bolukbasi, Kai-Wei Chang, James Zou, Venkatesh Saligrama, and Adam Tauman Kalai. 2016. Man is to computer programmer as woman is to homemaker? debiasing word embeddings. In *NIPS*.

Alexis Buettgen, Rachel Gorman, Marcia Rioux, Kuhu Das, and Soumya Vinayan. 2015. Employment, poverty, disability and gender: A rights approach for women with disabilities in india, nepal and bangladesh.

Census. 2011. *Measurement of Disability through Census National Experiences.*

Alison Croft. 2013. Promoting access to education for disabled children in low-income countries: Do we need to know how many disabled children there are? *International Journal of Educational Development*, 33(3):233–243. Educating the poorest.

Ranjita Dawn. 2014. "our lives, our identity": women with disabilities in india. *Disability and rehabilitation*, 36(21):1768–1773.

Jacob Devlin, Ming-Wei Chang, Kenton Lee, and Kristina Toutanova. 2018. Bert: Pre-training of deep bidirectional transformers for language understanding. *arXiv preprint arXiv:1810.04805*.

Bishnu Maya Dhungana. 2006. The lives of disabled women in nepal: vulnerability without support. *Disability & Society*, 21(2):133–146.

Emily Dinan, Angela Fan, Adina Williams, Jack Urbanek, Douwe Kiela, and Jason Weston. 2019. Queens are powerful too: Mitigating gender bias in dialogue generation. *CoRR*, abs/1911.03842.

Lucas Dixon, John Li, Jeffrey Sorensen, Nithum Thain, and Lucy Vasserman. 2018. Measuring and mitigating unintended bias in text classification. In *Proceedings of the 2018 AAAI/ACM Conference on AI, Ethics, and Society*, AIES '18, page 67–73, New York, NY, USA. Association for Computing Machinery.

Brooke Erin Duffy. 2015. Gendering the labor of social media production. *Feminist Media Studies*, 15(4):710–714.

Brooke Erin Duffy and Emily Hund. 2019. Gendered visibility on social media: Navigating instagram's authenticity bind. *International Journal of Communication*, 13:20.

Lata Dyaram and Suresh V. 2020. Workplace disability inclusion in india: review and directions.

Katie Ellis and Gerard Goggin. 2013. Disability and social media. In *The social media handbook*, pages 134–151. Routledge.

Liam French and Jill M Le Clair. 2018. Game changer? social media, representations of disability and the paralympic games. In *The Palgrave handbook of paralympic studies*, pages 99–121. Springer.

Michele Friedner. 2017. How the disabled body unites the national body: disability as 'feel good'diversity in urban india. *Contemporary South Asia*, 25(4):347–363.

Sahaj Garg, Vincent Perot, Nicole Limtiaco, Ankur Taly, Ed H. Chi, and Alex Beutel. 2019. Counterfactual fairness in text classification through robustness. In *Proceedings of the 2019 AAAI/ACM Conference on AI, Ethics, and Society*, AIES '19, page 219–226, New York, NY, USA. Association for Computing Machinery.

Nora E Groce, Gayatri Kembhavi, Shelia Wirz, Raymond Lang, Jean-François Trani, and Maria Kett. 2011. Poverty and disability – a critical review of the literature in low and middle-income countries. *WGSRN: Other Gender & Development (Sub-Topic).*

Saad Hassan, Matt Huenerfauth, and Cecilia Ovesdotter Alm. 2021. Unpacking the interdependent systems of discrimination: Ableist bias in NLP systems through an intersectional lens. In *Findings of the Association for Computational Linguistics: EMNLP 2021*, pages 3116–3123, Punta Cana, Dominican Republic. Association for Computational Linguistics.

Bronwyn Hemsley, Stephen Dann, Stuart Palmer, Meredith Allan, and Susan Balandin. 2015. "we definitely need an audience": experiences of twitter, twitter networks and tweet content in adults with severe communication disabilities who use augmentative and alternative communication (aac). *Disability and rehabilitation*, 37(17):1531–1542.

Ben Hutchinson, Vinodkumar Prabhakaran, Emily Denton, Kellie Webster, Yu Zhong, and Stephen Denuyl. 2020. Social biases in NLP models as barriers for persons with disabilities. In *Proceedings of the 58th Annual Meeting of the Association for Computational Linguistics*, pages 5491–5501, Online. Association for Computational Linguistics.

Jens Ineland, Stefan Gelfgren, and Coppélie Cocq. 2019. Negotiating authority: Disability, interactions and power relations on twitter. *Scandinavian Journal of Disability Research*, 21(1):238–249.

Syed Salma Jameel. 2011. Disability in the context of higher education: Issues and concerns in india. *Electronic Journal for Inclusive Education*, 2:3.

Sophie Jentzsch, Patrick Schramowski, Constantin Rothkopf, and Kristian Kersting. 2019. Semantics derived automatically from language corpora contain human-like moral choices. In *Proceedings of the 2019 AAAI/ACM Conference on AI, Ethics, and Society*, AIES '19, page 37–44, New York, NY, USA. Association for Computing Machinery.

Mali Jin, Daniel Preotiuc-Pietro, A. Seza Doğruöz, and Nikolaos Aletras. 2022. Automatic identification and classification of bragging in social media. In *Proceedings of the 60th Annual Meeting of the Association for Computational Linguistics (Volume 1: Long Papers)*, pages 3945–3959, Dublin, Ireland. Association for Computational Linguistics.

Aasha Kapur Mehta and Amita Shah. 2003. Chronic poverty in india: Incidence, causes and policies. *World Development*, 31(3):491–511. Chronic Poverty and Development Policy.

Priyanka Karmakar. 2021. Missing daughters: Social perceptions and treatment of the girl child in india.

Arun Kumar, Deepa Sonpal, and Vanmala Sunder Hiranandani. 2012. Trapped between ableism and neoliberalism: Critical reflections on disability and employment in india. *Disability Studies Quarterly*, 32.

S. G. Leveille, H. E. Resnick, and J. Balfour. 2000. Gender differences in disability: Evidence and underlying reasons. *Aging Clinical and Experimental Research*, 12(2):106–112.

Shahar Levy, Koren Lazar, and Gabriel Stanovsky. 2021. Collecting a large-scale gender bias dataset for coreference resolution and machine translation. In *Findings of the Association for Computational Linguistics: EMNLP 2021*, pages 2470–2480, Punta Cana, Dominican Republic. Association for Computational Linguistics.

Yinhan Liu, Myle Ott, Naman Goyal, Jingfei Du, Mandar Joshi, Danqi Chen, Omer Levy, Mike Lewis, Luke Zettlemoyer, and Veselin Stoyanov. 2019. Roberta: A robustly optimized bert pretraining approach. *arXiv preprint arXiv:1907.11692*.

Kelly Mack, Emma McDonnell, Dhruv Jain, Lucy Lu Wang, Jon E. Froehlich, and Leah Findlater. 2021. What do we mean by "accessibility research"? a literature survey of accessibility papers in chi and assets from 1994 to 2019. In *Proceedings of the 2021 CHI Conference on Human Factors in Computing Systems*, CHI '21, New York, NY, USA. Association for Computing Machinery.

Islay Mactaggart, Hannah Kuper, G. V. S. Murthy, Jayanthi Sagar, Joseph Oye, and Sarah Polack. 2016. Assessing health and rehabilitation needs of people with disabilities in cameroon and india. *Disability and Rehabilitation*, 38(18):1757–1764. PMID: 26680511.

Benjamin W Mann. 2018. Rhetoric of online disability activism:# cripthevote and civic participation. *Communication Culture & Critique*, 11(4):604–621.

Mary L McHugh. 2013. The chi-square test of independence. *Biochemia medica*, 23(2):143–149.

Nilika Mehrotra. 2021. Emergent Disability voices on Social Media during COVID -19 times.

George A. Miller. 1995. Wordnet: A lexical database for english. *Commun. ACM*, 38(11):39–41.

Dibyendu Mishra, Ronojoy Sen, and Joyojeet Pal. 2021. Sporting the government: Twitter as a window into sportspersons' engagement with causes in india and usa. *arXiv preprint arXiv:2109.07409*.

Fallon R Mitchell, Paula M van Wyk, and Sara Santarossa. 2021. Curating a culture: The portrayal of disability stereotypes by paralympians on instagram. *International Journal of Sport Communication*, 14(3):334–355.

Daniel Mont, Natasha Layton, Louise Puli, Shivani Gupta, Abner Manlapaz, Kylie Shae, Emma Tebbutt, Irene Calvo, Mahpekay Sidiqy, Kudakwashe Dube, and Ulamila Kacilala. 2021. Assistive Technology during the COVID-19 Global Pandemic: The Roles of Government and Civil Society in Fulfilling the Social Contract. *International Journal of Environmental Research and Public Health*, 18(22):12031.

Dat Quoc Nguyen, Thanh Vu, and Anh Tuan Nguyen. 2020. Bertweet: A pre-trained language model for english tweets. *arXiv preprint arXiv:2005.10200*.

Itto Outini. 2020. The Impact of Social Media on the Social Lives of People with Visual Impairment (Facebook Groups as a Case Study). *Graduate Theses and Dissertations*.

Joyojeet Pal, Ana Maria Huaita Alfaro, Tawfiq W. Ammari, Sidharth Chhabra, and Meera Lakshmanan. 2017. Representation, Access and Contestation: Facebook and Vision Impairment in Jordan, India, and Peru. Accepted: 2017-02-15T11:54:26Z Publisher: The Critical Institute.

Joshua R Pate, Robin Hardin, and Brody Ruihley. 2014. Speak for yourself: analysing how us athletes used self-presentation on twitter during the 2012 london paralympic games. *International Journal of Sport Management and Marketing*, 15(3-4):141–162.

Mónica Pinilla-Roncancio, Islay Mactaggart, Hannah Kuper, Carlos Dionicio, Jonathan Naber, G.V.S. Murthy, and Sarah Polack. 2020. Multidimensional poverty and disability: A case control study in india, cameroon, and guatemala. *SSM - Population Health*, 11:100591.

Shanya Sharma, Manan Dey, and Koustuv Sinha. 2021. Evaluating gender bias in natural language inference. *CoRR*, abs/2105.05541.

Russell Shuttleworth, Nikki Wedgwood, and Nathan J Wilson. 2012. The dilemma of disabled masculinity. *Men and masculinities*, 15(2):174–194.

Maya Thomas and Maliakal Joseph Thomas. 2002. Status of women with disabilities in south asia. *Selected readings in community-based rehabilitation, series*, 2.

Kim Toffoletti. 2018. Sport, postfeminism and women with disabilities: Female paralympians on social media. In *New Sporting Femininities*, pages 253–275. Springer.

Kim Toffoletti and Holly Thorpe. 2018. Female athletes' self-representation on social media: A feminist analysis of neoliberal marketing strategies in "economies of visibility". *Feminism & Psychology*, 28(1):11–31.

Twitter. More on restricted use cases – twitter developers.

Cynthia Van Hee, Els Lefever, and Véronique Hoste. 2018. SemEval-2018 task 3: Irony detection in English tweets. In *Proceedings of The 12th International Workshop on Semantic Evaluation*, pages 39–50, New Orleans, Louisiana. Association for Computational Linguistics.

Aditya Vashistha, Edward Cutrell, Nicola Dell, and Richard Anderson. 2015. Social Media Platforms for Low-Income Blind People in India. In *Proceedings of the 17th International ACM SIGACCESS Conference on Computers & Accessibility*, ASSETS '15, pages 259–272, New York, NY, USA. Association for Computing Machinery.

Ashish Vaswani, Noam Shazeer, Niki Parmar, Jakob Uszkoreit, Llion Jones, Aidan N Gomez, Łukasz Kaiser, and Illia Polosukhin. 2017. Attention is all you need. *Advances in neural information processing systems*, 30.

Zeerak Waseem and Dirk Hovy. 2016. Hateful symbols or hateful people? predictive features for hate speech detection on Twitter. In *Proceedings of the NAACL Student Research Workshop*, pages 88–93, San Diego, California. Association for Computational Linguistics.

Jieyu Zhao, Subhabrata Mukherjee, Saghar Hosseini, Kai-Wei Chang, and Ahmed Hassan Awadallah. 2020. Gender bias in multilingual embeddings and cross-lingual transfer. *CoRR*, abs/2005.00699.

11 Appendix

12 Disability Related Keywords

"deaf", "mute", "blind", "one legged","disabled", "disability", "handicap", "crippled", "low vision", "visually impaired", "Hearing impairment", "Locomotor disability", "Attention Deficit Hyperactivity Disorder", "ADHD", "Muscular Dystrophy", "Hard of Hearing", "Parkinson's Disease", "dwarf", "short stature", "accessibility", "braille", "sign language", "autism", "dyslexia", "dysgraphia", "dyscalculia", "dyspraxia", "aphasia", "dysphagia", "multiple sclerosis", "cerebral palsy", "genetic disorders", "arthritis", "heart failure", "insanity", "mental illnesses", "depression", "bipolar disorder", "paralysis", "wheelchair", "hearing aid", "epilepsy", "chronically ill", "down's syndrome", "retard", "Asperger Syndrome", "Alzheimer's" .

Gender	#Followers	#Tweets	Mention of Disability/Profession in Bio
Female	34.4k	6308	Para badminton player
Female	81k	977	Bomb Blast Survivor
Female	19k	1699	Amputee climb Mt Everest
Female	61.6k	6445	Paralympian
Female	1055	14400	Crip, queer artist, consultant
Female	270	1780	Author I Blogger
Female	7363	576	Deaf chess champion
Female	267	934	Gay, resentful
Female	309	996	Lifestyle blogger
Female	23.1k	28700	Autistic actor
Female	128	765	Law Student
Female	70	972	Mrs India 2021
Female	1055	14400	Crip, queer artist, consultant
Female	270	1780	Author I Blogger
Female	890	56500	Lawyer, Comedian
Female	407	853	Traveller
Female	71	42	Disability Inclusion Facilitator
Female	11.3k	1400	Managing Director,@Jindal$_{S}AW$
Female	521	3897	activist, comedian, writer
Female	388	61	Paralympian
Female	49k	235	Paralympian
Female	62	94	Indian Para Athlete
Female	1245	762	researcher, artist, and author
Female	629	390	Chief Content Officer
Female	403	136	Deaf Woman pursuing Law
Female	193	67	International Tennis Player
Female	865	1828	Aspiring Biologist
Male	1062	4253	Writer. Poet. Disabled.
Male	7437	25900	Disability Rights Defender
Male	5992	6445	Indian Para Swimmer
Male	151	724	an atheist, fan of test cricket
Male	2604	3364	Lawyer, Rhodes Scholar
Male	387	545	Para Archer
Male	28.5k	600	Javelin Thrower Paralympic
Male	96	507	Professor, Research Scholar
Male	80	51	deaf, Indian sign language
Male	51	71	Deaf Postal Assistant
Male	110	63	Deaf
Male	150	254	lawyer
Male	524	2357	L-Vision,(Blind) student
Male	750	10400	Deaf journalist
Male	197	530	visually impaired athlete

Table 5: Details of the Disabled Twitter Handles of India considered for our study.

Topic-aware Multimodal Summarization

Sourajit Mukherjee[1] Anubhav Jangra[1] Sriparna Saha[1] Adam Jatowt[2]
[1]Indian Institute of Technology Patna, India
{mailsourajit25, anubhav0603, sriparnasaha}@gmail.com
[2]University of Innsbruck, Austria
adam.jatowt@uibk.ac.at

Abstract

Multimodal Summarization (MS) has attracted research interest in the past few years due to the ease with which users perceive multimodal summaries. It is important for MS models to consider the topic a given target content belongs to. In the current paper, we propose a topic-aware MS system which performs two tasks simultaneously: differentiating the images into "on-topic" and "off-topic" categories and further utilizing the "on-topic" images to generate multimodal summaries. The hypothesis is that, the proposed topic similarity classifier will help in generating better multimodal summary by focusing on important components of images and text which are specific to a particular topic. To develop the topic similarity classifier, we have augmented the existing popular MS data set, MSMO, with similar "on-topic" and dissimilar "off-topic" images for each sample. Our experimental results establish that the focus on "on-topic" features helps in generating topic-aware multimodal summaries, which outperforms the state of the art approach by 1.7% in ROUGE-L metric.

1 Introduction

Due to the continuous growth of multimedia content, users often look for ways to read and go through only the crucial information content, and to avoid redundancy as much as possible. To cater to this need for concise information availability, automatic summarization systems are the need of the hour.

Extensive research works have produced summaries of a single modality like text (Gambhir and Gupta, 2017; Jangra et al., 2020a) or video (Apostolidis et al., 2021). However, researchers have also demonstrated that users are more satisfied with multimodal summaries than uni-modal summaries (Zhu et al., 2018). Thus, generating output summaries of different modalities like text and images makes sense. Images play essential roles in helping users understand the text and make the summary more attractive, contextualized, and complete. Topic information is crucial for correctly identifying pictures and text as a part of a multimodal summary. However, existing work (Jangra et al., 2021a) in the field of multimodal summarization has not yet utilized the sample's topic information to improve the multimodal summary quality.

Figure 1: In this example we select two images to be part of the pictorial summary. Using topic information, i.e., "sport", the model can decide that the images (1) and (2) are highly related to "sport" topic as compared to others, and hence increase their probability of being used in pictorial part of the final summary.

In this paper, we introduce *Topic-aware Multimodal Summarization (TMS)* where multimodal summaries consisting of texts and images are generated by also focusing on topic-centric information. Incorporating topic information of the source content aids the summarization process because the generated multimodal summary also considers the key elements of that topic. For example the

Findings of the Association for Computational Linguistics: AACL-IJCNLP 2022, pages 387–398
November 20–23, 2022. ©2022 Association for Computational Linguistics

summary of an article in the "sport" topic should highlight how a player scored a goal in a football match as a part of the text summary, and the images of the player as a part of the image summary (as shown in Fig. 1). In contrast, the multimodal summary of any article belonging to the "travel" topic should highlight details of the place mentioned, and the image summary should showcase the images of that place. Thus different topics may require different kinds of focus.

In our experiments we have investigated the following research objectives: i) the significance of the topic similarity classifier with respect to the combination of different modalities, ii) the impact of using similar "on-topic" image feature vectors instead of zero-padded vectors for samples having limited number of in-article images and iii) the comparison with respect to the existing state-of-the-art technique.

The key contributions of our work are as follows:

1. To the best of our knowledge, this is the first study where topic information is integrated with multimodal summary generation to improve the performance.

2. The existing MSMO data set is augmented with "on-topic" and "off-topic" images to perform an auxiliary task of topic similarity identification from images.[1]

3. A multi-task learning approach is proposed which solves simultaneously the two tasks:

    - classification of in-article images into "on-topic" and "off-topic" categories
    - generation of multimodal summary.

    The first task is our auxiliary task to extract more useful features from image and text modalities which in turn can help in generating better multimodal summaries.

2 Related Works

Multimodal Summarization has gained in popularity in the recent years due to the enhanced quality and user experience it is able to offer. Jangra et al. (2021a) provided an overview of the recent developments in the field of Multimodal Summarization. The summarization process can produce a single modality output (Chen and Zhuge, 2018; Palaskar et al., 2019; Li et al., 2018; Khullar and Arora, 2020) or a multi-modal output (Zhu et al., 2018; Jangra et al., 2020b,c, 2021b). In our work we focus on the latter case, and we have considered the MSMO model (Zhu et al., 2018) as the baseline which produces multi-modal output summary in the form of text and images. One of the recent works inspired by the MSMO model is (Zhu et al., 2020); however, unlike our model, it does not focus on producing topic-aware summaries. Zhu et al. (2020) also used an extended version of the MSMO dataset for training its image selection module in a supervised fashion. In contrast, we have used an unsupervised approach similar to MSMO for training our model's image selection module. Training our model using the extended dataset used by Zhu et al. (2020) might produce better results in the future.

Recently, Transformer-based models like MTMS (Ye et al., 2021) and CtnR (Zhang et al., 2021) were developed based on the MSMO dataset. However, these models either produce text-only summaries using multimodal input or use different input parameter sizes (max. encoder length, decoder length, max. number of images, etc.) for training the model. Thus because of these factors, we have not considered these Transformer-based models as a baseline for comparison. Furthermore, MTMS also uses 80% of the test data for fine-tuning its model with the image-saliency-based loss. Our model does not require using any segment of the test data for training purposes.

Multi-task learning (MTL) involves sharing representations between related tasks which helps in achieving better performance in the target task. Earlier MTL has been used for producing both textual (Nishino et al., 2019; Isonuma et al., 2017) and multimodal summaries (Zhao et al., 2016). Taking inspirations from these works we have used MTL for making our summarization model topic-aware.

Producing multimodal summaries, which relate well with the topic they belong to, helps users get a better understanding of the actual content. Earlier, research has been done in developing systems that produce multimodal summaries related to a specific topics like sports (Tjondronegoro et al., 2011; Sanabria et al., 2019), movies (Evangelopoulos et al., 2013) or E-commerce (Li et al., 2020) but those works have used datasets which are specific

[1] The extended dataset and our model's code is available at github.com/mailsourajit25/Topic-Aware-Multimodal-Summarization

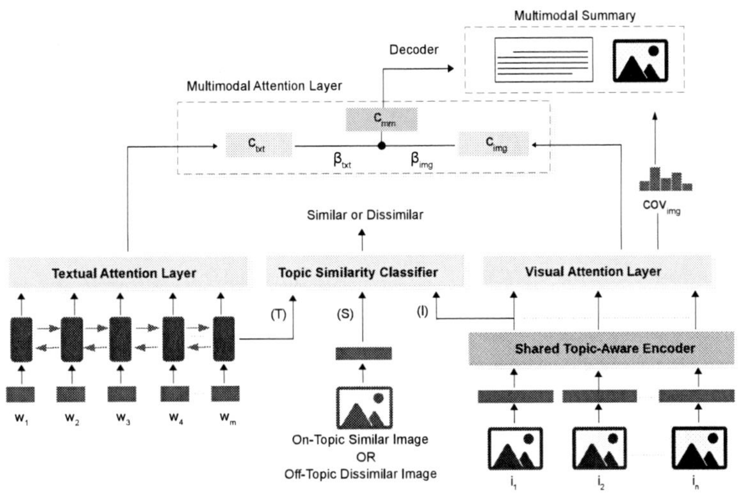

Figure 2: Proposed Architecture. The label (T) is the text encoder's last time-step output, (I) is the projected in-article image feature vector and (S) is the corresponding similar/dissimilar image feature vector, to be passed as input into the topic similarity classifier.

to a single particular topic. We are the first to introduce a model that not only can produce topic-aware multimodal summaries, but is also trained using a topic-generic dataset.

3 Our Model

3.1 Problem Definition

TMS task is defined as follows: Given a multimodal input $\{T, I\} \in D$, where T is a text article having W words, I is the set of in-article images and D is the topic of the article, the task is to create a multimodal topic-aware summary $\{T', I'\}$ highly related to the topic D and reflecting the content of $\{T, I\}$. The textual summary T' is composed of W' words such that $|W'| < |W|$. The pictorial summary I' such that $|I'| \leq |I|$ represents the set of recommended images extracted from I.

3.2 Model Architecture

Our model is a multi-task learning model that is trained to perform summarization as well as topic similarity identification. It is composed of a Bi-directional LSTM based text encoder for encoding the textual part of the input and a unidirectional LSTM based summary decoder. The image part of the input is encoded using a VGG19-based (Simonyan and Zisserman, 2015) image encoder which has been pretrained on ImageNet dataset (Deng et al., 2009). Zhu et al. (2018) passed the encoded images through a projection layer to project them into same dimension as text. We have re-defined the image projection layer as the **shared topic-aware encoder** because it is now shared between the classifier and the MSMO model. Previous researches (Zhu et al., 2020; Li et al., 2018) have shown that global features are more effective compared to local features. Hence in this paper, we have extracted the $4,096$ dimensional global features of the pre-softmax fully-connected layer denoted by g. These vectors are projected into the same dimension of textual context vector, using the following equation: $g^* = W_I^2(W_I^1 g + b_I^1) + b_I^2$, where W_I^1, b_I^1, W_I^2 and b_I^2 are trainable parameters. The output of the shared topic-aware encoder is branched off into two directions as shown in Fig. 2. One part is passed into the topic similarity classifier (discussed in Sec. 3.3) for topic similarity identification and the other one to the visual attention layer for the summarization task.

Next, the textual context vector c_{txt}^t is computed from the textual attention layer (Bahdanau et al., 2016; Luong et al., 2015), and c_{img}^t from visual attention layer (Li et al., 2018). These context vectors are then passed to the multimodal attention layer (Zhu et al., 2018) which combines the visual and textual attentions together to produce the multimodal context vector, c_{mm}^t, given as the weighted sum of c_{txt}^t and c_{img}^t. During decoding, the summary decoder takes as input the previously predicted word and c_{mm}^t to predict the next word. Further, in order to prevent repeated attention, we compute textual and visual coverage vectors, cov_{txt}^t and cov_{img}^t, as the sum of the respective attention weights over the previous decoding steps.

Our summary decoder is based on Pointer Generator Network (PGN) (See et al., 2017). It can decide whether to generate words from a fixed vocabulary or rather to copy words from the source while constructing the summary for a given input text. Finally, the loss at a time step t is given as the summation of the negative log likelihood of the target word, w_t, and the textual coverage loss $L_{txt}^{cov} = \sum_i min(\alpha_i^t, cov_i^t)$ and the visual coverage loss $L_{img}^{cov} = \sum_j min(\alpha_j^t, cov_{img,j}^t)$, where α_i^t and α_j^t are textual and visual attention weights, respectively.

$$L_t = -\log p_{w_t} + L_{txt}^{cov} + L_{img}^{cov} \quad (1)$$

Image Decoding: The visual coverage scores cov_{img}^t for every image at the last decoding timestep, are used to select the most relevant images representing the pictorial summary of the source. A higher coverage score indicates greater relevance.

3.3 Topic Similarity Classifier (TSC)

The topic similarity classifier helps the model to also consider the topic information while calculating attention for both image and text. The target output for the classifier is labelled as (topic) "similar" when similar "on-topic" images are passed as input while it is labelled as (topic) "dissimilar" when "off-topic" images are passed as input into the classifier (as shown in Fig. 2). The other inputs to the classifier are the text encoder's last time step output and the in-article image features. The topic similarity classifier is used only during training the model. During testing, the trained weights of the shared topic-aware encoder and the text encoder help the model in extracting topic-centric information. Thus, the classifier performs an auxiliary task of topic similarity classification during training that should aid the shared topic-aware encoder and the text encoder to learn and extract topic-related information during the encoding process. This would have impact on the visual and textual attention layers as now the model will provide more attention on images and text which are more related to the topic that the article belongs to. The classifier is defined as follows:

$$O_{TSC}^{sim} = \sigma(W_{txt}h_{txt} + W_s h_{img}^{sim} + W_{img}h_{img}) \quad (2)$$

$$O_{TSC}^{dissim} = \sigma(W_{txt}h_{txt} + W_s h_{img}^{dissim} + W_{img}h_{img}) \quad (3)$$

where W_{txt}, W_s and W_{img} are trainable parameters having dimensions $\mathbb{R}^{1\times d_{enc}}$, $\mathbb{R}^{1\times 4096}$ and $\mathbb{R}^{1\times d_{enc}}$. Here d_{enc} denotes the dimension of the Bi-LSTM based text encoder. O_{TSC}^{sim} and O_{TSC}^{dissim} denote the classification outputs of the classifier when we pass as input the VGG19-based feature vectors, h_{img}^{sim}, and h_{img}^{dissim}, of the similar and dissimilar images, respectively. h_{txt} denotes the hidden state output for the last time step of the text encoder. h_{img} represents the projected feature vectors of the in-article images obtained after passing through the shared topic-aware encoder. The classifier loss is defined as follows:

$$L_{TSC} = BCELoss([O_{TSC}^{sim}, O_{TSC}^{dissim}], [y^{sim}, y^{dissim}]) \quad (4)$$

where $BCELoss$ refers to binary cross-entropy loss. y^{sim} and y^{dissim} refer to the true labels for the classifier. Finally, the total loss for our model, with λ_{TSC} as classifier weight is computed as:

$$L = -\log p_{w_t} + L_{txt}^{cov} + L_{img}^{cov} + \lambda_{TSC}L_{TSC} \quad (5)$$

4 Experimental Settings

4.1 Dataset

The MSMO dataset (Zhu et al., 2018) is the only large-scale dataset best-suited for the task defined in Sec. 3.1. It was originally constructed using news articles collected from the *Daily Mail* website . It contains 293,965 samples in the train set, 10,355 samples in the validation and 10,261 samples in the test set. Each sample contains a multi-sentence news article (720 tokens on average), the set of multiple image and caption pairs (6 pairs on average) and the manually-written[2] multi-sentence highlights of each article (70 tokens on average). Furthermore, every multi-sentence article has a title and a body. We have considered the body of every article as the source text. To train our model using the topic similarity classifier, we need a similar "on-topic" image and a dissimilar "off-topic" image for every in-article image of the train set. To cater to this need for training our model, we have augmented the training set of the MSMO dataset.

Proposed Dataset Augmentation: For augmentation, we first determined the "topic" of each sample (or news article) from its URL. The URL path contains the name of the category or the topic to which the article belongs. The URL path also includes the name of the sub-topic of the article. Although the sub-topic is a better representation of an article's

[2]Created by *Daily Mail (http://www.dailymail.co.uk).*

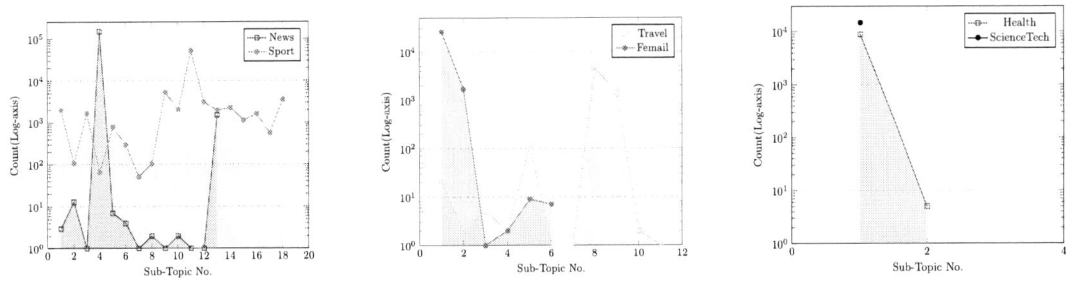

(a) "News" and "Sport" (b) "Femail" and "Travel" (c) "Health" and "ScienceTech"

Figure 3: Sub-Topic Count Distributions for different Topics. For the "sport" topic, sub-topics having count smaller than 50 are not shown in the plot.

category, we found an uneven count distribution of the number of samples belonging to each sub-topic (as shown in Fig. 3). Even the total number of sub-topics for different topics varied from being as high as 87 for the "sport" topic to just 1 for the "ScienceTech" topic. The irregular sub-topic count and uneven count distribution would pose a difficulty in finding similar images for every sample. Hence we decided to find topic-wise similar/dissimilar images for every sample instead of doing it sub-topic-wise.

We generated Universal Sentence Encoder (USE) embeddings (Cer et al., 2018) for the title of every article and grouped all samples into their respective topics. For topics having less than 5,000 samples, we grouped them under the "Others" category. To find similar images for a sample belonging to a certain topic, we compared its USE-based title embeddings with the title embeddings of 20,000[3] other randomly chosen samples belonging to the same topic by comparing their cosine similarity scores. The samples with the highest cosine-similarity scores were chosen and at most 10 images from these articles were selected as "On-Topic" - similar images. Table 1 discusses the details of the topic-wise cosine similarity scores in the augmented dataset.

Furthermore, we have also extracted the publication dates of the articles so that, in the future, we could use this augmented dataset to find similar images using temporal similarity. Temporal search can provide an alternate means of finding similar images faster by searching for similar articles within a specific time range before or after the target article's publication date (assuming that similar news articles get published often on consecutive days). Hence articles missing timestamp in-

[3] Limited number of comparisons were done to reduce the search space for generating similar images faster.

Topic	Sample Count (SC)	Mean Sim. Score	Sim. Score Std. Dev.	SC in Test Set
News	150551	0.535	0.073	5105
Sport	79098	0.671	0.098	2605
Femail	26983	0.550	0.083	971
Travel	6261	0.515	0.077	162
ScienceTech	14592	0.552	0.097	408
Health	8815	0.534	0.074	334
Others	6920	0.523	0.117	266

Table 1: Augmented Dataset: Similarity score statistics

formation were not considered, leading to 293,220 samples in the train set. We focused however on the title-based search in our work as it seemed more intuitive concerning our model architecture.

For finding dissimilar images for a sample belonging to a certain topic, we randomly picked 10 images from samples belonging to a different topic. In all the experiments, at most 10 in-article images were considered per sample such that for each in-article image, only one similar and one dissimilar image were taken during the classification task (Sec. 3.3).

4.2 Compared Methods

To evaluate the performance of our model, we have compared its performance with the following baselines:

- MSMO (**ATG, ATL HAN**): Zhu et al. (2018) proposed the ATG, ATL and HAN models, which uses the global, local and hierarchical image features, respectively, for the multi-modal abstractive summarization task.
- GuideRank (**GR**): We have also considered an extractive summarization baseline GuideRank (Li et al., 2016, 2017) which employs LexRank (Erkan and Radev, 2011) along with a guidance mechanism. In this approach, the captions rank the accompanying sentences based on relatedness. After using GR to estab-

lish the ranks of the sentences and captions, we remove sentences that satisfy the minimum length requirement as a text summary by the text's rating. Next, we pick the image whose caption ranks first among the captions to obtain the visual summary.

The previous researches (Zhu et al., 2018; Li et al., 2018) have already established that global image features perform better than local and hierarchical features in the multimodal summarization task. Hence we consider only the ATG model as a baseline for comparing the topic-wise results (Sec. 5.2) and human-evaluation results (Sec. 5.3).

We have performed experiments testing the following models:

- **TSC-MSMO-TIS:** This model consists of inputs (T), (I) and (S) as shown in Fig. 2.
- **TSC-MSMO-IS:** We have fed only (I) and (S) as input into the TSC.
- **TSC-MSMO-TS:** We have used (T) and (S) as input into the TSC.
- **TSC-MSMO-SIMPAD-TIS:** We have kept the inputs to the classifier unchanged, but if any sample has less than 10 images, then instead of padding with zero vector we replaced those with the similar "on-topic" images. All of these architecture changes were done during training the models.

4.3 Hyper-parameters and Evaluation Metrics

For training our $0.5M$ parameter models, we have considered 400 textual tokens and ten images per sample. Our models were trained for $255,000$ iterations (around 13 epochs for a batch size of 16) without considering coverage loss, followed by coverage loss for extra $45,000$ iterations. We have considered a vocabulary size of 50000 tokens. Early stopping was used by observing the running average of the loss on the validation set. For decoding our summaries, we have used a beam-search decoder with a beam length of 4. During decoding, we considered the maximum size of decoded tokens to be 120 and the minimum as 35. Our rest of the hyper-parameters regarding learning rate, word-embedding dimensions and LSTM-hidden unit dimensions are as reported in See et al. (2017). Although we have considered $\lambda_{TSC} = 1$, for all our experiments but to study its impact, we have experimented with different weights for our best-performing model (Sec. 5.1).

Model	R-1	R-2	R-L	IP
ATG (Zhu et al., 2018)	40.63	18.12	37.53	59.28
ATL (Zhu et al., 2018)	40.86	18.27	37.75	62.44
HAN (Zhu et al., 2018)	40.82	18.30	37.70	61.83
GR (Li et al., 2016)	37.13	15.03	30.21	61.70
TSC-MSMO-IS	41.03	18.77	37.90	63.93
TSC-MSMO-TS	41.0	18.70	37.87	63.8
TSC-MSMO-TIS	40.79	18.55	37.65	**64.13**
TSC-MSMO-SIMPAD-TIS	**41.42**	**19.06**	**38.17**	63.81

Table 2: Results on the Test set. We skipped the articles for which no relevant image labels were available resulting into evaluation of $9,851$ articles from the test set.

λ_{TSC}	R-1	R-2	R-L	IP
0	40.63	18.12	37.53	59.28
0.5	40.79	18.57	36.67	**64.45**
1	**41.42**	**19.06**	**38.17**	63.81
1.5	40.95	18.68	37.92	63.99

Table 3: Impact of changing classifier weight (λ_{TSC}) on *TSC-MSMO-SIMPAD-TIS* model's performance.

For evaluation of the textual summaries we have considered ROUGE (Lin, 2004). The official ROUGE script is used to report all of our ROUGE scores. For assessing the images recommended by the model as the pictorial summary we have used Image Precision (IP) defined by Zhu et al. (2018).

5 Quantitative Analysis

5.1 Overall Results

From Table 2, we can see that all the different model variants have outperformed the baselines. The *TSC-MSMO-SIMPAD-TIS* model has performed well in ROUGE-related metrics but did not perform as well as the *TSC-MSMO-TIS* in the IP metric. Using similar image feature vectors instead of zero-padded vectors during training has helped the *SIMPAD* model gain better textual understanding through the multimodal attention layers. However, using zero padded image vectors during testing did not support the model score well in the IP metric. Furthermore, the improved performance of the *TSC-MSMO-IS* in both ROUGE and IP metrics compared to the other non-*SIMPAD* variants supports the conclusion that the classifier works well when only image features are passed for classification.

The *TSC-MSMO-TIS* model also shows a marginal drop in the ROUGE-L score. The reason behind it may be that passing both textual and image features make it difficult for the classifier to decide whether to focus more on improving the "image" encoder or the "textual" encoder since the target labels (similar/dissimilar) of the classifier depend on the augmented "images". The improved performances of the non-*TIS*-based models also suggest the benefit of experimenting with the *SIMPAD* versions of those models in the future.

To verify the effectiveness of *TSC*, we have experimented by adjusting its weight λ_{TSC}, as shown in Table 3. Although for $\lambda_{TSC} = 0.5$, we get a higher IP value, but a reduced weight on the classifier decreases the ROUGE score. Hence $\lambda_{TSC} = 1$ is a better choice giving good values for both IP and ROUGE metrics.

	Femail			
Model	R-1	R-2	R-L	IP
ATG (Zhu et al., 2018)	**37.52**	**15.49**	**33.92**	46.09
TSC-MSMO-IS	36.74	14.81	33.16	46.26
TSC-MSMO-TS	36.99	15.06	33.55	**46.45**
TSC-MSMO-TIS	36.69	14.84	33.16	46.05
TSC-MSMO-SIMPAD-TIS	37.50	15.37	33.85	46.01

Table 4: Topic-wise results on the test set for the "Femail" topic.

	Others			
Model	R-1	R-2	R-L	IP
ATG (Zhu et al., 2018)	**34.13**	**13.92**	**31.02**	54.52
TSC-MSMO-IS	32.74	12.53	29.68	53.71
TSC-MSMO-TS	32.49	12.22	29.27	53.73
TSC-MSMO-TIS	31.89	11.81	29.05	**55.02**
TSC-MSMO-SIMPAD-TIS	32.80	12.54	29.50	54.15

Table 5: Topic-wise results on the test set for the "Others" topic.

	Health			
Model	R-1	R-2	R-L	IP
ATG (Zhu et al., 2018)	**42.04**	**19.89**	**39.15**	82.82
TSC-MSMO-IS	40.66	18.78	37.68	83.18
TSC-MSMO-TS	41.50	19.31	38.49	**83.89**
TSC-MSMO-TIS	41.36	19.24	38.33	82.49
TSC-MSMO-SIMPAD-TIS	41.69	19.25	38.55	83.28

Table 6: Topic-wise results on the test set for the "Health" topic.

5.2 Topic-wise Results

As a part of the experimental analysis, we have also computed results for different topics by different models. Except for "Femail"[4] (Table 4), "Health" (Table 6) and "Others" (Table 5) topics, the majority of the variants of the proposed model outperform the *MSMO-ATG* model in topic-wise results. A possible reason behind the poor performance of our model is that the topics "Femail" and "Health" consist of a high count of samples (the high spikes shown in Fig. 3b and 3c) belonging to a "Others" sub-topic. The "Others" sub-topic indicates a collection of multiple sub-topics within a topic. Furthermore, the "Others" topic being composed of numerous topics, implicitly contains various subtopics. Multiple sub-topics make it difficult for our title-based similarity search to find good quality similar images for the classifier hence leading to poor performance.

[4]A topic in DailyMail that covers news related to fashion, shopping, etc.

	News			
Model	R-1	R-2	R-L	IP
ATG (Zhu et al., 2018)	44.55	21.61	41.20	63.1
TSC-MSMO-IS	44.42	21.63	41.15	63.75
TSC-MSMO-TS	44.51	21.64	41.21	63.8
TSC-MSMO-TIS	44.25	21.44	40.93	**64.15**
TSC-MSMO-SIMPAD-TIS	**44.78**	**21.91**	**41.39**	63.89

Table 7: Topic-wise results on the test set for the "News" topic.

	Sport			
Model	R-1	R-2	R-L	IP
ATG (Zhu et al., 2018)	37.11	15.16	34.30	68.52
TSC-MSMO-IS	37.10	15.21	34.35	**68.57**
TSC-MSMO-TS	36.7	14.85	33.96	68.11
TSC-MSMO-TIS	36.49	14.75	33.76	68.51
TSC-MSMO-SIMPAD-TIS	**37.43**	**15.44**	**34.54**	68.05

Table 8: Topic-wise results on the test set for the "Sport" topic.

Major improvements are seen for "News" (Table 7), "Sports" (Table 8), "Travel" (Table 9), and "ScienceTech" (Table 10) topics. Even though the highest spike in the sub-topic sample count plot for the "news" topic (Fig. 3a) corresponds to the "Others" sub-topic, our model still performed well. The reason is that the high sample count within the "news" topic (as shown in Table 1) helped our title-based similarity find good-quality images for the classification task. Moreover, it is also observed that the models *TSC-MSMO-TS* and *TSC-MSMO-SIMPAD-TIS* have performed poorly only for the "Travel" topic as compared to other topics due to smaller training data available for the travel topic as it could be seen from Table 1. Thus data abundance in a particular topic plays an important role in improving the performance of our model.

5.3 Human Evaluation

We describe in this section the results of human evaluation of our proposed approach. For this, we employed three graduate student annotators to evaluate the multi-modal summaries produced by our best-performing model. We chose 100 random articles from the test set for the evaluation task. We then asked the annotators to judge the multi-modal

Model	Travel			
	R-1	R-2	R-L	IP
ATG (Zhu et al., 2018)	35.71	15.97	32.69	51.76
TSC-MSMO-IS	35.73	15.54	32.71	53.44
TSC-MSMO-TS	35.12	15.26	32.53	50.58
TSC-MSMO-TIS	**36.53**	**16.35**	**33.62**	**55.66**
TSC-MSMO-SIMPAD-TIS	36	16.37	33.17	52.27

Table 9: Topic-wise results on the test set for the "Travel" topic.

Model	ScienceTech			
	R-1	R-2	R-L	IP
ATG (Zhu et al., 2018)	41.29	20.23	38.41	72.94
TSC-MSMO-IS	41.65	**20.61**	**38.77**	73.53
TSC-MSMO-TS	41.42	20.15	38.48	72.8
TSC-MSMO-TIS	**41.73**	20.39	38.70	**73.92**
TSC-MSMO-SIMPAD-TIS	41.67	20.52	38.69	73.07

Table 10: Topic-wise results on the test set for the "ScienceTech" topic.

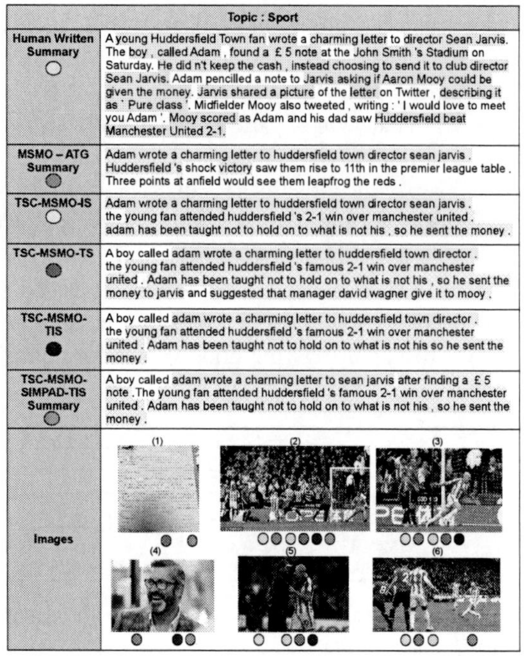

Figure 4: Topic: "Sport" Example Summaries comparison with Baseline. The circular colour codes corresponding to each category is used to represent the image selected as pictorial summary. The Green textual highlights refer to well-summarized content covering the major points of actual summary (highlighted in blue). The yellow highlights indicate extractive textual output.

summaries based on the following criteria: (1) *Coverage*: where the model-generated textual summary is compared with the actual textual summary to check if the major points are adequately covered. (2) *Grammar*: where we investigate whether the model-generated textual summary is semantically correct. (3) *Topic-Aware-Text*: where we analyze whether the model-generated textual summary follows the suitable writing style such that it reflects the topic it belongs to. For example, a "sport"-topic summary should cover player names, whereas a "ScienceTech" topic summary should explain scientific facts using scientific terms. (4) *Topic-Aware-Image*: with this measure, we check whether the images selected by our model reflect the topic or not. For example, a "sport" topic pictorial summary should select pictures of players rather than spectators watching the game, whereas a "ScienceTech" topic pictorial summary should highlight the scientific event correctly.

It is difficult to judge the topic-aware criterion for samples belonging to topics like "news" or "others" due to its multiple sub-topics. So, the annotators were instructed to judge the topic-aware summary quality based on the "topic" they could determine from the title of the sample. For each evaluation criterion, the annotators were instructed to give a score from 1 (minimum) to 5 (maximum) to multimodal summaries.

Model	Coverage	Grammar	TA-Text	TA-Image
ATG (Zhu et al., 2018)	3.71	**4.42**	4.12	4.09
TSC-MSMO-SIMPAD-TIS	**3.83**	4.38	**4.33**	**4.47**

Table 11: Human evaluation results. Here TA denotes Topic-Aware.

As it can be seen from Table 11 there is a 3.2% increase in "Coverage" score, 5.1% increase in Topic-Aware-Text score, and 9.2% increase in Topic-aware-Image scores. The higher ratings of the topic-aware metrics and the rise in coverage-related metrics indicate that topic-awareness helps cover the major points discussed in the article. A minor decrease (0.9%) in the "grammar" related score can be due to some punctuation errors.

6 Qualitative Analysis

As shown in Fig. 4[5], the textual summary produced by the baseline *ATG* model could not cover the content related to sending the letter well. In contrast, our best-performing model *TSC-MSMO-SIMPAD-TIS* captured the details of why the boy had sent the letter and gave insights into the match scores due to focusing on "sport"-topic-related features. Our *TSC-MSMO-SIMPAD-TIS* model selected the image of the letter (Image No. (1) in Fig. 4) as

[5]More examples are shown in Appendix A.1

part of the pictorial summary. Although the letter image was not in the human-annotated pictures list, its selection complements our textual summary well. The generated multimodal output indicates that the model maintains a balance between topic awareness and content relevance while producing the output. The balanced output may be because the classifier and the other summarizing components were given equal weights in the final loss function. The images chosen by the other *TSC*-variants and the baseline *ATG* were also not bad. In the given example, 4 images were chosen as part of the pictorial summary.

A significant limitation of our work, is the highlighted extractive textual summaries (Fig. 4) that resulted from using a PGN-based decoder. However, there are few extractive elements in the human written summaries, as seen from the blue highlighted text. Thus, the model learns this extractive behavior from the training data itself. Another limitation, as seen from the topic-wise results (Sec. 5.2), is the dependence on data size for producing good quality output. The presence of low-sample-count sub-topics further adds to the problem of finding good "On-topic"-similar images for the classifier, thus leading to a deterioration in the quality of the summary produced by our model.

7 Conclusion and Future Study

Multimodal summaries help users absorb rich multimedia knowledge by generating brief and pertinent summaries. Adding topic information helps our model learn the different representation styles of various topics resulting in better quality summaries. The improvement in ROUGE and IP scores in the overall test set and the topic-wise segments for all our experiments indicate that making the model learn topic-related information helps produce better quality multimodal summaries. Furthermore, our experiments also established that using similar image features instead of the zero-padded vectors for samples having lesser in-article images does help in producing better summaries.

In a future study, we can find similar images using temporal information already present in our augmented dataset. Exploration of other techniques like comparing image-image, image-caption, or image-title embeddings for finding similar photos can also be done. A novel dataset can be created with lesser sub-topics and well-defined topics for studying our topic-based summarization technique.

7.1 Acknowledgement

Dr. Sriparna Saha gratefully acknowledges the Young Faculty Research Fellowship (YFRF) Award, supported by Visvesvaraya Ph.D. Scheme for Electronics and IT, Ministry of Electronics and Information Technology (MeitY), Government of India, being implemented by Digital India Corporation (formerly Media Lab Asia) for carrying out this research.

References

Evlampios Apostolidis, Eleni Adamantidou, Alexandros I Metsai, Vasileios Mezaris, and Ioannis Patras. 2021. Video summarization using deep neural networks: A survey. *Proceedings of the IEEE*, 109(11):1838–1863.

Dzmitry Bahdanau, Kyunghyun Cho, and Yoshua Bengio. 2016. Neural machine translation by jointly learning to align and translate.

Daniel Cer, Yinfei Yang, Sheng yi Kong, Nan Hua, Nicole Limtiaco, Rhomni St. John, Noah Constant, Mario Guajardo-Cespedes, Steve Yuan, Chris Tar, Yun-Hsuan Sung, Brian Strope, and Ray Kurzweil. 2018. Universal sentence encoder.

Jingqiang Chen and Hai Zhuge. 2018. Extractive text-image summarization using multi-modal rnn. In *2018 14th International Conference on Semantics, Knowledge and Grids (SKG)*, pages 245–248, Guangzhou, China. IEEE, IEEE.

Jia Deng, Wei Dong, Richard Socher, Li-Jia Li, Kai Li, and Li Fei-Fei. 2009. Imagenet: A large-scale hierarchical image database. In *2009 IEEE Computer Society Conference on Computer Vision and Pattern Recognition (CVPR 2009), 20-25 June 2009, Miami, Florida, USA*, pages 248–255, Miami, Florida, USA. IEEE Computer Society.

Günes Erkan and Dragomir R. Radev. 2011. Lexrank: Graph-based lexical centrality as salience in text summarization. *CoRR*, abs/1109.2128.

Georgios Evangelopoulos, Athanasia Zlatintsi, Alexandros Potamianos, Petros Maragos, Konstantinos Rapantzikos, Georgios Skoumas, and Yannis Avrithis. 2013. Multimodal saliency and fusion for movie summarization based on aural, visual, and textual attention. *IEEE Transactions on Multimedia*, 15:1553–1568.

Mahak Gambhir and Vishal Gupta. 2017. Recent automatic text summarization techniques: a survey. *Artificial Intelligence Review*, 47(1):1–66.

Masaru Isonuma, Toru Fujino, Junichiro Mori, Yutaka Matsuo, and Ichiro Sakata. 2017. Extractive summarization using multi-task learning with document classification. In *Proceedings of the 2017 Conference on*

Empirical Methods in Natural Language Processing, EMNLP 2017, Copenhagen, Denmark, September 9-11, 2017, pages 2101–2110, Copenhagen, Denmark. Association for Computational Linguistics.

Anubhav Jangra, Raghav Jain, Vaibhav Mavi, Sriparna Saha, and Pushpak Bhattacharyya. 2020a. Semantic extractor-paraphraser based abstractive summarization. In *Proceedings of the 17th International Conference on Natural Language Processing (ICON)*, pages 191–199, Indian Institute of Technology Patna, Patna, India. NLP Association of India (NLPAI).

Anubhav Jangra, Adam Jatowt, Mohammed Hasanuzzaman, and Sriparna Saha. 2020b. Text-image-video summary generation using joint integer linear programming. In *Advances in Information Retrieval - 42nd European Conference on IR Research, ECIR 2020, Lisbon, Portugal, April 14-17, 2020, Proceedings, Part II*, volume 12036 of *Lecture Notes in Computer Science*, pages 190–198. Springer.

Anubhav Jangra, Adam Jatowt, Sriparna Saha, and Mohammad Hasanuzzaman. 2021a. A survey on multi-modal summarization. *CoRR*, abs/2109.05199.

Anubhav Jangra, Sriparna Saha, Adam Jatowt, and Mohammad Hasanuzzaman. 2020c. Multi-modal summary generation using multi-objective optimization. In *Proceedings of the 43rd International ACM SIGIR conference on research and development in Information Retrieval, SIGIR 2020, Virtual Event, China, July 25-30, 2020*, pages 1745–1748. ACM.

Anubhav Jangra, Sriparna Saha, Adam Jatowt, and Mohammed Hasanuzzaman. 2021b. Multi-modal supplementary-complementary summarization using multi-objective optimization. In *SIGIR '21: The 44th International ACM SIGIR Conference on Research and Development in Information Retrieval, Virtual Event, Canada, July 11-15, 2021*, pages 818–828. ACM.

Aman Khullar and Udit Arora. 2020. MAST: multi-modal abstractive summarization with trimodal hierarchical attention. *CoRR*, abs/2010.08021.

Haoran Li, Peng Yuan, Song Xu, Youzheng Wu, Xiaodong He, and Bowen Zhou. 2020. Aspect-aware multimodal summarization for chinese e-commerce products. In *The Thirty-Fourth AAAI Conference on Artificial Intelligence, AAAI 2020, The Thirty-Second Innovative Applications of Artificial Intelligence Conference, IAAI 2020, The Tenth AAAI Symposium on Educational Advances in Artificial Intelligence, EAAI 2020, New York, NY, USA, February 7-12, 2020*, pages 8188–8195, New York, NY, USA. AAAI Press.

Haoran Li, Jiajun Zhang, Yu Zhou, and Chengqing Zong. 2016. Guiderank: A guided ranking graph model for multilingual multi-document summarization. In *Natural Language Understanding and Intelligent Applications - 5th CCF Conference on Natural Language Processing and Chinese Computing, NLPCC 2016, and 24th International Conference on Computer Processing of Oriental Languages, ICCPOL 2016, Kunming, China, December 2-6, 2016, Proceedings*, volume 10102 of *Lecture Notes in Computer Science*, pages 608–620. Springer.

Haoran Li, Junnan Zhu, Tianshang Liu, Jiajun Zhang, and Chengqing Zong. 2018. Multi-modal sentence summarization with modality attention and image filtering. In *Proceedings of the Twenty-Seventh International Joint Conference on Artificial Intelligence, IJCAI 2018, July 13-19, 2018, Stockholm, Sweden*, pages 4152–4158, Stockholm,Sweden. ijcai.org.

Haoran Li, Junnan Zhu, Cong Ma, Jiajun Zhang, and Chengqing Zong. 2017. Multi-modal summarization for asynchronous collection of text, image, audio and video. In *Proceedings of the 2017 Conference on Empirical Methods in Natural Language Processing*, pages 1092–1102, Copenhagen, Denmark. Association for Computational Linguistics.

Chin-Yew Lin. 2004. ROUGE: A package for automatic evaluation of summaries. In *Text Summarization Branches Out*, pages 74–81, Barcelona, Spain. Association for Computational Linguistics.

Thang Luong, Hieu Pham, and Christopher D. Manning. 2015. Effective approaches to attention-based neural machine translation. In *Proceedings of the 2015 Conference on Empirical Methods in Natural Language Processing, EMNLP 2015, Lisbon, Portugal, September 17-21, 2015*, pages 1412–1421, Lisbon, Portugal. The Association for Computational Linguistics.

Toru Nishino, Shotaro Misawa, Ryuji Kano, Tomoki Taniguchi, Yasuhide Miura, and Tomoko Ohkuma. 2019. Keeping consistency of sentence generation and document classification with multi-task learning. In *Proceedings of the 2019 Conference on Empirical Methods in Natural Language Processing and the 9th International Joint Conference on Natural Language Processing, EMNLP-IJCNLP 2019, Hong Kong, China, November 3-7, 2019*, pages 3193–3203, Hong Kong, China. Association for Computational Linguistics.

Shruti Palaskar, Jindrich Libovický, Spandana Gella, and Florian Metze. 2019. Multimodal abstractive summarization for how2 videos.

Melissa Sanabria, Frédéric Precioso, and Thomas Menguy. 2019. A deep architecture for multimodal summarization of soccer games. In *Proceedings Proceedings of the 2nd International Workshop on Multimedia Content Analysis in Sports*, pages 16–24.

Abigail See, Peter J. Liu, and Christopher D. Manning. 2017. Get to the point: Summarization with pointer-generator networks. In *Proceedings of the 55th Annual Meeting of the Association for Computational Linguistics, ACL 2017, Vancouver, Canada, July 30 - August 4, Volume 1: Long Papers*, pages 1073–1083, Vancouver, Canada. Association for Computational Linguistics.

Karen Simonyan and Andrew Zisserman. 2015. Very deep convolutional networks for large-scale image recognition.

Dian Tjondronegoro, Xiaohui Tao, Johannes Sasongko, and Cher Han Lau. 2011. Multi-modal summarization of key events and top players in sports tournament videos. In *IEEE Workshop on Applications of Computer Vision (WACV 2011), 5-7 January 2011, Kona, HI, USA*, pages 471–478, Kona, HI, USA. IEEE Computer Society.

X. Ye, Z. Yue, R. Liu, and Q. Lu. 2021. Mtms: A fact-corrected summarization model based on multitask learning and multimodal fusion. In *2021 2nd International Conference on Big Data & Artificial Intelligence & Software Engineering (ICBASE)*, pages 238–247, Los Alamitos, CA, USA. IEEE Computer Society.

Chenxi Zhang, Zijian Zhang, Jiangfeng Li, Qin Liu, and Hongming Zhu. 2021. Ctnr: Compress-then-reconstruct approach for multimodal abstractive summarization. In *2021 International Joint Conference on Neural Networks (IJCNN)*, pages 1–8.

Sicheng Zhao, Hongxun Yao, Sendong Zhao, Xuesong Jiang, and Xiaolei Jiang. 2016. Multi-modal microblog classification via multi-task learning. *Multimedia Tools and Applications*, 75(15):8921–8938.

Junnan Zhu, Haoran Li, Tianshang Liu, Yu Zhou, Jiajun Zhang, and Chengqing Zong. 2018. MSMO: multimodal summarization with multimodal output. In *Proceedings of the 2018 Conference on Empirical Methods in Natural Language Processing, Brussels, Belgium, October 31 - November 4, 2018*, pages 4154–4164, Brussels, Belgium. Association for Computational Linguistics.

Junnan Zhu, Yu Zhou, Jiajun Zhang, Haoran Li, Chengqing Zong, and Changliang Li. 2020. Multimodal summarization with guidance of multimodal reference. *Proceedings of the AAAI Conference on Artificial Intelligence*, 34(05):9749–9756.

A Appendices

A.1 Sample Summaries

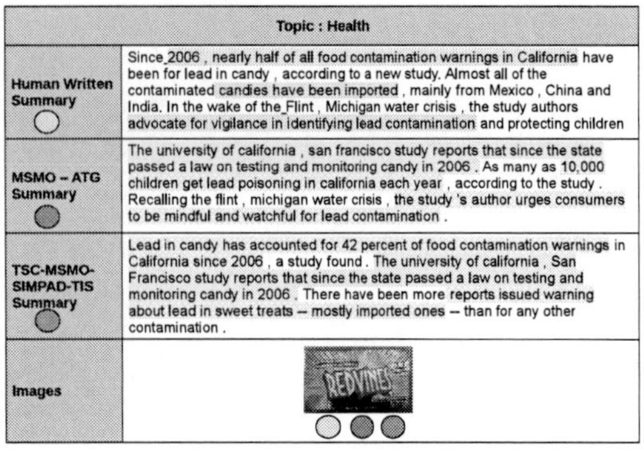

Figure 5: **Example 1:** Comparison between Multimodal summary generated by our best performing model TSC-MSMO-SIMPAD-TIS and the baseline for a sample belonging to "Health" topic. Only one image is part of the sample, and it is selected as the pictorial summary

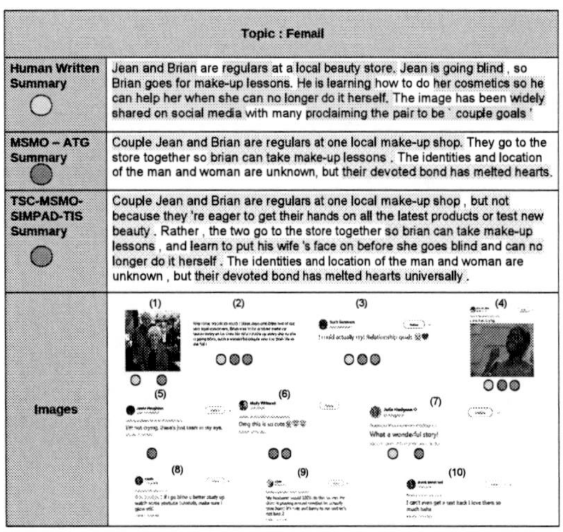

Figure 6: **Example 2:** Comparison between Multimodal summary generated by our best performing model TSC-MSMO-SIMPAD-TIS and the baseline for a sample belonging to "Femail" topic. Only one image is part of the sample, and it is selected as the pictorial summary

As shown in the 1st example (Fig. 5) our *TSC-MSMO-SIMPAD-TIS* model's summary stated the exact percentage of lead contamination (42%). In contrast, the human summary has stated: "nearly half" to explain the lead contamination rate. The *ATG* model covered facts regarding the number of children affected each year. However, it missed the detail that the "imported"-candies were mostly contaminated and should be avoided. This fact was covered well by our proposed model's textual summary.

In the 2nd example (Fig. 6), the textual summary produced by our *TSC-MSMO-SIMPAD-TIS* model was able to capture the significant reason why the couple went to the make-up-shop. The reason that Brian's wife would be going blind was not covered in the textual summary by *ATG* model. Further in the pictorial summary, although the *ATG* model chose good images of the tweets but missed the picture of the couple (Image no. (1) in Fig. 6), which our model chose.

ArgGen: Prompting Text Generation Models for Document-Level Event-Argument Aggregation

Debanjana Kar *
IBM Research
Bengaluru, India
debanjana.kar1@ibm.com

Sudeshna Sarkar and **Pawan Goyal**
IIT Kharagpur
Kharagpur, India
{sudeshna, pawang}@cse.iitkgp.ac.in

Abstract

Most of the existing discourse-level Information Extraction tasks have been modeled to be extractive in nature. However, we argue that extracting information from larger bodies of discourse-like documents requires more natural language understanding and reasoning capabilities. In our work, we propose the novel task of document-level event argument aggregation which generates consolidated event-arguments at a document-level with minimal loss of information. More specifically, we focus on generating precise document-level information frames in a multilingual setting using prompt-based methods. In this paper, we show the effectiveness of prompt-based text generation approach to generate document-level argument spans in a low-resource and zero-shot setting. We also release the first of its kind multilingual event argument aggregation dataset that can be leveraged in other related multilingual text generation tasks as well: `https://github.com/DebanjanaKar/ArgGen`

1 Introduction

Discourse-based Information Extraction (IE)is a well-explored NLP task. Most of these works (Yang et al., 2018; Zheng et al., 2019) rely on extractive approaches to mine relevant event-argument spans for specific argument roles. However, there are two main challenges in this effort. First, extractive argument spans may miss implicit information at a document-level. For example in Figure 1, the *Time* mentions in the document include the publishing date of the document and the day of the week the event occurred. An extractive approach will not be able to accurately determine the date of the event. We aim to address this challenge using a conditional text generation approach. Second, sentence-level argument mentions in the document are often scattered and may contain similar yet distinct information. For example, the *Casualties* argument mentions like 'kill 37', 'At least 37 civilians', 'killed several people, including militants' in the example (Figure 1) contain repetitive but slightly distinct information. An extractive method extracting such document level arguments may again miss key information as they employ elimination strategies to select the key argument mention at the document level. The approach we propose addresses this challenge by leveraging argument specific prompts with conditional text generation methods.

DOC: July 1, 2007, Sunday. Airstrikes in Helmand kill 37. Kabul. International airstrikes against the Taliban have killed civilians in Afghanistan again. At least 37 civilians were killed when a NATO-led coalition airstrike struck Helmand on Saturday morning. A military spokesman said the warplanes were sent to Helmand after a long battle between the joint forces and the Taliban. The bombing also killed several people, including militants. A joint operation in Afghanistan has killed at least 300 people this year.

TIME: 30 June 2007 Saturday morning.

PLACE: Helmand, Afghanistan.

CASUALTIES: at least 37 civilians of Helmand along with some militants were killed.

AFTER EFFECTS: N.A.

REASON: long battle against the Taliban.

PARTICIPANT: NATO-led joint forces and the Taliban..

Figure 1: Illustrative example of the Event Argument Aggregation Task. The sentence-level event argument mentions have been highlighted in the document with colours corresponding to their argument roles (like TIME, PLACE). Multiple sentence-level arguments in the same colour in the document indicate high redundancy of information for that particular argument role.

In this paper, we provide a fresh perspective to discourse-based IE and propose the task of Event Argument Aggregation. Event Argument Aggregation is a challenging natural language understanding task that aims to consolidate document-level structured information from given unstructured text. Closely related to the task of document-level event argument extraction, event argument aggregation emphasizes on filtering redundant and irrelevant

* Work done as a student at IIT Kharagpur

Findings of the Association for Computational Linguistics: AACL-IJCNLP 2022, pages 399–404
November 20–23, 2022.

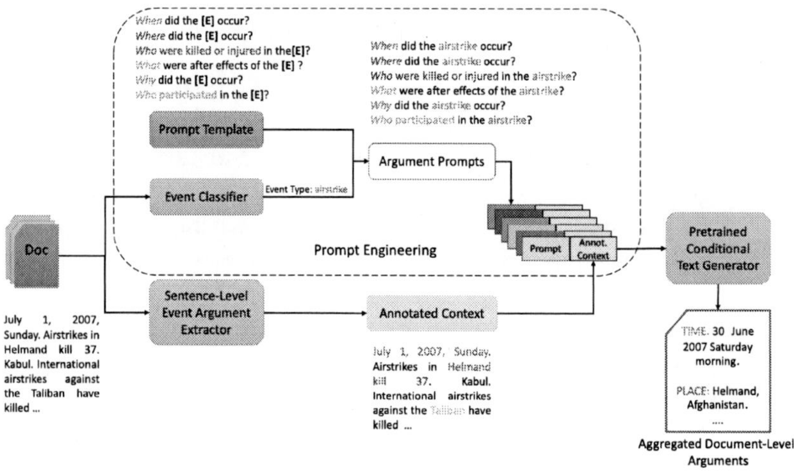

Figure 2: Illustration of the architecture for training our desired event-argument generation model.

argument mentions to generate precise document-level information frames. In our work, we focus on producing the document-level information frames using prompt-based generative approaches.

In our work, we adopt (Du and Cardie, 2020; Feng et al., 2020)'s idea of reducing our related task of Document-Level Event Argument Aggregation to that of Natural Language Question Answering. A very recently published work related to the task of Event Argument Generation is that of (Li et al., 2021). Like our approach, they too employ conditioned text generation to generate document-level event arguments. However, the argument spans they extract at a document level are much shorter and explicit in nature than our argument mentions. Prompt-based methods have recently gained popularity in a number of related tasks like entity extraction(Wang et al., 2022), question answering(Liu et al., 2022) and text generation(Li et al., 2022). In this paper, we show the effectiveness of prompt-based methods to aggregate event-arguments at a document-level. We evaluate our models on low-resource settings as well as more challenging zero-shot settings. We discuss and analyse the effectiveness of the proposed model in the following sections.

The key contributions of our work are enumerated as follows: i) We propose a fresh perspective to discourse-based IE through our proposed task of Event Argument Aggregation. ii) We are the first to explore prompt-based conditional text generation to aggregate event-arguments at a document level. Our proposed model provides state-of-the-art results on this task. iii) We are the first to release an annotated, multilingual event-argument aggregation dataset. The corpus consists of 346 annotated documents in English, Hindi and Bengali.

2 Event-Argument Aggregation

In this section, we detail the approaches we propose for the task of Document-Level Event Argument Aggregation. The framework primarily involves three steps: i) MRC Pre-training, ii) Prompt Engineering, iii) QA-based Argument Generation.

2.1 MRC Pre-training

For the model to generate informative aggregated argument mentions at a document-level from scattered sentence-level argument mentions (as demonstrated in Fig 2), the model requires strong comprehension and reasoning capabilities. For example, given the publishing date of the article and the day of the week on which the event occurred, the model should be able to comprehend and render the correct date of the event which is not explicitly mentioned in the input document. This requirement for infusing natural language understanding and reasoning capacities in the model necessitates the machine reading comprehension (MRC) pre-training step in our proposed approach. MRC usually comprises of NLP tasks like question-answering, textual-entailment, numerical reasoning, etc. We pre-train our model on an amalgamated QA dataset (Multi_QA, Section 3.1) which consists of reasoning QA data samples in English along with other QA data samples in Hindi and Bengali. The conditional text generator we use for this task is a transformer-based encoder-decoder ar-

Dataset	DROP	MLQA	XQuAD	TyDI	Multi_QA
#Train	77409	4918	96340	3585	1,82,252
#Test	9536	507	2374	113	12,530
Q Len	10.83	9.31	11.01	5.61	10.78
A Len	1.38	3.62	3.91	3.78	2.77
P Len	202.44	155.24	136.86	87.23	165.70

Table 1: Dataset Statistics for the amalgamated QA corpus Multi_QA along with it's constituent datasets. The first two rows enumerate the number of train test instances across the datasets. *Q, P, A Len* refer to the average lengths of Questions, Passage and Answers respectively.

chitecture which takes as input an input passage P and a query q, and is trained to generate an answer a of abstractive nature. We use the multilingual variant of the T5 model as our backbone model for this task. After training the small and base variants of mT5 and mBART-50, we find that mt5-base performs the best with an F1-score of 62.45%

2.2 Prompt Engineering

Prompting the QA-based argument aggregator is fairly intuitive. Given the argument roles, we design templates for the prompts like *When did [E] happen?* where $[E] \in$ disaster-based events like $\{earthquake, flood, terrorist\_attack, ..\}$. Since the number of argument-roles are limited, we manually define the prompts instead of generating them automatically for greater accuracy. We define our prompts using 5W words (*When, Where, What, Who, Why*) and it has been observed empirically that the prompts with 5Ws work better in such QA-based frameworks(Liu et al., 2022). To fill the event mask $[E]$ in the prompt, we define a document classifier which identifies the event type of the document. A classification head on top of multilingual BERT is trained iteratively to map the correct event-type to the input document instance. Since for each of m argument roles, we define a specific prompt, we hence refer to the prompts as *Argument Prompts*.

2.3 QA-based Argument Generation

Given a document, we parse the document to annotate sentence-level argument mentions. We extract sentence-level argument information from the document using the state-of-the-art event argument extraction method for this dataset (Kar et al., 2020). It uses causal knowledge structures to accurately detect the low-resource event argument mentions in the document's sentences. We mark the sentence-level argument spans in the document with special argument role tokens to generate our annotated context. We avoid marking duplicate argument mentions and mentions with very similar surface form in the document to curtail redundancy in the model. Using fuzzy string match techniques (Levenshtein, 1965), we only mark the longer argument span in case of redundancy. The annotated context is concatenated with an argument-specific prompt and used as the input to the pre-trained conditional text generator. The conditional text generator, pre-trained with an MRC objective in the previous step, is fine-tuned with few examples to generate the desired document-level aggregated argument mentions for a specific argument role. Our results and analysis in the following sections highlight that our proposed framework effectively generates meaningful aggregated argument mentions even after seeing only a few examples for each language.

3 Dataset

In the sections to follow, we discuss the details of the datasets we created for i) the MRC pretraining task and ii) Multilingual Event Argument Aggregation (*ArgGen* dataset).

3.1 MRC Pretraining Dataset

Most of the works in the domain of Natural Language Question Answering are of extractive nature. However, for the task of MRC Pretraining (as discussed in Section 2.1), we required an abstractive multilingual question answering dataset. We curate such a dataset by collating the following datasets: i) DROP Dataset (Dua et al., 2019) which is an abstractive, reasoning QA dataset with a special focus on numerical reasoning; ii) Hindi annotated instances of MLQA (Lewis et al., 2020) and XQuAD (Artetxe et al., 2020) datasets and iii) Bengali annotated instances from TyDi QA dataset (Clark et al., 2020). Although the multilingual datasets collated are extractive in nature, we use them in generative pretraining along with the abstractive DROP

Dataset	Eng.	Ben.	Hindi	Multi
# Docs	129	75	142	346
#Train Inst.	619	360	681	1660
#Test Inst.	155	90	171	416
Avg. Ans Len	7.2	9.3	11.0	9.3
Avg. Pas. Len	209.8	142.1	296.8	230.8

Table 2: Dataset Statistics for the ArgGen corpus. The terms *Multi, Inst., Ans, Pas.* refers to Multilingual, Istances, Answer and Passage in the table. Eng. and Ben. refer to English and Bengali respectively.

dataset so that the model doesn't learn to reason in a singular language resulting in a bias. The statistics of the amalgamated QA dataset *Multi_QA* [1] is given in Table 1.

3.2 ArgGen Dataset

We curate the first multilingual event argument generation dataset in English and two morphologically rich Indian languages, Hindi and Bengali. The dataset consists of abstractive aggregated argument mentions for each of the six argument roles, that is, *Time, Place, Casualties, After Effects, Reason, Participant*, in three different languages. While we use the same English documents as those used in the *ArgFuse* dataset (Kar et al., 2021), we source the Hindi and Bengali documents from reputed news websites. The news articles have been crawled from different time periods (2016-2020) to have diversity in the event types of the documents. [2]

For each document, the topic or event of the document is annotated. The documents cater specifically to the disaster domain and can correspond to 32 event types at a fine grain level and 12 event types at a coarse level. For a given document in the corpus, for each of the six argument roles, the annotator was asked to compose an aggregated argument mention in his/her own words. The aggregated argument mention should consolidate all available information from the given passage and present an informative, yet precise piece of text. All argument roles may not be populated for each and every document. Such roles are then filled with an 'N.A.' value. The corpus was annotated by two linguistic experts with good knowledge about data curation and had working/native proficiency in the

Model	Scores		
	R-L	MTR	BScr
English			
GPT-2	36.12	10.22	75.7
mT5-base	32.91	6.78	74.9
Our model	58.24	18.94	84.4
Bengali			
mT5-base	6.05	10.26	64.9
Our model	32.22	21.09	77.4
Hindi			
mT5-base	28.40	3.31	71.6
Our model	18.71	2.89	68.6
Multilingual			
mT5-base	44.03	13.53	74.7
Our model	39.75	9.85	77.6

Table 3: Document-Level Event-Argument Generation Results across languages (train and test languages are same). R-L, MTR and BScr denote ROUGE-L, METEOR Scores and BERTScore respectively as %.

languages of the documents. The statistics of the dataset is presented in Table 2. While we have create a low-resource multilingual NLG dataset, we have observed that our Hindi and Bengali corpus comprise of more challenging aggregated argument mentions.

4 Discussion

We have used mT5-base[3] (Xue et al., 2021) model at the core of our experiments. In Table 3, we present our event argument generation results across languages using ROUGE-L, METEOR [4] and BertScore [5]. We find that the results improve by a major margin by following our pretraining + finetuning recipe, infused with sentence-level argument information. However, given the model is trained on a large amount of English corpus, we find the best results being reported for English. We report the importance of each of the elements proposed in our framework in Table 4. We can observe that pre-training our model on reasoning data helps a lot in improving the generation capabilities of the model. Infusion of argument prompts can also be observed as a major point of guidance for the model. This highlights and justifies the necessity of our proposed pipeline framework instead of an end-to-end one.

[1]We access all the constituent datasets of Multi_QA from `https://www.tensorflow.org/datasets/catalog/overview`

[2]`https://www.anandabazar.com/`, `https://epaper.bhaskar.com/`

[3]`https://huggingface.co/google/mt5-base`

[4]`https://github.com/Maluuba/nlg-eval`

[5]`https://github.com/Tiiiger/bert_score`

BertScore	English	Bengali	Hindi	Multilingual
English	84.4	69.5	63.9	75.2
Bengali	68.3	77.4	62.7	69
Hindi	67.1	62.1	68.6	68.7
Multilingual	92.7	83.3	71.6	77.6

ROUGE-L	English	Bengali	Hindi	Multilingual
English	58.2	14.9	0.3	30.6
Bengali	31.8	32.2	1.9	24.4
Hindi	20.4	5.7	18.7	20.8
Multilingual	79.1	53.2	28.4	39.8

Figure 3: Crosslingual & Multilingual Analysis of Event Argument Generation using our model on ArgGen. The y-axis & x-axis labels correspond to the language of the training and test sets respectively where all scores are reported as %. The spectrum of values is represented with various shades, with the minimum values highlighted using peach and the maximum values highlighted using violet.

We present our results of the crosslingual and multilingual analysis in Figure 3. We analyse both at the surface level and at the contextual level using ROUGE-L and BERTScore respectively. We observe that for all the test cases, both at the surface-level as well as contextual, the model trained on the multilingual corpus performs the best. This can be regarded to the fact that the multilingual corpus with the combined, enlarged count of training samples provides the model a scope to train on additional data and learn from a variety of samples from different languages in a common embedding space. We also find that English, among all the other languages reports the best performance. We attribute this to i) the bias in training data of the core model for English compared to the other languages and ii) most of the aggregated mentions in the English corpora are of extractive nature, thus making it easier for the model to generate. The Hindi and Bengali corpus comprises of more challenging aggregated argument mentions which require advanced reasoning capabilities. We also find that Hindi reports the poorest performance compared to all the languages. We observed that the i) mT5-base model itself performs poorly when fine-tuned on the Hindi corpora, ii) our large Hindi pre-training corpora is of extractive nature. Although our Bengali pre-training corpora is also of extractive nature, the size of the data is lower by many orders compared to the Hindi corpora and hence we do not see such drastic effects. Our hypothesis is that i) It would help to pretrain on multilingual reasoning dataset of abstractive nature like DROP instead of large multilingual corpora of extractive nature, ii) for complex generation corpora like the Hindi corpora, larger and more complex models can help learn the synthesis better.

Setting	ROUGE-L	METEOR
Our model	58.24	18.94
- MRC pre-training	32.91	7.38
- argument prompts	31.62	9.56

Table 4: Ablation Study on the English corpus of ArgGen.'−' represents minus a particular setting. Scores have been reported as %.

5 Conclusion

We have presented *ArgGen*, a low-resource, prompt-based multilingual framework which aggregates event argument mentions at a document-level. We have also presented a fresh perspective in the domain of multilingual IE through our proposed challenging task of document-level event argument aggregation. We provide access to a novel multilingual event argument aggregation dataset which can also be leveraged for other related natural language generation tasks: `https://github.com/DebanjanaKar/ArgGen`. Our proposed model not only generates syntactically and semantically relevant aggregated argument mentions but demonstrates similar effectiveness in a zero-shot setting as well. In the future, we want to explore this task across more languages and documents.

References

Mikel Artetxe, Sebastian Ruder, and Dani Yogatama. 2020. On the cross-lingual transferability of monolingual representations. In *Proceedings of the 58th Annual Meeting of the Association for Computational Linguistics*, pages 4623–4637, Online. Association for Computational Linguistics.

Jonathan H. Clark, Eunsol Choi, Michael Collins, Dan Garrette, Tom Kwiatkowski, Vitaly Nikolaev, and Jennimaria Palomaki. 2020. TyDi QA: A benchmark for information-seeking question answering in typologically diverse languages. *Transactions of the Association for Computational Linguistics*, 8:454–470.

Xinya Du and Claire Cardie. 2020. Event extraction by answering (almost) natural questions. In *Proceedings of the 2020 Conference on Empirical Methods in Natural Language Processing (EMNLP)*, pages 671–683, Online. Association for Computational Linguistics.

Dheeru Dua, Yizhong Wang, Pradeep Dasigi, Gabriel Stanovsky, Sameer Singh, and Matt Gardner. 2019. DROP: A reading comprehension benchmark requiring discrete reasoning over paragraphs. In *Proceedings of the 2019 Conference of the North American Chapter of the Association for Computational Linguistics: Human Language Technologies, Volume 1 (Long and Short Papers)*, pages 2368–2378, Minneapolis, Minnesota. Association for Computational Linguistics.

Rui Feng, Jie Yuan, and Chao Zhang. 2020. Probing and fine-tuning reading comprehension models for few-shot event extraction.

Debanjana Kar, Sudeshna Sarkar, and Pawan Goyal. 2020. Event argument extraction using causal knowledge structures. In *Proceedings of the 17th International Conference on Natural Language Processing (ICON)*, pages 287–296.

Debanjana Kar, Sudeshna Sarkar, and Pawan Goyal. 2021. ArgFuse: A weakly-supervised framework for document-level event argument aggregation. In *Proceedings of the 4th Workshop on Challenges and Applications of Automated Extraction of Socio-political Events from Text (CASE 2021)*, pages 20–30, Online. Association for Computational Linguistics.

Vladimir I. Levenshtein. 1965. Binary codes capable of correcting deletions, insertions, and reversals. *Soviet physics. Doklady*, 10:707–710.

Patrick Lewis, Barlas Oguz, Ruty Rinott, Sebastian Riedel, and Holger Schwenk. 2020. MLQA: Evaluating cross-lingual extractive question answering. In *Proceedings of the 58th Annual Meeting of the Association for Computational Linguistics*, pages 7315–7330, Online. Association for Computational Linguistics.

Junyi Li, Tianyi Tang, Jian-Yun Nie, Ji-Rong Wen, and Xin Zhao. 2022. Learning to transfer prompts for text generation. In *Proceedings of the 2022 Conference of the North American Chapter of the Association for Computational Linguistics: Human Language Technologies*, pages 3506–3518, Seattle, United States. Association for Computational Linguistics.

Sha Li, Heng Ji, and Jiawei Han. 2021. Document-level event argument extraction by conditional generation. In *Proceedings of the 2021 Conference of the North American Chapter of the Association for Computational Linguistics: Human Language Technologies*, pages 894–908, Online. Association for Computational Linguistics.

Andy T. Liu, Wei Xiao, Henghui Zhu, Dejiao Zhang, Shang-Wen Li, and Andrew Arnold. 2022. Qaner: Prompting question answering models for few-shot named entity recognition.

Yufei Wang, Can Xu, Qingfeng Sun, Huang Hu, Chongyang Tao, Xiubo Geng, and Daxin Jiang. 2022. PromDA: Prompt-based data augmentation for low-resource NLU tasks. In *Proceedings of the 60th Annual Meeting of the Association for Computational Linguistics (Volume 1: Long Papers)*, pages 4242–4255, Dublin, Ireland. Association for Computational Linguistics.

Linting Xue, Noah Constant, Adam Roberts, Mihir Kale, Rami Al-Rfou, Aditya Siddhant, Aditya Barua, and Colin Raffel. 2021. mT5: A massively multilingual pre-trained text-to-text transformer. In *Proceedings of the 2021 Conference of the North American Chapter of the Association for Computational Linguistics: Human Language Technologies*, pages 483–498, Online. Association for Computational Linguistics.

Hang Yang, Yubo Chen, Kang Liu, Yang Xiao, and Jun Zhao. 2018. DCFEE: A document-level Chinese financial event extraction system based on automatically labeled training data. In *Proceedings of ACL 2018, System Demonstrations*, pages 50–55, Melbourne, Australia. Association for Computational Linguistics.

Shun Zheng, Wei Cao, Wei Xu, and Jiang Bian. 2019. Doc2EDAG: An end-to-end document-level framework for Chinese financial event extraction. In *Proceedings of the 2019 Conference on Empirical Methods in Natural Language Processing and the 9th International Joint Conference on Natural Language Processing (EMNLP-IJCNLP)*, pages 337–346, Hong Kong, China. Association for Computational Linguistics.

Hierarchical Processing of Visual and Language Information in the Brain

Haruka Kawasaki[1], Satoshi Nishida[2], and Ichiro Kobayashi[1]
[1]Ochanomizu University, Japan
[2]Center for Information and Neural Networks,
National Institute of Information and Communications Technology, Japan
[1]{g1820509, koba}@is.ocha.ac.jp
[2]s-nishida@nict.go.jp

Abstract

In recent years, many studies using deep learning have been conducted to elucidate the mechanism of information representation in the brain under stimuli evoked by various modalities. On the other hand, it has not yet been clarified how we humans link information of different modalities in the brain. In this study, to elucidate the relationship between visual and language information in the brain, we constructed encoding models that predict brain activity based on features extracted from the hidden layers of VGG16 for visual information and BERT for language information. We investigated the hierarchical characteristics of cortical localization and representational content of visual and semantic information in the cortex based on the brain activity predicted by the encoding model. The results showed that the cortical localization modeled by VGG16 is getting close to that of BERT as VGG16 moves to higher layers, while the representational contents differ significantly between the two modalities.

1 Introduction

In recent years, many studies have been conducted to elucidate the information representation mechanisms of the human brain using deep learning. Studies using convolutional neural networks (CNNs) have confirmed the hierarchical processing of visual information in the brain (Yamins et al., 2014; Eickenberg et al., 2017). In addition, studies using deep learning models that deal with language have confirmed that it is possible to model the representation of semantic information in the brain (Nishida et al., 2021). However, most studies are conducted separately, and the similarities and differences in the brain information representation of both modalities have not been sufficiently discussed.

With this background, the objective of this study is to investigate on how the information localization and representation of both modalities are related to each other in the brain – we particularly aim to investigate the hierarchical characteristics of the cortical localization and representation contents of visual and language information in the cerebral cortex by using representational similarity analysis (RSA) (Kriegeskorte et al., 2008).

2 Related research

In pioneering work in modeling brain representations using deep learning, Yamins et al. (2014) showed that there is homology between hierarchical information representations in the human cortex under visual stimuli and those in CNNs, and Güçlü and van Gerven (2015) showed that complexity gradually increases with higher layers in hierarchical processing. In a study using functional magnetic resonance imaging (fMRI) and magnetoencephalography, Cichy et al. (2016) used deep learning model to show that spatio-temporal dynamics in the human brain cortex during visual object recognition is a hierarchical response. Eickenberg et al. (2017) have revealed the functional organization of the visual cortex of the human brain by analyzing brain activity with the aid of a deep learning model. Nonaka et al. (2021) introduced the brain hierarchy score, which indicates the degree of hierarchical response based on encoding and decoding to brain activity, and discussed what kind of deep learning models accurately represent the structure of the visual cortex of the human brain, showing that deep learning models with high accuracy in image identification do not necessarily represent the behavior of the visual cortex of the human brain.

On the other hand, in a study that models brain representations from semantic features of language, Huth et al. (2012) used fMRI to observe brain activity of subjects watching a two-hour natural video and labeled them using 1705 WordNet (Fellbaum, 1998)-based categories for objects and actions in the video, showing that these categories are not represented in specific brain regions but as locations

Findings of the Association for Computational Linguistics: AACL-IJCNLP 2022, pages 405–410
November 20–23, 2022.

in a continuous semantic space. Huth et al. (2016) constructed semantic maps in brain regions from brain activity induced by natural speech stimuli, and found that in most regions of the semantic system, there are specific semantic regions and groups of related concepts. Nishida et al. (2021) clarified that quantitative modeling of meaning using word2vec (Mikolov et al., 2013) and other methods is an effective means of estimating language activity in the brain through comparison with semantic structures evaluated from human behavior. Jain and Huth (2018) introduced LSTM (Hochreiter and Schmidhuber, 1997) to extract vectors for each word, used them in their encoding model, and achieved more accurate estimation than conventional models. In recent years, the construction of computational models that explain language processing properties in the brain using distributed semantic representations has played an important role. In this context, Sun et al. (2021) scrutinized the still unexplored relationship between the brain representation of sentences and distributed representations, and whether the linguistic features captured by distributed representations can better explain the correlation between brain activities in which sentences are given as linguistic stimuli, and showed the characteristics of distributed representations and their effectiveness.

Most of the above studies have explored the properties of visual and semantic brain processing separately. Therefore, the hierarchical processing from visual to semantic information in the brain is not well understood. In this study, we construct and compare encoding models based on these two different modalities, and investigate the characteristics of information localization and information representation content in the hierarchical processing of visual and semantic information.

3 Brain information analysis with RSA

3.1 Overview

Figure 1 illustrates an overview of our study. Firstly, we use fMRI to collect brain activity data while subjects are watching movies with either fixation or free viewing. We then extracted image features from the images cropped from the movies given to the subjects as stimuli using VGG16 (Simonyan and Zisserman, 2014) and linguistic features from the annotations assigned to the images using BERT (Devlin et al., 2019).

To predict the brain activity from the features extracted by those deep learning models, we construct encoding models using Ridge linear regression. Then, to investigate the hierarchical characteristics of cortical localization and representational contents of visual and linguistic information on the cerebral cortex, we apply RSA to analyzing the brain states predicted by the encoding models.

3.2 Encoding model

In this study, we employ the method by Naselaris et al. (2011) for the construction of encoding models. When constructing the encoding model, the target feature space and brain activity patterns are linearly regressed, and weights are learned so that the measured brain activity patterns and predicted brain activity patterns are close. The constructed encoding model is then applied to the evaluation data, and the prediction accuracy is evaluated. In general, Ridge liner regression is used as the regression method, and by observing the regression coefficients, it is possible to observe the behavior with respect to voxels.

3.3 Representational Similarity Analysis

RSA is a framework for characterizing representations of various modalities by representational dissimilarity matrices (RDMs) and comparing RDMs. An RDM is a matrix that allows us to retrieve the representational distance (or dissimilarity) of each modality. The dissimilarity in our study is calculated by correlation distance (1 - Pearson's correlation coefficient). Creating RDMs makes us possible to measure things that cannot be directly measured for similarity. In addition, RSA has the property that it does not require the definition of mappings, which is necessary when directly comparing activity patterns.

4 Experiments

We have conducted the following three experiments to investigate whether or not:(i) predictable brain regions are similar to both vision and language stimuli; (ii) cortical localization patterns are similar; (iii) representational content is similar. The numbers on the right side of Figure 1 correspond to the numbers of the experiments.

4.1 Experimental settings

fMRI data Brain activity data were obtained by fMRI at the Center for Information and Neural Networks, National Institute of Information and

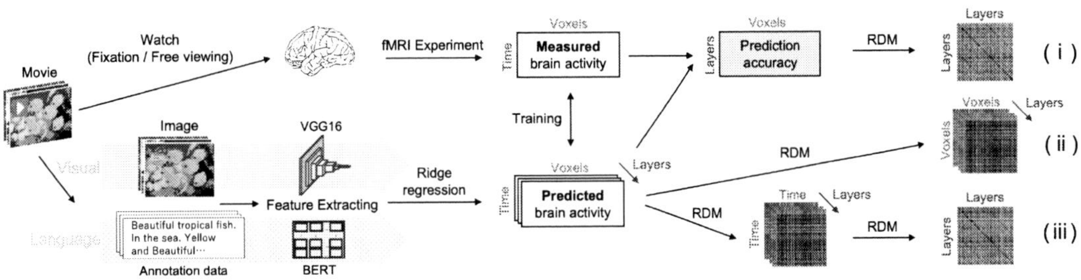

Figure 1: An overview of the experiments

Communications Technology (NICT). The brain activity data were collected by fMRI which is a 3T MRI (Siemens MAGNETOM Prisma), and the imaging parameters are TR 1 second and voxel size $2 \times 2 \times 2$mm. T1 structural images were also taken separately from the fMRI images, and were registered with the fMRI images using FreeSurfer (Dale et al., 1999). Only the voxels of the cerebral cortex extracted by this method were used in the analysis. Seven subjects (three males and four females, mean age 24.1 years) participated in the fMRI experiment. The experimental protocol was approved in advance by the Ethics Review Committee and Safety Review Committee of NICT, and written consent was obtained from all subjects before the experiment. Each subject watched a 2 hour 40 minutes compiled movie with sound in the fixation condition (gazing at a fixed point of view in the center of the screen) and the free viewing condition (moving the gaze freely). Of the 2 hours and 40 minutes of data obtained in each condition, 2 hours were used as training data for the model. The remaining 40 minutes of data consisted of four repetitions, which were averaged to 10 minutes and used as the evaluation data for the model.

Annotation data To extract linguistic features from the movies, we obtained written scene descriptions from five to six annotators for each one-second video scene. The annotators were native speakers of Japanese and did not participate in the fMRI experiment.

Encoding models for the experiments The same method was used to create encoding models based on image features and language features. A total of 40 encoding models were constructed using the features extracted from each of the VGG16 (using 8 layers) and BERT (12 layers in total) under fixation and free viewing conditions. A model that predicts the time series of brain activity using the time series of features as explanatory variables was trained by Ridge regression. In order to take into account the hemodynamic delay in the responses, we regressed the fMRI-observed brain activity data with the 3, 4, 5, and 6 seconds precedence features. In addition, 10-split cross-validation was conducted by shuffling the training data with 50 chunks, and the regularization term with the best average correlation coefficient was adopted. Using the learned encoding models, we evaluated the prediction accuracy of each voxel by obtaining Pearson's correlation coefficient between the predicted and measured fMRI signals to the same stimuli. In doing so, we rejected voxels with significant p-values ($p < 0.05$) corrected for false discovery rate.

4.2 Experimental results

In the following, we indicate total number of layers as n_layers, total number of voxels as n_voxels. We employ the rejected voxels with significant p-value in at least one of the 40 encoding models as the data used in all the following experiments.

(i) Predictable regions This analysis was performed to determine the similarity of brain regions that can be predicted by a total of 40 encoding models using features extracted from all targeted hidden layers of VGG16 and BERT as input. Prediction accuracies of all encoding models were used to create an RDM ($n\_layers \times n\_layers$) for each subject and averaged over all subjects. The upper figure of Figure 2 shows the RDM of ($n\_layers \times n\_layers$) and the lower figure shows it compressed into ($n\_layers \times 3$) using multi-dimensional scaling (MDS) and plotted on a 3-dimensional space. The closer the models are displayed to each other, the more similar brain regions they can predict. Both VGG16 and BERT are color-coded in the fixation and free viewing conditions, and visualized in a total of four colors according to the deep learning models and its conditions. The lighter colors indicate the lower layers and the darker colors the higher layers, and the numbers next to the dots indicate the number of the layer. From this result, it can be seen that brain regions where models are predictable become similar to that of BERT as the hierarchy of VGG16 increases from lower to higher layers.

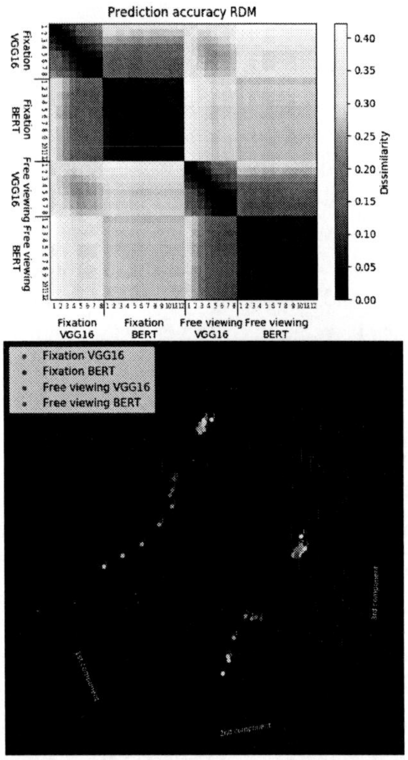

Figure 2: Similarity of predictable brain regions by the models

(ii) Cortical localization patterns We performed this analysis to see the similarity of cortical localization patterns for the VGG16 high layers and BERT. The brain activity predicted by each encoding model ($time \times n\_voxels$) was used to create an RDM ($n\_voxels \times n\_voxels$) of each layer for each subject. Figure 3 shows the visualization results of the predicted brain activity of one subject from the 8th layer, the highest layer among the targeted layers in VGG16 and the 12th layer of BERT under free viewing conditions. The RDM is reduced in dimensionality by uniform manifold approximation and projection (UMAP), and the colors are plotted on a flat map of the cortex created by means of Pycortex[1], with the colors of near objects being close to each other and distant objects being far apart. The results show that the pattern of similarity of the contents of voxel-wise information representation in the cortex is similar between the higher layer of VGG16 and that of BERT.

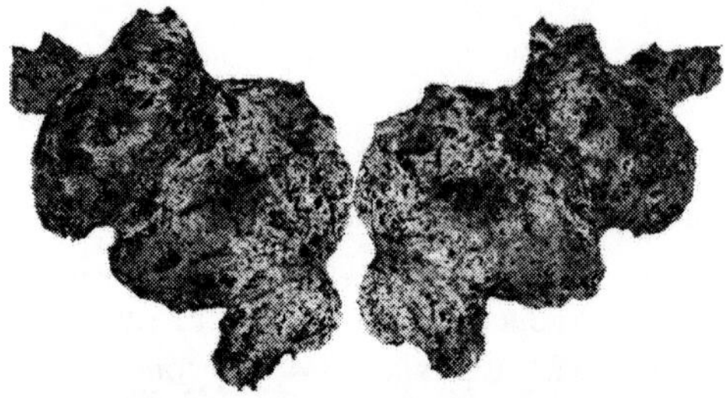

Layer 8 of VGG16 under free viewing

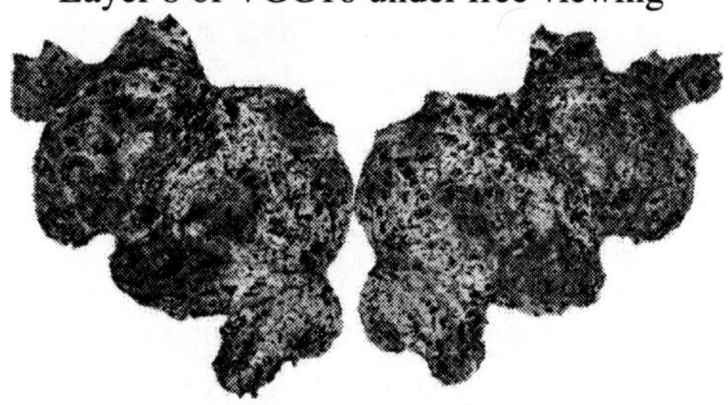

Layer 12 of BERT under free viewing

Figure 3: Similarity of cortical localization patterns

From (i) and (ii), we find that cortical localization becomes more similar to BERT as one moves from the lower to higher layers of VGG16. We now perform the experiment (iii) to see if the representational content also approaches BERT as one moves from the lower to higher levels of VGG16.

(iii) Representational content We performed this analysis to determine the similarity of representational content for 40 encoding models. Using the predictions of brain activity, we created RDMs of ($time \times time$) for each encoding model. All of these RDMs were then used to create an RDM of ($n\_layers \times n\_layers$) for each subject and averaged over all of them. Figure 4 shows the RDM among layers of VGG16 and BERT in terms of representational contents and the result of dimensionality reduction of the RDM with MDS and visualization on a 3-dimensional space. Figure coloring is the same as (i) of 4.2. From this result, it can be seen that there is a significant difference in the representation content between VGG16 and

[1]https://github.com/gallantlab/pycortex

BERT regardless of the fixation or free viewing conditions.

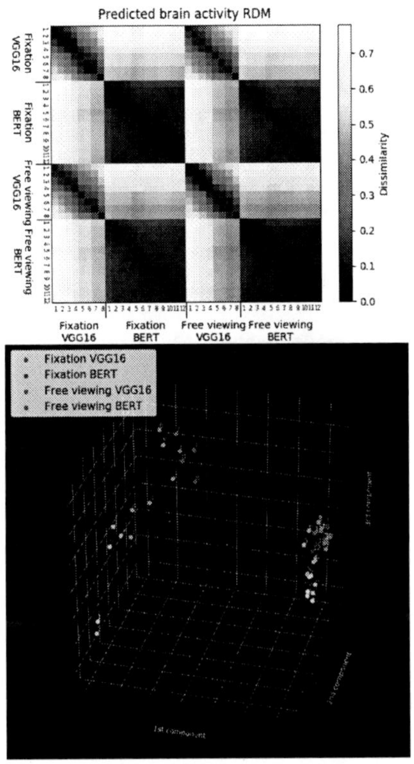

Figure 4: Similarity analysis of representation content

5 Discussion

In the experimental result of (i), we investigated the predictable regions of both models using RSA and found that the cortical localization becomes similar to that of BERT as VGG16 moves from lower to higher layers. In addition, from the result of the experiment (ii), it is observed that the pattern of similarity of information representation content is similar between the higher layer of VGG16 and that of BERT. We therefore estimated that the representational content in the two models is similar. However, from the result of experiment (iii), it was found that there is a significant difference in the representational content that can be modeled by VGG16 and BERT. In other words, our results suggest that VGG16 and BERT represent different brain information even in the same higher sensory cortex.

6 Conclusions

In this study, we have investigated the the hierarchical characteristics of cortical localization and representational content of visual and linguistic information on the cerebral cortex by means of RSA using prediction accuracy and contents. As a result, in the analysis of cortical localization using prediction accuracy, we found that VGG16, i.e., CNNs dealing with image features, was able to model the hierarchy in the cortical localization in the brain, and as it moved from lower to higher layers, it was able to predict brain regions closer to those predicted by BERT, i.e., DNNs dealing with linguistic features. Furthermore, in the analysis of information representation content with predicted brain activity, it was found that the higher layers of VGG16 can model complex cortical localization patterns in the cortex as well as BERT. However, we found a large gap between VGG16 and BERT in the comparison of the representational contents between the layers. These results suggest that visual information is represented in the same brain regions as linguistic information as it becomes more complex (e.g., category selection regions in the temporal cortex), but even within the same brain regions, there are significant differences between visual and linguistic information, and that modeling with VGG16 and BERT alone is not sufficient to fill in these differences. When cortical localization is similar between different modalities, we generally tend to conclude that the representational contents between them are also similar, but the results of this study suggest that the similarity relationship does not necessarily hold, which has an important message to encourage rethinking of the results of previous studies that tackle to elucidate brain information representation for different modalities based solely on the prediction accuracy of brain activity information. Based on this, we intend to continue to elucidate the characteristics between modalities.

References

Radoslaw Martin Cichy, Aditya Khosla, Dimitrios Pantazis, and Aude Torralba, Antonio an d Oliva. 2016. Comparison of deep neural networks to spatio-temporal cortical dynamics of human visual obj ect recognition reveals hierarchical correspondence. *Scientific Reports*, 6(1):27755.

Anders M Dale, Bruce Fischl, and Martin I Sereno. 1999. Cortical surface-based analysis: I. segmentation and surface reconstruction. *Neuroimage*, 9(2):179–194.

Jacob Devlin, Ming-Wei Chang, Kenton Lee, and Kristina Toutanova. 2019. BERT: Pre-training of deep bidirectional transformers for language understanding. In *Proceedings of the 2019 Conference of the North American Chapter of the Association for Computational Linguistics: Human Language Technologies, Volume 1 (Long and Short Papers)*, pages 4171–4186, Minneapolis, Minnesota. Association for Computational Linguistics.

Michael Eickenberg, Alexandre Gramfort, Gaël Varoquaux, and Bertrand Thirion. 2017. Seeing it all: Convolutional network layers map the function of the human visual system. *Neuroimage*, 152:184–194.

Christiane Fellbaum, editor. 1998. *WordNet: An Electronic Lexical Database*. Language, Speech, and Communication. MIT Press, Cambridge, MA.

Umut Güçlü and Marcel A J van Gerven. 2015. Deep neural networks reveal a gradient in the complexity of neural representations across t he ventral stream. *The Journal of neuroscience : the official journal of the Society for Neuroscience*, 35(27):10005–10014.

Sepp Hochreiter and Jürgen Schmidhuber. 1997. Long short-term memory. *Neural Computation*, 9(8):1735–1780.

Alexander G Huth, Wendy A de Heer, Thomas L Griffiths, and Jack L Theunissen, Frédéric E andĜallant. 2016. Natural speech reveals the semantic maps that tile human cerebral cortex. *Nature*, 532(7600):453–458.

Alexander G Huth, Shinji Nishimoto, An T Vu, and Jack L Gallant. 2012. A continuous semantic space describes the representation of thousands of object and action categories across the human brain. *Neuron*, 76(6):1210–1224.

Shailee Jain and Alexander Huth. 2018. Incorporating context into language encoding models for fmri. In *Advances in Neural Information Processing Systems*, volume 31. Curran Associates, Inc.

Nikolaus Kriegeskorte, Marieke Mur, and Peter Bandettini. 2008. Representational similarity analysis - connecting the branches of systems neuroscience. *Frontiers in Systems Neuroscience*, 2:4.

Tomas Mikolov, Ilya Sutskever, Kai Chen, Greg S Corrado, and Jeff Dean. 2013. Distributed representations of words and phrases and their compositio nality. In *Advances in Neural Information Processing Systems*, volume 26. Curran Associates, Inc.

Thomas Naselaris, Kendrick N. Kay, Shinji Nishimoto, and Jack L. Gallant. 2011. Encoding and decoding in fmri. *NeuroImage*, 56(2):400–410.

Satoshi Nishida, Antoine Blanc, Naoya Maeda, Masataka Kado, and Shinji Nishimoto. 2021. Behavioral correlates of cortical semantic representations modeled by word vectors. *PLoS Computational Biology*, 17(6):e1009138.

Soma Nonaka, Kei Majima, Shuntaro C Aoki, and Yukiyasu Kamitani. 2021. Brain hierarchy score: Which deep neural networks are hierarchically brain-like? *iScience*, 24(9):103013.

Karen Simonyan and Andrew Zisserman. 2014. Very deep convolutional networks for large-scale image recognition. *CoRR*, abs/1409.1556.

Jingyuan Sun, Shaonan Wang, Jiajun Zhang, and Chengqing Zong. 2021. Neural encoding and decoding with distributed sentence representations. *IEEE Trans. Neural Networks Learn. Syst.*, 32(2):589–603.

Daniel L. K. Yamins, Ha Hong, Charles F. Cadieu, Ethan A. Solomon, and James J. Seibert, Darren an d DiCarlo. 2014. Performance-optimized hierarchical models predict neural responses in higher visual cortex. *Proceedings of the National Academy of Sciences*, 111(23):8619–8624.

Differential Bias: On the Perceptibility of Stance Imbalance in Argumentation

Alonso Palomino[1] **Martin Potthast**[1] **Khalid Al-Khatib**[2] **Benno Stein**[3]

[1] Leipzig University `<first>.<last>@uni-leipzig.de`
[2] University of Groningen `khalid.alkhatib@rug.nl`
[3] Bauhaus-Universität Weimar `benno.stein@uni-weimar.de`

Abstract

Most research on natural language processing treats bias as an absolute concept: Based on a (probably complex) algorithmic analysis, a sentence, an article, or a text is classified as biased or not. Given the fact that for humans the question of whether a text is biased can be difficult to answer or is answered contradictory, we ask whether an "absolute bias classification" is a promising goal at all. We see the problem not in the complexity of interpreting language phenomena but in the diversity of sociocultural backgrounds of the readers, which cannot be handled uniformly: To decide whether a text has crossed the proverbial line between non-biased and biased is subjective. By asking "Is text X more [less, equally] biased than text Y?" we propose to analyze a simpler problem, which, by its construction, is rather independent of standpoints, views, or sociocultural aspects. In such a model, bias becomes a preference relation that induces a partial ordering from least biased to most biased texts without requiring a decision on where to draw the line. A prerequisite for this kind of bias model is the ability of humans to perceive relative bias differences in the first place. In our research, we selected a specific type of bias in argumentation, the stance bias, and designed a crowdsourcing study showing that differences in stance bias are perceptible when (light) support is provided through training or visual aid.

1 Introduction

Bias is a multifaceted phenomenon that can be wittingly or unwittingly introduced into language. Walton (1999) traces the term's history with argumentation and concludes that bias implies one-sidedness. Van Laar (2007) distinguishes two forms of biased argumentation, namely the exclusion of arguments of the pro or con position ("stance bias") and the exclusion of arguments discussing a certain aspect (frame) that is relevant to an issue. Figure 1 illustrates the spectrum of stance balance from a one-sided (left) to a balanced (right) situation. In between, an argument may be perceived as one-sided (biased) despite the inclusion of arguments from the other side if no sufficient balance is maintained. Nevertheless, a cleverly chosen stance imbalance can also serve as a rhetorical device for persuasion (Walton, 1999). Regardless of the actual balance of their arguments, both sides may accuse the other of bias due to one-sidedness.

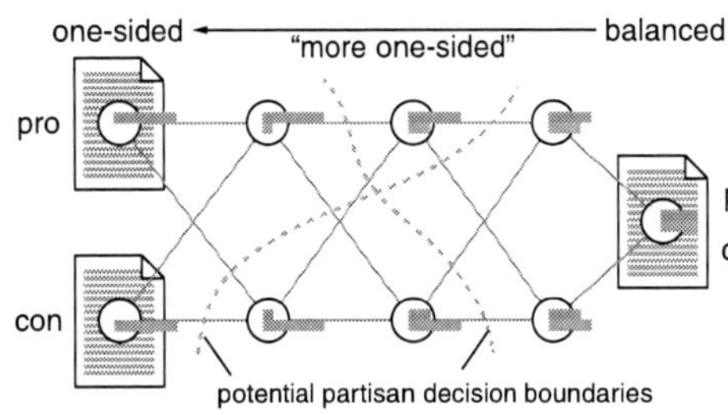

Figure 1: Stance bias induces a partial ordering of argumentations, the extremes being purely one-sided (left) or perfectly balanced (right). Where supporters of one side or the other draw the line between biased and non-biased depends on their degree of conviction.

The diversity of sociocultural backgrounds, environmental conditioning, or educational attainment makes it difficult to treat bias as an absolute concept for binary classification, except for extreme cases. Granted, when focusing on the relation between texts regarding their bias, one takes a step back both in terms of problem difficulty and predication. But, trying to model the "differential nature of bias" (differential bias) is a valid strategy to eliminate individual, subjective factors. By developing a measure of argumentative balance with respect to the stance (stance balance) that induces a partial ordering of argumentative texts, a gradual preference relation as shown in Figure 1 is established. As a consequence, the evaluation of one-sidedness cannot be decided for a single text but is constrained to insights from answers to the question: "Is text X more [less, equally] one-sided than text Y?"

Findings of the Association for Computational Linguistics: AACL-IJCNLP 2022, pages 411–421
November 20–23, 2022.

Using stance as an example, we investigate for the first time the extent to which differential bias is perceptible to human annotators—an important prerequisite for practical applications of debate technologies. Based on a model differential stance bias (Section 3), 720 human preference judgments are collected in a carefully designed crowdsourcing study (Section 4). Our analysis of the judgments shows that extreme imbalance is perceptible, whereas more subtle imbalance is not unless (mild) training is provided (Section 5).[1] This result is important for annotating language bias in general, for argument search engines, and for developing curricula for argument analysis (Section 6).

2 Related Work

After a brief review of research on bias in natural language processing (NLP), we survey bias and one-sidedness in argumentation, and the application of pairwise judgments in corpus construction.

2.1 Bias in Natural Language Processing

Blodgett et al. (2020) survey 146 papers that study various forms of bias, finding that "quantitative techniques for measuring or mitigating 'bias' are [often] poorly matched to their motivations." Sheng et al. (2021) survey 90 papers on societal biases in language generation that tackle gender, profession, race, religion, and sexuality, among which gender bias stands out as the most frequently studied form of bias. The literature review of 61 papers by Sun et al. (2019) focuses explicitly on recognizing and mitigating gender bias in NLP, concluding that the subfield still lacks a shared understanding, standardization, as well as evaluations that demonstrate the generalizability of current techniques. Shah et al. (2020) study bias formally and focus on how and where it is introduced into an NLP pipeline (e.g., semantic bias in embeddings, label and selection bias in data sources). Their survey of 93 papers overviews suggested countermeasures. Bender and Friedman (2018) proposes the use of "data statements" as a means to raise awareness of ethical issues among authors, which the ACL board has meanwhile taken up, and Hovy and Spruit (2016) outlines the ethical implications and impacts NLP systems have on society.

Although (social) bias has attracted much attention, to the best of our knowledge, only Spliethöver and Wachsmuth (2020) explicitly study social biases in argumentation, showing that current argument corpora are biased "in favor of male people with European-American names." However, two types of non-social biases have been studied more in-depth because of their relevance for argumentation: cognitive biases and one-sidedness bias.

2.2 Cognitive Biases in Argumentation

Huang et al. (2012) show that exposing decision makers—who exert confirmation bias via selective reading habits—to counterarguments will improve their decision outcomes. Wright et al. (2017) propose a visual "argument mapping" aid for intelligence analysts, which organizes arguments and counterarguments to better manage cognitive biases such as confirmation bias, anchoring, framing effects, and neglect of probability. These biases have recently also been studied by Kiesel et al. (2021), who discuss the challenges and opportunities of developing argumentative conversational search engines. For educators who teach argument evaluation, Diana et al. (2019, 2020) develop a measure that predicts if student assessments of argument strength are affected by confirmation bias; the measure is based on the alignment of individuals' values with values in political arguments. (Amorim et al., 2018) find that confirmation bias impacts peer-evaluation of student essays, which then propagate into automatic essay scoring systems.

2.3 One-Sidedness Bias in Argumentation

The following studies are of particular relevance to our contributions because of their focus on perceptions of bias in argumentation. Walton (1999) and Van Laar (2007) argue that bias in argumentation implies one-sidedness because a biased argumentation typically fails to be balanced, favoring one side of a topic, aspect, or stance over others. One-sidedness is a phenomenon that influences the perception of information seekers: Schlosser (2011) and Chen (2016) investigate the relation between reviewers' expertise, their bias, and product type when evaluating the utility of online product feedback. The authors observe that customers typically consider one-sided reviews more helpful than two-sided reviews because, in one-sided reviews, users usually consider aspects such as the expertise of the reviewer to be more significant in their purchase decision. Wolfe et al. (2013) analyze the process of students in understanding one-sided arguments: In two experiments that focus on measuring read-

[1] Code and data: https://github.com/webis-de/AACL-22

ing times and analyzing how students summarize neutral texts, the authors find that the processing of one-sided arguments is based on a "belief bias." Kienpointner and Kindt (1997) study one-sidedness of argumentation to understand the antagonistic climate of political debates about political assylum. They examine which aspects are included or excluded (global bias) and what strategies are used to address certain aspects (local bias).

Operationalizations of one-sidedness in argumentation have been contributed by Potthast et al. (2018) and Kiesel et al. (2019), who study writing-style-based approaches in order to detect hyperpartisan news; they organized a shared task that received more than 40 submissions. Stab and Gurevych (2016) choose a semantics-based approach to predict the presence or absence of opposing arguments in an argumentative text. Both approaches target only the extreme cases of one-sidedness (i.e., only pro or only con arguments; see Figure 1 on the far left). More generally, Küçük (2021) formulates the problem (without its operationalization) of predicting the ratio of pro, con, and neutral stances in argumentative corpora. Our work complements theirs by first answering the question whether stance bias can be perceived at all.

2.4 Relative Judgments in Argumentation

Kienpointner and Kindt (1997) point out that argument bias assessment requires judgment in relation to the argumentative context because of their complex properties. Lacking an objective reference, another piece of argumentation can be used instead. Two recent studies follow this approach: Habernal and Gurevych (2016) propose the task of predicting the convincingness of arguments, where given a pair of arguments with the same stance on an issue, the more convincing one must be chosen. From many such comparisons a global ranking can be statistically derived. Gienapp et al. (2020) apply the same approach to annotate argument quality while minimizing the number of comparisons required.

Beyond argumentation, (Howcroft et al., 2020) employ a relative judgment of summaries to rank them based on quality criteria, such as fluency and readability. Simpson et al. (2019) utilize pairwise comparisons to infer labels for humorous and metaphoric texts, and Gooding et al. (2019) do so to annotate words. Cattelan (2012) survey such analyses beyond NLP and computer science.

Text X on "Tidal Energy"	Text Y on "Tidal Energy"
Anchors of tidal energy systems can damage ecosystems. They might damage salt marshes, estuaries, and near-shore reefs, or alter the natural processes that maintain ocean and coastal ecosystems, such as the movement of sand, silt, animals, and larvae. Some fishing communities worry that their fishing grounds could be disturbed. Toxic hydraulic fluids might leak. Tidal energy could disrupt local fishing industries. While there may still be some concerns regarding the safety and local environmental impact of nuclear energy, nuclear energy releases 0-emissions and so is an important part of the fight against global warming. It should be pushed forward; tidal energy should not "replace" it. There is only one major tidal generating station in operation. This is a 240 megawatt station at the mouth of the La Rance river estuary on the northern coast of France (a large coal or nuclear power plant generates about 1,000 MW of electricity). Tidal energy generates very little energy comparatively.	Many forms of energy have potential environmental impacts. The focus should be on designing regulations that minimize or eliminate these impacts. Regulations can minimize the environmental impact of tidal energy. Bays and estuaries are always naturally "flushed" or cleansed and replenished by tide-waters flowing in and out. To the extent that tidal energy impairs the natural flows of these tides, it impairs this natural "flushing" mechanism. This can alter and even destroy an ecosystem. Tidal energy can slow the movement of water in a bay or estuary, which reduces the amount of kinetic energy and causes the body of water to freeze-over more often or for longer periods of time. This has consequences for marine eco-systems.Tidal energy can lead to undesirable prolonged winter icing. Offshore turbines do not alter the flow of tides as much as barrages can, so they have a smaller environmental impact. Offshore turbines don't hampert he flow of tides.

Figure 2: Which of the two argumentations (X vs. Y, left vs. right) is more biased? Answer is given below.

3 Measuring Differential Bias Perception

To measure the perceptibility of differential stance bias in argumentation in a controlled environment, we develop a basic experiment as shown in Figure 2. For two argumentations, X and Y, on the same topic, the central question to participants is: "Which of the two argumentations is more biased?" With a corpus of topic-labeled arguments at hand, the construction of pairs of argumentations for a given topic is straightforward. First, the number of pro arguments for X and Y is selected, each ranging from zero to four arguments. A corresponding number of pro arguments are randomly selected and randomly assigned to the available slots. Then, the remaining slots are randomly filled with random con arguments on the same topic. The two argumentations are shown side by side to be read one after the other and then compared. No 1:1 correspondence is to be assumed between arguments at the i-th position, $i = 1, \ldots, 4$, and therefore arguments are not aligned across argumentations.

Alternative experimental setups were explored as part of a pilot study to find the simplest ("atomic") setup to investigate our experiment variables of interest. In the following, an overview these variables is given (D = dependent, I = independent, C = controlled, U = uncontrolled):

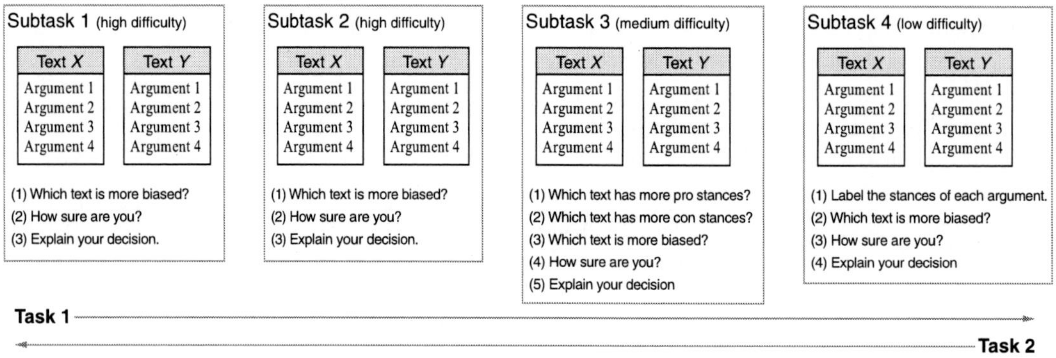

Figure 3: Two tasks organize the experiments in decreasing and increasing order of difficulty, respectively.

D perceptibility of differential stance bias

I_1 differential stance bias: 3 levels
I_2 difficulty: low, medium, high
I_3 participant training: autodidact vs. trained
I_4 participant expertise: stance labeling accuracy
I_5 participant confidence: 3-level self-assessment

C_1 argumentation length: 4 arguments each
C_2 argument length: 2-3 sentences each
C_3 argument frames: all arguments from 1 frame
C_4 order effects I: random order of arguments
C_5 order effects II: no textual coherence
C_6 opinion diversity: 9 participants per topic

U_1 stance perceptibility: e.g., explicit vs. implicit
U_2 other language biases: e.g., at the lexical level

Key to measuring D, the perceptibility of differential stance bias, is a model for independent variable I_1: Let X denote an argumentation on a given topic that argues pro or con a proposition, where $X = X^+ \cup X^-$ is the union of a set of pro arguments X^+ and con arguments X^-, so that $X^+ \cap X^- = \emptyset$. The stance balance δ between pro and con arguments in X is measured as the absolute size difference between X^+ and X^-:

$$\delta(X) = \big||X^+| - |X^-|\big|.$$

The closer δ is to 0, the more balanced the two sides are in X. Given a second argumentation Y, $|X| = |Y|$, the differential stance bias can then be quantified as the absolute difference between the stance balance scores of X and Y:

$$\Delta(X,Y) = |\delta(X) - \delta(Y)|.$$

The closer Δ is to 0, the less strong the differential bias is between X and Y. Given the designated argumentation length of $|X| = |Y| = 4$, the image of both δ and Δ is $\{0, 2, 4\}$.

Consider the "Tidal Energy" example in Figure 2: Argumentation X is an extreme case with only con arguments, argumentation Y is the balanced case with two pro (first, fourth) and two con arguments (second, third). This yields $\delta(X) = 4$ and $\delta(Y) = 0$ and thus $\Delta(X,Y) = 4$, the maximum possible differential bias in this setting. It follows that X is more biased than Y. Suppose Y consists of only pro arguments instead $(\delta(Y) = 4)$: Although X and Y argue exclusively on either the pro or the con side, both argumentations are equally imbalanced, so that $\Delta(X,Y) = 0$. The intermediate case of $\Delta(X,Y) = 2$ results when Y includes three pro and a single con argument or vice versa.

Regarding independent variable I_2 (see Figure 3), high difficulty means no indication is given about argument stance or stance balance before asking which of the two argumentations is more biased. Medium difficulty means we first ask which argumentation contains more pro arguments and which contains more con arguments before asking to select the more biased one—a subtle hint at stance balance. Low difficulty means the stance of each argument has to be labeled first as pro, neutral, con, or unknown, coloring each argument according to the chosen label. In this way, stance is strongly emphasized when answering the question which argument is more biased.

Experiments are presented in either decreasing (Task 1) or increasing (Task 2) order of difficulty (I_3; see Figure 3). Task 2 is also preceded by an explanation of the importance of stance balance in relation to bias, as well as an admission test for argument stance labeling that must be successfully completed. Note the different learning experiences participants have as they move through the two tasks. Two groups of participants are distinguished (I_4): those who succeed in stance labeling and those who get it wrong more than once. Also, participants are asked to self-assess their confidence (I_5).

The variables C_1-C_6 are tightly controlled by setting a specific value or by introducing diversity through randomization. Text lengths (C_1 and C_2) are kept as short as possible, and each argument has a similar length to the others, so that confounding by length differences is avoided.C_3 specifically avoids mixing up stance bias with Van Laar's second type of one-sidedness in argumentation with respect to topic frames. C_5 is due to the requirement to generate argumentative texts rather than reusing existing ones, although the texts are generally not extremely incoherent either. Variables beyond our control include the difficulty of distinguishing pro and con stances in the argument corpus (some arguments are more subtly pro or con than others; U_1), and (social) language biases that may be due to word choice (U_2). Nevertheless, we manually checked for hate speech and removed corresponding arguments, as well as analyzed for biased terminology using dictionaries.

4 Crowdsourcing Study

Our crowdsourcing study implements the assessment of the perceptibility of differential stance bias on Amazon Mechanical Turk (MTurk). We give an overview of the task design and its instantiation using an argument corpus.

4.1 Argument Corpus

Arguments from the Webis-Argument-Framing-19 corpus (Ajjour et al., 2019) were used to populate the tasks. It includes 12,000 arguments on 465 topics sourced from debatepedia.org. Each argument is labeled with its topic, pro or con stance, and frame. Table 1a shows three examples. Topics with fewer than 8 arguments of comparable length available with the same frame label were excluded (C_2, C_3). From the remaining topics, 40 argument pairs were randomly generated (see Figure 2). Table 1b shows the distribution of argument pairs across the six differential bias cases implied by our model (I_1).

To exercise "limited control" over possible linguistic biases (U_2), we use the Linguistic Inquiry and Word Count (LIWC) 2022 (Tausczik and Pennebaker, 2010),[2] a dictionary-based tool for identifying psycholinguistic, thematic, and tonal properties of language. All selected arguments score low on tone and swearing. Nevertheless, we manually reviewed each argument for quality and to ensure that they do not contain offensive language.

[2]https://www.liwc.app/

4.2 Study Execution

We created 20 "Human Intelligence Tasks" (HITs) on MTurk, 10 for each of the two tasks, and distributed the 40 argument pairs to them as subtasks (see Figure 3). A total of 571 workers participated, each of whom was allowed to participate only once. Repeated participation would have undermined the learning experience of a task and thus the results achieved. One task took 45 minutes and was paid at 6 USD or 8 USD per hour.

The tasks are implemented in the form of a dialog, one subtask per step. For quality control (see below) JavaScript code was inserted to monitor the workers. As in Figure 2, a pair of arguments was presented side by side in columns as titled boxes with borders. The dialog could only be worked through forward, using JavaScript to ensure that workers complete a subtask first before moving on. Moving back was prevented retrospective revisions, which is particularly relevant for Task 1, where subtasks are arranged in decreasing order of difficulty (I_2). Since nine workers (C_6) worked independently on the same subtask, the arguments in each argumentation X and Y were randomly shuffled for each worker (C_4).

The following measures were taken for quality control: (1) work times: exclusion of workers who took less than 3 minutes to read instructions or less than 8 minutes to complete a subtask; (2) MACE score (Hovy et al., 2013): exclusion of workers whose score is below 80%; (3) approval rate: exclusion of workers whose MTurk approval rate was below 90%; and (4) language proficiency: exclusion of workers who submitted many grammatical or spelling errors or random text in the mandatory comment fields for decision rationales in each subtask. For Task 2, an admission test had to be passe. Finally, we ensured that each task contained subtasks with ($\Delta(X, Y) = 0$) and without ($\Delta(X, Y) > 0$) differential stance bias. In this way, workers who are able to distinguish the two types can be distinguished from those who cannot.

(a)

Labels		Argument
Topic:	Abortion	No individual has rights over another individual. Therefore, a fetus cannot be said to have an inviolable right to a woman's body and sustenance from that body. A woman can, therefore, decide to deprive the fetus of the usage of her body (abortion). A fetus cannot have a right to a woman's body to sustain its life.
Stance:	Pro	
Frame:	Fetus rights	
Topic:	Death penalty	The U.N. does not support the death penalty. In all the courts we have set up (U.N. officials) have not included death penalty. United Nations oppose the death penalty.
Stance:	Con	
Frame:	Internat. law	
Topic:	Capitalism vs. Socialism	This type of helpful framework neglects appeals for human rights and any other framework of deontology, morality, ethics, etc. Capitalism can embrace the utilitarian framework while not precluding any form of decision calculus in policymaking to protect human rights. Socialist leadership cannot protect human rights effectively.
Stance:	Pro	
Frame:	Rights	

(b)

Differential Bias		Experiments	
$\Delta(X,Y)$	$\delta(X){:}\delta(Y)$	HITs	Workers
0	0:0	6	54
0	2:2	7	63
0	4:4	6	54
2	2:0 / 0:2	7	63
2	4:2 / 2:4	7	63
4	4:0 / 0:4	7	63

(c)

Bias	Precision		Accuracy
$\delta(X){:}\delta(Y)$	Pro	Con	
0:0	0.80	0.90	0.84
2:2	0.80	0.66	0.77
4:4	0.61	0.40	0.62
4:2 / 2:4	0.44	0.35	0.44
4:0 / 0:4	0.80	0.62	0.76
2:0 / 0:2	0.52	0.60	0.55
Avg.	0.66	0.59	0.66

Table 1: (a) Examples of arguments from the top three most frequent topics in the Webis-Argument-Framing-19 corpus. (b) The stance distributions and the number of instances considered for the crowdsourcing study. (c) The crowd worker precision and accuracy for labeling pro/con arguments.

5 Results and Analysis

This section reports workers' perception accuracy for differential stance bias with respect to the independent variables discussed in Section 3.

5.1 Perceptibility of Differential Stance Bias

Table 2a shows workers' overall perception accuracy of differential stance bias (I_1). Argument pairs without differential stance bias $\Delta(X,Y) = 0$) are less well perceived as such, with an average of 0.42 in Task 1 and 0.57 in Task 2, than argument pairs with differential stance bias ($\Delta(X,Y) > 0$; average of 0.55 in Task 1 and 0.72 in Task 2). The highest accuracy is obtained for the 2:0 / 0:2 distribution (0.56 and 0.76 in Tasks 1 and 2) and the lowest for the 0:0 distribution (0.46 and 0.51 in Tasks 1 and 2). The higher a differential stance bias, the easier it is for workers to perceive it.

Furthermore, we find that workers who are successful at labeling the stance of individual arguments (I_4; part of subtasks of low difficulty) are also more successful at perceiving differential stance bias. Table 1c shows the workers' precision and accuracy for stance labeling. Only the pro and con arguments are displayed. Workers who could not decide (label "unknown") or label an argument as neutral are excluded from further analysis, since all arguments are either pro or con. An average accuracy of 0.62 is achieved for stance labeling, ranging from 0.44 to 0.84 depending on the differential bias distribution. Table 2d shows that workers with high competence in stance labeling (accuracy > 0.7) achieve a perception accuracy for differential stance bias of 0.59 in Task 1 and 0.67 in Task 2, but workers with low competence achieve only 0.31 in Task 1 and 0.42 in Task 2.

An examination of whether workers' educational attainment (collected by questionnaire) affects perception accuracy is negative. The highest degrees attained are high school (20%), bachelor (60%), and master or higher (20%), and the Pearson correlations range from -0.08 to 0.0 for Task 1 and 0.01 to 0.0 for Task 2.

5.2 Dependence on Difficulty and Training

Table 2c shows perception accuracy as a function of difficulty (I_2) and difficulty order (I_3). In both tasks, perception accuracy increases the lower the difficulty of the subtask. The accuracy at high difficulty is 0.38 for Task 1 and 0.58 for Task 2. Accuracy at medium difficulty is 0.55 for Task 1 (0.17 improvement over high difficulty) and 0.67 for Task 2 (0.09 decrease below high difficulty). At low difficulty, workers achieve the highest accuracy of 0.64 in Task 1 and 0.74 in Task 2. Although an improvement in perception accuracy can be observed between high and low difficulty, workers in

(a)

Differential Bias		Accuracy per Subtask and Difficulty							
$\Delta(X,Y)$	$\delta(X){:}\delta(Y)$	1.1	1.2	1.3	1.4	2.1	2.2	2.3	2.4
0	0:0	0.27	0.33	0.58	0.66	0.60	0.55	0.42	0.50
0	2:2	0.33	0.28	0.56	0.57	0.62	0.67	0.56	0.54
0	4:4	0.11	0.36	0.44	0.64	0.70	0.64	0.52	0.50
2	2:0 / 0:2	0.41	0.60	0.55	0.68	0.88	0.86	0.62	0.70
2	4:2 / 2:4	0.44	0.44	0.55	0.65	0.77	0.69	0.66	0.59
4	4:0 / 0:4	0.45	0.55	0.68	0.70	0.88	0.66	0.75	0.66

(b)

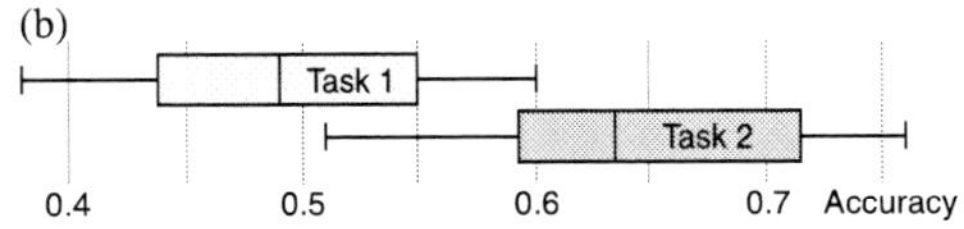

(c)

Average Accuracy per Task and Subtask Difficulty							
Sec.	Type	Acc.	Δ Acc.	Sec.	Type	Acc.	Δ Acc.
1.1 / 1.2	1	0.38	0.00	2.1	3	0.74	0.00
1.3	2	0.55	0.17	2.2	2	0.67	−0.07
1.4	3	0.64	0.09	2.3 / 2.4	1	0.58	−0.09

(d)

Differential Bias		Accuracy per Worker Competence Level															
		Task 1								Task 2							
		Low				High				Low				High			
$\Delta(X,Y)$	$\delta(X){:}\delta(Y)$	1.1	1.2	1.3	1.4	1.1	1.2	1.3	1.4	2.1	2.2	2.3	2.4	2.1	2.2	2.3	2.4
0	0:0	0.11	0.00	0.18	0.28	0.37	0.55	0.66	0.53	0.55	0.44	0.33	0.24	0.61	0.63	0.55	0.66
0	2:2	0.14	0.33	0.42	0.11	0.44	0.22	0.52	0.55	0.43	0.25	0.22	0.12	0.70	0.65	0.50	0.55
0	4:4	0.00	0.26	0.33	0.24	0.68	0.44	0.66	0.48	0.50	0.33	0.48	0.44	0.62	0.55	0.66	0.58
2	2:0 / 0:2	0.20	0.44	0.55	0.35	0.72	0.66	0.63	0.68	0.66	0.60	0.50	0.54	0.80	0.75	0.58	0.72
2	4:2 / 2:4	0.48	0.45	0.42	0.28	0.55	0.77	0.60	0.66	0.52	0.57	0.55	0.33	1.0	0.88	0.70	0.66
4	4:0 / 0:4	0.55	0.36	0.48	0.60	0.66	0.62	0.74	0.76	0.61	0.46	0.56	0.20	0.75	0.68	0.68	0.64
Average		0.25	0.31	0.40	0.31	0.57	0.54	0.63	0.61	0.54	0.44	0.40	0.29	0.74	0.69	0.61	0.63

Table 2: Perception accuracy of differential stance bias (a) dependent on subtask, and subtask difficulty (high: 1.1, 1.2, 2.1, and 2.2; medium: 1.3 and 2.3; low: 1.4 and 2.4), (b) dependent on task, (c) dependent on task and subtask difficulty, and (d) dependent on worker competence at argument stance labeling.

Task 1 seem to be confused by the change from high to medium difficulty. However, the relative improvement in accuracy between high and low difficulty is the same for both tasks.

The perception accuracy differs in absolute terms between Task 1 (high to low difficulty) and Task 2 (training, then low to high difficulty). Table 2b shows that workers achieve an accuracy of 0.38 to 0.60 with an average of 0.52 in Task 1 and an accuracy of 0.51 to 0.76 with an average of 0.64 in Task 2. This accuracy difference (about 0.15) suggests that there is a positive effect of training workers to perform more difficult subtasks, rather than expecting them to detect differential stance bias off hand. The difference is significant according to Welch's t-test, with a test statistic of 4.28 and a p value of 0.001.

5.3 Worker Confidence and Feedback

Participants had to self-assess their confidence in each subtask as "very sure," "reasonably sure," and "uncertain" (I_5). When workers gave either of the first two self-assessments, they have higher perception accuracies, albeit dependent on of the presence of differential stance bias. For Task 1, an accuracy of 0.58 is achieved in cases with differential stance bias, and an accuracy of 0.69 for Task 2. The lowest accuracies are observed when workers self-assess their confidence as "not sure", where the accuracy falls to 0.42 in Task 1 and 0.65 in Task 2.

For a qualitative assessment of the workers' abilities, we asked them to justify their decision as to which of the two argumentations is more biased. In reviewing the collected justifications, we found that some workers cited other types of bias in addition to stance bias. Table 3 shows selected justifications of the workers on subtasks with different differential bias distributions, depending on whether the workers chose the more biased argumentation correctly, or incorrectly. While one worker argues about the emotional tone of the argument chain on a subtask with differential bias distribution of 4:4, another worker addresses the factuality of the arguments on a subtask with a distribution of 4:0/0:4.

Differential Bias		Decision Justification		
$\Delta(X,Y)$	$\delta(x):\delta(y)$	Topic	Correct	Incorrect
0	0:0	Globalization	I'm not completely sure about the second paragraph in text X but I think overall both texts have 2 con and 2 pro paragraphs: X: pro-con-con-pro Y: con-pro-con-pro	It is a complex issue and at least one argument on both texts could be constructed as in favor or against globalization, depending on the reader's initial stance.
0	2:2	Adult Incest	Both texts have pros and cons regarding incest.	Text Y features three pro arguments, whereas text X has an equal share of pro and con arguments.
0	4:4	Animal Testing	Both X and Y have an even amount of pro and con arguments. The first argument in Y is in a slight gray area, but it seems to be against the spirit of animal testing overall so. I counted it as a con.	X favors the side of animal life being sacred more and a more emotional argument chain
2	2:0 / 0:2	Banning Cell Phones in Cars	Y posts three points on the good cellphones in cars can do and though it does present the cons they are vastly outweighed in the argument	Because X is more pro arguments
2	4:2 / 2:4	Tidal Energy	Text Y is more one-sided as it explains more cons of tidal energy than pros of it, whereas text X has an equal number of pros and cons.	Y is talking about megawatts and energy and anchors and cables while X speaks in a Reader's Digest form that most are able to understand
4	4:0 / 0:4	Atheism	X only makes arguments against atheism and tries to justify acts of religion. Y gives quite logical arguments and doesn't seem to be very one sided.	X seems more to add their own opinion, while Y explains more of the facts.

Table 3: Examples of worker decision justifications dependent on differential bias.

Some workers base their decisions on the perceived degree of subjectivity or objectivity of their arguments. Others argue about the constructiveness, persuasiveness, rationality, and verifiability of the arguments. Comparing the justifications in Task 1 with those in Task 2, many workers in Task 1 stick to their initial explanations used in the first subtasks. In contrast, workers in Task 2 more often realize that the study is about stance balance.

6 Conclusions and Future Work

How one-sided can an argumentation be without this one-sidedness going unnoticed? In political debates, parties often accuse each other of one-sidedness. An advanced debating skill hence is to subtly shift the balance of an argumentation so that it goes unnoticed, especially by potential voters. But political debate is perhaps only one of the most extreme cases in which skewed argumentation can be found, as Kienpointner and Kindt (1997) point out in their in-depth analysis of letters to the editor regarding the topic of political asylum. We believe that a perfectly balanced argument is the exception rather than the rule because, after all, the goal is to convince the audience of one's own opinion. For this reason, audiences must try to be alert to (subtle) manipulation opportunities, and here formal training to detect differences in stance bias seems a promising future direction. The results of our study indicate that differences in stance bias are perceptible, and even more so when (as in our crowdsourcing setting) workers are trained with a visual aid in the form of green/red signals that emphasize the stance of the arguments. In an online setting where arguments are read at leisure, a tool that highlights the distribution of stances could help readers make more informed decisions, not to mention formal training in the context of a debate.

Our study further demonstrates, to our knowledge for the first time, the viability of assessing bias via relative judgments rather than absolute ones. In this regard, we focus on stance bias for its ease of operationalization. It is likely that many other types of bias can be similarly addressed in future work, although not all of them can be operationalized as easily as in our study. In any case, the obvious benefits of reducing the subjective bias of annotators certainly justify further investigation and the development of a theory in this direction. This should, of course, include research on the interactions of biases, since not all biases can be easily controlled. For instance, some workers based their judgments not only on differences in stance, but also pointed to other language properties that, in their opinion, made one argumentation seem more one-sided than another. Although we took great care to exclude examples of language bias, subtle biases may still have been present in our sample. A straightforward and fascinating application of our differential bias model is to extend it to the study of frame bias.

Ethical Statement

Our study involved human annotators recruited via the Amazon Mechanical Turk (MTurk) crowdsourcing platform. In accordance with fair compensation guidelines for crowd workers, we ensured an appropriate hourly rate. As is common with Mturk, some worker accounts attempted to submit fake data. We reviewed all cases that met our study's exclusion criteria regarding rejection of submitted work. As part of the quality control process, in addition to open rejection, we also introduced "internal rejection," which resulted in acceptance of the submitted work with full payment but exclusion from our analysis. We decided to play it safe and discard internally in ambiguous cases. All workers were informed about the study and agreed to the quality controls and compensation conditions before work began.

One limitation of our study is that it focuses on differences between stance biases. We are aware that several factors play a role in making an argumentation biased such as the frame of an argumentation, logical connections between arguments, (lack of) cohesion and strength of arguments, or social biases resulting from loaded language. However, it remains an open problem to define the semantics of these biases. Of course, laboratory experiments are always limited in this or similar ways, and our experiment is no different. We do not foresee any unethical uses of our results or its underlying tools, but hope that it will contribute to advancing the discourse on bias, and help to depart from from absolute bias claims.

References

Yamen Ajjour, Milad Alshomary, Henning Wachsmuth, and Benno Stein. 2019. Modeling Frames in Argumentation. In *2019 Conference on Empirical Methods in Natural Language Processing and 9th International Joint Conference on Natural Language Processing (EMNLP 2019)*, pages 2922–2932. ACL.

Evelin Amorim, Márcia Cançado, and Adriano Veloso. 2018. Automated Essay Scoring in the Presence of Biased Ratings. In *Proceedings of the 2018 Conference of the North American Chapter of the Association for Computational Linguistics: Human Language Technologies, NAACL-HLT 2018, New Orleans, Louisiana, USA, June 1-6, 2018, Volume 1 (Long Papers)*, pages 229–237. Association for Computational Linguistics.

Emily M. Bender and Batya Friedman. 2018. Data Statements for Natural Language Processing: Toward Mitigating System Bias and Enabling Better Science. *Trans. Assoc. Comput. Linguistics*, 6:587–604.

Su Lin Blodgett, Solon Barocas, Hal Daumé III, and Hanna M. Wallach. 2020. Language (Technology) is Power: A Critical Survey of "Bias" in NLP. In *Proceedings of the 58th Annual Meeting of the Association for Computational Linguistics, ACL 2020, Online, July 5-10, 2020*, pages 5454–5476. Association for Computational Linguistics.

Manuela Cattelan. 2012. Models for paired comparison data: A review with emphasis on dependent data. *Statistical Science*, 27(3):412–433.

Ming-Yi Chen. 2016. Can Two-sided Messages Increase the Helpfulness of Online Reviews? *Online Information Review*, 40(3):316–332.

Nicholas Diana, John C. Stamper, and Ken Koedinger. 2019. Predicting Bias in the Evaluation of Unlabeled Political Arguments. In *Proceedings of the 41th Annual Meeting of the Cognitive Science Society, CogSci 2019: Creativity + Cognition + Computation, Montreal, Canada, July 24-27, 2019*, pages 1640–1646. cognitivesciencesociety.org.

Nicholas Diana, John C. Stamper, and Ken Koedinger. 2020. Towards Value-Adaptive Instruction: A Data-Driven Method for Addressing Bias in Argument Evaluation Tasks. In *CHI '20: CHI Conference on Human Factors in Computing Systems, Honolulu, HI, USA, April 25-30, 2020*, pages 1–11. ACM.

Lukas Gienapp, Benno Stein, Matthias Hagen, and Martin Potthast. 2020. Efficient Pairwise Annotation of Argument Quality. In *58th Annual Meeting of the Association for Computational Linguistics (ACL 2020)*, pages 5772–5781. Association for Computational Linguistics.

Sian Gooding, Ekaterina Kochmar, Advait Sarkar, and Alan Blackwell. 2019. Comparative judgments are more consistent than binary classification for labelling word complexity. In *Proceedings of the 13th*

Linguistic Annotation Workshop, pages 208–214, Florence, Italy. Association for Computational Linguistics.

Ivan Habernal and Iryna Gurevych. 2016. Which argument is more convincing? analyzing and predicting convincingness of web arguments using bidirectional LSTM. In *Proceedings of the 54th Annual Meeting of the Association for Computational Linguistics (Volume 1: Long Papers)*, pages 1589–1599, Berlin, Germany. Association for Computational Linguistics.

Dirk Hovy, Taylor Berg-Kirkpatrick, Ashish Vaswani, and Eduard H. Hovy. 2013. Learning Whom to Trust with MACE. In *Human Language Technologies: Conference of the North American Chapter of the Association of Computational Linguistics, Proceedings, June 9-14, 2013, Westin Peachtree Plaza Hotel, Atlanta, Georgia, USA*, pages 1120–1130. The Association for Computational Linguistics.

Dirk Hovy and Shannon L. Spruit. 2016. The Social Impact of Natural Language Processing. In *Proceedings of the 54th Annual Meeting of the Association for Computational Linguistics, ACL 2016, August 7-12, 2016, Berlin, Germany, Volume 2: Short Papers*. The Association for Computer Linguistics.

David M. Howcroft, Anya Belz, Miruna-Adriana Clinciu, Dimitra Gkatzia, Sadid A. Hasan, Saad Mahamood, Simon Mille, Emiel van Miltenburg, Sashank Santhanam, and Verena Rieser. 2020. Twenty years of confusion in human evaluation: NLG needs evaluation sheets and standardised definitions. In *Proceedings of the 13th International Conference on Natural Language Generation*, pages 169–182, Dublin, Ireland. Association for Computational Linguistics.

Hsieh-Hong Huang, Jack Shih-Chieh Hsu, and Cheng-Yuan Ku. 2012. Understanding the Role of Computer-mediated Counter-argument in Countering Confirmation Bias. *Decision Support Systems*, 53(3):438–447.

Manfred Kienpointner and Walther Kindt. 1997. On the problem of bias in political argumentation: An investigation into discussions about political asylum in germany and austria. *Journal of pragmatics*, 27(5):555–585.

Johannes Kiesel, Maria Mestre, Rishabh Shukla, Emmanuel Vincent, Payam Adineh, David Corney, Benno Stein, and Martin Potthast. 2019. SemEval-2019 Task 4: Hyperpartisan News Detection. In *13th International Workshop on Semantic Evaluation (SemEval 2019)*, pages 829–839. Association for Computational Linguistics.

Johannes Kiesel, Damiano Spina, Henning Wachsmuth, and Benno Stein. 2021. The Meant, the Said, and the Understood: Conversational Argument Search and Cognitive Biases. In *3rd Conference on Conversational User Interfaces (CUI 2021)*, New York. ACM.

Dilek Küçük. 2021. Stance Quantification: Definition of the Problem.

Martin Potthast, Johannes Kiesel, Kevin Reinartz, Janek Bevendorff, and Benno Stein. 2018. A Stylometric Inquiry into Hyperpartisan and Fake News. In *56th Annual Meeting of the Association for Computational Linguistics (ACL 2018)*, pages 231–240. Association for Computational Linguistics.

Ann E. Schlosser. 2011. Can Including Pros and Cons Increase the Helpfulness and Persuasiveness of Online Reviews? The Interactive Effects of Ratings and Arguments. *Journal of Consumer Psychology*, 21(3):226–239.

Deven Shah, H. Andrew Schwartz, and Dirk Hovy. 2020. Predictive Biases in Natural Language Processing Models: A Conceptual Framework and Overview. In *Proceedings of the 58th Annual Meeting of the Association for Computational Linguistics, ACL 2020, Online, July 5-10, 2020*, pages 5248–5264. Association for Computational Linguistics.

Emily Sheng, Kai-Wei Chang, Prem Natarajan, and Nanyun Peng. 2021. Societal Biases in Language Generation: Progress and Challenges. In *Proceedings of the 59th Annual Meeting of the Association for Computational Linguistics and the 11th International Joint Conference on Natural Language Processing, ACL/IJCNLP 2021, (Volume 1: Long Papers), Virtual Event, August 1-6, 2021*, pages 4275–4293. Association for Computational Linguistics.

Edwin Simpson, Erik-Lân Do Dinh, Tristan Miller, and Iryna Gurevych. 2019. Predicting humorousness and metaphor novelty with Gaussian process preference learning. In *Proceedings of the 57th Annual Meeting of the Association for Computational Linguistics*, pages 5716–5728, Florence, Italy. Association for Computational Linguistics.

Maximilian Spliethöver and Henning Wachsmuth. 2020. Argument from Old Man's View: Assessing Social Bias in Argumentation. In *7th Workshop on Argument Mining*, pages 76–87. Association for Computational Linguistics.

Christian Stab and Iryna Gurevych. 2016. Recognizing the Absence of Opposing Arguments in Persuasive Essays. In *Proceedings of the Third Workshop on Argument Mining, hosted by the 54th Annual Meeting of the Association for Computational Linguistics, ArgMining@ACL 2016, August 12, Berlin, Germany*. The Association for Computer Linguistics.

Tony Sun, Andrew Gaut, Shirlyn Tang, Yuxin Huang, Mai ElSherief, Jieyu Zhao, Diba Mirza, Elizabeth M. Belding, Kai-Wei Chang, and William Yang Wang. 2019. Mitigating Gender Bias in Natural Language Processing: Literature Review. In *Proceedings of the 57th Conference of the Association for Computational Linguistics, ACL 2019, Florence, Italy, July 28- August 2, 2019, Volume 1: Long Papers*, pages 1630–1640. Association for Computational Linguistics.

Yla R Tausczik and James W Pennebaker. 2010. The psychological meaning of words: Liwc and computerized text analysis methods. *Journal of language and social psychology*, 29(1):24–54.

Jan Albert Van Laar. 2007. One-Sided Arguments. *Synthese*, 154(2):307–327.

Douglas Walton. 1999. *One-sided Arguments: A Dialectical Analysis of Bias*. SUNY Press.

Michael B. Wolfe, Shawna M. Tanner, and Andrew R. Taylor. 2013. Processing and Representation of Arguments in One-Sided Texts About Disputed Topics. *Discourse Processes*, 50(7):457–497.

William Wright, David Sheffield, and Stephanie Santosa. 2017. Argument Mapper: Countering Cognitive Biases in Analysis with Critical (Visual) Thinking. In *21st International Conference Information Visualisation, IV 2017, London, United Kingdom, July 11-14, 2017*, pages 250–255. IEEE Computer Society.

BEAMR: Beam Reweighing with Attribute Discriminators for Controllable Text Generation

David Landsman
The Vanguard Group

Jerry Zikun Chen
The Vanguard Group

Hussain Zaidi
The Vanguard Group

{david_landsman, jerry_chen, hussain_zaidi}@vanguard.com

Abstract

Recent advances in natural language processing have led to the availability of large pre-trained language models (LMs), with rich generative capabilities. Although these models are able to produce fluent and coherent text, it remains a challenge to control various attributes of the generation, including sentiment, formality, topic and many others. We propose a Beam Reweighing (BEAMR) method, building on top of standard beam search, in order to control different attributes. BEAMR combines any generative LM with any attribute discriminator, offering full flexibility of generation style and attribute, while the beam search backbone maintains fluency across different domains. Notably, BEAMR allows practitioners to leverage pre-trained models without the need to train generative LMs together with discriminators. We evaluate BEAMR in two diverse tasks: sentiment steering, and machine translation formality. Our results show that BEAMR performs on par with or better than existing state-of-the-art approaches (including fine-tuned methods), and highlight the flexibility of BEAMR in both causal and seq2seq language modeling tasks.

1 Introduction

Text generation has improved significantly in recent years due to architectural advances in deep learning (namely, the transformer architecture and attention mechanism (Vaswani et al., 2017)) and training paradigms, allowing practitioners to train large language models on vast, unlabelled corpora, and transfer knowledge between various domains.

Controllable text generation involves generating text according to specific requirements, which may include a specific topic (Baheti et al., 2018), attribute (Goswamy et al., 2020), reward signal (Tambwekar et al., 2019), or other potential constraints. This task presents significant challenges, as large, unlabelled corpora are unlikely to be sufficient for learning domain-specific, controllable characteristics, and thus transferring knowledge becomes substantially more difficult. Moreover, due to the growing size of recent language models it is also less feasible to train and finetune them for many different controllable dimensions.

Recent work in controllable text generation involves various ways of incorporating desired attributes into the text generated by the base LM. Many approaches (Yang and Klein, 2021; Liu et al., 2021; Ghazvininejad et al., 2017) rely directly on decoding-time strategies in order to steer the generation towards a desired attribute. However, these approaches typically rely on token-level decoding which can result in various disfluencies in the output (e.g., repetition) (Holtzman et al., 2020) or limited generalizability due to tight coupling between the generation and attribute models. Several works (Dathathri et al., 2020; Keskar et al., 2019; Krause et al., 2020; Zeldes et al., 2020; Khalifa et al., 2021) attempt to tune a portion of the base LM in order to steer it towards a desired attribute. This tuning is either performed directly on the LM (i.e. via a fine-tuning stage), or using an auxiliary attribute model and applying gradient perturbations to LM latent states.

In this work, we propose a simple and robust decoding-based approach to controllable text generation, allowing practitioners to leverage existing, pre-trained, generative LMs and existing attribute models. Our method first uses the beam search algorithm to propose fluent and relevant candidates for a given input prompt from a generative language model. Subsequently, the candidates are scored by a discriminative model trained for a particular attribute (e.g., sentiment analysis, emotion detection, or topic classification). The candidate scores produced by beam search are combined with the scores from the discriminative model to produce a distribution over the candidates. We then sample

Findings of the Association for Computational Linguistics: AACL-IJCNLP 2022, pages 422–437
November 20–23, 2022. ©2022 Association for Computational Linguistics

a single candidate generation from this distribution. Our method solves some of the existing issues in controllable text generation approaches, by (1) leveraging beam search to produce more fluent and relevant candidates, (2) expanding the generalizability of controllable generation via a custom similarity measure that can be selected based on the discriminative model, and (3) eliminating the need for tight coupling between the generative and discriminative models by reweighing at the natural language level, agnostic to the tokenization scheme, thereby allowing practitioners to leverage strong models for generation and scoring.

We perform several experiments with our approach, compare to several state-of-the-art methods for controllable text generation and show that BEAMR is generalizable to various LMs and target applications. First, we experiment with controlling the sentiment of generations using an attribute model finetuned for sentiment analysis. We then highlight the generalizability of the BEAMR method by applying it to the sequence-to-sequence task of adjusting the formality of text translated from Spanish to English. In sentiment steering experiments, BEAMR outperforms the SOTA DExperts model (Liu et al., 2021) in positive steering, and offers good control ability in negative steering, while significantly outperforming all baselines in terms of fluency. We perform a human evaluation study on the sentiment steering task which aligns with the observations from automated evaluations. In machine translation formality experiments, BEAMR outperforms the FUDGE baseline in both translation accuracy and formality score. Hyperparameter experiments with BEAMR in both tasks highlight potential tradeoffs between fluency and attribute control.

2 Background

Generative language models learn to produce a distribution for the next token in a sequence given past context as input. Given a prompt sequence of tokens, $\mathbf{c}_t = \{x_1, x_2, \ldots, x_t\}$ where $x_i \in \mathcal{V}$ and $\mathcal{V}$ is a vocabulary of tokens, we can produce a distribution $p(x \mid \mathbf{c}_t)$ for the next token in the sequence,

$$\begin{aligned} \mathbf{o}_t &= f_\theta(\mathbf{c}_t) \\ p(x \mid \mathbf{c}_t) &= \text{softmax}(\mathbf{o}_t) \end{aligned} \quad (1)$$

where $\mathbf{o}_t$ is the logit vector given by a LM f_θ. Using the distribution in Eqn. (1) there are several common methods of generating a continuation of the prompt $\mathbf{c}_t$.

Greedy. In this approach, tokens are generated by iteratively choosing the most likely token from $p(x \mid \mathbf{c}_t)$, and updating the prompt $\mathbf{c}$.

Beam Search. In this approach, a set of most likely candidates are maintained at each timestep. First, K possible tokens are sampled or selected from $p(x \mid \mathbf{c}_t)$. At each subsequent step, beam search expands the search space to K^2 possible hypotheses, before pruning back down to K based on the likelihood of the candidates. For a given candidate $\mathbf{b}_t = \{b_1, b_2, \ldots, b_t\}$, the likelihood is computed as

$$\ell(\mathbf{b}_t) = \sum_{j \leq t} \log p(b_j \mid \mathbf{b}_{<j}) \quad (2)$$

Diverse Beam Search. Vijayakumar et al. (2018) proposed a modified version of beam search in order to produce more diverse candidates. They divide the set of all candidates into G disjoint groups, and incorporate a group dissimilarity metric into the likelihood calculation.

3 Beam Reweighing

We propose to modify the beam search algorithm by reweighing the candidate likelihoods in order to control a diverse set of attributes of the text, such as sentiment, formality, emotion or topic. Our method first decodes a set of K candidates, using diverse beam search (Vijayakumar et al., 2018) to improve variety among the candidates. The candidates are then scored using an attribute model. We then reweigh their likelihoods $\ell(\mathbf{b})$ with the attribute scores s and apply a softmax transformation to produce a reweighed candidate distribution $\tilde{p}$, encoding fluency and attribute characteristics. The reweighed distribution is used to sample a single candidate.

More formally, let $B_j = \{\mathbf{b}^1, \ldots, \mathbf{b}^K\}$ denote the set of candidates for iteration j of BEAMR and $\mathbf{b}^k \in B_j$ denote the kth candidate, with likelihood $\ell(\mathbf{b}^k)$. Let $g_\phi : \mathcal{P}(\mathcal{V}) \to \mathbb{R}^m$ represent a discriminator for an m-dimensional attribute. Given a target attribute vector $\mathbf{a} \in \mathbb{R}^m$, we compute a score for candidate $\mathbf{b}^k$:

$$\begin{aligned} d_k &= \mathcal{D}(g_\phi(\mathbf{b}^k), \mathbf{a}) \\ s(\mathbf{b}^k, \mathbf{a}) &= \left(1 + d_k + \left|\min_k d_k\right|\right)^\gamma \end{aligned} \quad (3)$$

where $\mathcal{D} : \mathbb{R}^m \times \mathbb{R}^m \to \mathbb{R}$ is an appropriate similarity measure and $\gamma > 0$ is a scaling hyperparameter. Note that Eqn. (3) ensures that the scores are an increasing function of γ, by transforming the output of $\mathcal{D}$ so that $\mathbb{R} \to [1, \infty)$ without changing the ranking order.

Combining the attribute score $s_k = s(\mathbf{b}^k, \mathbf{a})$ with the likelihood $\ell(\mathbf{b}^k)$ gives us a reweighed distribution $\tilde{p}$ over B_j:

$$\tilde{p}_k = \mathrm{softmax}(\ell(\mathbf{b}^k) + s_k) \quad (4)$$

A candidate can then be sampled from this distribution, $\mathbf{b} \sim \tilde{p}$. This formulation is akin to a product of experts model (Hinton, 2002; Welling, 2007) treating the LM f_θ as a linguistic expert and the discriminator g_ϕ as an attribute expert. Figure 1 presents a diagram of the BEAMR procedure. The detailed pseudo-code for a single iteration of BEAMR is presented in Algorithm 1.

Algorithm 1 Beam Reweighing

procedure BEAMR($x, \mathbf{a}; \mathcal{D}, K, T, \gamma$)
  $\{\mathbf{b}\}_k \leftarrow$ DIVERSEBS($x; f_\theta, T, K$)
  for $k \leftarrow 1, K$ **do**
    $p_k = \ell(\mathbf{b}_k)$
    $d_k = \mathcal{D}(g_\phi(\mathbf{b}_k), \mathbf{a})$
  end for
  for $k \leftarrow 1, K$ **do**
    $s_k = (1 + d_k + |\min_k\{d\}_k|)^\gamma$
    $\tilde{p}_k = \mathrm{softmax}(p_k + s_k)$
  end for
  $\tilde{x} \sim \{\tilde{p}\}_k$
  return $x \oplus \tilde{x}$
end procedure

3.1 Generalizability of Beam Reweighing

Our formulation of BEAMR is flexible enough to accommodate a variety of possible attributes and discriminator models, including both continuous and categorical attributes. This can be achieved via the choice of the similarity measure $\mathcal{D}$.

Continuous Attribute. The simplest case of a continuous attribute is $m = 1$, where $y = g_\phi(\mathbf{b})$ is a regression score, such as a sentiment between -1 (negative) and 1 (positive). In this case we can take $\mathcal{D}$ to be a standard similarity measure on $\mathbb{R}$, such as the inverse of L_1 or L_2 metrics, namely, $\mathcal{D}(y, a) = |y - a|^{-1}$ or $\mathcal{D}(y, a) = \|y - a\|_2^{-1}$, where a is the target attribute score.

Categorical Attribute. For categorical attributes with $m > 1$, such as emotion classes (e.g., joy, anger, fear and surprise), $g_\phi(\mathbf{b})$ produces a vector of logits $\mathbf{y} \in \mathbb{R}^m$. In this case $\mathbf{a}$ is a one-hot encoding of the target class $c \in \{1, \ldots, m\}$, and so we can take $\mathcal{D}$ to be negative cross-entropy,

$$\mathcal{D}(\mathbf{y}, \mathbf{a}) = \log\left(\frac{\exp(y_c)}{\sum_{i=1}^{m}\exp(y_i)}\right) \quad (5)$$

Multiple Attributes. In the case that we want to control the generated text according to multiple attributes, for example, joy and surprise, we can reframe the problem as a multi-label prediction problem. Given a classifier g_ϕ that produces a vector of independent logits $\mathbf{y} \in \mathbb{R}^m$, and a target binary vector $\mathbf{a} \in \{0, 1\}^m$ such that $a_i = 1 \ (1 \le i \le m)$ for the desired attributes, we can take $\mathcal{D}$ to be the average of negative binary cross-entropy across the attributes,

$$\mathcal{D}(\mathbf{y}, \mathbf{a}) = \frac{1}{m}\sum_{i=1}^{m} a_i \log\sigma(y_i) + (1 - a_i)\log(1 - \sigma(y_i)) \quad (6)$$

where $\sigma(\cdot)$ is the sigmoid function.

4 Evaluation

We conduct several experiments in order to evaluate BEAMR against SOTA controllable generation approaches, in various applications. We focus on (1) a sentiment steering task, whereby we generate positive or negative continuations to a variety of prompts (including positive, negative and neutral prompts), and (2) a machine translation formality task, whereby input sentences are translated to English and the translations are adjusted in order to improve the formality of the text, whilst maintaining the original meaning. We detail the relevant datasets, baselines and metrics for each experiment. We also conduct an analysis of hyperparameter selection for both tasks.

4.1 Sentiment Steering

We focus on the task of controlling the sentiment (positive or negative) of generated text, given a short prompt as input. For this experiment, we closely follow the experimental setup outlined in Liu et al. (2021). We evaluate two variants of BEAMR: (1) using the base GPT-2 large model and (2) using the appropriate finetuned expert model from DExperts (Liu et al., 2021).

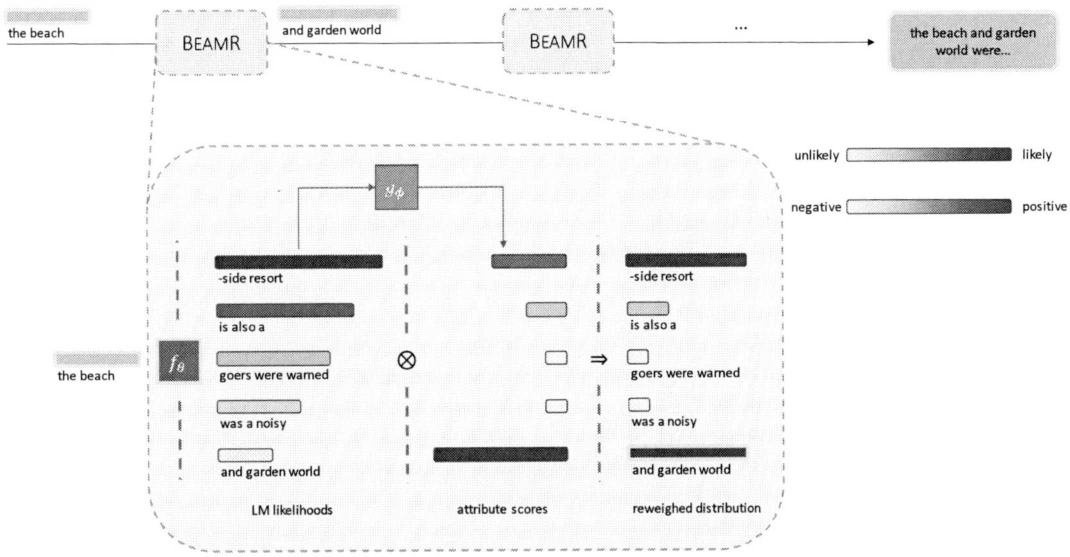

Figure 1: Illustration of BeamR method. An input prompt is fed into a generative LM (f_θ). Leveraging the diverse beam search algorithm, several candidate generations are produced, together with their likelihoods (depicted in blue). Candidates are then scored using a scoring LM (g_ϕ), a similarity measure $\mathcal{D}$, and the desired target attribute (e.g., positive sentiment). The scores produce an attribute distribution over the candidates (depicted in green). The candidates' original likelihoods are reweighed with the attribute distribution to produce $\tilde{p}$, and a single candidate $b \sim \tilde{p}$ is sampled (e.g. "and garden world"). Note that darker hues and longer bars indicate more probable candidates according to each distribution.

4.1.1 Datasets

We use the prompts dataset provided by Liu et al. (2021), originally collected from OpenWebText Corpus (OWT) (Gokaslan and Cohen, 2019). We use the same selections of 250 positive, 250 negative and 500 neutral prompts from Liu et al. (2021) as in their PPLM evaluation. For each prompt, we generate 25 continuations and score them using the default DistilBERT sentiment classifier.

4.1.2 Baselines

We consider the same baselines as outlined in Liu et al. (2021). **GPT-2** (Radford et al., 2019) is used without any steering towards a particular sentiment. **PPLM** (Dathathri et al., 2020) is used together with a sentiment classifier trained on SST-5 (Socher et al., 2013). **CTRL** (Keskar et al., 2019) is used by providing "Reviews" as the control code combined with a rating of 1.0 for negative steering and 5.0 for positive steering. CTRL's original training included examples from Amazon Reviews. **GeDi** (Krause et al., 2020) is used with the original sentiment-conditioned LMs, originally trained on IMDb movie reviews. **DExperts** using both positive and negative expert LMs is used. We present the results from the large version of DExperts.

4.1.3 Metrics

In our evaluation, we focus on several key metrics: steering ability, fluency, diversity and relevance.

Automated Evaluation. We use the DistilBERT sentiment classifier to evaluate the **steering ability** by computing the proportion of continuations for each type of prompt that succeed in generating the desired sentiment. We evaluate the **fluency** of the generations by computing the average perplexity under a base GPT2-XL model. We evaluate the **diversity** by computing the number of unique n-grams (Dist-1, 2 and 3 scores) (Li et al., 2016) across the generations of each prompt.

Human Evaluation. Although automated evaluation is easy to perform, it may not accurately reflect human judgments, especially for fluency and relevance metrics (Hashimoto et al., 2019; Liu et al., 2017). To that end, we design a human evaluation study to evaluate **steering ability**, **fluency** and **relevance**. We separately evaluate positive and negative steering. We randomly sample 10 neutral and 10 positive/negative prompts for each experiment. For each pair of models for comparison (i.e. BEAMR paired with another baseline, such as GPT-2, CTRL, DExperts, etc.), we sample 3 generations per model. We conduct human evaluations on the

Amazon Mechanical Turk (MTurk) platform, with 5 MTurk workers answering 3 questions about each pair of generations:

1. Which generation is more positive (resp. negative)?
2. Which generation is more fluent?
3. Which generation is more relevant to the prompt?

For each question workers may choose one of the models in the pair, or report that both models equally exhibit the characteristic in question. We compute 95% simultaneous confidence intervals (Goodman, 1965) for all three multinomial proportions for each pair of models and each question. We also perform a Z-test on the difference in proportions between the models in each pair.

4.1.4 Results

Automated Evaluation. Tables 1a and 1b show the results of the sentiment-based steering task for positive and negative steering, respectively. BEAMR scores in the top 2 models in terms of steering ability in all but one experiment, and outperforms DExperts in producing positive generations for neutral prompts. Noticeably, BEAMR struggles to achieve the steering ability of DExperts when tasked to produce negative generations for positive prompts. This may be explained by the fact that DExperts better incorporates negative tokens into its generation via its negative expert, whereas BEAMR is less likely to sample negative tokens from the base generation LM. In order to confirm this intuition, we also present results from BEAMR using the negative and positive experts as the generation model. We see that combining BEAMR with an expert model finetuned on the appropriate sentiment greatly improves performance and outperforms DExperts in both types of steering.

We also see that BEAMR outperforms all other models in terms of perplexity. The low perplexity of BEAMR compared to other methods may be explained by the fact that it utilizes beam search and reweighs candidate sequences of tokens, rather than reweighing individual tokens. Previous work (Holtzman et al., 2020) has shown that beam search leads to lower perplexity, although it tends to degenerate to repetition. BEAMR avoids repetition by performing separate iterations of beam search with shorter candidate lengths and introducing additional variability by utilizing a diversity measure (Vijayakumar et al., 2018) and sampling from the candidate distribution. It is important to note that combining BEAMR with a finetuned expert model increases the perplexity of the generations, likely due to a shift in the language distribution between the finetuned expert model and the base GPT-2 model.

BEAMR also performs competitively in terms of diversity, suggesting that it is able to produce varied generations that on the whole achieve the correct sentiment. Overall, these results highlight that BEAMR can achieve a good balance between generating the correct sentiment and producing fluent text.

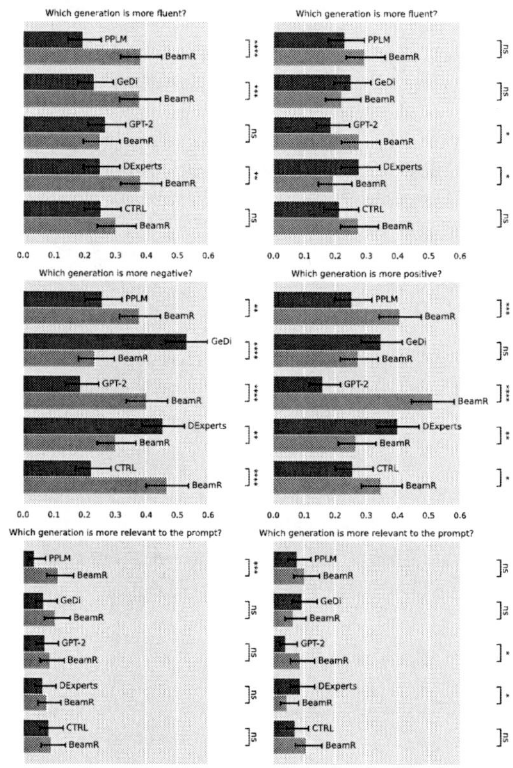

ns: $p \leq 1.00$
*: $1 \times 10^{-2} < p \leq 5 \times 10^{-2}$
**: $1 \times 10^{-3} < p \leq 1 \times 10^{-2}$
***: $1 \times 10^{-4} < p \leq 1 \times 10^{-3}$
****: $p \leq 1 \times 10^{-4}$

Figure 2: Results of human evaluations in sentiment steering experiment. For clarity, responses from options 'Equally positive/negative/fluent/relevant' are not shown. 95% simultaneous confidence intervals for multinomial proportion estimates are shown in black. Significance results from Z-test of the difference between multinomial proportions are shown at the edges of the plot, with corresponding legend below plot.

Model	% Positive Sentiment ↑		Perplexity ↓	Diversity (n-gram) ↑		
	Neutral Prompts	Negative Prompts		Dist-1	Dist-2	Dist-3
GPT-2	50.03	0.00	**29.04**	0.58	0.85	0.84
PPLM	52.69	8.72	135.55	0.61	0.86	0.85
CTRL	60.77	18.02	44.17	0.51	0.83	0.86
GeDi	85.61	26.54	55.21	0.57	0.80	0.79
DExperts	94.79	**34.93**	47.62	0.56	0.83	0.83
BeamR	**95.26**	30.34	**19.62**	0.53	0.82	0.84
BeamR + Positive Expert	**98.87**	**74.37**	51.4	0.56	0.84	0.85

(a) Positive Steering

Model	% Positive Sentiment ↓		Perplexity ↓	Diversity (n-gram) ↑		
	Neutral Prompts	Positive Prompts		Dist-1	Dist-2	Dist-3
GPT-2	50.03	100.00	**28.94**	0.58	0.85	0.87
PPLM	39.05	89.74	181.79	0.63	0.87	0.86
CTRL	37.94	80.98	37.04	0.50	0.83	0.85
GeDi	9.06	40.00	80.64	0.63	0.84	0.82
DExperts	**3.27**	**38.37**	45.16	0.60	0.83	0.82
BeamR	5.86	72.86	**23.45**	0.55	0.84	0.84
BeamR + Negative Expert	**1.99**	**28.42**	53.29	0.57	0.85	0.85

(b) Negative Steering

Table 1: Results of sentiment steering experiment. Given a neutral, negative or positive prompt, the models are tasked with producing positive or negative generations. **% Positive Sentiment** is computed as the average percentage of positive generations out of 25 total generations for each prompt. **Perplexity** is the average conditional perplexity of generations given the prompt, using a GPT2-XL model. **Diversity** is measured using the average number of distinct uni/bi/tri-grams in the generations for each prompt. Top 2 results are bolded.

Human Evaluation. Figure 2 presents the results of human evaluation on the sentiment steering task. We see that BEAMR significantly outperforms PPLM, GeDi and DExperts in **fluency** for negative steering, and otherwise performs on par with other models. BEAMR significantly outperforms PPLM, GPT-2 and CTRL in both negative and positive **steering ability**. On the other hand, GeDi and DExperts outperform BEAMR in steering ability, particularly in the negative steering experiment, which may support our earlier observations. BEAMR performs on par with other models in terms of relevance.

Effects of Hyperparameters. We conducted additional experiments to quantify the effect of the scaling hyperparameter γ and beam length T on both positive and negative steering, in terms of steering ability and fluency. Figure 3 in the Appendix Section A.3.1 presents the plots of % Positive Generations vs. Perplexity for varying settings of γ and T. As we might expect, increasing γ allows BEAMR to reach the desired sentiment in a higher proportion of generations. Moreover, increasing the beam length T leads to a lower perplexity, signifying more fluent generations.

4.2 Machine Translation Formality

In this set of experiments, we focus on the task of controlling the formality of English text that has been translated from Spanish. Unlike the sentiment steering task in Section 4.1 where BEAMR was applied to a causal language model, this involves applying BEAMR to a seq2seq translation model, thus further exhibiting the generalizability of our method. We follow the experimental setup outlined in Yang and Klein (2021).

4.2.1 Datasets

We use the Fisher and CALLHOME corpus (Post et al., 2013) of Spanish and English transcribed conversations, using the Spanish sentences as input to the Marian Spanish-to-English machine translation model (Junczys-Dowmunt et al., 2018). We leverage the pretrained formality classifier provided by Yang and Klein (2021) as the attribute model for BEAMR. The classifier was trained on the Entertainment/Music portion of the GYAFC formality corpus (Rao and Tetreault, 2018). For this experiment, BEAMR uses the Marian model as the generative LM (f_θ) and the pretrained FUDGE classifier as the attribute model (g_ϕ).

4.2.2 Baselines

We consider the same baselines as in Yang and Klein (2021). **MarianMT** base model is used to generate translations, without any steering towards more formal text. **T5** style transfer model (Raffel et al., 2020) is finetuned on the GYAFC corpus (Entertainment/Music portion) and applied post-hoc to the output of MarianMT translations. **FUDGE** classifier is used to guide the translations of MarianMT in a token-by-token manner.

4.2.3 Metrics

For evaluation, we consider two important criteria: translation accuracy and formality. We evaluate the **translation accuracy** by computing the BLEU score between the generations and the gold-standard translations provided in the Fisher/CALLHOME corpus (Post et al., 2013). We evaluate the **formality** using a pretrained formality classifier provided by Yang and Klein (2021) that has been trained on the Family/Relationships portion of GYAFC (Rao and Tetreault, 2018).

4.2.4 Results

Table 2 presents the results of the translation formality experiment. Notably, combining an unfinetuned Marian model and FUDGE with BEAMR, we achieve a higher BLEU score and a higher formality score than FUDGE, signifying more formal translations which are closer to the gold standard. Similarly, with a Marian model that was finetuned on the Fisher training set, we see that BEAMR can reach FUDGE's BLEU score while also achieving a higher formality score.

Model	Unfinetuned		Finetuned	
	BLEU ↑	Form. ↑	BLEU ↑	Form. ↑
Marian	16.98	0.45	**22.03**	0.41
+ T5	7.87	**0.96**	9.63	**0.97**
+ FUDGE	17.96	0.51	**22.18**	0.48
+ BeamR	**18.47**	**0.63**	21.14	**0.63**

Table 2: Results for the machine translation formality task. Given a sentence in Spanish, the models are tasked to produce a formal English translation. **BLEU** measures the accuracy of translation via n-gram precision. **Form.** is the average formality score provided by the FUDGE classifier trained on the Family/Relationships portion of the GYAFC dataset. Top results are bolded.

Effects of Hyperparameters. We conducted additional experiments to understand the effects of varying scaling hyperparameter γ and beam length T on the quality and formality of translations. Figures 4a and 4b in the Appendix Section A.3.2 present BLEU vs. formality score with varying T and γ, respectively.

We can see that varying γ allows for a trade-off between formality and translation accuracy. Namely, increasing γ improves formality score but decreases BLEU score. We also see trends in formality and translation accuracy when changing T. For shorter beam lengths, BEAMR makes locally optimal choices for formality, but suffers a significant decrease in BLEU score when considering the full translation. This hints at a similar behaviour as observed in sentiment steering (Section 4.1), namely that leveraging beam search can improve the quality of generation while leaving ample room for control.

5 Related Work

Recent methods in controllable text generation (Weng, 2021) may be categorized under decoding methods and tuning methods. Roughly speaking, decoding methods apply controllable characteristics only at the output distribution of a LM, while tuning methods additionally attempt to encode controllable characteristics into the generative LM itself, by tuning either some or all of its parameters.

5.1 Decoding methods

Decoding methods are applied to produce text output from an autoregressive generative language model. We first outline several general approaches to decoding from language models.

Typical decoding is done by sampling from the next token distribution, or picking the most likely token. However, these approaches lead to undesired output (Holtzman et al., 2020): sampling may lead to the model producing gibberish while greedy decoding often leads to repetitions. Several basic approaches have been proposed to tackle these issues, including top-k sampling (Fan et al., 2018), top-p sampling (Holtzman et al., 2020) and repetition-penalized sampling (Keskar et al., 2019). An alternative approach is the beam search algorithm (Graves, 2012) which maintains a collection of k best sequences at each time step. In order to promote more diversity in the generated candidates, Vijayakumar et al. (2018) proposed a diverse beam search algorithm, which splits the candidates into separate groups and enforces a dissimilarity metric across the groups.

Several approaches have been explored to

guide decoding according to a particular attribute. Ghazvininejad et al. (2017) modify the beam search algorithm to incorporate weighted feature functions during each step. They use several manually designed feature functions including custom word-lists, repetition penalty, and alliteration metrics for the problem of poetry generation. More recently Liu et al. (2021); Yang and Klein (2021) have proposed leveraging multiple language models to re-rank hypotheses according to a particular attribute. Liu et al. (2021) achieves this by fine-tuning generative language models on appropriate subsets of a dataset (e.g., training experts on toxic and non-toxic subsets of a dataset) and combining token-level distributions from the original language model and expert models. The downside of this approach is that it requires annotated data and additional training of the expert models, which may not be available for resource-constrained scenarios and domains. Yang and Klein (2021) propose to use a binary classifier trained for a particular task, to reweigh the token-level distribution produced by a generative LM. They highlight the flexibility of their approach in a variety of experiments, including couplet generation and topic control. Our method differs from and improves on FUDGE in several key ways, by:

- Applying reweighing to beam-level decoding thereby avoiding typical disfluency and repetition issues from token-level decoding mentioned in Holtzman et al. (2020)
- Allowing for the choice of a custom similarity measure $\mathcal{D}$ appropriate for the discriminator (e.g., regressor, classifier), thereby offering precise control of the desired target attribute value
- Removing the requirement of shared tokenization between the generative LM and the discriminator and instead reweighing natural language hypotheses, thereby improving generalizability to different LMs

5.2 Tuning methods

The majority of recent work on controllable text generation has focused on fine-tuning some or all of the parameters of a generative language model.

Keskar et al. (2019) train a transformer model (CTRL) to learn a conditional distribution over the data. By prepending different control codes (for instance, "Wikipedia" or "Reviews") to raw text from different sources (Wikipedia, or Amazon Reviews, respectively), it learns to associate certain types of text with the control codes. At inference time, CTRL interprets the first token in the prompt to be a control code, and can thus generate text in the corresponding style.

Dathathri et al. (2020) proposed Plug-and-Play Language Models (PPLM), a method to steer a subset of the parameters of a generative language model according to a lightweight auxiliary attribute model. They achieve this via backpropagation of the attribute model loss gradient into the past attention key-value pairs of a transformer-based language model. They experiment with simple attribute models consisting of a bag-of-words to encourage the LM to use words from the bag, as well as simple classifiers (e.g., sentiment) trained on top of the generative LM representations.

Zeldes et al. (2020) briefly describe a method to shift the output distribution of a generative language model using an auxiliary model. They combine the logits of both models and train them in tandem to maximize the likelihood of a certain attribute.

Our method is inspired by PPLM and also resembles a decoding method (Zeldes et al., 2020), whereby we similarly propose to control the output distribution of the generative language model. However, unlike those methods, we do not require that the generative and auxiliary models be trained together. In fact, our method is flexible and robust to the choice of the generative and auxiliary attribute models and can leverage pre-trained models, avoiding the need to re-train one or both of the models.

6 Conclusion

We present a simple and modular decoding-based approach to controllable generation, BEAMR. BEAMR combines a generative LM with an attribute discriminator and leverages beam search decoding in order to steer generated text to the desired target attribute. We show the results of BEAMR in two diverse tasks: sentiment-based steering, and machine translation formality steering. Our results from automated evaluations show that BEAMR outperforms strong baselines for both tasks, and human evaluations for sentiment steering further support this.

Noticeably, BEAMR struggles with negative sentiment steering, especially when compared to GeDi and DExperts. We hypothesize this may be due to GeDi and DExperts having direct access to class-conditioned distributions in their generation. Namely, GeDi trains a class-conditioned LM using control codes and anti-control codes (including `<negative>`) and DExperts trains separate expert and anti-expert LMs on subsets of the data (including an anti-expert trained on negative-only text). Future work on BEAMR may incorporate additional sources of language and attribute information to address this shortcoming.

BEAMR offers a great deal of flexibility by allowing us to plug different and independent generative LMs and attribute discriminators (with potentially different tokenization schemes). Moreover, BEAMR generalizes beyond classification tasks to any type of discriminator by appropriately selecting a similarity measure. Leveraging beam search for text decoding from a LM, BEAMR's generations avoid some of the typical problems with token-based decoding (such as repetition or disfluencies). Our work highlights that strong controllable text generation can be achieved by mixing together large pre-trained generative and discriminative models, with a flexible backbone offered by BEAMR, without sacrificing fluency.

7 Ethics of Controllable Text Generation

Usage of large language models for text generation can pose various risks, including producing harmful content or misinformation (Sheng et al., 2020; Gehman et al., 2020; Wallace et al., 2021). Controllable text generation may create additional risks if used maliciously. However, it can also help researchers and practitioners avoid the biases learned by large language models and reduce the aforementioned risks (Liu et al., 2021; Dathathri et al., 2020). Therefore, we believe advancing research in controllable text generation is valuable in order to understand the pitfalls of large language models and develop strong measures to prevent harmful content generation.

Human evaluation experiments were conducted on the Amazon Mechanical Turk platform, and evaluators were compensated above the federal minimum wage in the country of residence (United States).

Acknowledgements

We thank Gerald Penn for his invaluable input and feedback in the early stages of the work. We also thank Komal Teru, Shakti Kumar, the anonymous reviewers and the area chair for their feedback and comments on the paper which greatly helped to improve the quality of the final version.

References

Ashutosh Baheti, Alan Ritter, Jiwei Li, and Bill Dolan. 2018. Generating More Interesting Responses in Neural Conversation Models with Distributional Constraints. *arXiv:1809.01215 [cs]*.

Sumanth Dathathri, Andrea Madotto, Janice Lan, Jane Hung, Eric Frank, Piero Molino, Jason Yosinski, and Rosanne Liu. 2020. Plug and Play Language Models: A Simple Approach to Controlled Text Generation. *arXiv:1912.02164 [cs]*.

Angela Fan, Mike Lewis, and Yann Dauphin. 2018. Hierarchical Neural Story Generation. *arXiv:1805.04833 [cs]*.

Samuel Gehman, Suchin Gururangan, Maarten Sap, Yejin Choi, and Noah A. Smith. 2020. RealToxicityPrompts: Evaluating Neural Toxic Degeneration in Language Models. In *Findings of the Association for Computational Linguistics: EMNLP 2020*, pages 3356–3369, Online. Association for Computational Linguistics.

Marjan Ghazvininejad, Xing Shi, Jay Priyadarshi, and Kevin Knight. 2017. Hafez: An Interactive Poetry Generation System. In *Proceedings of ACL 2017, System Demonstrations*, pages 43–48, Vancouver, Canada. Association for Computational Linguistics.

Aaron Gokaslan and Vanya Cohen. 2019. OpenWebText Corpus.

Leo A. Goodman. 1965. On Simultaneous Confidence Intervals for Multinomial Proportions. *Technometrics*, 7(2):247–254.

Tushar Goswamy, Ishika Singh, Ahsan Barkati, and Ashutosh Modi. 2020. Adapting a Language Model for Controlled Affective Text Generation. In *Proceedings of the 28th International Conference on Computational Linguistics*, pages 2787–2801, Barcelona, Spain (Online). International Committee on Computational Linguistics.

Alex Graves. 2012. Sequence Transduction with Recurrent Neural Networks. *arXiv:1211.3711 [cs, stat]*.

Tatsunori B. Hashimoto, Hugh Zhang, and Percy Liang. 2019. Unifying Human and Statistical Evaluation for Natural Language Generation. *arXiv:1904.02792 [cs, stat]*.

Geoffrey E. Hinton. 2002. Training Products of Experts by Minimizing Contrastive Divergence. *Neural Computation*, 14(8):1771–1800.

Ari Holtzman, Jan Buys, Li Du, Maxwell Forbes, and Yejin Choi. 2020. The Curious Case of Neural Text Degeneration. *arXiv:1904.09751 [cs]*.

Marcin Junczys-Dowmunt, Roman Grundkiewicz, Tomasz Dwojak, Hieu Hoang, Kenneth Heafield, Tom Neckermann, Frank Seide, Ulrich Germann, Alham Fikri Aji, Nikolay Bogoychev, André F. T. Martins, and Alexandra Birch. 2018. Marian: Fast Neural Machine Translation in C++. In *Proceedings of ACL 2018, System Demonstrations*, pages 116–121, Melbourne, Australia. Association for Computational Linguistics.

Nitish Shirish Keskar, Bryan McCann, Lav R. Varshney, Caiming Xiong, and Richard Socher. 2019. CTRL: A Conditional Transformer Language Model for Controllable Generation. *arXiv:1909.05858 [cs]*.

Muhammad Khalifa, Hady Elsahar, and Marc Dymetman. 2021. A Distributional Approach to Controlled Text Generation. *arXiv:2012.11635 [cs]*.

Ben Krause, Akhilesh Deepak Gotmare, Bryan McCann, Nitish Shirish Keskar, Shafiq Joty, Richard Socher, and Nazneen Fatema Rajani. 2020. GeDi: Generative Discriminator Guided Sequence Generation. *arXiv:2009.06367 [cs]*.

Jiwei Li, Michel Galley, Chris Brockett, Jianfeng Gao, and Bill Dolan. 2016. A Diversity-Promoting Objective Function for Neural Conversation Models. *arXiv:1510.03055 [cs]*.

Alisa Liu, Maarten Sap, Ximing Lu, Swabha Swayamdipta, Chandra Bhagavatula, Noah A. Smith, and Yejin Choi. 2021. DExperts: Decoding-Time Controlled Text Generation with Experts and Anti-Experts. *arXiv:2105.03023 [cs]*.

Chia-Wei Liu, Ryan Lowe, Iulian V. Serban, Michael Noseworthy, Laurent Charlin, and Joelle Pineau. 2017. How NOT To Evaluate Your Dialogue System: An Empirical Study of Unsupervised Evaluation Metrics for Dialogue Response Generation. *arXiv:1603.08023 [cs]*.

Matt Post, Gaurav Kumar, Adam Lopez, Damianos Karakos, Chris Callison-Burch, and Sanjeev Khudanpur. 2013. Improved speech-to-text translation with the Fisher and Callhome Spanish-English speech translation corpus. In *Proceedings of the 10th International Workshop on Spoken Language Translation: Papers*, Heidelberg, Germany.

Alec Radford, Jeffrey Wu, Rewon Child, David Luan, Dario Amodei, and Ilya Sutskever. 2019. Language models are unsupervised multitask learners. *OpenAI blog*, 1(8):9.

Colin Raffel, Noam Shazeer, Adam Roberts, Katherine Lee, Sharan Narang, Michael Matena, Yanqi Zhou, Wei Li, and Peter J. Liu. 2020. Exploring the Limits of Transfer Learning with a Unified Text-to-Text Transformer. *arXiv:1910.10683 [cs, stat]*.

Sudha Rao and Joel Tetreault. 2018. Dear Sir or Madam, May I introduce the GYAFC Dataset: Corpus, Benchmarks and Metrics for Formality Style Transfer. *arXiv:1803.06535 [cs]*.

Elizabeth Salesky, Matthias Sperber, and Alexander Waibel. 2019. Fluent Translations from Disfluent Speech in End-to-End Speech Translation. In *Proceedings of the 2019 Conference of the North American Chapter of the Association for Computational Linguistics: Human Language Technologies, Volume 1 (Long and Short Papers)*, pages 2786–2792, Minneapolis, Minnesota. Association for Computational Linguistics.

Emily Sheng, Kai-Wei Chang, Prem Natarajan, and Nanyun Peng. 2020. Towards Controllable Biases in Language Generation. In *Findings of the Association for Computational Linguistics: EMNLP 2020*, pages 3239–3254, Online. Association for Computational Linguistics.

Richard Socher, Alex Perelygin, Jean Wu, Jason Chuang, Christopher D. Manning, Andrew Ng, and Christopher Potts. 2013. Recursive Deep Models for Semantic Compositionality Over a Sentiment Treebank. In *Proceedings of the 2013 Conference on Empirical Methods in Natural Language Processing*, pages 1631–1642, Seattle, Washington, USA. Association for Computational Linguistics.

Pradyumna Tambwekar, Murtaza Dhuliawala, Lara J. Martin, Animesh Mehta, Brent Harrison, and Mark O. Riedl. 2019. Controllable Neural Story Plot Generation via Reinforcement Learning. *arXiv:1809.10736 [cs]*.

Ashish Vaswani, Noam Shazeer, Niki Parmar, Jakob Uszkoreit, Llion Jones, Aidan N. Gomez, Lukasz Kaiser, and Illia Polosukhin. 2017. Attention Is All You Need. *arXiv:1706.03762 [cs]*.

Ashwin K. Vijayakumar, Michael Cogswell, Ramprasath R. Selvaraju, Qing Sun, Stefan Lee, David Crandall, and Dhruv Batra. 2018. Diverse Beam Search: Decoding Diverse Solutions from Neural Sequence Models. *arXiv:1610.02424 [cs]*.

Eric Wallace, Shi Feng, Nikhil Kandpal, Matt Gardner, and Sameer Singh. 2021. Universal Adversarial Triggers for Attacking and Analyzing NLP. *arXiv:1908.07125 [cs]*.

Max Welling. 2007. Product of experts. *Scholarpedia*, 2(10):3879.

Lilian Weng. 2021. Controllable neural text generation. *lilianweng.github.io*.

Thomas Wolf, Lysandre Debut, Victor Sanh, Julien Chaumond, Clement Delangue, Anthony Moi, Pierric Cistac, Tim Rault, Rémi Louf, Morgan Funtowicz, Joe Davison, Sam Shleifer, Patrick von Platen, Clara Ma, Yacine Jernite, Julien Plu, Canwen Xu, Teven Le Scao, Sylvain Gugger, Mariama Drame,

Quentin Lhoest, and Alexander M. Rush. 2020. HuggingFace's Transformers: State-of-the-art Natural Language Processing. *arXiv:1910.03771 [cs]*.

Kevin Yang and Dan Klein. 2021. FUDGE: Controlled Text Generation With Future Discriminators. *Proceedings of the 2021 Conference of the North American Chapter of the Association for Computational Linguistics: Human Language Technologies*, pages 3511–3535.

Yoel Zeldes, Dan Padnos, Or Sharir, and Barak Peleg. 2020. Technical Report: Auxiliary Tuning and its Application to Conditional Text Generation. *arXiv:2006.16823 [cs, stat]*.

A Appendix

A.1 Implementation Details

All experiments were conducted on a single NVidia Tesla T4 GPU. Transformers package (Wolf et al., 2020) version 4.8 was used to implement all algorithms and experiments. Table 3 presents average amount of time to run each experiment.

Experiment	Avg. Time (in minutes)
Sentiment Steering	1.19 per batch of 8
Machine Translation Formality (Training)[1]	1.22 per epoch (20 epochs)
Machine Translation Formality (Inference)	0.0033 per 1 generation

[1] Corresponds to training of the FUDGE classifier on the Entertainment/Music portion of the GYAFC formality corpus (Rao and Tetreault, 2018)

Table 3: Average time taken (per example or per epoch) to run each experiment in Section 4.

A.2 Hyperparameters

A.2.1 Sentiment Steering

Table 4 presents the full hyperparameter configurations for the sentiment steering task in Section 4.1.

Name	Values
Generation Model	GPT2-Large (774M params.)
Discriminator Model	DistilBERT (66M params.)
Generation Length	20
Temperature	1.0
Diversity Penalty	10.0
Scaling (γ)	$\{1, 2, \mathbf{3}\}$
Beam Length (T)	$\{1, 3, 5, \mathbf{7}\}$
Number of Candidates (K)	5
Beam Length Penalty	1.0
Batch Size	8

Table 4: Models and hyperparameters used for sentiment steering experiments with BEAMR. Best-found hyperparameters are bolded, where applicable.

A.2.2 Machine Translation Formality

Table 5 presents the full hyperparameter configurations for the machine translation formality task in Section 4.2.

Name	Values
Generation Model	MarianMT (74M params.)
Discriminator Model	FUDGE (~2M params.)
Generation Length	512
Temperature	0.5
Diversity Penalty	10.0
Scaling (γ)	$\{1, 2, \mathbf{3}, 4\}$
Beam Length (T)	$\{1, 3, 5, 7, \mathbf{10}\}$
Number of Candidates (K)	5
Beam Length Penalty	1.0
Batch Size	1

Table 5: Models and hyperparameters used for machine translation formality experiments with BEAMR. Best-found hyperparameters are bolded, where applicable.

A.3 Additional Experiments

This section contains additional results for the experiments in Sections 4.1 and 4.2.

A.3.1 Sentiment Steering Hyperparameters

Figure 3 shows the results of hyperparameter experiments from 4.1.

A.3.2 Machine Translation Formality Hyperparameters

Figures 4a and 4b show the results of beam length (T) and scaling hyperparameter (γ) experiments (resp.) from 4.2.

A.3.3 Visualization of Reweighing

In order to better understand the effects of the reweighing step in Eqn. (4), we selected a prompt from the sentiment steering task, and ran BEAMR to get 15 generations for each set of hyperparameters $(\gamma, T) \in \{0.1, 0.3, 1, 3\} \times \{3, 5, 7, 15\}$.

Figure 5 shows the average candidate, attribute and reweighed distributions across 15 generations, from a single step in the BeamR algorithm. We see that for small values of $\gamma < 1$, the reweighed distributions closely resemble the original candidate distributions while the attribute distribution is almost flat. When $\gamma \geq 1$, we see the reweighed distributions take the shape of the attribute distributions, signifying a stronger effect of the attribute score. We also see some effect of the beam length hyperparameter on the reweighing. In particular, for small T, the reweighed distributions closely match the attribute distributions, however as T increases, there is a larger gap between the distributions. This gap is offset by increasing the value of γ.

A.4 Qualitative Examples

A.4.1 Sentiment Steering

Tables 6a and 6b show some qualitative examples from positive and negative steering (resp.) comparing BEAMR and baseline models.

A.4.2 Machine Translation Formality

Table 7 shows some qualitative examples comparing BEAMR and FUDGE with reference translations (Salesky et al., 2019).

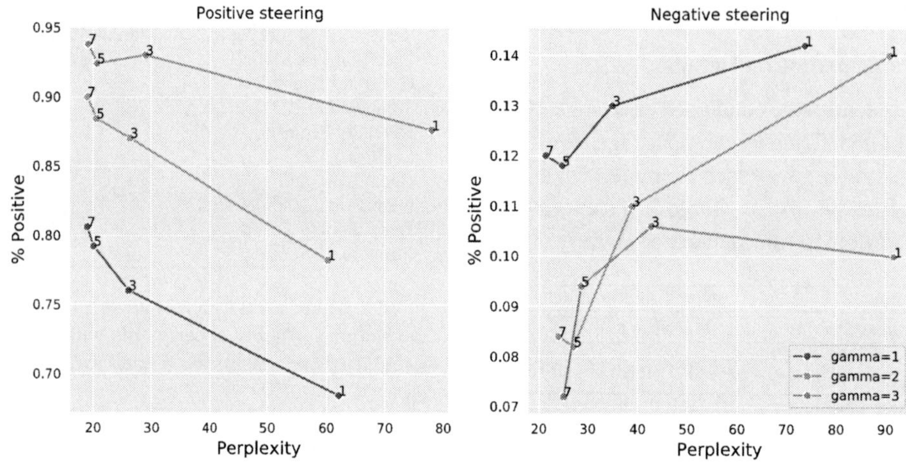

Figure 3: Results of hyperparameter experiments in sentiment steering task. Different coloured lines correspond to different values of scaling hyperparameter γ. Points labelled on the lines correspond to different values of beam length hyperparameter T.

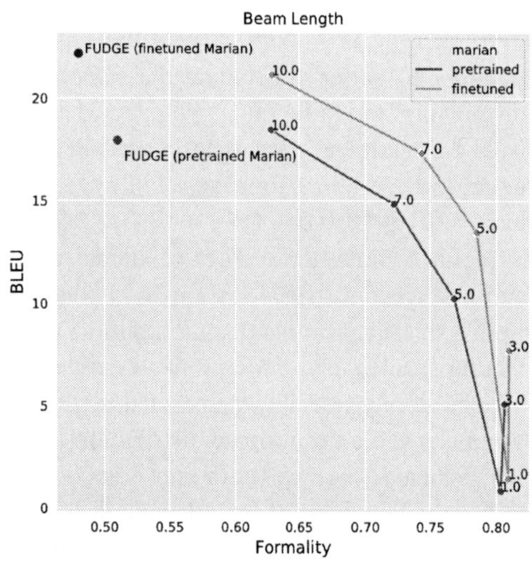

(a) Effect of beam length hyperparameter T on BLEU and Formality scores.

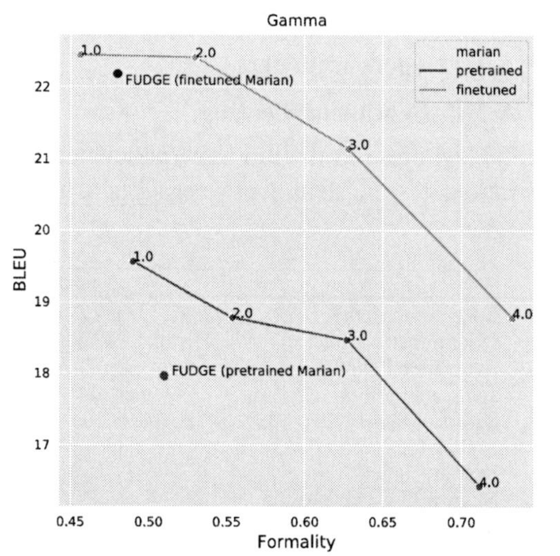

(b) Effect of scaling hyperparameter γ on BLEU and Formality scores.

Figure 4: Results of hyperparameter experiments in machine translation formality task. Different coloured lines correspond to pretrained or finetuned versions of the MarianMT model.

A.5 Human Evaluation

Figure 6 shows an example screenshot of the human evaluation instructions from MTurk.

A.6 Dataset Details

Table 8 presents the size of datasets used in our experiments in Section 4.

Dataset	Label	Number of examples
Sentiment Prompts	Positive	250
	Neutral	500
	Negative	250
GYAFC Inference (Ent./Music)	Formal	50967/1019/1000 (train/test/val.)
	Informal	50967/1332/1000
GYAFC Evaluation (Fam./Relation.)	Formal	51595/1082/1000
	Informal	51595/1416/1000

Table 8: Dataset sizes used for experiments in Section 4.

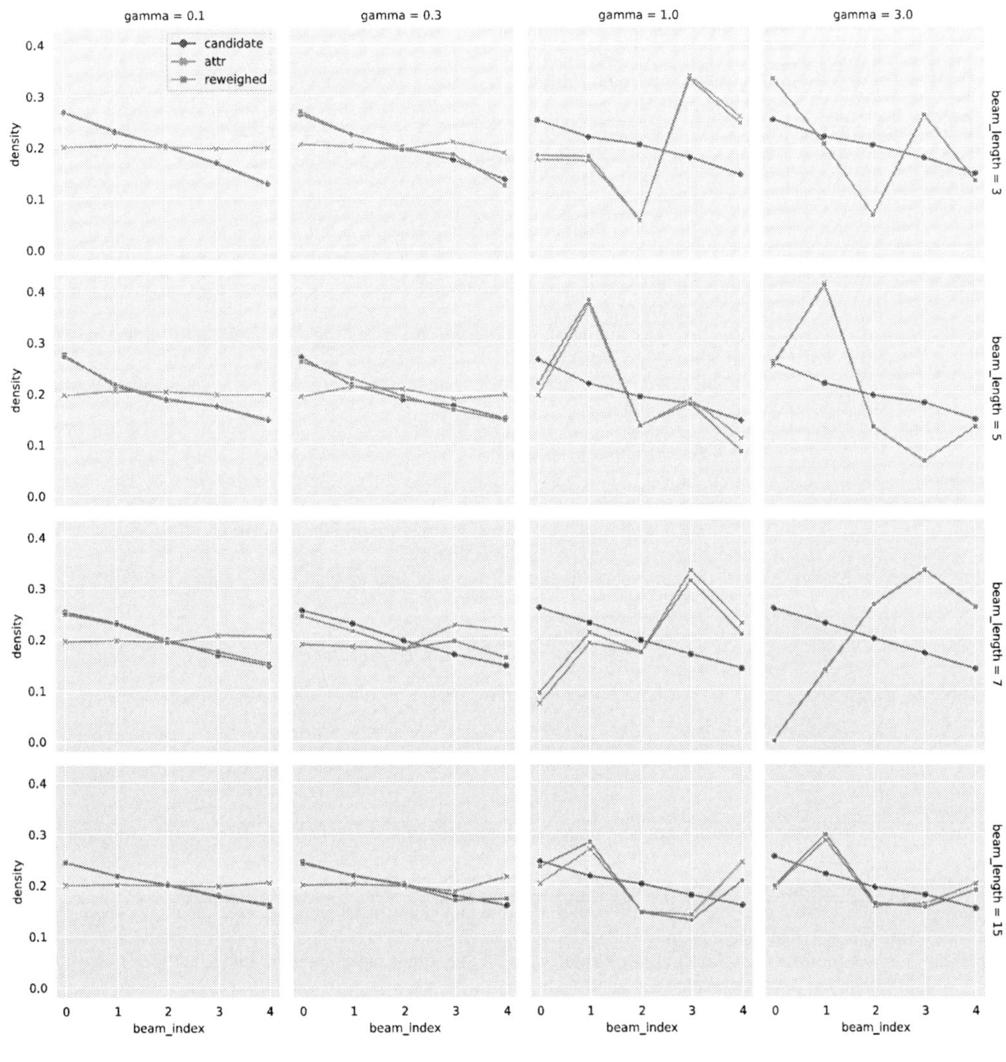

Figure 5: Comparison of differences between candidate, attribute and reweighed distributions from a single iteration of BEAMR for different combinations of scaling and beam length hyperparameters. Each point corresponds to the average density across 15 generations for a selected prompt.

Prompt: Until then, we should start

Model	Generation
GPT-2	Until then, we should start| collaborating. I'd love it if you could set up a foundation with the common interests of digital creators
PPLM	Until then, we should start| thinking of this awkwardness as largely just an blessings-and-worries life being shaped out
CTRL	Until then, we should start| by looking at the overall performance of both systems. If you want to know what makes one better than another,
GeDi	Until then, we should start| enjoying each other very much! :)\n\n\nThank you so much for visiting our shop! Happy New
DExperts	Until then, we should start| by appreciating the powerful sights and sounds of Japan's ancient forests and take pleasure in sampling traditional food
BeamR	Until then, we should start| the new year with a simple message of gratitude for the world we have. As we open our hearts
BeamR + Positive Expert	Until then, we should start| by acknowledging that the remarkable success of former boxing champion Mike Tyson's trilogy with Evander Holyfield

(a) Positive Steering

Prompt: Until then, we should start

Model	Generation
GPT-2	Until then, we should start| collaborating. I'd love it if you could set up a foundation with the common interests of digital creators
PPLM	Until then, we should start| thinking about scaling any application down.\n\n\nWhat a stubborn jerk!\n\n\nFigure this out if
CTRL	Until then, we should start| considering that this book was just a vehicle for his message - the Bible is God's Word, and it is
GeDi	Until then, we should start| testing for other reasons. Unfortunately, the lack of function over multiple visits is what makes this test bad
DExperts	Until then, we should start| loading vanilla content from somewhere else. The only solution is to dump something in oblivion.\n\n\n
BeamR	Until then, we should start| investing in fixing problems.\n\n\nUnfortunately the agenda to make the world go green is destroying the economy
BeamR + Negative Expert	Until then, we should start| thinking of this as just another lame, uninspired, and under-the-radar procedural,"

(b) Negative Steering

Table 6: Example generations from sentiment steering task, comparing BEAMR with baseline methods.

Spanish	si hay gente no que decir que no no hagan suficientes películas pero hacen tantas que no hay que ir a ver todas es es
Reference	There are so many movies made, you don't have to see them all.
Marian	yes, there are people that don't want to say that they don't make enough movies, but they make so many that you don't have to go see all of them, is, is
FUDGE	yes there are people that don't want to say that they don't make enough movies but they make so many that you don't have to go see all of them is is
BeamR	If there are people, right?, who want to stop making enough movies, but they make so many movies that you don't have to watch. It is

Spanish	también el veinti y el veintinueve también yo me acuerdo que más o menos en la misma vez se me acuerdo que están toda la misma fecha
Reference	Also the twenty nine. I remember that everybody were there in the same date
Marian	also on the twenty-nine and the twenty-nine also I remember that more or less at the same time I remember that they were all the same date
FUDGE	also on the twenty- and the twenty-nine also I remember that more or less at the same time I remember that they were all the same date
BeamR	Also, on the twenty-ninth, I also remember that more or less at the same time, I remember that they were all the same date.

Table 7: Example translations from machine translation formality task, comparing FUDGE and BEAMR with reference translations (Salesky et al., 2019).

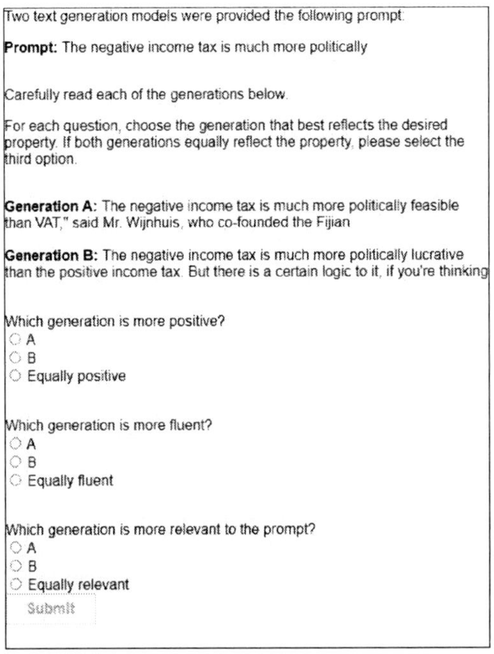

Two text generation models were provided the following prompt:

Prompt: The negative income tax is much more politically

Carefully read each of the generations below.

For each question, choose the generation that best reflects the desired property. If both generations equally reflect the property, please select the third option.

Generation A: The negative income tax is much more politically feasible than VAT," said Mr. Wijnhuis, who co-founded the Fijian

Generation B: The negative income tax is much more politically lucrative than the positive income tax. But there is a certain logic to it, if you're thinking

Which generation is more positive?
- ○ A
- ○ B
- ○ Equally positive

Which generation is more fluent?
- ○ A
- ○ B
- ○ Equally fluent

Which generation is more relevant to the prompt?
- ○ A
- ○ B
- ○ Equally relevant

Submit

Figure 6: Example of human evaluation instructions from MTurk experiments. For negative steering, the first question is phrased: "Which generation is more negative?"

R&R: Metric-guided Adversarial Sentence Generation

Lei Xu[1], Alfredo Cuesta-Infante[2], Laure Berti-Equille[3], Kalyan Veeramachaneni[1]
[1] MIT LIDS [2] Universidad Rey Juan Carlos [3] IRD
leix@mit.edu alfredo.cuesta@urjc.es laure.berti@ird.fr
kalyanv@mit.edu

Abstract

Adversarial examples are helpful for analyzing and improving the robustness of text classifiers. Generating high-quality adversarial examples is a challenging task as it requires generating fluent adversarial sentences that are semantically similar to the original sentences and preserve the original labels, while causing the classifier to misclassify them. Existing methods prioritize misclassification by maximizing each perturbation's effectiveness at misleading a text classifier; thus, the generated adversarial examples fall short in terms of fluency and similarity. In this paper, we propose a rewrite and rollback (R&R) framework for adversarial attack. It improves the quality of adversarial examples by optimizing a critique score which combines the fluency, similarity, and misclassification metrics. R&R generates high-quality adversarial examples by allowing exploration of perturbations that do not have immediate impact on the misclassification metric but can improve fluency and similarity metrics. We evaluate our method on 5 representative datasets and 3 classifier architectures. Our method outperforms current state-of-the-art in attack success rate by +16.2%, +12.8%, and +14.0% on the classifiers respectively. Code is available at https://github.com/DAI-Lab/fibber

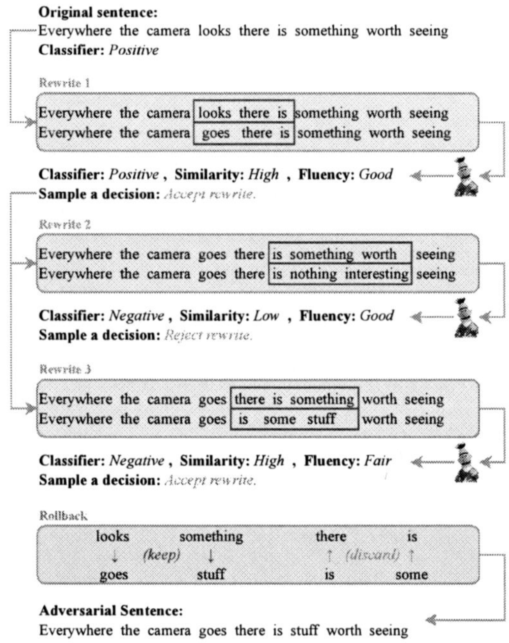

Figure 1: R&R generates adversarial examples by rewrite and rollback. The rewrite step explores possible perturbations stochastically and is guided by similarity metric and fluency metric to ensure better quality of the example. The rollback operation further improves the similarity.

1 Introduction

Recently, adversarial attacks in text classification have received a great deal of attention. Adversarial attacks are defined as subtle perturbations in the input text such that a classifier misclassifies it. They can serve as a tool to analyze and improve the robustness of text classifiers, thus being more and more important because security-critical classifiers are being widely deployed (Wu et al., 2019; Torabi Asr and Taboada, 2019; Zhou et al., 2019).

Existing attack methods either adopt a synonym substitution approach (Jin et al., 2020; Zang et al., 2020) or use a pre-trained language model to propose substitutions for better fluency and naturalness (Li et al., 2020; Garg and Ramakrishnan, 2020; Li et al., 2021). They follow a similar framework: first, construct some candidate perturbations, and then, use the perturbations that most effectively mislead the classifier to modify the sentence. This process is repeated multiple times until an adversarial example is found. This framework prioritizes misclassification by picking perturbations that most effectively mislead the classifier. Despite the success in changing the classifier prediction, it has two main disadvantages. First, it is prone to modify words that are critical to the sentence's meaning which decreases the similarity and is more likely

Findings of the Association for Computational Linguistics: AACL-IJCNLP 2022, pages 438–452
November 20–23, 2022. ©2022 Association for Computational Linguistics

to change the true label of the sentence, or introduce low-frequency words causing the fluency to decrease. Second, some perturbations do not have immediate impacts on misclassification, but can trigger it when combined with other perturbations, and these frameworks cannot find adversarial examples with these perturbations.

To overcome these problems, the attack method needs to consider fluency, similarity, and misclassification jointly, while also efficiently exploring various perturbations that do not show direct impacts on the latter. We define a critique score that combines fluency, similarity and misclassification metrics. Then, we present our design for a Rewrite and Rollback framework (R&R) which optimizes this score to generate better adversarial examples. In the rewrite stage, we explore multi-word substitutions proposed by a pre-trained language model. We accept or reject a substitution according to the critique score. We can generate a high-quality adversarial example after multiple iterations of rewrite. Rewrite may introduce changes that do not contribute to misclassification and may also reduce similarity and fluency. Therefore, we periodically apply the rollback operation to reduce the number of modifications without changing the misclassification result. Figure 1 illustrates the process using an example.

2 Problem Formulation

Let $\mathbf{x} = x_1, \ldots, x_l$ be a sentence of length l, y be its classification label, and $f(\mathbf{x})$ be a text classifier that predicts a probability distribution over classes. The objective of an attack method $\mathcal{A}(\mathbf{x}, y, f)$ is to construct $\mathbf{u} = u_1, \ldots, u_{l'}$ satisfying 3 conditions:

$$\begin{cases} \mathbf{u} \text{ is misclassified, i.e., } f(\mathbf{u}) \neq y, \\ \text{Human considers } \mathbf{u} \text{ as a fluent sentence,} \\ \text{Human considers } \mathbf{u} \text{ to be semantically similar to } \mathbf{x}. \\ \text{Human considers } \mathbf{u} \text{ preserves the true label } y. \end{cases}$$

where l' is the length of the adversarial sentence. However, this formulation requiring human evaluation is intractable for large-scale data. Therefore, we approximate the sentence fluency with the perplexity of the sentence. It is defined as

$$\text{ppl}(\mathbf{x}) = \exp\big[-\tfrac{1}{l}\textstyle\sum_{i=1}^{l}\log p(x_i|x_1\ldots x_{i-1})\big],$$

where $p(x_i|x_1 \ldots x_{i-1})$ is measured by a language model. Low perplexity means the sentence is predictable by the language model, which usually indicates the sentence is fluent. Sentence similarity can be quantified as $\cos\big(H(\mathbf{x}), H(\mathbf{u})\big)$, where $H(\cdot)$ is a pre-trained sentence encoder that encodes the meaning of a sentence into a vector. We assume that high sentence similarity implies preservation of the sentence label. Thus, finding the adversarial sentence $\mathbf{u}$ is formulated as a multi-objective optimization problem as follows:

$$\begin{aligned} &\text{Construct } \mathbf{u} = u_1, \ldots, u_{l'} \text{ to minimize ppl}(\mathbf{u}) \\ &\quad\text{and maximize } \cos\big(H(\mathbf{x}), H(\mathbf{u})\big) \\ &\quad\text{subject to } f(\mathbf{u}) \neq y. \end{aligned}$$

We use a fine-tuned BERT-base model (Devlin et al., 2019) to measure perplexity and use Unversal Sentence Encoder (USE) (Cer et al., 2018) to measure sentence similarity. Ultimately, fluency, similarity, and the preservation of original label need to be verified by humans. We discuss human verification in Section 4.

Threat Model. We assume the attacker can query the classifier for the prediction (i.e., the probability distribution over all classes). But they do not have knowledge on architecture of the classifier nor query for the gradient. They can also access some unlabeled text in the domain of the classifier.

3 Metric-Guided Rewrite and Rollback

In this section, we first give an overview, then introduce the rewrite and rollback components respectively. Finally, we give a summary of pre-trained models used in the framework.

3.1 Overview

R&R contains the rewrite and rollback steps. In the rewrite step, we randomly mask several consecutive words, and compute a *proposal distribution*, which is a distribution over the vocabulary on each masked position defined as Eq. (1). We construct a multi-word substitution[1] for the masked positions according to the distribution, then compute the *critique score* defined as Eq. (3)-(5). If the score increases, we accept the substitution. If the score decreases, we accept it with a probability depending on the degree of decrease. The rewrite step contains randomness to encourage exploration of different modifications, while the critique score will guide the rewritten sentence to a high-quality adversarial

[1]The number of words in each substitution, the number of rewrite steps between two rollback steps, the maximum number of rewrite steps, and the batch size are hyperparamters.

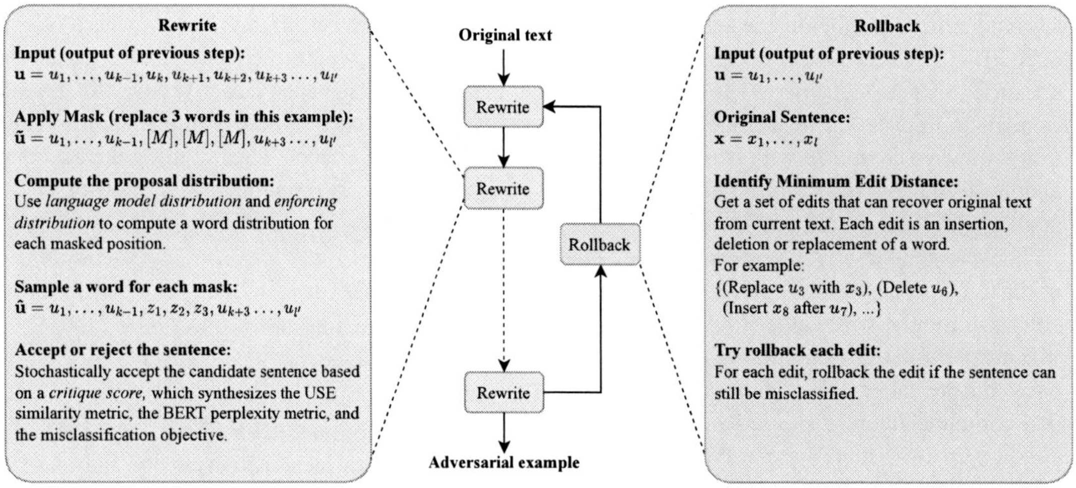

Figure 2: R&R Framework.

example. After several steps of rewriting[1], we apply a rollback operation on the sentences that have already been misclassified to reduce the number of changes introduced in the rewriting. In the rollback step, we identify a minimum set of edits required to change the current sentence back to the original sentence. We rollback an edit if it does not affect the misclassification.

We implement the framework to simultaneously rewrite a batch of sentences. We make multiple copies of an input text and create a batch[1]. The proposal distributions and critique scores for these copies can be computed in parallel on a GPU, while the randomness in the rewrite step leads to different rewritten sentences. The loop terminates when either the maximum number of rewrite steps is reached[1] or half of the sentences in the batch are misclassified. Figure 2 shows the R&R framework.

3.2 Rewrite

In each rewrite, we mask then substitute a span of words. It is composed of the following steps.

Apply mask in the sentence. First, we randomly pick m consecutive words in the sentence, and replace them with t mask, where t can be m, $m-1$, or $m+1$ meaning *replace*, *shrink*, and *expand* operation respectively. Compared with CLARE (Li et al., 2021) which masks one word at a time (i.e., $m = 1$), masking multiple words can make it easier to modify common phrases. We use $\tilde{\mathbf{u}}$ to denote the masked sentence.

Compute proposal distribution. Then, we compute proposal distribution for t masks in the sentence. This distribution assigns a high probability to words that can construct a fluent and legitimate paraphrase. Let $z_1, \ldots z_t$ be the words to be placed at the masked positions. The distribution is

$$p_{\text{proposal}}(z_i|\tilde{\mathbf{u}}, \mathbf{x}) \propto p_{\text{lm}}(z_i|\tilde{\mathbf{u}}) \times p_{\text{enforce}}(z_i|\tilde{\mathbf{u}}, \mathbf{x}) \tag{1}$$

where p_{lm} is a *language model distribution* that give high probability to words that can make a fluent sentence, and p_{enforce} is the *enforcing distribution*, which give high probability to words that can lead to semantically similar sentences. p_{lm} and p_{enforce} should be considered as two different weights of words and are multiplied together to get p_{proposal} so that if either p_{lm} or p_{enforce} is low, the word will have low probability in p_{proposal}. This is a desired property because we want the adversarial sentence to have good fluency (i.e., high p_{lm}) and high similarity (i.e., high p_{enforce}). p_{lm} is computed by sending $\tilde{\mathbf{u}}$ into BERT and taking the predicted word distribution on masked positions. Depending on the position, the word distributions for t masks are different. The enforcing distribution is measured by word embeddings. We use the sum of word embeddings $R(\mathbf{u}) = \sum_{u_k} E(u_k)$ as a sentence embedding, where $E(\cdot)$ is the counter-fitted word embedding (Mrkšic et al., 2016). Then we define the enforcing distribution as

$$p_{\text{enforce}}(z_i|\tilde{\mathbf{u}}, \mathbf{x}) \propto \exp\big[w_{\text{enforce}} \times (\cos(R(\mathbf{x}) - R(\tilde{\mathbf{u}}), E(z_i)) - 1)\big]. \tag{2}$$

w_{enforce} is a hyper-parameter with a positive value. Larger w_{enforce} penalizes more on dissimilar words. The exp ensures the value to be positive thus the values can be converted to a probability distribution over words. We use the conventional cosine similarity to compute the distance of two vectors. If the embedding of a word $E(z)$ perfectly aligns with the sentence representation difference $R(\mathbf{x}) - R(\tilde{\mathbf{u}})$, it gets the largest probability. The enforcing distribution aims at making the candidate modification more similar to the original sentence. Note that enforcing distribution is identical on all t masks.

Sample a candidate sentence. We sample a candidate word for each masked position by $z_i \sim p_{\text{proposal}}(z_i|\tilde{\mathbf{u}}, \mathbf{x})$. We do not consider the effect of sampling one word on other masked positions (i.e., we do not recompute proposal distribution for the remaining masks after sampling a word) because language model distribution already considers the position of the mask and assigns a different distribution for each mask, meanwhile recomputing is inefficient. We use $\hat{\mathbf{u}}$ to denote the candidate sentence.

Critique score and decision function. We decide whether to accept the candidate sentence using a decision function. The decision function computes a heuristic critique score

$$C(\mathbf{u}) = \big(w_{\text{ppl}} \min(1 - \text{ppl}(\mathbf{u})/\text{ppl}(\mathbf{x}), 0) \quad (3)$$

$$+ w_{\text{sim}} \min(\cos\big(H(\mathbf{u}), H(\mathbf{x})\big) - \phi_{\text{sim}}, 0) \quad (4)$$

$$+ w_{\text{clf}} \min(\max_{y' \neq y} f(\mathbf{u})_{y'} - f(\mathbf{u})_y, 0)\big) \quad (5)$$

Eq. (3) penalizes sentences with high perplexity, where $\text{ppl}(\mathbf{x})$ is perplexity measured by a BERT model. Eq. (4) penalizes sentences with sentences with cosine similarity lower than ϕ_{sim}, where $H(\cdot)$ is the sentence representation by USE. Eq. (5) penalizes sentences that cannot be misclassified where $f(\mathbf{u})_y$ means the log probability of class y predicted by the classifier. w_{ppl}, w_{sim} and w_{clf} are hyperparameters.

The decision is made based on

$$\alpha = \exp[C(\hat{\mathbf{u}}) - C(\mathbf{u})]. \quad (6)$$

If $\alpha > 1$, the decision function accepts $\hat{\mathbf{u}}$; otherwise it accepts $\hat{\mathbf{u}}$ with probability α. The computation of α is motivated by the Metropolis–Hastings algorithm (Hastings, 1970) (See Appendix A). The critique score is a straightforward way to convert the multi-objective optimization problem into a single objective. Although it introduces several hyperparameters, R&R is no more complicated than conventional methods, which also require hyperparameter setting.

3.3 Rollback

In the rollback step, we eliminate modifications that do not correct the misclassification. It contains the following steps.

Find a minimum set of simple edits. We first find a set of simple edits that change the current rewritten sentence back to the original sentence. Simple edits mean the insertion, deletion or replacement of a single word, which is different from the modification in the rewrite step.

Rollback edits. For each edit, if reverting it does not correct the misclassification, then we revert the edit. For convenience, we scan each word in the sentence from right to left, and try to rollback each edit. Note that rollback may introduce grammar errors, but they can be fixed in future rewrite steps.

3.4 Vocabulary Adaptation

Computing p_{propose} is challenging because of the inconsistent vocabulary. The counter fitted word embeddings in $p_{\text{enforce}}(\cdot)$ works on a 65k-word vocabulary, while the BERT language model used in $p_{\text{lm}}(\cdot)$ uses a 30k-word-piece vocabulary which contains common words and affixes. Rare words are handled as multiple affixes. For example "hyperparameter" does not appear in the BERT vocabulary, so it is handled as "hyper", "##para", and "##meter". Since the BERT model is more complicated, we keep it as is and transfer word embeddings to BERT vocabulary. We train the word-piece embeddings as follows. Let $\mathbf{w} = \{w_1, \ldots, w_L\}$ be a plain text corpus tokenized by words. Let $T(w)$ be word-piece tokenization of a word. Let $E(w)$ be the original word embeddings and $E'(x)$ be the transferred embeddings on word-piece. We train the word-piece embeddings E' by minimizing the absolute error $\sum_{w \in \mathbf{w}} ||E(w) - \sum_{x \in T(w)} E'(x)||_1$. We initialize E' by copying the embedding on words shared by two vocabularies and set other embeddings to 0. We optimize the absolute error using stochastic gradient descent. In each step, we sample 5000 words from $\mathbf{w}$, then update E' accordingly. Figure 9 in Appendix illustrates the algorithm.

3.5 Summary of pre-trained models in R&R

In R&R, we employ several pre-trained models. Choices are made according to the different characteristics of these pre-trained models.

BERT for masked word prediction and perplexity. Because BERT is originally trained for masked word prediction, it can predict the word distribution given context from both sides. Thus, BERT is preferable for generating p_{lm}. Estimating the perplexity for a sentence requires BERT to run in decoder mode and be fine-tuned. Perplexity can also be measured by other language models such as GPT2 (Radford et al., 2019). We use BERT mainly for the consistent vocabulary with p_{lm}.

Word embedding and USE for similarity. Word embedding is more efficient as it only computes the sum of vectors and cosine similarity. In enforcing distribution, we need to replace the selected position with all possible z's and measure the similarity, so we use word embeddings for efficiency. In the critique score, only the proposal sentence needs to be measured, so we can afford more computation time of USE.

4 Experiments

We conducted experiments on a wide range of datasets and multiple victim classifiers to show the efficacy of R&R. We first evaluate the quality of adversarial examples using automatic metrics. Then, we conducted human evaluation to show the necessity to generate highly similar and fluent adversarial examples. Finally, we conduct an ablation study to analyze each component of our method, and discuss defense against the attack.

Datasets. We use 3 conventional text classification datasets: topic classification, sentiment classification, and question type classification. We also use 2 security-critical datasets: hate speech detection and fake news detection. Dataset details are given in Table 1.

Name	#C	Len	Description
AG	4	43	News topic classification by Zhang et al. (2015).
MR	2	32	Moview review dataset by Pang and Lee (2005).
TREC	6	8	Question type classification by Li and Roth (2002).
HATE	2	23	Hate speech detection dataset by Kurita et al. (2020).
FAKE	2	30	Fake news detection dataset by Yang et al. (2017). We use the first sentence of the news for classification.

Table 1: Dataset details. #C means number of classes. Len is the average number of words in a sentence.

Victim Classifiers. For each dataset, we use the full training set to train three victim classifiers: (1) BERT-base classifier (Devlin et al., 2019); (2) RoBERTa-large classifier (Liu et al., 2019), and (3) FastText classifier (Joulin et al., 2017).

	AG	MR	TREC	HATE	FAKE
BERT-base	92.8	88.2	97.8	94.0	81.2
RoBERTa-large	92.7	91.6	97.3	95.0	75.5
FastText	89.2	79.5	85.8	91.5	72.4
Log Perplexity	3.38	5.27	3.91	3.56	4.92

Table 2: Accuracy of 3 classifers and sentence log perplexity on the clean test set.

Baselines. We compare our method against two strong baseline attack methods: TextFooler (Jin et al., 2020) and CLARE (Li et al., 2021).

Hyperparameters. In R&R, we use the BERT-base language model for p_{lm}. For each dataset, we fine-tune the BERT language model using 5k batches on the training set[2] with batch size 32 and learning rate 0.0001, so it is adapted to the dataset. We set the enforcing distribution hyper-parameters $w_{\text{enforce}} = 5$. The decision function hyper-parameters $w_{\text{ppl}} = 5$, $w_{\text{sim}} = 20$, $\phi_{\text{sim}} = 0.95$, $w_{\text{clf}} = 2$. To generate each paraphrase, we set maximum rewrite iterations to be 200, and replace a 3-word span in each iteration. We implement R&R in a 50-sentence batch and apply early-stop when half of the batch are misclassified. We apply rollback operation every 10 steps of rewrite. Then, we return the adversarial example with the best critique score.

Hardware and Efficiency. We conduct experiments on Nvidia RTX Titan GPUs. We measure the efficiency using average wall clock time. On the MR dataset, one attack on a BERT-base classifier using R&R takes 15.8 seconds on average. CLARE takes 14.4 seconds on average. TextFooler is the most efficient algorithm which takes 0.45 seconds.

Automatic Metrics. We evaluate the efficacy of the attack method using 3 automatic metrics:

Similarity (↑): We use Universal Sentence Encoder to encode the original and adversarial sentence, then use the cosine distance of two vectors to measure the similarity. We set a similarity threshold at 0.95, so the similarity of a legitimate adversarial example should be greater than 0.95.

Log Perplexity (↓) shows the fluency of adversarial sentences.

Attack success rate (ASR) (↑) shows the ratio of correctly classified text that can be successfully

[2]We use the plain text to fine-tune the language model, and do not use the label. In the threat model, we assume the attacker can access plain text data from a similar domain.

	Attack	AG ASR	AG Sim	AG PPL	MR ASR	MR Sim	MR PPL	TREC ASR	TREC Sim	TREC PPL	HATE ASR	HATE Sim	HATE PPL	FAKE ASR	FAKE Sim	FAKE PPL
BERT	TextFooler	16.8	**0.98**	4.00	26.0	0.97	5.92	1.8	**0.97**	5.30	30.6	0.97	**3.53**	29.9	**0.98**	5.44
	CLARE	28.8	0.97	**3.60**	48.4	0.97	5.70	2.5	0.96	5.58	31.0	0.97	3.99	48.9	**0.98**	**5.02**
	R&R (Ours)	**54.1**	**0.98**	3.64	**63.4**	**0.98**	**5.36**	**10.8**	**0.97**	**5.29**	**55.3**	**0.98**	4.06	**57.0**	**0.98**	5.05
RoBERTa	TextFooler	15.6	**0.98**	5.21	18.0	**0.97**	6.06	0.4	0.96	7.09	24.0	**0.98**	4.20	26.6	**0.98**	5.45
	CLARE	23.3	0.97	5.24	45.9	**0.97**	5.67	2.5	**0.97**	6.53	35.7	0.97	4.37	46.0	**0.98**	**5.20**
	R&R (Ours)	**41.2**	**0.98**	**3.73**	**48.5**	**0.97**	**5.53**	**12.5**	**0.97**	**5.17**	**55.7**	0.97	**4.07**	**59.6**	**0.98**	5.25
FastText	TextFooler	25.8	**0.98**	4.16	33.1	**0.98**	5.85	6.5	**0.98**	5.04	21.7	**0.98**	**3.44**	35.3	**0.98**	5.46
	CLARE	28.9	0.97	3.91	41.5	0.97	5.79	8.5	0.97	6.06	35.6	0.97	4.24	76.0	**0.98**	5.15
	R&R (Ours)	**37.8**	**0.98**	**3.84**	**48.9**	**0.98**	**5.48**	**44.1**	**0.98**	**4.68**	**53.3**	**0.98**	4.03	**76.4**	**0.98**	**5.10**

Table 3: Automatic evaluation results. "Sim" and "PPL" represent similarity measured by USE and the log perplexity measured by BERT respectively.

attacked.

Human Metrics: Automatic metrics are not always reliable. We use Mechanical Turk to verify the similarity, fluency, and whether the label of the text is preserved with respect to human evaluation.

Sentence similarity (↑): Turkers are shown pairs of original and adversarial sentences, and are asked whether the two sentences have the same semantic meaning. They annotate the sentence in a 5-likert, where 1 means strongly disagree, 2 means disagree, 3 means not sure, 4 means agree, and 5 means strongly agree.

Sentence fluency (↑): Turkers are shown a random shuffle of adversarial sentences, and are asked to rate the fluency in a 5-likert, where 1 describes a bad sentence, 3 describes a meaningful sentence with a few grammar errors, and 5 describes a perfect sentence.

Label match (↑): Turkers are shown a random shuffle of adversarial sentences and are asked whether it belongs to the class of the original sentence. They are asked to rate 0 as disagree, 0.5 as not sure, and 1 as agree.

We sample 100 adversarial sentences from each method, and each task is annotated by 2 Turkers. We do not annotate label matches on the FAKE dataset because identifying fake news is too challenging for Turkers. We require the location of the Turkers to be in the United States, and their Hit Approval Rate to be greater than 95%. The screenshots of the annotation tasks are shown on Figure 7 in Appendix.

Examples. Table 4 shows some examples. We find R&R makes natural modifications to the sentence and preserves the semantic meanings.

Original (prediction: Technology): GERMANTOWN , Md . A Maryland - based private lab that analyzes criminal - case DNA evidence has fired an analyst for allegedly falsifying test data .
Adversarial (prediction: Business): GERMANTOWN , Md . A Maryland - based bio testing company that analyzes criminal - case DNA evidence has fired an analyst for allegedly falsifying test data .

Original (prediction: Sport): LeBron James scored 25 points , Jeff McInnis added a season - high 24 and the Cleveland Cavaliers won their sixth straight , 100 - 84 over the Charlotte Bobcats on Saturday night .
Adversarial (prediction: World): LeBron James scored 25 points , Jeff McInnis added a season - high 24 and the Cleveland Cavaliers won their sixth straight , 100 - 84 Saturday over the visiting Charlotte Bobcats on Saturday night ..

Original (prediction: Negative): don ' t be fooled by the impressive cast list - eye see you is pure junk .
Adversarial (prediction: Positive): don ' t be fooled by this impressive cast list - eye see you is pure junk .

Original (prediction: Ask for description): What is die - casting ?
Adversarial (prediction: Ask for entity): What is the technique of die - casting ?

Original (prediction: Toxic) go back under your rock u irrelevant party puppet
Adversarial (prediction: Harmless) go back under the rock u irrelevant party puppet

Table 4: A few adversarial examples generated by R&R with the perturbation in red.

4.1 Is R&R effective in attacking classifiers?

Table 3 shows the ASR of R&R and baseline methods (with a rigorous 0.95 threshold on similarity). R&R achieves the best ASR on all datasets and across all classifiers. The average improvement compared with the CLARE baseline is +16.2%, +12.8%, +14.0% on BERT-base, RoBERTa-large and FastText classifiers respectively. This means that with the same rigorous similarity threshold, R&R is capable of finding more adversarial ex-

	AG			MR			TREC			HATE			FAKE	
	S.	F.	M.	S.	F.	M.	S.	F.	M.	S.	F.	M.	S.	F.
TextFooler	3.93	3.58	0.90	3.3	3.49	**0.92**	3.25	2.88	0.88	3.76	3.61	0.46	3.58	3.58
CLARE	3.75	3.65	0.93	2.44	3.33	0.74	3.00	3.00	0.75	**3.89**	**4.41**	**0.81**	3.67	3.65
R&R (Ours)	**4.12**	**3.87**	**0.99**	**3.48**	**3.61**	0.85	**3.59**	**3.14**	**0.89**	3.59	3.94	0.76	**3.81**	**3.87**

Table 5: Human evaluation. "S.", "F." and "M." represents the similarity, fluency and label match annotated by human.

amples, i.e. for some text, R&R can find adversarial examples with a similarity higher than 0.95 while baseline methods cannot. We further measure whether R&R can outperform baselines with less rigorous similarity thresholds. On Figure 3, we set different thresholds and show the corresponding ASR. We observe that the curves of R&R are above the baseline curves in most cases, showing that R&R outperforms baselines on most threshold settings. It means R&R can achieve a higher ASR with various different similarity thresholds.

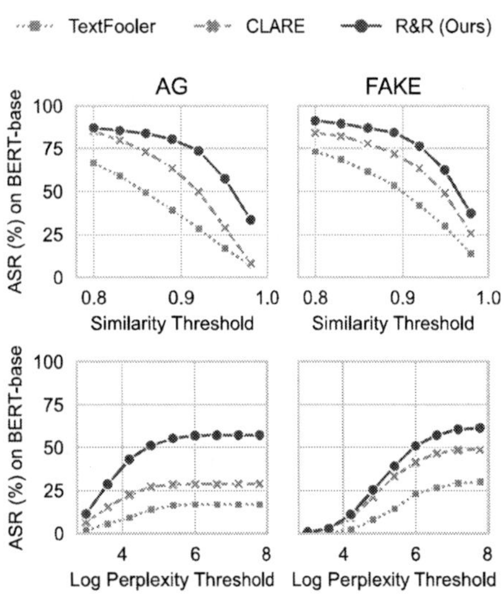

Figure 3: Attack success rate with respect to different similarity and perplexity constraints on BERT classifier. When evaluating different similarity thresholds, we do not set thresholds on perplexity. When evaluating perplexity thresholds, we fix the similarity threshold to 0.95. See Figure 8 in Appendix for other datasets and classifiers.

4.2 Does R&R generate semantically similar and fluent adversarial sentences?

Table 3 shows the USE similarity metric and log perplexity fluency metric (with a rigorous 0.95 threshold on similarity). Since we already apply a high threshold to ensure the adversarial examples are similar to the original sentences, the similarity metrics do not show significant differences. On AG, MR, TREC and FAKE datasets and 3 classifiers (a total of 12 settings), R&R outperforms baseline methods in 9 cases. This shows R&R keeps sentence fluency as high as baseline methods do, and does not sacrifice sentence fluency for higher ASR. The only failure case is on the HATE dataset, where TextFooler outperforms R&R in perplexity. Further investigation shows that it is because of the perplexity of the original sentence. If the original sentence has high perplexity, the corresponding adversarial sentence is likely to have high perplexity. It is possible that the original sentences that R&R succeeds on have higher perplexity than those successfully attacked by TextFooler. Therefore, we compute the average log perplexity for original sentences that are successfully attacked, and find that it is 3.24 for TextFooler and 3.94 for R&R. So TextFooler achieves low perplexity because it succeeds on original sentences with low perplexity while failing on those with higher perplexity.

USE similarity and log perplexity are proxy measures. To verify them, human annotations are needed. Table 5 shows the human evaluation results. R&R outperforms baselines on similarity and fluency on 4 datasets. This shows that by optimizing the critique score, R&R improves the similarity and fluency of adversarial sentences. Our method fails on the HATE dataset despite good automatic metrics. We hypothesize that this dataset collected from Twitter is more noisy than the others, causing the malfunction of automatic similarity and fluency metrics.

4.3 Do adversarial sentences preserve the original labels?

Preserving the original label is critical for an adversarial sentence to be legitimate. Table 5 also shows the human evaluation on label match. At least 76% of adversarial examples generated by R&R preserves the original label thus being legitimate. We also find that the label match is task dependent.

Preserving original labels on AG dataset is easier than others, while the HATE dataset is the most challenging one.

4.4 How does each component in R&R contribute to the good performance?

We conduct ablation study on AG and FAKE datasets to understand the contribution of stochastic decision function, and periodic rollback.

Decision Function In the Rewrite stage, we use a stochastic decision function based on the critique score. One alternative can be a deterministic greedy decision function, which accepts a rewrite only if the rewrite increases the critique score. Figure 4 shows the ASR with respect to different similarity thresholds. We find that the stochastic decision function outperforms the greedy one. We interpret the phenomenon as the greedy decision function gets stuck in local maxima, whereas the stochastic one can overcome this issue by accepting a slightly worse rewrite.

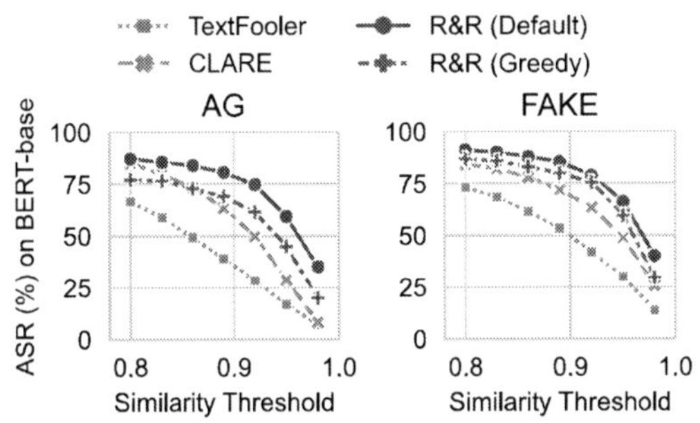

Figure 4: The ASR of R&R using different decision settings. "Greedy" means using a greedy decision function, which accepts a rewrite only if it has a higher critique score.

Rollback We apply rollback periodically during the attack. We compare it with two alternatives: (1) no rollback (NRB) which only uses rewrite to construct the adversarial sentences, and (2) single rollback (SRB) which applies rollback once on the NRB results. Figure 5 shows the result. We find that rollback has a significant impact. NRB performs the worst. Without rollback, it is difficult to get high cosine similarity when many words in the sentence have been changed. Single rollback increases the number of overlapped words, which usually increases the similarity measurement. By periodically applying the rollback, the rollbacked sentence can be further rewritten to improve the similarity and fluency metrics, thus yielding to the best performance.

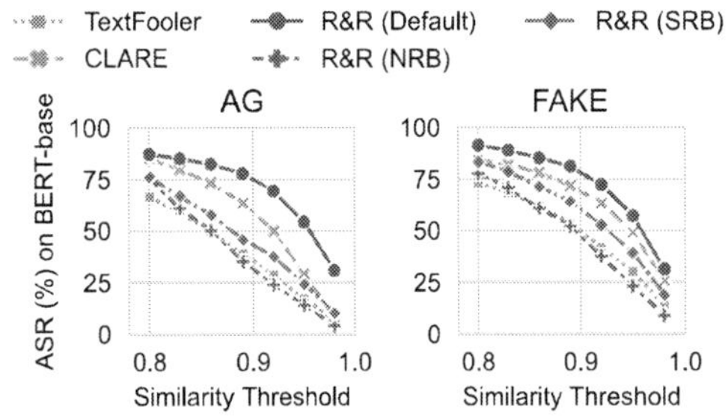

Figure 5: The ASR of R&R using different rollback settings. "NRB" means no rollback operation and "SRB" means single rollback.

Multiple-Word Masking In the Rewrite stage, we mask a span of multiple words in each iteration. Intuitively, when using a smaller span size, the masked words are easier to predict. The proposal distribution will assign high probability to the original words at masked positions. Therefore, the candidate sentences are likely to be identical to the original sentence, thus limiting the number of perturbations explored. When the span is large, predicting words becomes more difficult. Thus, we can sample different candidate sentences. But it is more likely to construct dissimilar or influential sentences. We vary the span size from 1, 2, 3, to 4 and show the results on Figure 6. We find that using span size 3 yields the best performance over most similarity thresholds.

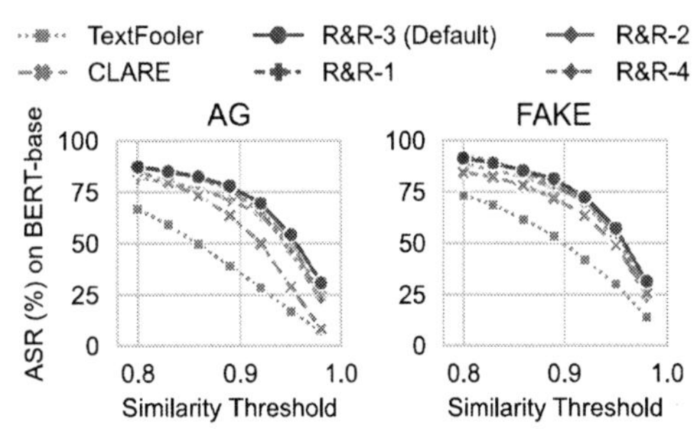

Figure 6: The ASR of R&R using different masking span sizes. R&R-1 to R&R-4 represent the span size of 1 to 4 respectively. We use span size 3 by default.

4.4.1 How do existing defense methods work against R&R?

We further explore the defense against this attack:

- Adversarial attack methods sometimes introduce outlier words to trigger misclassification. Therefore we follow Qi et al. (2020) and apply a perplexity-based filtering to eliminate outlier words in sentences. We generate adversarial sentences on vanilla classifiers, then apply the filtering.
- SHIELD (Le et al., 2022) is a recently proposed algorithm that modifies the last layer of a neural network to defend against adversarial attack. We apply this method to classifiers and attack the robust classifier.

	AG		FAKE	
	+Filter	+SHIELD	+Filter	+SHIELD
TextFooler	6.2	8.2	13.8	16.7
CLARE	5.6	18.2	19.0	51.1
R&R (ours)	**22.3**	**30.6**	**23.1**	**59.4**

Table 6: The ASR of attack methods when applying the perplexity-based filtering (Filter) and the SHIELD defense on the BERT classifier.

Table 6 shows the ASR of attack methods with a defense applied. We show that existing defense methods cannot effectively defend against R&R. It still outperforms baselines in ASR by large margin.

5 Related Work

Several recent works proposed word-level adversarial attacks on text classifiers. This type of attack misleads the classifier's predictions by perturbing the words in the input sentence. TextFooler (Jin et al., 2020) shows the adversarial vulnerability of the state-of-the-art text classifiers. It uses heuristics to replace words with synonyms to mislead the classifier effectively. It relies on several pre-trained models, such as word embeddings (Mrkšic et al., 2016), part-of-speech tagger, and Universal Sentence Encoder (Cer et al., 2018) to perturb the sentence without changing its meaning. However, simple synonym substitution without considering the context results in unnatural sentences. Several works (Garg and Ramakrishnan, 2020; Li et al., 2020, 2021) address this issue by using masked language models such as BERT (Devlin et al., 2019) to propose more natural word substitutions. Our method also belongs to this category. But R&R does not maximize the efficacy of each perturbation, instead it allows exploring combinations of perturbations to generate adversarial examples with high similarity with the original sentence. Besides word-level attacks (Zang et al., 2020; Ren et al., 2019), there are also character-level attacks which introduce typos to trigger misclassification (Papernot et al., 2016; Liang et al., 2017; Samanta and Mehta, 2018), and sentence-level attacks which attack a classifier by altering the sentence structure (Iyyer et al., 2018). Zhang et al. (2020) gives a comprehensive survey on such attack methods. Other work on robustness to adversarial attacks in NLP includes robustness of the machine translation models (Cheng et al., 2019), robustness in domain adaptation (Oren et al., 2019), adversarial examples generated by reinforcement learning (Wong, 2017; Vijayaraghavan and Roy, 2019), and certified robustness (Jia et al., 2019). Adversarial attack libraries (Morris et al., 2020; Zeng et al., 2021) are also developed to help future research.

6 Conclusion

In this paper, we formulate the textual adversarial attack as a multi-objective optimization problem. We use a critique score to synthesize the similarity, fluency, and misclassification objectives, and propose R&R that optimizes the critique score to generate high-quality adversarial examples. We conduct extensive experiments. Both automatic and human evaluation show that the proposed method succeeds in optimizing the automatic similarity and fluency metrics to generate adversarial examples of higher quality than previous methods.

Ethical Considerations

In this paper, we propose R&R to generate adversarial sentences. Like all other adversarial attack methods, this method could be abused by malicious users to attack NLP systems and obtain illegitimate benefits. However, it is still necessary for the research community to develop methods to exploit all vulnerabilities of a classifier based on which more robust classifiers can be developed.

Acknowledgments

Alfredo Cuesta-Infante has been funded by the Spanish Government research project MICINN PID2021-128362OB-I00.

References

Daniel Cer, Yinfei Yang, Sheng-yi Kong, Nan Hua, Nicole Limtiaco, Rhomni St. John, Noah Constant, Mario Guajardo-Cespedes, Steve Yuan, Chris Tar,

Brian Strope, and Ray Kurzweil. 2018. Universal sentence encoder for english. In Proceedings of the Conference on Empirical Methods in Natural Language Processing: System Demonstrations.

Yong Cheng, Lu Jiang, and Wolfgang Macherey. 2019. Robust neural machine translation with doubly adversarial inputs. In Proceedings of the Annual Meeting of the Association for Computational Linguistics.

Jacob Devlin, Ming-Wei Chang, Kenton Lee, and Kristina Toutanova. 2019. Bert: Pre-training of deep bidirectional transformers for language understanding. In Proceedings of the Annual Conference of the North American Chapter of the Association for Computational Linguistics.

Siddhant Garg and Goutham Ramakrishnan. 2020. Bae: Bert-based adversarial examples for text classification. In Proceedings of the Conference on Empirical Methods in Natural Language Processing and the International Joint Conference on Natural Language Processing.

W Keith Hastings. 1970. Monte carlo sampling methods using markov chains and their applications.

Mohit Iyyer, John Wieting, Kevin Gimpel, and Luke Zettlemoyer. 2018. Adversarial example generation with syntactically controlled paraphrase networks. In Proceedings of the 2018 Conference of the North American Chapter of the Association for Computational Linguistics: Human Language Technologies, Volume 1 (Long Papers).

Robin Jia, Aditi Raghunathan, Kerem Göksel, and Percy Liang. 2019. Certified robustness to adversarial word substitutions. In Proceedings of the Conference on Empirical Methods in Natural Language Processing and the International Joint Conference on Natural Language Processing.

Di Jin, Zhijing Jin, Joey Tianyi Zhou, and Peter Szolovits. 2020. Is bert really robust? natural language attack on text classification and entailment. In Proceedings of the AAAI Conference on Artificial Intelligence.

Armand Joulin, Édouard Grave, Piotr Bojanowski, and Tomáš Mikolov. 2017. Bag of tricks for efficient text classification. In Proceedings of the 15th Conference of the European Chapter of the Association for Computational Linguistics: Volume 2, Short Papers, pages 427–431.

Keita Kurita, Paul Michel, and Graham Neubig. 2020. Weight poisoning attacks on pretrained models. In ACL.

Thai Le, Noseong Park, and Dongwon Lee. 2022. Shield: Defending textual neural networks against multiple black-box adversarial attacks with stochastic multi-expert patcher. In Proceedings of the 60th Annual Meeting of the Association for Computational Linguistics (Volume 1: Long Papers), pages 6661–6674.

Dianqi Li, Yizhe Zhang, Hao Peng, Liqun Chen, Chris Brockett, Ming-Ting Sun, and William B Dolan. 2021. Contextualized perturbation for textual adversarial attack. In Proceedings of the 2021 Conference of the North American Chapter of the Association for Computational Linguistics.

Linyang Li, Ruotian Ma, Qipeng Guo, Xiangyang Xue, and Xipeng Qiu. 2020. Bert-attack: Adversarial attack against bert using bert. In Proceedings of the Conference on Empirical Methods in Natural Language Processing and the International Joint Conference on Natural Language Processing.

Xin Li and Dan Roth. 2002. Learning question classifiers. In COLING 2002: The 19th International Conference on Computational Linguistics.

Bin Liang, Hongcheng Li, Miaoqiang Su, Pan Bian, Xirong Li, and Wenchang Shi. 2017. Deep text classification can be fooled. In Proceedings of the International Joint Conferences on Artificial Intelligence.

Yinhan Liu, Myle Ott, Naman Goyal, Jingfei Du, Mandar Joshi, Danqi Chen, Omer Levy, Mike Lewis, Luke Zettlemoyer, and Veselin Stoyanov. 2019. Roberta: A robustly optimized bert pretraining approach. arXiv preprint arXiv:1907.11692.

John Morris, Eli Lifland, Jin Yong Yoo, Jake Grigsby, Di Jin, and Yanjun Qi. 2020. Textattack: A framework for adversarial attacks, data augmentation, and adversarial training in nlp. In Proceedings of the Conference on Empirical Methods in Natural Language Processing: System Demonstrations.

Nikola Mrkšic, Diarmuid OSéaghdha, Blaise Thomson, Milica Gašic, Lina Rojas-Barahona, Pei-Hao Su, David Vandyke, Tsung-Hsien Wen, and Steve Young. 2016. Counter-fitting word vectors to linguistic constraints. In Proceedings of NAACL-HLT.

Yonatan Oren, Shiori Sagawa, Tatsunori B Hashimoto, and Percy Liang. 2019. Distributionally robust language modeling. In Proceedings of the Conference on Empirical Methods in Natural Language Processing and the International Joint Conference on Natural Language Processing.

Bo Pang and Lillian Lee. 2005. Seeing stars: Exploiting class relationships for sentiment categorization with respect to rating scales. In Proceedings of the Annual Meeting of the Association for Computational Linguistics.

Nicolas Papernot, Patrick McDaniel, Ananthram Swami, and Richard Harang. 2016. Crafting adversarial input sequences for recurrent neural networks. In Proceedings of the IEEE Military Communications Conference.

Fanchao Qi, Yangyi Chen, Mukai Li, Yuan Yao, Zhiyuan Liu, and Maosong Sun. 2020. Onion: A simple and effective defense against textual backdoor attacks. arXiv preprint arXiv:2011.10369.

Alec Radford, Jeffrey Wu, Rewon Child, David Luan, Dario Amodei, and Ilya Sutskever. 2019. Language models are unsupervised multitask learners. OpenAI Blog.

Shuhuai Ren, Yihe Deng, Kun He, and Wanxiang Che. 2019. Generating natural language adversarial examples through probability weighted word saliency. In Proceedings of the Annual Meeting of the Association for Computational Linguistics.

Suranjana Samanta and Sameep Mehta. 2018. Generating adversarial text samples. In Proceedings of the European Conference on Information Retrieval.

Fatemeh Torabi Asr and Maite Taboada. 2019. Big data and quality data for fake news and misinformation detection. Big Data & Society, 6(1):2053951719843310.

Prashanth Vijayaraghavan and Deb Roy. 2019. Generating black-box adversarial examples for text classifiers using a deep reinforced model. In Proceedings of the European Conference on Machine Learning and Principles and Practice of Knowledge Discovery in Databases.

Catherine Wong. 2017. Dancin seq2seq: Fooling text classifiers with adversarial text example generation. arXiv preprint arXiv:1712.05419.

Liang Wu, Fred Morstatter, Kathleen M Carley, and Huan Liu. 2019. Misinformation in social media: definition, manipulation, and detection. ACM SIGKDD Explorations Newsletter.

Fan Yang, Arjun Mukherjee, and Eduard Dragut. 2017. Satirical news detection and analysis using attention mechanism and linguistic features. In EMNLP.

Yuan Zang, Fanchao Qi, Chenghao Yang, Zhiyuan Liu, Meng Zhang, Qun Liu, and Maosong Sun. 2020. Word-level textual adversarial attacking as combinatorial optimization. In Proceedings of the 58th Annual Meeting of the Association for Computational Linguistics.

Guoyang Zeng, Fanchao Qi, Qianrui Zhou, Tingji Zhang, Zixian Ma, Bairu Hou, Yuan Zang, Zhiyuan Liu, and Maosong Sun. 2021. OpenAttack: An open-source textual adversarial attack toolkit. In Proceedings of the 59th Annual Meeting of the Association for Computational Linguistics and the 11th International Joint Conference on Natural Language Processing: System Demonstrations.

Wei Emma Zhang, Quan Z Sheng, Ahoud Alhazmi, and Chenliang Li. 2020. Adversarial attacks on deep-learning models in natural language processing: A survey. ACM Transactions on Intelligent Systems and Technology.

Xiang Zhang, Junbo Zhao, and Yann LeCun. 2015. Character-level convolutional networks for text classification. In Proceedings of the Conference on Advances in Neural Information Processing Systems.

Zhixuan Zhou, Huankang Guan, Meghana Moorthy Bhat, and Justin Hsu. 2019. Fake news detection via NLP is vulnerable to adversarial attacks. In Proc. of the 11th Int. Conf. on Agents and Artificial Intelligence, ICAART'19.

A Relation to Metropolis-Hastings Sampling

Metropolis-Hastings sampling (MHS) (Hastings, 1970) is a Markov-chain Monte Carlo (MCMC) for generating independent unbiased samples from a distribution. Assume we have a target distribution of sentences $p_{\text{target}}(\mathbf{u}|\mathbf{x}, y)$ such that legitimate adversarial sentences of $\mathbf{x}$ have high probability, while other sentences (could be a meaningless sequence of words) have low probability, we may attempt to solve the adversarial attack problem by MHS. Because we are likely to get an adversarial sentence of $\mathbf{x}$ by drawing samples from $p_{\text{target}}(\mathbf{u}|\mathbf{x}, y)$. To apply MHS, we need to choose a transition probability $p_{\text{transition}}(\hat{\mathbf{u}}|\mathbf{u}, \mathbf{x}, y)$ that defines the probability to transit from one sentence to the next sentence in the MCMC. Then the MHS has following steps:

1. Start with $\mathbf{u} = \mathbf{x}$.
2. Get a candidate $\hat{\mathbf{u}} \sim p_{\text{transition}}(\hat{\mathbf{u}}|\mathbf{u}, \mathbf{x}, y)$.
3. Compute
$$\alpha = \frac{p_{\text{target}}(\hat{\mathbf{u}}|\mathbf{x}, y) p_{\text{transition}}(\mathbf{u}|\hat{\mathbf{u}}, \mathbf{x}, y)}{p_{\text{target}}(\mathbf{u}|\mathbf{x}, y) p_{\text{transition}}(\hat{\mathbf{u}}|\mathbf{u}, \mathbf{x}, y)}. \quad (7)$$
4. With probability $\min(\alpha, 1)$, use $\hat{\mathbf{u}}$ as new $\mathbf{u}$ and go to step 2; otherwise use the previous $\mathbf{u}$ and go to step 2.
5. After sufficient iterations, $\mathbf{u}$ is a sample drawn from $p_{\text{target}}(\mathbf{u}|\mathbf{x}, y)$. Note that MHS needs a lot of iterations considering the huge space of all sentences.

The rewrite step in R&R is similar to MHS, if we consider $\exp[C(\mathbf{u})]$ as the unnormalized target distribution[3] and $p_{\text{proposal}}(\cdot)$ as the transition probability. The definition of α in Eq. (6) and Eq. (7) is one significant difference, where R&R only uses target distribution and omits the transition probability. We find omitting it can make the sampling bias towards sentences with higher probability in target distribution (i.e., sentences with higher critique score), which benefits the adversarial attack efficacy.

[3] We apply the exponential function to make sure the probability mass is positive.

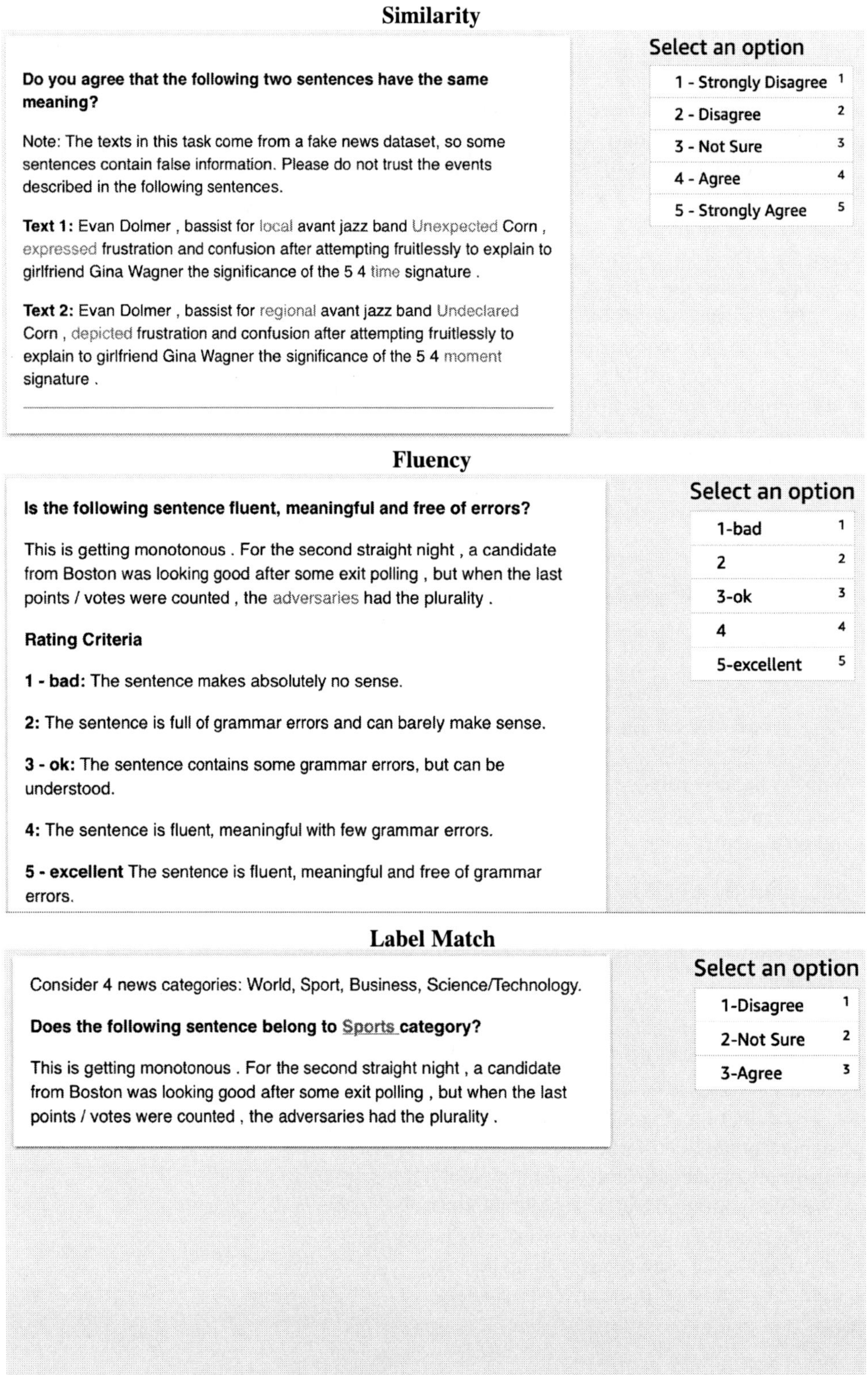

Similarity

Do you agree that the following two sentences have the same meaning?

Note: The texts in this task come from a fake news dataset, so some sentences contain false information. Please do not trust the events described in the following sentences.

Text 1: Evan Dolmer , bassist for local avant jazz band Unexpected Corn , expressed frustration and confusion after attempting fruitlessly to explain to girlfriend Gina Wagner the significance of the 5 4 time signature .

Text 2: Evan Dolmer , bassist for regional avant jazz band Undeclared Corn , depicted frustration and confusion after attempting fruitlessly to explain to girlfriend Gina Wagner the significance of the 5 4 moment signature .

Select an option

1 - Strongly Disagree 1
2 - Disagree 2
3 - Not Sure 3
4 - Agree 4
5 - Strongly Agree 5

Fluency

Is the following sentence fluent, meaningful and free of errors?

This is getting monotonous . For the second straight night , a candidate from Boston was looking good after some exit polling , but when the last points / votes were counted , the adversaries had the plurality .

Rating Criteria

1 - bad: The sentence makes absolutely no sense.

2: The sentence is full of grammar errors and can barely make sense.

3 - ok: The sentence contains some grammar errors, but can be understood.

4: The sentence is fluent, meaningful with few grammar errors.

5 - excellent The sentence is fluent, meaningful and free of grammar errors.

Select an option

1-bad 1
2 2
3-ok 3
4 4
5-excellent 5

Label Match

Consider 4 news categories: World, Sport, Business, Science/Technology.

Does the following sentence belong to Sports category?

This is getting monotonous . For the second straight night , a candidate from Boston was looking good after some exit polling , but when the last points / votes were counted , the adversaries had the plurality .

Select an option

1-Disagree 1
2-Not Sure 2
3-Agree 3

Figure 7: The screenshots of MTurk tasks.

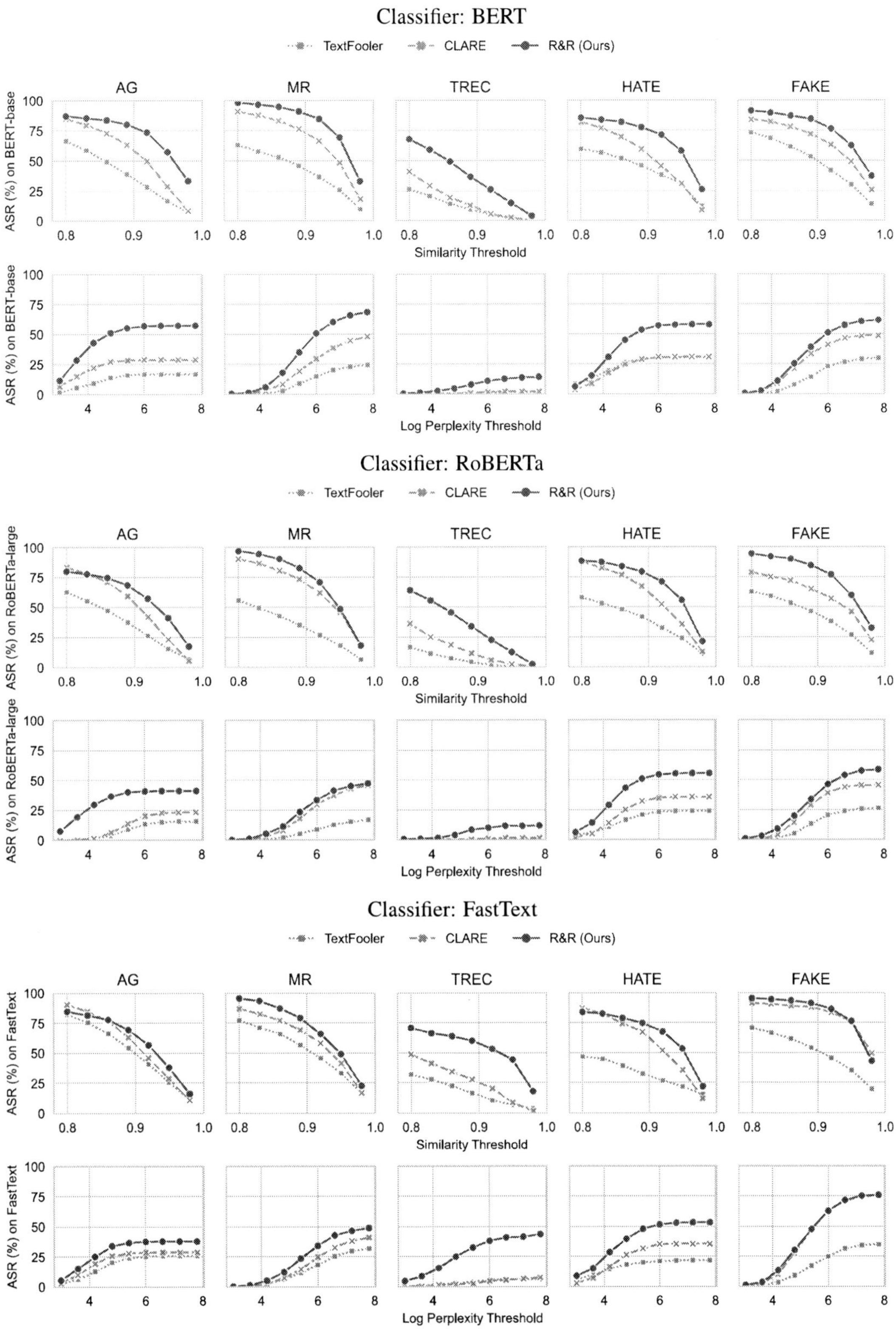

Figure 8: Attack success rate with respect to different similarity and perplexity constraints. When evaluating different similarity thresholds, we do not set thresholds on perplexity. When evaluating perplexity thresholds, we fix the similarity threshold to 0.95.

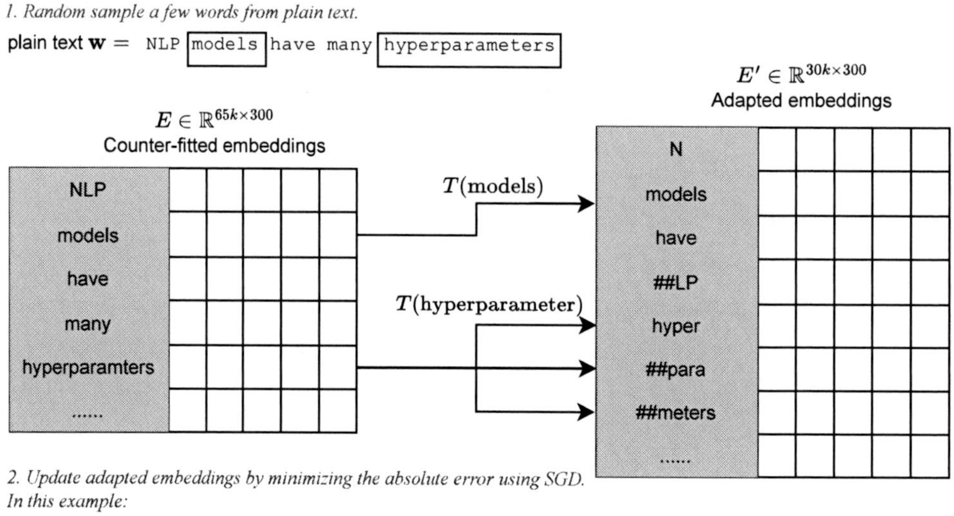

$$\begin{aligned} \text{minimize } & \left|E(\text{hyperparameters}) - E'(\text{hyper}) - E'(\#\#\text{para}) - E'(\#\#\text{meters})\right| \\ & + \left|E(\text{models}) - E'(\text{models})\right| \end{aligned}$$

Figure 9: One learning step of vocabulary adaptation algorithm. The plain text has only 5 words in this example, but it has much more words in real datasets. We illustrate by sampling only 2 words from plain text, while we sample 5000 words in practice.

A Simple yet Effective Learnable Positional Encoding Method for Improving Document Transformer Model

Guoxin Wang, Yijuan Lu, Lei Cui, Tengchao Lv, Dinei Florencio, Cha Zhang
Microsoft Corporation
{guow,yijlu,lecu,tengchaolv,dinei,chazhang}@microsoft.com

Abstract

Positional encoding plays a key role in Transformer-based architecture, which is to indicate and embed token sequential order information. Understanding documents with unreliable reading order information is a real challenge for document Transformer models. This paper proposes a simple and effective positional encoding method, learnable sinusoidal positional encoding (LSPE), by building a learnable sinusoidal positional encoding feed-forward network. We apply LSPE to document Transformer models and pretrain them on document datasets. Then we finetune and evaluate the model performance on document understanding tasks in form, receipt, and invoice domains. Experimental results show our proposed method not only outperforms other baselines, but also demonstrates its robustness and stability on handling noisy data with incorrect order information.

1 Introduction

Document understanding (in some context known as Document intelligence, Document AI) aims to extract, recognize, and understand information from document images. The performance of document understanding model is largely benefited from recent development of large scale pre-training technique on cross-modality data and effective transformer architectures (Cui et al., 2021). Document Transformer Model, e.g. LayoutLM (Xu et al., 2020b), is pretrained from visually-rich document data which consists of text, layout, and visual information based on Transformer architecture (Shaw et al., 2018). Recently, Xu et al. (2020a); Hong et al. (2021); Appalaraju et al. (2021); Li et al. (2021a) propose various approaches to further improve the performance of Transformer models on more challenging document understanding tasks.

Different from recurrent and convolutional based structures, Transformer based model does not encode relative or absolute position information explicitly since it is solely based on order-invariant attentional mechanism. In the original Transformer architecture (Vaswani et al., 2017), both learnable vector embedding and sinusoidal function are introduced as positional encoding methods for capturing positional information from input tokens. In order to improve positional representation ability, Shaw et al. (2018); Huang et al. (2020); He et al. (2021); Chi et al. (2021) introduce several relative position strategies into attention computation steps in the Transformer. Along with sequential reading order from text, visually-rich documents contain more spatial information of text blocks which poses a greater challenge to understand rich semantic and spatial relationship information at the same time. To obtain text blocks from document images, current off-the-shelf methods are borrowing results from existing Optical Character Recognition (OCR) engine while the reading order of text blocks is mostly arranged by a heuristic manner, top-to-bottom and left-to-right (Clausner et al., 2013; Wang et al., 2021). For documents with complex layout, such as forms, invoices, or receipts, the performance of reading order is not consistent which always leads to irrelevant or embarrassing predictions (Cui et al., 2021). Moreover, existing Document Transformer Models suffer from huge performance degradation on noisy data with unreliable reading order information (Hong et al., 2021). Therefore positional encoding plays an essential role in document Transformer models, which is to encode position embedding from data with inherent reading or spatial information. Thus, it is crucial to improve the robustness and learnability of position encoding methods, and therefore boost the model performance on noisy data with unreliable order and spatial information.

In this paper, we propose a learnable sinusoidal position encoding method, $LSPE$, by building a learnable fully connected feed-forward sinusoidal positional encoding network. And we apply it to

Findings of the Association for Computational Linguistics: AACL-IJCNLP 2022, pages 453–463
November 20–23, 2022.

represent multidimensional position information in the document Transformer model. Compared with current discrete embedding layer in the Transformer model, our method is numeric continuous for position scales which could improve positional representation of relative positions or distances between spatial elements. Our approach keeps the advantage of extrapolability from sinusoidal function which could extend to longer position than training cases. In addition, we build a learnable sinusoidal position network, which helps the pretrained language model to be easily adapted to various downstream tasks effectively.

We pretrain LayoutLM with various positional encoding methods and other baselines. Then we evaluate and compare the models' performance on document understanding downstream tasks. Experimental results show that our $LSPE$ method significantly outperforms other baselines and recent document language models on FUNSD, SROIE and our in-house invoice datasets. In addition, we evaluate the model robustness on noisy data by utilizing global and local shuffling augmentation strategies. Our method shows stable performance than other positional encoding methods with unreliable reading order information. Furthermore, we visualize and analyze similarity of positional representation of each method from 1D to 2D positional embedding of our pretrained models.

In summary, our contributions could be highlighted as follows: 1) We propose a simple and effective learnable positional encoding method with better learnability and extrapolability. It can be applied to any transformer based models to help them better encode and understand positional information. 2) We pretrain document Transformer models with $LSPE$ and other methods, and evaluate model performance on document understanding tasks. Experimental results show our proposed method outperforms other baselines and recent SOTA approaches on FUNSD, SROIE, and a large-scale invoice dataset.3) By the ablation study of employing global and local block shuffling augmentations, our method demonstrates optimal performance and robustness on noisy data with unreliable reading order information. Finally, our pretrained models with implementation of position encoding code will be publicly available.[1]

[1] `https://aka.ms/DocLPE`

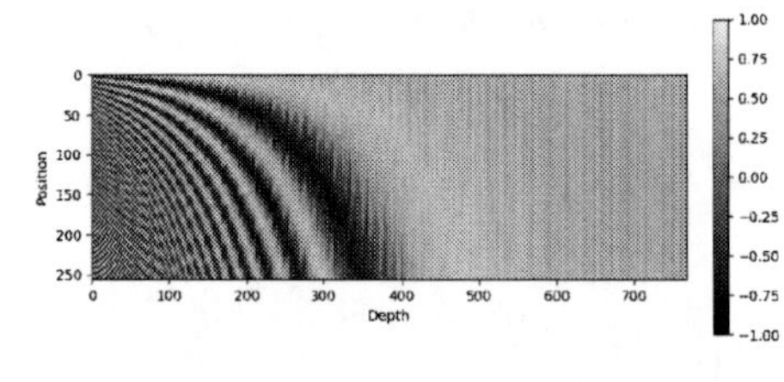

Figure 1: Visualization of 768-dimensional sinusoidal positional encoding for sequence with the maximum length of 256. Each position row p represents the embedding vector $PE_{sine}(p)$ as positional representation.

2 Background

Positional Encoding Methods in Transformer In the original proposal of Transformer architecture (Vaswani et al., 2017), both learnable vector and sinusoidal function are introduced as positional encoding methods and perform nearly identically in their downstream tasks. Although sinusoidal version with predefined wavelength has unique extrapolability which allows to encode longer sequential position than pre-training samples, it does not always perform well on downstream tasks (Shaw et al., 2018), due to the lack of learnability and flexibility. In practical, most pretrained language models, (e.g. (Devlin et al., 2018; Liu et al., 2019)), utilize learnable vector embedding (Gehring et al., 2017) as positional representation. Recently, several approaches are proposed to enhance positional representation by adding relative position information into attention score computation stage to improve performance of Transformer based models (Shaw et al., 2018; Huang et al., 2020; Dai et al., 2019; Dufter et al., 2021). By leveraging relative positional encoding and other advanced pretraining techniques, He et al. (2021) and Chi et al. (2021) achieve state-of-the-art performance on multiple nature language understanding tasks. Li et al. (2021b) explore the position encoding method in vision domain and propose a learnable Fourier feature to enhance positional encoding in Transformer. It outperforms other methods on both accuracy and convergence speed with vision transformer (Dosovitskiy et al., 2020) based model. Since it is nontrivial to modify or replace backbone of model structure during fine-tuning stage, some research works propose auxiliary tasks (Wang et al., 2019; Pham et al., 2021) or data augmentation approaches (Wei and Zou, 2019; Dai and Adel, 2020) to leverage absolute or relative position information without modifying model structure.

Document Transformer Models In document understanding area, LayoutLM (Xu et al., 2020b) utilizes the pretrained language model to resolve document understanding tasks, and achieves state-of-the-art performance on multiple document understanding benchmarks. To represent 2D position embedding, it decouples the x- and y- axes of text bounding box and sums up positional representations from each dimension independently. LayoutLMv2(Xu et al., 2020a) introduces spatial-aware self-attention mechanism to enhance the layout representation from both 1d and 2d relative position bias. BROS(Hong et al., 2021) uses relative position information in attentional mechanism along with absolute positional encoding from sinusoidal function, which perceives more spatial layout information. Li et al. (2021a) utilizes shared position information in the text blocks as position representation which further improves entity extraction performance by understanding cell information from layout. Appalaraju et al. (2021) proposes an End-to-End Transformer based model with 1D relative position embedding in attentional mechanism.

Document Understanding Tasks RVL-CDIP (Harley et al., 2015) is a document classification dataset with 400K gray-scale English document images in 16 document categories. This dataset is a subset of IIT-CDIP (Lewis et al., 2006) and has been widely used for pre-training language model purpose. Entity extraction is a classic and essential task in nature language understanding. It is to locate the boundary of entities and assign predefined classes to them. There are several popular benchmarks, consisting of multi-modality information with text, layout, and visual, to evaluate the performance of visually-rich document understanding. FUNSD (Guillaume Jaume, 2019) is a form understanding dataset for key-value extraction research [2] with 199 English forms. SROIE (Huang et al., 2019) and CORD (Park et al., 2019) are receipt understanding datasets to extract related entity types in English. XFUND (Xu et al., 2021) is an extended multi-lingual FUNSD dataset, which contains visually-rich documents in seven commonly-used languages.

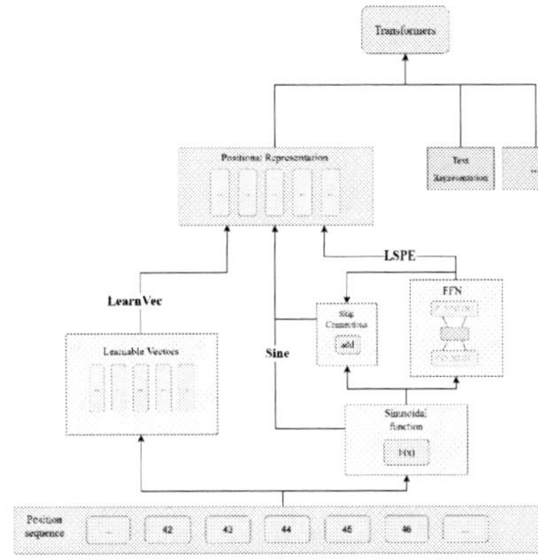

Figure 2: Flow of four positional encoding methods in Transformer based architecture: learnable vector embedding ($LearnVec$), sinusoidal positional encoding ($Sine$), learnable sinusoidal positional encoding ($LSPE$) and $LSPE_{SC}$ with skip connection structure.

3 Methodology

In this section, we formulate our positional encoding method $LSPE$ and introduce its applications on document transformer based language models. In order to evaluate its robustness and stability on noisy data with unreliable order information, we introduce two augmentation strategies: global and local text-block shuffling during fine-tuning stage.

3.1 Learnable Sinusoidal Positional Encoding

Positional representation is utilized as an inductive bias of positional relevance information by positional encoding function (PE) in Transformer model (Vaswani et al., 2017). Sinusoidal positional encoding is originally proposed and employed in attentional mechanism as better extrapolability and spatial correlation from the clean mathematical definition. Figure 1 shows the heatmap of sinusoidal positional encoding method. The hidden representation of position p in a sequence could be computed as Equation 1 for hidden dimension d, where D donates the size of positional representation:

$$
\begin{aligned}
PE_{sine}(p, 2d) &= sin\frac{p}{10000^{2d/D}} \\
PE_{sine}(p, 2d+1) &= cos\frac{p}{10000^{2d/D}}
\end{aligned} \tag{1}
$$

In practical applications, some pretrained Transformer language models (Gehring et al., 2017; Devlin et al., 2018; Liu et al., 2019; Xu et al., 2020b; Dosovitskiy et al., 2020) treat each position index p as a discrete learnable embedding vector

[2] More license and term of use information at https://guillaumejaume.github.io/FUNSD/work/

($LearnVec$) by learning from pre-training and fine-tuning data. This approach is generic and effective to adapt pretrained Transformer models to specific domains and tasks with various behavior of spatial sensitivity. However, for more challenging tasks, such as document understanding tasks, the performance of document Transfomer models with existing positional encoding approach drops significantly on noisy data with unreliable order information (Hong et al., 2021).

We propose a learnable sinusoidal positional encoding ($LSPE$) method by building a fully connected feed-forward sinusoidal position network, which consists of two linear transformations with $GeLU$ (Hendrycks and Gimpel, 2020) as activation function σ in between as:

$$\begin{aligned} FFN(x) &= \sigma(xW_1 + b_1)W_2 + b_2 \\ PE_{LSPE}(p) &= FFN(PE_{sine}(p)) \end{aligned} \quad (2)$$

Skip connection is a generic strategy to sum the input and output representation from a computational unit with a skip edge. In transformer based models, (He et al., 2020) propose a residual attention layer, which has shown some regularization effects that could stabilize training and benefit fine-tuning stages. Inspired by this, we conduct the skip connection strategy in $LSPE$ module as a variant of our method. It could be formulated as eq.3.

$$PE_{LSPEsc}(p) = PE_{sine}(p) + PE_{LSPE}(p) \quad (3)$$

Figure 2 visualizes the flow of our proposed method and baselines in this paper. Compared with discrete embedding, our method extends from sinusoidal function and treats position index as a continuous-valued vector which allows the model to extrapolate to longer length from training cases. Meanwhile, the learnable FFN component boosts the learnability and flexibility of positional representation for multidimensional spatial information.

3.2 Positional Representation in Document Transformer Language Model

Distinct from nature language data which only consist of 1D order information, visually-rich document data require more model capacity to represent both 1D and 2D positional information from individual element. Given token x_i series from a document D, let p_i donate 1D position index and b_i as $((x_0, y_0), (x_1, y_1))$ present the bounding box in normalized 2D coordinate system.

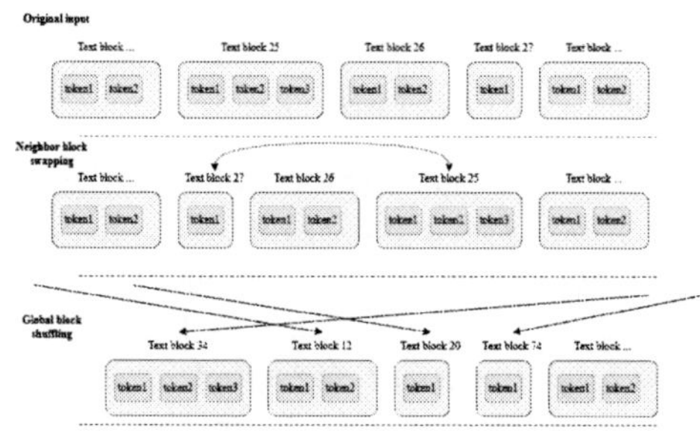

Figure 3: An example of text block shuffling augmentation methods, Neighbor Block Swapping and Global Block Shuffling.

As a general and commonly used pre-trained model for Document AI, LayoutLM (Xu et al., 2020b) utilizes independent 2D spatial embedding layers along with 1D position embedding initialized from pretrained BERT (Devlin et al., 2018) to represent positional information. Its composed positional representation R_i is computed via:

$$\begin{aligned} \mathcal{R}_i^{2D} &= \sum_{j=0}^{k} (PE_x(x_j) + PE_y(y_j)) \\ \mathcal{R}_i &= PE_{1d}(p_i) + \mathcal{R}_i^{2D} \end{aligned} \quad (4)$$

Where k donates the count of points in the bounding box, and PE_{1d}, PE_x, PE_y are the positional encoding methods for 1D order and 2D spatial information separately. The original positional encoding of LayoutLM is a learnable embedding which is identical to $PE_{LearnVec}$ at section 3.1 in this paper. The composed positional representation will be summed up with text embedding and token type embedding vectors as input of Transformer.

3.3 Text Block Shuffling Augmentations

In practical, understanding documents with incorrect reading order is a real challenge for document Transformer model which always leads to irrelevant or embarrassing error results. We introduce two text block shuffling augmentation methods: **Global Block Shuffling** and **Neighbor Block Swapping**, to simulate the noisy reading order scenario as shown in Figure 3. We apply these shuffling methods on text block level to a document, and keep the relative word order in the same text block. Text block is defined as a group of continual words in a spatial region (or a line of words).

In the **Global Block Shuffling**, we obtain the block information for each token, and shuffle the order of block index but keep the relative token order of internal OCR line. In the **Neighbor Block Swapping**, each text block is swapped to its neighbor block randomly, and the distance d of swapped block pairs follows a normal distribution function $\mathcal{N}(0, \sigma^2)$.

The intuition of applying augmentation methods on text block level is to generate samples which are closed to error cases in real-world document understanding applications, and the text block information could be obtained from OCR engines.

4 Experiments

We apply four positional encoding methods ($LearnVec$, $Sine$, $LSPEsc$, $LSPE$) to a representative transformer based model: LayoutLM without visual feature. We conduct pretraining and finetuning on these models to identify the affect of different positional encodings to the performance of transformers on document understanding tasks.

4.1 Pretraining

We pretrain LayoutLM with four positional encoding method as well as baseline methods on a 1M random subset of IIT-CDIP (Lewis et al., 2006) pretraining data set. The name of positional encoding method is used to indicate the pretrained model in the result table.

All pretraining jobs run on 8 NVIDIA Tesla V100 32GB GPUs with approximately 150 hours for each job. The pretraining hyper-parameters are shown in Table 6. The pretrained models are initialized from Bert-base-uncased except for specified positional encoding weights.

4.2 Experimental Settings

Then we fine-tune and evaluate the performance of our pretrained models on three datasets: FUNSD (Guillaume Jaume, 2019), SROIE (Huang et al., 2019), and an In-house Invoice Dataset, which are benchmark datasets for entity extraction in form, receipt, and invoice domains.

FUNSD [3] consists of noisy scanned documents. There are 149 scanned forms for training and 50 scanned forms for testing with more than 31K words, 9.7K entities, and 5.3K relations in combination. For more fair comparison, we refer the evaluation results from LayoutLM, DocFormer, and BROS with the same text and spatial features as input and similar model size architecture. The evaluation result of LayoutLMv2 is conducted by the same settings of our methods but without visual feature inputs.

SROIE [4] attracts a lot of attention from both research and industry community as an open-source OCR and information extraction benchmark for receipt understanding. The dataset consists of 626 receipt images for training and 347 receipt images for testing with four predefined entities which are $company$, $date$, $address$, and $total$. There is no post-processing strategy before evaluation as we tend to compare the performance gap caused by different positional encodings only. We also experiment with official pretrained LayoutLM and LayoutLMv2[5] on the same fine-tuning hyperparameters but without visual feature inputs for a fair comparison.

In-house Invoice Dataset To further evaluate the effectiveness of our positional encoding method on large scale document understanding tasks, we collect a large English inovice dataset with 24175 training and 643 testing invoices and 14 annotated fields. We test our approach on this in-house invoice dataset. (More detailed information of dataset and evaluation results are listed in Appendix A).

We use entity recognition evaluation metrics including entity-level precision, recall, and F1-score for each experiment with the default settings of seqeval package (Nakayama, 2018).

4.3 Experimental Results

As shown in Table 1, on FUNSD dataset, our $LSPE$ model achieves 82.04 F1-score and outperforms other baseline methods. The $Sine$ model achieves low performance and $LSPE_{SC}$ is worse than $LSPE$ which indicates the sinusoidal function cannot represent layout positional information with skip connection structure. The small performance gap between our $LearnVec$ and official LayoutLM model with shared model structure might be from different pretraining data and settings since our pretraining experiments run on a 1M subset training data and fewer pretraining steps.

We observe similar trend on SROIE as shown in Table 2. $LSPE$ model achieves F1 score of 93.87 with text and spatial features. With larger scale of training size on SROIE, the performance gap is narrowed down between $LearnVec$ and $LSPE$ in the testing dataset.

These results illustrate the effectiveness of our $LSPE$ on document understanding tasks with dif-

[3] https://guillaumejaume.github.io/FUNSD

[4] https://github.com/zzzDavid/ICDAR-2019-SROIE

[5] https://github.com/microsoft/unilm/tree/master

ferent data scale. And the ability of positional representation affects the final performance significantly on document understanding models.

Method	P(%)	R(%)	F1(%)
$LayoutLM$(2020b)	75.97	81.55	78.66
$DocFormer$(2021)	77.63	83.69	80.54
$BROS$(2021)	80.56	81.88	81.21
$LayoutLMv2_{base}$(2020a)	80.26	83.26	81.73
$LearnVec$	75.97	80.04	77.95
$Sine$	72.8	77.24	74.95
$LSPE_{SC}$	78.25	82.79	80.46
$LSPE$	80.4	83.74	**82.04**

Table 1: Entity level evaluation results on FUNSD dataset. All models utilize input features of text and spatial information with "Base" model size architecture. The evaluation result of $LayoutLMv2$ is reproduced without visual inputs.

Method	P(%)	R(%)	F1(%)
$LayoutLM_{base}$	91.4	94.24	92.8
$LayoutLMv2_{base}$	92.3	94.16	93.22
$LearnVec$	92.57	94.31	93.43
$Sine$	87.72	90.06	88.87
$LSPE_{SC}$	89.89	92.87	91.35
$LSPE$	92.94	94.81	**93.87**

Table 2: Results on SROIE datasets. All above experiments are fine-tuned with the same hyper-parameter setting and training environments. We evaluate the official $LayoutLM_{base}$ and $LayoutLMv2_{base}$ on the same settings without visual features.

4.4 Ablation Study

In real-world application, the reading order of text blocks is not always reliable and consistent. The incorrect reading order harms the performance of existing document language models and leads to embarrassing error of predictions in downstream tasks. We conduct three ablation experiments to simulate the impact of such error with the following augmentation methods.

Neighbor Block Swapping and Global Block Shuffling We apply these methods to training data only during fine-tuning which simulates impact of incorrect block order data. The testing set is kept as original which allows us to compare the performance with original reading order in Table 1. The σ of neighbor block swapping is set to 1 in all experiments. Note that the augmentation methods in this paper require block information of each token, and that might cause leaking of block boundary information during the model training indirectly. Besides of data impact, the model receives inconsistent reading order during training and it might benefit the evaluation performance by eliminating the over-fitting from 1D positional embedding, and tent to learn more information of relative token order inside block and 2D spatial information.

In Table 3, with synthetic noisy data generated by two augmentation methods, our $LSPE$ method shows better performance than existing discrete $LearnVec$ embedding and sinusoidal function $Sine$ consistently on FUNSD data. Similar observations can be found on the In-house Invoice dataset in Appendix A. The global block shuffling is harmful for all positional encoding methods while the performance impact of neighbor block swapping is marginally. The discrete positional encoding method shows more sensitive with significant performance drop by global block shuffling augmentation.

Removing 1D Position Input We throw the 1D positional input and only consider the 2D positional representation $\mathcal{R}^{2D}$ in eq. 4 in composed positional representation for both training and testing datasets. The model does not receive word order information on both text block and sub-token levels. We refer the performance result from BROS (Hong et al., 2021) with similar settings for comparison.[6]

On FUNSD dataset, we observe a significant performance degradation across all positional methods in Table 4. The $LearnVec$ leads a huge drop from approximately 79% to 49% on F1 score which indicates the discrete 2D embedding is not well represented without optimal order information. The continuous 2D positional encoding methods perform better relatively. $LSPE_{SC}$ performs the best with only 2.67% F1 drop, and keeps a reasonable performance even with none order information.

From Table 5, we observe our $LSPE$ model achieves 89.98 F1 score with 3.89% absolute drop (4.14% relatively) from Table 2. The performance of $LSPE_{SC}$ drops 3.2% relatively which shows better robustness on such extreme condition. There is significant performance regression with discrete $LearnVec$ method on this receipt understanding data set. The $LSPE_{SC}$ performs better with global block shuffling method on the FUNSD dataset which might be beneficial from regularization ad-

[6] Result from text line in their ablation study paragraph

Method	Neighbor Block Swapping			Global Block Shuffling		
	P(%)	**R**(%)	**F1**(%)	**P** (%)	**R**(%)	**F1** (%)
$LearnVec$	76.43	79.49	77.93	72.32	69.78	71.03
$Sine$	73.77	78.24	75.94	74.1	74.99	74.54
$LSPE_{SC}$	78.72	81.79	80.23	77.09	80.14	**78.59**
$LSPE$	79.9	82.14	**81.01**	78.03	78.34	78.18

Table 3: Comparison on **FUNSD** dataset for four positional encoding methods by applying **Neighbor Block Swapping** and **Global Block Shuffling** on training dataset. Evaluation results clearly demonstrate our methods show stable and robustness under unreliable order information.

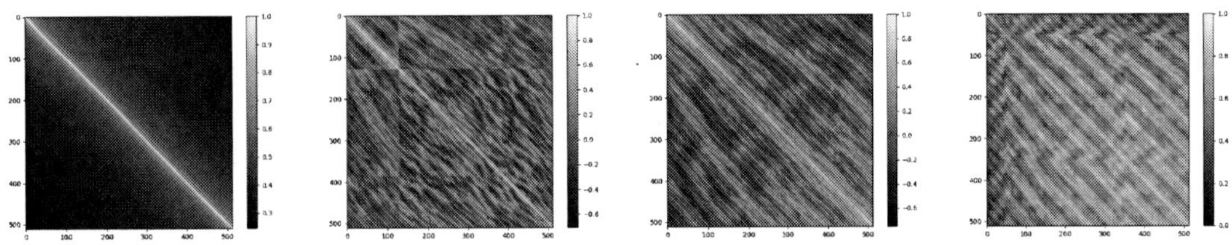

(a) $Sine$ (b) official $BERT$ (c) $LearnVec$ (d) $LSPE$

Figure 4: Similarity of 1D position embedding from pretrained $Sine$, official BERT, $LearnVec$, $LSPE$ models.

vantage of skip connection structure. Similar observations can be found on the In-house Invoice dataset in Appendix A.

Ablation study results further prove that better learnability and spatial correlation of positional representation are essential factors of existing document Transformer model. By comparing with other positional encoding methods and other recent pretrained Transformer based solutions, our methods demonstrate optimal performance and robustness on noisy data with unreliable order information.

Method	P(%)	R(%)	F1(%)
$BROS$(2021)	–	–	70.07
$LearnVec$	44.66	54.63	49.14
$Sine$	69.4	73.74	71.5
$LSPE_{SC}$	75.71	79.99	**77.79**
$LSPE$	72.2	77.19	74.61

Table 4: Experimental results by removing 1D position inputs on training and testing sets of FUNSD. The BROS performance is referenced from their ablation study with similar experimental setting.

5 Position Embedding Similarity Analysis

To further investigate what Transformer encoders capture about positions after pretraining, we visualize the position-wise cosine similarity of each position embedding (Wang and Chen, 2020) in the pretrained models. Figure 4 shows the position-wise cosine similarity of 1D position embedding in our pretrained models with $Sine$, $LearnVec$, $LSPE$ and in the official BERT model. The point at (i, j) indicates the similarity between the i-th position and the j-th position. (i and j are from 0 to 512). First, with regard to $Sine$, we can only observe that embedding vectors are similar to the positions nearby. Both Bert and $LearnVec$ can observe similar embedding vectors nearby, but have no or very limited explainable patterns in long-term relations. Our $LSPE$ shows obvious periodic patterns along with position orders, which displays its embedding can actually capture the meanings of positions in the long-term relations.

Method	P(%)	R(%)	F1(%)
$LearnVec$	75.12	79.18	77.1
$Sine$	83.71	87.03	85.34
$LSPE_{SC}$	87.46	89.41	88.42
$LSPE$	87.9	92.15	**89.98**

Table 5: Experimental results by removing 1D position inputs on training and testing sets of SROIE. The $LSPE$ achieves best performance and $LSPE_{SC}$ keeps lowest relative performance drop with this extra settings.

The 2D positional representation plays an essential role in document Transformer models with spatial information. Figure 5 shows position-wise cosine similarity of each position embedding of

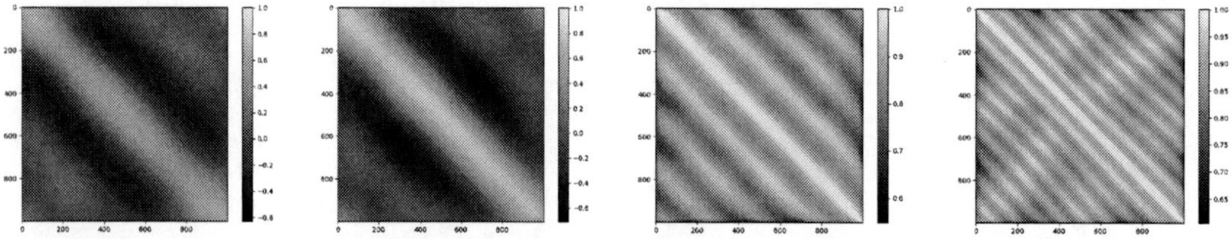

(a) PE_x of $LearnVec$ (b) PE_y of $LearnVec$ (c) PE_x of $LSPE$ (d) PE_y of $LSPE$

Figure 5: Similarity of x and y axes in 2D positional embedding from our pretrained $LearnVec$ and $LSPE$ models.

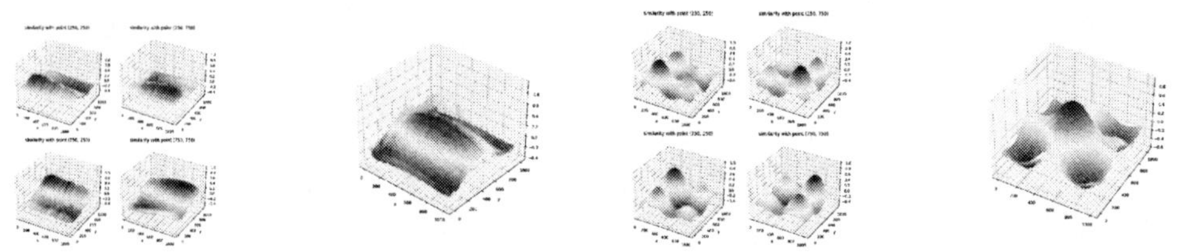

(a) official $LayoutLM$ (b) $LearnVec$

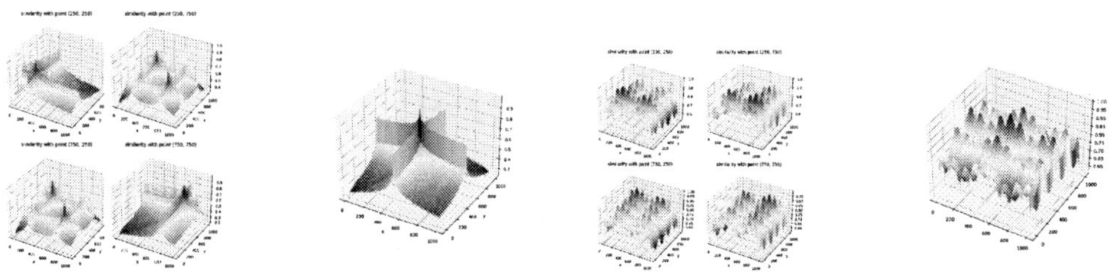

(c) $Sine$ (d) $LSPE$

Figure 6: Similarity of 2D positional representation on 5 fixed points ((250, 250), (250, 750), (750, 250), (750, 750), (500, 500)) to the rest positions from official LayoutLM and $LearnVec$, $Sine$, $LSPE$ positional encoding methods.

x- and y- axes in 2D positional embedding in our petrained $LearnVec$ and $LSPE$ models. We can find our $LSPE$ has obvious periodic patterns along with both x- and y- position orders in the long-term relations than the $LearnVec$, which can mostly capture similar embeddings nearby.

Figure 6 demonstrates the position-wise cosine similarity of $\mathcal{R}^{2D}$ representation of five specific points to the rest positions in our pretrained models and in the official LayoutLM. $Sine$ captures close similar embeddings only, where its 2D similary map decays rapidly from central point and shows sharp edge on the border. The official LayoutLM model shows boarder vision horizontally with proper spatial correlation, but still fail to capture long-term relations. Our $LSPE$ shows higher wave frequency on both x- and y- axes which tend to capture the long distance signals with obvious periodic pattern.

6 Conclusions

In this paper, we propose a simple but effective learnable positional encoding method $LSPE$ to improve the positional representation in Transformer based models. By building a sinusoidal position feed-forward network, our method has better learnability and extrapolability in position representation. Experimental results on FUNSD, SROIE and an in-house Invoice datasets clearly show the effectiveness of our method on document understanding tasks. By leveraging global and local shuffling augmentation methods and removing order information from inputs, we demonstrate our method substantially outperforms other positional encoding methods on noisy data with unreliable reading order.

For future research, we will employ and evaluate our method on other tasks or modalities such as Vision Transformer (Dosovitskiy et al., 2020).

References

Srikar Appalaraju, Bhavan Jasani, Bhargava Urala Kota, Yusheng Xie, and R Manmatha. 2021. Docformer: End-to-end transformer for document understanding. *arXiv preprint arXiv:2106.11539*.

Zewen Chi, Shaohan Huang, Li Dong, Shuming Ma, Saksham Singhal, Payal Bajaj, Xia Song, and Furu Wei. 2021. Xlm-e: Cross-lingual language model pre-training via electra.

Christian Clausner, Stefan Pletschacher, and Apostolos Antonacopoulos. 2013. The significance of reading order in document recognition and its evaluation. In *2013 12th International Conference on Document Analysis and Recognition*, pages 688–692. IEEE.

Lei Cui, Yiheng Xu, Tengchao Lv, and Furu Wei. 2021. Document ai: Benchmarks, models and applications. *arXiv preprint arXiv:2111.08609*.

Xiang Dai and Heike Adel. 2020. An analysis of simple data augmentation for named entity recognition.

Zihang Dai, Zhilin Yang, Yiming Yang, Jaime Carbonell, Quoc V. Le, and Ruslan Salakhutdinov. 2019. Transformer-xl: Attentive language models beyond a fixed-length context.

Jacob Devlin, Ming-Wei Chang, Kenton Lee, and Kristina Toutanova. 2018. Bert: Pre-training of deep bidirectional transformers for language understanding. *arXiv preprint arXiv:1810.04805*.

Alexey Dosovitskiy, Lucas Beyer, Alexander Kolesnikov, Dirk Weissenborn, Xiaohua Zhai, Thomas Unterthiner, Mostafa Dehghani, Matthias Minderer, Georg Heigold, Sylvain Gelly, et al. 2020. An image is worth 16x16 words: Transformers for image recognition at scale. *arXiv preprint arXiv:2010.11929*.

Philipp Dufter, Martin Schmitt, and Hinrich Schütze. 2021. Position information in transformers: An overview. *Computational Linguistics*, pages 1–31.

Jonas Gehring, Michael Auli, David Grangier, Denis Yarats, and Yann N Dauphin. 2017. Convolutional sequence to sequence learning. In *International Conference on Machine Learning*, pages 1243–1252. PMLR.

Jean-Philippe Thiran Guillaume Jaume, Hazim Kemal Ekenel. 2019. Funsd: A dataset for form understanding in noisy scanned documents. In *Accepted to ICDAR-OST*.

Adam W Harley, Alex Ufkes, and Konstantinos G Derpanis. 2015. Evaluation of deep convolutional nets for document image classification and retrieval. In *International Conference on Document Analysis and Recognition (ICDAR)*.

Pengcheng He, Xiaodong Liu, Jianfeng Gao, and Weizhu Chen. 2021. Deberta: Decoding-enhanced bert with disentangled attention.

Ruining He, Anirudh Ravula, Bhargav Kanagal, and Joshua Ainslie. 2020. Realformer: Transformer likes residual attention. *arXiv preprint arXiv:2012.11747*.

Dan Hendrycks and Kevin Gimpel. 2020. Gaussian error linear units (gelus).

Teakgyu Hong, DongHyun Kim, Mingi Ji, Wonseok Hwang, Daehyun Nam, and Sungrae Park. 2021. {BROS}: A pre-trained language model for understanding texts in document.

Zheng Huang, Kai Chen, Jianhua He, Xiang Bai, Dimosthenis Karatzas, Shijian Lu, and CV Jawahar. 2019. Icdar2019 competition on scanned receipt ocr and information extraction. In *2019 International Conference on Document Analysis and Recognition (ICDAR)*, pages 1516–1520. IEEE.

Zhiheng Huang, Davis Liang, Peng Xu, and Bing Xiang. 2020. Improve transformer models with better relative position embeddings.

David Lewis, Gady Agam, Shlomo Argamon, Ophir Frieder, David Grossman, and Jefferson Heard. 2006. Building a test collection for complex document information processing. In *Proceedings of the 29th annual international ACM SIGIR conference on Research and development in information retrieval*, pages 665–666.

Chenliang Li, Bin Bi, Ming Yan, Wei Wang, Songfang Huang, Fei Huang, and Luo Si. 2021a. Structurallm: Structural pre-training for form understanding. *arXiv preprint arXiv:2105.11210*.

Yang Li, Si Si, Gang Li, Cho-Jui Hsieh, and Samy Bengio. 2021b. Learnable fourier features for multi-dimensional spatial positional encoding.

Yinhan Liu, Myle Ott, Naman Goyal, Jingfei Du, Mandar Joshi, Danqi Chen, Omer Levy, Mike Lewis, Luke Zettlemoyer, and Veselin Stoyanov. 2019. Roberta: A robustly optimized bert pretraining approach. *arXiv preprint arXiv:1907.11692*.

Hiroki Nakayama. 2018. seqeval: A python framework for sequence labeling evaluation. Software available from https://github.com/chakki-works/seqeval.

Seunghyun Park, Seung Shin, Bado Lee, Junyeop Lee, Jaeheung Surh, Minjoon Seo, and Hwalsuk Lee. 2019. Cord: A consolidated receipt dataset for post-ocr parsing. In *Workshop on Document Intelligence at NeurIPS 2019*.

Thang M. Pham, Trung Bui, Long Mai, and Anh Nguyen. 2021. Out of order: How important is the sequential order of words in a sentence in natural language understanding tasks?

Peter Shaw, Jakob Uszkoreit, and Ashish Vaswani. 2018. Self-attention with relative position representations. *arXiv preprint arXiv:1803.02155*.

Ashish Vaswani, Noam Shazeer, Niki Parmar, Jakob Uszkoreit, Llion Jones, Aidan N Gomez, Lukasz Kaiser, and Illia Polosukhin. 2017. Attention is all you need. *arXiv preprint arXiv:1706.03762*.

Wei Wang, Bin Bi, Ming Yan, Chen Wu, Zuyi Bao, Jiangnan Xia, Liwei Peng, and Luo Si. 2019. Structbert: Incorporating language structures into pre-training for deep language understanding.

Yu-An Wang and Yun-Nung Chen. 2020. What do position embeddings learn? an empirical study of pre-trained language model positional encoding. *arXiv preprint arXiv:2010.04903*.

Zilong Wang, Yiheng Xu, Lei Cui, Jingbo Shang, and Furu Wei. 2021. Layoutreader: Pre-training of text and layout for reading order detection.

Jason Wei and Kai Zou. 2019. Eda: Easy data augmentation techniques for boosting performance on text classification tasks. *arXiv preprint arXiv:1901.11196*.

Yang Xu, Yiheng Xu, Tengchao Lv, Lei Cui, Furu Wei, Guoxin Wang, Yijuan Lu, Dinei Florencio, Cha Zhang, Wanxiang Che, et al. 2020a. Layoutlmv2: Multi-modal pre-training for visually-rich document understanding. *arXiv preprint arXiv:2012.14740*.

Yiheng Xu, Minghao Li, Lei Cui, Shaohan Huang, Furu Wei, and Ming Zhou. 2020b. Layoutlm: Pre-training of text and layout for document image understanding. In *Proceedings of the 26th ACM SIGKDD International Conference on Knowledge Discovery & Data Mining*, pages 1192–1200.

Yiheng Xu, Tengchao Lv, Lei Cui, Guoxin Wang, Yijuan Lu, Dinei Florencio, Cha Zhang, and Furu Wei. 2021. Layoutxlm: Multimodal pre-training for multilingual visually-rich document understanding.

A More Information on Training Hyperparameters

Pretraining We use PyTorch on Nvidia Tesla V100 GPU for all pretraining experiments. The training hyperparameters is listed in Table 6.

Finetuning For finetuning tasks, we use standard cross-entropy loss on the task-specific classification head layers over pretrained document transformer model outputs. To make fair comparisons on various positional encoding methods, we use same hyperparameters, same training data, and same running environment for each task. The learning rate is set to 3e-5 for FUNSD and 2e-5 for SROIE task with linear decay, and 10% of total steps are used for warm-up purpose. We use max_steps as $2k$ for FUNSD and $1.5k$ for SROIE task, and report the evaluation results on the finetuned models. We average evaluation results with different initial seeds to eliminate bias of shuffling augmentations.

Parameter Name	Value
max_steps	500K
per_device_train_batch_size	12
gradient_accumulation_steps	4
max_seq_length	512
max_2d_position_embeddings	1024
learning_rate	7e-5
warmup_ratio	0.1
fp16	true
fp16_backend	amp
fp16_opt_level	O1

Table 6: Pretraining hyperparameters for document Transformer model with our positional encoding methods.

Field Name	Training entity count	Testing entity count
BillingAddress	7515	198
CustomerAddress	19317	529
CustomerID	24927	643
DueDate	16319	701
InvoiceDate	26043	676
InvoiceNumber	21441	558
PONumber	2106	56
ShippingAddress	2486	74
Subtotal	6207	169
TotalInvoiceAmount	31075	853
TotalTax	11178	308
VendorAddress	29811	787
VendorName	45685	1208

Table 7: Per field statistics of Invoice dataset.

B Evaluation Result of In-house Inovice Dataset

To further analyze the effectiveness of various positional encoding methods on larger scale document understanding tasks, we collect a large English inovice dataset with 14 fields listed in Table 7. There are 24175 and 643 invoice documents in its training and testing sets.

We finetune the same pretrained document Transformer models from section 4.1 with $LearnVec$ and $LSPE$ positional encoding methods on this invoice dataset, and report their F1-Score in Table 8 with various 1D position inputs. We also apply global and neighbor shuffling augmentation methods on the training dataset from section 3.3. Then we evaluate the F1-Score performance on the testing dataset. $LSPE$ model shows consistent evaluation result and outperforms the baseline method on the original position inputs, no positional inputs, and various shuffling augmentation methods. The evaluation result clearly illustrates the effectiveness and robustness of $LSPE$ on handling unreliable reading order issues.

Model	Original 1D Position	No 1D Position	Global Shuffling	Neighbor Swapping
$LearnVec$	91.66	86.55	87.09	90.39
$LSPE$	92.17	92.27	92.16	91.71

Table 8: F1-Score comparison on the in-house **Invoice** testing dataset for two positional encoding methods, $LearnVec$ and $LSPE$, with **Original 1D Position**, **No 1D Position** inputs and applying **Neighbor Block Swapping** and **Global Block Shuffling** on the training data set.

MMM: An Emotion and Novelty-aware Approach for Multilingual Multimodal Misinformation Detection

Vipin Gupta*[,1], Rina Kumari*[,1], Nischal Ashok[2], Tirthankar Ghosal[3], Asif Ekbal[1]
[1]Indian Institute of Technology Patna, India
[2]UMass Amherst, Massachusetts, United States
[3]Institute of Formal and Applied Linguistics, MFF, Charles University, Czech Republic
{vipingupta1907,rinakri08,nischal.ashok09,asif.ekbal}@gmail.com
ghosal@ufal.mff.cuni.cz

Abstract

The growth of multilingual web content in low-resource languages is becoming an emerging challenge to detect misinformation. One particular hindrance to research on this problem is the non-availability of resources and tools. Majority of the earlier works in misinformation detection are based on English content which confines the applicability of the research to a specific language only. Increasing presence of multimedia content on the web has promoted misinformation in which real multimedia content (images, videos) are used in different but related contexts with manipulated texts to mislead the readers. Detecting this category of misleading information is almost impossible without any prior knowledge. Studies say that *emotion-invoking and highly novel* content accelerates the dissemination of false information. To counter this problem, here in this paper, we first introduce a novel multilingual multimodal misinformation dataset that includes *background knowledge* (from authentic sources) of the misleading articles. Second, we propose an effective neural model leveraging *novelty detection* and *emotion recognition* to detect fabricated information. We perform extensive experiments to justify that our proposed model outperforms the state-of-the-art (SOTA) on the concerned task [1].

1 Introduction

Fast adoption of social media platforms have promoted people to knowingly or unknowingly subscribe, create and share misleading, fake, and irrelevant information which consists of various attributes like title, text information, visual information, etc. These attributes may contain false or misleading information. The news or stories having false information is called misinformation. In recent years, we observe substantial advancements in automatic fake news detection. However, most of these are targeted to resource-rich language like English. When it comes to the scenario of (relatively) low-resource Indian languages like Hindi, Bengali and Tamil, the amount of research is insignificant, primarily due to the unavailability of data and other associated resources. With the advancement of multimedia news on the internet, news containing same (non-novel) image with different (novel) text influences the fake news on social media to mislead the newsreaders. Since the image looks authentic and aligns with the new text, it becomes very challenging to detect this category of fake news. The implication of misinformation detection with novelty detection and emotion recognition was first presented by MIT Scholars[2]. Novelty refers to the extent to which news readers encounter unfamiliar news, which may include some element of surprise. In this work, we take forward the misinformation work on the shoulder of novelty detection via entailment task with emphasis to textual similarity measures. Literature also suggest that novel and emotion invoking contents in the news articles act as fuel for the rapid dissemination (Kumari et al., 2021a),(Kumari et al., 2021b) and (Kumari et al., 2022).

Although people have performed an extensive investigation in different dimensions of misinformation detection, however, a very few mechanisms have focused on novelty and emotion aware misinformation detection with background knowledge for the relatively low-resource languages. We make an attempt to address these challenges by creating important resources and effective baseline. We first introduce a novel multilingual multimodal misinformation dataset for the Indian languages like Hindi, Bengali and Tamil. The instances (here, in-

* corresponding author

[1]Code and Data is available here: 1. https://www.iitp.ac.in/~ai-nlp-ml/resources.html#MMM_Dataset, 2. https://github.com/vipingupta1907/MVEN

[2]https://news.mit.edu/2018/study-twitter-false-news-travels-faster-true-stories-0308

Findings of the Association for Computational Linguistics: AACL-IJCNLP 2022, pages 464–477
November 20–23, 2022.

stance means a single claim may be real or fake) in each language are different, meaning the same instance will not be present in more than one language. During training the model, we mix the instances of all the three languages which makes it multilingual. We further design a deep learning-based misinformation detection model using novelty detection and emotion recognition as the assisting tasks.

The major contributions offered in this article are as follows:

- We create a novel multilingual multimodal misinformation dataset for Indian languages, which is, to the best of our knowledge, the very first attempt toward creating the corpus for multimodal misleading information detection where the same image is used in a different context to convey false information.

- We propose a multilingual multimodal framework using novelty and emotion recognition as the assisting tasks for misinformation detection, where the main task is to check whether the same image has been published earlier in a different context in other languages.

- We perform zero-shot experiments on our proposed architecture to demonstrate the robustness of our model on the unseen languages at the training time and obtain encouraging performance.

2 Related Work

The concept of misinformation or fake news detection has started in early 2010, as social media started to have an immense impact on people's views. Shu et al. (2017) has introduced one of the first extensive studies for misinformation detection on social media. It has described the fact-checking methodologies as verification of the hypothesis made in a news article to judge if the claim is true or not. The work presented in FakeDetector (Zhang et al., 2020) introduces a deep diffusive network model to detect fake news by learning the representations of news articles, creators, and subjects simultaneously.

Shu et al. (2019) introduced a sentence-comment co-attention sub-network which learns and captures check-worthy sentences and user comments jointly to explain why a particular news piece is detected as fake. People have organized many challenges for fake news detection that introduce several novel mechanisms. A competition *The Fake News Challenge (FNC)*[3] introduced a few works (Slovikovskaya and Attardi, 2020), (Chaudhry et al., 2017) for stance detection which are useful to understand attitudes expressed in texts. Stance detection means the detection of relative perspective of two text fragments. The stance detection justifies whether the news article agrees, disagrees, discusses or is unrelated to the news title. If the news article disagrees or is unrelated to the news title, it indicates a high probability of the news to be fake. Few notable works, such as Yin and Roth (2018) and Nie et al. (2019) verify the human generated claims as fake or real. The mechanism presented by Saikh et al. (2020) depicts a word attention-based deep learning model for automatic fake news detection.

The work explored in Jin et al. (2017) combines the textual, visual, and social context features using an attention mechanism for fake news prediction. In continuation to it, EANN (Wang et al., 2018), VAE (Khattar et al., 2019) and SpotFake Singhal et al. (2019) have introduced deep learning-based models and justified that the model is efficient in handling newly emerged events better than the existing methods. The research explored in (Kumari and Ekbal, 2021; Wu et al., 2021; Song et al., 2021) have given attention to feature fusion along with the feature extraction mechanisms and proved that the model's performance also depends upon the semantic interaction between different modalities. The method explored in Zhang et al. (2021) has taken the first step to find the credibility of previously published news articles on the same events as the background knowledge by introducing the Supervised Contrastive Learning (SCL) (Zhang et al., 2021).

One of the promising works (Abonizio et al., 2020) in multilingual misinformation detection explores language-independent fake news detection, which successfully differentiate fake, satirical, and legitimate news across three different languages. Another multilingual work presented in Guibon et al. (2019) uses the convolutional neural network (CNN) to detect fake news with satire on a multilingual dataset. The works presented in (Li et al., 2020b; Glenski et al., 2019) are the major contributors for multilingual multimodal misinformation detection. They first introduced a dataset which

[3]http://www.fakenewschallenge.org/

includes the instances in languages other than English.

Our work is different from the prior works in the perception that (i). we create a Multilingual Multimodal Misinformation (MMM) dataset with background knowledge for relatively low-resource Indian languages which includes the data instances in Hindi, Bengali and Tamil; and (ii). we design a novelty and emotion aware multimodal multilingual framework for misinformation detection.

3 Data Description and Analysis

Several resources like Twitter (Boididou et al., 2015), Weibo (Jin et al., 2017), TI-CNN (Yang et al., 2018), Fauxtography (Zlatkova et al., 2019), Fakeddit (Nakamura et al., 2020), NewsBag (Jindal et al., 2020), etc. are very eminent to study multimodal misinformation detection problems. People have introduced CoAID (Cui and Lee, 2020), MMCoVaR (Chen et al., 2021) and ReCOVery (Zhou et al., 2020) to tackle the misinformation during COVID-19 infodemic. Aforesaid datasets are only available in English language. Very few datasets such as ArCOV-19 (Haouari et al., 2021) and CHECKED (Yang et al., 2021) are available in the languages other than English. MM-COVID (Li et al., 2020a), MuMiN (Nielsen and McConville, 2022) and FactDRIL (Singhal et al., 2021) are the multilingual multimodal misinformation datasets. However, these datasets do not include background information (where and in which context the news has been published first) of the news articles, which are crucial for misleading misinformation detection. Therefore, we prepare a novel Multilingual Multimodal Misinformation (MMM) dataset which includes 10,473 samples. The developed dataset contains the instances from three different Indian languages *viz.* Hindi, Bengali and Tamil. Each instance of the dataset is in the form of source-target pair. Target is the combination of multimodal Hindi, Bengali and Tamil language instances which claim any information or news. The source is the related background information extracted from different websites corresponding to the target.

3.1 Data Collection

Our prepared dataset contains multimedia news disseminated across the country which are mostly centered around the politics, covid-19, social, health and religion domains. We collect the target instances of our *MMM* dataset in following steps:

Fake Instance Collection: We consider the FactDRIL (Singhal et al., 2021) dataset to prepare fake instance in our dataset. FactDRIL is a multilingual multimodal misinformation repository collected from Indian fact checking websites like *althindi, boomlive, newschecker, etc.*, which includes the instances of claim and their investigations in 13 low-resource Indian languages along with the English language. We only consider the multimodal instances from *Hindi, Bengali* and *Tamil* languages to prepare our dataset. We form a set of target samples by combining these instances which includes the fake claim and image URL pair and assign fake label to all instances.

Real Instance Collection: To collect real data instances, we choose two trusted news websites such as *News18* and *Abplive*. Then we crawl all the pages having general-domain national news and scrape all the news article URLs using request module and beautifulsoup[4] library of python. Using the news article URLs, we again webscrape main news content and image associated with the news articles. We collect only Hindi instances from Abplive website and Hindi, Bengali, Tamil instances from the News18 website. At last, we assign real label to each instance. We collect the background information for each multimodal instance of the target sample set in the following steps:

Source Information Extraction The target instance may have more than one image URL. We use OpenAI CLIP Model (Radford et al., 2021) with Multilingual Knowledge Distillation (MKD) (Reimers and Gurevych, 2020) to find the most relevant image among all the target images. Thus, we keep only single image URL corresponding to each target instance. After that, we perform Google reverse image search using all target image URL to retrieve the source information. We extract all the URLs of sources that contain text or image information related to the target image. Now, we send a get request to all URLs of the sources and then extract the text and images present on that particular source. If there is no source information available, we discard these target instances. In order to make the dataset multimodal, we also discard all the source-target pairs without images. In case of source texts in languages other than the respective target text language, we translate the source text into the target text language using googletrans

[4]https://pypi.org/project/beautifulsoup4/

python library [5]. In order to gather authentic background knowledge, the source itself must be highly credible. So, we evaluate the source credibility in the next step.

Credible Source Selection It is not necessary that the entire news article includes false content, instead that some small portion of the news may have false information. We assume that some websites always publish true news. On the other hand, some websites always publish false news. The trusted news website may also have some misinformation but they are very rare and unintentional. During collection of background information of each instance, we had gone through multiple websites. As per the above discussion, these websites may also contain misinformation. So to consider the source information only from the trusted websites, we have used MediaBias scores of different websites and eliminated the information obtained from non-trusted websites. Here, we use MediaBias score to determine the credibility of the websites from where we collect the data. We don't use this MediaBias score for the credibility checking of the instance. MediaBias assigns a class among the six classes *viz.* very high, high, primarily factual, mixed, low, and very low. We consider maximum four source information only from *very high, high, and primarily factual class.* We limit the number of sources to four because each target instance has, on average, four multimodal source information. We extract textual information from credible websites and save all the images present on these websites. For each instance, we have up to 4 sources where each source has some piece of text and a list of images. We consider the piece of text as the source text. Although the main purpose of this step is to shorten the background information up to four, however some target instances are also removed due to the low credibility of the source. By doing so, we extract textual information from credible source websites and save all the images present on them. Thus we discard all the source information extracted from low credible source websites.

Source Image Selection In this step, we remove all the images having dimension less than 50x50 from the list of images corresponding to each source and subsequently remove the unimodal source information again. We keep only one source image, which is approximately identical to the target image but may have some subtle difference since, our research attempts to detect fake news using non-novel images and novel text. We utilize VGG16 (Simonyan and Zisserman, 2014) and compute cosine similarity to find the similarity between target and source image. As a final step, we preserve only the most similar image from each source.

[5]https://pypi.org/project/googletrans/

3.2 Data Annotation

Since we create the *MMM* dataset by collecting real samples from the trusted news sources and fake samples from the existing FactDrill repository, we directly assign the labels as real and fake, respectively. The purpose of the annotation is to keep the source information if it is relevant to the corresponding target instance. Otherwise, it is discarded. Thus, we label every instance with either *yes* or *no*. All instances with *yes* labels are included in the dataset and other instances with *no* label are discarded from the dataset. It is solely based on the textual content of the source and target instances. In addition to automatic annotation, we also perform human annotation to check the quality of automatic annotation.

Automatic annotation We consider two types of annotations for each source-target pair of our MMM dataset:

(i). In the first annotation type, we assign the label of the source-target pair similar to the target label. If the target label is fake, we assign the label as fake and if the target data label is real, we assign the real label to the source-target pair instance. Thus, it is entirely based on the target data label and completely automatic.

(ii). In the second annotation type, we assign the label as" yes" if the source is relevant to the target; otherwise, we assign a label as "no". This annotation is based on the threshold value. To compute the threshold value, we perform Named Entity Recognition (NER) on both source text (S) and target texts (T). The threshold is the ratio of *the number of common entities present in source and target text and the number of entities present in the target text.* We define it as shown in Equation 1, where R represents the ratio or threshold. With the help of this threshold value, we find the semantic similarity between source and target text. For this purpose, we make a hypothesis that if the threshold value is greater than 0.5, it may have semantic similarity to some extent. By following this hypothesis, we fix the threshold as 0.5. We assign the label as "yes" for the source having a maximum threshold value if it is greater than 0.5. For other sources, we assign the label "no".

$$R = \frac{|S \cap T|}{|T|} \quad (1)$$

Human annotation We check the quality of automatic data annotation by performing human annotations for 500 instances of Hindi, Bengali and Tamil languages each. We randomly choose these 500 instances from each language in equal proportionate from fake and real classes. Each instance contains an ID, target-image-URL, target-text, source-URL, source-text, source-image-URL, and source reliability. We provide the selected instances of Hindi and Bengali to native Hindi and Bengali speakers who are proficient in reading, writing, and speaking. Due to the non-availability of Tamil native speakers, we first translated 500 instances of the Tamil language into English. We then provided these translated instances to three English speakers for the annotation. All three annotators are asked to do the following things: (i). Google the target Image URL and open the image in the browser; (ii). Read source-text and find that (a). Source text is related to the image or gives some description of the target image; (b). Source text gives any background information about the target image. If any one of the above points ((a) and (b)) is true, assign the label as "yes"; otherwise, assign the label as "no".

We compute the agreement between the automatic and all three human annotations for the 500 instances of each language using Cohen's Kappa coefficient (Cohen, 1960). On average, our dataset has 91.27%, 89.5% and 86.3% agreement on Hindi, Bengali and Tamil languages, respectively, indicating a high automatic data annotation quality.

3.3 Data Statistics

In order to create the *MMM* dataset, data instances were collected from Hindi, Bengali, and Tamil languages. We propose a corpus of 10,473 samples having 5630 real and 4840 fake samples. To build the train and test sets, we split the data in an 80:20 ratio. Table 1 outlines the complete data statistics and distribution of MMM dataset. The dataset is organized in a structured way inside the main folder 'Data' to make them more accessible to researchers. Inside this data directory, there are four folders *viz.* Source, Source Image, Target, and Target Image, and all these 4 folders have 3 sub directories: Hindi, Bengali, and Tamil. The source folder subdirectories contain CSV files corresponding to the language of the source information. All CSV files include attributes such as ID, Number of sources, Source URL, Source text, Image URL, and Reliability. Source Image folder sub-directories contain the source images corresponding to the source language. Target folder sub-directories contain the CSV files corresponding to the language of target information and contain information about the target instance, such as ID, Target URL, Target text, Image URL, and Label. Target Folder subdirectories contain the target image.

Dataset	Total	Real	Fake
Hindi	7163	3563	3600
Bengali	1543	1005	538
Tamil	1767	1065	702
MMM	10473	5633	4840

Table 1: *MMM* dataset statistics and distribution

4 Proposed Model

In this section, we present a brief description of the proposed framework. The overall model is shown in Figure 1 which consists of three components: *Novelty Detection, Image Emotion Prediction, and Misinformation Detection*. Below, we discuss all these three components in details.

4.1 Novelty Detection

We perform a novelty detection task using SCL to find high-level semantic interaction within target and source multimodal news pairs and extract the novelty-aware multimodal feature representations from these news pairs. As discussed below, we give the multimodal source and target as input to the model. We encode the text data using pre-trained MultilingualBERT model (Devlin et al., 2018) and extract the 768-dimensional textual feature representations. To encode the visual data, we use ResNet18 (He et al., 2016) and concatenate the textual and visual features to obtain the multimodal feature representations. We employ two fully connected layers over the encoded source and target representations to project them in a 128-dimensional latent space. Now, we train the model using contrastive learning so that the target representation attracts the source representation if both are of the same class; otherwise, the target repeals the source representation. We optimize the contrastive loss function, similar to Khosla et al. (2020)

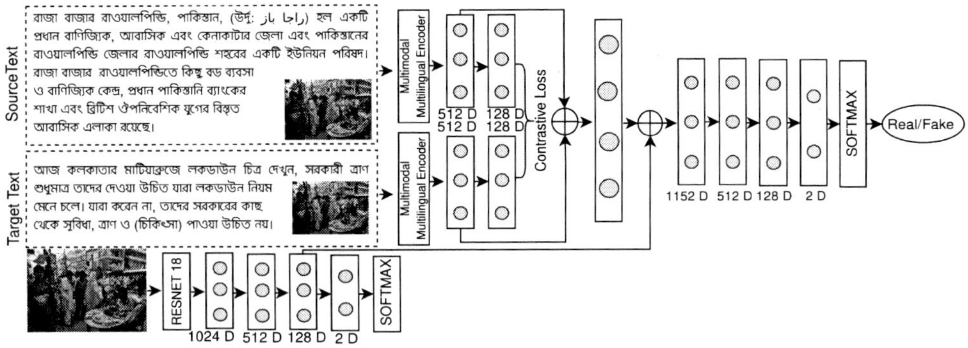

Figure 1: Proposed multilingual multimodal misinformation detection model

to train the novelty model. We mathematically define the loss function in Equation 2. Here, I is the set of indices of the target (anchor); P is the set of positive samples (samples of the same class of anchor), τ is a scalar parameter.

$$L_{SCL} = \sum_{i \in I} \frac{-1}{|P(i)|} \sum_{p \in P(i)} log \frac{exp(\frac{z_i \cdot z_p}{\tau})}{\sum_{a \in A(i)} exp(\frac{z_i \cdot z_p}{\tau})} \quad (2)$$

4.2 Image Emotion Prediction

Emotional appeal in the news content plays an inevitable role for the spread of false information. A number of prior works on misinformation detection have investigated textual emotions but the visual emotion is still under-explored. In the era of multimedia information, visual emotion convince people to believe in false information much compared to the textual emotion. Motivated by this, we design a neural network-based visual emotion classification model to obtain the emotion-aware visual feature representation. For pre-training this network, we use the combined form of UnbiasedEmo (Panda et al., 2018) and ArtPhoto (Machajdik and Hanbury, 2010) datasets. The instances of the combined datasets are associated with six emotion labels *viz.* joy, love, sadness, fear, surprise, and anger. The study presented by MIT scholars has proved that false rumors usually inspire replies expressing greater surprise, fear and disgust. On the other hand, the true stories inspire greater sadness, anticipation, joy, and trust. Motivated by this investigation, we have kept surprise, fear and disgust in one group and sadness, anticipation, joy, and trust in another group. Categorizing these emotions reflects the news characteristics, which shorten the decision boundary. The dataset that we are using for visual emotion prediction is also highly imbalanced. This is also a major reason for grouping the emotion instances into binary classes. For our experiments, we follow Kumari et al. (2021a) to consider two emotion labels, *emotion true* which is formed by combining joy, love, and sadness labels; and *emotion false* which is formed by the combination of fear, surprise, and anger. Given a set of n images I = (I1, .., In), and their emotion labels EL = (EL1, .., ELn), we encode each image ELi using ResNet18 to the model and pass this encoded image representation through a Multilayer Perceptron (MLP) network that consists of two hidden layers with 1024 and 512 neurons and one output layer with two neurons and a softmax classifier function. Since the number of instances in each emotion class is not balanced, we optimize the weighted cross-entropy loss during training. After training this emotion model, we predict the emotion labels of images present in the developed dataset.

4.3 Misinformation Detection

After pre-training the novelty model, we extract the 512-dimensional feature representations for the source and target then concatenate them to obtain multimodal representation. We project this fused representation into 512-dimensional feature space and use it as a novelty-aware multimodal feature representation to develop our fake news detection model. We also extract 512-dimensional emotion-aware visual feature representations from a pre-trained image emotion model. At last, we concatenate novelty and emotion-aware representations.

After obtaining novelty-aware multimodal representation and emotion-aware visual representation, we concatenate and pass them to MLP that contains two hidden layers and an output layer with a softmax function to classify the news as fake or real. We optimize the cross-entropy loss to train our fake news detection model.

5 Experiments and Results

This section presents experimental setup, baseline, results, case studies and error analysis.

5.1 Experimental Setup

We perform all the experiments with one NVIDIA GeForce RTX GPU and 11GB of RAM using the Pytorch library. We train the baseline models for 100 epochs using the Adam optimizer with 128 batch size. We pre-train the contrastive learning framework for 1000 epochs using LARS optimizer for Stochastic Gradient Descent (SGD) with 512 batch size, which takes approximately 10 minutes. The emotion model is pre-trained using Adam optimizer with 128 batches in 10 minutes, with 100 epochs. We train the final proposed model using the Adam optimizer for 100 epochs for a batch size of 128 which takes approximately 15 minutes.

5.2 Baselines and Comparing Systems

We design some baseline models for validating the performance of our proposed model. We show the results of the proposed and baseline models in Table 3. Apart from these, we also implement the state-of-the-art systems like MLBViT and EANN for the comparison where we feed target text and target image in multimodal feature extractor and use MultilingualBert in place of Text-CNN. We show the results of these comparing systems in Table 2.

Model	Hindi		Bengali		Tamil		MMM	
	FS	Acc	FS	Acc	FS	Acc	FS	Acc
MLBViT	.723	.735	.748	.758	.743	.752	.775	.780
EANN	.833	.822	.845	.856	.870	.883	.855	.868
MVEN	**.939**	**.938**	**.946**	**.945**	**.946**	**.946**	**.955**	**.956**

Table 2: Results of comparing systems. Here, MVEN is our proposed *Multilingual + VisualEmo + Novelty* model; MLBViT: *MultiLingualBert + Vision Transformer*

MLBERT+ResNet: We encode textual and visual information of target using pre-trained MultilingualBERT (Devlin et al., 2018) and pre-trained ResNet18 model (He et al., 2016), respectively. We concatenate the textual and visual representations to obtain multimodal representations and pass this target multimodal representation to MLP network that consists of two hidden layers and one output layer with a softmax function.

MLBERT+ResNet (WBG): We encode the textual and visual information for source and target both similar to the previous baseline model. We concatenate source and target multimodal representation and pass it to MLP network that consists of two hidden layers and one output layer with a softmax classifier function. Thus, in this baseline we also consider source information along with the target information.

Unimodal + VisualEmo: In this model, we encode the target text information using Multilingual-BERT and compute target image emotion using the method, similar to proposed model. We pass the textual representation and emotion aware visual representation to MLP network for the final classification.

Multimodal + VisualEmo: In visualEmo model, we compute the visual emotion similar to the previous baseline. We pass this emotion aware visual representation and source multimodal representation to MLP with Softmax classifier function for the final classification.

Multimodal + Novelty: In novelty model, we implement the proposed framework without emotion module. We apply SCL between source and target multimodal representation to compute the novelty aware representation. We only pass the novelty aware multimodal representation to the MLP with Softmax classifier function.

5.3 Results and Discussion

The results of the baseline models and our proposed model are shown in Table 3. We report the result for our developed *MMM* dataset and also for Hindi, Bengali and Tamil language dataset separately. As shown in Table 3, the *Multilingual + ResNet (WBG)* model performs better than the *Multilingual + ResNet* model for all the datasets which show the importance of background knowledge. *Multimodal + VisualEmo* model produces better results than *Multilingual + ResNet* model. In addition, the *Multimodal + VisualEmo* model performs better than the *Unimodal + VisualEmo* model. The above three factors assist us in concluding that background knowledge, emotion, and multimodality effectively help in fake news prediction. In comparison to the background knowledge framework, we obtain a 2.46 accuracy improvement when we use the *Multimodal + Novelty* model. We can therefore prove that our contrastive learning methodology helps to detect fake news. Compared

Model	Dataset	Fake F1	Real F1	Acc	WA	Model	Dataset	Fake F1	Real F1	Acc	WA
MLBERT + ResNet	Hindi	0.668	0.722	0.697	0.695	**MLBERT + ResNet(WBG)**	Hindi	0.876	0.889	0.876	0.883
	Bengali	0.627	0.813	0.751	0.734		Bengali	0.866	0.879	0.867	0.873
	Tamil	0.666	0.812	0.759	0.750		Tamil	0.872	0.885	0.873	0.880
	MMM	0.703	0.765	0.737	0.737		MMM	0.886	0.901	0.886	0.895
Unimodal + VisualEmo	Hindi	0.813	0.837	0.819	0.826	**Multimodal + VisualEmo**	Hindi	0.861	0.874	0.860	0.868
	Bengali	0.791	0.817	0.799	0.805		Bengali	0.840	0.859	0.848	0.851
	Tamil	0.801	0.826	0.807	0.841		Tamil	0.846	0.836	0.833	0.846
	MMM	0.808	0.851	0.834	0.830		MMM	0.857	0.858	0.857	0.857
Multimodal + Novelty	Hindi	0.919	0.928	0.914	0.925	**Multimodal + VisualEmo + Novelty**	Hindi	0.934	0.942	0.938	0.939
	Bengali	0.900	0.917	0.904	0.910		Bengali	0.939	0.950	0.945	0.946
	Tamil	0.902	0.911	0.899	0.905		Tamil	0.940	0.951	0.946	0.946
	MMM	0.907	0.926	0.910	0.920		MMM	**0.949**	**0.960**	**0.956**	**0.955**

Table 3: Results of the proposed model and its ablated versions. Here, *Multimodal + VisualEmo + Novelty* is our proposed model; F1: F1 score, Acc: Accuracy, MA: Macro Average, WA: Weighted Average.

to the *Multilingual + ResNet* baseline model, our final proposed model (*Multimodal + VisualEmo + Novelty*) achieves 21.77 accuracy improvement. Hence, our final proposed architecture that utilizes novelty and emotion outperforms all of the baselines and produces the most effective results. We also obtain an 8.8 accuracy improvement over the EANN model.

McNemar significance test (Pembury Smith and Ruxton, 2020) is a well-known statistical test to analyze statistical significance of the differences in classifier's performance. In our work, we also want to prove that the proposed model is comparatively significant with a larger margin than the baseline models. Therefore, we use the McNemar significance test to compute the significance difference between our proposed model and EANN model and obtain p-values 7.3*E-3 that are less than the threshold p-value i.e. 0.05 for rejection of the null hypothesis. It shows that our result is significant.

5.4 Case Studies and Error Analysis

We perform a detailed analysis in Figure 2 to show the efficacy of our background knowledge, novelty, emotion and multi-modality. First example shows that concatenation of background Knowledge (source text) with target text help the model to predict accurately. In the second example, source text and target text describe that location of target image is Pakistan and Kolkata, respectively. This mismatch in location is easily detected by *Multimodal + Novelty* model which use supervised contrastive learning. In the third example, emotion of target image is joy which is more inclined towards real news so the proposed model with novelty and emotion predicts it accurately. In the last example, visual features of target and source images with source and target text help the model to predict accurately which shows how significant the role multi-modality plays.

We show some examples in Figure 3, which are misclassified by our proposed model. For the first example, the target image shows Avni Chaturvedi, but the target text claims that the image shows Urvisha Jariwala, which is incorrect. *Multimodal + Novelty* model focuses solely on novelty and capture the mismatch in source and target text and correctly predicts fake news, but *Multimodal + VisualEmo + Novelty* model gives the wrong prediction because emotion associated with this image is joy which is an attribute of true news, so it misleads the model. In the second example, the model with novelty and emotion performs better than with model that doesbackground knowledge (WBG) model. Novelty emotion model can flag this news as fake based on the source text collected which clearly states that the original image was an old image and taken in 2014s. However, the mismatch between source and target text is not noticeable with background knowledge model, resulting in incorrect predictions. For the last example, *Multimodal + VisualEmo* model performs well than our proposed model. With novelty and emotion, we see that the source text and target text both give some information about covid-19 but the source text has some additional information about the election while the target text gives more emphasis on symptoms which mislead the model and contrastive learning takes it away from the main subject.

6 Conclusion

In this paper we solve the problem of multilingual multimodal misinformation detection in three Indian languages, Hindi, Bengali and Tamil. Now-a-days, same image is used in different textual context to mislead the reader. To address this problem, first, we have created our Multilingual Multimodal Misinformation dataset and then we

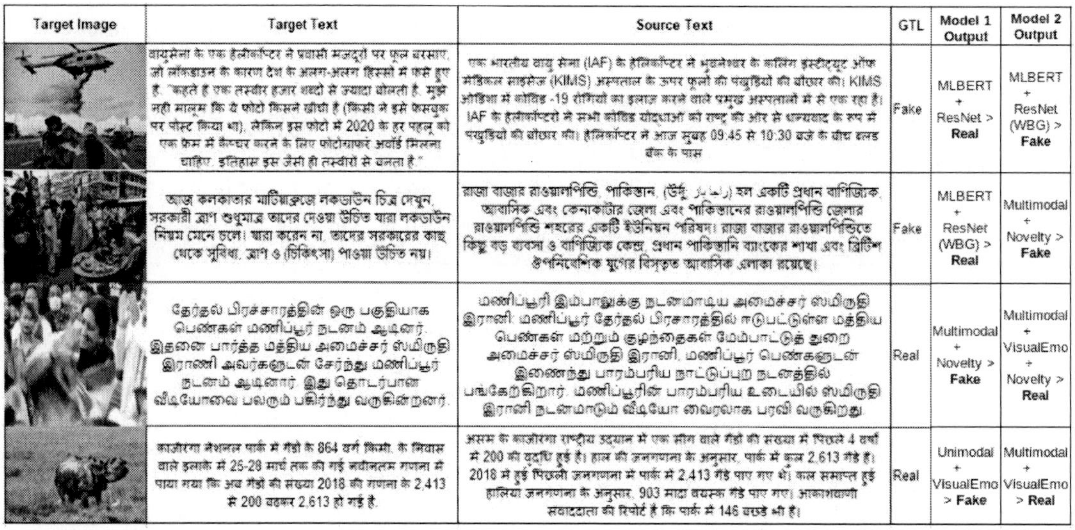

Figure 2: Some case studies where model 2 correctly classifies the misinformation. Here, GTL: Ground Truth Label, Model 1 Output and Model 2 Output are the different models output shown in that particular column.

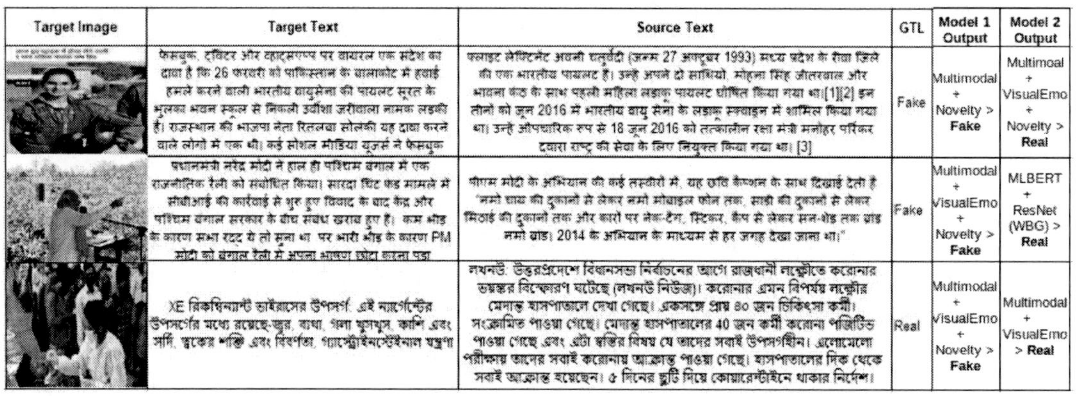

Figure 3: Error analysis on some examples which are misclassified.

have performed experiments on Multilinguality, Background knowledge, Emotion, Multimodality and Novelty to see the effect. We have built a novel framework based on novelty and emotion which outperform all the baseline and state-of-the-art models. Further, We want to extend our current work in following direction to prevent the spread of misinformation: (i). by including additional low-resources language; (ii). by addressing cross-lingual and code-mixed based resources and mechanisms; and (iii). by incorporating explainability in the model.

Ethical Declaration

We have developed our dataset using publicly available information on different websites. Our use of those data has adhered to the policy guidelines and has not caused any copyright issues. During the creation of our dataset, we collected news articles and related information that did not contain any sensitive information. We will make the data available only for research purposes after signing an agreement.

Acknowledgments

This reserach is partially supported by the project "HELIOS - Hate, Hyperpartisan, and Hyperpluralism Elicitation and Observer System", sponsored by Wipro. We thank all the anonymous reviewers for their insightful suggestions. We also sincerely thank Tanik Saikh for his contribution in data annotation of Bengali Language. All the research work was carried out at AI-ML-NLP research lab, IIT Patna.

References

Hugo Queiroz Abonizio, Janaina Ignacio de Morais, Gabriel Marques Tavares, and Sylvio Barbon Junior. 2020. Language-independent fake news detection: English, portuguese, and spanish mutual features. *Future Internet*, 12(5):87.

Christina Boididou, Katerina Andreadou, Symeon Papadopoulos, Duc-Tien Dang-Nguyen, Giulia Boato, Michael Riegler, Yiannis Kompatsiaris, et al. 2015. Verifying multimedia use at mediaeval 2015. *MediaEval*, 3(3):7.

Ali K Chaudhry, Darren Baker, and Philipp Thun-Hohenstein. 2017. Stance detection for the fake news challenge: identifying textual relationships with deep neural nets. *CS224n: Natural Language Processing with Deep Learning*.

M Chen, X Chu, and KP Subbalakshmi. 2021. Mm-covar: Multimodal covid-19 vaccine focused data repository for fake news detection and a baseline architecture for classification.

Jacob Cohen. 1960. A coefficient of agreement for nominal scales. *Educational and psychological measurement*, 20(1):37–46.

Limeng Cui and Dongwon Lee. 2020. Coaid: Covid-19 healthcare misinformation dataset. *arXiv preprint arXiv:2006.00885*.

Jacob Devlin, Ming-Wei Chang, Kenton Lee, and Kristina Toutanova. 2018. BERT: pre-training of deep bidirectional transformers for language understanding. *CoRR*, abs/1810.04805.

Maria Glenski, Ellyn Ayton, Josh Mendoza, and Svitlana Volkova. 2019. Multilingual multimodal digital deception detection and disinformation spread across social platforms. *arXiv preprint arXiv:1909.05838*.

Gaël Guibon, Liana Ermakova, Hosni Seffih, Anton Firsov, and Guillaume Le Noé-Bienvenu. 2019. Multilingual fake news detection with satire. In *CICLing: International Conference on Computational Linguistics and Intelligent Text Processing*.

Fatima Haouari, Maram Hasanain, Reem Suwaileh, and Tamer Elsayed. 2021. Arcov19-rumors: Arabic covid-19 twitter dataset for misinformation detection. In *Proceedings of the Sixth Arabic Natural Language Processing Workshop*, pages 72–81.

Kaiming He, Xiangyu Zhang, Shaoqing Ren, and Jian Sun. 2016. Deep residual learning for image recognition. In *Proceedings of the IEEE conference on computer vision and pattern recognition*, pages 770–778.

Zhiwei Jin, Juan Cao, Han Guo, Yongdong Zhang, and Jiebo Luo. 2017. Multimodal fusion with recurrent neural networks for rumor detection on microblogs. In *Proceedings of the 25th ACM international conference on Multimedia*, pages 795–816.

Sarthak Jindal, Raghav Sood, Richa Singh, Mayank Vatsa, and Tanmoy Chakraborty. 2020. Newsbag: A multimodal benchmark dataset for fake news detection.

Dhruv Khattar, Jaipal Singh Goud, Manish Gupta, and Vasudeva Varma. 2019. Mvae: Multimodal variational autoencoder for fake news detection. In *The World Wide Web Conference*, pages 2915–2921.

Prannay Khosla, Piotr Teterwak, Chen Wang, Aaron Sarna, Yonglong Tian, Phillip Isola, Aaron Maschinot, Ce Liu, and Dilip Krishnan. 2020. Supervised contrastive learning. *Advances in Neural Information Processing Systems*, 33.

Rina Kumari, Nischal Ashok, Tirthankar Ghosal, and Asif Ekbal. 2021a. Misinformation detection using multitask learning with mutual learning for novelty detection and emotion recognition. *Information Processing & Management*, 58(5):102631.

Rina Kumari, Nischal Ashok, Tirthankar Ghosal, and Asif Ekbal. 2021b. A multitask learning approach for fake news detection: Novelty, emotion, and sentiment lend a helping hand. In *2021 International Joint Conference on Neural Networks (IJCNN)*, pages 1–8. IEEE.

Rina Kumari, Nischal Ashok, Tirthankar Ghosal, and Asif Ekbal. 2022. What the fake? probing misinformation detection standing on the shoulder of novelty and emotion. *Information Processing & Management*, 59(1):102740.

Rina Kumari and Asif Ekbal. 2021. Amfb: Attention based multimodal factorized bilinear pooling for multimodal fake news detection. *Expert Systems with Applications*, 184:115412.

Yichuan Li, Bohan Jiang, Kai Shu, and Huan Liu. 2020a. Mm-covid: A multilingual and multimodal data repository for combating covid-19 disinformation. *arXiv preprint arXiv:2011.04088*.

Yichuan Li, Bohan Jiang, Kai Shu, and Huan Liu. 2020b. Toward a multilingual and multimodal data repository for covid-19 disinformation. In *2020 IEEE International Conference on Big Data (Big Data)*, pages 4325–4330. IEEE.

Jana Machajdik and Allan Hanbury. 2010. Affective image classification using features inspired by psychology and art theory. In *Proceedings of the 18th ACM international conference on Multimedia*, pages 83–92.

Kai Nakamura, Sharon Levy, and William Yang Wang. 2020. Fakeddit: A new multimodal benchmark dataset for fine-grained fake news detection. In *Proceedings of the 12th Language Resources and Evaluation Conference*, pages 6149–6157.

Yixin Nie, Haonan Chen, and Mohit Bansal. 2019. Combining fact extraction and verification with neural semantic matching networks. In *Proceedings of the AAAI Conference on Artificial Intelligence*, volume 33, pages 6859–6866.

Dan Saattrup Nielsen and Ryan McConville. 2022. Mumin: A large-scale multilingual multimodal fact-checked misinformation social network dataset. *arXiv preprint arXiv:2202.11684*.

Rameswar Panda, Jianming Zhang, Haoxiang Li, Joon-Young Lee, Xin Lu, and Amit K Roy-Chowdhury. 2018. Contemplating visual emotions: Understanding and overcoming dataset bias. In *Proceedings of the European Conference on Computer Vision (ECCV)*, pages 579–595.

Matilda QR Pembury Smith and Graeme D Ruxton. 2020. Effective use of the mcnemar test. *Behavioral Ecology and Sociobiology*, 74(11):1–9.

Alec Radford, Jong Wook Kim, Chris Hallacy, Aditya Ramesh, Gabriel Goh, Sandhini Agarwal, Girish Sastry, Amanda Askell, Pamela Mishkin, Jack Clark, et al. 2021. Learning transferable visual models from natural language supervision. In *International Conference on Machine Learning*, pages 8748–8763. PMLR.

Nils Reimers and Iryna Gurevych. 2020. Making monolingual sentence embeddings multilingual using knowledge distillation. In *Proceedings of the 2020 Conference on Empirical Methods in Natural Language Processing (EMNLP)*, pages 4512–4525.

Tanik Saikh, Arkadipta De, Asif Ekbal, and Pushpak Bhattacharyya. 2020. A deep learning approach for automatic detection of fake news. *arXiv preprint arXiv:2005.04938*.

Kai Shu, Limeng Cui, Suhang Wang, Dongwon Lee, and Huan Liu. 2019. Defend: Explainable fake news detection. In *25th ACM SIGKDD International Conference on Knowledge Discovery and Data Mining, KDD 2019*, pages 395–405. Association for Computing Machinery.

Kai Shu, Amy Sliva, Suhang Wang, Jiliang Tang, and Huan Liu. 2017. Fake news detection on social media: A data mining perspective. *ACM SIGKDD explorations newsletter*, 19(1):22–36.

Karen Simonyan and Andrew Zisserman. 2014. Very deep convolutional networks for large-scale image recognition. *arXiv preprint arXiv:1409.1556*.

Shivangi Singhal, Rajiv Ratn Shah, Tanmoy Chakraborty, Ponnurangam Kumaraguru, and Shin'ichi Satoh. 2019. Spotfake: A multi-modal framework for fake news detection. In *2019 IEEE Fifth International Conference on Multimedia Big Data (BigMM)*, pages 39–47. IEEE.

Shivangi Singhal, Rajiv Ratn Shah, and Ponnurangam Kumaraguru. 2021. Factorization of fact-checks for low resource indian languages. *arXiv preprint arXiv:2102.11276*.

Valeriya Slovikovskaya and Giuseppe Attardi. 2020. Transfer learning from transformers to fake news challenge stance detection (fnc-1) task. In *Proceedings of The 12th Language Resources and Evaluation Conference*, pages 1211–1218.

Chenguang Song, Nianwen Ning, Yunlei Zhang, and Bin Wu. 2021. A multimodal fake news detection model based on crossmodal attention residual and multichannel convolutional neural networks. *Information Processing & Management*, 58(1):102437.

Yaqing Wang, Fenglong Ma, Zhiwei Jin, Ye Yuan, Guangxu Xun, Kishlay Jha, Lu Su, and Jing Gao. 2018. Eann: Event adversarial neural networks for multi-modal fake news detection. In *Proceedings of the 24th acm sigkdd international conference on knowledge discovery & data mining*, pages 849–857.

Yang Wu, Pengwei Zhan, Yunjian Zhang, Liming Wang, and Zhen Xu. 2021. Multimodal fusion with co-attention networks for fake news detection. In *Findings of the Association for Computational Linguistics: ACL-IJCNLP 2021*, pages 2560–2569.

Chen Yang, Xinyi Zhou, and Reza Zafarani. 2021. Checked: Chinese covid-19 fake news dataset. *Social Network Analysis and Mining*, 11(1):1–8.

Yang Yang, Lei Zheng, Jiawei Zhang, Qingcai Cui, Zhoujun Li, and Philip S Yu. 2018. Ti-cnn: Convolutional neural networks for fake news detection. *arXiv preprint arXiv:1806.00749*.

Wenpeng Yin and Dan Roth. 2018. Twowingos: A two-wing optimization strategy for evidential claim verification. In *Proceedings of the 2018 Conference on Empirical Methods in Natural Language Processing*, pages 105–114.

Jiawei Zhang, Bowen Dong, and S Yu Philip. 2020. Fakedetector: Effective fake news detection with deep diffusive neural network. In *2020 IEEE 36th International Conference on Data Engineering (ICDE)*, pages 1826–1829. IEEE.

Wenjia Zhang, Lin Gui, and Yulan He. 2021. Supervised contrastive learning for multimodal unreliable news detection in covid-19 pandemic. *arXiv preprint arXiv:2109.01850*.

Xinyi Zhou, Apurva Mulay, Emilio Ferrara, and Reza Zafarani. 2020. Recovery: A multimodal repository for covid-19 news credibility research. In *Proceedings of the 29th ACM International Conference on Information & Knowledge Management*, pages 3205–3212.

Dimitrina Zlatkova, Preslav Nakov, and Ivan Koychev. 2019. Fact-checking meets fauxtography: Verifying claims about images. In *Proceedings of the 2019 Conference on Empirical Methods in Natural Language Processing and the 9th International Joint Conference on Natural Language Processing (EMNLP-IJCNLP)*, pages 2099–2108.

A Data Statistics

We have also computed the average and median length of the source and target text for Hindi, Bengali, Tamil and MMM datasets shown in Table 4. The average target text length of the Tamil language is smaller than other languages.

B Data Collection Flow Diagram

Figure 4 shows the complete data preparation flow diagram we have followed to collect background knowledge. We collect the target instances of our *MMM* dataset using the following flow diagram:

C Multilingual analysis

We also tested the trained model on language which is not included in the training process, as a zero-shot experiment. For this, we make three groups of dataset *Hindi+Bengali*, *Bengali+Tamil*, *Tamil+Hindi* and train the model on each group. Finally, we test the model on different combination of unseen and seen language. This experiment shows that the model can be generalized for an unseen language also by using language-independent features.

1.) Firstly, we test the model on Tamil, Hindi, and Bengali languages, which the model does not see during training. This experiment shows that the model can also be generalized for an unseen language by using language-independent features. The first section of Table 5 *Multilingual training with Monolingual testing on unseen language* shows the model's performance is the least when it is evaluated on the test set of Tamil data. This is because Hindi and Bengali belong to the same language family, i.e., the Indo-Aryan language family. In contrast, Tamil belongs to the Dravidian language family, resulting in less generalization of the model.

2.) We also test the model with test data, having all three language. It means this time; we consider both seen language and unseen language. The second section of Table 5 *Multilingual training with Multilingual testing on seen and unseen language* shows that model is performing slightly better than the first section of table 5 because training data include seen language also.

3.) The third section of Table 5 depicts the results for *Multilingual training with Monolingual testing on seen language*. Here, we train the model in two-step *viz.* i). We train the model with three language groups having two languages in each group and train the model with each group's language, respectively and ii). we train the model with all three languages and feed monolingual test data for all three languages.

D Translated version of case studies and error analysis

We have also translated case studies and error analysis into English language in Figure 5 and Figure 6 respectively so that everyone can understand it.

Dataset	Length	Target	Source_1	Source_2	Source_3	Source_4
Hindi	Average	103.22	1668.44	779.52	637.48	586.46
	Median	26	805.5	576	540	479
Bengali	Average	68.69	1964.26	584	471.07	403.81
	Median	12	772	396	367	302
Tamil	Average	37.43	1298.07	518.2	487.31	380.61
	Median	8	512	281	268	217
MMM	Average	87.93	1650.59	710.7	590.41	528.27
	Median	22	743.5	509	469	402

Table 4: Dataset statistics on Source and Target text length

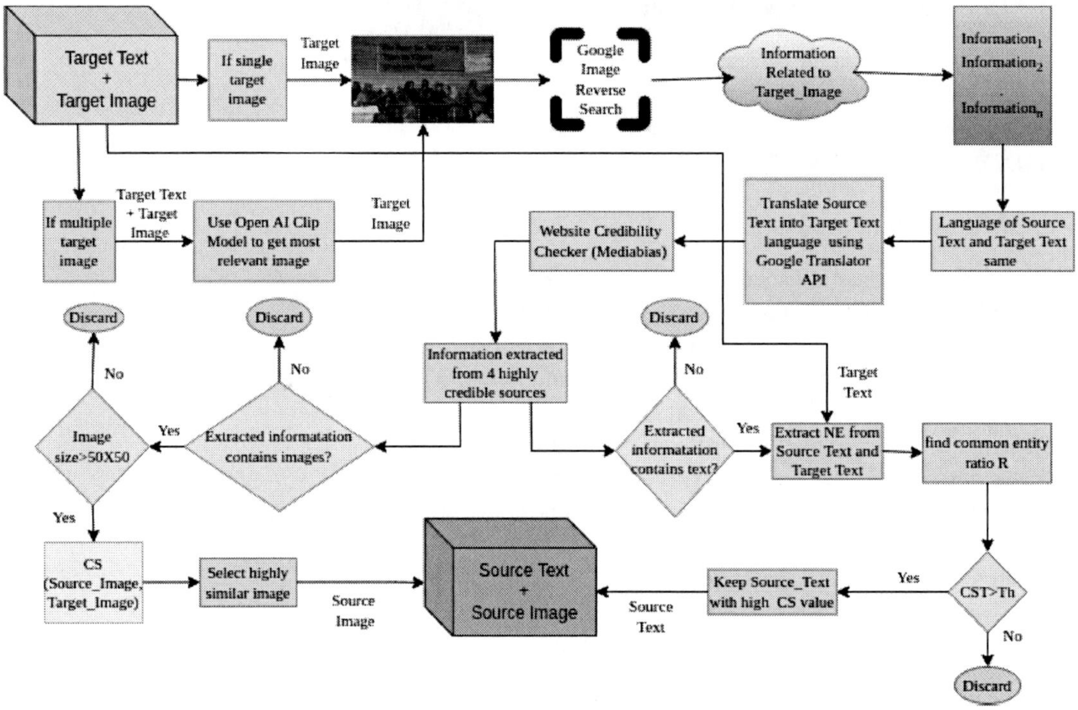

Figure 4: Flow diagram to collect source information from each target instance

Target Image	Target Text (Translated)	Source Text (Translated)	GTL	Model 1 Output	Model 2 Output
	An Air Force helicopter showered flowers on migrant laborers who have become firm in different parts of the country due to the lockdown. It is said that a picture speaks more than a thousand words, I don't know who took this photo (somebody posted it on Facebook, but this photo should get the Photographer Award for capturing every aspect of 2020 in one frame) History is made from such pictures.	An Indian Air Force (IAF) helicopter showers flower petals over the Kalang Institute of Medical Sciences (KIMS) Hospital in Bhubaneswar. KIMS has been one of the major hospitals in Odisha treating COVID 19 patients. IAF helicopters showered vertical showers of thanks on behalf of the nation to all the covid warriors. Helicopters from 09.45 am to 10:30 am today near Lad Bank	Fake	MLBERT + ResNet > **Real**	MLBERT + ResNet (WBG) > **Fake**
	View Lockdown Images Today in Martiaktje, Kolkata Government knowledge should be given only to those who follow the lockdown rules. Those who do not, should not get benefits, food and (treatment) from the government.	Raja Bazar Rawalpindi Pakistan, (Urdu 1961) is a major commercial residential and a union council of Rawalpindi city in Kenakartar district and Rawalpindi district of Pakistan. Raja Bazar in Rawalpindi Some major business and commercial centers include branches of major Pakistani banks and extensive residential areas dating back to the British colonial era.	Fake	MLBERT + ResNet (WBG) > **Real**	Multimodal + Novelty > **Fake**
	Women perform Manipur dance as part of election campaign. Seeing this Union Minister Samruti Irani danced Manipur along with them. Many people are sharing the related video.	Minister Smriti danced to Manipuri Imphal Irani Manipur Election Campaign Union Women and Child Development Minister Smriti Irani participates in a traditional folk dance with Manipur women. A video of Smriti Irani dancing in traditional Manipur attire is going viral.	Real	Multimodal + Novelty > **Fake**	Multimodal + VisualEmo + Novelty > **Real**
	In Kaziranga National Park, the latest census of 864 sq km inhabited by pits from March 25-28 found that the number of pits has now increased by 200 to 2,613 from 2,413 in the 2018 census.	In Assam's Jarga National Park, the number of one-sug-shaped pits has increased by 200 in the last 4 years. According to the most recent census, there are a total of 2,613 pits in the park. In the last census conducted in 2018, 2.413 rhinos were found in the park. According to the most recent census that ended yesterday, 903 female adult litters were found. All India Radio reporter reports that there are also 146 calves in the park.	Real	Unimodal + VisualEmo > **Fake**	Multimodal + VisualEmo > **Real**

Figure 5: Some case studies where model 2 correctly classifies the misinformation. Here, GTL: Ground Truth Label, Model 1 Output and Model 2 Output are the different models output shown in that particular column.

Train	Test	Fake P	Fake R	Fake F1	Real P	Real R	Real F1	Acc	MA	WA
Multilingual training with Monolingual testing on unseen language										
H+B	T	0.880	0.871	0.875	0.893	0.900	0.896	0.894	0.886	0.885
B+T	H	0.892	0.889	0.891	0.907	0.910	0.908	0.918	0.899	0.903
T+H	B	0.878	0.868	0.873	0.890	0.899	0.894	0.906	0.884	0.883
Multilingual training with Multilingual testing on seen and unseen language										
H+B	H+B+T	0.9305	0.915	0.920	0.925	0.942	0.934	0.927	0.927	0.927
B+T	H+B+T	0.935	0.904	0.919	0.922	0.941	0.931	0.926	0.925	0.926
T+H	H+B+T	0.9297	0.899	0.914	0.917	0.942	0.930	0.923	0.922	0.923
Multilingual training with Monolingual testing on seen language										
H+B	H	0.937	0.941	0.939	0.950	0.946	0.948	0.944	0.944	0.944
H+B	B	0.936	0.931	0.933	0.942	0.935	0.943	0.939	0.938	0.939
B+T	B	0.935	0.919	0.925	0.944	0.968	0.956	0.942	0.940	0.941
B+T	T	0.931	0.920	0.925	0.933	0.942	0.938	0.932	0.932	0.932
T+H	H	0.936	0.925	0.931	0.938	0.947	0.942	0.937	0.936	0.937
T+H	T	0.930	0.915	0.923	0.929	0.936	0.933	0.930	0.928	0.930
H+B+T	H	0.951	0.931	0.941	0.957	0.972	0.964	0.954	0.953	0.952
H+B+T	B	0.952	0.936	0.944	0.947	0.957	0.952	0.949	0.948	0.948
H+B+T	T	0.9526	0.946	0.949	0.955	0.962	0.958	0.954	0.953	0.954

Table 5: Results on a different combination of training and testing language; Here P, R, F-S are Precision, Recall and F1 score, respectively; Acc: Accuracy, MA: Macro Average, WA: Weighted Average; H:Hindi, B:Bengali, T:Tamil

Target Image	Target Text (Translated)	Source Text (Translated)	GTL	Model 1 Output	Model 2 Output
	A viral message on Facebook, Twitter and WhatsApp claims that the Indian Air Force pilot who carried out the air strikes in Pakistan's Balakot on February 26 is a girl named Urvasha Jariwala, who came out of Bhulka Bhawan school in Surat. Rajasthan's BJP leader Ritlawa Solko was one of the many social media users who made this claim on Facebook.	Flight Lieutenant Avani Chaturvedi (born 27 October 1993) is an Indian pilot from Rewa district, Madhya Pradesh. She was declared the first woman fighter pilot along with two of her teammates, Mohana Singh Jiterwal and Bhawna Kath. [1][2] All three were inducted into the fighter squadron of the Indian Air Force in June 2016. He was formally appointed to serve the nation by Defense Minister Manohar Parrikar on 18 June 2016. [3]	Fake	Multimodal + Novelty > **Fake**	Multimoal + VisualEmo + Novelty > **Real**
	Prime Minister Narendra Modi recently addressed a political rally in West Bengal. Relations between the Center and the West Bengal government have deteriorated following the controversy that started with the CBI action in the Saradha chit fund case. It was heard that the meeting was canceled due to less crowd, but due to the huge crowd, PM Modi had to rote his speech in the Bengal rally.	This image appears with the caption in many pictures of PM Modi's campaign. From NaMo tea stalls to NaMo mobile phones, from saree shops to sweet shops and from neck-tag sticker camps to sun-shades on cars, the brand was to be seen everywhere through the NaMo brand 2014 campaign.	Fake	Multimodal + VisualEmo + Novelty > **Fake**	MLBERT + ResNet (WBG) > **Real**
	Symptoms of XE Recombinant Virus Symptoms in infants include fever, sore throat, cough and runny nose, skin rash and discoloration, and gastrointestinal distress.	Ahead of assembly elections in Lucknow Uttar Pradesh, there was a terrible outbreak of corona in the capital Lucknow (Lucknow News). Such disaster of corona was seen in Lucknow Medanta Hospital. Around 40 medical personnel together. found infected. 40 employees of Medanta Hospital have been found corona positive and it is a relief that all of them are asymptomatic. All of them were found to be infected with corona in a random test. Everyone has been affected by the hospital. Ordered to stay in quarantine with 5 days leave.	Real	Multimodal + VisualEmo + Novelty > **Fake**	Multimodal + VisualEmo > **Real**

Figure 6: Error analysis on some examples which are misclassified.

Adversarial Sample Generation for Aspect based Sentiment Classification

Mamta and **Asif Ekbal**
Department of Computer Science and Engineerng
Indian Institute of Technology Patna, India
{mamta_1921cs11, asif}@iitp.ac.in

Abstract

Deep learning models have been proven vulnerable towards small imperceptible perturbed input, known as adversarial samples, which are indiscernible by humans. Initial attacks in Natural Language Processing perturb characters or words in sentences using heuristics and synonyms-based strategies, resulting in grammatical incorrect or out-of-context sentences. Recent works attempt to generate contextual adversarial samples using a masked language model, capturing word relevance using leave-one-out (LOO). However, they lack the design to maintain the semantic coherency for aspect based sentiment analysis (ABSA) tasks. Moreover, they focused on resource-rich languages like English. We present an attack algorithm for the ABSA task by exploiting model explainability techniques to address these limitations. It does not require access to the training data, raw access to the model, or calibrating a new model. Our proposed method generates adversarial samples for a given aspect, maintaining more semantic coherency. In addition, it can be generalized to low-resource languages, which are at high risk due to resource scarcity. We show the effectiveness of the proposed attack using automatic and human evaluation. Our method outperforms the state-of-art methods in perturbation ratio, success rate, and semantic coherence.

1 Introduction

Sentiment analysis is a well-established area in Natural Language Processing (NLP), and finds its applications in recommendation systems, national security-sensitive applications, curating online trends, etc. (Pang et al., 2002; Bakliwal et al., 2013; Kumar et al., 2019; Mamta et al., 2020, 2022b). Considering sentiment alone can only provide high-level insights, not sufficing to analyze reviews containing multiple attributes, known as aspects. Aspect level sentiment analysis (ABSA) provides more fine-grained information by classifying the sentiment towards a specific aspect of the product (Pontiki et al., 2014).

Recently, deep learning and transformer-based approaches have obtained state-of-the-art results in numerous classification applications such as emotion, sarcasm detection, etc. including ABSA (Wang et al., 2016; Liu et al., 2019; Akhtar et al., 2016a; Mamta et al., 2022a; Sun et al., 2019; Xu et al., 2019). However, these classification algorithms can be easily fooled by maliciously crafted (adversarial) examples (Miyato et al., 2016; Li et al., 2020b). Adversarial examples expose the system vulnerabilities and also help to improve the robustness of the model. The adversarial sample generation has been extensively explored to assess the resilience of the neural model, in the field of computer vision (Szegedy et al., 2013; Kurakin et al., 2016; Chakraborty et al., 2018). It has shown improvement in the robustness and generalized capability of the model via adversarial training (Goodfellow et al., 2014). The generation of such out-of-distribution samples against NLP models is more challenging than computer vision due to the discrete nature of text. In addition, semantic consistency and grammatical accuracy of generated adversarial samples should also be preserved.

Initial attempts to attack NLP models have shown to adapt the fast gradient sign methods (FGSM) (Goodfellow et al., 2014) and Generative Adversarial Networks (GANs) based methods from computer vision, to apply perturbations on the embedding space of the text (Papernot et al., 2016; Miyato et al., 2016; Zhao et al., 2017). There is, however, a difficulty in mapping perturbed continuous embedding space to discrete token space in these methods. There are prior works which explored character-level and word-level perturbation algorithms using synonym replacement and language model based approaches (Liang et al., 2017; Ebrahimi et al., 2017; Alzantot et al., 2018; Zhang et al., 2020a). Recent studies have revealed the vul-

Findings of the Association for Computational Linguistics: AACL-IJCNLP 2022, pages 478–492
November 20–23, 2022.

nerability of BERT-based (Bidirectional Encoder Representations from Transformers) text classification models in a black box setting using synonyms-based (Jin et al., 2020) and masked-language model (BERT-MLM) based approaches (Garg and Ramakrishnan, 2020; Li et al., 2020b; Mondal, 2021; Zhang et al., 2021).

Most existing attack methods are primarily focused on text classification, including document level sentiment classification and other question answering tasks. However, in the context of ABSA, these algorithms lack the design to maintain semantic coherency with the actual example, which is the foremost requirement of adversarial examples. For example, consider the example from SemEval laptop dataset, *Thanks for great service and shipping!* Adversarial example generated by SOTA method for aspect *service* is *Thanks for continued concern and shipping!* It is clear from the example that the overall semantics and aspect term have been changed. To maintain the semantic coherency with the actual example, aspect term should not be changed. Additionally, the presence of multi-word aspects in the sentence presents another challenge to preserve the semantics. For example, *quick and has built in virus control.* Here, the sentiment towards aspect *built in virus control* is positive. The adversarial example generated by SOTA method is *quick and has flaws in virus control*, which fails to preserve the semantic coherency and aspect term.

A recent attempt was made to attack the ABSA classifier by adding misspellings and punctuation to the actual sentences in the black-box setting (Hofer et al., 2021). These perturbations, however, can fool the classifier, but lack semantic and grammatical correctness. Moreover, these modifications may also be corrected by grammar or spelling checkers, thus increasing the likelihood of an attack failure. These approaches measure the word saliency by removing it from the sentence and calculating the drop in probability of correct class prediction (LOO). Almost all the efforts have been directed towards high-resource languages such as English. There has been no work on exposing vulnerabilities in low-resource NLP models, which are at high risk due to resource scarcity in low-resource languages. The existing ABSA attack is only applicable to the English language, as it uses language-specific rules and dictionaries. For example, the letter e can be replaced by 3 (homoglyphs) or s with 5.

To address these limitations, we propose an adversarial example generation algorithm designed for ABSA for a given aspect. Our proposed method is not dependent on the language-specific rules; hence, it can be generalized to low-resource languages with some optimizations. Our proposed algorithm applies perturbations at the word level by exploiting the model explainability technique, SHAP (SHapley Additive exPlanations) (Lundberg and Lee, 2017). We extend SHAP to BERT based ABSA task by incorporating aspect information so that it can generate word saliency scores according to the given aspect. SHAP considers various combination of words to determine the word importance, unlike in earlier attempts where importance is dependent on only one word. Moreover, our proposed algorithm can generate adversarial samples for single word and multi-word aspect terms.

We summarize the contributions of our work as follows:

- We propose an algorithm to generate adversarial samples for the ABSA task, utilizing the model explainability to better rank the words for their importance.
- The proposed algorithm has higher semantic similarity and grammatical correctness than the existing attacking algorithm by introducing ABSA specific components to preserve both single word and multi-word aspect terms.
- It achieves a higher attack success rate with fewer perturbations using model explainability technique and the proposed perturbation scheme.
- The proposed algorithm uses language independent rules and can be generalized to low-resource languages with some optimizations. This is first attempt to attack a low-resource ABSA model. We demonstrate it by performing experiments on the Hindi language.

2 Related Work

Generating the adversarial examples against neural models to assess resilience of the model has been explored extensively in the field of computer vision (Nguyen et al., 2015; Chakraborty et al., 2018; Miyato et al., 2018; Guo et al., 2020). However, attempts to expose the vulnerabilities of NLP models are relatively few (Zhang et al., 2020b). Initial attempts to attack NLP models adapt the FGSM (Goodfellow et al., 2014) from computer vision.

The key idea is to apply small perturbations to the embedding space of text (Papernot et al., 2016; Miyato et al., 2016) in the direction of the gradient. GANs (Zhao et al., 2017) based method are also explored by applying perturbations in the latent space. However, these approaches often lack in semantic correctness (Jin et al., 2020; Garg and Ramakrishnan, 2020). Subsequently, several methods focused on character level and word level perturbations in white box (Liang et al., 2017; Ebrahimi et al., 2017) or black box setting (Gao et al., 2018). The generated adversarial samples are easily identifiable by human and also lacks the grammatical correctness and semantic coherency with the seed sentences. To maintain grammatical correctness and semantic consistency, Li et al. (2018) proposed to perturb important words with the top *k* words obtained from the Glove embedding vectors. Authors also explored synonyms (Ren et al., 2019) and language model (Alzantot et al., 2018; Zhang et al., 2020a) based approaches for perturbations. Morris et al. (2020) introduced TextAttack to implement adversarial attacks in Python. It is composed of four basic components: a goal function, a set of constraints, a transformation, and a search method. TextAttack implements a wide range of adversarial attacks and supports a variety of datasets and models, such as BERT and transformer-based models.

2.1 Attacks on BERT

With the huge success of BERT for text classification in NLP, few attempts have been made to expose the vulnerabilities of recently risen BERT models (Sun et al., 2020). Jin et al. (2020) is first to propose a black-box algorithm to attack the BERT model with the help of closet synonyms. But it can lead to unnatural sentences because the synonym may not fit the context of sentence. To overcome this limitation, authors (Garg and Ramakrishnan, 2020; Li et al., 2020b; Mondal, 2021; Li et al., 2020a) proposed to use masked language model (BERT or Roberta) for replacements or insertions. The importance of each word is identified, as done in the previous black-box approaches (LOO). Relevant to our current work is the work done in (Hofer et al., 2021) which is first to attack aspect based sentiment classification model where character-level transformation are applied to generate adversaries against BERT. The importance of each word is calculated as done in (Garg and Ramakrishnan, 2020; Li et al., 2020b). However, the generated adversarial examples lack the semantic consistency due to mis-spellings.

Literature survey reveals that most of the efforts of attacking NLP models are for text classification, including document/sentence level sentiment classification tasks which lack the design to maintain semantic coherency with the seed sentence for ABSA task. The existing attack on ABSA uses language dependent rules and dictionaries, which can not be adapted to the Hindi language. In our work, we propose an attacking algorithm for aspect-based sentiment classification to address these limitations that can be generalized to low-resource languages. It uses SHAP, which is language independent component for word importance ranking, BERT-MLM, which can be applied to several languages, replace and insert operations which are language independent rules.

3 Threat Model

Our target model is a BERT based ABSA classifier. The adversary aims to generate adversarial samples against the target model due to their huge success in many NLP tasks, including ABSA (Liu et al., 2019; Xu et al., 2019; Sun et al., 2019).

Adversary's knowledge: The adversary has the black-box access of the target model. It queries the target model to get the prediction vector. The adversary does not have access to the data used to train the target model, rather it owns some test samples of similar distribution, which are used for the adversarial sample generation against the target model.

Adversary's goal: Given an input sentence S, consisting of n tokens $w_1, w_2, w_3, \ldots, w_n$ with m aspects asp = $asp_1, \ldots, asp_m$, where asp_i = $w_{s_i}, \ldots, w_{s_i+l_i}$ (contiguous subsequence of words from S), with ground truth sentiment label y_{asp_i} towards aspect asp_i, and a target model $M(S, asp_i) = y_{asp_i}$. Here l_i is the number of words in the asp_i (m and $l \geq 1$) and s_i is the starting index of asp_i. The goal of the adversary is to perform an un-targeted attack, i.e., find adversarial sample S_{adv} for aspect asp_i, causes M to perform misclassification, i.e., $M(S_{adv}, asp_i)! = y_{asp_i}$. At the same time, S_{adv} should satisfy the following properties: i). S_{adv} should be semantically similar to S. This is achieved by $sim(S, S_{adv}) > \epsilon$, where sim is cosine similarity and ϵ is the threshold value. ii). S_{adv} should be grammatically correct.

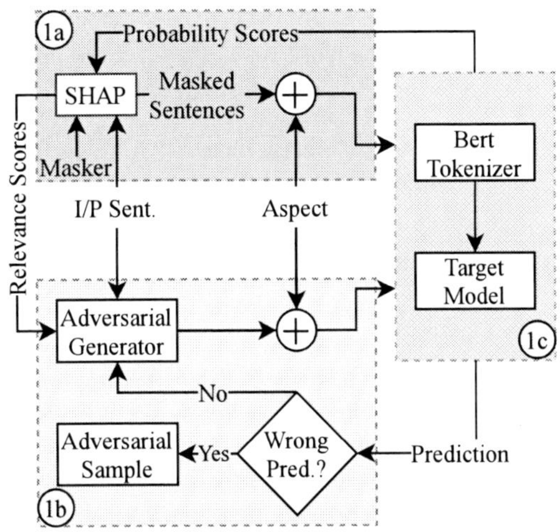

Figure 1: Proposed attack

iii). $HumanPred(S_{adv}, asp_i = y_{asp_i})$, where $HumanPred$ is classification by human. iv). S_{adv} should preserve the aspect asp_i for which the opinion is expressed. [1]

4 Methodology

We present model interpretable attack algorithm to generate high quality adversarial examples to assess the robustness of ABSA model by applying perturbations at the word-level. The detailed architecture of our proposed approach is depicted in Figure 1. There are 3 main components, *viz.* word saliency generator (1a), adversarial generator (1b) and the target model (1c). First, the saliency generator uses the model interpretation technique (SHAP) (Lundberg and Lee, 2017) to score the relevance of tokens in the input sentence for a given aspect. Relevance scores are used by the adversarial generator to generate the adversarial samples by applying perturbations at the word level. It runs iteratively until the generated adversarial sample is able to fool the target model.

4.1 Word saliency generator

Our first step is to find the contribution of each word for the final prediction. In general, word importance is computed as the difference between a prediction for a given sentence S (with n words) and the expected prediction when the word w_j is not present in S and replaced by $[MASK]$. It is described in Equation 1.

$$\phi_j(S) = M(w_1, \ldots, w_n) - E[M(w_1, \ldots, w_{j-1}, [MASK], w_{j+1} \ldots, w_n)] \quad (1)$$

We use Shapely algorithm, inspired by coalitional game theory, to determine the relevance of each word in a given sentence, against the target model. Shapley calculates the relevance score for each word based on possible coalitions for a particular prediction. Equation 2 explains the computation using a value function, which calculates the feature importance over the difference in prediction with or without w_j, over all combinations. It is the shapley value of a feature calculated as the contribution to the payout, weighted and summed over all possible feature value combinations.

$$\phi_j(\mathrm{w}) = \sum_{Q \subseteq S \setminus j} \frac{|Q|!(|S|-|Q|-1)!}{|S|!} \left(\mathrm{v}_{(Q \cup \{j\})}(w) - \mathrm{v}_Q(\mathrm{w})\right) \quad (2)$$

$v_Q(w)$ (value function) is the payout function for coalitions of players (feature values), which denotes the influence of a subset of feature values. It generalizes (Equation 1), in the following form

$$\mathrm{v}_Q(w) = \mathbb{E}\left[M \mid W_i = w_i, \forall i \in Q\right] - \mathbb{E}[M] \quad (3)$$

Where M provides the prediction over the set of features provided, S is the complete set of features, $Q \in S$ is a subset of features, and $|\cdot|$ is the size of feature set (Štrumbelj and Kononenko, 2014).

To adapt SHAP for the BERT based ABSA task, we implement a custom function for pre-processing the input data to obtain the predictions from the target model. In addition, we create an explicit word masker to tokenize the sentence into sentence fragments consisting of words, which serves as a basis for word masking in SHAP (here mask refers to hiding a particular word from the sentence). The input sentence along with the designed masker is passed to SHAP, generating various masked combinations of the sentence. These masked sentence fragments are concatenated with the input aspect with the help of CLS and SEP tokens ($[CLS]$ sentence $[SEP]$ aspect $[SEP]$) and further passed to the BERT tokenizer. Concatenation of aspect to masked sentence helps for better prediction scores, and in turn helps Shapley to focus on words which are relevant for sentiment classification of the given aspect. BERT tokenizer converts the words to subwords and generates input, segment, and mask embeddings for

[1] Suppose we have three aspect terms ($asp1$, $asp2$, asp) in the sentence ($sent$), then we have defined tuples like ($sent$, $asp1$), ($sent$, $asp2$), ($sent$, $asp3$). Our framework attempts to generate 3 adversarial examples (one for each aspect).

each subword unit and generate final representation by performing summation of all the three embeddings (Devlin et al., 2018). Finally, this combined representation of these vectors for each masked version is passed to the target model to obtain the output probabilities, which are further returned to SHAP to obtain the relevance of each word for the final prediction. This whole process is illustrated in Figure 1 (1a).

Algorithm 1 Adversarial Sample Generation

Input: Text Sentence S = $w_1, w_2, ..., w_n$, label y, importance_scores I, aspect asp, threshold ϵ, Prb$_{actual}$
Output: Adversarial Text Sentence S_{adv}

1: Initialization: $S_{adv} \leftarrow S$
2: Create $W_{context}$ and W_{aspect}
3: Remove stop words from I
4: **for each** word $w_k \in$ descending order of I **do**
5:     **if** $w_k \in W_{context}$ **then**
6:         replace w_k in S by $[MASK]$
7:     **else if** $w_k \in W_{aspect}$ **then**
8:         **if** $len(W_{aspect}) == 1$ **then**
9:             insert $[MASK]$ at start/end of w_k
10:         **else if** $len(W_{aspect}) > 1$ **then**
11:             insert $[MASK]$ at start/end of multi-word aspect asp
12:         **end if**
13:     **end if**
14:     find CANDIDATES for $[MASK]$ using BERT-MLM
15:     Success={}; ProbRed= {}
16:     **for** $c_j \in$ CANDIDATES **do**
17:         $S' \leftarrow$ Replace w_k with c_j in S_{adv}
18:         $y_j \leftarrow M(S')$
19:         $Prb_j \leftarrow M_{y_j}(S')$
20:         **if** (($\cos(S', S) > \epsilon$) and ($y_j \neq y$)) **then**
21:             Success[c_j] = $\cos(S', S)$
22:         **else if** (($\cos(S', S) > \epsilon$) and ($Prb_j < Prb_{actual}$)) **then**
23:             ProbRed[c_j] = $Prb_{actual} - Prb_j$
24:         **end if**
25:     **end for**
26:     **if** $len(Success) > 0$ **then**
27:         $S_{adv} \leftarrow$ replace $[MASK]$ in S with candidate word having the highest cos value
28:     **else if** $len(ProbRed) > 0$ **then**
29:         $S_{adv} \leftarrow$ replace $[MASK]$ in S with word which generates the lowest probability for y
30:     **end if**
31: **end for**

4.2 Adversarial generator

After finding relevance scores, we iteratively perturb the words in descending order of their relevance scores until the attack is successful. We create two different sets of words for aspect W_{aspect} and contextual words $W_{context}$. Let's consider an example sentence, "boot time is super fast, around anywhere from 35 seconds to 1 minute", with aspect boot time. Here W_{aspect} = (boot, time) and $W_{context}$ = (is, super, fast, around, anywhere, from, 35, seconds, to, 1, minute). At a given position in the sentence, we apply two kinds of perturbations, depending on the word type. The detailed process of generation is illustrated in Algorithm 1.

Contextual words perturbations: We perform a replace operation to perturb the contextual words in order to generate semantically coherent and grammatically correct sentences (lines 4-6). For each sentence, we opt not to perturb the stop words as they may affect the grammatical correctness of the sentence. Let w_k be the word to be perturbed in a sentence S. We apply a mask operation at k^{th} position so that later we can replace it with another word that satisfies the properties of the adversarial example. Mask operation at w_k is applied as follows: $S = w_1, ..., w_{k-1}, [MASK], w_{k+1}, .., w_n$.

Aspect terms: If the word w to be perturbed is an aspect term, then we do not perform a replace operation; instead, we change the context around the aspect term by inserting a token in front or end of it. We do so to preserve aspect terms of the sentence, which is essential to preserve semantics of the sentence (lines 7-13). Let, w_k is the word for perturbation. Then, there are two cases,
i). w_k is complete aspect term asp, then mask operation is applied as follows:
$S = w_1, ..., w_{k-1}, [MASK], w_k, w_{k+1}, .., w_n$.
ii). If the aspect term is the multi-word aspect, and w_k is one of its words, then we insert $[MASK]$ in front of the first word of the aspect term to preserve the complete aspect term. Let us say asp consists of w_{k-1} and w_k words, then mask operation is applied as follows:
$S = w_1, ..., [MASK], w_{k-1}, w_k, ..., w_n$.

After applying the mask operation, this masked sentence is fed into BERT-MLM following Garg and Ramakrishnan (2020); Li et al. (2020b) to generate top j CANDIDATES for the masked position. It ensures that the generated sentence preserves fluency and is grammatically correct. Furthermore, BERT-MLM considers the whole context when predicting the masked word; hence, the predicted word is context-aware. While replacing the contextual word, we omit the candidate words with different Part-of-speech (POS) tag than that of w_k to ensure grammatical correctness.

Semantic preservation: BERT-MLM generates contextual candidate words, but does not assure semantic similarity with the actual sentence. We use the cosine similarity metric to measure the similarity between adversarial and actual sentence (for each candidate) (Morris et al., 2020). We use Sentence Transformer to generate sentence representations (Reimers and Gurevych, 2019a, 2020). All the candidate words having cosine similarity above the threshold ϵ and are able to mislead the target model are added to the **Success**, and candidates which reduces the probability of actual class are added to **ProbRed** (lines 15-25).

4.3 Final adversarial sample

The candidate word that can successfully mislead the ABSA classifier with the highest semantic similarity score with the seed sentence or generate the lowest probability of actual class is chosen for final adversary generation (lines 26-30). The steps are repeated until the adversarial example can fool the target model.

5 Experimental Setup

We use BERT-base and BERT-base-multilingual as target models for English and Hindi, respectively. For adversarial example generation, we set the value of top candidates j to 50 and the threshold value ϵ to 0.8. To identify the POS tags, we use stanfordnlp library [2] for English and Hindi.

Datasets: To evaluate our proposed attack, we use the following ABSA datasets:

- **SemEval-14 laptop dataset**: This dataset is released as part of a shared task on ABSA (Pontiki et al., 2014) and consist of reviews from the laptop domain.
- **ABSA Hindi dataset:** Hindi ABSA dataset was released by Akhtar et al. (2016a) containing reviews from 12 domains. We use the 70%, 20%, and 10% split for train, test, and validation as done in Akhtar et al. (2016b).

The datasets are annotated with four classes, *viz.*, positive, negative, neutral, and conflict. Both the datasets contain fewer instances of conflict class. So, we focus on 3 classes by excluding the conflict class. (more details are present in A.1)

Baselines: We define the following baselines:

- **Baseline 1 (Li et al., 2020b)**: Baseline 1, BERT-attack, uses BERT-MLM to perturb the words using replace operation and used LOO for word importance ranking.
- **Baseline 2 (Garg and Ramakrishnan, 2020)**: Baseline 2, BAE, uses BERT-MLM to perturb the words using replace and insert operations, where word importance is calculated using LOO method. It performs insert operation after the replace operation.
- **Baseline 3 (Li et al., 2018):** Baseline 3, Textbugger, uses character-level and word-level perturbations. It searches for nearest neighbors in the embedding space using Glove model. Like baseline 1 and 2, it does not make any difference in the type of words (context words or aspect terms).
- **Baseline 4:** We extend the baseline 1 to Hindi ABSA setting. We use mBERT-MLM for word perturbation against the target model.
- **Baseline 5:** A state-of-the-art model proposed by Hofer et al. (2021) to attack an English ABSA model. It uses leetspeak (LEET), common mis-spellings (TYPO), or misplaced commas (PUNCT) to generate the adversarial examples. We implement all the three methods of attack for English. Their proposed LEET and TYPO are only applicable to English languages. However, the PUNCT attack can be applied to the Hindi language.
- **Baseline 6:** Baseline 6 extends baseline 2 to Hindi ABSA setting.

Baseline 1, 2, and 3 are originally proposed for text classification tasks. We extend them to an ABSA task by passing a pair of input containing sentence and aspect separated by $[SEP]$ token. We implement baseline 2 and 3 using TextAttack framework.

Evaluation metrics: To measure the effectiveness of the attack, we calculate (i). *Before-attack-accuracy and After-attack-accuracy* (*BA* and *AA*): The Before-attack-accuracy is estimated on the test set, and After-attack-accuracy is calculated on the adversarial test set; (ii). *Attack success rate (SR):* the percentage of adversarial examples that can successfully attack the target model; (iii). *Perturbation ratio (PR):* the ratio of words perturbed in the sentence to the total number of words in the sentence ; and (iv). *Semantic similarity (SS):* this is computed between the adversarial and actual sentence using the cosine similarity metric, which makes use of Sentence transformers (Reimers and Gurevych, 2019b) to generate sentence representations. In

[2]https://stanfordnlp.github.io/stanfordnlp/

Method	BA	AA	SR	PR	SS	ATCR
English						
b1	76.82	26.67	65.57	15.4	0.89	20.42
b2		22.06	70.68	14.51	0.83	25.53
b3		22.22	70.46	16.8	0.85	29.32
LEET		57	25	-	0.70	9.41
TYPO		59	22.5	-	0.61	10.30
PUNCT		69	10	-	**0.97**	-
Ours		**11.02**	**87.09**	**13**	0.92	**0**
Hindi						
b4	74.71	32.53	57.74	17	0.80	27.38
PUNCT		70.4	8.5		**0.97**	-
b5		28.00	62.05	16.2	0.83	-
Ours		**20.4**	**73.51**	**15**	0.89	**0**

Table 1: Experimental results. Here, b1: baseline 1, b2: baseline 2, b3: baseline 3, b4: baseline 4, and baseline 5 (LEET, TYPO, PUNCT), b5: baseline 5

Language	Type	GC	SP	HP
English	Baseline 1	4.1	3.7	71%
	Our	4.3	4.2	80%

Table 2: Human evaluation

Language	Ranking	AA	PR
English	random	33.90	21
	LOO	26.67	14.9
	SHAP	11.02	13
Hindi	random	48.00	24
	LOO	29.81	16.5
	SHAP	20.40	15

Table 3: Ablation experiment results

Setup	BA	AA	PR
English (10% adv)	76.81	20.63	14
(50% adv)	76.76	21.11	15
(100% data)	75.71	37.14	16
Hindi (10% data)	75.05	32.65	16.2
(50% data)	74.63	34.35	18.5
(100% data)	74.94	39.22	20

Table 4: Adversarial training results

addition to this, we also compute (v). Aspect terms change ratio (*ATCR*), which is defined as the ratio of the number of sentences where the aspect terms have been changed to the total number of sentences. We define this metric to illustrate the need for special design for ABSA adversarial generation.

6 Experimental Results and Analysis

Experimental results for both the languages for all the metrics are summarized in Table 1. We observe that our proposed attack outperforms all the baselines in terms of attack success rate, perturbation ratio, and semantic similarity. For English language, success rate of our model is higher than the other baselines by 21.52-77.09%. Our model achieves an average semantic similarity of 0.92 with actual sentences, higher than all the baselines except baseline 3-PUNCT. The semantic similarity of baseline 3-PUNCT is higher because it adds only comma after an important word. However, its success rate is only 10%, least among other attacks. ATCR ratio is highest for baseline 3. LEET and TYPO has less ATCR ratio, but their attack success rate (SR) is very less. Our proposed method is able to preserve the aspect terms, so ATCR ratio is 0%. In addition to this, our proposed method requires a few perturbations to execute a successful attack.

The same phenomenon is observed for Hindi. Our proposed attack method achieves 15.77-65.01% higher success rate than the other baselines. Notably, our method also outperforms baseline 1 and baseline 3-PUNCT in attack success rate. It requires fewer average modifications to input text compared to baseline 2. It needs to perturb only an average of 15% of the words to perform a successful attack. However, baseline 2 perturbs 17% of the words in input space.

Human evaluation: We also perform human evaluation to see the effectiveness of our proposed attack. We randomly select 100 samples from English language for baseline 1 (the strongest baseline) and our proposed attack. A total of 3 linguists (annotators) having post graduate level experience, with good knowledge of English and Hindi from India were employed for annotations. They were advised to mark the (i). grammatical correctness score (GC) on the scale of 1-5, (ii). sentiment class towards given aspect to evaluate the human prediction consistency (HP), and (iii). semantic preservation score (SP) on the scale of 1-5 to see whether they retain the meaning of actual sentences or not. For HP metric, annotators were asked to write the overall polarity of the adversarial sample in 3 categories *viz.* neutral, negative, and positive. They were provided with gold labeled samples to gain deep understanding of sentiment labels before actual annotations. Further, they were also advised to refrain from being biased towards either a specific demographic area, religion, or ethnicity while annotating the samples. Results are shown in Table

	Sentence	Aspect	Model Output
Actual	the apple engineers have not yet discovered the delete key	delete key	negative
Baseline 1	the **security authorities** have not yet **announced** the delete key		neutral
Ours	the apple engineers have not **until** discovered the **standard** delete key		neutral
Actual	air has higher resolution but the fonts are small	fonts	negative
Baseline 1	air has **more** resolution but the **applications** are **tiny**		negative
Ours	air has higher resolution but the **available** fonts are **tiny**		positive
Actual	i was given a demonstration of windows 8	windows 8	neutral
Baseline 1	i was given a demonstration of windows 8		neutral
Ours	i was given a demonstration of **the** windows 8		positive

Table 5: Adversarial samples generated by different methods

2. We observe that our proposed method obtains higher GC, HP, and SP scores than the baseline 1, illustrating the fact that our generated adversarial samples are more semantically coherent and grammatically correct.

Ablation study: We perform an ablation experiment to observe the effectiveness of the saliency generator in our proposed method and observe the change in after-attack accuracy and perturbation rate when it is removed. First, we rank the words in random order and then, use LOO method for word ranking. Table 3 shows the results for both the languages. We observe that there is an increment in after-attack accuracy and perturbation ratio for English as well as Hindi language (more ablation experiments are present in A.2).

Adversarial training: We observe the model robustness with adversarial training as a defence mechanism, using our proposed algorithm to generate adversarial samples for training data, followed by fine-tuning the target model on the combined original training data and adversarial training data. We design three strategies here: (i). actual training data + randomly sampled 10% adversarial data, (ii). actual training data + randomly sampled 50% adversarial data, (iii). actual training data + complete adversarial data. After fine-tuning the target model, we attack the target model with the proposed algorithm. Results for both the languages are shown in Table 4. We observe that the after attack accuracy and perturbation ratios are increased after adversarial training. This illustrates that the model becomes more robust against adversarial attacks as more adversarial examples are added to the training set. It can be also observed that the adversarial training reduces the actual test accuracy of the target model by a small percent, i.e., 1% in case of the English language, which is in line with Jia et al. (2019). However, in the case of Hindi, almost no drop in accuracy is observed; instead, the accuracy is increased by 0.34%. This demonstrates that our proposed algorithm can be used to improve the robustness of ABSA models.

Detailed analysis: For detailed qualitative analysis, we manually analyze the adversarial samples generated by baseline 1 and our proposed attack. As our saliency generator finds relevance of every word by considering various combinations, so it can decide better order of word perturbations. Examples 1 and 2 illustrate the importance of our saliency generator. In example 1, both the attack strategies successfully fools the classifier. But our proposed attack can generate a semantically similar example with fewer perturbations. Here, baseline 1 perturbs 3 words. However, our proposed attack perturbs one contextual word and alters the context around multi-word aspect term to perform a successful attack. This illustrates the improvement using SHAP scores compared to the method used in Garg and Ramakrishnan (2020); Li et al. (2020b). In example 2, baseline 1 performs an unsuccessful attack even by perturbing 3 words, including aspect word. On the top, changing the aspect *fonts* to *application* alters the semantics of the sentence. Our proposed method preserves the aspect information and requires only 2 modifications to execute a successful attack. In example 3, baseline 1 cannot find appropriate replacements to fool the target model. However, our method is able to fool the target model by inserting word *the* in front of the multi-word aspect term (more detailed qualitative analysis for all the baselines is present in section A.3).

7 Conclusion

In this paper, we have presented an effective algorithm to generate adversarial examples for assessing the resilience of the BERT based aspect based sentiment classification model. To generate adversarial examples, we exploit the model's explainability to identify the word saliency. We propose replace operation for contextual words and insert operation for aspect term to generate more semantically similar sentences. We have evaluated our proposed algorithm on two benchmark datasets, English and Hindi. Extensive experiments and human evaluation show that our proposed algorithm outperforms the state-of-art attack methods in success rate, perturbation ratio, and semantic preservation.

In our current work, we have evaluated the robustness of the sentiment classification task only. In future, we would extend this work to evaluate the robustness of both aspect term extraction and sentiment classification.

Acknowledgements

Asif Ekbal acknowledges the Young Faculty Research Fellowship (YFRF), supported by Visvesvaraya Ph.D. scheme for Electronics and IT, Ministry of Electronics and Information Technology (MeitY), Government of India, being implemented by Digital India Corporation (formerly Media Lab Asia).

References

Md Shad Akhtar, Asif Ekbal, and Pushpak Bhattacharyya. 2016a. Aspect based sentiment analysis in hindi: resource creation and evaluation. In *Proceedings of the Tenth International Conference on Language Resources and Evaluation (LREC'16)*, pages 2703–2709.

Md Shad Akhtar, Ayush Kumar, Asif Ekbal, and Pushpak Bhattacharyya. 2016b. A hybrid deep learning architecture for sentiment analysis. In *Proceedings of COLING 2016, the 26th International Conference on Computational Linguistics: Technical Papers*, pages 482–493.

Moustafa Alzantot, Yash Sharma, Ahmed Elgohary, Bo-Jhang Ho, Mani Srivastava, and Kai-Wei Chang. 2018. Generating natural language adversarial examples. In *Proceedings of the 2018 Conference on Empirical Methods in Natural Language Processing*, pages 2890–2896, Brussels, Belgium. Association for Computational Linguistics.

Akshat Bakliwal, Jennifer Foster, Jennifer van der Puil, Ron O'Brien, Lamia Tounsi, and Mark Hughes. 2013. Sentiment analysis of political tweets: Towards an accurate classifier. Association for Computational Linguistics.

Anirban Chakraborty, Manaar Alam, Vishal Dey, Anupam Chattopadhyay, and Debdeep Mukhopadhyay. 2018. Adversarial attacks and defences: A survey. *arXiv preprint arXiv:1810.00069*.

Jacob Devlin, Ming-Wei Chang, Kenton Lee, and Kristina Toutanova. 2018. Bert: Pre-training of deep bidirectional transformers for language understanding. *arXiv preprint arXiv:1810.04805*.

Javid Ebrahimi, Anyi Rao, Daniel Lowd, and Dejing Dou. 2017. Hotflip: White-box adversarial examples for text classification. *arXiv preprint arXiv:1712.06751*.

Ji Gao, Jack Lanchantin, Mary Lou Soffa, and Yanjun Qi. 2018. Black-box generation of adversarial text sequences to evade deep learning classifiers. In *2018 IEEE Security and Privacy Workshops (SPW)*, pages 50–56. IEEE.

Siddhant Garg and Goutham Ramakrishnan. 2020. Bae: Bert-based adversarial examples for text classification. *arXiv preprint arXiv:2004.01970*.

Ian J Goodfellow, Jonathon Shlens, and Christian Szegedy. 2014. Explaining and harnessing adversarial examples. *arXiv preprint arXiv:1412.6572*.

Pengxin Guo, Yuancheng Xu, Baijiong Lin, and Yu Zhang. 2020. Multi-task adversarial attack. *arXiv preprint arXiv:2011.09824*.

Nora Hofer, Pascal Schöttle, Alexander Rietzler, and Sebastian Stabinger. 2021. Adversarial examples against a bert absa model–fooling bert with l33t, misspellign, and punctuation. In *The 16th International Conference on Availability, Reliability and Security*, pages 1–6.

Robin Jia, Aditi Raghunathan, Kerem Göksel, and Percy Liang. 2019. Certified robustness to adversarial word substitutions. *arXiv preprint arXiv:1909.00986*.

Di Jin, Zhijing Jin, Joey Tianyi Zhou, and Peter Szolovits. 2020. Is bert really robust? a strong baseline for natural language attack on text classification and entailment. In *Proceedings of the AAAI conference on artificial intelligence*, volume 34, pages 8018–8025.

Sudhanshu Kumar, Mahendra Yadava, and Partha Pratim Roy. 2019. Fusion of eeg response and sentiment analysis of products review to predict customer satisfaction. *Information Fusion*, 52:41–52.

Alexey Kurakin, Ian Goodfellow, Samy Bengio, et al. 2016. Adversarial examples in the physical world.

Dianqi Li, Yizhe Zhang, Hao Peng, Liqun Chen, Chris Brockett, Ming-Ting Sun, and Bill Dolan. 2020a. Contextualized perturbation for textual adversarial attack. *arXiv preprint arXiv:2009.07502*.

Jinfeng Li, Shouling Ji, Tianyu Du, Bo Li, and Ting Wang. 2018. Textbugger: Generating adversarial text against real-world applications. *arXiv preprint arXiv:1812.05271*.

Linyang Li, Ruotian Ma, Qipeng Guo, Xiangyang Xue, and Xipeng Qiu. 2020b. Bert-attack: Adversarial attack against bert using bert. *arXiv preprint arXiv:2004.09984*.

Bin Liang, Hongcheng Li, Miaoqiang Su, Pan Bian, Xirong Li, and Wenchang Shi. 2017. Deep text classification can be fooled. *arXiv preprint arXiv:1704.08006*.

Xiaodong Liu, Pengcheng He, Weizhu Chen, and Jianfeng Gao. 2019. Multi-task deep neural networks for natural language understanding. *arXiv preprint arXiv:1901.11504*.

Scott M Lundberg and Su-In Lee. 2017. A unified approach to interpreting model predictions. In *Proceedings of the 31st international conference on neural information processing systems*, pages 4768–4777.

Mamta Mamta, Asif Ekbal, and Pushpak Bhattacharyya. 2022a. Exploring multi-lingual, multi-task, and adversarial learning for low-resource sentiment analysis. *ACM Trans. Asian Low-Resour. Lang. Inf. Process.*, 21(5).

Mamta Mamta, Asif Ekbal, Pushpak Bhattacharyya, Tista Saha, Alka Kumar, and Shikha Srivastava. 2022b. HindiMD: A multi-domain corpora for low-resource sentiment analysis. In *Proceedings of the Thirteenth Language Resources and Evaluation Conference*, pages 7061–7070, Marseille, France. European Language Resources Association.

Mamta Mamta, Asif Ekbal, Pushpak Bhattacharyya, Shikha Srivastava, Alka Kumar, and Tista Saha. 2020. Multi-domain tweet corpora for sentiment analysis: Resource creation and evaluation. In *Proceedings of the 12th Language Resources and Evaluation Conference*, pages 5046–5054, Marseille, France. European Language Resources Association.

Takeru Miyato, Andrew M Dai, and Ian Goodfellow. 2016. Adversarial training methods for semi-supervised text classification. *arXiv preprint arXiv:1605.07725*.

Takeru Miyato, Shin-ichi Maeda, Masanori Koyama, and Shin Ishii. 2018. Virtual adversarial training: a regularization method for supervised and semi-supervised learning. *IEEE transactions on pattern analysis and machine intelligence*, 41(8):1979–1993.

Ishani Mondal. 2021. Bbaeg: Towards bert-based biomedical adversarial example generation for text classification. *arXiv preprint arXiv:2104.01782*.

John X Morris, Eli Lifland, Jin Yong Yoo, Jake Grigsby, Di Jin, and Yanjun Qi. 2020. Textattack: A framework for adversarial attacks, data augmentation, and adversarial training in nlp. *arXiv preprint arXiv:2005.05909*.

Anh Nguyen, Jason Yosinski, and Jeff Clune. 2015. Deep neural networks are easily fooled: High confidence predictions for unrecognizable images. In *Proceedings of the IEEE conference on computer vision and pattern recognition*, pages 427–436.

Bo Pang, Lillian Lee, and Shivakumar Vaithyanathan. 2002. Thumbs up?: sentiment classification using machine learning techniques. In *Proceedings of the ACL-02 conference on Empirical methods in natural language processing-Volume 10*, pages 79–86. Association for Computational Linguistics.

Nicolas Papernot, Patrick McDaniel, Ananthram Swami, and Richard Harang. 2016. Crafting adversarial input sequences for recurrent neural networks. In *MILCOM 2016-2016 IEEE Military Communications Conference*, pages 49–54. IEEE.

Maria Pontiki, Dimitris Galanis, John Pavlopoulos, Harris Papageorgiou, Ion Androutsopoulos, and Suresh Manandhar. 2014. SemEval-2014 task 4: Aspect based sentiment analysis. In *Proceedings of the 8th International Workshop on Semantic Evaluation (SemEval 2014)*, pages 27–35, Dublin, Ireland. Association for Computational Linguistics.

Nils Reimers and Iryna Gurevych. 2019a. Sentence-bert: Sentence embeddings using siamese bert-networks. In *Proceedings of the 2019 Conference on Empirical Methods in Natural Language Processing*. Association for Computational Linguistics.

Nils Reimers and Iryna Gurevych. 2019b. Sentence-bert: Sentence embeddings using siamese bert-networks. *arXiv preprint arXiv:1908.10084*.

Nils Reimers and Iryna Gurevych. 2020. Making monolingual sentence embeddings multilingual using knowledge distillation. In *Proceedings of the 2020 Conference on Empirical Methods in Natural Language Processing*. Association for Computational Linguistics.

Shuhuai Ren, Yihe Deng, Kun He, and Wanxiang Che. 2019. Generating natural language adversarial examples through probability weighted word saliency. In *Proceedings of the 57th annual meeting of the association for computational linguistics*, pages 1085–1097.

Erik Štrumbelj and Igor Kononenko. 2014. Explaining prediction models and individual predictions with feature contributions. *Knowledge and information systems*, 41(3):647–665.

Chi Sun, Luyao Huang, and Xipeng Qiu. 2019. Utilizing bert for aspect-based sentiment analysis via constructing auxiliary sentence. *arXiv preprint arXiv:1903.09588*.

Lichao Sun, Kazuma Hashimoto, Wenpeng Yin, Akari Asai, Jia Li, Philip Yu, and Caiming Xiong. 2020. Adv-bert: Bert is not robust on misspellings! generating nature adversarial samples on bert. *arXiv preprint arXiv:2003.04985*.

Christian Szegedy, Wojciech Zaremba, Ilya Sutskever, Joan Bruna, Dumitru Erhan, Ian Goodfellow, and Rob Fergus. 2013. Intriguing properties of neural networks. *arXiv preprint arXiv:1312.6199*.

Yequan Wang, Minlie Huang, Xiaoyan Zhu, and Li Zhao. 2016. Attention-based lstm for aspect-level sentiment classification. In *Proceedings of the 2016 conference on empirical methods in natural language processing*, pages 606–615.

Thomas Wolf, Lysandre Debut, Victor Sanh, Julien Chaumond, Clement Delangue, Anthony Moi, Pierric Cistac, Tim Rault, Rémi Louf, Morgan Funtowicz, et al. 2019. Huggingface's transformers: State-of-the-art natural language processing. *ArXiv*, pages arXiv–1910.

Hu Xu, Bing Liu, Lei Shu, and Philip S Yu. 2019. Bert post-training for review reading comprehension and aspect-based sentiment analysis. *arXiv preprint arXiv:1904.02232*.

Huangzhao Zhang, Hao Zhou, Ning Miao, and Lei Li. 2020a. Generating fluent adversarial examples for natural languages. *arXiv preprint arXiv:2007.06174*.

Wei Emma Zhang, Quan Z Sheng, Ahoud Alhazmi, and Chenliang Li. 2020b. Adversarial attacks on deep-learning models in natural language processing: A survey. *ACM Transactions on Intelligent Systems and Technology (TIST)*, 11(3):1–41.

Xinze Zhang, Junzhe Zhang, Zhenhua Chen, and Kun He. 2021. Crafting adversarial examples for neural machine translation. In *Proceedings of the 59th Annual Meeting of the Association for Computational Linguistics and the 11th International Joint Conference on Natural Language Processing (Volume 1: Long Papers)*, pages 1967–1977.

Zhengli Zhao, Dheeru Dua, and Sameer Singh. 2017. Generating natural adversarial examples. *arXiv preprint arXiv:1710.11342*.

A Appendix

A.1 Experimental setup

To implement our model, we use the Python-based library Pytorch [3] and Hugging face implementation of BERT (Wolf et al., 2019). Target model for English (BERT-base) uses 12 layers of transformers block with a hidden size of 768 and number of self-attention heads as 12. It has 110M trainable parameters. Multilingual BERT is pre-trained on 104 languages including Hindi. Input consists of two segments, first contains the sentence and second part consists of aspect term, both are separated by $[SEP]$ tokens. We use the BertAdam optimizer to optimize the network weights based on the categorical cross entropy. The hyper-parameters of BERT are also fine-tuned for both the languages on the respective task datasets. We split 15% of the training data into validation set, used for fine-tuning the hyper-parameters. We show the dataset statistics in Table 7. We use the grid search to find the best set of hyper-parameters. All the hyper-parameters, along with the best set, are shown in Table 6. All the computations are performed on the Nvidia929GeForce GTX 1080 GPU with 12 GB memory.

Hyper-parameter	Values	Best
Learning rate	2e-5,3e-5,5e-5	3e-5
Batch size	8,16,32	16
Epochs	2,3,5	3

Table 6: Hyper-parameter values

A.2 More ablation studies

To investigate the performance of two perturbations, when applied individually, we carried out two ablation experiments where we (i). Perform only replace operation on contextual words and aspect words are left unchanged; (ii). Perform only insert operation for aspect words, and contextual words are not modified. Results are shown in Table 8. We observe that the after attack accuracies are changed to 26.23% and 51.47% only for replace operation and insert operation, respectively. The attack success rate for insert operation is very low as it only changes the context of aspect terms. By combining these two types of operations, our proposed method achieves a higher success rate.

[3]https://pytorch.org/

Dataset	Type	Samples	aspects	Pos	Neg	Neu	Con
SemEval	Train	3045	2458	987	866	460	45
	Test	800	654	341	128	169	16
Hindi	Total	5417	4509	1986	569	1914	40

Table 7: Data Statistics for English and Hindi datasets. pos: positive, neg: negative, neu: neutral, con: conflict

Language	Operation	AA	SR
English	Insert	51.47	40.42
	Replace	26.23	70.333
	Both	**11.02**	**87.09**

Table 8: Ablation experiments: Insert and replace operation

We also investigate the importance of POS constraints by removing them (for replace operation). We observe that removing the POS constraint increases the success rate to 89.93% and lowers the after attack accuracy to 10.63%. We manually analyze a few adversarial samples, which reveals that the removal of POS constraints affects the grammatical correctness of the sentence. So, the POS constraint step is to assure grammatical correctness.

Further, we replace the Stanford POS-tagger with NLTK POS-tagger [4] to observe the effect on the after attack accuracy and success rate of the model. NLTK POS-tagger yields the after attack accuracy of 17.6% with attack success rate of 77.25%.

A.2.1 Effect of semantic similarity constraint

To maintain semantic consistency with the original sentence, we preserve aspect terms and apply textual similarity constraint ($sim(S, S_{adv}) > \epsilon$). We ablate the textual similarity constraint ($sim(S, S_{adv}) > \epsilon$) to measure its effectiveness. Instead, we randomly choose a word from the set of candidates that can either decrease the classification probability or fool the classifier. We observe that removing semantic constraints decreases textual similarity to 0.82 (from 0.92) and increases the attack success rate to 89.22% (from 87.09%). It can also be observed that attacking a model without semantic similarity constraint (threshold constraint) becomes easier. However, the decline in the average semantic similarity between actual sentences and corresponding adversarial sentences indicates that there is a deterioration in the quality of generated examples. Examples shown in Table 9 demonstrate this fact. Although the generated adversarial sample can fool the classifier (model output changed to negative), it does not preserve the actual semantics and the original label (changed to negative) of the actual sentence.

[4] https://www.nltk.org/

A.2.2 Comparison of different similarity functions

We experimented with different similarity functions to observe the affect on attack accuracy and success rate. We measured semantic similarity with Jaccard similarity measure and Euclidean distance. For the Jaccard similarity measure and Euclidean distance measure, we set the threshold to 0.8 and 0.8 (1 - Euclidean distance), respectively. Results for both measures are shown in Table 10. Jaccard metric reduces the attack success rate to 58%. Similarly, Euclidean distance also reduces the attack success rate 31.35%.

A.2.3 Effect of threshold values

To study the effect of threshold values on attack success rate and semantic similarity, we perform various experiments with different values of ϵ. Results are shown in Table 11. We observe a trade-off between semantic similarity and attack success rate. With the increase in ϵ, semantic similarity increases, but the attack success rate decreases. The threshold value of 0.80 yields the attack success rate of 87.09% and semantic similarity of 0.92. However, the threshold value of 0.95 reduces the attack success rate to 56.35% and increases the semantic similarity to 0.973.

A.3 More qualitative Analysis

We further analyze the outputs of all the baselines for detailed analysis. Examples are shown in Tables 12 and 13. As indicated in example 1, baseline 1 violates semantic consistency (property 1), grammatical correctness due to incorrect article usage (property 2), and human predictions (property 4). Baseline 2 violates properties 1 and 2. Baseline 3 and LEET introduce misspellings, which also lacks semantic consistency. LEET replaces the word **excellent** with **3xc311nt**, which has no semantics. However, our proposed approach satisfies all the properties to execute a successful attack.

For example 2, the aspect term is **heat output**. BERT-attack (baseline 1) and BAE (baseline 2) require two perturbations and performed replace operation to execute a successful attack. However, the semantics of the original sentence are altered (property 1). Similarly, baselines 3 and LEET also lack

	Sentence	Aspect	Model Output	Human Pred.
Actual	the nicest part is the low heat output and ultra quiet operation	heat output	pos	pos
Adversarial (without constraint)	the **lowest** part is the low heat output and ultra quiet operation		neg	neg
Adversarial (with constraint)	the **best** part is the low heat output and ultra quiet operation		neg	neg

Table 9: Qualitative analysis of adversarial attacks with and without the semantic similarity constraint (threshold on cosine similarity). Here, pos: positive and neg: negative.

Language	Measure	AA	SR
English	Jaccard	32.53	58
	Euclidean distance	53.17	31.35
	Cosine	11.02	87.09

Table 10: Results on different similarity measures

Language	ϵ	AA	SR	SS
English	0.80	11.02	87.09	0.92
	0.82	16.98	82.60	0.925
	0.85	20.47	77.32	0.936
	0.87	23.65	74.84	0.944
	0.90	26.98	69.02	0.954
	0.92	31.75	63.40	0.964
	0.95	38.25	56.35	0.973

Table 11: Effect of threshold values

semantic consistency. Our proposed method requires only one perturbation and generates a more semantically coherent sentence than other baselines.

Similarly, baselines 1, 2, and 3 have altered the aspect term **compact computing** in example 3, affecting the semantic consistency (property 1). LEET and baseline 3 are also not able to maintain semantic consistency. However, our proposed approach preserves the aspect term and requires only 1 perturbation (insert operation) to execute a successful attack.

Example 4 also indicates that baseline 1 and baseline 2 cannot preserve property 1 (semantic consistency) and property 3 (human label prediction). However, the adversarial sentences generated by our proposed method satisfy all the properties of adversarial examples.

This detailed qualitative analysis illustrates that our proposed approach generates more grammatical and semantically coherent sentences with fewer perturbations than other baselines.

	Sentence	Aspect	Model Output	Human Pred.
Actual	they don't just look good; they deliver excellent performance	performance	pos	pos
baseline 1	they don't just look good; they deliver **an** performance		neg	neu
baseline 2	they don't just look good; they deliver **bad** performance		neg	neg
baseline 3	they don't just look good; they deliver **excelt** performance		neg	neu
LEET	they don't just look good; they deliver **3xc3113nt** performance		neg	neu
PUNCT	they don't just look good; ,they deliver excellent performance		neg	pos
Ours	they don't just look good; they deliver **good** performance		neu	pos
Actual	the nicest part is the low heat output and ultra quiet operation	heat output	pos	pos
baseline 1	the nicest part is the low heat output and **over** quiet **division**		neg	pos
baseline 2	the nicest part is the low heat output and ultra **weak reduced**		neg	pos
baseline 3	the nicest part is the low heat output and ultra **quit operaton**		neg	pos
LEET	the **nic35t** part is the low heat output and ultra quiet operation		neg	pos
PUNCT	the nicest **,** part is the low heat output and ultra quiet operation		neg	pos
ours	the **best** part is the low heat output and ultra quiet operation		neg	pos
Actual	the mac mini is probably the simplest example of compact computing out there	compact computing	pos	pos
baseline 1	the mac mini is probably the simplest **member** of **convex** computing out there		neg	aspect changed
baseline 2	the mac mini is probably the simplest example of **hard** computing out there		neg	aspect changed
baseline 3	the mac mini is **probabl** the **simpest** example of **pact** computing out there		neu	aspect changed
LEET	the mac mini is probably the simplest **3xampl3** of compact computing out there		neu	pos
PUNCT	the mac mini is probably the simplest**,** example of compact computing out there		pos	pos
Ours	the mac mini is probably the simplest example of **any** compact computing out there		neg	pos

Table 12: Detailed qualitative analysis of different methods. Here, pos: positive, neg: negative, neu:neutral

	Sentence	Aspect	Model Output	Human Pred
Actual	it is very easy to integrate bluetooth devices, and usb devices are recognized almost instantly	integrate bluetooth devices	pos	pos
baseline 1	it is very **hard** to integrate bluetooth devices, and usb devices are recognized almost instantly		neg	neg
baseline 2	it is very **hard** to integrate bluetooth devices, and usb devices are recognized almost instantly		neg	neg
baseline 3	it is very **uncomplicated** to integrate bluetooth devices, and usb devices are recognized almost instantly		neg	pos
LEET	it is very **345y** to integrate bluetooth devices, and usb devices are recognized almost instantly		pos	neu
PUNCT	it is very **easy,** to integrate bluetooth devices, and usb devices are recognized almost instantly		pos	pos
ours	it is very **basic** to integrate bluetooth devices, and usb devices are recognized almost instantly		neg	pos

Table 13: Detailed qualitative analysis of different methods. Here, pos: positive, neg: negative, neu:neutral

Author Index